Handbook of
Social Psychology

Edited by

John Delamater

University of Wisconsin
Madison, Wisconsin

Springer

John Delamater
University of Wisconsin
Madison, WI
USA

Library of Congress Control Number: 2006924283

ISBN-10: 0-387-32515-8
ISBN-13: 978-0387-32515-6

Printed on acid-free paper.

Printed in the United States of America.   (IBT)

9 8 7 6 5 4 3 2 1

springer.com

Contributors

Josh Ackerman, Center for Learning and Teaching Excellence, Arizona State University, Tempe, Arizona 85287

Mark M. Bernard, School of Psychology, Cardiff University, Cardiff, Wales, UK CF10 3YG

Peter J. Burke, Department of Sociology, University of California-Riverside, Riverside, California 92521

Karen S. Cook, Department of Sociology, Stanford University, Stanford, California 94305

Shelley J. Correll, Department of Sociology, University of Wisconsin-Madison, Madison, Wisconsin 53706

William A. Corsaro, Department of Sociology, Indiana University, Bloomington, Indiana 47405

Donna Eder, Department of Sociology, Indiana University, Bloomington, Indiana 47405

Diane H. Felmlee, Department of Sociology, University of California-Davis, Davis, California 95616

Laura Fingerson, Department of Sociology, University of Wisconsin-Milwaukee, Milwaukee, Wisconsin 53201

Michael A. Hogg, School of Psychology, University of Queensland, Brisbane, QLD 4072, Australia

Judith A. Howard, Department of Sociology, University of Washington, Seattle, Washington 98195

Howard B. Kaplan, Department of Sociology, Texas A&M University, College Station, Texas 77843

Sandi Kawecka Nenga, Department of Sociology, Indiana University, Bloomington, Indiana 47405

Douglas Kenrick, Psychology Department, Arizona State University, Tempe, Arizona 85287

Susan Ledlow, Center for Learning and Teaching Excellence, Arizona State University, Tempe, Arizona 85287

Kathryn J. Lively, Department of Sociology, Indiana University, Bloomington, Indiana 47405

Karen Lutfey, Department of Sociology, University of Minnesota, Minneapolis, Minnesota 55455

Michelle A. Luke, School of Psychology, Cardiff University, Cardiff, Wales, UK CF10 3YG

Gregory R. Maio, School of Psychology, Cardiff University, Cardiff, Wales, UK CF10 3YG

Douglas W. Maynard, Department of Sociology, University of Wisconsin-Madison, Madison, Wisconsin 53706

Jane D. McLeod, Department of Sociology, Indiana University, Bloomington, Indiana 47405

Karen Miller-Loessi, Department of Sociology, Arizona State University, Tempe, Arizona 85287

John Mirowsky, Department of Sociology, Ohio State University, Columbus, Ohio 43210

Jeylan T. Mortimer, Department of Sociology, University of Minnesota, Minneapolis, Minnesota 55455

James M. Olson, Department of Psychology, University of Western Ontario, London, Ontario, Canada N6A 5C2

Terri L. Orbuch, Department of Sociology, Oakland University, Rochester, Michigan 48309

Timothy J. Owens, Department of Sociology and Anthropology, Purdue University, West Lafayette, Indiana 47907

John N. Parker, Department of Sociology, Arizona State University, Tempe, Arizona 85287

Anssi Peräkylä, Department of Sociology and Social Psychology, University of Tampere, Tampere, Finland

Daniel G. Renfrow, Department of Sociology, University of Washington, Seattle, Washington 98195

Eric Rice, Department of Sociology, Stanford University, Stanford, California 94305

Cecilia Ridgeway, Department of Sociology, Stanford University, Stanford, California 94305

Deana A. Rohlinger, Department of Sociology, University of California-Irvine, Irvine, California 92697

Catherine E. Ross, Population Research Center, University of Texas, Austin, Texas 78712

David A. Snow, Department of Sociology, University of California-Irvine, Irvine, California 92697

Susan Sprecher, Department of Sociology and Anthropology, Illinois State University, Normal, Illinois 61790

Jan E. Stets, Department of Sociology, University of California-Riverside, Riverside, California 92521

Sheldon Stryker, Department of Sociology, Indiana University, Bloomington, Indiana 47405

Kevin D. Vryan, Department of Sociology, Indiana University, Bloomington, Indiana 47405

Preface

THE VISION

This *Handbook* is one tangible product of a lifelong *affaire*. When I was re-introduced to social psychology, as a first-semester senior psychology major, it was "love at first sight." I majored in psychology because I wanted to understand human social behavior. I had taken an introductory sociology course as a freshman. The venerable Lindesmith and Strauss was our text, and I enjoyed both the text and the course. I thought at the time that it was the *psychology* of the material that attracted me. Two years later, after several psychology courses, I walked into social psychology, and realized it was the *social* that attracted me. I never looked back. Later in that semester I quizzed my faculty mentors, and learned that there were three places where I could get an education in *social psychology*: at Stanford with Leon Festinger, at Columbia, and at Michigan, in the joint, interdisciplinary program directed by Ted Newcomb. Fortunately, I arrived in Ann Arbor in the fall of 1963, and spent the next four years taking courses and seminars in social psychology, taught by faculty in both the sociology and psychology departments. I especially value the opportunity that I had to learn from and work with Dan Katz, Herb Kelman, and Ted Newcomb during those years.

These experiences shaped my intellectual commitments. I am convinced that social psychology is best approached with an interdisciplinary perspective. I bring such a perspective to my research, undergraduate training, and mentoring of graduate students. I do not believe that social psychology is the only relevant perspective, but I do believe that it is essential to a complete understanding of human social behavior.

As I completed my graduate work, I was fortunate to obtain a position in the University of Wisconsin Sociology Department. At that time, there were two other faculty members there who had earned degrees in the joint program at Michigan, Andy Michener and Shalom Schwartz. The three of us did much of the teaching in the social psychology area, graduate and undergraduate. We shared the view that social psychology is an interdisciplinary field, that combining relevant work by persons working in psychology and in sociology leads to a more comprehensive understanding. We viewed social psychology as an empirical field; theory, both comprehensive and mid-range, is essential to the development of the field but so is empirical research testing and refining those theoretical ideas. We believed that research employing all types of methods, qualitative and quantitative, make an important contribution.

What, you ask, is the relevance of this personal history? The answer is that it is the source of the vision that guides my work. You will see this vision of the field reflected in various ways throughout this Handbook.

I was very pleased when the Social Psychology Section of the American Sociological Association decided to sponsor the volume, *Social psychology: Sociological perspectives*, edited by Rosenberg and Turner. I felt that there was a need for such a volume that could be used as a textbook in graduate courses. Following its publication in 1981, I used the book regularly in my graduate course. According to Cook, Fine, and House, it "became the textbook of choice for many sociologists teaching graduate courses in social psychology" (1995, p. ix). The need for an updating and expansion of that volume to reflect new trends in our field led the Section to commission a new work, published as *Sociological perspectives in social psychology* in 1995. I used this book in graduate courses for several years. By 2001 I felt that a new edition was needed. Conversations with members and officers of the Social Psychology Section indicated that the Section had no plans to commission such a book. At about this time Howard Kaplan, general Editor of this series of Handbooks, invited me to edit a volume on social psychology. And here it is. The editors of the two books commissioned by the Social Psychology Section graciously donated some of the royalties to the Section. I will donate to the Section one-half of any royalties from the sales of this Handbook.

THE GOALS

My goals as editor are similar to those of my distinguished predecessors, including Morris Rosenberg, Ralph Turner, Karen Cook, Gary Fine, and Jim House. I have also relied on the *Handbooks of social psychology*, which draw together work in our field from a more psychological perspective, in both my research and teaching. Now in the fourth edition, published in 1998, it convinced me of the value of a volume that can serve as a sourcebook for researchers and practitioners. One goal in preparing this *Handbook* is to provide such a sourcebook, or "standard professional reference for the field of social psychology" (Gilbert, Fiske, & Lindzey, 1998, p. xi). A second goal is to provide an opportunity for scholars in the field to take stock of and reflect on work in their areas of expertise. Authors were invited not only to draw together past work, but also to identify limitations in and to point to needed future directions. Third, I hope that this volume will serve as the "textbook of choice" for graduate courses for the next several years.

THE FIELD OF SOCIAL PSYCHOLOGY

Social psychology is a major subfield within sociology. The principal journal in the area, *Social Psychology Quarterly* (originally called *Sociometry*), was founded in 1937, and is one of only six journals published by the American Sociological Association. Sociologists share this field with psychologists. This has led to diverse views of the relationship between psychological and sociological social psychology. Twenty-five years ago, a widely held view was that these subfields were relatively distinct, that each was a distinctive "face" with its own core questions, theory, and methods (House, 1977). It is certainly true that there are differences in core questions; a comparison of the Table of Contents of the *Handbook of social psychology*

(1998) and *Sociological perspectives on social psychology* (1995) will make clear these differences. Psychologists often emphasize processes that occur inside the individual, including perception, cognition, motivation, and emotion, and the antecedents and consequences of these processes. In analyzing interaction, their focus is often on how aspects of self, attitudes, and interpersonal perception influence behavior. Sociologists have traditionally been more concerned with social collectivities, including families, organizations, communities, and social institutions.

Social psychology is the study of the interface between these two sets of phenomena, the nature and causes of human social behavior (Michener & DeLamater, 1999). Both intra-individual and the social context influence and are influenced by individual behavior. The *core concerns* of social psychology include:

- the impact of one individual on another
- the impact of a group on its individual members
- the impact of individuals on the groups in which they participate, and
- the impact of one group on another.

Given this set of concerns, I share Cook, Fine, and House's (1995) view that social psychology is interdisciplinary, that it involves and requires a synthesis of the relevant work in the two disciplines on which it draws. The apparent division into "two social psychologies" reflects in part the bureaucratic structure of the modern American university, including the division of knowledge by departments, and the practice of requiring a faculty member to have a single "tenure home." I do not believe that there are insurmountable differences in theory, method, or substance between the work of psychological and sociological social psychologists. The so-called "cognitive revolution" brought to the fore in psychology the same processes traditionally emphasized by symbolic interaction theory, identity theory, and the dramaturgical perspective in sociology.

One facet of social psychology within sociology is a set of theoretical perspectives. Rosenberg and Turner (1981) included chapter-length treatment of four theories: symbolic interaction, social exchange, reference group, and role theory. Cook, Fine, and House (1996) did not include a section devoted to theory, using instead an organization based on substantive areas. I have included a section on theory, with chapters on symbolic interaction, social exchange, expectation states, social structure and personality, and the evolutionary perspectives. The differences in the topics of theoretical chapters between Rosenberg and Turner and this Handbook reflect the changes in the field in the last two decades of the 20th century. Although it remains a useful metaphor, the role perspective *qua* theory has not flourished. Renewed interest in cognitive processes and their social context, and the development of social identity theory, has recast some of the concerns of the reference group perspective. Expectation states theory has become a major perspective, reflecting the continuing incremental and innovative theoretical development and research activities of a new generation of social psychologists. The rapid development of evolutionary perspectives and their application to such topics as interpersonal attraction, mate selection, family, and sexuality are the most visible changes to have occurred in the field.

Another facet is the methods we use to gather empirical data. Those who share(d) the "two social psychologies" view point(ed) to the dominance of the experiment in psychological social psychology, and of the survey in sociological social psychology. While there was a pronounced difference in this regard in the 1970s and 1980s, that difference has narrowed greatly in the past decade. Researchers, whether psychologists or sociologists, interested in areas such as prejudice and racism, mental health, and adult personality have always relied heavily on surveys. Recent developments in the analysis of data and the increasing use of longitudinal designs have enhanced our ability to test causal models with survey data; the experimental method is no longer the only way to study causality. Furthermore, the use of the experiment by sociologically oriented social psychologists is increasing, particularly in research on expectation states and exchange theory. This development is welcomed by those of us who believe that problems are best studied using multiple methods. Finally, there has been a renaissance in the use of systematic observation by sociologically oriented researchers. Thus in 2002, social psychologists from both sides of the aisle are using surveys, experiments, and observational methods, and learning from each other how to improve these techniques.

At the same time, social psychology remains well integrated into the larger discipline of sociology. We share the use of the theories and methods described above with other sociologists. In our research and writing, we focus on topics that are of interest and in some cases central to the discipline: life-course analyses, social networks, socialization, status, stereotyping, and stigma, to name a few. Work by social psychologists is integral to most of the other major subfields in sociology: collective behavior and social movements, development, deviance, emotion, health, language, and social stratification. The relevance of social psychology to these topics is made clear in many of the chapters that follow.

THIS HANDBOOK

The topic outline for this *Handbook* is the result of a variety of input. I began by looking in detail at the outlines of four previous handbooks. I noted the frequency with which topics appeared, and developed an initial list of more than 25 topics. The sifting and winnowing of the list benefited greatly from input from the graduate student and faculty participants in the Social Psychology Brownbag/Seminar and other faculty members at the University of Wisconsin. Howard Kaplan also reviewed the outline. The Table of Contents contains all of the topics on my final list, save one. Despite repeated efforts, I was unable to find someone to author a chapter on the social psychology of race and gender.

Section I of the book contains five chapters, each of which presents a theoretical perspective basic to contemporary social psychology. They include symbolic interaction theory, expectation states theory, social exchange theory, the social structure and personality perspective, and evolutionary theory. Section II includes three chapters looking at developmental and socialization processes across the life of the person. Reflecting the divisions of the research literature, these chapters focus on childhood, adolescence, and adulthood, respectively. Section III contains chapters on major topics that are associated primarily with the person, including self, language, social cognition, values and attitudes, and emotions. Section IV includes chapters on interpersonal phenomena, including attraction and relationships, small groups, social networks, and the impact of structural location on psychological processes. The last section includes chapters discussing the contributions of social psychology to topics of general interest to sociologists, including deviant behavior, intergroup relations, collective behavior and social movements, and the study of cultural variation.

On the whole, the process of inviting persons to contribute to the *Handbook* went smoothly because most of the persons I approached agreed to contribute. In some cases, they added the writing of a chapter for the *Handbook* to an already long list of commitments, and I am very grateful for their willingness to do so. I believe that in many cases, accepting my invitation reflects the person's sense that this is an important undertaking. Of the 38 contributors to this Handbook, 28 are new in the sense that they did not contribute to Cook, Fine, and

House. I invited more senior persons to collaborate with a younger scholar in writing their chapters, and many of them did so. I am delighted at the inclusion of so many members of the cohort recently entering the field.

In common with other recent Handbooks, this one has some limitations. Because it is a single volume, unlike Gilbert, Fiske, and Lindzey, some tough choices were necessary with regard to topics. Not included in this volume are chapter-length treatments of some important areas, including aging, ethnography, sexuality, social constructionism, and social psychology of organizations, of work. This volume does not include chapters on research methods. I considered this choice carefully, and I concluded that I wanted to use the pages to cover substantive topics, that there are other good sources of information on the methods *qua* methods. A second limitation arises from the page limit imposed on authors; the target was 40 manuscript pages, including references. This, of course, forced authors to omit some topics and abbreviate coverage of others.

In their preface, Rosenberg and Turner characterized sociological social psychology as "having reached the late adolescent stage of development; as such, it is heir to the various identity crises that so often characterize that developmental stage. This volume, we hope, will assist it in discovering and establishing that identity" (1981, p. xxxiv). Fourteen years later, in their Introduction, Cook, Fine, and House stated "we have grown as a field and become more integrated into the discipline" (1995, p. xii), and suggested that the field had reached early middle age. In light of the fact that only eight years has passed since then, and of the continued growth, emergence of new areas of work, and increasing integration captured in these pages, we cannot have grown much older. I foresee a long and healthy midlife.

Contents

PART I

THEORETICAL
PERSPECTIVES

CHAPTER 1

The Symbolic Interactionist Frame

SHELDON STRYKER

KEVIN D. VRYAN

THE IMAGERY, PREMISES, AND CONCEPTUALIZATIONS OF SYMBOLIC INTERACTIONISM

This chapter reviews symbolic interactionism, a framework or perspective composed of an imagery and conceptualizations in terms of which this imagery is expressed, as well as a set of initiating premises from which questions of social psychology can be pursued. The forerunners, early formulators, and current users share in important degree elements of the framework; they also in important degree differ in their imagery of, language describing, and premises about human beings, society, the relation of society and human beings, and the nature of human action and interaction. We begin our review by discussing underlying commonalities of most who see their social psychological work as stemming from symbolic interactionism. We hold for later discussion that differentiates social psychologists sharing the underlying commonalities.*

Imagery

From the perspective of symbolic interactionism, *society* is a web of communication or interaction, the reciprocal influence of persons taking each other into account as they act.

---

*Inevitably, this chapter draws heavily on the authors' previous work (esp. Stryker, 1981), not departing from that work simply for the sake of being different. It reflects, however, an updating of that prior work through substantive changes in ideas, the existence of a second author, and changes in the relevant literature.

SHELDON STRYKER AND KEVIN D. VRYAN • Department of Sociology, Indiana University, Bloomington, Indiana 47405

Handbook of Social Psychology, edited by John Delamater. Kluwer Academic/Plenum Publishers, New York, 2003.

Interaction is *symbolic*, proceeding in terms of meanings persons develop in interaction itself. The environment of action and interaction of humans is symbolically defined. Persons interact using symbols developed in their interaction, and they act through the communication of these symbols. Society is a term summarizing such interaction; subparts of society designate the settings in which interaction takes place. In this image, social life is a thoroughly dynamic process. Neither society nor its subparts exist as static entities; rather, these are continuously created and recreated as persons act toward one another. Social reality is a flow of events involving multiple persons. Just as society derives from the social process, so do people: both take on meanings that emerge in and through social interaction. Since both derive from the social process, neither society nor the individual possess reality that is prior to or takes precedence over the other. Society, as a web of interaction, creates persons; but the actions of persons create, through interaction, society. Society and person are two sides of the same coin, neither existing except as they relate to one another.

The symbolic capacity of humans implies they have minds and think, they manipulate symbols internally. They can think about themselves and in so doing come to have a self both shaped by the social process and entering into the social process. Thinking occurs in the form of internal conversation making use of symbols that develop out of the social process. Mind and self arise in response to interruptions in the flow of activities—or problems—and involve formulating and selecting among possible courses of action to resolve the problems. Choice is part of the human condition, its content contained in the subjective experience of the person emerging in and through the social process. Consequently, in order to comprehend human behavior, sociology must come to terms with the subjective experience of persons studied and incorporate that experience into accounts of their behavior. Part of that subjective experience, important for choices made, is the experience of self.

This imagery contains the idea that, individually and collectively, humans are active and creative, not only responders to external environmental forces. The environments in which they act and interact are symbolic environments; the symbols attaching to human and non-human environments are produced in interaction and can be manipulated in the course of interaction; thought can be used to anticipate the effectiveness of alternatives for action intended to resolve problems; and choice among alternative courses of action is a feature of social conduct. Thus, human social behavior is at least in degree indeterminate as a matter of principle (and not incomplete knowledge), since neither the course nor the outcomes of social interaction are completely predictable from factors and conditions that precede that interaction.

Premises*

As Snow (2001, p. 368) observes, a wide variety of persons who see their work as symbolic interactionist accept Blumer's (1969, pp. 2–6) specification of the three basic premises or principles of the frame. This appears to be true for those who accept the methodological dicta (see below) Blumer takes as necessary implications of those premises and those who, like the authors of this chapter, do not believe his methodological dicta are necessitated by the

---

*Three "versions" of the premises are provided because they differ in an important respect. For Blumer, the premises are what *define* symbolic interactionism, Stryker's premises reflect what persons presenting themselves as symbolic interactionists have in common, while Snow's cover the range of ideas in the collective work of contemporary interactionism.

premises. The three premises* on which symbolic interactionism rests—that is, the principles that are of defining significance for the frame—are, according to Blumer: (1) human beings act toward things—physical objects, other humans, categories of humans, institutions, ideals, activities of others, and situations encountered—on the basis of the meanings that the things have for them; (2) meanings arise in the process of interaction between people, that is, the meanings of things are social products growing out of how persons act toward one another with regard to the things; and (3) the use of meanings occurs through a process of interpretation in which actors communicate with themselves, selecting, checking, regrouping, transforming, and using meanings to form and guide their actions and interactions in situations in which they find themselves.

Stryker (1988), drawing on Blumer's treatment, gives these premises a somewhat different, albeit closely related, cast. He asserts that the premises shared among symbolic interactionists are: (1) an adequate account, whether explanation or simply understanding, of human behavior must incorporate the point of view of actors engaged in the behavior; (2) social interaction—the social process in Mead's terms—is fundamental, with both self and social structure emergent from interaction; and (3) persons' *reflexivity*, their responses to themselves, link larger social processes to the interactions in which they engage.

Believing Blumer's three principles do not adequately describe the tenets of the symbolic interactionist frame because they fail to explicitly articulate ideas implicit in them, Snow (2001) suggests a broader, more inclusive set of four "cornerstone" principles that better embrace the range of work symbolic interactionists do. By going beyond identifying meaning and interpretation as the orienting concerns of symbolic interactionism, Snow contends this set is not subject to criticisms levied at Blumer's conception of the frame (e.g., by Fine, 1992; Huber, 1973; Stryker, 1988).

The first and most basic of the set is the principle of interactive determination, asserting that understanding objects of analysis (self, identities, roles, organizational practices, etc.) cannot be achieved fully by considering only qualities intrinsic to them. Rather, understanding requires that the interactional contexts ("web of relationships") in which they are embedded be considered as well. The priority accorded this principle reflects Snow's argument that it is required to fully appreciate the remaining three principles, that the meaning and implications of other principles of symbolic interactionism result importantly from the interactional contexts in which they are embedded and from which they emerge.

The remaining members of Snow's symbolic interactionist principles are symbolization, emergence, and human agency. The principle of symbolization indicates that events, conditions, artifacts, individuals, aggregations of individuals, and other features of people's environments take on meanings and become objects for persons that elicit feelings and actions. He notes that this principle is the heart of Blumer's conception of symbolic interactionism and is typically taken as the focal concern of the framework. However, he asserts, too heavy an emphasis on the generation and imputation of meanings and on related interpretive processes can give rise to two related errors: seeing symbolization as always problematic, and seeing persons as continuously involved in trying to make sense of their worlds. Both errors fail to recognize how often symbols and meanings reflect cultural and organizational contexts. Otherwise stated, Snow's assertion is that symbolization, meanings, and interpretations are often givens in interaction embedded in social and cultural structures.

Nevertheless, symbolization is often at least in degree problematic, and Snow's principle of emergence focuses attention on the side of social life in which it is. When habit does

---

*Blumer terms these premises "simple," but they are complex in their implications.

not guide behavior, when social change makes previously operative meanings rooted in existing social and cultural contexts insufficient or ineffective in dealing with issues arising in interaction, new cognitive and affective states as well as new states of social relationships can give rise to new symbolizations. As Snow notes, these emergent new meanings and interpretations can depart from, challenge, and potentially transform existing structures and cultures.

The principle of human agency attends to humans as active and willful players constructing their lines of action. Not necessarily dismissive of structural and cultural constraints, symbolic interactionists tend to see such constraints as circumstances human actors take into account rather than determinants of lines of action. This formulation opens the way to viewing constraints as variably effective in closing off or in enabling particular lines of action—in short, as under some circumstances effectively determining or precluding actions and under other circumstances being of minimal import with respect to actions. As Snow states the matter: structural and cultural constraints and the behaviors they prescribe are sometimes taken for granted and routinized, and when they are the issue of agentic action fade into the background. When, however, the taken for granted and routinized are disrupted, the agency comes to the foreground as persons seek corrective or remedial actions.

Neither Stryker nor Snow see their descriptions of the frame as incompatible with Blumer's statement of its three premises. The former, who has strenuously rejected the methodological inferences Blumer draws from these meta-theoretical premises (see Stryker, 1980, 1988, and the discussion of these inferences below), finds the premises a reasonable statement of what symbolic interactionists can agree to. Snow sees his elaboration of the principles of symbolic interactionism as at least implicitly in Blumer's premises.

Conceptualizations

The symbolic interactionist imagery and underlying premises described above incorporate many of the concepts of the framework. Central is *meaning*, conceptualizations of which begin with the social act, behavior of at least two persons taking each other into account in the process of resolving some issue or problem. Social acts occur over time, and so allow the appearance of gestures, parts of a social act that indicate other parts of the act still to come. Vocal sounds, facial expressions, bodily movements, clothing, and so forth allow actors to anticipate one another's further actions; they are gestures. Gestures implying the "same" future behavior to those emitting and those perceiving them are *significant symbols*. When symbolized, things, ideas, and relationships between things and ideas enter people's experience as objects whose meanings, developing from social interaction, become their social reality. These meanings may not be identical among participants in social acts, but human communication and interaction presuppose the existence of sufficiently shared meanings.

As anticipations of the future course of acts, symbols underwrite plans for action, organizing behavior with reference to what they symbolize. To interact with others in a coherent, organized way, meanings need to be at least tentatively assigned to the situations in which persons find themselves and to the parts of those situations. Without such *definitions of the situation*, behavior is likely to be random or disorganized. Tentative definitions may hold indefinitely, or they may be revised as interaction unfolds and early definitions prove insufficient to allow the interaction to proceed in a satisfactory manner.

In general, and from the point of view of those involved in them, the most relevant aspects of situations requiring definition are who or what persons—self and other(s)—in the situation are, and what the situation of action itself may be. Defining the situation itself imposes limits on the kinds of people that can enter them, and in that sense, has primary import. Perhaps most often institutional parameters and the physical locations characteristic of these—is the table around which people are located in a seminar room at a university or in a dining room in a home?—are basic to emergent definitions. But institutions and physical locations allow great variation in the kinds of people entering them—the seminar room may be the scene of a dissertation defense or a discussion in an undergraduate honors class; the family dining table may be scene of a Thanksgiving dinner or a family conference about what to do about a wayward family member—and specifying the point or purpose of interaction may be critical to how interactants define themselves and others in particular situations.

Typically, others in the situation are defined by locating them in recognized social categories of actors representing the kinds of persons it is possible to be in a society: male or female, young or old, employed or unemployed, parent or child. Locating others in this way provides cues to their behavior in the form of expectations on the basis of which an actor can organize his/her own behavior with reference to the others. Expectations attached to social categories are *roles*.* Often situations allow or even require locating others in more than a single category and so open the possibility that conflicting expectations of others emerge and no clear means of organizing responses are available. Similarly, defining oneself in a situation involves locating oneself in socially recognized categories, and can involve locating oneself in multiple categories, with comparable consequences.

To respond reflexively to oneself by classifying and defining who one is, is to have a *self*. The meaning of self, like the meaning of any significant symbol, develops in and through interaction, and self, like any significant symbol, implies a plan of action. This is not to say that all social behaviors are to be understood as self-directed: much social behavior is based on habit (e.g., Camic, 1986) and ritual (e.g., Goffman, 1967), and self enters only when behavior becomes problematic for one reason or another. Nor is it to say that self-awareness is always present in social interaction: the effects of self-processes below the level of awareness may well have substantial impact on social behavior.

Role-taking refers to a process by which persons anticipate responses of others, in effect putting themselves in the place of others to see the world as they do. Prior experience with those others, knowledge of the social categories in which they are located, and symbolic cues emerging in interaction provide tentative definitions and expectations that are validated and/or reshaped in interaction. Role-taking permits anticipating and monitoring the consequences for interaction of one's own actions, and allows the redirection of those actions as useful or necessary. Interaction, sometimes predominately, also reflects *role-making* (Turner, 1962), modifying or creating roles by devising performances responsive to roles imputed to others. Role-making occurs when roles lack concreteness or consistency but actors must nevertheless organize their behavior on the assumption that they are unequivocal.

Especially in complex, highly differentiated societies, meanings are not likely to be shared in detail by parties to interaction, and indeed meanings held by some may contradict meanings held by others. To the extent that meanings are not shared, inaccuracy in role-taking and difficulty in role-making are likely to occur, complicating social interaction. Implied in these assertions is that smooth and cooperative relationships do not necessarily

---

*Many interactionists avoid the language of "role," believing the term implies fixed, static normative demands for behavior belied by the fluidity and creativeness of ongoing social life. The concept nevertheless is implied in interactionist work and provides a useful way of visualizing the link between social structure and social person central to some contemporary interactionist theory (see below).

follow from accurate role-taking or from role-making processes; conflict may well be sharpened by or result from accuracy.*

THE FOCUS OF THIS CHAPTER

Generally, treatments of symbolic interactionism use the language of "symbolic interaction *theory*." Conventional, that language promises something other than is delivered here. As our chapter title announces, our topic is a theoretical *framework* or *perspective*, a set of ideas about some part of the social world, about what that part of the world consists of and how it is made up, about how to investigate that part of the world. Some view symbolic interactionism as a perspective or framework underlying sociology in general (e.g., see Blumer, 1969; Maines, 2001). While there is some justification for this view, we discuss symbolic interactionism as a set of ideas especially applicable to a sociological social psychology, defined broadly as the study of the interplay between society and individual.[†] Further, some who see their work as symbolic interactionist disdain the objective of achieving theoretical generalizations about the relations of society and individual, questioning—even denying—the ability of scholars to produce objective knowledge. Perhaps most (including those working from versions of the frame stemming from very different epistemological and methodological positions[‡]) take the ultimate task of sociology and social psychology to be the development and test of theory. In this chapter, we do not discuss in detail interactionist work that rejects theoretical development as its goal.

The foregoing implies an important but often ignored distinction between "theory" and "theoretical framework" (or "perspective").[¶] The distinction is between a set of ideas intended as an explanation of some particular aspect of the empirical social world (theory) and the imagery, premises, and conceptualizations underlying that explanation (theoretical framework). Or, to use the slightly different and expanded terms of an earlier treatment of symbolic interactionism (Stryker, 1981, p. 27, footnote 3): "A theory, in a technical sense, is a set of propositions about some part of the empirical world specifying how this part presumably works, emerging from a set of assumptions or postulates and from a set of concepts used to describe the part of the world the theory purports to explain, and open to checking against empirical observations of that world."

This does not imply the lesser import of an underlying frame. There are virtually unlimited ways of viewing the empirical social world, and without some frame or another, a researcher faces a potentially bewildering range of possibilities. Indeed, to proceed without at least an implicit frame is a literal impossibility. The imagery, premises, and conceptualizations making up a theoretical frame give direction to inquiry. In short, a frame precedes theorization, suggesting some social phenomena in need of explanation, providing a sense of

---

*A persistent criticism of symbolic interactionism through the years refers to its ostensible inability to deal with conflict in social relationships and interaction. That criticism rests on a failure to understand these points as well as a simplistic view of the concept of meaning.

†"Society" here is a gloss for all relatively stable patterns of social (joint) interaction and relationships, and incorporating close examination of micro-social processes (Stryker, 2001a).

‡See, for example, the individual essays by Anselm Strauss (1994, pp. 3–8), Sheldon Stryker (1994, pp. 9–20), and Carl Couch (1994, pp. 21–34) in Volume 16 of *Studies in Symbolic Interaction*.

¶Contemporary recognition of this distinction and its import, coming from opposite poles of the sociological spectrum, can be found in Maines (2001) and Jasso (2001).

what is relevant and important to observe, and offering ideas about how concepts may interrelate to form an explanation of the phenomena of interest.

Frameworks are necessarily partial in focus. Being explicit about a frame underlying an inquiry has the virtue of revealing the strengths of the frame in generating theory and research. Equally important, it reveals the limitations of the frame by informing us about what is outside the frame's focus and, therefore, perhaps overlooked or discounted in its problem formulation, conceptualizations, and explanations, as well as the empirical evidence it pursues. There is another virtue in being explicit about the theoretical frame underlying specific inquiries: a frame can serve to tie individual theories together. Empty of an understanding of the frame joining individual theories, the latter are likely to develop on an ad hoc basis, in forms particular to the unique character of the empirical events being theorized, and thus limited in their more general meaning and significance.*

Frameworks are not themselves directly subject to empirical test, and so cannot be said to be true or false. Rather, they are to be judged by their fertility in producing theories consistent with empirical evidence. A framework that produces no empirically testable and ultimately tested theories has no value for sociology or social psychology, for we will never know if such a framework represents our creative imaginations or the social life we seek to understand. There are, indeed, testable and, in reasonable degree, tested theories that derive from a symbolic interactionist framework.† Historically, however, symbolic interactionists have spent more of their energies debating the virtues of preferred variations and providing illustrative applications of the frame, rather than in deriving and testing explanatory theories. More recently, there has been considerable movement toward correcting that imbalance.

There are a variety of perspectives in use among sociologists doing social psychology;‡ why should this volume devote a chapter to symbolic interactionism? The frame developed largely in the work of sociologists, and historically it has been prominent among frames used by sociological social psychologists. Of greater import, however, the frame brings into focus the unique contributions of sociology to social psychology: distinctive and valuable theoretical understanding of the impact of individuals' locations in patterned social settings and relationships on social interactions, social constructions, and social persons,¶ as well as the reciprocal impact of interactions, constructions, and individuals on social settings and relationships.

We continue our treatment of symbolic interactionism by examining the philosophic context from which the frame emerged, paying particular attention to a philosopher–psychologist, George Herbert Mead, whose writings** undergird all subsequent developments of the frame. We next attend to scholars who moved what Mead had to say into sociology and were, in that sense, early proponents of the frame, paying particular attention to Robert Park, Herbert Blumer,

---

*It seems to us that contemporary psychological social psychology and the Group Processes field tend to proliferate special theories of a wide range of phenomena whose relationship to one another remains relatively underdeveloped.

†Examples include the labeling theory of deviance (e.g., Lemert, 1951; Becker, 1963), identity theory (e.g., Stryker, 1968, 1980), and affect control theory (Heise, 1979).

‡Apart from the frames treated as "Theoretical Orientations" in this volume, an earlier treatment of "sociological social psychology" (Rosenberg and Turner, 1981) included chapters on social exchange theory, reference group theory, and role theory, as well as symbolic interactionism. More recent treatments have included group processes and social structure and personality along with symbolic interactionism (Stryker, 2001a).

¶In our judgment, if sociologists do not deal with the impact of social structures on social psychological processes, no one else will. The language used here, "social person," is, from the perspective of symbolic interactionism, redundant: the person is necessarily social.

**Actually, Mead wrote very little for publication. Much of his thought appears in volumes of his lectures edited and published by his students (e.g., Mead, 1934).

and Manford Kuhn. Then we turn to presenting contemporary variations in the frame, concluding with a discussion of the mutual relevance of its variants.

THE PHILOSOPHIC CONTEXT OF
SYMBOLIC INTERACTIONISM

"Symbolic interactionism" is a term invented by Herbert Blumer (1937) to describe a set of ideas largely developed in the post-World War I context of the University of Chicago's Department of Sociology. Strongly resonating with the ideas of 18th century Scottish Moral Philosophers, including Adam Smith, Adam Ferguson, and David Hume (see Bryson, 1945), symbolic interactionism has been more directly influenced by the peculiarly American philosophy of *pragmatism*.*

Maines (2000, pp. 2218–2219) offers a succinct summary of the main ideas of pragmatism, and suggests their sources in a neo-Hegelian emphasis on dialectic processes that rejected dualistic views placing mind in opposition to body, the subjective in opposition to the objective, and the individual in opposition to the social; an evolutionary, Darwinian, emphasis on emergence of new forms through variations in the old, differentially adaptive and adjusted to changes in environmental circumstances; and a behavioristic emphasis on understanding and reality as rooted in persons' conduct. Among the main ideas are:

> First, humans are active, creative organisms, empowered with agency rather than passive responders to stimuli. Second, human life is a dialectical process of continuity and discontinuity and therefore is inherently emergent. Third, humans shape their worlds and thus actively produce the conditions of freedom and constraint. Fourth, subjectivity is not prior to social conduct but instead flows from it. Minds (intelligence) and selves (consciousness) are emergent from interaction and exist dialectically as social and psychical processes rather than only as psychic states …. Eighth, human nature and society exist in and are sustained by symbolic communication and language. (Maines, 2000, pp. 2218–2219)

Of particular import for the ways in which the symbolic interactionist perspective developed were the late 19th-century and early 20th-century works of William James, John Dewey, and, most important of all, George Herbert Mead. James (1890), essentially neglected by sociologists given to symbolic interactionist ideas through about two thirds of the 20th century, was "rediscovered" in the last third by way of a key idea that is of strategic significance in contemporary formulations of those ideas. Sharing the then current view of humans as creatures of instinct, James argued that instincts are transitional and modifiable through the development of habits providing memories of prior experience, pointing to the impact of society (as well as biology) on human behavior. He saw human experience as a continuous flow rather than a sequence of discrete states, and he presented an analysis of consciousness as a continuous process. Emerging from consciousness is self, all that individuals can call their own, including self as knower (the *I*) and self as known (the *Me*). James continued his analysis by distinguishing four distinct types of self: material, spiritual, social, and

---

*Our discussion of pragmatism and pragmatic philosophers is selective, the selection a function of our immediate needs in presenting the symbolic interactionist frame. For a brief, excellent introduction to pragmatism and a bibliography dealing with the relations of pragmatism and sociology more generally, see Maines (2000); see also Shalin (1986) and Joas (1993).

pure ego. The social self, in particular, has an empirical source in the recognition given the person by others. Indeed, James asserted that a person:

> ... has as many social selves as there are individuals who recognize him.... But as the individuals who carry the images fall naturally into classes, we may practically say that he has as many different social selves as there are distinct *groups* of persons about whose opinions he cares. (James, 1890, p. 294; italics in original)

In this passage, James prepared the way for viewing the self as multifaceted and as the product of a heterogeneously organized society, a view that, as suggested, has been neglected (and so unexploited) in interactionist theories incorporating self until recently (see below).

Fundamental to Dewey's pragmatism is a view of mind as instrumental, itself emerging from his emphasis on evolution involving a process of human adjustment to environmental conditions. Mind (thinking) arises in that adjustment process (Dewey, 1930). Thinking or

> ... deliberation is a dramatic rehearsal (in imagination) of various competing lines of action.... It is an experiment in making various combinations of selected elements ... to see what the resultant action would be like if it were entered upon. (1930, p. 190)

Mind, according to Dewey, arises through conduct, emerging from actions taken to resolve problems. Raising the question of what constitutes a "stimulus" to behavior (Dewey, 1896), he argued that stimuli are defined in the context of action and neither exist prior to nor are causes of action, for example, a needle in a haystack cannot be a stimulus to behavior outside the context of someone searching for it. "The world that impinges on our senses is a world that ultimately depends on the character of the activity in which we are engaged and changes when that activity is altered" (Stryker, 1980, p. 26). This argument makes action fundamental to human behavior, social or not, and underlies Strauss' (1994, p. 4) assertion that the interactionism of its University of Chicago-linked practitioners is grounded in Dewey's (and Mead's) theory of action, a theory that describes a sequence of action: ongoing, blocked, deliberation about alternative possibilities of action, and then continued action.

Mead was Dewey's contemporary and collaborator at the Universities of Michigan and then Chicago. However, he moved their jointly developed ideas in ways that made him the pre-eminent philosophic precursor of symbolic interactionism. His was a creative synthesis that, indeed, drew heavily upon Darwinian evolution and pragmatism but included the idea from German Romantic philosophers such as Fichte and Hegel that persons, as selves, determine what the world is for them. From the psychologist Wilhelm Wundt, he took the concept of gesture, developing through that concept the idea that gestures were the mechanisms through which mind, self, and society emerged from social interaction. And from the work of the behavioristic psychologist John Watson, he regarded the psychological principle of reinforcement as sound.

Incorporating the natural selection theoretical notion of the necessity of adaptation to ensure survival, Mead saw evolution as bringing into existence the mind and self that characterize human beings, and he argued that what held for the species held for individual members of the species. Individuals, that is, deal with whatever may block their ongoing behavior by exercising mind, internally manipulating symbols to try out alternative ways to get around or otherwise rid themselves of those blockages. Humans can also respond to themselves reflexively—adopting perspectives that allow them to step outside of themselves, so to speak, and see themselves as objects—in order to react to whatever they may be doing in the ways they can react to other persons or things. In short, given that they have selves, they can treat themselves as objects and they can communicate with themselves. These distinctive human possibilities—mind and self—Mead saw as having their source in ongoing social processes of interaction in which people need one another in order to build solutions to problems that face them. Actions take time to occur, and early stages of actions—one's own as well as those of others—can be used to predict the later stages yet to occur. The mutual need for others as resources in arriving at effective problem solutions, he argued, implies that people must take others into account as they construct solutions, and they do so by taking the attitude or role of others, anticipating these others' responses to potential lines of action. Taking others into account is made possible by communicating with these others, and people communicate by developing in and through interaction significant symbols, gestures whose meaning—implications for the future course of their action—is shared in reasonable measure, thus making predicting one another's ongoing acts possible. Cooperation based on communication via significant symbols is a requisite for human survival.

Three implications worth noting are contained in the foregoing: (1) Organized society is a continuous process of routinization or institutionalization of solutions to collective problems, and society undergoes continuous change as new problems emerge in a physical or social environment and are dealt with by participants. (2) Both mind and self are intrinsically social phenomena. This is because both come into being—indeed, can only exist—in and through the process of communicating via significant symbols. (3) Social life is modeled on scientific method, that is, on systematically examining proposed solutions to problems until a successful solution is found; and the actor is modeled on the scientist conducting an experiment.* This model of the actor tends to neglect affect or emotion in human behavior, a neglect currently being addressed by interactionists.

Thus, for Mead, social interaction or process is fundamental, and from that interaction or process emerge both society and self. Indeed, society is for him an ongoing social process writ large, and the basic dictum of his social psychology is to start with that ongoing social process. The self, as an emergent from that social process, must reflect—and indeed, it must incorporate—that process. It does so most directly through the part of the self that Mead, recalling James, calls the *Me*, anticipated responses to oneself of what he called the "generalized other." Alternatively phrased, it is the organized attitudes or social roles of others with whom one interacts that become this part of self. The *Me* and the *I*, the other part of self, make up the person or personality as these develop via the social process. The *I* represents responses to the organized attitudes of others, and is used by Mead to deal with the spontaneity and creativity he believed to be an intrinsic part of human experience.† However, neither creativity nor spontaneity occur outside the social process. Social control, expressed through the *Me*, is a necessary condition for their appearance in action. In brief, social control and self-control are co-emergents from society. Finally, while the self is a product of society, the self, through an internal *I–Me* dialectic, continuously reacts to the society that shapes it. Consequently, society is never fixed; it is continuously being created and recreated. Social order and social change are together aspects of a larger social process.

---

*While this description resembles rational actor (or rational choice) theoretical models, a key difference is that these models assume an actor who has in hand a set of goals and means of achieving goals, while symbolic interactionists see both goals and means as emergents from interaction and subject to change in the course of interaction. Another distinction is that rational actor theorists adopt methodological individualism, while interactionists do not examine the individual in isolation from interactive and social contexts.

†Mead tended to a view of the *I* as pure impulse and essentially not further analyzable. An alternative view bringing spontaneity and creativity into the domain of social science is to view the *I* as the memory of former *Me*'s, that is, as the residue of prior social experience reacting to the other's expectations in the moment.

LINKAGES OF PRAGMATISM AND SOCIOLOGY: THE EARLY DEVELOPMENT OF SYMBOLIC INTERACTIONISM IN SOCIOLOGY

Not surprisingly, philosophic pragmatism had an early impact on American sociology. We will explore that impact through the work of two sets of sociologists, an earlier set comprised of Charles Horton Cooley, William Isaac Thomas, and Robert E. Park, and a somewhat later set comprised of Herbert Blumer, Everett Hughes, and Manford Kuhn. It is the work of these sociologists that brings us into the symbolic interactionism of modern sociology.*

The Early Set: Cooley, Thomas, Park

A contemporary of Dewey and Mead at the University of Michigan who was influenced by and influenced both (Miller, 1973, pp. xix–xx), Cooley began his academic career as an economist in the Department of Economics and Sociology and became a sociologist when offered an opportunity to teach in that field. His dissertation (Cooley, 1894) dealing with railroad transportation as a material link generating economic organization incorporated a discussion of communication as the "psychical" link generating social organization. That idea served as his prime bridge to sociology and social psychology. Indeed, his central sociological ideas all have a "psychical" quality.

The mental and subjective are, Cooley asserted, the special concern of sociology, for they are distinctively social. A person exists for another only in the latter's personal idea of the former. Society is a relation among personal ideas in one person's mind, as the contact and reciprocal influence of ideas having names (I, Peter, Deanna, etc.), and in another's mind as an equivalent similar set of ideas. Thus, the imaginations people have of one another are the solid facts of society (Cooley, 1902, pp. 26–27). While this conception of society may seem to require autobiography as the method of sociology, Cooley called for "sympathetic introspection," with the sociologist using sympathy (or empathy) to imagine the lives of persons studied.

Since persons exist in the observer's imagination, and since society is the imagination of a set of persons, persons and society are the distributive and collective aspects of the same thing, respectively—in Cooley's words, two sides of the same coin. Thus, a self cannot be distinct from others; it is a social product, defined and developed in social interaction. Specifically, it is the product of "the looking glass self," a process involving three main components: impressions we have of how we appear to others, impressions of these others' assessments of us, and our feelings (e.g., pride or shame) deriving from those imaginations. "We always imagine, and in imagining, share the judgments of the other mind" (Cooley, 1902, pp. 152–153).

Cooley held an organic conception of social life, seeing all aspects as linked just as all components of an organism are connected. Especially important, however, to self-development and to the ties people have to larger social organization are primary groups, defined by intimacy, face-to-face relations, and cooperation. Such groups form the social nature and ideals of a person and are the source of more complex relationships. He saw the groups that

---

*These two sets are highly selective, inadequate were we writing a history of symbolic interactionism but useful for the story we seek to tell in this chapter.

dominate childhood experience—family, play group, and neighborhood group—as most significant since childhood is the period when people are most open and plastic.*

Cooley's conception of society and others as existing only in a person's imagination may seem to imply an individualistic, idealistic, and subjectivist perspective on which a social psychology cannot be built. Indeed, Mead (1930; 1934, p. 224) took Cooley to task for what he termed the latter's "mentalism," which Mead saw as reducing social reality to the subjectivity of individual minds.† That charge is denied by Schubert (1998) who argues it does not hold since Cooley builds society into mind. More important, Cooley's work, relatively neglected (compared with Mead) by early symbolic interactionists, has won renewed attention because his sensitivity to affect as a defining element in self resonates with contemporary social psychology's interest in emotion.

"... (I)f men define situations as real, they are real in their consequences" (Thomas & Thomas, 1928, p. 572). This aphorism, the source of symbolic interactionism's prime—often misunderstood—methodological rule, is itself a major but not the sole reason for noting W. I. Thomas' contribution to forming this framework. With the pragmatists, Thomas took sociology's task to be examining the adjustive responses of people and groups to other people and groups. Adjustive responses occur in situations, objective circumstances in which persons and groups are embedded. The same objective circumstances, however, often do not lead to the same behavioral responses because subjective components of people's experience—definitions of the situation—intervene. The "total situation" that must be taken into account by analysts of persons' and groups' adjustive behaviors must include both the objective and verifiable situation *and* the situation as it is defined or interpreted by the persons and groups involved (Thomas, 1927; Thomas & Thomas, 1928).

As Volkart (1951) notes, Thomas shifted his conceptualization of the situation often.‡ In his classic study, with Znaniecki, of the adjustment of Polish peasant immigrants to their new lives in America, situations were characterized as involving values and attitudes:

> ... (1) the objective conditions under which the individual or society has to act, that is, the total-ity of values—economic, social, religious, intellectual, etc.—which at the given moment affect directly or indirectly the conscious status of the individual or the group, (2) the pre-existing atti-tudes of the individual or group which at the given moment have an actual influence upon his behavior, and (3) the definition of the situation, that is, the more or less clear conception of the conditions and consciousness of the attitudes. (Thomas & Znaniecki, 1918–1920, Vol. 1, p. 68)

However Thomas conceptualized the term, it invariably contained the dual reference to objective circumstances and subjective responses of persons and groups to those objective circumstances. In short, while some have used Thomas' concept of definition of the situation to deny the relevance of objective facts of social situations for the behavior of persons and groups, his own formulation of the idea does not support this view.

Though apparently seriously overlooked in critical appraisals of his foundational work on human ecology, there are clearly important elements of pragmatism in Robert E. Park's sociological perspective (Maines, 2001). Not generally seen as relevant to the development of symbolic interactionism, he becomes relevant through his central position on the faculty of

---

*Since Cooley's characterization of family, play group, and neighborhood as primary groups was developed, sociologists have been forced to recognize that primary *relations* are not necessarily present in these groups.

†A reading of Cooley shared by one of the present authors (Stryker, 1981) in an earlier chapter on the topic of symbolic interactionism.

‡Sociology has still not arrived at a generally accepted conceptualization of the situation. For a recent attempt to do so, see Seeman (1997).

the University of Chicago during its early development and by his influence on generations of sociologists through that position, as well as through his co-authorship of a classic text that helped shape the discipline of sociology in the United States (Park & Burgess, 1922). A student of William James at Harvard who studied for a short time with Georg Simmel in Germany, he taught at Chicago when Mead's influence there was strong. That influence was manifest in his insistence that communication was foundational to society and his further insistence that shared meaning both derived from interaction and was essential for communication. Accentuating his relevance is work that serves as a bridge between the social psychological writings of Mead and conceptions of social structure, with the concept of role playing a crucial aspect of the bridge. The following passage could serve as the introduction to some contemporary developments in symbolic interactionism.

> The conceptions which men form of themselves seem to depend upon their vocations, and in general upon the role they seek to play in communities and social groups in which they live, as well as upon the recognition and status which society accords them in these roles. (Park, 1955)

Bridges to the Recent Past and Present: Blumer, Kuhn, Hughes

Undoubtedly the single most influential voice shaping the sense of the symbolic interactionist perspective among most sociologists belongs to Herbert Blumer. In part, Blumer's influence reflects the fact that he inherited the University of Chicago's tradition of sociology and social psychology stemming from Mead. In part, it reflects his role as the strongest advocate for that position through a time—roughly, the 1930s through the 1960s—when it was superceded by an ascendant structural-functionalism that dominated sociology both intellectually and institutionally and was taken to deny fundamentals of the symbolic interactionist frame. Blumer's work maintained the pragmatic emphases on social change and social process, on the Dewey–Mead theory of action, and on the centrality of meaning and actors' definitions or interpretations in both individual and collective social behavior.[*] Further, Blumer articulated a symbolic interactionism containing strong humanistic elements, and so attracted sociologists who rejected a structural-functionalism they regarded as seeing humans as puppets of social structure and that was seen as "scientistic" as a by-product of that view.

Blumer believed that the symbolic interactionism he articulated was entirely consonant with Mead's thought (Blumer, 1980) and that it implied a set of methodological requirements.[†] With respect to his impact on the way in which symbolic interactionism as a social psychological framework has developed—our concern in this chapter—it is the methodological implications he drew from Mead that are most important.[‡] Blumer asserted that pursuing

---

[*] See Maines (2001), esp. Introduction to part I: "Theoretical Concerns" (pp. 31–35) and chapter 3. For diverse but mostly supportive views of Blumer's work, see "Special Issue on Herbert Blumer's Legacy" edited by Gary Alan Fine (*Symbolic Interaction 11*(1), Spring 1988).

[†] Blumer's more polemical methodological moments are exemplified in a book (1969) that incorporates a series of earlier publications. Some have pointed out that elsewhere Blumer was catholic in his methodological views (e.g., see Maines, 2001).

[‡] Maines (2001) makes a strong argument that Blumer's substantive work is important and has been grossly neglected. A clear distinction between a sociology and a social psychology is untenable, a division of labor reflected in this volume's focus on the latter justifies our focus on Blumer's influential methodological arguments vis-à-vis symbolic interactionism. It is only fair to note that Stryker (1980, 1988) has been and is strongly critical of those methodological arguments.

the goal of general, predictive theory in sociological research is futile given the centrality of meanings, and consequently of definitions and interpretations of the situations people find themselves in, for subjects' actions. He sees persons as actively and continuously constructing behaviors in the course of ongoing interaction itself, and he takes such perpetual construction as characteristic of all social life. Thus, the meanings, definitions, and interpretations basic to social interaction undergo continuous reformulation in the course of the interaction itself. They are emergent and subject to moment-to-moment change, and so do not have the generality required of theoretical concepts in terms of which predictive theories are developed. They do not and cannot represent the emergent meanings, definitions, and interpretations of actors constructing their lines of interaction. Blumer concludes from this argument that it is possible for sociologists to achieve after-the-fact understandings of social behavior that has occurred but cannot develop general theoretical explanations that predict social behavior, whether individual or collective.

This argument is metatheoretical, specifying a conceptual framework. As any framework, it has methodological consequences. First, it implies that sociologists waste their time when they undertake research that starts from an existing theory (since existing theory must use concepts that came before the new research) and that derives hypotheses anticipating outcomes of social behavior from existing theory. Second, it implies that a research method that does not involve direct examination of the empirical world—that does not focus directly on actors' meanings, definitions, and interpretations as these emerge in ongoing, naturally occurring interaction (e.g., experimental or survey methods)—cannot generate meaningful data and necessarily lacks validity. Third, it underwrites a denial of the value for sociology of mathematical and statistical manipulation of quantitative data, the argument being that such data are necessarily empty of the meanings that constitute the essential character of sociological phenomena. Fourth, it leads to minimizing the impact of social organization and social structure, at least within modern society, on social action, to seeing organization and structure as merely frames within which action takes place rather than as shaping action. Indeed, Blumer argues that seeking to link social behavior to elements of structure—role requirements, expectations, situational demands, and so forth—is inconsistent with recognizing that the human being is a constantly defining and interpreting creature.

Conventional sociological methodology and methods found wanting, Blumer proposes "exploration" and "inspection" as appropriate research methods. Exploration uses any ethical procedure that allows moving from a broad focus to a narrower understanding of how a problem of interest is to be posed, gathering appropriate data for pursuing this problem, and developing the conceptual tools that might be useful. It may involve, Blumer suggests, observation, interviewing, listening to conversations, life histories, letters, diaries, public records, and arranging for what today are called "focus groups" made up of people well-informed about the sphere of life being studied. In the process of attending to such materials, the researcher develops, tests, and revises images, beliefs, and conceptions of what is under scrutiny through direct observation, through posing questions sensitizing the researcher to new and different perspectives, and by recording observations that challenge working conceptions or that are odd and interesting but whose relevance is unclear.

Inspection is the procedure intended to meet the requirement of scientific analysis for identifying clear, discriminating analytic elements and isolating relationships between these elements. It aims to unearth generic relationships, sharpen the connotative reference of conceptions, and formulate theoretical propositions. Like exploration, inspection is a flexible procedure—imaginative, creative, free to change—and it involves a close, shifting examination of analytic elements used for analysis (e.g., integration), looking at analytic elements in different ways, from different angles, and with different questions in mind.*

Manford Kuhn's view of symbolic interactionism contrasts starkly with that of Blumer, and is close in spirit to the view underlying this chapter in that he aspired to precisely articulated theoretical generalizations and their rigorous test while using a symbolic interactionist frame (e.g., Kuhn & McPartland, 1954). To emphasize that aspiration and differentiate it from Blumer, he labeled his frame "self-theory." Agreeing with the pragmatic philosophers and sociologists who argued that social structure is created, maintained, and altered through symbolic interaction, he asserted that structure, once created, constrains further interaction. To implement that insight, he brought elements of role theory and reference group theory into his framework, adopting the former's conceptions of social structure as composed of networks of positions in structured relations among people and of role expectations as associated with these positions.

Emphasizing that the relation of role expectations and behavior is loose, Kuhn saw more determinacy in the relation of self, rather than role expectations, to behavior. He proposed that self be conceptualized as a plan of action, assimilating Mead's idea that self is an object and that objects are attitudes or plans of action. Indeed, precisely because self *is* a plan of action, it is the most significant object to be defined in a situation: to know an actor's self is to have the best available index of that actor's future behavior.

Central to Kuhn's theorizing is the concept of core self, a stable set of meanings attached to self providing stability to personality, continuity to interactions, and predictability to behavior. However, stability is relative. The role-taking process allows for creativity as does the self-control made possible by that process. Further, according to Kuhn, the self is comprised of a large variety of component parts, including status identifications, role expectations, preferences and avoidances, personal attributes and traits, self-enhancing evaluations, areas of threat to and vulnerability of self, and patterns of selection of reference groups. This complexity also admits slippage in the relation of social structure and self; the person is not a social automaton.

Defining self as plan of action, conceptualizing core self as having stability, and accepting Mead's equation of attitude and plan of action provided a rationale for the Twenty Statements Test (TST), measuring self-attitudes in response to the question "Who Am I?" Not particularly successful and at least partially discredited (Tucker, 1966), the failure of the particular instrument does not invalidate Kuhn's more general methodological stance. That stance, oriented to what Blumer called conventional science, calls for the development of general propositions from which specific hypotheses can be deduced and tested. If tests support the hypotheses, theory useful in explaining and predicting behavior in social interaction results. The road to explanatory and predictive theory is through sound measurement of the concepts embodied in general propositions with which the researcher begins. Clear, precise concepts are required for sound measurement. Kuhn sees no contradiction between the kinds of concepts entailed in symbolic interactionism and meeting the requirements of sound scientific measurement or developing general explanatory theories of social behavior subject to the test of rigorous empirical examination.

Everett Hughes' significance as a bridge from "founders" to contemporary symbolic interactionism can be presented succinctly. That significance stems not from a conceptual or theoretical contribution to the frame. It stems rather from his courses at the University of

---

*Exploration and inspection are clearly valuable tools for the development of concepts and theory, but fall short with respect to the task of testing theory.

Chicago in which graduate students interested in symbolic interactionist ideas became convinced of the value of fieldwork in pursuing those ideas.

THE SYMBOLIC INTERACTIONIST FRAME: VARIATIONS*

The contrasting views of Blumer and Kuhn, both deriving from earlier writings of Mead and other pragmatic philosophers, demonstrate the obvious: no single version of the frame guides the work of all who identify as symbolic interactionists. The premises reviewed above set general boundaries for dealing with social psychological questions. However, each leaves open important issues with respect to what to study, objectives of such study, how to conceptualize what is studied and its constituent parts, and methods by which topics of interest are studied.[†]

The Goals of Interactionist Analyses

One contemporary derivative of the frame, briefly referred to below, rejects the possibility of building general, predictive, research-based social psychological theory. As this suggests, there are important differences among symbolic interactionists in the goals of their work. For some, the continuously constructed character of interaction and the continuously emergent nature of society and self from interaction imply that social organization and self lack the constancy necessary to produce useful general concepts and to allow theory developed in one research project to be applied in later research. What these do imply to them is that social life is unpredictable and a goal of developing and testing general theories of social psychological phenomena cannot succeed. We can only describe interaction as it occurs and understand particular social events after their occurrence. Others argue that there is sufficient constancy and continuity in social life to warrant reasonable empirical generalizations going beyond particular situations of interaction. Implied is that concepts useful in understanding one situation can be useful for understanding other situations and, therefore, it is reasonable to seek to develop and test predictive explanations of social behavior (Heise, 1986; Kuhn, 1964; Stryker, 1980). These two very different senses of symbolic interactionist goals are in turn linked to a number of other variations.

Process versus Structure

Interactionists vary in the degree to which they introduce social structural concepts into their analyses. Some hold that actors' interpretations and definitions of situations, specified in the premises as powerful sources of lines of action, continuously undergo reformulation in the immediate situation of interaction. The fluidity claimed for definitions of the situation is extended to social life in general, suggesting that interaction may be reasonably described only as it unfolds. An important consequence of such views is that the relevance for social

---

*Much of this section is adapted from Stryker (2000).
[†]A similar set of dimensions is discussed in Vryan, Adler, and Adler (forthcoming) in relation to symbolic interactionist treatments of identity.

psychological analyses of concepts representing social structure and concepts imported from prior analyses of interaction is downplayed (Glaser & Strauss, 1967). Others believe including social structure in the study of social psychological processes is essential to the purposes of a sociological social psychology (Stryker & Burke, 2000). Conceptualizing social structure as relatively stable patterns of social interaction and social relationships, they see these patterns as constraints on actors' definitions, making for enough stability or continuity in definitions to justify using structural concepts in social psychological analyses.*

Whose Perspective?

Some argue that only perspectives of participants in social interaction are relevant to understanding their interaction, that introducing the perspective of sociological observers of the interaction prevents understanding. Consequently, they seek to minimize or eliminate the voices of observers in description and analysis, privileging accounts provided by those who are studied. Others argue that actors' definitions must be considered when seeking to explain their behavior but do not in themselves constitute explanations (Burke, 1991).

The Significance of Self

Interactionists vary in how they understand the relation of self to social structure and social interaction. For some, self is an "uncaused cause." That is, self, initially an emergent from society, becomes over time free of the constraints of social structure and a more rather than less independent source of social behavior (McCall & Simmons, 1978). For others, social organization and structure, born of prior interaction and the residual of that interaction, serves to initiate processes that result in persons with selves built in its image. Self is thus seen as a conduit through which prior organization and structures reproduce themselves rather than a source of social behavior (Goffman, 1974). Closely related are differences in the degree to which self is taken to be the source of creativity and the novel in social life, the degree to which creativity and novelty in social life are deemed highly probable rather than simply possible, and the degree to which social life is continuously constructed anew or reproduces previously existing patterns.

Phenomenology or Behaviorism?

The intellectual heritage of symbolic interactionism contains two parts in tension with, if not strongly opposed to, one another. Some emphasize the behavioristic part of that heritage and so focus on how concerted lines of social action are constructed through interaction, with little attention to persons' internal symbolic processes (Couch, Saxton, & Katovich, 1986; McPhail & Rexroat, 1979). Others concentrate attention on the internal, subjective worlds of the actors they study.

---

*"Structure" has diverse meanings for sociologists, ranging from macro-level social structure external to particular interactions (e.g., Stryker, 1980), to the structure of interactions themselves (e.g., Goffman, 1974), to intrapsychic cognitive structures that are formed in and affect interaction (e.g., Burke & Reitzes, 1981).

Methodological Predilections

While historically methodological predilections and preferences have been of perhaps primary importance in distinguishing among work done by scholars identified as holding a symbolic interactionist perspective, these seem to be becoming less important with the passage of time. Nevertheless, for some, the ideas of symbolic interactionism require a commitment to qualitative methods of research. Short of that extreme, many symbolic interactionists hold that the most useful methods of pursuing such ideas are naturalistic, that is, their strong preference is for ethnography, participant observation, and unstructured intensive interviewing. One consequence of this preference is that the locus of research tends to be small sets of interactants; another is that analytic procedures tend to be qualitative. Other interactionists accept the utility of a wider range of social science methods (Heise, 1979), including the quantification of data and statistical analyses. In practice, their method of choice will often be the sample survey and the quantitative analysis methods appropriate to survey data.

The variations are clearly not independent of one another. Those emphasizing the fluidity of social interaction and the situated character of definitions are also likely to emphasize the shifting character of social organization and structure, the absence of constraints on self in organizing behavior, creativity and novelty in social life, the way perspectives of observers contaminate descriptions of social interaction, the phenomenologies of actors, the irrelevance of a priori theory and conceptualizations, description and understanding as the goals of symbolic interactionist efforts, and qualitative research as the way to achieving these goals. Similarly, the opposing poles of the variations tend to hang together.

Our discussion of variations has posed these as stark contrasts that speak more to the history of the framework than to its present, more to the extreme stances characteristic of earlier arguments than to positions taken by contemporary interactionists. The labels "Chicago school" and "Iowa school" are commonly used in the literature describing approaches within symbolic interactionism and are associated with, respectively, qualitative methods and emphases on process and fluidity on the one hand, and, on the other hand, quantitative methods and emphases on structure and constancy. While historically there are bases for such distinctions, they represent rhetorical positions infrequently found in extreme form in the empirically based work of interactionists. Logic does not compel either-or choices among the poles of the various continua discussed. Stability and change, and social construction and reproduction, are all observable features of social life. Phenomenologies of persons, including their selves and their definitions, impact their behaviors, but phenomenologies are in part consequences of people's locations in social structures. Social life may be in principle "undetermined," but both self and social structure do constrain behavior. If these assertions hold, generalized concepts are potentially useful and general theory can be formulated and tested. Work using either qualitative methods or quantitative methods can be strategic in achieving this goal. Indeed, many symbolic interactionists have moved to positions recognizing the utility of work that at an earlier point they were likely to define as in opposition to their own and to dismiss for that reason.*

Still, current work stemming from the symbolic interactionist frame reflects the past. Scholars have described the varieties of this work variously, and have offered anywhere from

---

*Perhaps this is, on a balance theory principle, because they now share common opposition from those who dismiss theoretical generalization as a meaningful possibility of their work.

2–15 variants (Reynolds, 1993, p. 73).* Here we discuss in detail two general forms—traditional symbolic interactionism and social structural interactionism—adding a very brief comment on a third form, postmodern symbolic interactionism, that remains largely undiscussed because it rejects the possibilities of achieving the objective knowledge of and theoretical generalizations about social life it has been the purpose of this chapter to advance. The label "traditional" intends only that the variations to which it refers are largely in the tradition of Blumer. The label "social structural" intends to convey only that variations it subsumes give greater emphasis to the role of social structures in constraining and facilitating social psychological events and processes than the more traditional variants.

Traditional Symbolic Interactionism

There are two somewhat distinctive strands of traditional symbolic interactionism. To a considerable extent, the earlier discussion of imagery characterizes both of these strands. To a lesser extent, the same may be said of the earlier discussion of concepts—a major exception is the concept of role, objected to because it is taken to imply fixed social structural properties inconsistent with the favored emphasis on process. The strands also share a methodological preference for small-scale studies using ethnographic, observational, and intensive interviewing techniques and qualitative methods of analysis. What differentiates the two is basically whether a commitment to developing generalizable theoretical explanations of social psychological processes and events exists. Work in the first strand tends to follow Blumer's methodological dicta. Such work frequently is used to illustrate a concept previously developed in the work of others or to present and illustrate a "new" concept deemed useful in achieving understanding of the situation being examined. Often, the situation examined is relatively unusual or exotic, and is deliberately approached without a priori conceptualization, rationalized by reference to a grounded theoretical approach (Glaser & Strauss, 1967). Typically, such work exhibits little or no interest in whether what is learned generalizes to other situations or other interactions. That is, work done from this version of the symbolic interactionist frame appears to take as its task thorough description of the situation being examined in its full particularities and achieving an understanding of the processes occurring in that situation. A contemporary argument for the value of work in the first strand of traditional symbolic interactionism can be found in Harris (2001), who argues that giving voice to the subjects of research and focusing on the particularities of their definitions and interpretations in developing accounts of their behavior is the distinctive mission of symbolic interactionist research. Whatever the intent of work done in this vein, if done well it can serve the ends of achieving theoretical generalization either through stimulating efforts by others to apply its concepts to new situations or by serving as evidence increasing (or decreasing) the plausibility of ideas proposed as theories with general applicability.

The second strand of traditional symbolic interactionism draws on Blumer as well. It also draws, perhaps more heavily and directly, on the pragmatic philosophers' theory of action stressing that action and interaction represent collective efforts to resolve problematic situations. A preference for qualitative analysis and data gathered in field settings owes much to the previously noted impact of Everett Hughes on generations of University of Chicago students (Strauss, 1994). Again, however, what firmly distinguishes this second strand of

---

*For example, in addition to the varieties we discuss here, some have referred to dramaturgy, ethnomethodology, and role theory as variants of symbolic interactionism.

traditional symbolic interactionism from the first is its commitment to general theory (Strauss, 1994). There is some irony in this observation. Many of the proponents, as well as opponents, of the grounded theory argument have read (or misread, see Charmaz, 1995) the major text (Glaser & Strauss, 1967) developing and popularizing that argument as calling for research that ignores prior theory and conceptualization, thus allowing fresh perceptions of the situation from which appropriate explanatory concepts and theory can emerge. The irony lies in recognizing that concepts and theory developed in that fashion often center on that which is particular or unique in the situation rather than on that which is general across situations. One more feature of this strand of traditional symbolic interactionism differentiates it from the more "Blumerian" strand: attention is given to social structure, albeit generally only to structural features of the concrete situations of action under examination (e.g., Adler & Adler, 1991; Katovich & Reese, 1987; Strauss, 1978).

Social Structural Symbolic Interactionism

This variant of symbolic interactionism is explicit about the need to incorporate all levels of social structure into social psychological analyses. It developed in response to critiques of the traditional symbolic interactionist frame (Gouldner, 1970; Huber, 1973) claiming an ideological bias resulting from a neglect of social structure (Stryker, 1980), and has been motivated by: (1) the sense that social psychological processes cannot be understood without locating those processes in their structural contexts, and (2) the belief that if sociologists do not deal with this task no one else will.

Structural symbolic interactionism incorporates in modified form ideas of traditional interactionism about the openness and fluidity of social interaction, self-direction, and human agency stemming from the symbolic capacities of humans. Modifications stress the constraints on openness and fluidity, self-direction, and agency that are inherent aspects of membership in society. For this purpose, it draws on structural role theory (Stryker, 1980, 2001b).* Its imagery asserts that person and society are constitutive of one another, but it nevertheless accords causal priority to society in the society–person relationship on the grounds that every historical person is at birth enmeshed in and cannot survive outside of pre-existent organized social relationships. Thus, for all practical purposes, "in the beginning there is society" (Stryker, 1997). That aphorism leads to other underlying arguments of structural interactionism. Human experience is socially organized, not random. Contemporary societies are composed of diverse congeries of subparts: role relationships, groups, networks, communities, institutions, strata. These subparts may be interdependent or independent, isolated from or closely related to one another, cooperative or conflicting. Experience is shaped by social locations and the relationships, groups, networks, communities, institutions, and strata of which individuals are a part. Social structures in general define boundaries, making it likely that those located within them will or will not have relations with particular kinds of others and interact with those others over particular kinds of issues with particular kinds of resources. Structures will also affect the likelihood that persons will or will not develop particular kinds of selves, learn particular kinds of motivations, and have available particular symbolic resources for defining situations they enter.

Interactionists in general hold that social life is constructed, open to reconstruction and radical change. Structural interactionists agree, but note that constructions are not necessarily

---

*What is called role theory is more reasonably termed a role theoretic framework.

ephemeral and are themselves constrained by objective features of the world, prior constructions, norm-based pressures from partners in interaction, and habit. Indeed, much interaction simply reproduces extant structures (see e.g., Burawoy, 1979). Thus, while humans are actors, their action does not necessarily result in changing the situations or larger structural settings in which they live their lives. We can expect social behavior to reflect a blend of construction and reproduction, change and stability, creativity and conformity. A major task becomes specifying the conditions making for varying degrees of one or the other. Serpe and Stryker (1987) show that students leaving home communities to enter a university in another community both seek to establish new ties reflecting as well as enabling the maintenance of existing salient identities *and* reorder the salience of their identities to reflect new social relationships established in the university.

The symbolic and subjective are central to social life, warranting attention to the impact of definitions, including self-definitions. Symbolic interactionism stresses that self, in particular, mediates the reciprocal relation of society to social behavior. Rooted in reactions of others, an existing self can interact dialectically with others' responses to allow some measure of independence from others' expectations. At the same time, the symbolic and subjective are variably constrained by persons' structural locations. Further, external realities impinge—sometimes strongly—on social behavior independently of definitions, including definitions of self (e.g., social class exerts its effects whether or not actors conceptualize themselves, others, or situations in class terms). The argument is that social psychology must see the symbolic and social structural as operating simultaneously in social behavior, and an adequate social psychological frame must provide a place for both. The theoretical task again becomes specifying the conditions affecting the "mix" of the two. The concept of role is basic to providing for social structure in social psychological analyses because that concept facilitates the integration of traditional interactionist and role theoretic ideas. By building "down" to the social person and "up" to units of social organization, it serves as a bridge linking person and society.

A summary statement of a structural frame can now be offered. Social behavior depends on a named or classified world providing the ends and means of action. That world also provides opportunities for action and conditions affecting the success or failure of action. Labels attached to objects in the physical and social environment relevant to action are learned in interaction as are their meanings. Among symbols learned are positions, "parts" of relatively stable, organized social relationships collectively representing the kinds of people it is possible to be in society, and roles, or behavioral expectations attached to positions. These expectations may be strongly normative or not, specific or general, clear or vague, narrowly or widely shared, and applicable to limited or large numbers and varieties of interactions.

Interacting persons recognize and label one another as occupants of positions, invoking linked expectations. They label themselves, invoking expectations for their own behavior. On entering situations, people define who they and others in the situation are and what the situation itself is, and they use these definitions to organize their behavior. Interaction can validate these definitions; it can also challenge them. Interactions are often venues for bargaining or conflict over alternative definitions, for battles over whose definitions will hold and organize the interaction. Early definitions constrain, and may determine, later definitions.* Behavior may depend on role-making. The degree to which roles are made or conform to extant definitions depends on characteristics of the social structures in which interaction occurs.

---

*Experimental research in the expectations states or status characteristics tradition, while not initiated from a structural interactionist perspective, nevertheless may be understood from this perspective.

Structural symbolic interactionism conceptualizes society as a complex, differentiated but organized mosaic of relationships, groups, networks, organizations, communities, and institutions intersected by encompassing structures of age, gender, ethnicity, class, religion, and so forth. People largely live their lives in relatively small, specialized networks of social relationships, doing so through roles attached to positions in these networks. The networks may be independent of one another or overlap, and they may hold compatible or conflicting behavioral expectations. Since self reflects society, selves incorporate the characteristics of society. They are complex, differentiated but organized structures whose essential subparts are identities, internalized expectations attached to roles played in networks of social relationships. Identities, each tied to a particular network of social relationships, also can reflect compatible or conflicting expectations. Possibilities for interpersonal and intrapersonal role and identity reinforcement or conflict are both present in social interaction and relationships; the degree to which each occur will reflect characteristics of ties between persons and social structures.

Postmodern Symbolic Interactionism

Some symbolic interactionists have been influenced in recent years by developments initiated outside of interactionism, most significantly feminism (e.g., Richardson, 1991), poststructuralism and postmodernism (e.g., Denzin, 1990; Plummer, 1990), and cultural studies (e.g., Denzin, 1992). These developments have led some to identify what Denzin (1996) has termed "crises of representation and legitimation," and also to experiments with unconventional, alternative modes of presentation of ideas (Denzin, 1996; Ellis & Bochner, 2000; Richardson, 1997). Whether these efforts represent expansions of or developments in the symbolic interactionist frame, are related to but separate from that frame (Musolf, 1993), or are irrelevant to that frame are questions for current debate. For reasons noted above, we have chosen not to enter this debate here. Nevertheless, insofar as they imply the need for greater reflexivity on the part of symbolic interactionist researchers of whatever stripe, perhaps in particular greater sensitivity to the possible confounding of their perspectives and those of their research subjects, attention to these efforts is warranted.

CONCLUDING REMARKS

Passion and polemics characterized debate among symbolic interactionists in the past. Today, polemics if not passions are more muted. This is no claim that total agreement prevails. The variations described above are all reflected in contemporary work, and recent debates between those influenced by postmodernism and those who retain more "realist" positions have initiated a new and heated polemic at times. However, an important shift seems to have occurred in how variations within interactionism are viewed. Varying preferences for imagery, conceptualization, problem selection, and methods introduce tensions. It is possible to view such tensions as requiring resolution by exclusionary choice: accepting one position and rejecting the other(s). It is also possible to recognize benefits deriving from variations within a broad interactionist perspective.* Symbolic interactionists, in important degree, have been

---

*At least this is the judgment of the authors of this chapter, one of whom has been a participant in the intra-interactionist debates for over 50 years.

moving from the former possibility to the latter, justifying optimism about the healthy continuation of the frame in the social psychological work of sociologists. These potential benefits are many. For one thing, variations in emphases serve to minimize the chances that unwarranted positions will prevail. For example, an overemphasis on structure will draw counters from those whose work focuses on process, and vice versa. A deterministic role-based account of findings of will give rise to an account that notes evidence of agency in the data.

Further, since one method does not fit all problems, absolute adherence to methodological preferences of any sort limits the range of problems that can be approached through the lens of symbolic interactionism. A truism is worthy of note here: every method has its virtues and its limitations. Ethnographic data and analyses have the not so inconsiderable virtue of providing for rich, in-depth information about and understanding of situations that can facilitate the generation of theory, particularly with respect to issues that are novel or about which little is known. Moreover, some aspects of social life of interest to sociologists may not be accessible via survey questions or other forms of non-naturalistic data gathering, or may not be amenable to quantification. At the same time, ethnographic data are at a disadvantage compared to survey research when interest is in testing the generality of a theoretical argument, in part because a focus on limited situations amenable to ethnographic observation can produce theoretical accounts that center on what is unique about a situation, and because emphasis on the unusual and a choice not to attempt to build broadly representative samples limits potential generalizability. Further, large-scale survey work permits the evaluation of multivariate models of complex data sets based on relatively representative samples of much larger groups of people. Some interactionists have begun to incorporate multiple methods in their work, drawing on the unique strengths of each (e.g., Fine, 1998).

Not too long ago, symbolic interactionism was written off as no longer being an influential perspective in sociological work (Mullins, 1973). Current work stemming from the frame testifies vigorously to the inaccuracy of that judgment. Deriving from a powerful philosophical and sociological tradition, the future of the frame in guiding the theorizing and research of sociologists doing social psychology is indeed bright.

ACKNOWLEDGMENT: Kevin D. Vryan's research was supported in part by NIMH training grant T32 MH14588.

REFERENCES

Adler, Patricia A., & Adler, Peter. (1991). *Backboards and blackboards: College athletes and role engulfment.* New York: Columbia University Press.

Becker, Howard S. (1963). *Outsiders: Studies in the sociology of deviance.* New York: Free Press.

Blumer, Herbert. (1937). Social psychology. In E. P. Schmidt (Ed.), *Man and society* (pp. 144–198). Englewood Cliffs, NJ: Prentice-Hall.

Blumer, Herbert. (1969). *Symbolic interactionism: Perspective and method.* Englewood Cliffs, NJ: Prentice-Hall.

Blumer, Herbert. (1980). Mead and Blumer: The convergent methodological perspectives of social behaviorism and symbolic interactionism. *American Sociological Review 45,* 409–419.

Bryson, Gladys. (1945). *Man and society: The Scottish inquiry of the eighteenth century.* Princeton, NJ: Princeton University Press.

Burawoy, Michael. (1979). *Manufacturing consent: Changes in the labor process under monopoly capitalism.* Chicago, IL: University of Chicago Press.

Burke, Peter J. (1991). Attitudes, behavior, and the self. In J. A. Howard & P. L. Callero (Eds.), *The self society interface: Cognition, emotion and action* (pp. 189–208). New York: Cambridge University Press.

Burke, Peter J., & Reitzes, Donald C. (1981). The link between identity and role performance. *Social Psychology Quarterly 44,* 83–92.

Camic, Charles. (1986). The matter of habit. *American Journal of Sociology 91*, 1039–1087.

Charmaz, Kathy. (1995). Grounded theory. In R. Harre, J. A. Smith, & L. Van Langenhore (Eds.), *Rethinking methods in psychology.* London, UK: Sage.

Cooley, Charles Horton. (1894). *The theory of transportation.* Baltimore, MD: American Economics Association.

Cooley, Charles Horton. (1902). *Human nature and the social order.* New York: Scribner's.

Couch, Carl J. (1994). Why I went into the laboratory: And, what we found. *Studies in Symbolic Interaction 16*, 21–34.

Couch, Carl J., Saxton, Stan L., & Katovich, Michael A. (1986). *Studies in symbolic interaction: The Iowa school.* Greenwich, CT: JAI Press.

Denzin, Norman K. (1990). The spaces of postmodernism: Reading Plummer on Blumer. *Symbolic Interaction 13*, 145–154.

Denzin, Norman K. (1992). *Symbolic interactionism and cultural studies: The politics of interpretation.* Oxford: Blackwell.

Denzin, Norman K. (1996). The epistemological crisis in the human disciplines: Letting the old do the work of the new. In A. Colby, R. Jessor, & R. A. Shweder (Eds.), *Ethnography and human development: Context and meaning in social inquiry* (pp. 127–151). Chicago, IL: University of Chicago Press.

Dewey, John. (1896). The reflex arc concept in psychology. *Psychological Review 3*, 357–370.

Dewey, John. (1930). *Human nature and conduct.* New York: Modern Library.

Ellis, Carolyn, & Bochner, Arthur P. (2000). Autoethnography, personal narrative, reflexivity: Researcher as subject. In N. K. Denzin & Y. S. Lincoln (Eds.), *Handbook of qualitative research* (pp. 733–768). Thousand Oaks, CA: Sage.

Fine, Gary Alan. (1992). Agency, structure, and comparative contexts: Toward a synthetic interactionism. *Symbolic Interaction 15*, 87–107.

Fine, Gary Alan. (1998). *Morel tales: The culture of mushrooming.* Cambridge, MA: Harvard University Press.

Glaser, Barney G., & Strauss, Anselm L. (1967). *The discovery of grounded theory: Strategies for qualitative research.* Chicago: Aldine.

Goffman, Erving. (1967). *Interaction ritual: Essays on face-to-face behavior.* New York: Pantheon Books.

Goffman, Erving. (1974). *Frame analysis: An essay on the organization of experience.* Cambridge, MA: Harvard University Press.

Gouldner, Alvin W. (1970). *The Coming Crisis in Western Sociology.* New York: Basic Books.

Harris, Scott R. (2001). What can interactionism contribute to the study of inequality? The case of marriage and beyond. *Symbolic Interaction 24*, 455–480.

Heise, David R. (1979). *Understanding events: Affect and the construction of social action.* New York: Cambridge University Press.

Heise, David R. (1986). Modeling symbolic interaction. In J. S. Coleman, S. Lindenberg, & S. Nowak (Eds.), *Approaches to social theory* (pp. 291–309). New York: Russell Sage Foundation.

Huber, Joan. (1973). Symbolic interaction as a pragmatic perspective: The bias of emergent theory. *American Sociological Review 38*, 274–284.

Irwin, John. (1977). *Scenes.* Beverly Hills, CA: Sage.

James, William. (1890). *Principles of psychology.* New York: Holt.

Jasso, Guillermina. (2001). Formal theory. In J. H. Turner (Ed.), *Handbook of sociological theory* (pp. 37–68). New York: Kluwer Academic/Plenum Publishers.

Joas, Hans. (1993). *Pragmatism and social theory.* Chicago, IL: University of Chicago Press.

Katovich, Michael A., & Reese II, William A. (1987). The regular: Full-time identities and memberships in an urban bar. *Journal of Contemporary Ethnography 16*, 308–343.

Kuhn, Manford H. (1964). Major trends in symbolic interaction theory in the past twenty-five years. *Sociological Quarterly V*, 61–84.

Kuhn, Manford H., & McPartland, Thomas S. (1954). An empirical investigation of self-attitudes. *American Sociological Review 19*, 68–76.

Lemert, Edwin. (1951). *Social pathology.* New York: McGraw-Hill.

Maines, David R. (2000). Pragmatism. In E. F. Borgatta & R. J. V. Montgomery (Eds.), *Encyclopedia of Sociology* (pp. 2217–2224). New York: Macmillan.

Maines, David R. (2001). *The faultline of consciousness: A view of interactionism in sociology.* Hawthorne, NY: Aldine de Gruyter.

McCall, George J., & Simmons, J. L. (1978). *Identities and interactions: An examination of human associations in everyday life.* New York: Free Press.

McPhail, C., & Rexroat, C. (1979). Mead vs. Blumer: The divergent methodological perspectives of social behaviorism and symbolic interactionism. *American Sociological Review 44*, 449–467.

Mead, George Herbert. (1930). Cooley's contribution to American social thought. *American Journal of Sociology 35*, 693–706.

Mead, George Herbert. (1934). *Mind, self and society*. Chicago: University of Chicago Press.

Miller, George A. (Ed.). (1973). *Communication, language, and meaning: Psychological perspectives*. New York: Basic Books.

Mullins, Nicholas C. (1973). *Theories and theory groups in contemporary American sociology*. New York: Harper and Row.

Musolf, Gil Richard. (1993). Some recent directions in symbolic interactionism. In L. T. Reynolds (Ed.), *Interactionism: Exposition and Critique* (3d ed., pp. 231–283). Dix Hills, NY: General Hall.

Park, Robert Ezra. (1955). *Society: Collective behavior, news and opinion, sociology and modern society*. Glencoe, IL: Free Press.

Park, Robert Ezra, & Burgess, Ernest W. (1922). *Introduction to the science of sociology*. Chicago, IL: University of Chicago Press.

Plummer, Ken. (1990). Staying in the empirical world: Symbolic interactionism and postmodernism: A response to Denzin. *Symbolic Interaction 13*, 155–160.

Reynolds, Larry T. (1993). *Interactionism: Exposition and critique* (3rd ed.). Dix Hills, NY: General Hall.

Richardson, Laurel. (1991). Speakers whose voices matter: Toward a feminist postmodernist sociological prax. In N. K. Denzin (Ed.), *Studies in symbolic interaction* (pp. 29–38). Greenwich, CT: JAI Press.

Richardson, Laurel. (1997). *Fields of play*. New Brunswick, NJ: Rutgers University Press.

Rosenberg, Morris, & Turner, Ralph H. (Eds.) (1981). *Social psychology: Sociological perspectives*. New York: Basic Books.

Schubert, Hans-Joachim. (1998). Introduction. In Charles Horton Cooley, *On self and social organization* (pp. 1–31). Chicago, IL: University of Chicago Press.

Seeman, Melvin. (1997). The elusive situation in social psychology. *Social Psychology Quarterly 60*, 4–13.

Serpe, Richard, & Stryker, Sheldon. (1987). The construction of self and the reconstruction of social relationships. *Advances in Group Processes 4*, 41–66.

Shalin, Dmitri N. (1986). Pragmatism and social interactionism. *American Sociological Review 51*, 9–29.

Snow, David A. (2001). Extending and broadening Blumer's conceptualization of symbolic interactionism. *Symbolic Interaction 24*, 367–377.

Strauss, Anselm L. (1978). *Negotiations: Varieties, contexts, processes, and social order*. San Francisco: Jossey-Bass.

Strauss, Anselm L. (1994). From whence to whither: Chicago-style interactionism. *Studies in Symbolic Interaction 16*, 3–8.

Stryker, Sheldon. (1968). Identity salience and role performance: The relevance of symbolic interaction theory for family research. *Journal of Marriage and the Family 30*, 558–564.

Stryker, Sheldon. (1980). *Symbolic interactionism: A social structural version*. Menlo Park, CA: Benjamin/Cummings.

Stryker, Sheldon. (1981). Symbolic interactionism: Themes and variations. In M. Rosenberg and R. H. Turner (Eds.), *Social psychology: Sociological perspectives* (pp. 3–19). New York: Basic Books.

Stryker, Sheldon. (1988). Substance and style: An appraisal of the sociological legacy of Herbert Blumer. *Symbolic Interaction 11*, 33–42.

Stryker, Sheldon. (1994). Identity theory: Its development, research base, and prospects. *Studies in Symbolic Interaction 16*, 9–20.

Stryker, Sheldon. (1997). "In the beginning there is society": Lessons from a sociological social psychology. In C. McGarty & A. Haslam (Eds.), *Message of social psychology: Perspectives on mind in society* (pp. 315–327). London: Blackwell.

Stryker, Sheldon. (2000). Symbolic interaction theory. In E. F. Borgatta & R. J. V. Montgomery (Eds.), *Encyclopedia of sociology* (pp. 3095–3102). New York: Macmillan Reference USA.

Stryker, Sheldon. (2001a). Social psychology. In P. B. Baltes & N. J. Smelser (Eds.), *International encyclopedia of the social and behavioral sciences* (pp. 14,409–14,413) Oxford, UK: Pergamon.

Stryker, Sheldon. (2001b). Traditional symbolic interactionism, role theory, and structural symbolic interactionism: The road to identity theory. In J. H. Turner (Ed.), *Handbook of sociological theory* (pp. 211–232). New York: Kluwer Academic/Plenum.

Stryker, Sheldon, & Burke, Peter J. (2000). The past, present, and future of an identity theory. *Social Psychology Quarterly 63*, 284–297.

Thomas, William I. (1927). The behavior pattern and the situation. *Publications of the American Sociological Society 22*, 1–14.

Thomas, William I., & Thomas, Dorothy S. (1928). *The child in America: Behavior problems and programs.* New York: Knopf.

Thomas, William I., & Znaniecki, Florian. (1918–1920). *The Polish peasant in Europe and America.* Chicago, IL: University of Chicago Press.

Tucker, Charles W. (1966). Some methodological problems of Kuhn's self theory. *Sociological Quarterly 7,* 345–359.

Turner, Ralph H. (1962). Role-taking: Process versus conformity. In A. M. Rose (Ed.), *Human behavior and social processes* (pp. 20–40). Boston: Houghton Mifflin Co.

Volkart, Edmund H. (Ed.). (1951). *Social behavior and personality: Contributions of W. I. Thomas to theory and social research.* New York: Social Science Research Council.

Vryan, Kevin D., Adler, Patricia A., & Adler, Peter. (forthcoming). Identity. In L. J. Reynolds & N. J. Herman (Eds.), *Handbook of symbolic interactionism.* Walnut Creek, CA: AltaMira.

CHAPTER 2

Expectation States Theory

SHELLEY J. CORRELL
CECILIA L. RIDGEWAY

INTRODUCTION

Women in work groups often feel that their ideas are ignored or mistakenly credited to one of their male coworkers. African Americans often say they feel that they have to perform twice as well as their white counterparts to be given the same level of recognition. The ideas of people who talk more in a group are often judged to be more valuable than those offered by less talkative members. People with more prestigious jobs are more likely to be chosen leader of a group, such as a jury, even when their job has little, if anything, to do with the task at hand. Women are more likely than men in a group to be interrupted. Ideas often "sound better" when offered by someone perceived to be attractive.

What all of these observations have in common is that some members of a group seem to have real advantages that are denied to others. They have more opportunities to speak, their ideas are taken more seriously, and they have more influence over other group members. In expectation states theory these hierarchies of evaluation, influence, and participation are referred to as the "power and prestige structure" or the "status structure" of the group. The theory seeks to explain how these inequitable structures emerge and are maintained, and how they are related to other aspects of inequality in society.

SHELLEY J. CORRELL • Department of Sociology, University of Wisconsin-Madison, 1180 Observatory Drive, Madison, Wisconsin 53706
CECILIA L. RIDGEWAY • Department of Sociology, Stanford University, 450 Serra Mall, Building 120, Room 160, Stanford, California 94305-2047

Handbook of Social Psychology, edited by John Delamater. Kluwer Academic/Plenum Publishers, New York, 2003.

HISTORY

Expectation states theory began as an effort to explain some of the most striking findings of Robert F. Bales' (1950) influential early studies of interpersonal behavior in small groups (Berger, Conner, & Fisek, 1974; Berger & Zelditch, 1998, pp. 97–113).

Bales (1950, 1970) recorded the interactions of homogeneous, initially leaderless decision-making groups of three to seven unacquainted Harvard sophomore males over multiple hour-long sessions. Despite the initial lack of group structure and the social similarities of the members, inequalities in interaction developed quickly, stabilized over the first session, and then guided interaction thereafter. If inequalities emerge quickly in unstructured groups of social equals, Bales (1950) reasoned, status hierarchies are very likely in any group.

The inequalities Bales observed consisted of four correlated behaviors: participation initiated, opportunities given to participate, evaluations received, and influence over others. Bales (1970) found, for instance, that groups developed a most talkative member who talked considerably more than the others in the group. This most talkative person was also the one addressed most often by the others. The more a person talked, compared to the others, the more likely he was to be rated by others has having the best ideas and doing the most to guide and influence the group. The founders of expectation states theory, Joseph Berger, Bernard Cohen, Morris Zelditch, and colleagues, sought to explain why these correlated inequalities, labeled the group's "power and prestige" (i.e., status) structure, emerge together and how this happens even in a group of social equals.

Berger and his colleagues were also influenced by two additional sets of early studies. One set demonstrated the power of status structures, once formed, to bias group members' evaluations of each other and their behavior in the group. Riecken (1958) showed that the same idea was rated as more valuable when it came from a talkative group member than from a less talkative one. Sherif, White, and Harvey (1955) demonstrated that group members overestimate the performance of high status members and underestimate the performance of low status members. Whyte (1943), in his classic study of a street corner gang, showed that group members actually pressured one another to perform better or worse to keep their performances in line with their status in the group.

Another influential set of early studies demonstrated that when members of a goal-oriented group differed in socially significant ways, the interactional status structures that emerged tended to reflect the social status attached to each member's distinguishing characteristics. Strodtbeck, James, and Hawkins (1957), for instance, found that mock jury members' occupational status and gender predicted how active and influential they became, how competent and helpful they were judged to be by others, and how likely they were to be chosen foreman of the jury. Yet, the question left unanswered was *how* this occurred.

These studies encouraged Berger and his colleagues to formulate expectation states theory as a theory of an underlying process that (1) accounts for the formation of interactional status structures and (2) can explain *how* these structures develop both in groups of social equals and in groups where people differ in socially significant ways (Berger et al., 1974; Berger, Fisek, Norman, & Zelditch, 1977; Berger & Zelditch, 1998). The way people's socially significant characteristics, such as race, gender, occupation, or age, shape their access to participation, influence, and positive evaluation is an important aspect of social stratification in society. As a consequence, although expectation states theory began by explaining status structures in homogeneous groups, its explanation of status structures among people with significant social differences has become the most highly developed and commonly used aspect of the theory.

AN OVERVIEW OF EXPECTATION STATES THEORY

Expectation states theory seeks to explain the emergence of status hierarchies in situations where actors are oriented toward the accomplishment of a collective goal or task. *Collective orientation* and *task orientation* are the scope conditions of the theory (i.e., the conditions under which the theory is argued to hold). Individuals are task oriented when they are primarily motivated towards solving a problem, and they are collectively orientated when they consider it legitimate and necessary to take into account each other's contributions when completing the task.

While not all groups have collective task orientations, groups that do are a part of everyday experiences in socially important settings such as work and school. Informal work groups, committees, sports teams, juries, student project groups, explicitly established work teams, and advisory panels are just a few examples. By contrast, people talking at a party or a group of friends having dinner generally lack these orientations and, therefore fall outside of the theory's scope.

The shared focus of group members on the group's goal (i.e., the collective orientation) generates a pressure to anticipate the relative quality of each member's contribution to completing the task in order to decide how to act. When members of the group, for whatever reason, anticipate that a specific individual will make more valuable contributions, they will likely defer more to this individual and give her or him more opportunities to participate. These implicit, often unconscious, anticipations of the relative quality of individual members' future performance at the focal task are referred to as *performance expectation states*.

Once developed, performance expectation states (hereafter, "performance expectations") shape behavior in a self-fulfilling fashion. The greater the performance expectation of one actor compared to another, the more likely the first actor will be given chances to perform in the group, the more likely she or he will be to speak up and offer task suggestions, the more likely her or his suggestions will be positively evaluated and the less likely she or he will be to be influenced when there are disagreements. The actor with the lower performance expectations, by contrast, will be given fewer opportunities to perform, will speak less and in a more hesitant fashion, will frequently have his or her contributions ignored or poorly evaluated, and will be more influenced when disagreements occur. In this way, relative performance expectations create and maintain a hierarchy of participation, evaluation, and influence among the actors that constitutes the group's status hierarchy, as depicted on the right side of Figure 2-1.

Given the importance of relative performance expectations for the formation of status hierarchies, it is crucial to specify how social factors influence the formation of the performance expectations themselves. As shown on the left side of Figure 2-1, expectation states theory posits three distinct processes. These involve: (1) socially significant characteristics (e.g., race, gender,

FIGURE 2-1. The formation of performance expectations and status hierarchies.

physical attractiveness), (2) social rewards, and (3) patterns of behavior interchange between actors. We describe these three processes next along with empirical evidence in regard to them.

Status Characteristics and Performance Expectations

Perhaps one of the most important ways that actors develop differentiated performance expectations is by using socially significant attributes of individuals, called *status characteristics,* to anticipate the quality of their future task performances. Status characteristics are attributes on which people differ (e.g., gender, computer expertise) and for which there are widely held beliefs in the culture associating greater social worthiness and competence with one category of the attribute (men, computer expert) than another (women, computer novice). Status characteristics can be either *specific* or *diffuse.* Specific status characteristics, such as computer expertise, carry cultural expectations for competence at limited, well-defined range of tasks and, consequently, only impact the formation of performance expectations in this limited range of settings. Diffuse status characteristics, on the other hand, carry very general expectations for competence, in addition to specific expectations for greater or lesser competence at particular tasks. They affect performance expectations across a wide range of settings.

Gender is an example of a diffuse status characteristic in the United States and elsewhere. Widely shared cultural beliefs about gender have been shown to include expectations that men are diffusely more competent at most things, as well as specific assumptions that men are better at some particular tasks (e.g., mechanical tasks) while women are better at others (e.g., nurturing tasks) (Conway, Pizzamiglio, & Mount, 1996; Wagner & Berger, 1997; Williams & Best, 1990).

It is useful to compare the cultural beliefs that constitute a status characteristic to group stereotypes and to social identity based on group categorization. It is well known that mere categorization encourages beliefs that favor one's own category over another (Brewer & Brown, 1998; Mullen, Brown, & Smith, 1992; Tajfel, 1978). Status beliefs, in contrast to ingroup favoritism, are social representations that *consensually* evaluate one category as more status worthy and competent than another. This means that rather than simply preferring one's own group, even those disadvantaged by a status belief accept, as a social fact, that the other group is socially evaluated as better than their own (Jost & Burgess, 2000; Ridgeway, Boyle, Kuipers, & Robinson, 1998; Ridgeway & Erickson, 2000).

As a set of evaluative beliefs about social categories, status beliefs form an element of many widely shared group stereotypes. Importantly, the status element of group stereotypes, if present, is fairly similar across stereotypes that otherwise differ dramatically in content (Conway et al., 1996; Jost & Banaji, 1994). For instance, the stereotypes of gender, of race/ethnic categories, and of occupations differ enormously in specific content. But each of these stereotype sets has in common a status element that associates greater worthiness and competence with one category of the distinction (men, whites, professionals) than another (women, people of color, blue-collar workers). Because of this similar status element, expectation states theory argues that otherwise very different social distinctions can have comparable effects on the organization of interactional status hierarchies.

In discussing status beliefs, we should be clear that we are not endorsing the content of these beliefs. Nor are we suggesting that the self-fulfilling consequences of status beliefs are inevitable. Instead, it is our contention that reducing social inequalities in everyday contexts requires first acknowledging that status beliefs exist and then attempting to understand and expose the inequitable processes they prime. It is to that task that we now turn.

STATUS CHARACTERISTICS THEORY.   Status characteristics theory is a formal subtheory of expectation states theory that seeks to explain *how* beliefs about status characteristics get translated into performance expectations, which in turn, shape the behaviors of individuals in a group (Berger et al., 1977; Webster & Foschi, 1988). Some refer to status characteristics theory as a *theory of status generalization*, which is the process of attributing specific abilities to individuals based on the status characteristics they posses.

At the heart of the theory is a set of five assumptions that link beliefs about status to behavior (Balkwell, 1991; Berger et al., 1977). According to the *salience* assumption, for any attribute to affect performance expectations, it must be socially significant for the actors in the setting. A status characteristic is salient if it either differentiates actors, or if actors believe that the characteristic is relevant to completing the group's task. Consequently, situational goals and the way actors compare one another on the characteristic impact how and if a status characteristic affects performance expectations. The same characteristic (e.g., having a college degree) can advantage an actor in one setting (with a less educated group), have no impact in another (in a group where all have university degrees), and disadvantage the actor in a third setting (with a more educated group). Importantly, this implies that no status characteristic advantages or disadvantages an actor in all settings. Whether the status beliefs culturally available to actors shape performance expectations in any actual setting depends on the structure of the local setting itself.

The second assumption is called the *burden of proof* assumption and concerns the way status characteristics that differentiate actors but are not initially relevant to the performance of the group's task impact the formation of performance expectations. Actors act as though the burden of proof rests with showing that a salient status characteristic should *not* be taken into account when forming performance expectations. All salient information is incorporated, unless something in the setting explicitly dissociates the status characteristic from the task. So, for example, if gender is salient in a setting it will differentiate the performance expectations for men and women even though gender itself is not relevant to the task at hand. It is through the burden of proof process that diffuse status characteristics such as gender, age, race/ethnicity, and social class have modest but pervasive effects on the status hierarchies that emerge across a large range of settings in which they have no obvious task relevance.

The *sequencing* assumption specifies what happens in the more complicated situation when actors either enter or leave an existing social setting. The main point is that no status or competence information is lost. The performance expectations that formed in one encounter carry over to the next encounter, even if the specific actors change. This assumption has been used to intervene in the status generalization process. For example, if a man observes a woman performing a task better than he does, this can positively impact the performance expectations he forms for women in future encounters (Pugh & Wahrman, 1983). The effect may wear off over time without a "booster" experience, however (Markovsky, Smith, & Berger, 1984).

The *aggregation* assumption explains how the status information associated with multiple characteristics is combined to form aggregated performance expectations. In actual groups, such as work groups or committees, people commonly differ from one another on several status characteristics at the same time, and often these multiple status characteristics generate inconsistent expectations for performance. For example, on a legal team, a member may be not only a Harvard trained lawyer, but also an African American woman. A distinctive advantage of status characteristics theory is it offers a procedure for making exact predictions for the order of performance expectations actors will construct from a given set of salient consistent and inconsistent status characteristics. To continue with our example, if another member of the legal team is a white man who attended a lower status law school and a third member is an African American man who attended the same lower status law school, the theory provides us with a method for incorporating all the salient status information (i.e., that based on gender, race, and school attended) to determine the order of performance expectations the team members will likely construct.

A principle of subset combining is used to calculate aggregated performance expectations (Berger et al., 1977). The first step involves combining all of the positive status information about an actor into one subset and all negative information into another. In the second step, positive and negative subsets are combined to form an overall expectation.

Two principles describe how consistent and inconsistent status information is combined. The *attenuation effect* assumes that additional consistent information is subject to a declining marginal impact. If we already know that a person is a Harvard trained lawyer, learning that he is also a white man will have only a slight positive effect on raising performance expectations for him.

The *inconsistency effect* assumes that a single piece of positive status information in a field of negatively evaluated characteristics will be accorded more weight than it would have if it were the only piece of status information present. If we already know that a person is an African American woman, the fact that she is also a lawyer will carry more weight than it would have in the absence of information about her ethnicity and gender.

The theory argues that these processes occur mostly outside the realm of conscious thought. It does not contend that people literally weight and combine multiple bits of information before acting. Instead, people act *as if* they went through this chain of reasoning. *As if* approaches are quite common in mathematical models of information processing. This approach is appropriate here since status characteristics theory is ultimately a theory of behavior, not thought.

The emphasis on behavior, not thought, allows the theory to explain how status generalization processes can occur pervasively in a society and not just among individuals with strong conscious prejudices. For example in the case of gender, we know that men often speak more frequently than women in mixed-sex groups (Aries, 1996; Ridgeway & Smith-Lovin, 1999). Explanations that focus on individual attitudes might conclude that this pattern is due to the fact that some men are sexist or that some women fear success. By contrast, status characteristic theory claims that the fact that men are generally believed to be more competent than women makes gender a salient status characteristic in mixed-sex situations and, therefore, impacts the performance expectations formed by *all* men and women in the setting, including non-sexist men and highly confident women.

Finally, the fifth assumption describes how aggregated performance assumptions are translated into behavior. Relative aggregated performance expectations for any two actors are compared. The higher the expectations that an actor holds for herself compared to another actor, the greater the expectation advantage she will have over the second actor. The greater the performance expectation advantage of one actor over another, the more likely the first actor will be to receive opportunities to act, the more likely she will be to accept the opportunity to act, the more positive will be the evaluation of her action, and the more likely she will be to reject influence when the two actors disagree.

GRAPH THEORETIC REPRESENTATION.   Status characteristics theory uses graph theory to represent its arguments in a way that allows precise predictions of behavior. These graphs are also useful for comparing one status situation to another. We provide a brief overview of this approach here. (For a more complete description see Berger et al., 1977.)

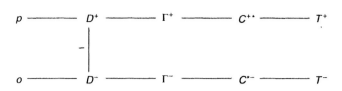

FIGURE 2-2. Graph theoretic representation of two actors differing on one diffuse status characteristic.

Signed graphs, like the one in Figure 2-2, link actors to expected task outcomes (positive or negative) through a series of paths. Since performance expectations are relative for each pair of actors in a setting, the structure represents the status situation for two actors, p (for self) and o (for other). Figure 2-2 depicts the relatively simple status situation where only one diffuse status characteristic, symbolized D, is salient in the setting. The positive sign attached to D for actor p indicates that p has the more valued state of the diffuse characteristic compared to actor o. For example, p might be a man interacting with a woman, o. A negative dimensionality line connects the two states of D. Since the actors possess oppositely valued states of D, the characteristic D *is salient in the setting*.

Proceeding to the right, the symbol Γ represents the expectation of an actor's general competence. Since actor p has the more valued state of D, the expectation for p's general competence is high relative to actor o. Higher expectations for general competence lead to higher expectations for competence at the group's focal task. The symbol C^* refers to the expectation for an actor's competence at a specific task. As the positive and negative signs attached to C^* indicate, the expectation for competence at the focal task is higher for actor p compared to actor o. This path exists because, as stated in the burden of proof assumption, a salient status characteristic is believed to be relevant unless it is somehow explicitly dissociated from the task at hand. T^+ refers to a successful task outcome, and T^- refers to an unsuccessful task outcome.

There are two paths linking actor p to expectations about his future task performance. The first is the path: p——D^+——Γ^+——C^+*——T^+ and the second path is: p——D^+——D^-——Γ^-——C^{*-}——T^-. Two important features of these paths are their lengths and their signs. Shorter paths have a greater impact on the magnitude of the expectation. Conceptually, as paths become longer it becomes harder for an actor to reason from the path to the task outcome. By simply counting the links between actor and task outcome, we determine that the first path diagramed above has a length of 4, compared to a length of 5 for the second path. The sign of the paths are determined by the method commonly used with signed graphs: We multiply the signs of the path by the sign of the task outcome to which the path leads. Doing so for the two paths above indicates that both are positive.

If we now apply the aggregation assumption, we first combine all like signed paths to compute the expectations for the positive and negative subset for actor p according to the formulas

$$e_p^+ = \{1 - [1 - f(i)] \cdots [1 - f(n)]\}; \tag{1a}$$

$$e_p^- = \{1 - [1 - f(i)] \cdots [1 - f(n)]\}; \tag{1b}$$

and then the aggregate expectation is represented by:

$$e_p = e_p^+ - e_p^-. \tag{2}$$

A similar calculation is made for actor o. Actor p's expectation advantage over actor o is simply the difference between their individual expectations $(e_p - e_o)$.

Values for $f(i)$ have been estimated empirically (Berger et al., 1977). Fisek, Norman, and Nelson-Kilger, (1992) have also derived a functional form for $f(i)$, which fits existing data well:

$$f(i) = 1 - \exp(2.618^{2-i}). \tag{3}$$

In Figure 2-2, actor p has two positive paths, one of length 4 and one of length 5, and no negative paths. Therefore, equation (1a) becomes:

$$e_p = \{ 1 - [1 - f(4)][1 - f(5)] - 0 \}. \tag{4a}$$

Likewise, actor o has two negative paths, one of length 4 and one of length 5 and no positive paths, making equation (1b)

$$e_o = 0 - \{ 1 - [1 - f(4)][1 - f(5)] \}. \tag{4b}$$

Using Fisek et al.'s derivation (equation [3] above), $f(4) = 0.1358$ and $f(5) = 0.0542$. Substituting these values into equations (4a) and (4b), $e_p = 0.1827$ and $e_o = -0.1827$, making the expectation advantage of actor p over actor o as 0.3653.

EMPIRICAL EVIDENCE. Status characteristics theory, and expectation states theory more generally, have been subjected to rigorous empirical evaluation, which has generated considerable evidence in support of the theory. Most of this evidence has come from social psychological experiments. Experiments afford the researcher the ability to isolate and manipulate variables of key theoretical interest, while controlling for potentially confounding factors. As such, experiments produce data that can more clearly establish the extent to which a change in an independent variable *caused* a change in the dependent variable, rather than being the result of some confounding or spurious factor.

The conceptual advances within status characteristics theory can largely be attributed to the reliance of researchers on a standardized experimental setting. This setting consists of a set of standardized procedures for introducing manipulations and operationalizations of key theoretical variables (e.g., status characteristics), assessing the effects of the independent variables on the dependent variable, which is usually a measure of social influence, and employing manipulations to achieve the scope conditions under which the theory is argued to hold (Troyer, 2001). By holding these aspects of the setting constant across studies whenever possible, the results that are produced can be compared across studies, which allows researchers to build on the results of others with confidence.

The standardized setting begins by instructing research participants that they are participating in a study designed to evaluate a "newly discovered skill." They are told that they will participate in a decision-making task with a "partner."* The task will evaluate their ability in regard to the skill. Several different "abilities" are commonly evaluated, including "contrast sensitivity ability," "meaning insight ability," and "spatial judgment ability." Participants are told that these skills are unrelated to known abilities, such as mathematical competence or artistic ability. These instructions and the use of a task associated with a fictitious ability are

---

*Quotes around phrases in this section indicate that the phrase represents an experimental deception. For example, the phrase "newly discovered skill" is communicated to the research participant. In actuality, the skills are usually fictitious. Likewise, "partners" are often computer programs, unbeknownst to the subject.

intended to keep participants from relying on prior beliefs about the skills when forming their expectations about competence at the task.

Before beginning the task, participants receive information about whether their partner is higher, lower, or equal status than they are. For example, if the subject is a college freshman, she might be told that her partner is a graduate student, a high school student, or another freshman. Importantly, research participants never see their partner since doing so could introduce other status information into the setting.

After introducing the manipulation of the key theoretical variable, which is the relative status of self and partner, participants learn that they will participate in several trials of the task with their partner. They are told that prior research establishes that groups have higher average scores on the task than individuals. For each trial, participants first make an individual choice about the best answer, then they are shown their partner's initial choice. Using this information, participants make a final choice about the best answer. They are told that their score will be based only on their final choices. This set of instructions is used to establish collective orientation by encouraging participants to consider the answers of their partner.

The feedback about the partner's initial choice is actually an experimental manipulation. Typically, on about 80% of the trials, the experimenter provides feedback that the partner has made a different initial choice than the participant. For these trials, the researcher is interested in whether the subject stays with his or her initial response or changes to match the partner's answer. When the subject makes a final choice that is the same as his or her initial choice, this is an operational measure of rejecting influence, one of the behaviors affected by having higher performance expectations relative to another actor in the setting. If the subject instead changes answers to agree with the partner, the subject is said to have been influenced by the partner, an event that the theory predicts is more likely when the partner is higher status relative to the participant. The dependent variable is the proportion of the trails that the subject stays with his or her initial response, abbreviated "P(s)" for "proportion of stay responses." The empirical prediction is that the higher the status of partner relative to self, the lower the P(s) value. In other words, higher status actors are more likely to reject influence.

Research relying on variants of this standardized setting has generated a substantial body of evidence that supports the theoretical account of the status generalization process. In a meta-analysis of studies involving a variety of diffuse (educational attainment, gender, military rank, race) and specific (pretest scores) status characteristics, Driskell and Mullen (1990) found support for the theory's central argument that external status affects power and prestige behaviors (influence, task contributions, etc.) indirectly through the performance expectations members form for one another rather than directly. Experiments also have demonstrated that, as the theory predicts, simple knowledge alone of an interactional partner's status characteristics relative to a participant's own is sufficient to affect willingness to accept influence from the partner in task settings (for gender, Pugh & Wahrman, 1983; race, Webster & Driskell, 1978; age, Freese & Cohen, 1973; educational attainment, Moore, 1968; specific abilities, Wagner & Berger, 1982; Webster, 1977). This occurs both when the status characteristic differentiates actors but is not initially task relevant (Moore, 1968; Pugh & Wahrman, 1983; Webster & Driskell, 1978) and when it is task relevant (Webster, 1977). Thus the impact of status characteristics on standing in interactional hierarchies does appear to be mediated by performance expectations and cannot be accounted for by assumptions about correlated differences in actors' behavioral assertiveness or nonverbal style.

Experiments also confirm the theory's prediction that task relevant status characteristics have a stronger impact on influence than do differentiating status characteristics that are not initially relevant to the task at hand (Wagner & Berger, 1982; Webster & Driskell, 1978). The differential impact of status characteristics based on their relevance to the task leads to some distinctive predictions of the theory. For instance, the theory predicts that in a mixed sex group with a gender-neutral task, men will have an advantage over women in participation and influence. If the task is a masculine typed one, men's advantage over women in these behaviors will be even greater. But if the task is a feminine typed one, women will have a modest advantage over men in participation and influence. A large body of research supports this pattern of behavioral inequalities in mixed sex contexts (for reviews, see Ridgeway, 2001a; Ridgeway & Smith-Lovin, 1999).

Experiments further confirm that people form influence hierarchies *as if* they were combining consistent and inconsistent status information, as predicted by the aggregation assumption (Webster & Driskell, 1978; Zelditich, Lauderdale, & Stublarec, 1980). There is evidence as well for the inconsistency effect. Recall that the addition of another status characteristic in a situation is argued to have a greater marginal impact on the status hierarchy if it is inconsistent, rather than consistent with other salient status information (Berger, Norman, Balkwell, & Smith, 1992; Norman, Smith, & Berger, 1988). Berger et al. (1992) compared the ability of subset combining to account for the interactional hierarchies participants in experiments formed from sets of consistent and inconsistent status information with three other information processing principles. They found that subset combining provided the best fit for the data. In a broader evaluation of status characteristic theory's ability to predict group status structures with its graph theoretic model of salience, relevance, and aggregation, Fisek et al. (1992) compared theoretical predictions to data from 24 experiments, reporting a good fit.

Rewards and Performance Expectations

Recall that expectation states theory posits three processes by which differentiated performance expectations emerge (see Figure 2-1). We have discussed at length the impact of salient status characteristics. We now turn to the other processes, beginning with the impact of socially valued rewards.

The theory argues that when a socially valued reward is distributed unequally among members of a group, the actors will infer performance expectations from their reward differences (Berger, Fisek, Norman, & Wagner, 1985). In this way, the differential distribution of rewards, like status characteristics, can actually create a status hierarchy among actors or modify positions in an existing hierarchy. In an experimental test of this argument, Cook (1975) showed that when a third party gave differential rewards to group members who had no other basis for evaluating their performances on a shared task, the members used the reward differences to infer ability differences. Harrod (1980) and Stewart and Moore (1992) showed that allocating differential pay levels to participants in an experiment created corresponding influence hierarchies among them during interaction. These results highlight how the power or good luck represented in the unequal possession of rewards generates status distinctions that are considered legitimate by those in the setting. By creating performance expectations, the unequal rewards appear to be "deserved" and, thus, justly bring respect, deference, and influence. Unequal rewards, according to the theory, combine with other factors, such as salient status characteristics, to determine the aggregated performance expectations that shape the behavioral status order in the setting.

In established hierarchies, actors' expectations for rewards in a task setting are interdependent with their expectations for performance and, consequently, with their positions in the status structure (Berger et al., 1985; Cook, 1975). It is a common observation in established hierarchies that valued rewards (pay, a corner office) tend to be distributed in accordance with rank and help maintain the relative power of those ranks (Homans, 1961). Because of the interdependence of performance and reward expectations, the theory predicts that when a status characteristic is salient in a setting, those disadvantaged by it will implicitly expect lower levels of rewards for themselves than will those advantaged by the characteristic. Research on women's lower sense of entitlement to rewards compared to men supports this prediction (Bylsma & Major, 1992; Jost, 1997; Major, McFarlin, & Gagnon, 1984).

Behavioral Interchange Patterns and Performance Expectations

In addition to status characteristics and rewards, a third factor that can have independent effects on performance expectations is the *behavioral interchange pattern* that develops among two or more actors (Fisek, Berger, & Norman, 1991; Skvoretz & Fararo, 1996). Such a pattern occurs between two or more actors when one engages in assertive, higher status behaviors (e.g., initiating speech, making a task suggestion, resisting change in the face of disagreement) that are responded to with deferential, lower status behaviors by the other actor(s) (e.g., hesitating to speak, positively evaluating the other's suggestion, changing to agree with the other). The more frequently these types of patterns are repeated between the actors, the more likely the actors are to view the behavioral patterns as cultural *status typifications*, which are shared beliefs about typical high-status–low-status, "leader–follower" behaviors. Following the common assumption that people speak up more confidently about things at which they are more expert, salient status typifications induce actors to assume that the more assertive actor is more competent at the task than the more deferential actor, creating differential performance expectations for them. In support of this argument, a variety of assertive verbal and nonverbal cues including taking a seat at the head of the table, having an upright, relaxed posture, speaking up without hesitation in a firm, confident tone, and maintaining more eye contact while speaking than listening have been shown in the United States to make an actor's ideas "sound better" and increase influence (for reviews see Dovidio & Ellyson 1985; Ridgeway, 1987; Ridgeway, Berger, & Smith, 1985).

Behavior interchange patterns shape performance expectations most powerfully among those actors in a group who are equals in both their external status characteristics and their reward levels, such as between two women in a mixed sex group (Fisek et al., 1991). Behavioral interchange patterns are the means by which expectation states theory accounts for the development of status structures in homogeneous groups like those studied by Bales (1950, 1970).

When actors differ in status characteristics, the differentiated performance expectations created by the status characteristics shape the actors' verbal and nonverbal assertiveness. Consequently, differences in status characteristics shape behavioral interchange patterns, as several studies have shown (Dovidio, Brown, Heltman, Ellyson, & Keating, 1988; Ridgeway et al., 1985; Smith-Lovin & Brody, 1989). In a clear demonstration of expectation states theory's predictions in this regard, Dovidio et al. (1988) showed that when mixed sex dyads shifted from a gender neutral task, where the man had a status advantage, to a feminine typed task, where the woman had a status advantage, the actors' participation rates and assertive nonverbal behaviors reversed from a pattern favoring the man to one favoring the woman. Thus, between actors who already differ on status characteristics, behavior interchange patterns often add little new information to the existing order of performance expectations.

Fisek et al. (1991) used the graph-theoretical methods described earlier to develop a model of how behavior interchange patterns combine with status characteristics and rewards to create an aggregated order of performance expectations for actors in the setting, which impacts the status structure of the group. They evaluated this model's ability to account for participation rates in unconstrained, face-to-face interaction by fitting it to several existing data sets including Bales' (1970) original data from 208 groups. The results supported the model. Skvoretz and Fararo (1996) updated the model to provide more detailed predictions about the dynamic evolution of status structures from combinations of status characteristics and behavioral interchange patterns. They similarly report a good fit of the model with participation data from six person groups that systematically varied in composition from all male to all female.

To this point, we have described the core ideas, assumptions, and scope conditions that constitute expectation states theory, experimental methods used to test it, and some of the key evidence that supports it. We now turn to some of the ways that the theory has been expanded.

THEORETICAL ADVANCES

Instead of seeing individuals as following rigid social scripts that dictate status relations, expectation states theory envisions individuals as possessing a basic vocabulary of cultural beliefs about the socially significant categories by which persons, settings, and events can be classified. When some of this cultural information is made salient by the particularities of a given situation, the theory assumes that individuals also possess shared rules for combining this information to generate a course of action toward self and others that is predictable, but nevertheless flexibly adjusted to the specifics of the situation at hand (Berger, Wagner, & Zelditch, 1992; Ridgeway & Smith-Lovin, 1994). As a result, people can respond even to unusual situations in a way that makes social sense to those present. Unfortunately, these socially sensible responses also reproduce, often inadvertently, society's meaningful axes of social inequality within the relationships among individuals.

This general metatheoretical image of how the cultural vocabulary of status beliefs shapes individual behavior and evaluations has guided recent advances in expectation states theory. Each of these advances seeks to account for the relationships between status beliefs and situational behavior across a wider range of contexts, social outcomes, and processes than that addressed by the original, core theory. In the following sections we describe some of these advances. Some retain the theory's focus on group status structures, but expand the aspects of these structures that the theory explains. For instance, double standards theory examines how status beliefs affect the inference of an actor's ability from performance. The theory of second order expectations addresses the impact on status relations of *other* people's situational expectations for an actor, rather than his or her own expectations. The theory of legitimation examines the impact of status beliefs on the authority of group leaders and the stability of status structures.

Other advances in expectation states theory reach beyond the focus on group status structures to examine a broader framework of status processes. Status construction theory asks how interactional encounters between people who differ on a socially recognized characteristic might create widely shared status beliefs about that characteristic. Other advances expand the scope conditions of expectation states theory to explain the impact of status beliefs on individual judgments and behavior on socially important tasks that are performed individually, rather than in groups, such as mental ability testing. We first review the theories that retain a focus on status structures and then discuss those that move beyond this focus.

Double Standards Theory

In the book, *Reflections of an affirmative action baby*, Carter (1993) describes one hurdle that African Americans face when they attempt to establish their competence in school or at work: "Our parents' advice was true: We really do have to work twice as hard [as whites] to be considered half as good" (p. 58). Carter describes a common observation by members of low status groups: Due to status beliefs that disadvantage them, they must actually perform at *higher* levels than members of high status groups to be judged as *equally* competent. More generally, the level of performance required for inferring ability varies with the status characteristics individuals possess.

In an extension of expectation states theory, Foschi (1989, 2000) incorporates insights from the psychological literature on attribution to account for these kinds of observations. She introduces "standards" as the mechanism by which actors attribute performance to ability. Foschi regards standards as a function of salient diffuse status characteristics that create differential performance expectations for actors. According to double standards theory, these differential performance expectations activate the use of different standards for attributing ability. When lower status individuals perform well at the group's task, their performances are critically scrutinized since a good performance is inconsistent with what was expected based on their position in the group's status hierarchy. When higher status individuals perform equally as well, their performances are consistent with status-based expectations and are, therefore, less scrutinized. Thus, those possessing the more valued state of a status characteristic are judged by a more lenient standard than are those with the more devalued state. As a result, equal task performances are more likely to be judged as indicative of ability when performed by a higher status member of the group.

The evidence supporting double standards theory ranges from accounts and descriptions, to results from surveys and experiments (for a review see Foschi, 2000). For example, in one experiment subjects in mixed sex dyads were informed that the group's task was one on which men generally perform better (Foschi, 1996). After completing this task, subjects were told that they scored in the mid range and either slightly higher or slightly lower than their opposite-sex partners. Subjects were then asked to estimate what percentage of questions the higher performing subject would need to have answered correctly in order to determine that s/he possessed task ability. As predicted, subjects set a significantly higher standard for ability when the better performer was a woman rather than a man. Biernat and Kobrynowicz (1997) report similar results for race as well as gender.

As with expectation states theory more generally, the predictions of double standards theory are dependent on features of the setting. For example, when gender is salient in the setting, the theory predicts that men will be held to a more lenient standard than women *either* when men are thought to be better at the task at hand or, according to the burden of proof assumption, when gender differentiates people in a setting but is not specifically linked to the task. If the setting is instead one where women are thought to be better at the task, the theory predicts that women would be judged by a more lenient ability standard.

Double standard theory shows that in addition to being given fewer opportunities to participate initially in the group, when lower status members do participate, their performances are evaluated by a stricter standard. This makes it difficult for competent performances by lower status members to be noticed as such, which further reduces their ability to achieve high status in the group.

Second Order Expectations

Status hierarchies have been shown to emerge in collectively oriented task groups because actors in the group develop differentiated performance expectations for themselves and their group mates. The performance expectations described in expectation states theory are *first order expectations:* they are the *personal* expectations an actor, *p*, holds for self and other, *o*. However, it is likely that the expectations actor *p* believes are held by *others* in the group also influence the emerging status structure. This idea has its roots in the long standing insight from social psychology that our perceptions of others' expectations influence our sense of self and our behavior in interaction (Cooley, 1902; Goffman, 1959; Mead, 1934). Recent theoretical elaborations in expectation states theory have sought to explain how these beliefs about others' expectations—called *second order expectations*—influence the power and prestige order of groups (Moore, 1985; Troyer & Younts, 1997; Webster & Whitmeyer, 1999).

Second order expectations refer, more specifically, to what an actor, *p*, believes that another in the situation, *o*, thinks about *p*'s and *o*'s relative abilities (Moore, 1985; Webster & Whitmeyer, 1999). Since people generally overestimate the extent to which others see things as they do (Marks & Miller, 1987), actors usually presume their own self–other expectations are shared by those in the situation and act on them accordingly (Troyer & Younts, 1997; Zelditch & Floyd, 1998). In this situation, second order expectations provide no new information. However, when second order expectations are communicated and they either conflict with first order expectations or are expressed when an actor has no self–other (first order) expectations, they will likely influence the first order expectations of actors in the setting and, consequently, the status structure of the group.

Consistent with these ideas Moore (1985) found that when participants in an experiment with no information about their competence compared to a partner heard their partner's views about their relative competence levels, these second order expectations shaped the first order expectations participants formed for themselves compared to the partner. Troyer and Younts (1997) showed that when group members receive second order expectations that conflict with their own first order expectations, they combine the information in the two sets of expectations to create aggregate, revised performance expectations that become the basis for their interaction in the group. They also found that in some instances, second order expectations actually had *more* influence than first order expectations in guiding interaction.

Drawing on previous research, Webster and Whitmeyer (1999) propose that the impact of another's second order expectations on *p*'s own expectations is a function of the performance expectations *p* holds for that other. Second order expectations communicated by an actor held in high regard will have a stronger impact than will expectations imputed by a less well regarded actor. Webster and Whitmeyer (1999) update expectation states theory's graph-theoretic model to show how second order expectations combine with all other salient status information to create the aggregate performance expectations upon which group members enact their status structure.

While social psychologists have long believed that our perceptions of others' expectations are important in making sense of self and guiding interaction, the incorporation of this insight into expectation states theory makes it possible to generate precise predictions about the relative impact of first and second order expectations in various settings. Consequently, this body of theoretical and empirical work not only represents an important elaboration of expectation states theory, but it also provides a systematic and empirically supported account of one of the key insights of social psychology.

Legitimacy

Empirical evaluations of expectation states theory have clearly demonstrated that individuals who posses a diffuse status characteristic that is devalued in society experience interactional disadvantages if the characteristic is salient in the setting. Women, people of color, or others with status disadvantages in society do nevertheless achieve high-ranking positions in status structures by acquiring advantaging status characteristics such as education and by their own successful task behaviors and performances in the context. Even when they gain a position of influence in the group, however, such people often encounter resistance from others when they attempt to go beyond persuasion to wield directive power over lower ranking members. An assistant professor in his late twenties, for instance, may encounter problems when he attempts to act authoritatively in a classroom filled with older adults. This resistance phenomenon has been most clearly documented in regard to gender. A wide variety of studies have shown that women leaders in mixed sex contexts in business and elsewhere are more likely than similar men to face resistive "backlash" and dislike when they assert directive authority over subordinates (Eagly & Karau, 2002; Rudman & Glick, 2001).

Expectation states theory conceptualizes the resistance faced by leaders who come from status disadvantaged groups as a problem in the *legitimation* of a status structure that puts these people ahead of those from more status advantaged groups (Berger, Ridgeway, Fisek, & Norman, 1998; Ridgeway & Berger, 1986). As Weber ([1918] 1968) observed, beyond persuasion and force, it is legitimacy that allows high-ranking members (i.e., leaders) of social hierarchies to issue directive commands and receive compliance. Since legitimacy underpins authority, it is important to the stability of social hierarchies of any kind including interpersonal status structures (Walker & Zelditch, 1993).

Expectation states theory argues that the status beliefs associated with diffuse status characteristics, in addition to affecting performance expectations, also provide outside cultural support for status hierarchies in which leaders are those with diffuse status advantages. This outside cultural support helps make the hierarchy seem "right" (Berger & Luckmann, 1966). More meritocratic leaders, however, who achieve their positions by demonstrating their skills in the situation despite low diffuse status do not have such added cultural support for their leadership to draw on. As a result, there is a lower likelihood that others in the situation will treat such meritocratic leaders as legitimate by willingly complying with their directive orders.

Specifically, the theory argues that when diffuse status characteristics are salient in a group context, the associated status beliefs implicitly cause members to expect that those advantaged by the diffuse characteristics will be more likely to occupy valued status positions in the group. When those advantaged by diffuse status do in fact become the high-ranking members, because members expected this to happen, they have a tendency to react as if this is what *should* have happened by treating the high-ranking members with honorific deference. If no one in the group challenges such honorific deference, others tend to assume it is appropriate and the hierarchy becomes implicitly legitimate so that compliance with the leader is expected (Berger et al., 1998; Ridgeway & Berger, 1986).

The more *comprehensive* a status structure is, in terms of the number of diffuse status characteristics that are salient, and the more *consistent* these status characteristics are with one another, the greater the likelihood that group members will legitimate a status structure that corresponds with their expectations for who should occupy high status positions (see Berger et al., 1998, for a graph-theoretic statement of the legitimation theory). In an experimental test of these ideas, Ridgeway, Johnson, and Diekema (1994) created status structures in which the high-ranking member was either advantaged by two diffuse status characteristics (age and education) or known to be highly skilled at the task (a specific status characteristic) but disadvantaged by education (a diffuse characteristic). Both these types of leaders were initially equally influential in their groups. Yet when the leaders attempted to go beyond persuasion to exercise dominant, directive power, group members, as the theory predicts, were significantly more likely to comply with status advantaged leader and to resist the meritocratic leader. Thus, group members were more likely to treat the diffuse status advantaged leaders as legitimate.

Status Construction Theory

Distinguishing characteristics such as occupation or race become status characteristics in a society when widely shared status beliefs develop that associate greater status worthiness and competence with those in one category of the characteristic than in another category. One of the ways that expectation states theory has broadened its focus in recent years has been to ask how such status beliefs develop.

As we have seen, status beliefs play an essential role in connecting the status organization of society as a whole with the status experiences of individuals. Yet, sociology has little systematic knowledge about how these beliefs develop, are maintained, or change. Weber ([1921] 1946) suggested many years ago that social groups commonly acquire an economic advantage first before acquiring high status in society. Yet even this observation fails to explain how a purely economic advantage is transformed into shared cultural beliefs about social status.

There are probably many ways that widely shared status beliefs form in societies. Status construction theory, however, asks whether the insights of expectation states theory can be used to explain at least some of these processes (Ridgeway, 1991, 2001b). Since expectation states theory has shown that status beliefs are at play in goal-oriented encounters among people, status construction theory asks if these same encounters might be a potent forum for the development and spread of new status beliefs or the maintenance or change of existing status beliefs.

Status construction theory begins with a simple suggestion. When people who differ on a socially recognized characteristic interact in regard to a shared goal, a status hierarchy will emerge among them as it does in almost all goal-oriented encounters. There is a chance, however, that the participants will associate the relative status each is accorded in this hierarchy with the characteristic that differentiates them, and form a fledgling status belief about the characteristic.

Whether these fledgling status beliefs are supported in future encounters and become stable status beliefs depends on the nature of the beliefs other people in other encounters are also forming about the same characteristic. If there is some factor that gives people in one category of the characteristic (call them As) a systematic advantage in gaining influence and esteem in encounters with people in another category of the characteristic (call them Bs), then the majority of encounters between As and Bs will induce their participants to form status beliefs that As are more worthy and competent than Bs. Since more people develop status beliefs favoring As rather than Bs under such circumstances, people who hold beliefs favoring As are more likely to have their beliefs supported in future encounters than are those who hold contrary beliefs. Also, when people who form a status belief in one encounter act on it in a subsequent encounter between As and Bs, there is a chance that they will "teach" their status belief to the others present by treating those others either deferentially or assertively according to the belief.

In this way, the initial small advantage for status beliefs favoring As rather than Bs is likely to spread and grow among people in the society. Under many circumstances, argues status construction theory, the eventual result will be widely shared status beliefs that As are more worthy and competent than Bs. Computer simulations of this process by which status beliefs spread through society suggest that, if people do form beliefs in encounters as the theory argues, then widely shared status beliefs would indeed be a logical result under many societal conditions (Ridgeway & Balkwell, 1997).

One factor that could give As an advantage in gaining influence and esteem in encounters with Bs is an economic advantage, as Weber suggested. As we have seen, differences in socially valued rewards such as pay or wealth tend to create corresponding differences in performance expectations that, in turn, create differences in influence and esteem in goal-oriented encounters. Therefore, if more As become economically advantaged in society than Bs, As will have a systematic advantage in gaining influence and esteem in the majority of encounters between As and Bs. As a result, widely shared status beliefs favoring As over Bs are likely to develop in the society. In this way, an economic advantage is transformed into cultural beliefs about the status of social groups.

To test whether people form status beliefs in this way, Ridgeway and colleagues (1998) told participants in an experiment that their partners differed from them in "personal response style." They were also told that they would be paid either more or less than their partners. While working on a decision task with their partners, influence hierarchies developed that corresponded to pay differences. After two such experiences, participants formed beliefs that "most people" see the typical person in the better paid response style group as more respected, more competent, more leader-like, higher status, but not as likeable as the typical person from the less well paid response style group. In other words, participants formed status beliefs favoring the economically advantaged response style group. Importantly, these status beliefs were consensual in that people from the less well paid group also agreed that most people see those from the better paid group as more respected and competent than those from their own group.

Economic advantages are one factor that can bias the development of status hierarchies between people who differ on a socially significant characteristic and cause status beliefs to form about the characteristic. Other factors, such as control of technology or valuable information (e.g., computer literacy), could have this effect as well, as long as these factors systematically bias the development of status hierarchies among people who differ on a characteristic. Webster and Hysom (1998), for instance, show how society's moral evaluations of homosexuality systematically bias the development of influence hierarchies between homosexuals and heterosexuals and foster status beliefs that disadvantage homosexuals in perceptions of worthiness and competence.

For widely shared status beliefs to develop in society, however, it is important not only that people form beliefs from their encounters, but also that they "teach" the beliefs to others by treating those others according to the beliefs in subsequent encounters. To examine this, participants in another experiment were again told that they differed from their partners in response style (Ridgeway & Erickson, 2000). While working on a task, the partners, who were confederates, treated the participants as if they held status beliefs about the difference by acting deferentially or assertively, causing influence hierarchies to form. After two such experiences, participants developed status beliefs about the response style groups that corresponded to their partner's treatment of them, confirming that status beliefs can be spread by acting on those beliefs. An additional experiment showed that third party participants who witnessed someone different from them defer to or assert influence over someone similar to them also acquired corresponding status beliefs, suggesting that encounters spread status beliefs widely (Ridgeway & Erickson, 2000).

Status construction theory and the evidence that supports it suggest that goal-oriented encounters between people who differ on socially significant characteristics are not only contexts where existing status beliefs are enacted, but also contexts where new status beliefs, perhaps about the digital divide, for instance, can take root and spread and existing status beliefs can be refreshed or, potentially, undermined.

Expanding the Scope Conditions

A growing body of empirical evidence suggests that status generalization processes occur in a broader range of settings than those defined by the scope conditions of expectation states theory (i.e., collectively oriented task groups). For instance, the settings where individuals take socially important mental ability tests, such as intelligence tests, SATs, and GREs, are highly task oriented but clearly lack collective orientation. Yet, Lovaglia and colleagues (Lovaglia, Lucas, Houser, Thye, & Markovsky, 1998) demonstrate that individuals randomly assigned to low status conditions in experiments scored lower on a test of mental ability than those assigned to high status conditions. They contend that any attempt to measure mental ability needs to account for the way that salient status processes actually interfere with test taking performance.

Similarly, psychologist Steele (1997) theorizes that individuals experience a self-evaluative threat in the presence of salient negative stereotypes about their group's intellectual ability. Through arousal, anxiety, and task-irrelevant processing, the threat of social devaluation interferes with intellectual functioning, leading to decreased test performance (Steele & Aronson, 1995). Steele shows, for example, that when a difficult, standardized verbal exam is described as diagnostic of ability, African American students perform more poorly than white students. However, when the same test is not characterized as ability-diagnostic, African American and white students perform at the same level.

Foschi and colleagues (Foschi, Lai, & Sigerson, 1994) also present evidence that expectation states theory may hold under a broader set of scope conditions. They consider a situation in which either male or female undergraduates act as evaluators who individually rate fictitious male and female job candidates for a summer internship job in engineering. When the male candidate was the slightly better candidate, the researchers found that male (although not female) evaluators rated him as more competent and chose him more often for the position than they did the female candidate when she had the slightly better record. These results suggest that, at least for male subjects, gender functioned as a diffuse status characteristic in this setting even though the setting did not involve a collectively oriented task group.

Correll (2001a), likewise, argues that salient beliefs about gender impact the standard individuals use to evaluate their own task ability in noncollective settings. She hypothesizes that cultural beliefs that men have more mathematical (but not verbal) ability, prime a status generalization process that causes men to use a more lenient standard than women to judge their own mathematical competence. She finds that, controlling for grades and test scores in mathematics, male high school students rate their own mathematical ability (but not verbal ability) higher than female students do. These results, like those of Foschi et al. (1994), imply that double standards theory, which is an extension of expectation states theory, holds in some noncollective settings.

What is the theoretical rationale for why status generalization would occur in these socially important, highly task oriented, but not collectively oriented settings? Recall that the reason why the theory has limited its scope to collectively oriented task groups is that in these groups individuals find it necessary to make *relative* anticipations of the likely task competence of group members. Importantly, the logic of the theory does not specifically require collective orientation as much as it requires individuals to consider themselves relative to another. Erickson (1998) has argued that whenever situational demands pressure actors to assess their task competence *relative* to others on a socially valid task, status processes should occur. While collectively oriented task groups readily create this pressure, settings where individuals engage in socially significant evaluative tasks, even if individually, also represent a setting where individuals are pressured to make relative assessments of their expected competence. Why is this so?

Individual evaluative tasks can provide the pressure to make relative assessments of competence in situations where actors know they will receive a socially important and socially valid performance evaluation. The use of evaluative tasks to rank individuals' performances is socially valid in the Weberian sense; that is, individuals expect *others* to accept the ranking as legitimate and, consequently, orient their behavior toward this expectation (see Weber [1918] 1968, pp. 31–33). The anticipation of this ranking creates a pressure for actors to assess their task competence relative to others who they imagine are also being or have been evaluated. This coordination of rank position requires evaluating oneself in relation to the social environment. However, the standards for what constitutes a competent performance are not usually clearly defined beforehand, and others' precise scores are rarely known. In this uncertain environment, salient status characteristics are available to influence performance expectations, as they do in collective task situations. Through the process of status generalization, individuals develop performance expectations for themselves that are consistent with their state on the salient status characteristic (Correll, 2001b; Erickson, 1998).

Assuming that a status characteristic is indeed salient in an individual evaluative setting, three theoretical predictions are implied. First, those with the more devalued state of the characteristic will perform less well on the task compared to those with the more valued state of the characteristic (cf. Lovaglia et al., 1998; Steele, 1997). Second, controlling for actual task performance, those with the more devalued state will evaluate their *own* task performance as less indicative of ability compared with the evaluations of those with the more valued state. Finally, when *others* evaluate the ability of high and low status actors, the same performance will be judged as more indicative of ability for high status actors (cf. Foschi et al., 1994).

In an experiment designed to meet Erickson's (1998) revised scope conditions and test the second of these predictions, Correll (2001b) compared how male and female subjects rated their competence at a "newly discovered ability" after taking a test purportedly designed to measure this ability. To make the test socially valid, participants were informed that the test was being considered for use in screening applicants for graduate school admissions. To make gender salient and task relevant, subjects in half of the conditions were told that men usually score higher on tests of the ability. To specifically disassociate gender from the task in the other conditions, subjects there were told that there is no gender difference in test scores. All subjects received the same slightly above average scores for their performance. In the first condition, where subjects had been told that males score higher on tests like the one they had just taken, male subjects rated their task ability significantly higher than female subjects did even though all subjects had received identical scores. In the gender irrelevant condition, no gender difference was found in how subjects rated their task ability. Since this experiment was specifically designed to meet the expanded scope conditions laid out by Erickson (1998), it provides the most convincing evidence to date that status processes occur in individual evaluative settings, settings that lack collective orientation.

Extending the scope conditions to include individual evaluative settings is an important advancement since this setting is both very common and highly consequential in its impact on educational and occupational attainment. It includes most standardized test settings, including those that are used to determine college, graduate school, and professional school admissions and those used for certification in a wide range of professional occupations. Expectation states theory has generated empirically supported propositions about how pre-existing inequalities are reproduced in collectively oriented task groups. This newer work in individual evaluative settings indicates that the impact of status processes on the reproduction of inequality is even more far reaching.

CONCLUSION

Expectation states theory is, in many ways, a textbook example of a theoretical research program. It is deductive, programmatic, formalized mathematically, cumulative, precise, and predictive; and its propositions have been subjected to rigorous evaluation. More importantly, however, it is a theory that illuminates core issues in social psychology and sociology more broadly. It is fundamentally a "macro–micro–macro" explanation about one way that categorical inequality is reproduced in society. Cultural beliefs about social categories at the macro level impact behavior and evaluation at the individual level, which acts to reproduce status structures that are consistent with pre-existing macro-level beliefs. Status structures in groups can be thought of as the building blocks of more macro-level structural inequalities in society. For example, to the extent that status processes make it less likely for women in work groups to emerge or be accepted as leaders, in the aggregate we will observe that more men than women hold leadership positions in organizations, a stratification pattern that is reproduced at least partially by the way macro-level beliefs impact individual behaviors and evaluations.

By focusing on the role of differentiated performance expectations, expectation states theory provides a unifying explanation for how reward structures, behavioral patterns, and macro-level beliefs about a diverse array of social categories produce similar effects on the organization of interactional status hierarchies, the building blocks of societal stratification. It helps us understand how inequitable structures emerge in these smaller structures, which increases our understanding of the emergence and reproduction of inequality in society more generally.

REFERENCES

Aries, E. (1996). *Men and women in interaction: Reconsidering the differences.* New York: Oxford.

Bales, R. F. (1950). *Interaction process analysis: A method for the study of small groups.* Reading, MA: Addison-Wesley.

Bales, R. F. (1970). *Personality and interpersonal behavior.* New York: Holt, Rinehart, and Winston.

Balkwell, J. W. (1991). From expectations to behavior: An improved postulate for expectation states theory. *American Sociological Review, 56,* 355–369.

Berger, J., Conner, T. L., & Fisek, M. H. (Eds.). (1974). *Expectation states theory: A theoretical research program.* Cambridge, MA: Winthrop.

Berger, J., Fisek, M. H., Norman, R. Z., & Wagner, D. G. (1985). The formation of reward expectations in status situations. In J. Berger & M. Zelditch (Eds.), *Status, rewards, and influence* (pp. 215–261). San Francisco: Jossey-Bass.

Berger, J., Fisek, M. H., Norman, R., & Zelditch, M. (1977). *Status characteristics and social interaction.* New York: Elsevier.

Berger, P., & Luckmann, T. (1966). *The social construction of reality.* New York: Doubleday.

Berger, J., Norman, R. Z., Balkwell, J. W., & Smith, L. (1992). Status inconsistency in task situations: A test of four status processing principles. *American Sociological Review, 57*, 843–855.

Berger, J., Ridgeway, C. L., Fisek, M. H., & Norman, R. Z. (1998). The legitimation and delegitimation of power and prestige orders. *American Sociological Review, 63*, 379–405.

Berger, J., Wagner, D., & Zelditch, M. (1992). A working strategy for constructing theories. In G. Ritzer (Ed.), *Metatheorizing* (pp. 107–123). Newbury Park, CA: Sage.

Berger, J., & Zelditch, M. (1998). *Status, power, and legitimacy: Strategies and theories.* New Brunswick, NJ: Transaction.

Brewer, M., & Brown, R. J. (1998). Intergroup relations. In D. T. Gilbert, S. T. Fiske, & G. Lindzey (Eds.), *Handbook of social psychology* (pp. 554–594). New York: McGraw-Hill.

Biernat, M., & Kobrynowicz, D. (1997). Gender and race-based standards of competence: lower minimum standards but higher ability standards for devalued groups. *Journal of Personality and Social Psychology, 72*, 544–557.

Bylsma, W., & Major, B. (1992). Two routes to eliminating gender differences in personal entitlement. *Psychology of Women Quarterly, 16*, 193–200.

Carter, S. L. (1993). *Reflections of an affirmative action baby.* New York: Basic Books.

Conway, M., Pizzamiglio, M. T., & Mount, L. (1996). Status, communality, and agency: Implications for stereotypes of gender and other groups. *Journal of Personality and Social Psychology, 71*, 25–36.

Cooley, C. H. (1902). *Human nature and the social order.* New York: Schribners.

Cook, K. S. (1975). Expectations, evaluations, and equity. *American Sociological Review, 40*, 372–388.

Correll, S. J. (2001a). Gender and the career-choice process: The role of biased self-assessments. *American Journal of Sociology, 106*, 1691–1730.

Correll, S. J. (2001b). *The gendered selection of activities and the reproduction of gender segregation in the labor force.* PhD dissertation, Department of Sociology, Stanford University.

Dovidio, J. F., & Ellyson, S. L. (1985). Patterns of visual dominance behavior in humans. In S. Ellyson & J. Dovidio (Eds.), *Power, dominance, and nonverbal behavior* (pp. 129–150). New York: Springer-Verlag.

Dovidio, J. F., Brown, C. E., Heltman, K. Ellyson, S. L., & Keating, C. F. (1988). Power displays between women and men in discussions of gender linked tasks: A multichannel study. *Journal of Personality and Social Psychology, 55*, 580–587.

Driskell, J. E., & Mullen, B. (1990). Status, expectations, and behavior: A meta-analytic review and test of the theory. *Personality and Social Psychology Bulletin, 16*, 541–553.

Eagly, A. H., & Karau, S. J. (2002). Role congruity theory of prejudice towards female leaders. *Psychological Review, 109*, 537–598

Erickson, K. G. (1998). *The impact of cultural status beliefs on individual task performance in evaluative settings: A new direction in expectation states research.* PhD dissertation, Department of Sociology, Stanford University.

Fisek, M. H., Berger, J., & Norman, R. Z. (1991). Participation in heterogeneous and homogeneous groups: A theoretical integration. *American Journal of Sociology, 97*, 114–142.

Fisek, M. H., Norman, R. Z., & Nelson-Kilger, M. (1992). Status characteristics and expectation states theory: A priori model parameters and test. *Journal of Mathematical Sociology, 16*, 285–303.

Foschi, M. (1989). Status characteristics, standards and attributions. In J. Berger, M. Zelditch, & B. Anderson (Eds.), *Sociological theories in progress* (pp. 58–72). Newbury Park, CA: Sage.

Foschi, M. (1996). Double standards in the evaluation of men and women. *Social Psychology Quarterly, 59*, 237–254.

Foschi, M. (2000). Double standards for competence: Theory and research. *Annual Review of Sociology, 26*, 21–42.

Foschi, M., Lai, L. & Sigerson, K. (1994). Gender and double standards in the assessment of job applicants. *Social Psychology Quarterly, 57*, 326–39.

Freese, L., & Cohen, B. P. (1973). Eliminating status generalization. *Sociometry, 36*, 177–193.

Goffman, E. (1959). *The presentation of self in everyday life.* New York: Doubleday.

Harrod, W. J. (1980). Expectations from unequal rewards. *Social Psychology Quarterly, 43*, 126–130.

Homans, G. C. (1961). *Social behavior: Its elementary forms.* New York: Harcourt Brace.

Jost, J. T. (1997). An experimental replication of the depressed-entitlement effect among women. *Psychology of Women Quarterly, 21*, 387–393.

Jost, J. T., & Banaji, M. R. (1994). The role of stereotyping in system-justification and the production of false consciousness. *British Journal of Social Psychology, 33*, 1–27.

Jost, J. T., & Burgess, D. (2000). Attitudinal ambivalence and the conflict between group and system justification in low status groups. *Personality and Social Psychology Bulletin, 26*, 293–305.

Lovaglia, M. J., Lucas, J. W., Houser, J. A., Thye, S. R., & Markovsky. B. (1998). Status processes and mental ability test scores. *American Journal of Sociology, 104*, 195–228.

Major, B., McFarlin, D., & Gagnon, D. (1984). Overworked and underpaid. *Journal of Personality and Social Psychology, 47*, 1399–1412.

Markovsky, B., Smith, L. F., & Berger, J. (1984). Do status interventions persist? *American Sociological Review, 49*, 373–382.

Marks, G., & Miller, N. (1987). Ten years' research on the false-consensus effect: An empirical and theoretical review. *Psychological Bulletin, 102*, 72–90.

Mead, G. H. (1934). *Mind, self and society.* Chicago: University of Chicago Press.

Moore, J. C. (1968). Status and influence in small group interactions. *Sociometry, 31*, 47–63.

Moore, J. C. (1985). Role enactment and self identity: An expectations states approach. In J. Berger & M. Zelditch (Eds.), *Status, rewards, and influence: How expectations organize behavior* (pp. 262–316). San Francisco: Jossey-Bass.

Mullen, B., Brown, R., & Smith, C. (1992). Ingroup bias as a function of salience, relevance, and status: An integration. *European Journal of Social Psychology, 22*, 103–122.

Norman, R. Z., Smith, L., & Berger, J. (1988). The processing of inconsistent status information. In M. Webster & M. Foschi (Eds.), *Status generalization: New theory and research* (pp. 169–187). Stanford, CA: Stanford University Press.

Pugh, M., & Wahrman, R. (1983). Neutralizing sexism in mixed-sex groups: Do women have to be better than men? *American Journal of Sociology, 88*, 746–762.

Ridgeway, C. L. (1987). Nonverbal behavior, dominance, and the basis of status in task groups. *American Sociological Review, 52*, 683–694.

Ridgeway, C. L. (1991). The social construction of status value: Gender and other nominal characteristics. *Social Forces, 70*, 367–386.

Ridgeway, C. L. (2001a). Gender, status, and leadership. *Journal of Social Issues, 57*, 627–655.

Ridgeway, C. L. (2001b). Inequality, status, and the construction of status beliefs. In J. Turner (Ed.), *Handbook of sociological theory*, (pp. 323–342). New York: Kluwer/Plenum.

Ridgeway, C. L., & Balkwell, J. (1997). Group processes and the diffusion of status beliefs. *Social Psychology Quarterly, 60*, 14–31.

Ridgeway, C. L., & Berger, J. (1986). Expectations, legitimation, and dominance behavior in groups. *American Sociological Review, 51*, 603–617.

Ridgeway, C. L., Berger, J., & Smith, L. (1985). Nonverbal cues and status: An expectation states approach. *American Journal of Sociology, 90*, 955–978.

Ridgeway, C. L., Boyle, E. H., Kuipers, K., & Robinson, D. (1998). How do status beliefs develop? The role of resources and interaction. *American Sociological Review, 63*, 331–350.

Ridgeway, C. L., & Erickson, K. G. (2000). Creating and spreading status beliefs. *American Journal of Sociology, 106*, 579–615.

Ridgeway, C. L., Johnson, C., & Diekema, D. (1994). External status, legitimacy, and compliance in male and female groups. *Social Forces, 72*, 1051–1077.

Ridgeway, C. L., & Smith-Lovin, L. (1994). Structure, culture, and interaction: Comparing two generative theories. *Advances in Group Processes, 11*, 213–239.

Ridgeway, C. L., & Smith-Lovin, L. (1999). The gender system and interaction. *Annual Review of Sociology, 25*, 191–216.

Rudman, L., & Glick, P. (2001). Prescriptive gender stereotypes and backlash against agentic women. *Journal of Social Issues, 57*, 743–762.

Riecken, H. W. (1958). The effect of talkativeness on ability to influence group solutions of problems. *Sociometry, 21*, 309–321.

Sherif, M. B., White, J., & Harvey, O. J. (1955). Status in experimentally produced groups. *American Journal of Sociology, 60*, 370–379.

Skvoretz, J., & Fararo, T. (1996). Status and participation in task groups: A dynamic network model. *American Journal of Sociology, 101*, 1366–1414.

Smith-Lovin, L., & Brody, C. (1989). Interruptions in group discussion: The effects of gender and group composition. *American Sociological Review, 54*, 424–435.

Steele, C. M. (1997). A threat is in the air: How stereotypes shape intellectual identity and performance. *American Psychologist, 52*, 613–629.

Steele, C. M., & Aronson, J. (1995). Stereotype threat and intellectual task performance of African Americans. *Journal of Personality and Social Psychology, 69*, 797–811.

Stewart, P. A., & Moore, J. C. (1992). Wage disparities and performance expectations. *Social Psychology Quarterly, 55*, 78–85.

Strodtbeck, F. L., James R. M., & Hawkins, C. (1957). Social status in jury deliberations. *American Sociological Review, 22,* 713–719.

Tajfel, H. (1978). *Differentiation between social groups.* London: Academic Press.

Troyer, L., & Younts, C. W. (1997). Whose expectations matter? The relative power of first-order and second-order expectations in determining social influence. *American Journal of Sociology, 103,* 692–732.

Troyer, L. (2001). Effects of protocol differences on the study of status and social influence. *Current Research in Social Psychology, 6,* 182–205. http: www.uiowa.edu/~grpprc

Wagner, D. G., & Berger, J. (1982). Paths of relevance and the induction of status-task expectancies. *Social Forces, 61,* 575–586.

Wagner, D. G., & Berger, J. (1997). Gender and interpersonal task behaviors: Status expectation accounts. *Sociological Perspectives, 40,* 1–32.

Walker, H. A., & Zelditch, M. (1993). Power, legitimacy, and the stability of authority: A theoretical research program. In J. Berger & M. Zeltditich (Eds.), *Theoretical research programs: Studies in the growth of theory* (pp. 364–384). Stanford, CA: Stanford Press.

Weber, M. ([1918] 1968). *Economy and society.* Edited by G. Roth & C. Wittich. Translated by E. Frischoff. New York: Bedminster.

Weber, M. ([1921] 1946). Class, status, and party. In H. Gerth and C. W. Mills (Eds. and trans.), *From Max Weber: Essays in sociology* (pp. 180–195). New York: Oxford University Press.

Webster, M. (1977). Equating characteristics and social interaction: Two experiments. *Sociometry, 40,* 41–50.

Webster, M., & Driskell, J. E. (1978). Status generalization: A review and some new data. *American Sociological Review, 43,* 220–236.

Webster, M., & Foschi, M. (1988). *Status generalization: New theory and research.* Stanford, CA: Stanford University.

Webster, M., & Hysom, S. J. (1998). Creating status characteristics. *American Sociological Review, 63,* 351–379.

Webster, M., & Whitmeyer, J. M. (1999). A theory of second-order expectations and behavior. *Social Psychology Quarterly, 62,* 17–31.

Whyte, W. F. (1943). *Street corner society.* Chicago: University of Chicago Press.

Williams, J. E., & Best, D. L. (1990). *Measuring sex stereotypes: A multination study.* Newbury Park, CA: Sage.

Zelditch, M., & Floyd, A. S. (1998). Consensus, dissensus, and justification. In J. Berger and M. Zelditch (Eds.), *Status, power, and legitimacy: Strategies and theories* (pp. 339–368). New Brunswick, NJ: Transaction Press.

Zelditch, M., Lauderdale, P., & Stublarec, S. (1980). How are inconsistencies between status and ability resolved? *Social Forces, 58,* 1025–1104.

CHAPTER 3

Social Exchange Theory

Karen S. Cook
Eric Rice

INTRODUCTION

Exchange theory has been one of the major theoretical perspectives in the field of social psychology since the early writings of Homans (1961), Blau (1964) and Emerson (1962, 1972). This theoretical orientation is based on earlier philosophical and psychological orientations deriving from utilitarianism on the one hand and behaviorism on the other. The vestiges of both of these theoretical foundations remain evident in the versions of exchange theory that are current today. In this chapter we will focus mainly on the theoretical contributions of exchange theory to the analysis of social psychological and sociological phenomena of importance in understanding the micro-level processes of exchange and the macro-structures they create in society.

While early debates focused on the nature of the actor that inhabits the world of social exchange few of these debates remain salient (see Ekeh, 1974; Heath, 1976). We discuss differences in the underlying models of the actor in the different variants of exchange theory, but we do not view these differences as critical to the major enterprise that has emerged over the last two decades, which has been the efforts of exchange theorists to understand the social structures created by exchange relations and the ways in which such structures constrain and enable actors to exercise power and influence in their daily lives. Whether these interactions are viewed as reciprocal exchanges or negotiated exchanges they are ubiquitous in social life and important to study.

One major hallmark of recent research on social exchange in the field of sociology is its attention to the links between social exchange theory and theories of social status, influence,

KAREN S. COOK AND ERIC RICE • Department of Sociology, Stanford University, Stanford, California 94305

Handbook of Social Psychology, edited by John Delamater. Kluwer Academic/Plenum Publishers, New York, 2003.

social networks, fairness, coalition formation, solidarity, trust, affect and emotion. We address these topics in our review of recent important contributions to exchange theory. Our review is organized topically. First, we provide an overview of the major theories of social exchange. Then we draw out some of the relevant distinctions between the different theoretical formulations. After this exercise we discuss the main topics of research that have been studied by the key contributors to the exchange tradition within the field of sociology over the past two decades. We conclude with a brief statement concerning directions for future research. In particular, we focus on the linkages between the exchange tradition of work in sociology and recent developments in related fields of inquiry such as economic sociology and social networks. In our view there are many important topics of research that have yet to be studied fully within the exchange tradition and that provide an exciting research agenda for the future.

SOCIAL BEHAVIOR AS EXCHANGE

For Homans (1961) the dominant emphasis was the individual behavior of actors in interaction with one another. His primary aim was to explain fundamental processes of social behavior (power, conformity, status, leadership, and justice) from the ground up. Homans believed that there was nothing that emerges in social groups that cannot be explained by propositions about individuals as individuals, together with the given condition that they happen to be interacting. In his effort to embrace this form of reductionism he parted company very clearly with the work of Peter Blau (1964) who built into his theory of social exchange and social structure an analysis of "emergent" properties of social systems.

Homans (1961, p. 13) defined social exchange as the exchange of activity, tangible or intangible, and more or less rewarding or costly, between at least two persons. Cost was viewed primarily in terms of alternative activities or opportunities foregone by the actors involved. Reinforcement principles derived from the kind of behaviorism popular in the early sixties (e.g., the work of B. F. Skinner) were used by Homans to explain the persistence of exchange relations. Behavior is a function of payoffs, whether the payoffs are provided by the nonhuman environment or by other humans. Emerson (1972a) subsequently developed a psychological basis for exchange based on these same reinforcement principles.

Homans explained social behavior and the forms of social organization produced by social interaction by showing how A's behavior reinforced B's behavior (in a two party relation between actors A and B), and how B's behavior reinforced A's behavior in return. This was the explicit basis for continued social interaction explained at the "sub-institutional" level. The existing historical and structural conditions were taken as given. Value is determined by the actor's history of reinforcement and thus also taken as a given at entry into an exchange relation. Homans' primary focus was the social behavior that emerged as a result of the social processes of mutual reinforcement (and the lack of it). Relations could also terminate on the basis of the failure of reinforcement.

Dyadic exchange, the main emphasis of his work, formed the basis for much of his theoretical consideration of other important sociological concepts such as distributive justice, balance, status, leadership, authority, power, and solidarity. Homans' work was often criticized for two main reasons: it was too reductionistic (i.e., it took the principles of psychology as the basis for sociological phenomena) and in analyzing the sub-institutional level of social behavior it underplayed the significance of the institutional as well as the social processes and structures that emerge out of social interaction. In this respect, it is somewhat ironic that one of Homans' lasting contributions to social psychology has been his early treatment of the issue of distributive justice in social exchange relations. The irony derives from the fact that Homans was explicitly much less interested in norms since he was preoccupied with the "sub-institutional" level of analysis in his study of elementary social behavior. His effort to focus on elementary behavior is derived in large part from his opposition to the heavily system-oriented and normative views of Parsons that held sway during the time that he wrote his treatise on social behavior. In his autobiography, Homans (1984) refers to Parsons main work on the social system as the "yellow peril." We discuss Homans' conception of distributive justice in greater detail in the section on fairness in exchange relations.

Homans' key propositions framed the study of social behavior in terms of rewards and punishments. Behavior that is rewarded in general continues (up to the limit of diminishing marginal utility). His first proposition, the success proposition, states that behavior that generates positive consequences is likely to be repeated. The second proposition, the stimulus proposition, states that behavior that has been rewarded on such occasions in the past will be performed in similar situations. The value proposition, the third proposition, specifies that the more valuable the result of an action is to an actor, the more likely that action is to be performed.

The fourth proposition, the deprivation–satiation proposition, qualifies the stimulus proposition introducing the general ideal of diminishing marginal utility: the more often a person has recently received a particular reward for an action, the less valuable is an additional unit of that reward. Finally, the fifth proposition specifies when individuals will react emotionally to different reward situations. People will become angry and aggressive when they do not receive what they anticipate. Homans (1974) later argues they can become angry when they do not receive a fair rate of return, introducing the normative concept of distributive justice into his analysis of dyadic exchange.

Blau, writing at about the same time, framed his micro-exchange theory in terms of rewards and costs as well, but took a decidedly more economic and utilitarian view of behavior rather than building upon reinforcement principles derived from experimental behavioral analysis. A key distinction between these two broad perspectives, as Heath (1976) points out, is whether the actor is forward-looking or backward looking in his determination of what to do next. Utilitarianism generally looks forward. Actors are viewed as acting in terms of anticipated rewards that benefit them and they tend to choose that alternative course of action that maximizes benefit (and minimizes cost, but see Molm, Takashashi, & Peterson, 2000). Reinforcement theories look backwards with actors valuing what has been rewarding to them in the past. The micro-level exchange theory in Blau's work is embryonic and underdeveloped though it is one of the first attempts to apply utilitarianism derived from economics to social behavior.

Blau viewed social exchange as a process of central significance in social life and as underlying the relations between groups as well as between individuals. He focused primarily on the reciprocal exchange of extrinsic benefits and the forms of association and emergent social structures that this kind of social interaction created. According to Blau (1964, p. 91): "Social exchange ... refers to voluntary actions of individuals that are motivated by the returns they are expected to bring and typically do in fact bring from others." In contrasting social and economic exchange he emphasizes the fact that it is more likely in social exchange for the nature of the obligations involved in the exchange to remain unspecified, at least initially. Social exchange, he argues, "involves the principle that one person does another a favor, and while there is a general expectation of some future return, its exact nature is definitely not stipulated in advance" (Blau, 1986, p. 93).

The first third of the book specifies the nature of the social processes that result in associations between individuals (e.g., attraction). Two conditions are defined as important in the assessment of whether or not the behavior involved leads to exchange. The behavior "must be oriented toward ends that can only be achieved through interaction with other persons, and it must seek to adapt means to further achievement of these ends" (Blau, 1986, p. 5). Social exchange processes give rise to differentiation in social status and power based on the dependence of some actors upon others for the provision of valued goods and services.

Much of the remaining focus of his book is on the structure of social exchange and emergent social processes at the group and organizational level, which we discuss in the next section of this chapter. His explicit attempt to build a theory of social structure on the basis of a micro-level theory of exchange was also influential in Emerson's work, though they used different theoretical strategies.

Emerson's important contributions to exchange theory are an interesting mix of the styles of work of both Homans and Blau. The behavioral underpinnings of his micro-level theory of exchange are based on reinforcement principles of the type that animated Homans work in the sixties. In Part I of his theory, Emerson takes the experimental analysis of behavior of Skinner and others as the basis for a formal theory of exchange behavior (see Emerson, 1972a). In Part II, he builds on the analysis of dyadic exchange to develop a framework for the analysis of exchange network structures (see Emerson, 1972b). This work is reviewed in our discussion of exchange and power, since power was the dominant emphasis of the early work on exchange structures. It was the main focus of the work of Blau and Emerson and until recently it has been the central topic of much of the empirical work on social exchange networks.

THE STRUCTURE OF SOCIAL EXCHANGE

One of the distinguishing features of Blau's (1964) influential book on social exchange is the primary emphasis on the structure of associations larger than the dyad. Blau's explicit aim was to develop a theoretical formulation that could form the basis for a theory of macro-social structures as well. His attempt to build links between a micro-sociological theory of behavior and a macro-social theory of social structure was in many respects prophetic of the sociological efforts in the 1980s and 1990s that emerged to examine more closely what came to be called the "micro–macro link" (Alexander, Munch, Smelsev, & Giesen, 1990; Huber, 1991).

In addition to the effort to build a macro-social theory of structure on the basis of a micro-social theory of behavior, Blau identified generic social processes and mechanisms that he viewed as operative at various levels of social organization. These included collective action, legitimacy, opposition, conflict, and cooperation. This work set the stage for a number of developments in exchange theory much later on collective action, coalition formation, justice and status, among others (see below), but Blau has never been given full credit for this broader influence, until quite recently.

Montgomery (1996), for example, reformulates Blau's (1964) model of social exchange to reflect the dynamic nature of interaction and the potential for opportunistic behavior. He demonstrates how social exchange may be formalized as a repeated game, and how game-theoretic models may be used to predict the stability of certain exchange network structures. Whereas Blau's (1964) theory could not explain the strong, reciprocal relationships in the workgroup advice network (Blau, 1955), Montgomery's model (1996) provides a plausible explanation. Montgomery's model only addresses the stability of the exchange network noted by Blau (1955) and does not address the emergence and possible transformation of this structure in real time. The primary emphasis in the work of Blau on exchange structures such as advice networks was on its causal link to the distribution of power and network influence.

EXCHANGE AND POWER

Starting with the early theoretical work of both Blau (1964, 1986) and Emerson (1962, 1972a,b) exchange research has focused on the connection between social structure and the use of power. Blau (1964) believed that inequality and power distributions were emergent properties of ongoing relations of social exchange. Inequalities, he argued, can result from exchange because some actors control more highly valued resources than do others. As a result, they incur social debts that are most easily discharged through the subordination of their social debtors. Blau (1964) argued that such relations of subjugation and domination took on a self-perpetuating character and formed the micro-foundations of power inequality.

For Emerson, the relationship between power and social structure was the central theoretical problem in social exchange theory. From his earliest work in social exchange, Emerson (1962) defined power in relational terms as a function of the dependence of one actor upon another. In a particular dyad (A, B) of exchanging partners, the power of one actor A over another actor B is a function of the dependence of B on A for valued resources and behaviors. Dependence and power are, thus, a function of the value one actor places on resources controlled by another and the relative availability of alternative sources of supply for those resources. This relational conception of power has two central features that helped to generate the large body of social exchange research that exists today. First, power is treated explicitly as relational, not simply the property of a given actor. Second, power is potential power and is derived from the resource connections among actors that may or may not be used.

It was Emerson's move to conceptualize power as a function of social relations that opened the door for the subsequent development of micro-theories connecting social networks to power. Like Blau (1964, 1986), Emerson viewed the fundamental task of social exchange theory to be the building of a framework in which the primary dependent variables were social structure and structural changes. He went on to expand his treatment of power and dependence as a function of social relations to an extensive theory of social exchange relations and outcomes (Emerson, 1972a,b). He argued that potential power was the direct effect of structural arrangements among actors who controlled valued resources (1972b). In his work with Cook (Cook & Emerson, 1978), Emerson brought social exchange theory into its contemporary empirical and theoretical domain. They argued and experimentally demonstrated that power was a function of relative dependence. Moreover, dependence was a feature of networks of interconnected exchange partners whose relative social power was the result of the shape of the social network and the positions they occupied (Cook & Emerson, 1978). While Cook and Emerson (1978) concerned themselves with other exchange outcomes, particularly commitment formation, it was the connection between the use of power and the structure of social networks that became the central focus of a new generation of social exchange theorists.

The most consistent finding among scholars working on social exchange is that relative position in a network of exchange relations produces differences in the relative use of power, manifest in the unequal distribution of rewards across positions in a social network (Cook & Emerson, 1978; Markovsky, Willer, & Patton, 1988; Skvoretz & Willer, 1993). While several competing micro-theories connecting network structure and power-use have emerged over the past two decades, all these competing perspectives converge on one point: "Power differentials between actors are related to differences in actor's positions in the network of exchange relations" (Skvoretz & Willer, 1993, p. 803). The theories, however, view different causal mechanisms as being at work in converting differentials in network position into differentials of power. The Graph-theoretic Power Index approach uses elementary theory and focuses on the role of exclusion in networks (Markovsky et al., 1988; Markovsky, Skvoretz, Willer, Lovaglia, & Erger, 1993; Skvoretz & Willer, 1993). Core theory borrows concepts and solutions from game theory and focuses on viable coalitions among partners (Bienenstock & Bonacich, 1992, 1993, 1997). Equi-dependence theory is based on power-dependence reasoning and centers on equilibrium points in which dependence between partners reaches a balance (Cook & Yamagishi, 1992). Finally, expected value theory is based on a probabilistic logic and looks at the expected value of exchanges weighted by their likelihood of occurrence* (Friedkin, 1992, 1993).

Bienenstock and Bonacich (1992, 1993, 1997) make arguments about how structural arrangements affect the frequency of exchange. They introduce the concept of the core, as developed by game theorists, into the context of social exchange. They argue that intuitively the core as a solution implies that "no group of players will accept an outcome if, by forming a coalition, they can do better" (Bienenstock & Bonacich, 1992). Not only do different network structures produce different power distributions, but also different cores or coalitions emerge as "solutions" to exchange. What this argument implies is that the structural arrangement of actors in relative position to one another can be an impetus for some sub-sets of actors to exchange more frequently than others. Indeed, Bienenstock and Bonacich (1993) are aware of this implication and test it explicitly, finding that the core typically made effective predictions about the frequency of exchanges as well as relative power differences.

Cook and Yamagishi (1992) also propose that structural arrangements can affect patterns of exchange among actors in a social network. They argue that exchanges proceed toward an equilibrium point where partners depend equally upon each other for valued resources. This equi-dependence principle has implications for partner selection. They argue that three different types of relations can emerge from a network of potential exchange relations (which they refer to as an opportunity structure). Exchange relations are those relations where exchanges routinely occur. Non-relations are potential partnerships within the network which are never used, and which if removed from the network do not affect the predicted distribution of power. Finally, latent relations are potential relations, which also remain unused but which if removed affect the subsequent predicted distribution of power across positions in the network.

Friedkin (1992, 1993) likewise argues that some relations are the focus of more frequent interaction than are others, depending upon the structure of alternative relations present in the exchange network. He views networks as a space for potential relations and calculates the probabilities that particular exchanges will occur. Payoffs are a function of the expected value of a particular exchange weighted by the probability of the occurrence of that exchange. For Friedkin, the fact that some relations are used more than others is central to his explanation for how power becomes differentially distributed across positions in a social network. Central to his theory of actor behavior in exchange networks are predictions about how often some exchange relations occur and, moreover, how some relations are more likely to occur within a given structure than are others.

As was the case for Expected Value Theory, the Graph-Theoretic Power Index (GPI) is explicitly concerned with predicting resource acquisition by actors in positions in networks of exchange. In so doing, GPI relies explicitly on the probability of particular partnerships being formed (see Markovsky et al., 1993, pp. 200–204 for a detailed explanation). Beyond

---

*For a detailed discussion of the relative merits of these theories and their predictive abilities see Skvoretz and Willer (1993). For thorough discussions of each of these alternative formulations see the Social Networks special issue edited by Willer (1992).

using the probability of an exchange occurrence in the GPI, Markovsky and his collaborators focus on the idea that some types of structures tend to have more of an impetus toward exclusion than do others. Some network structures can be characterized as weak-power networks and others as strong-power networks. The essential difference between these two types of networks is that strong-power networks include positions that can exclude particular partners without affecting their own relative power or benefit levels. One implication of this distinction is that strong-power networks will tend to have lower levels of commitment than will weak-power networks, because strong-power structures allow the arbitrary exclusion of some partners (Markovsky et al., 1993) facilitating power use.

Molm (1990, 1997a; Molm, Peterson, & Takahashi, 1999) formulated a different conceptualization of the connection between social structure and the use of power. Molm started with Emerson's two central propositions: power is relational and power is a function of dependence. But Molm's program of research took a distinct direction from the other positional theories of social exchange. First, Molm focused on exchanges that are not negotiated, but are reciprocal acts of contingent giving (Molm 1990, 1994, 1997a,b). In reciprocal exchange, actors do not bargain over the division of a finite pool of resources (or a fixed range of positive returns), rather exchange is a process of "gift-giving" or the simple act of the provision of a valued resource or service and exchange relationships develop over time through repeated acts of reciprocal giving. The failure of reciprocity results in infrequent exchange. Second, power is not solely tied to the legitimate use of authority. Power may take the form of coercion or punishment (Molm, 1990, 1994, 1997). Whereas the other theories view the use of power as wielding structural influence through the threat and/or practice of exclusion from exchange (especially when there is a power-imbalance in the network), Molm considers how actors may impose punitive sanctions or negative outcomes on one another. The threat or practice of exclusion is most effective in networks in which there is a large power difference between the actors. And, actors who are most dependent (least powerful) are most likely to be excluded from exchange in certain networks (e.g., networks in which there is a monopoly structure).

Molm's extensive research on non-negotiated or reciprocal exchange has produced important contributions to the understanding of the connections between social structure and the use of power (for a thorough review of this body of research, see Molm, 1997). First, Molm's work demonstrates that not all types of power use are primarily structurally motivated (Molm, 1990, 1994). While exclusion can produce the unconscious use of reward power in negotiated exchange contexts (Molm, 1990), punishment power is used more sparingly. Second, power use can have strategic motivations. Punishment power may not be used frequently but when it is, it is usually employed purposively to influence the future actions of one's exchange partners (Molm, 1990, 1994). Third, her work provides an analysis of the alternative sources of power. Power use in the form of punishment is distinct from power use in the form of the differential distribution of rewards. Finally, her line of research shows how coercive power is connected to and limited by the structures of dependence. Dependence upon rewards is the primary force in exchange relations, motivating both the use of punishment and reward power (Molm, 1990).

EXCHANGE AND FAIRNESS

Normative constraints on the exercise of power in exchange relations often include assessments of fairness, feelings of obligation, and interpersonal commitments. In a subsequent section we discuss the research on the emergence of commitments in exchange relations and networks. Here we focus on fairness and its role in the analysis of social exchange. Both Homans (1961) and Blau (1964) included a conception of fair exchange in their theoretical formulations. For Homans distributive justice exists when rewards align with investments, except where participation in the exchange involves costs beyond those investments. Taking costs into account, Homans (1961) suggests that distributive justice is obtained when the profits (rewards minus costs) of two actors are equal.

Blau addressed norms of fairness as determinants of the "proper" exchange rates. Norms of fair exchange develop over time, Blau argues, to regulate social exchange and to eliminate continuous negotiation and conflict over fair returns.* The conception of fairness and distributive justice in dyadic exchange was expanded in Homans' work to include indirect exchange involving three or more parties. The notion of indirect exchange and the evaluations of exchange relations by third parties were important in the development of Blau's more macro-level theory of exchange and legitimacy.

Cook and Emerson (1978) demonstrated in their work on exchange networks that equity concerns could limit the potentially exploitative use of power by power-advantaged actors (i.e., those with a positional advantage in a network of exchange relations). Once actors in the networks they studied were informed of consequential inequalities in the distribution of profit in the network subsequent exchange reflected a reduction in the nature of the demands made by the powerful actors in their exchanges and an increase in the demands of the less powerful actors. The power differences alone did not operate to justify the inequalities that emerged. Cook and Hegtvedt (1986) show that power disadvantaged actors view inequality in the distribution of profits resulting from exchange as more unfair than do those who have advantageous power positions in the network and who benefit from these positions in terms of higher rates of return.

Molm (1988) has also studied the role of fairness concerns in the exercise of power in relatively small exchange networks. In her research, the type of power the actor has (reward power or coercive power) does seem to influence the perceived fairness of their partners' power use strategies. Molm, Quist, and Wiseley (1994), for example, find that those who are the recipients of coercion feel that the use of power is fairer when the power user was power advantaged in the network than when she was power-disadvantaged. Thus, fairness judgments are affected not only by the power of the power-wielder, but also by the level of power of the recipient of the power use. Molm (1988) reports that fairness judgments also vary by the type of power being used—reward power versus coercive power. Coercive power is used much less frequently in power-imbalanced relations and is likely to evoke strong fairness judgments when exercised. In fact the norm against the use of coercive power appears to be quite strong in exchange settings. Molm argues that this is because of the fear that the use of coercive power to bring a partner's exchange behavior into line with expectations may have negative consequences, perhaps even termination of the relationship. This finding explains why coercive power is used much less frequently. When it is used, however, Molm's work suggests that it can be a fairly effective mechanism for aligning the interests of the parties to the exchange relation. In this research, tradition fairness judgments were based on individuals' own conceptions of justice and they extended beyond the evaluation of the outcomes to the exchange. They included the strategies actors used to obtain exchange outcomes.

The early exchange formulation of distributive justice produced by Homans was subsequently criticized by a number of authors (e.g., Berger, Zelditch, Anderson, & Cohen, 1972; Jasso, 1980) for focusing only on local comparisons (to one's exchange partner or those

---

*Thibaut and Kelley (1959) viewed norms such as fairness as constraints on the exercise of interpersonal power.

similarly situated in an exchange network) rather than referential comparisons (to groups or classes of actors). This criticism led to the development of several alternative justice formulations, the most significant of which is the one developed over the past two decades by G. Jasso (1980, 1986, 1998).

For Jasso, justice is an evaluation of what one receives in exchange or in an allocation more generally in comparison with a standard or expectation regarding one's "just share." The formulation is represented as: $JE = \ln$ (actual share/just share). The logarithm is taken of the ratio of the actual share to the just share to represent the empirical fact that individuals react more strongly to under reward (i.e., receiving less than one expects based on the just share) than to over reward (i.e., receiving more than one anticipated based on the just share). What is expected can be based on either a local comparison, an aggregate set of comparisons, comparison with a group, or with an abstract standard or principle (e.g., equal shares for all). Jasso argues that things like crime rates and collective action in the form of strikes or revolutions are often consequences of perceived injustices among individuals and members of various social groups. Her theory allows for the prediction of differential rates of responses to types of injustice based on the aggregate levels of perceived injustice in the relevant social group or society.

Various recent empirical tests (see Jasso, 2001) of some of these predictions provide some support for Jasso's "new" theory of distributive justice. In the next section we address the role of emotions in exchange relations. Ironically, the introduction of fairness conceptions into exchange theory by the early theorists placed emphasis upon the emotional side of exchange. That actors could view their exchange as unfair or unjust and react negatively with anger was one of the reasons Homans included fairness as a relevant concept in his formulation of dyadic exchange. Actors who receive what they anticipate, he argues, feel their exchange was just. Actors who do not react with either the positive emotion of guilt (when receiving more than they expect) or the negative emotion, anger (when receiving less than they expect). Jasso makes a similar argument concerning the emotions that attend receiving or not receiving the "just share."

EMOTION AND EXCHANGE

Recent work on the role of emotion in social exchange represents a distinct move away from the traditional focus on structural determinants of exchange outcomes, although it returns to some of the topics included in the work of the early exchange theorists, including the emotions associated with fairness in exchange relations. Much of the actual empirical work on exchange over the past 20 years investigates specifically how the social structure affects the outcomes of exchange such as power-use and commitment. The bulk of this research has shown that actors who are simply pursuing their own interests can unknowingly generate inequities in the distribution of resources and pattern exchange relations such that certain relations within an opportunity structure are favored over others, with little or no self-conscious intention of creating either outcome. This newer stream of research begins to explore the emotional consequences of social exchange processes and the role that certain emotions play in the structuring of the network of exchange relations.

Lawler and his collaborators (Lawler & Yoon, 1993, 1996; Lawler, Yoon, & Thye, 2000) have developed a theory, which they refer to as Relational Cohesion Theory, to explain how emotional responses to exchange relationships affect exchange outcomes. Molm and her collaborators (Molm et al., 1999, 2000) have likewise begun to explore the role of emotions in exchange, but focus more on affect as an outcome of exchange rather than a factor guiding exchange outcomes. While these two bodies of research each present a step away from the predominantly structural concerns of many recent exchange researchers (e.g., Markovsky et al.; Beinenstock & Bonacich; Cook et al.) the move to include affect as a concern in social exchange has deep connections to classical exchange theory. Blau (1964) was particularly concerned with the emergent properties of exchange relations. He argued that ongoing relationships of social exchange develop intrinsic value to exchange partners over time, a central concern of Relational Cohesion Theory (Lawler & Yoon, 1996, 1998; Lawler et al., 2000). Moreover, Emerson (1972b) theorized explicitly about trust, liking and commitment as emergent outcomes of successful exchange relations, all outcomes studied by Molm and her colleagues (Molm et al., 1999, 2000). We will discuss each line of research in turn, focusing on the key theoretical contributions to exchange theory.

Relational Cohesion—Lawler's Approach to Emotion

Relational Cohesion Theory is based on the premise that emotion is a proximal mechanism in the exchange process, mediating the effects of structural arrangements on behavioral outcomes. The basic model which Lawler and Yoon (1993, 1996, 1998) originally proposed argued for a simple causal chain: structural power positively affects the frequency of exchanges between actors, which in turn results in the development of positive everyday emotions (e.g., liking, satisfaction) which in turn positively affects relational cohesion which positively affects behavioral outcomes such as commitment to the relation. It is important to note their focus on the relation as the unit of theoretical and empirical analysis. Lawler and Yoon (1993, 1996, 1998) repeatedly stress that central to this process is the idea that actors come to see an ongoing exchange relationship as an object toward which they develop emotional responses. They are careful to point out that each effect in the chain is dependent upon the previous step. It is only relational cohesion that is expected to have a direct effect on commitment behaviors. All other variables work through relational cohesion.

Their early work generated a great deal of empirical support for many aspects of the theory (Lawler & Yoon, 1993, 1996, 1998). Exchange partners expressed positive emotions about their relationships and these positive emotions increased commitment to these relations. Two unanticipated results, however, have led to subsequent modifications of their theory. First, they found that perceptions of uncertainty and the frequency of exchange have enduring independent effects on relational cohesion and commitment (Lawler & Yoon, 1996). Second, when social network structures were added to their empirical tests, the effects of relational cohesion became more complex. In egalitarian relationships (i.e., equal power), they found that affect acted in accordance to their theory. But in power imbalanced dyads, relational cohesion had a positive effect on commitment for powerful actors but a negative effect on commitment for less powerful members of the dyad (Lawler & Yoon, 1998). This latter finding revealed that individual actors within a given relationship might have different orientations toward the relationship, violating the relational focus of the theory.

These empirical outcomes have led to a subsequent modification of the basic model proposed in the original theoretical formulation (Lawler et al., 2000). Lawler and his colleagues now acknowledge that two parallel processes affect the development of relational cohesion, one emotional and the other more cognitive. Actors are motivated to form commitments as a way of reducing uncertainty. They argue that this cognitive process is one of boundary defining, in which individuals who are interested in reducing the possibilities of a loss by increasing the predictability of exchange outcomes come to see relations as distinct social entities. The emotional aspect of exchange is a social bonding process in which the relation becomes an object of intrinsic or expressive value. As was the case with their earlier formulation, this more refined model also finds empirical support, with one important caveat. The independent effect of "predictability," the proximate cognitive causal mechanism, has no direct effect on cohesion, but perplexingly from the theory's standpoint has a strong independent effect on commitments.

Molm's Analysis of Affect in Exchange Relations

Molm and her collaborators (Molm et al., 1999, 2000), while having an equally keen interest in the connections between affect and commitment in social exchange, have a markedly different conception of the social psychological processes at play. For them, affect is not a proximal mechanism promoting commitment to particular relations. In their theory, emotion is an outcome of the exchange process generated largely by commitments to exchange relations. It is structural arrangements, not emotional mechanisms that are responsible for differences in commitment behaviors across different social structures. Affect, they argue, is driven by both the form of exchange (i.e., reciprocal or negotiated) and the level of behavioral commitment induced by the shape of available alternatives to exchange in a social network (Molm et al., 2000).

Central to Molm and her colleagues' theory is the delineation of commitment into two distinct components, one behavioral and the other affective. The behavioral aspect of commitment focuses on the patterns of exchange found in networks of social exchange, in which actors choose to interact repeatedly with one another rather than with their available alternatives. The affective component, however, is concerned with the emotional bonds that develop from repeated experiences with successful exchanges between the same partners. This aspect of commitment shares many similarities with Lawler et al. (2000) "social bonding" aspect of relational cohesion, but there is a critical distinction that must be made between the bonding in each of these two theories. In Relational Cohesion Theory, "social bonding" centers around a relation as a social object, whereas Molm and her colleagues discuss emotion directed toward a particular partner not the relation or group.

Molm et al. (1999) argue that the social psychological mechanisms responsible for each of the two kinds of commitment are different. Behavioral commitment is determined by the structure of relations. Large power imbalances lead to low levels of commitment, while balanced relations promote commitment behaviors (Molm et al., 2000; see also Cook & Emerson, 1978). Affective commitment, however, is a function of two influences: the type of exchange and the level of behavioral commitment. In reciprocal exchanges, as opposed to negotiated exchanges, there are great uncertainties surrounding the outcome of exchanges; partners are not obligated to return non-negotiated gifts. This relative lack of certainty leads actors to develop feelings of trust and other positive affective orientations toward their partners as successful exchange relations emerge. Moreover, as the level of behavioral commitment increases, so too does an actor's level of positive affect toward her partner.

There are two important distinctions to be made between these two theories of emotion in social exchange. First, as we have already mentioned, Molm and her colleagues see affect directed toward particular partners whereas Lawler and his collaborators stress the centrality of the exchange relation as the object of affect. While each camp is careful to distinguish their unit of analysis, it is not entirely clear that such distinctions are critical. For one, Lawler and Yoon (1998) have themselves found looking at actor-specific, relational affect to be empirically and theoretically fruitful, despite their careful use of relations and not individuals as the main unit of analysis in their theory. Moreover, in practice actors may have great difficulty separating affect directed toward a relation from affect directed toward a partner. The second difference may be more critical. Molm et al. (2000) see affect as an outcome, whereas Lawler et al. (2000) view affect as a proximal mechanism. When emotion is taken to be an outcome, structural issues still dominate theorizing, as Molm and her colleagues are careful to point out. When emotion becomes a causal mechanism, however, structural arrangements can then become outcomes. If emotion dictates patterns of behavior to the extent that alternative relations atrophy and cease to become viable exchange alternatives, the shape of the social networks of exchanging actors can be altered. While Lawler and his collaborators continue to find enduring independent effects for factors outside of relational cohesion, their theoretical orientation may provide crucial insights into the dynamic linkages between structure and action.

COMMITMENT TO EXCHANGE RELATIONS

Like many other research topics within exchange theory, the earliest work on commitment formation was largely focused on examining how commitments were affected by structural arrangements between actors (Cook & Emerson, 1978; Cook, Emerson, Gillmore, & Yamagishi, 1983; Markovsky et al., 1988). Connections to other social psychological concepts such as social uncertainty (Cook & Emerson, 1984; Kollock, 1994; Yamagishi, Cook, & Watabe, 1998) or affect (Lawler & Yoon, 1998; Lawler et al., 2000; Molm et al., 2000) were later developments and refinements. In the earliest experimental work on social exchange (Cook & Emerson, 1978; Stolte & Emerson, 1977), researchers have been interested in actor's commitments to particular relations within an opportunity structure of alternative relations. Cook and Emerson (1978) originally described commitment within the context of social exchange as "an interpersonal attachment leading persons to exchange repeatedly with the same partners." For them, commitment was defined in pure behavioral terms, as the frequency to exchange with a given partner relative to all available exchange opportunities. They found that power-use and commitment were inversely related. Commitments, moreover, have been shown to be a function of the distribution of power throughout an exchange network (Markovsky et al., 1988; Lawler & Yoon, 1998). Markovsky and his collaborators argue that some network structures (which they refer to as strong-power networks) allow exclusion in any given round without reducing the rates of exchange for the non-excluded members. Commitments in such network structures are rare. Take, for example, three actors connected in a line, A to B to C. Actor B is pulled equally toward and away from each A and C. Alternatively, some network structures promote commitments. The classic, "kite-shaped" network of four persons (one actor with three alternatives, two with two alternatives—one other and the central actor—and a third actor connected only to the central actor) promotes commitment between the central actor and the actor with only one alternative, and a second committed relation between the remaining two actors (Lawler & Yoon, 1998; Skvoretz & Willer, 1993).

While commitment has been shown to be a function of power-use (Cook & Emerson, 1978) as well as the distribution of power in a network (Markovsky et al., 1988), the focus of most research within social exchange theory on the concept of commitment has linked commitment to social uncertainty.* The conceptualization of uncertainty, however, has undergone some modification over the past 20 years. Initially, Cook and Emerson (1984, p. 13) argued "uncertainty refers to the subjective probability of concluding a satisfactory transaction with any partner" (italics in original). They found that greater uncertainty led to higher levels of commitment with particular exchange partners within an opportunity structure. Actors formed these commitments, they argued, because it increased the frequency of completed exchanges, thereby increasing an actor's overall level of benefit. While this conceptualization of uncertainty would be picked up by Markovsky and his collaborators in their work on exclusion, most other social exchange theorists opted for a new conceptualization of social uncertainty (Markovsky et al., 1988, 1993).

Recently research within exchange theory has conceptualized social uncertainty as the probability of suffering from acts of opportunism imposed by one's exchange partners (Kollock, 1994; Rice, 2002; Yamagishi et al., 1998). Within this new line of research, social uncertainty has also been shown to promote commitment formation (Kollock, 1994; Rice, 2002; Yamagishi et al., 1998). Commitments in all of these studies are examined in environments that allow actors to cheat one another in their exchanges. As such, commitments to specific relations are a viable solution to the problem of uncertainty in these environments. If an actor or subset of actors within a given opportunity structure proves themselves to be a trustworthy exchange partner, continued exchanges with that partner provides a safe haven from opportunistic exchangers. Such commitments, however, have the drawback of incurring sizable opportunity costs in the form of exchange opportunities foregone in favor of the relative safety of commitments.

In Kollock's initial study connecting opportunistic uncertainty and commitment, actors exchanged in two different environments. In one environment (low uncertainty) the true value of goods being exchanged was known, while in the other (high uncertainty) environment the true value of goods was withheld until the end of the negotiations. He found that actors had a greater tendency to form commitments in the higher uncertainty environment. Moreover, actors were willing to forgo more profitable exchanges with untested partners in favor of continuing to transact with known partners who have demonstrated their trustworthiness in previous transactions (i.e., they did not misrepresent the value of their goods).

Yamagishi et al. (1998) further explored the connections between uncertainty and commitment, deviating from Kollock's experimental design but coming to similar conclusions. In their experiment, actors are faced with the decision of remaining with a given partner or entering a pool of unknown potential partners. They employed several modifications of this basic design, but in each instance the expected value of exchange outside the existing relation was higher than the returns from the current relation. They found that actors were willing to incur sizeable opportunity costs to reduce the risks associated with opportunism. Moreover, they found that uncertainty in either the form of an uncertain probability of loss or an unknown size of loss were each able to promote commitments between exchange partners.

Recent work by Rice (2002) has attempted to bridge this early work on uncertainty as the probability of finding an exchange partner with uncertainty as environments that allow opportunism. In both the Kollock (1994) and Yamagishi et al. (1998) studies, exchange occurs among actors in environments which allow for the potential for opportunism, but where actors are guaranteed of finding an exchange partner on every round. In Rice's (2002) design, actors exchange in two different environments: one that allows actors to renege on their negotiated

---

*Recent research has also demonstrated the strong connection between affect directed at exchange partners or exchange relations and commitments. This research is reviewed in the section titled "Emotion and Exchange."

exchange rates (high uncertainty) and one where negotiations are binding (low uncertainty). Exchange, however, also occurs within two different network structures: a complete network where all actors can always find a partner, and a T-shaped network, where two actors are excluded from exchange every round. He found that uncertainty promoted commitment in the complete network, but not in the T-shaped (strong-power) network. Commitments, he argued, are viable solutions to uncertainty in networks that do not force exclusion. In networks that do force exclusion, the structural pull away from commitment is sufficiently intense as to undermine the propensity to form commitments. Whereas the earlier work of Kollock and Yamagishi and his collaborators suggested that actors would incur sizeable opportunity costs to avoid potentially opportunistic partners, Rice's (2002) work suggests that such tendencies can be muted by particularly deterministic network structures.

Rice (2002), moreover, expands the work on social uncertainty in exchange by exploring how commitment relates to other exchange outcomes, such as the distribution of resources across relations and within networks as a whole. He argues that commitments will reduce the use of power in imbalanced networks, resulting in a more egalitarian distribution of resources across different positions in a network. In networks where power between actors is unequal, power-advantaged actors have relatively better opportunities for exchange than their power-disadvantaged partners. These superior alternatives are the basis of power-advantaged actor's power. If, as uncertainty increases, power-advantaged actors form commitments with power-disadvantaged actors, they erode the very base of their power. Forming commitments entails ignoring potential opportunities. Alternative relations are the basis of structural power and as these relations atrophy, the use of power and the unequal distribution of resources will be reduced.

Recent research results on exchange under social uncertainty indicate a strong tendency for actors to incur large opportunity costs by forming commitments to achieve the relative safety or certainty of ongoing exchange with proven trustworthy partners (Kollock, 1994; Rice, 2002; Yamagishi et al., 1998). In addition to these opportunity costs Rice (2002) argues that commitments may also have unintended negative consequences at the macro level of exchange. Actors tend to invest less heavily in their exchange relations under higher levels of uncertainty. Moreover, acts of defection in exchange while producing individual gain, result in a collective loss, an outcome common in prisoner's dilemma games. Both processes reduce the overall collective gains to exchange in the network as a whole. So while there is a socially positive aspect to uncertainty, in so far as commitments increase feelings of solidarity (e.g., Lawler & Yoon, 1998) and resources are exchanged more equally across relations (Rice, 2002), there is the attendant drawback of reduced aggregate levels of exchange productivity and efficiency.

EXCHANGE, POWER AND STATUS RELATIONS

In recent work, Thye and others have made explicit linkages between current theories of exchange and theories of status. Although both Homans and Blau included considerations of status processes centrally in their original formulations of exchange the empirical research on exchange since the 1980s shifted attention to power processes primarily independent of status dynamics. After two decades of concentrated work on the role of network structure as a determinate of power in exchange networks it thus appears that status processes have been given the short shrift. In addition, some of the most developed theoretical formulations on status dynamics in social relations during this same time period have given much less attention to power than originally implicated in earlier work. For example, the earliest formulations of expectations states theory in sociology (e.g., Berger et al., 1972) presented status as a clear determinant of the observable power and prestige order within a group. Status in this sense is viewed as a cause of differences in power and influence in society. In contrast, the exchange formulation of power dynamics focused more attention on the structural and locational causes of power differences. The location of an actor in a network was viewed as the key determinant of an actor's power and influence (in the form of control over needed resources such as knowledge, information or goods and services at her disposal).

The interesting feature of the most recent work by Thye (2000) and Lovaglia (1994, 1995), among others, is that they are attempting to produce a conception of composite power—power that is determined by both location in a structure of exchange relations and power that is derived from the status of the actors in a hierarchy of status relations. Specifically, power in this framework is conceived as a structural potential that enables some actors to earn favorable resource distributions at the expense of others. The status of the actors in the exchange is viewed as having influence on the perceived value of the resources to be exchanged. Resources (e.g., goods and services) associated with high status actors are perceived to be of higher status value than those of low status actors and this valuation is symmetric. That is, both low and high status actors have the same view (i.e., view high status actors' resources as more valuable). Thye's (2000) findings indicate that there is a preference for interaction with high status actors in exchange networks of equal power. Even in unequal power networks status confers an advantage on high status actors. High status actors were more actively sought after as exchange partners and received more favorable exchange rates in both equal and unequal (weak) power networks.

This research begins the interesting task of determining the separate effects of status and power differentials. What are the mitigating effects of positional power or status when the two are not consonant? How does low status affect the relative power of an actor with high positional power or vice versa? The findings Thye (2000) reports suggest that there is an interesting combinatorial effect of status and positional power in exchange networks in which weak power differences exist. The relatively high status actors in lower power positions exercised more power and were preferred exchange partners more often than in networks in which there is no status distinction among the actors in the network, only positional differences. The effort to link attributional and positional determinants of power is an important direction for new research in exchange network theory. It might also draw on significant developments in network methods (Faust & Wasserman, 1992) that allow the analysis of positional and attributional factors as predictors of network level events and processes. As Thye (2000, p. 426) concludes, "further research is needed to determine exactly how levels of power and status differentially affect the tendency to seek partners for exchange." Another topic of research that crosses research traditions in social psychology is the work on collective action. In the next section we discuss some of the links between research on social dilemmas and collective action in exchange networks.

COLLECTIVE ACTION AND SOCIAL EXCHANGE

Research on social exchange has many theoretical ties to the enormous body of research on social dilemmas (for a thorough review of this research see, e.g., Yamagishi, 1995). The theoretical problems, however, faced by theorists of power and dependence generate a unique perspective on the problems of collective action in exchange (e.g., Cook & Gillmore, 1984; Leik, 1992; Lawler et al., 2000). As with most collective action problems, actors in social exchange contexts face the competing pressures of satisfying self-interest and the provision of collective goods (see Yamagishi, 1995 for a review of social dilemma research in sociology). Moreover, while many exchanges are the outcome of explicit negotiations, many exchanges occur within contexts in which there is no guarantee that partners will fulfill their obligations (Kollock, 1994; Molm, 1997a,b; Yamagishi et al., 1998). Such uncertainties characterize a great many exchanges outside of the laboratory context (Heckathorn, 1985). Heckathorn has argued that exchanges in the "real world" are thus the product of two factors: the explicit negotiation over social goods and the individual decision to abide by the terms of trade. He claims that social exchange thus entails not only the bargaining over social goods, but also the playing out of a prisoner's dilemma concerning the fulfillment of social obligations.

The dynamics of power and dependence within networks of exchange partners create additional problems of collective action that cannot be characterized as a prisoner's dilemma. Power inequality creates strains in exchange relations and provides an impetus toward structural changes, creating problems of collective action unique to exchange contexts (Cook & Gillmore, 1984; Emerson, 1972b; Lawler & Yoon, 1998). Before turning to empirical work on such collective action problems within exchange it is necessary to briefly review Emerson's (1972b) ideas concerning power balancing mechanisms, for this theory constitutes the intellectual basis for this work. Emerson argued that reciprocity was a core feature of exchange relations over the long term and that ongoing exchange relations could be characterized as relations in which a balance of power existed. Power imbalances, he argued, were a temporary state of social relations, which generated strains in exchange relations that must be resolved. He claimed that four distinct "balancing" operations existed which would stabilize relationships. Within the context of a given dyadic relation, if the dependence of an actor A for good y (controlled by actor B) is greater than B's dependence on A for good x (controlled by actor A), there are four possible outcomes: First, there can be a decrease in the value of good y for actor A, called "withdrawal." Second, there can be an increase in the value of x for actor B, called "status-giving." Third, there can be an increase in the number of alternatives open to A, called "network extension." Fourth, there can be a reduction in the number of alternatives open to B, called "coalition formation." Note that the first two mechanisms concern changes in value whereas the second two focus on structural change. With the exception of Emerson (1987) exchange theorists have focused their energies on exploring the latter two outcomes.

The work on coalition formation (Cook & Gillmore, 1984) has empirically demonstrated that power imbalances do promote the formation of coalitions. In a network in which there are power imbalances, some actors can be characterized as power-advantaged while others are power-disadvantaged. In simple hierarchical network structures in which one power-advantaged actor exchanges with a number of power-disadvantaged actors, a coalition of all power-disadvantaged actors against the power-advantaged actor will balance power in the network (Cook & Gillmore, 1984). Those coalitions that do not include all disadvantaged actors will not attain power-balance because the power-advantaged actor still possesses alternatives to the coalition. Moreover, coalitions that include all power-disadvantaged actors tend to be stable over time, as Emerson (1972b) would argue they should. Coalitions, however, that do not include all disadvantaged actors tend to deteriorate over time.

The tensions generated by power inequality can also result in network extension. Power-disadvantaged actors rather than banding together to form coalitions to balance power, may alternatively seek out new relations, thus also reducing their dependence upon a given actor for valued resources. This solution to power balance has been less thoroughly explored by exchange researchers, but warrants a brief discussion none-the-less.

Recently Leik (1992) proposed a theory of network extension and contraction based upon the theoretical principles of the GPI model developed by Network Exchange Theory (e.g., Markovsky et al., 1988, 1993; Willer & Anderson, 1981). He argues that so long as actors are assumed to be trying to maximize their power vis-à-vis their partners, power-advantaged actors will attempt to reduce linkages between partners in an effort to consolidate their power while power-disadvantaged actors will attempt to create new linkages in order to increase their power. He goes on to explain that such a theory requires that actors have a great deal of information and strategic savvy: "Without sufficient information and the savvy to utilize it, neither the weak nor the strong will be able to perceive the advantage of linkage changes" (Leik, 1992, p. 316). Recent empirical work by Lawler and Yoon (1998), however, suggests that emotional responses to inequality may be sufficient to motivate network extension. While Lawler and Yoon are explicitly concerned with developing a theory of relational cohesion based upon affect directed toward exchange relations (see the discussion of this work above), their empirical work sheds light on issues of network extension. Toward the end of their experiment, actors are freed from the constraints of their initial network of exchange relations and allowed to interact with every other participant. Actors in relations that can be characterized as power balanced continued to seek out one another in exchange. Power-advantaged actors, likewise continued to solicit exchanges from their disadvantaged partners, whereas the disadvantaged attempted to form new relations with other participants who had not been previously exploitative (Lawler & Yoon, 1998). Thus, the negative affect directed toward a power-advantaged actor by a power-disadvantaged partner in concert with the low levels of reward accrued by power-disadvantaged actors seems sufficient to motivate network extension.

Beyond the issues of power-balancing operations and prisoner's dilemma features of exchange relations, a third type of collective action problem has arisen in recent research in social exchange: generalized exchange. Generalized exchange encompasses those social exchange relations in which one actor gives resources to another, but where such resources are reciprocated not by the recipient but rather a third party (Molm & Cook, 1995). These exchange relations inherently involve a minimum of three actors. Moreover, there is no one-to-one correspondence between what two actors directly give to and receive from one another. There have been several recent attempts to explain how such complex exchange systems may emerge (Bearman, 1997; Takahashi, 2000; Ziegler, 1990).

Generalized exchange, like coalition formation, presents a collective action problem unique to work on social exchange. First, the fact that all generalized exchange systems require a minimum of three actors means that coordination problems are likely. Because actors are not simply trading across a particular dyad, they must rely on the goodwill of a third-party, over whom they have no immediate control. Second, such unilateral gift giving opens systems of generalized exchange to free riders. Without immediate guarantees of reciprocity or mutually contingent exchanges, actors can shirk their social responsibilities and reap the rewards of systems of unilateral gift giving by receiving rewards and refusing to pass on rewards to others. This conflict between group and self-interest means that generating and maintaining collective action is difficult (Takahashi, 2000). Takahashi (2000) demonstrates that pure generalized exchange may emerge among self-interested actors in social systems where actors have some information about the behaviors of their immediate "neighbors." His solution, like many solutions to the problem of the evolution of cooperation in systems of repeated prisoner's dilemmas relies on the existence of network structures that provide some sort of localized information and accountability (e.g., Axlerod, 1984; Macy & Skvoretz, 1998).

FUTURE DIRECTIONS: LINKAGES TO
ECONOMIC SOCIOLOGY AND THE STUDY
OF NETWORKS

While exchange theorists for the past few decades have been primarily experimentalists, there is certainly room for exchange theory to make more meaningful ties to other sub-fields on the broader canvas of sociological research. The best candidate for such a venture seems to be the emerging field of economic sociology. Exchange theory and economic sociology focus on a similar set of core theoretical issues. Both fields balk at the notion that individual motives (or the mere aggregation of individual motives) can properly explain transactions between social actors. Moreover, both sub-fields theorize extensively about the role of networks of ongoing relations in exchange. We will argue in this section that a marriage of these two fields would greatly benefit each. First, we discuss the reasons for the development of each field in isolation from the other. We then focus on the theoretical overlap in the work of "embeddedness" and Relational Cohesion Theory and argue that each field can benefit from exposure to the other. Finally, we provide two illustrations of this argument by looking through the lens of exchange theory at recent studies within economic sociology of the credit card market in Russia and of emerging business relations that extend beyond familial and friendship ties in this transitional economy.

The separation of these two sub-fields is likely due to the conflation of several issues. First, early theorists of social exchange were careful to make the distinction between economic and social exchange. This focus, however, has slowly receded as work in exchange theory has become increasingly abstracted and the exchange of resources under study are now typically concrete and quantifiable objects. Second, exchange theory is often aligned with rational choice theory (Blau, 1964; Bienenstock & Bonacich, 1992; Heckathorn, 1984) and economic sociologists often use rational choice theory as a theoretical foil against which to argue their more "social" theories. But even when exchange theory is founded in operant psychology (e.g., Emerson, 1972a; Molm, 1994), connections between the two sub-fields are rare. This separation can most readily be attributed to methodological divides. Exchange theorists tend to generate a priori predictions that they test in laboratory experiments, whereas economic sociologists favor ex post explanations and empirical field research. Such differences in style have caused these two fields to develop in relative isolation.

Research on "embeddedness" shares a great deal of intellectual common ground with contemporary work in social exchange. Exchanges are rarely purely economic; rather they often are "embedded" in networks of ongoing social relations. This last claim is the central claim of economic sociology and the focus of much of the theoretical and empirical research. Uzzi (1996) argues that "embeddedness" has profound behavioral consequences, affecting the shape of exchange relations and the success of economic ventures. "A key behavioral consequence of embeddedness is that it becomes separate from the narrow economic goals that originally constituted the exchange and generates outcomes that are independent of the narrow economic interest of the relationship." (Uzzi, 1996, p. 681). The recent work by Lawler and Yoon (1996, 1998) and Lawler et al. (2000) mirrors this set of theoretical concerns. They argue that as exchange relations emerge actors develop feelings of relational cohesion directed toward the ongoing exchange relation. These feelings of cohesion result in a wide variety of behaviors which extend beyond the "economic" interests of the relationship, such as gift-giving, forming new joint ventures across old ties, and remaining in a relationship despite the presence of new, potentially more profitable partnerships.

There is great mutual benefit to be derived from increased attention to research done in each field. Exchange theorists can benefit from the rich tapestry of "real" world (i.e., non-laboratory) exchange contexts studied by economic sociologists. While great theoretical advances have been made in exchange theory within the context of experimental work, any sociological theory worth its salt must also speak to empirical phenomenon outside of the laboratory. Moreover, new insights and new theoretical directions are likely to be uncovered by a renewed focus on the kinds of exchanges that can be studied outside of the experimental setting. Economic sociology would likewise benefit from the work of exchange theorists, particularly in so far as exchange theory provides easily derivable and testable predictions for actor behavior under exchange. Moreover, exchange theorists have conducted research on the effects of a number of interesting variables that often go overlooked by economic sociologists, such as the use and distribution of power and cohesion within relationships.

To illustrate the potential value of such a marriage, we discuss how two recent studies within economic sociology relate to recent work in exchange theory and explore the possibilities for new research generated by such an examination. Recently in one study Guseva and Rona-Tas (2001) have compared the credit card markets of post-Soviet Russia and the United States. They are concerned with how credit lenders in each country manage the uncertainties of lending credit. In the United States, they argue, credit lending is a highly rationalized process that converts the uncertainty of defaulting debtors to manageable risk. Lenders take advantage of highly routinized systems of scoring potential debtors, through the use of credit histories and other easily accessed personal information. This system allows creditors in the United States to be open to any individuals who meet these impersonal criteria.

In Russia, creditors must reduce uncertainties through personal ties and commitments. Defaulting is an enormous problem in Russia, aggravated by the fact that credit information such as that used by American lenders has, until quite recently, been unavailable. To overcome these uncertainties Russian banks seeking to establish credit card markets must use and stretch existing personal ties. Loan officers make idiosyncratic decisions about potential debtors, based largely on connections to the banks, or known customers of the bank. In this way defaulting debtors cannot easily disappear, as they can be tracked through these ties.

Viewed through the lens of recent theorizing on the connections between uncertainty and commitments, these different strategies seem quite reasonable. As discussed earlier, exchange theorists have repeatedly shown that as uncertainty increases, commitments to specific relations likewise increases (Cook & Emerson, 1984; Kollock, 1994; Yamagishi et al., 1998). In the case of credit card markets, it is clear that the United States presents an environment of relatively low uncertainty, compared to the high-levels of uncertainty present in Russia. Exchange theory argues therefore that commitments will be greater in Russia, which is exactly the case. Lending is facilitated by existing commitments to the banks or the bank's known customers. While such theoretical confluence is interesting, it is in generating new insights that one can see the value of examining this situation through the lens of exchange theory. Rice (2002) in his work on exchange under uncertainty argues that network structure will intervene in the process of commitment formation. This insight suggests that sociologists ought to ask how different shaped networks of potential debtors and lenders in Russia affect the use of commitments to procure credit? Rice also argues that uncertainty, while promoting commitment simultaneously reduces the overall level of exchange in networks; this is yet another outcome observed in the Russian credit card market, but one largely ignored by Guseva and Rona-Tas (2001). It is this aspect of the problem that is recently addressed to some extent in another study by Radaev (2002) on the emergence of reputational systems in Russia. Finally, Yamagishi and his collaborators (Yamagishi et al., 1998) argue that uncertainty can stem from either the probability of loss or the size of loss. Another question that should be raised in this context is how the size of loss, not just the potential for loss relates to the behaviors observed in the Russian versus the American credit card markets.

This examination, however, is not a one sided affair, benefiting only economic sociology. Exchange theorists also can learn from this example. Exchange theory tends to focus on commitments as an outcome, not as a social mechanism. In the case of the Russian credit card market, existing commitments provide a mechanism through which network structures are expanded and changed. This raises the issue of how commitments may in turn create opportunities for network expansion and/or reduction. Similarly, in the context of credit card markets, there are two distinct roles, creditors and debtors. Exchange theory, with the exception of Kollock's (1994) work, does not focus on the explicit context of buying and selling. Exchanges are studied among actors who divide, give or trade resources with other actors who are engaged in an identical task. Much of the world of economic transactions, however, does not occur in such contexts, rather buying and selling are the primary modes of exchange. Exchange theorists if they are to speak to economic sociologists and inform economic research must develop a more explicit and rigorous theory of exchange across roles of this type.

In another recent study of emerging markets for non-state businesses in Russia, Radaev (2002) investigates the mechanisms and institutional arrangements that help actors cope with the uncertainty and opportunism common in such an uncertain environment. Two features of the situation are significant. Under uncertainty actors turn to interpersonal ties involving trust and greater certainty to produce some security in the context of high levels of opportunism. This is the behavior that is documented also by Guseva and Rona-Tas (2001) discussed previously.

In documenting the uncertainty of business relations in Russia, respondents to the surveys Radaev (2002) conducted indicated how important honesty and trustworthiness were in business partners. This result is driven by the fact that there are frequent infringements of business contracts creating both risk and high levels of uncertainty. Half of the respondents admitted that contract infringements were quite frequent in Russian business in general and a third of the respondents had had a high level of personal experience with such infringements. This degree of opportunism creates barriers to the formation of reciprocal trust relations. Widespread distrust exists of newcomers to the market but reliable partners are viewed as more trustworthy.

In this climate commitment is clearly the most predictable response to uncertainty as in the case of Kollock's (1994) rubber markets and the credit card market discussed by Guseva and Rona-Tas (2001). Another reason for the uncertainty is that the existing institutions lack credibility and legitimacy. Dispute resolution is not effectively managed by the courts and business contracts are not secured by existing institutions. To cope with this fact the business community creates closed business networks with reputation systems that define insiders and outsiders. This system is based on information obtained from third parties, but more importantly on common face-to-face meetings between potential partners.

In a 1993 survey conducted by Radaev the emerging networks of entrepreneurs in Russia primarily included personal acquaintance (42%), friends and their relatives (23%) and relatives (17%). This fact reflects the reality discussed in the work of Guseva and Rona-Tas (2001) on the credit card market in Russia. Only a small percentage (11%) of the business contacts in 1993 were new or relatively new acquaintances. More recently, however, the move is away from affect-based commitment and trust to reputation-based trust as the networks formed purely on the basis of acquaintance, kin ties or friendship have tended to fall apart due to inefficiency. The relatively closed business networks that have emerged to replace the older "familial" and friendship ties provide better information about the trustworthiness of the partners and their competence. Within exchange theory the formation of commitment and trust networks (see also Cook & Hardin, 2001) in the face of uncertainty provide theoretical support for the evidence provided by Radaev (2003) and others on the recent emergence of business networks in Russia. This argument is also consistent with Rice's (2002) argument that commitments can have negative aggregate level consequences in terms of productivity and efficiency in exchange systems.

These concluding remarks identify only some of the ways in which exchange theory can inform recent empirical work in what has come to be called economic sociology. Topics that have returned to center stage on the agenda for future research in the exchange theory tradition such as trust, emotion, affect, fairness, strategic action, commitment and reputational networks all have potential applications in the analysis of the emergence of exchange networks in countries with transitional economies as well as in other types of economies as evidenced by the work of many economic sociologists (e.g., Uzzi, Granovetter, etc.). Moving from closed groups to more open networks of trade mirror some of the processes identified by Emerson (1972) as important for study from an exchange perspective contrasting group-level exchange systems (productive exchange in corporate groups) with network-level exchange. In addition, the return to the study of the significant differences between social processes (e.g., power, justice, and commitment) involved in different types of exchange, negotiated, reciprocal, and generalized exchange (Molm, 1988, 1990, 1994) has the potential to provide new insights into a variety of emergent forms of exchange under different circumstances. For example, under conditions of uncertainty, negotiated, binding exchange is likely to emerge before reciprocal (most often, non-binding) exchange because reciprocal exchange involves a greater degree of uncertainty. Reciprocal exchange, as Molm and her coauthors (Molm et al., 1999, 2000) have documented, generally requires more trust since the terms of exchange are not simultaneously negotiated and opportunism is possible. This research has the potential to produce a theoretical basis for the empirical work on the development of various economic sectors as well as for the study of the Internet and its consequences for the world of trade.

Exchange theory provides a general analytic approach to a wide array of social processes that are central to sociological inquiry at various levels. We have provided not only an introduction to the current status of this work, but also a window into the ways in which it continues to produce important insights into the world around us as the social, political, and economic landscape continues to change, often more rapidly than our theories do.

ACKNOWLEDGMENT: The authors would like to acknowledge the assistance of Alexandra Gerbasi in the production of this chapter and the support of Russell Sage Foundation and Stanford University.

REFERENCES

Alexander, Jeffery, Munch, Richard, Smelser, Neil, & Giesen, Bernhard. (1990). *The micro–macro link*. Berkeley: University of California Press.

Axelrod, Robert. (1984). *The evolution of cooperation*. New York: Basic Books.

Blau, P. M. (1955). *The dynamics of bureaucracy*. Chicago: University of Chicago Press.

Blau, P. M. (1964). *Exchange and power in social life*. New York: Wiley.

Blau, P. M. (1986). *Exchange and power in social life* (2nd printing). New Brunswick, NJ: Transaction Books.

Bearman, Peter. (1997). Generalized exchange. *American Journal of Sociology, 102*, 1383–1415.

Berger, Joseph, Cohen, Bernard, & Zelditch, Morris, Jr. (1972). Status characteristics and social interaction. *American Sociological Review, 37*, 241–255.

Berger, Joseph, Zelditch, Morris, Jr., Anderson, Bo, & Cohen, Bernard. (1972). Structural aspects of distributive justice: A status value formation. In Joseph Berger, Morris Zelditch Jr., & Bo Anderson (Eds.), *Sociological theories in progress*. Boston: Houghton Mifflin.

Bienenstock, Elisa Jayne, & Bonacich, Phillip. (1992). The core as a solution to exclusionary networks. *Social Networks, 14*, 231–243.

Bienenstock, Elisa Jayne, & Bonacich, Phillip. (1993). Game-theory models for exchange networks: Experimental results. *Sociological Perspectives, 36*, 117–135.

Bienenstock, Elisa Jayne, & Bonacich, Phillip. (1997). Network exchange as a cooperative game. *Rationality and Society, 9*, 937–965.

Cook, Karen S., & Emerson, Richard M. (1978). Power, equity and commitment in exchange networks. *American Sociological Review, 43*, 721–739.

Cook, Karen S., & Emerson, Richard M. (1984). Exchange networks and the analysis of complex organizations. *Research in the Sociology of Organizations, 3*, 1–30.

Cook, Karen S., Emerson, Richard M., Gillmore, Mary R., & Yamagishi, Toshio. (1983). The distribution of power in exchange networks: Theory and experimental results. *American Journal of Sociology, 89*, 275–305.

Cook, Karen S., & Gillmore, Mary R. (1984). Power, dependence and coalitions. In E. J. Lawler (Ed.), *Advances in group processes* (pp. 27–58). Greenwich, CT: JAI Press.

Cook, Karen S., & Hardin, Russell. (2001). Norms of cooperativeness and networks of trust. In M. Hechter & K.-D. Opp (Eds.), *Social norms* (pp. 327–347). New York: Russell Sage Foundation.

Cook, Karen S., & Hegtvedt, Karen A. (1986). Justice and power: An exchange analysis. In H. W. Bierhoff, Ronald L. Cohen, & Jerald Greenberg (Eds.), *Justice in social relations* (pp. 19–41). New York: Plenum.

Cook, Karen S., & Yamagishi, Toshio. (1992). Power in exchange networks: A power-dependence formulation. *Social Networks, 14*, 245–265.

Ekeh, Peter. (1974). *Social exchange theory: The two traditions*. Cambridge: Harvard University Press.

Emerson, Richard. (1962). Power-dependence relations. *American Sociological Review, 27*, 31–41.

Emerson, Richard. (1972a). Exchange theory, Part I: A psychological basis for social exchange. In Joseph Berger, Morris Zelditch Jr., & B. Anderson (Eds.), *Sociological theories in progress* (pp. 38–57). Boston: Houghton Mifflin.

Emerson, Richard. (1972b). Exchange theory, Part II: Exchange relations and networks. In Joseph Berger, Morris Zelditch Jr., & B. Anderson (Eds.), *Sociological theories in progress* (pp. 58–87). Boston: Houghton Mifflin.

Emerson, Richard. (1987). Toward a theory of value in social exchange. In Karen S. Cook (Ed.), *Social exchange theory* (pp. 11–58). Newbury Park, CA: Sage.

Faust, Katherine, & Wasserman, Stanley. (1992–1993). Centrality and prestige: A review and synthesis. *Journal of Quantitative Anthropology, 4*, 23–78.

Friedkin, Noah E. (1992). An expected value model of social power: Predictions for selected exchange networks. *Social Networks, 14*, 213–229.

Friedkin, Noah E. (1993). An expected value model of social exchange outcomes. In Edward J. Lawler (Ed.), *Advances in group processes* (pp. 163–93). Greenwich, CT: JAI Press.

Guseva, Alya, & Rona-Tas, Akos. (2001). Uncertainty, risk, and trust: Russian and American credit card markets compared. *American Sociological Review, 66*, 623–646.

Heath, Anthony F. (1976). *Rational choice and social exchange: A critique of exchange theory*. Cambridge: Cambridge University Press.

Heckathorn, Douglas D. (1984). A formal theory of social exchange: Process and outcome. *Current Perspectives in Social Theory, 5*, 145–180.

Heckathorn, Douglas D. (1985). Power and trust in social exchange. In Edward J. Lawler (Ed.), *Advances in group processes* (pp. 143–167). Greenwich, CT: JAI Press.

Homans, G. C. (1961). *Social behavior and its elementary forms*. New York: Harcourt, Brace and World.

Homans, G. C. (1974). *Social behavior and its elementary forms*. New York: Harcourt, Brace and World.

Homans, G.C. (1984). *Coming to my senses: The autobiography of a sociologist*. New Brunswick, NJ: Transaction Books.

Huber, Joan. (1991). *Macro–micro linkages in sociology*. Newbury Park, CA: Sage.

Jasso, Guillermina. (1980). A new theory of distributive justice. *American Sociological Review, 45*, 3–32.

Jasso, Guillermina. (1986). A new representation of the just term in distributive justice theory: Its properties and operation in theoretical derivation and empirical estimation. *Mathematical Sociology, 12*, 251–274.

Jasso, Guillermina. (1998). Studying justice: Cross-country data for empirical justice analysis. *Social Justice Research, 11*, 193–209.

Jasso, Guillermina. (2001). Rule finding about rule making: Comparison processes and the making of rules. In M. Hechter & K.-D. Opp (Eds.), *Social norms* (pp. 348–393). New York: Russell Sage Foundation.

Kollock, Peter. (1994). The emergence of exchange structures: An experimental study of uncertainty, commitment, and trust. *American Journal of Sociology, 100,* 313–45.

Lawler, Edward J., & Yoon, Jeongkoo. (1993). Power and the emergence of commitment behavior in negotiated exchange. *American Sociological Review, 58,* 465–481.

Lawler, Edward J., & Yoon, Jeongkoo. (1996). Commitment in exchange relations: Test of a theory of relational cohesion. *American Sociological Review, 61,* 89–108.

Lawler, Edward J., & Yoon, Jeongkoo. (1998). Network structure and emotion in exchange relations. *American Sociological Review, 63,* 871–894.

Lawler, Edward J., Yoon, Jeongkoo, & Thye, Shane R. (2000). Emotion and group cohesion in productive exchange. *American Journal of Sociology, 106,* 616–657.

Leik, Robert K. (1992). New directions for network exchange theory: Strategic manipulation of network linkages. *Social Networks, 14,* 309–323

Lovaglia, Michael J. (1994). Relating power to status. *Advances in Group Processes, 11,* 87–111.

Lovaglia, Michael J. (1995). Power and status: Exchange, attribution, and expectation states. *Small Group Research, 26,* 400–426.

Macy, Michael W., & Skvoretz, John. (1998). The evolution of trust and cooperation between strangers: A computational model. *American Sociological Review, 63,* 638–660.

Markovsky, Barry, Willer, David, & Patton, Travis. (1988). Power Relations in Exchange Networks. *American Sociological Review, 5,* 101–117.

Markovsky, Barry, Skvoretz, John, Willer, David, Lovaglia, Michael J., & Erger, Jeffrey. (1993). The seeds of weak power: An extension of network exchange theory. *American Sociological Review, 58,* 197–209.

Molm, Linda. (1988). The structure and use of power: A comparison of reward and punishment power. *Social Psychology Quarterly, 51,* 108–122.

Molm, Linda. (1990). Structure, action, and outcomes: The dynamics of power in social exchange. *American Sociological Review, 55,* 427–447.

Molm, Linda. (1994). Is punishment effective? Coercive strategies in social exchange. *Social Psychology Quarterly, 57,* 75–94.

Molm, Linda. (1997a). *Coercive power in social exchange.* Cambridge: Cambridge University Press.

Molm, Linda. (1997b). Risk and power use: Constraints on the use of coercion in exchange. *American Sociological Review, 62,* 113–133.

Molm, Linda, & Cook, Karen S. (1995). Social exchange and exchange networks. In Karen S. Cook, Gary Alan Fine, & James S. House (Eds.), *Sociological perspectives on social psychology* (pp. 209–235). Boston: Allyn & Bacon.

Molm, Linda, Peterson, Gretchen, & Takahashi, N. (1999). Power in negotiated and reciprocal exchange. *American Sociological Review, 64,* 876–890.

Molm, Linda, Quist, Theron M., & Wiseley, Phillip A. (1994). Imbalanced structures, unfair strategies: Power and justice in social exchange. *American Sociological Review, 49,* 98–121.

Molm, Linda, Takahashi, N., & Peterson, Gretchen. (2000). Risk and trust in social exchange: An experimental test of a classical proposition. *American Journal of Sociology, 105,* 1396–1427.

Montgomery, J. (1996). The structure of social exchange networks: A game-theoretic reformulation of Blau's Model. *Sociological Methodology, 26,* 193–225.

Radaev, Vadim. (2002). Entrepreneurial strategies and the structure of transaction costs in Russian business. *Problems of Economic Transition, 44,* 57–84.

Radaev, Vadim. (2003). Coping with distrust and contract infringement in the emerging Russian markets. In Russell Hardin (Ed.), *Distrust.* New York: Russell Sage Corporation, in press.

Rice, Eric R. W. (2002). *The effect of social uncertainty in networks of social exchange.* Unpublished Ph.D. dissertation.

Skvoretz, John, & Willer, David. (1993). Exclusion and power: A test of four theories or power in exchange networks. *American Sociological Review, 58,* 801–818.

Stolte, John R., & Emerson, Richard M. (1977). Structural inequality: Position and power in network structures. In Robert L. Hamblin & John H. Kunkel (Eds.), *Behavioral theory in sociology* (pp. 117–138). New Brunswick, NJ: Transaction Books.

Takahashi, N. (2000). The emergence of generalized exchange. *American Journal of Sociology, 105,* 1105–1134.

Thibaut, John W., & Kelley, Harold H. (1959). *The social psychology of groups.* New York: Wiley.

Thye, Shane R. (2000). A status value theory of power in exchange relations. *American Sociological Review, 65,* 407–432.

Uzzi, Brian. (1996). The sources and consequences of embeddedness for the economic performance of organizations: The network effect. *American Sociological Review, 61,* 674–698.

Willer, David, & Anderson, Bo. (1981). *Networks, exchange and coercion: The elementary theory and its applications.* New York: Elsevier.

Yamagishi, Toshio. (1995). Social Dilemmas. In Karen S. Cook, Gary Alan Fine, & James S. House (Eds.), *Sociological perspectives on social psychology.* Boston: Allyn & Bacon.

Yamagishi, Toshio, Cook, Karen S., & Watabe, M. (1998). Uncertainty, trust and commitment formation in the United States and Japan. *American Journal of Sociology, 104,* 165–194.

Ziegler, R. (1990). The Kula: Social order, barter and ceremonial exchange. In M. Hechter, K.-D. Opp, & R. Wippler (Eds.), *Social institutions: Their emergence, maintenance and effects.* New York: Aldine de Gruyter.

CHAPTER 4

Social Structure and Personality

JANE D. MCLEOD

KATHRYN J. LIVELY

Social structure and personality (SSP) research is concerned with the relationship between macro-social systems or processes and individual feelings, attitudes, and behaviors. It is considered a perspective or framework rather than a theoretical paradigm because it is not associated with general theoretical claims that transcend specific substantive problems. Rather, it provides a set of orienting principles that can be applied across diverse substantive areas. These principles direct our attention to the hierarchically organized processes through which macrostructures come to have relevance for the inner lives of individual persons and, in theory, the processes through which individual persons come to alter social systems.

Although the SSP name implies an exclusive focus on social structures, SSP research is concerned more broadly with social systems, sets of "persons and social positions or roles that possess both a culture and a social structure" (House, 1981, p. 542). Whereas House (1981) notes that social structure can be used to refer to "any or all aspects of social systems," he and other SSP researchers define social structure more precisely as "a *persisting* and bounded *pattern* of social relationships (or pattern of behavioral intention) among the units (persons or positions) in a social system" (House, 1981, p. 542, emphasis in the original). This definition encompasses features of the macro-social order such as the structure of the labor market and systems of social stratification as well as processes such as industrialization. In contrast, culture is used in SSP research to refer to "a set of cognitive and evaluative beliefs— beliefs about what is or what ought to be—that are shared by the members of a social system and transmitted to new members" (House, 1981, p. 542). The distinction between structure and culture is not always maintained in practice (a point we discuss in more detail later), but

JANE D. MCLEOD • Department of Sociology, Indiana University, Blommington, Indiana 47405
KATHRYN J. LIVELY • Department of Sociology, Dartmouth College, Hanover, New Hampshire 03755
Handbook of Social Psychology, edited by John Delamater. Kluwer Academic/Plenum Publishers, New York, 2003.

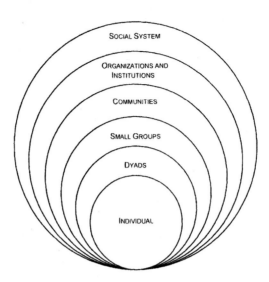

FIGURE 4-1. The Social Structure and Personality Framework.

it is nevertheless useful analytically to separate the effects of constraints that emanate from the societal infrastructure and those that depend on the internalization of values and ideals by societal members.

SSP researchers adopt a similarly broad conception of personality, as "stable and persisting psychological attributes" (House, 1981, p. 527), which encompasses a wide variety of psychological dispositions as well as attitudes, emotional states, self-perceptions, and cognitive schemas. Although not considered personality as such, researchers within the SSP tradition have extended their interests to include behavioral outcomes such as educational attainment and crime (e.g., Hagan & Palloni, 1990; Sewell, Haller, & Ohlendorf, 1970), as well as other indicators of individual functioning such as health states and outcomes (Williams, 1990). Because of these extensions, some people refer to the field more generically as "social structure and the individual."

The SSP perspective conceives of the social world as a set of embedded circles, with the individual at the core surrounded by progressively larger and more complex social groupings, including dyads, small groups, communities, organizations and institutions, and finally the larger social system (see Figure 4-1).* In much the same way that one can peel away layers of an onion to reveal the inner core, SSP researchers attempt to trace the processes through which components of the social system influence individuals and through which individuals affect social systems. Although SSP studies rarely examine the linkages between every layer with equal care, they are distinguished by their simultaneous consideration of multiple hierarchically organized features of the social environment.

While the SSP framework promotes a holistic vision of social life, SSP studies typically focus on the relevance of specific features of a social system for its members. Thus, represented under the SSP rubric we find such diverse topics as the implications of work environments for personality and health (Kohn & Schooler, 1983), the intergenerational transmission of educational attainment (see Kerckhoff, 1995 for a review), and the relationship between racial inequality and racial attitudes (Bobo, Oliver, Johnson, & Valenzuela, 2000). As these illustrative examples suggest, most SSP studies take stratification as their starting point, adhering to

*This figure is based on McLeod's notes from a graduate course on social structure and personality taught by Jim House.

House's (1977) dictum to focus on social "phenomena or problems ... having some ultimate applied value" (pp. 172–173).

Described in this way, SSP seems indistinguishable from the broader sociological project concerned with the social causes and consequences of human behavior. Where SSP differs is in its commitment to incorporating psychological processes into sociological research, and its adherence to a set of specific methodological and theoretical principles for analyzing the relationship between macro and micro phenomena. We begin our chapter with a description and illustration of these principles. Then, because the success of SSP research depends on its ability to apply these principles in research practice, we review each principle in depth.

KEY PRINCIPLES OF SSP RESEARCH

Social structure and personality research can be traced back to Comte, Marx, Weber, and Durkheim, each of whom was centrally concerned with the relationship between societies and individual psychology (see House, 1981 for a detailed review). Later studies in this tradition drew on anthropological, psychological, and psychiatric insights to posit national differences in personality characteristics derived from differences in child-rearing practices (e.g., Adorno, Frenkel-Brunswik, Levinson, & Sanford, 1950; Gorer, 1943). The framework came into its own, however, in the work of Inkeles and his colleagues on modernization and modernity (Inkeles, 1969; Inkeles & Smith, 1974). They used survey data from six developing counties to investigate the convergence hypothesis—"that the standardized institutional environments of modern society induce standard patterns of response, despite the countervailing randomizing effects of persisting traditional patterns of culture" (1960, p. 1). Inkeles argued that the new structures of industrializing societies become incorporated into the self-systems of their members through an implicit learning process whereby men begin to see the world in a new way. Inkeles's empirical analyses documented mean differences in psychological modernity* between societies that were substantially explained by differences in education, factory experience, mass media exposure, urban residence, and possession of consumer goods. Research on modernization remains vibrant (see, e.g., Inglehart & Baker, 2000), if controversial—a testament to the strength of Inkeles's approach.

Inkeles believed that sociological analysis was impossible in the absence of systematic and explicit attention to psychological processes (Inkeles, 1959). However, despite his efforts to create a coherent field of research based on that claim, SSP research floundered in the years that followed, fragmented by both the increasing substantive specialization within sociology and sociologists' long-standing resistance to psychological theories. In response to both of these challenges, House (1981) presented a conceptualization of social structure and personality research that focused on the analytic commonalities of diverse substantive projects, and called for the integration of sociological and psychological social psychology.

Drawing on Inkeles's work, House advanced three theoretical and methodological principles that guide SSP research. The first, the components principles, stipulates that researchers identify the specific components of the social system that are most relevant to understanding the phenomenon of interest. The second, the proximity principle, directs our attention to the proximate social experiences through which macro-social structures impinge on individual lives, in particular, micro-interactions and small-group processes. The third, the psychological principle, demands a thorough understanding of individual psychology so as to

---

*Modernity was defined as a cluster of psychological attributes including openness to new experience, the assertion of independence from traditional authorities, belief in the efficacy of science and medicine, and ambition.

allow a more precise accounting of the specific mechanisms through which macro-social structures and proximal experiences are processed and incorporated by individuals. House's three principles remain the most coherent and influential statement of the SSP framework to date.

Perhaps more than any other program of research, Kohn and Schooler's (1983) research on work and personality illustrates these principles. In a series of projects extending over almost two decades, Kohn, Schooler, and their colleagues have advanced the claim that occupational conditions importantly explain social structural differences in values, attitudes, and psychological well-being (e.g., Kohn & Schooler, 1983; Kohn & Slomczynski, 1990; Naoi & Schooler, 1990). In adherence to the components principle, Kohn and colleagues distinguish two major dimensions of social structure—social stratification and social class. Social stratification refers to the hierarchical ordering within society based on power, privilege, and prestige, whereas social class refers to groups defined in terms of their relationship to the means of production and their control over the labor of others (Kohn, Naoi, Schoenbach, Schooler, & Slomczynski, 1990). Kohn and colleagues identify occupational conditions, particularly opportunities to exercise self-direction on the job, as the primary explanation for the association of class and stratification with psychological functioning, thereby addressing the proximity principle. Finally, with respect to the psychological principle, they invoke a learning generalization process to account for the relationship between occupational self-direction and diverse aspects of psychological functioning (e.g., orientations to self and others, intellectual flexibility, well-being) in other areas of their lives. According to their findings, persons in higher status positions evidence greater intellectual flexibility, more self-confidence, more self-directedness, and less conservatism because their everyday occupational experiences demand those orientations.

As this example illustrates, the three principles of SSP research highlight potential linkages between sociological social psychology and the broader concerns of sociology and cognate disciplines. The components principle links SSP research with the long tradition of research and theorizing regarding the nature of social structure within sociology. The proximity principle focuses the SSP lens on the traditional concerns of symbolic interactionists, exchange theorists, and other researchers interested in networks and small groups. Finally, the psychological principle serves as a natural point of contact between sociological social psychologists and psychological social psychologists (Stryker, 1977), a contact that has recently been strengthened by developments in research on self and in social cognition (e.g., Hollander & Howard, 2000; Morgan & Schwalbe, 1990).

These linkages have proven more difficult to achieve in practice than in theory, in part, because of the way in which the SSP framework has traditionally been operationalized. With respect to linking with the broader discipline of sociology, the deterministic conceptualization of social structure that guides most SSP research is out of sync with recent theoretical developments within sociology regarding the relationship between structure and human agency. With respect to linking with other traditions within sociological social psychology, the reliance of SSP research on quantitative, survey-based techniques has limited its ability to operationalize the interactional processes that lie at the heart of other traditions. Finally, SSP researchers do not appear to have fully embraced theories from psychology and other disciplines concerned with individual functioning (e.g., psychiatry, medicine), perhaps because of continued concern about psychologization or because of organizational and institutional barriers to interdisciplinary collaboration.

We elaborate these points in our review of the three orienting principles of SSP research. We describe the basic tenets of each principle, the ways these principles have been applied in research, and their potential to encourage communication between social psychologists and the broader discipline of sociology, and among the different "faces" of social psychology (House, 1977). Our review identifies gaps between each principle and research practice, as well as promising new directions for research.

THE COMPONENTS PRINCIPLE: SOCIAL STRUCTURE, CULTURE, AND AGENCY

The components principle directs researchers to identify those aspects of the social system that are most relevant to understanding the process of interest. In House's (1981) account, this requires a detailed description of the social structure, position, or system of interest, as well as an adjudication of the components of the social system that affect proximal social environments and individual responses most strongly. The same principle can be applied to the study of culture specifying, for example, which of the many differences between nations or groups account for cross-cultural variations in psychological functioning. The identification of relevant components can be driven by a priori theoretical decisions (as when researchers study the effects of a specific component of stratification, such as education, on individual functioning; Ross & Wu, 1995) or can be determined empirically (as in studies that evaluate the relative importance of income, education, occupational prestige, and other indicators of socioeconomic position for health; Williams & Collins, 1995).

SSP researchers conceive of social structure within a structuralist tradition, as an external, objective force that has a determinative influence over feelings and actions. More specifically, social structures are seen as shaping opportunities, which, in turn, constrain individual responses (Rubinstein, 2001). Kohn, Schooler, and their colleagues (e.g., Kohn & Schooler, 1983; Kohn et al., 1990), for example, argue that social stratification and social class determine opportunities for occupational self-direction and, thereby, values and intellectual functioning. Whereas structural symbolic interactionism emphasizes the limits that social structures place on possibilities for interaction (i.e., what persons are brought together in what settings) and on the situational definitions that can be invoked in interaction (Stryker, 1980), SSP adds a concern with the material resources and limits associated with different social structural positions, independent of individuals' perceptions (Fine's [1991] obdurate realities).

Within SSP research, social structure is most often operationalized with variables denoting individual positions within social hierarchies. Socioeconomic stratification, for example, is represented by income, education, and occupational prestige, racial stratification by individuals' self-reported (or sometimes attributed) primary racial identification, and gender by a variable indicating whether the participant is (or is seen as) biologically male or female. This approach can be criticized on two points. First, it ignores the relational nature of inequality, which depends on patterned distributions of power, resources, and privileges among sets of actors (Hollander & Howard, 2000). While there are exceptions to this criticism (e.g., studies of the individual implications of racial inequality: Bobo et al., 2000), SSP researchers do not typically incorporate power, domination, and oppression into their empirical analyses of system components. Second, variable-based operationalizations assume implicitly that persons who occupy equivalent status positions share common experiences, thereby forestalling analysis of individual resistance and change. Because lived experiences of domination and oppression vary among persons with equivalent status characteristics, status characteristics are meso-level proxies for macro-level structures.

Relatedly, systems of stratification depend on mutually reinforcing structures and ideologies that are not easily disentangled. Racial inequality, for example, has been conceptualized as a system that subjugates some population groups to others based on the identification of presumed physical differences and the association of those differences with ideologies of inferiority and superiority (Anderson, 1990a; Feagin & Booher Feagin, 1999; Williams & Williams-Morris, 2000). This system is manifested in myriad differences in the institutional, interactional, and psychological experiences of members of different racial and ethnic groups, all of which are interdependent. Whereas a traditional SSP analysis might choose a single component of racial inequality on which to focus, or might attempt to estimate the independent effects of multiple components, racial inequality may affect individuals in a holistic fashion that defies disaggregation (Bobo et al., 2000).

House (1981) identified two key dilemmas in SSP research that underly these comments: how to distinguish structure from culture, and how to incorporate human agency into explanations for the relationship between structure and individual outcomes. Recent theoretical developments within sociology suggest that these two dilemmas are linked, and have common origins in structuralist conceptions of social structure. In the remainder of this section, we review traditional SSP approaches to conceptualizing the distinction between culture and structure, and the relevance of human agency for the relations between macro and micro-phenomena. We then introduce more recent conceptualizations, and discuss the implications of these new conceptualizations for SSP research. In brief, we contend that these new conceptualizations create unique opportunities for linkages between SSP and other areas of sociology, including other traditions within social psychology. Moreover, SSP research could assist in the refinement of these conceptualizations if it were more explicitly oriented toward them.

The Distinction between Culture and Structure

SSP research maintains a long-standing conviction in the importance of distinguishing the structural and cultural origins of feelings, attitudes, and behaviors. The conceptual distinction between structure and culture can be traced back at least to the work of Marx and Weber whose relative emphasis on material and ideological interests has been the source of continuing discussion and debate (e.g., Alexander, 1984; Rubinstein, 2001). This distinction also served as a focal point of Inkeles's research on modernization, and received substantial discussion in House's (1981) review of the field.

Structural explanations emphasize current material conditions of life as they constrain and enable action and thereby generate characteristic psychological and behavioral responses. In contrast, cultural explanations attribute persisting patterns of behavior to beliefs and values that are transmitted to members of the social system through socialization. In a stark example of the distinction between these approaches, the culture of poverty thesis ultimately attributes the intergenerational persistence of poverty to the socialization of poor children into maladaptive psychological and behavioral patterns that diminish their abilities to take advantage of opportunities that become available to them (e.g., Lewis, 1968). In contrast, structural explanations attribute the intergenerational persistence of poverty to the persistence of blocked opportunity structures in impoverished areas (e.g., Liebow, 1967). Both types of explanations see individual behavior and psychology as the product of constraining features of the social order, but they differ in the nature of the constraints that are presumed most relevant.

As suggested, the choice between cultural and structural origins is often cast as either-or; therefore, a central goal of analysts has been to determine which of these broad components of the social system has most influence over societal members. Even explanations that allow for the importance of both cultural and structural processes choose between one or the other as the ultimate determinant. For example, Wilson (1987, 1991) offers a more nuanced under-standing of ghetto life by attributing the marginal economic position of ghetto residents to both macro-economic conditions that block opportunities for legitimate, stable employment and the formation of a social milieu that fosters a collective sense of futility among ghetto residents. Although Wilson does acknowledge that futility can be conceived as a cultural value that is learned and shared, he ultimately attributes futility to socially structured lack of opportunity.*

Despite the analytic appeal of the structure–culture distinction, some sociological theorists question its utility (see Rubinstein, 2001 for a review). Noting that culture has a constraining, quasi-external nature similar to that of structure, some theorists merge their definitions, effectively asserting that the two cannot be distinguished either conceptually or empirically (e.g., Hays, 1994; Wuthnow, Hunter, Bergeson, & Kurzweil, 1984). In a slightly different argument, Rubinstein (2001) contends that culture, structure, and agency are mutually constitutive. In essence, he suggests that while each has an independent influence on action, each is also partially determined by the others and none holds a superior position of influence.†

Although different, both arguments imply that it may be more difficult to distinguish cul-tural and structural effects in practice than in theory. In particular, Rubinstein's claim implies that it may be more fruitful to study how culture and structure relate to each other, and how both respond to human agency, rather than attempting to determine their relative primacy. These relationships are visible in high relief at the locus of decision-making and action, where individuals define their interests, identify alternative courses of action, experience emotions and desires, and respond. Rubinstein's emphasis on studies of decision-making echoes House's (1995) call for renewed attention to the nature of social action by SSP researchers (see Alexander & Wiley, 1981; and Shanahan, 2000). Analyses of decision-making and action have the potential to reveal how structure and culture become embedded in proximal environ-ments and individual psyches, and how they shape choice and action, while also allowing for the possibility that actors have autonomy. To date, SSP researchers have shied away from these types of analyses, perhaps because of concerns that they underemphasize structural constraints

---

*Although different in substantive focus, cross-cultural research within social psychology also attempts to distin-guish the structural and cultural processes that shape individual psychology. In a recent extension of Inkeles and Smith's (1974) work, Inglehart and Baker (2000) use data from three waves of the World Values Survey to test two opposing hypotheses: that values converge as a result of modernization, and that traditional values persist in the face of economic and political change. They conclude that both processes occur. Values change in marked and pre-dictable ways with industrialization and the later shift to a postindustrial economy. At the same time, distinctive cul-tural traditions (operationalized as Protestant, Orthodox, Islamic, and Confucian) persist even in the face of economic change. In sum, "(e)conomic development tends to push societies in a common direction, but rather than converging, they seem to move on parallel trajectories shaped by their cultural heritages" (p. 49). Inglehart and Baker's attempt to measure culture directly contrasts with most studies of cross-cultural variation in attitudes or other psychological dispositions that use nation-states as proxies for culture, leaving the specific cultural elements that distinguish nations underspecified (see Miller-Loessi, 1995 for a review).

†For example, Rubinstein contends that culture guides actors' identification of the opportunities available to them (e.g., racial intermarriage is not a realistic option for members of the Ku Klux Klan) and shapes judgments about the utility of pursuing alternative options. Actors are creative when interpreting culture, and can reappropriate cul-ture to new ends (as in Sewell's [1992] transposition of schema), but culture is not infinitely malleable. Structures contstrain the cultural interpretations that actors can apply and thereby limit strategic innovation. Moreover, shared values and beliefs define what is seen as desirable and useful, but do not serve strictly utilitarian ends. Schooler (1994) contends that there is a lag between psychological change, structural change, and cultural change such that psychological-level phenomena change more quickly than social structures, which, in turn, change more quickly than culture. This cultural "time lag" creates discrepancies among cultural values, social structural imperatives, and the desires of individuals. Schooler has more faith than Rubinstein that these discrepancies will ultimately be resolved through cultural and structural change, but his basic notion of cultural lag conforms to Rubinstein's interpretation.

(Kohn, 1989) and overemphasize culture (House, 1995). While recognizing these risks, we suggest that they have two related strengths. First, they remedy SSP's overly deterministic conceptualization of structure without denying its centrality to human action. Second, they serve as a means to explore the effects of micro-experiences on macro-structures—a long-neglected part of the SSP agenda. We elaborate these points in a discussion of the ways in which human agency has been incorporated into previous SSP research.

Human Agency

The question of how to conceptualize and operationalize the role of action, choice, and agency in the face of structural and cultural constraints has received substantial attention from sociological theorists (e.g., Emirbayer & Mische, 1998; Giddens, 1976; Sewell, 1992). While this is a question that applies across diverse areas of sociology, it begs close attention from SSP researchers because of their desire to make specific claims about the effects of structures on individuals, and of individuals on structures. Two common SSP approaches to addressing this question are the analysis of selection effects and studies of the role of agency in the life course. Both approaches highlight the influence of individual traits or actions on the proximal environments that people occupy. SSP researchers have also considered the more general question of the reciprocal relations between micro- and macro-phenomena, particularly in analyses of social movements. These analyses bring SSP research more in line with developments in sociological theory regarding the dynamic, dualistic nature of social structure.

SELECTION EFFECTS.   Relationships between social structural conditions and individual outcomes may reflect the effects of structural conditions on individuals, but may also result from nonrandom selection of individuals into those conditions. A classic example in medical sociology is the relationship between socioeconomic status (SES) and mental health. Whereas low SES is associated with life conditions that diminish mental health, mental health problems may also impede socioeconomic attainment. Thus, observed associations between SES and mental health may reflect either social causation or social selection (Miech, Caspi, Moffitt, Wright, & Silva, 1999; Wheaton, 1978).

Analyses of selection effects rely on longitudinal data or instrumental variable techniques to discern the relative strength of the competing processes. Selection processes may occur as a result of conscious decisions on the part of the individual (e.g., a person with severe depression seeks a job with lower demands), but also through unconscious person-environment adaptations (e.g., as when persons with severe depression and their employers gradually adjust work performance expectations) and the actions of others (e.g., a person with severe depression is fired for failing to meet job expectations). Thus, selection effects incorporate both more and less than is implied by the concept of human agency.

THE LIFE COURSE.   The life course paradigm offers an alternative conceptualization of the role of human agency in social life that incorporates the possibility of selection effects but adds to that an analysis of individual propensities, behaviors, and actions that propel and sustain life course development. In Elder's (1997) words, "(p)eople bring a life history of personal experiences and dispositions to each transition, interpret the new circumstances in terms of this history, and work out lines of adaptation that can fundamentally alter the life course" (p. 957). Thus, the life course paradigm emphasizes both the historical embeddedness of individual experience and individual contributions to life course construction. These emphases are consistent with, but go beyond, the SSP paradigm as it is traditionally conceived (Elder, 1981).*

Empirical research validates the general claim that people select and create environments that shape their future life course. Assortative processes, in which people select situations that reinforce preexisting dispositions, have been observed in studies of behavioral continuities, attitudes, and personality (Alwin, Cohen, & Newcomb, 1991; Caspi & Herbener, 1990; Caspi, Bem, & Elder, 1989). People also make conscious decisions to change their lives in order to improve their conditions or to realize desired selves (Kiecolt & Mabry, 2000; Shanahan, 2000) within perceived constraints. This research demonstrates that assortative processes and motivated action merit empirical investigation in their own right, as important influences on the structure of individual lives, rather than as mere statistical nuisances (Thoits, 1995).

MICRO–MACRO EFFECTS. Analyses of selection processes and life course development extend micro-effects into proximal environments, but do not offer an account of the processes that link interpersonal environments to macro-social structures. This additional step is essential if SSP research is to fulfill its stated mission to analyze the effects of individuals on social systems as complement to its analyses of the effects of social systems on individuals. The micro–macro link has been most fully elaborated by social movements researchers. They trace the effects of individual predispositions and actions on macro social change through analyses of the processes by which individuals become attracted and committed to social movements, and the subsequent influence of social movements on the larger social structure (see Snow & Oliver, 1995 for a review). Although the complete pathway of micro–macro influence cannot be established within any specific study, it can be constructed from the cumulative findings of research in this area.

Important for our purposes here, recent research in social movements highlights the reciprocal relations between psychological attributes (cognitions, affect, values, identities) and social movement participation (see Snow & Oliver, 1995, for a review). For example, drawing on classic SSP research on the relationship between social class and efficacy (e.g., Kohn, 1969, 1983), Sherkat and Blocker (1994) show that social class and gender differences in activist participation can be explained by differences in religiosity, personal efficacy, and parental socialization into protest activities (operationalized with parent's own participation). Furthermore, even when controlling factors that predict protest movement participation, participation was associated with liberal political orientations, nontraditional religious orientations, later age at marriage, and selection into "new class" occupations (e.g., social worker, journalist, academic) seventeen years later (Sherkat & Blocker, 1997).

The notion that macro structures and individual actions are mutually relevant and reinforcing also appears in other areas of SSP research. For example, Bobo and colleagues (2000) propose that racial inequality, racial residential segregation, and negative intergroup attitudes are mutually constitutive.

> The persistence of racial residential segregation deepens the overlap between economic disadvantage and race and ethnicity by serving to concentrate high rates of poverty and unemployment in communities of color. Racial residential segregation in turn, is reinforced by group identities and negative racial attitudes—which are made harder to transform in a positive way while groups remain economically unequal and residentially separated. Such conditions provide both the kernel of truth and the motivation to sustain mutual suspicion and hostility. (p. 31)

---

*Life course theorists also define the life course as a social structure itself by conceptualizing the life course as "age-graded life patterns embedded in social institutions and subject to historical change" (Elder & O'Rand, 1995, p. 453).

They provide support for their claim through analyses of survey and Census data from Los Angeles County. One study in their volume finds, for example, that despite substantial racial residential segregation, there are few racial and ethnic differences in housing expenditures, knowledge of housing costs, or housing tastes. Rather, preferences for integration with respect to specific other groups (e.g., White preferences for integration with Blacks) were most strongly predicted by negative stereotypes of those groups. Moreover, in contradiction to theories of prejudice, increased residential contact with Blacks diminished rather than increased White preferences for integration (Charles, 2000).

These efforts to elaborate the micro–macro interface are in accord with recent theoretical developments regarding the nature of social structure. For over two decades, Giddens (e.g., 1976, 1984), Alexander (1982, 1984), Bourdieu (1977), and Sewell (1992), among others have devoted substantial attention to the question of how to theorize social structure in a way that allows actors some autonomy. Whereas their specific arguments are quite different, they share a common underlying conceptualization of structure and agency as dualistic. "Structures shape people's practices, but it is also people's practices that constitute (and reproduce) structures" (Sewell, 1992, p. 4). In other words, social actors are constrained by the structures in which they are embedded, but they also reproduce those structures through their actions (as when people "do gender" (West & Zimmerman, 1987) or "do difference" (West & Fenstermaker, 1995)). Moreover, within the constraints of their lives, actors can apply cultural schema and resources creatively to change structures (Callero, 1994).

This dualistic conceptualization of structure represents a more radical departure from the traditional SSP conceptualization than the claim that structures and individuals have reciprocal effects. Not surprisingly, then, empirical research that engages dualistic conceptualizations of structure (e.g., Burawoy, 1982; Pierce, 1995; West & Zimmerman, 1987) is conducted by scholars who would not identify with SSP and who, in fact, see their work as remedial to SSP's determinism. Is there a place for SSP research in these developments? We believe that there is, if SSP researchers orient themselves more explicitly toward analyses of process in proximal environments, and broaden their empirical base to incorporate the insights of experimental and ethnographic research (House, 1995).

FROM MACRO TO MICRO AND IN BETWEEN: THE PROXIMITY PRINCIPLE

The proximity principle asserts that the effects of social structures, positions, and systems are transmitted to individuals through stimuli that impinge directly on the individual via, "the smaller structures and patterns of intimate interpersonal interaction or communication that constitute the proximate social experiences and stimuli in a person's life" (House, 1981, p. 540). The proximity principle serves as the means by which SSP researchers trace the effects of macro-social experiences on individuals. It could, in theory, serve the same for analyses of the effects of micro-social experiences on macro-social structures but that possibility is rarely realized in practice. Because the proximity principle is concerned with the proximal experiences of individuals—the contexts in which individuals experience social structure—this component provides a natural link to other areas within sociological social psychology (e.g., symbolic interactionism, exchange theory).

The meso-structures and processes that are the focus of the proximity principle traverse multiple levels of social life, including everything from dyads to small groups to formal organizations. Each level encompasses multiple, multidimensional contexts that define the settings in which macro-conditions derive tangible and symbolic reality for individuals.* We define contexts broadly as the locations defined by geography, function, and interpersonal relations in which tasks are accomplished and interpersonal exchanges occur. The importance of any particular context for individual functioning depends on its relationship to other contexts, both those that exist in a hierarchically superior position (as a community would to an individual family) and those with which it overlaps (such as work organizations and families). To date, SSP researchers have given much more attention to interactions between personal status characteristics and proximal environments when predicting individual outcomes (e.g., gender differences in the effects of substantive complexity on psychological functioning; Miller, Schooler, Kohn, & Miller, 1983) than to interactions across domains of life (such as between school experiences and relations with peers). In contrast, developmental psychologists emphasize the inherent contingencies in meso-level processes (e.g., families matter differently in different cultural and community contexts) and the need to move beyond linear, additive models (Boyce et al., 1998; Bronfenbrenner, 1979)—emphases that SSP researchers would do well to adopt.

Until recently, school, work, and family contexts have received the most sustained attention from SSP researchers. This focus is not surprising given the amount of time that individuals spend within these contexts, and the functions they perform for individual survival (Parsons & Smelser, 1956). Family, school, and work organizations are primary sites of socialization and value transmission for children and adults and are also the source of valued network ties. Accordingly, they have been invoked as relevant proximal environments in research on stratification and mobility (Kerckhoff, 1995), the intergenerational transmission of crime (Hagan & Palloni, 1990), and the effects of economic conditions on individual functioning (Elder, 1974; McLeod & Shanahan, 1993; Menaghan, 1991; Parcel & Menaghan, 1994).

Hearkening back to the concerns of early Chicago school sociology, neighborhoods and communities have become increasingly prominent in research on race and economic stratification in recent years. Following from Wilson's (1987) and Massey and Denton's (1993) analyses of racial residential segregation, analysts have charted the damaging effects of race- and class-based segregation on job outcomes, patterns of childbearing and marriage, and psychological well-being, among other outcomes (Anderson, 1990b; Connell & Halpern-Felsher, 1997; Crane, 1991; McLeod & Edwards, 1995). Neighborhoods represent a set of physical and environmental conditions, with implications for health and development, as well as social contexts that facilitate or impede social interactions of various types. For example, Sampson, Raudenbush, and Earls (1997) conclude that the effects of neighborhood-level economic disadvantage and instability on violent crime are largely mediated by collective efficacy (social cohesion among neighbors). Many cities organize social services at the community or neighborhood level, giving neighborhoods added relevance as the sites at which resources are distributed.

Proximal contexts can be characterized by structures of interpersonal relations (which include social networks as well as roles, role partners, and role sets), as well as by the nature and content of context-based interpersonal interactions. Further consideration of each reveals potential linkages between SSP and other social psychological traditions. We emphasize symbolic interactionism and its offshoots here because it is strongest where SSP research is weakest, in particular, in its emphasis on proximal environments as contexts for day-to-day

---

*We use the term context purposefully because it is broad enough to encompass both functionally specific domains (Parsons & Smelser, 1956) as well as historical epochs, geographically defined areas such as neighborhoods, and particular organizations. The important point here is that contexts are often embedded and mutually reinforcing.

interactions, its greater sensitivity to the social construction of diffuse status characteristics, and its recognition of human agency. However, similar possibilities for integration exist with respect to exchange theory.

The Structure of Interpersonal Relations

The two most common sociological approaches to conceptualizing the structure of interpersonal relations are as social networks or as social roles.

SOCIAL NETWORKS. Social network conceptualizations emphasize the structural connections—the presence or absence of links—among individuals or groups. Common network concepts such as density (the degree of overlap among the links within a given domain), reciprocity (whether exchanges occur in both directions across a link), and multiplexity (whether a given link involves an exchange of more than one function or activity) further specify the nature of the connections among groups of individuals and the possible pathways for the exchange of information and resources. The concept of social support, particularly popular among health researchers, highlights the content of social networks and their provision of caring and instrumental assistance (House, Umberson, & Landis, 1988; Turner & Turner, 1999).

Networks play an important role in social movements as conduits for information, resources, and affect, and as bridges between diverse individuals and groups (see Snow & Oliver, 1995 for a review). The bridging functions of social networks have also been used by stratification researchers to understand how individuals become linked to jobs both in the United States and abroad (Bian, 1997; Bian & Ang, 1997; Granovetter, 1973). Social networks constitute the structural basis for social capital, and serve as pathways for the transmission of values, attitudes, and behaviors (Alwin et al., 1991; Matsueda & Heimer, 1987; Newcomb, 1963; Patterson, DeBaryshe, & Ramsey, 1989). Homophily in social networks both reflects and reproduces social hierarchies (Bobo, Johnson, & Suh, 2000; Johnson, Farrell, & Stoloff, 2000) placing social networks at the center of research on social inequality. In short, networks are important to SSP research inasmuch as the structure and content of social networks may change in response to macro-structures and processes, and because networks serve as points of entrée through which macro-structures infiltrate individual lives (as in Katz & Lazersfeld's 1955 study of the transmission of media reports to individual political attitudes through network-based opinion leaders).

SOCIAL ROLES. Although the concept of role also implies links among individuals, it focuses on the social expectations associated with specific structural positions rather than on the presence or absence of interactional links between specific individuals. In its most traditional or structuralist form, a social role refers to the behavioral expectations that are associated with, and emerge from, identifiable positions in social structure (e.g., Merton, 1957). The role of mother, for example, carries with it normative expectations that shape role occupants' actions. As this example suggests, the traditional conceptualization views social roles as existing prior to specific interactions and serving as constraints on behavior.

This conceptualization of roles has motivated SSP research on structurally based variation in role occupancy and role expectations as determinants of individual functioning. Role allocation, or the availability of roles to different societal members, has structural origins as well as psychological effects, giving it central relevance as a mediational process in

SSP research. Drawing on traditional sociological interests in the fit (or lack thereof) between structural requirements and individual personality (e.g., Marx's alienation, Durkheim's anomie), SSP researchers have studied the implications of role incongruity, role conflict, and role overload for physical and mental health and for deviant behavior (Merton, 1957; Thoits, 1983). There is also a well-established literature on multiple role occupancy and well-being that tests the competing hypotheses that multiple roles offer greater potential for self-actualization (Linville, 1987) and that multiple roles create tension and stress (Thoits, 1983), with recent research suggesting that their effects are contingent on role quality and role salience (Hyde, Delamater, & Durik, 2001; Hyde, Delamater, & Hewitt, 1998). However, beyond these specific lines of research, role theory is not commonly invoked within SSP.

Traditional role theory has been repeatedly criticized for its lack of attention to individual agency. In response, several attempts have been made to revitalize our understanding of role and, therefore, role theory through the introduction of interactionist principles. The first of these theoretical innovations shifted the conceptualization of role-based human behavior from role-playing to role-making (Stryker & Statham, 1985; Turner, 1962). The concept of role-making emphasizes situational dynamics, bargaining, and personal control in role-based behavior. In essence, the interactionist conceptualization views individuals as creative negotiators of role expectations within specific interactions. More recently, Callero (1994) extended this argument further by introducing the notion of role-using, which begins from the premise that roles are not bundles of rights and obligations but cultural objects that serve as resources in interaction.

The unique contribution of Callero's conceptualization is his contention (borrowed from Baker & Faulkner, 1991) that roles do not have a preexisting reality but, rather, become real as they are enacted in the context of specific interactions. At the same time, roles have independent symbolic and cognitive realities, named variously "typifications" (Hewitt, 1991; Schutz, 1970) or "gestalts" (Turner, 1978) that transcend specific pragmatic applications. These symbolic realities involve generalized images of what it means to hold specific role positions that can be used by individuals as identity claims (as when a woman asserts her identity as a mother) but also to claim resources (e.g., assistance with child rearing) and to understand behaviors or feelings (e.g., men can invoke the role of mother to explain their nurturing behaviors even if they cannot claim the role). Roles as cultural objects shape cognition (motherhood implies a certain perspective or orientation to the social world) and influence behavior, although in a negotiated rather than deterministic way.

The astructural conceptualization of role that Callero (1994) offers is not easily reconciled with the structuralist biases of SSP research. They nevertheless find common ground in questions about the processes through which roles are claimed and the consequences of role claims for interactions within specific settings. As Callero notes, roles are not uniformly available as identity claims. Men cannot claim the role of mother, and most of us will never have access to the role of U.S. senator (although the role of U.S. senator is available as a cultural object to understand the political system). Beyond Heiss's (1981) discussion of the effects of socialization and prior interactions on consensus vs. dissensus of role definitions, however, the structural bases for the success and failure of role claims have received relatively little empirical attention. This disconnect suggests one potential area of convergence between SSP researchers and interactionist role theory, especially in light of the early theoretical discussions of status inconsistency that address the interaction of diffuse status characteristics, such as race and gender, and particular role-identities (Hughes, 1945). The distinction between role-based self-identifications, pragmatic role enactment, and roles as cultural objects would also help SSP researchers better specify the components of the social system that are most consequential for individual functioning.*

On a more general level, the roles-as-resources perspective would allow SSP researchers to address better the interrelations of culture, structure, and agency (Rubinstein, 2001). By acknowledging the cultural component of roles, new approaches to role theory invite inquiry into the relationships among social structural positions, behavioral expectations, and broader cultural trends, as well as the links between structured roles and culturally based prestige, status, and power. In addition, if we accept the notion that roles are resources that can be used for action, they offer one avenue through which to address processes of social change and the responsiveness of social structure to individual agency.

Interpersonal Processes

SSP researchers often invoke socialization as an explanation for the effects of social positions on feelings, attitudes, and behaviors. Socialization-based explanations appear in research on gender (Beutel & Marini, 1995), child development (Corsaro & Eder, 1995), work and occupations (Kohn & Schooler, 1983), deviance (Krohn, 1999; Matsueda, 1988), and, somewhat less commonly, social movements (Snow & Oliver, 1995). These explanations resonate with the early traditions of SSP research and remain very popular in contemporary research. Despite the availability of careful research on socialization processes (see Corsaro & Eder, 1995, for a review), however, socialization is often treated as a fall-back explanation in SSP research—something that explains whatever cannot be explained by other mechanisms.

The nature and quality of interpersonal interactions within (and across) domains have also been implicated in the relations between social systems and individuals. For example, numerous studies demonstrate the mediating role of marital relations, parent–child interactions, and the development of trust between neighbors in the relationship between economic deprivation and individual well-being (e.g., Conger et al., 1992; Elder, 1999; Sampson, Raudenbush, & Earls, 1997). Work conditions shape interpersonal interactions in the workplace (Hochschild, 1983; Lively, 2001) but also at home (Menaghan, 1991). In sum, socially structured conditions influence interactions with intimates (as evidenced in the association of social support with gender and class; Turner & Marino, 1994), as well as with strangers (as evidenced in mundane acts of racism; Feagin, 1991). These interactions, in turn, affect attitudes, feelings, and behaviors (e.g., House et al., 1988; Williams & Williams-Morris, 2000), often reinforcing the social order from which they are derived.

Whereas SSP researchers have been reasonably successful at identifying the interactional correlates of social structural positions, they have been less successful at analyzing the processes that account for them. Research in the symbolic interactionist and status characteristics traditions complements SSP research by focusing specifically on those processes, each

---

*Whereas this approach could be usefully applied to organizational roles, its benefits are perhaps most clear in the case of diffuse status characteristics such as race and gender. By considering the independent and interactive contributions of structural position (e.g., power, status) and cultural understandings, SSP researchers would be better able to move away from variable-oriented analyses toward more dynamic, contextual conceptualizations and, thereby, to converse with research on gender and race conducted within other social psychological (and feminist) traditions.

with a unique emphasis. Recent interactionist studies on emotional labor performed by service workers (Hochschild, 1983) and on more general face-to-face interactions (Maynard, 1991; West & Fenstermaker, 1995; West & Zimmerman, 1987), link the interactional patterns that exist within dyads, small groups, and formal organizations to larger social structures of race, class, and gender. West and Zimmerman (1987), for example, demonstrate that gender is both expressed and reproduced in interaction. Specifically, they find that men are more likely than women to begin conversations, to monopolize talk time, and to interrupt. West and Zimmerman contend that gendered behavioral expectations lead women to be more passive in interaction than men and that women, themselves, assist in the reproduction of gendered stereotypes and male dominance through their passivity. Similarly, researchers who study emotional labor have shown that female workers are more likely than men to engage in emotional labor, which further perpetuates the expectation that women are caretakers, as well as norms regarding the inappropriateness of female anger (Pierce, 1995). While these interactionist studies provide insightful accounts of the ways in which larger social structures affect individuals more proximally, they often lack the careful consideration given to the relative effects of culture and of structure deemed necessary by SSP researchers.

Status characteristics theory supplements those accounts with an explanation for how, and why, status structures that occur in socially heterogeneous groups often reflect the larger social structures within which they are embedded. Specifically, status characteristics theory proposes that status characteristics, when salient in the situation, create performance expectations in goal-oriented settings and these expectations, in turn, shape the actors' behavior and rank in the power and prestige order (Berger, Cohen, & Zelditch, 1972; Berger, Fisek, Norman, & Zelditch, 1977; Ridgeway & Walker, 1992; Webster & Foschi, 1988). Individuals with devalued statuses are less able than others to assume leadership roles and participate actively, and their contributions to the task are evaluated less positively. Even when diffuse status characteristics such as race and gender are not directly *relevant* to the task at hand, they become salient in mixed group settings (Ridgeway & Diekema, 1989; Ridgeway & Walker, 1992; Tannen, 1995).*

These theoretical traditions hold promise for SSP research because they offer accounts of the processes through which the larger social structure impinges upon interactional opportunity structures, normative expectations, and individual behaviors. The narrow scope of status characteristics theory (confined to task-oriented groups) limits the domains to which it can be applied directly, but its convergence with ethnographic analyses of the reproduction of hierarchy (Lively, 2000; Ollilainen, 2000; Pierce, 1995) implies a more general process that has relevance for interactions within other groups such as formal organizations and dyads. Each of these traditions, in turn, would benefit from a stronger linkage with SSP research. In particular, they, like most interactionist studies, assume the presence of structure (or structures) without having clearly explicated the nature of the structures or the specific components of the structures that impinge upon interactions. Gendered expectations, for example, could have their origins in cultural assumptions, the traditional distribution of roles by sex, or,

---

*Although Ridgeway and Walker (1992) offer status characteristics theory as an explanation for the reproduction of status hierarchies within small groups, they acknowledge that the reproduction is not perfect. Because people are complex packages of skills and status characteristics, the status structures people construct through interaction are aggregates: weighted averages of a sort. As a result, people *may* experience power and prestige hierarchies that "*challenge* their usual expectations for individuals with given diffuse status characteristics" (Ridgeway & Walker, 1992, p. 294). The imperfect relationship between societal stratification and group-based status structures suggests the potential for individuals to create expectations that result in individual-, group-, and societal-level change.

in some cases, biological distinctions that preclude role occupancy. Careful attention to the components of macro-structures, encouraged by the SSP framework, would allow scholars working within these traditions to develop more precise theories about the macro-structural origins of the group-based processes they observe.

In sum, adherence to the proximity principle requires attention to the range of life domains that are implicated as well as to their organization, content, and implied interactional processes. Because of its unique position as a link between macro and micro worlds, the proximity principle offers SSP researchers an opportunity to converse with other traditions in sociological social psychology, as well as to engage broader disciplinary debates about the relative importance of structure and agency in human behavior. The potential insights from this type of integration are manifold, but it will require a willingness to move back and forth between the positivistically oriented large-scale quantitative analyses that have historically characterized SSP research and the case-based insights of experimental and ethnographic researchers (see Mueller, Mulinge, & Glass, 2002).

THE PSYCHOLOGICAL PRINCIPLE

The psychological principle stipulates that we examine the psychological mechanisms through which proximal structures and processes affect individual attitudes, feelings, and behaviors. In other words, it is not enough to understand how macro-structures shape the proximal environments of individuals; we have to also understand how those environments become integrated into individual thoughts and actions. The expansion of the SSP perspective into health research implies a broadening of this principle, to incorporate an understanding of how proximal environments affect physiological functioning and "get under the skin" (Taylor, Repetti, & Seeman, 1997). Although efforts to bring psychology and biology into SSP studies are linked, they are not inseparable. The mechanisms that link some environmental characteristics (e.g., chronic stress) to physiology are psychologically mediated, but other environmental characteristics (e.g., environmental toxins) have effects that transcend cognition.

In an early statement of the relevance of personality for sociology, Inkeles (1959) argued that sociological analysis is incomplete without a general theory of personality. While most SSP researchers accept Inkeles's directive to explicitly analyze psychological processes, most have rejected the stringent assumptions implicit in general theories of personality or basic human needs. Rather, they posit specific psychological processes, such as social comparisons (Rosenberg & Pearlin, 1978) and identity-based processes (Stryker, 1980) that link features of proximal social environments to individual thoughts, feelings, and behaviors. These processes focus on the ways in which proximal environments are perceived by, and come to have meaning for, individuals.

Despite the centrality of the psychological principle to the success of the SSP framework, it is the principle that is least often realized in practice. Many SSP analyses rely on naïve theories of psychological process, or assume the existence of hypothesized processes from the association of specific proximal conditions with individual outcomes. We urge greater attention to the work of psychologists by SSP researchers, both for the sake of improving SSP analyses and of creating greater integration between the two disciplines. In this section, we highlight two areas of research, both of which focus on meaning and perception, in which we see convergence between the concerns of sociologists and psychologists: social cognition and self. We then describe recent research on health that highlights the potential of interdisciplinary research on the links between macro-social structures and individual biology.

Social Cognition

Theories of social cognition represent one point of entrée into the question of meaning. Social cognition dominates the field of psychological social psychology, but has been virtually absent from SSP research.*

Social cognition refers to "structures of knowledge, the processes of knowledge creation, dissemination, and affirmation, the actual content of that knowledge, and how social forces shape each of these aspects of cognition" (Howard, 1995, p. 91). Cognitive structures, or schema, influence what we attend to, what we remember, and our inferences about others (Hollander & Howard, 2000). Studies of social cognition, therefore, focus on how information is organized and stored in memory, the processes that link information with social experience in memory, and how experience, in turn, alters the stored information (Morgan & Schwalbe, 1990).

According to Howard (1994) cognitions are inherently social and context-dependent. Echoing dualistic conceptualizations of structure and agency, Howard claims that social structure and cognition are mutually constitutive. The categories that we use to store information, and the accessibility and salience of those categories to cognition, depend on both socially and culturally constructed boundaries and on the situational imperatives of the setting in which cognition occurs.

Focusing on the social nature of cognition highlights the potential contributions of social cognition research to the study of inequality—a topic clearly relevant to SSP researchers. Certain characteristics (e.g., gender) lend themselves to social differentiation and categorization, which reinforce group boundaries. Selective information processing (of which social categorization is one such example) leads persons to see out-group members are less differentiated than in-group members, a perceptual bias that favors more extreme evaluations of out-group members (Deschamps, 1983). More generally, social categories underpin processes of attribution, self-evaluation, and the like in ways that contribute to the legitimation of social hierarchies based on group level identities, or characteristics, such as race, class, gender, sexual orientation, and the like (Della Fave, 1980). A focus on these types of processes when studying stratification would enhance our understanding of the psychological mechanisms through which stratified social orders come to have meaning for individuals, and shape social interactions so as to reify existing inequality.

Self

Theories of social cognition can also be used to merge sociological and psychological understandings of self. Self is a central concept in both sociology and psychology, although its specific conceptualizations and uses differ. Self and self-processes are often invoked by sociologists to explain the influence of proximal experiences on psychological well-being, for example, Rosenberg and Pearlin's use of reflected appraisal to link social class to self-esteem (also see Gecas and Seff's (1990) discussion of other self-processes to explain the specific effects of occupation and work conditions on self-esteem). These types of explanations are invoked increasingly in research on social movements as researchers attempt to discern the motivations, emotions, cognitions, and the like, that motivate individuals' entrance into,

---

*While social cognition has been absent in SSP, this is not necessarily true for other traditions within sociological social psychology. See Morgan and Schwalbe (1990) and Howard (1994, 1995) on the potential of social cognition to facilitate communication between various psychological and sociological traditions.

participation in, and exit out of particular involvements (Goodwin, Jasper, & Polletta, 2000; Granberg & Brown, 1989; Oliver & Johnston, 2000; Sherkat & Blocker, 1994).

Although definitions of self vary even among sociologists, the concept of self is "often used generically to refer to all of the *products* or consequences" (Gecas & Burke, 1995, p. 42) of the reflexivity between self as subject and self as object. The most common operationalizations of self measure aspects of self-concept (i.e., self-esteem and self-efficacy) or of identities (linked to roles, memberships, categories, and character traits). Sociological conceptualizations of self emphasize the relationships among different components of self (as in identity hierarchies) and the embeddedness of self within social situations and structures, offering a natural linkage to the proximal environments that interest SSP researchers.*

Early work in psychology conceptualized self as an attributional system, operationalized with measures of self-awareness (Duval & Wicklund, 1972), self-monitoring (Snyder, 1974), and so on. More recent work, however, has developed a model of self as a cognitive system of self-schemas (or prototypes) that processes self-relevant information (Kihlstrom & Cantor, 1984; Markus, 1977; see Linville & Carlston, 1994, for a review). According to the latter, self determines which aspects of the social environment are taken into account, how they are interpreted, and how we respond (Morgan & Schwalbe, 1990).

Despite their differences, sociological and psychological conceptualizations of self share the beliefs that there are multiple selves (organized hierarchically around social roles, personal identities, or interactional contexts), that self-knowledge can be gained through social interaction as well as self-observation, and that self-motives (e.g., self-verification, self-enhancement, self-consistency) contribute to stability in self over time. Moreover, both are based on fundamentally cognitive models of human behavior, in which persons make attributions about the environment in order to organize and understand it. These commonalities suggest the possibility for interdisciplinary collaboration on questions of how proximal social structures shape self-relevant interactions and how those interactions become integrated into self-structures.

Sociologists' emphasis on the social structural and interactional origins of the self complements psychologists' more nuanced and comprehensive theoretical understanding of internal self-processes. Morgan & Schwalbe (1990) elaborate this complementarity in a discussion of the analogous concepts of role-based identities and self-schemas. Both refer to aspects of self-organization that facilitate processing of incoming social information. They differ in that role-based identities are defined as deriving from formally defined roles (e.g., parent, worker) whereas self-schemas are more often defined in terms of individual traits (e.g., hard-working vs. lazy). Linking these two concepts theoretically would yield benefits for both psychology and sociology. Schema-based models of self could be used to extend sociological theories regarding the implications of the self for behavior by specifying the processes through which the self shapes attentional processes, and through which environmental experiences are integrated into self-knowledge and guide behavior. In complement, sociological theories of role-based identities have the potential to reveal the origins of self-schema in status hierarchies, social networks, and other socially patterned interactions.

As a specific example of the convergence of these approaches, we consider the concept of identity salience. Identity theory contends that role-based identities are organized hierarchically according to their commitment and salience. The underlying proposition is that identities

---

*This conceptualization of self derives from Stryker's theory of Structural Symbolic Interaction (1980). To the degree that sociologists view self as a reflection of a differentiated society, they also view the self as differentiated. Although most symbolic interactionists would argue that there is no "real" self, or that there are as many selves as there are roles, or role partners, structural symbolic interactionists argue that the stability we typically encounter in self is attributable to individuals' patterned involvement with social networks and their positions within the existing social structure.

to which individuals are more committed (either affectively or by virtue of social network structure) are more salient (i.e., more likely to be invoked) and have greater influence on behavior (see Chapter 2 in this volume for a more complete discussion). The question that remains is: *How and why* does identity salience influence behavior? Self-schema theories provide precise models for the processing of self-relevant information that could help answer this question. According to these models, information that pertains to self-domains that are well-developed (i.e., schematized) receives greater attention and is assimilated into existing cognitive structures more rapidly than information that pertains to self-domains that are less well-schematized. Furthermore, information that is accessible to memory has a stronger effect on behavior than information that is not. Based on those findings, one might hypothesize that salient identities have stronger effects on behaviors because they facilitate the ease and rapidity with which individuals process self-relevant information.

Whereas several theorists have argued convincingly for the integration of sociological and psychological theories of self and identity (Alexander & Wiley, 1981; Morgan & Schwalbe, 1990; Stryker, 1983; Stryker & Burke, 2000), integration at the empirical level is less well-developed. Promising areas of interdisciplinary collaboration include studies of the self in social movements (Stryker, Owens, & White, 2000) and of social identity (Tajfel & Turner, 1986). With respect to the former, psychological and sociological social psychologists move easily within each other's literatures, and have developed convergent explanations for the effect of consistency between self-views and movement identities on movement participation (see, e.g., Pinel & Swann, 2000 on the links between identity theory and self-verification theory). With respect to the latter, psychologists have begun to incorporate social networks into their theories of how group-based identities are developed and how they influence behavior (e.g., Deaux & Martin, 2001), borrowing from identity theory. These "collaborations" demonstrate the increased sensitivity of each discipline to the insights of the other, but rarely involve the development of common research agendas. The organizational, disciplinary, and methodological barriers to interdisciplinary research remain substantial impediments to truly interdisciplinary research (Stryker, 1983).

Biology

The promise of interdisciplinary collaboration between the social, behavioral, and biological sciences can be seen in the active project concerning the effects of socioeconomic status and race on health. Drawing on perspectives from stress research (Pearlin, 1999), and using SSP as an organizing framework, researchers interested in the effects of stratification on health have developed comprehensive conceptual models that trace the effects of macro-structures on individuals through intervening experiences in proximal environments (e.g., families, social networks, communities) and, importantly, through the relevance of those proximal environments for physiological functioning. Although the hypothesized linkages have not all been established empirically, early results are encouraging.

In one specific example of this type of model, Williams and Williams-Morris (2000) trace the effect of racism on individual health through the mediating experiences of low socioeconomic status, discrimination, and ego identities. As the authors note, racism is a system that involves an ideology of inferiority accompanied by individual-level prejudice and discrimination. Moreover, racism is not independent of other social institutions but, rather, transforms those institutions so that the entire social system becomes racialized. Racism becomes relevant for individual health through multiple pathways including: (1) the effects of discrimination, blocked opportunities, and social isolation on the socioeconomic attainment of racial minority groups, (2) residential segregation of minority groups in economically deprived neighborhoods, (3) individual experiences of discrimination, and (4) the internalization of stigma and racial inferiority. Furthermore, these studies have found that discrimination influences cardiovascular reactivity and blood pressure, suggesting one mechanism by which macro-environments get "under the skin" of individuals.

In a similar vein, Taylor, Repetti, and Seeman (1997) review research demonstrating links between environmental experiences, stress, and physiological responses, which suggests that chronically challenged physiological systems experience cumulative damage (a build-up of allostatic load) with implications for physical functioning. For example, persistently conflictual marital interactions are associated with greater cardiovascular and neuroendocrine reactivity and lower immune function (Kiecolt-Glaser, Malarkey, Cacioppo, & Glaser, 1994). Moreover, drawing the connection between mind and body, research suggests that negative emotions suppress immune function and may increase risk of heart attacks because of activation of the sympathetic-adrena-medullary system (see Taylor et al., 1997, for a review of relevant research). While neither of these approaches has been entirely successful at tracing the full set of linkages from the macro-environment to individual outcomes, both suggest the promise of interdisciplinary collaboration in research on social location, personality, behavior, and health.

Even as progress is made in this regard, there remain undercurrents of dissatisfaction among sociologists, who often feel that their contributions are overlooked or devalued by researchers from other disciplines. Schwartz (1999), for example, claims that sociological theories of mental illness are often deemphasized in favor of psychology and biology, an observation that echoes Kohn's (1989) concern with the increasing psychologization within social psychology. Sociological stress researchers have also decried the shift in emphasis away from the structural origins of stress to the processes through which stress comes to have psychological relevance for individual behavior and outcomes (Pearlin, 1989).

Although we are sympathetic to these arguments, we are less concerned than our colleagues about the future of sociology in these types of projects, particularly given that psychologists and health researchers, alike, have become more, rather than less, aware of the importance of social context in the last twenty years (Deaux, 2000; Ryff, 1987; Taylor et al., 1997). While there is always the danger that psychologists will psychologize social processes, that danger has not yet been fully realized. Moreover, linking the project of sociological relevance exclusively to the identification of macro-origins of individual outcomes cedes little of social life to sociology, and minimizes the importance of proximal social interactions as meso-level instantiations of macro-structures.

CONCLUSION

As we describe it here, SSP is a perspective of paradoxes. Seemingly central to sociological interest in the macro–micro link (e.g., Alexander, Geisen, Münch, & Smelser, 1987; Huber, 1990), it is not a key contributor to those developments and is often explicitly cited as irrelevant (Hollander & Howard, 2000). Whereas SSP is the social psychological paradigm that best explicates the need for simultaneous consideration of multiple levels of social life, the most innovative multilevel research is being conducted by persons who do not explicitly pledge allegiance to the SSP paradigm. Finally, although SSP is now routinely accepted as one of the three faces of social psychology (House, 1977), it is virtually invisible in sociological social psychology textbooks (with the notable exception of Michener & Delamater, 1999) and in *Social Psychology Quarterly*, the flagship journal of the discipline.

As Kohn (1989) notes, SSP is a "quintessentially sociological" project. What distinguishes the SSP approach from the more general disciplinary project of macro–micro linkage is its adherence to its three orienting principles. Among extant approaches to macro–micro analysis, SSP offers the most explicit prescription for research, demanding careful attention to the structure and content of social relations and social processes at multiple levels of analysis. However, whereas the SSP framework provides scholars with a useful orientation to analyzing macro–micro relations it does not, in and of itself, offer a specific explanation for how and why those relations exist. As a result, SSP researchers rely on theories and research from other theoretical traditions within sociology and psychology, some of whose basic assumptions conflict with those of the SSP framework. This conflict is particularly evident in the increasing complexity and nuance in sociologists' conceptions of social structure, culture, and human agency as they contrast with the more deterministic conceptions of social structure in SSP research.

SSP is an inherently integrative framework. It brings together the contributions of structural sociologists, sociologists of culture, and social psychologists within both sociology and psychology. This integration cannot be accomplished within a single study but, rather, depends on the cumulative development of knowledge within specific substantive areas. By implication, contributions to SSP may come from people who do not explicitly identify as adherents to the tradition as well as from those who do. SSP researchers build on those contributions to develop models of social life that attend simultaneously to multiple levels of analysis.

The successful realization of SSP depends on our abilities to work with other disciplines concerned with psychological and biological processes, such as psychology, neurobiology, medicine, and public health. Without precise models of the mechanisms by which proximal environments influence individual thoughts and actions, the SSP framework cannot achieve the disciplinary integration to which it aspires. These collaborations depend, in turn, on finding points of intellectual convergence and identifying organizational forms and funding mechanisms that permit such collaborations to flourish. At the individual level, this means that sociologists and psychologists must work consciously and intentionally to overcome personal and departmental biases against the incorporation of competing theoretical paradigms into their work. At the institutional level, universities must continue to support interdisciplinary academic and research centers that bring together scholars from diverse disciplines concerned with common substantive problems.

ACKNOWLEDGMENTS: Our work on this chapter was supported by NIMH training grant T32 MH14588 (Jane D. McLeod, Principal Investigator). We thank Bernice Pescosolido and John Delamater for helpful comments on an earlier draft.

REFERENCES

Adorno, T., Frenkel-Brunswik, E., Levinson, D. J., & Sanford, R. N. (1950). *The authoritarian personality*. New York: Harper.

Alexander, C. N., & Wiley, M. G. (1981). Situated activity and identity formation. In M. Rosenberg & R. H. Turner (Eds.), *Social psychology: Sociological perspectives* (pp. 269–289). New York: Basic Books.

Alexander, J. C. (1982). *Theoretical logic in sociology: Positivism, presuppositions, and current controversies*. Berkeley: University of California Press.

Alexander, J. C. (1984). Social-structural analysis: Some notes on its history and prospects. *Sociological Quarterly, 25*, 5–26.

Alexander, J. C., Geisen, B., Münch, R., & Smelser, N. J. (Eds.). (1987). *The micro–macro link*. Los Angeles, CA: University of California Press.

Alwin, D. F., Cohen, R. L., & Newcomb, T. M. (1991). *Aging, personality, and social change: Attitude persistence and change over the life-span*. Madison, WI: University of Wisconsin Press.

Anderson, E. (1990a). *Streetwise: Race, class, and change in an urban community*. Chicago, IL: University of Chicago Press.

Anderson, E. (1990b). Neighborhood effects on teenage pregnancy. In C. Jencks & P. E. Peterson (Eds.), *The urban underclass* (pp. 375–398). Washington, DC: The Brookings Institution.

Baker, W. E., & Faulkner, R. R. (1991). Role as resource in the Hollywood film industry. *American Journal of Sociology, 97*, 279–309.

Berger, J., Cohen, B. P., & Zelditch, M. (1972). Status characteristics and social interaction. *American Sociological Review, 56*, 355–369.

Berger, J., Fisek, M. H., Norman, R. Z., & Zelditch, M. (1977). *Status characteristics in social interaction: An expectations states approach*. New York: Elsevier.

Beutel, A. M., & Marini, M. M. (1995). Gender and values. *American Sociological Review, 60*, 436–448.

Bian, Y. (1997). Bringing strong ties back in: Indirect ties, network bridges, and job searches in China. *American Sociological Review, 62*, 366–385.

Bian, Y., & Ang, S. (1997). Guanxi networks and job mobility in China and Singapore. *Social Forces, 75*, 981–1005.

Bobo, L. D., Johnson, D., & Suh, S. A. (2000). Racial attitudes and power in the workplace: Do the haves differ from the have-nots? In L. D. Bobo, M. L. Oliver, J. H. Johnson, Jr., & A. Valenzuela, Jr. (Eds.), *Prismatic metropolis: Inequality in Los Angeles* (pp. 491–522). New York: Russell Sage Foundation.

Bobo, L. D., Oliver, M. L., Johnson, J. H., Jr., & Valenzuela, A., Jr. (Eds.). (2000). *Prismatic metropolis: Inequality in Los Angeles*. New York: Russell Sage Foundation.

Bourdieu, P. (1977). *Outline of a theory of practice*. Cambridge, UK: Cambridge University Press.

Boyce, W. T., Frank, E., Jensen, P. S., Kessler, R. C., Nelson, C. A., Steinberg, L., & The MacArthur Foundation Research Network on Psychopathology and Development. (1998). Social context in developmental psychopathology: Recommendations for future research from the MacArthur Network on Psychopathology and Development. *Development and Psychopathology, 10*, 143–164.

Brofenbrenner, U. (1979). *The ecology of human development: Experiment by nature and design*. Cambridge, MA: Harvard University Press.

Burawoy, M. (1982). *Manufacturing consent: Changes in the labor process under monopoly capitalism*. Chicago, IL: University of Chicago Press.

Callero, P. L. (1994). From role-playing to role-using: Understanding role as resource. *Social Psychology Quarterly, 57*, 228–243.

Caspi, A., & Herbener, E. S. (1990). Continuity and change: Assortative marriage and the consistency of personality in adulthood. *Journal of Personality and Social Psychology, 58*, 250–258.

Caspi, A., Bem, D. J., & Elder, G. H., Jr. (1989). Continuities and consequences of interactional styles across the life course. *Journal of Personality, 57*, 375–406.

Charles, C. Z. (2000). Residential segregation in Los Angeles. In L. D. Bobo, M. L. Oliver, J. H. Johnson, Jr., & A. Valenzuela, Jr. (Eds.), *Prismatic metropolis: Inequality in Los Angeles* (pp. 167–219). New York: Russell Sage Foundation.

Conger, R. D., Conger, K. J., Elder, G. H., Jr., Lorenz, F. O., Simons, R. L., & Whitbeck, L. B. (1992). A family process model of economic hardship and adjustment of early adolescent boys. *Child Development, 63*, 526–541.

Connell, J. P., & Halpern-Felsher, B. L. (1997). How neighborhoods affect educational outcomes in middle childhood and adolescence: Conceptual issues and an empirical example. In J. Brooks-Gunn, G. J. Duncan, & J. L. Aber (Eds.), *Neighborhood poverty: Context and consequences for children* (Vol. 1) (pp. 174–199). New York: Russell Sage Foundation.

Corsaro, W. A., & Eder, D. (1995). Development and socialization of children and adolescents. In K. S. Cook, G. A. Fine, & J. S. House (Eds.), *Sociological perspectives on social psychology* (pp. 421–451). Boston, MA: Allyn and Bacon.

Crane, J. (1991). Effects of neighborhoods on dropping out of school and teenage childbearing. In C. Jencks & P. E. Peterson (Eds.), *The urban underclass* (pp. 299–320). Washington, DC: The Brookings Institution.

Deaux, K. (2000). Surveying the landscape of immigration: Social psychological perspectives. *Journal of Community and Applied Social Psychology, 10*, 421–431.

Deaux, K., & Martin, D. (2001). *Which context? Specifying levels of context in identity processes*. Paper presented at the Indiana Conference on Identity Theory, April 27–29, 2001, Bloomington, IN.

Della Fave, L. R. (1980). The meek shall not inherit the earth: Self-evaluation and the legitimacy of stratification. *American Sociological Review, 45*, 955–971.

Deschamps, J. (1983). Social attribution. In J. Jaspars, F. D. Fincham, & M. Hewstone (Eds.), *Attribution theory and research: Conceptual, developmental, and social dimensions* (pp. 223–240). New York: Academic Press.

Duval, S., & Wicklund, R. W. (1972). *A theory of objective self-awareness*. New York: Academic Press.

Elder, G. H., Jr. (1974). *Children of the Great Depression: Social change in life experience*. Chicago: University of Chicago Press.

Elder, G. H., Jr. (1981). History and the life course. In D. Bertaux (Ed.), *Biography and society* (pp. 77–115). Beverly Hills, CA: Sage.

Elder, G. H., Jr. (1997). The life course and human development. In R. M. Lerner (Ed.), *Handbook of child psychology: Volume 1. Theoretical models of human development* (pp. 939–991). New York: Wiley.

Elder, G. H., Jr. (1999). *Children of the Great Depression: Social change in life experience* (25th anniversary edition). Boulder, CO: Westview.

Elder, G. H., Jr., & O'Rand, A. M. (1995). Adult lives in a changing society. In K. S. Cook, G. A. Fine, & J. S. House (Eds.), *Sociological perspectives on social psychology* (pp. 452–475). Boston, MA: Allyn and Bacon.

Emirbayer, M., & Mische, A. (1998). What is agency? *American Journal of Sociology, 103*, 962–1023.

Feagin, J. R. (1991). The continuing significance of race: Antiblack discrimination in public places. *American Sociological Review, 56*, 101–116.

Feagin, J. R., & Booher Feagin, C. (1999). Theoretical perspectives in race and ethnic relations. In F. L. Pincus & H. J. Ehrlich (Eds.), *Race and ethnic relations: Contending views on prejudice, discrimination, and ethnoviolence* (2nd ed.) (pp. 41–59). Boulder, CO: Westview.

Fine, G. A. (1991). On the macrofoundations of microsociology: Constraint and the exterior reality of structure. *The Sociology Quarterly, 32*, 161–177.

Gecas, V., & Burke, P. J. (1995). Self and identity. In K. S. Cook, G. A. Fine, & J. S. House (Eds.), *Sociological perspectives on social psychology* (pp. 41–67). Boston, MA: Allyn and Bacon.

Gecas, V., & Seff, M. A. (1990). Social class and self-esteem: Psychological centrality, compensation, and the relative effects of work and home. *Social Psychology Quarterly, 53*, 165–173.

Giddens, A. (1976). *The new rules of sociological method.* New York: Basic Books.

Giddens, A. (1984). *The constitution of society: Outline of the theory of structuration.* Berkeley, CA: University of California Press.

Goodwin, J., Jasper, J. M., & Poletta, F. (2000). The return of the repressed: The fall and rise of emotions in social movements theory. *Mobilization, 5*, 65–84.

Gorer, G. (1943). The concept of national character. *Science News, 18*, 105–123.

Granberg, D., & Brown, T. A. (1989). Affect and cognition in politics. *Social Psychology Quarterly, 52*, 171–182.

Granovetter, M. S. (1973). The strength of weak ties. *American Journal of Sociology, 78*, 1360–1380.

Hagan, J., & Palloni, A. (1990). The social reproduction of a criminal class in working-class London, circa 1950–1980. *American Journal of Sociology, 96*, 265–299.

Hays, S. (1994). Structure and agency and the sticky problem of culture. *Sociological Theory, 12*, 57–72.

Heiss, J. (1981). Social roles. In M. Rosenberg & R. H. Turner (Eds.), *Social psychology: Sociological perspectives* (pp. 94–129). New York: Basic Books.

Hewitt, J. P. (1991). *Self and society* (5th ed.). Boston: Allyn and Bacon.

Hochschild, A. R. (1983). *The managed heart: The commercialization of human feeling.* Berkeley: The University of California Press.

Hollander, J. A., & Howard, J. A. (2000). Social psychological theories on social inequalities. *Social Psychology Quarterly, 63*, 338–351.

House, J. S. (1977). The three faces of social psychology. *Sociometry, 40*, 161–177.

House, J. S. (1981). Social structure and personality. In M. Rosenberg & R. H. Turner (Eds.), *Social psychology: Sociological perspectives* (pp. 525–561). New York: Basic Books.

House, J. S. (1995). Social structure, relationships, and the individual. In K. S. Cook, G. A. Fine, & J. S. House (Eds.), *Sociological perspectives on social psychology* (pp. 387–395). Boston, MA: Allyn and Bacon.

House, J. S., & Mortimer, J. (1990). Social structure and the individual: Emerging themes and new directions. *Social Psychology Quarterly, 53*, 71–80.

House, J. S., Umberson, D., & Landis, K. (1988). Structures and processes of social support. *Annual Review of Sociology, 14*, 293–318.

Howard, J. A. (1994). A social cognitive conception of social structure. *Social Psychology Quarterly, 57*, 210–227.

Howard, J. A. (1995). Social cognition. In K. S. Cook, G. A. Fine, & J. S. House (Eds.), *Sociological perspectives on social psychology* (pp. 90–117). Boston, MA: Allyn and Bacon.

Huber, J. (1990). Macro–micro links in gender stratification. *American Sociological Review, 55*, 1–10.

Hughes, E. C. (1945). Dilemmas and contradictions of status. *American Journal of Sociology, 50*, 353–359.

Hyde, J. S., Delamater, J. D., & Durik, A. M. (2001). Sexuality and the dual-earner couple, part II: Beyond the baby years. *Journal of Sex Research, 38*, 10–23.

Hyde, J. S., Delamater, J. D., & Hewitt, E. C. (1998). Sexuality and the dual-earner couple: Multiple roles and sexual functioning. *Journal of Family Psychology, 12*, 354–368.

Inkeles, A. (1959). Personality and social structure. In R. K. Merton, L. Broom, & L. S. Cottrell, Jr. (Eds.), *Sociology today* (pp. 249–276). New York: Basic.

Inkeles, A. (1960). Industrial man: The relation of status to experience, perception, and value. *American Journal of Sociology, 66,* 1–31.

Inkeles, A. (1969). Making men modern: On the causes and consequences of individual change in six developing countries. *American Journal of Sociology, 75,* 208–225.

Inkeles, A., & Smith, D. H. (1974). *Becoming modern: Individual change in six developing countries.* Cambridge, MA: Harvard University Press.

Inglehart, R., & Baker, W. E. (2000). Modernization, cultural change, and the persistence of traditional values. *American Sociological Review, 65,* 19–51.

Johnson, J. J., Jr., Farrell, W. C., Jr., & Stoloff, J. A. (2000). African American males in decline: A Los Angeles case study. In L. D. Bobo, M. L. Oliver, J. H. Johnson, Jr., & A. Valenzuela, Jr. (Eds.), *Prismatic metropolis: Inequality in Los Angeles* (pp. 315–337). New York: Russell Sage Foundation.

Katz, E., & Lazersfeld, P. F. (1955). *Personal influence.* Glencoe, IL: Free Press.

Kerckhoff, A. C. (1995). Social stratification and mobility processes: Interaction between individuals and social structures. In K. S. Cook, G. A. Fine, & J. S. House (Eds.), *Sociological perspectives on social psychology* (pp. 476–496). Boston, MA: Allyn and Bacon.

Kiecolt, J. K., & Mabry, J. B. (2000). Agency in young adulthood: Intentional self-change among college students. *Advances in Life Course Research, 5,* 181–205.

Kiecolt-Glaser, J. K., Malarkey, W. B., Cacioppo, J. T., & Glaser, R. (1994). Stressful personal relationships: Immune and endocrine function. In R. Glaser & J. Kiecolt-Glaser (Eds.), *Handbook of human stress and immunity* (pp. 321–339). San Diego, CA: Academic.

Kihlstrom, J. F., & Cantor, N. (1984). Mental representations of the self. In L. Berkowitz (Ed.), *Advances in experimental social psychology, 2,* 2–48. New York: Academic.

Kohn, M. L. (1969). *Class and conformity: A study in values.* Homewood, IL: Dorsey.

Kohn, M. L. (1989). Social structure and personality: A quintessentially sociological approach to social psychology. *Social Forces, 68,* 26–33.

Kohn, M. L., & Schooler, C. (1983). *Work and personality: An inquiry into the impact of social stratification.* Norwood, NJ: Ablex.

Kohn, M. L., & Slomczynski, K. M. (1990). *Social structure and self-direction: A comparative analysis of the United States and Poland.* Cambridge, MA: Basil Blackwell, Inc.

Kohn, M. L., Naoi, A., Schoenbach, C., Schooler, C., & Slomczynski, K. M. (1990). Position in the class structure and psychological functioning in the United States, Japan, and Poland. *American Journal of Sociology, 95,* 964–1008.

Krohn, M. D. (1999). Social leaning theory: The continuing development of a perspective. *Theoretical Criminology, 3,* 462–476.

Lewis, O. (1968). *La vida: A Puerto Rican family in the culture of poverty—San Juan and New York.* New York: Vintage.

Liebow, E. (1967). *Tally's corner: A study of Negro streetcorner men.* Boston: Little, Brown.

Linville, P. W. (1987). Self-complexity as a cognitive buffer against stress-related illness and depression. *Journal of Personality and Social Psychology, 52,* 663–676.

Linville, P. W., & Carlston, D. E. (1994). Social cognition of the self. In P. G. Devine, D. L. Hamilton, & T. M. Ostrom (Eds.), *Social cognition: Impact on social psychology* (pp. 144–193). New York: Academic Press.

Lively, K. J. (2000). Reciprocal emotion management. *Work and Occupations, 27,* 32–63.

Lively, K. J. (2001). Occupational claims to professionalism: The case of paralegals. *Symbolic Interaction, 24,* 343–366.

Markus, H. (1977). Self-schemata and processing information about the self. *Journal of Personality and Social Psychology, 35,* 63–78.

Markus, H., & Nurius, P. (1987). Possible selves: The interface between motivation and the self-concept. In K. Yardley & T. Honess (Eds.), *Self and identity: Psychosocial perspectives* (pp. 157–172). New York: John Wiley & Sons Ltd.

Massey, D. S., & Denton, N. A. (1993). *American apartheid: Segregation and the making of the underclass.* Cambridge, MA: Harvard University Press.

Matsueda, R. L. (1988). The current state of differential association theory. *Crime and Delinquency, 34,* 277–306.

Matsueda, R. L., & Heimer, K. (1987). Race, family structure, and delinquency: A test of differential association and social control theories. *American Sociological Review, 52,* 826–840.

Maynard, D. W. (1991). Interaction and asymmetry in clinical discourse. *American Journal of Sociology, 97,* 448–495.

McLeod, J. D., & Edwards, K. (1995). Contextual determinants of children's responses to poverty. *Social Forces, 73,* 1487–1516.

McLeod, J. D., & Shanahan, M. J. (1993). Poverty, parenting, and children's mental health. *American Sociological Review, 58,* 351–366.

Menaghan, E. G. (1991). Work experiences and family interaction processes: The long reach of the job? *Annual Review of Sociology, 17,* 419–444.

Miech, R. A., Caspi, A., Moffitt, T. E., Wright, B. E., & Silva, P. A. (1999). Low socioeconomic status and mental disorders: A longitudinal study of selection and causation during young adulthood. *American Journal of Sociology, 104*, 112–147.

Merton, R. K. (1957). The role-set: Problems in sociological theory. *British Journal of Sociology, 8*, 106–120.

Michener, H. A., & Delamater, J. D. (1999). *Social Psychology*, 4th edition. Orlando, FL: Harcourt Brace.

Miller, J., Schooler, C., Kohn, M. L., & Miller, K. A. (1983). Women and work: The psychological effects of occupational conditions. In M. L. Kohn & C. Schooler (Eds.), *Work and personality: An inquiry into the impact of social stratification* (pp. 195–216). Norwood, NJ: Ablex.

Miller-Loessi, K. (1995). Comparative social psychology: Cross-cultural and cross-national. In K. S. Cook, G. A. Fine, & J. S. House (Eds.), *Sociological perspectives on social psychology* (pp. 396–420). Boston, MA: Allyn and Bacon.

Morgan, D. L., & Schwalbe, M. L. (1990). Mind and self in society: Linking social structure and social cognition. *Social Psychology Quarterly, 53*, 148–164.

Mueller, C. W., Mulinge, M., & Glass, J. (2002). Interactional processes and gender workplace inequalities. *Social Psychology Quarterly, 65*, 163–185.

Naoi, M., & Schooler, C. (1990). Psychological consequences of occupational conditions among Japanese wives. *Social Psychology Quarterly, 53*, 100–116.

Newcomb, T. M. (1963). Persistence and regression of changed attitudes: Long-range studies. *Journal of Social Issues, 19*, 3–14.

Oliver, P. E., & Johnston, H. (2000). What a good idea; Ideologies and frames in social movement research. *Mobilization, 5*, 37–54.

Ollilainen, M. (2000). Gendering emotions, gendering teams: Construction of emotions in self-managing teamwork. In N. M. Ashkanasy, C. E. J. Hartel, & W. J. Zerbe (Eds.), *Emotions in the workplace* (pp. 82–96). Westport, CT: Quorum Books.

Parcel, T. L., & Menaghan, E. G. (1994). *Parents' jobs and children's lives.* New York: Aldine de Gruyter.

Parsons, T., & Smelser, N. J. (1956). *Economy and society: A study in the integration of economic and social theory.* New York: Free Press.

Patterson, G. R., DeBaryshe, B. D., & Ramsey, E. (1989). A developmental perspective on antisocial behavior. *American Psychologist, 44*, 329–335.

Pearlin, L. I. (1989). The sociological study of stress. *Journal of Health and Social Behavior, 30*, 241–256.

Pearlin, L. I. (1999). Stress and mental health: A conceptual overview. In A. V. Horwitz & T. L. Scheid (Eds.), *A handbook for the study of mental health: Social contexts, theories, and systems* (pp. 161–175). New York: Cambridge University Press.

Pierce, J. L. (1995). *Gender trials: Emotional lives in contemporary law firms.* Berkeley, CA: University of California Press.

Pinel, E. C., & Swann, W. B., Jr. (2000). Finding the self through others: Self-verification and social movement participation. In S. Stryker, T. J. Owens, & R. W. White (Eds.), *Self, identity, and social movements* (pp. 132–152). Minneapolis, MN: University of Minnesota Press.

Ridgeway, C., & Diekema, D. (1989). Dominance and collective hierarchy formation in male and female task groups. *American Sociological Review, 54*, 79–93.

Ridgeway, C. L., & Walker, H. A. (1992). Status structures. In K. S. Cook, G. A. Fine, & J. S. House (Eds.), *Sociological perspectives on social psychology* (pp. 281–310). Boston: Allyn and Bacon.

Rosenberg, M., & Pearlin, L. I. (1978). Social class and self-esteem among children and adults. *American Journal of Sociology, 84*, 53–77.

Ross, C. E., & Wu, C. (1995). The links between education and health. *American Sociological Review, 60*, 719–745.

Rubinstein, D. (2001). *Culture, structure, and agency: Toward a truly multidimensional society.* Thousand Oaks, CA: Pine Forge Press.

Ryff, C. D. (1987). The place of personality and social structure research in social psychology. *Journal of Personality and Social Psychology, 53*, 1192–1202.

Sampson, R. J., Raudenbush, S. W., & Earls, F. (1997). Neighborhoods and violent crime: A multilevel study of collective efficacy. *Science, 277*, 918–924.

Schooler, C. (1994). A working conceptualization of social structure: Mertonian roots and psychological and sociocultural relationships. *Social Psychology Quarterly, 57*, 262–273.

Schutz, A. (1970). *On phenomenology and social relations.* Chicago: University of Chicago Press.

Schwartz, S. (1999). Biological approaches to psychiatric disorders. In A. V. Horwitz & T. L. Scheid (Eds.), *A handbook for the study of mental health: Social contexts, theories, and systems* (pp. 79–103). New York: Cambridge University Press.

Sewell, W. H., Jr. (1992). A theory of structure: Duality, agency, and transformation. *American Journal of Sociology, 98*, 1–29.

Sewell, W. H., Haller, A. O., & Ohlendorf, G. W. (1970). The educational and early occupational status attainment process: Replication and revision. *American Sociological Review, 35,* 1014–1027.

Shanahan, M. J. (2000). Pathways to adulthood in changing societies: Variability and mechanisms in life course perspective. *Annual Review of Sociology, 26,* 667–692.

Sherkat, D., & Blocker, J. T. (1994). The political development of sixties' activists: Identifying the influence of class, gender, and socialization on protest participation. *Social Forces, 74,* 821–841.

Sherkat, D., & Blocker, J. T. (1997). Explaining the political and personal consequences of protest. *Social Forces, 75,* 1049–1070.

Snow, D. A., & Oliver, P. E. (1995). Social movements and collective behavior: Social psychological dimensions and considerations. In K. S. Cook, G. A. Fine, & J. S. House (Eds.), *Sociological perspectives on social psychology* (pp. 571–599). Boston, MA: Allyn and Bacon.

Snyder, M. (1974). Self-monitoring of expressive behavior. *Journal of Personality and Social Psychology, 30,* 526–537.

Stryker, S. (1977). Developments in "two social psychologies": Toward an appreciation of mutual relevance. *Sociometry, 40,* 145–160.

Stryker, S. (1980). *Symbolic interactionism: A social structural version.* Menlo Park, CA: Benjamin/Cummings.

Stryker, S. (1983). Social psychology from the standpoint of a structural symbolic interactionism: Toward an inter-disciplinary social psychology. *Advances in Experimental Social Psychology, 16,* 181–218.

Stryker, S., & Burke, P. J. (2000). The past, present, and future of an identity theory. *Social Psychology Quarterly, 63,* 284–297.

Stryker, S., & Statham, A. (1985). Symbolic interaction and role theory. In G. Lindzey & E. Aronson (Eds.), *Handbook of social psychology: Theory and method (Vol. I)* (pp. 311–377). New York: Random House.

Stryker, S., Owens, T. J., & White, R. W. (Eds.). (2000). *Self, identity, and social movements.* Minneapolis, MN: University of Minnesota Press.

Tajfel, H., & Turner, J. C. (1986). The social identity of intergroup behavior. In S. Worchel & W. G. Austin (Eds.), *Psychology of intergroup relations* (2nd ed.) (pp. 7–24). Chicago: Nelson-Hall.

Tannen, D. (1995). *Talking from 9 to 5: Women and men in the workplace: Language sex and power.* New York: Avon Books.

Taylor, S. E., Repetti, R. L., & Seeman, T. (1997). Health psychology: What is an unhealthy environment and how does it get under the skin? *Annual Review of Psychology, 48,* 411–447.

Thoits, P. A. (1983). Multiple identities and psychological well-being: A reformulation and test of the social isolation hypothesis. *American Sociological Review, 48,* 174–187.

Thoits, P. A. (1995). Stress, coping, and social support processes: Where are we? What next? *Journal of Health and Social Behavior, Special Issue,* 53–79.

Turner, R. H. (1962). Role-taking: Process v. conformity. In A. M. Rose (Ed.), *Human behavior and social processes* (pp. 20–40). Boston: Houghton Mifflin.

Turner. R. H. (1978). Role and the person. *American Journal of Sociology, 84,* 1–23.

Turner, R. J., & Turner, J. B. (1999). Social integration and support. In C. S. Aneshensel & J. C. Phelan (Eds.), *Handbook of the sociology of mental health* (pp. 301–320). New York: Kluwer/Plenum.

Turner, R. J., & Marino, F. (1994). Social support and social structure: A descriptive epidemiology. *Journal of Health and Social Behavior, 35,* 193–212.

Webster, M., Jr., & Foschi, M. (1988). *Status generalization: New theory and research.* Stanford, CA: Stanford University Press.

West, C., & Fenstermaker, S. (1995). Doing difference. *Gender & Society, 9,* 506–513.

West, C., & Zimmerman, D. H. (1987). Doing gender. *Gender & Society, 1,* 125–151.

Wheaton, B. (1978). The sociogenesis of psychological disorder: Reexamining the causal issues with longitudinal data. *American Sociological Review, 43,* 383–403.

Williams, D. R. (1990). Socioeconomic differentials in health: A review and redirection. *Social Psychology Quarterly, 53,* 81–99.

Williams, D. R., & Collins, C. (1995). US socioeconomic and racial differences in health: Patterns and explanations. *Annual Review of Sociology, 21,* 349–386.

Williams, D. R., & Williams-Morris, R. (2000). Racism and mental health: The African American experience. *Ethnicity & Health, 5,* 243–268.

Wilson, W. J. (1987). *The truly disadvantaged: The inner city, the underclass and public policy.* Chicago: University of Chicago Press.

Wilson, W. J. (1991). Studying inner city social dislocations: The challenge of public agenda research. *American Sociological Review, 56,* 1–14.

Wuthnow, R., Hunter, J., Bergeson, A., & Kurzweil, E. (1984). *Cultural analysis.* Boston: Routledge & Kegan Paul.

CHAPTER 5

Evolutionary Social Psychology

Adaptive Predispositions and Human Culture

Douglas Kenrick

Josh Ackerman

Susan Ledlow

> The conventional wisdom in the social sciences is that human nature is simply the imprint of an individual's background and experience. But our cultures are not random collections of arbitrary habits. They are canalized expressions of our instincts. That is why the same themes crop up in all cultures—themes such as family, ritual, bargain, love, hierarchy, friendships, jealousy, group loyalty, and superstition ... Instincts, in a species like the human one, are not immutable genetic programs; they are pre-dispositions to learn. (Ridley, 1996)

Social psychologists have generated a wealth of fascinating empirical findings on topics ranging from altruism and aggression through stereotyping and xenophobia. Yet a recurrent criticism of the field is the lack of a cohesive theoretical framework to incorporate these diverse snapshots of empiricism. Part of the appeal of an evolutionary perspective is its capacity to organize these findings, and to integrate the insights of psychology, sociology, and anthropology with those of the other life sciences. Another part of its appeal is its ability to provide answers to interesting questions that are not easy to address from traditional social science perspectives. For example: Why is the distinction between "Us" and "Them" universal? In selecting a mate, why are men generally more attuned to physical attractiveness and women to social status? Why do age preferences in mate choice over the lifespan violate the homogamy principle in a patterned and

Douglas T. Kenrick, Josh M. Ackerman, and Susan E. Ledlow • Department of Psychology, Arizona State University, Tempe, Arizona 85287

Handbook of Social Psychology, edited by John Delamater. Kluwer Academic/Plenum Publishers, New York, 2003.

universal way? Why are stories about "wicked step-parents" found in many different cultures? Why are some characteristics universally treated as stigmas? Why is investment by fathers, normally rare in mammals, found in all human societies?

In spite of its theoretical promise and an increasing body of empirical research, evolutionary social psychology remains misunderstood. This chapter provides an overview of current research and theory on evolutionary psychology, explores some implications for research on cultural and group processes, and addresses some recurrent criticisms and misconceptions.

GENERAL PRINCIPLES OF EVOLUTIONARY MODELS

Evolutionary theorists assume that human beings share certain characteristics with other animals by virtue of either common descent (e.g., with great apes such as chimpanzees) or common ecological demands (e.g., with other groups of living mammals such as wolves or baboons). Observations across the spectrum of living organisms have yielded a number of powerful general principles, which are now being used to expand our understanding of human social behavior. In this section, we summarize the concepts of natural selection, inclusive fitness, life history strategies, differential parental investment, and sexual selection.

Natural Selection: Morphology and Behavior by Adaptive Design

Darwin's (1859) original theory of natural selection was based on three interlinked concepts: variability within a species, inheritance of traits by offspring, and differential reproduction. Within any species, individuals vary in traits relevant to survival and reproduction. For example, a trait that helps an animal run faster than others of its same species will assist in escaping predators, and therefore living longer and producing more offspring than others without that trait.

Physical innovations such as a whale's flipper or a bat's wing only help the animal survive and reproduce because they co-evolved with central nervous systems capable of producing particular behaviors adapted to the animal's particular environment. Imagine a whale trying to hunt flying insects at night, or a bat trying to sift plankton from the ocean, for instance. Besides their wings, however, bats have inherited complex neural machinery designed to fit a particular behavioral repertoire. Because they must locate moving prey in the dark, bats have a large portion of their brains dedicated to analyzing the sonar-like echoes of the specialized sounds they emit. On the other hand, humans have brain mechanisms specially designed to analyze binocular color vision, which assists in locating and tracking prey or estimating ripeness of fruit on a distant limb.

Despite the very different ecological demands on whales, bats, and humans, they also share certain behavioral programs by virtue of common descent and common ecological pressures. For example, all mammalian females nurse their young. Most species of whales and bats, like humans, congregate in large groups, a behavioral adaptation that has some adaptive advantages—avoiding predators or searching for scattered food sources, for example, but also some disadvantages—such as increased intraspecies competition and disease (Alcock, 1998). Group aggregation, like most behavioral tendencies, is found when advantages outweigh disadvantages (more likely in prey than in predator species, e.g., and less likely in species who eat food that can be defended in small territories). Besides those adaptations shared by common descent or common ecological demands, some are uniquely designed to solve particular problems encountered by a given species (e.g., flying ability in bats, but not in other mammals).

Modern evolutionary theorists assume that many features related to human cognition, motivation, and behavior were designed through natural selection. For example, much as the bird of paradise has inherited dazzling plumage and associated courtship displays, humans have inherited a larynx along with a brain designed to easily learn to communicate using language (Pinker, 1994).

From an evolutionary perspective, the first question one asks about a morphological or behavioral feature is: What is its function? A baby's crying would have served to alert its mother to the child's immediate needs, and its smiling and cooing to cement the mother–infant bond, for example. From the mother's perspective, the bond would have served to increase the survival rates of her offspring (Zeifman & Hazan, 1997).

Because humans have lived in small, kin-based groups for over three million years (Foley, 1989), it is assumed that many features of human cognition and behavior were designed to solve the problems of living in such groups (Kenrick, Sadalla, & Keefe, 1998). For example, humans around the world have well-articulated vocabularies for describing the extent to which another person is cooperative or dominant, and it has been suggested that this is because our ancestors' survival and reproduction would have been served by knowledge of those who were reliable allies or leaders (White, 1980). Similarly, people are very good at solving normally difficult logical problems when they are framed in terms of detecting cheaters in social situations, and it has been suggested that this ability was likewise well-fitted to the demands of living in human ancestral groups (Tooby & Cosmides, 1992).

It is important to note that evolutionary theorists do not assume that humans or other organisms inherit some capacity to determine in advance which behavioral strategy will be adaptive, and thereby proceed through life as "fitness-maximizing" machines. Instead, it is assumed that organisms inherit specific behavioral mechanisms designed to increase the probability of solving recurrent problems confronted during the ancestral past. For example, animals whose ancestors ate fruit are sensitive to sweetness, and find it reinforcing; animals whose ancestors were purely carnivorous do not. Generally, sweetness sensitivity led our human ancestors to eat ripe, rather than unripe, fruit (the latter having less nutritional value, and higher toxin content). While evolutionary psychologists typically begin by investigating a behavior's function, it is not always assumed that the particular behavior in question continues to be adaptive in the human-altered modern world. Because natural selection operates over the long haul, whereas human culture and technology can change rapidly, modern humans likely possess some characteristics that are less than perfectly suited for current environments. For a diabetes-prone individual with unlimited access to chocolate bars and ice cream, the sweetness-seeking mechanism might shorten his or her lifespan; however, it would, on average, have helped his or her *ancestors* survive to reproductive age.

Inclusive Fitness: Why Humans Everywhere are Concerned with the Distinction between Kin and Non-Kin

While Darwinian theory revolutionized the natural sciences, its focus on individual reproductive success could not account for the persistence of behaviors in which one individual sacrificed his or her reproductive success for the sake of another individual. Altruistic acts such as sacrificing one's life for a child, or refraining from mating in order to help care for the offspring of others (common among many social insects), would seem likely to be replaced by more selfish behaviors that led to successful reproduction. This dilemma was resolved when biologists began to understand processes of genetic inheritance. W. D. Hamilton (1964) explained that any gene in an individual may be propagated by that individual directly or by a related individual who shares that gene. More closely related individuals are more likely to share the gene and are also more likely to exhibit altruistic behaviors towards each other. Because closely related individuals share common genes, altruistic inclinations could be selected if on average, they led organisms to act in ways that maximized the genetic payoff (e.g., risking one's own life to save three brothers). While classical fitness had been calculated based only on the number of offspring an individual produced, inclusive fitness is calculated in terms both of direct reproduction and indirect replication of genes gained through assistance to kin. The biological literature abounds with descriptions of altruistic acts among related animals (Alcock, 1998; Trivers, 1985). This does not mean that humans, or any other animals, consciously decide to assist kin because it maximizes their own fitness. Proximate mechanisms such as familial love incline people to help relatives; inclusive fitness theory merely explains how such a behavior could develop and be sustained in a species.

Alarm calls in various rodents offer good examples of kin altruism (Hoogland, 1983; Sherman, 1977). Upon sighting predators such as hawks, ground squirrels risk their own lives by making an alarm call that warns neighbors to take cover. However, their alarm calling is socially contingent, and from a genetic perspective, actually selfish: It is much more likely when the animals are in the vicinity of close kin as opposed to unrelated squirrels. Another common example of kin altruism is known as "helping at the nest"—a phenomenon in which adult offspring help care for relatives' offspring. For example, when they are unable to find a suitable location to mate on their own, white-fronted bee-eaters delay mating to help both younger siblings and more distant relatives who inhabit the same communal nest. The likelihood that a bird will aid a relative can be modeled with extreme precision to Hamilton's laws of inclusive fitness. Full siblings are the most likely to be helped; distant relatives are the least likely. Emlen (1997) notes that over 90% of bird and mammal species living in multigenerational families show this cooperative breeding behavior.

In humans as well, resources and assistance are often provided by close kin. According to kin selection theory, we should help siblings, parents, and offspring (who share on average 0.50 of our genes) more often than aunts and uncles or nieces and nephews (all sharing about 0.25 of our genes). Aunts and uncles (especially on the mother's side) tend to invest effort in helping a woman raise her children (Gaulin, McBurney, & Brademan-Wartell, 1997). Grandparents, again more so on the maternal side, are particularly likely to invest in children (Euler & Weitzel, 1996). There is, in general, a propensity to support relatives of many types, although close relatives are usually favored over more distant ones. The fact that helping is more likely from a mother's relatives is also consistent with notions of inclusive fitness: Paternity always carries some degree of uncertainty, so although the mother's relatives can always be certain they are helping kin, the father's cannot.

In times of real need, it is often kin, and not friends, that people call upon for assistance and support. In a series of experiments, Burnstein, Crandall, and Kitayama (1994) asked participants to imagine that they were in a burning building and given a choice of which one family member to save. Grandparents were more likely to be helped in everyday situations, but in life-and-death situations, helping for grandparents as well as cousins decreased in favor of more assistance for siblings who were not past the age of reproductive viability (younger siblings). Under the collective threat of war, people rely increasingly on relatives rather than the friends or neighbors they turn to for everyday support (Shavit, Fischer, & Koresh, 1994). In a multicultural study, there were some cultural differences in the composition of support networks, but regardless of ethnicity, the person most likely to care for a mentally ill person was a female relative (Guarnaccia & Parra, 1996).

On the other side of the equation, non-relatives often suffer neglect and abuse. Anderson, Kaplan, and Lancaster (1997) found that genetic children were 5.5 times more likely than stepchildren to receive money for college expenses. Of even greater concern, children living with a stepparent are approximately 40 times more likely to suffer physical abuse than those living with two genetic parents (Daly & Wilson, 1985) and 40–100 times more at risk of homicide (Daly & Wilson, 1988). These figures hold even when controlling for factors such as socioeconomic status. In short, social relationships in humans, like those in other animals, are greatly influenced by genetic relationships between the actors.

Life History Strategies: When and How to Reproduce?

A life history is a genetically organized plan for allocating resources over the lifespan. Individual animals have a finite amount of time and energy to invest in growth, maturation and reproduction before they die. Life history theory assumes that natural selection operates on the timing of allocation of effort to these processes (Crawford & Anderson, 1989; Stearns, 1976). For example, an animal could invest all its energy over a prolonged period into somatic effort (bodily growth and maintenance) while delaying expenditures of energy for reproductive effort (mating and parenting). If the animal, therefore, becomes larger, stronger, and healthier than competitors, it may eventually leave more offspring, and its developmental gamble would have then paid off. On the other hand, in a different environment, those rivals who begin reproducing right away might leave more offspring than the animal who delays reproduction and dies before leaving viable offspring.

Organisms show an amazing array of life history patterns. One small mammal from Madagascar begins reproducing a few weeks after birth (Quammen, 1996). Elephants, on the other hand, take decades to reach sexual maturity, and then carry each fetus for over a year (Daly & Wilson, 1983). Variations in rate and timing of maturity, and relative amount of effort invested in somatic versus reproductive effort are related to ecological conditions in a species' evolutionary past. For example, animals whose newborns are subject to heavy predation, like wildebeests, may reproduce *en masse* on one day of each year, thus reducing their individual risk of losing individual offspring to predators, who can only attack a few of the helpless offspring at one time.

Primates in general reach sexual maturity later and live longer than other mammals of similar size. Compared with other primates, humans have four unique life history characteristics: (1) a very long life span, (2) an extended period of offspring dependence, (3) reproductive support by older post-reproductive individuals, and (4) male help in caring for offspring (Hill & Kaplan, 1999). Hill and Kaplan (1999) argue that species such as humans, whose food is varied and difficult to obtain, delay reproduction to acquire the knowledge and skills needed to successfully forage. In hunter-gatherer groups, older females who are slightly more vigorous, despite declining fertility, often provide foods such as tubers and berries to enhance the survivorship of grandchildren while allowing the mothers of those offspring to begin a new pregnancy sooner (Hawkes, 1999).

Another characteristic of human life-history is lifelong relationships between related individuals of both sexes. Among our closest relatives, the chimpanzees (*Pan paniscus*), females disperse from the group at sexual maturity, and have no further contact with related individuals with whom they grew up. In all human societies, individuals of both genders maintain relationships with kin of both genders, even if they are not in physical proximity (Rodseth, Wrangham, Harrigan, & Smuts, 1991).

Life-history theory offers insights into a number of social psychological phenomena. For example, in a wide variety of human societies, the long delay in reproduction is more pronounced for males, who must generally accumulate status and resources before attracting a mate (Hill & Kaplan, 1999). This may be associated with a general female tendency to prefer older rather than younger partners. A sex difference in the age of preferred mates, in fact, appears in all human cultures examined thus far (Kenrick & Keefe, 1992; Otta, Queiroz, Campos, daSilva, & Silveira, 1998). The general pattern is that females of all ages generally prefer older males, whereas males change their relative preferences as they age. Young men are attracted to women older than themselves, men in their twenties are attracted to women their own age, and older men are interested in younger women (Kenrick, Yabrielidis, Keefe, & Cornelius, 1996). It appears that women in the years of peak fertility are attractive to men in all cultures (Kenrick & Keefe, 1992). Because of intrinsic differences in the costs of reproduction for males and females, some of the most theoretically important within-species differences cut along the lines of sex, a topic to which we now turn.

Differential Parental Investment: Sex Differences and Similarities in Reproductive Strategy

The question of how much to invest in offspring is a key part of the life-history strategy. Resources invested in one offspring exact costs to the parent's ability to invest in others (Trivers, 1985). In reptiles, birds, and mammals, there is an initial sex difference in parental investment stemming from the fact that eggs are more nutritionally expensive than sperm. In most mammals, the initial expense of producing a large nutritionally rich egg (as in reptiles and birds), are drastically increased because the fertilized egg develops inside the mother's body (in most mammals). After birth, mammalian females invest further by nursing their young for some time—a year or more in some species. In over 95% of mammalian species, males invest no more direct nutritional resources than the calories required to produce and deposit sperm (Clutton-Brock, 1991).

Parental investment is correlated with selectivity in choosing a mate. Because females generally tend to invest more, they are generally more demanding shoppers in the mating marketplace. Consider spending money from a bank account as an analogy for investing resources in reproduction (Kenrick & Trost, 1996). Imagine men and women each have bank account balances of $1,000 when they reach reproductive age. Women are required to spend at least $100 on every child they bear, while men can spend as little as 10 cents or as much as $100. For a man, the low cost (or 10 cent) option involves only as much energy as it takes to have sex. Under this circumstance, a male need not be selective about partners, because he has almost nothing to lose by mating with anyone. Contrast this with the woman, whose minimum required investment is $100, which is a significant portion of her total bank account. She is not likely to spend that $100 on just anyone. In return for her higher investment, she will demand a mate of high quality, to ensure that her few precious offspring have a good chance at survival and reproduction. When men decide to invest more than the minimum in their offspring, their choices follow the same pattern as women: men desire a high quality partner in return for larger investments (Kenrick, Sadalla, Groth, & Trost, 1990; Kenrick, Groth, Trost, & Sadalla, 1993).

Given an opportunity to make the minimum investment in offspring, a man could afford to be less selective in choosing partners. But most men will find few takers for such a low offer. Because females are selective, a male must demonstrate qualities that make him a better deal than other males. These might be better genes than his competitors, signaled by a relatively more robust and symmetrical physical appearance, or extraordinary skills (Gangestad & Thornhill, 1997; Miller, 1999). Or the male might show a willingness to match some of the female's investments with investments of his own, such as nest building and providing her with nutrition.

There are species in which males invest in the offspring as much as, if not more than, females. The male seahorse carries the fertilized eggs in a pouch and then cares for the newborns, freeing the female to invest energy in a new family. Like male humans who invest $100 rather than a dime, male seahorses are more selective about the females with which they will mate, and females in such species may compete with one another for the male's attentions (Trivers, 1985).

Thus, parental investment leads to at least two general regularities in animal behavior. First, there is a direct link between the amount of resources invested by a given sex and that sex's selectiveness in choosing mates. Second, to the extent that members of one sex make investments, and are therefore selective, members of the other sex will compete with one another, and hence show sexually selected traits. For example, in monogamous species, males and females tend to be similar in size and appearance. In polygynous species, where one male mates with several females, males tend to be larger and to possess decorative or defensive features, such as peacocks' feathers or bucks' antlers. The reason for this is related to the principles we discussed previously. Males in monogamous species make high investments of effort and resources in the offspring, often matching those of the females. Males in polygynous species make less direct investment in any given female or her offspring, and hence are subject to strong sexual selection pressures, as females pick males with traits suggesting superior genes. Polygynous males must, therefore, make higher investments in features that females find attractive.

Because humans are mammals, there is a large initial discrepancy in parental investment. Consistently, there is abundant data that men given the opportunity are, compared with women, more likely to accept a low cost sexual opportunity (e.g., Buss & Schmitt, 1993; Clark & Hatfield, 1989; Kenrick et al., 1990). But unlike 95% of other mammals, human males often invest heavily in their offspring, with long-term marriage bonds being universal across human societies (Broude, 1994; Daly & Wilson, 1983). Parental investment theory would lead to the prediction that males will have minimal criteria for engaging in casual sexual relationships, but will become increasingly selective about partners for long-term relationships (Kenrick et al., 1990). Consistently, males surveyed about criteria for one-night stands expressed standards considerably below those of females, and were willing to have sex with a partner whose intelligence was considerably lower than they would require in a dating partner. However, males' minimum standards for marriage partners were much more similar to those of females (e.g., both sexes insisted on someone considerably above average in intelligence for a spouse).

With regard to criteria such as status and wealth in a mate, however, men's standards are still lower than those of women, and for characteristics related to physical attractiveness, men sometimes have higher standards than women. These differences are consistent with research and theory on sexual selection, to which we now turn.

Sexual Selection: Mate Choice, Status, and Attractiveness

Sexual selection was a concept advanced by Charles Darwin to explain the evolution of sex-based characteristics that did not, at first glance, seem to make sense from the perspective of *natural* selection. Traits such as peacock's feathers seem to directly reduce survival. Large colorful male animals are likely to die earlier: Their showy displays are not only physiologically costly to maintain, but are also like neon signs that draw the attention of hungry predators. If selection favors characteristics well suited to survival, how could such traits have ever evolved? The answer is that these characteristics helped ancestral animals acquire more mates than their less colorful or smaller-antlered competitors. The bottom line of selection is not survival, but reproduction. Traits that predispose an individual to live long without reproducing do not get replicated. Alternatively, traits that enhance successful mating, even if they impose a potential survival cost, can be selected if the mating enhancement is enough to compensate for their costs on longevity.

Sexual selection can be further divided into *intrasexual* and *intersexual selection*. Intrasexual selection refers to competition within one's own sex for mates, and encompasses features such as large size or weapons of defense such as large antlers. In many species, physically dominant males are disproportionately successful in leaving offspring (Hrdy, 1999). In some species, such as elephant seals, *Mirounga angustirostris* (Stewart & Huber, 1993), only the strongest male in a particular group gets to mate at all. Intersexual selection, also known as mate choice, refers to success in *attracting* members of the opposite sex.

Darwin believed sexual selection most commonly results from *female choice* of males. For example, a female fruit fly chooses her mate by his dancing ability. Dancing ability is a proxy for overall health and vigor, so those male fruit flies that can't keep up with her elaborate dance are not chosen as mates. Females' choices therefore influence not only their own reproductive success but also the evolution of males (Maynard Smith, 1955).

There is evidence that female choice operated in human evolution. Adult males are about 30% heavier, due in part to larger upper body muscles and in part to longer bodies (males are about 10% taller). Male and female humans also mature at different rates. Although both sexes delay maturity for over a decade, males typically reach puberty later than do females, and continue to grow for several years longer. Knowing nothing else about this species, a biologist would observe these physical differences as the marks of sexual selection (Geary, 1998). The extent of the discrepancies suggests a species whose ancestors were somewhat polygynous, and in which males competed with one another for females. However, human males are not immensely larger than females, as is found in highly polygynous species, like elephant seals and baboons, where males are several times larger. The degree of difference instead suggests a species that was only mildly polygynous (Daly & Wilson, 1983).

In species in which males invest in the offspring, male choice may also exert sexual selection pressures on females. As we noted earlier, men are indeed selective when it comes to choosing long-term mates. Given that each sex would be expected to choose partners on characteristics that enhanced reproductive success, some of the selection criteria should be the same for both sexes. For example, both men and women preferentially choose partners manifesting traits (such as symmetry) that are correlated with "good" genes, often indicating longevity, reproductive viability, and parasite resistance (Gangestad, 1994; Thornhill & Gangestad, 1994). However, human males and females contribute different resources to the offspring, and would be expected to value potential correspondingly different traits. Because females contribute direct physical resources, carrying the fetus and nursing the offspring, males would be expected to value characteristics that tend to be correlated with fertility, such as health and physical traits typical of women who have reached puberty but not yet borne children (Cunningham, Druen, & Barbee, 1997; Kenrick & Keefe, 1992; Singh, 1993). Because males contribute indirect resources, such as material goods and protection, females would be expected to place more emphasis on characteristics associated with financial success and social status (e.g., Sadalla, Kenrick, & Vershure, 1987). Consistent with these expectations, research conducted across different cultures has shown that females place more importance on the status of a mate while males place more value on a mate's attractiveness (Broude, 1994; Buss, 1989; Townsend & Wasserman, 1998). Some of the cues linked to successful reproduction are behavioral, and may require inferences about underlying personality traits, such as fidelity or agreeableness (Kenrick & Trost, 1996).

MIND, LANGUAGE, AND CULTURE

It is a rare social scientist who rejects Darwinian theory as an explanation of whale's flippers or bat's wings, yet many still question its relevance to human social behavior. Some believe that an evolutionary approach provides an incompatible alternative to the cultural, cognitive, or learning-based approaches most familiar to social scientists. Others believe that biological and social approaches are not actually incompatible, but represent different "levels of analysis" which, like a topographical map and a subway map, are appropriately explored independently of one another. Still others grant that an evolutionary analysis is relevant and useful when applied to some "simple behaviors" such as initial attraction and aggression, but fail to see its relevance to complex group level phenomena such as intergroup stereotyping, social identity, or culture. In this section, we argue that an evolutionary perspective is neither incompatible with, nor independent of, the study of culture, learning, or cognition. Instead, these perspectives are mutually informative and all essential to a full understanding of the roots of human social behavior. The characteristics that make humans unique, including the capacity for language, thought, and the creation of culture, can be fully understood only in light of the powerful evolutionary forces that shaped human nature. What humans are inclined to learn, what humans are inclined to think about, and the cultural norms that humans create are all indirect products of the adaptive pressures that shaped the human mind. In this section, we first consider the evidence for adaptive biases in learning, then we consider human language as a model of how genetic and cultural forces mutually construct and constrain one another. We also consider some ways in which evolutionary analyses may be applied to other group-level phenomena, including social identity and intergroup relations.

Adaptively Prepared Learning

For decades, social scientists were mired in the nature–nurture controversy, wed to the idea that "learning" and "instinct" were alternatives—that animals either learned their habitual behaviors or inherited them in programs written before birth. Researchers in the field of learning and cognition have, in recent decades, shed these old dichotomous ways of thinking. One of the most useful constructs to emerge from this controversy is the notion of "preparedness"—the idea that organisms are often predisposed to learn some associations more easily than others (e.g., Ohman & Mineka, 2001; Rozin & Kalat, 1971; Seligman & Hager, 1972). The best-known example comes from research on food aversion. Rats exposed to novel foods and later made nauseous learn in one trial to avoid those foods in the future

(Garcia & Koelling, 1966). This aversive learning is difficult to extinguish, and does not follow normal principles of classical conditioning. For example, it does not require multiple trials and it can occur when the novel taste stimulus and the nausea response are separated by hours (rather than the usual milliseconds required for "normal" classical conditioning). Furthermore, rats cannot learn to associate nausea to visual stimuli, but only to taste stimuli. Human beings likewise are subject to one-trial conditioning when novel tastes are followed by later nausea (Seligman & Hager, 1972). Animals such as rats and humans, who sample widely from a range of potentially toxic plant substances, are "prepared" to quickly learn associations between novel tastes and nausea, in order to protect them from eating potentially poisonous foods more than once.

Ohman and Mineka (2001) review evidence that fear responses involve just such an innate prepared system. For example, the lower brain centers associated with fear have a powerful directive effect on cortical processing, and are difficult to override consciously (most people have difficulty picking up a snake, for example, even after they have been convinced it is non-poisonous). But although some of the triggers for fear responses may be innate (snakes, wasps, or large spiders), most of them are learned (the face of the neighborhood bully, or the characteristics of members of "enemy" groups). Importantly, this fear learning is itself "prepared," in that it is markedly easier to learn, and harder to extinguish, avoidance responses to some cues than others (e.g., angry as opposed to happy faces, dogs as opposed to flowers).

Preparedness applies to more complex forms of learning as well. For example, the human brain is particularly prepared to learn a spoken language. Infants are born especially sensitive to human vocal patterns, and predisposed to emit all the phonemes of human language. During the first few years of life, despite their generally undeveloped state of cognitive development and lack of formal training in grammar, they learn the local argot to a level of perfection that will not be possible at any later time in life (Pinker, 1997). Highly intelligent adult Americans who move to Germany still speak the new language with noticeable imperfections decades later, while their 4-year-old children, barely able to tie their own shoelaces or learn simple addition and subtraction, manage to converse in complex and fluent German prose.

As in the case of language, evolution-based sex differences in behavior need not be "hard-wired" at birth. Instead, the sexes may be simply be "prepared" to have different learning experiences. For example, simple differences in size, upper body development, and testosterone levels, may combine to make aggressiveness more appealing and rewarding for males than for females. And differences in estrogen and oxytocin levels may combine to make close social relationships more rewarding for females. Thus, even though some gender differences in social behavior are found across a wide array of animal species, this does not imply that they arise "independent" of experience. The sexes may simply enter the world biologically prepared to experience slightly different events, and the societies constructed by adult members of this particular species may further reinforce, channel, and facilitate those differential learning experiences.

The Construction of Culture

Evolutionary theorists would not deny that humans have complex cultures, and that these vary from time to time and place to place. Furthermore, some of the variations are the products of arbitrary historical accident, such as whether one eats with a fork, chopsticks, or one's left hand. However, an evolutionary analysis of culture begins with the assumption that many important cultural norms are not arbitrary, but products of an interaction between flexible evolved psychological mechanisms and local ecological conditions. Evolved preferences and capacities simply influence the menu of likely cultural practices (Fiske, Kitayama, Markus, & Nisbett, 1998). Language provides a perfect model—no one argues that there is an evolved genetic tendency to speak Italian as opposed to Dutch—if two Venetian newlyweds move to Amsterdam, their children will speak perfect Dutch. Yet, no other species is capable of conversing in any human language, and human languages the world over share many features, such as similar levels of grammatical complexity (Pinker, 1997). Thus, human language is best understood as an innate predisposition to absorb certain kinds of cultural information. Without either the innate predisposition or the cultural context, language could not exist.

Part of the evolutionary program has been a search for common features that link human cultures the world over (Brown, 1991; Rosch, 1973). For example, all human cultures have systems for reckoning kinship, and norms for differential treatment of individuals according to kinship status (Daly, Salmon, & Wilson, 1997). All human cultures have long-term marital bonds between males and females who share parenting responsibilities (Broude, 1994; Daly & Wilson, 1983). The latter fact is neither necessary nor obvious, in that it does not apply to 95% of other mammalian species (Geary, 1998). Older men in all human cultures are attracted to women who are younger than themselves (Harpending, 1992; Kenrick & Keefe, 1992; Otta et al., 1998). Adult males are more likely to kill one another than are adult females in all human societies (Daly & Wilson, 1988). Mothers spend much more time in childcare than do fathers in all human societies (Geary, 1998). All human cultures also have status hierarchies, divisions between ingroups and outgroups, and many other common features (Brown, 1991). And facial signals that communicate anger and disgust are recognized by people in all cultures (Ekman & Friesen, 1971).

To point out common cultural features is not to imply that humans construct their cultures robot-like, according to a rigid genetic program. These cultural similarities exist alongside many cultural variations. Consider the case of the Tiwi. In this aboriginal Australian group, a young man often marries a much older woman (Hart & Pillig, 1960). Among traditional Tiwi, all women were required to be married. Widows re-married at their husband's gravesites, and infant girls were betrothed at birth. Men were not required to be married, and because the society was polygynous, many men remained single for a good portion of their lives. There were two ways for a man to get a wife—to have an older married man betroth his infant girl to cement an alliance, or to marry an older widow to gain her resources, while cementing an alliance with her sons. As it turns out, traditional Tiwi men married older women not because of a reversal of normal attraction preferences, but as a pathway to gaining the younger wives, they found most desirable (Hart & Pillig, 1960). Rather than being completely arbitrary, Tiwi mating patterns manifest an interplay between general human mating preferences and a particular social ecology.

Indeed, some of the most interesting questions at the interface of evolutionary biology and the social sciences involve a search for the precise ecological conditions under which cultural practices will vary. For example, most human marriages are monogamous, although a majority of cultures permit polygyny (one man and more then one wife), and a few permit polyandry (one woman and more than one husband). When biologists find variations across species in behavior, they search for correlations with ecological factors (Alcock, 2001). These include factors relevant to survival and reproduction, such as the type and spatial distribution of food resources, population density and distribution (e.g., small groups, large herds, isolated mating pairs), proximity to kin, and sex ratios of mating age adults. For example, polyandry in birds is often found under conditions of extreme resource scarcity, and males who share a partner are often brothers (Daly & Wilson, 1983). Similarly, one can search across human cultures for ecological factors associated with variations in cultural practices, such as marital arrangements. This search has yielded some interesting regularities (Crook & Crook, 1988). For example, polyandry, though rare, is associated with conditions of extreme resource scarcity (as found in the high Himalayas) under which survival rates for children of single males and their wives are low. In Nepal and a few other places, several brothers often combine their resources and marry a single wife, increasing survival rates for resultant children. On the other hand, extreme polygyny (harems) is correlated with ecological conditions including: (1) steep social hierarchy, (2) generally rich environment allowing higher status families to accumulate vast wealth, (3) occasional famines so lower status families face possibilities of starvation (Crook & Crook, 1988). Under these circumstances, a woman who absorbs the cost of sharing a wealthy husband reaps a survival insurance policy for herself and resultant children.

Due to warfare, migration, and random historical and geographic variations, there are sometimes relatively more available females than males in the pool of eligible mates, or the converse. Guttentag and Secord (1983) found that a surplus of women (putting men in a "buyers' market") is associated with later marriage, more divorce, and permissive sexual norms. A surplus of men, on the other hand, is associated with male commitment to more stable monogamous relationships. Again, variations in ecological circumstances (sex ratios) seem to interact with innate predispositions (sex differences in inclinations toward unrestricted mating) to result in meaningful patterns at the societal level. By searching for interactions between local conditions and individual-level predispositions, we may develop a fuller picture of the emergence of cultural practices (Gangestad & Buss, 1994; Kenrick, Li, & Butner, 2003). Following ecological research in biology and anthropology, it might be profitable to begin the focus on large-scale factors directly related to survival and reproduction (distribution and abundance of resources, kin proximity, population density, sex ratios of mature adults in the local environment, and so on).

Intra- and Intergroup Relationships

Anthropological and archaeological data suggest that the context for human evolution has always involved small groups of related individuals. Data from historical and modern hunter-gatherers suggest that these groups were comprised of 20–30 individuals at the lower end, up to a few hundred individuals in richer environments (Barnard, 1999). While hunter-gatherer bands might may coalesce into larger groups seasonally, small groups are and were more often the norm. The typical size for hunter-gatherer bands is about 50–80 people (Maryanski & Turner, 1992). These bands occupy relatively large and exclusive territories through which they migrate to exploit resources. Compared with agricultural and industrial societies, life in hunter-gatherer bands is characterized by relatively less steep social hierarchies (although mature adults and males tend to hold relatively higher status positions across human societies). Ties of kinship (whether actual or fictive) are extended to almost all in the local band (Barnard, 1999; Maryanski & Turner, 1992).

While our human and proto-human ancestors foraged (or at least scavenged) for several million years, plant cultivation is, in evolutionary perspective, a recent phenomenon, beginning only about 10,000 years ago (Maryanski & Turner, 1992). Modern, industrial, anonymous society represents only a small slice of our evolutionary history. In the ancestral world, an unknown individual was a potential enemy—perhaps someone encroaching on our band's hunting and gathering territory. Although some traditional groups do establish cordial exchange relationships, trading goods with members of other groups, outsiders may also bring increased threats of kidnapping, rape, or, homicide (Chagnon, 1988; Radcliffe-Brown, 1913).

The data on hunter-gatherers has led some to suggest that humans are cognitively inclined to divide other people into "in-group" and "out-group" (Krebs & Denton, 1997; Wilson, 1978). Because out-group members did not always pose threats, and could sometimes offer rewards, a simplistic inclination to reject and avoid such individuals under all circumstances would have not have been as adaptive as a more flexible response system. Schaller (2003) and his colleagues have conducted a series of studies suggesting that circumstances associated with increasing danger in ancestral environments can enhance group stereotypes associated with threat. For example, Canadian students showed exaggerated perceptions of the hostility and untrustworthiness of Iraqis and African Americans, and less favorable attitudes toward immigration, when rating the out-group members in a darkened room (likely to have been associated with increased danger in the ancestral environment). Darkness increased stereotyping only for threat-relevant characteristics (e.g., dangerous), and not for other stereotypical traits (e.g., lazy). This research is typical of recent evolutionarily inspired work—rather than presuming inflexible mechanisms "hard-wired" at birth, this modern work posits cognitive mechanisms that respond in adaptive and flexible ways to environmental variations (c.f., Kenrick, 1994; Kenrick, Neuberg, Zierk, & Krones, 1993).

Because in-group members would have been connected by genetic relatedness and long-term reciprocal exchanges, relationships within groups in traditional human societies would have been more trusting, and characterized by communal exchange of goods rather than market-like reciprocal exchange (Fiske, 1992). Evolutionary analyses of social stigmatization processes have suggested that stigmas often involve threats to group welfare, with particular distaste for individuals who violate principles of fair sharing or group welfare, such as cheaters, free riders, sociopaths, and carriers of communicable pathogens (Kurzban & Leary, 2001; Neuberg, Smith, & Asher, 2000). Consistent with this analysis, a series of experiments by Cosmides and Tooby (1992) suggest that people are especially good at solving otherwise difficult logical problems if the problems are framed so they involve catching cheaters on social contracts.

Besides this nascent work on stereotypes and intergroup relations, there have been evolutionary analyses of other topics relevant to group researchers, including cooperation, leadership, and sexual harassment in organizations (e.g., Brewer, 1997; Caporael & Baron, 1997; Kenrick, Trost, & Sheets, 1996). Unlike the research on aggression or mating strategies, evolutionary analyses of group processes have only begun to explore the implications of adaptationist thinking, and a great deal more research is required. However, the human mind was designed in the context of group living, and increased understanding of any cognitive or learning biases that affect processes within and between groups could have socially important implications.

WHY DON'T SOCIAL SCIENTISTS TAKE FULLER ADVANTAGE OF MODERN EVOLUTIONARY THEORY?

An evolutionary approach to social behavior is based on a pair of rather unremarkable premises. First, animals' physical and behavioral structures evolved through the process of natural selection. Second, human behavior can be better understood if the social scientist's empirical and theoretical toolbox included the sorts of functional analyses that have proved so useful in understanding the social arrangements of ants, bee-eaters, and chimpanzees. Indeed, it would be quite remarkable if *Homo sapiens* were the one species to which evolutionary theory is irrelevant. The evolutionary perspective has already yielded increased understanding of a number of human behaviors, such as nepotism and gender differences in sexual selectivity, and we believe many more insights would follow if students were better trained in evolutionary principles, and more research efforts were directed toward understanding the interaction of genes, culture, and cognition. Yet, as we indicated earlier, many social scientists continue to be reluctant to incorporate evolutionary perspectives into their models (Badcock, 2000; LoPreato & Crippen, 1999). Lee Ellis (1996) goes so far as to suggest that many social scientists suffer from "biophobia."

There are a number of concerns and misconceptions that have kept social scientists from taking full advantage of an evolutionary perspective, and these have been addressed in great detail elsewhere (Alcock, 2001; Buss & Kenrick, 1998). In this section, however, we consider five important concerns about evolutionary theory: that it is reductionistic; that it implies that evolved mechanisms are unchangeable; that it implies that evolved mechanisms are "natural" and therefore good or moral; that its hypotheses are untestable; and, that its explanations are post hoc.

The concerns about reductionism stem from a perception that the aim of evolutionary analyses is to isolate the particular genes for various social behaviors. This misconception is perhaps understandable in light of the fact that natural selection indeed operates on genetic predispositions (Alcock, 2001). One of the most popular books on sociobiology was in fact titled *The Selfish Gene* (Dawkins, 1989). While it is true that evolutionary analyses assume cross-generational transmission of genetically based traits, it does not follow that most evolutionary researchers (1) assume single genes for each and every social behavior, (2) assume that genes (singly or in combination) do not interact with the environment, or (3) are more interested in studying genes than in studying the environments within which genetic predispositions unfold. By analogy, consider that, although any cognitive psychologist interested in memory must assume brain cells capable of storing information, most have absolutely no interest in locating the neurons wherein memories are stored. Most evolutionary researchers who study behavior are curious about the functional relationships between behaviors and changes in the environment, and are in fact no more interested in particular genes than cognitive psychologists are interested in particular neurons (c.f., Alcock, 2001). For example, a researcher interested in sexual selection and its relation to differential parental investment would examine the correlation between male parental care and female competition over males (Geary, 1998). A researcher interested in inclusive fitness and prosocial behavior might examine the correlation between helping in communally nesting birds and the relatedness between helping providers and recipients (Emlen, Wrege, & DeMong, 1995).

Even Richard Dawkins, author of the *Selfish Gene*, has been quite explicit in explaining that single genes do not determine anything except in interaction with other genes and developmental experience (Dawkins, 1982, 1989). Genes interact with other genes to produce cells, which interact with other cells to produce organs, which interact with other organs to produce organisms, which interact with one another to produce emergent social structures such as ant colonies, chimpanzee dominance hierarchies, the Bon Jovi fan club, and the European Union. We believe that individual social traits can only be fully understood when considered in light of emergent group phenomena, and that conversely, emergent group phenomena can only be understood in light of the characteristics of the individuals involved. Indeed, one of us has elsewhere argued for an integration of evolutionary psychology with the insights and methods of complexity theory, which, as the study of emergent phenomena, is anything but reductionist (Kenrick et al., 2003).

Related to the concern about genetic reductionism is the assumption that to admit a behavior is linked to evolved mechanisms is to say it is unchangeable. But as we discussed, the model of psychological mechanisms held by evolutionary psychologists and biologists is not one of determinism, but rather of "if-then" decision-rules that are inherently flexible and dynamically linked to the environment (Alcock, 2001; Kenrick, 1995; Kenrick et al., 2003). As discussed earlier, evolved fear responses and poison-avoidance mechanisms are characterized not by inflexibility, but by especially rapid learning (Garcia & Koelling, 1966; Ohman & Mineka, 2001).

Perhaps stemming from this concern about inflexible genes is the naturalistic fallacy— the error of jumping from what is to what ought to be. But a moments' reflection refutes that line of reasoning. For example, natural selection has led to viruses that destroy their host's immune systems and to insects whose offspring, after hatching from eggs laid inside paralyzed prey, eat their way out. Biologists indeed view such behaviors as products of natural selection, but certainly do not claim they are therefore "good." Likewise, to say that past evolutionary pressures contributed to the tendency for humans to be xenophobic, or for males to be relatively more violent than females, is not to imply that prejudice or male violence should be encouraged. To understand the roots of a behavior is not to condone it, but to be in a better position to intervene. An excellent example comes from research on PKU, a disease in which a genetic predisposition leads to an inability to metabolize certain proteins present in milk, and consequent mental retardation. Understanding these links led not to passive acceptance, but to a simple intervention—removing milk from these childrens' diets effectively prevents retardation (Alcock, 2001).

One application of the naturalistic fallacy is the belief that evolutionary explanations of sex differences are sanctions for a social system in which women are oppressed. Besides the fact that such a belief confuses causal explanation with prescription, the sexism accusation is worth re-examining for other reasons (Gowaty, 1997; Kenrick, Trost, & Sheets, 1996). Indeed, according to most evolutionary models, many gender differences in behavior and morphology are driven by *female choice*—selective females choose amongst males, who compete amongst themselves for the attentions of those selective females. Studies of other primates, for example, suggest that females have at least as much power as males in making reproductive decisions, and in influencing the course of evolutionary history (Hrdy, 1999; Small, 1993). As compared to a view of females as helpless pawns of norms created by powerful males, the evolutionary model may be, contrary to popular opinion, more flattering to both sexes.

Another concern is that evolutionary hypotheses are not falsifiable. Part of the concern here can be clarified by considering the distinction between research predictions and the underlying theoretical assumptions on which they are based (Alcock, 2001; Buss, 1999; Schaller & Conway, 2000). For example, based upon evolutionary assumptions regarding an association between parental investment and selectiveness in choosing mates, one of us predicted that men and women would differ greatly in their standards for short-term sexual partners (where the two sexes differ greatly in expected parental investment), but would become increasingly similar in their standards for long-term relationship partners (where the two sexes differ less in expected parental investment) (Kenrick et al., 1990, 1993). That research prediction could very easily have been disproved. The fact that the data were consistent with the hypotheses, on the other hand, does not prove every step in the underlying logic. Perhaps the observed sex difference was due to sex-role socialization processes unique to the Western society in which the data were collected, for example. To address that alternative possibility, cross-cultural data would be necessary (see Kenrick & Keefe, 1992, for an example of this approach). However, even cross-cultural data do not definitively prove or disprove broad underlying theoretical assumptions. Broad theoretical notions, such as differential parental investment, generate diverse predictions and rest upon nomological networks of different sources of data (such as developmental findings, physiological research, and cross-species comparisons of species in which males and females vary in their relative amounts of parental investment, Geary, 1998). Those broad assumptive networks ultimately stand or fall to the extent that scientists find them useful for generating new predictions, parsimonious in integrating existing findings, and so on (Ketelaar & Ellis, 2000).

A related and final concern is that evolutionary hypotheses are simply post-hoc re-explanations of obvious social phenomena (such as sex differences in mate preferences). But evolutionary models have in fact been useful in leading researchers to look beyond the obvious. Consider one supposedly well-known sex difference—females generally marry relatively older males; males generally marry relatively younger females. Evolutionary theorists explained this apparent discrepancy in terms of a sex difference for desired commodities in partners. Because ancestral females contributed bodily resources to their offspring, and males contributed indirect resources, females were selected to value male partners for their resources, which generally increase with age; males were selected to value females for fertility, which generally decreases with age (Symons, 1979). A reasonable alternative explanation is that such sex differences result from cultural norms—men prefer younger women because they *should* prefer younger and less powerful mates (e.g., Deutsch, Zalenski, & Clark, 1986). If children could be socialized to follow such a seemingly obvious norm, why posit evolutionary explanations that assume pressures from a past that we cannot directly observe? Part of the answer is that an evolutionary life-history perspective leads to novel predictions (Kenrick & Keefe, 1992). For example, that model assumes that age-linked changes in mate choice will be the same across cultures, because females in all cultures bear the children and go through an age-linked decline in fertility (terminating in menopause), whereas males in all cultures contribute indirect resources, which tend to increase with age. Another differential prediction from an evolutionary perspective is that males will change their age preferences as they age; with the preference for relatively younger females pronounced only amongst older males (for teenage males, older females are *more* fertile). Because younger males tend to be more attuned to sex-role norms (Deutsch et al., 1986), the evolutionary prediction that younger males will show *less* of the "sex-typed" preference for younger (and less powerful) partners is at odds with a perspective focusing on sex-role socialization in our culture. Across a number of societies, these evolutionary predictions were corroborated—males' tendency to prefer younger females becomes more pronounced with age (Kenrick & Keefe, 1992), and teenage males are strongly attracted to females *above* their own age (Kenrick et al., 1996). Thus, the presumed common knowledge of normative sex differences in age preference was erroneous, and an evolutionary perspective led to a better understanding of the phenomenon.

CONCLUSION

We have argued that the evolutionary perspective to social psychology is not untestable, not reductionist, not a theory about rigid genetic determinism, not a justification for the status quo, and not incompatible with sociocultural or cognitive analyses. What it is, instead, is a set of ideas that have proved quite useful in generating novel hypotheses, and parsimoniously connecting findings from very different domains ranging from mate choice and family relationships to aggression and intergroup relations. Adopting an evolutionary perspective can help us appreciate not only the common threads that bind the people in our culture to those in other cultures, but also, beyond that, to the other species with which we share the earth. Taking this broad perspective, however, also makes us aware of the vast reaches of our own ignorance. As yet, we know very little about how evolved psychological mechanisms inside individuals develop, or how they influence, and are influenced by, the complex cultures that humans construct. Bringing light to these questions will require a fuller integration of all the different theoretical perspectives on human social behavior.

REFERENCES

Alcock, J. (1998). *Animal behavior: An evolutionary approach* (6th ed.). Sunderland, MA: Sinauer.

Alcock, J. (2001). *The triumph of sociobiology.* New York: Oxford University Press.

Anderson, J. G., Kaplan, H. S., & Lancaster, J. B. (1997, June). *Paying for children's college: The paternal investment strategies of Albuquerque men.* Paper presented at the Ninth Annual Conference of the Human Behavior and Evolution Society, University of Arizona, Tucson, AZ.

Badcock, C. (2000). *Evolutionary psychology: A critical introduction.* Cambridge, UK: Polity.

Barnard, A. (1999). Modern hunter-gatherers and early symbolic culture. In R. Dunbar, C. Knight, & C. Power (Eds.), *The evolution of culture: An interdisciplinary view.* New Brunswick, NJ: Rutgers University Press.

Broude, G. J. (1994). *Marriage, family, and relationships: A cross cultural encyclopedia.* Santa Barbara, CA: ABC-CLIO.

Brewer, M. B. (1997). On the social origins of human nature. In C. McGarty & S. A. Haslam (Eds.), *The message of social psychology: Perspectives on the mind in society* (pp. 54–62). Oxford: Blackwell.

Brown, D. E. (1991). *Human universals.* New York: McGraw Hill.

Burnstein, E., Crandall, C., & Kitayama, S. (1994). Some neo-Darwinian decision rules for altruism: Weighing cues for inclusive fitness as a function of the biological importance of the decision. *Journal of Personality and Social Psychology, 67*(5), 773–789.

Buss, D. M. (1989). Sex differences in human mate preference: Evolutionary hypothesis tested in 37 cultures. *Behavioral and Brain Sciences, 12*, 1–49.

Buss, D. M. (1999). *Evolutionary psychology: The new science of the mind.* Boston, MA: Allyn & Bacon.

Buss, D. M., & Kenrick, D. T. (1998). Evolutionary social psychology. In D. T. Gilbert, S. T. Fiske, & G. Lindzey (Eds.), *Handbook of social psychology* (4th ed., pp. 982–1026). New York: Oxford.

Buss, D. M., & Schmitt, D. P. (1993). Sexual strategies theory: An evolutionary perspective on human mating. *Psychological Review, 100*, 204–232.

Caporael, L. R., & Baron, R. M. (1997). Groups as the mind's natural environment. In J. A. Simpson & D. T. Kenrick (Eds.), *Evolutionary social psychology* (pp. 317–344). Hillsdale, NJ: Erlbaum.

Chagnon, N. (1988). Life histories, blood revenge, and warfare in a tribal population. *Science, 239*, 985–990.

Clark, R. D., & Hatfield, E. (1989). Gender differences in receptivity to sexual offers. *Journal of Psychology and Human Sexuality, 2*, 39–55.

Clutton-Brock, T. H. (1991). *The evolution of parental care.* Princeton, NJ: Princeton University Press.

Cosmides, L., & Tooby, J. (1992). Cognitive adaptations for social exchange. In J. H. Barkow, L. Cosmides, & J. Tooby (Eds.), *The adapted mind* (pp. 163–228). New York: Oxford University Press.

Crawford, C. B., & Anderson, J. L. (1989). Sociobiology: An environmentalist discipline. *American Psychologist, 44*, 1449–1459.

Crook, J. H., & Crook, S. J. (1988). Tibetan polyandry: Problems of adaptation and fitness. In L. Betzig, M. Borgerhoff Mulder, & P. Turke (Eds.), *Human reproductive behavior: A Darwinian perspective* (pp. 97–114). Cambridge: Cambridge University Press.

Cunningham, M. R., Druen, P. B., & Barbee, A. P. (1997). Angels, mentors, and friends: Tradeoffs among evolutionary, social, and individual variables in physical appearance. In J. Simpson & D. T. Kenrick (Eds.), *Evolutionary social psychology* (pp. 109–141). Hillsdale, NJ: Erlbaum.

Daly, M., & Wilson, M. (1983). *Sex, evolution, and behavior* (2nd ed.). Belmont, CA: Wadsworth.

Daly, M., & Wilson, M. (1985). Child abuse and other risks of not living with both parents. *Ethology and Sociobiology, 6*, 197–210.

Daly, M., & Wilson, M. (1988). *Homicide.* New York: Aldine deGruyter.

Daly, M., Salmon, C., & Wilson, M. (1997). Kinship: The conceptual hole in psychological studies of social cognition and close relationships. In J. A. Simpson & D. T. Kenrick (Eds.), *Evolutionary social psychology* (pp. 265–296). Mahnaw, NJ: Lawrence Erlbaum Associates.

Darwin, C. (1859). *The origin of species by natural selection or the preservation of favoured races in the struggle for life.* London: Murray.

Dawkins, R. (1982). *The extended phenotype.* San Francisco: Freeman.

Dawkins, R. (1989). *The selfish gene* (2nd ed.). Oxford: Oxford University Press.

Deutsch, F. M., Zalenski, C. M., & Clark, M. E. (1986). Is there a double standard of aging? *Journal of Applied Social Psychology, 16,* 771–775.

Ellis, L. (1996). A discipline in peril: Sociology's future hinges on curing its biophobia. *American Sociologist, 27,* 21–41.

Ekman, P., & Friesen, W. V. (1971). Constants across cultures in the face and emotion. *Journal of Personality and Social Psychology, 17*(2), 124–129.

Emlen, S. T. (1997). The evolutionary study of human family systems. *Social Science Information, 36*(4), 563–589.

Emlen, S. T., Wrege, P. H., & DeMong, N. J. (1995). Making decisions in the family: An evolutionary perspective. *American Scientist, 83,* 148–157.

Euler, H. H., & Weitzel, B. (1996). Discriminating grandparental solicitude as a reproductive strategy. *Human Nature, 7,* 39–59.

Fiske, A. P. (1992). The four elementary forms of sociality: Framework for a unified theory of social relations. *Psychological Review, 99*(4), 689–723.

Fiske, A. P., Kitayama, S., Markus, H. R., & Nisbett, R. E. (1998). The cultural matrix of social psychology In D. T. Gilbert, S. T. Fiske, & G. Lindzey (Eds.), *Handbook of social psychology* (5th ed., Vol. II, pp. 915–982). New York: McGraw-Hill.

Foley, R. (1989). The evolution of hominid social behavior. In V. Standen & R. Foley (Eds.), *Comparative socioecology.* Oxford: Blackwell Scientific Publications.

Gangestad, S. W. (1994). Sexual selection and physical attractiveness: Implications for mating dynamics. *Human Nature, 4*(3), 205–235.

Gangestad, S. W., & Buss, D. M. (1994). Pathogen prevalence and human mate preferences. *Ethology and Sociobiology, 14*(2), 89–96.

Gangestad, S., & Simpson, J. A. (1990). Toward an evolutionary history of female sociosexual variation. *Journal of Personality, 58,* 69–96.

Gangestad, S. W., & Thornhill, R. (1997). Human sexual selection and developmental stability. In J. A. Simpson & D. T. Kenrick (Eds.), *Evolutionary social psychology* (pp. 169–196). Hillsdale, NJ: Erlbaum.

Garcia, J., & Koelling, R. A. (1966). Relation of cue to consequence in avoidance learning. *Psychonomic Science, 4,* 123–124.

Gaulin, S. J. C., McBurney, D. H., & Brademan-Wartell, S. L. (1997). Matrilateral biases in the investment of aunts and uncles. *Human Nature, 8,* 139–151.

Geary, D. C. (1998). *Male, female: The evolution of human sex differences.* Washington, DC: American Psychological Association.

Gowaty, P. A. (Ed.). (1997). *Feminism and evolutionary biology: Boundaries, intersections, and frontiers.* New York: Chapman and Hall.

Guarnaccia, P. J., & Parra, P. (1996). Ethnicity, social status, and families' experiences of caring for a mentally ill family member. *Community Mental Health Journal, 32*(3), 243–260.

Guttentag, M., & Secord, P. F. (1983). *Too many women? The sex ratio question.* Beverly Hills, CA: Sage.

Hamilton, W. D. (1964). The genetical evolution of social behavior. I, II. *Journal of Theoretical Biology, 7,* 1–52.

Harpending, H. (1992). Age differences between mates in Southern African pastoralists. *Behavioral and Brain Sciences, 15,* 102–103.

Hart, C. W., & Pillig, A. R. (1960). *The Tiwi of North Australia.* New York: Holt, Rinehart, & Winston.

Hawkes, K. (1999). Grandmothering and the evolution of *homo erectus. Journal of Human Evolution, 36,* 461–485.

Hill, K., & Kaplan, H. (1999). Life history traits in humans: Theory and empirical studies. *Annual Review of Anthropology, 28,* 397–430.

Hoogland, J. L. (1983). Nepotism and alarm calling the black-tailed prairie dog (*Cynomys ludovicianus*). *Animal Behavior, 31,* 472–479.

Hrdy, S. H. (1999). *Mother Nature: A history of mothers, infants, and natural selection.* New York: Pantheon Books.

Kenrick, D. T. (1994). Evolutionary social psychology: From sexual selection to social cognition. In M. P. Zanna (Ed.), *Advances in experimental social psychology: Vol. 26* (pp. 75–122). San Diego, CA: Academic Press.

Kenrick, D. T. (1995). Evolutionary theory versus the confederacy of dunces. *Psychological Inquiry, 6*, 56–61.

Kenrick, D. T., Gabrielidis, C., Keefe, R. C., & Cornelius, J. (1996). Adolescents' age preferences for dating partners: Support for an evolutionary model of life-history strategies. *Child Development, 67*, 1499–1511.

Kenrick, D. T., Groth, G. R., Trost, M. R., & Sadalla, E. K. (1993). Integrating evolutionary and social exchange perspectives on relationships: Effects of gender, self-appraisal, and involvement level on mate selection criteria. *Journal of Personality and Social Psychology, 64*, 951–969 .

Kenrick, D. T., & Keefe, R. C. (1992). Age Preferences in mates reflect sex differences in human reproductive strategies. *Behavioral and Brain Sciences, 15*, 75–133.

Kenrick, D. T., Li, N. P., & Butner, J. (2003). Dynamical evolutionary psychology: Individual decision-rules and emergent social norms. *Psychological Review, 110*, 3–28.

Kenrick, D. T., Neuberg, S. L., Zierk, K. L., & Krones, J. M. (1994). Evolution and social cognition: Contrast effects as a function of sex, dominance, and physical attractiveness. *Personality & Social Psychology Bulletin, 20*, 210–217.

Kenrick, D. T., Sadalla, E. K., Groth, G., & Trost, M. R. (1990). Evolution, traits, and the stages of human courtship: Qualifying the parental investment model. *Journal of Personality, 58*, 97–117.

Kenrick, D. T., Sadalla, E. K., & Keefe, R. C. (1998). Evolutionary cognitive psychology: The missing heart of modern cognitive science. In C. Crawford & D. Krebs (Eds.), *Handbook of evolutionary psychology* (pp. 485–514). Mahwah, NJ: Erlbaum.

Kenrick, D. T., & Trost, M. R. (1996). The evolutionary psychology of relationships. In S. Duck (Ed.), *Handbook of personal relationships*. Orlando, FL: Academic Press.

Kenrick, D. T., Trost, M. R., & Sheets, V. L. (1996). Power, harassment, and trophy mates: The feminist advantages of an evolutionary perspective. In D. M. Buss & N. M. Malamuth (Eds.), *Sex, power, conflict: Evolutionary and feminist perspectives* (pp. 29–53). New York: Oxford University Press.

Ketelaar, T., & Ellis, B. J. (2000). Are evolutionary explanations unfalsifiable? Evolutionary psychology and the Lakatosian philosophy of science. *Psychological Inquiry, 11*, 1–21.

Krebs, D. L., & Denton, K. (1997). Social illusions and self-deception: The evolution of biases in person perception. In J. A. Simpson & D. T. Kenrick (Eds.), *Evolutionary social psychology* (pp. 21–48). Mahwah, NJ: Erlbaum.

Kurzban, R., & Leary, M. R. (2001). Evolutionary origins of stigmatization: The functions of social exclusion. *Psychological Bulletin, 127*, 187–208.

LoPreato, J., & Crippen, T. (1999). *Crisis in sociology: The need for Darwin.* London: Transaction.

Maryanski, A., & Turner, J. H. (1992). *The social cage: Human nature and the evolution of society.* Stanford, CA: Stanford University Press.

Maynard Smith, J. (1955). Fertility, mating behavior, and sexual selection in Drosophila subobscura. *Genetics, 54*, 261–279.

Miller, G. F. (1999). *The mating mind: How sexual choice shaped the evolution of human nature.* New York: Doubleday.

Neuberg, S. L., Smith, D. M., & Asher, T. (2000). Why people stigmatize: Toward a biocultural framework. In T. F. Heatherton & R. E. Kleck (Eds.), *The social psychology of stigma*. New York: The Guilford Press.

Ohman, A., & Mineka, S. (2001). Fear, phobias and preparedness: Toward an evolved module of fear and fear learning. *Psychological Review, 108*(3), 483–522

Otta, E., Queiroz, R. D. S., Campos, L. D. S., daSilva, M. W. D., & Silveira, M. T. (1998). Age differences between spouses in a Brazilian marriage sample. *Evolution and Human Behavior, 20*, 99–103.

Pinker, S. (1994). *The language instinct: How the mind creates language.* New York: William Morrow.

Pinker, S. (1997). *How the mind works.* New York: Norton.

Quammen, D. (1996). *The song of the dodo: Island biogeography in an age of extinction.* New York: Scribner.

Radcliffe-Brown, A. (1913). Three tribes of Western Australia. *Journal of the Royal Anthropological Institute, 43*, 143–194.

Ridley, M. (1996). *The origins of virtue: Human instincts and the evolution of cooperation.* New York: Viking.

Rodseth, L., Wrangham, R. W., Harrigan, A. M., & Smuts, B. B. (1991). The Human Community as a Primate Society. *Current Anthropology, 32*(3), 221–254.

Rosch, E. H. (1973). Natural categories. *Cognitive Psychology, 4*, 328–350.

Rozin, P., & Kalat, I. W. (1971). Specific hungers and poison avoidance as adaptive specializations of learning. *Psychological Review, 79*, 259–276.

Sadalla, E. K., Kenrick, D. T., & Vershure, B. (1987). Dominance and heterosexual attraction. *Journal of Personality & Social Psychology, 52*, 730–738.

Schaller, M. (2003). Ancestral environments and motivated social perception: Goal-like blasts from the evolutionary past. In S. J. Spencer, S. Fein, M. P. Zanna, & J. M. Olson (Eds.), *Motivated social cognition: The Ninth Ontario Symposium.* Mahwah, NJ: Erlbaum.

Schaller, M., & Conway, L. G., III. (2000). The illusion of unfalsifiability and why it matters. *Psychological Inquiry, 11*(1), 49–52.

Seligman, M. E. P., & Hager, J. L. (1972). Biological boundaries of learning. The sauce-bearnaise syndrome. *Psychology Today, 6*, 59–61, 84–87.

Shavit, Y., Fischer, C. S., & Koresh, Y. (1994). Kin and non-kin under collective threat: Israeli networks during the Gulf War. *Social Forces, 72*(4), 1197–1215.

Sherman, P. W. (1977). Nepotism and the evolution of alarm calls. *Science, 197*(4310), 1246–1253.

Singh, D. (1993). Adaptive significance of female physical attractiveness: Role of waist-to-hip ratio. *Journal of Personality & Social Psychology, 65*, 293–307.

Small, M. F. (1993). *Female choices: Sexual behavior of female primates*. Ithaca, NY: Cornell University Press.

Stearns, S. C. (1976). Life history tactics: A review of the ideas. *The Quarterly Review of Biology, 51*, 3–47.

Stewart, B. S. & Huber, H. R. (1993). Mirounga angustirostris. *Mammalian Species, 449*, 1–10.

Symons, D. (1979). *The evolution of human sexuality*. New York: Oxford University Press.

Thornhill, R., & Gangestad, S. W. (1994). Human facial beauty: Averageness, symmetry, and parasite resistance. *Human Nature, 4*(3), 237–269.

Tooby, J., & Cosmides, L. (1992). The psychological foundations of culture. In J. Barkow, L. Cosmides, & J. Tooby (Eds.), *The adapted mind: Evolutionary psychology and the generation of culture*. New York: Oxford University Press.

Townsend, J. M., & Wasserman, T. (1998). Sexual Attractiveness: Sex differences in assessment and criteria. *Evolution and Human Behavior, 14*, 171–191.

Trivers, R. L. (1985). *Social evolution*. Menlo Park: Benjamin/Cummings.

White, G. M. (1980). Conceptual universals in interpersonal language. *American Anthropologist, 82*, 759–781.

Wilson, E. O. (1978). *On human nature*. Cambridge, MA.: Harvard University Press.

Zeifman, D., & Hazan, C. (1997). Attachment: The pair in pair bonds. In J. Simpson & D. T. Kenrick (Eds.), *Evolutionary social psychology*. Hillsdale, NJ: Erlbaum.

PART II

DEVELOPMENT AND SOCIALIZATION

CHAPTER 6

Development and Socialization in Childhood

WILLIAM A. CORSARO
LAURA FINGERSON

In recent years, we have seen important changes in the conceptualization of early child development and socialization in psychology, sociology, and anthropology. In general, these changes involve more of a focus on children's agency in the socialization process, more concern for the importance of social context, and agreement that children's experiences beyond their early years in the family (especially their interactions and experiences with peers) are in need of more careful theoretical development and empirical research. Also, at least in sociology and anthropology, there is a recognition that children both affect and are affected by society and culture. This recognition has led to more appreciation of the creativity and autonomy of children's peer cultures and to the awareness that the quality of children's lives, even in their first years, is enriched or constrained by power relations, and social and economic policies.

In this chapter we begin by differentiating various approaches within and across disciplines in terms of their emphasis on individual as opposed to collective aspects of human development. Here we stress that the theories, which focus on individual human development can complement sociological theories of the collective development of humans. We believe, however, that sociology must continue the recent attempt to build a new sociology of childhood and children that sees interaction in social context and groups or cohorts of children as the basic units of analysis. We then expand on this point by an examination of a variety of methods currently employed to study children's lives. After these discussions we turn to the

WILLIAM A. CORSARO • Department of Sociology, Indiana University, Ballantine Hall 744, 1020 E. Kirkwood Avenue, Bloomington, IN 47405   LAURA FINGERSON • Department of Sociology, University of Wisconsin-Milwaukee, P.O. Box 413, Milwaukee, Wisconsin 53201

Handbook of Social Psychology, edited by John Delamater. Kluwer Academic/Plenum Publishers, New York, 2003.

major section of our chapter, which reviews and evaluates research on children's everyday experiences in the family, school, peer cultures, and broader society. We conclude the chapter with a brief discussion about the future of childhood and childhood research.

PSYCHOLOGICAL THEORIES OF HUMAN DEVELOPMENT

Theories of human development in psychology are primarily concerned with intraindividual change—the individual child's acquisition of skills and knowledge and general adaptation to the environment. However, psychological theories vary regarding: (1) their perception of individuals as active or passive; (2) the importance they place on biological factors, the social environment, and social interaction; and (3) their conception of the nature of development or change. Here we consider three recent theoretical approaches that have important implications for sociological approaches to childhood socialization.

Cognitive Developmental Theory

Recent work in cognitive developmental theory centers around refinements and extensions of Piagetian (1950) theory, which advocates a more active view of the child. Several theorists argue that early interpretations of Piaget's work concentrate on the details of stages in cognitive development at the expense of an understanding of the theory they were intended to illustrate. Tesson and Youniss (1995) argue that Piaget did not place great importance on the stages, and in his later work investigated the interrelationship between the logical and the social qualities of thinking. Expanding on this later work, they argue that Piagetian operations enable children to make sense of the world as a set of possibilities for action and thereby they can build a framework within which these possibilities may be envisioned (Tesson & Youniss, 1995). Thus, Piaget attributes agency to children and further argues that children's symmetrical relations with each other were more conducive to the development of operations than the authoritative relations with adults, which primarily involved unilateral constraint. Tesson and Youniss (1995) then link this aspect of Piaget's thinking to social theorists such as Giddens in that Piaget sees structure as dynamic and mobile, not simply as constraining.

Systems Theories of Human Development

Lerner (1998) argues that mechanistic and atomistic views of the past have been replaced by dynamic models that stress the synthesis of multiple levels of analysis. An excellent recent example of dynamic systems theory can be seen in the work of Thelen and Smith. Thelen and Smith criticize studies of human development, which strive to discover invariants, that is, programs, stages, structures, representations, schemas, and so forth that underlie performance at different ages. They argue that this approach uses the metaphor of a machine and that "knowledge is like the unchanging 'innards' of the machine, and performance subserves the more permanent structure" (Thelen & Smith, 1998, p. 568).

Thelen and Smith offer instead the image of a mountain stream to capture the nature of development. They note that there are patterns in a fast-moving mountain stream with water flowing smoothly in some places, but nearby there may be a small whirlpool or turbulent eddy while in other parts of the stream there may be waves or spray. These patterns may occur for hours or even days, but after a storm or a long dry spell, new patterns may emerge. The mountain stream metaphor captures development as something formed or constructed by its own history and system-wide activity (Thelen & Smith, 1998). Here we get a direct focus on processes while outcomes are important primarily as part of further developing processes. The key strength of Thelen and Smith's systems approach is that it captures the complexity of real-life human behavior in physical, social, and cultural time and context. In this way, it is similar sociocultural approaches to human development to which we now turn.

Sociocultural Theories

Sociocultural theorists refine and extend central concepts in the work of the Russian psychologist Lev Vygotsky (Rogoff, 1990; Wertsch, 1998). Two of Vygotsky's concepts are of key importance: "semiotically mediated activity" and "the zone of proximal development." According to Vygotsky, human activity is inherently mediational in that it is carried on with language and other cultural tools. A significant proportion of children's everyday mediated activities take place in the zone of proximal development: "the distance between the actual developmental level as determined by independent problem solving and the level of potential development as determined through problem solving under adult guidance or in collaboration with more capable peers" (Vygotsky, 1978, p. 86). Rogoff, Mosier, Mistry, and Göncü (1989) argue that interactions in the zone of proximal development and culture enable children to participate in activities that would be beyond their own capabilities by using cultural tools that themselves must be adapted to the specific activity at hand. Thus, the model of development is one in which children gradually appropriate the adult world through the communal processes of sharing and creating culture with adults and each other.

The sociocultural work of Rogoff and her colleagues is much in line with the systems theory of Thelen and Smith in developmental psychology and the interpretive approach to socialization in sociology, we will discuss below. Rogoff (1996) argues that changes or transitions in children's lives can be best examined by asking how children's involvements in the activities of their community change, rather than focusing on change as resulting from individual activity. To capture the nature of children's involvements or changing participation in sociocultural activities, Rogoff suggests that they be studied on three different planes of analysis: the community, the interpersonal, and the individual. Rogoff notes, however, that these processes cannot be analyzed as separate planes of analysis, but rather that all must be studied together with shifting foci (from background to foreground) through a community, interpersonal, or individual analytic lens (Rogoff, 1996). In line with this view of change Rogoff introduces the notion of "participatory appropriation" by which she means that "any event in the present is an extension of previous events and is directed toward goals that have not yet been accomplished" (Rogoff, 1995, p. 155). Thus, previous experiences in collectively produced and shared activities are not merely stored in memory as schema, plans, goals, and so forth and called up in the present, rather the individual's previous participation contributes to and prepares or primes the event at hand by having prepared it.

SOCIOLOGICAL THEORIES OF SOCIALIZATION AND THE SOCIOLOGY OF CHILDHOOD

When discussing human development, sociologists normally use the term *socialization*. Their definitions of socialization stress the ways in which the individual learns to fit into society. However, in recent years there has been a movement to refine or even replace the term "socialization" in sociology because it has an individualistic and forward-looking connotation that is inescapable (Corsaro, 1997; James, Jenks, & Prout, 1998; Qvortrup, 1991; Thorne, 1993). These authors offer instead interpretive-reproductive theories that present a new sociology of children and childhood where children's own cultures are the focus of research, not the adults they will become. In this section we trace the development of these new approaches as refinements of earlier theoretical work on socialization in sociology,

Macrolevel Approaches to Socialization

Inkeles (1986) argues that socialization is a functional requisite of society and that the overwhelming majority of other requisites (e.g., role differentiation and assignment, shared cognitive orientations) are dependent on adequate socialization. The major spokesperson of this functionalist perspective, Talcott Parsons, envisioned society as an intricate network of interdependent and interpenetrating roles and consensual values (Parsons & Bales, 1955). The entry of the child into the system is problematic because although she has the potential to be useful to the continued functioning of the system, she is also a threat until she is socialized. Parsons likened the child to "a pebble 'thrown' by the fact of birth into the social 'pond' " (Parsons & Bales, 1955, pp. 36–37). The initial point of entry—the family—feels the first effects of this "pebble," and as the child matures the effects are seen as a succession of widening waves that radiate to other parts of the system. In a cyclical process of dealing with problems and through formal training to follow social norms, the child eventually internalizes the social system (Parsons & Bales, 1955).

Functionalist theorists are criticized for their overconcentration on outcomes of socialization, deterministic views of society, and underestimation of the agency of social actors. A recent and innovative macro, or structural, perspective of childhood can be seen in the work Qvortrup (1991, 1994) whose approach is based on three central assumptions: (1) childhood constitutes a particular structural form; (2) childhood is exposed to the same societal forces as adulthood; and (3) children are themselves co-constructors of childhood and society. By childhood as a social form, Qvortrup means it is a category or a part of society like social class, gender, and age groups. In this sense children are incumbents of their childhoods. Because childhood is interrelated with other structural categories, the structural arrangements of these categories and changes in these arrangements affect the nature of childhood. In modern societies, for example, changes in social structural arrangements of categories like gender, work, family, and social class have resulted in many mothers working outside the home and their children both taking on more household work and also spending more of their time in institutional settings, such as day care centers and after school programs, that did not exist in the past (Qvortrup, 1994). Finally, while acknowledging the historical trend of an increasing sentimentalism and overprotectiveness of children as noted by Zelizer (1985) and others, Qvortrup challenges the accompanying claim that children have moved from being useful to useless. On the contrary, children have always been useful and it is instead the nature of their contributions to society that have changed (Qvortrup, 1991). For example, children's schooling is not a break from the past when children worked on farms, in factories, and on the street, but it is a continuation of children's work in that it is an investment in the future economic health of any modern society (Qvortrup, 1994).

At a more intermediate level, analysis of socialization processes can be seen in work on social structure and personality, and the life course. This work often escapes the deterministic nature of traditional macro theories by documenting how specific features of social structure affect interaction in various contexts of socialization (Elkin & Handel, 1989; Gecas, 1981; Elder, 1994, 1998). For example, Elder (1994) argues that transitions in the life course are always embedded in trajectories that give them a distinct form and meaning. The life course approach, thus, overcomes the static nature of cross-sectional studies and captures the complexity of socialization across generations and key historical periods.

To date, work on the life course seldom addresses the life transitions of young children. One reason for this neglect may be, as Elder suggests, the loss of interest in childhood socialization in sociology. However, Elder refers to the limits of traditional neo-behavioristic and psychoanalytic views of socialization, which stress the importance of experiences in early childhood for adult personality and social life. As we shall see shortly, interpretive approaches to socialization, especially their focus on children's life transitions, offer opportunities for fruitful cross-fertilization between the two approaches.

Interactionist Approaches to Socialization

Interactionist approaches stem primarily from the social philosophy of G. H. Mead (1934). Mead saw the genesis of self-consciousness as starting with the child's attempts to step outside him or herself by imitating others, and reaching completion when the child, through participation in games with rules, acquires the ability to take on the organized social attitudes of the group. However, in Mead's stages in the genesis of self, children acquire more than a sense of self, they also appropriate conceptions of social structure and acquire a collective identity.

Surprisingly there has been little research by symbolic interactionists on early socialization. In one exception, Denzin (1977) studied early childhood and argued that socialization "from the standpoint of symbolic interactionism, represents a fluid, shifting relationship between persons attempting to fit their lines of action together into some workable, interactive relationship" (1977, p. 2). From this perspective, Denzin studied the worlds of childhood in the preschool and family. However, there has been no real research tradition or theoretical innovation on children and childhood from Denzin's work.

Other symbolic interactionists have been more persistent in the theoretical and empirical work on young children and preadolescents. Spencer Cahill, Gary Fine, and Patricia and Peter Adler, for example, carried out a number of studies on children and preadolescents, which we discuss below.

Interpretive Approaches to Children's Socialization and the New Sociology of Childhood

Interpretive theorists view socialization as not only a matter of adaptation and internalization, but also a process of appropriation, reinvention, and reproduction. Central to this view and a new sociology of childhood is the appreciation of the importance of collective, communal activity—how children negotiate, share, and create culture with adults and each other (Corsaro, 1992, 1997; James et al., 1998).

In line with these assumptions regarding interpretive collective activity, Corsaro (1997) offers the notion of *interpretive reproduction*. The term "interpretive" captures innovative and creative aspects of children's participation in society. Children produce and participate in their own unique peer cultures by creatively appropriating information from the adult world to address their own peer concerns. The term "reproductive" captures the idea that children do not simply internalize society and culture, but also actively contribute to cultural production and change. The term also implies that children are, by their very participation in society, constrained by the existing social structure and by social reproduction.

Children's participation in cultural routines is a central element of the interpretive approach. Routines are recurrent and predictable activities that are basic to day-to-day social life. The habitual, taken-for-granted character of routines provides actors with the security and shared understanding of belonging to a cultural group (Giddens, 1984). On the other hand, this very predictability empowers routines, providing frames with which a wide range of cultural knowledge and skills can be produced, displayed, and interpreted (Goffman, 1974). Interpretive reproduction views children's evolving membership in their culture as reproductive rather than linear. According to the reproductive view, children strive to interpret or make sense of the adult culture, and in the process they come to produce their own peer cultures (Corsaro, 1997; Corsaro & Eder, 1990). Appropriation of aspects of the adult world is creative in that it both extends or elaborates peer culture (transforms information from the adult world to meet the concerns of the peer world) and simultaneously contributes to the reproduction of the adult culture (Corsaro, 1997; Qvortrup, 1991).

This process of creative appropriation is in line with Giddens' notion of the duality of social structure, in that "the structural properties of social systems are both medium and outcome of the practices they recursively organize" (Giddens, 1984, p. 25). We can see that the notion of interpretive reproduction and the stress on children's agency is much in line with the Tesson and Youniss's (1995) reconceptualization of Piagetian theory, Thelen and Smith's (1998) system approach, and sociocultural theory. Further, James et al. (1998) argue that making connections between interpretive views of socialization to broader theoretical views in sociology in the work of Giddens and others will give childhood a social status in its own right, with its own agendas. Without this connection to general sociological theory, they argue, childhood will "be condemned to remain, as in the past, simply an epiphenomenon of adult society and concern" (James et al., 1998, p. 197). It is with these goals and the development of an extensive body of empirical research (which we discuss below) that the new sociology of childhood will become entrenched as a key area in the social sciences.

CONVERGENCE IN THEORIES OF HUMAN DEVELOPMENT AND CHILDHOOD SOCIALIZATION

Our review of psychological and sociological theories of human development reveals several important trends. First, in recent theories children are seen as active agents who are influenced by and influence others. The trend is seen in the theoretical approaches of sociocultural, systems, life course, and interpretive theories. This active view of children can also be seen in the refinement and expansion of more traditional orientations (cognitive developmental, reproductive, and interactionist). Second, there has been growing appreciation of the fact that development is a lifelong process. Here systems and life course theorists go beyond the identification of the form and function of developmental changes over the life course. These theorists challenge end-stage models by stressing the importance of interindividual variability and plasticity. Similarly, interpretive reproduction argues that collective social processes among peers (over the full life course including early childhood) is essential for the development of humans and social reproduction. Third, there is an increasing recognition of the importance of context (physical, societal, and sociocultural) for human development. In psychology, context at different levels is central to systems theories and sociocultural theory. These theories call for a movement away from searching for underlying competencies or causes of human development (at the genetic or cognitive level) and stress the importance of direct studies of developmental processes over time and space to identify how developmental processes are constructed by their own history and system-wide activity. In sociology, there has long been an emphasis on the effects of social structure and historical context on developmental outcomes as seen in the work on social structure and personality and life course theory. Interpretive theory refines these views by arguing that children live their lives and contribute to social reproduction in the present, while at the same time acquiring cultural knowledge and skills that prepare them for the future.

METHODS IN RESEARCHING CHILDREN'S LIVES

What are some of the special issues in doing social psychological research with children? Some investigators argue that children themselves are not unique in comparison with adults, rather, methods studying any group should include a rigorous application of techniques applied to that group with special attention to the group's specific needs and particularities (Christensen & James, 2000). They make the point that children are a diverse group and any method should be examined in the context of that diversity, not, as is frequently done, only by age.

A key methodological issue is conducting research *with* children, rather than *on* them (O'Kane, 2000). This position stresses the importance of hearing children's own voices and recognizing that they are the most knowledgeable and most experienced in their own lives. In order to respect the rights of children and include them as active participants in the research, Roberts (2000) outlines ten questions investigators should ask. These include institutional review board issues of consent, confidentiality, privacy, benefits, and selection as well as broader ethical issues such as ensuring that research funding comes from pro-child organizations, including children in the design and implementation of the research, and working for a positive impact of the results on children's lives. In this review we concentrate on methods most used in social psychological studies of children's development: ethnographies, interviews, surveys and demographic methods, and nontraditional methods.

Ethnography

Ethnography is an especially good method for studying young children because many features of their interactions and cultures are produced and shared in the present and cannot easily be obtained by way of interviews or surveys. Three central features of ethnography with young children are that it be sustained and engaged, microscopic and holistic, and flexible and self-corrective (Gaskins, Miller, & Corsaro, 1996). Ethnography usually involves prolonged fieldwork in which the researcher gains access to a group and carries out intensive observation for a period of months or years. The value of prolonged observation is that the ethnographer discovers what daily life is like for members of the group—their physical and institutional settings, their daily routines, their beliefs and values, and the linguistic and other semiotic systems that mediate all these contexts and activities.

In his work on peer culture, Corsaro conducted six intensive studies of peer interaction and culture over the course of an academic year in preschool settings in the United States and Italy. In several of these projects, he returned for shorter periods to observe some members of the children's groups who spent successive years in the preschool and in others he continued ethnographic observation as children made the transition from preschool to elementary school and throughout elementary school (Corsaro, 1985, 1993; Corsaro & Molinari, 2000a,b). The sustained nature of these and other ethnographic studies of young children (Evaldsson, 1993; Goodwin, 1990; Thorne, 1993) documents crucial changes and transitions in children's lives, which is essential for understanding socialization as a process of production and reproduction.

To ensure that ethnographic interpretations are culturally valid, they must be grounded in an accumulation of the specifics of everyday life. But simply describing what is seen and heard is not enough, as ethnographers must engage in a process of "thick description" (Geertz, 1973). This mode of interpretation goes beyond the microscopic examination of actions to their contextualization in a more holistic sense, to capture successfully actions and events, as they are understood by the actors themselves. For example, Corsaro documents through observation and audiovisual records that preschoolers often resist the access of peers into established play routines. At the level of thin description (and from an adult perspective), this behavior is seen as a refusal to share. However, given features of preschool settings, Corsaro interprets this behavior as the "protection of interactive space" and argues that it was not that children did not want to share. Instead, they wanted to keep sharing the fragile play activities that they knew from experience were often easily disrupted by the entry of others (Corsaro, 1997).

It is the essence of ethnography that it is a feedback method in which initial questions may change during the course of inquiry. This flexibility in inquiry is accompanied by self-correction when the ethnographer searches for additional support for emerging hypotheses, including negative cases, which can lead to refinements and expansion of initial interpretations. It is this feature of ethnography that fits with our earlier discussion of research *with* rather than *on* children. Over the course of research, children, like adult ethnographic informants, come to reflect on the nature of the ethnography and its place in their lives. For example, in Corsaro's (Corsaro & Molinari, 2000b) work with Italian preschoolers, the children often wanted to display their art and literacy skills by drawing and printing in his notebook. Given Corsaro's interest in literacy in the children's preparation for and transition to first grade, the children were in fact inscribing Corsaro's field notes directly.

Individual and Group Interviewing

Ethnography explores how children act; their everyday play and talk. Interviews allow researchers access to how children perceive their actions and their worlds. Eder and Fingerson (2002) contend that using individual and group interviews with children is one of the strongest methods of exploring children's own interpretations of their lives. Using interviews, Eder and Fingerson further argue, researchers can study topics in children's lives that are highly salient, yet are not discussed in everyday interactions, such as divorce, family relationships, violence, or other sensitive issues. However, researchers must be aware that, as with any other research method, the power imbalance between the researcher and respondent is heightened because of the age and status difference. Ways of reducing this power difference include group interviewing, creating a natural context, using multiple methods, and engaging in reciprocity.

For example, Mayall (2000) uses the "research conversation" to learn about children's health and health care. She engaged small groups of 5–9-year-old children in conversations during the children's everyday school activities. The children were thus comfortable in their familiar setting and were engaging in discussions similar to their own conversations Mayall heard in the school's classrooms and corridors. The children were responsible for the agenda and controlled the pace and direction of the conversation. In this way, Mayall was able to understand the issues important to the children, rather than the children responding to questions based on what was important to Mayall.

In L. Davies's (1983) research on children's understandings of gender, she held "study groups" of fifth and sixth graders. The groups met once per week for $1\frac{1}{2}$ hr for over 12 months. Activities included discussion, sharing photos of family, taking pictures with disposable cameras, making collages, reading traditional and feminist stories, and writing stories and autobiographies. Through this wide variety of activity, the children explored their discourses of gender from multiple angles.

Methods of sociolinguistics analysis are ideally suited for interview and ethnographic data as they explore children's structures of talk and how this talk shapes and is shaped by their social interactions. Sociolinguistics is based on tenets of symbolic interactionism in that it is through interaction that we learn to understand and interpret our social worlds. Several researchers of children have used sociolinguistic methods effectively to explore how children use talk to define and interpret their worlds such as James's (1995) empirically based link between identity, social class, and language, Greenwood's (1998) analysis of preadolescents' dinner table conversations, and Hoyle's (1998) exploration of register and footing in children's imaginary role play.

Surveys and Demographic Research

Much social psychological research on children focuses on ethnography, participant observation, and interviewing. However, there are also important surveys and demographic studies of children. In detailed reviews of the methodological and empirical literature, Scott (1997, 2000) outlines the benefits of using children in quantitative research and cites several research studies using such methods. Scott finds that children, even younger children, are good questionnaire respondents if they are asked about events that are meaningful in their lives. Children can be willing and able to answer questions about their experiences if the response alternatives are appropriate and ordered well. Additionally, children are motivated to give truthful and careful answers if there is a good relationship between the interviewer and child and if the child feels secure in the confidentiality of the responses.

Specific issues that need to be addressed, however, include language use, literacy, and cognitive development. Pretests of the survey instrument are particularly important in research on children to ensure that the children's understanding of a question is the same as the researcher intended. One way of developing good instruments is through the use of focus group interviewing to elicit children's ideas, language, and uncover what is most salient to them. Scott (2000) argues that until recently, children have been neglected from survey research and instead, their parents or teachers have responded for them. This not only eliminates the children's own voices but also gives researchers false data as adult respondents do not always give the same responses their children would.

Children from age 11 and up are particularly able to respond to standardized questionnaire instruments (Scott, 2000). Scott lists several successful surveys interviewing children in Britain. Included in the methods of data collection are a Walkman tape self-administered questionnaire (ages 11–15), face-to-face interviews (ages 12–19), diaries (ages 9–15), and self-completion written interviews (school-age children). She also finds that telephone inter-viewing is effective with children ages 11 and older and has high hopes for Computer Assisted Personal Interviewing (CAPI) for even younger respondents. CAPI, in particular, can incor-porate both visual and audio stimuli that decrease the need to rely only on verbal or written questions and answers.

Demographic studies relying on census data have been essential in documenting changes in family structure and children's lives. The work of Hernandez (1995), in particular, has been important in the United States because he uses the child (rather than the family) as the unit of analysis to describe profound changes in families and childhood over the last 150 years. In addition, several authors have worked with large-scale survey data sets involving the direct participation of children [the 1997 Child Development Supplement (CDS) of the Panel Study of Income Dynamics (PSID) which is a 30-year longitudinal survey of men, women, and the families in which they reside (see Hofferth and Sandberg, 2001)] or reports by parents and other caretakers about the quality of life of children in the United States (the PSID, National Child Care Survey 1990 and the Profile of Child Care Settings in 1989–1990, see Hofferth, 1995). The collection and analysis of large-scale survey data sets and census data both in the United States and in other countries are essential to gauge the effects of globaliza-tion on children's lives, welfare, and social trajectories to adulthood.

Nontraditional Methods in Studying Children

Williams and Bendelow (1998) find that although research data can be gathered from tradi-tional methods, such as ethnography and surveys, there is a need in childhood research to develop and practice "child-centered" methods in order to encourage children to present their own images and representations of their lives.

Several researchers, including Williams and Bendelow, use drawing to elicit stories and understandings of children's everyday lives. For example, Holmes (1995) asked children to draw self-portraits while telling her about what they were drawing to understand how kinder-gartners construct race and ethnicity. She argues that through drawing, children can express themselves on subjects and ideas they have difficulty conveying verbally to adults, such as complex notions of race. Christensen and James (2000a) use drawing to explore similarities and differences in 10-year-olds' daily experiences and organization of their time. The children were given a piece of paper inscribed with a large circle titled, "My Week." Then, they were asked to divide the circle to represent their weekly activities and how much time they spent in each activity. They were given complete freedom to fill in the circle however they felt best represented their experiences. During the activity, which was completed in small groups, the researchers were both present and had a tape recorder running. Christensen and James thus collected a wide variety of data that was meaningful to each child, both on the paper draw-ings and in their dialogue about the process of doing the activity.

Children can also be used as research assistants and informants, helping the adult inves-tigator with interviews, understanding children's local culture, and analyzing the data. Thus, the children become co-producers of the data and findings. Alderson (2000) argues that in research, children are an underestimated and underused resource. Our understandings of chil-dren's lives can be significantly enhanced as children know their own cultures, views, and experiences better than adult researcher. Adults not only have their outsider status to over-come in understanding children's worlds, but also their inherent power difference (Eder & Fingerson, 2002). Children-as-researchers can gain access to respondents unavailable or unknown to adults, they become more involved and invested in the quality of the data being gathered, and can serve as validity-checkers to adults' interpretations and findings. The child-researchers themselves can gain more skills and confidence as a result of the collaboration.

For example, in her empirical work, Alderson (2000) explores children's everyday projects that they do in school as sources of data, such as a project where 9–11-year-olds ran small group brainstorming sessions to design a pond for their school playground. In her ethnography of Black males' experiences in elementary school, Ferguson (2000) uses Horace, age 12, as a research assistant. Horace both helps Ferguson understand aspects of the boys' cultures, music, and worlds that were otherwise inaccessible to her and he helps her design the topics for her interviews with other boys. As an insider, Horace knew about aspects of his culture that were most salient to him and his peers. Similarly, in his study of street children in Brazil, Hecht (1998) uses children as interviewers. He found they asked questions he would not have thought about and received responses that he would not have been able to elicit as an adult and an outsider. The child-interviewers had a deep understanding of street life and could connect with other street children on a level inaccessible to Hecht.

Traditional ethnographers attempt to become a member of children's peer cultures. However, some researchers use their own children as research participants thereby blending the parent and researcher roles (which can lead to role conflict). Greenwood (1998) set up tape recorders in her home for one year to record her three children and their guests. She contends that one of the benefits of such recording is that there were no adults in the room and the recorder was out of sight of the children. Thus, she feels she was able to gather more "natural" interaction data than with other methods. Hoyle (1998) also uses her own children to gather sociolinguistic data as she analyzed the play of her son and his two friends in her home.

Adler and Adler (1998) call this practice "PAR," or "parents as researchers" and use this method as the basis of their research on preadolescent culture and identity. They argue that there are three primary benefits to such research. First, parents can gain access to children's worlds through their own children, who thereby act as informants. Second, the role of "parents" is an existing social role with which children are already very familiar. In other research settings, such as ethnography in a classroom, researchers must spend time explaining their unique role as not a teacher, but clearly not a child. Third, parents have easy access to a variety of children's settings in their recreational and social lives such as the home, playground, and school. Adler and Adler spent most of their research time observing their children and their interactions with their friends from their home or in a park, often without the children noticing the Adlers were there.

Ethical Issues in Researching Children's Lives

In addition to ethical issues of power and representation already discussed, doing research with children has Institutional Review Board (IRB) implications. With the tightening of IRB standards for research with human subjects, research with children has undergone even higher scrutiny. IRB rules vary from institution to institution and even federal requirements are changing rapidly, but one consistent and most important feature is the requirement of active parental consent. Such consent forms usually contain guarantees of privacy (through the use of cover names and restrictions on the display of audiovisual data) and give parents the right to inspect field notes and audiovisual data upon request and to demand that certain data not be included in analysis. Previously, negative consent could be obtained whereby a letter was sent home to the parents and if they did not want their child to participate, they could send a negative reply. Currently, active consent is required whereby each child must have a signed consent form in order to participate in research. For example, when conducting research in a classroom, each child's parent/guardian must sign an informed consent form, which, in addition to the guarantees discussed above, details the research plan and provides contact information for the researcher and the research institution's IRB (often, if the child is 10 years old or younger, her or his own signature is not required, although we believe the child's own consent is a necessary step). If any of the children do not have signed consent forms, they must be excluded from all data collection whether it be from field notes, audio, or video recordings. Although this safeguards children's and parents' rights, requiring active consent makes ethnography in particular a much more difficult research endeavor. It also means that ethnographers or interviewers may have to sacrifice important data collection opportunities (e.g., alter or restrict field notes or stop videotaping if a child without consent enters an interactive event). However, most ethnographers have little trouble dealing with these challenges given the large amount of rich data that they normally collect in intensive fieldwork.

One strategy some researchers have employed to work around this requirement is using their own children, often along with children of friends and neighbors, as research participants. However, the PAR strategy (discussed above) is one of the most widely critiqued methods of studying children. Parents can frequently face ethical and role conflicts in deciding what events are public and therefore available to be recorded as data versus what events are private and confined to the parental role. Additionally, traditional ethnographers, for example, attempt to see the world through the children's eyes and become a member of children's cultures as much as possible. Parents, on the other hand, ethically cannot easily cross the boundary between child and adult to become "one of the kids" as they are in a supervisory position.

As in any research, unanticipated ethical issues will arise even after fulfilling IRB requirements. Such unforeseen problems can often be the case in sociological studies of young children, especially given the subtle implications of the power differential between adults and children and the fact that children are an understudied group. For this reason, those who carry out ethnographies, interviews, or surveys with children should carefully document the research process as it unfolds and pay special attention to unanticipated ethical problems. When they occur, researchers should discuss decisions in dealing with them with IRBs, parents and other gatekeepers, and children themselves. Also researchers should discuss such issues in as much detail as possible (while preserving privacy) in research reports so that other researchers can gain from their experience.

CONTEXTS OF SOCIALIZATION

Children in the Family

In reviewing research on children in the family, we first consider more traditional studies in psychology and sociology that focus on how various parent–child interactions or parenting styles affect developmental outcomes. We then turn to more recent and often cross-cultural research that directly explores children's place and activities in the family.

Most studies on family socialization concentrate on developmental outcomes. For example, there is a long history of research on attachment and emotional bonding (Bowlby, 1980). Attachment remains a controversial issue as researchers continue to debate the effects of early child care on attachment and children's emotional and social development (see Belsky, 1988; Clarke-Stewart, 1989). Another line of research focuses on the role of parenting styles on children's developmental outcomes. Baumrind (1989) finds that parents who were authoritative (neither permissive or authoritarian) in their discipline styles tended to have children who did well in school and got along better with other children and adults. Baumrind's findings are similar to those of the sociologist, Kohn (1969), who contends that middle- and upper-class parents who value curiosity, consideration of others, and happiness (as compared to working- and lower-class parents who value obedience, conformity, and good manners) have children who are more successful in school and later in life.

Recently, this and similar work on parental effects on children's outcomes has come under attack for its mixed and generally weak findings of parental influence on personality, its failure to take genetic effects into account, and its underestimation of the influence of peers (Harris, 1998). For example, in both Baumrind and Kohn's work, the findings held mainly for White middle- and working-class children and not for other ethnic groups including Asian and African Americans (Rosier & Corsaro, 1993; Steinberg, Dornbusch, & Brown, 1992). Harris (1998) points to work in behavioral genetics, which claim that around 50% of personality outcomes can be linked to genetic factors and the remaining 50% to the environment. The surprising part of this work is that when behavioral geneticists went on to study the effects of shared (in the family) and nonshared environments (outside the family), they consistently found that growing up in the same home and being reared by the same parents had little or no affect on the adult personalities of siblings (Harris, 1998; Plomin & Daniels, 1987) nor did birth order have any significant effects (Dunn & Plomin, 1990; also see work by sociologists such as Freese, Powell, & Steelman, 1999). Returning to Baumrind's study, for example, Harris points to the fact that parenting styles can be a result of temperament and other genetic traits and that parents can use different styles with different children in the same family.

Given the findings from behavioral genetics, anthropology, and sociology on peer group interaction, Harris claims that peers are more important than parents in regard to developmental outcomes. She does, however, qualify that parents have important effect on their children's behavior *within* the family. Overall, Harris' argument and group socialization theory, most especially its emphasis on the importance of social context, is quite similar to sociocultural, life course, and interpretive theories of socialization we discussed earlier.

Harris's emphasis on the importance of parents' effects on the way their children behave in the family early and later in life and that children affect parenting styles is in line with recent important work on family interaction. The most well-known work in this area is that of Dunn (1988) who uses a combination of observational and interview methods to capture key processes in children's socioemotional development between the ages of 1 and 3. Dunn finds rapid growth in the assertive and resistant behavior of children in their second year in interaction with parents and siblings. These behaviors lead to conflicts and emotional displays by which the children gained some sense of control over their parents. According to Dunn, self-assertiveness is driven by young children's desire to be active and effective members of family life.

Many important studies of adult–child interaction in the family focus on children's development of communicative competence. For example, Miller (1986) examines narrative practices or stories family members use to create, interpret, and project culturally constituted images of self. In a study of middle-class Taiwanese and American families, Miller and her colleagues found that both families routinely engaged in personal storytelling with their young children about a variety of positive and negative events. However, the Taiwanese often used stories of children's misdeeds as an opportunity to impart moral and social standards by publicly shaming the child to some degree. American families, on the other hand, played down the seriousness of children's transgressions and even recast some of them as strengths rather than faults (Miller, Wiley, Fung, & Liang, 1997). In related work, Pontecorvo, Fasulo, and Sterponi (2001) studied Italian debate or *discussione* in family settings. Using conversational analysis they demonstrated how parents and children work collaboratively to establish a sense of moral meaning and social order. Particularly striking in their analysis is how the children were very active agents in talk, using discursive contributions to shape the structure and thematic content of parental talk and socialization.

Finally, work in non-Western societies in line with the sociocultural approach in psychology discussed earlier, finds quite different patterns of parenting compared to Western cultures. Consider again the stress on attachment and bonding between mother and child for healthy emotional development in American society. In a study of the Efe of northeastern Zaire, Tronick, Morelli, and Winn (1987) found a distinctive pattern of multiple caretaker childcare. Efe infants spend much time away from their mothers, who return to work in the fields only a few days after giving birth. At the work site, child-care responsibilities are shared by several women, including the mother, who nurse or suckle a fussy infant. The authors see beneficial physical, emotional, and social outcomes of multiple care giving in that it functions "to teach infants about culturally appropriate styles of interactions as well as to expose infants to the culture's valuation of cooperation, mutual support, and gregariousness" (Tronick, Morelli, & Winn, 1987, p. 103).

Similar patterns of multiple care giving, most especially of young children by older siblings and peers, can be seen in other parts of Africa (Harkness & Super, 1992; Nsamenang, 1992). In the East African countries of Kenya, Tanzania, and Uganda, for example, infants as young as 1–3 months are often turned over to child nurses, usually young girls between 6 and 10 years of age. These child nurses serve as primary caregivers as the mothers normally return to full-time agricultural work. These caretaking practices may seem neglectful by Western standards. However, child nurses and mothers are quite indulgent as the African babies receive three times the amount of attention (total minutes of attention) of American babies, whereas the rate of attention (how frequently attention was given in a specified time span) in both samples were similar (Harkness & Super, 1992, p. 453). Furthermore, as Harkness and Super note, "it would be unthinkable in the East African context for a baby to cry itself to sleep; this U.S. custom is considered abusive by East Africans" (1992, p. 453).

Overall these comparative studies of family interaction, most especially involving the care and development of young children, shows the diversity of family values and practices. We also see in such comparative work that the nature of siblings and the peer group can vary in important ways. In these African societies and in many developing countries, siblings and older peers take an active role in caretaking and the peer group itself is of mixed-age children. Age segregation in the school and peer group in Western societies leads to quite different patterns of interaction and development as we will discuss shortly.

Children in School

There is a vast literature on children and schooling that is far beyond what we can address in this chapter. Here, we focus on recent research that explores young children's transition from the home or preschool to formal schooling and early literacy development.

Children's entry into elementary school is a critical transition in their lives. It is particularly important because the attitudes and reputations established in the early grades may follow children through their many years of formal schooling (Ladd & Price, 1987). Recent theoretical perspectives in psychology offer ecological and systems-based models to the transition, which focus on contexts (family, classroom, community, peer group) and connections among contexts (e.g., family and school relations) rather than only looking at children's individual skills (Rimm-Kaufman & Pianta, 2000). Sociologists take a somewhat similar approach at both the macro- and micro-levels of analysis. Entwisle and Alexander (1999) ask how early schooling provides advantages for some children and disadvantages for others that reinforce inequalities in the U.S. stratification system. These authors assert that schools themselves are not so much the problem, but rather the distribution of resources across families and communities in preparing children for formal schooling. They especially note the lack of good preschools for impoverished 3- and 4-year olds and underdeveloped kindergarten programs.

Rosier's (2000) ethnographic study of nine African American families living in poverty as their children moved from preschool to formal schooling capture many of the challenges the lack of resources Entwisle and Alexander emphasize regarding the educational transitions of poor children. Rosier finds that the families have high educational goals for their children and that parents supported educational activities in the home. However, most of the children in these families had difficult transitions to formal schooling because of: poverty and family instability; mis-communications between parents and teachers; teachers' underestimation of children's academic skills; and difficulties in peer interactions for the children who were bussed from primarily African American preschools to predominately White elementary schools.

From a more micro perspective, Corsaro and Molinari (2000a) carried out a longitudinal ethnography of Italian children's transition from the final year of publicly funded preschool to their first months of formal schooling. As they made the transition with the children, the researchers found both formal school organization and activities as well as more informal routines in the peer and school culture "primed" the children for a smooth transition to first grade. The notion of priming, where past events prepare children in making transitions, has much in common with Thelen and Smith's systems theory, which stresses the need for how previous developmental processes help organize future ones. In their Italian study, Corsaro and Molinari (2000a) identify how patterns in priming for transitions can be more important than children's internalized representations of elementary school in the actual transition. The authors also place their findings in the context of American school systems and suggest how the United States could learn from the Italian experience.

Early childhood literacy is dependent on preschool experience and successful transition to elementary school. Recent work on literacy is based on models that stress social context and children's active participation with teachers and peers. In an innovative study, Dyson (1997) finds that second and third grade children showed great interest and improved learning in reading and writing instruction when they can use popular culture (cartoons and comics), which are part of peer culture. Corsaro and Nelson (in press) expand on Dyson's work and find that 5- and 6-year-old children's spontaneous written production (e.g., writing names, letters to friends, stories, and drawings) contributes to children's acquisition of literacy. They also find that children often take literacy knowledge and skills they were recently exposed to in structured lessons and use, refine, and expand them in peer interaction.

There are many recent ethnographies of the nature of children's lives in elementary school. In a study of a British primary school, Filer and Pollard (2000) study assessments of children in the classroom. They find that contrastive forms of teachers' language in assessing students promoted or inhibited their responses. In this way, in line with the theoretical work of Bernstein (1996), they identify processes of cultural reproduction stemming from students' access to culturally specific patterns of interactions used in teacher assessments (see Plank, 2000, for a similar study of teaching styles and peer relations in Wisconsin).

In related work in a more positive vein and based on sociocultural theory, Rogoff, Tukanis, and Bartlett (2001) carried out a collaborative research-teacher study of an innovative project school in Utah. Based on Rogoff's notion of collaborative participation at multiple levels (school, community, research-team, and students) the study documents how learning as a community involves people learning together in purposeful activities, with mutual responsibilities, shared decision making, and motivation based on shared interests and objectives.

CHILDREN'S EVERYDAY EXPERIENCES IN PEER CULTURES

Earlier, we noted that the interpretive approach to childhood socialization maintains that children creatively appropriate information from the adult world to produce their own unique peer cultures. Although a wide range of features of children's peer cultures have been identified, two central themes consistently appear: children make persistent attempts to *gain control* of the their lives and to *share* that control with each other. In the preschool years children have an overriding concern with social participation and with challenging adult authority. In elementary school such challenging of adult authority persists, but there is also a gradual movement toward social differentiation within the peer group. This differentiation is marked by negotiations and conflicts as children attempt to gain control over the attitudes and behaviors of peers.

Children's Friendships

As Winterhoff (1997) argues, two metatheoretical assumptions underlie most of the research on children's friendships. The first, "friendship as outcome" assumption sees relationships as if they were static entities and often strives to identify a universal definition of friendship. The second, "friendship as process" assumption sees friendships as socially constructed and seeks to identify patterns and variations in their collective construction over time and across sociocultural settings.

Although the outcome approach dominated most of the theory and early research on children's friendships in developmental psychology, many developmental psychologists have begun to question this dominance and argue for the potential of the process approach (consider our earlier discussion of Tesson & Youniss, 1995). However, it is recent theory and research on children's friendships and peer relations in sociology and anthropology that have fully developed the importance of the process approach. Most of this research has been ethnographic and conducted in educational settings with a focus on friendship processes in classrooms and on playgrounds and in other peer settings (Corsaro, 1985; Evaldsson, 1993; Rizzo, 1989). However, there have also been ethnographic studies of children's friendship processes in homes, neighborhood, and community organizations (Adler & Adler, 1998; Fine, 1987; Goodwin, 1990).

Many recent studies have been comparative in that they examine children's friendships across age, gender, class, race and ethnicity, and cultural groups. All of the studies are longitudinal in that children are observed or interviewed over several months or years. Surprisingly a good deal of work on children's friendships documents the importance of discussion, debate, and conflict. For example, Corsaro (1994) has found that Italian and African American preschool children often forge and develop friendship ties through debates and teasing, while White middle-class American preschool children are highly sensitive to such activities. On the other hand, the middle-class American children are quick to use the denial of friendship ("I won't be your Buddy," or "You can't come to my birthday party," if you do not play with me or play the way I like). In his study of middle-class first grade American children, Rizzo (1989) found that when the children noticed problems in their friends' behaviors, they insisted that their friends change their behavior. Such challenges often led to emotional disputes. Rizzo argued that such disputes not only helped the children obtain a better understanding of what they could expect from each other as friends, but also brought about personal reflection, resulting in the children's development of unique insight into their own actions and roles as friends.

In work on elementary school children Adler and Adler (1998) found different levels of cliques (popular, wannabes, middle group of friends, and isolates) with a great deal of competition, conflict, and manipulation within the popular group and between the popular and other groups. On the other hand, the middle circle of friends (usually 3–5 children in overlapping groups) tended to be less competitive and were emotionally supportive of each other. Overall, we see that children's collective actions (often including conflict) is central to the development of children's conceptions of friendship and their friendship activities and relations.

Children's Bodies and Nonverbal and Verbal Play Routines

Williams and Bendelow (1998) contend that children's bodies are absent in much of the adult-oriented sociological work on the body, and the work that has been done is directed at children rather than based in children's own knowledge and experience. Prout (2000) additionally argues that childhood and the body are each topics that have experienced recent growth in sociological interest, but there has been little contact between these two fields. This is due to how sociologists have traditionally addressed the body and also a lack of recognition of children's agency and distinct childhood cultures (James, 2000). To date, we know relatively little of children's own experiences of their bodies.

Children experience and understand their bodies in ways significantly different from adults. Bodily change in childhood is a salient marker not only of a childhood identity itself, but also a marker of different ages in the structural placement in childhood (James, 2000). James argues that the body, in particular, represents the passage of time for children as the body grows and develops at a much more accelerated pace than the adult body. For example, James finds in her ethnographic fieldwork among children ages 4 through 9 that height is a significant marker of age and status. The children use height to mark their social rank within the larger group and their progress toward being an adult, a position of power and maturity. Additionally, James finds that the children are involved in "body work," as they constantly negotiate the presentation of their bodies, their bodies' actions, and their bodies' appearances. Children work both to make themselves appear taller and to stay within the cultural prescriptions of thinness.

In schooling, children's bodies are ordered and controlled. In preschools, Martin (1998) uncovers a hidden school curriculum designed to control children's bodily practices. Teachers require that children walk properly and quietly down the hall, sit up straight, and try not to fidget. Simpson (2000) finds that children's bodies are perceived as dangerous and troublesome and thus many school rules are designed to control students' bodies and their attentions. Further, when kids misbehave in school, their bodies are used in the punishment. For example, a child who was talking while the students were lining up for the dining room was punished by being made to stand in the main passage with his back to the rest of the school. He was bodily put on display. In this way, Simpson contends that the body is central to power relations among children and between children and adults in the schools. For children in school, being invisible, unnoticed, and just a part of the group means they have managed to stay out of trouble.

Children also use their bodies, bodily functions, and bodily waste products to resist authority. For example, children tell dirty jokes, disobey the dress code, and use taboo bodily waste to shock teachers and other adults. Simpson relates one incident where a boy deliberately stabbed himself with a pencil to draw blood so he could leave the classroom lesson and visit the nurse. Resistance to the "boredoms" of school lessons is well documented (Best, 1983; Everhart, 1983), but in this case it is the body that is directly used as the object of resistance.

Orchestrated and repeated body movements—often seen as just running around—are accepted routines in the peer culture of young children. Several studies identify such routines among toddlers (Corsaro & Molinari, 1990; Mussati & Panni, 1981). One example, "the little chairs routine," captures the flavor of primarily nonverbal play among toddlers (Corsaro & Molinari, 1990). The routine took place regularly in a large room in an Italian *asilo nido* (preschool for 2- and 3-year-olds). In the routine the children appropriate the small chairs they sit on for snacks and other activities to create their own activity. The children begin by pushing the little chairs to the center of the room to make a long line from one wall to a small platform sitting against the opposite wall. Once the line is finished, the children are careful to make sure the chairs are together and the line is straight. Then the children walk across the room from chair to chair—sometimes swaying and saying "I'm falling! I'm falling," but always keeping their balance—until they reach the platform and jump down. They then run back to the other side of the room to take another turn. During the routine the teachers want the children to be careful, but they rarely intervene and only when they fear an injury might occur. An important feature of toddler routines like the "little chairs" is their simple and primarily nonverbal participant structure, which consists of a series of orchestrated bodily actions. The structure also incorporates the option of frequent recycling, which allows the children to begin and end participation (with some entering and others leaving) and to embellish certain features of the routine like the swaying and pretending to lose their balance.

In terms of gender, Thorne (1993) finds that children use differences between their bodies as ways to tease the other sex and highlight the differences between the sexes. She contends that power differences between fourth and fifth grade boys and girls are communicated and learned through social interaction focusing on the body. She talks about "gender play," which is where children use the frame of "play" as a cover for serious, gender-based messages about sexuality and aggression. Examples of gender play include bra-snapping and "cooties" rituals. These types of gender games show a specific construction of femininity and womanhood, which is based on female pollution and a subordination of female maturity. This highlights the social power differences between boys and girls as learned through body-based social interaction. Similarly, Martin (1998) shows that in preschools, children use their physical bodies to divide themselves up into gendered groupings whose bodily practices differ.

Children's Fantasy Play

Numerous studies document the complexity of children's fantasy play. In his work, Corsaro (1985) identifies the complex language and paralinguistic skills children exhibit in fantasy play events. He also identifies three underlying themes in their play (lost–found, danger–rescue, and death–rebirth), which enable children to address important emotional concerns in their lives. Sawyer (1997) and Goldman (1998) offer detailed sociolinguistic studies of pretend play in which they reveal its poetic qualities. Sawyer, relying on work in metapragmatics, impressively identifies the improvisational nature of a group of American children's play comparing it with improvisation jazz and theater. Goldman studied Huli children of

Papua New Guinea and demonstrates how pretense is socially mediated and linguistically constructed viewing the children's play as oral poetry. These studies and other work on children's fantasy play leads to the argument that such play demonstrates improvisational skills that surpass those of most older children and adults. This contention is novel for theories of development because it suggests that some skills may deteriorate with age due to a lack of opportunities for refinement and sharpening (a process of "use it or lose it").

Young children's dramatic role play can be differentiated from fantasy play in that the children take on real roles that exist in society such as mothers, fathers, police, firefighters, and so on. Role play is especially popular among preschool children. In role play, children have a clear sense of status as power and authority over others, which is clearly displayed in the children's actions and language in the play (e.g., high use of imperatives, heavy stress and intonation with commands, threats of punishment) (Anderson, 1990; Corsaro, 1985). On the other hand, children sometimes show confusion about role relations. For example, Corsaro (1985) videotaped an episode of role play where the children began with a husband and wife, and two pet kitties. The husband and wife display stereotypic role relations as the husband moves furniture while the wife cleans. Both husband and wife discipline the kitties for being in the way and peeing on the floor. One boy who tired of being a kitty suggested there be two husbands and the original husband quickly agreed and they jumped around shouting: "We need two husbands!" and "Husbands! Husbands!" The wife, however, was not sure about this and suggested that the boy who wanted to be husband be a grandma instead. He refused and the wife pleaded: "You can't marry two husbands." The boys responded that they would marry themselves. In the end, the wife became a kitty who was bossed around by the two husbands (Corsaro, 1985, pp. 101–105).

Children's Experience of Gender, Race, and Social Class

GENDER.   Gender, along with age, is one of the first classifications children learn. In contrast with the more ambiguous and complex categories of race, ethnicity, religion, and social class, gender is highly visible. Children learn gender through language, interactions, and discourse with each other and with adults (Connell, 1987; B. Davies, 1989; Fernie, Davies, Kantor, & McMurray, 1993). Children learn that having a gendered body is a positive social achievement through age and maturity. Being called a "big boy" or "big girl" is positive feedback while being called a "baby," is tied to negative sanctions (Cahill, 1987). Similarly, in elementary school, teachers and other adults use gendered terms consistently to mark out groups of students, often during episodes of social control (Thorne, 1993).

For boys, both younger and older, masculinity is characterized by a focus on toughness and aggression, which also translates into competition for higher social status and social power (Adler & Adler, 1998; Fine, 1987). Fine (1987), in his ethnography of Little League Baseball teams, finds that not only is it important for boys to be tough and aggressive, but also to belittle and separate themselves from anything that was younger, weaker or feminine. In Messner's (2000) research on 4–5-year-old soccer players, by teasing the girls' team and their unique expressions of femininity and soccer, the boys distance themselves from that construction and define themselves as more masculine and aggressive soccer players. According to Adler and Adler (1998), toughness and masculinity for elementary school boys includes disobeying adult rules and receiving disciplinary actions. Boys who are constantly in trouble receive greater social status from their male peers. Masculinity also includes being a "ladies man," which implies not only being popular with one girl, but with several.

Masculinity is marked and defined in opposition to femininity. B. Davies (1989) finds that preschool children place utmost importance on accurate gender definitions for themselves and their peers. These gender categories, created and sustained by the children's narrative structures, are mutually exclusive, opposite, absolutely rigid, and impenetrable. Additionally, being correctly gendered and adhering to these gender prescriptions is of vital importance for social and emotional survival in the preschool. The discourses available to children do not include any variation, merging, or challenge of different gendered characteristics or practices. Children who "correctly" follow the forms of masculinity and femininity are rewarded with high status and popularity.

As Davies read feminist stories to preschoolers, she learns that even when presented with alternate discourses, it is hard for children to imagine, much less accept, and practice, any alternative to their existing dualistic gender order. Some children might be interested in doing things assigned to the other gender, but they are constrained by their gender categories and the threat of peer sanctions. To keep peers in-line, Davies finds the preschoolers engage in "category-maintenance work." Similar to Thorne's (1993) concept of "border work" among elementary school students, discussed above, such interactions serve to reinforce and maintain the gender boundaries.

Among kindergartners, Holmes (1995) finds that gender identity is the ultimate mechanism for social differentiation. Gender schemas organize children's thoughts, attitudes, and heavily influence their everyday social behavior. For example, gender is often used as a basis for inclusion or exclusion in a play group. In their social interactions, the kindergartners define and explore gender appropriate behavior and sanction, often through teasing, those kids who do not comply.

Evaldsson (1993) finds a great deal of cross-gender interaction among Swedish 7–10-year-olds during play in their after school program. However these games, such as "tunnel of love" in jump rope and playing "fortune tellers" were often sexually charged. Among fifth and sixth graders, B. Davies (1993) also finds a preoccupation with romance and sexuality as any interaction between boys and girls is automatically laden with heterosexual meanings, whether intended or not. One of the girls in her data wanted to borrow a pencil from a boy, but knew she should not because it would be interpreted as if she had romantic and sexual interest in the boy.

Two different approaches characterize the study of gender in childhood. Lever's (1976) study on "Sex differences in children's play," exemplifies the socialization model as it is applied to empirical research by finding that children's play is primarily designed to socialize children into adult roles. In particular, she argues that boys' and girls' play are significantly different and each leads participants to the development of different social skills and capacities for different, gender-based, adult roles. Boys' play prepares them for the public world of competitive work, and girls' play socializes them into private roles of motherhood and domesticity. Gilligan (1982) also follows a gender-difference model finding that girls and boys go through different moral developments that lead to an emphasis on connectedness, cooperation, and mutuality for girls, and an emphasis on separateness, competition, and independence among boys.

There are many critiques of such "gender-difference" approaches, which attack not only their interpretations of the data and assumptions of rigid gender differences, but also their adherence to the socialization model. Lees (1993), in particular, critiques socialization models in general because they cannot account for change. For example, how can gender roles change if they are merely learned from adults? How can boys and girls choose and successfully negotiate different roles than the ones they were socialized for?

Following an interpretive approach, Thorne (1993) and Goodwin (2003) advocate approaching children from a non-gendered, contextual approach where researchers look for patterns and themes among all the children and then see if any parse out by gender, or by other differences. They believe that when researchers enter the field expecting gender difference, they will significantly limit their ability to see similarities among girls and boys. Messner (2000) follows this stance as he explores not simply why boys and girls are different, but under what conditions children constitute themselves as separate, gendered, oppositional groups (see Aydt & Corsaro, 2002, for a similar approach looking at differences in gender play across cultures).

In Goodwin's (1990) investigation of talk among 6- through 14-year-old Black children, she finds that girls and boys each have complex, role taking games, and experience conflict and status ranking in their everyday play. For example, in hopscotch, girls negotiate for power and status as they disagree about rules, hopscotch moves, and interpretations of those moves. Theoretically, both Goodwin (1990, 2003) and Thorne (1993) note that power and gender are negotiated by children through social interaction, not simply through socialization and imitating adult behaviors. Thorne, in her research on White elementary school children, provides the example of giving "cooties," where through play, boys and girls learn the complex rules of who has cooties, who can give cooties, how to prevent cooties, and who is more polluting.

Recent comparative research shows that children of various cultures differ in their construction of gender concepts and behavior. Goodwin (1998) finds that African American and Latina girls value ritualized conflict and they frequently argue about the interpretation of the rules of the games. Kyratzis and Guo (2001) find cross-cultural differences in the gendered speech patterns of preschoolers in the United States and China. They found that among American children, boys tend to be more assertive than girls in same-sex interactions, but in China girls are more assertive with one another than boys. However, context is important in determining who dominates cross-sex interaction. Chinese boys take the lead in discussions regarding work, but Chinese girls dominate when relationships and courtship is the theme. Both Chinese girls and American boys freely use bold, directive speech when they disagreed with their classmates while American girls use mitigated, discourse during disputes.

RACE. Race, although just as integral to children's identities, is a much more complex construct than gender as racial and ethnic categories are not as clear cut. Many investigators assume that children have temporary or naive views on race and ethnicity until at least age 7 or 8. In his research, Sacks (2001) finds that not until age 7 or 8 do children differentiate and label others on the basis of perceived race, and thus argues that racial issues are not relevant to the peer cultures of young children. Using a developmental-based approach, he attributes 4-year-olds' use of racist terminology to modeling adult behavior. However, Sacks compares the children's understanding of race to the adult concept of race, rather than children's own possible constructions of race. Additionally, Tynes (2001) finds that children under the age of 10 are often confused when asked "What race or color do you consider yourself" leading her to conclude that their racial constructions and identities are not yet developed. She argues that children see skin color as only one of many different physical characteristics people have, not as a basis for hierarchical stratification.

Holmes (1995) advocates using an ethnographic approach when studying race and ethnic concepts in young children as opposed to most previous research that is based on experiments or in other contrived and structured settings. By studying children in their own environments, in her case, the classroom, Holmes is able to use children's own language and their own interactions to understand how they construct race. In contrast to developmental research, she finds skin color is a dominant feature in how kindergartners see themselves. In particular, she finds "White" is the default race, even among children, as White children rarely mention skin color while Black children clearly emphasize their Black skin.

Based on their interpretive research on preschool children ages 3–5, Van Ausdale and Feagin (2001) find that even very young children use race and ethnicity as identifying and stratifying markers and that they are salient features of children's cultures. The children they observed use racial and ethnic concepts to structure their play as a means to exclude and/or include children and as a means of controlling their environments and peer interactions. Rather than using an adult-based understanding of race, Van Ausdale and Feagin find that children develop, through social interaction, their own complex and intricate constructions and uses of race and ethnicity based on the color of their skin, the languages they speak, and how they understand their parents' color and race.

Children also use such concepts to define their own identities and the identities of those around them (Holmes, 1995; Van Ausdale & Feagin, 2001). Holmes concludes that kindergartners' racial categories are fixed and unconditional. People are in one category or another and the members of one group are homogeneous. Van Ausdale and Feagin, however, find that among preschoolers, ideas of race are more fluid and flexible and the children try to understand not only single race markers, but also their peers of "mixed" heritage. Not all children fit into one category or the other, rather, there are multiple categories and children move from one to another depending on the situation.

For example, one 4-year-old girl in their study was born in Africa of a White American father and a Black African mother. Corinne was very aware of her mixed ancestry and stressed both her American and African heritage to other children and adults. Her fellow students often challenged Corinne. One White boy denied Corrine's father was White even when the father came to the school and verified that he was Corinne's father and that her mother was African. Adults also frequently challenged Corinne. New teachers and visitors to the school often corrected Corinne when she claimed to be African, and would say: "Your mommy and daddy's ancestors came from Africa, but you are African American." At one point, Corinne got so frustrated that she retorted: "No, you don't get it, I'm from Africa. My daddy is from here" (Van Ausdale & Feagin, 2001, p. 85).

Van Ausdale and Feagin also find that adults did not believe the children made the negative racial remarks and slurs that the researchers recorded and denied children had any real understanding of such speech. Van Ausdale and Feagin argue adults misunderstand and underestimate young children's understanding and use of racial attitudes because they believe that children can not be racist. However, seeing children as simply racist misses the point. Given the pervasive racism that exists in American society it is not surprising that young children—in line with an interpretive approach to childhood socialization—observe, experience and absorb racial thinking, discourse and behavior and use such knowledge in their everyday lives (Van Ausdale & Feagin, 2001).

SOCIAL CLASS. As with gender and race, children show an awareness of social class and class differences from a young age. In a comparative study of role play, Corsaro finds key differences in the children's conceptions of their place in society and their future as adults. The upper-class White children construct play in which they see themselves as adults who have efficacy in the present and optimism about their futures. In contrast, the poor African American children constructed play themes that reflect the hardships their parents endure and display a resolution to the fact that overcoming such challenges is unlikely (Corsaro, 1993).

Working-class and middle-class students experience school in different ways as their schools are structured according to different principles. L. Davies (1989) finds that in the preschools she observed, the working-class students' time and space is more structured, their free play is under control of the teachers, and the teachers are more authoritarian in their interactions with the students. In contrast, the middle-class preschool children have more freedom, the emphasis is on children developing their own play and routines, and the teachers actively encourage autonomy. Evaldsson (1993) finds similar patterns in two Swedish after-school centers for children ages 7 through 10. The two centers she observed are in the same urban area, yet the center catering to working-class families focuses on order and control of children handed "top-down" from teachers while the middle-class center emphasizes children's own role in creating and sustaining classroom order.

In addition to experiences in schooling, class also affects children's language use. James (1995) finds that there are strong links between social class and language use in Britain as the language children use identifies their speech community. Corsaro (1994) conducted comparative study of language and friendship and finds that the Italian and African American children use more dramatic and teasing language styles while the White American middle-class children use a style where they try to avoid or mitigate conflict. However, the White American middle-class children show more negative emotional reactions to conflict and language slights ("You're not my friend"), while the Italian and African American children engage in oppositional talk and debates with rare displays of negative emotions or threats.

Children's Experience of Health and Well-Being

Similar to work on the body, most research in health has focused on adult perspectives and not on what children themselves know, believe, or want to know about health and the body (Williams & Bendelow, 1998). In their research, by having children draw and talk about what cancer means to them, Williams and Bendelow give voice to children's own concerns, feelings, and emotions. Children experience health, well being, and illness in unique ways that stem from their peer cultures and everyday lives. Christensen and Prout (1999) contend that in terms of everyday sickness, children develop elaborate cultural performances. Children frequently talk about bodily phenomena and understand what is happening with their bodies collectively. Bleeding or tissue swelling is something to be shown off, looked at, and shared with the group. For example, in her research on Danish 6–13-year-olds, Christensen (2000) found that during minor accidents in school, teachers responded with alarm and concern, and worked immediately to clean the wound and cover it with a bandage. The injured child, in contrast, might often magnify the extent of the injury as the other children gather around to investigate the wound.

Additionally, rather than being concerned about the body part that might be affected, such as a cut arm, children emphasize their own actions and the actions of others, such as in what circumstances the arm was cut or how their social activities might be changed because of the cut (Christensen, 2000). Christensen finds that children see sickness as a disruption to their daily routines and wellness, as one 7-year-old says, "to do as I usually do." For children, the body is not a bounded object, but rather is experienced through continuous action and interaction.

CHILDREN'S INTERACTIONS WITH LARGER STRUCTURES

Children's interactions in and contributions to macro levels of society and culture are key aspects of the new sociology of childhood. Here we discuss children's symbolic and material culture, children's involvement in work and the economy, poverty, and children's rights as citizens.

Children's Symbolic and Material Culture

In children's everyday lives, they not only base their cultures on interactions with peers, family, and school, but also in the larger worlds of symbolic and material culture. This includes the media and popular culture such as mythical figures related to holidays (like Christmas and Easter), television, movies, advertisements, and books. Many studies of children's symbolic and material culture focus primarily on the content and features of toys, texts, films, or ritual events (Kinder, 1999; Steinberg & Kincheloe, 1997; see Seiter, 1993; Tobin, 2000, for exceptions to this trend). However, as with other realms of children's lives, it is important to recognize children as actively engaged with media and larger material culture.

For example, Clark (1995) went directly to children and parents to explore the rituals and meanings of Santa Claus, the Tooth Fairy, and the Easter Bunny. Clark's findings and analysis regarding the retrospective and prospective features of the Tooth Fairy ritual are especially interesting. In retrospectively celebrating the loss of the tooth shortly after it has occurred, the ritual also marks the beginning of an occurrence that will have may repetitions (the loss of additional teeth in exchange for money from the Tooth Fairy). In this way the ritual encourages children's awareness of ongoing transitions in their lives and helps prepare them for these changes. The children, who are in kindergarten and first grade, valued the power and independence that money from the Tooth Fairy can provide. As one child observes, "I like carrying around my own money. I feel more grown up and special" (Clark, 1995, p. 19).

In a study of children and media, Fingerson (1999) finds that preadolescent girls are active in television viewing, rather than simply accepting media messages passively. The girls use their own experiences to critically evaluate television families and they actively assess various aspects of the program that are most salient to them. Additionally, and most importantly, watching television, for these girls is a pro-social way of sharing experiences that can be later used to build talk, foster social interaction, and enhance social relationships.

Children's Work and Economy

Children are often seen by adults in contemporary society as nonproductive and dependent as childhood is constructed as freedom from the responsibilities of work (Morrow, 1995). Although young children's work in developed societies does not contribute to the current economy (such as their schooling work), research indicates that children contribute a great deal to their own family economy and the larger arenas of work and labor (see Hine, 1999, for a history of children's work). Examples of children's work include childcare, contributions to family business, household chores, and employment in part-time jobs in the labor market (for older children, in particular). Solberg (1997) finds that as children's work in and outside the home increases over time, parents begin to see their children as more capable and independent.

In the United States, informal paid work often begins before adolescence as children begin their work in the home or the neighborhood, such as babysitting, mowing lawns, shoveling snow, cooking, cleaning, and other localized duties (Fine, Mortimer, & Roberts, 1990). This work is often conducted in the presence of or supervised by adults. By the time they are 12, most children start working for pay outside their homes. Interestingly, those children from more affluent backgrounds (middle class or higher) are more likely to work for pay than those in poorer areas (Fine et al., 1990; Morrow, 1995). These children have more opportunities to work in their local areas, their families might expect them to work as part of their moral upbringing, and they might have incorporated values of consumerism that would require their own source of income.

Morrow (1995) contends that children's work can be classified into four general categories: wage labor, marginal economic activities (e.g., babysitting, car washing, odd self-employment jobs), non-domestic family labor (e.g., helping in family businesses), and domestic labor. For example, Song (1996) finds that in Chinese take-out restaurants in Britain, children are actively engaged in the family business as they contribute substantial amounts of labor and assistance. Duties, that often depend on age and maturity, include working at the counter, taking customer orders, messengering between the counter and the kitchen, and cleaning. Some children also help with food preparation, cooking, and have increased domestic responsibility to free up the parents' time for the business.

Children in Poverty

Child poverty is an overwhelming problem in developing countries often resulting in the exploitation of children as underpaid workers or indentured servants, prostitutes, and as pawns in drug trafficking. As a result, children are not only exploited, but are also the victims of abuse and violence. In the wealthy nations of the world, children are rarely shot on the streets for being poor, nor are they allowed to be sold into indentured servitude. The majority of children in Western industrialized societies live in relative comfort with high aspirations and bright futures. Even so, many poor children live in the modern industrialized world, and a significant number live in impoverished and dangerous environments.

Childhood poverty varies across wealthy nations, but the richest nation in the world, the United States, has one of the highest child poverty rates. Although the U.S. rate has dropped recently from over 20% in 1991 to around 17% in the year 2000, it is more than twice as high as many European countries (including France, Germany, and the Netherlands) and 4–8 times as high as Northern European and Scandinavian countries (Belgium, Switzerland, Norway, Denmark, Sweden, and Finland, see Bradbury & Jäntti, 2001; Rainwater & Smeeding, 1995). These high rates of poverty in the United States compared to most of Western Europe also do not take into account programs for families with children like universal health care, paid maternity and family leave, and government funded child care and early education. These programs exist throughout Europe, but are sorely lacking in the United States. The lack of health care for over 14% of American children from working families is especially shameful in the United States, which provides universal health care regardless of income for all those over 65.

Sadly, living in poverty and becoming a victim of abuse or violent crime are interrelated for many American children (see Ambert, 1995; Males, 1996). Although there has been a recent drop in violent crime, homicide and victim of violent crime rates for children and youth are staggering when compared to other modern societies. In fact, there has been a trend in the United States in which rates of victims of violent crime for the younger age groups (12–15 and 16–19) have become higher than the 20–24 age group and much higher than other older age groups. This U.S. trend toward a lack of a fair distribution of resources by age and the resulting consequences is even more troubling given demographic shifts of increased elderly and fewer children.

Children's Rights

Although there is little empirical work in the area of children's rights, the philosophical and theoretical discussions are rich and lead to promising areas of research (see Archard, 1993, for an extensive review). In the United States and in most Western countries, children are not afforded the same rights as adults. Rights denied include the right to own property, to work, to vote, to choose one's guardian, and to make sexual choices (Archard, 1993). Following socialization approaches, children are constructed as developmentally and socially incomplete and thus not capable of holding such rights. Children's liberationists, based in a movement with roots in the 1960s, believe that children should have these rights and any right that an adult has. Opponents of increased children's rights argue that children need to be protected from the adult world and the decisions and responsibilities of that world. In dominant adult culture, childhood is seen as a time of innocence, a time free from responsibility and conflict, and a time dominated by play (Lansdown, 1994).

However, Lansdown finds that children themselves feel powerless and with little control over their lives, but this is a result of a structural vulnerability and not inherent to their age and developmental stage. This structural condition, Thorne (1987) argues, masks the ways in which adults abuse and exploit children, such as in governmental policies that contribute to the high rates of child poverty. Although not directly advocating a platform of children's rights, some researchers such as Thorne find that children, like women, are a minority group in society and we need to rethink our ideological constructions of them (Alanen, 1994; Oakley, 1994). Lansdown further contends that we need to recognize children as participants in society with their own needs and rights.

One way of documenting how children conceptualize and negotiate their rights is by exploring forms of resistance to dominant adult-based structures. For example, there are many examples of girls and boys resisting dominant sexuality and gender norms, even as early as pre-school (Anyon, 1983; Brown, 1998; Lee & Sasser-Coen, 1996; Messner, 2000). Messner (2000) explores gender construction and boundary maintenance among 4–5-year-old girls and boys in a youth soccer organization. Although the boys taunt the girls who were dancing and playing in celebration of their self-named team "Barbie Girls," the girls ignore them. When the boys invaded their space, the girls chased them off. The girls celebrate themselves and girl power and do not succumb to pressure from the boys to be quiet and passive in a traditionally male-dominated sports realm. Children also directly resist adult-based structures such as schools. For example, B. Davies (1982) finds elementary school children resist teachers and the school structure as they engage in their own agendas of learning and socialization. She shows evidence of children mocking teachers and other caretakers as well as questioning the teachers' methods.

Future research can explore what children want in terms of rights. Do children in fact desire more rights? What happens in circumstances where they gain rights? In thinking about the political implications, Roche (1996) argues that we must be careful with the language and implications of children's rights. What about the wide variety of children's cultures? For example, how do we account for the variety in children's notions of family life? Children live in vastly different households and communities with different boundaries of authority and responsibility. Children thus may make varying demands for their rights specifically in terms of their own education, health, family, and guardianship. Full children's rights can seem to be a "never-never-land" sort of place. Regardless, children's rights in regard to the most serious issues of equitable distribution of resources in society must be addressed by representatives of children or children themselves. How we do this might be difficult, but it must be done.

THE FUTURE OF CHILDHOOD

Much of the recent research in childhood focuses on children as agents in their own right, rather than as products of their parents or as adults-in-the-making. This recognition leads to a new sociology of children and childhood that documents children's rich peer cultures, the complexity of their evolving membership in their cultures, and their contribution to social reproduction and change. The new sociology of children and childhood also establishes childhood as a social form that must be conceptualized in time and place, most especially regarding power relations in a local and global sense.

Given the vast problems of poverty, disease, abuse, and violence toward children in developing societies and many industrialized countries, the rights of children as citizens must be established and maintained. The growing demographic changes of increasing life spans and falling birthrates in Western industrialized societies is accompanied by an uneven distribution of material, social, and economic resources (Peterson, 1999; Sgritta, 1994). Now, more than ever, is the time to appreciate and invest in children. All too often, individuals and societies try to justify their actions in terms of their effects on children's futures as adults. This focus on the future, on what our children will become, often blinds us to how we treat and care for our children in the present. Enriching the lives of all our children will produce productive adults and will enable our children to participate actively and fully in their own childhoods and to contribute to the quality of adult life. For this reason, we must realize and remember that the future of childhood is the present.

REFERENCES

Adler, P. A., & Adler, P. (1998). *Peer power: Preadolescent culture and identity.* New Brunswick, NJ: Rutgers, University Press.

Alderson, P. (2000). Children as researchers: The effects of participation rights on research methodology. In P. Christensen & A. James (Eds.), *Research with children: Perspectives and practices* (pp. 241–257). London: Falmer Press.

Alanen, L. (1994). Gender and generation: Feminism and the "child question." In J. Qvortrup, M. Bardy, G. Sgritta, & H. Wintersberger (Eds.), *Childhood matters: Social theory, practice, and politics* (pp. 27–42). Brookfield, VT: Ashgate Publishing Company.

Ambert, A. (1995). Toward a theory of peer abuse. In N. Mandell (Ed.), *Sociological studies of children* (vol. 7, pp. 177–205). Greenwich, CT: JAI Press.

Andersen, E. (1990). *Speaking with style: The sociolinguistic skills of children.* New York: Cambridge University Press.

Anyon, J. (1983). Intersections of gender and class: Accommodation and resistance by working-class and affluent females to contradictory sex-role ideologies. In S. Walker & L. Barton (Eds.), *Gender, Class & Education* (pp. 19–38). Sussex, England: Falmer Press.

Archard, D. (1993). *Children: Rights and childhood.* London: Routledge.

Aydt, H., & Corsaro, W. (2002). Differences in children's construction of gender across culture: An interpretive approach. Unpublished paper.

Baumrind, D. (1989). Rearing competent children. In W. Damon (Ed.), *Child development today and tomorrow* (pp. 349–378). San Francisco: Jossey Bass.

Bernstein, B. (1996). *Pedagogy, symbolic control and identity.* London: Taylor & Francis.

Best, R. (1983). *We've all got scars: What boys and girls learn in elementary school.* Bloomington, IN: Indiana University Press.

Belsky, J. (1988). The "effects" of infant daycare reconsidered. *Early Childhood Research Quarterly, 3,* 235–272.

Bowlby. J. (1980). *Attachment and loss, 3. Loss: Sadness and depression.* New York: Basic Books.

Bradbury, B., & Jämtti, M. (2001). Child poverty across twenty-five countries. In B. Bradbury, S. P. Jenkins, & J. Micklewright (Eds.), *The dynamics of child poverty in industrialized countries* (pp. 62–91). New York: Cambridge University Press.

Brown, L. (1998). *Raising their voices: The politics of girls' anger.* Cambridge, MA: Harvard University Press.

Cahill, Spencer E. (1987). Language practices and self-definition: The case of gender identity acquisition. *Sociological Quarterly, 27,* 295–311.

Christensen, P., & James, A. (2000). Childhood diversity and commonality: Some methodological insights. In P. Christensen & A. James (Eds.), *Research with Children: Perspectives and practices.* London: Falmer Press.

Christensen, P., & Prout, A. (1999). The cultural performance of children's everyday sickness. Paper Presented in Sociology Departmental Colloquium. Indiana University.

Christensen, P. (2000). Childhood and the cultural constitution of vulnerable bodies. In A. Prout (Ed.), *The body, childhood and society* (pp. 38–59). New York: St. Martin's Press.

Clark, C. D. (1995). *Flights of fancy, leaps of faith*. Chicago: University of Chicago Press.

Clarke-Stewart, A. (1989). Infant day care: Maligned or malignant? *American Psychologist, 44*, 66–73.

Connell, R. (1987). *Gender and power: Society, the person and sexual politics*. Stanford, CA: Stanford University Press.

Corsaro, W. (1985). *Friendship and peer culture in the early years*. Norwood, NJ: Ablex.

Corsaro, W. (1992). Interpretive reproduction in children's peer cultures. *Social Psychology Quarterly, 55*, 160–177.

Corsaro, W. (1993). Interpretive reproduction in children's role play. *Childhood, 1*, 64–74.

Corsaro, W. (1994). Discussion, debate, and friendship: Peer discourse in nursery schools in the US and Italy. *Sociology of Education, 67*, 1–26.

Corsaro, W. (1997). *The sociology of childhood*. Thousand Oaks, CA: Pine Forge Press.

Corsaro, W., & Eder, D. (1990). Children's peer cultures. *Annual Review of Sociology, 16*, 197–220.

Corsaro, W., & Molinari, L. (1990). From *seggiolini* to *discussione*: The generation and extension of peer culture among Italian preschool children. *International Journal of Qualitative Studies in Education, 3*, 213–230.

Corsaro, W., & Molinari, L. (2000a). Priming events and Italian children's transition from preschool to elementary school: Representations and actions. *Social Psychology Quarterly, 63*, 16–33.

Corsaro, W., & Molinari, L. (2000b). Entering and observing in children's worlds: A reflection on a longitudinal ethnography of early education in Italy. In P. Christensen & A. James (Eds.), *Research with children: Perspectives and practices* (pp. 179–200). London: Falmer Press.

Corsaro, W. A., & Nelson, E. (in press). Children's collective activities in early literacy in American and Italian preschools. *Sociology of Education*.

Davies, B. (1982). *Life in the classroom and playground: The accounts of primary school children*. Boston: Routledge and Kegan Paul.

Davies, B. (1989). *Frogs and snails and feminist tales: Preschool children and gender*. Boston: Allen & Unwin.

Davies, B. (1993). *Shards of glass: Children reading and writing beyond gendered identities*. Cresskill, NJ: Hampton Press.

Davies, L. (1983). Gender, resistance and power. In S. Walker & L. Barton (Eds.), *Gender, class & education* (pp. 39–52). Sussex, England: Falmer Press.

Denzin, N. (1977). *Childhood socialization*. San Francisco: Jossey-Bass.

Dunn, J. (1988). *The beginnings of social understanding*. Cambridge, MA: Harvard University Press.

Dunn, J., & Plomin, R. (1990). *Separate lives: Why siblings are so different*. New York: Basic Books.

Dyson, A. (1997). *Writing superheroes: Contemporary childhood, popular culture, and classroom literacy*. New York: Teachers College Press.

Eder, D., & Fingerson, L. (2002). Interviewing children and adolescents. In J. F. Gubrium & J. A. Holstein (Eds.), *Handbook of interview research* (pp. 181–201). Thousand Oaks, CA: Sage Publications.

Elder, G. (1994). Time, human agency, and social change: Perspectives on the life course. *Social Psychology Quarterly, 57*, 4–15.

Elder, G. (1998). *Children of the great depression* (25th Anniversary ed.). New York: Harper and Collins.

Elkin, F., & Handel, G. (1989). *The child and society: The process of socialization* (5th ed.). New York: Random House.

Entwisle, D., & Alexander, K. (1999). Early schooling and social stratification. In R. Pianta & M. Cox (Eds.), *The transition to kindergarten* (pp. 13–38). Baltimore, MD: Brookes.

Everhart, R. (1983). *Reading, writing and resistance: Adolescence and labor in a junior high school, critical social thought*. Boston: Routledge and Kegan Paul.

Evaldsson, A. (1993). *Play, disputes and social order: Everyday life in two Swedish after-school centers*. Linköping, Sweden: Linköping University.

Ferguson, A. (2000). *Bad boys: Public schools in the making of black masculinity*. Ann Arbor: University of Michigan Press.

Fernie, D., Davies, B., Kantor, R., & McMurray, P. (1993). Becoming a person in the preschool: Creating integrated gender, school culture, and peer culture positionings. *Qualitative Studies in Education, 6*, 95–110.

Filer, A., & Pollard, A. (2000). *The social world of pupil assessment: Processes and contexts of primary schooling*. London: Continuum.

Fine, G. (1987). *With the boys: Little league baseball and preadolescent culture*. Chicago: University of Chicago Press.

Fine, G., Mortimer, J., & Roberts, D. (1990). Leisure, work, and the mass media. In S. S. Feldman & G. R. Elliott (Eds.), *At the threshold: The developing adolescent* (pp. 225–253). Cambridge: Harvard University Press.

Fingerson, L. (1999). Active viewing: Girls' interpretations of family television programs. *Journal of Contemporary Ethnography, 28,* 389–418.

Freese, J., Powell, B., & Steelman, L. (1999). Rebel without a cause or effect: Birth order and social attitudes. *American Sociological Review, 64,* 207–231.

Gaskins, S., Miller, P. J., & Corsaro, W. A. (1992). Theoretical and methodological perspectives in the interpretive study of children. In W. Corsaro & P. J. Miller (Eds.), *Interpretive approaches to children's socialization* (pp. 5–23). San Francisco: Jossey-Bass.

Geertz, C. (1973). *The interpretation of cultures.* New York: Basic Books.

Gecas, V. (1981). The contexts of socialization. In M. Rosenberg & R. Turner (Eds.), *Social psychology: Sociological perspectives* (pp. 165–199). New York: Basic Books.

Giddens, A. (1984). *The constitution of society.* Oxford, UK: Polity Press.

Gilligan, C. (1982). *In a different voice: Psychological theory and women's development.* Cambridge, MA: Harvard University Press.

Goffman, E. (1974). *Frame analysis.* New York: Harper & Row.

Goldman, L. R. (1998). *Child's play: Myth, miimesis and make-believe.* New York: Oxford.

Goodwin, M. H. (1990). *He-said-she-said: Talk as social organization among black children.* Bloomington, IN: Indiana University Press.

Goodwin, M. H. (1998). Games of stance: Conflict and footing in hopscotch. In S. Hoyle & C. T. Adger (Eds.), *Language practices of older children* (pp. 23–46). New York: Oxford.

Goodwin, M. H. (2003). The relevance of ethnicity, class, and gender in children's peer negotiations. In Janet Holmes & Miriam Meyerhoff (Eds.), *Handbook of language and gender.* London: Blackwell.

Greenwood, A. (1998). Accomodating friends: Niceness, meanness, and discourse norms. In S. M. Hoyle & C. T. Adger (Eds.), *Kids talk: Strategic language use in later childhood.* New York: Oxford University Press.

Harkness, S., & Super, C. (1992). Shared child care in East Africa: Sociocultural origins and developmental consequences. In M. Lamb, K. Sternberg, C. Hwang, & A. Broberg (Eds.), *Child care in context: Cross cultural perspectives* (pp. 441–459). Hillsdale, NJ: Lawrence Erlbaum.

Harris, J. (1998). *The nurture assumption.* New York: Free Press.

Hecht, T. (1998). *At home in the street: Street children of northeast Brazil.* Cambridge: Cambridge University Press.

Hernandez, D. (1995). *America's children: Resources from family, government and the economy.* New York: Russell Sage.

Hine, T. (1999). *The rise and fall of the American teenager.* New York: Harper Collins.

Hofferth, S. (1995). Caring for children at the poverty line. *Children and Youth Services Review, 17,* 61–90.

Hofferth, S., & Sandberg, J. (2001). How American children spend their time. *Journal of Marriage and the Family, 63,* 295–308.

Holmes, R. M. (1995). *How young children perceive race* (vol. 12) J. H. Stanfield, II. (Ed.). Thousand Oaks, CA: Sage.

Hoyle, S. M. (1998). Register and footing in role play. In S. M. Hoyle & C. T. Adger (Eds.), *Kids talk: Strategic language use in later childhood* (pp. 47–67). New York: Oxford University Press.

Inkeles, A. (1986). Society, social structure, and child socialization. In J. Clausen (Ed.), *Socialization and society* (pp. 73–129). Boston: Little Brown.

James, A. (1995). Talking of children and youth: Language, socialization, and culture. In V. Amit-Talai & H. Wulff (Eds.), *Youth cultures: A cross-cultural perspective* (pp. 43–62). London: Routledge.

James, A. (2000). Embodied being(s): Understanding the self and the body in childhood. In A. Prout (Ed.), *The body, childhood and society* (pp. 19–37). New York: St. Martins Press.

James, A., Jenks, C., & Prout, A. (1998). *Theorizing childhood.* New York: Teachers College Press.

Kinder, M. (Ed.). (1999). *Kids' media culture.* Durham, NC: Duke University Press.

Kohn, M. (1969). *Class and conformity: A study in values.* Homewood, IL: Dorsey.

Kyratzis, A., & Guo, J. (2001). Preschool girls' and boys' verbal conflict strategies in the United States and China. *Research on Language and Social Interaction, 34,* 45–74.

Ladd, G., & Price, J. (1987). Predicting children's social and school adjustment following the transition from preschool to kindergarten. *Child Development, 58,* 1168–1189.

Lansdown, G. (1994). Children's rights. In B. Mayall (Ed.), *Children's childhoods: Observed and experienced* (pp. 33–44). London: Falmer Press.

Lee, J., & Sasser-Coen, J. (1996). *Blood stories: Menarche and the politics of the female body in contemporary society.* New York: Routledge.

Lees, S. (1993). *Sugar and spice: Sexuality and adolescent girls.* London: Penguin Books.

Lerner, R. (1998). Theories of human development: Contemporary perspectives. In R. Lerner (Ed.), *Handbook of Child Psychology* (vol. 1, pp. 1–24). New York: Wiley.

Lever, J. (1976). Sex differences in the games children play. *Social Problems, 23*, 478–487.

Males, M. (1996). *The scapegoat generation.* Monroe, ME: Common Courage Press.

Martin, K. A. (1998). Becoming a gendered body: Practices of preschools. *American Sociological Review, 63*, 494–511.

Mayall, B. (2000). Conversations with children: Working with generational issues. In P. Christensen & A. James (Eds.), *Research with children: Perspectives and practices* (pp. 120–135). London: Falmer Press.

Mead, G. H. (1934). *Mind, self, and society.* Chicago: University of Chicago Press.

Messner, M. A. (2000). Barbie girls versus sea monsters: Children constructing gender. *Gender & Society, 14*, 765–784.

Miller, P. (1986). Teasing as language socialization and verbal play in a white, working class community. In B. Schieffelin & E. Ochs (Eds.), *Language and Socialization Across Cultures* (pp. 199–212). New York: Cambridge University Press.

Miller, P., Wiley, A., Fung, H., & Liang, C. (1997). Personal storytelling as a medium of socialization in Chinese and American families. *Child Development, 68*, 557–568.

Morrow, V. (1995). Invisible children? Toward a reconceptualization of childhood dependency and responsibility. In N. Mandell (Ed.), *Sociological studies of children* (vol. 7, pp. 207–230). Greenwich, CT: JAI Press.

Mussati, T., & Panni, S. (1981). Social behavior and interaction among day care center toddlers. *Early Child Development and Care, 7*, 5–27.

Nsamenang, A. (1992). Early childhood care and education in Cameroon. In M. Lamb, K. Sternberg, C. Hwang, & A. Broberg (Eds.), *Child care in context: Cross cultural perspectives* (pp. 441–449). Hillsdale, NJ: Lawrence Erlbaum.

Oakley, A. (1994). Women and children first and last: Parallels and differences between children's and women's studies. In B. Mayall (Ed.), *Children's childhoods: Observed and experienced* (pp. 13–32). London: Falmer Press.

O'Kane, C. (2000). The development of participatory techniques: Facilitating children's views about decisions which affect them. In P. Christensen & A. James (Eds.), *Research with children: Perspectives and practices* (pp. 136–159), & London: Falmer Press.

Parsons, T., & Bales, R. (1955). *Family, socialization, and interaction process.* New York: Free Press.

Piaget, J. (1950). *The psychology of intelligence.* London: Routledge & Kegan Paul.

Peterson, P. (1999). *Gray dawn.* New York: Random House.

Plank, S. (2000). *Finding one's place: Teaching styles and peer relations in diverse classrooms.* New York: Teachers College Press.

Plomin, R., & Daniels, D. (1987). Why are children in the same family so different from one another? *Behavioral and Brain Sciences, 10*, 1–60.

Pontecorvo, C., Fasulo, A., & Sterponi, L. (2001). Mutual apprentices: The making of parenthood and childhood in family dinner conversations. *Human Development, 44*, 340–361.

Prout, A. (2000). Childhood bodies: Construction, agency and hybridity. In A. Prout (Ed.), *The body, childhood and society* (pp. 1–18). New York: St. Martin's Press.

Qvortrup, J. (1991). Childhood as a social phenomenon: An introduction to a series of national reports. *Eurosocial Report No. 36.* Vienna, Austria: European Centre for Social Welfare Policy and Research.

Qvortrup, J. (1994). Childhood matters: An introduction. In J. Qvortrup, M. Bardy, G. Sgritta, & H. Wintersberger (Eds.), *Childhood matters: Social theory, practice, and politics* (pp. 1–23). Brookfield, VT: Ashgate Publishing Company.

Rainwater, L., & Smeeding, T. (1995). Doing poorly: The real income of American children in a comparative perspective. Luxembourg Income Study Working Paper Number 127. Walferdange, Luxembourg.

Rimm-Kaufman, S. & Pianta, R. (2000). An ecological perspective on the transition to kindergarten: A theoretical framework to guide empirical research. *Journal of Applied Developmental Psychology, 21*, 491–511.

Rizzo, Thomas A. (1989). *Friendship development among children in school.* Norwood, NJ: Ablex.

Roberts, H. (2000). Listening to children: And hearing them. In P. Christensen & A. James (Eds.), *Research with children: Perspectives and practices* (pp. 225–240). London: Falmer Press.

Roche, J. (1996). The politics of children's rights. In J. Brannen & M. O'Brien (Eds.), *Children in families: Research and policy* (pp. 26–40). London: Falmer Press.

Rogoff, B. (1990). *Apprenticeship in thinking: Cognitive development in social context.* New York: Oxford University Press.

Rogoff, B. (1995). Observing sociocultural activity on three planes: Participatory appropriation, guided participation, and apprenticeship. In J. V. Wertsch, P. Del Río, & A. Alvarez (Eds.), *Sociocultural studies of mind* (pp. 139–164). New York: Cambridge University Press.

Rogoff, B. (1996). Developmental transitions in children's participation in sociocultural activities. In A. Sameroff & M. Haith (Eds.), *The five to seven year shift* (pp. 273–294). Chicago: University of Chicago Press.

Rogoff, B., Mosier, C., Mistry, J., & Göncü, A. (1989). Toddlers' guided participation in cultural activity. *Cultural Dynamics, 2,* 209–237.

Rogoff, B., Tukanis, C., & Bartlett, L. (2001). *Learning together: Children and adults in a school community.* New York: Oxford.

Rosier, K. (2000). *Mothering inner-city children: The early school years.* New Brunswick, NJ: Rutgers University Press.

Rosier, K., & Corsaro, W. (1993). Competent parents: Complex lives. *Journal of Contemporary Ethnography, 22,* 171–204.

Sacks, C. H. (2001). Interracial relationships and racial identity processes in an urban mother-and-child rehabilitation program. *Sociological Studies of Children and Youth, 8,* 43–68.

Sawyer, R. K. (1997). *Pretend play as improvisation.* Mahwah, NJ: Lawrence Erlbaum.

Scott, J. (1997). Children as respondents: Methods for improving data quality. In L. Lyberg, P. Biemer, M. Collins, E. D. Leeuw, C. Dippo, N. Schwarz, & D. Trewin (Eds.), *Survey Measurement and Process Quality* (pp. 331–350). New York: John Wiley & Sons.

Scott, J. (2000). Children as respondents: The challenge for quantitative methods. In P. Christensen & A. James (Eds.), *Research with children: Perspectives and practices* (pp. 98–119). London: Falmer Press.

Sgritta, G. (1994). The generational division of welfare: Equity and conflict. In J. Qvortrup, M. Bardy, G. Sgritta, & H. Wintersberger (Eds.), *Childhood matters: Social theory, practice, and politics* (pp. 335–362). Brookfield, VT: Ashgate Publishing Company.

Seiter, E. (1993). *Sold separately: Parents & children in consumer culture.* New Brunswick, NJ: Rutgers University Press.

Simpson, B. (2000). Regulation and resistance: Children's embodiment during the primary–secondary school transition. In A. Prout (Ed.), *The body, childhood and society* (pp. 60–78). New York: St. Martin's Press.

Solberg, A. (1997). Negotiating childhood: Changing constructions of age for Norwegian children. In A. James & A. Prout (Eds.), *Constructing and reconstructing childhood: Contemporary issues in the sociological study of childhood* (pp. 34–62). London: Falmer Press.

Song, M. (1996). "Helping out": Children's labour participation in Chinese take-away business in Britain. In J. Brannen & M. O'Brien (Eds.), *Children in families: Research and policy* (pp. 101–113). London: Falmer Press.

Steinberg, L. Dornbusch, S., & Brown, B. (1992). Ethnic differences in adolescent achievement: An ecological perspective. *American Psychologist, 47,* 723–729.

Steinberg, S., & J. Kincheloe (Eds.). (1997). *Kinder-culture: The corporate construction of childhood.* Boulder, CO: Westview Press.

Tesson, G., & Youniss, J. (1995). Micro-sociology and psychological development: A sociological interpretation of Piaget's theory. In A. Ambert (Ed.), *Sociological studies of children* (vol. 7, pp. 101–126). Greenwich, CT: JAI Press.

Thelen E., & Smith, L. (1998). Dynamic systems theories. In R. Lerner (Ed.), *Handbook of child psychology* (vol. 1, pp. 563–634). New York: Wiley.

Thorne, B. (1987). Re-visioning women and social change: Where are the children? *Gender & Society, 1,* 85–109.

Thorne, B. (1993). *Gender play: Girls and boys in school.* New Brunswick, NJ: Rutgers University Press.

Tobin, J. (2000). *"Good boys don't wear hats": Children's talk about the media.* New York: Teachers College Press.

Tronick, E., Morelli, G., & Winn, S. (1987). Multiple caretaking of Efe (Pygmy) infants. *American Anthropologist, 89,* 96–106.

Tynes, S. R. (2001). The colors of the rainbow: Children's racial self-classification. *Sociological Studies of Children and Youth, 8,* 69–85.

Van Ausdale, D., & Feagin, J. (2001). *The first R: How children learn race and racism.* Lanham, MD: Rowan & Littlefield.

Vygotsky, L. (1978). *Mind in society.* Cambridge, MA: Harvard University Press.

Wertsch, J. (1998). *Mind as action.* New York: Oxford University Press.

Williams, S. J., & Bendelow, G. A. (1998). Malignant bodies: Children's beliefs about health, cancer and risk. In S. Nettleton & J. Watson (Eds.), *The body in everyday life* (pp. 103–123). London: Routledge.

Winterhoff, Paul A. (1997). Sociocultural promotions constraining children's social activity: Comparisons and variability in the development of friendships. In J. Tudge, M. Shanahan, & J. Valsiner (Eds.), *Comparisons in human development: Understanding time and context* (pp. 222–251). New York: Cambridge University Press.

Zelizer, V. (1985). *Pricing the priceless child: The changing social value of children.* New York: Basic Books.

CHAPTER 7

Socialization in Adolescence

DONNA EDER
SANDI KAWECKA NENGA

Early investigations of adolescent socialization envisioned adolescents passively and individually receiving knowledge and skills from adults. More recently, scholars have argued that adolescent socialization is an active, collective process in which adolescents interact with each other and adults to "produce their own worlds and peer cultures, and eventually come to reproduce, to extend, and to join the adult world" (Corsaro & Eder, 1995, p. 444). Here, we review different theoretical approaches scholars have used to study adolescent socialization. Then, we discuss research on adolescent socialization within the contexts of family, school, and peer groups.

THEORETICAL PERSPECTIVES

Life Course

One theoretical perspective shaping investigations into adolescence is the life course perspective. This perspective views individuals as moving through different stages of the life course on a trajectory marked by events. Events mark the transition from one life stage to another, and significant events, known as turning points, signal drastic changes in individual trajectories. Individuals move into, through, and out of adolescence, and this movement may be punctuated by key events such as the first day at middle school, first job, graduation, and first sexual experience. Life course scholars scrutinize both the sequence and timing of such

DONNA EDER AND SANDI KAWECKA NENGA • Department of Sociology, Indiana University, Bloomington, IN 47405-7103

Handbook of Social Psychology, edited by John Delamater. Kluwer Academic/Plenum Publishers, New York, 2003.

key events. For example, they may question how an adolescent whose first work experience is at 14 before leaving school fares compared to an adolescent whose first work experience is at 18 after leaving school (Elder, 1974, 1985a).

To capture the intersection of history and biography, life course scholars use three concepts: age, period, and cohort. As the example above suggests, life course scholars assume that the *age* of an individual at the time of a key event can change the experience and consequences of that event. Second, the historical context affects the nature of key events, and life course scholars assume that adolescents in different historical *periods* will experience the same event differently. An adolescent whose first job is during World War II, for example, will have a different experience than an adolescent whose first job is during the 1990s. The third concept, *cohort*, is often inextricably tangled with period and age. Cohorts refer to groups of age peers and are often referred to as a generation, as in Generation X (Giele & Elder, 1998). The shared experience of a peer group entering the workforce at the same time may also affect an individual's experience of a first job.

Life course scholars investigating adolescence most commonly focus on the transition from adolescence to adulthood. The key events marking this transition include leaving school, leaving a childhood home, full-time employment, marriage, and parenthood (Shanahan, 2000). Life course scholars in this area have examined such varied topics as the sequence of school leaving, work, and marriage (Modell, 1989), trajectories into and out of juvenile delinquency (Sampson & Laub, 1993), and the timing of war mobilization for young men (Elder, 1987). Because of its longitudinal approach, the life course perspective is useful for overcoming the static portrait painted by cross-sectional studies and capturing the complexities of socialization over time. Although life course studies need not focus on outcomes, many do conceptualize the teenager as a future adult and focus largely on how various events in adolescence impact adult outcomes.

Social and Cultural Reproduction

Another theoretical perspective which influences research on adolescent socialization is the social and cultural reproduction perspective. This approach emphasizes the strong influence of social class, ethnicity, and gender on adolescents' experiences as mediated through school and family processes. Bowles and Gintis (1976) focused primarily on the role of schooling in their initial development of the social reproduction of class differences. According to them, schooling socializes students differently based on their social class background, preparing them for their place in the occupational hierarchy. While students from lower class backgrounds are more likely to be taught conformity and subordination to authority, students from higher class backgrounds are more likely to be taught how to internalize norms and affiliate with others. Importantly, all students are taught to view social hierarchies as normative through routine participation in curriculum tracking, ability grouping, and other academic ranking practices. Differential effects by social class might occur across schools as well as within schools in the form of different experiences in curriculum tracks (Metz, 1978; Oakes, 1985). Later research using this approach was applied to gender and ethnic differences in formal and informal schooling (Kessler, Ashenden, Connell, & Dowsett, 1985; MacLeod, 1995; Valenzuela, 1999).

Cultural reproduction theory—also known as cultural capital theory—emphasizes differences that students bring *to* the school setting as a result of unequal access to cultural resources ranging from certain communication styles to museum visits and music lessons

(Bourdieu & Passeron, 1977). According to Bourdieu and Passeron, school personnel view certain cultural styles as more legitimate and, without realizing it, teachers tend to give preference to students who use these styles. In this way, schools again play a crucial role in reproducing current social inequities.

Early research on this theory focused primarily on younger students, showing how teachers reproduce ethnic inequality by focusing on certain communication styles when evaluating students' performances or assigning them to ability groups (Heath, 1983; Philips, 1972). Other research found strong social class differences in parental involvement in schooling due to a variety of factors from intimidation to lack of participation in informal networks (Lareau, 1989). At the high school level, DiMaggio (1982) found that participation in prestigious status cultures had a positive impact on grades. Specifically, he found that students who perform, attend arts events, and express greater interest in the arts were more likely to have higher academic grades.

While this theory illuminates how structural factors unequally affect adolescents' lives, it has been criticized for its overly deterministic view of society as well as for underestimating the active and innovative capabilities of adolescents (Corsaro & Eder, 1995; Mehan, Hubbard, & Villanueva, 1994). This perspective fails to show how other school practices besides tracking can counteract structural inequalities, and it cannot account for the reflexive relationship between social constraints and social agency.

Subcultural Approaches

Subcultural approaches to adolescent socialization provide one account of the relationship between social constraints and social agency. Parsons (1951) first introduced the term "youth subculture" to characterize the distinctive and often oppositional values, ideas, and symbols shared by adolescents. Throughout the 20th century, American scholars typically used the concept to explain juvenile delinquency committed by male, urban, underclass teenagers (Brake, 1985; Epstein, 1994).

In the 1970s, scholars at the Birmingham Centre for Contemporary Cultural Studies (CCCS) took the term in a new direction. Groups of working-class teenage boys in Britain wearing flamboyant, recognizable styles had caught the scholarly eyes of CCCS researchers. The groups, including punks, mods, and teddy boys, defined themselves using clothing, music, and argot. Their rebellious and creative styles appeared to challenge, if only obliquely, dominant ideas and values (Hebdige, 1979).

Drawing on Marxist thought, CCCS scholars theorized the conditions under which such oppositional styles formed. They defined subcultures as "meaning systems, modes of expression or lifestyles developed by groups in subordinate structural positions in response to dominant meaning systems, and which reflect their attempt to solve structural contradictions arising from the wider societal context" (Brake, 1985, p. 8). Subcultures, in this approach, arise in response to two adult cultures: the hegemonic culture representing the interests of the dominant class, and the "parent" culture of working-class adults. The clash between these two adult cultures creates the structural, material, and ideological contradictions to which subcultures respond. The subcultural response, in this theory, is always consciously oppositional. Youth use cultural elements, such as music, fashion, and language, to satirize and resist the dominant cultures' values.

For example, Willis' (1981) ethnography of a group of working-class boys documents the "lads'" subculture. The high school is part of the hegemonic culture and reinforces values such as diligence, deference, and respect. The "parent" culture of working-class adults promotes values such as chauvinism, toughness, and street smarts. Caught between these two cultures, the lads develop a counter-school culture which uses cigarettes, alcohol, and clothing to mark their opposition to school authority and to gain informal control over their routines and spaces. Willis (1981) documents how the counter-school culture actually facilitates working-class lads' movement into working-class jobs and the reproduction of shopfloor culture, belying the potential resistance of the subculture.

Subcultural analyses often focus more on the group than the individual, and groups are presented as internally homogenous and easily distinguished from one another. Wulff (1988) has argued that this approach obscures the commonalities between groups and the considerable diversity within groups. She views culture as something that is *distributed* among people in a group, with some individuals reflecting certain meanings more strongly through their personalities than other individuals.

The initial focus on subcultural resistance may have been facilitated by the early tendency of CCCS scholars to conduct semiotic analyses of the most visible youth subcultures. McRobbie (1991) critiqued the prominence of boys in subcultural work, resulting from boys' ability to congregate in public places like streets, and suggested that girls develop less visible subcultures centered in more private spaces such as bedrooms and youth clubs. More recent ethnographic work has examined the ways in which subcultural activity is tied to nondeviant behavior and consumer culture as well as resistance (Epstein, 1998; Gaines, 1991; Gelder & Thornton, 1997).

Interpretive

The interpretive approach to adolescent socialization emphasizes the collective, public nature of developing cultural meanings. Growing out of interactionist approaches that showed how meanings are defined and shaped within social interaction (Mead, 1934), the interpretive perspective adds an important structural component by examining the reflexive relationship between structure and agency (Cicourel, 1974; Corsaro, 1985; Giddens, 1984). This approach views adolescents as active agents, capable of constructing their own shared understandings. This means that adolescents do not passively conform to the roles and norms of adults or to structural inequalities in schooling, but that they challenge them while creating their own social identities and subcultures.

As in the life course approach, interpretive approaches note that individuals participate in different subcultures at each stage of life. However, the interpretive approach sees development as a productive–reproductive process rather than a linear one (Corsaro, 1985; Corsaro & Eder, 1995). While adolescents draw upon their own experiences in earlier childhood cultures, they, in turn, shape and influence the childhood cultures of those younger than them. Likewise, adolescents' cultural knowledge reflects the beliefs of the adult world while also containing unique interpretations which have the potential of influencing adult culture.

Adolescents' participation in cultural routines is an essential aspect of the interpretive approach. Because routines, such as greetings, insult exchanges, and gossip, are recurrent and predictable activities, they provide actors with the security and shared understanding of belonging to a cultural group (Giddens, 1984). At the same time, this very familiarity provides frames in which a range of cultural knowledge can be explored, displayed, and interpreted (Giddens, 1984; Goffman, 1974). Research has shown how the predictable nature of routines allows children to participate readily in conversations with peers while providing opportunities for embellishments and creative adaptations (Corsaro, 1985; Corsaro & Rizzo, 1988). Adolescents use familiar language routines of gossip, insulting, teasing, and collective narratives both to reproduce adult beliefs as well as to creatively explore new meanings regarding gender and other aspects of adolescent life (Eder, Evans, & Parker, 1995; Everhart, 1983; Labov, 1972; Shuman, 1986).

This approach goes beyond other longitudinal perspectives such as the life course approach by focusing on the processes by which meanings are constructed at different stages of the life course. It emphasizes the collective, emergent nature of the socialization process. The interpretive perspective also addresses some of the limitations of reproduction theories. While acknowledging the impact of structural factors on adolescents' lives, it allows for the possibility of adolescents and other social agents taking an active role in counteracting or modifying structural forces. Finally, while the interpretive approach is similar in many respects to subcultural perspectives, this approach considers a variety of responses to social structure besides oppositional and resistance practices. Although we see the interpretive approach as the most useful approach to the study of adolescents, we do not see these four theoretical approaches as incompatible. Each perspective can draw on the strengths of others. For example, research using the interpretive perspective is strongest when it considers key transitions and processes over time as the life course perspective does, variation within and between groups as subcultural approaches do, and structural factors related to inequality as the social and cultural reproduction approach does.

SOCIALIZATION IN THE FAMILY

Research on adolescent socialization in the family is largely focused on how parenting produces academic and psychological outcomes. Although the influence of parents begins to decrease during early adolescence, most adolescents continue to report high levels of attachment to parents (Kandel & Lesser, 1972; Youniss & Smollar, 1985). The type of influence and level of attachment varies depending on parenting styles and the parent's gender. In addition, recent studies have examined how socioeconomic status (SES), ethnicity, and family structure play a role in strengthening or weakening parental influence.

Certain parenting styles have been found to influence adolescents' academic achievements and self-confidence. Parental monitoring and efforts to include adolescents in joint decision making increases academic performance (Dornbusch, Ritter, Leiderman, Roberts, & Fraleigh, 1987). In addition, participation in joint decision making enhances adolescents' self-confidence (Grotevant & Cooper, 1986). A democratic, rather than authoritarian, parenting style leads to adolescents having the best sense of parental expectations as well as considering the expectations to be neither too high nor too low (Elder, 1985b).

Youniss and Smollar (1985) identified several differences in the ways fathers and mothers relate to their adolescent daughters and sons, leading to different levels and forms of attachment. Their findings revealed that most father–daughter interactions are asymmetrical and consist of rule making, rule enforcing, and giving advice and practical information. In contrast, daughters are more likely to confide in personal matters with their mothers, receiving personal as well as practical advice. The most common type of interaction between fathers and sons involve recreational or work-related instrumental activities, showing that sons benefit by having more shared interests with their fathers than do daughters. Sons, like daughters, are more likely to confide in their mothers.

Researchers have expanded the study of family socialization to include differences by social class. Past research has shown that socioeconomic status is strongly related to parents' involvement in elementary school children's education, with middle-class parents participating more than working-class parents (Lareau, 1989). However, in a study at the junior high level Sui-Chu and Willms (1996) found only small effects of SES on parents' discussion of school activities, contact with school personnel, and participation in school events. They found no difference by social class in parental supervision of adolescents' school work.

Sui-Chu and Willms' (1996) study of eighth grade students also dispels the belief that non-White parents are generally less involved in their children's schooling than White parents. They found that Black parents had slightly higher levels of supervision of school work, discussion of school activities with adolescents, and contact with school personnel than White parents, while being similar to Whites in school participation. Hispanic parents had slightly higher levels of supervision of school work than White parents and were similar on other measures of school involvement. Interestingly, while Asian parents also had higher levels of supervision of school work than White parents, they were lower than Whites on the other measures of school involvement. However, the overall picture is one in which parents of all races have approximately equal levels of school involvement.

Other studies using more in-depth methods report similar findings and provide a broader understanding of the differential effects of ethnicity on parenting. A case study of a Vietnamese American family found that language and cultural barriers often deter parents from greater school involvement (Phelan, Davidson, & Yu, 1998). At the same time many Vietnamese American adolescents' high academic achievement is influenced by the strong value which parents place on the "learned individual" as well as by an ethic of bringing honor to one's family through academic performance. Another case study of three African American families found that the adolescent from a middle-class family had a closer fit with school values than did those from working-class families. The family of one working-class female valued cooperation over individual pursuits while the family of a working-class male pressured him to not "sell out" by speaking standard English (Hemmings, 1998).

More research is needed on other ways in which race influences adolescent socialization in the family. The few studies that have examined this topic suggest that some Asian families have much greater concern about supervising the social life of their daughters than their sons, often restricting their freedom so that they feel they are missing out on important social events. This has been found among Vietnamese Americans in the United States (Phelan et al., 1998) as well as among Sikhs living in Britain (Hall, 1995). These studies suggest that such cultural differences in parenting contribute to adolescents' difficulties communicating with parents and greater reliance on friends for support. In contrast, some Mexican girls report extremely close friendships with their mothers and discuss the same topics with them that they do with peers (Phelan et al., 1998). Further research is needed to understand how ethnicity enhances or weakens communication between adolescents and their parents, and how these patterns reflect differences between family and peer cultures.

Finally, there is a growing body of research on the influence of family structure on adolescents' academic achievements and other aspects of their well-being. Among the benefits of having a two-parent household was the greater likelihood of parental involvement in school and supervision of homework (McLanahan, 1985; Sui-Chu & Willms, 1996). However, the belief that adolescents benefit from having a same-sex single parent has been challenged by a study which found few differences between adolescents raised by a same-sex versus opposite-sex parent (Powell & Downey, 1997). The only negative effects of an opposite-sex parent were a greater likelihood of dropping out of school for boys and a greater likelihood of smoking and having a weaker locus of control for girls.

While the presence of many siblings in a family has been found to be a strain on the financial and personal resources of parents, the results depend on a variety of factors. The overall effect of more siblings is lower grades, test scores, and rates of college attendance, although this effect is stronger if the siblings are brothers (Downey, 1995; Powell & Steelman, 1990). In addition, because first born children are more likely to talk to their parents about school while latter born children are more likely to receive financial assistance for post-secondary schooling, the impact of siblings varies by birth order (Powell & Steelman, 1993).

The research reviewed here focused primarily on how parenting affects adolescents. Less is known about the *experiences* of adolescents with siblings and other family members. In one of the few studies of sibling relations, Handel (1986) found that solidarity between siblings is enhanced when they perceive they are being treated equitably. However, he also found that equity among siblings is continually challenged by age differences and the tendency for some siblings to want to exercise power over others. More research is needed to understand how adolescents interact with parents, siblings, and other relatives.

SOCIALIZATION IN SCHOOLS

The Transition to Middle and Junior High School

For most adolescents school settings are an important context for developing friendships and social skills as well as for academic learning. As students move from elementary into middle or junior high schools they are suddenly confronted with a much larger group of same-age peers, averaging five times greater in size (Simmons & Blyth, 1987). Middle and junior high students have lower self-esteem, less stable self-images, and greater self-consciousness than do younger or older youth (Simmons, Rosenberg, & Rosenberg, 1973). Simmons and Blyth (1987) found that girls who entered a junior high in 7th grade have much lower self-esteem compared to those who remained in elementary school settings. Both boys and girls are less likely to participate in extracurricular activities in the junior high setting as compared to the elementary school setting. Other research has found that the effects of entry into junior high school are most negative for children who lack stable friendships during this transition (Berndt, 1989).

Simmons and Blyth (1987) also examined the long-term consequences of attending a junior high instead of remaining in an elementary school. Students who attended a junior high continue to show similar disadvantages in high school compared to those who remained in elementary schools, with girls having lower self-esteem and both girls and boys being less likely to participate in extracurricular activities. Although one could argue that an early transition into a large school environment might better prepare students for later transition into high school, their findings support the interpretation that this transition may come too soon developmentally or be so stressful that it puts students at a disadvantage for their next transition.

The Social Worlds of Middle School

In-depth studies of middle schools offer additional understanding as to why this type of environment may be disadvantageous for adolescents, especially for girls (Eder, 1985; Eder et al., 1995; Merten, 1997). The large number of same-age peers along with the limited number of extracurricular activities promotes a unidimensional hierarchy of cliques. Since status at this age is based on "being known" by peers, students who participate in activities that draw large groups of spectators are much more visible than other students. In middle school, and in many high schools, male athletics provide boys with both visibility and status (Cusick, 1973; Eder & Parker, 1987; Karweit & Hansell, 1983). Due to the large number of spectators at male athletic events, female cheerleaders also have increased visibility and status (Eder et al., 1995; Merten, 1997). In addition, girls are able to gain entry into elite groups through friendships with popular girls and through their attractiveness to high status boys.

This focus on social relations as an important avenue for status for girls as compared to boys may help explain why both junior high and middle school environments lead to lower self-esteem in girls but not boys. Since girls rely in part on friendships to gain status, while boys rely on athletic achievements, it is not surprising that girls become increasingly concerned with being well-liked when they enter middle or junior high school. Because social status is so closely tied to friendships, girls who become popular often become the targets of negative sentiment when they fail to respond to all the overtures they receive (Eder, 1985a; Eder et al., 1995). This cycle of popularity means that even popular girls face negative sentiments that could prove harmful to their self-images.

In addition, Merten's (1997) research in an upper middle-class suburb found that junior high popular girls direct much of their hostile or mean behavior toward other girls in the high status group rather than toward students outside the group. In this school the competition for social status was very strong. As certain girls advanced in the social hierarchy, other high status girls sought to undermine their new status through a variety of indirect but hostile behaviors. Because of their high status these girls were able to get away with considerable meanness and even received peer support, showing how junior high girls can transfer popularity into a form of social power.

While females appear to show the most negative consequences from attending junior high or middle schools, both females and males later complain about the extreme hierarchal nature of this environment. They report that because only a small number of students can join the elite groups, everyone else feels like "dweebs" or social failures (Kinney, 1993). This is partly due to the fact that there are fewer extracurricular activities available per student at middle school than in the upper grades of elementary school or in most high schools (Kinney, 1993; Simmons & Blyth, 1987). Also, both males and females show a drop in social competence upon entry into junior high and while self-esteem was found to rebound by the end of seventh grade for these students, feelings of social competence did not (Eccles, Wigfield, Flanagan, Miller, Reuman, & Yee, 1989).

Middle and junior high school environments appear to increase social anxieties for many students. However, the students who may be most negatively affected are those who fail to form friendships with their peers. Those students who are perceived to be unattractive, less intelligent (typically those in special education), and/or deviant in regard to gender roles often may not be accepted by their peers for fear of being associated with these perceived undesirable characteristics (Eder et al., 1995; Evans & Eder, 1993). These students are often the targets of considerable ridicule as other students try to establish greater social distance from them or use them as outlets to help relieve their own sense of social inadequacy.

Research indicates that different middle school structures can produce very different social environments with important implications for intergroup contact. Damico and Sparks (1986) compared two middle schools, one in which students were stratified by grade and ability level and one in which the students were randomly assigned to learning teams which were diverse in terms of grade, ability, race, and gender. Also, in the latter school classroom instruction consisted of a combination of multi-task, individual, and cooperative learning as compared to the use of a recitation format in the more traditional school. White students in the traditionally structured school interacted less with Black students than they did in the school with mixed teams. In the mixed-team school, Whites talked to Blacks as much as they talked to other Whites and had more cross-racial friendships. The nature of talk between races was also more reciprocal in this school, whereas in the traditional school Blacks talked to whites more often than Whites talked to Blacks.

In another study of a Mexican middle school, Levinson (1998) found few social divisions in peer groups due to both organizational practices and school discourses promoting solidarity. Students in this school were assigned to small groups of 36–45 students that were designed to be heterogeneous by academic ability, social class, ethnicity, and gender. The students stayed with these groups for 3 years for most of their classes as well as for many extracurricular activities. The teachers continually spoke of the need to help each other academically and socially and in other ways emphasized the importance of group solidarity. While a few friendships formed around social class and ethnic backgrounds, most of the lasting friendships were formed in these small groups and transcended boundaries of social class and ethnicity. More research is needed to examine the implications of different organizational practices in middle school for both intergroup contact and students' academic and emotional experiences.

The Social Worlds of High School

By high school, clearly defined subcultures exist including "preppies" or "jocks," "druggies" or "burnouts," "normals," and "grits" to name a few (Eckert, 1989; Kinney, 1999; Lesko, 1988). Some of these subcultures such as "preppies" continue to rely on school activities for their visibility and are viewed by school staff and certain students as the elite group. However, by high school there is much less consensus about peer values and many other groups claim elite status either through visibility in dress and behavior ("druggies," "headbangers," "punks," and "hippies") or through participation in other school activities ("normals," "band people," and "politicos") (Kinney, 1993, 1999; Larkin, 1979).

Subcultures of resistance play a greater role at the high school level. Willis (1981) found that working-class boys in England place more value on fighting skills, humor, and defiance of authority. As they continued to seek greater control over time and space, informal peer groups became the center of their interest and excitement while at school. Studies of female subcultures have found that working-class girls, as compared to boys, tend to engage in less overt and visible acts of resistance, such as skipping school and classes, reading magazines and passing notes during class, and goofing off when the teacher is gone (Griffin, 1985; Wulff, 1988). Instead of valuing academics, they tend to value nonconformity, excitement, pleasure, and being "grown-up" (i.e., being sexually developed, having boyfriends, and having more adult responsibilities).

Besides resisting the adult academic culture of school, other subcultures resist the *social* norms of the school-sponsored elite groups, viewing these students as being overly materialistic and too concerned with social trends (Eckert, 1988; Kinney, 1999; Lesko, 1988). The resistance of social as well as academic norms contributes to the more complex social hierarchies found in many large high schools. These diverse subcultures and stratification processes may help prepare adolescents for the complex stratification processes of adult life in which there also are elite groups, as well as many subcultures, which resist the values of elite groups and mainstream culture.

Many subcultures within schools are segregated by social class and ethnicity. However, some high school subcultures provide opportunities for adolescents to cross racial and social class boundaries (Gotto, 1997; Hemmings, 1998; Proweller, 1998). Because of the diversity across subcultures, Gotto (1997) found that Chinese Americans' experience in high school reflects the subcultures they join. While some Chinese American students join racially homogeneous peer groups and focus primarily on academic performance, others form friendships with African Americans and Latinos often through shared participation in sports. For these latter students who came in contact with an anti-academic subculture, being able to move across social groups was more salient than economic mobility.

By high school, the role of extracurricular activities is more complex with important implications for students' sense of belonging and self-esteem. Because athletics and certain social activities continue to provide students with visibility, adolescents throughout the United States tend to place more importance on athletic and social success than on academic success (Brown, 1990; Brown & Lohr, 1987; Goldberg & Chandler, 1989). In their comparison of Danish and American youth, Kandel and Lesser (1972) found that leading crowds were less prominent in Danish high schools, which did not offer extracurricular activities. Also, Danish youth were more likely to want to be remembered as being brilliant students than were the American youth in their study. However, in a study of Australian schools which did offer athletic activities, values promoted through football, such as aggression and toughness, were more salient than academic values, even in the upper-class schools (Kessler et al., 1985).

Extracurricular activities provide students with resources besides visibility, such as special privileges and greater control over time and space (Eckert, 1988). Typically, White middle-class students are most likely to benefit from these privileges (Eckert, 1988; Lesko, 1988). However, in certain urban settings, lower class African American boys were found to be more involved in schools than were lower class White boys through their greater participation in athletics (MacLeod, 1995).

The complexity of extracurricular activities at the high school level is also affected by the wider range of activities offered, providing more students with an opportunity to demonstrate leadership or social competence. For example, in his study of a suburban high school, Larkin (1979) found three distinct elite groups based on their participation in athletics and cheerleading, in student government, and in academic activities. Increased opportunities for involvement at the high school level not only change the basis and nature of status processes, they also help restore the self-esteem of adolescents who felt socially inadequate in middle school (Kinney, 1993, 1999). Through involvement in one of the many available activities, more students are able to feel like they are part of a meaningful social group and develop new social competencies.

Structural factors in high schools, such as the demographic composition, also shape student identities and peer groups. Wexler's (1992) comparative study of three high schools examined how social class composition shaped students' sense of self. Students at a working-class high school were subject to excessive control and discipline by teachers whose work had been routinized and who burned out quickly. Instead of developing a sense of self in relation to caring adults, students focused on creating self-images based on material items such as cars and money. At a professional middle-class high school, students faced intense pressure to get into college and a highly structured educational experience led by teachers who were isolated within academic departments. Wexler charges that these students develop a sense of professionalism about their work, but never develop a sense of self in relation to the larger school or society. Students at the underclass high school Wexler observed experienced tracking and discipline as moral judgments of their self-worth. Students responded by working to reaffirm their self-worth. The racial as well as social class composition of a school can impose certain definitions on students. For example, the elite high school Horvat and Antonio (1999) studied created rituals and rules based on the assumption that all students were White and wealthy. The organizational practices of that high school imposed an "outsider" identity on African American students.

What effect does school context have on the formation of peer group hierarchies? It is not as simple as arguing that, for example, class or racial homogeneity minimize hierarchy. Student hierarchies have been reported at elite academies (Horvat & Antonio, 1999; Proweller, 1998), Catholic high schools (Lesko, 1988), racially homogenous public schools (Valenzuela, 1999), and poor, racially diverse public schools (Hemmings, 1998; Mirón & Lauria, 1998). The groups in these hierarchies may break down into recognized categories, such as Lesko's (1988) "rich and populars," "mellows," and "burnouts," or they may break down into groups by immigrant status, as in Valenzuela's (1999) Latino high school. In many high schools, the hierarchy of groups is arranged along race and class lines (Brantlinger, 1993; Eckert, 1989).

A few recent studies have identified schools where hierarchies, class conflict, and racial tensions are minimal. Some are cases where egalitarianism is evident only on the surface level. For example, the teens at Proweller's (1998) elite girls' academy reported that they have forged such a strong school-based identity that race and class differences did not matter. Race and class did matter, however, in the formation of peer groups. The highest status group was all-White and composed of young women from the wealthiest families although the other two groups were more diverse in terms of race and class. Similarly, Hemmings' (1998) description of two high-achieving African American students at an urban high school with high academic standards revealed a veneer of egalitarianism. The college prep orientation of the high school created a common culture of academic values, language, and the arts. Within this common culture, though, the peer groups were ranked hierarchically by race and class.

Still other cases suggest that egalitarianism can run much deeper. Bettis (1996) described an urban, poor, and racially diverse public high school that lacked a peer group hierarchy. She argued that deindustrialization in the community created a sense of liminality for these students. As the manufacturing jobs in the area disappeared, students at this high school developed a common sense of hopelessness. This, combined with a poor academic reputation, created a communal underdog spirit at the high school that facilitated a collective identity rather than peer group hierarchies. In this liminal period, Bettis argued that racial categories are more fluid, allowing students to claim different parts of multiracial identities over time. With less fixed racial identities, Bettis suggested that racial tension is less prominent in the high school. Mirón and Lauria (1998) reported an egalitarian social world at a different kind of high school, a racially homogenous African American urban magnet school. This high school created a culture where students and teachers mutually strived for a quality education. The high school fostered a sense of Black pride among the students, a caring atmosphere, and cooperation among students. Peer groups formed around extracurricular activities but were not stratified.

Taken together, these studies suggest that schools can impose different identities on students and produce very different peer cultures. Creating a common culture and common school identity seem crucial to reducing social hierarchies among students. However, it is not yet clear why some high schools develop only a veneer of egalitarianism while other schools actually break down hierarchies.

In summary, school settings vary greatly in their impact on students' social experiences. Since many middle schools promote a unidimensional status hierarchy due to limited activities, visibility among peers is often an all-too-scarce resource. High schools have a greater variety of activities which enhance students' self-esteem and sense of belonging. While a few high schools lack social hierarchies altogether, most have a complex status structure with multiple subcultures, many of which resist the official academic and/or social values. More research is needed to better understand the wide range of social experiences and the ways organizational practices at both middle school and high school levels impact these experiences.

SOCIALIZATION IN PEER GROUPS

Peer Relations

Peer relations increase in salience and complexity during adolescence as best friendships become more valued and youth reach out to a wider circle of friends. Many adolescents report that their best friendships are characterized by acceptance, understanding, self-disclosure, and mutual advice (Giordano, 1995; Wulff, 1995; Youniss & Smollar, 1985). Adolescents tend to discuss their problems, feelings, fears, and doubts with best friends rather than parents, and close friendships provide an important opportunity to develop greater self-knowledge through mutual reflection. A study based on high school yearbooks found that best friends also emphasized shared memories and, in many cases, believed that surviving fights and difficulties together had strengthened their friendships (Giordano, 1995). In addition, ethnographies by Wulff (1995) and Merten (1997) indicate that being willing to share secrets and knowing what to keep secret were important ways in which adolescent girls identified their best friends.

The importance of intimacy and openness in friendship increases during adolescence, while the importance of friendship choices based on popularity decreases (Youniss & Smollar, 1985). Loyalty and commitment also become more salient in later adolescence, especially among working-class youth (Bigelow & LaGaipa, 1980; Eckert, 1988; Lesko, 1988). While loyalty and commitment lead to more stable friendships in later adolescence, the structure of certain high schools can lead to less stable friendships. In a study of a working-class neighborhood school in Montreal, Amit-Talai (1995) found that security concerns led administrators to shorten leisure time at school, leading students to develop and change friendships according to changes in their academic and extracurricular schedules.

Peer relations also become increasingly complex in later adolescence as youth become more cognizant of social class, racial, and gender tensions in the larger society. In some public high schools high-income students are viewed as being socially exclusive, materialistic, and snobbish by other students (Brantlinger, 1993; Kinney, 1999). While high-income students deny being elitist, they do report giving in to peer pressure in their selection of friends. In a study of a private girls' school Proweller (1998) found that the students in groups with mixed social class backgrounds viewed those in the elite clique as being motivated entirely by self-interest and as having a sense of entitlement that allowed them to "walk all over people" (Proweller, 1998, p. 77).

Racial differences between African Americans and European Americans serve as the basis for ongoing tensions and fights in many public schools, disrupting the academic atmosphere (Hemmings, 1998; Mirón & Lauria, 1998). In other public schools, Vietnamese Americans and Mexican Americans reported that their White friends frequently make fun of recent Asian immigrants and Mexican Americans, calling them stupid and putting them down in other ways (Phelan, Davidson, & Yu, 1993, 1998). In the private school Proweller (1998) studied, racial tensions also existed. While Blacks felt that White students did not want to hear their perspectives in class, Whites felt that they could not express their opinions without being labeled racist. However, because violence was not tolerated in this predominantly upper middle-class environment, Proweller notes that Black students were able to more openly express their views on racism without fearing violent reprisals.

Even in environments where racial tensions exist, both Whites and Blacks take on aspects of the others' culture. In Proweller's (1998) study, Whites viewed Black styles as being more exotic and sensual, freeing them from the constraints of a White, middle-class culture while Blacks saw White styles as being more accepted in this academic setting. Both Whites and Blacks were criticized by peers for acting "White" (as Blacks) or "Black" (as Whites). However, in Wulff's (1995) study of an interracial group of friends there was little tension between races and no negative reaction to adopting each other's styles of dress and appearance. Instead, this group of teenage girls cultivated an aesthetic of ethnic equality through their clothing, jewelry, hairstyle, make-up, and music.

Gender tensions can also emerge in early adolescent peer culture where sexual aggression is often part of routine activities such as insulting, teasing, and story-telling (Eder et al., 1995). While medium status boys were less likely to engage in aggressive sexual talk than were high and low status boys, they were generally unsuccessful in challenging the sexist behavior of their peers. Stein (1993) also found sexual harassment to be a frequent occurrence in schools across the country. Both studies found a link between sexual aggression and bullying behavior in which boys as well as girls were targeted.

In contrast, Kenway and Willis (1998) found that only a minority of boys had a tough, misogynist stance in their study of Australian youth. Most boys found male banter and name-calling to be a source of embarrassment and frustration, while others were preoccupied with trying to avoid being victims of verbal and physical violence themselves. Some boys in their study expressed a sense of injustice, believing that teachers and administrators tend to discipline boys more than girls for rowdy behavior.

Adolescent girls respond to boys' sexually aggressive talk and behavior in a variety of ways. A few girls report such instance to authorities, while others find creative ways of joking back or diffusing the aggressive tone (Eder et al., 1995). However, most girls end up resigning themselves to this behavior, often with a certain degree of resentment (Stein, 1993). Many girls also feel that subtle pressures to "get a man" can undermine their female friendships. Again, some girls respond to this by developing creative strategies to maintain the intimacy of these friendships (Griffin, 2000; Hey, 1997). Girls' friendships also are threatened by labels of "lezzie" or "lesbian," restricting the degree to which girls can openly express passionate feelings for each other. In response to this, some girls openly negotiate the physical expressions they consider appropriate for friendships and those which they will avoid (Hey, 1997).

In summary, adolescents' relations with peers reflect their growing concerns with mutual support and openness. At the same time, social class, racial, and gender tensions often emerge during adolescence as students begin to interact with peers from different backgrounds and reproduce some of the power inequities of the larger society. More research is needed to show how adolescents respond to some of these tensions by forming groups that cross race and class boundaries and by finding creative strategies for avoiding or confronting social labeling and aggressive behavior.

Social Identities

Stemming from a focus on identity politics in the larger society, researchers have sought to disentangle the complex threads of racial identities among youth within Western societies.

For many youth the salience of ethnic and racial identities increased during the 1970s and 1980s and remained strong throughout the 1990s. For other youth, embedded identities—those situated in particular roles or relationships within their community—gained greater importance as they placed more emphasis on shared interests than on shared racial backgrounds.

Racial identity has been the basis for an oppositional stance among certain youth in which their values, norms, and styles of interaction run counter to those of mainstream culture. This stance is more predominant among "involuntary minorities"—those who were conquered, colonized, or enslaved and never chose to become part of the United States—as compared to "voluntary minorities"—those who chose to immigrate to the United States (Ogbu & Simmons, 1999). According to Ogbu and Simmons, involuntary minorities include American Indians, Mexican Americans, and African Americans, who came as slaves. Because of their long history with discrimination and lack of choice about participation in American society, involuntary minorities believe learning White ways is detrimental to their ethnic identity and have therefore developed a collective identity defined by its opposition to White identity. This has led some Black students and Mexican Americans to avoid achieving academically or speaking standard English except when necessary, viewing both as "acting White" (Fordham, 1999; Valenzuela, 1999). For some Black youth, racial and social class identities are so intertwined that oppositional behaviors include those behaviors which oppose middle-class as well as White norms, such as loud talking, impolite behavior, and distinct modes of dress (Cousins, 1999).

The term "oppositional" as applied to American Indians has been challenged by Deyhle (1995) who claims that Navajo youth are not reacting in opposition to White culture so much as claiming a separate identity that preceded colonization by Whites. For many Navajo youth, their social identity is tied closely with family and a collective rather than individual sense of success. Deyhle (1995) found that while some Navajo youth assimilate White values and others reject school norms, the youth that are most successful academically are those who remain involved in traditional culture. These youth have found a way to honor both cultures by drawing on the strengths of each and, according to Deyhle, have "accommodated without assimilating."

This practice of accommodation without assimilation has been studied among other involuntary minorities. In their study of several untracked California high schools, Mehan et al. (1994) found that programs aimed at bringing underachieving minorities into college tracks provided these youth with opportunities to form peer cultures that supported both their academic interests and their cultural identities. They also found that many of the students who did well in these programs maintained a critical consciousness about race that formerly has been associated with minority youth who reject school. Other recent research has found that high-achieving African American youth are often more likely to use "race dominant" discourse, seeing race as constraining life chances in multiple domains, than are lower achieving youth (O'Connor, 1999). This also challenges the view that a politically aware consciousness is tied to low school performance for involuntary minorities.

According to Hemmings (2000), some youth now participate in what she refers to as "post-oppositional identity work." In a study of a working-class racially mixed school, Hemmings found certain peer cliques to be social spaces for positive identity work. In one group, a Black female leader encouraged her racially diverse friends to come to terms with their true identities regarding sexual preferences, academic ability, and parenthood. At the same time, this group developed norms about accepting differences in others and reconciling with social worlds they had once opposed, such as school and home.

Other research has found that for some youth, ethnic identities are not as salient in the 1990s. Many inner city youth are now seeking a sense of personal efficacy and a sense of belonging by joining youth organizations such as dance troupes, Boys' and Girls' Clubs, and athletic teams (Heath & McLaughlin, 1993). For these youth, ethnicity is important only as it functions within a host of embedded identities such as being a player on a team or the sibling of a gang member. Also, youth leaders often seek to bring youth together around shared artistic and athletic interests that transcend ethnicity.

The nonschool nature of these peer groups is critical since in schools many youth are labeled based on what they are not, while in community organizations the focus is on what they are (Heath & McLaughlin, 1993). In these activities, adolescents interact with younger peers, often as mentors, which further enhances their sense of self-worth and belonging. Those involved in dance and theater also benefitted from opportunities to perform on stage as well as to explore their ethnic past through dramatic performances (Ball & Heath, 1993). In a study of an inner city art center, youth did not feel they needed to abandon their ethnic identities but were able to develop a stronger acceptance and appreciation of differences in this nonschool setting (Fine, Weis, Centrie, & Roberts, 2000).

More research is needed to better understand the complex nature of ethnic identities among youth. New concepts may also be needed to capture the persistence of certain cultures such as American Indians and which allow for multiple identities. In particular, more research is needed on youth organizations to determine the conditions under which they foster solidarity and acceptance of diversity.

Language Activities and Discourse Processes

Ethnographers and sociolinguists have examined the discourse processes by which adolescents create peer cultures and express group identities. Willis (1981) was one of the first to show that informal group interaction and humor are essential elements for creating and maintaining a subculture. Language activities, such as insulting, teasing, story-telling, and gossip, are crucial for culture production since it is through language that shared interpretations develop. Adolescents also use language to express various social identities, including that of being an adolescent, along with ambivalences related to these identities.

Although most research on insulting has involved Black male adolescents (Goodwin, 1990; Labov, 1972), others have studied White males and Black and White working-class females (Everhart, 1983; Goodwin, 1990). Studies of ritual insulting have shown how being able to interpret insults as playful and responding with more clever or elaborate insults are essential skills for successful participation in certain subcultures. Youth who lack these skills are more likely to become targets of serious ridicule or physical attacks as the conflict escalates (Everhart, 1983; Labov, 1972). On the other hand, by responding playfully to insults, a sense of solidarity based on shared interpretation is developed (Everhart, 1983). Because many Whites are less familiar with challenges and insults, Schofield (1989) found they often interpreted these acts as being aggressive rather than playful. This led to the belief by Whites that African Americans are "tough" and "aggressive" while African Americans came to view Whites as being "easily bullied."

Another form of group humor that has been studied is playful teasing. Here again, interpreting teasing remarks as playful and responding in kind are essential skills (Eder, 1991). Teasing is more loosely structured than ritual insulting, allowing for collaborative participation which can build solidarity among the "teasers" as well as the targets. While there is a loose structure and familiarity to teasing routines, they also allow novel responses given their playful, humorous nature. A study of teasing at different age levels found that it is not until early adolescence that most children realize teasing can be playful and is a way to mark and strengthen friendships (Mills, 2001). Older adolescents are even more sophisticated, adjusting their teasing remarks to their friends' needs and sensitivities (Emihovich, 1998; Mills, 2001).

Story-telling is also a common activity among adolescents taking a variety of forms including fight stories and collaborative narratives. Since stories are based on past experiences, full participation depends on shared experiences among group members. Shuman (1986) found that the females who had the most knowledge about a fight were entitled to tell fight stories and only those who were close friends were allowed to hear certain fight stories, such as those involving family disputes (Goodwin, 1990; Labov, 1972). Storytelling in peer culture is often collaborative (Eder, 1988; Goodwin, 1990) with collaboration serving both to strengthen group ties and allow for the development of shared perceptions and orientations.

Although gossip is a common activity among adolescents, it has not been adequately studied. In a study of younger adolescents, Eder and Enke (1991) found that the structure of gossip makes it difficult to challenge negative evaluations once the initial evaluation has been supported. This means that early adolescents are likely to engage in considerable negative evaluation in order to participate in this common activity. Parker and Gottman (1989) found that gossip was primarily used for group solidarity and communication of norms in early adolescence, but that in later adolescence, gossip provided an entry into the psychological exploration of the self. In another study of older adolescent females, Fine (1986) found that gossip was used primarily to clarify moral concerns and values. The females Fine studied were concerned with reaching consensus and they minimized potential conflict by expressing counter views in ways that allowed their views to be easily modified.

Language is also a means for adolescents to express group identities. Kelle (2001) found that 9- to 12-year olds look to changes in their peers' practices related to gender relations as a way to express entry into adolescence, using terms such as "further developed" versus "childish." Ambivalence about this new identity is revealed by describing it in both positive terms ("cool") and negative ones ("wishing to be older than they are"). Girls also use discourse to develop and share knowledge about their identities as females as they relate to new concerns regarding sexuality and menstruation (Emihovich, 1998; Fingerson, 2001). Fingerson (2001) found that older adolescents tell narratives about strategies for hiding menstrual products at school as well as about occasions where they flaunted them, reflecting the ambivalence of some girls regarding the strong privacy norms for a naturally occurring female experience.

Recent studies of marking racial identities through language show that for some youth like many Puerto Rican Americans and African Americans code-switching across languages and dialects is an important way to indicate their dual identities (Fordham, 1999; Zentella, 1998). At the same time, some African American youth reported not liking code-switching because "you can't tell whether she's White or Black" (Fordham, 1999, p. 284). More research is needed to show how non-White youth use language to mark their racial identities and how they deal with different perceptions of the use of code-switching and other identity markers.

These recent studies on age, gender, and racial identities show the value of examining discourse processes to capture the meaning and ambivalence around such identities in adolescence. Also, while a number of studies examined the way in which language activities convey concerns and values related to gender in adolescence, more research is needed to show how racial concerns and stereotypes become shaped and reproduced through daily language activities in adolescence.

Media

On average, adolescents in the United States use media nearly 7 hr per day (Roberts, 2000). Media use studies suggest that early adolescents tend to watch television with siblings and parents, and that older adolescents spend more time listening to music alone and with friends; adolescents are also likely to read print media (Larson, Kubey, & Colletti, 1989; Roberts, 2000). Early studies of adolescent media were content analyses aimed at identifying messages of violence and sexism. These studies assumed that adolescents would internalize these messages unadulterated. With the rise of cultural studies and audience reception research, scholars of media and adolescence have begun to ask whether adolescents actually receive the messages discerned in content analyses and how adolescents use media to produce identity. These studies generally focus on how *individuals* decode messages from *one* type of media and produce identity. Rarely do studies examine how adolescents *in groups* appropriate *multiple* types of media for identity production and use in peer cultures.

MAGAZINES. McRobbie's (1991) landmark study of the British girls' magazines *Jackie* and *Just Seventeen* in the 1970s and 1980s detailed how the magazines presented a feminine sphere of fashion, beauty, pop rock, and romance that constructed problems as personal, rather than structural. United States fashion magazines through the 1990s also reinforced hegemonic ideas of heterosexual romance and female beauty (Carpenter, 1998; Durham, 1998).

Many early adolescent girls accept and use the messages promulgated by fashion magazines. Duke and Kreshel (1998) found that White girls relied heavily on magazines' advice on how to obtain boys' approval, act in romantic situations, and analyze beauty. The Asian Canadian girls Gonick (1997) interviewed were so heavily invested in hegemonic ideas of beauty and heterosexual romance that they forcefully rejected alternative magazines such as *New Moon* and *Sassy*. By mid-adolescence, girls personally reject the beauty images in these magazines, but the images continue to powerfully shape girls' self-concepts because girls believe that *others* accept the magazine images (Milkie, 1999). In addition, Durham's (1999) ethnographic investigation demonstrated that eighth grade girls reinforced hegemonic ideas of beauty and heterosexual romance with images from other print media, the Internet, and music television.

TELEVISION. Adolescents draw on television programs and advertising to generate heterosexual, racial, and gender identities. Pasquier (1996) suggested that French adolescents use teen series, such as the American *Beverly Hills 90210* and the French show *Helen and the Boys*, as a nonthreatening introduction to the world of heterosexual relationships. The French adolescents in her survey preferred storylines about romantic–but not sexual–relationships that take place within a group of friends and disparaged characters who promoted themselves at the expense of the group. Adolescent viewers of *90210* in the United States also focused on relationships during focus group discussions (Granello, 1997). While younger viewers virtually ignored the heterosexual relationships on *90210* in favor of friendships, older viewers extensively discussed *90210*'s male–female relationships.

Adolescents' discussions of television programs play an important role in racial and gender identity construction as well. During small group discussions in school, teenaged Asian girls in Britain compared and contrasted themselves to Asian soap opera characters. In doing so, these girls constructed a hybridized British Asian identity for themselves (Barker, 1997). Similarly, Black adolescent boys in Canada used Black celebrity athletes in sneaker commercials as a reference point for identity construction (Wilson & Sparks, 1996). In focus groups, these teens expressed both masculine and Black identities through affiliation with celebrity athletes' basketball playing style and athletic apparel. In a group interview conducted during a larger ethnographic study, a group of eighth grade boys who discussed movies shown on cable television collectively valued aggressive behavior, identified with images of sexually aggressive men, and applied media stereotypes of women to girls they knew (Milkie, 1994).

MUSIC.   Given the media attention to violent and sexist lyrics in rap and heavy metal music, there are surprisingly few content analyses of song lyrics (Friesen & Helfrich, 1998). Instead, more attention has been paid to how adolescents use music to produce individual identities and to define subcultures. Listening to music affects teenagers' emotions, and in turn, adolescents use these emotions to imagine identities they might adopt. Girls who listened to Top 40 music with friends and boys who listened to heavy metal or hard rock reported positive emotions (Larson, 1995). Boys who listened to heavy metal, in particular, stated that it calmed them and relieved feelings of anger and frustration (Arnett, 1991). Adolescents used the emotional images projected in music, such as the rescued lover and the powerful hero, to imagine themselves in a range of roles and identities (Larson, 1995). The African American teens in Dimitriadis' (2001) study suggested adolescents use music to index actual identities as well as possible ones. These teens used Southern rap to construct a sense of Southern values and identity and to mark their own relationship to the South.

Sociological research on adolescents and music often examines the role of music in defining subcultures. Typically, cultural studies scholars link a subculture to music, and then submit the subculture's clothing and music to textual analysis (Thornton, 1997). Ethnographic investigations focus instead on the role of music within a group. For example, a group of interracial friends in South London created a subcultural norm of ethnic equality; they then used music to remind themselves of the history of Black girls and to reinforce their group's value of ethnic equality (Wulff, 1995). The burnouts Gaines (1991) studied in New Jersey used heavy metal to mark the boundaries of their group and address the social constraints of the New Jersey suburbs: the teens' dismal occupational future as blue-collar jobs disappear, the perpetual nothing-to-do and nowhere-to-go of suburbia, and overregulation by adults. These two examples suggest that music can be an avenue of agency, resistance, and social change for teens.

In sum, adolescents draw on media like magazines, television, and music for images and emotions they use to construct gendered, racial, and sexual identities. As active consumers of media, teens may use media to reinforce conventional ideas of gender and heterosexuality. However, some teens may use media as an avenue for resistance and the creation of new identities. A more contextual understanding of these identity processes, and the conditions under which each occur, could be developed by studying how teens embed media in peer cultures and how the identities teens generate from media shift over time.

Sexuality

Toward the end of elementary school, children become increasingly interested in dating and romance (Reynold, 2000; Thorne, 1993). The imperative to engage in heterosexual romance and sexual behavior is so strong during adolescence that several scholars use Adrienne Rich's (1980) term "compulsory heterosexuality" to characterize the sexual atmosphere teenagers face (Martin, 1996; Morris & Fuller, 1999). Although much of the research on adolescent sexuality is grounded in demographic and life course perspectives, a body of research using cultural reproduction and interpretive perspectives has illuminated some aspects of this sexual atmosphere. Teenagers' sexual cultures reflect the broader culture's power dynamics, structures of gender relations, and values of hierarchy, competition, and romance.

Against this backdrop, many adolescent boys learn to view girls in terms of sexual conquest. In early adolescence, teenage boys discuss girls primarily in terms of "how far they got" with them sexually (Fine, 1987; Parker, 1991). Boys learn not to let girls replace other boys as the focus of their attention, and emphasize the importance of the male peer group (Fine, 1987). In later adolescence, many boys state that they want girlfriends for friendship and sex, but that they do not want romance or intense, emotional intimacy with their girlfriends (Martin, 1996). Working-class boys often tell stories emphasizing their sexual experiences. Many view girls as sexual objects and in general see them as weak, indirect, and sexually passive (Willis, 1981). Boys, as well as girls, use the labels "slut," "whore," or "slag" to control female sexual behavior. These labels are applied to any girl who is sexually promiscuous, even though such behavior is viewed as acceptable for boys (Griffin, 1985; Lees, 1993; Wulff, 1988).

Teenage girls, however, tend to view boys primarily in terms of heterosexual, monogamous romance rather than sex. Some girls come to believe in the importance of "being in love continually" and are always searching for new targets for their romantic feelings (Simon, Eder, & Evans, 1992). Many White working-class girls develop a culture of romance as part of their resistance to middle-class academic norms (Griffin, 1985; McRobbie, 1991). Although not all girls participate in the culture of romance, female adolescents of all classes at least hope to find "true love" with a boy (Martin, 1996; Thompson, 1995). Asian and African American girls, however, tend to be more critical of romance ideals and are less concerned with getting a boyfriend (Griffin, 1985). Unlike boys, there is some evidence that girls will value boyfriends more than their female peer groups. Feminist scholars in the United Kingdom described dating patterns where girls replaced female friends with boyfriends in the 1970s, girls tried but ultimately failed to keep female friends once they had boyfriends in the 1980s, and finally were more successful keeping female friends while dating boys in the 1990s (Morris & Fuller, 1999). It is not clear, however, whether these dating patterns were empirically present or the result of researcher emphasis.

These ideas of heterosexuality form the context in which teenagers experience sex. Boys who have had sex for the first time report that it made them feel grown up, masculine, and sexually agentic. Boys often imply, rather than discuss, sexual pleasure (Martin, 1996). Girls who have had heterosexual sex for the first time tell their stories as if they were sexually passive and often use the phrase "it just happened." Some girls have sex because they are afraid of losing their true love, and many girls have sex because they are coerced. Afterward, many girls report feeling confused and uncertain about their sexual experiences. Sexual pleasure is not a part of many girls' sexual stories (Martin, 1996; Thompson, 1995). Many teenage girls do experience sexual desire and pleasure, however (Tolman, 1994). Middle-class girls, especially popular ones, tend to be less susceptible to notions of true love and less likely to fuse romantic love and sex (Thompson, 1995). Lesbian teens' first experiences of sex with men are similar to those of heterosexual girls; their first experiences of sex with *women* are more positive and sexually pleasing (Thompson, 1995).

In their experiences with love, dating, romance and sex, teenagers reproduce some of the most stereotypical aspects of heterosexuality. Many teenage boys learn to sexually objectify girls and to keep their distance in relationships. Many teenage girls are steeped in a culture of romance, are sexually passive, and experience sex without sexual pleasure. We need more research grounded in cultural reproduction and interpretive perspectives to understand how adolescents reproduce and challenge sexual inequality. In particular, future research should investigate when and how teenagers are able to produce alternative forms of heterosexuality and disrupt the compulsory heterosexuality now characterizing adolescence.

DIRECTIONS FOR FUTURE RESEARCH IN ADOLESCENT SOCIALIZATION

The research reported in this chapter offers some insights into the meaning of adolescence as viewed from different theoretical perspectives. As mentioned earlier, a life course approach views adolescence as it is embedded in individual trajectories. Life course scholars focus on the structural precursors of events during adolescence. The cultural reproductive perspective also examines social structures in adolescence and views adolescents as being shaped through factors such as race, gender, and social class. In the review of research on family and schools we saw how structural factors, such as family composition and school contexts, shape adolescent trajectories and identities in school. More research is needed to identify other variations in parenting practices and school contexts and how they might limit or expand the range of social identities that adolescents can assume. At the same time, researchers in this area need to be careful not to presume that adolescents respond passively to these constraints.

In contrast, for those with a subcultural perspective the meaning of adolescence is often one of resistance to White and other mainstream cultures. In this review we found many examples of Black youth and other youth of color adopting oppositional identities and practices. More research is needed to examine such practices for other groups such as gay, lesbian, and bisexual youth. Also, ways in which non-mainstream youth come to accommodate multiple perspectives while remaining politically aware need further study.

The interpretive perspective encourages the study of *how* various meanings of adolescence are constructed. One especially intriguing area of study is how adolescents transcend the social constraints of adult worlds. Several studies have shown that youth can lead the way in modeling new modes of acceptance and even appreciation of diversity. More research is needed on the creative ways in which adolescents construct ethnic and other social differences, embrace their own, often multiple, identities, and develop greater tolerance of others' identities. This perspective reminds us that adolescents have their own separate culture—one that is not completely free of adult norms and yet with the potential to shape them.

As the research on peer groups continues to expand and diversify, we saw more examples of how peer groups counteract rather than simply reproduce structural factors related to gender, race, and class. More research is needed to show how certain school practices like detracking create peer groups that support multiple identities. At the same time, more research is also needed showing how effective youth leaders have the agency to move beyond oppositional practices through informal and formal mentoring.

We also saw some common factors that minimize a sense of social hierarchy both in and outside of schools. Hierarchies among peer groups were less common when schools or youth organizations created a common identity which emphasized the similarities among youth rather than their differences. We need to further our understanding of when and how certain contexts produce a focus on social equality for youth rather than social inequality. With this increased knowledge we could then promote more contexts in which youth experience the benefits of more egalitarian structures.

Our review focused on the areas of family, school, and peer groups because the bulk of current research on adolescent socialization occurs within these contexts. To some degree the focus on family and school was influenced by early, more passive, theories of socialization in which youth were viewed as being shaped by adult forces (Lesko, 2001). It also reflects an earlier focus on outcomes rather than socialization processes, trying to determine the extent to which efforts to influence youth were succeeding or failing. Theories with a more active view of youth have included peer groups, but most of these studies still occur in school settings where, as some researchers claim, adolescents are still largely labeled based on what they are not rather than on what they are (Heath & McLaughlin, 1993).

It is essential to study adolescents outside of family and school settings in a variety of contexts, including paid and unpaid work. A recent study of Puerto Rican youth at work found that adolescence is a time for shaping career identities that often began as early as childhood based on unique talents or powerful life experiences (Munoz, 1995). Puerto Rican youth in this study were motivated to solve social problems or to help Puerto Ricans, often by being liaisons for other youth. This made their work more meaningful and as a result they felt more confident, competent, and independent. More studies such as this are needed to better understand how paid work settings can both motivate and empower youth. Also, even though service learning projects and community leadership programs are growing in frequency, we know little about how youth who serve as mentors, counselors, or advocates for others shape their own lives as well as the lives of others.

Finally, we want to note that only a few researchers studied youth in multiple contexts, showing difficult as well as smooth transitions across family, school, and peer groups. Sociologists tend to shape their research agendas by focusing on a particular social institution and this has the unfortunate consequence of compartmentalizing the experiences of youth. Anthropologists have recently offered several important examples of understanding youth culture as a whole, especially for youth from a variety of ethnic backgrounds. Drawing on cultural pluralism—a theory of group relations that promotes cultural diversity—these researchers are attempting to identify ways youth can retain ethnic subcultures while operating within other cultural systems (Hemmings, 1998; Phelan et al., 1993, 1998).

Stratified social systems, such as those reviewed in this chapter, often constrain identity choices and set the stage for conflicts between parents, schools, and friends. As a result, for many non-mainstream youth, the boundaries between these domains are difficult to pass (Hemmings, 1998; Phelan et al., 1998). For other youth, the boundaries are described as being "manageable." Some bi-racial youth, for example, have found ways to value both Mexican and Anglo cultures, although stereotypes on both sides may limit the closeness of friendships at school or in the community (Phelan et al., 1998). Other youth, like Sikh teenagers in Britain, change their behavior according to the context they are in, acting the most English in school and the most Indian at home and the temple (Hall, 1995). School practices that support the aspirations of minority youth can also promote smooth transitions between family, school, and peers (Mehan et al., 1994; Phelan et al., 1998).

Over the years the research in this area has come to replace a view of adolescents as passively adopting societal norms and beliefs with a view of adolescents as actively constructing their social worlds. We see this already in much of the research on peer socialization where youth are shown as leaders in modeling new modes of interracial acceptance and friendships. By expanding the research on youth to settings beyond family and school, we are likely to see even more evidence of ways in which youth become empowered and find meaningful roles in their communities. Also, by studying adolescent socialization across multiple contexts, we will better understand youth as integrators of meaning and experience. This will further add to our knowledge of youth as active agents in the socialization process.

REFERENCES

Amit-Talai. (1995). The Waltz of Sociability: Intimacy, dislocation and friendship in a Quebec high school. In V. Amit-Talai & H. Wulff (Eds.), *Youth cultures: A cross-cultural perspective* (pp. 144–165). London, New York: Routledge.

Arnett, J. (1991). Adolescents and heavy metal music. *Youth & Society, 23*, 76–98.

Ball, A., & Heath, S. B. (1993). Dances of identity: Finding an ethnic self in the arts. In S. B. Heath & M. W. McLaughlin (Eds.), *Identity and inner-city youth: Beyond ethnicity and gender* (pp. 69–93). New York: Teachers College Press.

Barker, C. (1997). Television and the reflexive project of the self: Soaps, teenage talk, and hybrid identities. *British Journal of Sociology, 48*, 611–628.

Berndt, T. J. (1989). Obtaining support from friends in childhood and adolescence. In D. Belle (Ed.), *Children's social networks and social supports* (pp. 308–331). New York: Wiley.

Bettis, P. J. (1996). Urban students, liminality, and the postindustrial context. *Sociology of Education, 69*, 105–125.

Bigelow, B. J., & LaGaipa, J. J. (1980). The development of friendship values and choice. In H. C. Foot, A. J. Chapman, & J. R. Smith (Eds.), *Friendship and social relations in children* (pp. 15–44). New York: Wiley.

Bourdieu, P., & Passeron, J.-C. (1977). *Reproduction in education, society, and culture.* (R. Nice, Trans.). Beverly Hills: Sage.

Bowles, S., & Gintis, H. (1976). *Schooling in capitalist America.* New York: Basic Books.

Brake, M. (1985). *Comparative youth culture: The sociology of youth cultures and youth subcultures in America, Britain, and Canada.* London and Boston: Routledge & Kegan Paul.

Brantlinger, E. A. (1993). *The politics of social class in secondary school: Views of affluent and impoverished youth.* New York and London: Teachers College Columbia University.

Brown, B. B. (1990). Peer groups and peer cultures. In S. S. Feldman & G. R. Elliott (Eds.), *At the threshold: The developing adolescent* (pp. 171–196). Cambridge, MA: Harvard University Press.

Brown, B. B., & Lohr, M. J. (1987). Peer group affiliation and adolescent self-esteem: An integration of ego-identity and symbolic interaction theories. *Journal of Personality and Social Psychology, 52*, 47–55.

Carpenter, L. M. (1998). From girls into women: Scripts for sexuality and romance in seventeen magazine, 1974–1994. *Journal of Sex Research, 35*, 158–168.

Cicourel, A. V. (1974). *Cognitive sociology: Language and meaning in interaction.* New York: Free Press.

Corsaro, W. A. (1985). *Friendship and peer culture in the early years.* Norwood, NJ: Ablex.

Corsaro, W. A., & Eder, D. (1995). Development and socialization of children and adolescents. In K. S. Cook, G. A. Fine, & J. S. House (Eds.), *Sociological perspectives on social psychology* (pp. 421–451). New York: Allyn & Bacon.

Corsaro, W. A., & Rizzo, T. A. (1988). Discussione and friendship: Socialization processes in the peer culture among Italian preschool children. *American Sociological Review, 53*, 879–894.

Cousins, L. (1999). "Playing between classes": America's troubles with class, race and gender in a Black high school and community. *Anthropology & Education Quarterly, 30*, 294–316.

Cusick, P. A. (1973). *Inside high school: The student's world.* New York: Holt, Rinehart, & Winston.

Damico, S. B., & Sparks, C. (1986). Cross-group contact opportunities: Impact on interpersonal relationships in desegregated middle schools. *Sociology of Education, 59*, 113–123.

Deyhle, D. (1995). Navajo youth and Anglo racism: Cultural integrity and resistance. *Harvard Educational Review, 65*, 4403–4444.

DiMaggio, P. (1982). Cultural capital and school success: The impact of status culture participation on the grades of U.S. high school students. *American Sociological Review, 47*, 189–201.

Dimitriadis, G. (2001). "In the clique": Popular culture, constructions of place, and the everyday lives of urban youth. *Anthropology & Education Quarterly, 32*, 29–51.

Dornbusch, S. M., Ritter, P. L., Leiderman, P. H., Roberts, D. F., & Fraleigh, M. (1987). The relation of parenting style to adolescent school performance. *Child Development, 58*, 1244–1257.

Downey, D. (1995). When bigger is not better: Family size, parental resources, and children's educational performance. *American Sociological Review, 60*, 746–761.

Duke, L. L., & Kreshel, P. J. (1998). Negotiating femininity: Girls in early adolescence read teen magazines. *Journal of Communication Inquiry, 22*, 48–71.

Durham, M. G. (1998). Dilemmas of desire: Representations of adolescent sexuality in two teen magazines. *Youth & Society, 29*, 369–389.

Durham, M. G. (1999). Girls, media, and the negotiation of sexuality: A study of race, class and gender in adolescent peer groups. *Journalism and Mass Communication Quarterly, 76*, 193–216.

Eccles, J. S., Wigfield, A., Flanagan, C. A., Miller, C., Reuman, A., & Yee, D. (1989). Self-concepts, domain values and self-esteem: Relations and changes at early adolescence. *Journal of Personality, 57*, 282–310.

Eckert, P. (1988). Adolescent social structure and the spread of linguistic change. *Language in Society, 17*, 183–208.

Eckert, P. (1989). *Jocks and burnouts: Social categories and identity in the high school.* New York: Teachers College Columbia University.

Eder, D. (1985). The cycle of popularity: Interpersonal relations among female adolescents. *Sociology of Education, 58*, 154–165.

Eder, D. (1988). Building cohesion through collaborative narration. *Social Psychology Quarterly, 51*, 225–235.

Eder, D. (1991). The role of teasing in adolescent peer culture. *Sociological Studies of Child Development, 4*, 181–197.

Eder, D., & Enke, J. L. (1991). The structure of gossip: Opportunities and constraints on collective expression among adolescents. *American Sociological Review, 56*, 494–508.

Eder, D., Evans, C. C., & Parker, S. (1995). *School talk: Gender and adolescent culture.* New Brunswick, NJ: Rutgers University Press.

Eder, D., & Parker, S. (1987). The cultural production and reproduction of gender: The effects of extracurricular activities on peer group culture. *Sociology of Education, 60*, 200–213.

Elder, G. H., Jr. (1974). *Children of the great depression: Social change in life experience.* Chicago: University of Chicago Press.

Elder, G. H., Jr. (1985a). Perspectives on the life course. In G. H. Elder, Jr. (Ed.), *Life course dynamics: Trajectories and transitions, 1968–1980* (pp. 23–49). Ithaca, NY: Cornell University Press.

Elder, G. H., Jr. (1985b). *Life course dynamics: Trajectories and transitions, 1968–1980.* Ithaca, NY: Cornell University Press.

Elder, G. H., Jr. (1987). War mobilization and the life course: A cohort of World War II veterans. *Sociological Forum, 2*, 449–472.

Emihovich, C. (1998). Bodytalk: Discourses of sexuality among adolescent African American girls. In S. M. Hoyle & C. T. Adger (Eds.), *Kids talk: Strategic language use in later childhood* (pp. 113–133). New York: Oxford University Press.

Epstein, J. S. (1994). Misplaced childhood: An introduction to the sociology of youth and their music. In J. S. Epstein (Ed.), *Adolescents and their music: If it's too loud, you're too old* (pp. xiii–xxxiv). New York and London: Garland.

Epstein, J. S. (1998). Introduction: Generation X, youth culture and identity. In J. S. Epstein (Ed.), *Youth culture: Identity in a postmodern world* (pp. 1–23). Malden, MA: Blackwell.

Evans, C., & Eder, D. (1993). "No exit:" Processes of social isolation in the middle school. *Journal of Contemporary Ethnography, 22*, 139–170.

Everhart, R. B. (1983). *Reading, writing, and resistance: Adolescence and labor in a junior high school.* Boston: Routledge.

Fine, G. A. (1986). The social organization of adolescent gossip: The rhetoric of moral evaluation. In J. Cook-Gumperz, W. A. Corsaro, & J. Streeck (Eds.), *Children's Worlds and Children's Language* (pp. 405–423). Berlin: Mouton.

Fine, G. A. (1987). *With the boys: Little league baseball and preadolescent culture.* Chicago: University of Chicago Press.

Fine, M., Weis, L., Centrie, C., & Roberts, R. (2000). Educating beyond the borders of schooling. *Anthropology & Education Quarterly, 31*, 131–151.

Fingerson, L. (2001). *Social construction, power, and agency in adolescents' menstrual talk.* PhD Thesis, Department of Sociology, Indiana University, Bloomington.

Fordham, S. (1999). Dissin' "the standard": Ebonics as guerilla warfare at Capital High. *Anthropology & Education Quarterly, 30*, 272–293.

Friesen, B. K., & Helfrich, W. (1998). Social justice and sexism for adolescents: A content analysis of lyrical themes and gender presentations in Canadian heavy metal music, 1985–1991. In J. S. Epstein (Ed.), *Youth culture: Identity in a postmodern world* (pp. 263–285). Malden, MA: Blackwell.

Gaines, D. (1991). *Teenage wasteland: Suburbia's dead end kids.* Chicago: University of Chicago Press.

Gelder, K., & Thornton, S. (1997). *The subcultures reader* (pp. xvi, 599). London and New York: Routledge.

Giddens, A. (1984). *The constitution of society: Outline of the theory of structuration.* Berkeley, CA: University of California Press.

Giele, J. Z., & Elder, G. H. Jr. (1998). Life course research: Development of a field. In J. Z. Giela & G. H. Elder, Jr. (Eds.), *Methods of life course research: Qualitative and quantitative approaches* (pp. 5–27). Thousand Oaks, CA: Sage.

Giordano, P. (1995). The wider circle of friends in adolescence. *American Journal of Sociology, 101*, 661–697.

Goffman, E. (1974). *Frame analysis: An essay on the organization of experience.* New York: Harper & Row.

Goldberg, A. D., & Chandler, T. J. L. (1989). The role of athletics: The social world of high school adolescents. *Youth & Society, 21*, 238–250.

Gonick, M. (1997). Reading selves, re-fashioning identity: Teen magazines and their readers. *Curriculum Studies, 5*, 69–86.

Goodwin, M. H. (1990). *He-said-she-said: Talk as social organization among Black children*. Bloomington, IN: Indiana University Press.

Gotto, S. (1997). Nerds, normal people, and homeboys: Accommodation and resistance among Chinese American students. *Anthropology & Education Quarterly, 28*, 70–84.

Granello, D. H. (1997). Using Beverly Hills, 90210 to explore developmental issues in female adolescents. *Youth & Society, 29*, 24–53.

Griffin, C. (1985). *Typical girls? Young women from school to the job market*. London and New York: Routledge & Kegan Paul.

Griffin, C. (2000). Constructions of sexuality in young women's friendships. *Feminism and Psychology, 10*, 227–245.

Grotevant, H. D., & Cooper, C. R. (1986). Individuation in family relationships: A perspective on individual differences in the development of identity and role-taking skill in adolescence. *Human Development, 29*, 82–100.

Hall, K. (1995). "There's a time to act English and a time to act Indian": The politics of identity among British–Sikh teenagers. In S. Stephens (Ed.), *Children and the politics of culture* (pp. 243–264). Princeton, NJ: Princeton University Press.

Handel, G. (1986). Beyond sibling rivalry: An empirically grounded theory of sibling relationships. *Sociological Studies of Child Development, 1*, 105–122.

Heath, S. B. (1983). *Ways with words: Language, life, and work in communities and classrooms*. Cambridge, New York: Cambridge University Press.

Heath, S. B., & McLaughlin, M. (1993). Ethnicity and gender in theory and practice: The youth perspective. In S. B. Heath & M. W. McLaughlin (Eds.), *Identity and inner-city youth: Beyond ethnicity and gender* (pp. 13–35). New York: Teachers College Press.

Hebdige, D. (1979). *Subculture: The meaning of style*. London: Methuen.

Hemmings, A. (1998). The self-transformation of African American achievers. *Youth & Society, 29*, 330–368.

Hemmings, A. (2000). Lona's links: Postoppositional identity work of urban youths. *Anthropology & Education Quarterly, 31*, 152–172.

Hey, V. (1997). *The company she keeps: An ethnography of girls' friendships*. Buckingham: Open University Press.

Horvat, E. M., & Antonio, A. L. (1999). "Hey, those shoes are out of uniform": African American girls in an elite high school and the importance of habitus. *Anthropology & Education Quarterly, 30*, 317–342.

Kandel, D. B., & Lesser, G. S. (1972). *Youth in two worlds*. San Francisco: Jossey-Bass.

Karweit, N., & Hansell, S. (1983). Sex differences in adolescent relationships: Friendship and status. In J. L. Epstein & N. Karweit (Eds.), *Friends in school: Patterns of selection and influence in secondary school* (pp. 115–130). New York: Academic.

Kelle, H. (2001). The discourse of "development": How 9- to 12-year-old children construct "childish" and "further developed" identities within their peer culture. *Childhood, 8*, 95–114.

Kenway, J., & Willis, S. (1998). *Answering back: Girls, boys, and feminism in schools*. London: Routledge.

Kessler, S., Ashenden, D. J., Connell, R. W., & Dowsett, G. W. (1985). Gender relations in secondary schooling. *Sociology of Education, 58*, 34–48.

Kinney, D. A. (1993). From nerds to normals: The recovery of identity among adolescents from middle school to high school. *Sociology of Education, 66*, 21–40.

Kinney, D. A. (1999). From "headbangers" to "hippies": Delineating adolescents' active attempts to form an alternative culture. *New Directions for Child and Adolescent Development, 84*, 21–35.

Labov, W. (1972). *Language in the inner city: Studies in the Black English vernacular*. Philadelphia: University of Pennsylvania Press.

Lareau, A. (1989). *Home advantage: Social class and parental involvement in elementary education*. Philadelphia: Falmer Press.

Larkin, R. W. (1979). *Suburban youth in cultural crisis*. New York: Oxford University Press.

Larson, R. (1995). Secrets in the bedroom: Adolescents' private use of media. *Journal of Youth and Adolescence, 24*, 535–550.

Larson, R., Kubey, R., & Colletti, J. (1989). Changing channels: Early adolescent media choices and shifting investments in family and friends. *Journal of Youth and Adolescence, 18*, 583–599.

Lees, S. (1993). *Sugar and spice: Sexuality and adolescent girls*. New York: Penguin Books.

Lesko, N. (1988). *Symbolizing society: Stories, rites and structure in a catholic high school*. New York, London: Falmer.

Lesko, N. (2001). *Act your age! A cultural construction of adolescence.* New York: Routledge.

Levinson, B. (1998). Student culture and the contradictions of equality at a Mexican secondary school. *Anthropology & Education Quarterly, 29,* 267–296.

MacLeod, J. (1995). *Ain't no makin' it: Aspirations and attainment in a low-income neighborhood.* Boulder, CO: Westview Press.

Martin, K. A. (1996). *Puberty, sexuality, and the self: Boys and girls at adolescence.* New York: Routledge.

McLanahan, S. (1985). Family structure and the reproduction of poverty. *American Journal of Sociology, 90.*

McRobbie, A. (1991). *Feminism and youth culture: From Jackie to Just Seventeen.* Boston: Unwin Hyman.

Mead, G. H. (1934). *Mind, self, and society.* Chicago: University of Chicago Press.

Mehan, H., Hubbard, L., & Villanueva, I. (1994). Forming academic identities: Accommodation with assimilation among involuntary minorities. *Anthropology & Education Quarterly, 25,* 91–117.

Merten, D. E. (1997). The meaning of meanness: Popularity, competition, and conflict among junior high school girls. *Sociology of Education, 70,* 175–191.

Metz, M. H. (1978). *Classrooms and corridors: The crisis of authority in desegregated secondary schools.* Berkeley, CA: University of California Press.

Milkie, M. (1994). Social world approach to cultural studies: Mass media and gender in the adolescent peer group. *Journal of Contemporary Ethnography, 23,* 354–380.

Milkie, M. A. (1999). Social comparisons, reflected appraisals, and mass media: The impact of pervasive beauty images on Black and White Girls' self-concepts. *Social Psychology Quarterly, 62,* 190–210.

Mills, C. B. (2001). *Being mean, having fun, or getting things done?: A developmental study of children's understanding of the forms and functions of teasing.* PhD Thesis, Department of Psychology, Purdue University, Lafayette.

Mirón, L. F., & Lauria, M. (1998). Student voice as agency: Resistance and accommodation in inner-city schools. *Anthropology & Education Quarterly, 29,* 189–213.

Modell, J. (1989). *Into one's own: From youth to adulthood in the United States, 1920–1975.* Berkeley: University of California Press.

Morris, K., & Fuller, M. (1999). Heterosexual relationships of young women in a rural environment. *British Journal of Sociology of Education, 20,* 531–543.

Munoz, V. I. (1995). *'Where something catches': Work, love and identity in youth.* Albany, NY: State University of New York Press.

Oakes, J. (1985). *Keeping track: How schools structure inequality.* New Haven: Yale University Press.

O'Connor, C. (1999). Race, class and gender in America: Narratives of opportunity among low-income African American youth. *Sociology of Education, 72,* 137–157.

Ogbu, J., & Simmons, H. (1999). Voluntary and involuntary minorities: A cultural–ecological theory of school performance with some implications for education. *Anthropology & Education Quarterly, 29,* 155–188.

Parker, J. G., & Gottman, J. M. (1989). Social and emotional development in a relational context: Friendship interaction from early childhood to adolescence. In T. J. Berndt & G. W. Ladd (Eds.), *Peer Relationships in Child Development* (pp. 95–131). New York: Wiley.

Parker, S. (1991). *Early adolescent male cultures: The importance of organized and informal sport.* PhD Thesis, Department of Sociology, Indiana University, Bloomington.

Parsons, T. (1951). *The social system.* Glencoe, IL: Free Press.

Pasquier, D. (1996). Teen series' reception: Television, adolescence, and culture of feelings. *Childhood, 3,* 351–373.

Phelan, P., Davidson, A. L., & Yu, H. C. (1993). Students' multiple worlds: Navigating the borders of family, peer and school cultures. In P. Phelan, A. L. Davidson, & H. C. Yu (Eds.), *Renegotiating Cultural Diversity in American Schools* (pp. 52–88). New York: Teachers College Press.

Phelan, P. (1998). *Adolescents' worlds: Negotiating family, peers, and school.* New York and London: Teachers College Press.

Philips, S. (1972). Participant structures and communicative competence: Warm Springs children in community and classroom. In C. B. Cazden, V. P. John, & D. Hymes (Eds.), *Functions of Language in the Classroom,* New York: Teachers College Press.

Powell, B., & Downey, D. (1997). Living in single-parent households: An investigation of the same-sex hypothesis. *American Sociological Review, 62,* 521–539.

Powell, B., & Steelman, L. C. (1990). Beyond sibship size: Sibling density, sex composition, and educational outcomes. *Social Forces, 69,* 181–206.

Powell, B., & Steelman, L. C. (1993). Doing the right thing: Race and parental locus of responsibility for funding college. *Sociology of Education, 66,* 223–244.

Proweller, A. (1998). *Constructing female identities: Meaning making in an upper middle class youth culture.* Albany: State University of New York Press.

Reynold, E. (2000). "Coming out": Gender, (hetero)sexuality and the primary school. *Gender and Education,* *12,* 309–326.

Rich, A. (1980). Compulsory heterosexuality and lesbian existence. *Signs, 5,* 631–660.

Roberts, D. F. (2000). Media and youth: Access, exposure, and privatization. *Journal of Adolescent Health, 27,* 8–14.

Sampson, R. J., & Laub, J. H. (1993). *Crime in the making: Pathways and turning points through life.* Cambridge, MA: Harvard University Press.

Schofield, J. W. (1989). *Black and White in school: Trust, tension, or tolerance?* New York: Teachers College Press.

Shanahan, M. J. (2000). Pathways to adulthood in changing societies: Variability and mechanisms in life course perspective. *Annual Review of Sociology, 26,* 667–692.

Shuman, A. (1986). *Storytelling rights: The uses of oral and written texts by urban adolescents.* Cambridge, UK: Cambridge University Press.

Simmons, R. G., & Blyth, D. A. (1987). *Moving into adolescence: The impact of pubertal change and school context.* New York: Aldine de Gruyter.

Simmons, R. G., Rosenberg, F., & Rosenberg, M. (1973). Disturbance in the self-image at adolescence. *American Sociological Review, 38,* 553–568.

Simon, R. W., Eder, D., & Evans, C. (1992). The development of feeling norms underlying romantic love among adolescent females. *Social Psychology Quarterly, 55,* 29–46.

Stein, N. (1993). No laughing matter: Sexual harassment in K-12 schools. In E. Buchwald (Ed.), *Transforming a rape culture* (pp. 313–314). Minneapolis: Milkweed Editions.

Sui-Chu, E. H., & Willms, J. D. (1996). Effects of parental involvement on eighth-grade achievement. *Sociology of Education, 69,* 136–141.

Thompson, S. (1995). *Going all the way: Teenage girls' tales of sex, romance, and pregnancy.* New York, NY: Hill and Wang.

Thorne, B. (1993). *Gender play: Girls and boys in school.* New Brunswick, NJ: Rutgers University Press.

Thornton, S. (1997). General introduction. In K. Gelder & S. Thornton (Eds.), *The subcultures reader* (pp. 1–7). London and New York: Routledge.

Tolman, D. L. (1994). Daring to desire: Culture and the bodies of adolescent girls. In J. M. Irvine (Ed.), *Sexual cultures and the construction of adolescent identities* (pp. 250–284). Philadelphia, PA: Temple University Press.

Valenzuela, A. (1999). *Subtractive schooling: U.S.–Mexican youth and the politics of caring.* Albany: State University of New York Press.

Wexler, P. (1992). *Becoming somebody: Toward a social psychology of school.* London and Washington, DC: Falmer Press.

Willis, P. E. (1981). *Learning to labor: How working class kids get working class jobs.* New York: Columbia University Press.

Wilson, B., & Sparks, R. (1996). "It's gotta be the shoes": Youth, race, and sneaker commercials. *Sociology of Sport Journal, 13,* 398–427.

Wulff, H. (1988). *Twenty girls: Growing up, ethnicity and excitement in a South London microculture.* Stockholm: University of Stockholm.

Wulff, H. (1995). Inter-racial friendship: Consuming youth styles, ethnicity and teenage femininity in South London. In V. Amit-Talai & H. Wulff (Eds.), *Youth cultures: A cross-cultural perspective* (pp. 63–80). London and New York: Routledge.

Youniss, J., & Smollar, J. (1985). *Adolescent relations with mothers, fathers and friends.* Chicago: University of Chicago Press.

Zentella, A. C. (1998). Multiple codes, multiple identities: Puerto Rican children in New York City. In S. M. Hoyle & C. T. Adger (Eds.), *Kids talk: Strategic language use in later childhood* (pp. 95–112). New York: Oxford University Press.

CHAPTER 8

Development and Socialization through the Adult Life Course

KAREN LUTFEY

JEYLAN T. MORTIMER

INTRODUCTION

The stability of society depends on the continual integration of new actors who are capable of maintaining, promoting, and modifying basic components of social life. The phenomenon of socialization is therefore critical to sociology. In this chapter, we consider varied definitions of socialization, how the concept is tied to fundamental sociological issues, and how its original conceptualizations provided a framework for later investigations. Specifically, we focus on socialization through the adult life course, with emphasis on heterogeneity and contingency in life experiences. To develop a theoretical and methodological perspective that is sensitive to temporality, we call attention to individuals' biographies and temporal orientations, as well as historical variability in the ways people adapt to new social roles and circumstances. While we touch on themes deriving from early work on childhood and adolescent socialization, our primary focus is on adult socialization, or that which occurs after the completion of general education, whether secondary school or college.

Socialization is the process by which individuals acquire social competence by learning the norms, values, beliefs, attitudes, language characteristics, and roles appropriate to their social groups (for other definitions, see Bush & Simmons, 1981, p. 134; Gecas, 2000, p. 2855; George, 1993, p. 353). It is central to role theory, which examines the links between

KAREN LUTFEY • Robert Wood Johnson Foundation Scholars in Health Policy Research Program, University of California-Berkeley and Department of Sociology, University of Minnesota   JEYLAN T. MORTIMER • Department of Sociology, University of Minnesota
Handbook of Social Psychology, edited by John Delamater. Kluwer Academic/Plenum Publishers, New York, 2003.

statuses and roles, or positions in social structure, and the behaviors appropriate for those specific status locations (for a discussion of role theory and life transitions, see George, 1993, pp. 354–356; Linton, 1936). Because it provides a mechanism for creating new social actors, understanding socialization is critical for assessing how actors enter, exit, and accommodate themselves to already-established status positions and roles; it is also key for explaining how requisite orientations and behaviors are transmitted to people who enter new roles as first-time incumbents (Bush & Simmons, 1981).

Furthermore, socialization is fundamental to debates about the reproduction of social order, and is therefore at the heart of perennial sociological questions. How does society reproduce itself, and how do individuals function in that process? Which societal functions are served by socialization? Similarly, questions about stability and change in individuals are tethered to socialization. Are personal and behavioral propensities formed entirely in childhood, or do processes of socialization continue throughout life? If core aspects of personality develop during childhood, which functions are served by socialization in adulthood?

The process of socialization has a dual locus. Some definitions are oriented to individuals; in these, socialization is seen as a means by which individuals learn how to participate in social life and to obtain their objectives in socially approved ways. Other definitions focus on groups and societies; from this perspective, socialization is a mechanism for furthering group goals and maintaining the overall health of a society. Following from these different emphases are two related problems: on the one hand, articulating processes of human development, and on the other, accounting for social continuity across generations. Resonating with these differences, early studies of childhood socialization provided an important foundation for studies of personality and social structure by focusing on interactions between individuals and the larger structures in which they are embedded (Benedict, 1938; House, 1981; Mead, 1928). Corsaro and Eder note that there has been a general tendency for sociologists to approach socialization at either the "macro" or "micro" level, implicitly emphasizing a distinction between individuals and social structures. They write, "since the mid-1980s there has been a growing dissatisfaction with the general acceptance of this bifurcation and a movement toward viewing socialization as a process of collective action and interpretive reproduction" (Corsaro & Eder, 1995, p. 424).

Building on this comment, we contend that such micro–macro bifurcation can be eroded by identifying some of the static assumptions underlying the concept of socialization and replacing them with a perspective that is sensitive to historical and life course temporality. Insofar as it is interested in changes associated with social transitions, role theory is necessarily associated with life course undertakings and it is the perspective we espouse here. At the same time, however, role theory's conceptualization of socialization is constrained by some of the same assumptions as current socialization research. It is our goal to identify some of these assumptions, discuss some of the research that has helped refine notions of socialization, and to articulate potential future directions for this area of work.

CHANGING CONCEPTUALIZATIONS OF SOCIALIZATION

In this section, we survey historical trends in the study of socialization. Specifically, we consider socialization's origins in functionalism; the subsequent shift to symbolic interactionist, active views of socializees; the historical focus on life-stage specific socialization; and finally, the focus on context-specific socialization. We suggest that these perspectives are static in that the charactéristics and prior experiences of socializees are not expected to differ in ways that would influence the socialization process. Instead, we call for a life course perspective on socialization that is sensitive to diverse manifestations of temporality.

Theoretical Development of Socialization

Early work on socialization focused on individual psychological progressions. Beginning with Freud's psychosexual stage theory, socializees were characterized as organisms moving through a linear series of developmental stages. While the progression could be potentially retarded or accelerated by environmental stimuli, inborn personality structures—id, ego, and superego—essentially propelled children through a series of psychological stages. Piaget's (1950) cognitive-developmental stage theory suggests more collective processes by pointing out that children move from one stage to the next as they learn to cognitively respond to environmental stimuli, including those provided by the social environment. Similarly, Vygotsky (1978) views the individual as actively engaged with his or her surroundings, and argues that movement from one stage to the next is contingent on social interaction with the environment.

Despite their focus on emergent psychological capacities, these approaches are compatible with functionalist assumptions that socialization serves the interests of the larger society by converting untrained children into competent adults capable of executing their roles and maintaining the existing social system. Furthermore, implicit in their focus on children is an assumption that preadult stages of development are important because they produce functioning adults, that such progression is a highly predictable process, and that there is a great deal of homogeneity among children.

Anthropologists, by contrast, have emphasized the transmission of culture. Mead (1928) and Benedict (1938), for example, were concerned with the ways in which culture affects life transitions, particularly from childhood or adolescence to adulthood. Over time, particularly through the development of symbolic interactionism (Blumer, 1969; Mead, 1934), sociologists have highlighted the distinctively social character of the socialization process. From their perspective, socialization occurs as individuals create and act upon definitions of their social situation that are jointly and collaboratively achieved with others. Thus, the individual socializee is viewed as highly active; personal changes hinge primarily on interaction with the social environment. Symbolic interactionism marks a significant departure from previous work by dismissing the notion of predetermined stages in favor of conceptualizing interaction, and the interpretation of interaction, as the driving force behind socialization. In this approach, actors are capable of shaping the conditions that influence their subsequent development rather than passively succumbing to a psychologically inborn progression of stages or simply responding to social stimuli. Accompanying this theoretical shift was a movement toward studying socialization as an ongoing, lifelong process, not limited to childhood. Interest in adult socialization grew, particularly that occurring in educational and occupational settings.

There is greater interest today in the processes through which socialization, writ large, lead to the transformation of society itself. However, as Bush and Simmons first noted in 1981, and Corsaro and Eder later corroborated (Corsaro & Eder, 1995, p. 424), sociologists still "tend to emphasize the ways in which the individual learns to fit into society." A secondary consideration is "how this process changes not only the individual but society as well" (Bush & Simmons, 1981, p. 135). A life course perspective on socialization draws attention to the mutually consequential interplay between individuals and social structure.

SOCIALIZATION AS LIFE-STAGE SPECIFIC.   While role theorists initially studied socialization in childhood and adolescence, subsequent research drew attention to socialization
after childhood (Brim & Wheeler, 1966; Mortimer & Simmons, 1978). Theoretically, this
change reflected broadening notions of what is accomplished through socialization, implying
that roles other than "adulthood" are appropriate for examination. Brim and Wheeler (1966),
for example, assert that socialization operates differently according to the life stage of the
socializee, both in terms of its *content* and the *context* in which it occurs. Childhood socialization, they argue, is focused primarily on providing socializees with basic values and motivations that will be generically appropriate to later tasks. For example, middle-class American
parents want their children to be independent and self-sufficient, able to meet the challenges
of higher level professional and managerial occupations; working class parents manifest
greater concern about obedience, preparatory to the kinds of non-supervisory, blue collar and
lower white collar occupations that they are likely to hold in the future (Kohn & Schooler,
1969; Alwin, 1989). By necessity, socialization during childhood cannot definitively prepare
children for the many varied social roles and unforeseeable life changes they will subsequently encounter. Socialization during adulthood, therefore, is oriented toward the acquisition of specific new skills and information, which can be integrated with the moral foundation
created in childhood (Brim & Wheeler, 1966; Mortimer & Simmons, 1978).

Socialization in adulthood differs from childhood socialization in several additional
ways. For children, socialization to adulthood places them in student roles, where they learn
about roles they will occupy in the future, but from which they are currently far removed.
Accordingly, the content of what is learned during childhood socialization is idealized, and
socializees assume a passive position in the process. By contrast, the greater social power and
influence adults hold in comparison to children contribute to a socialization process wherein
they are active rather than passive. Socialization occurring in adulthood pertains to roles in
which socializees are incumbent, such as the spousal role. By extension, adults' initial
attempts to enact their roles are likely to be far more consequential. A new manager must
"learn the ropes" while simultaneously exercising authority and making decisions that are
likely to be quite consequential for subordinates and for the organization itself.

As a result, adults are often socialized in ways that are qualitatively distinct from children's
experiences. Many adult roles, for example, do not require socializees to first assume the role
of learner; instead, they learn about specific roles while simultaneously occupying them, as with
socialization to marriage, parenthood, new work positions, or widowhood. Adults may also be
subject to resocialization, a mechanism by which society can exert control over actors who do
not exhibit appropriate social competence. Most notably, resocialization occurs in the context of
deviance and correctional institutions, attempting to create or restore socializees' proper values
and moral orientations to society by limiting their social activity (Brim & Wheeler, 1966, p. 39;
Mortimer & Simmons, 1978, p. 435). Finally, adult socialization is tied to a broader range of
socializing organizations than childhood socialization, where socializees are primarily affected
by their families, schools, and peers. For adults, socialization occurs in a wide array of work,
educational, civic, and other settings, where the purported goal may or may not be training for
adults to assume new roles (Brim & Wheeler, 1966, p. 68). Some of these socializing organizations have been extensively studied, a point we return to below.

SOCIALIZATION AS CONTEXT-SPECIFIC.   In addition to concerns with life stages of socializees, socialization research has been particularly attentive to how features of socialization
contexts influence outcomes. Family contexts, for example, are essential to the successful
primary socialization of children; it is among families that children develop physically and

cognitively,[1] and acquire the sense of social self and language skills that are required for interaction with others and for effective adaptation to future adult roles (Corsaro & Eder, 1995; Gecas, 1981). Furthermore, it is through family socialization that children learn about sex, age, and family roles they will assume later in life. In the absence of these basic socialization processes, as with, for example, feral children, children are profoundly disadvantaged (Gecas, 2000, pp. 2856–2857).

Extensive research on families as contexts for socialization indicates that parents exert a robust influence on children, extending through adolescence and into adulthood. To a lesser degree, and with less consensus among findings, siblings are also important agents of childhood socialization (Dunn & Kendrick, 1982; Sulloway, 1996). Specifically, parental support and control are critical if children are to identify with and internalize parental values, attitudes, and beliefs (Gecas, 2000, p. 2857). Following from our earlier discussion of unidirectional assumptions in developmental stage theories, much of the existing literature on parental socialization of children assumes that the influence operates in one direction—from parents to children, and not the reverse. In more recent decades, however, it has become clear that parents and children affect one another reciprocally, and such bidirectional models of influence have been studied extensively (Corsaro & Eder, 1995; Gecas, 1981, 2000). Increased interest in adult socialization, however, has broadened the previous, nearly exclusive focus on families as settings for socialization.

As institutions charged with helping children acquire knowledge and skills they will need as competent adults, schools are, by definition, critical contexts for socialization, and they have been studied extensively as such. It is in schools that children's academic performances are labeled and evaluated in comparison to their peers, which contributes to children's developing senses of identity and self-concept. As in family contexts, children in school settings are not just passive recipients of socialization, but are differentially responsive to their social environments. Based on their perceptions of how others think of them, children may learn to embrace or distance themselves from the student role, consequently shaping further the perceptions of their teachers and peers. If, for example, students perceive that teachers have labeled them as "underachievers" or "slow learners," they may be more likely to behave in ways that corroborate that perception; by contrast, students labeled "gifted" or "intelligent" may more readily embrace academic performance as an activity boosting their self-concepts (Rosenthal & Jacobson, 1968).

More broadly, school as a context for socialization can be seen as accomplishing something more general than teaching socializees specific skills and knowledge that build on their primary socialization. Dreeben (1968), for example, characterizes schools as critical linkages between families and other institutions, suggesting that their central goal is teaching children how to move successfully from their private family lives to the public political and occupational settings in which adults live. As adults, socializees must have the psychological capacities to conduct themselves appropriately in multiple settings which will place varied demands on them, and school offers an important environment for learning how to accomplish that.

For Dreeben, organizational features of schools, including the demands they place on students, generate normative outcomes consistent with this ability to transition among institutions. Unlike families, where helping others is fully accepted in virtually all circumstances, pupils must learn to do much of their school work "on their own," and to be evaluated, at least some of the time, for their individual efforts. Behaviors that are appropriate, even encouraged, in the family setting may be regarded with suspicion or disdain at school, interpreted as "cheating." Children who learn to act independently as well as cooperatively will be able to adjust more readily to adult roles that place a premium on either one, or both, of these capacities. Similarly, children learn in school that students of the same age are treated alike, attending the same grades irrespective of their races, religions, or personality traits. According to Dreeben, enactment of this universalistic principle in the school setting prepares young people for their future adult roles as citizens in democratic states.

OCCUPATIONAL SOCIALIZATION.   In modern societies, occupational roles largely determine individuals' positions in the status hierarchy and lifestyle, as well as affecting many of the most basic routines and challenges of everyday life. Because of this centrality, sociological interest in socialization after childhood has come to focus on socialization to work, including that which occurs in preparatory institutions, such as technical institutes and professional schools, and that taking place on the job (Mortimer & Lorence, 1995). Studies of socialization to work have followed two distinct tracks. The first examines particular socialization content and processes in distinct occupational settings. Socializees learn the special subcultures of the occupations for which they are being prepared, including incentives for and markers of success, attitudes toward coworkers, customers and clients, and special world views. Interest focuses on what is needed— in terms of skills, knowledge, and behaviors—for socializees to function as full and effective occupational incumbents. Thus, there are case studies of socialization pursuant to becoming a physician (Becker, Geer, Hughes, & Strauss, 1961; Merton, Reader, & Kendall, 1957), psychiatrist (Light, 1980), policeman (Hopper, 1977), clergyman (Schoenherr & Greeley, 1974), and sociologist (Wright, 1967). The second track is less interested in how individuals must change for effective work performance in particular occupational roles, and more focused on how work experiences influence basic attitudes, values, and ways of conceiving the self that affect all aspects of everyday life. Rather than examining particular occupations, such as minister or teacher, this second perspective conceptualizes the job in terms of critical dimensions, such as autonomy, the routinization of tasks, pressures, and stressors in the work setting, or intrinsic and extrinsic rewards.

This second approach is exemplified by Kohn and Schooler's "generalization model" and empirical studies of change in worker orientations and values in response to the structural imperatives of their work (Kohn & Schooler, 1983). Research focuses on the features of work that have the greatest significance for personal development. Kohn and Schooler emphasize opportunities for occupational self-direction, as indicated by substantive complexity in relation to data, people and things, variety, complex organization, and an absence of close supervision. They found that men whose work was more self-directed emphasized self-direction rather than conformity in their values for their children. These men also had higher self-esteem, more responsible moral standards, greater trust of others, and were more open to change than men whose work lacked self-directed features (Kohn & Schooler, 1969). Subsequent longitudinal studies demonstrated that substantively complex work also fostered psychological change, especially intellectual flexibility, among men (Kohn & Schooler, 1973, 1983). Following Kohn and Schooler's pathbreaking studies, the model was extended to women, paid work of adolescents (Mortimer & Finch, 1996), school work of children, work of homemakers, and to people in diverse national contexts, including Poland, the Ukraine, and Japan (for a summary of this work, see Miller, 1988). For example, learning opportunities at work have been found to foster the development of occupational reward values, promoting vocational development (Mortimer & Finch, 1996). More recent investigation focuses on possible interactions between work experiences and personal characteristics, and how the latter may influence responsiveness to work. These characteristics include age—that is, whether work experience has stronger effects on younger than on older workers (Lorence &

Mortimer, 1985), gender, and ethnicity (for a review, see Mortimer & Lorence, 1995). However, the greater emphasis in this area has been on uniformities, not differences, in the ways workers respond to their jobs (Kohn & Schooler, 1983).

CURRENT THEMES AND OPPORTUNITIES FOR EXPANDING CONCEPTUALIZATIONS OF SOCIALIZATION

To the extent that socialization research has focused on life stages and major socialization contexts, heterogeneity, on at least two dimensions, is inadequately addressed. Here, we consider some of the potential limitations arising from these approaches, and develop a life course perspective on socialization that is more sensitive to diverse life course experiences and to the historically changing socialization experiences of individuals. First, we suggest that life-stage specific and context-specific approaches to socialization are rather static in that prior experiences of socializees are not expected to influence the socialization process. By not attending to differences in when socialization occurs in the life span and in historical time, existing work ignores the increasingly individualistic character of the life course (Shanahan, 2000). It also assumes a high level of continuity among socializees, socializers, and the organizational contexts in which they interact. Particularly in light of widespread societal changes in recent decades, it is important for socialization researchers to recognize that contexts are changing, and that shifts in the character of role incumbency require new adaptations of socializees and socializers. Assumptions of uniformity across social contexts and time may inhibit our ability to understand how socializees, even when considered "successful" in the socialization process, may be inadequately prepared for what they will encounter in their changing social worlds.

Moreover, socialization research has focused on normative events in socializees' lives. Clearly, it is important and theoretically fruitful to examine life transitions that are expected and common to large segments of the population. There is good coverage in the socialization literature of roles and role transitions that are highly prevalent (e.g., family member, student, worker, spouse, or parent), normative, anticipated, and considered to have positive implications for individuals. Studying how children are socialized by their families and schools to become adults, for example, is critical for understanding how these experiences of socialization operate in the lives of almost all people. Similarly, examination of how people are socialized to occupational settings or to adult family roles yields highly generalizable information about how these processes affect the majority of socially functioning adults. In light of the extensive body of literature that has been generated on these topics, however, it is also important to consider the assumptions underlying these research strategies, and their implications for future work. Paralleling the early developmental stage theories of socialization, this focus on normativity treats socialization as a process that prepares people to behave in ways that are functional for society. While such research has been essential for the development of socialization theory to date, we suggest that future work would benefit from the incorporation of more diverse types of socialization processes, roles, and transitions.

What can we learn by studying non-normative socialization? While we know that effective socialization to motherhood benefits society by enhancing mothers' mental health, marital stability, and the socialization of children, we know less about, for example, socialization to the non-normative but increasingly common role of chronic illness sufferer. By continuing to focus on highly traditional forms of socialization, we may forego a clearer understanding of universal processes at work in socialization to both normative and non-normative roles. We also forego the recognition and understanding of important differences in processes of socialization across situations. Systematic consideration of variation in socialization—in terms of roles, content, and context—can enrich our current knowledge and provide a strong theoretical foundation for future studies.

To this end, this chapter develops a life course perspective on socialization that is sensitive to the many ways in which temporality shapes socialization. Rather than examining substantive contexts and various life stages separately from one another, it is important to consider theoretical commonalities shared by these diverse areas of study. Through the recognition of individualization and destructuration in life course studies, socialization research can move forward under a conceptual umbrella that extends the notions of context and life stage. Here, we examine three ways in which a life course perspective on socialization could expand our knowledge of the topic: through consideration of socializees' individual biographies; socializers' temporal orientations; and historical variability in socialization.

Importance of Socializees' Individual Biographies

SENSITIVITY TO INCREASING DIVERSITY OF LIFE COURSE TRAJECTORIES. Stage-specific socialization theories assume, to a greater or lesser extent, a uniform life course. That is, individuals are seen as progressing from one life stage to another in a fairly uniform manner, undergoing socialization processes specific to each stage. Childhood socialization in the family gives way to socialization in the peer group as children grow older; the organization of the school functions as a major socialization context for children and adolescents; the work setting assumes priority at a subsequent stage. This familiar conceptualization of the life course is now being challenged by increasing diversity and unpredictability of life course trajectories in modern societies. For example, the transition from adolescence to adulthood has become prolonged and individualized as people stay in school longer and postpone family formation (Shanahan, 2000). At the same time, markers of adulthood are less likely to be achieved in an orderly and predictable fashion (e.g., leaving home, followed by full-time work, marriage, and parenthood). Instead of a unidirectional predictable movement from one stage to another, there are more frequent delays, reversals, or changes in direction. Young people leave home to establish an independent residence only to return again at a subsequent time; they are more likely than in prior cohorts to have children prior to marriage; they move between school and work, dropping out of college for the labor force, only to return to acquire further educational credentials.

Contemporary adulthood, at least in some respects, is therefore less predictable than formerly. As job and career changes are propelled by technological advances (Buchmann, 1989), persons seeking new occupational knowledge and skills—whether through vocational or professional schools, liberal arts colleges, general educational credentials, or other venues—may be diverse in age, as well as in work and life experience. Similarly, persons remarrying following divorce or widowhood are likely to experience entry to their new family roles in ways that are different from that of persons entering first marriages, given the more complex relational structure to which they must adapt (with stepchildren and other new relatives). These considerations give rise to some fundamental questions about variability in socialization processes and outcomes that are dependent on individual biography.

These types of differences in socializees' individual biographies impact their socialization experiences in several ways, including their capacity for socialization, their ability to adapt to socialization settings, and their orientation toward socialization. We begin by calling attention to the ways socializees' prior life experiences influence their capacity to engage socialization processes. Despite the diversity in life course trajectories, and the demonstrated relationship among many earlier and later life events, relatively little is known about how individual biographies are connected to socialization processes. Instead, much of the existing socialization literature assumes that prior life experiences are not critical for understanding socialization. Corsaro and Eder (1995, p. 444) suggest that, with respect to childhood socialization, "instead of focusing on the autonomous child on a lonely journey in which s/he must first learn and then use the skills and knowledge of his/her culture ... (we) focus on children's negotiations with others." While our focus differs from that of Corsaro and Eder in that we are more broadly concerned with a life course perspective than interpretive approaches to socialization, we agree with their point about the importance of viewing socializees as *active participants* in socialization processes. Furthermore, we wish to elaborate the importance of contingency in socialization, a theme which remains implicit in Corsaro and Eder's discussion. In addition to contingencies arising from interaction among socializees and their interpretation of culture, we also observe that socialization across the life course is shaped in part by individuals' biographies. Prior life experience, in other words, shapes what individuals bring to a situation and their capacity to learn.

PRIOR LIFE EXPERIENCES. Extensive life course research has explored the potential impact of early life events on subsequent life course trajectories of individuals (George, 1993, pp. 363–364). For example, Brown and Harris (1978) found that the loss of a parent in childhood predicts later clinical depression, lower socioeconomic achievement, and lower quality marriages in adulthood. Children's experiences in starting school have been found to impact their later achievement (Alexander & Entwisle, 1988); early onset of mental illness is associated with lower academic achievement, lower occupational prestige, and increased unemployment (Turnbull, George, Landerman, Swartz, & Blazer, 1990); and early choices regarding family and career predict retirement income (O'Rand, 1988).

Previous research considers ways socialization can go awry, and how society can manage deviant behavior through social control, punishment, and resocialization of socializees who exhibit problem behavior or incompetence. Likely attributable, at least in part, to the long-term focus on childhood socialization in the extant literature, there is little systematic attention to variation among individuals prior to the socialization experience that is the object of study, and how this variation may lead to differential responses to quite similar situations. If early biographical experiences—for example, family dysfunction—disrupt the acquisition of basic social skills, individuals may respond ineffectually to later socialization. While life course perspectives have considered how early events affect achievement and other outcomes, such a perspective has not been well integrated into socialization research: how and why do socializees vary in their preparedness for socialization?

In one exceptional study, Tallman, Gray, Kullberg, and Henderson (1999) examined the effects of the composition of the family of origin on socialization to marriage to examine how past biographical experiences can shape later socialization processes. Using a sample of newly married couples, they explored patterns of conflict that varied depending on whether both spouses came from intact families, both were from divorced families, or one was from a divorced family and the other was from an intact one. They predicted that spouses would replicate conflict patterns exhibited in their families of origin if those learned patterns of behavior were reinforced in their current marriage environment. If such behaviors are not reinforced by a spouse, there is a potential for new behavioral patterns to emerge. Based on this principle, they predicted, and found, that when both partners are from divorced families, couples will have the highest levels of marital conflict over time, collectively replicating distrusting and conflict behaviors learned in their families of origin. For similar reasons, newlyweds from intact families exhibited the lowest level of conflict. Couples in which one person was from a divorced family and the other from an intact family had the highest potential for new behavior, and, in fact, gravitated over time to a lower conflict (and more gratifying) style of interaction.

Depending on their prior experience, socializees' capacities for learning may differ along multiple dimensions, including receptivity, level of engagement, and readiness for socialization. Responses to college professors as socializers in the context of higher education may vary according to high school experiences, to prior courses, or to previous programs of study. Socialization to new romantic relationships may be affected by experiences with previous partners. Which circumstances led the socializee to his or her current situation? Is the attendee of an Alcoholics Anonymous (AA) meeting there for the first time, or following prior attendance and subsequent relapses? Is the person there of his or her own volition, at the urging of a spouse, or because it has been mandated as part of legal sentencing following an arrest? Like students who use procrastination or nonparticipation as failure-avoiding strategies in school (Covington & Beery, 1976; Gecas, 2000, p. 2859), so could a potential socializee at an AA meeting disengage from the setting because of the biographical circumstances that resulted in attendance in the first place.

Furthermore, socializees may have developed self-concepts based on past biographical experiences that affect their responses to socialization. From a symbolic interactionist perspective, self-concepts are based on actors' understandings of others' perceptions of them, and actors are therefore motivated to behave in ways that reinforce the identities they wish to maintain. Students who have developed self-concepts as intelligent people in high school, for example, may be motivated to behave in ways that confirm that identity when they arrive in college. Because the new socialization setting is highly consistent with positive components of their self-concept, they may respond differently than someone in the same situation who developed a negative self-concept as a result of early educational experiences. In sum, rather than seeing socializees as passive recipients of socialization, attention to biographical differences calls attention to how past experiences may act synergistically with socialization in the present.

TEMPORAL ORIENTATIONS.   Beyond a basic capacity for socialization, individuals' temporal orientations, especially their future referents, are also likely to shape their adaptations to socialization settings. Orientations to the future, tied to expectations for life plans and attainment, vary by the life stage of the actor and may account for differences in adaptation to socialization contexts. Using the case of the person attending an AA meeting, adaptation to the setting may differ according to whether the end goal is long-term sobriety or short-term satisfaction of legal requirements for probation. Current work on socialization, however, often orients to such differences in terms of functional outcomes—the person who aspires only to meet legal requirements, and resumes drinking after doing so, would likely be characterized as having failed to be properly socialized by the organization. The individual, however, would likely evaluate his or her AA participation as a success. By considering differences among socializees in terms of their own temporal orientations and expectations for the future, as opposed to researchers' or organizations' expectations, we can generate more nuanced interpretations of socialization outcomes. Instead of assuming uniformity among socializees, we encourage assessment of outcomes in terms of diverse personal goals and expectations.

The amount of time socializees anticipate spending in a particular role may also be linked to socialization processes. As longevity increases, people may expect to spend a larger portion of their lives in statuses assumed by the elderly, such as retirement or widowhood. For example, as child-raising occupies a progressively smaller portion of the life span, socialization for the parenting role may diminish in importance. Similarly, socialization for retirement may assume greater salience as that phase occupies a longer portion of the life span. Changes in life course patterns have been accompanied by the emergence and growth of new roles, or at least reconceptualizations of existing ones. Differences between "traditional" and "nontraditional" students, for example, imply variation in socialization to the student role; similarly, the proliferation of temporary or "contingent" employment contributes to increasingly diverse expectations for time spent in roles as well as trajectories once those roles are entered (Kalleberg, Reskin, & Hudson, 2000). As new role conceptualizations take hold, systematic differences among cohorts may also emerge.

In addition to these culturally based temporal expectations, social psychological literature identifies additional features as shaping actors' temporal orientations and receptivity to socialization. Markus and Nurius (1986), for example, introduce the notion of "possible selves" as a form of self-knowledge pertaining to how people think about their potential and their future, both in terms of what they would like to become and what they fear becoming:

> The possible selves that are hoped for might include the successful self, the creative self, the rich self, the thin self, or the loved and admired self, whereas the dreaded possible selves could be the alone self, the depressed self, the incompetent self, the alcoholic self, the unemployed self, or the bag lady self. (Markus & Murius, 1986, p. 954)

This self-knowledge, Marcus argues, is essentially a manifestation of long-term cognitive goals. Based on past experience, possible selves function as incentives for future behavior, thereby linking actors' individual biographies to their receptivity to socialization.

Clausen (1991) considers adolescent planful competence as another social psychological characteristic that shapes life course trajectories in ways related to socialization. He argues that, compared to peers who are not planfully competent, adolescents who are able to rationally and thoughtfully consider educational and career decisions are more likely to make decisions they are happy with in the long term, and they are more likely to be rewarded for those choices and the planfulness that produced them. As a result, these adolescents will exhibit less personality change over the life course. Most importantly, however, Clausen contends that people must exhibit such competence very early in life to reap the benefits as adults. This work implicates temporality in individuals' biographies in at least two ways: first, activities early in the life course of these adolescents impact their later achievement; and, second, the very nature of their mental orientation implies a serious, highly contemplative, future-oriented temporality. Both in terms of their lived pasts and their approaches to the future, biography is intimately connected to how people learn and think about their environments, and how they respond to socialization opportunities and constraints.

Arguably, the articulation of possible selves, and the exercise of planful competence, is linked to the structure of opportunities in subsequent stages of life. In general, socializees will be more engaged in the process of socialization when they see a connection between their performance in that setting and future valued outcomes. To the extent that socializees can visualize, and understand, the character of subsequent role demands, and the knowledge and skills that are necessary to enact them competently, their possible selves become more complex and differentiated, and their plans more detailed and realistic. Accordingly, Schneider and Stevenson (1999) worry that contemporary American students' exclusive interest in getting into college, and the absence of serious consideration of occupational choice, reduces the psychological relevance of higher education to future outcomes. The lack of connection between education and desired outcomes increases the likelihood of both a lack of commitment to the educational process once they are accepted into college and consequent floundering between schools, majors, and other programs of study. In the process, higher educational resources may not be optimally utilized.

Macroinstitutional contexts of socialization may have features that highlight socialization outcomes for socializees, thereby influencing their motivation and involvement in the socialization process. In contrasting the school to work transition for the non-college bound in the United States and Germany, Mortimer and Krüger (2000) illustrate the importance of structural bridges in affecting the psychological orientations of socializees. In the United States, there is little connection between high school grades and vocational outcomes, and motivating involvement of non-college youth in their programs of study is quite problematic. In Germany, in contrast, non-college youth are motivated to do well in their apprenticeships and their related coursework because these are integrated by design and clearly linked to longer term objectives. Those young people who do well in the school-based component of their apprenticeship have more knowledge and skills that are applicable to the problems and tasks that they encounter in their apprentice position in the work setting. And those who do better in their apprentice placements are more likely to be retained by their employers and to succeed in passing certifying examinations that will allow entry to other employing organizations. Linkages between schools and employers in Japan similarly strengthen motivation on the part of the less academically oriented students (i.e., those who are not oriented to college) to do well in school (Rosenbaum & Kariya, 1991).

Overall, increase in the diversity of lived trajectories means that people are exercising more options and exhibiting a greater diversity of temporal orientations. Aspirations and expectations for the future, in combination with the amount of time people anticipate spending in the roles for which they are being prepared, need to be further examined as factors influencing socialization, both in terms of its content and the receptivity of socializees. In addition, prior biographical experiences and macroinstitutional contexts of socialization need to be considered as potentially influencing socialization processes.

CONCURRENT LIFE EXPERIENCES.   Concurrent life experiences also influence actors' orientations toward socialization by shaping their self-concepts, goals, and expectations for future trajectories. Adolescents' selection of work activities during high school clearly illustrates this principle. Adolescents from less advantaged family backgrounds tend to seek work during high school in order to learn new skills, acquiring human capital through early work experience (Mortimer, 2003). They tend to have high school work trajectories that are more time-consuming, financially rewarding, and stressful, but ones that also involve more advancement opportunities. A different strategy is apparent, however, for adolescents who have greater resources that enable higher educational attainment. Ninth graders who come from more advantaged family backgrounds, and those who have stronger intrinsic motivation to their schoolwork upon entry to high school, obtain work experiences during the following 3 years that are less involving and demanding and that enable them to participate in extracurricular activities and a diverse array of other activities besides work. They are also more likely to save at least some of their earnings for college. Given the diverse life experiences and orientations of adolescents, and the varying meanings of their work experience, it may be concluded that adolescent work functions differently for varying groups of teenagers.

Socialization contexts may also have different meanings according to whether socializees experience asynchronies in their concurrent role trajectories. Burton (Burton, Obeidallah, &

Allison, 1996), for example, has studied precocious adulthood in poor minority populations, as children are socialized to behave like adults at home, assuming major family responsibilities, while being socialized to behave like children at school. More generally, being a novice in one socialization context while having senior status in a concurrent one may impact several aspects of socialization, including actors' compliance with socializers and their capacity to fulfill socializers' expectations. In Burton's study, precocious children fulfilling adult roles at home often had trouble completing their homework, exacerbating struggles to meet teachers' expectations for their student roles.

This issue is related to the broader concept of status incongruence or inconsistency (Dogan, 2000). That is, persons whose positions in hierarchies of status, rewards, and responsibility are inconsistent, whether in family, school, work, or other settings, are likely to respond differently to socialization attempts, as well as other life experiences, from those whose statuses are similar. As socializees receive inconsistent reactions across their incongruent roles, they may experience increased distress. In turn, such distress could prompt socializees to improve such situations by increasing the level or salience of more valued statuses and decreasing that of less valued statuses—and in this process, become less receptive to some types of socialization. For example, Dogan (2000) reports that highly educated young people in Western European countries whose educational credentials are not matched by the occupations they have been able to find constitute a " 'reserve army' of alienated people" (2000, p. 3051); in one sense, Dogan describes a population resistant to socialization to employment status that is incongruent with their educational credentials. Socializees could also manage status inconsistency through, for example, collective action (e.g., by joining a political movement) or individual efforts (e.g., by educational accomplishments fostering mobility).

Under conditions of status inconsistency, however, responses are likely to depend on the particular configuration of age, education, occupational status, and ethnic backgrounds of the socializer(s) and socializee. For example, a 45-year-old senior personnel manager who returns to business school for an MBA is likely to be less impressed by the 28-year-old instructor (despite that instructor's PhD) than the recent college graduate with little work experience who is pursuing the same advanced degree. Sometimes status inconsistencies between role partners can provide the impetus for rejection of long-term patterns of socialization and traditional role allocation in favor of new innovations. For example, Atkinson and Boles (1984) found that wives in their study who were occupationally superior to their husbands became what the authors called "senior partners," reversing traditional division of labor and achievement patterns within their families. Husbands assisted their wives by doing much household work and by providing emotional support.

Furthermore, people may simultaneously occupy both normative and non-normative or deviant status positions; this is a unique type of status inconsistency that could have distinct effects on socialization. Studies of health and illness, for example, have generated extensive literature addressing how people are socialized to identities as people with chronic or terminal illness (Charmaz, 1991), parents of seriously ill children (Davis, 1991), or as infertile people (Greil, 1991). For most people, chronic health problems arise in the midst of their "normal" lives, as they are suddenly challenged with managing a new, deviant role while simultaneously remaining responsible for their concurrent, normative roles. Precisely because people with chronic illness are not able to subscribe to a traditional, inherently temporary "sick role" (Parsons, 1951), they are concurrently identified as both normal and deviant. This dual identity often increases the difficulty they have in either their socialization to the sick role or with their abilities to maintain their original roles, such as spouse, parent, friend, or worker. For people suffering from terminal illness or for those who act as caregivers to the terminally ill, socialization involves learning about a role that will be occupied, by definition, on a temporary basis, but still poses grave challenges for integration with concurrent roles. Charmaz (1991) describes how chronically ill persons move from a state of intrusion, during which symptoms disrupt conventional roles, to a state of immersion, at which point these roles must be relinquished to enable one's full energies to be devoted to managing the illness itself. Furthermore, for people who have suffered with chronic illness for long periods of time, the role as chronic illness sufferer can also function as previous experience affecting socialization to new roles, as discussed above. In the larger societal context of changing family roles, extended life spans, and increased prevalence of age-related illnesses, health-related identities once considered highly deviant are becoming more common. We need to better understand how people are socialized to those situations as well as how they manage tension among concurrent social roles.

Importance of Socializers' Temporal Orientations

Appreciating temporality in socialization requires attention to how socializers' temporal orientations impact their expectations about, and experience with, socializing others. We begin by considering how socializers' temporal orientations shape their expectations for socializees' capacities for socialization, as well as the length and desirability of their probable trajectories in a role. In their classic study *Pygmalion in the classroom*, Rosenthal and Jacobson (1968) examined how expectations for behavior, in this case, teachers' expectations for students, can function as self-fulfilling prophecies. When teachers in their study used randomly selected test scores, which they believed to be true student scores, to predict those students who would experience intellectual growth spurts over the following academic year, their predictions were quite accurate. The authors argue that their assessments of the students helped produce the very outcomes they foresaw.

Socializers' roles in assessing socializees and shaping their outcomes have been well-studied in the social psychological literature, but the importance of these temporal aspects is not always well integrated into socialization research. For example, educators try to assess students' cognitive ability; police, judges, and parole board members try to assess defendants' guilt, innocence, or degree of rehabilitation; advice-givers try to assess recipients' current states of knowledge; and other service providers try to assess laypersons' motivation and competence vis-à-vis particular behaviors. At the same time, salient characteristics of socializees, such as intelligence, guilt, innocence, motivation, and competence are generally treated as phenomena residing entirely within the individual.

These attributions, however, are likely to be collectively constructed in interactions between socializers and socializees, rendering the perspectives of socializers critical to understanding socialization processes. In their work on standardized educational testing, for example, Maynard and Marlaire (1992) use conversation analysis to examine videotaped data of teachers administering test questions to children. They find that student–teacher interaction does not function as a neutral conduit through which children convey their knowledge. Instead, there is an interactional substrate through which testers provide, and students respond to, cues about correct responses to questions—in essence, educators teach students how to successfully take standardized tests while they are administering them. Resonating with Rosenthal and Jacobson's work, this microinteractionalist approach articulates additional mechanisms by which socializers affect socialization processes. In similar ways, additional conversation analytic studies have examined how socialization occurs in and through interaction, including, for example, how 911 call-takers train callers to provide information that facilitates the dispatch of emergency services (Whalen & Zimmerman, 1998; Whalen, Zimmerman, & Whalen, 1988). Additionally, Lutfey and Maynard (1998) have studied how physicians attempt to socialize patients to their new prognoses as "terminally ill" by introducing interactionally delicate topics of death, dying, and hospice care.

Finally, socializers' previous experiences with socializing others to a particular role may shape socialization outcomes. In studies of socialization to the roles of medical student and physician (Becker et al., 1961; Hafferty, 1991), past experiences of attending physicians contribute to the process of socializing neophyte medical practitioners, both in terms of what they learn directly from their supervisors and how students learn to socialize one another. For example, seasoned practitioners' past experiences with cadavers is critical for teaching new students how to handle this aspect of medical school: because they know their teachers have, at some point in their own educational trajectories, had to become comfortable with dissecting humans, students are socialized to model that behavior themselves. Furthermore, new students form inferences as they learn about their instructors' experiences in the practice of medicine. They conclude that if they are not successful in learning to deal with cadavers and other unpleasantries, they will be fundamentally unsuccessful at practicing medicine at all.

Consideration of temporality in the process of socialization draws attention to sequences of interaction as the process unfolds. Drawing again from Corsaro and Eder's (1995) discussion of interpretation, interaction, and reproductive processes in socialization, we invoke studies of interaction to understand the dynamic, contingent, and temporal aspects of socialization. While microinteractional studies are not common among life course scholars, they are potentially illuminating of socialization processes. Microinteractionists' concerns with conceiving actors as active instead of passive; attending to the roles of socializers as well as socializees; assuming and integrating diversity of prior biographies and future trajectories; and understanding contingency are shared by scholars of the life course who are sensitive to socialization research. More generally, interactional and observational studies provide a methodological mechanism for understanding how socialization is accomplished and how the diverse parties participate in it.

Historical Variability

A life course perspective on socialization also implies consideration of how the contexts and meanings of socialization have changed over time. Attention should be directed to historical variation among numerous phenomena: the attitudes of both socializers and socializees, the conceptualization of life course stages, demographic changes and the interpersonal dynamics of socialization, all of which may influence socialization processes and outcomes.

For example, contexts of socialization often change over time in response to historical processes. Family structures have changed immensely over the last several decades as a result of economic shifts, changing expectations about life styles, family life, and women's roles. The roles of "woman," "spouse," "mother," and "worker" have changed in combination with one another as women have returned to work outside the home and the traditional breadwinner–homemaker model of marriage has become less common. Over the past half-century there has been an increase in dual income marriages, divorced families, single-parent families, and blended families. As more women work outside the home, formal child care becomes increasingly prevalent, and children are more involved in after-school activities. The contexts in which primary socialization occurs thus change in important ways.

Similarly, school contexts continue to change along with these shifts in family structure, as well as in response to large-scale political and social changes, as exemplified by school desegregation in the 1950s. The most dramatic change in the educational context during the past several decades is the expansion of higher education, prompted by shifts in the occupational structure and the growing affluence of the population. Almost two thirds of recent cohorts of U.S. high school graduates go on to some form of post-secondary education (Kerckhoff, 2002). Exposure to higher education has been linked to manifold socialization outcomes, including a wide range of values and attitudes, the propensity for civic involvement, and health (Pallas, 2000).

Historical trends also implicate changes in the features of cohorts. Alwin (1989) finds that changes in conformity and autonomy values are predicted in part by cohort, particularly whether parents were born before or after the Great Depression. More broadly, socialization research would benefit from considering several aspects of cohorts in their historical contexts to learn how socialization is affected. Cohort size, for example, may influence expectations for opportunities as they are shaped by economic circumstances, demographic patterns, political situations, presidential administrations, or public policy programs.

As we discussed earlier, increased individualization of life course trajectories is tied to socialization and to historical change. Especially in light of demographic shifts involving women who increasingly move in and out of family, education, and work contexts, it is important to consider how such changes affect socialization. Furthermore, historical changes in roles and institutions can generate time lags between configurations of roles that exist when people are socialized and new combinations of roles once people come to occupy them. Such a lag is illustrated, for example, in Conley's (1998) description of her experiences as the first tenured female neurosurgeon in the United States. Her socialization experience was very painful for reasons that she attributes to gender stratification in her area of expertise, where her role as female neurosurgeon was poorly clarified and not previously experienced by any of her coworkers. Because of the conflicting role expectations arising from "neurosurgeon" and "woman," it was difficult and anomic for her and her coworkers to integrate her role into the existing setting. As people from different historical cohorts, or even contemporaries, interpret these roles differently, there is a potential for conflicting expectations and friction in socialization.

Cultural and attitudinal changes also vary historically, and may shape the content of socialization. Alwin (1989), for example, finds that there have been significant changes in the qualities that Americans value in their children from the years 1964 to 1984. While parents used to emphasize obedience or conformity, as manifested by children obeying parents, having good manners, and conforming to sex roles, they have more recently considered autonomy or self-direction to be more desirable qualities, as indicated by exhibiting good judgment, honesty, responsibility, and consideration toward others. Alwin suggests that such changes are linked to cultural changes in school socialization, but may also be related to family-level characteristics such as religious orientation. Values and expectations also evolve with large-scale cultural changes, as illustrated in the generational challenge to authority that occurred in the 1960s, when students demanded representation on key college committees. As actors' individual and cultural values and attitudes change over time, so do socialization processes evolve.

NEW DIRECTIONS FOR SOCIALIZATION RESEARCH

In summary, we call for greater attention to socialization in a life course perspective. Historically, conceptualizations of socialization have changed and developed in several important ways: socializees are viewed as active, interactive actors instead of passive recipients of information in a relatively deterministic developmental model; socialization is seen as a lifelong process not necessarily bound to specific life stages; socialization is seen as occurring in a variety of contexts beyond family and school; and broader social contexts are seen as critical for understanding socialization over time. While early work focusing on roles occupied by large segments of the population is methodologically and theoretically important for yielding generalizable analyses about experiences familiar to many people, we call for an extension of socialization research to more divergent and temporally diverse circumstances. We suggest that by attending to the many ways temporal issues shape socialization processes and outcomes, we can significantly develop and refine the strong research foundation that already exists on this topic. Furthermore, sensitivity to temporal aspects of socialization will help maintain a unified theoretical foundation for studies focusing on various contents and contexts of socialization. Specifically, we identify three fruitful areas for increased attention: socializees' individual biographies in socialization; socializers' temporal orientations; and historical variation that potentially shapes several aspects of socialization.

More generally, we also suggest that sociological notions of socialization could be broadened to include a more diverse array of roles, transitions, events, and conditions. Future work could benefit from deeper consideration of non-normative, unexpected, or stigmatizing roles or circumstances to which people must be socialized—which may include the disappearance of roles or circumstances to which a socializee is already accustomed. Particularly in a historical period witnessing an increasing diversity in life course trajectories, people are often forced to adjust to changes that are much less common, not generally anticipated at all, and therefore not necessarily attached to a normative role concept. By studying the vast assortment of non-normative socialization processes occurring daily, we can better understand socialization to changing, emergent, and inconsistent roles, as well as more traditional roles and life course trajectories.

Future socialization research would also benefit from increased attention to the characteristics of socialization settings that are linked to individual outcomes. In his 1981 discussion of social structure and personality, House (1981, pp. 540–541) asserts that sociologists need to better understand psychological theories in order to successfully articulate linkages between social systems and changes in individual-level behaviors and attitudes. In addition to psychological processes, he suggests that research would benefit from increased attention to both the components of social structure and the proximal linkages operating between individual personalities and the social systems in which they develop. We concur with this assessment, and suggest that socialization research would also benefit from improved understandings of the mechanisms through which large-scale social structures are connected to individual-level phenomena. For example, educational attainment is often linked to diverse outcomes without explicit attention to how and why such links occur (Pallas, 2000). In fact, Pallas contends, "the very plausibility of [widely established] accounts [for why schooling is associated with a range of adult outcomes] has had the unintended consequence of dissuading researchers from filling in the gaps that remain in this literature" (2000, p. 522). In similar ways, socialization research would benefit from a re-orientation to intermediate processes.

It is important for sociological social psychologists to consider how studies of socialization have permeated various substantive areas, and to integrate this work across subareas based on commonalities in their theoretical underpinnings. Without systematic consideration of connections among these substantive areas, socialization studies—which are so theoretically essential to sociology—could potentially dissipate across subfields in ways that would detract from the large body of work that has already been done. Maintaining awareness of how socialization studies may exist across substantive areas is important for building on the strong foundation already in place as well as protecting the conceptual unity of future work.

There is also a need to connect socialization research with broader sociological concerns about macro–micro linkages, the exercise of agency, and individuals' strategizing as it is related to their biographies. According to Shanahan (2000), life course studies of the transition to adulthood are largely organized around two themes: (1) increased variability in trajectories, both historically and in ways patterned by socioeconomic status, gender, and race; and (2) examination of transition behaviors as developmental processes. He argues that research would benefit from joining these lines of inquiry because it would facilitate an examination of "interplay between agency and social structures in the shaping of lives" (Shanahan, 2000, p. 667). Resonating with our earlier discussion, such attention to multiple levels of analysis would facilitate the development of more temporally sensitive, nuanced, multifaceted approaches to socialization.

REFERENCES

Alexander, K. L., & Entwisle, D. R. (1988). Achievement in the First Two Years of School: Patterns and process. *Monographs of the Society for Research in Child Development, 53*(2), 1–139.

Alwin, D. F. (1989). Changes in qualities valued in children in the United States, 1964–1984. *Social Science Research, 18*, 195–236.

Atkinson, M. P., & Boles, J. (1984). WASP (wives as senior partners). *Journal of Marriage and the Family, 46*(4), 861–870.

Becker, Howard S., Geer, Blanche, Hughes, Everett C., & Strauss, Anselm L. (1961). *Boys in white: Student culture in Medical School*. Chicago: University of Chicago Press.

Benedict, Ruth. (1938). Continuities and discontinuities in cultural conditioning. *Psychiatry, 1*(2), 161–167.

Blumer, Herbert. (1969). *Symbolic interactionism: Perspective and method*. Englewood Cliffs, NJ: Prentice Hall.

Brim, Orville G., & Wheeler, Stanton. (1966). *Socialization after childhood: Two essays*. New York: Wiley.

Brown, G. W., & Harris, T. O. (1978). *Social origins of depression: A study of psychiatric disorder in women*. New York: Free Press.

Buchmann, Marlis. (1989). *The script of life in modern society: Entry into adulthood in a changing world*. Chicago: University of Chicago Press.

Burton, Linda M., Obeidallah, Dawn A., & Allison, Kevin. (1996). Ethnographic insights on social context and adolescent development among inner-city African-American teens. In R. Jessor, A. Colby, and R. A. Shweder (Eds.), *Ethnography and Human Development: Context and Meaning in Social Inquiry* (pp. 395–418). Chicago: University of Chicago Press.

Bush, Diane Mitsch, & Simmons, Roberta G. (1981). Socialization processes over the life course. In M. Rosenberg & R. Turner (Eds.), *Social psychology: Sociological perspectives* (pp. 133–164). New York: Basic Books.

Charmaz, Kathy. (1991). *Good days, bad days: The self in chronic illness and time*. New Brunswick: Rutgers University Press.

Clausen, J. S. (1991). Adolescent competence and the shaping of the life course. *American Journal of Sociology, 96*(4), 805–842.

Conley, Frances K. (1998). *Walking out on the boys*. New York: Farrar, Straus, & Giroux.

Corsaro, William A., & Eder, Donna. (1995). Development and socialization of children and adolescents. In K. S. Cook, G. A. Fine, & J. S. House (Eds.), *Sociological perspectives on social psychology* (pp. 421–451). Boston: Allyn & Bacon.

Covington, Martin V., & Beery, Richard G. (1976). *Self-worth and school learning*. New York: Holt, Rinehart, & Winston.

Davis, Fred. (1991). *Passage through crisis: Polio victims and their families*. New Brunswick: Transaction.

Dreeben, Robert. (1968). *On what is learned in school*. Reading, MA: Addison-Wesley.

Dunn, J., & Kendrick, C. (1982). *Siblings: Love, envy, and understanding*. London: Grant McIntyre.

Erckhoff, Alan C. (2002). The transition from school to work. In J. T. Mortimer and R. Larson (Eds.), *The changing adolescent experience: Societal trends and the transition to adulthood*. New York: Cambridge University Press.

Gecas, Viktor. (1981). Contexts of socialization. In M. Rosenberg & R. H. Turner (Eds.), *Social psychology: Sociological perspectives* (pp. 165–199). New York: Basic Books.

Gecas, Viktor. (2000). Socialization. In E. F. Borgatta (Ed.), *Encyclopedia of sociology* (pp. 2855–2864). Detroit: Macmillan.

George, Linda K. (1993). Sociological perspectives on life transitions. *Annual Review of Sociology, 19*, 353–373.

Greil, Arthur. (1991). *Not yet pregnant: Infertile couples in contemporary America.* New Brunswick, New Jersey: Rutgers University Press.

Hafferty, Frederic. (1991). *Into the valley: Death and the socialization of medical students.* New Haven: Yale University Press.

Hopper, Marianne. (1977). Becoming a Policeman: Socialization of cadets in a Police Academy. *Urban Life, 6*(2), 149–170.

House, James S. (1981). Social structure and personality. In M. Rosenberg & R. Turner (Eds.), *Social psychology: Sociological perspectives* (pp. 525–561). New York: Basic Books.

Kalleberg, A. L., Reskin, B. F., & Hudson, K. (2000). Bad jobs in America: Standard and nonstandard employment relations and job quality in the United States. *American Sociological Review, 65*(2), 256–278.

Kohn, Melvin L., & Schooler, Carmi. (1969). Class, occupation, and orientation. *American Sociological Review, 34*(5), 659–678.

Kohn, Melvin L., & Schooler, Carmi. (1973). Occupational experience and psychological functioning: An assessment of reciprocal effects. *American Sociological Review, 38*(1), 97–118.

Kohn, Melvin L., & Schooler, Carmi. (1983). *Work and personality: An inquiry into the impact of social stratification.* Norwood, NJ: Ablex.

Light, Donald. (1980). *Becoming psychiatrists: The professional transformation of self.* New York: W.W. Norton.

Linton, Ralph. (1936). *The study of man.* New York: D. Appleton-Century.

Lorence, Jon, & Mortimer, Jeylan T. (1985). Job involvement through the life course: A panel study of three age groups. *American Sociological Review, 50*(5), 618–638.

Lutfey, Karen, & Maynard, Douglas W. (1998). Bad news in Oncology: How physician and patient talk about death and dying without using those words. *Social Psychology Quarterly, 61*(4), 321–341.

Markus, Hazel, & Nurius, Paula. (1986). Possible selves. *American Psychologist, 41*(9), 954–969.

Maynard, Douglas W., & Marlaire, Courtney L. (1992). Good reasons for bad testing performance: The interactional substrate of educational exams. *Qualitative Sociology, 15*(2), 177–202.

Mead, G. H. (1934). *Mind, self, and society.* Chicago: University of Chicago Press.

Mead, Margaret. (1928). *Coming of age in Samoa.* New York: Harper Collins.

Merton, R. K., Reader, G. C., & Kendall, P. (1957). *The student physician: Introductory studies in the sociology of medical education.* Cambridge, MA: Harvard University Press.

Miller, Joanne. (1988). Jobs and work. In N. J. Smelser (Ed.), *Handbook of sociology* (pp. 327–359). Newbury Park, CA: Sage.

Mortimer, Jeylan T. (2003). *Working and growing up in America.* Cambridge, MA: Harvard University Press.

Mortimer, Jeylan T., & Finch, Michael D. (1996). *Adolescents, work, and family: An intergenerational developmental analysis.* Thousand Oaks, CA: Sage.

Mortimer, Jeylan T., & Krüger, Helga. (2000). Pathways from school to work in Germany and the United States. In M. Hallinan (Ed.), *Handbook of the sociology of education* (pp. 475–497). New York: Kluwer Academic/Plenum.

Mortimer, Jeylan T., & Lorence, Jon. (1995). Social psychology of work. In K. S. Cook, G. A. Fine, & J. S. House (Eds.), *Sociological perspectives on social psychology* (pp. 497–523). Boston: Allyn & Bacon.

Mortimer, Jeylan T., Pimentel, Ellen E., Ryu, Seongryeol, Nash, Katherine, & Lee, Chaimun. (1996). Part-time work and occupational value formation in adolescence. *Social Forces, 74*(4), 1405–1418.

Mortimer, Jeylan T., & Simmons, Roberta G. (1978). Adult socialization. *Annual Review of Sociology, 4*, 421–454.

O'Rand, A. M. (1988). Convergence, institutionalization, and bifurcation: Gender and the pension acquisition process. *Annual Review of Gerontology and Geriatrics, 8*, 132–155.

Pallas, Aaron M. (2000). The effects of schooling on individual lives. In M. T. Hallinan (Ed.), *Handbook of the sociology of education* (pp. 499–525). New York: Kluwer Academic/Plenum.

Parsons, Talcott. (1951). *The social system.* Glencoe: Free Press.

Piaget, Jean. (1950). *The psychology of intelligence.* London: Routledge & Paul.

Rosenbaum, James E., & Kariya, T. (1991). Do school achievements affect the early jobs of high school graduates in the United States and Japan? *Sociology of Education, 64*(2), 78–95.

Rosenthal, Robert, & Jacobson, Lenore. (1968). *Pygmalion in the classroom.* New York: Holt, Reinhart, & Winston.

Schneider, Barbara, & Stevenson, David. (1999). *The ambitious generation: America's teenagers, motivated but directionless.* New Haven: Yale University Press.

Schoenherr, R. A., & Greeley, A. M. (1974). Role commitment processes and the American catholic priesthood. *American Sociological Review, 39*(3), 407–426.

Shanahan, Michael J. (2000). Pathways to adulthood in changing societies: Variability and mechanisms in life course perspective. *Annual Review of Sociology, 26*, 667–692.

Sulloway, Frank J. (1996). *Born to rebel: Birth order, Family dynamics, and creative lives.* New York: Pantheon Books.

Tallman, Irving, Gray, Louis N., Kullberg, Vicki, & Henderson, Debra. (1999). The intergenerational transmission of marital conflict: Testing a process model. *Social Psychology Quarterly, 62*(3), 219–239.

Turnbull, J. E., George, L. K., Landerman, R., Swartz, M. S., & Blazer, D. G. (1990). Social outcomes related to age of onset among psychiatric disorders. *Journal of Consulting and Clinical Psychology, 58*, 832–839.

Vygotsky, L. S. (1978). *Mind in society: The development of higher psychological processes.* Cambridge, MA: Harvard University Press.

Whalen, Jack, & Zimmerman, Don H. (1998). Observations on the display and management of emotion in naturally occurring activities: The case of "hysteria:" in calls to 9-1-1. *Social Psychology Quarterly, 61*(2), 141–159.

Whalen, Jack, Zimmerman, Don H., & Whalen, Marilyn R. (1988). When words fail: A single case analysis. *Social Problems, 35*(4), 335–361.

Wright, Charles R. (1967). Changes in the occupational commitment of graduate sociology students. *Sociological Inquiry, 37*(1), 55–62.

PART III

INTRAPERSONAL PROCESSES

CHAPTER 9

Self and Identity

TIMOTHY J. OWENS

Self and identity may be two of the most popular concepts in social psychology. Nearly every area of social psychology touches on some aspect of a person's self or identity, or on a group's identity. The most cursory glance at a library's card catalog or a bookstore's holdings show that self and identity have enormous popularity among academic researchers and the general public.

The prominence of self and identity research in sociology and psychology traces first to James's (1890) original and incisive treatment followed by some early and important efforts by sociologists (Cooley, 1902; Thomas & Znaniecki, 1918) and philosophers (i.e., Mead, 1934). Still, thorough and empirically oriented work on self and identity did not flourish until sociology's post–World War II renaissance as a methodologically rigorous science (Martindale, 1981) and psychology's cognitive revolution in the 1950s (Gardner, 1985).

Theory and research on self and identity, though nearly 60 years old by the 1950s, was still in its infancy, if the bulk of publications is any indication. This is especially true for identity. As the figures that follow show, journal articles, authored books, and dissertations with self or identity in their titles or abstracts grew exponentially from the 1950s to the present. According to PsycINFO (American Psychological Association, 2002),* 2,820 journal articles on the self were published from 1950 to 1959; 5,894 from 1960 to 1969; 18,706 during the 1970s; 38,096 during the 1980s; and a whopping 70,781 from 1990 to the present. With respect to identity, the 1950s saw 190 articles; the 1960s 687; the 1970s 2,268; the 1980s 5,029; and the 1990s to the present 11,166.

Dissertations and books on self or identity also exploded during this time period. For dissertations on the self, 7,759 were approved between 1950 and 1979, with the number

---

*At this time, Sociological Abstracts on-line only extends back to 1974.

TIMOTHY J. OWENS • Department of Sociology and Anthropology, Purdue University, West Lafayette, IN 47907-1365

Handbook of Social Psychology, edited by John Delamater. Kluwer Academic/Plenum Publishers, New York, 2003.

nearly quadrupling to 28,753 since 1980 alone (with 20,190 appearing since 1990). At the same time, 925 authored books on the self were produced from 1950 to 1989 and 2,902 in the 12 years since 1990. Identity shows a similar pattern. There were 541 dissertations on identity approved between 1950 and 1979, 974 in the 1980s, and an additional 3,802 generated since 1990. Among books, 223 were published from 1950 to 1989 and 834 since 1990. These figures show the concepts' enduring vitality and increasing popularity. Since dissertations are indispensable vehicles for future research, the data indicate that theory and research on self and identity will continue their vigorous representation in the literature.

SELF AND IDENTITY: SOME DISTINCTIONS AND DEFINITIONS

Self and identity are complementary terms with much in common. They are nevertheless distinct. Their complementarity sometimes comes at the cost of imprecision and confusion, especially in how they are similar though distinct. Self actually subsumes identity, just as self also subsumes self-concept. It is a matter of the hierarchical ordering of the concepts, with fine, though valid, distinctions. Nevertheless, I must attempt to differentiate and then define self and identity, even though James warned us over a century ago that selfhood (including identity) is "the most puzzling puzzle with which psychology has to deal" (James, 1890, p. 330). The central quality that distinguishes self from identity is that the self is a *process and organization born of self-reflection* whereas identity is a *tool* (or in some cases perhaps a stratagem) by which individuals or groups categorize themselves and present themselves to the world.

Sniderman (1975) has observed that a person's definition of the self is often a function of one's temperament and professional inclination. "In general," he writes, "the more abstract the meanings assigned to the idea of the self, the more agreement there appears to be, and the more specific the operational definitions, the more disagreement there appears to be" (Sniderman, 1975, p. 25). Following this, I define the self as: *an organized and interactive system of thoughts, feelings, identities, and motives that (1) is born of self-reflexivity and language, (2) people attribute to themselves, and (3) characterize specific human beings.* In contemporary psychology, self is generally conceptualized as a set of cognitive representations reflecting a person's personality traits, organized by linkages, across representations created by personal experience or biography. It is sometimes extended to include things besides trait attributes, such as social roles, and even identities (see Thoits, 1995). Here the self is a cognitive structure incorporating elements such as intelligent, persevering, and honest, or perhaps, rich, Catholic, and Australian.

Historically the self was of foremost concern to theologians, philosophers (going back to antiquity), and men and women of letters. Questions of the self that have occupied humans for millennia include: Who am *I*? Why am *I* here? What does *my* life mean? Where did *I* come from? Why have good (or bad) things happened to *me*? Am *I* a good person? Am *I* capable of change? Am *I* loved? Can *I* love? Do *I* love? And what makes me, *me* and you, *you*? All of these questions imply a self.

Although philosophy and theology still wrestle with these questions, the contemporary yeoman's service on exploring the self has largely been in the hands of social scientists (most notably sociologists, psychologists, and political scientists). And while this is not the proper venue to explore the self's many constituencies, meanings, and nuances, the interested reader would benefit from overviews by Diggory (1966), Wylie (1979), Gergen (1971), Burns (1979) or Rosenberg (1979). Suffice it to say here that research on the self has long fascinated social scientists, at least since Cooley (1902) outlined the "looking-glass self" and James (1890) and Mead (1934) distinguished the "I" from the "me": or, the self as subject and object or knower and known. The key is human reflexivity, or the ability to view oneself as an object capable of being not just apprehended, but also labeled, categorized, evaluated, and manipulated. Moreover, reflexivity hinges on language, any language—whether emanating from a broader culture's written or non-written language (e.g., Russian and Hmong, respectively) or a sub-culture's argot (e.g., Ebonics). In short, the reflexive self allows people to view themselves from an external point of view, just as other people might view them through varying degrees of detachment (Mead, 1934). Additionally, since the self can reflect back on itself, it is an integral part of many features we associate with being human. Namely, the ability to plan, worry about personal problems, ruminate about past actions, lament present circumstances, or be envious of others.

Identity is subsumed within the broader concept of self and is a newer entrant to social psychology. Regardless, it has been used variously in the English language since the fourteenth century. Unlike self, the etymology and definition of identity is quintessentially relational.* The *Oxford English Dictionary* (1999) suggests that the modern term "identity" came from the Latin *idem* (same) and *identidem* (over and over again, repeatedly). These have subsequently combined to mean being "side-by-side with those of 'likeness' and 'oneness.' " In contemporary social psychology, the concept of identity retains these earlier notions while also explicitly employing relatedness. Identity can thus be broadly defined as: *categories people use to specify who they are and to locate themselves relative to other people* (Michener & Delamater, 1999). In this sense, identity implies both a distinctiveness (I am not like them or a "not-me") and a sameness as others (I am like them or a "me-too") (McCall, in press; see also Burke & Tully, 1977; James, 1890).†

Referring to James's observation of the "puzzling puzzle," it is worth noting that at least part of the puzzlement regarding self and identity is now caused by sometimes careless, imprecise, and indiscriminate employment of these ubiquitous terms. This partly stems from failure to adequately specify their complex meanings. At one extreme, self and identity are simply used as synonyms. At the other, they represent alternative uses of words from well-established social science concepts such as culture, ethnicity, or group. The apparent cause is a failing to recognize that there is a difference between self and identity concepts with respect to levels of analysis, whether an individual, a social category or collectivity, or a whole society (Stryker, Owens, & White, 2000a). A related tendency is to use conceptions of self and identity appropriate to analyses on one level as though they were equally appropriate to analyses at other levels. This state of affairs, as Stryker (2000) points out, reflects by turns the imprecise relationship of personal identities and identities defined in categorical or collective terms, as well as between the self and identities of whatever variety. Other problems exist too: using the same term to mean different things, and failing to be aware of ambiguous overlaps among a variety of conceptualizations of self and identity. Thoits and Virshup (1997) have attempted to make some order of the confusion.

---

*Although its typical definition is not explicitly relational, the self is nevertheless relational as well since it arises from and is developed and sustained by human interaction (Mead, 1994).

†A useful alternative definition of identity is provided by Hewitt (1979, p. 91): "the person's biographical sense of relationship to the others with whom he has been and is customarily associated." Biography in this sense has four inter-related meanings (Hewitt, 1979, pp. 84–85). First, people have memories of past roles, successes and failures, and hopes and disappointments that are situated in time and place. Second, these memories are used by individuals to locate themselves with reference to others. Third, by evoking such memories, people define themselves as persons. Last, peoples' biographies are constructed both by their own hand as well as by the people and situations that surround them.

SELF AND SELF-CONCEPT

Having previously defined self in abstract terms and reviewed general aspects of identity, I now move to another fundamental aspect of the self: self-concept, or how we envisage and perceive our self. Self-concept is inextricably tied to the "I–me" dualism found in the self and may be defined as: *the totality of an individual's thoughts and feelings about a particular object—namely, his or her self* (Rosenberg, 1979). The "I–me" dualism has other implications as well. The self-concept includes cognition and emotion since it is both an object of perception and reflection and an emotional response to that perception and reflection. As a product of its own objectification, it requires individuals (i.e., subjects, "knowers," or "I's") to stand outside themselves and react to themselves as detached objects of observation (i.e., objects, the known, or "me's"). Accepting that the self may be both subject and object serves as the rationale for conducting studies of the self-concept (Rosenberg, 1979), which I now take up.

Self-Concept Theory

According to Rosenberg (1979, pp. 62–77), four broad principles form the basis of support for "most of the theoretical reasoning employed in the literature to understand the bearing of interpersonal and social structural processes on the self-concept" (p. 62). However, he also warns, as have others, that the proper application of these general principles is necessary to advance our efforts to explain diverse phenomena with respect to self-concept (particularly, though not limited to, self-esteem). The four principles of self-concept development are reflected appraisals, social comparisons, self-attributions, and psychological centrality. The principle of *reflected appraisals* is central to the symbolic interactionist's insistence that the self is a social product derived from the attitudes that others have toward one's self and that one eventually comes to see him- or herself as others do, à la Meadian self theory and Cooley's looking-glass self (1902). Through *social comparisons*, people judge and evaluate themselves in comparison to particular individuals, groups, or social categories. Two self-reference bases establish social comparisons: criteria and normative. Criteria bases come into play when, for example, people compare themselves to others in terms of superiority or inferiority, or better or worse on some criteria of interest. Normative comparison bases fall along dimensions of deviance or conformity, or believing one is generally in harmony and agreement with others or in disharmony and opposition to them. *Self-attribution* holds that individuals draw conclusions about themselves by observing their own actions and their outcomes (e.g., dull, well-liked, unattractive, funny). Finally, the principle of *psychological centrality* holds that the self is an interrelated system of hierarchically organized components, with some attributes and identities more important to the self than others are. Psychological centrality (or importance) helps protect peoples' self-concepts by pushing potentially damaging self-attributes and identities to the periphery of the self system, while holding enhancing attributes closer to the center. The principle of psychological centrality is perhaps the most abstract of the four principles; however, it might also be the most consequential for the nature and character of one's self and self-concept. Psychological centrality points directly to the *structure* of the self, which is as complex as any phenomenon in science. Empirical research on the role of this principle in particular has not received the attention it deserves, earlier work stemming from Kuhn and McPartland's (1954) Twenty Statements Test and Marsh and associates more recent work on the multidimensional self (e.g., Marsh, Byrne, & Shavelson, 1992; Marsh, Craven, & Debus, 1998) not withstanding.

According to self-concept theory, as one observes, evaluates, and ultimately draws conclusions about one's self, two key motives work in service of protecting and maintaining the present self-concept: self-esteem and self-consistency (Rosenberg, 1979). The self-esteem motive provokes individuals to think well of themselves (e.g., Allport, 1961; Kaplan, 1975). Indeed, many self-theorists regard this motive as universally dominant in the human motivational system (James, 1890; Kaplan, 1975; Rosenberg, 1979). As Rosenberg puts it:

> The self-esteem motive rests on its own foundation; high self-esteem is innately satisfying and pleasurable, low self-esteem the opposite. A major determinant of human thought and behavior and a prime motive in human striving, then, is the drive to protect and enhance one's self-esteem. (1979, p. 57)

On the other hand, the self-consistency motive (Lecky, 1945) asserts that people struggle to validate their self-concepts, even when they are negative.

> The individual sees the world from his own viewpoint, with himself as the center. Any value entering the [value] system which is inconsistent with the individual's valuation of himself cannot be assimilated; it meets with resistance and is, unless a general reorganization occurs, to be rejected. This resistance is a natural phenomenon; it is essential for the maintenance of individuality. (Lecky, 1945, p. 153)

Swann (1983, 1996) has incorporated the spirit of self-consistency into self-verification theory. Self-verification theory is organized around three basic assumptions with respect to self-conceptions (Swann calls them self-views). First, at the most basic level self-concepts help guide people's behaviors. Second, à la Mead, they enable people to anticipate other's reactions to their own behaviors. Third, they help organize people's notions of reality. Not surprisingly, the upshot is that once people become confident of their self-conceptions, they work to confirm them—whether positive or negative, well-founded or not. In the process, people strive to refute information that disconfirms their self-conceptions. In a somewhat counterintuitive twist, self-verification theory also predicts that people with negative self-conceptions often prefer negative evaluations from others, especially if their negative self-conceptions are held firmly or in the extreme. An exception is if the person with a negative self-concept is in or wants a longer-term relationship with a negative evaluator. In this case the other's negative evaluations are not generally favored (Swann, Milton, & Polzer, 2000).

SELF-CONCEPT AS SOCIAL PRODUCT AND SOCIAL FORCE.   Although the idea that self and society are twinborn (i.e., cocreated) traces to Cooley (1909) and Mead (1934) and has thus been an axiom of symbolic interactionism for decades, Rosenberg (1981) helped codify the notion more recently. As he rightfully saw it, at first blush the self-concept seems for many to be a quintessentially psychological phenomenon. However, accepting that self and society are twinborn and that the self-concept is both a social product and a social force, one can readily see its importance and relevance for sociology: it is not present at birth, it arises out of interaction, and myriad social factors help in its formation.

The self-concept not only incorporates the individual's location in the social structure but is also affected by it. In this more sociological sense, self-concept (like self generally) is a social creation molded by a person's interactions with others, his or her past and ongoing affiliations and experiences within and across social contexts and institutional affiliations, and his or her location within culture and social structure. In short, the self—and thus the self-concept—is a social *product*. This vein of self-concept research tends to be studied more by social psychologists in sociology than psychology. Recent examples of self-concept as a social product include Ge, Elder, Regnerus, and Cox's (2001) study of adolescent overweight and its deleterious effect on self-image; Haj-Yahia's (2001) examination of the corrosive effect of wife abuse on a victim's sense of self; Schnittker's (2001) research on acculturation and neighborhood ethnic composition on the self-esteem of Chinese immigrants; and Thoits and Hewitt's (2001) investigation of the salutary effect that volunteer work can have on the self.

On the other hand, once a person has a self-concept, it has important consequences for action on both the individual (e.g., Baumeister, Smart, & Boden, 1996) and group levels (e.g., Swann et al., 2000). In these cases, the self-concept exerts a twofold influence. First, it influences the individual's cognitions, emotions, and behaviors. Second, it can influence the groups to which a person belongs as well as the society as a whole through the manifestation of social problems linked to the self-concept. In short, the self—and by extension the self-concept—is a social *force*. Recent examples of self as a social force include Nyamathi, Longshore, Keenan, Lesser, and Leake's (2001) study of the protective effect of a positive self-concept on daily alcohol use among homeless women; Parker's (2001) examination of the role of self-concept in task performance; Peltzer, Malaka, and Phaswana's (2001) research on self-concept's role in substance use; and Tarrant, North, and Hargreaves's (2001) investigation of the role of self-concept in in-group favoritism and out-group prejudice (where people with lower self-esteem tend to think twice before discriminating against out-group members). A number of studies incorporate both the self as a social force and a social product. Recent examples include Clay-Warner's (2001) study of the interrelation of self and perceived injustice; Kiecolt and Mabry's (2000) examination of the processes of self-change among men and women; Rosenberg and Owens's (2001) research on the causes and consequences of low self-esteem; and Wright, Gronfein, and Owens's (2000) investigation of the reciprocal effects of social rejection and the self-concept among the severely mentally ill.

SELF-PRESENTATION THEORY: EXPLICITLY LINKING SELF-CONCEPT AS A SOCIAL PRODUCT AND A SOCIAL FORCE. The theoretical basis for contemporary theory and research on self-presentation is derived from Goffman's (1959) landmark dramaturgical analysis of social relations and interactions in daily life and to a lesser degree Jones's (1964, pp. 40ff.) work on self-presentation as an aspect of ingratiation.* Goffman's basic premise is that some of the most illuminating insights about social behavior can be revealed by careful and detailed analysis of people's everyday—and especially public—behaviors.† As he saw it, people are "actors" (his stage allegory is intentional) who assume roles that they perform for "audiences" in social situations. In so doing, both the actor and the audience cocreate a "definition of the situation." This definition, fashioned through the process of interaction and negotiation, guides the actor's performance and the meanings the audience attribute to it. Actors' role performances are guided by the impressions they wish to impart to one another or to the audience and are codified in what Goffman termed their "impression management tactics" (Goffman, 1959). In short, through impression management an individual actor seeks to make some desired impression on others. Consequently, it is in the actor's interest to attempt

---

*Although Goffman (1959) was clearly on the scene first, Jones's (1964) study of self-presentation (i.e., impression management) helped launch self-presentation research among psychological social psychologists. I believe Leary (1996, p. 8) erroneously suggested that Jones was unaware of Goffman's (1959) work when he started his research on self-presentation and published his findings in 1964. Jones (1964) in fact cites Goffman.

†This stood in especially stark contrast to the insistence of many psychologists that such insights could only come from a detailed knowledge of people's inner motives and personalities.

to control others and their responses to his or her behavior. This control is sought by trying to influence the definition of the situation under which all the actors (and the audience) putatively operate. People not only formulate impressions, consciously or otherwise, but project those impressions with the goal of having others "voluntarily" come to the conclusions they desire.

Taking a cue from Goffman, Schlenker (1980, p. 6) defines impression management as *"the conscious or unconscious attempt to control images that are projected in real or imagined social interactions"* (emphasis in the original). However, when the projected image refers to the self, it is called *self-presentation,* in accordance with Jones's (1964) terminology, which was itself adopted directly from Goffman's (1959) *The Presentation of Self in Everyday Life* (Jones & Pittman, 1982, p. 231). Jones (1964) defined self-presentation within the context of an ingratiation tactic. On one hand, he believed self-presentations are "communications which are explicitly self-descriptive ('I am the kind of person who...')" and on the other as "more indirect communicative shadings which convey the same kind of information about how a person wishes to be viewed by others" (Jones, 1964, p. 40).

It is the self-presentation aspect of impression management that seems to have captured the attention of many psychological social psychologists, particularly in the association between self-presentations, the self-concept, and behavior. Reminiscent of reflected appraisals discussed earlier, Schlenker (1980) refined the definition of self-presentation to: the attempt to influence how real or imagined others "perceive our *personality traits*, abilities, intentions, behaviors, attitudes, values, physical characteristics, social characteristics, family, friends, job, and possessions" (p. 6, emphasis added). In doing so, self-presentations reflect back upon the actor and influence how the actor sees and defines him- or herself. More recently, Leary (1996) has extended the notion of self-presentation by asserting that an overall self-presentational motive lies beneath practically every aspect of interpersonal life (p. xiii). This overall motive has been further refined into two subcomponents: impression motivation (how much a person is concerned with controlling how they are perceived in a situation) and impression construction (the actual image a person wants to convey) (Leary & Kowalski, 1990). In addition, the content of an individual's self-presentations is shaped by five factors: "their self-concepts, constraints imposed by salient social roles, their desired and undesired identity images, the values of the people to whom they are impression-managing, and the current and potential nature of their public images" (Nezlak & Leary, 2002, p. 212).

Self-presentation is a special class of impression management. However, the precise demarcation between the two concepts (like many of the other "puzzling puzzles" regarding the self) is murky. Part of the problem stems from a habit many writers on self-perception have of using the term interchangeably with its cognate—impression management. The other is drawing distinctions that sometimes seem based as much as anything on disciplinary boundaries and methodological preferences. For example, Leary (1996) says that while Goffman was "an astute observer of human behavior with the ability to see processes of social life in new ways and to describe them in an engaging fashion" (p. 8) his "work was more akin to social anthropology than sociology" (p. 7) much less psychology. Moreover, Goffman reported essentially "anthropological field observations in narrative essays ... and tried to *persuade* his readers of his insights through observations and anecdotes" (p. 9, emphasis in the original). Jones on the other hand, "tried to confirm or disconfirm particular theoretical ideas through controlled experimentation" (Leary, 1996, p. 8).

Discipline and methodological issues aside, what distinguishes Goffmanesque research on impression management and Jonesian research on self-presentation is where and how "the situation" and "the self" are emphasized. Goffman emphasized how actors project a definition of the situation and how each actor subjectively perceives and responds to the emergent definition and the situation. One the other hand, Jones and his associates and heirs examine "attempts on the part of the actor to shape others' *impressions of his personality*" (Jones & Pittman, 1982, p. 231, emphasis added). The latter, while certainly of interest to Goffman, was secondary to his main analytic goal.

Contemporary self-presentation researchers are interested in the problematic aspects of self-presentation for the group as well as the individual. For example, being too concerned with the impression one is making in a given situation may affect psychological outcomes such as increasing the actor's level of anxiety or influence behavioral outcomes such as successful task performance (Leary, 1996). More recently, self-presentation research has been extended beyond the laboratory (Nezlak & Leary, 2002) by examining how personality variables influence the impressions people want to construct in everyday life. Among their more interesting findings is the relation of positive and negative self-evaluations and the self-presentation motive. In a sample of college students, women with more negative self-evaluations were more self-presentationally motivated than women with more positive self-evaluations; the reverse was observed among men. Culos-Reed, Brawley, Martin, and Leary (2002) used survey methods to assess the self-presentational versus health-related motives of patients receiving cosmetic surgery for either vein problems (varicose or spider) or severe acne. They found, among other things, that patients who underwent the surgery primarily for self-presentational reasons tended to exercise less and have higher public self-consciousness than more frequent exercisers.

SOME NEW AND UNDER-RESEARCHED CONCEPTS IMPORTANT TO THE SELF MATTERING

One of the most under-researched ideas in self and identity research involves Rosenberg and McCullough's (1981) concept of mattering. Turning Sullivan's (1953) concept of significant others on its head, while also taking a cue from Durkheim ([1897] 1951), mattering is defined as "the degree to which we feel we feel we matter to others ...." and command "the interest or notice of another person" (Rosenberg & McCullough, 1981, pp. 163–164). Perhaps the only thing more depressing than dying "unmourned is to die unloved" (p. 164). While Rosenberg and McCullough view mattering in a more positive light, if we follow this logic to its extreme, there is much in the literature to suggest also that some people would rather be despised than forgotten. That is, to matter, even if negatively or harshly, to another is an important human need.

According to Rosenberg and McCullough (1981), mattering is founded on three components: attention, importance, and dependence. Attention refers to the joy we feel at being the *object* of a significant other's attention and the gloom we feel when there is no one out there for whom we matter. Importance refers not only to being the object of another person's attention, but also of *concern* to them. They care about us. Dependence refers to the belief that others *rely* on us to fill some great or small need in their lives (e.g., school teachers who believe their pupils need and rely on them, a sick friend who needs our aid). Mattering, however, transcends the cognitive and emotional lives of individuals. It is also implicated in the very fabric of social life and social structure. "Mattering represents a compelling social obligation and a powerful source of social integration: we are bonded to society not only by virtue of our dependence on others but on their dependence on us" (Rosenberg & McCullough, 1981, p. 165).

Although there have been relatively few publications on mattering, this may be changing. A number of dissertations using the concept have been produced: one in the 1980s, five in the 1990s, and three since 2000 alone (American Psychological Association, 2002). Chapters and articles on mattering are also beginning to appear more frequently. Two notable examples are Taylor and Turner's (2001) examination of mattering and depression in the general adult population and Pearlin and LeBlanc's (2001) research on the psychological consequences of loss of mattering among Alzheimer's caregivers. Taylor and Turner's (2001) study of over 1,300 Canadians found through cross-sectional analysis that mattering is inversely related to depression for men and women alike. However, when personal resources, social support, and demographic factors were controlled, mattering remained protective only for women. That is, the more women felt they mattered to others (e.g., were important to others, would be missed if they went away, have others who depend on them) the lower their reported depressive symptomatology. Longitudinal data supported this general conclusion and also showed that changes in mattering over time predicted changes in depression, but again only for women.

Extending Rosenberg and McCullough (1981) in a new direction, Pearlin and LeBlanc (2001) focus on a dependence aspect of mattering and the psychological impact of a sudden *loss* of profound mattering. They examined 555 familial caregivers of people with Alzheimer's disease who received residential care at Time 1 (of five interview-points). Loss of mattering was measured with a four-item Likert scale that included such questions as how much the caregiver missed having someone to whom they were important and to whom their care was appreciated (even if the object of care could not show it). Acknowledging that a sense of mattering should contribute to general well-being, Pearlin and LeBlanc found that its absence had modestly negative consequences for the self as manifested by lowered self-esteem, a diminished sense of personal mastery, and increased depression. Interestingly, among the spouses of Alzheimer's patients who died during the study period, the correlation between the loss of mattering and dating or remarriage a year later was $-.41$ ($p < .001$). They also found that gender was predictive of a loss of mattering (in the direction of women), when a variety of sociodemographic, role-related characteristics of the caregiver, and social supports for the caregiver role were controlled.

Comfort with the Self

The idea of comfort with the self comes from Roberta Simmons's (2001) posthumously published work of the same title. While unable to completely explicate this potentially important concept before her untimely death, she was able to link being comfortable or uncomfortable with the self with the cueing function of emotion. She believed that people comfortable with who they are and with a world that allows them to enact that self get reflected appraisals indicating that no major alteration in their self is necessary. The self they present to the world is okay. However, people who feel uncomfortable with themselves are being cued that a change in self or their situation may be necessary, lest they continue their undesirable emotional state (p. 198).*

Simmons (2001) saw three aspects of comfort with the self: (1) the *absence* of negative emotions regarding oneself,† (2) feeling familiar with oneself and at ease and at home when

---

*This line of reasoning is very much in step with affect control theory, discussed later, even though there is no evidence that she was drawing on it.

†Note that this aspect of comfort with the self is very much in line with Rosenberg's (1965, 1979) conceptualization of self-esteem. A detailed examination of his original Guttman scale of self-esteem revealed that he saw self-esteem not so much as the presence of positive thoughts and feelings regarding oneself. Instead, self-esteem is the absence, in varying degrees, of self-condemning thoughts and feelings. Consequently, high self-esteem people are not necessarily full of self-congratulations but instead reject, again in varying degrees, self-condemnation (see Owens & King, 2001, for a more complete discussion).

thinking about oneself, and (3) having low to moderate emotional arousal with respect to the self. Concerning the latter, one is comfortable when experiencing neither high positive emotions nor elevated negative emotions regarding the self. However, she does not advocate an ever-contented self. Comfort is also time-bound and punctuated by periods of high arousal and discomfort. These stave off boredom and complacency while also motivating people to make necessary life changes and transitions (e.g., the transition to adulthood and for some parenthood). Finally, comfort is a binary condition: one is either in a state of comfort in a situation or not. She did not see it as a matter of degree.

Call and Mortimer (2001) recently examined Simmons's notion of comfort and extended it to four key arenas in the world of adolescents: family, school, peer group, and work. In contrast to Simmons's work on comfort with the self, Call and Mortimer emphasize areas of comfort. These are viewed as places where people can relax and rejuvenate themselves while also steadying themselves for the stresses engendered in other life contexts.

IDENTITY

We turn now to an examination of another essential aspect of the self—identity. This section focuses on three key aspects of identity in contemporary social psychology—personal, social, and collective. Along the way I note some important points of convergence and divergence among the three forms. Oddly, because of historical terminology, theoretical development of personal identity—or identities attached to individuals—is largely the province of sociologists. In what seems counterintuitive, theoretical development of social and collective identity—or identities based on group-level characteristics—has chiefly been the bailiwick of psychologists, although sociologists are increasingly making contributions (e.g., Jasper, 1997; Stryker, Owens, & White, 2000b; Subramaniam, 2001; Taylor, 1996; White, 2001) What differentiates personal identities from social and collective identities is that personal identities are both attached to individuals (e.g., their traits, unique identifiers, personality characteristics) and are internalized by them. Alternatively, social identities tend to attach to groups while collective identities tend to attach to demographic categories. Moreover, the internalization of an identity is a definitional requirement of personal identity but not of social or collective identity. A number of recent articles and books compare and contrast various forms and uses of identity, including Côté and Levine (2002); Owens and Aronson (2000); Stets and Burke (2000); Stryker et al. (2000b); and Thoits and Virshup (1997).

The somewhat confusing nomenclature regarding the three forms of identity under discussion arose, in part, because personal identity as used by McCall and Simmons (1966) and with variation by Stryker (1968) predated the terms collective and social identities in the literature. As for personal identity, which has two meanings, the variant employed by Stryker (1968, 1980) and his associates might be more aptly termed *structural* identity for reasons discussed in the next section. Nevertheless, all three streams of identity (personal, social, and collective) take it as axiomatic that the human mind classifies and categorizes those parts of reality that enter into its experience. This profound cognitive tapestry begins when an infant is born into a set of social relations or a unit of social structure that labels, classifies, and demarcates the world into socially defined categories (e.g., mama, dada, choo-choo) and continues throughout his or her life course (e.g., immigrant, iron worker, grandmother, war veteran). I begin with the most sociologically rooted of the identities—personal—and then move on to discuss social and collective identities in turn.

Identities Based on Individual-Level Characteristics

PERSONAL IDENTITY. Like other "puzzling puzzles" of self and identity, the concept of personal identity, like identity perspectives in general, suffers somewhat from multiple though related usages. In the first usage, outlined by McCall and Simmons (1966) and specifically termed "personal identity," the concept comes closest to its denotative meaning. Here personal identity refers to unique individuals in relation to various categories.

> Personal identities serve as the pegs upon which social identities and personal biographies can be hung. If an individual could not be recognized from one occasion to another as the same person, no stable social relationships could be constructed, and therefore there would be no social identities at all. Both types of identification are vitally important in the process of human interaction. (McCall & Simmons, 1966, p. 65)

Thus, in McCall and Simmons's use of the term, personal identities are indeed *personal*. Thoits and Virshup (1997) concur. They treat personal identities as unique identifiers (still social in origin but more specific and less generic/categorical than social and collective identities). Examples of unique identifiers would include such things as I am Tim Owens; I am Gene and Clary's son; I graduated from Minneapolis' Patrick Henry High; I am married to Susan Burns. I am a Vietnam-era veteran.

In the second view, McCall and Simmons's basic definition of identity is retained but sharpened by rendering it emphatically structural (Stryker, 1968, 1980). According to Stryker (1980, p. 60) "identities are 'parts' of self [constituting] internalized positional designations ... [that] exist insofar as the person is a participant in structured role relations" (Stryker, 1980, p. 60).* Here one's identity is tied to specific social networks such as a family, work crew, friendship group, or the Riverside PTA, rather than to grosser social groupings such as Arab, Catholic, woman, or African American (as in social identity and collective identity). As employed through Stryker's (1980) identity theory (described later), personal identities carry expectations with respect to present and future interaction with role-related others. This facet of identity has been significantly developed over the past several decades through the work of the "Indiana School" of symbolic interactionism (Ervin & Stryker, 2000; Stryker, 1968, 1980; Stryker & Burke, 2000; Stryker & Serpe, 1994; Stryker & Statham, 1985). In this application, identity salience (the probability of an identity's enactment), and commitment (ties to and affect for others in one's role-related social networks) are intrinsically linked and situated in role-choice behavior. Indeed, the very notion of identity in symbolic interactionism connotes an intimate linkage between self and role (Burke & Tully, 1977) such that human beings are confronted regularly with choices between alternative commitments and actions (Stryker, 1980).

As used by sociological social psychologists, personal identity theory is derived from general principles of symbolic interactionism and the influence of Mead (1934). Four premises underlie the general theory (Stryker, 1991, pp. 22–24). First, people are actors and reactors. Second, human action and interactions are shaped substantially by the definitions the actors derive from the situation and these definitions are based on shared meanings that arise as people interact with one another. Third, the meanings people attribute to themselves, and thus their self-concepts, are crucial to the process that produces their actions and interactions. Fourth, like other meanings, self-conceptions are molded in the course of interaction with others and are largely the outcomes of others' responses to the person.

---

*I place Stryker in the individual-based identity category with caution. As mentioned earlier, his view of identity is actually *structural* and thus bridges individual and group-based identities. However, given the importance of role-relatedness in his conceptualization, and because individuals are attached to roles, his categorization makes sense here.

Motivation in the context of personal identity theories has been a central concern to many theorists (e.g., Foote, 1951; Heise, 1979; MacKinnon, 1994; McCall & Simmons, 1966; Stryker, 1968) and is implicit in much of what I have to say with respect to identity and role. However, due to space limitation I will not give it a formal assessment here. Suffice it to say that much of the current thinking about motivation vis-à-vis identity stems from Foote (1951). He attempted to clarify several strands of role theory by rejecting motivation theories and accounts based on biological determinism ("the person impelled from within") and cultural determinism ("the person driven from without") in favor of a *social* psychology of motivation (p. 21). Taking Cooley's (1902) idea of self and society as twinborn ("One has no identity apart from society; one has no individuality apart from identity," p. 21) Foote's influential initial statement toward a theory of situated motivation is based upon language and identification. Briefly, language is seen as a powerful ingredient in motivation because it helps shape behavior by enabling individuals to meaningfully construe and label their past actions in order to formulate present and future outcomes. Identification means "appropriation of and commitment to a particular identity or series of identities (p. 17) and is used to illuminate the process people use to link themselves and others to groups. Together, this means people have multiple identities and their identities give their behavior meaning and purpose. (See MacKinnon [1994, pp. 50–63] for an extended treatment.)

I turn now to two well-established strains of personal identity theory in sociology (McCall and Simmons's role-identity theory and Stryker's identity theory as it is simply called) and two more recent extensions (Heise's affect control theory and Burke's identity control theory).

ROLE-IDENTITY THEORY.   McCall and Simmons (1966) define role-identity, the central concept in their theory, in dramaturgical language as the character and the role that individuals devise for themselves when occupying specific social positions. In addition, role-identity stems from the "imaginative view [a person has] of himself *as he likes to think of himself being and acting* as an occupant of a position" (p. 67, emphasis in the original). Here role-identities serve as the primary source of a person's action plans (à la Mead, 1934) and thus influence his or her everyday life (McCall & Simmons, 1966). This influence is manifested in a number of other ways (McCall & Simmons, 1966, pp. 69–70). First, recalling our discussion of reflected appraisals and self-attributions, the contents of a person's role-identities constitute the materials by which a person appraises (and possibly corrects) his or her actual role performances. Second, via the "me," role-identities provide a frame of reference for assessing one's thoughts and feelings regarding an associated role performance. Third, role-identities "give the *meaning* to our daily routine, for they largely determine our interpretations of the situations, events, and other people we encounter" (pp. 69–70, emphasis in the original). Finally, because role-identities provide us with plans of action and classification systems, they also help determine the objects in our environment, the labels we give them, and their meanings. All this adds up to a view of people capable of creativity and improvisation in the performance of their roles yet still guided by the overall requirements of their social position. This commingling of individuality, idiosyncrasy, and impulsiveness with behavior constrained by social convention occurs through a dialog between the "I" and the "me" bounded by the broad dictates of one's role-identity.

Since people have multiple role-identities that vary and compete within and across social situations, an important theoretical problem in McCall and Simmons's role-identity theory is to explain which role-identities people value most and will thus attempt to perform. They argue that the multiplicity of role-identities organized within the self and their probable activation is predicated on a hierarchy of prominence. And the prominence itself is predicated on a number of factors the individual must weigh in terms of how his or her self-concept links to a role-identity. First and foremost, is the degree of commitment one has to a particular role-identity and by extension how much of his or her self-esteem is bound to its successful activation (pp. 77–78). Second, when musing about one's ideal self vis-à-vis a particular role-identity, how much has the person's heretofore overt actions generally comported with performing the role-identity and living up to one's ideal self? Third, how does the person believe his or her significant others will evaluate and appraise the role when and if it is activated? Last, how much reward has the person gotten from a role-identity's prior activation.

IDENTITY THEORY. Identity theory à la Stryker (Stryker, 1968, 1980, 1987; Stryker & Statham, 1985) shares the symbolic interactionist assumption that humans have the possibility of choice, even though choices are constrained by the situation (i.e., social structure and social interaction).* Humans are thus proactive and not merely reactive. More specifically, his theory focuses on the reciprocal relationship between the individual and the larger social structure and the interactions between sets of individuals and society. Stryker's identity theory sees the self as consisting of a hierarchical ordering of identities, with each identity differentiated according to its *salience* and one's *commitment* to his or her role relations. Thus, one is committed not to an identity but to relationships with respect to which the identity is pertinent. Although somewhat akin to McCall and Simmons's hierarchy of prominence,[†] Stryker's (1980) identity salience hierarchy refers to the ordering of identities into a hierarchy in such a way that the higher the positioning of a particular identity, the higher the probability of its activation.

Identity salience is defined as the *probability* of a particular identity being invoked by self or others within or across social situations (Stryker, 1980). However, while an identity is often invoked willfully, it need not always be. Relationship commitment focuses on a person's *position* in a network of social relations and is marked by two general dimensions (Stryker & Serpe, 1994). The first, interactional commitment, is the extensiveness of interactions in a social network to which one belongs by virtue of having an identity. Extensiveness in turn is operationalized as the number of persons one interacts with and the amount of time, energy, and resources one expends in the social network by way of a particular identity. The second, affective commitment, marks the emotional significance that others in a social network have for a person via his or her particular identity. While interactional and affective commitments are related, Stryker and Serpe (1994) argue they are nevertheless theoretically and empirically independent.

To illustrate how salience and commitment are related to identity (under the rubric of role-choice behavior), I paraphrase Stryker's (1980) example of a question posed by identity theory: Why does one parent, given a free weekend, spend it playing golf with friends while another takes his or her children to the zoo (1980, pp. 59–60)? In terms of salience, perhaps they went to the zoo the week before (i.e., the parent identity was recently activated) or maybe the person has a semi-frequent weekend golf outing with the group? On the other hand, perhaps the group also includes important business or professional contacts, thus suggesting the golfer identity is embedded in more than one social network. For example, the person's golfer

---

*Stryker's theory stems from structural symbolic interactionism (1980) in contrast to processual symbolic interactionism á la Blumer (Meltzer & Petras, 1970).

[†]It should be noted that Stryker's (1968) identity theory was developed without foreknowledge of McCall and Simmons or their 1966 book. Indeed, Stryker's 1968 article, which laid out the basic parameters of his theory, was originally presented at a 1966 plenary session of the American Sociological Association's Section on the Family. After delivering it, George McCall approached Stryker and said, "You've just given our book!" (S. Stryker, personal communication, September 17, 2002).

identity might be invoked at work on Monday morning by being told that someone in the golf group made a hole-in-one, thus excluding the person from a group experience that will no doubt be discussed at work for years. However, commitment is also relevant. Are the golfers casual friends or strong ones? Have they known and liked each other for years? How much would losing or disappointing this group trouble the golfer? In the sense used here, an identity's salience tends to be initiated prior to commitment, but the exact causal ordering is debatable. For example, Stryker and Serpe (1994) show that prior commitment impacts salience at Time 2, and Time 2 salience impacts commitment. The strength of the former relationship, however, was greater. Another part of the answer to the family versus golf choice resides in acknowledging that this aspect of identity theory is bounded by a scope condition recognizing that the theory only applies to those situations where alternative courses of action are reasonably open to the actor. Thus, a single parent without access to a baby-sitter or ready cash may be precluded from even trying to invoke the golfer identity.

Identity salience with respect to commitment begins with a self composed, in part, of a number of identities, with each corresponding to a role the individual plays.* In this formulation, identities differ in their salience in the self-system, such that identity salience is dependent on how much allegiance one has to a particular identity and how positive one's evaluation of the identity is. Consider the weekend golfer again. The person's parent role may be highly salient because of strong attachment to it (emotionally and structurally via commitment). If so, the person will likely accommodate that role and heighten its priority among his or her constellation of role-based identities and their associated obligations. Put differently, the activation of a particular role-identity, predicated on its salience, will influence the person's other obligations and thus role choices, including circumscribing choices.

Finally, an important conceptual elaboration and distinction has been made between identity theory's use of salience and our previous discussion of self-concept theory's principle of psychological centrality. Stryker and Serpe (1994) show that while the phenomena are substantially independent of each other, they are also related. Salience is the likelihood that a given identity will be invoked and is strongly influenced by social network and other structural constraints on the individual. On the other hand, psychological centrality—or importance—is the *personal value* one places on an identity, thus tapping into the person's subjective feelings of what is most important to his or her conceptions of self. Ervin and Stryker (2001) have recently noted that the two concepts differentially reflect the amount of influence a particular role may have on an individual's life. Even though the concepts' effects may often be quite similar, when the effects of salience and centrality are in opposition or conflict, distinguishing their differential effects can provide insight into why people continue to perform roles that they personally dislike. Distinguishing salience and centrality may also be a key to refining hypotheses pertaining to the relationship between role-specific and global self-esteem (Ervin & Stryker, 2001), an important avenue of research deserving of more attention (some recent exceptions include Ervin & Stryker, 2001, and especially Rosenberg, Schooler, Schoenbach, & Rosenberg, 1995).

AFFECT CONTROL THEORY: LINKING IDENTITY PROCESSES TO EMOTION, AND BEHAVIOR. Since its inception in the 1970s (Heise, 1977, 1979) and its elaboration, codification, and maturation in the 1980s and 1990s (e.g., MacKinnon, 1994; Smith-Lovin &

---

*This recalls James's (1890) observation that a person *"has as many social selves as there are persons who recognize him* and carry an image of him in their mind" (p. 294, emphasis in the original).

Heise, 1988) affect control theory (hereafter ACT) has become one of the most vigorously researched and systematic identity-based theories in sociological social psychology. It also promises to be one of the most cross-cultural. As MacKinnon (1994) explains, ACT is true to its symbolic interactionist roots, particularly Mead (1934) but does not accept his ideas wholesale. On the one hand, ACT claims to formalize Mead's (1934) theory of the mind as an internal process of cybernetic feedback and control, as well as his conception of social interaction as an ongoing process of mutually adjusted responses among interactants in a situation. In addition, ACT holds fast to Mead's insistence on the primacy of language, particularly his argument that language initiates our shared objects of consciousness through the process of social categorization (a theme revisited in the discussion of social and collective identities, below). ACT also accepts that these social cognitions form the basis of both intersubjectivity and coordination in social interaction. However, "contrary to Mead's view that the affective associations of social cognitions are individual or idiosyncratic rather than social," ACT views them as "more or less shared by members of the same culture or subculture" (MacKinnon & Bowlby, 2000, p. 44).* The latter are termed *cultural* or *fundamental sentiments* in ACT parlance (Heise, 1979; Smith-Lovin & Heise, 1988). We return to these shortly.

At the core of the theory is the deflection between fundamental sentiments and transient (situational) feelings produced by an interactional event. The theory predicts interpersonal interactions and their emotional ramifications for individuals from deflections between fundamental sentiments and the transient feelings produced by a social event (its unit of analysis). Interactions are viewed within an A-B-O model consisting of an *a*ctor (e.g., a mother), the actor's *b*ehavior (e.g., scolding), and the *o*bject of the behavior (e.g., her daughter) (see Heise, 1979). However, ACT is not simply a conceptual framework. It also consists of a set of mathematical models simulating social interaction, emotional response to events, and labeling and attribution processes.

Along with ideas from symbolic interactionism, the threads of two key principles run though ACT: the principle of *affective reaction* and, not surprisingly, the principle of *affect control* (Heise, 1979). The affective reaction principle asserts that people respond affectively to interactional events (e.g., having a chance meeting on the street with an old friend generates *transient feelings* for the actor, behavior, and object-person in the event). On the other hand, the affect control principle asserts that actors construct and interpret events so as to confirm *cultural sentiments* (broadly shared affective meanings by members of a given culture) for each component of an event. For example, the chance meeting noted previously may start with an acknowledgment of the old friend through a recognizing smile followed by a warm handshake or hug and concluding with some thoughtful catching up on each other's lives. The emotions experienced and displayed by interactants may thus be joy, warmth, and concern.

---

*This observation is predicated on MacKinnon's (1994) thesis that "Mead maintained that the natural function of language is to convey the cognitive meaning of adjustive responses, not to express emotional states (p. 67). MacKinnon (1994, pp. 65ff.) continues that for Mead, language, mind and consciousness, self, individual and social acts, are strictly cognitive phenomena; otherwise, in his view, they would not be social. In this regard, Mead attempted to build a social psychology that could not be reduced to individual or general psychology. Emotion could not be part of this social psychology because in his view emotion is an individual rather than a social phenomenon. Therefore, he relegated emotion to a "second kind of consciousness," one that is individual and subjective, as compared to "reflective consciousness," which is cognitive and social (MacKinnon, 1994, p. 71). Consequently, Mead relegated the affective dimension of self-concept to the nonsocial "I" of the self, thereby reducing self-concept to self-image and ignoring an affective phenomena such as self-esteem altogether. In short, Mead considered emotion as an individual phenomenon, a matter of individual or general psychology, rather than a social psychology (MacKinnon, 1994 and N. J. MacKinnon, personal communication, September 18, 2002).

The discrepancy between deep-seated cultural sentiments (e.g., how one *should* feel when meeting an old friend) and one's event-specific transient feelings (perhaps dread of having to stop and appear happy and concerned about someone else when you have other, more pressing things on your mind) is defined as *affective deflection*. It is important to note that in some rare cases ACT predicts *positive* emotion from deflection. This could occur when an actor is treated *better* on the evaluation dimension than his or her identity meanings would lead the person to expect. For example, Robinson and Smith-Lovin (1992) found that people who think they are terrible public speakers but who get a very positive evaluation on a speech feel positive emotion, but then choose to interact with a more negative evaluator in order to confirm their poor speechmaker identity meanings (cf. Swann et al., 2000).

In terms of measurement, Heise's ACT is highly indebted to Osgood's research on semantic differentials (Osgood, May, & Miron, 1975; Osgood, Suci, & Tannenbaum, 1957). This is especially true of the three universal dimensions of affective meaning he identified: *e*valuation (good, nice versus bad, awful), *p*otency (powerful, strong versus powerless, weak), and *a*ctivity (lively, young versus quiet, old). The affective meanings of objects—whether a physical entity like a terrycloth robe, a political entity like the United Nations, or a social status like mother—are then codified in a unique EPA profile.

Springboarding from Mead's theory of mind and self, Osgood's pioneering work on object-meaning measurement, McCall and Simmons's role-identity theory (discussed earlier), and Powers's (1973) cognitive control theory of perception, ACT was initially published in *Behavioral Science* (Heise, 1977). Shortly afterwards Heise framed his theory with a set of six propositional statements (Heise, 1979, p. 3). MacKinnon (1994, pp. 15–40) has retained ACT's essential structure from Heise (1979) and its elaboration in Smith-Lovin and Heise (1988) but detailed it with set of 24 propositional statements. They are organized under seven fundamental ACT themes: (1) symbols, language, and affective meaning; (2) cognitive constraints; (3) affective response and control—the core of Heise's theory; (4) event assessment; (5) event production; (6) emotions; and (7) cognitive revisions (e.g., labelings and attributions). Each theme incorporates three or four propositions.

Due to space limitations, I collapse ACT into three broad propositional statements (see also Heise, 2002; and for a mathematical and technical account see Heise, 1988). First, people behave so as to experience sentiments consistent with the identities they are trying to confirm in a situation (i.e., their situated identities) and the emotions they experience signal the extent to which they have been successful or unsuccessful in doing so. In this regard ACT distinguishes between general affective responses (e.g., a fundamental sentiment measured by an EPA profile) evoked through cognition (e.g., the thought of one's mother generally evokes evaluative feelings of goodness and moderate feelings of potency and activity) and the specific, ephemeral, affective experiences commonly known as *emotions* (e.g., happy, sad, angry, afraid). The latter are treated by ACT as affectively rich cognitive signals that tell the actor whether or not identity-confirmation or disconfirmation is taking place as a consequence of an event.* For example, during an annual performance appraisal meeting, a supervisor may criticize a subordinate's work. This, then, constitutes a concrete event. However, according to ACT, the emotional response of the subordinate to the criticism (e.g., gratitude, simmering

---

*According to ACT, fundamental sentiments are established by one's culture and possess a high degree of stability across situations and events. This stability has been convincingly demonstrated in empirical work showing virtually identical EPA profiles from repeated samples from the same population (MacKinnon, 1994, p. 22). Naturally, however, different cultures will likely have different EPA profiles for the same object even though the sentiment *dimensions* of evaluation, potency, and activity will be the same.

rage) depends on the generalized affective *meanings* embodied in the two role-identities present in the interactional situation. For instance, supervisors are supposed to be especially frank in such situations and subordinates receptive to criticism aimed at improving their job performance. Still, people impute meanings to the situation that generate event-specific feelings or transient impressions. Subsequent events may change the feelings in the direction of closer proximity to the fundamental sentiments. The supervisor may later praise the subordinate for other things done well thus reinforcing the definition of the situation as a balanced appraisal of one's *job performance* (i.e., work identity) and not an attack based on other identities (e.g., being an older worker or member of an ethnic minority). On the other hand, the deflection of transient impressions from fundamental sentiments may increase if the subordinate considers that the supervisor's observations and comments are illegitimate (i.e., identity-disconfirming).

Second, if, through action, a person is unable to maintain situationally appropriate feelings, the person will reformulate his or her definition of the situation to bring feelings and definitions into alignment. This can be seen by the ACT proposition that minimizing deflection (the discrepancy between fundamental sentiments for identities and the transient impressions created by events) is a general incentive in human behavior, with identity-confirmation being an important instance of this general incentive. Third, a person's emotions in a given situation signal the relationship between his or her experiences in the situation (derived from both proximate and distal stimuli) and the person's definition of the situation (see Smith-Lovin & Heise, 1988).

ACT has had a number of recent applications and extensions. For instance, Rashotte (2002) used ACT to examine nonverbal behavior within the context of speech and action (e.g., laughing, leaning back, speaking in a monotone). By focusing on the impressions created by specific nonverbal behavior, rather than simply the emotions they generated, she has identified distinct cultural meanings and impressions that a number of nonverbal behaviors have on the people who view them. She plans to extend the present study of American college students to other social settings such as business, politics, or sales relationships. Interesting cross-cultural work is also being conducted by ACT researchers. Smith, Matsuno, and Ike (2001) recently compared the mental processes that Americans and Japanese employ when socially constructing perceptions of people. Not surprisingly, in the Japanese social context men and women are much more segregated from each other than their American counterparts. More significantly, they demonstrated that unlike Americans, Japanese are more apt to make distinctions between personal modifiers of emotional expression (e.g., thrilled, disgusted), trait dispositions (e.g., brave, rude), and status characteristics (e.g., male, poor) when apprehending a role-identity. In addition, Japanese are particularly concerned with maintaining psychological consistency and congruency when viewing and assessing role-identities and personal modifiers. In an experimental mock jury trial, Tsoudis and Smith-Lovin (1998) used ACT to predict the impact of perpetrator and victim emotion displays on jurors' (the experimental subjects') judgments about the others' identities and the recommended punishment of the perpetrator. The experimenters used actual trial transcripts (modified to elicit particular emotion displays by the victim and perpetrator) from two violent crimes, an armed robbery of a restaurant resulting in two victims being shot and a vicious street mugging with a lead pipe. They found, among other things, that the recommended sentences the "jurors" gave the perpetrators was determined by both the *identities* they imputed to the victim and the perpetrator and their judgments of the severity of the criminal *behavior* as revealed by the trial transcripts. Finally, Willigan and Heise (Shin, 2002) are embarking on a landmark sociological study of Navajo subjective culture using ACT.

IDENTITY CONTROL THEORY. Burke and associates (Burke, 1991; Burke & Reitzes, 1991; Burke & Stets, 1999) have for several years been developing a theory very much in the tradition of ACT, which they first termed a cybernetic control model of identity processes. Later in the 1990s it started to be informally called identity control theory, especially by ACT researchers. By the early 2000s the term identity control theory (hereafter ICT) was formally integrated into the literature (Stets & Tsushima, 2001). I will henceforth call it by its shorter and more descriptive name: ICT. Like its predecessor ACT, Burke's ICT has important implications for behavior and emotion. The primary focus of Burke's ICT, like Heise's ACT but unlike Stryker's (structural) identity theory, is on the *internal* dynamics of self-processes (Stryker & Burke, 2000). However, unlike ACT, ICT predicts a negative emotion from a discrepancy (Stets & Tsushima, 2001). Stets and Burke (2002, p. 139) write, "any discrepancy between perceived self-in-situation meanings and identity standard meanings...reflects a problem in verifying the self, and as a result of this the individual experiences negative emotional arousal such as depression and distress...anger...and hostility." As discussed earlier, ACT allows for positive emotion in some cases of deflection. (ICT's "discrepancy" is equivalent to ACT's "deflection.") Both theories, however, are keenly interested in the operation of cybernetic controls (or feedback loops) within the individual and between an individual and his or her social situation (per Powers, 1973).

ICT has its roots in structural symbolic interactionism (Stryker, 1980) and owes part of its intellectual lineage to such previously discussed sociological works as McCall and Simmons's (1966) role-identity theory; Stryker's (1968) identity theory; and Heise's (1979) ACT (the latter contention is discussed below). ICT, like ACT, also draws heavily on the work of Osgood et al. (1957) and Powers's (1973) cognitive control theory of perception. Unlike ACT, however, ICT explicitly incorporates ideas from Swann's (1983) self-verification theory (previously discussed). In accordance with identity theory, ICT also emphasizes the importance of understanding identity not as an individual's state or trait characteristic but as a continuous process. As Burke (1991) writes, "An identity process is a *continuously operating, self-adjusting,* feedback loop: individuals continually adjust behavior to keep their reflected appraisals congruent with their identity standards or references (p. 840, emphasis in the original). Like general symbolic interactionism, an identity is viewed as a set of meanings applied to the self in a social role or social situation. These meaning-sets both define and act as a standard or reference for who one is.

When an identity is activated a feedback loop with four components is also established (Burke, 1991, pp. 837–838). While this interaction of person (via identity) and social situation is important in Burke's model, the heart of the model is that people act in such a way as to counter any disturbance to their perceived (in the situation) self-meanings (identities). Although ICT has many nuances and layers that the interested reader may investigate in a fuller treatise on the subject (notably Burke, 1991; Stryker & Burke, 2000), for our purposes the following summary from Stryker and Burke (2000) is sufficient. The model consists of four key components: (1) the *identity standard*, which is "the set of (culturally prescribed) meanings" (p. 287) individuals hold, is defined as a person's role-identity in a situation;* (2) a person's *perception* of self-relevant meaning within the situation, "matched by the dimensions of meaning in the identity standard" (p. 287); (3) the *comparator* that compares

---

*Burke notes that these meanings are not completely prescribed by culture, which he claims "is true of ACT, but learned and developed by each person in interaction with others" (P. J. Burke, personal communication, September 4, 2002). This is not entirely correct. According to Heise (personal communication, January 13, 2003) "the notion of prescription is foreign to ACT because the individual always is creating action from the inside out. The individual is trying to confirm all the meanings in the situation, not follow rules or orders." Thus, "culture is a useful generalization in ACT but as quick as we analyze it, culture comes down to interactions with others and the kind of aggregate interactional effects that Cecilia Ridgeway or Noah Friedkin write about."

the perceived situational meanings in (#2) with those held in the identity standard in (#1); and (4) *outputs* or the individual's behavior or activity resulting from the discrepancy between the standard in (#1) and perceptions in (#2). That is, through learning, behaviors are chosen that result in changes in the environment such that perceptions from (#1) are brought into closer accord with the standards in (#2).

A simple example will help illustrate how the model works. Recalling the scenario outlined earlier of a female supervisor and a male subordinate engaged in a performance appraisal meeting, let's examine the identities and the situation through the lens of ICT. This time we will focus on the supervisor, a woman, and just the potency component of her supervisor identity (per the earlier discussion of Osgood et al.) as powerful. And while my language may suggest to some that I am describing a linear process, I am not. It is simply a pedagogical device. Indeed, while the actors in my scenario perceive they also act, and vice versa. In "phase" one ([1], the identity standard) the supervisor criticizes her male subordinate's work just as she did before, thus activating the power dimension of *her* supervisor identity standard. (Naturally the other person's identity standard as a subordinate employee is also activated.) Note that a person has an identity standard for how potent they *think* they are and they *behave* so as to help ensure their perceptions of themselves in the situation are as powerful as their identity standard tells them they are. In "phase" two ([2], perceptions), the subordinate, for illustration sake, responds to the criticism by angrily standing up and glaring at the supervisor. His behavior thus serves as an input to the supervisor. In "phase" three ([3], the process of comparison), the supervisor, through the reflected appraisals she perceives from her subordinate in "phase" two, may determine that the powerfulness of her supervisor identity standard legitimately criticizing a subordinate is being undermined. Thus, a discrepancy has occurred between her supervisor identity standard and the perceptions arising in the situation. That is, the comparator signals a disconfirmation when the perception and standard are different. The comparator thus outputs the magnitude of the discrepancy, which is zero when they are the same. In "phase" four ([4], outputs) she may *react* in a number of subtle or overt ways in an attempt to reestablish the power dimension of her supervisor identity. Indeed, ICT suggests she will act in whatever way she can to reduce the discrepancy (within the constraints of maintaining other identities as well—e.g., as a lawful person, an honest person, a female, a professional, and so on). For example, she might tell him to sit down; explain her reasoning and why she is standing by it; or give a knowing gesture indicating that, yes, she knows such news is sometimes hard to accept, but it's her job (role-identity) to do and his to respectfully listen to it. It also warrants reiterating that ICT would assert that the identity standard exists, the perceptions are ongoing, and consequently the comparator's output is ongoing, as too is the behavioral response to the comparator's output.

While Burke's erstwhile cybernetic model of identity processes originally appeared in the literature in an examination of commitment to the student role (Burke & Reitzes, 1991), and aspects of it were anticipated somewhat by Burke and Tully's (1977) work on the gender roles of school children, nowhere in the latter is the language of cybernetic control used nor is Powers (1973) cited. However, in 1980, Burke first appears to invoke the language of control of feedback and cites Powers even though the latter were not central to the paper's overall theme. By 1991, Burke (1991) and Burke and Reitzes (1991) had finally drawn together the strands of his nascent ICT appearing in the literature over the previous decade into focused treatments. But it was his 1991 *American Sociological Review* article that truly sharpened ICT (called in that piece a "control-system view of identity process" [Burke, 1991, p. 838]) considerably over Burke and Reitzes (1991) earlier in the year and placed it firmly in the literature.

ICT has produced a number of interesting and innovative applications and connections to other concepts and theories too numerous to review here. To name just a few of ICT's offerings over the past decade and more, Burke (1991) posed it as a challenge to prevailing views of stress as the result of too many role demands on a person. Burke and Reitzes (1991) linked ICT to an investigation of how college students use cognitive commitment (the rewards, costs, and value of being a college student) and socioemotional commitment (interpersonal ties to others while being a student) to instill the student role and social structure with self-meanings and motives. Within an ICT framework, Burke and Stets recently (1999) illustrated how self-processes can influence social structure. Stets and Tsushima (2001) have also expanded ICT into an examination of the moderating influence of group-based identities and role-based identities on how people experience and cope with the strong emotion of anger.

Identities Based on Group-Level Characteristics

SOCIAL IDENTITY.   There are two broad ways to view social identity. One stems from the sociological social psychology strain of labeling theory represented by Goffman (1963) and the other from European psychological social psychology represented by Tajfel (1981). I begin with a discussion of the origins and various meanings of social identity in sociology and psychology. However, because the aspect of social identity research inspired by Tajfel's initial formulation is currently on the ascendancy in the social sciences, I will focus more on it than social identity research stemming from Goffman's work.

In the sociological sense, one's social identity is derived from the groups, statuses, and categories to which individuals are *socially recognized* as belonging. It is one of their labels. The world thus encounters the individual—and the individual the world—in varying categorical terms: WASP, nun, Ojibwe, tramp. This can be illustrated by comments reported in the *New York Times* by former U.S. Ambassador to Switzerland, Madeleine Kunin, about being Jewish in Switzerland versus the United States (Sciolino, 1997). In her 1985 inaugural speech as Governor of Vermont, Kunin willingly mentioned several of her social identities: the first *woman* to serve as *governor* in that state as well as the third *Democrat* since the Civil War and the second governor of *European birth*. Mentioning that she was also the first *Jewish* governor did not occur to her (Sciolino, 1997, p. A3). Later, as an ambassador, she lamented that her social identity as a Jew was repeatedly invoked by the Swiss press where in "Switzerland my Jewishness is more visible" (p. A3). (This was particularly true because of the ongoing scandal linking Swiss banks to the Nazis and the banks' seizure of Holocaust victims' deposits.)

Social identity in the sense used by psychological social psychologists is a bedrock of social identity theory (see Tajfel, 1981; Tajfel & Turner, 1986) and approaches the issue differently from the way sociologists have traditionally used the term. Yet social identity researchers from both sociology and psychology agree that people can accept or reject social definitions that are applied to them, even if others hold opposing views. However, rather than focus on attempts to apply an identity from the outside, as in sociological labeling theory,* psychologists who use social identity theory see social identity more as a cognitive *tool* individuals use to partition, categorize, and order their social environment and their own place in it. This leads social identity theorists to a particular interest in examining the effect of specific group memberships on how people define themselves. When the "tool" and self-definition aspect of social identity are combined, it can lead to explanations of intergroup conflict and competition. This aspect of the theory is based, in part, on the self-esteem motive discussed

*I recognize the phenomenon of self-labeling as well, but here it is secondary to my main argument.

earlier. One way people sometimes seek to lift their self-esteem is by being part of a distinctive in-group, like a winning team; another is by emphasizing the positive qualities of one's in-group while denigrating the qualities of some out-group (e.g., Nazis denigrating Jews and Gypsies).

Indeed, social identity theory was originally developed to explain prejudice and large-scale conflict among religious, ethnic, and political/national groupings.* As such, social identity theory revolves around a keen interest in social problems stemming from in-group/out-group categorizations (see Stryker et al., 2000a). However, Tajfel (1981) was also determined to use social identity theory to develop a more *social* social psychology as a counter to the individualist bias he saw in American psychology (Thoits & Virshup, 1997). Part of his vexation with overly individualistic social psychology, was its inability to explain large-scale social calamities like the Holocaust without resorting to psychological reductionism. He found such explanations patently unsatisfactory because they not only collapsed personality differences and studies of national character, but because they also tend to smugly dismiss societal-level variables (Tajfel, 1981).

Social identity theory incorporates self-categorization theory (Turner, Hogg, Oakes, Reicher, & Wetherell, 1987), which shows how cognitive processes allow people to simplify the world of social and nonsocial stimuli into separate groups of like and unlike stimuli. More specifically, self-categorization theory's goal is to make social identity (the aspect of self derived from group memberships) not only the "social-cognitive basis of group behaviour" but also the mechanism that makes such behavior possible (Turner et al., 1987, p. ix). In addition, by asserting that "self-categorizations function at different levels of abstraction," the theory casts group and individual behavior in terms of the self (Turner et al., 1987, p. ix). This goal is derived from a tripartite view of self-categorizations moving from least to most abstract (Turner et al., 1987, p. 45). The "subordinate level" encompasses personal self-categorizations based on particular individuals comparing and contrasting themselves to members of some in-group. For example, this could happen when Gene Doe, an insurance agent, compares himself to other insurance agents, not just along lines of sales success, but in terms of how good they are with people or how concerned they are about other people's welfare. The "intermediate level" encompasses a person's in-group–out-group categorizations based on perceived social similarities and differences of some in-group versus some out-group. For example, the insurance agent may see his sales vocation as an honorable profession but that of used-car sales-people as somewhat disreputable. The "superordinate level" of self-categorizations is based on the perceived common features of human beings *sui generis* versus other life forms. Perhaps Gene Doe is a pacifist and vegetarian because he believes humans, endowed by the same creator, ought never to kill each other, while also refusing to eat meat because he feels it is wrong to take advantage of lesser animals. Incorporating self-categorization theory into social identity theory, however, effectively collapses "group" and "social category."

For Tajfel (1981), social identity theory starts by assuming the primacy of the mind and then defines social identity as:

> that *part* of an individual's self-concept which derives from his knowledge of his membership in a social group (or groups) together with the value and emotional significance attached to that membership .... [T]he assumption is made that, however rich and complex may be the individuals' view of themselves in relation to their surrounding world ... *some* aspects of that view are contributed by the membership of certain social groups or categories. Some of these memberships are more salient than others; and some may vary in salience in time as a function of a variety of social situations. (p. 255, emphases in the original)

---

*This practical aspect of social identity theory owed to Tajfel's experience in World War II as a European Jew and refugee, being his family's lone Holocaust survivor, and his eventual immigration to and university education in Britain (Tajfel, 1981, pp. 1–2).

By extrapolation, social identity can be seen as encompassing two interrelated dimensions: the group-level (including social structural characteristics of a social identity) and the individual-level desires, motives, and actions derived from a social identity. However, Tajfel's motivation was not to explain intergroup conflict and competition through intraindividual and interpersonal process; it was by exploring between-*group* psychological processes.

People not only take in the overall cultural evaluations of groups (e.g., status, prestige, worth), they also vary in the degree of legitimacy they afford those cultural evaluations. Taylor's (1996, 2000) study of the emergence of a social identity among women in a postpartum depression self-help group is illustrative. She shows that the women in her study perceived a high degree of generalized stigma because of the ambivalent, sometimes hostile, and even homicidal feelings they had toward their newborns.* That is, the women grew to perceive themselves as an in-group at odds with an out-group—established medicine. Many of the mothers took solace in their newfound social identity as a mother with a recognizable problem rather than bad or perhaps wicked mothers, as they saw the aloof male dominated medical establishment defining them (Taylor, 2000). Thus, a person might well see and understand the lower standing and possible contempt of his or her group from the broader culture's or another group's viewpoint yet attach little or no legitimacy to the evaluation. And according to Tajfel (1981), the most positive reaction to finding oneself a member of an undervalued social group is to take social action that expresses the needs of one's in-group to some out-group(s). This transformation is well-illustrated in Taylor's (1996, 2000) study. Once the individual women started to realize that there were others in the same predicament and started forming a social identity around postpartum depression, they were in a position to work with other mothers to redress their grievances and advocate for their numerous needs. Enter collective identity.

COLLECTIVE IDENTITY. Although a relatively recent concept in the social science literature, and one originating in psychological social psychology, some early sociologists anticipated collective identity. Marx's "class consciousness," Durkheim's ([1897] 1951) "collective conscience," and Giddings's (1898) "consciousness of kind" are notable. And while a consensus of meaning surrounding collective identity has yet to clearly form, I will examine the concept and a theory closely associated with the pioneering work of Alberto Melucci (1989, 1996), a European psychological social psychologist. Melucci sees collective identity as an important conceptual tool for understanding the micro development of sociopolitical collective action and social movements. For him, it represents a process of agentic action rather than a social actor's trait. As such, it is a process by which a set of individuals interact to create a shared identity and action system that is cognitively and emotionally framed through active relationships with others (1989, pp. 34–35). He defines collective identity as:

> an interactive and shared definition produced by a number of individuals (or groups at a more complex level) and concerning the *orientations* of action and the *field* of opportunities and constraints in which the action is to take place. By "interactive and shared" I mean that these elements are constructed and negotiated through a recurrent process of activation of the relations that bind actors together. (Melucci, 1996, p. 70, emphases in the original)

His research program includes three key features that orient the research and shape subject selection: (1) the collectivity has continuity over time and tries to adapt to its social

---

*The recent case of infanticide by the Texas mother of five, Andrea Yates, and her documented history of postpartum depression (and psychosis) is a case in point, including her and her husband's alleged difficulty in getting appropriate and sympathetic professional care.

and political environment; (2) the collectivity is differentiated and distinguished with respect to other collectivities; and (3) the collectivity is able to recognize itself and be recognized by others (Melucci, 1996, pp. 70–71). In this sense, collective identity is purposefully constructed and negotiated through a repeated activation of the relationships that link particular individuals to particular groups. Polletta and Jasper (2001) make a useful elaboration. Collective identity is an "individual's cognitive, moral, and emotional connection with a broader community, category, practice, or institution" (p. 285). In addition, since a collective identity is a "perception of a shared status or relation," it may be imagined or experienced directly (p. 285). Unlike social identity, which is essentially an individual-level concept based on the supposed characteristics of some group or category to which one is attached, collective identity is a distinctively group-level concept referring to the *processes* by which an action-oriented group comes to identify itself.* Consequently, collective identity is not only derived from the process of interaction, but from the repeated identity activations a group undergoes as it negotiates its self-identification.

Sociologists and social movements researchers from other disciplines were attracted to collective identity as a response to gaps they saw in resource mobilization and political process models of social movements (Polletta & Jasper, 2001). They use it to address four important concerns (Polletta & Jasper, 2001, p. 284). (1) Why people become political actors when they do. (2) Why people are in fact motivated to act to redress a collective grievance or oppose the *status quo*. Understanding collective identity promises to shed light on the "pleasures and obligations that actually persuade people to mobilize," rather than having researchers simply concentrate on material incentives for people to do so (p. 284). (3) If people choose to participate because it also corresponds to their personal identities, then assessing the nature of their collective identity can be helpful in understanding the forms of protest they employ. (4) Collective identity can illuminate how culture effects social movements. Taken as a whole, collective identity is the only one of the three forms under consideration with an express interest in linking micro motives and interactions with macro behavior.

Recalling the "not-me" aspect of identity discussed earlier, it should be noted that collective identities can and frequently are identities attached to membership in collectivities defined in contrast to or in opposition with other collectivities. Put differently, collective identity often implies direct opposition to the dominant order. Melucci (1989, p. 35) holds that social movements build "submerged networks" of political culture that are interwoven with everyday life and provide new expressions of identity that challenge dominant representations of the social and political *status quo* (see Britt & Heise, 2000, for an illustration). As Pizzorno (1978) suggests, the purposeful and expressive disclosure to others of one's subjective feelings, desires, and experiences surrounding a social identity can result in gaining recognition and influence in subsequent collective action via the building of a collective identity. One thing that makes the concept of social identity so interesting to social movements researchers, is that a social identity can transition into a collective identity by the process of group members sharing with each other cognitive and emotional aspects of a social identity, which in turn may get mobilized into action through the rise of a particular collective identity.

If one wanted to study the collective identity of labor activists, for instance, one would likely start by going to an appropriate union directly and studying the actions and sentiments of its members in an effort to understand the shared meanings and collective behavior of the

*Social identities are to individuals what collective identities are to groups. As such, the women in Taylor's (1996) study have individual social identities as women with potentially malevolent postpartum depression, while they have a collective identity as a group of women fighting together for the rights and needs of women everywhere so afflicted.

group. The next step, as Taylor and Whittier (1995) and Klandermans (1997) illustrate, often is to define the collectivity of interest by contrasting it to its perceived opposition (e.g., management or perhaps other unions believed to be ineffectual or corrupt). However, in order to understand a person's social identity as a labor activist, the investigator would do well to measure not only how the activist evaluates his or her union identity and its relative importance, but also how he or she perceives relevant others evaluate and judge it. Finally, if one wanted to address the personal identity of a labor activist, via Stryker's structuralist framework, an important first step would be to assess the salience of the members labor activist identities, thus grappling with the probability of it being activated within and across its possessors' various other role-identity situations (e.g., family, church, recreation, work setting). In this context, one would also be interested in the degree of affective and interactional commitment the unionists have to their labor activist identity.

CONCLUSION

At the start of this chapter, I showed the tremendous rise in self and identity research over the past 50 years, and its veritable explosion in the past 20. This unmitigated ascendancy, however, can be seen as a blessing and a curse. It is a blessing because theoretical and empirical work has enriched our knowledge of self and identity beyond anything the early theorists could envisage while successfully establishing both ideas in the social science literature—particularly in sociology and psychology. Self and identity researchers have also been linking the concepts to macro phenomenon such as social movements and collective behavior, thus placing the concepts in new and exciting literatures while also expanding avenues of future research. However, it may also be something of a curse. As noted throughout the chapter, the "puzzling puzzle" that James noted with respect to the self persists today. Some of it stems from the self's sheer complexity. Fair enough. But some is also due to awkward disciplinary boundaries, reinvention and redundancy, and alternative terminology for equivalent concepts and theories. Other problems stem from imprecise employment of the concepts and confusion over their similarities, differences, and proper applications. Some of this can be resolved by addressing the congruities and incongruities of sociological and psychological approaches to self and identity. There are signs of such intellectual pluralism but more work is needed.

Looking back across this chapter, several general points seem to have emerged. First, self and identity's theoretical landscape is rich and varied. While more theoretical work is in the offing, there are a number of well-constructed theories addressing everything from affect, self-presentation, and identity enactment to social network views of identity and the self as a social force. Second, even though we have a number of theories of self and identity, we have not been as successful as we could be in linking our theoretical research to the practical problems of everyday life. There are exceptions, of course, but self and identity research could do more by way of addressing social stratification, mental heath, and social well-being. Moreover, the time seems methodologically and theoretically ripe to better integrate life course concepts and longitudinal data into our research. Third, I have noted several human motivations with respect to the self (e.g., self-esteem, self-consistency, self-presentation). What we do not know is their relative importance to the self and their relative implications for action. It seems that more theoretical and empirical clarity is necessary before more motivations are proffered. Finally, it seems clear that self and identity approaches are moving vigorously into interesting research areas. The challenge will be to remain theoretically grounded; increase interdisciplinary appreciation and work; emphasize social problems more; and continue linking to new areas, especially at the macro level.

ACKNOWLEDGMENTS: I wish to thank Peggy Thoits, Sheldon Stryker, Mangala Subramaniam, Lynn Smith-Lovin, Neil MacKinnon, and Peter Burke for commenting on portions of earlier drafts.

REFERENCES

Allport, G. W. (1961). *Pattern and growth in personality*. New York: Holt, Rinehart and Winston.

American Psychological Association. (2002). *PsycINFO*. Washington, DC.

Baumeister, R. F., Smart, L., & Boden, J. M. (1996). Relation of threatened egotism to violence and aggression: The dark side of high self-esteem. *Psychological Review, 103*, 5–33.

Britt, L., & Heise, D. (2000). From shame to pride in identity politics. In S. Stryker, T. J. Owens, & R. W. White (Eds.), *Self, identity, and social movements* (pp. 252–268). Minneapolis: University of Minnesota Press.

Burke, P. J. (1980). The self: Measurement requirements from an interactionist perspective. *Social Psychology Quarterly, 43*, 18–29.

Burke, P. J. (1991). Identity processes and social stress. *American Sociological Review, 56*, 836–849.

Burke, P. J., & Reitzes, D. C. (1991). An identity theory approach to commitment. *Social Psychology Quarterly, 54*, 239–251.

Burke, P. J., & Stets, J. E. (1999). Trust and commitment through self-verification. *Social Psychology Quarterly, 62*, 347–366.

Burke, P. J., & Tully, J. T. (1977). The measurement of role/identity. *Social Forces, 55*, 880–897.

Burns, R. B. (1979). The self concept in theory, measurement, development, and behaviour. London: Longman.

Call, K. T., & Mortimer, J. T. (2001). *Arenas of comfort: A study of adjustment in context*. Mahmah, NJ: Lawrence Erlbaum.

Cambridge Scientific Abstracts. (2002). *SocioFile/Sociological Abstracts*. San Diego, CA.

Clay-Warner, J. (2001). Perceiving procedural injustice: The effects of group membership and status. *Social Psychology Quarterly, 64*, 224–238.

Cooley, C. H. (1902). *Human nature and the social order*. New York: Charles Scribner's Sons.

Cooley, C. H. (1909). *Social organization: A study of the larger mind*. New York: Schocken Books.

Cote, J. E., & Levine, C. G. (2002). *Identity formation, agency, and culture: A social psychological synthesis*. Mahwah, NJ: Lawrence Erlbaum.

Culos-Reed, S. N., Brawley, L. R., Martin, K. A., & Leary, M. R. (2002). Self-presentation concerns and health behaviors among cosmetic surgery patients. *Journal of Applied Social Psychology*, (32), 560–569.

Diggory, J. C. (1966). *Self-evaluation: Concepts and studies*. New York: John Wiley & Sons.

Durkheim, E. (1951). *Suicide*. Glencoe, Il: Free Press.

Ervin, L., & Stryker, S. (2000). Theorizing the relationship between self-esteem and identity. In T. J. Owens, S. Stryker, & N. Goodman (Eds.), *Extending self-esteem theory and research: Sociological and psychological currents* (pp. 29–55). New York: Cambridge University Press.

Foote, N. N. (1951). Identification as the basis for a theory of motivation. *American Sociological Review, 16*, 14–21.

Garder, H. (1985). *The mind's new science: A history of the cognitive revolution*. New York: Basic Books.

Ge, X., Elder, G. H., Jr., Regnerus, M., & Cox, C. (2001). Pubertal transitions, perceptions of being overweight, and adolescents' psychological maladjustment: Gender and ethnic differences. *Social Psychology Quarterly, 64*, 363–375.

Gergen, K. J. (1971). *The concept of self*. New York: Holt, Rinehart, and Winston.

Giddings, F. H. (1896). *The principles of sociology: An analysis of the phenomena of association and of social organization*. New York: Macmillan.

Goffman, E. (1959). *The presentation of self in everyday life*. Garden City, NY: Doubleday.

Goffman, E. (1963). *Stigma: Notes on the management of spoiled identity*. New York: Simon & Schuster.

Haj-Yahia, M. M. (2001). Implications of wife abuse and battering for self-esteem, depression, and anxiety as revealed by the second Palestinian national survey on violence against women. *Journal of Family Issues, 21*, 435–463.

Heise, D. R. (1977). Social action as the control of affect. *Behavioral Science, 22*, 163–177.

Heise, D. R. (1979). *Understanding events: Affect and the construction of social action*. New York: Cambridge University Press.

Heise, D. R. (1988). Affect control theory: Concepts and models. In L. Smith-Lovin & D. R. Heise (Eds.), *Analyzing social interaction: Research advances in affect control theory* (pp. 1–33). New York: Gordon and Breach.

Heise, D. R. (2002). *Affect control theory*. Web site: URL http://www.indiana.edu/~socpsy/ACT/

Hewitt, J. P. (1979). *Self and society: A symbolic interactionist social psychology.* Boston: Allyn and Bacon.

James, W. (1890). *The principles of psychology.* New York: Henry Holt.

Jasper, J. M. (1997). *The art of moral protest: Culture, biography, and creativity in social movements.* Chicago: University of Chicago Press.

Jones, E. E. (1964). *Ingratiation.* New York: Appleton-Century-Crofts.

Jones, E. E., & Pittman, T. S. (1982). Toward a general theory of strategic self-presentation. In J. Suls (Ed.), *Psychological perspectives on the self* (Vol. 1, pp. 231–262). Hillsdale, NJ: Lawrence Erlbaum.

Kaplan, H. B. (1975). *Self-attitudes and deviant behavior.* Pacific Palisades, CA: Goodyear.

Kiecolt, K. J., & Mabry, J. B. (2000). Agency in young adulthood: Intentional self-change among college students. *Advances in Life Course Research, 5,* 181–205.

Klandermans, B. (1997). *The social psychology of protest.* Oxford, UK: Blackwell Publishers.

Kuhn, M. H., & McPartland, T. S. (1954). An empirical investigation of self-attitudes. *American Sociological Review, 19,* 69–76.

Leary, M. R. (1996). *Self-presentation: Impression management and interpersonal behavior.* Boulder, CO: Westview.

Leary, M. R., & Kowalski, R. M. (1990). Impression management: A literature review and two-component model. *Psychological Bulletin, 107,* 34–47.

Lecky, P. (1961). *Self-consistency: A theory of personality.* New York: Island Press.

MacKinnon, N. J. (1994). *Symbolic interaction as affect control.* Albany, NY: State University of New York Press.

MacKinnon, N. J., & Bowlby, J. W. (2000). The affective dynamics of stereotyping and intergroup relations. *Advances in Group Processes, 17,* 37–76.

Marsh, H. W., Byrne, B. M., & Shavelson, R. J. (1992). A multidimensional, hierarchical self-concept. In T. M. Brinthaupt & R. P. Lipka (Eds.), *The self: Definitional and methodological issues* (pp. 44–95). Albany, NY: State University of New York Press.

Marsh, H. W., Craven, R., & Debus, R. (1998). Structure, stability, and development of young children's self-concepts: A multicohort-multioccasion study. *Child Development, 69,* 1030–1053.

Martindale, D. (1981). *The nature and types of sociological theory* (2nd ed.). Boston: Houghton Mifflin.

Marx, K. (1978). Economic and philosophical manuscript of 1844. In R. C. Tucker (Ed.), *The Marx-Engels reader* (2nd ed., pp. 66–132). New York: W. W. Norton.

McCall, G. J. (in press). The me and the not-me: Positive and negative poles of identity. In P. J. Burke, T. J. Owens, R. T. Serpe, & P. A. Thoits (Eds.), *Advances in identity theory and research.* New York: Kluwer/Plenum.

McCall, G. J., & Simmons, J. L. (1966). *Identities and interaction.* New York: Free Press.

Mead, G. H. (1934). *Mind, self, and society from the standpoint of a social behaviorist.* Chicago: University of Chicago Press.

Meltzer, B. M., & Petras, J. W. (1970). The Chicago and Iowa schools of symbolic interactionism. In T. Shibutani (Ed.), *Human nature and collective behavior: Papers in honor of Herbert Blumer* (pp. 3–17). Englewood Cliff, NJ: Prentice-Hall.

Melucci, A. (1989). *Nomads of the present: Social movements and individual needs in contemporary society.* Philadelphia: Temple University Press.

Melucci, A. (1996). *Challenging codes: Collective action in the information age.* Cambridge: Cambridge University Press.

Michener, H. A., & Delamater, J. D. (1999). *Social psychology* (4th ed.). Fort Worth, TX: Harcourt Brace.

Nezlek, J. B., & Leary, M. R. (2002). Individual differences in self-presentational motives in daily social interaction. *Personality & Social Psychology Bulletin, 28,* 211–223.

Nyamathi, A., Longshore, D., Keenan, C., Lesser, J., & Leake, B. D. (2001). Childhood predictors of daily substance use among homeless women of different ethnicities. *American Behavioral Scientist, 45,* 35–50.

Osgood, C. E., May, W. H., & Miron, M. S. (1975). *Cross-cultural universals of affective meaning.* Urbana, IL: University of Illinois Press.

Osgood, C. E., Suci, G. J., & Tannenbaum, P. H. (1957). *The measurement of meaning.* Urbana, IL: University of Illinois Press.

Owens, T. J., & Aronson, P. J. (2000). Self-concept as a force in social movement involvement. In S. Stryker, T. J. Owens, & R. W. White (Eds.), *Self, identity and social movements* (pp. 132–151). Minneapolis: University of Minnesota Press.

Owens, T. J., & King, A. B. (2001). Measuring self-esteem: Race, ethnicity, and gender considered. In T. J. Owens, S. Stryker, & N. Goodman (Eds.), *Extending self-esteem theory and research: Sociological and psychological currents* (pp. 56–84). New York: Cambridge University.

Parker, R. J. (2001). The effects of evaluative context on performance: The roles of self- and social-evaluations. *Social Behavior & Personality, 29,* 807–822.

Pearlin, L. I., & LeBlanc, A. J. (2001). Bereavement and the loss of mattering. In T. J. Owens, S. Stryker, & N. Goodman (Eds.), *Extending self-esteem theory and research: Sociological and psychological currents* (pp. 285–300). New York: Cambridge University Press.

Peltzer, K., Malaka, D., & Phaswana, N. (2001). Psychological correlates of substance use among South African university students. *Social Behavior & Personality, 29,* 799–806.

Pizzorno, A. (1978). Political science and collective identity in industrial conflict. In C. Crouch & A. Pizzorno (Eds.), *The resurgence of class conflict in Western Europe since 1968* (pp. 277–298). New York: Holmes and Meier.

Polletta, F., & Jasper, J. M. (2001). Collective identity and social movements. *Annual Review of Sociology, 27,* 283–305.

Powers, W. T. (1973). *Behavior: The control of perception.* Chicago: Aldine.

Rashotte, L. S. (2002). What does that smile mean? The meaning of nonverbal behaviors in social interaction. *Social Psychology Quarterly, 65,* 92–102.

Robinson, D. T., & Smith-Lovin, L. (1992). Selective interaction as a strategy for identity maintenance: An affect control model. *Social Psychology Quarterly, 55,* 12–28.

Rosenberg, M. (1965). *Society and the adolescent self-image.* Princeton, NJ: Princeton University Press.

Rosenberg, M. (1979). *Conceiving the self.* New York: Basic Books.

Rosenberg, M. (1981). The self-concept: Social product and social force. In M. Rosenberg & R. H. Turner (Eds.), *Social psychology: Sociological perspectives* (pp. 593–624). New York: Basic Books.

Rosenberg, M., & McCullough, B. C. (1981). Mattering: Inferred significance and mental health among adolescents. *Research in Community and Mental Health, 2,* 163–182.

Rosenberg, M., & Owens, T. J. (2001). Low self-esteem people: A collective portrait. In T. J. Owens, S. Stryker, & N. Goodman (Eds.), *Extending self-esteem theory and research: Sociological and psychological currents* (pp. 400–436). New York: Cambridge University Press.

Rosenberg, M., Schooler, C., Schoenbach, C., & Rosenberg, F. (1995). Global self-esteem and specific self-esteem: Different concepts, different outcomes. *American Sociological Review, 60,* 141–156.

Schlenker, B. R. (1980). *Impression management: The self-concept, social identity, and interpersonal relations.* Monterey, CA: Brooks/Cole.

Schnittker, J. (2001). Acculturation in context: The self-esteem of Chinese immigrants. *Social Psychology Quarterly, 65,* 56–76.

Sciolino, E. (1997, October). A careful dance for U.S. envoy in Switzerland. *New York Times,* p. A3.

Shin, J. H. (2002, December). Willigan and Heise Study Navajo social interaction and culture. *Footnotes,* p. 7.

Simmons, R. G. (2001). Comfort with the self. In T. J. Owens, S. Stryker, & N. Goodman (Eds.), *Extending self-esteem theory and research: Sociological and psychological currents* (pp. 198–222). New York: Cambridge University Press.

Smith, H. W., Matsuno, T., & Ike, S. (2001). The affective basis of attributional processes among Japanese and Americans. *Social Psychology Quarterly, 64,* 180–194.

Smith-Lovin, L., & Heise, D. R. (Eds.). (1988). *Analyzing social interaction: Research advances in affect control theory.* New York: Gordon & Breach.

Sniderman, P. M. (1975). *Personality and democratic politics.* Berkeley, CA: University of California Press.

Stets, J. E., & Burke, P. J. (2000). Identity theory and social identity theory. *Social Psychology Quarterly, 63,* 224–237.

Stets, J. E., & Burke, P. J. (2002). A sociological approach to self and identity. In M. R. Leary & J. P. Tangney (Eds.), *Handbook of self and identity* (pp. 128–152). New York: Guilford Press.

Stets, J. E., & Tsushima, T. M. (2001). Negative emotion and coping responses within identity control theory. *Social Psychology Quarterly, 64,* 283–295.

Stryker, S. (1968). Identity theory and role performance. *Journal of Marriage and the Family, 30,* 558–564.

Stryker, S. (1980). *Symbolic interactionism: A social structural version.* Menlo Park, CA: Benjamin Cummings.

Stryker, S. (1987). The vitalization of symbolic interactionism. *Social Psychology Quarterly, 50,* 83–94.

Stryker, S. (1991). Exploring the relevance of social cognition for the relationship of self and society: Linking the cognitive perspective and identity theory. In J. A. Howard & P. L. Callero (Eds.), *The self-society dynamic: Cognition, emotion, and action* (pp. 19–54). New York: Cambridge University Press.

Stryker, S. (2000). Identity competition: Key to differential social movement participation? In S. Stryker, T. J. Owens, & R. W. White (Eds.), *Self, identity and social movements* (pp. 21–40). Minneapolis: University of Minnesota.

Stryker, S., & Burke, P. J. (2000). The past, present, and future of an identity theory. *Social Psychology Quarterly, 63,* 284–297.

Stryker, S., & Serpe, R. T. (1994). Identity salience and psychological centrality: Equivalent, overlapping, or complementary concepts? *Social Psychology Quarterly, 57,* 16–35.

Stryker, S., & Statham, A. (1985). Symbolic interaction and role theory. In L. Gardner & E. Aronson (Eds.), *Handbook of social psychology* (3rd ed., pp. 311–378). New York: Random House.

Stryker, S., Owens, T. J., & White, R. W. (2000a). *Self, identity, and social movements*. Minneapolis, MN: University of Minnesota Press.

Stryker, S., Owens, T. J., & White, R. W. (2000b). Social psychology and social movements: Cloudy past and bright future. In S. Stryker, T. J. Owens, & R. W. White (Eds.), *Self, identity and social movements* (pp. 1–17). Minneapolis, MN: University of Minnesota.

Subramaniam, M. (2001). Translating participation in informal organizations into empowerment: Women in rural India. Unpublished doctoral dissertation, University of Connecticut, Storrs.

Sullivan, H. S. (1953). *The interpersonal theory of psychiatry*. New York: Norton.

Swann, W. B., Jr. (1996). *Self-traps: The elusive quest for higher self-esteem*. New York: W. H. Freeman.

Swann, W. B., Jr. (1983). Self-verification: Bring social reality into harmony with the self. In J. M. Suls & A. G. Greenwald (Eds.), *Social psychological perspectives on the self* (Vol. 2, pp. 33–66). Hillsdale, NJ: Lawrence Erlbaum.

Swann, W. B., Jr., Milton, L. P., & Polzer, J. T. (2000). Should we create a niche or fall in line? Identity negotiation and small group effectiveness. *Journal of Personality & Social Psychology, 79*, 238–250.

Tajfel, H. (1981). *Human groups and social categories: Studies in social psychology*. Cambridge: Cambridge University Press.

Tajfel, H., & Turner, J. C. (1986). The social identity theory of intergroup behavior. In S. Worchel & W. G. Austin (Eds.), *Psychology of intergroup relations* (2nd ed., pp. 7–24). Chicago: Nelson-Hall.

Tarrant, M., North, A. C., & Hargreaves, D. J. (2001). Social categorization, self-esteem, and the estimated musical preferences of male adolescents. *Journal of Social Psychology, 141*, 565–581.

Taylor, J., & Turner, R. J. (2001). A longitudinal study of the role and significance of mattering to others for depressive symptoms. *Journal of Health and Social Behavior, 42*, 310–325.

Taylor, V. (1996). *Rock-a-by baby: Feminism, self-help, and postpartum depression*. New York: Routledge.

Taylor, V. (2000). Emotions and identity in women's self-help movements. In S. Stryker, T. J. Owens, & R. W. White (Eds.), *Self, identity, and social movements* (pp. 271–299). Minneapolis, MN: University of Minnesota Press.

Taylor, V., & Whittier, N. E. (1995). Analytical approaches to social movement culture: The culture of the women's movement. In H. Johnston & B. Klandermans (Eds.), *Social movements and culture* (pp. 163–187). Minneapolis: University of Minnesota Press.

Thoits, P. A. (1995). Social psychology: The interplay between sociology and psychology. *Social Forces, 73*, 1231–1243.

Thoits, P. A., & Hewitt, L. N. (2001). Volunteer work and well-being. *Journal of Health & Social Behavior, 42*, 115–133.

Thoits, P. A., & Virshup, L. K. (1997). Me's and we's: Forms and functions of social identities. In R. D. Ashmore & L. Jussim (Eds.), *Self and identity: Fundamental issues* (Vol. 1, pp. 106–133). New York: Oxford University Press.

Thomas, W. I., & Znaniecki, F. (1918). *The Polish peasant in Europe and America*. Boston: G. Badger.

Tsoudis, O., & Smith-Lovin, L. (1998). How bad was it? The effects of victim and perpetrator emotion on responses to criminal court vignettes. *Social Forces, 77*, 695–722.

Turner, J. C., Hogg, M. A., Oakes, P. J., Reicher, S. D., & Wetherell, M. S. (1987). *Rediscovering the social group: A self-categorization theory*. Oxford, UK: Basil Blackwell.

White, R. W. (2001). Social and role identities and political violence: Identity as a window on violence in Northern Ireland. In R. D. Ashmore & L. Jussim (Eds.), *Social identity, intergroup conflict, and conflict reduction* (Vol. 3, pp. 133–158). London: Oxford University Press.

Wright, E. R., Gronfein, W. P., & Owens, T. J. (2000). Deinstitutionalization, social rejection, and the self-esteem of former mental patients. *Journal of Health and Social Behavior, 41*, 68–90.

Wylie, R. C. (1979). *The self-concept: Theory and research on selected topics* (Rev. ed.). Lincoln, NE: University of Nebraska Press.

CHAPTER 10

Language and Social Interaction

Douglas W. Maynard
Anssi Peräkylä

At least since Aristotle, language has been seen as distinctively human in its complexity. Ethologists have increased our appreciation of how other mammals—dolphins, chimpanzees, gorillas, and so on—employ sounds to signal one another in sophisticated ways, but humans, in conducting their everyday affairs, rely on spoken and gestural forms of intercourse to an unparalleled degree (Eibl-Eibesfeldt, 1989). Despite the centrality of language use in human society, social psychology textbooks often ignore the topic (Clark, 1985, p. 179), and when they do pay attention it is to regard language as a mode of communication or a vehicle whereby humans transmit information, including ideas, thoughts, and feelings, from one to another.

A variety of philosophers and social scientists regard the view of language as primarily communicative in function as the "conduit metaphor" (Reddy, 1979). This metaphor is rooted in the commonsensical notion that, through speech, one person conveys information by inserting it into words and sending them along a communicative channel. People receive the words at the other end and extract the encoded thoughts and feelings from them. The conduit metaphor reinforces an idea that problems of meaning in human society are essentially *referential* or concerned with how concepts correspond to or represent reality, and that language operates to make propositions about the world (Pitkin, 1972, p. 3). Instead of using the conduit metaphor and referential approach to meaning, scholars recently have approached language as a medium of organized social activity, in which words are "performatives" (Austin, 1962) or "deeds" (Wittgenstein, 1958, para. 546). It is partly through language that humans "do" the social world, even as the world is confronted as the unquestioned background or condition for activity. The conduit metaphor and "picture book" view of language, rather than the

DOUGLAS W. MAYNARD • Department of Sociology, University of Wisconsin-Madison, Madison, Wisconsin 53706
ANSSI PERÄKYLÄ • Department of Sociology and Social Psychology, University of Tampere, Tampere, Finland

Handbook of Social Psychology, edited by John Delamater. Kluwer Academic/Plenum Publishers, New York, 2003.

more dynamic or activist approach, still heavily influence social psychological theory and research, however. This chapter begins with a review of general statements in social psychology about language, then examines language as action and the philosophical and social scientific background to this perspective. We review the so-called *mapping problem* or the question of how utterances become linked to social actions. Rule-based answers to this question include sociolinguistics and discourse analysis. In other perspectives—the frame analysis of Goffman, and discursive psychology—rules play a less dominant role. Finally, we discuss ethnomethodology and conversation analysis, in which rules are altogether abandoned as explanatory resources and investigators connect language to action through other means, such as the sequential organization of talk.

LANGUAGE IN SOCIAL PSYCHOLOGY

There are two main disciplinary "branches" to the field of social psychology—the psychological and the sociological (House, 1977). Along the psychological branch, it has been traditional to employ the conduit model of language. For example, a frequent topic along this branch is that of *persuasion*, and the well-known Yale communication model (Hovland, Harvey, & Sherif, 1953) poses a basic question about it: "Who says what to whom by what means?" This model, which has been modified by more recent, cognitively oriented models such as the elaboration likelihood and heuristic and systematic models (Chaiken, 1987; Petty & Cacioppo, 1986), includes four factors that are important to achieving persuasion— a communicator or source, a message, an audience, and a channel through which the message is conveyed. When, for example, audience members perceive a source as credible and trustworthy, they are more likely to be persuaded by what the source says. Over the years, such public figures as (in the United States) Eleanor Roosevelt, Ronald Reagan, and Bill Clinton have been seen as examples of persuasive source figures. Other "source" features including likeability, attractiveness, and expertise also affect how audiences evaluate messages. Besides features of a source, researchers have studied characteristics of messages (capacity to arouse emotion or fear, quantity and timing of messages, discrepancy between message and target's own position, etc.), targets (mood, motivation, etc.) and situations for their influence on persuasiveness.

In the sociological branch of social psychology, symbolic interactionists have been most concerned with language. This is no doubt due to the influence of Mead (1934), who originated the suggestion that humans employ *significant symbols* that, when emitted by one party, elicit the same response in that party as in the party to whom the symbol is directed. This suggestion assumes significance in a larger context than social psychology, however. Sociologists regard communication as achieving a solution to "the problem of meaning," which Weber (1947) long ago identified as being at the core of social action, for the defining criterion of such action is that it is a product of the interactive interpretations of society's members. When Mead (1934) proposed the existence of significant symbols and the capacity for "taking the role of the other," it seemed to represent a clear statement of how humans could form common understandings, produce mutual and complementary stances within what he called the "social act," and also thereby provide for larger patterns of social life.

From ideas like Mead's and a more general concern with the problem of meaning, it is easy to see how social psychologists moved to the conduit metaphor when discussing human language, seeing it as a repository of significant symbols in which people package their ideas and feelings. Significant symbols include not only words but gestures as well, although there are two views of gestural communication. In one view, gestures are substituted for words. Thus, a hand wave stands for "hello," a green light suggests "go," a beckoning arm signifies "come on," and so on (Hertzler, 1965, pp. 29–30). In the other view, gestures occupy a different "channel of communication" than words—a nonverbal one. In either view, because of the presumption that gestures encode referential meaning, the conduit metaphor is preserved. Although it is recognized that gestures and words are arbitrary and conventional and that they take on different senses according to the context in which they appear, individuals' ability to encode their own experiences with words and gestures inexorably leads actors to share the same mental attitudes or states and to agree upon reference (Hewitt, 1997, pp. 30–38), which makes collaborative activity possible.

An influential variant of the communicational view of language is the famous Sapir–Whorf, or linguistic relativity, hypothesis. Benjamin Whorf, a student of the anthropologist Edward Sapir, studied the languages of American Indians and other groups, and argued that these languages conditioned the members' life experiences. As a straightforward example (Whorf, 1956, p. 216) observes that the Hopi language has one word for everything that flies (except birds, which form another category), whereas English has separate nouns for insect, airplane, aviator, and so on. Thus, according to Whorf (1956, p. 218), actors "dissect" the world "along lines laid down by our native languages." Despite the relativity it implies, the Whorfian hypothesis is compatible with the conduit metaphor and communicational view of language in that it proposes the very source of an individual's experience.* Once individuals have learned the group's language, they have acquired the symbolic means for having emotions, beliefs, perceptions, and so on and transmitting them to one another.

Of course, most social psychologists argue that language and experience reciprocally influence one another. Nevertheless, in studies where language is a prominent variable, it remains as a relatively static repository of meanings† that either conditions or is conditioned by those social factors of interest to the investigator. Later, we show that in traditional studies, social structure is often conveyed by the conduit of communication. Overall, then, language has been important to social psychology because it represents a vital medium whereby actors can communicate with one another and thereby set up joint projects according to preexisting social arrangements. In this view, the manipulation of significant symbols is a precursor to action and behavior is the product of linguistically achieved common understandings. A different view of language sees it as co-constitutive of social activity. That is, language and action are facets of a single process that participants collaboratively organize through their practices of speech and gesture.

LANGUAGE AND ACTION

The conduit metaphor implies that language is largely a vehicle whereby interactants make propositions about the world. From this perspective, which is explicit or implicit in traditional social psychological research on language, problems of meaning involve how well linguistic concepts refer to, correspond with, or represent reality, including internal thoughts and feelings.

---

*The Whorfian hypothesis suggests an iconic relation between language and thought—that is, that language determines thought. Early on, Lenneberg (1953) and Brown (1958) pointed out the logical flaws in this proposition. For a more recent critique, see Pinker (1994, chapter 3).

†This is true, as Boden (1990, p. 245) remarks, even in symbolic interactionist studies, which, despite interest in people's *defining* activities, have accorded language very little direct attention.

A different idea— that language is a site of social activity—stems from developments in what is called ordinary language philosophy. A variety of scholars, including Austin, Ryle, Searle, and Wittgenstein, take the position that problems of meaning and reference in traditional philosophy—and, by extension, issues concerning how and under what conditions interactants communicate effectively with one another—can be fruitfully recast through investigation of ordinary language. This means avoiding the abstracting and generalizing process whereby words serve to reference or point to objects and situating words in orderly contexts to appreciate how words achieve actions.

Speech Act Theory

The title of John Austin's famous book, *How to Do Things with Words*, conveys the essence of speech act theory. Austin (1962, p. 12) questions "an old assumption in philosophy" that to say something is to state something in a propositional sense. Sentences that convey referential information, in Austin's words, form *locutionary* acts, but many utterances do not describe or report anything. That is, they do not state anything and cannot be evaluated for their truth, but rather are *illocutionary* performances.* Examples, paraphrased from Austin (1962, p. 5), are:

> "I do" (take this woman to be my lawful wedded wife) (as uttered during a marriage ceremony)
> "I name this ship the *Queen Elizabeth*" (as uttered when smashing the bottle against the stem)
> "I give and bequeath my watch to my brother" (as occurring in a will)
> "I bet you it will rain tomorrow"

Such utterances do not report or describe what a person is doing; they achieve a designated activity, such as promising, naming, giving, or betting.

As Austin (1962, p. 100) reflected on the characteristics of performatives or illocutionary acts, he came to view locutionary acts in a new way. He proposed that the "occasion of an utterance matters seriously" and that to understand how it functions, the "context" in which it is spoken must be investigated together with the utterance itself (Austin, 1962, p. 98). That is, when we examine the *occasion* of locutionary or statement-like acts, we see that speakers are *using* them to ask or answer a question, give assurance or a warning, announce a verdict or intent, and so on. Accordingly, so-called "statements" also occur as some specific action— they are performative rather than referential. The lesson for the "communicational" view of language is that the locutions through which persons provide information about their thoughts, feelings, and ideas occur as part of some context of acting and are, like promising, naming, giving, and so on, illocutionary:

> What we need to do for the case of stating, and by the same token, describing and reporting, is to take them a bit off their pedestal, to realize that they are speech-acts no less than all these other speech-acts that we have been mentioning and talking about as performative. (Austin, 1961, pp. 249–250)

---

*Austin (1962, p. 102) also discusses "perlocutionary acts," or utterances that are consequential in particular ways for the behavior of persons to whom they are directed, but this type need not concern us here. The distinction between illocutionary and perlocutionary acts is hazy (Levinson, 1983, p. 287).

Thus, Austin abandons the dichotomy between locutionary and illocutionary acts "in favor of more general families of related and overlapping speech acts."

One of Austin's successors, Searle (1969, pp. 16–17), more forcefully states that the "unit of linguistic communication is not, as has generally been supposed, the symbol, word, or sentence ... but rather the production of the symbol or word or sentence in the performance of a speech act," and that a theory of language, therefore, needs a theory of action. For Searle, this theory is one in which a set of underlying, constitutive rules specifies how speech acts can be accomplished.

Both Austin (1962) and Searle (1969) attempt to come to grips with the well-known problem in the philosophy of language that a sentence with a given reference and predication can have an assortment of meanings. In terms of speech act theory, the "same" utterance can perform a variety of different speech acts. Searle's (1969, pp. 70–71) classic example is a wife reporting to her husband at a party, "It's really quite late":

> That utterance may be at one level a statement of fact; to her interlocutor, who has just remarked on how early it was, it may be (and be intended as) an objection; to her husband it may be (and be intended as) a suggestion or even a request ("Let's go home") as well as a warning ("You'll feel rotten in the morning if we don't").

Among speech act theorists, linking a given or "same" utterance to specific actions may involve what Austin (1962, pp. 15–24) called "felicity conditions," or the set of circumstances that allow for the successful completion of a performative. Thus, for an act of promising to be effective, Austin (1962, pp. 21–22) suggests that the promisor must intend to promise, have been heard by someone, and be understood as promising. Incorporating and correcting theories of meaning (Grice, 1957; Strawson, 1964) that, somewhat like Austin, are based on speakers' intentions, Searle (1969, 1975) provides a sophisticated system of rules whereby the "direct" or "indirect" action a given sentence is intended to initiate can be consummated. For example, rules or conventions, according to Searle (1969, pp. 57–61) specify how an uttered promise is produced, what the preparatory conditions are (e.g., that the promise stipulates an act for someone that would not occur in the normal course of events), that the speaker intends to do the act as an obligation, and that the hearer recognizes the utterance as it was meant. These rules can be related to what Grice (1975) has called "conversational implicature," a set of maxims that underlie and provide for the cooperative use of language (Levinson, 1983, p. 241).

Language as a Form of Life

Another important figure, and perhaps the most influential, in the ordinary language tradition is Ludwig Wittgenstein, who in his own early work was deeply committed to logical positivism and the idea that the function of language is to represent objects in the world. Subscribing to the referential approach to meaning, Wittgenstein thought that the fundamental question about language was the truth or falsity of its propositions. The philosopher's main task was to translate complex sentences into their elementary units in order to assess its truth or falsity (Pitkin, 1972, pp. 27–28). Later, Wittgenstein disavowed this approach and any rule-based approach to language, instead urging the examination of language *practice*—how actors employ words and sentences in concrete situations. Thus, in *Philosophical Investigations* and other posthumous publications, Wittgenstein (1958) argues that language, rather than being a vehicle for naming things, conveying information, or even enacting intentions according to rules, is an *activity* or *form of life* in its own right. For example, to analyze a single word in the language, and propose that there is a single definable class of phenomena to which it refers is to neglect that the word can be a wide variety of things depending on the various roles it plays in a multiplicity of *language games* (Wittgenstein, 1958, para. 24). Consider the word "hello," which we might define as a *greeting*. However, its status as a greeting depends on *where*, in a developing conversation, the item occurs (Schegloff, 1986). When a party uses the word after picking up a ringing telephone, the activity it performs is *answering* a summons rather than greeting the caller. Subsequently, there may be an exchange or sequence of salutations, and in *that* context "hello" does perform greeting. To discover the meaning of a word, then, it is not possible to rely on ostensive or demonstrative or any other fixed definitions; one must examine the *contexts of use*. When contexts of use are similar, then words may be said to share what Wittgenstein (1958, para. 67) called "family resemblances." It is in the actual practice of placing words in particular contexts that such resemblances can be traced and the lexical and other components of language appreciated as a form of life.

This emphasis on actual practice differs significantly from speech act theory, especially that of Searle. In Wittgenstein's view, just as the word *hello* might appear in a variety of language games, so might the word *promise*, but rather than deriving its meaning from some underlying constitutive rules, the illocutionary force of the utterance in which it appears derives from its pragmatics, including both vocal and nonvocal signaling as it occurs within the patterning or "grammar" of diverse language games. From this perspective, an investigator would eschew attempts to derive the rules of illocutionary force or to obtain access to speaker intentions and instead would maintain an interest in the overt expressions and acts through which a word such as "promise" comes to life. Linguistic competence, in other words, consists not in following rules to realize intent but in systematically relating given lexical items to other pieces of vocal and bodily conduct that signal how such items are produced and understood.

The "Mapping" Problem

According to the speech act theorists, the language that humans use can help constitute an infinite variety of social actions (1969, p. 23). Austin (1962, p. 150) suggests that there are on the order of a thousand or so actions, while Wittgenstein (1958, para. 23) proposes that there are "innumerable" activities in which language plays a part, including but by no means limited to "ordering, describing, reporting, speculating, presenting results, telling a story, being ironic, requesting, asking, criticizing, apologizing, censuring, approving, welcoming, objecting, guessing, joking, greeting." This list can be indefinitely extended and shows that, as all the speech act theorists would argue, the communicative function of language, wherein people refer to objects and report their thoughts or feelings about them in a verifiable way, is only one among many modes of linguistic usage.*

When social scientists regard language in this dynamic sense, as intimately bound with action, a seemingly simple problem still looms large for the investigator: How are we to know what the illocutionary force of an utterance is? It is not tenable that the performative aspect of an utterance is somehow built into its form, for the reason stated above—the "same" utterance can perform a variety of acts. Put differently, the "form" of a sentence or utterance is often misleading about its status as an activity. For example, Levinson (1983, p. 275) mentions *imperatives*, which, despite their grammatical structure as commands or requests, rarely

---

*In Katriel and Philipsen's (1990) study, informants use "communication" in contrast to "small talk" to depict speech in relationships that are "close ... supportive," and "flexible."

appear as such in natural conversation. Rather, they occur "in recipes and instructions, offers (*Have another drink*), welcomings (*Come in*), wishes (*Have a good time*), curses and swearings (*Shut up*), and so on ... ." That is, the linguistic form is subordinated to social action and interaction (Ochs, Schegloff, & Thompson, 1996). As Levinson (1983, p. 274) nicely formulates the problem of knowing the illocutionary force of an utterance, it is one of *mapping* speech acts onto utterances as they occur in actual contexts. As we have seen, in ordinary language philosophy, there are two main solutions to this mapping problem, one being the rule-based approach of Austin, Searle, Grice and others, and the other being the practice-based approach of Wittgenstein. In contemporary social science, we also find these two approaches.

SOCIOLINGUISTICS AND
DISCOURSE ANALYSIS

Although a number of sociologists, anthropologists, and linguists have affiliated with the term *sociolinguistics*, it is, as its name implies, a field linked to linguistics proper. Pioneers in sociolinguistics, such as Gumperz (1972), Hymes (1974), and Labov (1972b), were wrestling with a legacy of theorizing about language that posited its fundamental forms as being cognitive or minded phenomena. This legacy started with Ferdinand de Saussure's (1962) famous distinction between *langue*, which comprises an underlying systematics across variations in social context, and *parole*, which consists of the actual speech that people produce. In de Saussure's (1962) view, the proper focus of study was *langue*, the idea being that human cognition was the seat of linguistic structures and categories that guided people's behavior. In contemporary times, Noam Chomsky (1965) has continued the cognitive legacy with his very influential notion of generative grammar, a set of psychologically based universal structures whose systematic transformations result in an infinite variety of human speech productions. With its emphasis on Cartesian mental properties, structural linguistics has always sought to decontextualize linguistic phenomena in favor of finding certain ideal properties of abstracted sentences. That is, the overwhelming tendency has been to view linguistic structure as extant outside of time and place and hence not subject to social influence.

Sociolinguists, following scholars such as Firth (1935), Malinowski (1923), and others, were utterly dissatisfied with such a view. As Hymes (1974, pp. 2–3) has argued, the frame of reference of the *social* scientific investigation of language could not be linguistic forms in themselves, and must substitute the community context as a frame. Indeed, Labov (1972b, p. xiii) resisted the term sociolinguistics because he could not conceive of linguistic theory or method that did *not* incorporate a social component. The social component would include cultural values, social institutions, community history and ecology, and so on (Hymes, 1974, p. 3). While sociolinguists agree that social influence is crucial to understanding linguistic structure, there are different perspectives on the relationship between society and language (Grimshaw, 1974) and different strategies for investigating this relationship. The earliest sociolinguistic studies used dialect surveys to study speech variation among social networks and communities, finding that dialect variables were an excellent gauge of both social class and ethnic identity (Gumperz & Hymes, 1972, p. 12).

Variation in linguistic patterns is a prominent theme in sociolinguistics. Besides dialect usage, another example of variation is *code switching* (Ervin-Tripp, 1972), or the manner in which members of a single community juxtapose, in the same situation, speech belonging to different grammatical systems (Breitborde, 1983; Fishman, 1983; Gumperz, 1982). When a group, such as African American, Spanish-speaking, or Hindi-speaking minorities in the

United States, is basically bilingual, the usual categories of class, ethnicity, education, and so on are not good predictors of code switching. Of course, survey studies can document situational (e.g., home vs. work) determinants of code switching in communities but are hard-pressed to explain within-situation exhibits of the phenomenon. *Interpretive sociolinguists* argue that code switching reflects speakers' ability to categorize situations, interlocutors, and social relationships and thereby to make inferences and judgments about the appropriate and relevant speech forms to produce. Whereas the presumption in sociolinguistic survey research is that language usage is normatively guided, interpretive studies propose that ethnographic investigation is necessary to define the *competence* with which interactants manipulate linguistic markers and devices to obtain their ordinary goals in everyday life (Gumperz, 1982, pp. 35–36):

> The analyst's task is to make an in depth study of selected instances of verbal interaction, observe whether or not actors understand each other, elicit participants' interpretations of what goes on, and then (a) deduce the social assumptions that speakers must have made in order to act as they do, and (b) determine empirically how linguistic signs communicate in the interpretation process.

These strategies are compatible with Hymes's (1974) comprehensive outline of the "ethnography of communication," a way of collecting, categorizing, and analyzing the action-oriented linguistic events in a particular community to answer the basic questions of what these events are and how they work.

Sociolinguistics has been occupied with numerous topics surrounding code switching, including second language learning and the relation of diverse languages to self concept, personality, and status attitudes. Other classic topics in sociolinguistics are language conflict, loyalty, and maintenance and the structure and organization of pidgin and creole languages. Grimshaw (1974, p. 80) reviews the early literature comprehensively and suggests that sociolinguistics is a "hybrid discipline" that is "largely atheoretical."

Related to sociolinguistics, and representing an effort to become more theoretically sophisticated about the relationship between language and society, is the general category of linguistic *discourse analysis*.* "Discourse" broadly includes both textual and spoken forms of language and refers to language production as it is organized external to the unitary sentence or clause (Stubbs, 1983). That is, discourse analysis is concerned with the orderly connections between clauses and sentences, rather than with the structuring of those units alone. Thus, as Coulthard (1977, p. 3) notes, discourse analysis overlaps partially with *pragmatics*, a subfield in linguistics that is distinguished from traditional concerns with syntax and semantics by the interest in how language users take the social context into account when producing and understanding speech forms. Discourse analysis, however, is multitopical and multidisciplinary, with scholars from anthropology, artificial intelligence, communications, philosophy, psychology, and sociology contributing to the enterprise (Stubbs, 1983; van Dijk, 1985).

One approach to discourse analysis is in Grimshaw's (1989) effort to transcend the linguistically oriented work of Labov and Fanshel (1977) by formalizing sociological variables as derived from a more inductive and ethnographic inquiry such as Cicourel's (1974) cognitive sociology. Grimshaw (1989) models the discourse process as involving

---

*The term "discourse analysis" can be used to refer to a number of quite different research traditions. Along with the linguistic discourse analysis discussed here, there is historical discourse analysis that usually focuses on written texts (Armstrong, 1983; Foucault, 1979), "critical discourse analysis" which combines social criticism with the analysis of textual material (Fairclough, 1992), and the social psychological discourse analysis that has come to be called "discursive psychology" and will be discussed later in this chapter.

a "source," or originator of some manipulative speech move, a "goal," or target of the move, an "instrumentality," which is the speech act itself, and a "result" or outcome that the source pursues. The particular speech act a source employs is constrained according to the three variables of power, affect, and utility. Power has to do with the relative statuses of parties, affect with the emotionality of their relationship, and utility with the value and costs to both the source and target of a speech act in achieving some result. Thus, Grimshaw's (1989, pp. 532–533) approach complements Labov and Fanshel's preoccupation with rules of *discourse* by emphasizing rules deriving from essentially social considerations of *appropriateness* as based on participants' cultural and social knowledge. A less formalistic approach to describing discourse and its social parameters—how discourse as action involves topic selection, overall or schematic organization, local meanings, choice of words, style, and rhetorical devices—can be found in van Dijk (1997). Viewing discourse as action, van Dijk (1997) also stresses the importance of context and power in the analysis of text and talk.

GOFFMAN AND FRAME ANALYSIS

Sociolinguistics and discourse analysis emphasize the importance of micro-analysis of minute particles of speech and single interactional events as a means for understanding the social dimensions of language use. Both areas invoke rule-like mechanisms for connecting social environments and structures to these particles and events. In Goffman (1983)'s work,* we begin to see less emphasis on the connective or even causal approach to rules and more concern with social actors' agency and rule usage. Rather than a broader social context, the corporeal "face to face" or "body to body" situation—whether in urban or in rural areas, in a business or in a family, and independent of socioeconomic class, gender or ethnic categories—should be the primary focus for understanding social interaction. That is, the same rules and conventions, applying to turn-taking, physical distance between speakers, and other matters, prevail in social interaction regardless its broader context. Or to take a more specific example: Goffman (1983) refers to a "contact" ritual, such as any service encounter where customers may form a queue as they await their turn at being helped. Although the queue could be organized according to externally structured attributes of involved parties (e.g., age, race, gender, or class), normal queuing "blocks" or filters out the effects of such variables in favor of an egalitarian, first-come, first-serve ordering principle.

Such an ordering principle belongs to what Goffman (1983) calls the "interaction order," which consists of "systems of enabling conventions, in the sense of ground rules for a game, the provisions of a traffic code, or the syntax of a language." The interaction order is a relatively autonomous order of organization both in relation to the broader social organization and to the psychological properties of the actors. Hence, Goffman wanted to promote it as a target of social scientific study in its own right. Although the interaction order consists largely of rules or conventions, violations do not threaten the game or the language as much as they serve as resources for accomplishing the very projects that adherence itself involves, including the definition of self and the creation or maintenance of social meaning (Goffman, 1971, p. 61):

> Given that a rule exists against seeking out a stranger's eyes, seeking can then be done as a means
> of making a pickup or as a means of making oneself known to someone one expects to meet but
> is unacquainted with. Similarly, given that staring is an invasion of information preserve, a stare

---

*For overviews see Drew and Wootton (1988), Burns (1992), and Manning (1992).

can then be used as a warranted negative sanction against someone who has misbehaved—the misbehavior providing and ensuring a special significance to overlong examination.

Actors, in this view, do not range between naive conformity and blatant rule breaking. Rules, says Goffman (1971, p. 61) make possible a *set* of "nonadherences," which, according to how we classify the interactional work they do, have a variety of meanings.* The interactional rules do not tightly constrain actions; they are more like rough guidelines that permit actors to accomplish a variety of social projects, depending on how they align themselves with respect to those rules or guidelines.

This point about actors' capacity for flexible alignment to rules is most fully developed in *Frame Analysis*, Goffman's (1974) major treatise on the "organizational premises" of ordinary activity, or, the "reality" of everyday experience. Much of everyday experience goes beyond literal activity and has numerous figurative aspects, which are especially visible in talk (Goffman, 1974, p. 502). In particular, Goffman (1974, chapter 13) argues that rather than using terms such as *speaking* and *hearing* to characterize the production and understanding of utterances, analysts must see how participants align themselves to those utterances. A speaker, for instance, may employ a variety of *production formats* when talking, so that he/she says something as *principal* (one whose position is represented in the talk) or as *animator* (who simply speaks the words representing another's position).

As principal or animator, one can also project a particular identity or figure (ranging from that of the speaker to identities of fictitious and actual others). Finally, a speaker can be a strategist who acts to promote the interests of an individual on whose behalf he/she is acting. In a way complementary to speakers, hearers also take up different alignments or participation statuses—ratified recipient, overhearer, eavesdropper, and so on. Eventually, Goffman (1979) referred to the frame analysis of talk as an investigation of the "footing" or stances that participants constantly change over the course of an utterance's production. Goffman's work on footing has been taken up in a variety of contemporary studies, including those on children's arguments (Goodwin, 1988; Goodwin, 1990), the news interview (Clayman, 1988), and the survey interview (Houtkoop-Steenstra, 2000).

DISCURSIVE PSYCHOLOGY

Discursive psychology is a European social psychological approach that focuses on language use, taking an "action oriented" understanding of language as its point of departure. This approach has been developed since the late 1980s, by scholars such as Billig (1987), Edwards (1997, 1992), Potter (1996, 1987) and Antaki (1994). In their writings, discursive psychologists strongly question the "cognitivist" presuppositions predominant in current psychology. The cognitivism attacked by discursive psychologists actually coincides with the "conduit metaphor." In cognitivism, "we start with a given, external world, which is then perceived and processed, and *then put into words*" (Edwards, 1997, p. 19). In this view, language is understood as a transparent medium used for transfer of ideas concerning the external reality and inner worlds of humans. To counter this, discursive psychologists study *accounts* and *accounting*—how everyday descriptions of people, their behavior, and their mental states are

---

*Indeed, actors' orientation to the interaction order remains moral, resting on commitments that in one way or another (through adherence or violation) enable the self to emerge and be preserved. On this point, see Goffman (1971, pp. 185–187); for secondary discussion, see Rawls (1987, pp. 42–44).

in themselves actions (Antaki, 1994). Descriptions are produced in particular occasions to do particular things, such as blaming, justifying, explaining, and so on (Buttny, 1993).

The work of discursive psychologists has drawn inspiration from the social studies of scientific knowledge: for example, Bloor (1976), Mulkay (1979), Woolgar (1988), and others, who sought to show that the "factuality" of scientific knowledge is embedded in a set of discursive and rhetorical practices. The discursive social psychologist examines how our mundane understanding of the world and people in it are similarly socially located in such practices (Edwards, 1997, pp. 51–83; Potter & Wetherell, 1987, pp. 146–155). As the last section of this chapter will make apparent, this research program is much in debt to Garfinkel's ethnomethodology. The themes of discursive psychology include *accounts of courses of action*, *accounts of mind*, and *accounts of identities*.

Accounts of Courses of Action

Everyday language use frequently involves descriptions of courses of action: accounts of the speaker's and others' ordinary conduct. Citing Schegloff (1989), and like Potter and Wetherell (1987, pp. 74–94), Edwards (1997, p. 8) points out that "accounts *of* actions are invariably, and at the same time, accounts *for* actions." Two distinct aspects of these accounts involve *scripts* and *dispositions* (Edwards, 1997, pp. 142–169). In describing events in terms of scripts, the speakers often implicitly (and sometimes explicitly) propose that what happened followed a routine pattern in the given circumstances. The course of action is then presented as expected, as ordinary, as "natural" one that follows a script. On the other hand, events can also be described as *breaches* from the script, as something unusual and not to be expected. When events are describing as breaches from the script, dispositions often come into play. Dispositions are "pictures" of the actor implied by the description of the course of action. Two relevant dimensions of dispositions include the personality and the moral character of the actor. Deviations from scripts are often linked to specific dispositions of the actor. However, scripted courses of action can also be linked to dispositions, not least to dispositions of "normality."

Cognitive social psychologists (Heider, 1958; Mandler, 1984; Shaver, 1983) also discuss scripts and dispositions, as principles that organize perception, inference, and memory. However, discursive psychologists take a unique approach to these phenomena. Unlike cognitivists, they emphasize that course-of-action descriptions are designed to *exhibit* the routine or breaching character of the events, and to build the corresponding disposition of the actor. Thus, in discursive psychology, scripts and dispositions are seen as *resources* used by speakers in pursuing their local interactional goals (Edwards & Potter, 1992, pp. 77–126).

Accounts of Mind

Description of mind is another facet of ordinary talk (Coulter, 1989). Discursive psychologists are interested specifically in the ways in which the participants' states of knowledge figure in talk (Edwards, 1997, pp. 114–141, 170–201). They examine how emotional and cognitive states are practically accomplished, and how local interactional goals are pursued in and through them. Cognitive states are achieved, for example, through the ways in which statements, stories and descriptions are designed and received in conversation. As conversation analysts (see the section below) have shown, speakers design their talk carefully to show their understanding of the recipients' prior knowledge, and correspondingly, the recipients show through their own action whether the things that were told were new information or already known by them (Sorjonen, 2001).

Discursive psychology also investigates descriptions of affect, or the ways in which speakers avow their own emotions and ascribe them to others. In line with other social constructionist approaches (Harré, 1986), research centers on the use of emotion *words* (rather than non-lexical expression of emotion), to show how they are used (Edwards, 1997, p. 170):

> in assigning causes and motives of action, in blamings, excuses, and accounts ... Emotional states
> may figure as things to be accounted for (in terms of prior causal events or dispositional tenden-
> cies, say), as accounts (of subsequent actions and events), and also as evidence of what kind of
> events or actions precede or follow them.

Thus, emotion descriptions are seen as an essential resource in accounting *of* and accounting *for* action. Moreover, as Edwards (1997, p. 171) points out, emotion descriptions are closely tied with scripts and dispositions. Emotion descriptions can be embedded on routine scripts (when a particular event, such as having a child, awakes a particular emotion, such as happiness). They can also be part of dispositions, for example, when a specific emotion, such as inclination towards jealousy, explains non-routine courses of action.

Accounts of Identity

Identity is the third central theme in discursive psychology. In and through their talk, speakers present themselves, those that they talk to, and those that they talk about, as having particular identities, as being particular persons and particular sorts of persons. Just like mental states discussed above, also the identity is, as Antaki and Widdicombie (1998, p. 1) put it, both an *achievement* and a *tool*: identity is achieved in and through the talk, and it is used as a tool in performing particular actions in talk. Or to put it in terms used by Edwards and Potter (1992, p. 192), "... detailed language of describing persons is a resource for action." For example, in blaming the other or in defending one's own (or the other's) actions, speakers ascribe and avow particular motives and personality features, and thereby construct identities (Potter & Wetherell, 1987, pp. 110–115).

Drawing on Sacks' work (see the section on conversation analysis below),* Antaki and Widdicombie (1998, pp. 3–6) emphasize the centrality of *categorization* in the construction of identity: "to have an identity" entails being "cast into a category with associated characteristics or features." Categories can, of course, be numerous, the most general ones including age, ethnic, gender and professional categories. In investigating categorization, Antaki and Widdicombie (1998) point out, a key challenge is to show how a particular categorization is *oriented to* by the interactants, and how this orientation is *consequential* for their joint courses of action.

"Description as action" is the primary topic of research in discursive psychology. Three broad and interrelated areas of description are accounts of courses of action, accounts of mind, and accounts of identities. In all these fields, discursive psychologists seek to show how the design and reception of descriptions contributes to particular social actions. This research program, of course, raises once again the above mentioned "mapping problem": on which

---

*For discussion of Sacks' work on membership categorization devices, see Hester and Francis (2000) and Watson (2000).

basis can we say that a particular type of description contributes to a particular social action? In recent years, the research methodology of discursive psychologists has come very close to that in ethnomethodology and conversation analysis. Therefore, the ways in which discursive psychology deals with the mapping problem are more or less the same as those in conversation analysis, and we can postpone the discussion on them until we have introduced conversation analysis in more detail.

ETHNOMETHODOLOGY AND CONVERSATION ANALYSIS

Ethnomethodology proposes that there is a self-generating order in everyday activities (Garfinkel, 1967) and takes a unique approach to the problem of mapping utterances onto actions in at least two ways. First, where Goffman's frame analysis relaxed the theoretical hold that rules could have in explaining linguistic conduct, ethnomethodology, arguing that rules can be treated as topics and features of the activities they are said to organize, utterly extricates rules from theory per se. That is, in ethnomethodology there is no attempt to explain linguistic or other behavior by reference to rules. Instead, the analytic tactic is to treat rules as *resources* for actors, who use them for various situated projects and ends of their own. Whether abstract conformity or deviance occurs has to do with what works to accomplish these projects and ends. It is not that behavior is unconstrained, disorderly, or arbitrary, but that rules, if they are operative at all, figure as part of actors' own practices of reasoning and ways of organizing a social setting. Members are artful *users* of rules, often invoking them in an ex post facto, rhetorical manner to describe the morality of some way of life. For example, jurors invoke legal standards to depict ex post facto how they arrived at a verdict, even when the route involved substantial common-sense, non-standardized reasoning (Garfinkel, 1967), residents at a halfway house use the "convict code" to account for disregard of the official ways of doing things (Wieder, 1974), and staff members at a social welfare agency get their "people processing" job done, in part, through departing from routine policies and still providing a "sense" of having conformed (Zimmerman, 1970). In language-oriented research, ethnomethodologists study how "normative assertions" (Maynard, 1985) operate in the context of already organized group activities to further such local purposes as accusing, competing, and according membership. Rules, to repeat, are features of actions rather than explanations for them.

Another unique aspect of ethnomethodological research is its concern with "indexical expressions" (Garfinkel, 1967; Garfinkel & Sacks, 1970), or utterances whose meaning and understandability depend on the context or circumstances in which they appear. That "deictic" utterances, such as "this," "that," "here," "there," and so on, assume particular meaning according to their speech environment is generally recognized, but Garfinkel (1967) argued that all talk is, without remedy, indexical and context-dependent. One major, orderly aspect of "context" is an utterance's sequential placement. Conversation analysis theorizes that an utterance's force as an action of a particular type derives from such placement (Heritage, 1984, p. 242; Maynard & Clayman, 1991, pp. 397–400). Thus, rather than linguistic or social rules, sequential organization has primary analytic utility in describing talk as action and its relation to "interaction" as well (Schegloff, 1991). Overall, ethnomethodology and conversation analysis have affinities with the Wittgensteinian "form of life" approach to the mapping problem, in which actual, orderly linguistic practice (rule usage and sequence organization) is brought to the fore of analytic inquiry.

With its commitment to the study of naturally occurring talk, conversation analysis in particular aims to rebuild sociology as a natural observational science (Sacks, 1984, 1992a). Indeed, in pursuing this goal, conversation analysts have generated a sizable research literature over the past 35 years (Clayman & Gill, Forthcoming; Goodwin & Heritage, 1990; Heritage, 1984, Chapter 8; ten Have, 1999). Furthermore, in maintaining a commitment to examining naturally occurring social action, conversation analysis avoids treating language as a variable to be manipulated, tested, or related to other variables. We explore the implications of this stance in the next section. Here, the point is that conversation analysts' major social scientific concern has been with endogenous (internally orderly) features of "talk-in-interaction" (Schegloff, 1991). There are three principal domains in which the analysis of endogenously structured conversation is grounded: the organization of sequences, turn taking, and repair.

Organization of Sequences

It is well established that conversational interaction occurs in a serial fashion, with participants taking turns in an A–B–A–B–A–B…ordering. However, parties collaboratively structure the ordering rather tightly. This structure is sequence organization, exemplified in the *adjacency pair*, which includes such conversational objects as question–answer, request–grant/refusal, and invitation–acceptance/declination sequences. Adjacency pairs have the following characteristics (Schegloff & Sacks, 1973): (1) they are a sequence of two-utterance length, which are (2) adjacent to one another, (3) produced by different speakers, (4) ordered as a first part and a second part, and (5) typed, so that a first part requires a particular second part or a range of second parts.

Moreover, adjacency pairs are characterized by "conditional relevance"—conditional on the occurrence of an item in the first slot, or first pair-part (e.g., the question), the occurrence of an item in the second slot, or second pair-part (e.g., the answer to the question), is expected and required. Consider an example of requesting (Wootton, 1981, p. 62, simplified):

    Child: Can I have a wee drink while I'm waiting?
    Mother: Yes, you can.

The absence of a second pair-part may occasion a repeat of the first pair-part and perhaps "warranted inferences" concerning coparticipants who seem nonresponsive (e.g., that they are being "evasive"). In the next example a child reissues the request for sweets when the mother does not respond to the first request. In other words, a response is expected, and when it does not occur it is *noticeably absent* (colons denote stretching of the preceding sound) (Wootton, 1981, p. 66, simplified):

    Child: Mom, I want some swee:::ties.
             [11.4 seconds silence]
    Child: I want so:me: swee::ties.
             [Child moves rapidly towards sweets; 2.5 seconds silence]
    Child: There's not any:::: …
             [Child finds no sweets in their normal location]
    Mother: You'll get some after.

The noticeable absence of the mother's reply is evident in the way the child pursues talk and moves toward the object of his request until the mother deals with it—that is, answers him.

That second pair-parts are required does not mean answers or replies always occur in a sequential position adjacent to the specific questions or requests (or first pair-parts) they are addressing. Often, participants produce *insertion sequences* between first and second pair-parts, as in invitation sequences, for example, where a recipient may need pertinent details before providing a reply (Schegloff, 1972, p. 78):

> A: Are you coming tonight?
> B: Can I bring a guest?
> A: Sure.
> B: I'll be there.

Additionally, when second pair parts do not occur, it may reflect other actions of the recipient, such as "ignoring" insistent demands, "snubbing," or otherwise resisting the initial action. Importantly, inferences concerning these kinds of other actions are made by the participants of interaction themselves, not, in the first place, by the analyst.

Turn-Taking Organization

The A–B–A–B serial ordering of sequences also involves a recurring transfer of speakership. The ordering of speaker change, as well as the size and content of a speaker's turn, is not predetermined in ordinary conversation but instead is free to vary (Sacks, Schegloff, & Jefferson, 1974). Moreover, change of speakership is so tightly articulated that both gap and overlap are minimized (see Lerner [1989] and Schegloff [2000] for elaboration on the social organization of overlap). Consider the following example, which exhibits extremely close turn transitions—the equal signs denote immediate "latching" of one utterance to the other (Jefferson, 1986, p. 154, simplified):

> EMMA: G'morning Letitia=
> LOTTIE: =uh How're YOU=
> EMMA:=   =FI:NE

This finely tuned coordination by participants is made possible through the projection of possible completion points in any one turn. Hearers anticipate exactly when speakers may complete a current utterance, which enables precision timing in the start of next turns.

The projection of a possible completion point is just one social organizational feature of turn taking, however, which relates to the issue of "who will speak next" on some occasion. To determine this, participants methodically allocate turns of talk through a set of ordered options, including current speaker selecting the next speaker, the next speaker self-selecting, or current speaker continuing to speak (Sacks et al., Schegloff, & Jefferson, 1974). Through projecting the completion points of current turns and precisely timing the start of new turns, participants achieve hearing and understanding as an ongoing feature of ordinary talk.

Organization of Repair

Given this elaborate and systematic organization of sequences and turns within sequences, how are interactional troubles managed? That is, how do participants handle errors, mishearings, glitches in turn transition, problems of meaning, and the like? The answer is that the turn-taking system itself provides resources for understanding as well as "repair" (Levinson,

1983, pp. 340–342; Schegloff, Jefferson, & Sacks, 1977). In coordinating exchange of speakership and tightly articulating sequences, participants display for one another their sense of a current vocal action in the very next turn at talk. Consider this as a "proof procedure": the second speaker's turn serves as a resource by which the first speaker may check whether a turn was heard correctly. In the next example, Marcia is, according to Schegloff (1992, p. 1301), explaining to her exhusband why their son is flying home rather than driving:

(1) MARCIA: …Becuz the top was ripped off of his car which is to say somebody helped themselves.
(2) TONY: Stolen.
(3) MARCIA: Stolen. Right out in front of my house.

In turn 2, Tony offers a candidate understanding ("stolen") of Marcia's ambiguous reference in turn (1) to the top being "ripped off" their son's car. Then, in turn (3), Marcia confirms Tony's candidate understanding. Had Tony not been correct in his understanding, this is a point at which Marcia could have repaired the trouble. In general, the third turn such as this is a slot that may be taken up with the business of repairing various interactional troubles (Heritage, 1984, pp. 254–258; Levinson, 1983, p. 340; Schegloff, 1992, p. 1302). This is not the first opportunity in the sequence for repair initiation, however, for participants might well repair their own utterances in their own first turn at talk or in the transition between turns. Indeed, as Schegloff (1992, pp. 1300–1301) notes about the above episode, Marcia appears to have used "which is to say somebody helped themselves" to clarify "ripped off," a phrase that could be ambiguous as between a literal meaning and an idiomatic expression for robbery. This is termed a "self-initiated self-repair." Also, in the second turn in the sequence it is possible for the second speaker to repair aspects of the first speaker's turn (Schegloff et al., 1977). Thus, turn taking and the organization of repair in the system of turn taking provide a structural basis for the achievement of intersubjectivity or mutual understanding (Sacks et al., 1974; Schegloff, 1992).

   The explication of these three domains of the social organization of conversation (sequences, turn taking, and repair) provides the basis for much of the vigorous research agenda in conversation analysis and has generated an expansive literature on talk in institutional and organizational settings. We now consider this literature, along with other research on the relation between language, action, and social structure.

LANGUAGE, ACTION, AND SOCIAL STRUCTURE

Thus far, we have concentrated on *interaction*, suggesting that social psychology benefits from understanding how parties use language in an immediate sense to perform joint endeavors of all sorts. Of course, as parties talk and gesture to one another, more than completely local interests and social organization may be at stake, and this means that questions regarding "social structure" come to the fore. Following Zimmerman and Boden's (1991) reflections on talk and social structure, there are three approaches to probing the interrelation of language, action, and social structure: macrodirectional, dialectical, and reflexive.

Macrodirectional Approach: Social Categories and Language Use

Investigators often see social structure as consisting of such forms as age, gender, class, and other sociodemographic categories, as well as culture, institutions, and complex organizations, which condition the use of language in specifiable ways. "In such a framework," Zimmerman and Boden (1991, p. 5) remark, "talk and, indeed, all interaction of actual actors in social situations is seen as a *product* of those social forces." This is the strategy in experimental and survey-based social psychology that examines how social structural arrangements *condition* language and social interaction, and emphasizes the relationship between social statuses or categories (e.g., race, gender, class, and age) and language. Perhaps the best known work in this area is that of Bernstein (1961, 1972), who proposed that middle and working-class children learn two very different linguistic "codes"—an "elaborated" and "restricted" code, respectively, with the features of each determined by the forms of social relations in different communities. Middle-class subcultures assert the primacy of the individual "I" over collective "we," which results in an elaborated code characterized by flexible organization and a range of syntactic options. In contrast, in working-class communities the collective "we" is used over the "I," and the result is a restricted, more rigid code with low levels of syntactic and vocabulary selection, and implicit rather than explicit meanings (Bernstein, 1972, pp. 475–476). These two class-based codes, Bernstein argues, help account for middle-class children's success and working-class children's lack of success in school.

Bernstein's argument generated a vigorous response. Portraying Bernstein's analysis of elaborated and restricted codes as a "deficit model," Labov (1972a) demonstrates that the "nonstandard English" spoken in U.S. African American communities is not "restricted" in its flexibility or range of options for syntax or vocabulary and, in certain ways, exhibits impressive linguistic, social, and cultural complexity and competence on the part of the speakers. More recently, Goodwin (1990) shows how skilled urban African American youth are in various linguistic activities (especially disputing) whereby they display and generate "character" and achieve localized social organization. Thus, Labov (1972a) has argued that there is no relationship between language use or the "codes" employed in poor and working-class African American communities and failure in school. Instead, "failure" may lay within the school as a social institution that does not adapt to the cultures of the diverse communities it serves. Controversy about whether linguistic repertoires represent "differences" or "deficits" continues (Baugh, 1999; Edwards, 1979; Giles & Robinson, 1990).

Studies of the relationship between language and social stratification are related to numerous comparisons of speech practice—based on cross-cultural, gender, and ethnic differences. Perhaps most prominent are investigations of linguistic divergences between women and men. Early research suggested that women are more expressive in intonation; that they use more adjectives and intensifiers, including so, *such, quite, vastly,* and *more;* that they make more precise determinations of color (Key, 1972); that they employ more fillers, such as *umh* and you *know;* and that they more often use affectionate address terms, such as *dear honey,* and *sweetie* (West & Zimmerman, 1985, p. 106). As it turns out, when researchers examine these items as simple markers or indicators of female speech, only two show any consistent patterning: compared to men, women produce speech in phonetically more correct forms (Thorne & Henley, 1975, p. 17) and vary their pitch and intonation more (West & Zimmerman, 1985, p. 107). Even the tradition of research on interruptions that West and Zimmerman (1983) initiated has shown few regular results (Aries, 1996), as other status and power differences (Kollock, Blumstein, & Schwartz, 1985) as well as processes intrinsic to the interaction (Okamoto & Smith-Lovin, 2001), including participation rates and manner (topic-changing behavior) may overshadow a characteristic such as gender. Still, differences between men's and women's speech appear to be enough for Tannen (1990) to propose that males and females speak different "genderlects." Consistent with this is evidence that females are more likely to interpret remarks *indirectly* rather than *directly* (Holtgraves, 1991), and that men may initiate more "unilateral" (as compared "collaborative") topic changes in interaction

(Ainsworth-Vaughn, 1992; West & Garcia, 1988). Research on linguistic differences based on gender, ethnicity, age, and other social categories has proliferated (Giles & Robinson, 1990) and no doubt will continue to do so.

Talk and Social Structure: Dialectics and Reciprocal Influence

A dialectical approach to talk and social structure involves social structure as cause *and* outcome of spoken interaction; language is the site of the production and reproduction of sociodemographic, cultural, institutional, and organizational forms characteristic of the overall society. It is therefore important to know both the local and broad context in which utterances occur, making it incumbent on the investigator to engage in ethnographic inquiry to complement the analysis of recorded speech. This premise is central to cognitive sociology (Cicourel, 1981), and it informs the work of students of talk in such institutional settings as preschools (Corsaro, 1979, 1996), schools (McDermott, Gospodinoff, & Aron, 1978; Mehan, 1979; Phillips, 1982), universities (Grimshaw, 1989), doctor's offices or hospitals (Cicourel, 1981; Fisher, 1983; Silverman, 1987; Strong, 1979; Waitzkin, 1991), and courts (Danet, 1980; Molotch & Boden, 1985). As an example of this approach, Mehan (1991) argues that the "social facts" of school systems derive from the "practical work" of educators engaged in interaction with students, parents, and other professionals in a series of "microevents" that occur in the classroom, testing sessions, and meetings. The dialectical approach is also compatible with the work of European theorists such as Bourdieu (1991), Giddens (1984), and Habermas (1979) and their concerns with language, ideology, and social reproduction.

Talk and Social Structure: Reflexivity between Interactional and Institutional Orders

A reflexive analysis of language, action, and social structure sees the interaction order and the institutional order having complex interrelationships not adequately described in causal or even reciprocally causal terms. The interaction order is comprised of mechanisms of turn taking and other sequential organizations, which provide the resources for producing and understanding what is being said and done in concert (Zimmerman & Boden, 1991, p. 9). As Goffman (1983) pointed out, the interaction order and its constituent devices are basic or primordial in the sense of underlying, preceding, being organized independently of any social structural context in which talk occurs, and being invariant although with sensitivity to historical and cultural variation.*

If the interaction order is primordial in this sense, it behooves investigators to analyze its workings as a prelude to explicating the use of language in institutional settings. When investigators do not do so, they risk attributing features of the talk to its institutional surround and missing both the bedrock of orderliness that makes it possible for participants to understand one another at all (no matter what the setting) and the ways in which they display the relevance of social structure through procedural "work" that is visible in the details of their talk (Schegloff, 1991). Conversation analysts, who take this position, have shown its implications in various ways. One implication is that the fundamental organization of conversational turn

_____

*See, for example, recent studies of Japanese talk-in-interaction and how basic turn design, turn-taking and other mechanisms are adapted to this language (Mori, 1999; Tanaka, 1999).

taking may be different in institutional as compared with ordinary settings. Thus, where in conversation turn size, turn content, and turn order are free to vary and are subject to local management, in settings such as courtrooms (Atkinson & Drew, 1979), the jury deliberation (Manzo, 1996), classrooms (McHoul, 1978; Mehan, 1979) and testing (Marlaire & Maynard, 1990), news interviews (Clayman & Heritage, 2002), clinical settings (Peräkylä, 1995), and the survey interview (Maynard, Houtkoop-Steenstra, Schaeffer, & Zouwen, 2002), this is not the case. Attorneys, teachers, newscasters, clinicians, or survey interviewers *ask* questions, and witnesses, students, interviewees, patients, or respondents must *answer*. From these elemental observations, a wide range of consequences follow in regard to how professionals, in collaboration with lay and other participants, organize such actions as accusing and denying in the courtroom, teaching, testing, and showing learning ability in the classroom, being "neutral" and expertly informative in the news interview, eliciting talk about delicate and sensitive personal matters in the clinic, or achieving the "standardization" of social measurement in the survey interview.*

It is not just alterations in turn taking that characterize institutional talk. Another implication of regarding conversation as primordial is that some mundane conversational sequences might be imported more or less wholesale as a resource for tasks that actors in institutional settings face recurrently. Thus, in medical settings, physicians and others are occupationally predisposed to having to deliver "bad news" in the form of diagnostic information. Maynard (1991) identified a *perspective display series* that, in ordinary conversation, involves one party asking another about some social object, whereupon the first party presents a report or assessment that is then regularly outfitted to agree with the second party's. This way of producing a report or assessment is an inherently cautious maneuver, in that a speaker can elicit, in a preliminary manner, some display from a recipient of how well the speaker's own information or opinion meshes with the recipient's. Overall, this means that the perspective display series permits delivery of such information or opinion in a way that proposes a mutuality of perspective between speaker and recipient. In medical settings, where severe illness and death are customary topics, the perspective display series and its orderly features can be adapted to handling these topics. Clinicians, rather than presenting a diagnosis or death announcement straightforwardly, often take the more circuitous route of eliciting the view of their recipient before reporting the bad news, and then agreeably shape the news to the recipient's knowledge and beliefs. At the very least, this works to promote the recipient's understanding of what may be technically difficult jargon or terminology. In addition, it co-implicates the recipient's perspective in the presentation of the news, so that clinicians can give a diagnosis in a publicly affirmative and nonconflicting manner.

Still another implication of treating conversation as a primordial backdrop to institutional language is that actors can change the ordering of intact sequences of talk in systematic ways. In a comprehensive analysis of openings to ordinary telephone calls, Schegloff (1986) distinguished four core opening sequences—the summons/answer sequence (consisting of a ringing phone and its answer), the identification/recognition sequence, the greeting, and the "how are you." After participants produce these four sequences, they enter into the "first topic" of the call. As Whalen and Zimmerman (1987) compared a corpus of calls to emergency ("9-1-1") dispatch centers with Schegloff's analysis, they noticed that the organization consisting of these four sequences was modified so that (a) identification of the

---

*For recent book-length treatments in which the reflexive approach to interactional an institutional orders informs the analysis, see Clayman and Heritage (2002), Heritage and Maynard (2003). For a secondary and general summary of the approach, see Arminen (Forthcoming).

dispatch center occurs as part of answering the summoning phone ring, and (b) the "first topic" (a request for assistance) occurs immediately after the summons answer sequence. Participants dispense with other forms of recognition, with greetings, and with "how are you's." Following Heritage (1984, pp. 238–240), Whalen and Zimmerman (1987) argue that (a) represents a *specialization* of ordinary conversational procedure, and (b) indicates a *reduction* of the core opening sequences.

Thus, the interaction order of talk, what Whalen and Zimmerman (1987) call an "interactional machinery," is intimately involved in the means whereby, in institutional settings, participants "exhibit for one another (and for the analyst) their appreciation of who, situationally speaking, they are, and what, situationally speaking, they are up to." That is, in and through modifications to the interaction order, participants also produce the institutional order. These orders are distinct and yet related in complex ways. A reflexive approach to language, action, and social structure, then, means understanding how sequential organization and other aspects of the interaction order can be deployed in ways that are sensitive to the contingencies and relevances of a society's organizational and institutional settings. This might be through alterations to turn taking, particularized adoption of ordinary conversational sequences and series, discrete changes to the ordering of sequences, and other procedural means yet to be discovered and analyzed.

CONCLUSION

Language is a primary medium of social behavior and, as such, deserves center stage in the panoply of social psychological topics. Indeed, other topics in social psychology, including exchange, bargaining, justice, socialization, deviance, health, ethnic relations, and collective behavior, necessarily involve interactive speech processes, which makes language use perhaps the most basic of social psychological phenomena. This is, we have argued, not so much because language is a vehicle of communication; rather, it is a resource for activity. One activity humans sometimes perform is "communicating" information of various kinds, but this is one among many other activities, such as arguing, promising, requesting, apologizing, joking, and greeting.

Influenced by ordinary language philosophy, recognizing that words do not have stable "meanings," and that the "same" utterance has different interpretations according to its context of use, language-oriented researchers therefore wrestle with the basic question of how utterances perform specifiable actions. Sociolinguists and discourse analysts answer this question in one way by suggesting that some combination of linguistic and social rules link words and activities together. This answer comes close to the theoretical model provided by the speech act theory of Austin and Searle. Frame analysts also presume some normative connection between utterances and actions, while giving freer rein to actors' strategic calculations and decision making in regard to rule adherence. Ethnomethodologists, conversation analysts, and discursive psychologists argue that in their ongoing conduct, participants themselves are users of rules who make normative assertions in the service of performing various activities. Rules, therefore, are only one possible facet of the practices whereby actors order speech productions to accomplish and understand the active force of these utterances. This way of solving the "mapping problem" is closer to Wittgenstein's idea of language games.

Moreover, in the conversation analytic view, importance is attached to how actors combine their utterances in a sequenced fashion. That is, the sequential organization of talk-in-interaction is a "primordial site of social action," which implies that this organization needs investigation and explication before the orderliness of conduct and action in institutional and other social structural arenas can be analyzed fully. This assertion implies a point of contact between conversation analysts and Goffman's concern with the interaction order. Among sociolinguists, discourse analysts, and cognitive sociologists, however, the argument is that participants' actions are not completely local in terms of either genesis or effect. It behooves the analyst to import the context or setting of talk enthnographically to analyze speech patterning and interactive order properly.

In short, the understanding of spoken language has moved from the conduit metaphor to an "action" orientation. Still, considerable controversy exists on how this orientation is best represented in theory and research. As this controversy continues, ever more realms of language use come under the social psychological microscope. To name just a few, these include discourse "marking" (Schiffrin, 1987; Sorjonen, 2001)—uses of "well ... and," "so," "y'know," and the like, idiomatic expressions (Drew & Holt, 1988; Kitzinger, 2000), gossip (Bergmann, 1993; Eder & enke, 1991; Goodwin, 1990), narrative (Labov, 1972a; Sacks, 1992b), puns and jokes (Sacks, 1992b), rhetoric (Atkinson, 1984; Billig, 1987), laughter (Glenn, 1995; Haakana, 2001; Jefferson, 1979; Lavin & Maynard, 2001), the intersection of grammar and interaction (Ochs et al., 1996) and numerous other aspects of the extraordinary human wealth represented in ordinary language, action, and social interaction.

REFERENCES

Ainsworth-Vaughn, N. (1992). Topic transitiions in physician-patient interviews: Power, gender, and discourse change. *Language in Society, 21*, 409–426.

Antaki, C. (1994). *Explaining and arguing: The social organization of accounts.* London: Sage.

Antaki, C., & Widdicombe, S. (1998). Identity as an achievement and as a tool. In C. Antaki & S. Widdicombe (Eds.), *Identities in talk.* London: Sage.

Aries, E. (1996). *Men and women in interaction: Reconsidering the differences.* Oxford: Oxford University Press.

Arminen, I. (Forthcoming). *Institutional interaction.* London: Sage.

Armstrong, D. (1983). *Political anatomy of the body.* Cambridge: Cambridge University Press.

Atkinson, J. M. (1984). *Our masters' voices: The language and body language of politics.* London: Methuen.

Atkinson, J. M., & Drew, P. (1979). *Order in court: The organisation of verbal interaction in judicial settings.* London: Macmillan.

Austin, J. L. (1961). *Philosophical papers.* London: Oxford University Press.

Austin, J. L. (1962). *How to do things with words.* Oxford: Oxford University Press.

Baugh, J. (1999). *Out of the mouths of slaves.* Austin: University of Texas Press.

Bergmann, J. R. (1993). *Discreet indiscretions: The social organization of gossip* (J. John Bednarz, Trans.). New York: Aldine De Gruyter.

Bernstein, B. (1961). Social structure, language and learning. *Educational Research, 3*, 163–176.

Bernstein, B. (1972). A sociolinguistic approach to socialization: With some reference to educability. In J. J. Gumperz & D. Hymes (Eds.), *Directions in sociolinguistics: The ethnography of communication* (pp. 465–511). New York: Holt, Rinehart & Winston.

Billig, M. (1987). *Arguing and thinking.* Cambridge: Cambridge University Press.

Bloor, D. (1976). *Knowledge and social imagery.* Chicago: University of Chicago.

Boden, D. (1990). People are talking: Conversation analysis and symbolic interaction. In H. Becker & M. McCall (Eds.), *Symbolic interaction and cultural studies* (pp. 244–273). Chicago: University of Chicago Press.

Bourdieu, P. (1991). *Language and symbolic power.* Cambridge, MA: Harvard University Press.

Breitborde, L. B. (1983). Levels of analysis in sociolinguistic explanation: Bilingual code switching, social relations, and domain theory. *International Journal of the Sociology of Language, 39*, 5–43.

Brown, R. (1958). *Words and things.* New York: Free Press.

Burns, T. (1992). *Erving Goffman.* London: Routledge.

Buttny, R. (1993). *Social accountability in communication.* London: Sage.

Chaiken, S. (1987). The heuristic model of persuasion. In M. P. Zanna, J. M. Olson, & C. P. Herman (Eds.), *Social influence: The ontario symposium* (Vol. 5). Hillsdale, NJ: Erlbaum.

Chomsky, N. (1965). *Aspects of the theory of syntax.* Cambridge, MA: MIT press.

Cicourel, A. V. (1974). *Cognitive sociology.* New York: Free Press.

Cicourel, A. V. (1981). Notes on the integration of micro- and macro-levels of analysis. In K. Knorr-Cetina & A. V. Cicourel (Eds.), *Advances in social theory and methodology: Toward an integration of micro- and macro-sociologies.* Boston: Routledge and Kegan Paul.

Clark, H. H. (1985). Language use and language users. In G. Lindzey & E. Aronson (Eds.), *The handbook of social psychology, volume 2* (pp. 179–231). New York: Random House.

Clayman, S. E. (1988). Displaying neutrality in television news interviews. *Social Problems, 35*(4).

Clayman, S. E., & Gill, V. T. (Forthcoming). Conversation analysis. In A. Bryman & M. Hardy (Eds.), *Handbook of data analysis.* Beverly Hills: Sage.

Clayman, S. E., & Heritage, J. (2002). *The news interview: Journalists and public figures on the air.* Cambridge: Cambridge University Press.

Corsaro, W. A. (1979). Young children's conception of status and role. *Sociology of Education, 55,* 160–177.

Corsaro, W. A. (1996). Transitions in early childhood: The promise of comparative, longitudinal ethnography. In R. Jessor, A. Colby, & R. A. Shweder (Eds.), *Ethnography and human development: Context and meaning in social inquiry* (pp. 419–456). Chicago: University of Chicago Press.

Coulter, J. (1989). *Mind in action.* Atlantic Highlands, NJ: Humanities Press.

Coulthard, M. (1977). *An introduction to discourse analysis.* London: Longman.

Danet, B. (1980). Language in the legal process. *Law and Society Review, 14,* 445–564.

Drew, P., & Holt, E. (1988). Complainable matters: The use of idiomatic expressions in making complaints. *Social Problems, 35,* 398–417.

Drew, P., & Wootton, A. (1988). *Erving Goffman: Exploring the interaction order.* Cambridge: Polity Press.

Eder, D., & Enke, J. (1991). The structure of gossip: Opportunities and constraints on collective expression among adolescents. *American Sociological Review, 56,* 495–508.

Edwards, D. (1997). *Discourse and cognition.* London: Sage.

Edwards, D., & Potter, J. (1992). *Discursive psychology.* London: Sage.

Edwards, J. (1979). *Language and disadvantage.* London: Arnold.

Eibl-Eibesfeldt, I. (1989). *Human ethology.* Hawthorne, NY: Aldine de Gruyter.

Ervin-Tripp. (1972). On sociolinguistic rules: Alternation and co-occurrence. In J. J. Gumperz & D. Hymes (Eds.), *Directions in sociolinguistics: The ethnography of communication.* New York: Holt, Rinehart & Winston.

Fairclough, N. (1992). *Discourse and social change.* Cambridge, England: Polity Press.

Firth, J. R. (1935). The techniques of semantics. *Transactions of the Philological society, 7,* 36–72.

Fisher, S. (1983). Doctor talk/patient talk: How treatment decisions are negotiated in doctor-patient communication. In S. Fisher & A. D. Todd (Eds.), *The social organization of doctor-patient communication* (pp. 135–157). Washington DC: Center for Applied Linguistics.

Fishman, J. (1983). Levels of analysis in sociolinguistic explanation. *International Journal of the Sociology of Language, 39.*

Foucault, M. (1979). *Discipline and punish: The birth of the prison.* New York: Random House.

Garfinkel, H. (1967). *Studies in ethnomethodology.* Englewood Cliffs, NJ: Prentice-Hall.

Garfinkel, H., & Sacks, H. (1970). On formal structures of practical actions. In J. D. McKinney & E. A. Tiryakian (Eds.), *Theoretical sociology* (pp. 337–366). New York: Appleton-Century Crofts.

Giddens, A. (1984). *The constitution of society.* Cambridge: Cambridge University Press.

Giles, H., & Robinson, W. P. (1990). Prologue. In H. Giles & W. P. Robinson (Eds.), *Handbook of language and social psychology* (pp. 1–8). New York: Wiley.

Glenn, P. (1995). Lauging at and laughing with: Negotiations of participant alignments through conversational laughter. In P. T. Have & G. Psathas (Eds.), *Situated order: Studies in the social organization of talk and embodied activities* (pp. 43–56). Washington DC: University Press of America.

Goffman, E. (1971). *Relations in public: Microstudies of the public order.* New York: Harper and Row.

Goffman, E. (1974). *Frame analysis: An essay on the organization of experience.* New York: Harper and Row.

Goffman, E. (1979). Footing. *Semiotica,* 1–29.

Goffman, E. (1983). The interaction order. *American Sociological Review, 48,* 1–17.

Goodwin, C. (1988). Participation frameworks in children's argument. In K. Ekberg & P. E. Mjaavatn (Eds.), *Growing into a modern world: Proceedings from an international interdisciplinary conference on the life and development of children in modern society* (pp. 1188–1195). Trondheim Norway: The Norwegian Centre for Child Research.

Goodwin, C., & Heritage, J. (1990). Conversation analysis. *Annual Review of Anthropology, 19,* 283–307.

Goodwin, M. H. (1990). *He-said-she-said: Talk as social organization among black children.* Bloomington: Indiana University Press.

Grice, H. P. (1957). Meaning. *Philosophical Review, 67*, 53–59.

Grice, H. P. (1975). Logic and conversation. In P. Cole & N. L. Morgan (Eds.), *Syntax and semantics, Vol. 3, Speech acts* (pp. 41–58). New York: Academic Press.

Grimshaw, A. (1989). *Collegial discourse: Professional conversation among peers.* Norwood, New Jersey: Ablex.

Grimshaw, A. D. (1974). Sociolinguistics. In I. D. S. Pool & W. Schramm (Eds.), *Handbook of communication* (pp. 49–92). Chicago: Rand McNally.

Gumperz, J. J. (1972). Introduction. In J. J. Gumperz & D. Hymes (Eds.), *Directions in sociolinguistics: The ethnography of communication* (pp. 1–25). New York: Holt, Rinehart & Winston.

Gumperz, J. J. (1982). *Discourse strategies.* Cambridge: Cambridge University Press.

Gumperz, J. J., & Hymes, D. (1972). *Directions in sociolinguistics: The ethnography of communication.* New York: Holt, Rinehart & Winston.

Haakana, M. (2001). Laughter as a patient's resource: Dealing with delicate aspects of medical interaction. *Text, 21*, 187–219.

Habermas, J. (1979). *Communication and the evolution of society.* Boston: Beacon Press.

Harré, R. (1986). An outline of the social constructionist viewpoint. In R. Harré (Ed.), *The social construction of emotions* (pp. 2–14). Oxford: Blackwell.

Heider, F. (1958). *The psychology of interpersonal relations.* New York: Wiley.

Heritage, J. (1984). *Garfinkel and ethnomethodology.* Cambridge, England: Polity Press.

Heritage, J., & Maynard, D. W. (Eds.). (2003). *Practicing medicine: Structure and process in primary care encounters.* Cambridge: Cambridge University Press.

Hertzler, J. O. (1965). *A sociology of language.* New York: Random House.

Hester, S., & Francis, D. (2000). Ethnomethodology, conversation analysis, and "institutional talk." *Text, 20*, 391–413.

Hewitt, J. P. (1997). *Self and society: A symbolic interactionist social psychology.* Boston: Allyn & Bacon.

Holtgraves, T. (1991). Interpreting questions and replies: Effects of face-threat, question form, and gender. *Social Psychology Quarterly, 54*, 15–24.

House, J. S. (1977). The three faces of social psychology. *Sociometry, 40*, 161–177.

Houtkoop-Steenstra, H. (2000). *Interaction and the standardized survey interview: The living questiionnaire.* Cambridge, UK: Cambridge University Press.

Hovland, C. I., Harvey, O. J., & Sherif, M. (1953). *Persuasion and communication.* New Have: Yale University press.

Hymes, D. (1974). *Foundations in sociolinguistics: An ethnographic approach.* Philadelphia: University of Pennsylvania Press.

Jefferson, G. (1979). A technique for inviting laughter and its subsequent acceptance/declination. In G. Psathas (Ed.), *Everyday language: Studies in ethnomethodology* (pp. 79–96). New York: Irvington.

Jefferson, G. (1986). Notes on "latency" in overlap onset. *Human Studies, 9*, 153–183.

Katriel, T., & Philipsen, G. (1990). "What we need is communication": "Communication" as a cultural category in some American speech. In D. Carbaugh (Ed.), *Cultural communication and intercultural contact* (pp. 77–93). Hilldale, NJ: Erlbaum.

Key, M. R. (1972). Linguistic behavior of male and female. *Linguistics, 88*, 15–31.

Kitzinger, C. (2000). How to resist an idiom. *Research on Language and Social Interaction, 33*, 121–154.

Kollock, P., Blumstein, P., & Schwartz, P. (1985). Sex and power in interaction: Conversational privileges and duties. *American Sociological Review, 50*, 34–46.

Labov, W. (1972a). *Language in the inner city: Studies in the black english vernacular.* Philadelphia: University of Pennsylvania Press.

Labov, W. (1972b). *Sociolinguistic patterns.* Philadelphia: University of Pennsylvania Press.

Labov, W., & Fanshel, D. (1977). *Therapeutic discourse: Psychotherapy as conversation.* New York: Academic Press.

Lavin, D., & Maynard, D. W. (2001). Standardization vs. Rapport: Respondent laughter and interviewer reaction during telephone surveys. *American Sociological Review, 66*, 453–479.

Lennenberg, E. H. (1953). Cognition and ethnolinguistics. *Language, 29*, 463–471.

Lerner, G. (1989). Notes on overlap management in conversation: The case of delayed completion. *Western Journal of Speech Communication, 53*, 167–177.

Levinson, S. C. (1983). *Pragmatics.* Cambridge: Cambridge University Press.

Malinowski, B. (1923). The problem of meaning in primitive societies. In C. K. Ogden & J. A. Richards (Eds.), *The meaning of meaning* (pp. 451–510). London: Kegan Paul.

Mandler, J. M. (1984). *Scripts, stories and scenes: Aspects of schema theory.* Hillsdale, NJ: Lawrence Erlbaum.

Manning, P. (1992). *Erving Goffman and modern sociology.* Stanford: Stanford University Press.

Manzo, J. (1996). Taking turns and taking sides: Opening scenes from two jury deliverations. *Social Psychology Quarterly, 59*, 107–125.

Marlaire, C. L., & Maynard, D. W. (1990). Standardized testing as an interactional phenomenon. *Sociology of Education, 63*, 83–101.

Maynard, D. W. (1991). Interaction and asymmetry in clinical discourse. *American Journal of Sociology, 97*, 448–495.

Maynard, D. W. (2003). *Bad news, good news: Conversational order in everyday talk and clinical settings*. Chicago: University of Chicago Press.

Maynard, D. W., & Clayman, S. E. (1991). The diversity of ethnomethodology. *Annual Review of Sociology, 17*, 385–418.

Maynard, D. W., Houtkoop-Steenstra, H., Schaeffer, N. C., & Zouwen, H. v. d. (Eds.). (2002). *Standardization and tacit knowledge: Interaction and practice in the survey interview*. New York: Wiley Interscience.

McDermott, R. P., Gospodinoff, K., & Aron, J. (1978). Criteria for an ethnographically adequate description of concerted activities and their contexts. *Semiotica, 24*, 245–275.

McHoul, A. (1978). The organization of turns at formal talk in the classroom. *Language in Society, 7*, 183–213.

Mead, G. H. (1934). *Mind, self, and society*. Chicago, IL: University of Chicago.

Mehan, H. (1979). *Learning lessons*. Cambridge, MA: Harvard University Press.

Mehan, H. (1991). The school's work of sorting students. In D. Boden & D. H. Zimmerman (Ed.), *Talk and social structure* (pp. 71–90). Cambridge, England: Polity Press.

Molotch, H. L., & Boden, D. (1985). Talking social structure: Discourse, domination and the watergate hearings. *American Sociological Review, 50*, 273–288.

Mori, J. (1999). *Negotiating agreement and disagreement in Japanese: Connective expressions and turn construction*. Amsterdam/Philadelphia: John Benjamins.

Mulkay, M. (1979). *Science and the sociology of knowledge*. London: Allen and Unwin.

Ochs, E., Schegloff, E. A., & Thompson, S. A. (Eds.). (1996). *Interaction and grammar*. Cambridge: Cambridge University Press.

Okamoto, D. G., & Smith-Lovin, L. (2001). Changing the subject: Gender, status, and the dynamics of topic change. *American Sociological Review, 66*, 852–873.

Peräkylä, A. (1995). *Aids counseling: Institutional interaction and clinical practice*. Cambridge: Cambridge University Press.

Petty, R. E., & Cacioppo, J. T. (1986). *Communication and persuasion*. New York: Springer-Verlag.

Phillips, S. (1982). *The invisible culture: Communication in classroom and community on the warm springs Indian reservation*. New York: Longman.

Pinker, S. (1994). *The language instinct: How the mind creates language*. New York: Harper Collins.

Pitkin, H. F. (1972). *Wittgenstein and justice: On the significance of Ludwig Wittgenstein for social and political thought*. Berkeley: University of California Press.

Potter, J. (1996). *Representing reality: Discourse, rhetoric, and social construction*. London: Sage.

Potter, J., & Wetherell, M. (1987). *Discourse and social psychology: Beyond attitudes and behavior*. London: Sage.

Rawls, A. W. (1987). The interaction order sui generis: Goffman's contribution to social theory. *Sociological Theory, 5*, 136–149.

Reddy, M. J. (1979). The conduit metaphor. In A. Ortony (Ed.), *Metaphor and thought* (pp. 284–324). Cambridge: Cambridge University Press.

Sacks, H. (1984). Notes on methodology. In J. M. Atkinson & J. Heritage (Eds.), *Structures of social action* (pp. 21–27). Cambridge, England: Cambridge University Press.

Sacks, H. (1992a). *Lectures on conversation (Vol. 1: Fall 1964–Spring 1968)*. Oxford, England: Basil Blackwell.

Sacks, H. (1992b). *Lectures on conversation (Vol. 2: Fall 1968–Spring 1972)*. Oxford: Blackwell.

Sacks, H., Schegloff, E. A., & Jefferson, G. (1974). A simplest systematics for the organization of turn-taking for conversation. *Language, 50*, 696–735.

Saussure, F. D. (1962). *Cours de linguistiqu generale*. Paris: Payot.

Schegloff, E. A. (1972). Notes on a conversational practice: Formulating place. In D. Sudnow (Ed.), *Studies in social interaction* (pp. 75–119). New York: Free Press.

Schegloff, E. A. (1986). The routine as achievement. *Human Studies, 9*, 111–151.

Schegloff, E. A. (1989). Reflections on language, development and the interactional character of talk-in-interaction. In M. Bornstein & J. S. Bruner (Eds.), *Interaction in human development* (pp. 139–153). New York: Erlbaum.

Schegloff, E. A. (1991). Reflections on talk and social structure. In D. Boden & D. H. Zimmerman (Eds.), *Talk and social structure* (pp. 44–70). Berkeley: University of California Press.

Schegloff, E. A. (1992). Repair after next turn: The last structurally provided for place for the defence of inter-subjectivity in conversation. *American Journal of Sociology, 95*(5), 1295–1345.

Schegloff, E. A. (2000). Overlapping talk and the organization of turn-taking for conversation. *Language in Society, 29*, 1–63.

Schegloff, E. A., Jefferson, G., & Sacks, H. (1977). The preference for self-correction in the organization of repair in conversation. *Language, 53*, 361–382.

Schegloff, E. A., & Sacks, H. (1973). Opening up closings. *Semiotica, 8*, 289–327.

Schiffrin, D. (1987). *Discourse markers.* Cambridge: Cambridge University Press.

Searle, J. R. (1969). *Speech acts: An essay in the philosophy of language.* Cambridge: Cambridge University Press.

Searle, J. R. (1975). Indirect speech acts. In P. Cole & J. L. Morgan (Eds.), *Syntax and semantics* (Vol. 3, pp. 59–82). New York: Academic Press.

Shaver, K. G. (1983). *An introduction to attribution processes.* Hillsdale, NJ: Lawrence Erlbaum.

Silverman, D. (1987). *Communication and medical practice.* London: Sage.

Sorjonen, M.-L. (2001). *Responding in conversation: A study of response particles in Finnish.* Amsterdam: Benjamins.

Strawson, P. F. (1964). Intention and convention in speech acts. *Philosophical Review, 73*, 439–460.

Strong, P. (1979). *The ceremonial order of the clinic.* London: Routledge.

Stubbs, M. (1983). *Discourse analysis.* Oxford: Blackwell.

Tanaka, H. (1999). *Turn-taking in Japanese conversation: A study in grammar and interaction.* Amsterdam/Philadelphia: John Benjamins.

Tannen, D. (1990). *You just don't understand: Women and men in conversation.* New York: William Morrow.

ten Have, P. (1999). *Doing conversation analysis.* London: Sage.

Thorne, B., & Henley, N. (1975). *Language and sex: Difference and dominance.* Rowley, MA: Newbury House.

van Dijk, T. (1997). Discourse as interaction in society. In T. V. Dijk (Ed.), *Discourse as social interaction.* London: Sage.

van Dijk, T. (Ed.). (1985). *Handbook of discourse analysis, volumes 1–4.* London: Academic Press.

Waitzkin, H. (1991). *The politics of medical encounters: How patients and doctors deal with social problems.* New Haven, Conn.: Yale University Press.

Watson, R. (2000). The character of "institutional talk": A response to Hester and Francis. *Text, 20*, 377–389.

Weber, M. (1947). *The theory of social and economic organization.* New York: Free Press.

West, C., & Garcia, A. (1988). Conversational shift work. *Social Problems, 35*, 550–575.

West, C., & Zimmerman, D. (1983). Small insults: A study of interruptions in cross-sex conversations with unacquainted persons. In B. Thorne, C. Kramarae, & N. Henley (Eds.), *Language, gender and society* (pp. 102–117). Rowley MA: Newbury House.

West, C., & Zimmerman, D. H. (1985). Gender, language and discourse. In T. A. V. Dijk (Ed.), *Handbook of discourse analysis, vol. 4* (pp. 103–124). London: Academic Press.

Whalen, M., & Zimmerman, D. H. (1987). Sequential and institutional contexts in calls for help. *Social Psychology Quarterly, 50*, 172–185.

Whorf, B. (1956). *Language, thought, and reality: Selected writings of Benjamin Lee Whorf.* Cambridge, MA: MIT Press.

Wieder, D. L. (1974). *Language and social reality.* The Hague: Mouton.

Wittgenstein, L. (1958). *Philosophical investigations.* Translated by G.E.M. Anscombe. New York: Macmillan.

Woolgar, S. (1988). *Science the very idea.* London: Ellis Horwood and Tavistock.

Wootton, A. J. (1981). The management of grantings and rejections by parents in request sequences. *Semiotica, 37*, 59–89.

Zimmerman, D. H. (1970). The practicalities of rule use. In J. Douglas (Ed.), *Understanding everyday life* (pp. 221–238). Chicago: Aldine.

Zimmerman, D. H., & Boden, D. (1991). Structure-in-action: An introduction. In D. Boden & D. H. Zimmerman (Eds.), *Talk and social structure* (pp. 3–21). Cambridge, UK: Polity Press.

CHAPTER 11

Social Cognition

Judith A. Howard
Daniel G. Renfrow

The turbulent months following the September 11 terrorist attacks on the World Trade Center and the Pentagon witnessed a backlash in discrimination and bias crimes targeting Arab Americans. Two months after the attacks, over 500 incidents of violence directed toward people of Middle-Eastern descent—including multiple murders—were reported to the American Arab Anti-Discrimination Committee (ADC). Dozens of individuals were forced to leave airplanes because other passengers or airline officials were afraid to fly with them. Perhaps the accounts receiving the most heated public discussion, however, were the institutionalized instances of racial profiling by law enforcement officers, acts permitted under the auspices of the U.S. Patriot Act enacted as part of America's *war on terrorism*.

Ethnicity of the target is the common denominator in each of these incidents. Bias crimes, such as those aimed at Arab Americans, illustrate social actors' reliance on cognitive structures—those based upon social categories such as race and ethnicity—in making social judgments. Reacting to the terrorist attacks, individuals relied on social information to make judgments about the cause of the attacks, evaluations of the people involved, generalizations of these evaluations to broader social categories, judgments of responsibility, and the appropriateness of retaliation. Racial stereotypes and the priming of these preconceptions played significant roles in generating these responses. Societal reactions to historical events such as these point to the social significance and consequences of cognition in everyday life.

Social cognition is one of the dominant substantive areas within social psychology. Psychologists, by and large, have done the theoretical, empirical, and applied work in this area. Cognition continues to provide the foundation for much of the work in developmental personality and clinical psychology (Schneider, 1991). Cognition is also making strides in

Judith A. Howard • University of Washington, Box 354345, Seattle, WA 98195-4345
Daniel G. Renfrow • Department of Sociology, University of Washington, Seattle, Washington 98195

Handbook of Social Psychology, edited by John Delamater. Kluwer Academic/Plenum Publishers, New York, 2003.

disparate fields such as the study of artificial intelligence (Dreyfus, 1992) and the study of language and discourse (Potter, 1998; van Dijk, 1996). Juxtaposed to this sustained psychological tradition, sociological work in the area emphasizes the more social aspects of cognition. In this chapter, we trace this sociological perspective in cognition.

We begin the chapter by defining key terms and reviewing the basic elements of social cognition. We relate social cognition to key psychological and sociological theories, linking a largely experimental research literature to sociological concerns and calling attention to other methodological techniques used in more recent research. Some significant topics receive little attention in this chapter. We do not address the relationships among cognition, affect, and behavior as they are discussed at length elsewhere in this volume. In the second part of the chapter, we address questions about what type of thinkers we are and about the epistemological status of thought, as well as the need to incorporate change and stability into cognitive models. In conclusion, we consider the sociological dimensions of social cognition, exploring its connections to interaction, social structure, and culture.

DEFINING SOCIAL COGNITION

How social scientists use the concept *social cognition* reflects the perspectives of their varied, relevant disciplines. Psychologists Fiske and Taylor (1991) use "social cognition" to refer to the process whereby "people make sense of other people and themselves," whereas sociologists move away from individualistic views of cognition and, instead, stress the social aspects of cognition more explicitly. Howard and Hollander (1997) suggest that cognition goes beyond intra-individual information processing; it is socially structured and transmitted, mirroring the values and norms of the relevant society and social groups. Condor and Antaki (1997) reflect an interdisciplinary orientation in their approach to cognition, moving away from the "mental processing of information" and toward a definition of cognition as the "social construction of knowledge." Borrowing from each of these traditions, we use social cognition to refer to structures of knowledge, the interpersonal processes of knowledge creation and dissemination (including the encoding, storage, retrieval, and activation of social information), the actual content of this knowledge, and the shaping of each of these aspects of cognition by social forces.

Relation of Social Cognition to Other Key Theoretical Paradigms

PSYCHOLOGICAL. Elements of social cognition can be seen in much of the psychological research throughout the twentieth century. Advances in cognitive psychology and computer technology during the 1970s and 1980s marked the beginning of a cognitive revolution (Schneider, 1991) and the *hybridization* of cognition across various sub-fields within the social sciences (Operario & Fiske, 1999). The growth of social cognition was a reaction to the earlier dominance of behaviorism, a reductionist model that does not capture the nuances of a wide range of social behaviors. Years of research witnessed the development of an increasingly more sophisticated cognitive model, from a *naïve scientist* model that used lay theories to explain the world to the *cognitive miser* model that focuses more on what people actually do when thinking (i.e., relying on mental shortcuts and categorizations) to more recent models of the *motivated tactician*, who uses multiple strategies based upon goals and motives (i.e., belonging, maintaining the self, etc.) (Operario & Fiske, 1999). While social cognition is only one of many theoretical perspectives and methodological toolkits within the psychological repertoire, its impact on social psychology has been extreme; contemporary social psychologists no longer question the idea that mental knowledge structures mediate between external stimuli and social action.

SOCIOLOGICAL. Social cognition can trace its roots to each of the classical lines of sociological theory. Work by Durkheim, Weber, and Marx, as well as the more contemporary theoretical traditions of phenomenology and symbolic interaction, laid the conceptual groundwork for much of the cognition research of today. Critical of psychology's reductionist tendencies, Durkheim (1898) argued for a theory of collective psychology. Foreshadowing Moscovici's (1981) concept of social representations, Durkheim suggested that people within social groups share a collective conscience, as well as common representations of this knowledge. Weber (1968) suggested that individuals attach subjective meaning to action, meaning that guides the operation of larger social systems. Contemporary views of cognitive structures, such as prototypes, share much in common with Weber's concept of "ideal types," or perfect forms. Marx's critique of industrialization focuses on the role of dominant ideologies in the preservation of social systems (Marx & Engels, 1947). Marx details a false consciousness whereby individuals buy into hegemonic belief systems, even when detrimental to their own positions within society. In some ways, this concept resembles the "mindlessness" of some cognitive processing (Langer, 1989). Each of these theoretical traditions constitutes part of the intellectual heritage of social cognition.

Both the *phenomenological* and *symbolic interactionist* traditions emphasize the impact of everyday activities on macro-level social actions, mining Weber's earlier concerns regarding the importance of subjective meaning in shaping the activities of everyday life. While phenomenologists ground the shaping and revision of schemas shared throughout communities in the workings of everyday activities, symbolic interactionists focus on the construction of knowledge and the creation of symbolic meaning, particularly as these relate to the construction of self. Mead (1934) held that significant symbols are created through conversations of gestures. Understanding these symbols permits individuals to take the role of the other—where they anticipate their own and others' responses to possible lines of action—and to direct their behavior accordingly, thereby producing minds and selves. Contextualizing these processes, Blumer (1969) emphasizes the importance of social context in shaping interpretations, marking cognition as fundamentally social. Goffman's (1959, 1963) work on self-presentation and impression management demonstrates how action can be motivated and directed by meaning attached to significant symbols. By understanding and skillfully manipulating these verbal and nonverbal gestures, social actors can fashion others' impressions. These early theorists contributed to a sociological tradition well suited for the further development and application of cognitive concepts. Contemporary theorists continue to explore the relationship between internal and external forces in decision-making and thought processes.

Social exchange theory applies economic models to decision-making processes in everyday encounters. Like behaviorism, social exchange theory assumes that social actors can be motivated by rewards, both material and symbolic, and deterred by punishment or costs (Blau 1964; Thibaut & Kelley, 1959). Here the exchange itself is the unit of analysis, rather than the individual. This perspective relies heavily upon memory and claims that we must understand consequences of prior behavior in order to make decisions about future behavior. Cognitive processing aids individuals in choosing between alternative outcomes. While social exchange theory can incorporate the positionality of the social actor—the idea that individuals are vying for resources in a system with differential opportunity structures—into interactions,

Howard and Hollander (1997) suggest the perspective glosses the complexities of cognitive processing (i.e., neglecting beliefs, attitudes, etc.).

Closely aligned with interactionist concerns with defining social situations, *expectation states theory* explores the processes whereby actors attempt to define their own and others' roles in task-oriented encounters and allocate status based upon these expectations and performance evaluations. Power and prestige rankings come from actors' expectations about their own and others' performances, as well as from the perceived value of these performances. Salient characteristics associated with social categorizations influence the rank ordering that is generated by this collective reward system. Even when socially evaluated characteristics are not important to the particular situation, they may still influence attributions. This perspective stems from the early work of Berger and colleagues (1974, 1977) and is further elaborated by Ridgeway (1991, 2000). Current research continues to demonstrate that expectation states, like many social psychological processes, tend to mirror and promote inequalities of the social context in which they occur (Cast, Stets, & Burke, 1999). Supported by predominantly laboratory-based research, expectation states and social exchange theories both leave sociologists questioning how well these theories can explain social interactions outside of artificially constructed contexts.

Any examination of social systems is relevant to themes of power, as social relationships are fundamentally based upon power. Yet, power is virtually absent from some of the more sociological strands of social psychology. *Critical social psychology* revisits many of the classic themes within the discipline and reexamines these central issues with an eye toward identifying the role of power, as well as multiple structures of powerlessness, in social processes. Illustrating this critique, Cherry (1995) uses the incident of the murder of Kitty Genovese and the line of bystander response research springing from her murder to demonstrate how gender, race, and social class have been neglected. Similarly, in a critical read of social psychology's treatment of race as a "natural" category, Leach (1998) claims the field's reliance on categorization reifies socially constructed categories such as race. From this perspective, the availability of the category itself may work toward reifying racism within our discipline. These critical social psychologists struggle with reconciling ideas about individual agency with notions about the constraints placed upon individuals by social systems (Ibanez, 1997). At the heart of critical social psychology, power shapes a sense of identity in everyday interactions and provides a context for information processing and behavior.

ELEMENTS OF SOCIAL COGNITION

Cognitive Structures

Social information must be represented in some mental form, whether sensory, verbal, or iconic. Social cognition emphasizes verbal representations of knowledge; it is these organized representations that provide the basis for cognitive structures. Early forms of these structures include beliefs, attitudes, and values. (Chapter 10 discusses these early structures in more detail.)

Contemporary views of cognitive structures follow the cognitive miser view of the human actor, suggesting that humans have cognitive limits. Because it is impossible to process all incoming information in a given situation, we develop systems of categorization. Zerubavel (1996) describes this categorization as a process of "lumping" and "splitting," where dissimilar information is split into distinct categories and similar information is lumped together into mental clusters. This process allows individuals to "sculpt" mental structures and thereby construct reality. Cognitive structures, therefore, are categories into which we sort incoming information. These structures are created through multiple experiences and function as interpretive frameworks for new information.

Individuals create *prototypes* by synthesizing their experiences with members of a social category into an average—albeit abstract—account of characteristics associated with that particular group (Cantor & Mischel, 1979). Drawing upon the example we use to introduce this chapter, accounts of racial profiling show how young men of apparent Middle-Eastern descent might be considered the prototype for the larger category "terrorist"—particularly in a climate of fear perpetuated by media reports. In short, prototypes are the central tendency of characteristics associated with members of a social group generated from experience. Another cognitive structure, *exemplars*, refers to actual cases that are representative of others—although not necessarily the perfect form. Understandings about these particular experiences are then extended to new situations. Fiske and Taylor (1991) suggest that exemplars are better predictors of attributions than are prototypes or schemas, because exemplars are actual instances, not averages or ideal types.

Schemas, on the other hand, act as everyday theories that shape how people view and use information. They are both abstract cognitive structures that represent organized knowledge about a concept or stimulus as well as mechanisms used in information processing (DiMaggio, 1997). Schemas allow individuals to apply social knowledge and to exert a degree of control over the social world by guiding our perceptions, memory, and inference processes. We develop person, role, and event schemas, as well as content-free schemas, which provide processing rules. *Person schemas* organize knowledge about particular individuals or specific types of people, usually emphasizing traits or personality categories. *Self-schemas*, a type of person schema garnering considerable attention in recent years, organize knowledge about one's self. A person might be self-schematic for one trait, nationalism for instance, but aschematic or lacking such information on another trait.

Role schemas are organized knowledge about the norms and expectations associated with particular social positions. Role schemas are mechanisms for stereotyping and intergroup prejudice and discrimination. Consequently role schemas have considerable sociological significance. *Event schemas* describe expected sequences in routinized, everyday events such as going to the market. Lindenfield (1994) illustrates how individuals rely on such sequences through his examination of verbal interactions at a public market in southern California. The scheme he outlines for a typical exchange entails three steps: an appeal or offer of service is made by the stand operator, which is followed by an order from the customer and then compliance on the part of the seller. Event schemas such as this one provide stage directions by designating who the actors are, what they do and when, where they stand, and what props they use during the encounter. Like other forms of event schemas, social scripts are organized into major scenes or subsets of actions. These lines of action are guided by particular goals—buying fruit at the market for instance—and thus are keys to understanding action.

Overlap and interaction among schemas are commonplace. The situation, for example, may influence person schemas. While we may expect our elected officials to be stubborn and uncompromising in serving their constituencies, we do not generalize these expectations to other situations—to their intimate relationships for example. Similarly, role schemas can shape person schemas because people rely on general expectations for particular social roles in making attributions about particular individuals. Furthermore, correlations between the content of different types of schemas vary depending, in part, on the salience of role information. In the context of a predominantly White school, African American and Hispanic students are much more likely to mention their ethnic group membership when responding to the question: who am I? than are White students (McGuire, McGuire, Child, & Fujioka, 1978). Social context can be tied to role salience, which in turn shapes social cognition.

Out of critiques portraying schemas as "asocial" and "decontextualized" snapshots missing historical and cultural contexts (Augustinos & Inness, 1990), scholars have identified other more fully social cognitive structures, such as Serge Moscovici's (1981) concept of social representations. These representations are not just opinions or attitudes, but commonsense theories about how the world works (Augustinos & Inness, 1990). Social representations are more social than schemas in that they are consensual and shared, created through interaction and communication (Augustinos & Inness, 1990), and because their contents are representations of the social world (Huguet & Latane, 1996). Although social representations are structural elements in the cognitive systems of individuals, the generation and communication of social representations are collective processes.

Social representations are more dynamic than schemata, being created and recreated through social interaction. This construct blurs the division between structure and process; representations are structures in the sense of being organized knowledge, but they are structures in process, continually transforming some forms of information into others. Through social representations, we make sense of the social world and communicate that sense to others. Social representations situate individuals in material space and provide codes allowing for communication and mastery of the social world. Unlike the more static concept schema, representations are dynamic and gain a "life force" of their own; on occasion, however, some representations may become reified (Augustinos & Inness, 1990). A review by Wagner et al. (1999) illustrates how abstract processes such as conception are objectified though the use of metaphors about gender, where sperms are personified in masculine terms (i.e., active, fast, and dominant) and the egg in feminine terms (i.e., passive, slow, and submissive). Conception itself remains intangible because it eludes observation, but through the use of gender stereotypes that connect the phenomenon with preexisting cultural "knowledge," the process becomes concrete and understandable. Martin (1991) details the use of similar metaphors about conception in scientific texts. Her feminist critique challenges such "scientific fairy tales," pointing to the egg's active role in conception, as well as emphasizing how naturalizing gender expectations and imagery at the cell level can have larger social implications.

Despite increased interest in this line of research in recent years—among European sociologists in particular—Moscovici's theory has come under attack (Potter & Litton, 1985). Some scholars question the concept of social representations itself, claiming it is far too vague to be useful. Augustinos and Inness (1990) suggest positivists also question Moscovici's laissez faire attitude toward research methodologies. Other criticisms concern the idea of consensus: How much variation is allowed, and how are groups distinguished from one another? Recent work by Huguet and Latane (1996) uses dynamic social impact theory to address these criticisms by specifying a mechanism for the spread and endurance of representations. They outline criteria for deciding whether or not a representation is shared, specifying when a group exists and indicating how disagreement and variation can fit into the social representation model. Nevertheless, the insistence of this concept on the significance of social interaction for the creation and transmission of cultural concepts is a major contribution to a sociological understanding of cognition.

Cognitive Processes

Cognitive processes rely upon organized knowledge, in the form of cognitive structures. Contemporary social psychologists' focus on cognitive processes, in part, has been due to technological advancements, which allow scientists to use computer simulations as a means of manipulating and understanding thought processes within the laboratory (Fiske & Taylor, 1991). More recent work on cognitive processes also relies on alternative methods such as motivated ethnography, interviews, focus groups, content analysis, and questionnaires to specify how social information is cognitively processed in real-world contexts (Wagner et al., 1999).

Information processing begins when some object, whether from the environment or the contents of our mind, becomes the focus of our *attention*. At this point, we select, identify, categorize, and assign meaning to the stimulus. While some object may capture our attention, the intensity of this focus varies across situations. Numerous stimuli compete for our attention at all times. We consciously decide what to attend to in some situations, but usually this occurs without conscious control on our part. Here, the pivotal issue becomes how we select what to attend to and what to ignore.

Contextual conditions may influence what we attend to. Salient stimuli—that is, those that stand out vis-à-vis others—are more likely to capture our attention. Visual characteristics, for example, may enhance the salience of a stimulus. A single white cloud in an otherwise empty, blue sky is likely to capture and hold our attention. Salience within social interactions, however, tends to depend on the social meaning attached to a particular trait. For instance, Secretary of State Colin Powell has garnered national attention because he is the first African American to be appointed to such an office in U.S. government. Salience, as this example shows, may be achieved by contrasting group memberships—that is, being African American in a predominantly White polity. Similarly, actions that contradict those we expect tend to be more salient than more normative actions. Charges that former President Clinton engaged in extra-marital relations with a White House intern caused a media sensation and non-partisan outrage, prompting much public discussion on the moral responsibilities of the Commander in Chief. When our expectations for actors in particular social roles are not met, such instances attract and hold our attention.

Accessibility of cognitive structures, the potential of available knowledge to be activated (Higgins, 2000), also influences our attention. Knowledge we engage with frequently is more accessible and thus more likely to be brought to our attention. Recently activated ideas show similar patterns. Through priming, socially significant categories influence social inferences. Using two similar studies, Levy (1996) primed negative and positive stereotypes about aging in an elderly sample. Those exposed to positive stereotypes performed better during memory exercises and displayed more positive views about aging and about self-efficacy compared to those primed with more negative attitudes. A follow-up study using a younger sample did not find similar patterns, suggesting that for this effect to hold, ideas about aging must be important to the individual's self-concept. Similarly, Gorham (1999) examines the influence of priming on racial stereotypes, finding that the process of priming makes the content of stereotypes available for future processing, which influences cognitive processes whether or not we believe the preconception. The effects of priming, therefore, may have real-world consequences.

Information about the social world is stored in *memory* and is available to be retrieved and used for future cognitive inferences. When we recall this information, we activate knowledge stored in our long-term memory and bring it into short-term memory, where we consciously attend to it. Mental schemas are relevant to memory in various ways: individuals recall information encoded into schemata quickly and accurately; information is recalled better when it is relevant to preexisting theories; and people may also falsely remember information relevant to schemas (DiMaggio, 1997). Because of this tendency to recall inaccurate information, assessing cognitive accuracy remains a major preoccupation of memory researchers. Information recall, however, improves when the reason for encoding and retrieving the information is more engaging and significant, when one empathizes with another and when one anticipates future interaction with others, pointing both to the importance of affect for understanding memory and to social influences on memory.

As with attention, studies illustrate how social context shapes human memory and how cognitive structures influence this process. C. Cohen (1981), for example, exposed subjects to a short video of a woman having a birthday dinner with her husband. When asked questions about the tape, subjects who thought the woman was a waitress remembered details consistent with her being a waitress, whereas subjects who were told she was a librarian later recalled details more consistent with stereotypes about librarians. Memory was supplemented by role schemas in both cases; even though details were not shown in the videotape, absent information was created and then "remembered" in light of existing schemas, suggesting how cognitive structures may influence recall. Similarly, social roles influence memory. Memory models, for the most part, focus on intra-individual storage of information. Wegner (1986), however, outlines how members of social groups divide cognitive labor, allocating information among members of a social group. Taken together, these studies point to how cognitive structures influence the encoding of social information and the retrieval of this information from memory, as individuals or as groups.

INFORMATION PROCESSING

Cognitive inferences require the evaluation of social information according to some set of rules and the formation of a social judgment (i.e., decisions, probability, cognitive evaluations, attributions of causality, and other attributes linked to social actors). *Gathering relevant information* is the first step of this process. Acting as cognitive misers, we generally do not gather all of the available, relevant information, but instead, we rely upon preexisting expectations and theories to select a sample of potentially relevant information. We tend to rely on our theories, rather than data, when we are confident in the theory, the theory is salient and the data are ambiguous. Because of the demands of cognitive efficiency, we generally are inattentive to sample size, and thus, we overestimate the reliability of our small sample of experiences, of contacts with objects, persons, and situations. Similarly, we tend to overlook the biases in samples. Our tendency to infer general principles on the basis of our friends is a common example. We also tend to underuse base-rate information. Hamill, Wilson, and Nisbett (1980) illustrate this reliance in their study of social judgments. Their subjects were influenced more by a single case study about a woman and her many children living a lavish lifestyle while on welfare, more so than base-rate information contradicting this account. Thus, our expectations about social groups may influence what information we gather. Moreover, patterns of information selection like these reflect and maintain prevailing societal patterns.

After we have gathered what we believe to be enough information, we make social inferences. Although some models of *information integration* assume we are capable of sophisticated and rational strategies in information processing, others tend to focus on biases in these processes. Still other models outline a series of *heuristics*, or cognitive shortcuts. Tversky and Kahneman (1974) have identified several prominent heuristics: representativeness (i.e., judging the probability of an event on the basis of its similarity to its parent population); availability (i.e., estimating frequency or probability by how easily instances are recalled), and anchoring and adjustment (i.e., reducing the ambiguity of a judgment by starting the process from a beginning reference point, or anchor, and then adjusting it to reach a final judgment based on our own experience). These heuristics simplify otherwise complex problem solving into more manageable mental tasks.

Heuristics assume that we need to reduce information, and thus our reliance upon them makes us vulnerable to their biases, a necessary evil according to the cognitive miser view. The violation of these key principles necessary for gathering accurate information has lead to research focusing on errors in cognitive processing. One requirement for making an accurate judgment is the capacity to assess covariation. Nisbett and Ross (1980) demonstrate, however, that humans do not assess covariation very accurately. When we expect to find a relationship between two variables, we tend to overestimate the strength of that relationship, perhaps creating an illusory correlation. This cognitive phenomenon is one of the bases of stereotyping. As an illustration, Hamilton and Gifford (1976) found that illusory correlations based on paired distinctiveness shape negative stereotypes of minority group members. Students in their sample were asked to make trait inferences about two hypothetical groups, attributions of group membership and estimates for the frequency of traits in each group. Their findings indicate that when both behavior and group membership are non-normative, individuals tend to perceive a correlation between them. These illusory correlations illustrate people's tendency to process information in ways that confirm prior expectations, often leading to cognitive errors and providing firm cognitive foundations for social prejudices.

The formation of causal or trait inferences follows the principles of *attribution*. First articulated by Heider (1958), *causal inferences* are judgments about what factors may have produced a particular outcome in some situation, whereas *trait inferences* assign particular characteristics to an individual. Kelley (1967, 1973), and Jones and Davis (1965) have extended and complicated Heider's original formulation. Both of their formal models begin with the assumption that the causes of behavior can be associated either with an individual actor, or with the situation or environment in which that behavior occurs. These models, however, depart from one another in their assumptions about the relationship between the individual and social factors.

Kelley's (1967, 1973) line of research improves our understanding of how and when individuals attribute causality to social actors or to the environment. He also theorizes how—when information is deficient—we make attributions by applying various causal schemas, or conceptions people have about how causes interact to produce specific effects. Jones and colleagues (1965, 1976) examine which circumstances lead individuals to make attributions of particular traits to an individual based upon his behavior. Such trait attributions are a function of our evaluations of the outcome associated with the behavior and the alternative behaviors available in the situation, as well as our a priori expectations about how the actor will act. We may have individualized, *target-based expectations* stemming from our knowledge of the actor's past behavior, in addition to more generalized, *category-based expectations* based on our knowledge of relevant social groups and social norms. In either case, we use information about the actor's own behavior and the behavior of others as the basis for making causal inferences.

In two related studies, Innman, Huerta, and Oh (1998) examine how power expectations associated with the race of a hypothetical perpetrator influence whether respondents perceive the individual's behavior as discriminatory. Behavior by individuals expected to be in control of the situation at hand tended to be seen as discriminatory, more so than behavior by individuals in groups not expected to be in control. Thus, Whites and racial minorities both were cast as discriminating in some situations and not in others—depending upon social expectations. A second study addresses why these high-status individuals are viewed as more discriminating and concludes that these decisions emerge from two independent processes. First, participants rely on expectations about the groups in the scenario; groups expected to be in power in a particular context are held more accountable for their behavior than others. Second, actions viewed as violating the norm of responsibility—that is, situations in which perpetrators are seen as hurting an individual of disadvantaged or marginal status—are deemed more malicious and discriminatory. Such findings suggest that people bring their own world knowledge to bear in making cognitive inferences.

The distinction between target- and category-based expectancies, between individual and group expectations, emphasizes the social significance of cognitive inferences, linking mental processing to behavior. If people internalize their group memberships, much individual behavior is guided by social norms for the relevant reference group. Furthermore, Oakes (1987) suggests that behavior can be explained in terms of people's collective properties, as well as their own characteristics. Interestingly enough, however, the attribution literature lacks a term to describe individual behavior that reflects an individual's group membership and values.

While Heider's model grounded cognitive processes in the activities of everyday life, emphasizing the more subjective aspects of attribution, subsequent attribution models assume that cognitive processing approximates scientific models of logic. Consequently these theories rely on normative criteria in assessing these processes; determining the extent to which laypeople deviate from these objective criteria has become a popular preoccupation among social psychologists. For example, the "fundamental attribution error," outlined by L. Ross (1977), suggests actors tend to attribute causality to people rather than the environment in which a behavior occurs. Additional research identifies actor–observer biases, where individuals involved in a situation tend to attribute causality to the environment, whereas observers tend to attribute causality to the actor (Nisbett & L. Ross, 1980; L. Ross, 1977). Individuals may underuse consensus information, or use the self to define consensus when we do use it. Such information can then be used to cast the self positively, or to denigrate one's self when it serves our purposes. At the group level, these patterns demonstrate a systematic tendency to attribute opinions implied by group decisions to the individual members of the group, even when the group decision was not made collectively (Allison & Messick, 1985). All of the problems associated with assessing covariation also shape attributions, because attributions rely on perceived patterns of covariation.

There is substantial empirical evidence of the effects of social categorization on attribution. Individuals not only sort information into distinct categories but they also make evaluations of these categories—evaluations that replicate societal power relations. Jost and Burgess (2000) found that low status individuals show less in-group favoritism and more in-group ambivalence than members of high status groups. High perceived legitimacy (in terms of socioeconomic success) of status differences led to increased out-group favoritism among the low status group and increased in-group favoritism among the high status group. System justification thus increases in-group ambivalence among low status groups and decreases ambivalence among high status groups. Furthermore, in experimentally manipulated situations, subjects who were assigned more powerful positions in task groups devote more attention to negative stereotypes about subordinates than those assigned subordinate positions (Rodriguez-Bailon, Moya, & Yzerbyt, 2000). An extension of this experiment manipulates perceptions about the legitimacy of this power and concludes that the threat to one's power—particularly power viewed as illegitimate—may influence individuals' impressions of subordinates in the direction of maintaining social inequalities. This line of research suggests that power arrangements, as well as consciousness of group power (Gurin, Miller, & Gurin, 1980), influence attributions by members of those groups and must be included in an explanation of those attributions.

In short, a comprehensive sociological perspective on attribution processes must specify how cognitive processing operates at multiple levels of analysis. At the micro level, the process of attribution relies on the social categorization of actors and perceivers. At the meso-level, behavior within organizations is fundamentally social, occurring in socially meaning-ful and interactive contexts; and at the level of social systems, attributions are shaped by the historical, economic, and political contexts of intergroup relations (Howard, 1990).

ISSUES IN SOCIAL COGNITION

We devote the remainder of this chapter to several significant questions in social cognition research. The first set of questions assesses the human thinker. What are the goals of thought, and how do we evaluate this process? Are accuracy, utility, or rationality appropriate or com-patible standards? Second, we discuss the epistemological status of thought, asking how much do we actively engage in thought? Is consciousness necessary for action? Next we address questions about the dynamics of cognition. Specifically, when and how do cognitions change? In our last section, we ask why sociologists should care about social cognition? That is, what is the significance of social categorization? What are the interactive, social structural, and cultural dimensions of social cognition?

What Kind of Thinker Are We?

The literatures reviewed here paint a rather schizophrenic portrait of the human thinker. While some cognitive models view social actors as methodical, rational thinkers, others portray indi-viduals as efficient, although flawed, information processors. To some degree, both views seem to be true, raising questions about the standards by which we should assess humans' cognitive abilities. For early models, following the naïve scientist view that assumes we are logical information processors, the logic and accuracy of social judgments are reasonable standards for assessing cognitive processing. In most situations, however, such objective standards do not exist—particularly if we define attributions as subjective judgments or evaluations—and accuracy seems an inappropriate rubric. Rather than accuracy and logic, what we can assess, however, is whether social judgments are adaptive or pragmatic.

Cognitive social psychologists have devoted substantial attention to cognitive errors and biases even though accuracy and logic fail to be appropriate standards for evaluating our thinking. *Cognitive errors*—such as the representativeness error and misattributions—are inaccurate predictions or judgments that depart from known facts, whereas *cognitive biases*—such as correspondence and accessibilities biases—are more systematic misrepresentations of otherwise plausible or logical attributions (see Higgins, 1998 for an overview of these errors and biases). However like most laboratory-based social psychological research, this line of research does not examine how people make social judgments in real-world situations. It should come as no surprise that in most studies of heuristics the researchers violate principles of social discourse. By presenting information that is neither informative nor relevant to the specific situation, studies provide results reflecting subjects' misapplication of communica-tion rules in artificially constructed scenarios (Schwarz, Strack, Hilton, & Naderer, 1991). Such findings and the existence of these cognitive errors and biases, however, do not mean we are necessarily faulty thinkers in everyday life, when the consequences are much more significant.

The need for efficiency, as well as other social motives, shapes our processing of social information. Fluid social interactions would be impossible if human actors were forced to process information without cognitive shortcuts. Heuristics and biases permit actors to limit the amount of data they must encode and process during an interaction, and thus, these facilitate inferential processes. Social motives, however, leave their influence on how we think. In fact, social motives may even lead us to adopt heuristics knowingly for interpersonal ends. Heimer (1988) demonstrates that individuals actively employ heuristics as rhetorical strategies to mold how the public views the importance of social problems. Such evidence portrays the human information processor as a motivated tactician, marking cognition as fundamentally pragmatic.

The Epistemological Status of Thought

A fundamental assumption of social cognition is that we actively engage in thought. Yet, considerable empirical evidence suggests otherwise, emphasizing our tendency toward *automatic* or involuntary thinking. Indeed a substantial amount of social information is encoded outside of our awareness through automatic processes. Habitual exposure to any stimulus is likely to curb active thinking and instead elicit automatic judgments. To revisit Gorham's (1999) work on media representations of race, repeated exposure to images germane to cultural stereotypes about race might lead to the automatic application of these characterizations in real life, a byproduct of "mindlessness" to borrow Langer's (1989) term. While mediated by the novelty or uniqueness of a situation and perceptions of costs, this mindless processing reduces our need to focus our attention, as well as our sensitivity to nuances in social encounters. DiMaggio's (1997) review suggests that automatic cognition relies heavily on schema and culture, whereas deliberative thinking tends to be the result of focused attention.

Given that much of our daily lives center around routinized activities, there clearly are a number of circumstances in which humans do not actively engage in thought, raising questions about what factors prompt active thinking. In novel situations for which we do not have preexisting theories or schemas, in high-effort situations in which reliance on habit or routine might prove costly, and in situations in which the outcomes are unexpected, especially when they are negative, people will actively and consciously think (Langer, 1989; Wong & Weiner, 1981). Individuals also tend to actively think when their attention is captured, when they are motivated, or when schemas are challenged. Attention increases when a problem arises in the interaction or actors become self-aware. Dijkesterhuis and van Knippenberg's (2000) work in the Netherlands, for instance, suggests the heightened self-focus produced by placing mirrors in front of their subjects can inhibit automatic stereotype activation. Motivation comes into play when the individual is dissatisfied with how things are proceeding, the status quo. In some situations, schemata do not work, so individuals engage active thinking to deal with the situation at hand.

Forces toward Cognitive Stability and Cognitive Change

As suggested by the concept of structure, cognitive structures tend to be stable. Change, while it is possible, occurs slowly. Newly gathered information is sorted into preexisting mental frameworks, but when this information is incongruent with these structures, our cognitive structures may be revised accordingly—either changing the content of our stored knowledge or the organization of such information. A. Miller and Hoffman (1999) examine stability and change in cognitive structures among White members of orthodox (e.g., Baptists, Fundamentalists, etc.) and progressive (e.g., Methodists, Presbyterians, etc.) religious groups. They test whether or not there is a "growing divisiveness" in orthodox and progressive attitudes toward issues like abortion and homosexuality, and find that there does not seem to be any real change. Pointing to key events of the 1970s and 1980s, Miller and Hoffman make the case that the distinctions between these two ideological positions have become more salient in the public sphere over the years, thereby polarizing group identification, but not fundamentally changing the underlying attitudes. While providing some evidence that the terms groups use to self-identify may change over time, their findings about the stability of attitudes point to the static nature of cognitive structures.

Concern for enduring changes in cognitive structures has lead social psychologists to focus on structures tied to how individuals view themselves, most notably the *self-concept* (see Chapter 10). While postmodernists view the self as process and, to a large degree, illusory, modern theorists tend to describe a more consistent self, one with a stable core. The contemporary self, thus merges this self, centered around a core set of elements with a phenomenal or experienced self that is fashioned by changes in social context. Salient characteristics of an audience or interactive group can alter the salience of self-relevant characteristics and hence influence their accessibility. Reoccurring shifts in the accessibility of information may lead to deeper, more enduring changes in self-concept. Looking from the outside inward, Hormuth (1990) attributes significant self-change to changes in the ecological system, drawing on an empirical study of the effects of physical relocation on the self-concept. M. Ross (1989), on the other hand, demonstrates that cognitive processes may bolster the primacy of the current self. Our current sense of self guides reinterpretation of the past. Such a perspective is consistent with Mead's view that the past and present, as well as goals for the future, emerge through our present realities.

These interpretations illustrate the dynamics of cognitive processes, those of attention, memory, and inference making, emphasizing how people may use temporal dimensions and expectations about change in their thinking. We engage in mental simulations, for example, constructing hypothetical scenarios about the future to predict outcomes in a given situation, and presumably adjusting our own behavior accordingly (Kahneman & Tversky, 1982). Simulations illustrate how individuals make comparisons, using time as a variable (i.e., comparing information at time 1 with similar information from time 2). These representations show the self in progress and may have motivational influences on inferences and behavior. M. Ross and Newby-Clark (1998) examine how people reconstruct pasts and construct futures based on theories of typical patterns of pasts and futures, rather than based on actual memories or "accurate" assessments of futures. In general, pasts receive mixed (both positive and negative) reviews, while futures receive "unequivocally positive" reviews. In terms of the past, M. Ross and Newby-Clark suggest that people are more likely to be critical of their past in situations in which implicit theories indicate there should be improvement in the characteristic over time or when the characteristic has little impact or relevance to their current sense of self. Individuals are more likely to enhance recollections of their past if normative temporal theories suggest a decline in the characteristic from then to now and when the characteristic has some impact or relevance to their current sense of self. People are more likely to focus on the positive aspects of their future. However, people who first consider negative events, subsequently take positive events less seriously. Predictions made through this process (i.e., first considering negative possibilities and then positive ones) tend to be more accurate, hinting that predictions may be self-fulfilling.

WHY SOCIOLOGISTS SHOULD CARE

What does social cognition offer sociologists? The social elements of psychological social psychology concern the content of social knowledge and how that knowledge is used. Social categorization constructs the social knowledge stored in particular cognitive structures, such as stereotypes or role schemas, and through categorization this social knowledge shapes social phenomena such as prejudice and discrimination. Cognitions are expressed through and shaped by social interaction and the symbolic, interactive, and communicative aspects of social cognition. Cognitions also underlie intergroup relations and social structures; they are created and processed both collectively as well as individually.

Intergroup Aspects of Cognition

Social categorization occurs in virtually all social encounters, whether we are aware of it or not. Tajfel, Billig, Bundy, and Flament (1971) demonstrate, time and time again, that people categorize others and themselves on the basis of trivial characteristics such as the tendency to over- or underestimate the number of dots on a dot counting test. Such group configurations—even those based on insignificant criteria—then figure prominently in decisions about the allocation of money and positive evaluations, often favoring in-group members over others. Similarly, members of a group tend to notice similarities among their own members, while being attentive to differences that distinguish them from the members of other groups. This selective information gathering allows us to generate more complex, highly detailed schemas about in-group members and less differentiated views about out-group members. Such variations in information, in turn, have an impact on the extremity of cognitive evaluations—the general rule being that more complex schemas often result in less extreme evaluations.

There is considerable evidence that social actors can and do categorize others, as well as ourselves, according to differences in a wide range of characteristics. Some characteristics trigger categorization more so than others. Highly visual differences among groups, for example, are likely to stimulate categorization. A prime illustration of this process is the controversial classroom experiment by Jane Elliott, where elementary school students were divided into two rank-ordered groups based upon eye color. On the first day of the experiment, the blue-eyed students held the privileged position, while the brown-eyed students were considered lesser in intelligence and humanity. This hierarchy was then reversed the following day, so that brown-eyed students moved to the privileged position. As this experiment on discrimination suggests, characteristics that have no inherent social meaning can become meaningful in particular social configurations, and they then may be used to define groups of people and used in making attributions about the members of those social groups. Ridgeway (1991, 2000), in a synthesis of Blau's (1977) structural theory and expectation states theory, theorizes on the maintenance of social inequality. She suggests that whenever a nominal distinction exists in conjunction with a noticeable difference in resources, the group with more resources will be assigned more status in society. This model assumes that a common set of goals is shared among groups. Belief formations, as well as status markers, are essential components of this process whereby status differentials gain social validity.

Categorization processes lead to the identification of social groups. Out of these group memberships, individuals gain a sense of identity. The self-concept is categorized or compartmentalized into social and personal identities, the relative salience of these depending on the accessibility of a category and the fit between the information present in a situation and the parameters of a stored category (Turner, 1987). Cultural boundaries between majority and minority groups also are principal components in determining the salience of category memberships (Tajfel, 1981). Such an emphasis on culture, as well as the content-based criteria of both structural and normative fit, underscore that the social content of categorization is crucial for understanding the salience of social categories and their effects.

The power arrangements that organize society are reflected in social categorizations. Individuals in positions of domination—that is, those members of groups with the discursive power to define, locate, and order others—conceive of themselves as outside any particular category (Deschamps, 1983). Their power affords them the privilege of defining themselves as specific, unique individuals, whereas members of dominated groups are viewed as undifferentiated representatives of their categories. Along these lines, and in keeping with social identity theory, social identities are likely to be more salient than personal identities for those who are dominated, not only in interactions with members of the dominant group but also within their own self-concepts. Personal identities, however, are more salient among members of dominant groups. Thus, power based upon social position has a major impact on social and self-categorizations.

In an empirical assessment of group consciousness, Gurin et al. (1980) compare group consciousness across superordinate and subordinate strata. Findings highlight that only along racial lines is group identification stronger for the subordinate stratum, with consciousness strongest among African Americans. Group consciousness was weakest among women and moderate among older people, and those in working-class positions. This study also illustrates the connection between categorization and attribution processes, as well as the possible link to social action. Both women and African Americans who look to structural explanations for gender and race disparities, tend to endorse collective action as a vehicle for overcoming these inequities, more so than those who blame their own group members. While several other studies attempt to explain identity-related action (McAdam, 1988; Snow, Burke, Worden, & Benford, 1986), the cognitive mechanism underlying these behaviors has not been specified, pointing to a direction for future research.

Cognition and Social Interaction

Cognition occurs during social interaction, as social actors play out cultural scripts. In these interactive contexts, actors actively search for meaning in the encounter—oftentimes forcing one another into negotiations to establish a joint definition for the situation. This process depends upon communication, both verbal and nonverbal, and as such, language can be seen as a product of cognitive processing of social information.

Several lines of research hint at the significance of interaction. Explanations of the risky shift phenomenon, which refers to attitude change in groups, point to the generation of persuasive arguments in a group that any one individual member might not have thought of. Social comparisons of one's own opinions with those of other group members can also generate attitude change. Both of these explanations assume some degree of communication in producing cognitive change. Group memory research suggests that groups may assign members roles in the cognitive processing of information, such that certain individuals are responsible for particular types of information (Wegner, 1986). The subsequent retrieval task requires communication of cognitions. Furthermore, these processes may influence social action, as interpretative frames communicated throughout groups prompt individuals to engage in collective activities (Snow et al., 1986). Each of these lines of research illustrates the implicit links between cognition and interaction.

Other researchers draw more explicit connections between cognition and interaction. Stryker and Gottlieb (1981), for example, focus on the interactive aspects of cognition in their attempt to examine attributive processes from a symbolic interactionist perspective. While attribution theories tend to view cognition as an intrapersonal phenomenon where individuals respond to objectively defined stimuli, symbolic interaction focuses on the interactive aspects of cognition and maintains that reality itself is socially defined and therefore indeterminate. Stryker and Gottlieb's (1981) critique of the cognitive paradigm suggests the need to devote more attention to interaction, if we are to understand attributive processes. Crittenden (1983) makes a similar point, linking research in labeling theory, accounts, and impression management to cognitive themes. In an empirical evaluation of the relationship between attribution and labeling, Howard and Levinson (1985) suggest that labeling can explain socially significant but anomalous attribution patterns: labels may be applied to actors in the absence of internal attributions of cause for behavior, pointing to reconsideration of the traditional dichotomy between internal and external attributions.

Impression management also plays an important role in attribution. In communicative interactions, social actors make claims, which ultimately may be instrumental in fashioning observers' attributional conclusions about a particular individual. Self-serving biases, those motivated by the desire to positively influence public evaluations or to "save face," may figure prominently in attributive processes, as well as guide behavior (Bradley, 1978; Lindenfield, 1994). At the individual level, impression management techniques may take the form of "passing," or masking stigmatized identities with more socially acceptable ones (Goffman, 1963; Renfrow, 2001). At the group level, as Pitchford's (2001) work on Welsh nationalists shows, impression management techniques may allow groups to challenge stereotypes and create new collective identities through a process of "image-making." Welsh nationalists employ historical and cultural symbols to create positive, alternative images of their group by linking claims about themselves to dominant values in society. These claims are met with resistance, and out of these conflicts new collective identities take shape, illustrating how groups engage in impression management techniques to overcome stigma.

Because of our reliance on language for communication during social encounters, language has become central to the study of attribution. We use language both to engage in self-interaction—that is, as a way of thinking about and dealing with ideas internally—and as a vehicle to communicate with others. Emphasizing the link between everyday communication in interaction and the development of everyday explanations, Hilton (1990) uses a conversational framework to demonstrate how causal explanations are hypothesized to occur through communication. Looking at the changing goals in everyday conversation and how these goals allow conversations to move away from prototypical scenarios, Lindenfield (1994) finds that actors may initiate an encounter with predetermined goals in mind (i.e., economic exchange) and in keeping with societal norms that govern such transactions, but conversations do not always follow the model. Thus, new goals (i.e., saving face) may take precedence and direct action. Undoubtedly, explanations are offered and sought when unexpected things occur; they can also serve to bolster preexisting expectations. Taken together, these studies show that ordinary language is fundamentally pragmatic.

Language is one of the primary tools of human communication and as such has an impact on social cognition. Semin (1995, 2000) argues that our limited knowledge about the connection between social behavior and intrapyschological processes is the result of our inability to use language as an analytic tool in social psychology. He urges us toward a shift from the individual as the unit of analysis to language, which would help create a more *social* social cognition. To illustrate the importance of language in understanding cognitive processes, he demonstrates how different types of words may trigger different types of cognitive responses: individuals recall certain word types (subject vs. object) in stimulus sentences more than others. Thus, understanding social interaction and how it is maintained depends upon our understanding of language properties.

Conversations that occur in social encounters are useful for studying causal attribution. According to Hewstone (1983), the strategies we use to describe events often carry implicit attributions. More precisely, the way we present a phenomenon in words often has implications for how the event is explained. Thus, person attributions, for example, are more likely to follow accomplishment and action verbs, whereas stimulus attributions are associated with emotion and opinion verbs. As instrumental social actors, we may deliberately choose our words in ways that allow us to manipulate other people's perceptions.

Furthermore, language can communicate information about social categories. Court transcripts illustrate this point, by showing that complainants using a "powerful" linguistic style were awarded higher damages (Lind, Erickson, Conley, & O'Barr, 1978). The size of this effect was largely determined by interactions between the gender of the lawyers and witnesses, and the linguistic styles they used. Moreover, Tajfel and Turner (1986) suggest that language aids social categorization because the terms we use to designate groups influence our perception of self and others. That is, the category labels we use to organize information—to sort individuals in this case—are artifacts of the language we use and, as such, are a linguistic accomplishment (Potter & Wetherell, 1987).

Thus, language provides the basis for both cognition and communication. Indeed, cognition, fundamentally, is communication. Through cognitive processing of social information, we are able to communicate with one another. These communications become part of our knowledge structures as well as a part of the larger cultural repertoires of society.

Individual and Social Structure

While language and communication emphasize both the intrapersonal and interactive components of social cognition, thoughts are also processed collectively at the macro level. The collective processes have a significant history in the sociological tradition, beginning with the work of Emile Durkheim. In his work on collective representations, Durkheim (1898) posited that social facts are independent of individual consciousness. Such representations, although they emerge from individual-level interactive contexts, are distinct from individual representations (Augustinos & Inness, 1990). Such social representations of knowledge are transformed into common-sense understandings through communicative interactions, in which individuals interpret the content of these representations by relying on socially meaningful categories (Hewstone, 1989). They provide a framework for the processing of information and the stimulation of cognitive inferences. Social representations also cast time as a variable, in contrast to the more static concept of schemas. Some representations tend to be distributed throughout society and across generations but at very slow rates—cultural representations for example—while others tend to spread rapidly but do not persist over time—for example, fashion trends (Sperber, 1985).

A prime example of this collective information processing includes societal accounts of social problems, such as racial and gender inequality, unemployment, and poverty. While most Western countries attribute unemployment to societal factors, half of Feagin's (1972) U.S. sample used individualistic explanations for poverty. The degree to which individualism influences societal accounts varies substantially by country, reflecting the need to incorporate the role of culture into our studies of cognitive processing (Pandey, Sinha, Prekash, & Tirupathi, 1982).

Cross-Cultural Perspectives

While the tide is beginning to turn, North America remains the focus of most social psychological research, embedding our knowledge of social processes in our own cultural understandings. Only in recent years, in the wake of what Parker (1989) calls the "crisis" years, have self-examination and disciplinary reflection impelled researchers to consider the cultural limitations of our social psychological understandings. Critiques following this move emphasize the role dominant ideologies in the United States have played in shaping the discipline (Sampson, 1977), while others suggest we treat our findings not as universal truths, but as unique historical events that are contingent upon specific social conditions (Gergen & Gergen, 1984). Both arguments have sparked research that explicitly tests the cross-cultural validity of key social psychological phenomena. Yet, building a cross-cultural focus is still one of the challenges facing social psychology today; it is essential in forging micro- macro-links (Cook, 2000).

One branch of cross-cultural research examines the consistency of cognitive structures across geographic space and national boundaries. Wagner and colleagues (1999) review Markova's recent work assessing whether or not the values of democracy and individualism (i.e., freedom, agency, and individual rights and responsibilities)—those rejected by many communist regimes—are endorsed by the residents of formerly communist countries, after the fall of these regimes. Findings suggest that these values, remnants of a shared European heritage, persist in these countries despite the intervention of communist ideologies. Such evidence suggests cognitive structures may be shared across cultures and that they endure over time.

J. Miller's (1984) comparative study of attributions follows a second line of research focusing on the influence of culture on cognitive processes, comparing attributions made by subjects in the United States and India. J. Miller found that as they become older, subjects in the United States tend to use dispositional attributions more so than Hindus, who tend to rely on predominantly contextual attributions. The cultural limitations of the fundamental attribution error—that is, the tendency of actors to attribute cause to individuals rather than to situations—are apparent from this study. Also noting cultural variation in social psychological processes, Shweder and Bourne (1982) demonstrate that adults in the West place emphasis on being an individual, whereas non-Westerners do not distinguish the person from the social role. Markus and Kitayama (1991) find a similar focus on the interdependence of roles in establishing personhood typical of many Asian cultures. These lines of research speak to the cultural boundedness of our key theories of attribution, each of which assumes the concept of a person distinct from his/her environment and other actors. While social actors in cultures throughout the world try to account for patterns in interpersonal communication and behavior, the explanations developed reflect their own culturally shared understandings. Current research continues to demonstrate that the Western world may be extreme in its individualistic emphasis on personality and individual capacities.

Cognition shapes and is shaped by interactions among social groups. As globalization and expansion bring social groups together, individuals are confronted with collective understandings much different than their own, at times leading to the assimilation of new ideas and ways of doing things into one's own cultural repertoire. If globalization tends to homogenize cultures, what are the implications for cognitive structures and processes? In a study of *glocalization*, the process through which commercial goods from abroad enter local cultures, Raz (1999) demonstrates that both the cultural materials transmitted, as well as the locality, are transformed. Raz's empirical work examines the transmission and adaptation of Disney institutional culture from the original Disneyland in California to Tokyo Disneyland. Drawing upon symbolic interaction, glocalization and the idea of looking-glass cultures, Raz outlines how the values of the Disney "smile factory" become part of institutional culture within the new locality through a process of Disney socialization. Furthermore, Raz describes how the new locality reshapes the imported cultural materials by examining how objects like Mickey Mouse are reinvented such that they become authentically Japanese in the minds of Japanese children. Such processes highlight the impact cross-cultural interaction has on social psychological processes.

As these studies illustrate, cross-cultural research in social cognition forces researchers to think about their own and other cultures and, at a more fundamental level, to define the concept of culture itself. An understanding of culture has not been necessary to study what are assumed to be cross-cultural similarities. Cross-cultural difference, however, can be understood only through a thorough understanding of the respective cultures at hand. Processes of globalization, as well as the impetus to reexamine the meaning of *culture*, make cross-cultural studies of social psychological processes such as cognition all the more important.

CONCLUSION

The social psychology of the 21st century is more sophisticated—both methodologically and theoretically—than ever before. Social cognition, the study of information processing and knowledge creation, continues to be one of the leading specialty areas within the discipline. Recent technological advancements allow social scientists to more fully explore the nuances of individual-level cognitive processing. Moreover, our willingness to embrace less traditional methodological approaches enhances our ability to assess the formation and dissemination of collective representations shared among particular societies. Increased attention to geographic areas beyond the borders of the United States plays an important role in shaping the future of social cognition, and social psychology in general, by assessing the influence of culture in thought processes.

While social cognition reflects its roots in the more psychological strands of social psychology, the study of cognition continues to feel the touch of more sociologically minded social scientists as well. Their major contribution is linking social behaviors, phenomena such as stratification, social movements, and intergroup relations, with individual thought, focusing on how cognitive processes allow individuals and groups to create, perpetuate, and justify the inequalities found in their society. The cognitive limitations of individuals under the rubric of cognitive efficiency lead social actors to rely on mental structures and common-sense theories to process information mindlessly. These mental shortcuts often make our judgments prone to numerous errors and biases, which play out in the social world through discriminatory behaviors such as racial profiling.

Moving away from this overly deterministic view of society, more critical social psychologists are beginning to emphasize the role social psychological knowledge can play in eradicating social problems such as race and gender inequalities by increasing our awareness of these tendencies. As research demonstrates, self-awareness, as well as motivations to change the status quo, disrupts the automatic processing of information, allowing individuals to think actively. Research agendas by Devine, Plant, and Harrison (1999)—who outline multiple avenues for negating negative attributions directed toward individuals living with AIDS—and G. Cohen, Steele, and Ross (1999)—who demonstrate that "wise" mentoring can overcome racialized reactions to criticism and challenge the learned helplessness of racial minorities—identify two fronts on which this battle must be fought and speak to social psychology's capacity to foster social change. How individuals will use this knowledge, what strategies they will use and what the outcomes will be, remain to be seen; we urge social psychologists and sociologists alike to use our research to promote the goals of social justice so crucial to the global future.

REFERENCES

Allison, Scott T., & Messick, David M. (1985). The group attribution error. *Journal of Experimental Social Psychology, 21*, 563–579.

Augustinos, Martha, & Inness, John Michael. (1990). Towards an integration of social representations and social schemas theory. *British Journal of Social Psychology, 29*(3), 213–231.

Berger, Joseph, Conner, Thomas L., & Fisek, M. Hamit. (1974). *Expectation states theory.* Cambridge, MA: Winthrop.

Berger, Joseph, Fisek, M. Hamit, Norman, Robert Z., & Zelditch, Morris, Jr. (1977). *Status characteristics in social interaction.* New York: Elsevier.

Blau, Peter M. (1977). *Inequality and heterogeneity: A primitive theory of social structure.* New York: Free Press.

Blau, Peter M. (1964). *Exchange and power in social life.* New York: Wiley.

Blumer, Herbert. (1969). *Symbolic interactionism: Perspective and method.* Englewood Cliffs, NJ: Prentice Hall.

Bradley, Gifford Weary. (1978). Self-serving biases in the attribution process: A reexamination of the fact or fiction question. *Journal of Personality and Social Psychology, 36*, 56–71.

Cantor, Nancy, & Mischel Walter. (1979). Prototypes in person perception. In L. Berkowitz (Ed.), *Advances in experimental social psychology* (vol. 12, pp. 3–52). New York: Academic.

Cast, Alicia D., Stets, Jan E., & Burke, Peter J. (1999). Does the self conform to the views of others? *Social Psychology Quarterly, 62*(1), 68–82.

Cherry, Frances. (1995). *The "stubborn particulars" of social psychology.* New York: Routledge.

Cohen, Claudia E. (1981). Person categories and social perception: Testing some boundaries of the processing effects of prior knowledge. *Journal of Personality and Social Psychology, 40*, 441–452.

Cohen, Geoffrey L., Steele, Claude M., & Ross, Lee D. (1999). The mentor's dilemma: Providing critical feedback across the racial divide. *Personality and Social Psychology Bulletin, 25*(10), 1302–1318.

Condor, Susan, & Antaki, Charles. (1997). Discourse studies: A multidisciplinary introduction. In Teun A. van Dijk (Ed.), *Discourse as structure and process* (pp. 320–347). London: Sage.

Cook, Karen S. (2000). Advances in the microfoundations of sociology: Recent developments and new challenges for social psychology. *Contemporary Sociology, 29*(5), 685–692.

Crittenden, Kathleen S. (1983). Sociological aspects of attribution. *Annual Review of Sociology, 9*, 425–446.

Deschamps, Jean-Claude. (1983). Social attribution. In J. Jaspars, F. D. Fincham, & M. Hewstone (Eds.), *Attribution theory and research: Conceptual, developmental and social dimensions* (pp. 223–240). New York: Academic.

Devine, Patricia G., Plant, E. Ashby, & Harrison, Kristen. (1999). The problem of "us" versus "them" and AIDS stigma. *American Behavioral Scientist, 42*(7), 1208–1224.

Dijkersterhuis, Ap, & van Knippenberg, Ad. (2000). Behavioral indecision: Effects of self-focus on automatic behavior. *Social Cognition, 18*(1), 55–74.

DiMaggio, Paul. (1997). Culture and cognition. *Annual Review of Sociology, 23*, 263–287.

Dreyfus, Hubert L. (1992). *What computers still can't do.* Cambridge, MA: MIT Press.

Durkheim, Emile. (1898). Representations individuelles et representations collectives. *Revue de Metaphysique et de Morale, 6*, 273–302.

Feagin, Joe. (1972). Poverty: We still believe that God helps them who help themselves. *Psychology Today, 6*, 101–129.

Fiske, Susan T., & Taylor, Shelley E. (1991). *Social cognition* (2nd ed.). New York: McGraw-Hill.

Gergen, Kenneth J., & Gergen, Mary M. (Eds.). (1984). *Historical social psychology.* Hillsdale, NJ: Erlbaum.

Goffman, Erving. (1959). *The presentation of self in everyday life.* Garden City, NY: Doubleday.

Goffman, Erving. (1963). *Stigma*. Englewood Cliffs, NJ: Prentice-Hall.

Gorham, Bradley. (1999). Stereotypes in the media: So what? *Howard Journal of Communications, 10(4)*, 229–247.

Gurin, Patricia, Miller, Arthur H., & Gurin, Gerald. (1980). Stratum identification and consciousness. *Social Psychology Quarterly, 43*, 30–47.

Hamill, R., Wilson, Timothy D., & Nisbett, Richard E. (1980). Insensitivity to sample bias: Generalizing from atypical cases. *Journal of Personality and Social Psychology, 39*, 578–589.

Hamilton, David L., & Gifford, R. K. (1976). Illusory correlation in interpersonal perception: A cognitive basis of stereotypic judgments. *Journal of Experimental Social Psychology, 12*, 392–407.

Heider, Fritz. (1958). *The psychology of interpersonal relations*. New York: Wiley.

Heimer, Carol A. (1988). Social structure, psychology, and the estimation of risk. *Annual Review of Sociology, 14*, 491–519.

Hewstone, Miles. (1983). The role of language in attribution processes. In J. Jaspars, F. D. Fincham, & M. Hewstone (Eds.), *Attribution theory and research: Conceptual, developmental, and social dimensions* (pp. 241–259). London: Academic.

Hewstone, Miles. (1989). *Causal attribution: From cognitive processes to collective beliefs*. Oxford, UK: Blackwell.

Higgins, E. Tory. (2000). Social cognition: Learning about what matters in the social world. *European Journal of Social Psychology, 30(1)*, 3–39.

Higgins, E. Tory. (1998). The aboutness principle: A pervasive influence on human inference. *Social Cognition, 16(1)*, 173–198.

Hilton, Denis J. (1990). Conversational processes and causal explanation. *Psychological Bulletin, 107*, 65–81.

Hormuth, Stefan E. (1990). *The ecology of the self: Relocation and self-concept change*. Cambridge, UK: Cambridge University Press.

Howard, Judith A. (1990). A sociological framework of cognition. *Advances in Group Processes, 7*, 75–103.

Howard, Judith A., & Hollander, Jocelyn. (1997). *Gendered situations, gendered selves*. Thousand Oaks, CA: Sage.

Howard, Judith A., & Levinson, Randy. (1985). The overdue courtship of attribution and labeling. *Social Psychology Quarterly, 48*, 191–202.

Huguet, Pascal, & Latane, Bibb. (1996). Social representations as dynamic social impact. *Journal of Communication, 46(4)*, 57–63.

Ibanez, Tomas. (1997). Why a critical social psychology? In Tomas Ibanez & Lupicinio Iniguez (Eds.), *Critical social psychology* (pp. 27–41). Thousand Oaks, CA: Sage.

Inman, Mary L., Huerta, Jennifer, & Oh, Sie. (1998). Perceiving discrimination: The role of prototypes and norm violation. *Social Cognition, 16(4)*, 418–450.

Jones, Edward E., & Davis, Keith E. (1965). From acts to dispositions: The attribution process in person perception. In L. Berkowitz (Ed.), *Advances in experimental social psychology* (vol. 2, pp. 220–266). New York: Academic.

Jones, Edward E., & McGillis, Dan. (1976). Correspondent inferences and the attribution cube: A comparative reappraisal. In J. H. Harvey, W. Ickes, & R. F. Kidd (Eds.), *New directions in attribution research* (Vol. 1, pp. 389–420). Hillsdale, NJ: Erlbaum.

Jost, John T., & Burgess, Diana. (2000). Attitudinal ambivalence and the conflict between group and system justification motives in low status groups. *Personality and Social Psychology Bulletin, 26(3)*, 293–305.

Kahneman, Daniel, & Tversky, Amos. (1982). The simulation heuristic. In D. Kahneman, P. Slovic, & A. Tversky (Eds.), *Judgment under uncertainty: Heuristics and biases* (pp. 201–208). New York: Cambridge University Press.

Kelley, Harold H. (1967). Attribution theory in social psychology. In D. Levine (Ed.), *Nebraska Symposium on Motivation* (vol. 15, pp. 192–240). Lincoln: University of Nebraska Press.

Kelley, Harold H. (1973). The processes of causal attribution. *American Psychologist, 28*, 107–128.

Langer, Ellen J. (1989). *Mindfulness*. Reading, MA: Addison-Wesley.

Leach, Colin Wayne. (1998). Toward a social psychology of racism? Comments on the parallels between social cognition and the "new racism" by N. Hopkins, S. Reicher and M. Levine. *British Journal of Social Psychology, 37(2)*, 255–258.

Levy, Becca. (1996). Improving memory in old age through implicit self-stereotyping. *Journal of Personality and Social Psychology, 71(6)*, 1092–1107.

Lind, E. A., Erickson, B. E., Conley, J., & O'Barr, W. M. (1978). Social attributions and conversational style in trial testimony. *Journal of Personality and Social Psychology, 36*, 1558–1567.

Lindenfield, Jacqueline. (1994). Cognitive processes and social norms in natural discourse at the marketplace. *Journal of Pragmatics, 22(5)*, 465–476.

Markus, Hazel, & Kitayama, Shinobu. (1991). Culture and the self: Implications for cognition, emotion, and motivation. *Psychological Review, 98*, 224–253.

Martin, Emily. (1991). The egg and the sperm: How science has constructed a romance based on stereotypical male–female roles. *Signs, 16*(3), 485–501.

Marx, Karl, & Engels, Friedrich. (1947). In R. Pascal (Ed.), *The German ideology.* New York: International.

McAdam, Doug. (1988). *Freedom summer.* New York: Oxford University Press.

McGuire, William J., McGuire, C., Child, P., & Fujioka, T. (1978). Salience of ethnicity in the spontaneous self-concept as a function of one's ethnic distinctiveness in the social environment. *Journal of Personality and Social Psychology, 36,* 511–520.

Mead, George Herbert. (1934). *Mind, self and society.* Chicago: University of Chicago Press.

Miller, Joan G. (1984). Culture and the development of everyday explanation. *Journal of Personality and Social Psychology, 46,* 961–978.

Miller, Alan S., & Hoffman, John P. (1999). The growing divisiveness: Culture wars or a war of words? *Social Forces, 78*(2), 721–745.

Moscovici, Serge. (1981). On social representations. In J. P. Forgas (Ed.), *Social cognition: Perspectives on everyday understanding* (pp. 181–209). London: Academic.

Nisbett, Richard E., & Ross, Lee. (1980). *Human inference: Strategies and shortcomings of social judgment.* Englewood Cliffs, NJ: Prentice Hall.

Oakes, Penelope. (1987). The salience of social categories. In J. C. Turner (Ed.), *Rediscovering the Social Group: A Self-Categorization Theory* (pp. 117–141). Oxford, UK: Blackwell.

Operario, Don, & Fiske, Susan. (1999). Social cognition permeates social psychology: Motivated mental processes guide the study of human social behavior. *Asian Journal of Social Psychology, 2*(1), 63–78.

Pandey, J., Sinha, Y., Prekash, A., & Triupathi, R. C. (1982). Right–left political ideologies and attributions of the causes of poverty. *European Journal of Social Psychology, 12,* 327–331.

Parker, Ian. (1989). *The crisis in modern social psychology—and how to end it.* London: Routledge.

Pitchford, Susan R. (2001). Image-making movements: Welsh nationalism and stereotype transformation. *Sociological Perspectives, 44*(1), 45–65.

Potter, Jonathan. (1998). Cognition as context (Whose context?). *Research on Language and Social Interaction, 31*(1), 29–44.

Potter, Jonathan, & Litton, Ian. (1985). Some problems underlying the theory of social representations. *British Journal of Social Psychology, 24,* 81–90.

Potter, Jonathan, & Wetherell, Margaret. (1987). *Discourse and social psychology: Beyond attitudes and behaviour.* London: Sage.

Raz, Aviad E. (1999). Glocalization and symbolic interactionism. *Studies in Symbolic Interaction, 22,* 3–16.

Renfrow, Daniel G. (2001). *Playing parts: An examination of "passing" in everyday life.* Paper presented at the Annual Meeting of the Pacific Sociological Association. San Francisco, CA.

Ridgeway, Cecilia. (2000). The formation of status beliefs: Improving status construction theory. *Advances in Group Processes, 17,* 77–102.

Ridgeway, Cecilia. (1991). The social construction of status value: Gender and other nominal characteristics. *Social Forces, 70,* 367–386.

Rodriguez-Bailon, Rosa, Moya, Miguel, & Yzerbyt, Vincent. (2000). Why do superiors attend to negative stereotypic information about their subordinates? Effects of power legitimacy on social perception. *European Journal of Social Psychology, 30*(5), 651–671.

Ross, Lee. (1977). The intuitive psychologist and his shortcomings: Distortions in the attribution process. In L. Berkowitz (Ed.), *Advances in experimental social psychology* (vol. 10, pp. 174–221). New York: Academic.

Ross, Michael. (1989). Relation of implicit theories to the construction of personal histories. *Psychological Review, 96,* 341–357.

Ross, Michael, & Newby-Clark, Ian R. (1998). Construing the past and future. *Social Cognition, 16,* 133–150.

Sampson, E. E. (1977). Psychology and the American ideal. *Journal of Personality and Social Psychology, 35,* 767–782.

Schneider, David J. (1991). Social cognition. *Annual Review of Psychology, 42,* 527–561.

Schwarz, Norbert, Strack, Fritz, Hilton, Denis, & Naderer, Gabi. (1991). Base rates, representativeness, and the logic of conversation: The contextual relevance of "irrelevant" information. *Social Cognition, 9,* 67–84.

Semin, Gun R. (2000). Agenda 2000—Communication: Language as an implementational device for cognition. *European Journal of Social Psychology, 30,* 595–612.

Semin, Gun R. (1995). Interfacing language and social cognition. *Journal of Language and Social Psychology, 14*(1–2), 182–194.

Shweder, R. A., & Bourne, E. J. (1982). Does the concept of the person vary cross-culturally? In R. S. Shweder & R. A. Levine (Eds.), *Culture theory: Essays on mind, self and emotion* (pp. 158–199). Cambridge, UK: Cambridge University Press.

Snow, David A., Burke, Rochford E. Jr., Worden, Steven K., & Benford, Robert D. (1986). Frame alignment processes, micromobilization, and movement participation. *American Sociological Review, 51*, 464–481.

Sperber, D. (1985). Anthropology and psychology: Towards an epidemiology of representations. *Man, 20*, 73–89.

Stryker, Sheldon, & Gottlieb, Avi. (1981). Attribution theory and symbolic interactionism: A comparison. In J. H. Harvey, W. Ickes, & R. F. Kidd (Eds.), *New directions in attribution research* (vol. 3, pp. 425–458). Hillsdale, NJ: Erlbaum.

Tajfel, Henri. (1981). *Human groups and social categories: Studies in social psychology.* Cambridge, UK: Cambridge University Press.

Tajfel, Henri, Billig, Michael., Bundy, R. P., & Flament, C. (1971). Social categorization and intergroup behavior. *European Journal of Social Psychology, 1*, 149–177.

Tajfel, Henri, & Turner, John C. (1986). The social identity theory of intergroup behavior. In S. Worchel & W. G. Austin (Eds.), *The psychology of intergroup relations* (pp. 7–24). Chicago: Nelson-Hall.

Thibaut, John W., & Kelley, Harold H. (1959). *The social psychology of groups.* New York: John Wiley.

Turner, John C. (1987). *Rediscovering the social group: A self-categorization theory.* New York: Blackwell.

Tversky, Amos, & Kahneman, Daniel. (1974). Judgment under uncertainty: Heuristics and biases. *Science, 185*, 1124–1131.

van Dijk, Teun A. (1996). Discourse, cognition and society. *Discourse and Society, 7(1)*, 5–6.

Wagner, Wolfgang, Duveen, Gerard, Farr, Robert, Jovchelovitch, Sandra, Lorenzi-Cioldi, Fabio, Markova, Ivana, & Rose, Diana. (1999). Theory and method of social representations. *Asian Journal of Social Psychology, 2(1)*, 95–125.

Weber, Max. (1968). *Economy and society.* New York: Bedminster.

Wegner, D. 1986. Transactive memory: A contemporary analysis of the group mind. In B. Mullen and G. R. Goethals (Eds.), *Theories of group behavior* (pp. 185–208). New York: Springer-Verlag.

Wong, P. T. P., & Weiner, Bernard. (1981). When people ask "why" questions, and the heuristics of attributional search. *Journal of Personality and Social Psychology, 40*, 650–663.

Zerubavel, Eviatar. (1996). Lumping and splitting: Notes on social classification. *Sociological Forum, 11(3)*, 421–433.

CHAPTER 12

Ideologies, Values, Attitudes, and Behavior

GREGORY R. MAIO
JAMES M. OLSON
MARK M. BERNARD
MICHELLE A. LUKE

History is replete with cases where people have worked hard as individuals and groups for causes they regarded as important; these efforts have ranged in intensity from simple letter-writing campaigns to extreme acts of violence. An example of the violent end of the spectrum occurred in the terror attacks on September 11, 2001. In the attacks, Muslim extremists killed thousands and sacrificed their own lives for a cause that the extremists regarded as important. Since then, public speculation about the reasons for the attacks has varied. Some explanations focus on psychological attributes of the extremists themselves. In particular, the extremists' actions have been regarded as an inevitable consequence of their peculiar mix of Islam and conservative ideology, their lack of respect for innocent human beings, and their hatred toward the United States. In other words, the extremists' behavior has been partly regarded as a product of their ideologies, values, and attitudes.

Such explanations do not apply only to acts of terror. These explanations can account for the behaviors of most people, in circumstances ranging from voting during elections to protesting at

GREGORY R. MAIO, MARK M. BERNARD, AND MICHELLE A. LUKE • School of Psychology, Cardiff University, Cardiff, Wales, UK CF10 3YG   JAMES M. OLSON • Department of Psychology, University of Western Ontario, London, Ontario, Canada N6A 5C2

Handbook of Social Psychology, edited by John Delamater. Kluwer Academic/Plenum Publishers, New York, 2003.

a rally. This chapter describes abundant social psychological research supporting the specula-tion that such behaviors and behaviors in general are influenced by three psychological constructs: ideologies, values, and attitudes. By the term "attitudes," we mean tendencies to evaluate an object positively or negatively (Bem, 1972; Eagly & Chaiken, 1998; Olson & Zanna, 1993; Petty, Wegener, & Fabrigar, 1997). Values are regarded as abstract ideals (e.g., freedom, helpfulness) that function as important guiding principles (Rokeach, 1973; Schwartz, 1992), and ideologies are systems of attitudes and values that are organized around an abstract theme (e.g., liberalism; Converse, 1964; McGuire, 1985). We will first discuss how these constructs are interrelated, followed by detailed descriptions of each construct and how they predict behavior. Finally, we will describe directions for future research.

CONCEPTUAL SIMILARITIES AND DIFFERENCES

Our definitions make evident that ideologies, values, and attitudes differ in levels of abstrac-tion. People can possess attitudes toward any concrete object (e.g., milk, pizza) or abstract issue (e.g., abortion, censorship) in their environment. In contrast, values focus entirely on abstract ideals, such as freedom, helpfulness, and equality. Ideologies are even more abstract than single values, because ideologies subsume sets of values and attitudes. For example, a liberal ideology may encompass the values of freedom and helpfulness, together with unfavorable attitudes toward censorship and reduced social spending. In addition, values and ideologies are more prescriptive than attitudes. For instance, people may not feel that they have an obligation to buy a flavor of ice cream that they like. In contrast, if people value helpfulness, they should feel obliged to help an ailing person (Feather, 1995; Maio & Olson, 1998). Similarly, people may feel duty-bound to vote in a manner that is consistent with their political ideologies.

Despite the differences between ideologies, values, and attitudes, they share several conceptual features. First, all of these constructs are evaluative—they reflect positivity or negativity toward an entity. Second, all of these constructs are subjective. That is, they reflect how a person sees the world and not necessarily how the world actually exists. For example, a person who values equality may desire equal treatment of others, even if such treatment is rare in the real-world. Third, all of the constructs may exist at nonconscious and conscious levels—they can be the focus of our attention on some occasions, but not on other occasions (see below). Finally, none of the constructs exist in isolation from each other. For example, people's ideologies should affect their values, which should shape their attitudes. Similarly, people's attitudes may influence their values, which may influence their ideologies. Thus, there are bidirectional causal influences between these constructs.

Although a particular concrete attitude may elicit changes in higher order values and ideologies, researchers have focused on the influences from the highest level of abstraction (ideologies) to the lowest level of abstraction (attitudes). This direction of influence is partic-ularly interesting because it would involve a mechanism wherein even small changes in the most abstract ideologies and values lead to numerous changes in related, lower level attitudes. This mechanism can be illustrated by considering the effects of changing the extent to which people value equality. If people begin to attach less importance to this value, they might change their attitudes toward a variety of issues, ranging from affirmative action to immigration quo-tas and attitudes toward equal rights organizations. This potential breadth of effects makes ideologies and values powerful constructs.

Ideologies

Conservatism and liberalism are the most commonly examined ideologies in social psychological research. These ideologies are theoretical constructions. Conservative ideologies are hypothesized to subsume attitudes and values that promote freedom and self-enhancement, whereas liberal ideologies are hypothesized to subsume attitudes and values that promote benevolence and universal rights (e.g., Kerlinger, 1984). If these hypotheses are correct, then people should tend to endorse either conservative attitudes or liberal attitudes, but not both.

Interestingly, however, people's actual conservative and liberal attitudes do not follow this simple pattern (Converse, 1964; Fleishman, 1986). People who endorse so-called conservative attitudes do not always disavow so-called liberal attitudes, and this lack of cohesion is most evident among people who lack knowledge about political issues (Lavine, Thomsen, & Gonzales, 1997; Lusk & Judd, 1988). Thus, the conservative–liberal ideology lacks empirical support for many people.

Are there ideologies that are more strongly substantiated? Researchers have found at least two distinct ideological dimensions within political attitudes: compassion versus competition and moral regulation versus individual freedom (e.g., Ashton, Danso, Maio, Esses, Bond, and Keung 2003; Boski, 1993; Ferguson, 1939). For example, Ashton et al. (2003) discovered these dimensions in analyses of Americans' responses to a 1996 Gallup Poll, which was designed to tap a variety of political attitudes. Favorable attitudes toward defense spending, imposing a minimum wage, and implementing busing to achieve racial balance in schools were among many attitudes that positively defined the compassion versus competition factor. Favorable attitudes toward a welfare cutoff after two years, the death penalty, and a freeze on immigration were among many attitudes that negatively defined this factor. The moral regulation versus individual freedom factor was positively defined by favorable attitudes toward a ban on abortions, prayer in public schools, and teaching creationism in schools (among other attitude items). Favorable attitudes toward doctor-assisted suicide, legalization of homosexual marriages, and legalization of marijuana were among many items that negatively defined this factor. Importantly, these researchers rediscovered the same dimensions in analyses of political attitudes outside of the United States, using many new attitude items that were not in the American Gallup poll.

It is also possible to discover important ideologies in nonpolitical attitudes. For example, intergroup attitudes may reflect several ideological dimensions, including multiculturalism versus color-blindness (Wolsko, Park, Judd, & Wittenbrink, 2000) and individualism versus communalism (Katz & Hass, 1988). In addition, diverse ideologies have been examined in studies of attitudes toward gender roles (Spence, 1993), body weight and obesity (Quinn & Crocker, 1999), ways of life (de St. Aubin, 1996), and violence (Cohen & Nisbett, 1994). Also, cross-cultural research has distinguished between ideologies that emphasize individual pursuits and ideologies that emphasize collective concerns (e.g., Triandis, 1995). As described in our concluding section, an important challenge for future research is to show how these various ideologies are interrelated.

Values

Many conceptualizations of values have been proposed (Rohan, 2000). Although these conceptualizations often regard values as abstract ideals that guide thoughts and behaviors, some of the models have demonstrated methodological problems (Kluckhohn & Strodtbeck, 1961; Morris, 1956), low contemporary relevance (Allport, Vernon, & Lindzey, 1960;

Bales & Crouch, 1969), a lack of reliability and validity (e.g., Harding & Phillips, 1986; Lorr, Suziedelis, & Tonesk, 1973), or have been investigated in primarily one applied context (e.g., consumer preferences; Kahle, 1996). Below, we focus on three models that have received extensive attention and support in studies of many value-relevant topics and across cultures.

INGLEHART. This model explicitly begins from both a psychological and sociological perspective. From a psychological perspective, Inglehart's (1971, 1997) model is based on Maslow's (1970) theory that people possess basic needs and distinct higher order needs. Basic needs are concerned with safety, survival, and sustenance, whereas higher order needs are concerned with belongingness, esteem, and self-fulfillment. From a sociological perspective, Inglehart argues that Western people's values have changed significantly since the beginning of the previous century. He claims that the rise of economic development and the rise of the welfare state has led to less obsession with materialistic needs, such as economic and physical security, and more concern about postmaterialistic needs, such as freedom, self-expression, and quality of life. Thus, people's values should reflect this change in emphasis.

Inglehart (1997) has tested this reasoning by asking participants from over 43 societies to rank several materialist values (e.g., fight crime, maintain economy) and postmaterialist values (e.g., give people more say in government decisions, protect free speech) according to their importance for their country. Factor analyses of participants' responses revealed a single dimension ranging from materialist to postmaterialist goals (Abramson & Inglehart, 1995). In addition, as predicted by Inglehart, people born before World War II attach more importance to materialist values than do people born after the war (Inglehart, 1997). Also, as expected, people who highly rank postmaterialist values are more favorable toward many socially oriented programs, such as employment equity for women, human rights, and participation in petitions (Inglehart, 1997).

ROKEACH. According to Rokeach (1973, p. 5), values are "enduring beliefs that a specific mode of conduct or end-state of existence is personally or socially preferable to an opposite or converse mode of conduct or end-state of existence." This definition makes clear several important features of Rokeach's model. First, whereas Inglehart focused on people's perceptions of the values that are important for society, Rokeach's definition explicitly suggested that values can refer to oneself or to others. For example, a person may believe that he or she should be helpful, but that society should be less concerned with being helpful.

Second, Rokeach's (1973) definition regards values as enduring beliefs. Values are stable because they are learnt in an absolute manner—we are taught to accept values without question (see also Maio & Olson, 1998). Nonetheless, Rokeach also argues that values can change as people learn to make decisions favoring one value over another. Thus, values are at least somewhat capable of change, despite their stability.

Third, Rokeach's (1973) definition distinguishes values that refer to modes of conduct from values that refer to end-states of existence. Values that refer to modes of conduct are labeled instrumental values, and examples include helpful, loving, and obedient. Values that refer to end-states of existence are labeled terminal values, and examples include an exciting life, a world of beauty, and wisdom. According to Rokeach, this distinction is fundamental to the study of values, and there may be important functional relations between instrumental and terminal values.

In addition to citing the above attributes in his definition of values, Rokeach suggested that values are central in cognitive networks of attitudes and beliefs (see also Rosenberg, 1960, 1968). In other words, a relatively small set of social values should influence a much larger set of attitudes. For example, people who value obedience should be more favorable toward a variety of obedience-promoting policies (e.g., censorship, tough policing) and behaviors (e.g., deference to an authority, group conformity) than people who do not value obedience. Consistent with this reasoning, rankings of the importance of values predict a large variety of attitudes and behavior (e.g., Maio, Roese, Seligman, & Katz, 1996), and an intervention that causes change in a target value can influence many attitudes that are relevant to the value (Bernard, Maio, & Olson, 2001). Also, priming a value makes accessible a variety of value-relevant attitudes (Gold & Robbins, 1979; Gold & Russ, 1977; see also Gilchrist, 1995; Thomsen, Lavine, & Kounios, 1996). In fact, this value centrality may cause values to be resistant to change, because change in one value can ricochet through many connected attitudes (Rosenberg, 1960).

Rokeach (1973) also emphasized the notion that values exist in systems and not as isolated entities. He proposed that people organize their values on a continuum from the least important to the most important. For this reason, he asked participants to rank a list of values in terms of their importance, similar to Inglehart's approach. This ranking task was performed separately for 18 instrumental and 18 terminal values. Using this approach, Rokeach found that participants' rankings of their instrumental and terminal values predict their attitudes toward a wide range of attitudes, including attitudes toward civil rights, international affairs, religion, and brands of detergent. Value rankings also predicted a range of behaviors, such as joining a civil rights organization, attending church, attending antiwar protests, and even returning borrowed pencils. Thus, this approach demonstrated predictive validity.

SCHWARTZ.   Most of Rokeach's (1973) tenets are accepted by Schwartz's (1992) model of values. Schwartz regards values as abstract ideals that are important guiding principles in one's life. Consequently, Schwartz's model is congruent with notions of value stability and centrality. In addition, Schwartz's model recognizes that personal and societal values can be examined.

Nevertheless, Schwartz (1992) forms a unique typology of values, which distinguishes between three universal requirements of human existence: needs of individuals as biological organisms, requisites of coordinated social interactions, and survival needs of groups. According to Schwartz, these needs become enshrined in values that express ten types of motivation: achievement, benevolence, conformity, hedonism, power, security, self-direction, stimulation, tradition, and universalism. As shown in Figure 12-1, these values can be plotted in a circumplex structure to form four higher order value domains: conservation, openness, self-enhancement, and self-transcendence. These four higher order domains, in turn, represent two basic dimensions of value conflict. One dimension contrasts conservation values (e.g., national security) against openness values (e.g., freedom), whereas the other dimension contrasts self-enhancement (e.g., power) against self-transcendence values (e.g., helpfulness). Thus, according to the model, people who attach high importance to conservation values tend to attach less importance to openness values, whereas people who attach high importance to self-enhancement values tend to attach less importance to self-transcendence values.

This model has been tested using more than 200 samples in over 60 countries (Schwartz, 1996). Because of statistical problems when analyzing value rankings (Kerlinger, 1973; see also Maio, Roese, Seligman, & Katz, 1996), Schwartz does not utilize the ranking procedure employed by Inglehart and Rokeach. Instead, Schwartz asks participants to rate 56 values on scales from -1 (unimportant) to 7 (extremely important). The rated values include many of the 36 values examined by Rokeach, in addition to numerous others proposed by Schwartz. Analyses of these ratings have revealed patterns of correlations between values that fit the

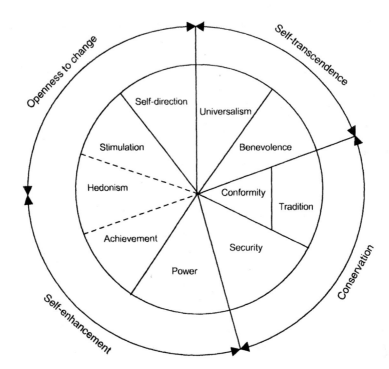

FIGURE 12-1. The circumplex model of values proposed by Schwartz. Congruent value domains (e.g., benevolence and universalism) are plotted adjacent to each other, whereas conflicting domains (e.g., benevolence and power) are plotted opposite to each other. In addition, the ten value types form four higher order domains that represent two dimensions of conflict among values. One dimension opposes conservation values and openness values, whereas the other dimension opposes self-enhancement and self-transcendence values.

circumplex structure predicted by Schwartz, such that ratings of opposing values in the model tend to be negatively correlated, whereas ratings of adjacent values in the model tend to be positively related (Schwartz, 1992, 1996). More importantly, opposing values tend to exhibit opposing relations with additional dependent variables, such as interpersonal cooperation, political party preference, readiness for social contact with an out-group, trust in institutions, attitudes toward charitable behavior, and concerns about society (Devos, Spini, & Schwartz, in press; Maio & Olson, 1995; Schwartz, 1996; Schwartz, Sagiv, & Boehnke, 2000). Thus, abundant evidence is consistent with Schwartz's typology.

Attitudes

Attitudes have been more extensively studied by social psychologists than have values and ideologies. Consequently, there are many well-founded conceptualizations of attitudes. These perspectives delineate the content of attitudes in memory (i.e., attitude structure) and the motivations that are served by attitudes (i.e., attitude function). Below, we provide a snapshot of these perspectives on attitude structure and attitude function.

ATTITUDE STRUCTURE.   There are four well-established perspectives on attitude structure (Olson & Maio, 2003). Two of these perspectives focus on the capacity of attitudes to express more basic psychological constructs, such as beliefs and emotions, and are labeled the three-component model and the belief-based model.

According to the three-component model, attitudes express feelings, beliefs, and past behaviors regarding an attitude object (Zanna & Rempel, 1988). For example, people might form a positive attitude toward participating in a rally for the environment because they enjoy rallies (affective component) and believe that the rally will help ensure more green spaces (cognitive component). More subtly, people might decide that they like to participate in the pro-environment rally because they can recall past occasions wherein they performed pro-environmental behaviors (behavioral component)—in this process, people deduce their attitude by recalling their past behavior relevant to the issue (Bem, 1972; Olson, 1990, 1992).

On the basis of the affective, cognitive, and behavioral components, people may form a general positive or negative evaluation that summarizes their responses. Once formed, these net evaluations may also shape the feelings, beliefs, and behaviors to make them more consistent with each other. Consequently, the specific components may become more similar in valence (i.e., negativity versus positivity) as experience with the attitude object increases (see Eagly & Chaiken, 1993). Thus, people who have positive attitudes toward an attitude object should often possess beliefs, feelings, and behaviors that are favorable toward the object, whereas people who have negative attitudes toward an attitude object should often possess beliefs, feelings, and behaviors that are unfavorable toward the object.

Based on this model, research sometimes assesses separately the overall attitude, attitude-relevant feelings, attitude-relevant beliefs, and attitude-relevant behaviors. The overall attitude can be measured using scales that ask respondents to indicate the extent to which they feel favorable versus unfavorable toward the attitude object (Bell, Esses, & Maio, 1996; Campbell, 1971; Haddock, Zanna, & Esses, 1994; Stangor, Sullivan, & Ford, 1991; Wolsko, Park, Judd, & Wittenbrink, 2000). The components can be assessed using open-ended measures that ask participants to list their emotions, beliefs, and behaviors regarding the attitude object (Esses & Maio, in press; Haddock & Zanna, 1998). Participants can then rate the desirability of each response using, for example, a 7-point scale from -3 (extremely unfavorable) to $+3$ (extremely favorable). The components can also be assessed using closed-ended measures that ask respondents to indicate the extent to which they experience specific emotions, beliefs, or behaviors (e.g., Crites, Fabrigar, & Petty, 1994; Luke & Maio, 2002).

Unlike the three-component model, the belief-based model suggests that attitudes are simply affective responses to an object that are influenced by beliefs alone (Fishbein, 1967; McGuire, 1960; Wyer, 1970). For example, people might like to participate in the pro-environment rally because they believe that the rally will increase the availability of public transport and that the rally will help build solidarity among environmentalists. Importantly, however, people may hold implicit expectancies about the likelihood that each belief is valid. For example, a person may be only 50% certain that the rally will help obtain more public transport, but 90% certain that rally will help build solidarity among environmentalists. According to the belief-based model, a belief (e.g., effect of the rally on availability of public transport) should have a weaker impact on attitudes when the belief is associated with weak expectancies (e.g., 50% certainty) than with strong expectancies (90% certainty).

This reasoning has been formalized in a well-known equation (Fishbein & Ajzen, 1975): $A = \sum b_i e_i$, where A is the total attitude toward the attitude object, b_i is the subjective belief that the object possesses attribute i (e.g., the probability that the rally will increase the availability of public transport), and e_i is the evaluation of attribute i (e.g., the positive value attached to public transport). Consequently, measures of attitude that are based on this perspective ask participants to consider a list of attributes of an attitude object and then, for each attribute, rate (1) the likelihood that the object possesses the attribute and (2) the desirability of the attribute. The probability ratings are often obtained using scales from -3 (very improbable) to 3 (very probable) or scales from 0 (not at all) to 1 (definitely). In contrast, the evaluative ratings are obtained using scales from -3 (e.g., very bad) to $+3$ (e.g., very good). To compute the overall attitude, the product of the probability and evaluative ratings is determined for each attribute, and the products are summed across the attributes.

Although the three-component model and the belief-based model describe the manner in which attitudes encompass feelings, beliefs, and/or behaviors, both models are relatively silent about the manner in which attitudes summarize negativity and positivity in memory. Two perspectives examine this issue. First, the unidimensional perspective regards attitudes as being bipolar evaluations, which express either negativity or positivity toward the attitude object. In other words, the unidimensional perspective assumes that attitudes subsume (1) negativity, (2) positivity, or (3) neither negativity nor positivity toward the attitude object. In accordance with this assumption, most traditional measures of attitudes ask participants to indicate their attitudes using scales that are anchored by a negative adjective at one end (e.g., bad) and a positive adjective at the other end (e.g., good). To obtain a total index of attitudes, responses are averaged across many different scales that are anchored by different bipolar adjective pairs (e.g., bad vs. good; negative vs. positive).

A more recent perspective, however, rejects the assumption that attitudes vary on a single dimension from negativity to positivity. Specifically, the bidimensional model proposes that attitudes subsume an evaluation that varies in negativity *and* an evaluation that varies in positivity. Consequently, according to this view, attitudes toward an object subsume (1) negativity, (2) positivity, (3) neither negativity nor positivity, and (4) both negativity and positivity. Thus, to measure attitudes from this perspective, the positive and negative responses must be assessed separately. For example, researchers can use a response scale from -3 (very bad) to 0 (neutral) and a separate response scale from 0 (neutral) to 3 (very good), rather than use a single scale from -3 (very bad) to 3 (very good) (Kaplan, 1972). Importantly, this separation of the negative and positive dimensions also facilitates the calculation of ambivalence, which is the simultaneous existence of negativity and positivity toward the attitude object (Kaplan, 1972; Maio, Bell, & Esses, 1996; Olson & Zanna, 1993).

Which of these four perspectives on attitude structure is most valid? Empirical evidence supports each of the perspectives to some extent. Consistent with the three-component model, people's feelings, beliefs, and behaviors toward an attitude object are correlated, but distinct (e.g., Breckler, 1984; Breckler & Wiggins, 1989; Crites et al., 1994; Haddock & Zanna, 1998; Trafimow & Sheeran, 1998). In addition, there are at least moderate correlations between attitudes and the expectancy-value products (e.g., Budd, 1986; Fishbein & Coombs, 1974; van der Pligt & de Vries, 1998), supporting the belief-based model. Also, the unidimensional model is supported by findings that unidimensional measures of attitude yield scores that significantly predict attitude-relevant behavior (Ajzen & Fishbein, 1977; Kraus, 1995), thereby establishing construct validity for these measures. Nonetheless, consistent with the bidimensional view, there are only moderate negative correlations between people's negativity and positivity toward a variety of attitude objects (e.g., Bell et al., 1996; Kaplan, 1972; Katz & Hass, 1988; Thompson, Zanna, & Griffin, 1995; cf. Jonas, Diehl, & Brömer, 1997).

Despite the evidence that all four perspectives are at least somewhat valid, it can be argued that the three-dimensional and bidimensional views are particularly strong. The primary support for this claim is the simple fact that these models are consistent with the data supporting the belief-based and unidimensional models, while also explaining data that cannot be explained by the belief-based and unidimensional models. For instance, the three-component model does not dispute the notion that the sum of evaluative beliefs contributes to a person's attitude. Nor does the bidimensional model assume that responses to unidimensional scales are invalid: negativity and positivity can be combined to yield some net evaluation for an attitude scale, even if the net evaluation belies latent negativity and positivity (Cacioppo, Gardner, & Berntson, 1997). In contrast, the belief-based and unidimensional models have not yet parsimoniously explained the effects of feelings and behaviors on attitudes and the low correlations between negativity and positivity.

ATTITUDE FUNCTION. In biological research, it is a truism that organic structures and their functions are inextricably linked. We expect that the structure and functioning of social attitudes are also closely intertwined. Nonetheless, early research on attitude structure proceeded largely independently of research on attitude functions, which are the psychological needs that attitudes fulfill (Maio & Olson, 2000).

Early theories suggested many important attitude functions (Katz, 1960; Smith, Bruner, & White, 1956). The object-appraisal function is often considered primary: It exists when attitudes serve to simplify interactions with the attitude object. This function is served by any attitude that can be easily retrieved from memory, regardless of whether the attitude is positive or negative. Consider a person who holds strong, easy-to-retrieve attitudes toward the candidates in an upcoming election. Presumably, this voter would have an easier time deciding which vote to make than a voter who holds no attitudes toward the candidates (Fazio, 2000). In other words, accessible attitudes are useful guides for decisions. Abundant evidence supports this view, because people spontaneously orient greater attention toward objects of their more accessible attitudes (Roskos-Ewoldsen & Fazio, 1992), and they exhibit lower physiological arousal when making decisions about the objects of their more accessible attitudes, presumably because the decisions are easier to make (Blascovich et al., 1993).

In addition, people may form and maintain attitudes because attitudes serve basic needs to experience emotion. There are many reasons to suspect that people have a basic need for emotional experiences, partly because emotions energize behavior and provide signposts for learning about our successes and failures (e.g., Damasio, 1994; Zajonc, 1980). Attitudes might help to fulfill this need for affect, in addition to helping simplify the cognitive need for object appraisal (Maio, Esses, & Olson, in press; Maio & Olson, 2000). Supporting this view, people who are high in the need for affect possess more extreme attitudes than people who are low in the need (Maio & Esses, 2001).

Other motivations are served by holding particular attitude positions, rather than by forming attitudes per se. For example, people dislike things that are harmful to them and like things that are beneficial, and this tendency has been labeled the utilitarian function of attitudes (Herek, 2000; Katz, 1960). In addition, people tend to like attitude objects (e.g., fashionable clothes) that are popular among people whom they admire, but not attitude objects that are unpopular (Smith et al., 1956; Snyder & DeBono, 1985), and this tendency has been labeled the social adjustment function of attitudes. Also, there is a value-expressive function: people tend to like objects that promote their personal values (e.g., a national flag), while disliking objects that threaten their values (Katz, 1960; Luke & Maio, 2002; Maio & Olson, 1994, 1995).

The value-expressive function of attitudes is particularly relevant to this chapter, because this function explicitly refers to the connection between values and attitudes. Nonetheless, the empirical study of this function is difficult, because values may occasionally function as post hoc justifications for attitudes, rather than as their psychological basis (Kristiansen & Zanna, 1988). Moreover, when causal influences of values do occur, the effects may be indirect or direct. In an indirect effect, values influence a target attitude indirectly through other attitudes. For instance, the value of helpfulness might cause a person to favor higher taxes, but only because these taxes might bolster social services, which the person also favors. In a direct effect, other attitudes do not mediate the effect of a value or ideology on the target attitude (e.g., the effect of the value of helpfulness on attitudes toward social services).

Research has used several techniques to examine the effects of values on attitudes. Some approaches measure or manipulate whether or not people are made aware that their attitude toward an issue (e.g., a designated smoking area) can express their values (Maio & Olson, 1994, 1995, 2000). In this research, when the value-expressive function has *not* been made salient, participants' value ratings have not predicted attitudes and behavioral intentions. When the value-expressive function has been made salient, however, people's judgments of the importance of values relevant to the attitude topic predict their attitudes and behavioral intentions. Moreover, these significant effects of values occur over and above value-justification effects (Maio & Olson, 1994), while accounting for variance in behavioral intentions beyond the level explained by the theory of reasoned action (Ajzen, 1985), which is described below (Maio & Olson, 1995). Thus, values can powerfully predict attitudes and intentions, at least when the values are consciously perceived as being relevant to the attitudes and intentions (see also Mellema & Bassili, 1995).

Formation of Ideologies, Values, and Attitudes

We have already commented on the interrelations among ideologies, values, and attitudes— each of these constructs influences and is influenced by each of the others. But how do the constructs initially form? That is, what are the sources of people's ideologies, values, and attitudes? And are the sources of the three constructs shared or distinct?

Ultimately, ideologies, values, and attitudes all rest on the three fundamental elements described earlier: feelings, beliefs, and past behavior. People evaluate particular ideologies, values, and attitude objects favorably or unfavorably because the target elicits positive or negative affect, people possess favorable or unfavorable beliefs about the target, and/or they recall behaving negatively or positively toward the target in the past (e.g., see Cacioppo, Marshall-Goodell, Tassinary, & Petty, 1992; Olson & Maio, 2003; van der Pligt & deVries, 1998). For example, individuals may value equality because they believe that equality is useful in society, feel badly when people are discriminated against, and/or recall behaving positively toward minority group members in the past. Because these three elements can combine to influence the formation of ideologies, values, and attitudes, it is vital to understand how the elements are acquired.

These elements can often be obtained from direct, personal experience with those objects. Feelings, in particular, are usually based on personal experience. People learn that apples taste good, that fire is hot, and that their mother cares for them by direct interaction with these objects and people. Direct experience is more important for attitudes, which are relatively specific and concrete, than for values and ideologies. The latter constructs rely to a greater extent on information obtained from others (indirect experience). We will discuss some implications of this direct–indirect experience factor shortly. For now, let us consider the sources of indirect information. Many people and organizations influence individuals' ideologies, values, and attitudes, including parents, peer groups, the educational system, religious institutions, and the mass media. We will highlight the role of two sources: parents and the media.

FAMILY TRANSMISSION. Parents are the primary source of information for the first few years of a child's life. Not surprisingly, therefore, researchers have found that children's attitudes and values correlate significantly with their parents' attitudes and values. For example, children's attitudes toward cigarette smoking have been found to be related to their parents' smoking attitudes and behavior (Chassin, Presson, & Sherman, 1984). Similarly, the attitudes of 18-year-old men and women toward the appropriate gender divisions of household duties (e.g., whether husbands should participate significantly in housework) have been shown to be related to their mother's gender role attitudes and to their father's actual participation in household tasks during their adolescence (Cunningham, 2001). In the domain of political attitudes, Jennings and Niemi (1968) found a strong relation between high school seniors' political party identification and the party identification of their parents.

Rohan and Zanna (1996) examined the similarity of the profile of values endorsed by children and their parents. Participants in this study consisted of male university students and their parents, all of whom completed Schwartz's (1992) value inventory. Participants reported their ratings of 10 value dimensions. The correlations between the ratings of children and their parents were highly significant (mean $r = 0.54$). The researchers also measured the right-wing authoritarianism (Altemeyer & Hunsberger, 1992) of the parents and found that *low* authoritarian parents yielded particularly strong correlations between their values and their children's values (the mean r for parents in the lower half of the sample in authoritarianism was 0.62). The authors speculated that the apparently greater influence of low right-wing authoritarian parents may have been due to their greater responsiveness as parents to their children's needs.

Nonetheless, the relations between parents' attitudes and children's attitudes are not always clear-cut. For instance, there is mixed evidence about the relations between parents' attitudes toward other ethnic groups and their children's attitudes (see Aboud & Doyle, 1996; and Towles-Schwen & Fazio, 2001). Towles-Schwen and Fazio (2001) suggested that these mixed findings may occur because children learn motivations to control prejudices, in addition to learning prejudicial attitudes themselves. Supporting this view, these researchers found that perceptions of parental prejudice and positive childhood experiences with Blacks both predicted adult participants' concern with appearing prejudiced toward Blacks. Thus, these findings highlight the need to consider how attitude-relevant motivations are acquired, in addition to the attitudes themselves.

MASS MEDIA. The mass media, especially television, have been indicted as having many undesirable attitudinal and behavioral effects on children and adults, producing such things as aggressive attitudes and behavior (e.g., Wood, Wong, & Chachere, 1991), undue fear of being a victim of random violence (e.g., Peterson & Zill, 1981), unrealistic standards of physical attractiveness (e.g., Silverstein, Perdue, Peterson, & Kelley, 1986), and deterioration of reading skills and creativity (e.g., Williams, 1986). Of course, the media can also have desirable effects, such as when they provide viewers with educational information, deliver news coverage to isolated communities, and keep politicians honest by reporting freely on decisions and actions. For better or worse, the media are an important source of information about many issues, places, and people—often the *only* source for far-off events.

One noteworthy effect of the media is that they "frame" issues, perhaps unintentionally, by emphasizing certain elements and downplaying other elements (Kinder, 1998). Thus, the media often "set the agenda" for the public by identifying issues that should be addressed (Cohen, 1963; Neuman, 1990). For example, energy shortages and arms control became high priority issues only after they attained prominence in newspaper and television coverage (Kinder, 1998). In this way, the media constitute important agents of socialization in our culture, helping to inculcate ideologies, values, and attitudes.

On the other hand, there may be a tendency to overrate media bias. Vallone, Ross, and Lepper (1985) found that pro-Arab students and pro-Israeli students each perceived television coverage of the Beirut massacre as being hostile to their own position and more sympathetic toward the other side, and this tendency has been dubbed the "hostile media" phenomenon (see also Zanna, Klosson, & Darley, 1976). In addition, people are particularly agreeable to the information that appears congenial to their point of view (Houston & Fazio, 1989; Lord, Ross, & Lepper, 1979). These tendencies to dismiss some media reports as "hostile" and to be more convinced by congenial reports may enable people to be at least somewhat resistant to media influence.

DIRECT VERSUS INDIRECT EXPERIENCE. We mentioned that ideologies, values, and attitudes can come either from direct, personal experience with an object or from indirect experience through other people and organizations. Researchers have proposed that this direct–indirect experience factor has significant implications for the resulting ideology, value, or attitude. For example, Fazio and Zanna (1981) found that attitudes based on direct experience with the attitude object were held more strongly and were more accessible (easier to retrieve) than attitudes based on indirect experience. Direct experience attitudes also predicted subsequent behavior better than did indirect experience attitudes (see also Doll & Ajzen, 1992).

Gilovich (1987) tested the interesting idea that, at least under certain conditions, attitudes based on indirect experience might be more polarized than attitudes based on direct experience. To test this hypothesis, participants either watched a videotape of an individual describing negative events in his/her life or listened to a tape-recorded description of the same individual made by someone who had watched the video. Results showed that the latter participants, who based their impressions on indirect information, reported more extreme attitudes toward the target person than did the former participants. Presumably, direct experience provided more detailed information about qualifications to the individual's central traits.

Thompson, Judd, and Park (2000) extended Gilovich's reasoning to the domain of group impressions (i.e., group stereotypes). Some participants read 45 sentences describing behaviors allegedly performed by members of a particular fraternity; the sentences produced a positive overall impression. Other participants were given only a written description of the fraternity that had been composed by someone who read the 45 sentences. Results showed that participants who based their attitudes on second-hand information reported more extreme (positive) ratings and estimated less variability within members of the fraternity than did participants who were exposed to the original set of behaviors. Thus, paradoxically, indirect experience can lead to attitudes that are more black-and-white than attitudes based on direct experience, even though the latter attitudes may be held more confidently and may predict behavior better.

CULTURAL DIFFERENCES. If ideologies, values, and attitudes develop through direct and indirect experience, then growing up in different cultures should produce differences in ideologies, values, and attitudes. Indeed, cultural differences in each of these constructs have been documented.

The best-known cultural difference studied by social scientists is one that exists between so-called "eastern" cultures, such as Japan, Korea, Malaysia, and "western" cultures, such as United States, Canada, Australia, and the United Kingdom. The difference involves the relative importance of individualist versus collectivist concerns. Eastern cultures tend to value interdependence and group harmony more than independence and individual achievement, whereas western cultures show the opposite pattern of values (e.g., Bochner, 1994; Markus & Kitayama, 1991; Triandis, 1995). Interestingly, although cultural differences in the relative importance placed on certain values are reliable, the interrelationships among values (i.e., the structure of values—the fundamental dimensions underlying values) are stable across cultures (e.g., Schwartz, 1992). It is also possible to view individualism versus collectivism as competing ideologies. The individualist ideology "gives priority to the separate, essentially nonsocial individual," and the collectivist ideology embraces "the idea that the individual is fundamentally interdependent with others" (Markus, Kitayama, & Heiman, 1996, p. 902).

Not surprisingly, individualist and collectivist cultures manifest a variety of differences in more specific attitudes and beliefs that are consistent with the differences in values. For example, attitudes toward marriage, love, the family, sex roles, social customs, expression of feelings, and many other issues have been shown to differ predictably across cultures (e.g., see Levine, Sato, Hashomoto, & Verman, 1995; Matsumoto, 1996; Triandis, 1994, 1995). Such differences document the systematic effects of environmental variables on attitudes and values (cf. Olson, Vernon, Harris, & Jang, 2001).

PREDICTION OF BEHAVIOR

The conceptual importance of ideologies, values, and attitudes rests, in significant part, on the assumption that these constructs influence behavior. Thus, many researchers have investigated the prediction of behavior and have identified variables that moderate relations between these constructs and behavior. Nonetheless, most of the research has examined attitude–behavior or value–behavior consistency. In the following sections, we briefly review some of this research.

Attitudes and Behavior

Investigations of attitude–behavior consistency have delineated some of the conditions under which attitudes predict behavior strongly. These conditions include attitudinal qualities, personality traits, situational variables, and methodological factors. Each category of variables is addressed in turn below.

ATTITUDINAL QUALITIES.   Certain kinds of attitudes predict behavior better than do other kinds of attitudes. For example, we have already noted that attitudes based on direct, personal experience with the attitude object predict behavior better than attitudes based on indirect experience (Doll & Ajzen, 1992; Fazio & Zanna, 1981). Fazio and Williams (1986) suggested that attitudes based on direct experience predict behavior better because they are more *accessible*—that is, they are more likely to be evoked spontaneously in the presence of the object (Higgins, 1996). Consistent with this reasoning, Fazio and Williams found that voters who were able to report their evaluations of political candidates quickly were subsequently more likely to vote for their preferred candidate (thereby behaving consistently with their attitude) than were voters who were slower to report their evaluations. Thus, attitudes high in accessibility predicted behavior better than did attitudes low in accessibility.

Another attitudinal quality that affects attitude–behavior consistency is *ambivalence*. As noted earlier, ambivalence refers to the simultaneous existence of negativity and positivity toward the attitude object (Kaplan, 1972; Olson & Zanna, 1993). Ambivalent attitudes yield lower correlations with behavior (e.g., Armitage & Conner, 2000), presumably because the negative and positive elements may each become salient at different times, producing inconsistent behavior. In line with this reasoning, MacDonald and Zanna (1998) found that priming either the negative or positive qualities of feminists led men with ambivalent attitudes toward feminists to behave very differently, whereas the behavior of men with nonambivalent attitudes was not affected by the priming manipulation.

An attitudinal quality similar to ambivalence is *evaluative–cognitive consistency* (cf. Maio, Esses, & Bell, 2000), which refers to the degree of consistency between the overall attitude (the evaluation) and the beliefs about the object (cognition). Attitudes that are high in evaluative–cognitive consistency are more predictive of behavior than are attitudes that are low in evaluative–cognitive consistency (e.g., Chaiken, Pomerantz, & Giner-Sorolla, 1995). Presumably, paralleling the explanation for ambivalence, when attitudes are low in evaluative–cognitive consistency, different contexts can make either the evaluation or the cognition salient, thereby inducing inconsistent behavior, whereas attitudes that are high in evaluative–cognitive consistency are not susceptible to such contextual effects.

A final attitudinal quality that has been related to attitude–behavior consistency is *embeddedness*. Attitude embeddedness, also called working knowledge, refers to the amount of attitude-relevant information that is linked to the attitude, including beliefs, memories, and expectations (Scott, 1968; Wood, 1982). Highly embedded attitudes are more resistant to change (e.g., Wood, Rhodes, & Biek, 1995) and more predictive of behavior (e.g., Kallgren & Wood, 1986) than are low embeddedness attitudes. Presumably, highly embedded attitudes provide the individual with confidence and/or knowledge to counteract situational variables that might otherwise lead to inconsistent behavior.

PERSONALITY TRAITS. Some people's actions accord with their attitudes more than do other people's actions. For example, *self-monitoring* (Snyder, 1987) refers to the extent to which individuals base their actions on internal or external cues. Low self-monitors use internal cues, such as their ideologies, values, and attitudes, to guide their behavior, whereas high self-monitors act on the basis of external cues, such as norms and other people's opinions. As would be expected given these definitions, low self-monitors exhibit stronger attitude–behavior consistency than do high self-monitors (e.g., Snyder & Kendzierski, 1982). Kardes, Sanbonmatsu, Voss, and Fazio (1986) found that low self-monitors have more accessible attitudes than high self-monitors, presumably because low self-monitors think about their attitudes more often. We noted in the preceding section that attitudes high in accessibility predict behavior better than attitudes low in accessibility.

Another personality variable that moderates attitude–behavior consistency is *private self-consciousness* (Fenigstein, Scheier, & Buss, 1975). Individuals who are high in private self-consciousness are more aware of their internal states, such as moods and attitudes, than are individuals who are low in private self-consciousness. As might be expected, the greater awareness of internal states by individuals high in private self-consciousness has been shown to be associated with stronger attitude–behavior consistency, compared to individuals low in private self-consciousness (e.g., Scheier, Buss, & Buss, 1978; Wicklund, 1982).

SITUATIONAL VARIABLES. Situational factors can either enhance attitude–behavior consistency or reduce it. For example, situational variables can increase the salience or accessibility of an attitude, and such "priming" will heighten the attitude's impact on behavior. Fazio, Chen, McDonel, and Sherman (1982) asked some participants to report their attitudes toward several types of puzzles a number of times, whereas other participants reported their attitudes only once. In a subsequent free time period, participants who had previously reported their attitudes several times behaved in accordance with their attitudes (i.e., played with positively evaluated puzzles more than with negatively evaluated puzzles) to a greater extent than did participants whose attitudes had not been primed. Thus, a situational manipulation of priming increased attitude–behavior consistency, presumably because primed attitudes became more accessible.

In contrast, situational variables can impair attitude–behavior consistency by introducing other motives or incentives for behavior. For example, strong situational norms can override attitudes, such as when individuals act courteously to disliked coworkers because of politeness norms. Many attitude theorists have recognized the importance of norms; for example, subjective norms (normative pressure to behave in certain ways because of others' expectations) were included as the only variable other than attitudes hypothesized to influence behavioral intentions in Fishbein and Azjen's (1975) *theory of reasoned action.* Similarly, Schwartz and Tessler (1972) showed that perceived moral obligations (one type of norm) predicted behavior independently from attitudes.

In addition, strong external incentives can affect behavior independently of attitudes. For example, large rewards or punishments for behaving in a certain way can overwhelm the effects of attitudes, such as when individuals engage in disliked behavior because they are being remunerated or when threat of physical harm coerces individuals to tolerate unacceptable treatment. Of course, these situational incentives are, in essence, rendering behavior nonvolitional—individuals really have no choice but to work to obtain the reward or avoid the punishment. Attitude theorists have long recognized that the influence of attitudes on behavior is limited largely to the domain of volitional actions (e.g., Eagly & Chaiken, 1993; Fishbein & Ajzen, 1975).

METHODOLOGICAL FACTORS.   Ajzen and Fishbein (1977) made an important methodological observation about attitude–behavior consistency. These authors argued that measures of attitudes and behaviors must be compatible in terms of their *specificity*—whether they reflect an entire category/domain of actions or just a single behavior. Attitudes toward objects (e.g., attitudes toward dairy products) should predict the class of actions, over time and settings, which are related to that object (e.g., a summary measure of the individual's dairy-related behaviors over a period of time). Composite measures of a class of actions are called *multiple-act behavioral criteria.* Ajzen and Fishbein argued that attitudes toward objects should *not* be expected to predict a single, isolated behavior very well (e.g., whether the individual buys ice cream on a particular trip to the shopping mall). Most attitudes of interest to social psychologists (e.g., attitudes toward objects, issues, and people) refer to targets that have categories of relevant actions. Thus, empirical investigations of attitude–behavior consistency should typically employ multiple-act behavioral criteria. Indeed, reviews of the extant literature show that, when measures of attitudes and behavior are compatible in terms of their specificity, attitude–behavior correlations are substantial (e.g., Kraus, 1995).

Lord, Lepper, and Mackie (1984) made another methodological point about attitude–behavior consistency that extended the compatibility idea just described. Specifically, these researchers hypothesized that attitudes will predict behavior toward *typical* instances or members of an attitudinal category better than behavior toward atypical instances or members. That is, prototypical exemplars of a category or group will elicit attitude-consistent behavior more than will unusual exemplars of a category or group. For example, Lord et al. found that participants' attitudes toward gay men predicted how they behaved toward a gay man who closely matched the stereotype better than how they behaved toward an atypical gay man. Thus, compatibility between the group stereotype and individual group members influenced attitude–behavior consistency. The authors labeled this finding a "typicality effect."

Values and Behavior

The effects of values on behaviors are occasionally weak (Kristiansen & Hotte, 1996), making it important to discover variables that moderate the relations between values and behavior. Many moderators of value–behavior consistency have been examined. Below, we will first describe the ways in which personality and situational variables affect value–behavior relations. We will then examine properties of values that moderate these relations.

PERSONALITY. According to Wojciszke (1987), people vary in idealism, which is the extent to which self-related ideals are valued and used to determine behavior. Theoretically, people who score higher in idealism should exhibit more value–behavior consistency, and Wojciszke (1989) has found such a pattern using both self- and peer-ratings of value-relevant behavior. Thus, idealism may be one trait that moderates value–behavior relations.

An additional relevant trait is self-monitoring. As described above, Snyder's (1987) theory of self-monitoring indicates that low self-monitors base their behaviors on their internal ideologies, values, and attitudes, whereas high self-monitors base their behaviors on external, social cues. The evidence described above indicates that self-monitoring does moderate the extent to which people utilize their attitudes, and some additional evidence is consistent with the hypothesis that self-monitoring moderates the extent to which people utilize their values. For example, DeBono (1987) predicted and found that low self-monitors were more persuaded by persuasive arguments that cited values than were high self-monitors, whereas high self-monitors were more persuaded by persuasive arguments that cited the popularity of the advocated position than were low self-monitors. Low self-monitors may also be more likely to see their values as being relevant to their attitudes and behavior (Kristiansen & Zanna, 1988; cf. Maio & Olson, 1994). Together, such evidence provides indirect support for the notion that value–behavior relations are stronger among low self-monitors.

SITUATION. Some situational factors can decrease the impact of values by reducing people's capacity to express their values in their behavior. For example, time pressure might cause people to temporarily ignore an important value, thereby reducing its impact on behavior. Consistent with this reasoning, Darley and Batson (1973) found that seminarians who were late to give a talk about the importance of helping others were less likely to help an ailing bystander than were seminarians who were on time. Thus, time pressure reduced the extent to which the seminarians' behavior was congruent with their salient value (i.e., helpfulness).

In general, however, behavior should be more congruent with a value when the value is made salient than when it is not made salient (Bargh & Barndollar, 1996; Maio & Olson, 1995; Verplanken & Holland, 2002). In addition, values may exert stronger effects in situations that elicit high self-focus or a need to promote self-esteem through affirmation of the cherished values (Verplanken & Holland, 2002).

VALUE QUALITIES. Although salient values may be more likely to influence behavior than nonsalient values, this effect should be particularly likely for values that are part of one's self-definition and identity. According to Verplanken and Holland (in press), values that are central to the self-concept should be particularly likely to influence how people perceive and interpret situations, thereby enhancing the impact of the values on subsequent behavior. In other words, values garner stronger motivational properties by being linked to the self. Across four experiments, Verplanken and Holland (in press) obtained evidence consistent with this reasoning: primed environmental values influenced behavior more strongly when the values were perceived as more closely connected to the person's sense of self.

Another important value quality is the extent to which they are embedded in argumentative support. Maio and Olson (1998) argued that values generally function as truisms, because they are endorsed highly but lack argumentative support. Several experiments have supported this hypothesis. For instance, participants who analyze reasons for values change their ratings of those values significantly more than participants in control conditions, and this finding should occur only if people lack prior cognitive support for this value (Maio & Olson, 1998).* In fact, the effect of analyzing reasons on values is eliminated when participants are first provided with an opportunity to learn arguments supporting their values (Maio & Olson, 1998). Also, people agree very highly with their values, list few reasons to support their values (and far fewer against the values), show weak relations between their reasons and their values, indicate strong positive feelings about their values, and exhibit strong relations between their feelings about the values and the importance of the values. Overall, these results are consistent with the hypothesis that values possess strong affective support, but not strong cognitive support.

The importance of this observation is highlighted by McGuire's (1964) hypothesis that truisms may act like paper tigers: They look tough but are easily crumpled. Consequently, if values function as truisms, their effects on behavior and their general resistance to change may be weaker than might otherwise occur. To address this issue, several experiments tested whether making salient cognitive support for a value increases pro-value behavior in situations that challenge the value, over and above the effect of making the value salient (Maio, Olson, Bernard, & Allen, 2001). For example, in one experiment, participants were given an incentive to discriminate in the minimal group paradigm (Tajfel, 1970). Results indicated that participants were less likely to discriminate in this situation after their reasons for valuing equality were made salient than after the value alone was made salient. In another experiment, a confederate requested extra participation in a lab experiment, even though participants were already committed to 20 unpaid hours. Results indicated that participants offered more help to the confederate after their reasons for valuing helpfulness were made salient than after the value itself was primed. Thus, the two experiments supported the hypothesis that cognitive support for values can motivate pro-value behavior in situations that present justification for ignoring the value.

Additional experiments have extended these findings by showing that argumentative support influences the resistance of values to change (Bernard et al., 2003). Specifically, in two experiments, we provided participants with the opportunity to generate or read arguments for and against the value of equality. We then exposed participants to an essay attacking the value of equality. This essay argued that equality is an unobtainable ideal, people are not actually equal, and real-world applications of the value of equality lead to incorrect decisions for business and government. Next, participants were asked to (1) rate their agreement with equality, (2) rate their attitudes toward a variety of issues pertaining to equality, and (3) rate the importance of five self-transcendence (including equality) and five openness values. Consistent with McGuire's (1964) research, we predicted and found that participants who received an opportunity to build arguments for the value of equality endorsed the value more strongly following the persuasive attack than did participants in a control condition. Moreover, there were similar effects on attitudes toward the equality-relevant issues and on the self-transcendence values. In addition, postattack ratings of the importance of equality statistically mediated the effects of the argumentative support on attitudes toward the

---

*This value change was bi-directional. That is, the reasons analysis did not consistently produce more extreme values—some participants became more extreme and others became less extreme (resulting in no difference in final values between conditions).

equality-relevant issues and on the self-transcendence values. Thus, the provision of argumentative support for a single value can have widespread repercussions for a whole range of relevant attitudes and values.

VALUES, ATTITUDES, AND CULTURAL ESTRANGEMENT

Ideologies, values, and attitudes should influence people's participation in society and their feelings of connection with society. In fact, many sociologists, philosophers, and psychologists suggest that a sense of cultural estrangement occurs when people feel that their values are discrepant from those of the society (e.g., Cozzarelli & Karafa, 1998; Fromm, 1941; Kenitson, 1965; Kohn & Schooler, 1983; Schacht, 1970; Seeman, 1975). Recently, social psychological research has begun to examine empirically the notion of cultural estrangement.

For example, Cozzarelli and Karafa (1998) used a variety of psychometric techniques to develop a new measure of cultural estrangement. Their measure contains two subscales: their "atypical" subscale assesses the extent to which people feel that their attitudes, beliefs, and values do not fit those of society, whereas their "misfit" subscale assesses a more general feeling of not fitting in with others. Using this cultural estrangement inventory and a few others (Kohn & Schooler, 1983; Maddi, Kobosa, & Hoover, 1979), it is now possible to look more closely at the social psychological predictors of cultural estrangement.

A good starting point is to test whether the subjective feelings of cultural estrangement are related to actual discrepancies between the values of self and the perceived values of society. This issue is important because people might report high feelings of cultural estrangement without thinking about *all* of their values. They might base their judgments on salient differences in a few specific types of values. For example, some people may feel estranged from society because they believe that people are too strongly driven by values capturing self-interest (e.g., self-enhancement values) and not enough by values promoting collective concerns (e.g., self-transcendence values). Others' sense of alienation may derive from different values. For example, some people may feel alienated because they believe that society cherishes openness values (e.g., freedom) and not conservative values (e.g., tradition). Is there a specific pattern of value discrepancies that drives the experience of cultural estrangement?

Moreover, people might construe high estrangement from perceived discrepancies between important political attitudes that they hold and the perceived political attitudes of the society. Given the links between attitudes and values that are described above, an important issue is whether values actually play a unique role in predicting estrangement. If values are uniquely tied to estrangement, then perceived value discrepancies should predict estrangement independently of perceived discrepancies in attitudes generally.

Bernard and Maio (2003) recently conducted a study addressing these questions. In this study, participants were given questionnaires to assess personal and societal values, personal and societal political attitudes, and personal and societal mundane attitudes. The measure of personal values asked each participant to rate the importance of 28 different social values, which were drawn from all four higher order domains represented in Shalom Schwartz's (1992) comprehensive value survey. The measure of personal political attitudes asked participants to rate their attitudes toward 28 different political issues examined in prior research on political attitudes (e.g., abortion, censorship; see Maio, Roese, Seligman, & Katz, 1996). The measure of mundane attitudes asked participants to rate their attitudes toward 28 different food and beverages, such as milk and pizza. The societal measures for each construct utilized the same questionnaires, except that participants were asked to rate society's values or attitudes. Finally, participants completed the measure of cultural estrangement that was developed by Cozzarelli and Karafa (1998).

Using these measures, we calculated the average of the absolute magnitude of the discrepancies (i.e., |personal − societal|) between (1) each pair of personal and societal values, (2) each pair of personal and societal political attitudes, and (3) each pair of personal and societal mundane attitudes. We then examined the correlations between these discrepancy scores and participants' cultural estrangement. As expected, the results indicated that cultural estrangement was higher among those participants who reported big value discrepancies than among those participants who reported small value discrepancies. A similar, but weaker, pattern occurred for the political attitude discrepancies. Also, when all three types of discrepancies were entered as predictors of cultural estrangement in a regression analysis, only the value discrepancy scores were significant predictors of cultural estrangement. Most importantly, as predicted by Keniston (1965), additional analyses of the algebraic discrepancies between the personal and societal values revealed that estrangement was highest among those participants who believed that societal values were more selfish and achievement oriented than their own values. Specifically, estrangement was higher among those people who believed that they considered the self-transcendence values to be more important than the society and the self-enhancement values to be less important than the society.

In sum, the above research has shown that perceived discrepancies between personal and societal values predict feelings of cultural estrangement over and above perceived discrepancies between personal and societal attitudes. In addition, the effect of values is driven by perceived differences in self-enhancement and self-transcendence values, and not by all values in general. Thus, cultural estrangement may be more closely linked to specific ideologies relevant to these values than to values and attitudes in general. This provocative hypothesis provides an interesting issue for future research.

FUTURE DIRECTIONS

As the field of social psychology has grown, social psychologists have focused their attention on increasingly basic and concrete levels of analyses. This trend has been particularly apparent in the study of ideologies, values, and attitudes. Although there is a critical mass of valuable research in all three domains, the amount of research on abstract ideologies and values is far outweighed by the amount of research on more specific and concrete attitudes.

This imbalance has revealed a lot of information about basic attitudinal processes, many of which also pertain to ideologies and values. Indeed, some of the most important and captivating research on attitudes has focused on attitudinal issues that are at the heart of issues addressed by ideologies and values (e.g., prejudice). For this reason, research should continue to explore connections between ideologies, values, and attitudes. For example, although ideologies are presumed to subsume patterns in values and attitudes, the extant research has focused primarily on detecting ideologies in patterns of attitudes, but not in patterns of values. One exception is found in the research by Ashton et al. (2003). This research discovered that the political ideologies of moral regulation and compassion (which were obtained from studies of political attitudes) were related to dimensions in social values that were predicted and found by Schwartz (1992). These researchers also obtained evidence that the political ideologies of moral regulation and compassion overlapped considerably with the cultural ideologies of horizontal and vertical individualism and communalism (Triandis, 1995). Thus, it is possible that moral regulation and compassion are basic ideologies, which meaningfully relate to both values and attitudes.

In addition, although research indicates that attitudes sometimes serve a value-expressive motivation, little is known about how *different* values influence and shape attitudes (Maio & Olson, 2000). Are attitudes stronger and more resistant to change when they serve to express self-enhancement values than self-transcendance values? This possibility is raised by findings that people tend to disregard important self-transcendence values when there is a strong motivation to pursue their own self-interest (Batson & Thompson, 2001). Thus, the self-enhancement motivation may be stronger, and attitudes tapping it may be more resistant to change.

Another interesting issue is whether the relations between values and estrangement differ across different societies. In an individualistic, European society (Britain), Bernard and Maio (2001) discovered that estrangement was higher among people who considered self-enhancement values to be less important or self-transcendence values to be more important. It is possible that these values possess a different relationship to estrangement in an Asian society, because many Asian cultures emphasize collectivist ideologies (Triandis, 1995). Specifically, estrangement might be higher among Asians who consider self-enhancement values to be more important and self-transcendence values to be less important. In general, the relationship between values and estrangement should depend on the prevailing cultural zeitgeist.

In all cultures, however, there are common interests in understanding how dominant ideologies and values influence important social problems. For example, social psychological research has begun to examine the costs and benefits of different ideologies on stereotypes and racial attitudes. In particular, Wolsko et al. (2000) contrasted two ideologies on race: multiculturalism and color-blindness. The multicultural ideology advocates recognizing and appreciating ethnic diversity, whereas the color-blind ideology advocates judging others solely as individuals. Wolsko et al. (2000) predicted and found that participants who had been asked to consider the strengths of the multicultural ideology subsequently reported more accurate stereotypes than participants who had been asked to consider the strengths of the color-blind ideology. In addition, participants who had considered the strengths of the multicultural ideology used the stereotypes more prudently in judgments of a target individual than did participants who had considered the strengths of the color-blind ideology. Based on these results and prior research (e.g., Brewer & Miller, 1988; Hewstone & Brown, 1986), Wolsko et al. concluded that a combination of multicultural and color-blind ideologies may be the best means to combat prejudice.

Nevertheless, the breadth of values and ideologies is their pitfall as well as their asset. As described by Fish (2000), there are many ways to interpret broad values and ideologies. For example, the value of equality may signify a variety of policy principles, including equality of opportunity to succeed, equality of outcomes for people occupying the same roles, equality of outcomes as a proportion of individuals' contributions, and equality of outcomes for individuals with the same level of need. Similarly, some people may view multiculturalism as actively promoting group differences, whereas others may perceive mutliculturalism as being indifferent to group differences. Such differences in construal remain an important issue in all research on ideologies, values, and attitudes.

In this chapter, we have attempted to describe how ideologies, values, and attitudes are formed and maintained in the human mind, while highlighting their functions and consequences. The evidence that we presented strongly supports the importance of these constructs for understanding social behavior and feelings about society. Indeed, the study of these constructs is one of the most important research agendas in the social sciences. Some of society's numerous attempts to codify basic values (e.g., equality, freedom), such as the Magna Carta, European Commission of Human Rights Act, and the United Nations Declarations of Human Rights, illustrate the importance of this agenda. These legal pronouncements have become gold standards for law, against which any case can be judged. It is therefore imperative that we understand how the average person understands and reasons about these basic ideals—ideals that guide and maintain civilization itself.

REFERENCES

Abramson, P. R., & Inglehart, R. (1995). *Value change in global perspective*. Ann Arbor: University of Michigan Press.

Aboud, F. E., & Doyle, A. B. (1996). Parental and peer influences on children's racial attitudes. *International Journal of Intercultural Relations, 20*, 371–383.

Ajzen, I. (1985). From intentions to actions: A theory of planned behavior. In J. Kuhl & J. Beckman (Eds.), *Action-control: From cognition to behavior* (pp. 11–39). Heidelberg: Springer.

Ajzen, I., & Fishbein, M. (1977). Attitude–behavior relations: A theoretical analysis and review of empirical research. *Psychological Bulletin, 84*, 888–918.

Allport, G. W., Vernon, P. E., & Lindzey, G. (1960). *Study of values. Manual and test booklet* (3rd ed). Boston, MA: Houghton-Mifflin.

Altemeyer, B., & Hunsberger, B. (1992). Authoritarianism, religious fundamentalism, quest, and prejudice. *International Journal for the Psychology of Religion, 2*, 113–133.

Armitage, C. J., & Conner, M. (2000). Attitude ambivalence: A test of three key hypotheses. *Personality and Social Psychology Bulletin, 26*, 1421–1432.

Ashton, M. C., Danso, H. A., Maio, G. R., Esses, V. M., Bond, M. H., & Keung, O. K. Y. (2003). *Two dimensions of political attitudes and their individual difference correlates: A cross-cultural perspective*, manuscript submitted for publication.

Bales, R., & Crouch, A. (1969). The value profile: A factor analytic study of value statements. *Sociological Inquiry, 39*, 3–17.

Bargh, J. A., & Barndollar, K. (1996). Automaticity in action: The unconscious as a repository of chronic goals and motives. In J. A. Bargh & P. M. Gollwitzer (Eds.), *The psychology of action: Linking cognition and motivation to behavior* (pp. 457–481). New York: Guilford Press.

Batson, D. C., & Thompson, E. R. (2001). Why don't moral people act morally? Motivational considerations. *Current Directions in Psychological Science, 10*, 54–57.

Bell, D. W., Esses, V. M., & Maio, G. R. (1996). The utility of open-ended measures to assess intergroup ambivalence. *Canadian Journal of Behavioural Science, 28*, 12–18.

Bem, D. J. (1972). Self-perception theory. In L. Berkowitz (Ed.), *Advances in experimental social psychology* (Vol. 6, pp. 1–62). San Diego, CA: Academic Press.

Bernard, M. M., & Maio, G. R. (2003). *Cultural estrangement: The role of social values*. Manuscript submitted for publication.

Bernard, M. M., Maio, G. R., & Olson, J. M. (2003). The vulnerability of values to attack: Inoculation of values and value-relevant attitudes. *Personality and Social Psychology Bulletin, 29*, 63–75.

Blascovich, J., Ernst, J. M., Tomaka, J., Kelsey, R. M., Salomon, K. L., & Fazio, R. H. (1993). Attitude accessibility as a moderator of autonomic reactivity during decision making. *Journal of Personality and Social Psychology, 64*, 165–176.

Bochner, S. (1994). Cross-cultural differences in self-concept: A test of Hofstede's individualism/collectivism distinction. *Journal of Cross-Cultural Psychology, 25*, 273–283.

Boski, P. (1993). Socio-political value orientations among Poles in presidential '90 and '91 elections. *Polish Psychological Bulletin, 20*, 551–567.

Breckler, S. J. (1984). Empirical validation of affect, behavior, and cognition as distinct components of attitude. *Journal of Personality and Social Psychology, 47*, 1191–1205.

Breckler, S. J., & Wiggins, E. C. (1989). Affect versus evaluation in the structure of attitudes. *Journal of Experimental Social Psychology, 25*, 253–271.

Brewer, M. B., & Miller, N. (1988). Contact and cooperation: When do they work? In P. A. Katz & D. A. Taylor (Eds.), *Eliminating racism: Profiles in controversy* (pp. 315–328). New York: Plenum Press.

Budd, R. J. (1986). Predicting cigarette use: The need to incorporate measures of salience in the theory of reasoned action. *Journal of Applied Social Psychology, 16*, 663–685.

Cacioppo, J. T., Gardner, W. L., & Berntson, G. G. (1997). Beyond bipolar conceptualizations and measures: The case of attitudes and evaluative space. *Personality and Social Psychology Review, 1*, 3–25.

Cacioppo, J. T., Marshall-Goodell, B. S., Tassinary, L. G., & Petty, R. E. (1992). Rudimentary determinants of attitudes: Classical conditioning is more effective when prior knowledge about the attitude stimulus is low than high. *Journal of Experimental Social Psychology, 28*, 207–233.

Campbell, A. (1971). *White attitudes toward Black people*. Ann Arbor: Institute for Social Research.

Chaiken, S., Pomerantz, E. M., & Giner-Sorolla, R. (1995). Structural consistency and attitude strength. In R. E. Petty & J. A. Krosnick (Eds.), *Attitude strength: Antecedents and consequences* (pp. 387–412). Mahwah, NJ: Erlbaum.

Chassin, L., Presson, C. C., & Sherman, S. J. (1984). Cigarette smoking and adolscent psychosocial development. *Basic and Applied Social Psychology, 5*, 295–315.

Cohen, B. (1963). *The press and foreign policy*. Princeton, NJ: Princeton University Press.

Cohen, D., & Nisbett, R. E. (1994). Self-protection and the culture of honor: Explaining Southern violence. *Personality and Social Psychology Bulletin, 20*, 551–567.

Converse, P. E. (1964). The nature of belief systems in mass publics. In D. E. Apter (Ed.), *Ideology and discontent* (pp. 206–261). New York: Free Press.

Cozzarelli, C., & Karafa, J. A. (1998). Cultural estrangement and terror management theory. *Personality and Social Psychology Bulletin, 24*, 253–267.

Crites, S. L., Fabrigar, L. R., & Petty, R. E. (1994). Measuring the affective and cognitive properties of attitudes: Conceptual and methodological issues. *Personality and Social Psychology Bulletin, 20*, 619–634.

Cunningham, M. (2001). The influence of parental attitudes and behaviors on children's attitudes toward gender and household labor in early adulthood. *Journal of Marriage and the Family, 63*, 111–122.

Damasio, A. (1994). *Descartes' error: Emotion, reason, and the human brain*. New York: Avon.

Darley, J. M., & Batson, C. D. (1973). From Jerusalem to Jericho: A study of situational and dispositional variables in helping behavior. *Journal of Personality and Social Psychology, 27*, 100–119.

DeBono, K. G. (1987). Investigating the social adjustive and value expressive functions of attitudes: Implications for persuasion processes. *Journal of Personality and Social Psychology, 52*, 279–287.

de St. Aubin, E. (1996). Personal ideology polarity: Its emotional foundation and its manifestation in individual value systems, religiosity, political orientation, and assumptions concerning human nature. *Journal of Personality and Social Psychology, 71*, 152–165.

Devos, T., Spini, D., & Schwartz, S. H. (in press). Conflicts among human values and trust in institutions. *British Journal of Social Psychology*.

Doll, J., & Ajzen, I. (1992). Accessibility and stability of predictors in the theory of planned behavior. *Journal of Personality and Social Psychology, 63*, 754–765.

Eagly, A. H., & Chaiken, S. (1993). *The psychology of attitudes*. Fort Worth, TX: Harcourt Brace Jovanovich.

Eagly, A. H., & Chaiken, S. (1998). Attitude structure and function. In D. T. Gilbert, S. T. Fiske, & G. Lindzey (Eds.), *The handbook of social psychology* (4th ed., Vol. 1, pp. 269–322). New York: McGraw-Hill.

Esses, V. M., & Maio, G. R. (2002). The benefits of open-ended measures for assessing attitude structure. In W. Stroebe & M. Hewstone (Eds.), *European review of social psychology* (Vol. 12, pp. 71–102). Chichester, UK: John Wiley & Sons.

Fazio, R. H. (2000). Accessible attitudes as tools for object appraisal: Their costs and benefits. In G. R. Maio & J. M. Olson (Eds.), *Why we evaluate: Functions of attitudes* (pp. 1–36). Mahwah, NJ: Erlbaum.

Fazio, R. H., Chen, J., McDonel, E. C., & Sherman, S. J. (1982). Attitude accessibility, attitude–behavior consistency, and the strength of the object-evaluation association. *Journal of Experimental Social Psychology, 18*, 339–357.

Fazio, R. H., & Williams, C. J. (1986). Attitude accessibility as a moderator of the attitude-perception and attitude–behavior relations: An investigation of the 1984 presidential election. *Journal of Personality and Social Psychology, 51*, 505–514.

Fazio, R. H., & Zanna, M. P. (1981). Direct experience and attitude–behavior consistency. In L. Berkowitz (Ed.), *Advances in experimental social psychology* (Vol. 14, pp. 161–202). San Diego, CA: Academic Press.

Feather, N. (1995). Values, valences, and choice: The influence of values on the perceived attractiveness and choice of alternatives. *Journal of Personality and Social Psychology, 68*, 1135–1151.

Fenigstein, A., Scheier, M. F., & Buss, A. H. (1975). Public and private self-consciousness: Assessment and theory. *Journal of Applied Psychology, 43*, 522–527.

Ferguson, L. W. (1939). Primary social attitudes. *Journal of Psychology, 8*, 217–223.

Fish, S. (1999). *The trouble with principle*. London, UK: Harvard University Press.

Fishbein, M. (1967). A consideration of beliefs, and their role in attitude measurement. In M. Fishbein (Ed.), *Readings in attitude theory and measurement* (pp. 257–266). New York: Wiley.

Fishbein, M., & Ajzen, I. (1975). *Belief, attitude, intention, and behavior: An introduction to theory and research*. Reading, MA: Addison-Wesley.

Fishbein, M., & Coombs, F. S. (1974). Basis for decision: An attitudinal analysis of voting behavior. *Journal of Applied Social Psychology, 4*, 95–124.

Fleishman, J. A. (1986). Types of political attitude structure: Results of a cluster analysis. *Public Opinion Quarterly, 50*, 371–386.

Fromm, E. (1941). *Escape from freedom*. New York: Avon.

Gilchrist, R. S. (1995). *An investigation of value accessibility and its role in the value–attitude relationship*. Unpublished doctoral dissertation. Department of Psychology, University of Western Ontario.

Gilovich, T. (1987). Secondhand information and social judgment. *Journal of Experimental Social Psychology, 23*, 59–74.

Gold, J. A., & Robbins, M. A. (1979). Attitudes and values: A further test of the semantic memory model. *Journal of Social Psychology, 108*, 75–81.

Gold, J. A., & Russ, R. C. (1977). A semantic memory approach to the conceptualization of attitudes and values. *Journal of Social Psychology, 102*, 233–240.

Haddock, G., & Zanna, M. P. (1998). On the use of open-ended measures to assess attitudinal components. *British Journal of Social Psychology, 37*, 129–149.

Haddock, G., Zanna, M.P., & Esses, V.M. (1994). The (limited) role of trait-laden stereotypes in predicting attitudes toward Native peoples. *British Journal of Social Psychology, 33*, 83–106.

Harding, S., & Phillips, D. (1986). *Contrasting values in Western Europe: Unity, diversity, and change*. London: Macmillan.

Herek, G. M. (2000). The social construction of attitudes: Functional consensus and divergence in the U.S. public's reactions to AIDS. In G. R. Maio & J. M. Olson (Eds.), *Why we evaluate: Functions of attitudes* (pp. 325–364). Mahwah, NJ: Erlbaum.

Hewstone, M., & Brown, R. J. (1986). Contact is not enough: An intergroup perspective on the "contact hypothesis." In M. Hewstone and R. J. Brown (Eds.), *Contact and conflict in intergroup encounters* (pp. 1–44). Oxford, UK: Blackwell.

Higgins, E. T. (1996). Knowledge activation: Accessibility, applicability, and salience. In E. T. Higgins & A. W. Kruglanski (Eds.), *Social psychology: Handbook of basic principles* (pp. 133–168). New York: Guilford.

Houston, D. A., & Fazio, R. H. (1989). Biased processing as a function of attitude accessibility: Making objective judgments subjectively. *Social Cognition, 7*, 51–66.

Inglehart, R. (1971). The silent revolution in Europe: Intergenerational change in post-industrial societies. *American Political Science Review, 65*, 991–1017.

Inglehart, R. (1997). *Modernization and postmodernization: Cultural, economic, and political change in 43 societies*. Princeton, NJ: Princeton University Press.

Jennings, M. K., & Niemi, R. G. (1968). The transmission of political values from parent to child. *American Political Science Review, 62*, 169–184.

Jonas, K., Diehl, M., & Brömer, P. (1997). Effects of attitude ambivalence on information processing and attitude–intention consistency. *Journal of Experimental Social Psychology, 33*, 190–210.

Kahle, L. R. (1996). Social values and consumer behavior: Research from the list of values. In C. Seligman, J. M. Olson, & M. P. Zanna (Eds.), *The psychology of values: The Ontario symposium* (pp. 135–152). Mahwah, NJ: Lawrence Erlbaum Assoc.

Kallgren, C. A., & Wood, W. (1986). Access to attitude-relevant information in memory as a determinant of attitude–behavior consistency. *Journal of Experimental Social Psychology, 22*, 328–338.

Kaplan, K. J. (1972). On the ambivalence-indifference problem in attitude theory and measurement: A suggested modification of the semantic differential technique. *Psychological Bulletin, 77*, 361–372.

Kardes, F. R., Sanbonmatsu, D. M., Voss, R. T., & Fazio, R. H. (1986). Self-monitoring and attitude accessibility. *Personality and Social Psychology Bulletin, 12*, 468–474.

Katz, D. (1960). The functional approach to the study of attitudes. *Public Opinion Quarterly, 24*, 163–204.

Katz, I., & Hass, R. G. (1988). Racial ambivalence and American value conflict: Correlational and priming studies of dual cognitive structures. *Journal of Personality and Social Psychology, 55*, 893–905.

Keniston, K. (1965). *The uncommited: Alienated youth in American society*. New York: Harcourt, Brace, & World.

Kerlinger, F. N. (1973). *Foundations of behavioral research* (2nd ed.). New York: Holt, Rhinehart & Winston.

Kerlinger, F. N. (1984). *Liberalism and conservatism: The nature and structure of social attitudes.* Hillsdale, NJ: Erlbaum.

Kinder, D. R. (1998). Opinion and action in the realm of politics. In D. T. Gilbert, S. T. Fiske, & G. Lindzey (Eds.), *The handbook of social psychology* (4th ed., Vol. 2, pp. 778–867). New York: McGraw-Hill.

Kluckhohn, F. R., & Strodtbeck, F. (1961). *Variations in value orientations.* Evanston, IL: Row, Peterson.

Kohn, M., & Schooler, C. (1983). *Work and personality: An inquiry into the impact of social stratification.* Norwood, NJ: Ablex.

Kraus, S. J. (1995). Attitudes and the prediction of behavior: A meta-analysis of the empirical literature. *Personality and Social Psychology Bulletin, 21,* 58–75.

Kristiansen, C. M., & Hotte, A. M. (1996). Morality and the self: Implications for the when and how of value–attitude–behavior relations. In C. Seligman, J. M. Olson, & M. P. Zanna (Eds.), *The psychology of values: The Ontario symposium* (pp. 77–106). Mahwah, NJ: Lawrence Erlbaum.

Kristiansen, C. M., & Zanna, M. P. (1988). Justifying attitudes by appealing to values: A functional perspective. *British Journal of Social Psychology, 27,* 247–256.

Lavine, H., Thomsen, C. J., & Gonzalez, M. H. (1997). The development of interattitudinal consistency: The shared-consequences model. *Journal of Personality and Social Psychology, 72,* 735–749.

Levine, R., Sato, S., Hashomoto, T., & Verman, J. (1995). Love and marriage in eleven cultures. *Journal of Cross-Cultural Psychology, 26,* 554–571.

Lord, C. G., Lepper, M. R., & Mackie, D. M. (1984). Attitude prototypes as determinants of attitude–behavior consistency. *Journal of Personality and Social Psychology, 46,* 1254–1266.

Lord, C. G., Ross, L., & Lepper, M. R. (1979). Biased assimilation and attitude polarization: The effects of prior theories on subsequently considered evidence. *Journal of Personality and Social Psychology, 37,* 2098–2109.

Lorr, M., Suziedelis, A., & Tonesk, X. (1973). The structure of values: Conceptions of the desirable. *Journal of Research in Personality, 7,* 137–147.

Luke, M. A., & Maio, G. R. (2002). *Humanity-esteem: Introducing the highest level of self-categorization.* Unpublished manuscript, Cardiff University.

Lusk, C. M., & Judd, C. M. (1988). Political expertise and the structural mediators of candidate evaluations. *Journal of Experimental Social Psychology, 24,* 105–126.

MacDonald, T. K., & Zanna, M. P. (1998). Cross-dimension ambivalence toward social groups: Can ambivalence affect intentions to hire feminists? *Personality and Social Psychology Bulletin, 24,* 427–441.

Maddi, S., Kobosa, S.C., & Hoover, M. (1979). An alienation test. *Journal of Humanistic Psychology, 19,* 73–76.

Maio, G. R., Bell, D. W., & Esses, V. M. (1996). Ambivalence and persuasion: The processing of messages about immigrant groups. *Journal of Experimental Social Psychology, 32,* 513–536.

Maio, G. R., & Esses, V. M. (2001). The need for affect: Individual differences in the motivation to approach or avoid emotions. *Journal of Personality, 69,* 583–616.

Maio, G. R., Esses, V. M., & Bell, D. W. (2000). Examining conflict between components of attitudes: Ambivalence and inconsistency are distinct constructs. *Canadian Journal of Behavioural Science, 32,* 58–70.

Maio, G. R., Esses, V. M., & Olson, J. M. (in press). The function-structure model of attitudes: Incorporating the need for affect. In G. Haddock & G. R. Maio (Eds.), *Perspectives on attitudes for the 21st Century.* London, UK: Psychology Press.

Maio, G. R., & Olson, J. M. (1994). Value–attitude–behavior relations: The moderating role of attitude functions. *British Journal of Social Psychology, 33,* 301–312.

Maio, G. R., & Olson, J. M. (1995). Relations between values, attitudes, and behavioral intentions: The moderating role of attitude function. *Journal of Experimental Social Psychology, 31,* 266–285.

Maio, G. R., & Olson, J. M. (1998). Values as truisms: Evidence and implications. *Journal of Personality and Social Psychology, 74,* 294–311.

Maio, G. R., & Olson, J. M. (2000). What is a value-expressive attitude? In G. R. Maio & J. M. Olson (Eds.), *Why we evaluate: Functions of attitudes* (pp. 249–269). Mahwah, NJ: Erlbaum.

Maio, G. R., Olson, J. M., Bernard, M., & Allen, L. (2001). Addressing discrepancies between values and behavior: The motivating effect of reasons. *Journal of Experimental Social Psychology, 37,* 104–117.

Maio, G. R., Roese, N. J., Seligman, C., & Katz, A. (1996). Ratings, rankings, and the measurement of values: Evidence for the superior validity of ratings. *Basic and Applied Social Psychology, 18,* 171–181.

Markus, H., & Kitayama, S. (1991). Culture and the self: Implications for cognition, emotion, and motivation. *Psychological Review, 98,* 224–253.

Markus, H., Kitayama, S., & Heiman, R. J. (1996). Culture and "basic" psychological principles. In E. T. Higgins & A. W. Kruglanski (Eds.), *Social psychology: Handbook of basic principles* (pp. 857–913). New York: Guilford Press.

Maslow, A. H. (1970). *Motivation and personality* (Rev. ed.). New York: Harper & Row.

Matsumoto, D. (1996). *Culture and psychology.* Pacific Groves, CA: Brooks/Cole.

McGuire, W. J. (1960). A syllogistic analysis of cognitive relationships. In C. I. Hovland & M. J. Rosenberg (Eds.), *Attitude organization and change: An analysis of consistency among attitude components* (pp. 65–111). New Haven, CT: Yale University Press.

McGuire, W. J. (1964). Inducing resistance to persuasion: Some contemporary approaches. In L. Berkowitz (Ed.), *Advances in experimental social psychology* (Vol. 1, pp. 191–229). New York: Academic Press.

McGuire, W. J. (1985). Attitudes and attitude change. In G. Lindzey & E. Aronson (Eds.), *Handbook of social psychology* (3rd ed., Vol. 2, pp. 233–346). New York: Random House.

Mellema, A., & Bassili, J. N. (1995). On the relationship between attitudes and values: Exploring the moderating effects of self-monitoring and self-monitoring schematicity. *Personality and Social Psychology Bulletin, 21,* 885–892.

Morris, C. W. (1956). *Varieties of human value.* Chicago, IL: University of Chicago Press.

Neuman, W. R. (1990). The threshold of public opinion. *Public Opinion Quarterly, 554,* 159–176.

Olson, J. M. (1990). Self-inference processes in emotion. In J. M. Olson & M. P. Zanna (Eds.), *Self-inference processes: The Ontario symposium* (Vol. 6, pp. 17–41). Hillsdale, NJ: Erlbaum.

Olson, J. M. (1992). Self-perception of humor: Evidence for discounting and augmentation effects. *Journal of Personality and Social Psychology, 62,* 369–377.

Olson, J. M., & Maio, G. R. (2003). Attitudes in social behavior. In T. Millon & M. J. Lerner (Eds.), *Handbook of psychology: Personality and Social Psychology* (Vol. 5, pp. 299–325). Hoboken, NJ: John Wiley & Sons.

Olson, J. M., Vernon, P. A., Harris, J. A., & Jang, K. L. (2001). The heritability of attitudes: A study of twins. *Journal of Personality and Social Psychology, 80,* 845–860.

Olson, J. M., & Zanna, M. P. (1993). Attitudes and attitude change. *Annual Review of Psychology, 44,* 117–154.

Peterson, J. L., & Zill, N. (1981). Television viewing in the United States and children's intellectual, social, and emotional development. *Television and Children, 2,* 21–28.

Petty, R. E., Wegener, D. T., & Fabrigar, L. R. (1997). Attitudes and attitude change. *Annual Review of Psychology, 48,* 609–647.

Quinn, D. M., & Crocker, J. (1999). When ideology hurts: Effects of belief in the Protestant Ethic and feeling overweight on the psychological well-being of women. *Journal of Personality and Social Psychology, 77,* 402–414.

Rohan, M. J., & Zanna, M. P. (1996). Value transmission in families. In C. Seligman, J. M. Olson, & M. P. Zanna (Eds.), *The psychology of values: The Ontario symposium* (Vol. 8, pp. 253–276). Mahwah, NJ: Erlbaum.

Rohan, M. (2000). A rose by any name? The values construct. *Personality and Social Psychology Review, 4,* 255–277.

Rokeach, M. (1973). *The nature of human values.* New York: Free Press.

Rosenberg, M. J. (1960). An analysis of affective-cognitive consistency. In C. I. Hovland & M. J. Rosenberg (Eds.), *Attitude organization and change: An analysis of consistency among attitude components* (pp. 15–64). New Haven, CT: Yale University Press.

Rosenberg, M. J. (1968). Hedonism, inauthenticity, and other goads toward expansion of a consistency theory. In R. P. Abelson, E. Aronson, W. J. McGuire, T. M. Newcomb, M. J. Rosenberg, & P. H. Tannenbaum (Eds.), *Theories of cognitive consistency: A sourcebook* (pp. 827–833). Chicago: Rand McNally.

Roskos-Ewoldsen, D. R., & Fazio, R. H. (1992). On the orienting value of attitudes: Attitude accessibility as a determinant of an object's attraction of visual attention. *Journal of Personality and Social Psychology, 63,* 198–211.

Schacht, R. (1970). *Alienation.* New York: Doubleday & Company.

Scheier, M. F., Buss, A. H., & Buss, D. M. (1978). Self-consciousness, self-report of aggressiveness, and aggression. *Journal of Research in Personality, 12,* 133–140.

Schwartz, S. H. (1992). Universals in the content and structure of values: Theoretical advances and empirical tests in 20 countries. In M. P. Zanna (Ed.), *Advances in experimental social psychology* (Vol. 25, pp. 1–65). San Diego, CA: Academic Press.

Schwartz, S. H. (1996). Value priorities and behavior: Applying the theory of integrated value systems. In C. Seligman, J. M. Olson, & M. P. Zanna (Eds.), *Values: The Ontario symposium* (Vol. 8, pp. 1–24). Mahwah, NJ: Erlbaum.

Schwartz, S. H., Sagiv, L., & Boehnke, K. (2000). Worries and values. *Journal of Personality, 68,* 309–346.

Schwartz, S. H., & Tessler, R. C. (1972). A test of a model for reducing measured attitude–behavior discrepancies. *Journal of Personality and Social Psychology, 24,* 225–236.

Scott, W. A. (1968). Attitude measurement. In G. Lindzey & E. Aronson (Eds.), *Handbook of social psychology* (2nd ed., Vol. 2, pp. 204–273). Reading, MA: Addison-Wesley.

Seeman, M. (1975). Alienation studies. *Annual Review of Sociology, 1,* 91–123.

Silverstein, B., Perdue, L., Peterson, B., & Kelley, E. (1986). The role of the mass media in promoting a thin standard of bodily attractiveness for women. *Sex Roles, 14,* 519–532.

Smith, M. B., Bruner, J. S., & White, R. W. (1956). *Opinions and personality*. New York: Wiley.

Snyder, M. (1987). *Public appearances, private realities*. New York: Freeman.

Snyder, M., & DeBono, K. G. (1985). Appeals to image and claims about quality: Understanding the psychology of advertising. *Journal of Personality and Social Psychology, 49*, 586–597.

Snyder, M., & Kendzierski, D. (1982). Acting on one's attitudes: Procedures for linking attitudes and behavior. *Journal of Experimental Social Psychology, 18*, 165–183.

Spence, J. T. (1993). Gender-related traits and gender ideology: Evidence for a multifactorial theory. *Journal of Personality and Social Psychology, 64*, 624–635.

Stangor, C., Sullivan, L. A., & Ford, T. E. (1991). Affective and cognitive determinants of prejudice. *Social Cognition, 9*, 359–380.

Tajfel, H. (1970). Experiments in intergroup discrimination. *Scientific American, 223*, 96–102.

Thompson, M. M., Zanna, M. P., & Griffin, D. W. (1995). Let's not be indifferent about (attitudinal) ambivalence. In R. E. Petty & J. A. Krosnick (Eds.), *Attitude strength: Antecedents and consequences* (pp. 361–386). Mahwah, NJ: Erlbaum.

Thompson, M. S., Judd, C. M., & Park, B. (2000). The consequences of communicating social stereotypes. *Journal of Experimental Social Psychology, 36*, 567–599.

Thomsen, C. J., Lavine, H., & Kounios, J. (1996). Social value and attitude concepts in semantic memory: Relational structure, concept strength, and the fan effect. *Social Cognition, 14*, 191–225.

Towles-Schwen, T., & Fazio, R. H. (2001). On the origins of racial attitudes: Correlates of childhood experiences. *Personality and Social Psychology Bulletin, 27*, 162–175.

Trafimow, D., & Sheeran, P. (1998). Some tests of the distinction between cognitive and affective beliefs. *Journal of Experimental Social Psychology, 34*, 378–397.

Triandis, H. (1994). *Culture and social behavior*. New York: McGraw-Hill.

Triandis, H. (1995). *Individualism and collectivism*. Boulder, CO: Westview Press.

Vallone, R. P., Ross, L., & Lepper, M. R. (1985). The hostile media phenomenon: Biased perception and perceptions of media bias in coverage of the Beirut massacre. *Journal of Personality and Social Psychology, 49*, 577–585.

van der Pligt, J., & de Vries, N. (1998). Belief importance in expectancy-value models of attitudes. *Journal of Applied Social Psychology, 28*, 1339–1354.

Verplanken, B., & Holland, R. W. (in press). Motivated decision making: Effects of activation and self-centrality of values on choices and behavior. *Journal of Personality and Social Psychology, 82*, 434–447.

Wicklund, R. A. (1982). Self-focused attention and the validity of self-reports. In M. P. Zanna, E. T. Higgins, & C. P. Herman (Eds.), *Consistency in social behavior: The Ontario symposium* (Vol. 2, pp. 149–172). Mahwah, NJ: Erlbaum.

Williams, T. (Ed.). (1986). *The impact of television: A natural experiment in three communities*. Orlando, FL: Academic Press.

Wojciszke, B. (1987). Idealism scale for the measurement of individual differences in regulatory functions of the ideal self. *Polish Psychological Bulletin, 18*, 325–333.

Wojciszke, B. (1989). The system of personal values and behavior. In N. Eisenberg, J. Reykowski, & E. Staub (Eds.), *Social and moral values: Individual and societal perspectives* (pp. 229–251). Mahwah, NJ: Lawrence Erlbaum.

Wolsko, C., Park, B., Judd, C. M., & Wittenbrink, B. (2000). Framing interethnic ideology: Effects of multicultural and color-blind perspectives on judgments of groups and individuals. *Journal of Personality and Social Psychology, 78*, 635–654.

Wood, W. (1982). Retrieval of attitude-relevant information from memory: Effects on susceptibility to persuasion and on intrinsic motivation. *Journal of Personality and Social Psychology, 42*, 798–810.

Wood, W., Rhodes, N., & Biek, M. (1995). Working knowledge and attitude strength: An information processing analysis. In R. E. Petty & J. A. Krosnick (Eds.), *Attitude strength: Antecedents and consequences* (pp. 455–487). Mahwah, NJ: Erlbaum.

Wood, W., Wong, F. Y., & Chachere, J. G. (1991). Effects of media violence on viewers' aggression in unconstrained social interaction. *Psychological Bulletin, 109*, 371–383.

Wyer, R. S., Jr. (1970). Quantitative prediction of belief and opinion change: A further test of a subjective probability model. *Journal of Personality and Social Psychology, 16*, 559–570.

Zajonc, R. B. (1980). Feeling and thinking: Preferences need no inferences. *American Psychologist, 35*, 151–175.

Zanna, M. P., Klosson, E. C., & Darley, J. M. (1976). How television news viewers deal with facts that contradict their beliefs: A consistency and attribution analysis. *Journal of Applied Social Psychology, 6*, 159–176.

Zanna, M. P., & Rempel, J. K. (1988). Attitudes: A new look at an old concept. In D. Bar-Tal & A. W. Kruglanski (Eds.), *The social psychology of knowledge* (pp. 315–334). Cambridge, England: Cambridge University Press.

CHAPTER 13

Emotions and Sentiments

Jan E. Stets

INTRODUCTION

Definitions

I begin with the classical theorist Cooley (1909, p. 177) who defined *sentiment* in this way: "By sentiment I mean *socialized* [my emphasis] feeling, feeling which has been raised by thought and intercourse out of its merely instinctive state and become properly human. It implies imagination, and the medium in which it chiefly lives is sympathetic contact with the minds of others." Sentiment is distinctly social. Gordon (1981) highlights this by identifying sentiment as a socially constructed combination of autonomic responses, expressive behaviors, and shared meanings usually organized around another person. As he writes, sentiment involves "combinations of bodily sensations, gestures, and cultural meanings that we learn in enduring social relationships" (Gordon, 1981, p. 563). For example, love is a sentiment that is characterized by autonomic symptoms such as the flow of adrenaline and increased heart rate, emerges with another we see as attractive, and may be expressed in gazing and smiling at the other. We learn through socialization the vocabulary to name our internal sensations given objects or events that we encounter, and we learn how to express them accordingly.*

The clearest definition of an *emotion* comes from Thoits' (1990) who indicates that an emotion has four interconnected components: (1) situational cues, (2) physiological changes, (3) expressive gestures, and (4) an emotion label that names the specific configuration of

---

*Others use the term, sentiments, particularly affect control theorists (Heise, 1979; Smith-Lovin, 1990). Similar to Gordon's definition, they see sentiments as providing cultural meanings as to how the self, others, and social actions in situations are to be interpreted.

Jan E. Stets • Department of Sociology, University of California, Riverside, CA, USA
Handbook of Social Psychology, edited by John Delamater. Kluwer Academic/Plenum Publishers, New York, 2003.

components.* Thoits contends that children learn the connection between these components by repeatedly being exposed to emotion labels from others when particular configurations of the components emerge in their own experiences. I think Thoits' definition of an emotion has all of the elements of a sentiment. While persons experience particular biological responses (including autonomic, chemical, and neural activity), it is to an object or event (situational cue) that is interpreted in a culturally laden manner. Further, our culture influences the gestures and label we will apply to the experience. Using Thoits' components of an emotion, let us consider fear. Physiologically, fear is associated with greater decreases in blood pressure and blood flow to the extremities (Levenson, 1992).[†] It is generally activated when there is an interpretation of potential harm in one's environment (Ekman & Friesen, 1975). So, when we see a bear in the woods, our culture informs us that a bear is dangerous and will likely harm us, our heart rate will increase, our hands will become warm, our body may begin to tremble, and we will culturally associate the entire experience with the emotion, fear.

While both Gordon and Thoits recognize the biological and cognitive aspects of experiences, they also recognize the social: the interpretation(s) made in the situation, the expressions and gestures, and the vocabulary/labels that are all learned through socialization. Given the similarity in how sentiments and emotions have been defined, I will use these terms interchangeably throughout this review to refer to experiences that result from the combined influences of the biological, the cognitive, and the social. I will be particularly attentive to the social.

Other terms appear in the literature on emotions. Among the most general is the term *affect*, which is "any evaluative (positive or negative) orientation toward an object" (Smith-Lovin, 1995, p. 118). This highlights the cognitive aspect of emotions and sentiments. *Moods* are "affective states without an object or without a specific object" (Frijda, 1993, p. 381). Compared to emotions, moods are usually longer in duration, lower in intensity, and more diffuse/global. Finally, there is the term *feeling,* which may be defined as the internal, subjective experience of an emotion that is unique to each person. I will use these terms less frequently in this chapter.

Primary and Secondary Emotions

Researchers in sociology and psychology have examined whether there is a small set of primary or basic emotions from which all other emotions are derived. One of the earliest arguments is that of the psychologist, Ekman. With Freisen, Ekman showed still photographs of facial expressions to observers in different cultures and then asked them to check from a list of emotions which ones they saw. Five emotions were recognized in the face in literate and preliterate societies: anger, fear, sadness, disgust, and happiness (Ekman & Freisen 1975).[‡] The universality of these facial expressions provided compelling evidence that these emotions are basic to humans. Four out of these five emotions are negative, suggesting that humans may be more attentive to negative than positive cues, perhaps because negative cues register

---

*Similarly, Averill (1980) sees emotions as *syndromes*, that is, a set of events that tend to occur together in a systematic fashion. The components include subjective experiences, expressive reactions, patterns of physiological responses, and coping reactions.

[†]Damage to the amygdala, the part of the limbic area where emotion is now thought to reside, appears to impair the activation of fear (Damasio, 1994; LeDoux, 1996).

[‡]A sixth emotion, surprise, which was originally identified as basic, turns out to be less convincing over time; evidence is not as firm that a unique facial expression can be identified (Ekman, 1992).

danger and impel us to respond. Recently, Ekman (1992) has discussed other characteristics of basic emotions including the fact that they have unique autonomic responses, they are quick in their onset, and they are brief in their duration.

In sociology, Kemper (1987) identified a set of primary emotions. His four primary emotions: anger, fear, depression, and satisfaction parallel Ekman's set of basic emotions. Kemper maintains that these emotions are fundamental because each has evolutionary survival value (e.g., fear and anger encourage individuals to respond quickly when they are in danger), they appear in the earliest stages of human development, they are universally recognized in the face, they have unique autonomic responses, and they emerge in social relations.

Kemper takes his analysis one step further by arguing that there is a second layer of emotions that stems from primary emotions, which he labels secondary emotions. These emotions are more socially constructed (unlike the primary emotions, which Kemper sees as innate). They are learned through socialization in connection with the primary emotions. For example, guilt is learned from the primary emotion fear. When a child commits a forbidden act, he fears punishment. Over time, a child learns that when he performs a bad act and he fears punishment, guilt is the emotion label he should invoke. Kemper further states that a *combination* of primary emotions can lead to secondary emotions. For example, fear and anger can lead to the secondary emotions of hate, jealousy, and envy.

A contemporary sociological view of primary emotions is in the work of Turner (2002), who provides his list of primary emotions: assertion–anger, aversion–fear, disappointment–sadness, and satisfaction–happiness. One sees parallels to Ekman's and Kemper's list. Turner discusses how each of these emotions is identifiable in different parts of the brain. For each of the four emotions, he identifies a list of additional emotions that are linked to these primary emotions along the dimension of intensity. For example, satisfaction–happiness of low intensity is serenity. Assertion–anger of moderate intensity is hostility. Disappointment–sadness that is of high intensity is sorrow. Further, Turner adopts Kemper's analogy of "mixing" primary emotions to arrive at a list of secondary emotions. For example, disappointment–sadness combined with lesser levels of satisfaction–happiness is solace and melancholy.

Another label for secondary emotions is *social* or *self-conscious* emotions (Tangney & Fischer, 1995). In addition to the recognition that they are socially constructed, social or self-conscious emotions emerge out of social interaction where there is some evaluation that is made of the self and/or other in the situation. Some of the more common self-conscious emotions that have been investigated include guilt, shame, embarrassment, empathy, and sympathy. I will discuss each of these later.

Emotion and Reason

Historically, emotion and reason were considered opposing forces in which cognition directed "rational action" and emotion directed "irrational action." This assumption is not as widely shared today with the development of important lines of research in areas such as neurology and human development among others, which, in my view, convincingly show how reasoning is intimately dependent upon emotion. For example, Damasio's (1994) work in neurology has shown that emotion is very important in decision-making. According to his somatic-marker hypothesis, when individuals experience neurological damage to selected areas of the prefrontal region of the brain, they lose the ability to experience feelings or sensations that mark specific actions as having particular negative outcomes. Having lost this "marker" or "alarm signal," individuals are unable to decide advantageously in situations involving risk and conflict. In human development, Greenspan (Greenspan & Benderly, 1997) links early emotional experiences to the growth of the mind. He argues that as children develop, sensory perception forms part of a dual code: children interpret phenomena in terms of its physical properties, but they also react to phenomena affectively. Greenspan maintains that to the extent that caregivers are inattentive to their children's emotional needs, the intellectual competence of their children can be compromised.

Emotions are an important source of information with individuals more or less skilled at processing this information. This skill has now been labeled *emotional intelligence* (Goleman, 1995).* A recent theory of emotional intelligence indicates that it encompasses four competencies: (1) perceiving and expressing emotion, (2) integrating emotion into thought, (3) understanding emotions, and (4) managing emotions (Mayer & Salovey, 1997). Emotional intelligence is very similar to the idea of *emotional competence* (Saarni, 1999). Some of the skills involved in emotional competence include: (1) an awareness of one's own and others emotional state, (2) the ability to use the vocabulary of emotion and expression available from one's culture, (3) the capacity for empathy and sympathy, (4) the ability to cope with aversive emotions and distressing circumstances, and (5) the capacity for emotional self-efficacy or living out one's personal theory of emotion.

Research on emotional intelligence informs us that we need to see emotion as guiding rational action in the same way that cognition does. To push this issue a little further, Frank (1988) reasons that if we assume a rational actor whose behavior is driven by immediate self-interest, what emotion resolves is that which the rational actor creates: the "problem of commitment" in society. Purely self-interested actors have difficulty committing to others because their chief concern is accruing immediate benefits. When emotions such as love and sympathy enter the scene, they help to regulate this self-interest and immediate self-gratification by fostering helping behavior. Over time, helping behavior is reciprocated, thereby producing a community of actors rather than a population of egoists. Frank further contends that individuals communicate their emotions in situations through subtle cues, and these cues serve as important markers for predicting how they will behave. Thus, it appears to be rational to attend to the emotional aspect of the human condition.

THEORIES ON EMOTIONS AND SENTIMENTS

Nonsociological Theories

EVOLUTIONARY.   The earliest scientific treatment of emotions can be traced to Darwin who published his now classic treatment on emotional expressions entitled, *The expression of the emotions in man and animals* (Darwin & Ekman, 1872). Darwin did not discuss emotions, but the *expressions* of emotions. He maintained that any expression had once been a part of actions that had purpose in our ancestors. Over time, these expressions became genetically retained in the absence of their purpose. For example, the open mouth and show of teeth that sometimes occurs when one is angry (Ekman & Friesen, 1975) reminds us of the bared-teeth grimace of an animal that is used to threaten an opponent that was originally part of the action

---

*Goleman (1995, p. 34) indicates that emotional intelligence includes "abilities such as being able to motivate oneself and persist in the face of frustrations; to control impulse and delay gratification; to regulate one's moods and keep distress from swamping the ability to think."

of actually biting another animal. Thus, emotional expressions were simply vestiges of old habits. Darwin believed that emotional expressions were universal. He was the first to study photographs of people to identify the commonality in various expressions. This served as the foundation for research on the universality of emotions through facial expressions (Ekman & Friesen, 1975).

BIOLOGICAL. While Darwin focused on emotional expressions, William James (1890) focused on the inner experience of emotion—one's feelings. He saw feelings as rooted in people's perceptions of changes in their bodily state. When a person perceived something in the environment, there was an immediate visceral change, for example, increases in sympathetic nervous system activity, which registered particular effects to the organs and other parts of the body. These physiological changes led one to link the bodily sensations to an emotion. Essentially the feedback from the body importantly influenced emotion. Around the same time, Lange (1885) proposed a similar theory on emotion. He emphasized the circulation of the blood, particularly vasomotor changes (changes in the muscles that constricted the blood vessels) as influencing emotional experiences. Given the similarity in approaches of James and Lange, the biological theory on emotion came to be known as the James–Lange theory. A review of research on autonomic activity and emotions does show some distinct differences, for example, anger is associated with an increase in heart rate while disgust shows a decrease in heart rate (Levenson, 1992).

PSYCHOANALYTIC. Like the biological view, the psychoanalytic perspective focuses on what is going on within the individual that influences emotions, but the emphasis is on psychological processes such as repression, projection, and displacement rather than physiological processes. Freud (1905) focused on anxiety and guilt. From his clinical practice, he saw these emotions as rooted in repressed illicit childhood sexual desires. Lewis (1987) has argued that rather than Freud focusing on the actual experiences of sexual abuse that his patients were recounting, he instead reframed their experiences in the form of unforbidden sexual longings. This reframing led him to anxiety and guilt while ignoring the important role of shame. Nevertheless, there is some value in Freud's thinking. As Turner (2002) argues, Freud brought out the idea that we can hide our emotions from ourselves, pushing them below a level of consciousness, that not only affects our own behavior but also how others act toward us.

COGNITIVE. The cognitive approach emphasizes the role of *judgments* in determining people's emotions. Early on, Arnold (1960) argued that emotion was an outcome of the *appraisal process*, that is, evaluating an object or event in terms of whether it was potentially harmful or beneficial to oneself. If the object were judged as potentially harmful, negative emotion would result; if judged as potentially beneficial, positive emotion would result. A contemporary view of Arnold's approach is in the work of Lazarus (1991) who maintains that we evaluate a stimulus in terms of its significance for our well-being, that is, whether it promotes or obstructs our goals. This is the *primary appraisal* phase. This is followed by the *secondary appraisal* phase, which involves coping. If individuals determine that their goals will be obstructed, coping involves strategies to manage or rid themselves of the negative emotion. If they think their goals will be facilitated, coping involves strategies to acquire further benefits.*

---

*Lazarus view stands in stark contrast to Zajonc's (2000) position that we should view cognition and emotion as operating independent of each other, on parallel, nonintersecting paths. He argues that emotion need not depend on cognition, and he turns to studies on the "mere exposure effect" as evidence for this. Individuals show a positive preference for phenomena they previously have been exposed to even without conscious recognition that they have

Mandler's (1975) theory of emotion assumes that emotion emerges when action that is guided by one's goals is *interrupted*. This interruption influences arousal of the sympathetic nervous system and signals to the individual that events in the environment require one's attention and adjustment. Importantly, this theory forms the basis of an analysis of emotion in identity theory; identity theory posits that negative emotional arousal is due to an interruption in achieving one's goal (Burke, 1991). Similarly, affect control theory (Heise, 1979; Smith-Lovin, 1990) and self-discrepancy theory (Higgins, 1987) maintain that an interruption in ongoing activity arouses emotion.

Research using the nonsociological theories have made important contributions to the study of emotions and sentiments. Physiological changes do occur in situations, and such changes may serve the survival interests of the actor, thus supporting the evolution of emotions. For example, the increase in heart rate observed in anger may supply an actor with the energy needed to prepare to attack an enemy or fend off an attack. There is a link between the body and emotion and neurological findings showing how emotion is tied to brain functioning further demonstrates this (Damasio, 1994; LeDoux, 1996). However, emotion is also influenced by thought, and how actors appraise situations will influence what they feel. Yet, how actors appraise situations, even how they appraise bodily changes, is influenced by culture. Individuals are socialized into what emotion label to apply to situations and to physiological changes. For this reason, emotions and sentiments are intimately social. They have no meaning until social actors give them meaning. It is societal members who provide a vocabulary as to what we are to feel, when, and how to express those feelings. It is here that we see the contribution of sociology to the study of emotion.

Sociological Theories[†]

CLASSICAL THEORISTS.   The concern with emotions and sentiments can be seen in the classic works of Marx, Weber, Durkheim, and Cooley. While Marx saw emotions as rooted in the economic structure of a society, Weber and Durkheim embedded emotions in the culture of a society (specifically religion), and Cooley saw sentiments as emerging out of face-to-face interaction. For Marx (Marx & Engels, 1848), capitalism and its system of exploitation of workers led workers to feel alienated. Through identification with other workers, feelings of solidarity could emerge and lead to a revolt against the system. Hochschild (1983) extends Marx' thesis by identifying alienation as further rooted in what individuals are to *feel* at work. While workers may be slaves to the labors of their job, there is further subjugation that involves emotional labor and control of the heart.

For Weber (1904–1905), the doctrine of Calvinism and the predetermination of one's fate in the afterlife created anxiety for people. To resolve this anxiety, people thought that if they strictly adhered to God's commands including being responsible, following their

---

(*contd.*)

seen it before. The difference in Lazarus and Zajonc's views (Lazarus, 1982; Zajonc, 1984) rests largely in how cognition and emotion are defined (Cornelius, 1996). Zajonc's contention that very little cognition precedes emotion and Lazarus' view that cognition in the form of appraisals precedes emotion may both be true given recent neurological evidence that the amygdala receives dual sensory inputs from the thalamus, the subcortical path, which allows the organism to detect threatening stimuli quickly, and the cortex, the cortical path that serves to more fully analyze the stimulus (LeDoux & Phelps, 2000).

[†]Others have reviewed the contributions of sociological theories to emotions and sentiments in more detail than I have space to do here (see especially Kemper, 1991a; Smith-Lovin, 1995).

vocation, and engaging in honest, hard work, perhaps they could alter the unalterable. This hard work served as an important motivator underlying capitalism. Durkheim (1912) located sentiments in religious worship. He argued that the celebration of rituals to honor the sacred generated collective emotional excitement. In turn, this built commitment and solidarity—the very foundations of a society. Collins (1990) draws on Durkheim's idea of ritual interaction and emotional excitement to build a theory of interactional ritual and emotional energy in modern organizations.

Cooley viewed sentiment or "socialized feeling" as emerging out of social interaction. As he stated, "it [Sentiment] implies imagination, and the medium in which it chiefly lives is sympathetic contact with the minds of others" (Cooley, 1909, p. 177). For Cooley, sentiment was shaped by one's culture. We learned to label our physiological arousal as it emerged out of relations with others. Gordon's (1990) work on *emotional culture* draws on Cooley.

MID-20TH CENTURY. By the mid-1900s, small group researchers began to attend to emotions. Bales (1950) brought emotion into problem-solving groups by identifying socio-emotional behaviors within a group, that is, action designed to manage interpersonal problems that emerged. Homans (1961) was interested in the problem of distributive justice: the distribution of rewards and costs between persons. He maintained that when people received a reward that was less than what they expected, they would display anger. When they received a reward that was more than what they expected, they would display guilt. Emotions such as anger and guilt continue to be examined in research on justice (Hegtvedt, 1990; Stets, 2003).

It is also important to mention the contributions of Goffman (1959) during this time. Goffman was interested in how individuals managed a favorable impression of themselves to others. When actors' presentations failed, when the identity they were claiming was challenged by some untoward behavior in the situation, actors suffered a "loss of face" and would experience embarrassment. Interactive strategies would follow to repair a discredited identity.* Goffman's work continues to be influential in modern research on embarrassment (Miller, 1996; Scheff, 1990).

CONTEMPORARY VIEWS. Current sociological research on emotions and sentiments can be divided into three broad areas: a social structural approach, a cultural perspective, and a symbolic interactionist framework. The social structural approach maintains that one's position in the social structure importantly influences emotions and sentiments. A cultural approach emphasizes the norms that shape emotion and sentiments. The symbolic interactionist perspective addresses how self-processes influence emotions.

Social Structural Approach. For Kemper (1991b), sentiments are rooted in the dimensions of power and status. Power entails getting what one wants despite opposition from the other. It is dominance and control over another to which the other submits to involuntarily. Status involves voluntarily submitting to another because he or she is judged as valuable. Kemper sees every exchange as taking place along the dimensions of power and status. In interaction, there may be a change (increase or decrease) in power, a change (increase or decrease) in status, or no change on each dimension. Emotions emerge when there is a change in power and status. For example, power gain instigates happiness while power loss generates fear. When

---

*Goffman's ideas have an affinity with Cooley's "looking-glass self," where individuals imagine how they appear to others, imagine how that appearance is judged by others, and feel pride or mortification depending upon whether that evaluation is good or bad. Cooley's mortification is echoed in Goffman's embarrassment.

the self is responsible for status gain, pride is felt, and when another is responsible for one's status gain, joy is experienced. When the self is the agent of status loss, it brings about shame, and when another is the agent of one's status loss, one feels anger. In general, power and status increases are associated with positive emotions while power and status decreases are associated with negative emotions.

Hegtvedt (1990) draws on Kemper's theory of emotions by examining the status structure of a relationship and how this influences emotional reactions to inequity in an impersonal exchange situation. When subjects' role-play characters in a vignette, those assigned to the power-advantaged position are more likely than those in a power-disadvantaged position to report positive emotions such as feelings of deservedness, particularly those who are equitably rewarded or over-rewarded. Power-advantaged occupants presumably see that they are entitled to rewards, even over-rewards. Indeed, they are less likely than power-disadvantaged occupants to report feelings of gratitude for a reward. Overall, this research is consistent with the idea that positive emotion is more likely to be tied to positions of power while negative emotions are more likely to be linked to positions of powerlessness.

Collins (1990) stratifies the social structure into *order-givers* and *order-takers* in organizations. Order givers are the established leaders in organizations. The order takers are the workers in organizations. Collins examines the emotions of order-givers and order-takers through the lens of a Durkheimian analysis. He argues that interaction in organizations is essentially formatted in a ritual manner. The order-givers, for example, the managers, provide information to workers, critically evaluate their performance, speak strongly about policies and future operations, and so forth. Since the order-givers are more committed to the organization (the object of their attention in the ritual), they are likely to derive *emotional energy* or intense enthusiasm from the interaction. Their positive feelings are also derived from the positive feedback that they get from the workers. Alternatively, the order-takers simply assent to the commands of the order-givers and are less likely to experience emotional energy because they do not value the organization to the extent that the order-givers do. In fact, they may feel resentment, indifference, boredom, in general, alienation, with the order-takers' commands. Outside of the ritual interaction, they may express feelings of anger (hostility turned outward) or depression (hostility turned inward). Once again, we see how persons in powerful positions are more likely to experience positive emotion while persons in less powerful positions are more likely to experience negative emotion.

In keeping with Collins' idea of the importance of ritual interaction for emotions, Smith-Lovin and Douglas (1992) examined the emotions that emerge from rituals in two religious groups. One religious group was created to serve the gay community while a second religious group was not. Their results showed how the gay church developed a positive interaction style that reaffirmed the homosexual identity, for example, religious figures and church members supported gays and were even playful with them, while the other church had developed a more negative interaction style in which, rather than embracing homosexuals, they distanced themselves from homosexuals, hoping that God would advise them on how to best serve homosexuals, thereby confirming the deviant status of homosexuals.

A Cultural Perspective.   If Kemper and Collins see emotions as derived from one's social structural standing, researchers within the cultural perspective see social norms as influencing sentiments. One's culture tells one what to feel in situations. Historical analyses of changing emotions, given the changing environmental context, provide some understanding of the role of culture. For example, researchers have outlined how the onslaught of industrialization and the separation of work from home influenced greater control of emotions such as anger at work and a freer expression of negative emotions at home (Stearns & Stearns, 1986). Other researches show that the rise of sibling jealousy in the early part of the 20th century occurred at a time when maternal intensity was on the rise thus exposing children to more affectionate mothers, more hospitals were being used for the delivery of infants which could heighten the felt threat to maternal affection by an older child, and small families were becoming increasingly common (Stearns, 1988).

A cultural perspective is seen in research on love that reveals how the modern version of love as in being expressive and dependent corresponded with the emergence of a capitalist economy (Cancian, 1987). With the division of labor, the image of love became intimately tied to the home and what women did while self-development and independence became tied to work and what men did. Love became feminized with an emphasis on private feelings, and self-development became masculinized. When women entered the labor force in growing numbers in the mid-20th century, the emphasis on self-development and independence came to be applied to men and women equally, but views of love remained feminized. Cancian has argued that feminized love became costly because it ignored the masculine, instrumental version of love. Similarly, she pointed out that self-development could be problematic if it did not involve interdependence and commitment—critical features for a successful marriage. Her resolution has been for individuals to adopt an androgynous version of love that recognizes the feminine *and* masculine versions of love.

This may be what is occurring in contemporary society. For example, Swidler (2001) has discussed how both men and women appear to hold two (conflicting) versions of love: the mythic, romantic view and prosaic, realistic view, and they use these different views in different contexts. When people are deciding whether to marry or stay married, they employ the mythic, romantic view. They ask themselves, "Do I really love this person?" When thinking about how to maintain their marriage, they use the prosaic, realistic view. They ask themselves, "What do I need to do in this relationship? What do I need to give and/or give up?" In this way, the different versions of love can coexist because they serve different purposes. The mythic version motivates one to enter a marriage and even remain in it when divorce is considered, and the prosaic version mobilizes one to routine action to maintain the marriage. More generally, the culture of love helps people enter into lines of action that link them to the institution of marriage.

Rather than there being two versions of love, Sternberg (1998) argues that there are multiple versions of love. He argues that people tend to fall in love, marry, and remain married to those whose story of love matches their own. Love stories may change over time, and if both partners' love story does not change at a similar point in time, it may threaten the stability of the marriage. Love stories are influenced by people's pasts, including what they did not get and what they now desire, as well as what they experienced and still want. However, love stories are formulated within a culture in which there is pressure (albeit, subtle) to create stories that are culturally acceptable.* Sternberg identifies five major kinds of love stories. I mention three. *Asymmetrical* stories are premised on complementary roles in the relationship such as one being the "teacher" and the other being the "student." *Object* stories involve the partner or *relationship* as a means toward some other end. In the collection story, a partner may be seen as part of a larger collection, while in the religion story, a relationship may be seen as a way to get closer to God. *Genre* stories emphasize the interaction style of the relationship. Thus, a war story involves partners "doing battle," while a humor story involves a lighthearted

---

*As Sternberg (1998, p. 43) remarks, "People may be executed in one time or place for a story—about adultery, for example—that in another time or place would scarcely raise an eyebrow."

relationship. For Sternberg, understanding individuals' relationships means getting at their story of love.

For Gordon (1990), we have an *emotional culture* that we take account of when we act. This emotional culture includes "emotion vocabularies (words for emotions), norms (regulating expression and feeling), and beliefs about emotions (e.g., the idea that 'repressed' emotion is disturbing)" (Gordon, 1990, p. 146). Gordon (1989a) identifies two different orientations within emotional culture: *institutional* and *impulsive* meanings of emotion. Institutional meanings of emotions are those experiences we have when we are in full control of our feeling and expression. We act in ways that maintain the norms and standards. Impulsive meanings of emotions are spontaneous, uninhibited expressions of emotion that are thought to reveal our deep, hidden self. Morgan and Averill's (1992) research on authenticity has an affinity with Gordon's thesis. Examining "ordinary" and "true/authentic" feelings (similar to Gordon's institutional and impulsive meanings of emotions, respectively), they find that "true/authentic" feelings are: (1) perceived as emerging from deep within individuals—a deeper source than ordinary feelings, (2) judged as more intense and painful than ordinary feelings, and (3) seen as outside of one's control compared to ordinary feelings.

Operating in a similar tradition, Hochschild (1983) states that culture plays a significant role in emotions to the extent that there are *feeling rules* or cultural standards regarding how we ought to feel in situations. When what we feel differs from the cultural expectations, we engage in *emotion management* to bring the emotion into better alignment with the rules and create a more socially acceptable response.* Emotion management can take the form of *surface acting* in which people change their outward appearance so that it is consistent with normative expectations, or *deep acting* in which people change their inner feelings to be consistent with an outward, normative appearance. Hochschild labels emotion management done for a wage *emotional labor*. She associates this type of labor particularly with middle-class service jobs in which workers must frequently interact with their clients such as flight attendants. These workers are socialized to remain pleasant and friendly despite demanding, even irate passengers. Similarly, Pierce (1995) shows how female paralegals in contemporary law firms are expected to stay calm and be comforting and deferential in the face of angry outbursts from trial attorneys.

Thoits (1990) takes Hochschild's theme of emotional management one step further. She contends that when felt emotions repeatedly fail to meet cultural expectations and management efforts become ineffective, *emotional deviance* has occurred, and this may be a sign of mental illness. Such persons may actually indicate to themselves that they have a mental problem if they persistently find themselves unable to manage counter-normative feelings. The source of emotional deviance may reside in inadequate socialization (as when a child is not taught the normative emotional responses in particular situations) or when one of the following structural conditions occurs: (1) multiple role occupancy, (2) subcultural marginality, (3) role transitions, and (4) rigid rules associated with rituals or restrictive roles.

The Symbolic Interactionist Framework.   While culture provides the vocabulary and norms for emotions and sentiments, actors are the carriers of these emotions. How emotions emerge

---

*Hochschild's emotion management is similar to the idea of *emotional display* or "the self-regulation of emotional exhibition for the purpose of producing intended effects on others' minds" (Rosenberg, 1990, p. 4). Rosenberg argues that we engage in emotional display to indicate to others that we are moral actors (we are sensitive to the emotions norms of society), and to get what we want (e.g., we may express anger in the hopes that a wrong will be corrected).

within actors (given what is important to them, what is salient to them, and what their standards are) is important to researchers within the symbolic interactionist framework. For example, early in the development of identity theory, a structural variant of the symbolic interactionist framework, researchers argued that if an important identity has been threatened (by others not supporting that identity), an individual would experience negative emotion (McCall & Simmons, 1978). Consistent with this, Ellestad and Stets (1998) found that when nurturing behavior was linked to fathering rather than mothering, women whose mother identity was more important reacted with jealousy. Since nurturance is tied more to the mother identity than the father identity, when fathers engaged in action that involved close, warm, and intimate interactions with a child, mothers perceived this as a threat in a domain that was important to their self-definition. They responded with negative emotion. Stryker (1987) has noted that identities that generate negative feelings should be less likely to be played out and move down in one's hierarchy of identities while identities that cause positive feelings should be played out more often and move up in one's identity hierarchy.

Burke (1991) sees emotions as stemming from the discrepancy between how people perceive themselves in a situation and their identity standard meanings. Continuous congruence between people's self-in-situation meanings and identity standard meanings (self-verification) results in positive emotion, and incongruence between the two (a lack of self-verification) registers negative emotion. For example, in examining the spousal identity for newly married couples during the first 3 years of marriage, Burke and Stets (1999) found that when the spouse confirms one's self-view (self-verification), it enhances each person's feelings of self-esteem and mastery and reduces depression and distress.

Affect control theory, another structural variant of the interactionist framework, is closely aligned to identity theory in its assumption on the relationship between identities and emotions (Heise, 1979; Smith-Lovin, 1990). According to this theory, emotion signals the extent to which events *confirm* or *disconfirm* one's identity in a situation. When an event confirms one's identity, the evaluation, potency, and activity of the emotions in the situation (transient impressions) roughly matches the evaluation, potency, and activity of (the fundamental sentiments associated with) the identity. When an event in a situation disconfirms one's identity by creating transient impressions that differ from the fundamental sentiments associated with the identity, a deflection has occurred. If transient impressions are more positive than the fundamental sentiments of the identity, one will feel more positive emotions while impressions that fall below the fundamental sentiments will produce more negative emotion.

In an interesting application of affect control theory to two support groups (divorce and bereavement), Francis (1997) found that support group leaders help to resolve identity deflections for individuals. Specifically, an event of divorce or death creates negative transient impressions in a situation that differs from the fundamental sentiments that one is a good person/spouse. The sufferers have resolved the deflection by giving themselves a negative identity (i.e., "bad acts are done to bad persons"). Group facilitators reduce the deflection and transform the experience into a positive one by first giving the sufferer a positive identity, and then shifting responsibility of the bad act onto the other (the spouse). The result is that the negative emotion and negative identity are eliminated.

While emotions help to sustain individuals, emotions also sustain social structure (Shott, 1979). Shott maintains that *role-taking* emotions serve as a mechanism for social control in society. These emotions involve putting oneself in the place of another and seeing the situation from the other's perspective. She identifies two types of role-taking emotions. *Reflexive* role-taking emotions are directed toward oneself when one commits a counter-normative act; they comprise the sentiments of guilt, shame, and embarrassment. *Empathic* role-taking emotions involve mentally placing oneself in another's position and feeling what the other feels; empathy and sympathy are good examples. Shott claims that because it is impossible for society to monitor and sanction everyone's behavior all of the time, social control is largely self-control through self-regulation. While reflexive role-taking emotions serve to keep individuals "in line," empathic role-taking emotions service others.

Emotions also have implications for society in Scheff's work (1990, 1997). Drawing on Durkheim and Cooley, Scheff sees emotion as expressing the nature of the social bond. He indicates that a secure social bond is one in which individuals experience *attunement*, that is, mutual understanding (Scheff, 1997). Threats to a secure bond can come from either the bond being too loose, leading to isolation, or too tight, resulting in engulfment. Emotion identifies the state of the social bond, for example, "pride signals an intact social bond; shame, a threatened one" (Scheff, 1990, p. 71). Pride signals solidarity and shame signals alienation (Scheff, 1997). Scheff maintains that shame may not be disruptive to social bonds as long as it is acknowledged. Borrowing from Lewis (1971), when shame is unacknowledged in the form of *undifferentiated* shame (labeling the painful feeling something else) or *bypassed* shame (attempting to avoid the pain), it becomes disruptive. Unacknowledged shame can set off a chain reaction both within an individual and between individuals in which the emotional arousal increases in intensity and duration, setting the stage for interpersonal conflict, even violence (Scheff & Retzinger, 1991).

SOCIALIZATION OF EMOTIONS AND SENTIMENTS

What influences individuals' emotional experiences and expressions? One answer to this question is socialization. There are two main approaches to the study of emotional socialization. The cognitive developmental approach focuses on how cognitive processes that develop in an age-related manner influence how children think about and respond to their own and others' emotions. The interactionist perspective broadly focuses on the role of culture in people's understanding of emotions and sentiments. There is an analysis of children's interactions with parents, educators, and peers that help formulate children's emotions.

Cognitive Developmental Approach

The cognitive approach focuses on internal mental processes that develop as a child ages and that mediate between the self and the emotional experience. For example, Lewis (2000a) provides a model of the emergence of different emotions over the first 3 years of life. He assumes that at birth, children show a tripartite division of pleasure, interest, and distress. By the first 6 months of life, children show signs of all the basic emotions: happiness, sadness, disgust, anger, fear, and surprise. During the second half of the second year of life, the emergence of consciousness gives rise to a second class of emotions, the self-conscious emotions such as embarrassment, envy, and empathy. By age 3, children have a sense of self and are able to evaluate their behavior against a standard. This evaluation gives rise to the self-conscious evaluative emotions such as pride, shame, and guilt. Thus, by age 3, a child's emotional life has become fairly well differentiated.

Hoffman (2000) has focused on the development of empathy in children. He is interested in *empathic distress*—the ability to feel what another feels in a situation—which serves as the basis for prosocial, moral action in situations. Hoffman links the development of empathy to a child's development of a sense of self, others, and the relationship between self and others. There are four stages in the development of self and other and, correspondingly, an increasing mastery for empathic distress. A precursor of empathic distress occurs in the initial stage of development with a *newborn's reactive cry*: upon hearing another infant cry, a child cries. This is mimicry. Early in the second year, children move to the *quasi-egocentric* stage where they begin to see that the distress of another may not be their own distress. This stage is more fully developed by the middle of the second year in what Hoffman labels *veridical empathic distress*. Children become aware that others have inner states (thoughts and feelings) and that another's inner states may be different from their own. The fourth stage occurs between the ages of 5 and 8 where children acquire *empathic distress beyond the situation*. By this time, children have reached the point of seeing themselves and others as having separate histories and identities, and that the feelings that another shows in a situation is to be put into the context of the other's larger life experiences. For example, if another person shows sadness, this may represent the other's chronically unpleasant life condition.

There is a broad array of issues on the developmental aspects of children's emotions. For example, some researchers have examined children's developmental understanding of mixed feelings, that is, that more than one emotion can be experienced at the same time in a situation (Harter & Whitesell, 1989). Others have studied the development of self-conscious emotions such as guilt (Bybee, 1998), pride, shame, and embarrassment (Griffin, 1995). For example, Griffin argues that it is not until age 7–8 that children are able to engage in thought that simultaneously considers one's feeling states and the judgments of others—such thought is relevant for experiencing self-conscious emotions. In three separate studies, Griffin finds that when children are put into hypothetical situations in which the actor's behavior exceeds or falls short of the social standard, older (and not younger) children feel pride (for exceeding the standard), and embarrassment or shame (for falling short of the expectation).

Interactionist Perspective

The interactionist perspective focuses on how emotions and sentiments develop out of interaction. For example, Gordon (1989b) maintains that an understanding of emotions in terms of the subjective experience, expressive behavior, situational appraisal, and so forth is learned in interpersonal transactions during socialization. Children are taught the cultural meaning of an emotion, and then they "act toward it—magnifying, suppressing, or simulating it in themselves, and evoking or avoiding it in other people" (Gordon, 1989b, p. 324).

Rather than children learning the emotion culture, Russell (1989) contends that children learn an *emotion script*. A script is "a knowledge structure for an event in which the event is thought of as a sequence of subevents" (Russell, 1989, p. 303). An emotion script would be a knowledge structure that identifies the antecedents and accompanying reactions. The script contains the essential features commonly associated with the emotion. Russell (1989, p. 303) provides an example of the prototypical case of anger: "You are working hard to get something you want. Someone intervenes to prevent you from having it. You stop and stare. You feel your heart pounding, your muscles tightening. You race forward, knocking the person to the ground." Russell maintains that part of a child's acquisition of emotions comes in caregivers making associations for the child, and labeling and interpreting the experience for the child.

Parents, particularly mothers, have a significant influence in emotional socialization. For example, some find that mothers who discuss emotions with their children, express predominately positive emotions with them, and respond to their emotions calmly and reassuringly raise children who are happier, more self-confident, better able to regulate their emotionally expressive behavior, and are socially more competent with their peers (Denham, Mitchell-Copeland, Strandberg, Auerbach, & Blair, 1997). Similarly, others maintain that parents whose interaction with children is warm and affectionate, non-derogatory (lacks parental criticism and mockery), involves scaffolding/praising (task instructions are provided in a simple and relaxed fashion and approval is offered when a child had done something right), and has emotion-coaching (parents value their children's emotional expressions and assist them with their emotions), raise children who are socially competent with their peers, are able to inhibit negative affect, and are better able to be cognitively attentive (Gottman, Katz, & Hooven, 1997).

Brody (2001) maintains that the different roles mothers and fathers play in the family may set in motion different patterns of emotional expression for daughters and sons. She finds that when fathers are more active in childrearing, children become less sex-role stereotyped in their emotional expressivity. Sons become more emotionally expressive than their male counterparts in traditional families, and daughters become more competitive and show less vulnerability to sadness and fear relative to their female counterparts in traditional families. Involved fathers may be less likely to gender stereotype their children, thereby inducing fewer self-fulfilling prophecies in their children's emotional development.

Other adults such as caretakers in day care or other institutions can exert their own influence on children's emotional development. For example, some find that day care providers fail to legitimize children's emotions (Leavitt & Power, 1989). Children's emotions are ignored; there is a lack of response to what they are expressing. What caregivers do address is children's display of appropriate emotional behaviors, regardless of what children are feeling on the inside, and whether these feelings are congruent with their emotional displays. This is consistent with Hochschild's (1983) argument that we socialize individuals to manage their emotions. The consequence of teaching emotion management is that authentic feelings get suppressed, and caregivers' relationships with the children are emotionally distant.

In striking contrast, research at a therapeutic nursery for emotionally and behaviorally disturbed young children shows how caretakers are very involved in teaching children about emotions (Pollak & Thoits, 1989). Caretakers make associations for children between situational stimuli and emotion words so that children can understand what they are feeling, and they make associations for children between expressive behaviors and emotion words so that they can understand what others are feeling. Caretakers are more elaborate in their instruction about emotion only when a child exhibits inappropriate feelings or behavior. They take corrective action when they witness a deviation from emotion norms.

Emotional socialization may also come from peers. For example, research finds that adolescent girls communicate normative information and reinforce feeling and expression norms to one another about romantic love (Simon, Eder, & Evans, 1992). Discourse strategies such as joking, teasing, gossip, and confrontation may be used to socialize each other regarding the relative importance of romantic love and the appropriate object of one's romantic feelings. Interestingly, this research also evidences that sometimes girls will resist the emotion norms surrounding romantic love, suggesting that socialization does not completely determine affect.

SOCIAL EMOTIONS: REFERENCING THE SELF, INTERACTION, AND SOCIETY

A growing literature is developing on emotions that are self-conscious. Some of the more common emotions that have been investigated are guilt, shame, embarrassment, empathy, and sympathy.* Like the basic emotions, most of these emotions are negatively valenced, again suggesting that humans are more attentive to negative cues than positive cues in their environment. Self-conscious emotions are *social emotions* (Barrett, 1995) for three reasons.

First, they reference the self in that a sense of self (seeing oneself as an object to one's own actions) is a necessary prerequisite. Lewis (2000b) makes clear the role of the self in self-conscious emotions by identifying these emotions as *evaluative*, that is, they emerge when persons evaluate their thoughts, feelings, or actions against the standards or goals that guide them.† In the evaluation process, individuals either hold themselves responsible for the outcomes being evaluated (an internal attribution), or do not hold themselves responsible (an external attribution). Further, individuals evaluate themselves in terms of global or specific attributions. Global self-attributions refer to the "whole self," the entire self is involved in the evaluation. Thus, one may identify herself as a "good person" in the case of pride or a "bad person" in the case of shame. Specific self-attributions refer to "specific features or actions of the self" (Lewis, 2000b, p. 624). One identifies having done a "bad thing" rather than being a "bad person."

The self-referential nature of self-conscious emotions also is revealed in the fact that they help in the development of the self to the extent that people learn about themselves through these emotions, including maintaining or modifying future actions. They aid in the acquisition of self-knowledge (Barrett, 1995). For example, if individuals harm others, the guilt that is experienced tells them that there is discomfort in hurting others, and that they have the power to control this behavior.

Second, these emotions are grounded in social interaction. They emerge out of interaction with at least one other actor, either real or imagined. This is evident during socialization, most importantly parent–child interactions, in which the self is taught the standards or rules that societal members live by (Barrett, 1995). Acquiring socially valued behaviors such as helping others rather than hurting them is most likely to emerge for children when they receive both parental support (children are accepted and find approval) and parental inductive control (children are listened to and reasoned with).

Beyond socialization, social emotions emerge out of interpersonal encounters. As Fischer and Tangney (1995, pp. 3–4) write, "Emotions such as shame, guilt, pride, and embarrassment are founded in social relationships, in which people not only interact but evaluate and judge themselves and each other. Self-conscious emotions are built on reciprocal evaluation and judgment. For example, people are ashamed or guilty because they assume that someone (self and/or other) is making a negative judgment about some activity or characteristic of theirs." Indeed, researchers have discussed self-conscious emotions such as guilt (Baumeister, Stillwell, & Heatherton, 1994) and embarrassment (Miller, 1996) as intimately *inter*personal.

Finally, social emotions reference society because they often stem from considering society's standards vis-à-vis one's own actions. Indeed, feeling these emotions reminds actors of society's standards. Social emotions also monitor one's own behavior when others are not able to monitor it for the person. This makes social order possible. Social emotions can even be used in the service of society, reintegrating people who are outcasts, thereby avoiding a

---

*Space limitations do not allow a review of all of the self-conscious emotions, thus some emotions are omitted such as jealousy and envy (Salovey, 1991), grief (Stroebe, Hansson, Stroebe, & Schut, 2001) and forgiveness (McCullough, Pargament, & Thoresen, 2000).

†In my view, the standards/goals that are used in the evaluation process are, in part, culturally derived. We are socialized into what we "should" do and how we "ought" to be. On the other hand, they are, in part, idiosyncratically formulated given our own values and ideals. This is consistent with Higgins' (1987) idea that the self has different domains (an actual self, an ought self, and an ideal self) and that these different domains serve as self-guides for behavior.

deviant master status. For example, Braithwaite (1989) argues that shaming can reintegrate offenders into a law-abiding community by directing the shaming at the evil of the act rather than the evil of the person and requiring the offender to engage in gestures or ceremonies of forgiveness. In general, social emotions reference the micro, meso, and macro levels of social life. Below I briefly discuss each of the more common social emotions.

Guilt

Guilt involves a sense of tension, remorse, and regret for having done a bad thing (Tangney, 1995). Guilt appears to be a moral emotion in that the feeling motivates the person to corrective action. One may confess, apologize, and/or repair the damage that was done. The focus is on the offending behavior, the misdeed that was perpetrated, and its harmful consequences. In feeling guilt, rather than the entire self being scrutinized, one's behavior is evaluated. Because global devaluations of the self are unlikely to emerge, the self readily navigates itself in a situation to take reparative action. One is able to remain engaged in the encounter, show empathy, and do something so that the transgression may be forgiven.

Hoffman (1998) indicates that the most effective parental discipline method for producing guilt in children is *induction*. Induction involves parental disapproval of a child's harmful acts, and then calling attention to both the victim's distress and the child's responsibility for causing the distress. Making the victim salient should arouse empathic distress in a child. After a child sees that he has caused the victim's distress, the self-blame should transform feelings of empathy into guilt. Parental disapproval reinforces this guilt. After several repetitions of transgression followed by induction, empathic distress, and guilt, a child forms a "Transgression → Induction → Guilt Script" (Hoffman, 1998, p. 101).

Often when we think of guilt, we think of that which happens to a person rather than that which happens between people. Baumeister and his colleagues (Baumeister et al., 1994) highlight the *inter*personal nature of guilt. They maintain that rather than guilt damaging interpersonal relationships, it actually protects and strengthens them. To illustrate this, they identify three interpersonal functions of guilt. First, when an individual hurts another in a relationship, the guilt motivates her to engage in reparative action. Asking for forgiveness and so forth lets the other know that he is valued.*

A second interpersonal function of guilt is that it serves as an influence technique. One person may get what he wants by making the other feel guilty. The person using guilt as an influence strategy lets the other know that a particular action (or inaction) will be hurtful. Thus, the potential transgressor avoids the behavior so as to avoid the aversive state of guilt. There may be potential costs to this. The potential offender may resent the use of guilt despite compliance. The potential victim may also feel "metaguilt" or guilt over inducing guilt in another.

Third, feelings of guilt redistribute negative affect in a relationship. When one commits a transgression, the offender may get what she wants while the victim suffers the negative consequences. Guilt reduces the benefits of the transgressor since not all of what is gained is positive. Additionally, if the victim sees that the transgressor feels guilty, this may make the victim feel better not only because the victim sees that the offender has also suffered, but also because the trangressor's guilt may signify that she does care about the victim.

---

*This is not to say that guilt does not benefit offenders. Guilt can teach individuals to change their behavior so as to avoid threatening valued social attachments.

In a broad sense, guilt helps to maintain civility in society. By taking responsibility for harmful acts, individuals honor personal commitments—the very foundation of society. As some have argued, "the more people are committed to a community of others (close relationships, family, or the larger community), the more likely they will be to experience guilt" (Lindsay-Hartz, De Rivera, & Mascolo, 1995, p. 292). And these researchers point out an interesting paradox. People such as sociopaths who are quite guilty in an objective sense experience very little guilt, while those who live their lives doing loving acts often experience immense guilt. It is the latter group who sees how their fellow humans fail—how a wrongful act could have been prevented if a person had acted differently.

Shame

Shame is a far more intense feeling than guilt primarily because the whole self is involved in the evaluation of some wrongdoing. There is a feeling of shrinking, feeling small, worthless, and powerless (Tangney, 1995). Rather than focusing on the behavior that caused the misdeed, the focus is on the self as some horrible agent.* This global devaluation results in the person wanting to hide, disappear, or escape the situation. Sometimes, shamed people feel anger and blame others for their shame-inducing experience. Indeed, this is at the heart of Scheff and Retzinger's (1991) "shame-anger cycle" that they identify in marriage.† The cycle begins when one (A) is insulted or rebuffed by another (B). B becomes the source of A's hurt (shame), and in response, A may return the insult with an insult (anger). B now sees A as the source of B's hurt, and B reacts with a stronger assault than the initial attack. The interaction continues with demeaning criticisms and insults leveled at each other, separating A and B further from each other. If this cycle spirals out of control, it can lead to interpersonal violence.

Shame experiences are more likely to involve the self being evaluated by others whereas guilt is more likely to involve a concern with one's effects on others. The more egocentric concern in shame and the more other-oriented concern in guilt echo Lewis' (1971) classic observation that in shame there is a focus on the self and in guilt there is a focus on one's behavior.‡ Given this egocentrism, rather than remaining interpersonally involved in encounters, feelings of shame lead to withdrawing from the relationship because of the painful feeling and the sense of exposure (Tangney, 1995). This fleeing response, or alternatively, a defensive, retaliative anger for having been shamed makes shame more difficult for interpersonal relationships since resolution may be more problematic.

---

*Tangney (1995) distinguishes between shame and low self-esteem by noting that shame is a relatively transient emotional experience that emerges from specific failures and transgressions whereas low self-esteem is a more enduring and global self-conception.

†When the *anger* in the shame–anger sequence is *directed at the self*, it leads to feelings of guilt (Scheff & Retzinger, 1991). For Scheff, guilt *is* shame/anger. The anger masks or covers up the shame, and in this sense, guilt is bypassed shame. Recently, Scheff remarked that guilt has a feeling of power associated with it that shame does not (Personal conversation, October, 2001). In guilt, one has a sense of power in being able to make amends, but there is also power in knowing that one can harm another; in shame, the self feels powerless rather than powerful. The self is unable and weak.

‡Higgins (1987) has theorized that a discrepancy in actual versus ideal self-guides will lead to shame while a discrepancy in actual versus ought self-guides will lead to guilt. Tangney and her colleagues (Tangney, Niedenthal, Cover, & Barlow, 1998) do not find support for this. Since shame involves global negative evaluations of the self, it is not clear why one type of self-guide discrepancy would be more vulnerable to shame than another. Furthermore, guilt focuses on a specific behavior, making self-guide discrepancies less relevant. Indeed, Tangney and her associates find that all types of self-discrepancies are related to shame.

Researchers have undertaken an analysis as to whether we experience more shame or guilt in American society. In a large-scale cross-cultural study in 37 countries, Wallbott and Scherer (1995) found that in collectivist cultures such as Brazil, Mexico, and Greece, shame *and* guilt were reported as less recent in one's experiences, were viewed as less immoral, and had fewer negative effects on an individual's self-esteem and interpersonal relationships compared to individualistic cultures such as the United States, Italy, and Sweden. In collectivist societies, shame appeared to be the more predominant emotion while in individualist societies, guilt seemed to be the more common emotion. Wallbott and Scherer point out that our white, Anglo-Saxon/Nordic living where the Protestant ethic of personal responsibility prevails likely encourages feelings of guilt compared to shame. It is possible that Americans feel shame but underreport it when asked about it. Indeed, Scheff (1990) argues that shame is low in visibility in our society because individuals hide it from others, ashamed of their state of shame.

Embarrassment

For years, embarrassment was seen as a mild form of shame (Miller, 1996). More recently, this view has been challenged (Miller & Tangney, 1994; Tangney, Miller, Flicker, & Barlow, 1996).* When Miller and Tangney (1994) asked subjects to recall three situations that caused embarrassment, and three other, different situations in which their strongest feeling was shame, they found that embarrassing situations were described as more likely to emerge in predicaments that were light-hearted and funny, whereas shameful episodes were seen as more serious events, laughter was rare, and persons often felt angry with themselves.

In embarrassment, *social evaluation* appears to be important. There is a concern as to what others are thinking given their *public* exposure of appearing inept (clumsy or forgetful). In shameful incidents, *self-evaluation* is more important. Shaming brings on the painful realization of one's own imperfections. Thus, the *private* aspect of the experience plays a larger role. In recalling embarrassing situations, embarrassed people bring up feelings of awkwardness whereas shameful people feel immoral and are likely to consider themselves bad people. While embarrassing situations signify a "temporary error" that the self had committed, shameful experiences identify "deep-seated flaws." In later work, Tangney and her associates (Tangney et al., 1996) add guilt to their analysis of shame and embarrassment. They report that both shame and guilt are experienced more intensely, more painfully, and are more lasting emotions that have moral implications compared to the less intense, less painful feeling of embarrassment.

While some argue that embarrassment follows from a *violation of conventions* whereas shame follows from a *violation of moral rules* (Keltner & Buswell, 1997), others challenge this distinction (Sabini, Garvey, & Hall, 2001). Sabini and his colleagues point out, for example, that tripping or falling is not so much a violation of convention as much as a failure at motor control. They argue that the distinction between shame and embarrassment is rooted in the appraisal process. Specifically, they find that when people believe that a *real flaw* of their self has been revealed, they experience shame, but when a flaw has been revealed and people *disagree that this flaw is real*, they report embarrassment. As they point out, "shame is tied to real flaws, whereas embarrassment is tied to apparent ones" (Sabini et al., 2001, p. 106).

---

*Scheff maintains that while shame and embarrassment result from an insecure bond, embarrassment is a more transient feeling than shame (Personal conversation, October, 2001).

Embarrassment may involve blushing, but it is more reliably characterized by looking away from others, smile controls, a lowering of the head, and facial touching (perhaps to hide a smile or hide the eyes to avoid eye contact) (Miller, 1996). People respond to their embarrassing experiences in a variety of ways. They may flee because the experience is too mortifying, act like nothing has happened, laugh at it, explain their behavior through excuses or justifications, or apologize to the offended party (Miller, 1996). The most common responses from audience members to an embarrassed actor are support and empathy.

Empathy

While some social psychologists conceptualize empathy as a cognitive process (Clark, 1997; Ickes, 1997) in that one "reads" another, others see empathy as an affective process in that one feels the way another feels (Hoffman, 2000). However, empathy can have both cognitive and affective components (Davis, 1996). Clark (1997) makes a useful distinction between *cognitive* empathy (recognizing that another is in difficulty), *physical* empathy (seeing another's emotional expressions and that inducing similar expressions in oneself), and *emotional* empathy (feeling emotions that refer to another's plight). Clark maintains that empathy usually begins cognitively and may never become emotional or physical.

Gender differences in empathy have captured some attention given the belief in "women's intuition." Most of the recent evidence shows no difference in empathy by gender. There is a difference when women are made aware that they are being evaluated on their empathic ability (Graham & Ickes, 1997). When women are told that the task that they are about to complete will assess their empathic capabilities, their motivation to be empathic increases, leading them to be more successful in this ability. As Graham and Ickes (1997) point out, although men are just as accurate as women in identifying another's thoughts and feelings, they may be less motivated to be accurate given their gender-role socialization. Men are less likely than women to be taught to be empathic toward others. In fact, Graham and Ickes (1997, p. 140) argue that because men are more likely to be in positions of power, they may be more likely to expect that others "'read their minds' without feeling any obligation to return the favor."

Research reveals that empathic people are more likely to be intelligent, open-minded, and demonstrate good psychological adjustment (Davis & Kraus, 1997), they are more likely to empathize with those who they like and who are similar to them demographically (Clark, 1997). Empathy has positive consequences for intimate relationships since it facilitates stability and satisfaction (Ickes & Simpson, 1997).

Empathy clearly benefits society. It promotes helping behavior and tends to inhibit aggressive behavior (Davis, 1996). It is congruent with the moral principles of caring and justice (Hoffman, 2000). As Clark (1997) points out, modernization has made empathy more difficult. Increasing differentiation, residential mobility, urbanization, pressures to compete and succeed, makes it difficult for one to see the problems of another and respond benevolently. Nevertheless, it is an expectation that we have of others, and it is promoted through the different institutions in our society, particularly the institution of religion.

Sympathy

Clark (1997) sees empathy as a necessary prerequisite for sympathy. For her, the sympathy sentiment is "other-targeted emotions corresponding specifically to the other's hurt or anguish or worry" (Clark, 1997, p. 44). Clark maintains that when one's empathy is emotional or physical rather than cognitive, sympathy is more likely to emerge. And like empathy, Clark does not find that the sympathy sentiment varies by gender. In her study, men and women reported similar levels of compassion. However, she did find that men and women subscribed to different "sympathy rules." Men had a tendency to conceal sympathy, even their own problems that might merit sympathy, because it was inconsistent with being masculine and was contrary to what was expected of them at their job. Thus, men felt more sympathy than they showed. Alternatively, women were more likely to display acts of sympathy when they felt it.

Clark examines sympathy from a survey of over 1,000 people in New Jersey, participant observation of sympathy from sidewalks and street corners to funeral homes, content analysis of acts of sympathy in the mass media such as in novels, etiquette books, and greeting cards, and in-depth interviews with over 50 other people. From these rich data sources, she identifies some interesting aspects of sympathy including *sympathy margins, sympathy etiquette,* and *using sympathy micropolitically.* Sympathy margins are lines of "sympathy credits" that sympathizers/socioemotional bankers extend to others. A small sympathy margin signifies a few credits while a large sympathy margin has many credits. Once these credit lines have been advanced, another can claim them, but once another "cashes in" on some or all of these credits in the margin, fewer credits are available for later misfortunes. When persons repeatedly request sympathy, they may be "overdrawing" on their account, this might lead to resentment on the part of the sympathizer, and the sympathizer may "close" the account.

Clark (1997, p. 159) rules of sympathy etiquette include: "(1) Do not make false claims, (2) Do not claim too much, for too long, or for too many problems, (3) Claim some sympathy to keep accounts open, and (4) Reciprocate to those who have given sympathy." While we can imagine sympathy under-investors, what Clark (1997, p. 153) calls an "emotional 'tightwad,'" there are also sympathy over-investors or individuals who provide sympathy frequently, perhaps as a way to help establish their moral worth.

Individuals do not always act sympathetic for benevolent reasons. Sympathy can also be used to maintain one's own position of power in an interaction, perhaps even raise one's position of power. This is using sympathy micropolitically. For example, people can demean others in the course of sympathizing with them, thereby highlighting or elevating their own superior place. Alternatively, sympathy might be used to reduce power differences, thereby raising the position of a weaker person. Of course, a stronger person might reject the sympathy of a weaker position in an attempt to protect their powerful place.

While sympathy may be used to manipulate another, perhaps far more important is the fact that sympathy is important in generating social bonds in society. Indeed, Clark maintains that the mere fact that people display sympathy forces them to interact with another. In turn, this interaction creates social integration and solidarity that otherwise might not have arisen. I would add that sympathy helps to restore some balance when individuals are unjustly treated. During those times, the sympathy that they receive from others may signal that humanity is still compassionate.

EMOTIONS AND SENTIMENTS IN
DEVELOPING THEORY AND RESEARCH

More attention is being given to the role of emotions and sentiments in social psychological theories and research. Affect control theory in the symbolic interaction tradition continues to remind us of the importance of sentiments in interaction, for example, how the display of sentiment in interaction can importantly influence one's outcomes. Heise (1989) maintains that when people display appropriate affect in a situation, it can lead to positive characterizations of the person, while the display of inappropriate affect can foster stigmatization. Thus, the negative implications of a deviant act can be forestalled by the appropriate display of shame by the offender. Indeed, Robinson, Smith-Lovin, and Tsoudis (1994) find that the display of remorse during a confession can decrease the severity of the sentence.

There are other theoretical and research traditions that have not characteristically examined emotion but are increasingly doing so in the course of their development. These include identity theory, exchange theory, and expectations states theory. I briefly discuss these developments because they are giving us further insights into the role of emotions and sentiments for the self and for interaction.

Identity Theory

In the identity cybernetic model, *any discrepancy* between perceived self-in-situation meanings and identity standard meanings reflect a problem in verifying the self and negative emotional arousal such as distress result (Burke, 1991). Further, *repeated interruptions* in the self-regulating identity process cause more negative emotions than occasional or infrequent interruptions. I examine the above two assumptions by studying the distributive justice process and individuals' emotional responses to injustice in a laboratory setting that simulates a work situation (Stets, 2003). If one translates the idea of a discrepancy into being over-rewarded or under-rewarded in a justice situation, negative emotion should result, and more intense negative emotion should occur as the inequitable distributive process persists.

I find that an identity discrepancy does not always lead to negative emotion. When one is over-rewarded, positive emotion results. When individuals receive rewards rather than punishments, their standard may quickly adjust in a positive direction to the new level if the over-reward is relatively small. If the discrepancy is large, though it is in a positive direction, it may lead to negative emotion because the size of the discrepancy makes it too difficult to self-verify. Thus, the degree of exceeding the standard may be important in determining the emotion. I also find that as the inequitable distributive process persists, individuals' emotions become less and not more intense. This suggests that individuals are changing their standards, adjusting them to the level of rewards they receive. In general, these unexpected findings have implications for modifying assumptions in identity theory about the relationship between identity expectations, emotion, and the repetitiveness of disrupting the identity process.

The strength or intensity of an emotional response to identity disconfirmation has also been examined in other recent work. Using a national probability sample, Tsushima and I find that more intense anger is associated with the lack of verification of *group-based* identities that are intimate such as the family identity that meet our need to feel valuable, worthy, and accepted (Stets & Tsushima, 2001). Less intense anger is associated with *role-based* identities that are less intimate such as the worker identity that fulfills our need to feel competent and effective. This finding supports Burke's (1991) hypothesis that greater distress will be felt when the self-verification process is interrupted by a significant other than a casual acquaintance. In general, Tsushima and I point to the relevance of incorporating group and role-based identities into our understanding of emotion within the identity control model.

Exchange Theory

In the same way that recent developments in identity theory have argued that identity verification leads to positive emotion, recent developments in exchange theory have argued that repeated exchange agreements lead to positive sentiments between actors. This is evident in Lawler and Yoon's theory of relational cohesion (1996). They argue that individuals are more likely to interact with those in which relative dependence is equal. However, what determines the cohesiveness of the unit is not so much the direct impact of the mutual dependence as much as the frequency of exchange agreements and the positive emotion that ensue. Repeated and successful exchange agreements generate an emotional "buzz" between actors in the form of satisfaction or excitement. These positive emotions lead to relational cohesion or the perception that one is part of a group. In turn, being a part of a group, individuals will be more willing to take risks or make sacrifices on behalf of the group. Ultimately, this leads to actors become committed to the exchange relations that comprise the group.

Clearly, not all exchanges constitute equal dependence. Some exchanges are imbalanced with one person have greater power than the other. There has been an increasing amount of evidence in the exchange tradition that those who occupy low positions of power in an exchange are more likely to experience negative emotions while those in high positions of power are more likely to experience positive emotions (Molm, 1997; Willer, Lovaglia, & Markovsky, 1997). Identity theorists studying family relations have found a similar pattern, that is, that the weaker party such as women and those with a low status occupation in a marriage are more likely to respond negatively while the stronger party such as men and those high in status occupation are more likely to respond positively (Stets, 1997; Stets & Burke, 1996). What this indicates is that one's position in an exchange may have more to do with how they feel than what others do to them.

Lawler and Thye (1999) discuss the fruitfulness of building emotional processes into exchange theorizing. They note that bringing in emotion will provide a richer understanding of social cohesion and solidarity. Emotions inform actors as to the likelihood of future exchanges with positive emotions signaling future benefits and negative emotions suggesting the threat of future relations. Given that commitment between actors makes social order possible, emotions may lie at the heart of the matter.

Expectations States Theory

Like exchange theorists, expectations states theorists have examined one's position of power in a group and the sentiments that ensue. For example, Ridgeway and Johnson (1990) argue that because high status persons in a group receive frequent positive feedback, they will be more likely to express positive emotions. However, if low status persons respond negatively to high status persons, high status persons will direct negative emotion to them in order to "keep them in their place." Low status persons will experience more negative feedback in groups. When low status persons oppose high status persons, they are less likely to express their negative emotions, in part, because low status persons see themselves as responsible for the opposition.* Ridgeway and Johnson's argument differs from exchange theorists since

---

*Lovaglia and Houser (1996) extend Ridgeway and Johnson's analysis by examining how emotional reactions to status influence the status hierarchy in groups. They find support for the idea that since positive emotion is compatible with high status, it decreases resistance to influence in a group, thereby reducing status differences among group members. On the other hand, negative emotion is compatible with low status, it increases resistance to influence in a group, thus increasing status differences among group members.

exchange theorists contend that low status persons often express their negative emotions in groups.

Ridgeway and Johnson's (1990) work suggests that status processes influence sentiment in groups. Driskell and Webster (1997) directly examine the relationship between status structures (who influences whom) and sentiment structures (who likes whom) in groups. They find that status affects sentiment but sentiment does not affect status. For example, while high status group members are judged more competent and are thus deferred to more in groups, they are also viewed as more likable. In this way, high status conveys an additional advantage. Interestingly, they find that while liking alone does not influence performance expectations, external status characteristics alone do. This indicates that status structures and not sentiment structures are a primary basis for influence in a group.

Contrary to Driskell and Webster's work, more recent research finds that sentiment structures do influence performance expectations (Shelly, 2001). Shelly finds that actors first develop feelings of liking and disliking toward others. Following these evaluations, they form performance expectations. Group members expect those they like to perform more competently than those they dislike. Thus, it is not simply status structures that influence a group but also sentiment structures.

CONCLUDING REMARKS

In my view, there is much for sociological social psychologists to contribute to this ever-growing field on emotions and sentiments. The proliferation of research on social emotions, that is, emotions that individuals feel when they take themselves as an object to their own actions, that occur in interaction, and that implicate society's standards is an area that sociologists need to be making more of a contribution. While we are gaining insights from researchers such as Scheff on shame and Clark on sympathy, there is a rich set of emotions that have yet to be examined up close. For example, identity theorists might want to extend the analysis of my work with (Stets & Tsushima, 2001) on group-based identities and role-based identities and emotion by studying whether the lack of verification of group-based identities such as the spousal identity influences feelings of jealousy and grief while the lack of verification of role-based identities such as the worker identity generates feelings of envy. While jealousy and grief share a feeling of loss of a significant other, envy occurs when a rival fares better than oneself. What is important here is whether particular social emotions are linked to specific identity discrepancies. Exchange theorists, particularly within the relational cohesion paradigm, may want to examine the conditions under which different social emotions emerge given the type of other that one has entered into an exchange (e.g., familiar/unfamiliar other, high/low status other) and the type of exchange (e.g., exchange of goods/services or affection/love). In other words, these exchange theorists may want to go beyond the pleasure/satisfaction and interest/excitement dimensions of emotions and examine how more complex, secondary emotions arise in exchanges.

Importantly, our development of knowledge on emotions and sentiments must be systematic and cumulative. We must be cognizant of research going on in other social science disciplines, even in the biological sciences, and find ways to make a contribution that is distinctively sociological. To do otherwise would be to miss out on an important opportunity to deepen our understanding of what it is we study.

ACKNOWLEDGMENTS: I would like to thank John Delamater, Tom Scheff, Lynn Smith-Lovin, and Jonathan Turner for their comments on an earlier version of this chapter.

REFERENCES

Arnold, M. B. (1960). *Emotion and personality, Vol 1, psychological aspects.* Oxford, England: Columbia University Press.

Averill, J. R. (1980). The emotions. In E. Staub (Ed.), *Personality: Basic aspects and current research* (pp. 134–199). Englewood Cliffs, NJ: Prentice-Hall.

Averill, J. R. (1982). *Anger and aggression: An essay on emotion.* New York: Springer-Verlag.

Bales, R. F. (1950). *Interaction process analysis; A method for the study of small groups.* Oxford, England: Addison-Wesley.

Barrett, K. C. (1995). A functionalist approach to shame and guilt. In J. P. Tangney & K. W. Fischer (Eds.), *The psychology of shame, guilt, embarrassment, and pride.* New York: Guilford.

Baumeister, R. F., Stillwell, A. M., & Heatherton, T. F. (1994). Guilt: An interpersonal approach. *Psychological Bulletin 115*, 243–267.

Braithwaite, J. (1989). *Crime, shame and reintegration.* Cambridge: Cambridge University Press.

Brody, L. (2001). *Gender, emotion, and the family.* Cambridge: Harvard University Press.

Burke, P. J. (1991). Identity processes and social stress. *American Sociological Review 56*, 836–849.

Burke, P. J., & Stets, J. E. (1999). Trust and commitment through self-verification. *Social Psychology Quarterly 62*, 347–366.

Bybee, J. (1998). The emergence of gender differences in guilt during adolescence. In J. Bybee (Ed.), *Guilt and children* (pp. 113–125). New York: Academic.

Cancian, F. M. (1987). *Love in America: Gender and self-development.* New York: Cambridge University Press.

Clark, C. (1997). *Misery and company: Sympathy in everyday life.* Chicago: University of Chicago Press.

Collins, R. (1990). Stratification, emotional energy, and the transient emotions. In T. D. Kemper (Ed.), *Research agendas in the sociology of emotions* (pp. 27–57). New York: State University of New York Press.

Cooley, C. H. ([1909] 1962). *Social organization.* New York: Scribner.

Cornelius, R. R. (1996). *The science of emotion: Research and tradition in the psychology of emotions.* Upper Saddle River, NJ: Prentice-Hall.

Damasio, A. R. (1994). *Descartes' error: Emotion, reason, and the human brain.* New York: G. P. Putnam.

Darwin, C., & Ekman, P. (1872). *The expression of the emotions in man and animals* (3rd ed.). London: Oxford University Press.

Davis, M. H. (1996). *Empathy: A social psychological approach.* Boulder, CO: Westview.

Davis, M. H., & Kraus, L. A. (1997). Personality and empathic accuracy. In W. Ickes (Ed.), *Empathic accuracy* (pp. 144–168). NY: The Guilford Press.

Denham, S. A., Mitchell-Copeland, J., Strandberg, K., Auerbach, S., & Blair, K. (1997). Parental contributions to preschoolers' emotional competence: Direct and indirect effects. *Motivation & Emotion, 21*, 65–86.

Driskell, J. E., & Webster, M. J. (1997). Status and sentiment in task groups. In J. Szmatka, J. Skvoretz, & J. Berger (Eds.), *Status, network, and structure: Theory development in group processes* (pp. 179–200). Stanford: Stanford University Press.

Durkheim, E. ([1912] 1965). *The elementary forms of the religious life.* New York: Free press.

Ekman, P. (1992). An argument for basic emotions. In N. L. Stein & K. Oatley (Eds.), *Basic emotions* (pp. 169–200). Hillsdale, NJ: Lawrence Erlbaum.

Ekman, P., & Friesen, W. V. (1975). *Unmasking the face: A guide to recognizing emotions from facial clues.* Oxford, England: Prentice-Hall.

Ellestad, J., & Stets, J. E. (1998). Jealousy and parenting: Predicting emotions from identity theory. *Sociological Perspectives 41*, 639–668.

Fischer, K. W., & Tangney, J. P. (1995). Self-conscious emotions and the affect revolution: Framework and overview. In J. P. Tangney & K. W. Fischer (Eds.), *Self-conscious emotions: The psychology of shame, guilt, embarrassment, and pride* (pp. 3–22). New York: Guilford.

Francis, L. E. (1997). Ideology and interpersonal emotion management: Redefining identity in two support groups. *Social Psychology Quarterly 60*, 153–171.

Frank, R. H. (1988). *Passions within reason: The strategic role of the emotions.* New York: W. W. Norton.

Freud, S. (1905). Jokes and the relation to the unconscious. *Standard edition* (Vol. 7). London: Hogarth.

Frijda, N. H. (1993). Moods, emotion episodes, and emotions. In L. Michael & J. M. Haviland (Eds.), *Handbook of emotions* (pp. 381–403). New York: Guilford.

Goffman, E. (1959). *The presentation of self in everyday life.* Garden City, NY: Doubleday.

Goleman, D. (1995). *Emotional intelligence.* New York: Bantam.

Gordon, S. L. (1981). The sociology of sentiments and emotion. In M. Rosenberg & R. H. Turner (Eds.), *Social psychology: Sociological perspectives* (pp. 562–592). New York: Basic Books.

Gordon, S. L. (1989a). Institutional and impulsive orientations in selectively appropriating emotions to self. In D. D. Franks & E. D. McCarthy (Eds.), *The sociology of emotions: Original essays and research papers* (pp. 115–135). Greenwich, CT: JAI.

Gordon, S. L. (1989b). The socialization of children's emotions: Emotional culture, competence, and exposure. In C. Saarni & P. L. Harris (Eds.), *Children's understanding of emotion* (pp. 319–349). Cambridge: Cambridge University Press.

Gordon, S. L. (1990). Social structural effects on emotions. In T. D. Kemper (Ed.), *Research agendas in the sociology of emotions* (pp. 145–179). Albany, NY: State University of New York Press.

Gottman, J. M., Katz, L. F., & Hooven, C. (1997). *Meta-emotion: How families communicate emotionally.* Hillsdale, NJ: Lawrence Erlbaum.

Graham, T., & Ickes, W. (1997). When women's intuition isn't greater than men's. In W. Ickes (Ed.), *Empathic accuracy* (pp. 117–143). New York: Guilford.

Greenspan, S. I., & Benderly, B. L. (1997). *The growth of the mind and the endangered origins of intelligence.* Cambridge: Perseus.

Griffin, S. (1995). A cognitive-developmental analysis of pride, shame, and embarrassment in middle childhood. In J. P. Tangney & K. W. Fischer (Eds.), *Self-conscious emotions: The psychology of shame, guilt, embarrassment, and pride* (pp. 219–236). New York: Guilford.

Harter, S., & Whitesell, N. R. (1989). Developmental changes in children's understanding of single, multiple, and blended emotion concepts. In C. Saarni & P. L. Harris (Eds.), *Children's understanding of emotion* (pp. 81–116). Cambridge: Cambridge University Press.

Hegtvedt, K. A. (1990). The effects of relationship structure on emotional responses to inequity. *Social Psychology Quarterly 53,* 214–228.

Heise, D. R. (1979). *Understanding events: Affect and the construction of social action.* Cambridge: Cambridge University Press.

Heise, D. R. (1989). Effects of emotion displays on social identification. *Social Psychology Quarterly 52,* 10–21.

Higgins, E. T. (1987). Self-discrepancy: A theory relating self and affect. *Psychological Review 94,* 319–340.

Hochschild, A. R. (1983). *The managed heart: Commercialization of human feeling.* Berkeley: University of California Press.

Hoffman, M. L. (1998). Varieties of empathy-based guilt. In J. Bybee (Ed.), *Guilt and children* (pp. 91–112). New York: Academic.

Hoffman, M. L. (2000). *Empathy and moral development: Implications for caring and justice.* New York, NY: Cambridge University Press.

Homans, G. C. (1961). *Social behavior: Its elementary forms.* New York: Harcourt Brace and World Inc.

Ickes, W. (1997). Introduction. In W. Ickes (Ed.), *Empathic accuracy* (pp. 1–16). New York: Guilford.

Ickes, W., & Simpson, J. A. (1997). Managing empathic accuracy in close relationships. In W. Ickes (Ed.), *Empathic accuracy* (pp. 218–250). New York: Guilford.

James, W. (1890). *Principles of psychology.* New York: Holt Rinehart and Winston.

Keltner, D., & Buswell, B. N. (1997). Embarrassment: Its distinct form and appeasement functions. *Psychological Bulletin 122,* 250–270.

Kemper, T. D. (1987). How many emotions are there? Wedding the social and autonomic components. *American Journal of Sociology 93,* 263–289.

Kemper, T. D. (1991a). An introduction to the sociology of emotions. In K. T. Strongman (Ed.), *International review of studies on emotion* (pp. 301–349). New York: John Wiley & Sons.

Kemper, T. D. (1991b). Predicting emotions from social relations. *Social Psychology Quarterly 54,* 330–342.

Lange, C. G. ([1885] 1922). The emotions: A psychophysiological study. In C. G. Lange & W. James (Eds.), *The emotions* (pp. 33–90). Baltimore: Williams & Wilkins.

Lawler, E. J., & Thye, S. R. (1999). Bringing emotions into social exchange theory. *Annual Review of Sociology 25,* 217–244.

Lawler, E. J., & Yoon, J. (1996). Commitment in exchange relations: Test of a theory of relational cohesion. *American Sociological Review 61,* 89–108.

Lazarus, R. S. (1982). Thoughts on the relations between emotion and cognition. *American Psychologist 37,* 1019–1024.

Lazarus, R. S. (1991). *Emotion and adaptation.* London: Oxford University Press.

Leavitt, R. L., & Power, M. B. (1989). Emotional socialization in the postmodern era: Children in day care. *Social Psychology Quarterly 52,* 35–43.

LeDoux, J. E. (1996). *The emotional brain: The mysterious underpinnings of emotional life.* New York, NY: Simon & Schuster.

LeDoux, J. E., & Phelps, E. A. (2000). Emotional networks in the brain. In M. Lewis & J. M. Haviland-Jones (Eds.), *Handbook of emotions* (pp. 157–172). New York: Guilford.

Levenson, R. W. (1992). Autonomic nervous system differences among emotions. *Psychological Science 3*, 23–27.

Lewis, H. B. (1971). Shame and guilt in neurosis. *Psychoanalytic Review 58*, 419–438.

Lewis, M. (2000a). The emergence of human emotions. In M. Lewis & J. M. Haviland-Jones (Eds.), *Handbook of emotion* (pp. 265–280). New York: Guilford.

Lewis, M. (2000b). Self-conscious emotions: Embarrassment, pride, shame, and guilt. In M. Lewis & J. M. Haviland-Jones (Eds.), *Handbook of emotion* (pp. 623–636). New York: Guilford.

Lindsay-Hartz, J., De Rivera, J., & Mascolo, M. F. (1995). Differentiating guilt and shame and the effects on motivation. In J. P. Tangney & K. W. Fischer (Eds.), *Self-conscious emotions: The psychology of shame, guilt, embarrassment, and pride* (pp. 274–300). New York: Guilford.

Lovaglia, M. J., & Houser, J. (1996). Emotional reactions and status in groups. *American Sociological Review 61*, 867–883.

Mandler, G. (1975). *Mind and emotion*. New York: Wiley.

Marx, K., & Engels, F. ([1848] 1959). The communist manifesto. In L. Feuer (Ed.), *Marx and Engels: Basic writings on politics and philosophy* (pp. 1–41). Garden City, NY: Doubleday.

Mayer, J. D., & Salovey, P. (1997). What is emotional intelligence? In P. Salovey & D. J. Sluyter (Eds.), *Emotional development and emotional intelligence: Implications for educators* (pp. 3–31). New York: Basic Books.

McCall, G. J., & Simmons, J. L. (1978). *Identities and interactions*. New York: Free.

McCullough, M. E., Pargament, K. I., & Thoresen, C. E. (Eds.). (2000). *Forgiveness: Theory, research, and practice*. New York: Guilford.

Miller, R. S. (1996). *Embarrassment: Poise and peril in everyday life*. New York: Guilford.

Miller, R. S., & Tangney, J. P. (1994). Differentiating embarrassment and shame. *Journal of Social & Clinical Psychology 13*, 273–287.

Molm, L. D. (1997). *Coercive power in exchange*. Cambridge: Cambridge University Press.

Morgan, C., & Averill, J. R. (1992). True feelings, the self, and authenticity: A psychosocial perspective. In D. D. Franks & V. Gecas (Eds.), *Social perspectives on emotion* (pp. 95–123). Greenwich, CT: JAI.

Pierce, J. L. (1995). *Gender trials: Emotional lives in contemporary law firms*. Berkeley: University of California Press.

Pollak, L. H., & Thoits, P. A. (1989). Processes in emotional socialization. *Social Psychology Quarterly 52*, 22–34.

Ridgeway, C. L., & Johnson, C. (1990). What is the relationship between socioemotional behavior and status in task groups? *American Journal of Sociology 95*, 1189–1212.

Robinson, D. T., Smith-Lovin, L., & Tsoudis, O. (1994). Heinous crime or unfortunate accident? The effects of remorse on responses to mock criminal confessions. *Social Forces 73*, 175–190.

Rosenberg, M. (1990). Reflexivity and emotions. *Social Psychology Quarterly 53*, 3–12.

Russell, J. A. (1989). Culture, scripts, and children's understanding of emotion. In C. Saarni & P. L. Harris (Eds.), *Children's understanding of emotion* (pp. 293–318). Cambridge: Cambridge University Press.

Saarni, C. (1999). *The development of emotional competence*. New York: Guilford.

Sabini, J., Garvey, B., & Hall, A. L. (2001). Shame and embarrassment revisited. *Personality & Social Psychology Bulletin 27*, 104–117.

Salovey, P. (Ed.). (1991). *The psychology of jealousy and envy*. New York: Guilford.

Scheff, T. J. (1990). *Microsociology: Discourse, emotion, and social structure*. Chicago: University of Chicago Press.

Scheff, T. J. (1997). *Emotions, the social bond, and human reality: Part/whole analysis*. Cambridge: Cambridge University Press.

Scheff, T. J., & Retzinger, S. M. (1991). *Emotions and violence: Shame and rage in destructive conflicts*. Lexington, MA: Lexington Books/D. C. Heath.

Shelly, R. K. (2001). How performance expectations arise from sentiments. *Social Psychology Quarterly 64*, 72–87.

Shott, S. (1979). Emotion and social life: A symbolic interactionist analysis. *American Journal of Sociology 84*, 1317–1334.

Simon, R. W., Eder, D., & Evans, C. (1992). The development of feeling norms underlying romantic love among adolescent females. *Social Psychology Quarterly 55*, 29–46.

Smith-Lovin, L. (1990). Emotion as the confirmation and disconfirmation of identity: An affect control model. In T. D. Kemper (Ed.), *Research agendas in the sociology of emotions* (pp. 238–270). Albany, NY: State University of New York Press.

Smith-Lovin, L. (1995). The sociology of affect and emotion. In K. S. Cook, G. A. Fine, & J. S. House (Eds.), *Sociological perspectives on social psychology* (pp. 118–148). Boston: Allyn & Bacon.

Smith-Lovin, L., & Douglas, W. (1992). An affect-control analysis of two religious groups. In V. Gecas, D. D. Franks et al. (Eds.), *Social perspectives on emotion* (Vol. 1, pp. 217–247). Greenwich, CT: JAI.

Stearns, C. Z., & Stearns, P. N. (1986). *Anger: The struggle for emotional control in America's history*. Chicago: University of Chicago Press.

Stearns, P. N. (1988). The rise of sibling jealousy in the twentieth century. In C. Z. Stearns & P. N. Stearns (Eds.), *Emotion and social change: Toward a new psychohistory* (pp. 193–222). New York: Holmes & Meier.

Sternberg, R. J. (1998). *Love is a story: A new theory of relationships*. London: Oxford University Press.

Stets, J. E. (1997). Status and identity in marital interaction. *Social Psychology Quarterly 60*, 185–217.

Stets, J. E. (2003). *Justice, emotion, and identity theory*. In P. J. Burke, T. J. Owens, R. T. Serpe, & P. A. Thoits (Eds.), Advances in identity theory and research. New York: Kluwer Academic/Plenum Publishers.

Stets, J. E., & Burke, P. J. (1996). Gender, control, and interaction. *Social Psychology Quarterly 59*, 193–220.

Stets, J. E., & Tsushima, T. (2001). Negative emotion and coping responses within identity control theory. *Social Psychology Quarterly 64*, 283–295.

Stroebe, M. S., Hansson, R. O., Stroebe, W., & Schut, H. (Eds.). (2001). *Handbook of bereavement research: Consequences, coping, and care*. Washington, DC: American Psychological Association.

Stryker, S. (1987). *The interplay of affect and identity: Exploring the relationships of social structure, social interaction, self, and emotion*. Chicago: American Sociological Association.

Swidler, A. (2001). *Talk of love: How culture matters*. Chicago: The University of Chicago Press.

Tangney, J. P. (1995). Shame and guilt in interpersonal relationships. In J. P. Tangney & K. W. Fischer (Eds.), *Self-conscious emotions: The psychology of shame, guilt, embarrassment, and pride* (pp. 114–139). New York: Guilford.

Tangney, J. P., & Fischer, K. W. (Eds.). (1995). *Self-conscious emotions: The psychology of shame, guilt, embarrassment, and pride*. New York: Guilford.

Tangney, J. P., Miller, R. S., Flicker, L., & Barlow, D. H. (1996). Are shame, guilt, and embarrassment distinct emotions? *Journal of Personality & Social Psychology 70*, 1256–1269.

Tangney, J. P., Niedenthal, P. M., Cover, M. V., & Barlow, D. H. (1998). Are shame and guilt related to distinct self-discrepancies? A test of Higgins's (1987) hypotheses. *Journal of Personality & Social Psychology 75*, 256–268.

Thoits, P. A. (1990). Emotional deviance: Research agendas. In T. D. Kemper (Ed.), *Research agendas in the sociology of emotions* (pp. 180–203). Albany, NY: State University of New York Press.

Turner, J. H. (2002). *Face-to-face: Towards a sociological theory of interpersonal behavior*. Stanford: Stanford University Press.

Wallbott, H. G., & Scherer, K. R. (1995). Cultural determinants in experiencing shame and guilt. In J. P. Tangney & K. W. Fischer (Eds.), *Self-conscious emotions: The psychology of shame, guilt, embarrassment, and pride* (pp. 465–487). New York: Guilford.

Willer, D., Lovaglia, M. J., & Markovsky, B. (1997). Power and influence: A theoretical bridge. *Social Forces 76*, 571–603.

Zajonc, R. B. (1984). On the primacy of affect. *American Psychologist 39*, 117–123.

Zajonc, R. B. (2000). Feeling and thinking: Closing the debate over the independence of affect. In J. P. Forgas (Ed.), *Feeling and thinking: The role of affect in social cognition* (pp. 31–58). New York: Cambridge University Press.

PART IV

INTERPERSONAL PROCESSES

CHAPTER 14

Attraction and Interpersonal Relationships

TERRI L. ORBUCH

SUSAN SPRECHER

INTRODUCTION

A growing body of research demonstrates that interpersonal relationships are central and significant to the lives of individuals (Berscheid, 1999; Campbell, Converse, & Rodgers, 1976; Myers & Diener, 1995). Satisfying relationships also have strong links to individuals' mental and physical well being. It is not surprising, then, that social psychologists have been interested in how these relationships are established and maintained and how and why they sometimes end.

The initial focus of relationship-oriented social psychologists was on the attraction process, primarily between strangers meeting for the first time (Berscheid & Walster, 1969, 1978). In the 1960s, which was a time of expansion for social psychology into new topics, the study of interpersonal attraction became recognized as a major subarea. By the 1980s, social psychologists also began to study more intense sentiments and phenomena experienced in actual relationships (friendships, dating relationships, marriages). Further, the context of a relationship and more specifically, the kind of relationship within which interaction takes place was recognized as an important influence on human social behaviors.

Research on attraction and interpersonal relationships has grown steadily since the 1960s. Although the contributions of social psychology to the science of interpersonal

TERRI L. ORBUCH • 530 Varner Hall, Department of Sociology, Oakland University, Rochester, MI 48309

SUSAN SPRECHER • Department of Sociology and Anthropology, Illinois State University, Normal, IL 61790

Handbook of Social Psychology, edited by John Delamater. Kluwer Academic/Plenum Publishers, New York, 2003.

relationships are not always distinguishable from the contributions of other disciplines, the discipline has played a central role in the development of the science of interpersonal relationships (Berscheid & Reis, 1998; Kelley et al., 1983). In addition, the science of interpersonal relationships has advanced the field of social psychology (Felmlee & Sprecher, 2000; Orbuch & Veroff, in 2002). For example, there have been advancements in many of the other topics covered in this Handbook as researchers began to examine these phenomena within the context of relationships. Yet, despite the growth of relationship science, only a limited number of reviews of the literature on attraction and interpersonal relationships by (and for) social psychologists exist in sociology.* Our goal for this chapter is to make sociological social psychologists more aware of the flourishing science of interpersonal relationships, in which social psychology has had a central role, and to highlight new ways that they may contribute to this area.

In the first section of this chapter, we summarize the early research on initial attraction and then discuss several new directions in attraction research since the mid-1980s. In the second section, we review some of the expansive social psychological literature on interpersonal (close) relationships. The majority of this work has focused on taking the pulse of the relationship (the assessment of interrelated but distinct concepts, such as, quality, stability, happiness, commitment) and then predicting what factors contribute to greater quality or more stable relationships. In the final section, we present several themes for further research on attraction and interpersonal relationships.

INTERPERSONAL ATTRACTION

The Concept of Attraction

Attraction is most often conceptualized as an attitude toward another, consisting of feelings, cognition (beliefs), and behaviors (e.g., Berscheid, 1985). Furthermore, attraction has generally been conceptualized as unidimensional, ranging from negative attraction (repulsion) to intense positive attraction. However, some leading scholars (Berscheid, 1985; Berscheid & Reis, 1998) have argued for conceptualizing attraction as consisting of two independent dimensions, one positive and the other negative. That is, a person can be both attracted to and repulsed by the other. The unidimensional approach to attraction, however, has been most popular, and hence little is known about the conditions under which people experience both negative and positive attitudes (i.e., ambivalence) for the same person. There also are different types of attraction that people can experience for another, including friendship attraction and sexual/romantic attraction (e.g., Sprecher & Duck, 1994), as well as different types of relationships (friendships vs. romantic relationships) in which attraction may be experienced.

Attraction has been operationalized in a variety of ways, although self-report measures are the most common. Generally, in studies that focus on assessing how much individuals are attracted to another after a brief interaction, several questions are asked, such as: "How much do you like ...?," "How much would you like to work with ...?," and "How much do you think you would like to be friends with ...?," with additional questions (e.g., "How much would you

---

*The social psychology of attraction and interpersonal relationships was not the topic of a chapter in the most recent volume of *Sociological perspectives on social psychology* (Cook, House, & Fine, 1999). The last Annual Review of Sociology Chapter to address interpersonal relationships was written by Philip Blumstein and Peter Kollock in 1988.

like to date ...?") sometimes asked when the other is opposite gender (e.g., Katz & Beach, 2000; Lindzey & Bryne, 1968; Sprecher, 1989). Much less often, attraction is measured unobtrusively, such as by the duration of eye gaze, the distance two people stand from each other, and the willingness to engage in altruistic behaviors toward the other (Webb, Campbell, Schwartz, & Sechrest, 1966).

The Social Context of Attraction

Attraction generally occurs between P (Person) and O (Other) only if there is mutual awareness and usually some minimal interaction between them. The conditions that bring P and O in mutual awareness and minimal interaction reside in the social context. People are members of families, neighborhoods, peer groups, work settings, and other institutional structures. The likelihood that two people will become aware of each other and have minimal interaction is determined, to some degree, by the social networks and other aspects of social contexts in which each person is embedded (Sprecher, Felmlee, Orbuch, & Willetts, 2002). For example, a large proportion of relationships begin through an introduction by a third party, who is often a friend (Laumann, Gagnon, Michael, & Michaels, 1994) and romantic partners and friends often know a member of their friend's or partner's network before they meet their friend or partner (Parks & Eggert, 1991). (For more information on social network influence, see Felmlee's chapter in this volume.)

The social context also provides norms, which dictate the characteristics that should be considered attractive in another and how the attraction process should unfold (Kerckhoff, 1974). For example, Prather (1990) asked college students about the messages that parents and others gave them concerning the type of person they should marry. Most of the messages focused on the potential mate's religious background, race, and social class or earning potential. In a study of adolescent female peer groups, Simon, Eder, and Evans (1992) found that female adolescents exchange messages that emphasize norms that stress the importance of entering romantic relationships, particularly those that are exclusive, monogamous, and heterosexual.

The Determinants of Attraction

The early research on attraction focused on identifying the "determinants" or "predictors" of attraction—the factors that lead a person to experience attraction toward another. The research often employed a bogus stranger paradigm conducted with college students (e.g., Byrne, 1971). The participants were presented with minimal information about another person, and asked how much they liked this person based on the information presented. Unbeknownst to the participants, they were participating in an experiment, and one or more variables were manipulated and the person or persons the participants were asked to evaluate generally did not exist. Get-acquainted interaction studies (e.g., Walster, Aronson, Abrahams, & Rottman, 1966) also were used, in which pairs of real people (strangers to each other) were allowed to interact and their liking for each other was assessed after the interaction and correlated with their perceptions of each other's characteristics and/or each person's social desirability as determined more objectively (by outsiders).

Based on results from the bogus stranger experiments, the get-acquainted interaction studies, and studies examining friendship choices in natural settings (e.g., Festinger,

Schachter & Back, 1950), four factors have often been identified as "predictors" or "determinants" of attraction: *proximity* (which includes not only geographical distance, but also interaction accessibility), *similarity* (or homogamy), *physical attractiveness* of the other, and *reciprocal liking*. Extensive research has demonstrated that these factors lead to attraction (for reviews, see Backman, 1981; Berscheid & Reis, 1998; Simpson & Harris, 1994). That is, high levels of these factors lead to more attraction than low levels or their opposites (e.g., dissimilarity). Several other factors also have been found to be associated with attraction, including "playing selectively hard to get" (easy to get for the target person but hard to get for everyone else) (e.g., Walster, Walster, Piliavin, & Schmidt, 1973), arousal from other sources such as exercising and emotional movies (e.g., White, Fishbein, & Rutstein, 1981), anxiety-provoking situations (e.g., Schachter, 1959), and repeated exposure (e.g., Moreland & Zajonc, 1982). Although not necessarily identified as a "predictor," *familiarity* is often referred to as "the most basic principle of attraction" (e.g., Bersheid & Reis, 1998), and can explain why some factors (e.g., proximity, mere exposure, similarity) lead to attraction.

Some writers who have reviewed the literature on attraction predictors (e.g., Simpson & Harris, 1994) have organized the determinants of attraction according to Kelley et al.'s (1983) model of causal conditions affecting close relationships. P variables are attributes of the person (e.g., readiness to become attracted); O variables are attributes of the other (e.g., physical attractiveness), P × O variables are unique to the association between P and O (e.g., similarity); and E variables refer to aspects of the social or physical environment (e.g., parental reactions). Most research on determinants of attraction has focused on O variables and P × O variables. For example, all of the major predictors of attraction referred to above are either O or P × O factors.

Attraction Theories

Various social psychological theories have been used to make predictions about whether a particular factor will lead to attraction or have been used to provide post hoc explanations for certain results. These theories include reinforcement–affect theory (e.g., Clore & Bryne, 1974; Lott & Lott, 1974), social exchange theory (Homans, 1961, 1974; Thibaut & Kelley, 1959), balance or cognitive consistency theory (Newcomb, 1971), and misattribution of emotions (Berscheid & Walster, 1974) or excitation transfer (Zillman, 1984). For example, according to the reinforcement and exchange approaches, similarity, proximity, physical attractiveness, and reciprocal liking and many other P, O, P × O, and E factors are reinforcing and rewarding (and not costly) and also are associated with access to other rewards (e.g., prestige). Thibaut and Kelley's (1959) exchange theory (see also, Rusbult's [1983] Investment model) would also suggest that rewards and costs have to be considered in a larger context. Attraction for another may be determined by how the rewards (minus costs) compare to a comparison level (what one expects to receive) and a comparison level for alternatives (the best other option available).

More recently, evolutionary principles also have been offered to explain the associations between some predictors (e.g., physical attractiveness, wealth) and attraction. According to this perspective, humans become attracted to those who they believe (subconsciously or consciously) will maximize the opportunities for conception, birth, and survival of their offspring (e.g., Buss, 1989). Another recent theory applied to explain attraction as well as more intense sentiments (falling in love) is Aron and Aron's (1986) self-expansion theory. These theorists argue that people have a desire to expand themselves (e.g., increase their self-efficacy) and will become attracted to those who have attributes or resources that are perceived to present opportunities to increase self-expansion.

New Directions in Attraction Research

Since the mid-1980s, attraction research has taken several new directions.

MULTIVARIATE APPROACHES. Research focused on identifying predictors of attraction has become more multivariate, which includes comparing the relative importance of various predictors of attraction, examining how predictor variables interact with each other in their influence on attraction, and testing possible mediating variables.

As an illustration, Sprecher (1989), using the bogus stranger paradigm, manipulated three characteristics of a bogus opposite-sex other: physical attractiveness, earning potential, and expressiveness (or openness). Although high levels of each of these characteristics were associated with more attraction than low levels, physical attractiveness had the strongest effect on attraction. In addition, a gender of partner × physical attractiveness × expressiveness interaction was found, in which men were more attracted to the high expressive target than the low expressive target only when she was also physically attractive. Women, however, were more attracted to high expressiveness in both physical attractiveness conditions, and in fact, especially when the target was unattractive. A similar gender of participant × physical attractiveness × earning potential interaction was found. Men were more attracted to a woman with high earning potential than low earning potential only if she was also attractive. Women expressed more attraction to a man when he had high rather than low earning potential in both physical attractiveness conditions, but especially if he was unattractive. These results suggest that determinants of attraction may interact with each other and with participant characteristics (gender) in complex ways, yet to be fully explored. Furthermore, in this same study, the participants were asked what factors affected their attraction for the bogus stranger and they reported that physical attractiveness was least important, which suggests that people may not be aware of what influences their attraction.

In a study of attraction choices in a naturalistic setting (a school system), Kubitschek and Hallinan (1998) examined the relative importance of and interactions among proximity, similarity, and status. They found that each variable affected attraction in the expected direction, but also found that the effects of proximity, similarity, and status depended on the level of the other two factors. In another study that considered multiple variables, Condon and Crano (1988) examined the degree to which the inference of a positive evaluation by the other mediates the similarity—attraction association. They conducted a bogus stranger experiment and manipulated the similarity of the bogus stranger (to the participant) and whether a positive evaluation was also received. Both the similarity of the stranger and the existence of a positive evaluation had positive effects on attraction. Using partial correlational techniques, the researchers found that the effect of similarity on attraction was mediated by "inferred evaluation" or how much they expected to be liked by the stranger. We anticipate more research in the future that examines the cognitive and affective processes that mediate the effects of predictors of attraction.

INDIVIDUAL DIFFERENCES IN THE PREDICTORS OF ATTRACTION. A second new direction of attraction research is the examination of whether the effects of certain predictors on attraction may be moderated by individual characteristics. Several studies, including those based on meta-analyses of previous studies, have found gender differences in the effects of predictors of attraction. In particular, men's attraction for another seems more affected than women's by the other's physical attractiveness (e.g., Feingold, 1991; Lundy, Tan, & Cunningham, 1998; Shaffer & Bazzani, 1997; Sprecher & Duck, 1994), whereas women's attraction has been found to be more affected than men's by quality communication (Sprecher & Duck, 1994), similarity in attitudes (Feingold, 1991), sense of humor (Lundy et al., 1998), and personality (Shaffer & Bazzini, 1997). We also referred above to how certain predictors of attraction may interact with each other in different ways for men versus women.

Differences in predictors of attraction based on an aspect of "the self" have also been examined. For example, Snyder, Berscheid, and Glick (1985) found that men who are high self-monitors (who change their behavior in different social situations) report they are more attracted to a good-looking woman who has an undesirable personality than to an unattractive woman who has a desirable personality, whereas just the reverse was found for men who are low self-monitors. (However, Schaffer and Bazzani [1997] asked participants to rate an array of opposite-sex individuals, and found minimal differences in the determinants of attraction based on the self-monitoring of the participants.)

Self-esteem has also been found to affect the degree to which certain factors, particularly positive evaluations by the other, affects attraction. Individuals high in self-esteem are particularly likely to become attracted to someone who provides positive evaluations and liking for them because it satisfies two motives—self-enhancement (seeking positive information about self to enhance self-esteem) and self-consistency (seeking feedback that is consistent with how they perceive themselves). For individuals low in self-esteem, however, these two motives may be incompatible when they receive approval and affection from another; hence, low self-esteem individuals may be more likely than those higher in self-esteem to reject another who offers approval and liking (e.g., Katz & Beach, 2000).

RELATIONAL HISTORY AS A PREDICTOR OF ATTRACTION.   Attraction research has also been extended to a consideration of characteristics in "O" other than obvious personal attributes such as physical attractiveness and personality. In particular, a target person's past relational behavior (e.g., sexual behavior) and relationship orientation have been examined as predictors of attraction. Research using the bogus stranger paradigm has found that a hypothetical stranger is liked more when he or she is presented as having little prior sexual experience and/or more restrictive sexual attitudes than when he or she is presented with having more extensive sexual experience and/or casual sexual attitudes (e.g., Bettor, Hendrick, & Hendrick, 1995; Sprecher, McKinney, & Orbuch, 1991). However, the effect of sexual experience on attraction depends on the relational context: Sexual experience leads to more attraction when the target person is being considered for a sexual relationship than for a marital relationship (e.g., Kenrick, Sundie, Nicastle, & Stone, 2001; Sprecher et al., 1991).

Other research has demonstrated that a bogus stranger presented as having a secure attachment style elicits more attraction than a person presented as having one of the insecure attachments styles (e.g., avoidant, preoccupied) (Chappell & Davis, 1998; Fraizer, Byer, Fischer, Wright, & DeBord, 1996). This research grows out of an extensive body of literature that links adult attachment style, believed to originate with early childhood experiences with caregivers, with relationship processes and outcomes (for a review, see Feeney, Noller, & Roberts, 2000).

THE COMPONENTS OF PHYSICAL ATTRACTIVENESS.   Another new direction of research is an identification of the specific features that are considered to be physically attractive and that lead to attraction. This research indicates that "baby-faced features" are considered attractive in women, whereas dominant features are considered attractive in men (Cunningham, 1986; Cunningham, Barbee, & Pike, 1990). For both sexes, symmetry (both sides of the face as mirror images of the other) and averaged faces are more attractive than asymmetrical faces and faces that are unusual (e.g., Grammer & Thornhill, 1994; Langlois, Roggman, & Musselman, 1994). People also tend to agree about what makes an attractive body, particularly in a woman. An "hourglass figure" with a waist about 30% smaller than the hips is considered attractive in a woman (Singh & Luis, 1995).

NONLINEARITY IN THE EFFECTS OF PREDICTORS OF ATTRACTION.   A fifth new direction of attraction research is the examination of the nonlinear relationship between predictor variables and attraction, or more generally an assessment of where along the full range of a variable is its effect on attraction. For example, a debate has emerged as to whether similarity leads to attraction or whether dissimilarity leads to repulsion. Rosenbaum (1986) has argued that dissimilarity leads to repulsion but that similarity does not lead to attraction. Byrne, Clore, & Smeaton (1986), in response, presented a two-step model of the attraction process. According to the model, individuals first reject those who are dissimilar, and then among those who remain, are attracted to those who are most similar.

More recently, Kenrick et al. (2001) found that some determinants of attraction, particularly level of past sexual experience and wealth, may have a nonlinear relationship with attraction. For example, above middle-class incomes, further wealth does not increase a man's attractiveness to college-age women. Furthermore, a man with one or a few past sexual partners is perceived to be more attractive than a man with zero partners, although a man who has had several prior sexual partners is perceived to be less desirable.

ATTRACTION FROM AN INSIDER PERSPECTIVE IN EXISTING RELATIONSHIPS.   A sixth new direction of attraction research is a focus on determinants of attraction from an insider's perspective and retrospectively; that is, people involved in intimate relationships have been asked why they became attracted to their partner or friend. Although people may under- or overestimate the effects of certain factors on their attraction (e.g., Sprecher, 1989), these accounts or explanations are important to examine because, as explained by Aron, Dutton, Aron, and Iverson (1989), they "probably represent to a significant degree the psychological reality at the time of the event, and this reality often underlies what people do" (p. 254). Insiders *say* that the most important reasons they become attracted to a person is the other's intrinsic characteristics (such as warmth and kindness) and the other's expressed liking (reciprocal liking) (Aron et al., 1989; Sprecher, 1998) and they rate external factors (e.g., social reactions, proximity) as relatively unimportant. In addition, this research has found that the importance of particular predictors of attraction depend somewhat on whether the context is a romantic relationship or a friendship. For example, physical attractiveness and other's liking were rated more important as determinants of romantic attraction than of friendship attraction (Sprecher, 1998).

Felmlee (1995, 1998) has extended the study of attraction based on an insider perspective by linking predictors of attraction to perceived reasons for breakup. She has identified what are called "fatal attractions." In this dark side to attraction, individuals are initially attracted to a partner because of certain desirable characteristics, but later an aspect of these qualities contributes to a breakup or a serious conflict. For example, an individual may be initially attracted to a partner because he is ambitious but later break up with him because he is always working. According to Felmlee's (1995, 1998) research, 30–45% of relationships result in a fatal attraction. People attracted to a dissimilar other or someone with a unique or extreme quality were more likely to have fatal attractions.

ATTRACTION OVER THE INTERNET. A seventh and just emerging new direction of research is to examine attraction over the Internet. That is, researchers have examined what factors lead to attraction when "meeting" for the first time on the Internet, and how these predictors differ from those important in face-to-face meetings. As part of a larger set of studies on relationship formation, McKenna, Green, and Gleasen (2002) found that strangers meeting for the first time on the Internet were more attracted to each other than people meeting for the first time face to face (how partners met was randomly assigned and controlled). In addition, they found that liking for a person met over the Internet was largely determined by the level and quality of conversation, whereas attraction in face-to-face settings was generally unrelated to the quality of conversation and presumably affected by what the researchers called "gating features," such as physical appearance.

Mate Selection Research

Research on mate selection is closely related to research on attraction because many factors considered to be determinants of attraction (e.g., physical attractiveness of the partner, similarity) are also investigated in mate-selection studies. In this approach, which first began by family sociologists in the 1930s and 1940s (e.g., Hill, 1945), participants (usually young, unmarried college students) are presented with a list of traits and asked to rate how important each trait would be for a mate or date to have. Although only a few such studies were conducted prior to 1985 (e.g., Hudson & Henze, 1969), this questionnaire approach has been used in numerous studies conducted by social psychologists in recent years. (Content analysis of personal want ads is another common method for examining mate preferences, e.g., Kenrick & Keefe, 1992).

The popularity of the mate selection preference studies is due in part to the development of the evolutionary theory of human behavior, which presents very clear predictions about gender differences in mate preferences. Evolutionary theorists (e.g., Buss, 1989) argue that as a consequence of the negligible amount of investment men must make to conceive and give birth to a child relative to women (e.g., Trivers, 1972), men and women have become genetically programmed to desire different traits in a partner. Men are predisposed to prefer mates with traits that signal their reproductive value (traits such as good looks and youth), and women are predisposed to prefer mates with traits that signal the potential for resource acquisition (traits such as ambition and status). Considerable research has found support for these predictions (Buss, 1989; Goodwin, 1990; Regan, 1998; Sprecher, Sullivan, & Hatfield, 1994), although the genders are more similar than different in that both rate physical attractiveness and resource characteristics lower than intrinsic characteristics such as honesty, kindness, and sense of humor.

Recent extensions of mate-selection research have examined how preferences depend on the particular type of relational context, including differences between short-term mating (sexual flings) and long-term mating (marriage) (e.g., Kenrick, Sadalla, Groth, & Trost, 1990; Regan, Levin, Sprecher, Christopher, & Cate, 2000), and between romantic relationships and friendships (e.g., Sprecher & Regan, 2002). Generally, similarities are found in preferences across types of relationships, although some differences also exist, including greater importance expressed for external attributes (e.g., physical attractiveness) in short-term sexual relationships than in long-term committed relationships.

Sociologists, feminists, and others have been critical of the evolutionary explanation for gender differences in mate preferences. Sociologists (e.g., Howard, Blumstein, & Schwartz, 1987) explain the same gender differences by pointing to different socialization and social opportunities experienced by men and women. This perspective, called the "social argument," "principles of social factors," "structural powerlessness hypothesis" and "socioeconomic explanation," argues that it is not surprising that women focus on the ability of a partner to provide resources because traditionally they have lacked social, educational, and economic means. Men, who have not had to worry about finding a partner who can provide resources, would have more freedom to choose a partner based on physical appearance and youth. This argument would predict that as conditions change, so would gender differences in mate preferences and/or what is found to be attractive in another. However, to date, no research has been conducted to provide a critical test of how changes in socioeconomic factors affect changes in traditional gender differences in what is preferred in a mate. However, Wiederman and Allgeier (1992) found, contrary to what might be predicted from the sociological argument, a modest positive correlation between women's expected income in the future and their importance ratings of "good financial prospects" in a partner. However, in support of the sociological perspective, Gangestad (1993) reanalyzed data collected from Buss (1989) on mate preferences in 37 cultures and reported that the more economic power women had, the more important they rated physical attractiveness in a partner (hence, when women do not have to worry about finding a partner with resources, they can focus on other attributes, including good looks).

Although attraction is important, maybe even necessary, for P and O to form a voluntary relationship (a friendship or romantic relationship), once the relationship is formed, many other processes will affect the likelihood that P and O stay in the relationship and are satisfied with it. We turn to those issues next.

INTERPERSONAL RELATIONSHIPS

The Concept of an Interpersonal (Close) Relationship

Individuals have various types of relationships (e.g., friendship, parent–child, neighbors, doctor–patient, marital), some of which may be intimate and close (e.g., parent–child, spouse–spouse) and others, which may not be intimate or as close (neighbor, teacher–student). However, most of the research on interpersonal relationships focuses on those relationships that are close, intimate, and interdependent (i.e., the behavior of each affects the outcomes of the other) (Berscheid, Snyder, & Omoto, 1989; Perlman & Fehr, 1987; Prager, 1995, 2000; Thibaut & Kelley, 1959). "Words such as love, trust, commitment, caring, stability, attachment, one-ness, meaningful, and significant, are often used to describe close relationships" (Berscheid & Peplau, 1983, p. 12). The majority of the work on relationships has focused on taking the pulse of the relationship (the assessment of interrelated but distinct concepts, such as quality, stability, happiness, commitment) and then predicting what factors contribute to greater stability or more satisfying relationships. Berscheid and Reis (1998) state that "no single question in relationship research has captured more attention than why one [relationship] endures and another dissolves" (p. 230).

Pulse of the Relationship

In the 1980s and 1990s, a large number of studies were conducted that conceptualized and measured the "pulse of a relationship." Many researchers were interested in taking the pulse of close relationships, particularly marriage, with a particular focus on understanding that "pulse" for its own sake but also for its link to numerous other processes inside or outside the individual (Bradbury, Fincham, & Beach, 2000). For example, in the early 1980s many researchers debated about whether relationship satisfaction or quality was a uni- or a multi-dimensional concept (Fincham & Bradbury, 1987; Glenn, 1990). Although many suggest that the unidimensional view is best suited for conceptualizing relationship *quality* (Fincham & Bradbury, 1987), there is now a growing appreciation for the view that there are distinctive evaluations of relationships that are highly related to one another. Fincham and Bradbury (1987) also make a distinction between the *quality* and *stability* of a relationship. They argue that the terms quality, satisfaction, adjustment, and distress are typically used interchangeably and refer to partners' evaluations of their relationship; stability is used to refer to the status of the relationship (intact or dissolved). The important distinction between the evaluation of a relationship (quality, well-being) and the status of the relationship (stability) has also been confirmed in other research as well (Crohan & Veroff, 1989; Veroff, Young, & Coon, 1997).

Similarly, Fletcher, Simpson and Thomas (2000) examined several different subjectively held evaluations that might be present in the minds of relationship partners, such as commit-ment, trust, passion, love, and satisfaction. They wanted to assess how these components were structured and interrelated. Using confirmatory factor analyses, they showed that all of these constructs have distinct, but clearly overlapping components. Fincham, Beach, and Kemp-Fincham (1997) further argued that it is important to measure both the positive and negative evaluations of a relationship as separate, although related, dimensions. They found that the two dimensions (positive and negative) have different correlates and account for unique variance in reported relationship behaviors and attributions. Thus, although common sense may define high satisfaction as the presence of positive and the absence of negative, there is now a "growing appreciation for the view that a satisfying relationship is not merely a relationship characterized by the absence of dissatisfaction. Factors that lead to relationship distress may not be the simple inverse of the factors that lead to a satisfying relationship" (Bradbury et al., 2000, p. 973).

New Directions in Research on Interpersonal Relationships

Given the growth of scientific work on interpersonal relationships, a summary of all the recent developments and advances in this area is too challenging a task for any one chapter. Thus, there are many possibilities of how to organize this section of the chapter.

First, reviews of the interpersonal relationship literature in the 1980s identified specific kinds of relationships (e.g., friendship, marriage, siblings) and organized the relevant rela-tional processes or findings within those relationship types. This framework often appears in textbooks and handbooks that are wedded to disciplinary boundaries. For example, sociolo-gists are particularly interested in research on marriage and the family, specifically the struc-tural and demographic correlates of these relations (Blood, 1967). Although a brief review of the current literature might suggest that the body of knowledge on interpersonal relationships is truly organized according to relationship type, Berscheid (1994) argues that most relation-ship scholars, "hope their efforts ultimately will result in a body of knowledge about the causal dynamics of relationships that will transcend relationship type" (p. 80).

Next, as social psychological research became more grounded in the life course approach in the late 1980s (Elder, 1994, 1995; Moen, 1995), relationship scholars began to address specific relational processes that were relevant at various stages of a relationship (e.g., attraction, development, maintenance, dissolution). Given the emphasis on the importance of examining relationships over time, reviews of the literature in the early 1990s (late 1980s) began to focus on relational processes within the various stages of a relationship—the development (attraction, sexuality), maintenance (love, quality, commitment) and dissolution (disengagement, adjustment, coping) of a relationship (e.g., Blumstein & Kollock, 1988; Orbuch, 1992).

The approach we take in this section reflects a recent transition in interpersonal relationship research, one which Bradbury (1998) suggests is a shift from studying only the qualities of individuals and their influence on relationships, to studying relationships over time in a fashion that will help *explain how* relationships succeed or fail. This shift in focus allows us to see new interconnections between the individual, the relationship, social interaction, culture, and social structure over time (Orbuch & Veroff, 2002). Thus, consistent with new developments in the literature (Bradbury, 1998), we review research aimed at examining social psychological variables that explain *how* relationship quality and stability change over time. Numerous social psychological variables have been significant to understanding variations in the well being and stability of relationships over time. Similar to Brofenbrenner's (1979) ecological framework, which argues that the meaning and implications of relationships cannot be fully understood without considering the multiple levels/ecologies within which the relationship resides, we organize these social psychological predictor variables according to three levels of analysis: individual or psychological factors, interpersonal or dyadic processes, and social contextual or systemic factors. Sarason, Sarason, and Pierce (1995) note that "either explicitly or implicitly, most research on personal relationships is directed at one of three levels of analysis: individual, dyadic, and systemic" (p. 615).

We recognize that it is not possible to review all of the relevant factors at each level, so within this framework, we focus on several new directions since the mid-1980s that we argue are most relevant to an audience of sociological social psychologists. We explicate these factors below taking account of the level of analysis in an ecological framework. However, before we begin, it is important to note that most of the current research on relationship well-being and stability has focused on dating and marital relationships (Berscheid & Reis, 1998). Although there are exceptions (friendship, parent–child relations), this limitation is inherent in the review below.

Individual Factors

There has been a great deal of research examining how qualities of the individual or personality traits influence individuals' behaviors and attributions in their relationships, which then lead to overall reports of relationship well-being or stability.

NEUROTICISM.   One personality trait that has received a great deal of attention is neuroticism (Karney & Bradbury, 1997). Chronically neurotic people are less satisfied with their relationships than those low on neuroticism. Further, Kelly and Conley (1987) found that levels of neuroticism prior to marriage (engagement) predicted partners' satisfaction levels after they were married. This research argues that negative outlooks make individuals nervous, fearful, and unhappy, which lead to unpleasant and unrewarding interactions, and then lower marital well-being or satisfaction (as cited in Brehm, Miller, Perlman, & Campbell, 2002).

ATTACHMENT STYLE.   Another individual factor that has been explored widely in the research on interpersonal relationships is attachment style. Attachment styles are conceptualized as individuals' past histories or global views of relationships. Many argue that attachment styles influence feelings, emotions, and behaviors within relationships (Hazan & Shaver, 1987, 1994), which then can determine the well-being and stability experienced in relationships. Early typologies of attachment used three categories of attachment (i.e., secure, avoidant, and anxious/ambivalent), which were identified initially in young infants' attachment to their primary caregivers (Bowlby, 1969). At first, researchers assumed that an individual's attachment style was fixed and could be predicted before the child was born by the mother's attachment style (Fonagy, Steele, & Steele, 1991). As researchers began to study adult attachment, they recognized that the categories of attachment style were more complex, and they have since been revised (i.e., secure, preoccupied, fearful, and dismissing) (Feeny et al., 2000). More recent provocative studies also indicate that attachment styles can be unlearned or can change over time given traumatic experiences or the loss of a relationship (Baldwin & Fehr, 1995). Other research shows that specific pairings of attachment styles in partners lead to happier and more stable relationships (Jones & Cunningham, 1996).

Interpersonal/Dyadic Factors

There is considerable debate about how to conceptualize a "relationship." According to Berscheid and Reis (1998) "relationship scholars differ on how much interaction between two people, and what kind of interaction, must take place before they are willing to say that two people are in a relationship" (p. 198). Nonetheless, relationship scholars have spent considerable time studying the effects of interactions and behaviors between the two members of a couple on relationship quality and stability. There are several new directions to summarize.

UNIT OF ANALYSIS. First, recent relationship research has become much more dyadic in nature whereby the relationship or dyad is the unit of analysis rather than the individual. This shift in the unit of analysis, both conceptually and methodologically, appears at all levels of analysis (of the ecological framework), but seemed most relevant in this section on dyadic-level factors. For example, Moen, Kim, and Hofmeister (2001) examined whether couples' *joint* employment/retirement circumstances (rather than individual employment/retirement situations) differentially predicted marital quality for men and women. In their study, a respondent's own retirement was predictive of marital quality for both men and women, however, the perceived discrepancy in employment status between husbands and wives also lead to high marital conflict (or low marital well-being), regardless of gender. Their findings support the importance of incorporating couples' *joint* work/retirement status and making the couple the unit of analysis (rather than the individual) in predicting the well-being of the dyad.

Veroff, Douvan, and Hatchett (1995; Orbuch, Veroff, & Holmberg, 1993) provide another example of how the dyad has become the focus, rather than the individual, of relationship research. These researchers asked couples to jointly tell the story of their relationship—from how they became a couple, decided to get married, experienced the wedding and honeymoon, and thought about the future. Their findings indicated that how much a wife/husband collaborates (a joint style of interaction—whether the couple agrees with each other, whether they jointly tell the story together, whether they assist each other in talk) with his/her spouse was a significant predictor of relationship well-being over time. The results suggest that only after we take account of the interaction that is jointly constructed by both spouses, can we truly understand and predict its import to the well-being of the relationship over time.

Gottman's sequential analysis (Gottman, 1979, 1994) with married couples, whereby he records the temporal sequence of interaction behaviors, is similar to the Veroff et al. (1995) focus above. Because relationship partners are interdependent, in order to fully understand Partner A's behavior in interaction with Partner B, one must also record the behavior of Partner B that preceded Partner A's behavior.

Recent research has also shifted from collecting information from only one individual in the dyad to acknowledging that data from both members of the couple is important in assessing the well-being of the relationship. Duck (1990) encourages relationship researchers not to label differences in perspectives between two members of a couple as error terms or undesired discrepancies in the data. Instead, researchers should appreciate inevitable differences in perspectives between two members of a couple. Currently, many relationship researchers collect direct information from both members of the dyad (and evaluate discrepancies and consistencies between partners) to adequately predict relationship well-being and stability. A recent edited book, "The developmental course of marital dysfunction" (Bradbury, 1998), highlights several longitudinal projects of marriage from a social psychological perspective. Most of these projects collect information from both members of the couple at more than one point in time and take the relationship as the unit of analysis, in order to explain *how* relationship quality and stability change over time.

MULTIVARIATE APPROACH. A second new direction, similar to developments in attraction research, is that research has become more multivariate in nature, including whether specific qualities of the dyad mediate or moderate the effect of other individual or structural variables on relationship outcomes.

For example, Amato and Rodgers (1997) revealed ways in which interpersonal problems experienced in marriage mediate some of the structural features found to be predictive of divorce. Further, Karney and Bradbury (1995; Bradbury, Cohan, & Karney, 1998) argued that positive marital adaptations in the early years provide critical supportive environments that lessen or override the likelihood that individuals' vulnerabilities (e.g., depression, anxiety, physical health, alcohol abuse) will affect marital well-being and stability. This argument is based on a vulnerability–stress–adaptation model. By understanding what adaptations in marriage are beneficial to individuals' mental and physical health over time, especially at times of stress, we can buffer the risk factors that may produce marital dissolution or divorce.

INTERACTION OF SELF AND OTHER. The third new direction in research on dyadic/interpersonal variables has been to apply symbolic interactionist concepts to the study of relationship well-being and stability. The basic tenets of symbolic interactionism are to understand the processes by which the self is created and individuals come to take on specific identities. Symbolic interactional perspectives (Stryker & Stratham, 1985), especially those informed by identity theory (Burke & Cast, 1997; Burke & Reitzes, 1991), view the self within a relational and interactional context; the self is created out of the perceptions of others with whom a person is in significant social interaction. These concepts and basic social psychological processes have been applied to the processes by which individuals' perceptions of partners change behaviors.

For example, recent research shows that evaluations of self and partner change over time, and this change can influence the well-being of the relationship. Murray, Holmes, and Griffin (1996) find that over time young married couples project their ideals onto their partners. These evaluations are often more positive than their partners' own view of themselves. Such illusion-making seems to have positive consequences for their partners, and the marriage can operate more effectively (Murray et al., 1996; Murray & Holmes, 1999). Sometimes, people can persuade their partners that they are the wonderful people others wish them to be. Further, Fletcher, Simpson, and Thomas (2001) argue that over time, people may change their ideals of what they want in a partner to fit the partner they actually have, which in turn makes them happier with their present relationship.

The same process may be involved in the phenomena that Bradbury and Fincham (1990) reported regarding the attributions that happily married spouses make about their partners' negative behaviors. These happily married spouses often think of these negative behaviors as situationally caused, rather than emanating from their partners. Further, happily married spouses often think that their spouse's positive behaviors are intentional, stable and global in nature. Bradbury and Fincham (1990) argue that happy people make attributions for their partner's behaviors that are relationship enhancing. In contrast, couples that are unhappy make attributions for their partners' behaviors that are distress maintaining.

Other researchers have used symbolic interactionist concepts to explain men's commitments to the fathering role and satisfaction with their father–child relationship (Ihinger-Tallmann, Pasley, & Buehler, 1993; Minton & Pasley, 1996). For example, Fox and Bruce (2001) presented findings, which show that identity salience (the importance of a man's paternal identity in relation to other identities) was an important predictor of men's fathering commitments to children, even after controlling for sociodemographic variables. Maurer, Pleck and Rane (2001) also demonstrated that the link between paternal identity and parental behavior was a function of perceived reflected appraisals; men's perceptions of their spouse's evaluation of self within the parental role predicted behavior in that father role.

Social Context Factors

Berscheid (1998) points out that most relationship research has yet to deal with the larger environmental or structural conditions that can be harmful or beneficial for a couple's well-being and stability. Yet, in the last decade, relationship scholars have begun to appreciate the notion that relationships are embedded within various social environments. They have begun to examine more closely the links between social contextual factors and relationship well-being and stability. Bradbury et al. (2000) note that in order to fully understand the interactions and behaviors that occur within relationships, we must account for the links between members in a relationship and the "sociocultural ecologies" that relationships reside in. These sociocultural ecologies are the norms, cultural meanings, settings, circumstances, or people outside the relationship that are likely to be important to couples and have influence on the functioning and success of that relationship (Berscheid & Reis, 1998; Bradbury et al., 2000; Sarason, Sarason et al., 1995).

SOCIAL NETWORKS.   One new direction in this area is to examine the influence of social networks of family and friends on relationship quality and stability (See Sprecher et al., 2002). The general notion that social networks are linked to the internal "pulse of the relationship" was first examined by Elizabeth Bott (1957, 1971). Her hypotheses, which argue that the qualities of networks determine segregated roles and other relationship processes, are still being examined in current work (See Milardo & Alan, 1996).

Further, although social networks can influence relationship well-being and stability in multiple ways (e.g., network overlap between partners is associated with greater relationship well-being, see Julien & Markman, 1991; Stein, Bush, Ross, & Ward, 1992), the majority of work focuses on the manner in which social networks can be a potential source of support for couples. Social support is just one of many small environmental impacts that can affect couples. For example, relationship research consistently finds that a couple's well-being can be enhanced by the assistance of others in the couple's environment, particularly family and friends who are close to the individuals or couple. Bryant and Conger (1999) found that relationship satisfaction was linked to positive support from the network for the relationship. Further, Veroff et al. (1995) provided evidence that in the first two years of marriage, interferences felt from friends and family were predictive of marital instability later in the marriage.

More recent findings by Timmer and Veroff (2000) also find that the cycle of divorce in couples who themselves have emerged from divorced families can be broken for some couples when there are close relationships established with in-laws. Research results also indicate that the link between close family ties and marital stability or quality may be more critical for husbands (Cotton, 1995; Milardo & Allan, 1996), African Americans (Stack, 1974; Staples & Johnson, 1993), and women with children (Huston & Vangelisti, 1995). Finally, support from social networks (instrumental and emotional support) has been found to be positively linked to parent–child relationship quality after divorce (McLanahan & Sandefur, 1994; Orbuch, Thornton, & Cancio, 2000).

THE SOCIAL CONSTRUCTION OF MEANING.   Another new direction is to examine the social context of the construction of meaning within relationships for relationship quality and stability through the use of a narrative or account approach. This narrative technique asks respondents (or couples) to tell stories of specific events or experiences in their relationships. Social psychologists propose that these reconstructive memories or stories (or accounts, narratives; see Orbuch, 1997) are embedded within sociocultural ecologies and are the outcomes of the process of meaning construction. According to Harvey, Weber, and Orbuch (1990) these accounts or narratives are like photo albums, they help us to organize our memories and understandings of important events and others surrounding our relational lives. Veroff, Sutherland, Chadiha, and Ortega (1993a) suggest that "direct questions can elicit historical truth to some extent, but they often engage much more of the person's social self-presentation and hence are primarily useful in understanding situations where self-presentations are particularly salient" (p. 439). In contrast, accounts or narratives, although not historical reality, are more likely to reveal non-conscious motives and meanings and to illuminate individuals' interpretations in a social, cultural, and personal context (Orbuch, 1997).

Consequently, an increasing number of relationship researchers have begun to use the narrative approach to gain a better understanding of relationships and relational processes over time (Stueve & Pleck, 2001; Surra, Batchelder, & Hughes, 1995; Veroff, Sutherland, Chadiha, & Ortega, 1993b). Systematic research has focused on the processes by which individuals construct these stories and on the recognition that stories formulate, control, and represent self, other, and relationships. Sternberg (1995) claims that people organize their views of relationships in story schemas; future relationships are then shaped and controlled through the process of storytelling. Other scholars argue that narratives are psychological realities in themselves that may have no historical reality, but the content (themes) of narratives and the style in which narratives are presented to others have significant implications for the future quality, stability, and behaviors within relationships (e.g., Buehlman, Gottman, & Katz, 1992).

Orbuch et al. (1993) have also used the couple narrative technique and found that both the content and style of storytelling is predictive of relationship quality over time. For example, they found that a positive non-romantic reconstruction of the flow of the couple's courtship in the first-year narrative was positively predictive of marital well-being 2 years later. They argued that when couples characterize their courtship as a highly romanticized story early on in marriage, this meaning has potential negative consequences to the marriage later on. They also found that for all but the Black husbands in their sample, the fact that the couple had some conflict in telling the courtship story in Year 1 (of their marriage) was predictive of less marital well-being in Year 3, than if the couple did not have this kind of conflict. Overall, these findings support a link between the content and style of storytelling and couples' relationship quality and stability over time.

More research is needed, however, to determine the causal connection between relationship well-being/stability and the construction of meaning (narratives). The meanings or stories that respondents/couples tell may be influenced by the psychological functioning of the couple/individual at the time of narration. Alternatively, the narrative itself (and the act of narration) may elicit or help construct the well-being or psychological functioning of the couple/individual.

ETHNICITY/RACE.   The third contextual factor that has received research attention recently is the context of ethnicity/race. McLoyd, Cauce, Takeuchi, and Wilson (2000) state that "by the year 2050, the U.S. population is expected to be 8% Asian American, 14% African American, 25% Hispanic, and 53% non-Hispanic White" (p. 1071). Given these demographic predictions, the new millennium will bring with it an increase in relationships whose members are from multicultural backgrounds. Nonetheless until recently, relationship research has not highlighted the cultural or racial/ethnic contexts of relational processes (McLoyd et al., 2000; Orbuch, Veroff, Hassan, & Horrocks, 2002). Gaines (1995) argues that ethnicity and related variables (e.g., culture, race), although neglected in previous relationship research, are now being recognized for their important role in relational processes.

In general, social psychologists and other social scientists have emphasized the structural rather than the cultural or interpersonal factors that may affect relational processes among various ethnic groups. For example, current research proposes several structural explanations to understand differential rates of marital quality and stability between African Americans and Whites (African Americans report less marital quality and greater marital instability than Whites). For some structuralists it is sufficient to argue that because African Americans are in many social group categories (low income, low occupational status, low education) that imply more disadvantages and injustices than Whites (e.g., job security is not as accessible to Black males as it is to White males in our society), they will, in turn suffer greater ongoing tensions than Whites and have fewer resources for stabilizing marriages (Orbuch et al., 2002). Such ongoing conflict with the external environment may carry over and affect the well-being and stability of African American marriages.

One specific structural explanation focuses on the sex ratio of Black males to females (Lichter, McLaughlin, Kephart, & Landry, 1992; Tucker & Mitchell-Kernan, 1995). The marriage market may be different for African Americans than for Whites because there is a smaller number of marriageable Black men than women. This situation increases the probability of unmarried Black females and decreases the number of possible husband–wife combinations (Staples & Johnson, 1993). The unbalanced marriage market also influences the degree to which Black men have a larger pool from which to choose a partner or mate, which may affect the selection of a mate or the likelihood that one stays within a marriage (Orbuch, Veroff, & Hunter, 1999). This unbalanced marriage market may be viewed as contributing to Blacks' lower marital stability and quality (Veroff et al., 1995).

Although not as dominant in the literature, other research has given attention to cultural factors beyond structure that may affect relational processes among various ethnic groups (Hunter & Davis, 1992; Orbuch et al., 1999). In general, these explanations focus on the context of a racial/ethnic culture, consisting of norms or expectations that determine the meaning of various interpersonal or relational factors (e.g., parental status, social network ties, conflict), which then have differential consequences for how these factors are related to relational outcomes (Adelmann, Chadwick, & Baerger, 1996; Orbuch et al., 1999). One specific explanation emphasizes that among African Americans and Whites, the cultural context may filter ways that men and women experience the power they have within their marriages (Hunter & Davis, 1992; Orbuch et al., 1999). Recent studies find that Black couples are more egalitarian than White couples in their attitudes toward women and gendered roles (Kamo & Cohen, 1998). Evidence also suggests that African American men place great value on the input of women and men inside and outside the home, perhaps in response to their lack of structural opportunities, and they are more likely than White men to criticize gender inequality and more traditional views of masculinity and femininity (Collins, 1990; Hunter & Sellers, 1998; Kane, 1992). Given these differential views of women and men and their import to the economic and psychological survival of the family, gender–power dynamics play different roles and meaning in the two cultures and lead to differential connections between these dynamics, and marital quality and stability.

Although current research has begun to highlight variations in relationship quality and stability by race/ethnicity, even this research is limited. This research is dominated by what Collins (1990) calls "a biracial or dichotomous thinking, where the normative work is conducted using European American relationships and the 'minority' perspective is represented via an examination of African American relationships" (as cited by McLoyd et al., 2000, p. 1071). Future relationship research must continue to explore relational processes in other ethnic/racial groups (e.g., Latino, Asian American, Native American, etc.).

CONCLUSIONS AND FUTURE RESEARCH DIRECTIONS

The social psychologists who have contributed to the study of attraction and interpersonal relationships have overwhelmingly come from the subfield of psychological social psychology. With a few exceptions (e.g., Burke, Conger, Felmlee, Glenn, Hallinan, Milardo, Kubitschek, Orbuch, Sprecher), the researchers cited earlier in this review are social psychologists housed in psychology departments. However, the research questions that have been investigated are not inherently more psychological than sociological. Some of the founding social scientists, such as Simmel (1950) and Moreno (1934) were concerned with attraction and close relationship issues, and thus it is this subdiscipline's mandate to continue research on the topic. In addition, sociological social psychologists have the theory, tools, and approaches to take the study of attraction and interpersonal relationships in new directions (Felmlee & Sprecher, 2000). We encourage more research by sociological social psychologists on the topics of attraction and interpersonal relationships and provide several suggestions for avenues of research.

First, we encourage more researchers to move from an examination of single predictors to an analysis of multiple factors that may interact to predict attraction or relationship outcomes. For example, we suggest that more research be conducted on social and physical environmental factors that influence attraction and relationship quality/stability, in interaction with individual and other social contextual factors. More specifically, how do attraction, relationship quality, commitment, and related phenomena between two people depend on the degree to which they are both in the same social network and/or share network members (see Felmlee, Chapter this volume) and does this vary by other individual or social contextual factors (e.g., physical attractiveness, age, gender, race). Similarly, research might examine how factors known to increase attraction or relationship stability are influenced by organizational structures in society. An example of such research is that by Kubitschek and Hallinan (1998) on how academic tracking in school systems influence the operation of similarity, proximity, and status on attraction choices. In addition, as researchers examine multiple levels of factors (individual, dyadic, social contextual) in predicting attraction and relational quality/stability, they should explain the processes by which these factors are interconnected. For example, what is the relative importance of dyadic variables (e.g., conflict, social support) given certain social contexts (e.g., gender, race) and particular enduring individual factors (e.g., personality, attachment styles) in explaining relationship outcomes? Does social support from a partner protect individuals from the stressors and external pressures of employment that can lead to increased levels of individual maladjustment and relationship instability over time? Are these dyadic variables important for different cultures, husbands and wives, and at all stages of a marriage? Questions also can be asked such as what predicts relationship stability or quality—is it the qualities of one partner, the other partner's qualities, or the particular combination (e.g., joint qualities, discrepancy between qualities) of partner and other qualities (Gonzalez & Griffin, 1999)? All of these suggestions use multiple levels of factors to examine attraction or other relationship outcomes.

Second, the existing work on attraction and interpersonal relationships has not sufficiently accounted for the influences of diverse socioeconomic backgrounds (e.g., class, ethnicity/race) as contributing influences. More research should be conducted to examine how attraction and relationship quality/stability, and the predictors of these processes, depend on cultural, subcultural, or class memberships. We encourage researchers to examine these diverse cultural memberships for *within* and *between* group differences. Most importantly however, is to remember that there are common as well as distinctive predictors across various cultural groups, and once distinctive predictors are found, we should also try to understand these distinctive patterns or results.

Third, research needs to be done on how the predictors of attraction and relationship outcomes may vary across the life course. The factors that contribute to attraction to a friend or romantic partner in middle and old age are not likely to be the same as those that contribute to attraction in young adulthood. Furthermore, the factors influencing relationship quality later in life may not be the same as those that are important early in life. For example, according to Carstensen's (1993) Socioemotional Selectivity theory, people in later life show a greater selectivity in social partners, preferring to a greater degree than young adults, those who are familiar and who provide positive emotional experiences.

Fourth, more qualitative research is needed on the processes of attraction and relationship outcomes. Qualitative research has been more common in sociological social psychology than in psychological social psychology, which has been dominated by quantitative, positivistic paradigms. Qualitative research would allow us to examine attraction and relationship development in naturalistic settings and from the participants' own perspectives and in their own words (see, e.g., Simon et al., 1992). There are a variety of qualitative approaches that can be used to examine these processes, but as we discussed previously, the narrative or accounts-as-stories method has become quite popular in the area of interpersonal relationships (Orbuch, 1997).

Fifth, more efforts need to be made to apply theories that are associated with sociological social psychologists to the study of attraction and other relationship processes. For example, as we noted above, identity theory is being applied to how the self changes in response to relationship partner, and how these changes affect both behaviors within and the well-being of interpersonal relationships. These same concepts and processes of identity theory (e.g., Stets & Burke, 2000) could be used to examine how P's and O's role identities, including the degree to which they are verified by each other and are similar to each other, influence attraction for each other (see Burke & Stets, 1999).

Lastly, additional efforts need to be made to utilize larger and more representative samples that are nonclinical and do not consist of only college students. Some of the empirical work examining interpersonal relationships, particularly parent–child and husband–wife dyads, has utilized at-risk or clinical samples of children, adolescents, and married couples instead of examining differences in developmental pathways that may exist for nonclinical and clinically referred samples. Further, the majority of the work on interpersonal relationships continues to examine individuals, typically college students, rather than both members of the dyad among non-college students. The samples that we use to examine attraction and relational outcomes, as well as reports from both members of the dyad, need to be considered seriously in future research.

REFERENCES

Adelmann, P. K., Chadwick, K., & Baerger, D. R. (1996). Marital quality of black and white adults over the life course. *Journal of Social and Personal Relationships, 13*, 361–384.

Amato, P. R., & Rodgers, S. T. (1997). A longitudinal study of marital problems and subsequent divorce. *Journal of Marriage and the Family, 59*, 612–624.

Aron, A., & Aron, E. (1986). *Love and the expansion of self: Understanding attraction and satisfaction.* New York: Hemisphere.

Aron, A., Dutton, D. G., Aron, E. N., & Iverson, A. (1989). Experiences of falling in love. *Journal of Social and Personal Relationships, 6*, 243–257.

Backman, C. W. (1981). Attraction in interpersonal relationships. In M. Rosenberg & R. H. Turner (Eds.), *Social Psychology: Sociological Perspectives* (pp. 235–268). New York: Basic Books.

Baldwin, M. W., & Fehr, B. (1995). On the instability of attachment style ratings. *Personal Relationships, 2*, 247–261.

Berscheid, E. (1994). Interpersonal relationships. *Annual Review of Psychology, 45*, 79–129.

Berscheid, E. (1998). A social psychological view of marital dysfunction and stability. In T. Bradbury (Ed.), *The developmental course of marital dysfunction* (pp. 441–460). New York: Cambridge University Press.

Berscheid, E. (1999). The greening of relationship science. *American Psychologist, 54*, 260–266.

Berscheid, E., & Peplau, L. A. (1983). The emerging science of relationships. In H. H. Kelley, E. Berscheid, A. Christensen, J. H. Harvey, T. L. Huston, G. Levinger, E. McClintock, L. A. Peplau, & D. R. Peterson, *Close relationships* (pp. 1–19). New York: W.H. Freeman.

Berscheid, E., & Reis, H. (1998). Attraction and close relationships. In D. T. Gilbert, S. T. Fiske, & G. Lindzey (Eds.), *The handbook of social psychology* (4th ed., pp. 193–281). New York: McGraw-Hill.

Berscheid, E., & (Hatfield) Walster, E. (1969, 1978). *Interpersonal attraction.* Reading, MA: Addison-Wesley.

Berscheid, E., Snyder, M., & Omoto, A. M. (1989). The Relationship Closeness Inventory: Assessing the closeness of interpersonal relationships. *Journal of Personality and Social Psychology, 57*, 792–807.

Berscheid, E., & Walster, E. (1974). A little bit about love. In T. Huston (Ed.), *Foundations of interpersonal attraction* (pp. 355–381). New York: Academic Press.

Bettor, L., Hendrick, S. S., & Hendrick, C. (1995). Gender and sexual standards in dating relationships. *Personal Relationships, 2*, 359–369.

Blood, R. O. (1967). *Love match and arranged marriage.* New York: Free Press

Blumstein, P., & Kollock, P. (1988). Personal relationships. *Annual Review of Sociology, 14*, 467–490.

Bott, E. (1957, 1971). *Family and social networks.* London: Tavistock.

Bowlby, J. (1969). *Attachment and loss: Vol. 1. Attachment.* New York: Basic Books.

Bradbury, T. N. (Ed.) (1998). *The developmental course of marital dysfunction*. New York: Cambridge University Press.

Bradbury, T. N., Cohan, C. L., & Karney, B. R. (1998). Optimizing longitudinal research for understanding and preventing marital dysfunction. In T. N. Bradbury (Ed.), *The developmental course of marital dysfunction* (pp. 279–311). New York: Cambridge University Press.

Bradbury, T. N., & Fincham, F. D. (1990). Attributions in marriage: Review and critique. *Psychological Bulletin, 103*, 3–33.

Bradbury, T. N., Fincham, F. D., & Beach, S. R.H. (2000). Research on the nature and determinants of marital satisfaction: A decade in review. *Journal of Marriage and the Family, 62*, 964–980.

Brehm, S. S., Miller, R. S., Perlman, D., & Campbell, S. M. (2002). *Intimate relationships*. Boston: McGraw Hill.

Brofenbrenner, U. (1979). *The ecology of human development: Experiments by nature and design*. Cambridge, MA: Harvard University Press.

Bryant, C. M., & Conger, R. D. (1999). Marital success and domains of social support in long-term relationships: Does the influence of networks members ever end? *Journal of Marriage and the Family, 61*, 437–450.

Buehlman, K. T., Gottman, J. M., & Katz, L. F. (1992). How a couple views their past predicts their future: Predicting divorce from an oral history interview. *Journal of Family Psychology, 5*, 295–318.

Burke, P. J., & Cast, A. D. (1997). Stability and change in the gender identities of newly married couples. *Social Psychology Quarterly, 60*, 277–290.

Burke, P. J., & Reitzes, D. C. (1991). An identity theory approach to commitment. *Social Psychology Quarterly, 54*, 239–251.

Burke, P. J., & Stets, J. E. (1999). Trust and commitment through self-verification. *Social Psychology Quarterly, 62*, 347–366.

Buss, D. M. (1989). Sex differences in human mate preferences: Evolutionary hypotheses tested in 37 cultures. *Behavioral and Brain Sciences, 12*, 1–49.

Byrne, D., Clore, G. L., & Smeaton, G. (1986). The attraction hypothesis: Do similar attitudes affect anything? *Journal of Personality and Social Psychology, 51*, 1167–1170.

Byrne, D. (1971). *The attraction paradigm*. New York: Academic Press.

Byrne, D., Ervin, C. R., & Lamberth, J. (1970). Continuity between the experimental study of attraction and real-life computer dating. *Journal of Personality and Social Psychology, 16*, 157–165.

Campbell, A., Converse, P. E., & Rodgers, W. L. (1976). *The quality of American life*. New York: Russell Sage Foundation.

Carstensen, L. L. (1993). Motivation for social contact across the life span: A theory of socioemotional selectivity. In J. E. Jacobs (Ed.), *Nebraska symposium on motivation* (pp. 209–254). Lincoln: University of Nebraska Press.

Chappell, K. D., & Davis, K. E. (1998). Attachment, partner choice, and perception of romantic partners: An experimental test of the attachment–security hypothesis. *Personal Relationships, 5*, 327–342.

Clore, G. L., & Byrne, D. (1974). A reinforcement–affect model of attraction. In T. L. Huston (Ed.), *Foundations of interpersonal attraction* (pp. 143–170). New York: Academic Press.

Collins, P. H. (1990). Black feminist thought: Knowledge, consciousness, and the politics of empowerment. *Perspectives on gender* (Vol. 2) Boston: Unwin Human.

Condon, J. W., & Crano, W. D. (1988). Inferred evaluation and the relation between attitude similarity and interpersonal attraction. *Journal of Personality and Social Psychology, 54*, 789–797.

Cotton, S. (1995). Support networks and marital satisfaction. Unpublished manuscript, Macquarie University, Sidney, Australia.

Crohan, S. E., & Veroff, J. (1989). Dimensions of marital well-being among White and Black newlyweds. *Journal of Marriage and the Family, 51*, 373–383.

Cunningham, M. R. (1986). Measuring the physical in physical attractiveness: Quasi-experiments on the sociobiology of female beauty. *Journal of Personality and Social Psychology, 50*, 925–935.

Cunningham, M. R., Barbee, A. P., & Pike, C. L. (1990). What do women want? Facialmetric assessment of multiple motives in the perception of male facial physical attractiveness. *Journal of Personality and Social Psychology, 68*, 261–279.

Elder, G. H. (1994). Time, human agency, and social change: Perspectives on the life course. *Social Psychology Quarterly, 57*, 4–15.

Elder, G. H. (1995). The life course paradigm: Social change and individual development. In P. Moen, G. H. Elder, & K. Luscher (Eds.), *Examining lives in context: Perspectives on the ecology of human development* (pp. 101–140). Washington, DC: American Psychological Association.

Feeney, J. A., Noller, P., & Roberts, N. (2000). Attachment and close relationships. In C. Hendrick & S. S. Hendrick (Eds.), *Close relationships: A sourcebook* (pp. 185–201). Thousand Oaks, CA: Sage.

Feingold, A. (1991). Sex differences in the effects of similarity and physical attractiveness on opposite-sex attraction. *Basic and Applied Social Psychology, 12*, 357–367.

Felmlee, D. H. (1995). Fatal attractions: Affection and disaffection in intimate relationships. *Journal of Social and Personal Relationships, 12*, 295-311.

Felmlee, D. H. (1998). "Be careful what you wish for...": A quantitative and qualitative investigation of "fatal attractions." *Personal Relationships, 5*, 235-253.

Felmlee, D., & Sprecher, S. (2000). Close relationships and social psychology: Intersections and future paths. *Social Psychology Quarterly, 63*, 365-376.

Festinger, L., Schachter, S., & Back, K. W. (1950). *Social pressures in informal groups: A study of human factors in housing.* New York: Harper & Brothers.

Fincham, F. D., Beach, S. R. H., & Kemp-Fincham, S. (1997). Marital quality: A new theoretical perspective. In R. J. Sternberg & M. Hojjat (Eds.), *Satisfaction in close relationships* (pp. 275-304). New York: Guildford Press.

Fincham, F. D., & Bradbury, T. N. (1987). The impact of attributions in marriage: A longitudinal analysis. *Journal of Personality and Social Psychology, 53*, 510-517.

Fletcher, G. J. O., Simpson, J. A., & Thomas, G. (2000). The measurement of perceived relationship quality components: A confirmatory factor analytic approach. *Personality and Social Psychology Bulletin, 26*, 340-354.

Fonagy, P., Steele, H., & Steele, M. (1991). Maternal representations of attachment during pregnancy predict the organization of infant-mother attachment at one year. *Child Development, 62*, 891-905.

Fox, G. L., & Bruce, C. (2001). Conditional fatherhood: Identity theory and parental investment theory as alternative sources of explanation of fathering. *Journal of Marriage and the Family, 63*, 394-403.

Frazier, P. A., Byer, A. L., Fischer, A. R., Wright, D. M., & DeBord, K. A. (1996). Adult attachment style and partner choice: Correlational and experimental findings. *Personal Relationships, 3*, 117-136.

Gaines, S. O. (1997). *Culture, ethnicity and personal relationship processes.* New York: Routledge.

Gaines, S. O., Jr., & Liu, J. H. (2000). Multicultural/Multiracial relationships. In C. Hendrick and S. S. Hendrick (Eds.), *Close relationships: A sourcebook* (pp. 97-108). Thousand Oaks, CA: Sage.

Gangestad, S. W. (1993). Sexual selection and physical attractiveness: Implications for mating dynamics. *Human Nature, 4*, 205-235.

Glenn, N. D. (1990). *Quantitative research on marital quality in the 1980's: A critical review. Journal of Marriage and the Family, 52*, 818-831.

Gonzales, R., & Griffin, D. (1999) Correlation models for dyad-level models: Models for the distinguishable case. *Personal Relationships*, 449-469.

Gottman, J. M. (1979). *Marital interaction: Experimental investigations.* New York: Academic Press.

Gottman, J. M. (1994). *What predicts divorce? The relationship between marital processes and marital outcomes.* Hillsdale, NJ: Erlbaum.

Grammer, K., & Thornhill, R. (1994). Human facial attractiveness and sexual selection: The role of averageness and symmetry. *Journal of Comparative Psychology, 108*, 233-242.

Harvey, J. H., Weber, A. L., & Orbuch, T. L. (1990). *Interpersonal accounts: A social psychological perspective.* Cambridge, MA: Blackwell.

Hatfield, E., & Sprecher, S. (1995). Men's and women's preferences in marital partners in the United States, Russia, and Japan. *Journal of Cross-Cultural Psychology, 26*, 728-750.

Hazan, C., & Shaver, P. (1987). Romantic love conceptualized as an attachment process. *Journal of Personality and Social Psychology, 52*, 511-524.

Hazan, C., & Shaver, P. (1994). Attachment as an organizational framework for research on close relationships. *Psychological Inquiry, 5*, 1-22.

Hill, R. (1945). Campus values in mate selection. *Journal of Home Economics, 37*, 554-558.

Homans, G. C. (1961, 1974). *Social behavior: Its elementary forms.* London: Routledge & Kegan Pual/New York: Harcourt, Brace, Jovanovich.

Howard, J. A. Blumstein, P., & Schwartz, P. (1987). Social or evolutionary theories? Some observations on preferences in human mate selection. *Journal of Personality and Social Psychology, 53*, 194-200.

Hudson, J. W., & Henze, L. P. (1969). Campus values in mate selection: A replication. *Journal of Marriage and the Family, 31*, 772-778.

Hunter, A. G., & Davis, J. (1992). Constructing gender: An exploration of Afro-American men's conceptualization of manhood. *Gender and Society, 6*, 464-479.

Hunter, A. G., & Sellers, S. L. (1998). Feminist attitudes among African-American men's conceptualization of manhood. *Gender and Society, 12*, 81-99.

Huston, T. L., & Vangelisti, A. L. (1995). How parenthood affects marriage. In M. A. Fitzpatrick (Ed.), *Explaining family interactions* (pp. 147-176). Thousand Oaks, CA: Sage.

Ihinger-Tallman, M., Pasley, K., & Buehler, C. (1993). Developing a middle-range theory of father involvement post-divorce. *Journal of Marriage and the Family, 14*, 550-571.

Jones, J. T., & Cunningham, J. D. (1996). Attachment styles and other predictors of relationship satisfaction in dating couples. *Personal Relationships, 3*, 387-399.

Julien, D., & Markman, H. (1991). Social support and social networks as determinants of individual and marital outcomes. *Journal of Social and Personal Relationships, 8*, 549–568.

Kamo, Y., & Cohen, E. L. (1998). Division of household work between partners: A comparison of Black and White couples. *Journal of Comparative Family Studies, 29*, 131–145.

Kane, E. W. (1992). Race, gender, and attitudes toward gender stratification. *Social Psychology Quarterly, 55*, 311–320.

Karney, B. R., & Bradbury, T. N. (1995). The longitudinal course of marital quality and stability: A review of theory, method, and research. *Psychological Bulletin, 118*, 3–34.

Karney, B. R., & Bradbury, T. N. (1997). Neuroticism, marital interaction, and the trajectory of marital satisfaction. *Journal of Personality and Social Psychology, 72*, 1075–1092.

Katz, J., & Beach, S. R. H. (2000). Looking for love? Self-verification and self-enhancement effects on initial romantic attraction. *Personality and Social Psychology Bulletin, 12*, 1526–1539.

Kelley, H. H., Berscheid, E., Christensen, A., Harvey, J. H., Huston, T. L., Levinger, G., McClintock, E., Peplau, L. A., & Peterson, D. R. (1983). Analyzing close relationships. In H. H. Kelley et al. (Eds.), *Close relationships* (pp. 29–67). New York: Freeman.

Kelly, E. L., & Conley, J. J. (1987). Personality and compatibility: A prospective analysis of marital stability and marital satisfaction. *Journal of Personality and Social Psychology, 52*, 27–40.

Kenrick, D. T., & Keefe, R. C. (1992). Age preferences in mate reflect sex differences in human reproductive strategies. *Behavioral and Brain Sciences, 15*, 75–133.

Kelley, H., & Thibaut, J.T. (1978). *Interpersonal relations: A theory of interdependence.* New York: Wiley.

Kenrick, D. T., Sadalla, E. K., Groth, G., & Trost, M. R. (1990). Evolution, traits, and the stages of human courtship: Qualifying the parental investment model. *Journal of Personality, 58*, 97–116.

Kenrick, D. T., Sundie, J. M., Nicastle, L. D., & Stone, G. O. (2001). Can one ever be too wealthy or too chaste? Searching for nonlinearities in mate judgment. *Journal of Personality and Social Psychology, 80*, 462–471.

Kerckhoff, A. C. (1974). The social context of interpersonal attraction. In T. L. Huston (Ed.), *Foundations of interpersonal attraction* (pp. 61–78). New York: Academic Press.

Kubitschek, W., & Hallinan, M. T. (1998). Tracking and students' friendships. *Social Psychology Quarterly, 61*, 1–15.

Langlois, J. H., Roggman, L. A., & Musselman, L. (1994). What is average and what is not average about attractive faces? *Psychological Sciences, 5*, 214–220.

Laumann, E. O., Gagnon, J. H., Michael, R. T., & Michaels, S. (1994). *The social organization of sexuality: Sexual practices in the United States.* Chicago: University of Chicago Press.

Lichter, D. T., McLaughlin, D. K., Kephart, G., & Landry, D. J. (1992). Race and retreat from marriage: A shortage of marriageable men? *American Sociological Review, 57*, 781–799.

Lott, A. J., & Lott, B. E. (1974). The role of reward in the formulation of positive interpersonal attitudes. In T. L. Huston (Ed.), *Foundations of interpersonal attraction* (pp. 171–189). New York: Academic Press.

Lundy, D. E., Tan, J., & Cunningham, M. R. (1998). Heterosexual romantic preferences: The importance of humor and physical attractiveness for different types of relationships. *Personal Relationships, 5*, 311–325.

McKenna, K. Y. A., Green, A. S., & Gleason, M. E. J. (2002). Relationship formation on the Internet: What's the big attraction? *Journal of Social Issues, 58*, 9–32.

McLananhan, S., & Sandefur, G. (1994). *Growing up with a single parent: What hurts, what helps.* Cambridge, MA: Harvard University.

McLoyd, V. C., Cauce, A. M., Takeuchi, D., & Wilson, L. (2000). Marital processes and parental socialization in families of color: A decade in review. *Journal of Marriage and the Family, 62*, 1070–1093.

Maurer, T. W., Pleck, J. H., & Rane, T. R. (2001). Parental identity and reflected-appraisals: Measurement and gender dynamics. *Journal of Marriage and the Family, 63*, 309–321.

Milardo, R. M., & Allan, G. (1996). Social networks and marital relationships. In S. Duck, K. Dindia, W. Ickes, R. Milardo, R. Mills, & B. Sarason (Eds.), *Handbook of personal relationships* (pp. 505–522). London: J. Wiley & Sons.

Minton, C., & Pasley, K. (1996). Fathers' parenting role identity and father involvement: A comparison of nondivorced and divorced, nonresidential fathers. *Journal of Family Issues, 17*, 26–45.

Moen, P. (1995). Gender, age, and the life course. In R. H. Binstock & L. George (Eds.), *Handbook of aging and the social sciences* (pp. 171–187). San Diego, CA: Academic Press.

Moen, P., Kim, J., & Hofmeister, H. (2001). Couples' work/retirement transitions, gender, and marital quality. *Social Psychology Quarterly, 64*, 55–71.

Moreland, R. L., & Zajonc, R. B. (1982). Exposure effects in person perception: Familiarity, similarity, and attraction. *Journal of Experimental Social Psychology, 18*, 395–415.

Moreno, J. L. (1934). *Who shall survive? A new approach to the problem of human interrelationships.* Washington, DC: Nervous and Mental Disease Publishing.

Murray, S. L., & Holmes, J. G. (1999). The (mental) ties that bind: Cognitive structures that predict relationship resilience. *Journal of Personality and Social Psychology, 77*, 1228–1244.

Murray, S. L., Holmes, J. G., & Griffin, D. W. (1996). The benefits of positive illusions: Idealization and the construction of satisfaction in close relationships. *Journal of Personality and Social Psychology, 70*, 79–98.

Myers, D. G., & Diener, E. (1995). *Who is happy? Psychological Science, 6*, 10–19.

Newcomb, T. M. (1971). Dyadic balance as a source of clues about interpersonal attraction. In B. I. Murstein (Ed.), *Theories of attraction and love* (pp. 31–45). New York: Springer.

Orbuch, T. L. (1992). *Close relationship loss: Theoretical perspectives.* New York: Springer.

Orbuch, T. L. (1999). People's accounts count: The sociology of accounts. *Annual Review of Sociology, 23*, 455–478.

Orbuch, T. L., & Eyster, S. (1997). Division of household labor among Black couples and White couples. *Social Forces, 76*(1), 301–322.

Orbuch, T. L., Thornton, A., & Cancio, J. (2000). The impact of divorce, remarriage and marital quality on the relationships between parents and their children. *Marriage and Family Review*, 221–246.

Orbuch, T. L., & Veroff, J. (2002). A programmatic review: Building a two-way bridge between social psychology and the study of the early years of marriage. *Journal of Social and Personal Relationships, 19*, 549–568.

Orbuch, T. L., & Timmer, S. G. (2001). Differences in his marriage and her marriage. In D. Vannoy (Ed.), *Gender Mosaics: Social Perspectives* (pp. 155–164), CA: Roxbury Press.

Orbuch, T. L., Veroff, J., Hassan, H., & Horrocks, J. (2002). Who will divorce: A 14-year longitudinal study of married black couples and White couples. *Journal of Social and Personal Relationships, 19*, 179–202.

Orbuch, T. L., Veroff, J., & Holmberg, D. (1993). Becoming a married couple: The emergence of meaning in the first years of marriage. *Journal of Marriage and the Family, 55*, 815–826.

Orbuch, T. L., Veroff, J., & Hunter, A. G. (1999). Black couples, White couples: The early years of marriage. In E. M. Hetherington (Ed.), *Coping with divorce, single parenting, and remarriage* (pp. 23–43), Mahwah, NJ: Erlbaum.

Parks, M. R., & Eggert, L. L. (1991). The role of social context in the dynamics of personal relationships. In W. Jones & D. Perlman (Eds.), *Advances in personal relationships* (vol. 2, pp. 1–34). London: Jessica Kinglsey.

Prager, K. J. (1995). *The psychology of intimacy.* New York: Guildford.

Prager, K. J. (2000). Intimacy in personal relationships. In C. Hendrick and S. S. Hendrick (Eds.), *Close relationships: A sourcebook* (pp. 229–242). Thousand Oaks, CA: Sage.

Prather, J. E. (1990). "It's just as easy to marry a rich man as a poor one!": Students' accounts of parental messages about marital partners. *Mid-American Review of Sociology, 14*, 151–162.

Regan, P. C. (1998). What if you can't get what you want? Willingness to compromise ideal mate selection standards as a function of sex, mate value, and relationship context. *Personality and Social Psychology Bulletin, 24*, 1288–1297.

Regan, P. C., Levin, L., Sprecher, S., Christopher, S., & Cate, R. (2000). Partner preferences: What characteristics do men and women desire in their short-term sexual and long-term romantic partners? *Journal of Psychology and Human Sexuality, 12*, 1–21.

Rosenbaum, M. E. (1986). The repulsion hypothesis: On the nondevelopment of relationships. *Journal of Personality and Social Psychology, 51*, 1156–1166.

Rusbult, C. E. (1983). A longitudinal test of the investment model: The development (and deterioration) of satisfaction and commitment in heterosexual involvement. *Journal of Personality and Social Psychology, 45*, 101–117.

Sarason, I. G., Sarason, B. R., & Pierce, G. R. (1995). Social and personal relationships: Current issues, future directions. *Journal of Social and Personal Relationships, 12*, 613–619.

Schachter, S. (1959). *The psychology of affiliation: Experimental studies of the sources of gregariousness.* Stanford, CA: Stanford University Press.

Shaffer, D. R., & Bazzini, D. G. (1997). What do you look for in a prospective date? Reexamining the preferences of men and women who differ in self-monitoring propensities. *Personality and Social Psychology Bulletin, 23*, 605–616.

Simmel, G. (1950). *The sociology of Georg Simmel*, translated by Kurt Wolff. New York: Free Press.

Simon, R. W., Eder, D., & Evans, C. (1992). The development of feelings norms underlying romantic love among adolescent females. *Social Psychology Quarterly, 55*, 29–46.

Simpson, J. A., & Harris, B. A. (1994). Interpersonal attraction. In A. L. Weber & J. H. Harvey (Eds.), *Perspectives on close relationships* (pp. 45–66). Needham Heights, MA: Allyn and Bacon.

Singh, D., & Luis, S. (1995). Ethnic and gender consensus for the effect of waist-to-hip ratio on judgments of women's attractiveness. *Human Nature, 6*, 51–65.

Snyder, M., Berscheid, E., & Glick, P. (1985). Focusing on the exterior and the interior: Two investigations of the initiation of personal relationships. *Journal of Personality and Social Psychology, 48*, 1427–1439.

Sprecher, S. (1989). The importance to males and females of physical attractiveness, earning potential, and expressiveness in initial attraction. *Sex Roles, 21*, 591–607.

Sprecher, S. (1998). Insiders' perspectives on reasons for attraction to a close other. *Social Psychology Quarterly, 61*, 287–300.

Sprecher, S., & Regan, P. (2002). Liking some things (in some people) more than others: Partner preferences in romantic relationships and friendships. *Journal of Social and Personal Relationships, 19*, 436–481.

Sprecher, S., & Duck, S. (1994). Sweet talk: The importance of perceived communication for romantic and friendship attraction experienced during a get-acquainted date. *Personality and Social Psychology Bulletin, 20*, 391–400.

Sprecher, S., Felmlee, D., Orbuch, T. L., & Willetts, M. C. (2002). Social networks and change in personal relationships. In A. Vangelisti, H. Reis, & M. A., Fitzpatrick (Eds.), *Advances in personal relationships: Vol. 2; Stability and change in relationship behavior* (pp. 257–284). Cambridge.

Sprecher, S., McKinney, K., & Orbuch, T. L. (1991). The effect of current sexual behavior on friendship, dating, and marriage desirability. *The Journal of Sex Research, 28*, 387–408.

Sprecher, S., Sullivan, Q., & Hatfield, E. (1994). Mate selection preferences: Gender differences examined in a national sample. *Journal of Personality and Social Psychology, 66*, 1074–1080.

Stack, C. B. (1974). *All our kin: Strategies for surviving in a Black community.* New York: Harper & Row.

Staples, R., & Johnson, L. B. (1993). *Black families at the crossroads.* New York: Jossey-Bass.

Stein, C. H., Bush, E. G., Ross, R. R., & Ward, M. (1992). Mine, yours and ours: A configural analysis of networks of married couples in relation to marital satisfaction and individual well-being. *Journal of Social and Personal Relationships, 9*, 365–383.

Sternberg, R. (1995). Love as a story. *Journal of Social and Personal Relationships, 12*, 541–546.

Stets, J. A., & Burke, P. J. (2000). Identity theory and social identity theory. *Social Psychology Quarterly, 63*, 224–237.

Stryker, S., & Stratham, A. (1985). Symbolic interactionism and role theory. In G. Lindzey & E. Aronson (Eds.), *Handbook of social psychology* (3rd ed., vol. 1, pp. 311–378). New York: Random House.

Stueve, J. L., & Pleck, J. H. (2001). Parenting voices: Solo parent identity and co-parent identities in married parents' narratives of meaningful parenting experiences. *Journal of Social and Personal Relationships, 18*, 691–708.

Surra, C. A., Batchelder, M. L., Hughes, D. K. (1995). Accounts and the demystification of courtship. In M. A. Fitzpatrick, A. L. & Vangelisti (Eds.), *Explaining family interactions* (pp. 112–141). Thousand Oaks, CA: Sage.

Thibaut, J. W., & Kelley, H. H. (1959). *The social psychology of groups.* New York: Wiley.

Timmer, S. G., & Veroff, J. (2000). Family ties and the discontinuity of divorce in Black and White newlywed couples. *Journal of Marriage and the Family, 62*, 349–363.

Trivers, R. L. (1972). Parental investment and sexual selection. In B. Campbell (Ed.), *Sexual selection and the descent of man 1871–1971* (pp. 136–179). Chicago: Aldine.

Tucker, M. B., & Mitchell-Kernan, C. (Eds.). (1995). *The decline in marriage among African Americans: Causes, consequences and policy implications.* New York: Russell Sage.

Veroff, J., Douvan, E., & Hatchett, S. (1995). *Marital instability: A social and behavioral study of the early years.* Westport, CN: Praeger.

Veroff, J., Sutherland, L., Chadiha, L., & Ortega, R. M. (1993a). Newlyweds tell their stories: A narrative method for assessing marital experiences. *Journal of Social and Personal Relationships, 10*, 437–457.

Veroff, J., Sutherland, L., Chadiha, L., & Ortega, R. (1993b). Predicting marital quality with narrative assessments of marital experience. *Journal of Marriage and the Family, 55*, 326–337.

Veroff, J., Young, A., Coon, H. (1997). The early years of marriage, In S. Duck (Ed.), *Handbook of personal relationships* (pp. 431–450). New York: Wiley.

Walster, E., Aronson, V., Abrahams, D., & Rottman, L. (1966). The importance of physical attractiveness in dating behavior. *Journal of Personality and Social Psychology, 4*, 508–516.

Walster, E., Walster, G. W., Piliavin, J., & Schmidt, L. (1973). "Playing hard-to-get": Understanding an elusive phenomenon. *Journal of Personality and Social Psychology, 26*, 113–121.

Webb, E. J., Campbell, D. T., Schwartz, R. D., & Sechrest, L. (1966). *Unobtrusive measures: Nonreactive research in the social sciences.* Chicago: Rand McNally.

White, G. L., Fishbein, S., & Rutstein, J. (1981). Passionate love: The misattribution of arousal. *Journal of Personality and Social Psychology, 41*, 56–62.

Wiederman, M. W., & Allgeier, E. R. (1992). Gender differences in mate selection criteria: Sociobiological or socio-economic explanation? *Ethology and Sociobiology, 13*, 115–124.

Zillman, D. (1984). *Connections between sex and aggression.* Hillsdale, NJ: Erlbaum.

CHAPTER 15

Interaction in Small Groups

Peter J. Burke

INTRODUCTION

In the early 1970s, the question "whatever happened to research on the group in social psychology" was raised (Steiner, 1974). A year earlier, small group research was declared dead in a chapter on small groups subtitled "the light that failed" (Mullins & Mullins, 1973). In the early 1980s, Rosenberg and Turner's coverage of the field of social psychology included a chapter on small groups by Kurt Back (1981), but almost all of the research cited was done before the mid to late 1950s. The more recent coverage of the field of social psychology did not include a chapter on group processes (Cook, Fine, & House, 1995). However, it did include a section under the rubric of social relationships and group processes in which seven chapters were placed. Small group research has not disappeared; rather, it has become ubiquitous, spread among a number of research issues (e.g., networks, exchange, bargaining, justice, group decision making, intergroup relations, jury studies, expectation states, minority influence, leadership, cohesion, therapy and self-analytic processes, and power and status) and disciplines (e.g., sociology, psychology, communications, organizational research) (Davis, 1996). In fact, research in all of these areas is active, though the outlets for such research are varied, and it is likely that no one is completely aware of the full range of activity.

On the other hand, research on groups has diminished in sociology as a result of the way in which much research on group processes is conducted. Following the insights of Zelditch (1969), laboratory practice in sociology has shifted from the earlier study of freely interacting persons in a group context to the study of particular processes, perceptions, and reactions that can often be studied on individuals within real or simulated social settings. This approach was often used in psychology from the early studies of Sherif on norms and the autokinetic effect (Sherif, 1936) and the Asch studies of conformity to group pressures (Asch, 1960), as

Peter J. Burke • Department of Sociology, University of California Riverside, Riverside, California, 92521-0419
Handbook of Social Psychology, edited by John Delamater. Kluwer Academic/Plenum Publishers, New York, 2003.

well as the work on "groups" by Thibaut and Kelley (1959). As sociologists began to focus experimentally more on particular processes such as status or exchange, studies of the group *qua* group declined, but did not disappear.

In the present volume, two of the most active areas of group research have been elevated to theoretical orientations (expectation states and social exchange theory), and two other areas have their own chapters (intergroup relationships and interaction in networks). Still, the area of small group interaction contains a wide and rich history and set of empirical works that I attempt to summarize in this chapter.

This chapter is broken down into three sections. In the first, I review some of the historical foundations of small group research. I then cover selected research on three issues, again examining some important historical landmarks as well as more current theory and research. These three issue areas are status, power, and leadership; group integration and cohesion; and interaction.*

EARLY BEGINNINGS

Among the earliest writings on the small group is the work of Georg Simmel who, in the late 1800s and early 1900s, was concerned with general principles of groups and group formation (Wolff, 1950). At one end of the size continuum, he focused on how two person groups (dyads) differed from individuals in isolation and how groups of three (triads) differed from dyads (Wolff, 1950). At a more general level, he analyzed how people affiliate into groups of all sizes and how those multiple group affiliations influence the individual (Simmel, 1955). He also analyzed small groups, large groups, issues of divisions in groups, of authority and prestige as well as of superordination and subordination (Wolff, 1950)—all matters that still concern researchers in small groups.

Another writer in the early 1900s was Charles H. Cooley with interests in the nature of the social order. His work on conceptualizing primary groups reflected a general concern about changes in society, and how what are now called primary relationships (person to person) were giving way to more impersonal role to role relationships, what are now called secondary relationships (Cooley, 1909).

Thrasher's (1927) study of gangs in Chicago in the early 1920s focused on groups and group processes in a natural habitat. With discussions of status and leadership, the structure of and roles in the gang, social control of members, Thrasher examined many of the same group processes that continue to occupy researchers (cf. Short & Strodtbeck, 1965).

The rise of group therapy in the military during World War Two to handle the large numbers of battle stressed soldiers, who could not be accommodated in traditional individual therapy, gave rise to the study of what came to be known as T-groups (for therapy groups and [leadership] training groups). The study of therapy groups produced a plethora of research on group processes and the relationship between group processes and therapeutic processes (Bion, 1961; Scheflen, 1974; Whitaker & Lieberman, 1967). Much of this work had psychoanalytic underpinnings, often focusing on member leader/therapist relations growing out of Freud's discussion of group psychology (Freud, 1959). The National Training

---

*A fourth area that is very active, especially in psychological social psychology is the area of intergroup processes based on social categorization theory and social identity theory (Hogg, 1996). Because this area is adequately covered in another chapter in this volume, I will not include it here.

Laboratory in Bethel, Maine, started by Kurt Lewin's Research Center for Group Dynamics, became the center for research on training groups (cf. Bennis, Benne, & Chin, 1961). This latter work also influenced Bales as he was working out the observational method of Interaction Process Analysis (Bales, 1950), though it had more influence in his later work examining the self-analytic group (Bales, 1970, 1999).

In the late 1940s and 1950s, there was a surge of work on small groups in psychology and sociology, such as William F. Whyte's (1955) study of a street corner gang, Moreno's (1951) research on sociometry (which began much of the current work on networks), and the work by Roethlisberger and Dixon (1970) on group processes in the bank-wiring room at the General Electric plant. Homans (1950) used several of these studies to generate principles of group interaction.

Today, much of the work in sociology can be traced back to the work of Robert F. Bales and his students in the Laboratory for Social Relations at Harvard, especially as this theoretical work was influence by the social systems approach of Talcott Parsons (e.g., Parsons, Bales, & Shils, 1953). Much of the work in psychology was built upon the work of Kurt Lewin and his students at the Research Center for Group Dynamics, first at MIT and then at the University of Michigan. Below, I briefly review earlier work within the framework of each of these "schools" and more current work that directly or indirectly has built on them. In addition to the two locations, each of these schools has had a number of distinctive features. The Harvard school tended to study intact groups freely interacting to solve a common problem. The Michigan school tended to study individuals in contrived social settings or groups that were constrained in some way to prevent free interaction. The Harvard school was interested in the development of social structure within the group. The Michigan school was interested in testing theoretical principles with controlled experiments. The Harvard school was made up primarily of sociologists. The Michigan school was made up primarily of psychologists.

The Harvard School

Research in the Harvard school was spear-headed in 1950 by the publication of *Interaction Process Analysis* (Bales, 1950). This book described a procedure for scientifically coding group interaction so that the objective study of group processes and structures could be conducted. This book, together with a series of publications that used the methodology, provided a new framework for systematically studying "whole" groups. The interaction process analysis (IPA) coding system was developed over several years of studying groups.

Behavior was broken down into *acts*, each defined as a simple sentence or its nonverbal equivalent. A person's turn at talk received one or more codes for each act, with a notation of who acted, to whom it was directed, and the sequence order of the acts. Each act was coded into one of 12 categories (see Figure 15-1). These were arranged into four symmetric groups: positive reactions and negative reactions (both representing socioemotional activity), and problem-solving attempts and questions (both representing instrumental activity).

The coding conventions called for every act to be classified into one of the categories, with ambiguous acts classified into the more extreme (toward categories 1 or 12) of the categories for which it might be relevant. This latter convention was to counter a bias in most coders that was less sensitive to the more emotional and extreme categories of action. With training, coders could achieve a high degree of reliability and agreement (Borgatta & Bales, 1953a).

Area	Type of Act
A. Positive Reactions	1 **Shows Solidarity,** raises other's status, gives help, reward 2 **Shows Tension Release,** jokes, laughs, shows satisfaction 3 **Agrees,** shows passive acceptance, understands, concurs
B. Problem-solving Attempts	4 **Gives Suggestion,** direction, implying autonomy for other 5 **Gives Opinion,** evaluation, analysis, expresses feeling, wish 6 **Gives Orientation,** information, repeats, clarifies, confirms
C. Questions	7 **Asks for Orientation,** information, repetition, confirmation 8 **Asks for Opinion,** evaluation, analysis, expression of feeling 9 **Asks for Suggestion,** direction, possible ways of action
D. Negative Reactions	10 **Disagrees,** shows passive rejection, formality, withholds help 11 **Shows Tension,** asks for help, withdraws "out of field" 12 **Shows Antagonism,** deflates other's status, defends or asserts self

FIGURE 15-1. Description of Bales' interaction process analysis (IPA) coding system.

As in many fields, the presence of a new methodology opens up a new line of research, and that was true in this case, with a significant increase in the amount of small group research published. It also opened the field of group research to several other systems for coding interaction that developed over the next several years (e.g., Borgatta & Crowther, 1965; Gottman, Markman, & Notarius, 1977; Mills, 1964). Many of the issues that were to occupy researchers in the following years were first explored using the IPA scoring system and post-discussion questionnaires on groups in the Harvard laboratory. These issues included the development of leadership status orderings (Bales, 1956, 1958; Borgatta & Bales, 1953b, 1956), leadership role differentiation (Bales, 1956; Borgatta, Bales, & Couch, 1954; Slater, 1955), and the phases in group development (Bales, 1953; Heinicke & Bales, 1953).

The Michigan School

The Center for the Study of Group Dynamics was formed under the guidance of Kurt Lewin at MIT. Later it was moved to Michigan, where its work began to receive attention with the publication of an edited collection of theory and research. Much of this collection grew out of research within the framework of the Michigan school, but it also drew on work that was being done in a number of places (Cartwright & Zander, 1953b).* This collection was

---

*The Harvard school had its own answer to this collection with the publication three years later of another edited collection of research on small groups (Hare, Borgatta, & Bales, 1955).

characterized by a strong theoretical focus and a commitment to careful experimental design to test hypotheses rather than to discover, or observe and document group phenomenon. Issues were often couched in the field theoretic approach of Lewin and included group cohesiveness, group pressures and standards, group goals and locomotion, the structural properties of groups, and group leadership.

The field theoretic approach, with it's view of groups as interdependences among individuals that are mediated by cognitions and perceptions (life-space), dominated this line of research (Lindenberg, 1997). Now classic studies collected into this volume include, among many others, selections from Festinger, Schachter, and Back's (1950) study of social pressures in the Westgate and Westgate West communities, Schachter's (1953) study of reactions to deviance in groups, Bavelas' (1953) study the effect of different communication structures on problem-solving ability in groups, and White and Lippitt's (1953) study of group members reactions to democratic, laissez-faire, and autocratic leaders. In addition to its experimental approach to testing theory, the Michigan school gave the evolving field of small group research an important approach to concepts such as cohesion and group structure in terms of interdependencies among individuals, and a cognitive focus that dominates much research today.

THREE FOCAL ISSUES

The critical issues that have influenced much of the work in the area of small groups within sociological social psychology are status and power, integration and cohesion, and interaction. The most influential issue in sociology has been research concerned with status and power, or as some prefer to label it, social inequality. Work on cohesion and interaction processes diminished, but in recent years has begun to increase. These three areas will be explored in the remaining parts of this chapter.

Status, Power, and Leadership

Since much of the work in sociology on status and power in groups can be traced back to the work of Bales, I begin this section with some background. Among the early work by the Bales group at Harvard were two papers that outlined interests in the development of structure and process in problem-solving groups. The first paper examined the phases task oriented groups went through in solving task problems (Bales & Strodtbeck, 1951). A second paper incorporated many of the results of the first paper and focused on the equilibrium problem in small groups (Bales, 1953). The equilibrium problem, from the functional perspective of Parsons and Bales (1953, p. 123), is the problem of establishing cyclic patterns of interaction that move the group forward to accomplish the task, and patterns of interaction that restore the internal socioemotional balance disturbed by the pursuit of the task.

Using data obtained through application of the IPA coding system, a number of empirical regularities were documented as evidence of the types of equilibria that a group maintained (Bales, 1953). There was a balancing of proaction (that initiated a new line of activity) and reaction (the first response to another actor). Among the reactions, positive reactions were seen to outnumber negative reactions. There was unequal participation of members. The most active members talked more to the group as a whole, and less active persons talked more to those ranked above them in participation than below them. Thus, persons who participated more also received proportionately more positive reactions. These patterns of participation produced a "fountain effect" with contributions going up the hierarchy and then sprinkling out on the group as a whole (Bales, Strodtbeck, Mills, & Roseborough, 1951).

It was also noted that there were phases in the type of activity that occurred over time. Activity in the problem-solving sequence moved from orientation to evaluation to control. Simultaneously, both positive and negative reactions built up over time with a final surge of positive reactions and joking toward the end. It was also observed that there was a differentiation of activity across persons, with some persons being more proactive and others being more reactive. The most active person was less well liked (and more disliked) than the next most active member. This led to ideas of a more active instrumental/adaptive specialist and a less active integrative/expressive specialist, each of whom fulfilled important functions in the group.

ROLE DIFFERENTIATION.   Bales and Slater (1955; Slater, 1955) formalized many of the above ideas in a study outlining this theory of leadership specialization or leadership role differentiation. This was an interesting issue that combined work on the status/power issue with work on the integration/cohesion issue.* Bales and Slater studied small, task-oriented, decision-making groups composed of male undergraduate students at Harvard. They gave members of each group a five page written summary of an administrative case problem and told them to consider themselves members of an administrative team and return a report to the central authority. The report was to contain their opinion as to why the persons involved in the case were behaving as they were, and their recommendation as to what the central authority should do about it. Bales and Slater coded the interaction in these groups using the IPA coding system described earlier. In addition, after the discussion, they gave forms to the members to rate each other in terms of liking and on the leadership activities of providing the best ideas and guiding the discussion.

Bales and Slater conceptualized the observed actions with their various qualities as emerging from a latent "social interaction system" that was differentiated in a number of ways. Proactions (initiation of new lines of activity) tended to be concentrated in the instrumental categories of giving suggestion, opinion, or information, while reactions tended to be concentrated in the expressive categories of showing agreement, disagreement, or tension release (e.g., laughter). Additionally, reactions, while often coming after proactions by another person, also tended to be differentiated in time. A larger proportion appeared toward the end of the meeting during a final period of laughing and joking, suggesting that the "latent state of the total system" varied over time.

Another type of differentiation was discovered in the data, which Bales and Slater (1955) described as a "separation [over time] of the rankings on likes from the rankings on other measured characteristics [task contributions]." Accompanying this separation of the best liked person from the person making the largest task contributions was a difference in the activities of these two persons. The best ideas person had an activity profile across the 12 IPA categories that was similar to the proactive profile, while the best liked person had an activity profile that was similar to the reactive profile.

Bales and Slater (1955) theorized that the differentiation of task and expressive leadership functions between two different group members was the result of several factors. First, the different types of activity reflected responses to the different demands on the group for solving both the instrumental problems relating the group to its environment and task conditions,

---

*According to the framework being used, these issues were problems that all groups (as social systems) needed to resolve (Parsons et al., 1953).

and the socioemotional problems of maintaining interpersonal relationships to keep the group intact. Second, these different activities were performed by different persons since the task specialist "tends to arouse a certain amount of hostility because his prestige is rising relative to other members, because he talks a large proportion of the time, and because his suggestions constitute proposed new elements to be added to the common culture, to which all members will be committed if they agree" (1955, p. 297). Liking, thus, becomes centered on a person who is less active and who can reciprocate the positive affect.

After these initial findings were reported, there was a flurry of publications in which the theory was both criticized and elaborated.* Some suggested that instrumental and expressive leadership may be more likely to reside in the same person in non-laboratory groups, thus indicating that leadership role differentiation may be conditional (Leik, 1963; Mann, 1961). Verba (1961) suggested that the conditionality depended upon the legitimacy of the task leader. His argument, elaborating on the suggestion of Bales and Slater, was that the negative reactions of the group members toward the task leader were brought about by non-legitimate task leadership. If the task leader were legitimate, such negative reactions would be less likely to occur. In a series of experiments Burke (1967, 1968, 1971) tested this idea and suggested an elaboration of the theory (Burke, 1974a).

Using better measures of socioemotional leadership activity and role-differentiation, strong experimental support for this theory about the effects of legitimation was found. Role differentiation did not tend to occur when the task leader was given positional legitimation by being appointed by the experimenter (Burke, 1968), nor did it occur when task activity was legitimated by providing strong motivation for the group members to accomplish the task (Burke, 1967). The incompatibility of the two types of activity was demonstrated, under conditions of low task legitimation, by a strong negative correlation between task performance and expressive performance for the task leader (Burke, 1968). Because role differentiation tends to occur only under conditions of low legitimation, it is not often observed in non-laboratory groups where legitimation tends to be higher.

STATUS STRUCTURES.   The study of the emergence of leadership structures out of freely interacting task-oriented groups described above, was taken up by other researchers who were interested in how such (task) status structures emerged in the first place and the impact that they had on group processes. With a systems understanding of the nature of groups and group interaction, Bales (1953) suggested that the differentiation was the result of both the task and socioemotional domains as well as their relationship. Others were interested in the mechanisms by which some individuals claimed and were granted more status and interaction time. The study of these status organizing processes showed that individuals over time came to have expectations about the future performances of group members (including themselves) based on perceptions of inequalities and differences in the characteristics upon which perceptions of status were based (Berger, Fisek, Norman, & Zelditch, 1977). Once formed, these expectations came to determine subsequent task related interactions among the group members.

---

*Criticisms included a critique of the way in which liking was measured (Riedesel, 1974), whether there was evidence of incompatibility of the two leadership roles (Lewis, 1972), whether differentiation of behavior between task and expressive specialists actually occurs (Bonacich & Lewis, 1973), and whether the results are generalizable to groups outside the laboratory (Leik, 1963; Mann, 1961; Verba, 1961).

The task related behaviors that were influenced by these status expectations (both for self and other) were the *performance outputs* (problem-solving attempts), *action opportunities* (questions), *communicated evaluations* (positive and negative reactions), and *influence* (acceptance or rejection of suggestions given disagreement) (Berger et al., 1977). Note that these categories of task related behaviors are (with the exception of the last) the categories of Bales' IPA coding system, which form a single cluster or correlated activity. The last category, influence or agreement and disagreement, was moved from the socioemotional areas (A and D in Bales' IPA) to the task area and came to play a significant role in the experimental procedures that developed to build and test the newly developing expectation states theory and status characteristics theory. The probability that one person deferred to another (accepted or agreed to the other's suggestion even when one privately disagreed with it) became the experimental (and theoretical) definition of status ordering; the more one deferred to another, the lower was one's status relative to the other. This probability of not deferring, called the probability of staying (with one's own opinion), was termed the P(s). In some ways, this was an unfortunate choice because, without knowing the reasons for the compliance, it confounded power and status (or prestige), which are only now beginning to be experimentally disentangled.* Additionally, by focusing exclusively on task status, omitting socioemotional considerations, the full interaction structure studied by Bales was neglected.

A second consequence of using P(s) as the outcome to be studied was that the study of a group process became the study of an individual perception/action. This meant that the experiments studying the impact of various factors on status required only individuals to be put into a situation in which their probability of deference, [1-P(s)], could be determined, and this was often, especially in more recent work, to synthetic or computer others with no group or interaction processes. As it developed, this line of work took the group out of group processes,† but it also set the precedent in sociology for the way in which laboratory work and theorizing was to be done. Because this work on status characteristics and expectation states is more fully described in another chapter in this volume, I will not discuss it further. However, a number of other theories about groups and group processes have evolved from the expectation states and status characteristics theories and traditions that are worth discussing more fully.

THEORIES OF LEGITIMATION.   As already mentioned, the issue of legitimation came up early in the work on leadership and was instrumental in understanding the conditions under which task and socioemotional leadership role differentiation occurred. In the work on expectation states and status characteristics theory, legitimation was taken for granted. Legitimation was one of the three bases of social power initially described by French and Raven (1960) (the others were reward power and coercive power). They defined legitimate power as the power that stems from internalized values in person A that dictates that person B has a legitimate right to influence person A, and that person A has an obligation to accept this influence. However, more recent research sees legitimacy as a property that can be applied to acts as well as persons and positions (Michener & Burt, 1975; Walker, Thomas, & Zelditch, 1986).

---

*Much of the early work talk about the "power and prestige" ordering of group members. The separation of these two concepts, for example, in the work of Lovaglia (1995b) and Thye (2000) is discussed later in this chapter.

†In fairness, as Zelditch (1969) points out, it is good experimental design to incorporate only those elements of the theory that need to tested, while controlling for everything else. Because status was defined in terms of the deferential response of an individual, this was appropriate. In more recent work to be discussed below, however, status processes are not treated solely in terms of individual responses. Interaction processes in freely interacting groups may become, once again, important.

Three sources of legitimation are distinguished: *endorsement* (from peers, or "validity" in the terminology of Dornbusch and Scott (1975)), *authorization* (from more powerful persons), and *propriety* (from the focal actor). Walker and his colleagues (Walker et al., 1986) showed that the effect of legitimation in the form of endorsement acts to stabilize a system of positions in a group (Berger, Ridgeway, Fisek, & Norman, 1998; Zelditch, 2001), a fact also reflected in Hollander's (1993) discussion of the importance of follower endorsement in understanding the relational nature of leadership (i.e., that leadership is a relationship not a personal characteristic).

Building upon this work on legitimacy, Ridgeway and Berger (1986) turned the question around to understand the way in which informal status structures come to be legitimated in groups. This was done by extending expectation states theory and viewing status (and the status order) as a reward, about which members come to have expectations. These expectations were derived from ideas in the general culture (referential structures) about the way in which rewards, including status, are normally distributed. Three types of referential structures were posited from expectation states theory: *categorical beliefs* (such as males having higher status than females), *ability structures* (suggesting that those with the highest ability have higher status), and *outcome beliefs* (suggesting that those who are successful have higher status). The theory went on to argue that legitimation would occur to the extent that the expectations based on the referential structures were consistent across dimensions, more differentiated, and shared and similarly responded to by others, thus validating them in the eyes of the focal person (cf. Ridgeway, Johnson, & Diekema, 1994).

These ideas provided the seed for the development of status construction theory (Ridgeway, 1991, 2001). Here the question was how do status characteristics (such as race and sex) come to have status value in the first place. The logic of the argument is that it occurred through much the same process that status structures come to be legitimated, only now with the focus on the status characteristic. The full argument is presented in the chapter on expectation states theory in this volume.

In most of the above research, status and power were not clearly separated. Recent research, however, is beginning more clearly to make that separation and to ask about the relationship between power and status (Lovaglia, 1995b; Thye, 2000; Willer, Lovaglia, & Markovsky, 1997). By bringing together two theoretical paradigms and experimental procedures (*power* as investigated in network exchange theory and *status* as investigated by expectation states theory) these two concepts are theoretically and experimentally related (Willer et al., 1997). Lovaglia (1995b) created power differences based on structural dependence and observed that those with more structural power were accorded more status in the sense that participants held expectations of higher ability for persons in the powerful positions. However, these expectations did not translate to increased behavioral influence. As pointed out by Willer and his associates (1997), emotion played a role in the translation of power to status. If negative emotional responses to power occur, these can prevent the attribution of status to the powerful person.

Thye (2000), in his status value theory of power, examined the reverse effect of status on power and found that persons with high status had more power in an exchange setting, and that this power resulted from the increase in attributed value of the resources held by a higher status person. From all of these results it is clear that while power and status are different, each can be derived from the other under certain conditions, but emotion plays an important role. And, since emotion is often a function of the legitimation of the powerful position/ person/act, the role of legitimation needs yet to be explored in this process. More is said on this later in the chapter in the section on status and emotion.

LEADERSHIP. When we shift focus from the entire status structure of the group to the top person and simultaneously shift from a structure to a process orientation, we move to the study of leadership. Leadership has been a central concern in the study of groups since the very early years, with much of the early focus on the traits of good leaders (e.g., Boring, 1945). However, as Bird (1950) and others have pointed out, almost no identified traits were replicated in more than a few studies. Research then turned to identifying leadership functions by examining what leaders actually do in groups, and how leadership is accomplished (Cartwright & Zander, 1953a). Lippitt and White (1943) examined the question of what leaders do when they studied the different climates that resulted from the different actions in which authoritarian, democratic, and laissez-faire leaders engaged. As pointed out by Burke (1966), however, the impact of these leadership styles depends heavily upon the expectation of the members. Leadership that is too directive or is not directive enough (relative to the expectations of the group members) leads to problems of tension, hostility, and absenteeism.

The second approach, asking how leadership is accomplished, was in some sense more fruitful as it allowed any group member to perform leadership functions. The work of Bales and his associates on leadership role differentiation may be seen in that light as it measured task leadership performance of all group members. By examining how leadership is accomplished, it became clear that the style and function of leadership were contingent on the type of group in which they occurred.

The most well-known theory of leadership was the contingency model of Fiedler (1978a), which sees leadership as a combination of personal and situational factors. Still somewhat of a trait theory, the model suggests that the traits necessary for effective leadership are contingent upon the circumstances of the group. Fiedler suggests there are two types of leaders: task-oriented leaders who more negatively evaluate their "least preferred co-worker" (LPC) and relationship-oriented leaders who more positively evaluate their LPC. This is viewed as a persistent trait of an individual, but its consequences depend upon the context in which leadership is exercised. Each type (high vs. low LPC) is predicted be effective under different conditions of situational control, which are a function of three factors: the leader's relations with the group (good vs. poor), the task structure (highly structured vs. less structured), and the leader's positional power (strong vs. weak). The various combinations of these three factors yield eight conditions with different degrees of situational control. By ordering the factors from most to least important, an ordering of the eight conditions of situational control is created. High LPC (task oriented) leaders are most effective in conditions of either high or low situational control, while low LPC leaders are most effective in situations of medium situational control.

While the specific predictions that Fiedler's theory makes about the effectiveness of task-oriented and relationship-oriented leaders have been born out in a number of tests (Strube & Garcia, 1981), two of the eight conditions, as noted by Fiedler (1978b), are less well supported. These conditions are the good leader–member relations, structured task, and weak leader position power, and its complete opposite, the poor leader–member relations, unstructured task and strong leader positional power. At this point, it is not fully clear why these two conditions work out less well, though it may have something to do with the relative importance of the three factors which serve to order the eight conditions (Singh, Bohra, & Dalal, 1979). Fiedler's theory suggested that the most important factor was leader–member relations, and the least important was the leader's positional power (Fiedler, 1978a). Singh and his associates (1979) suggest there is evidence that this suggested order may be incorrect. By changing importance of the factors, the two cases are less anomalous, though it is not clear theoretically why either order is to be preferred.

Hollander (1958; Hollander & Julian, 1969) developed a more process oriented view of leadership that aimed to understand how the leader can be both a person who pushes the group in new and innovative directions and be a person who upholds the group norms. His idea is that leadership is a relationship between leader and followers. He developed the idea of "idiosyncrasy credit," viewed as an index of status. Leaders develop credit while interacting with other group members over time by adhering to the group norms and by identifying strongly with the group. This credit can then be used later when the leader engages in idiosyncratic behavior to push the group in new directions. In a sense, idiosyncrasy credit is the legitimacy (endorsement) which the leader can gain or lose by their behavior.

This idea of idiosyncrasy credit was more fully developed in later work which focused directly on the issue of the leader's legitimacy, which was derived from his or her prior acceptance in the process of emerging as leader (Hollander, 1993; Julian, Hollander, & Regula, 1969). Three basic sources of legitimacy were seen as important in group member's accepting a leader. The leader's competence and task success were two factors that increased the legitimacy of the leader (thus, forecasting Ridgeway and Berger's (1986) theory on the sources of legitimation). However, these two factors interacted in a complex fashion with the third factor, election versus appointment of the leader, which can be seen to reflect what Zelditch and Walker (1984) called endorsement and authorization (Julian et al., 1969). For elected leaders, there was low satisfaction with an incompetent leader, irrespective of the leader's success or failure. For successful leaders, however, there was satisfaction only for the competent. Among appointed leaders, the pattern shifted. There was satisfaction with successful leaders, whether or not they were competent, while competence moderated the satisfaction with leaders who failed, with the more competent still enjoying some satisfaction among the members.

A very different approach to the study of leadership was initiated by Moreno (Moreno & Jennings, 1960) in the context of what he called *sociometry*, or the measurement of social configurations (see also the chapter on social networks in this volume). Based on the idea that there are positive and negative connections between persons in groups (each based on particular criteria, e.g., live with, work with, play with, etc.), sociometry maps these connections by asking group members to select (or reject) others based on the criteria. Additional information is gathered to help understand the pattern of choices and help draw conclusions from those patterns. Some people are chosen by a lot of others, some are chosen by no others, some are rejected. Those who are relatively over chosen may be considered to be leaders in this approach (Jennings, 1950). It is stressed in this approach that it is not just the pattern of choices that is important, but understanding the basis of that pattern (e.g., the characteristics of the chooser and chosen).

This approach to the identification of individuals in different positions within a group (e.g., stars or isolates) found acceptance in therapeutic (e.g., Passariello & Newnes, 1988), organizational (e.g., Patzer, 1976), and educational settings (e.g., Hallinan & Smith, 1985). In more mainstream sociology, this approach moved away from notions of leadership and developed into the study of formal networks (White, Boorman, & Breiger, 1976) as well as the study of larger social networks and the ways people are tied into them (examples include Burt & Janicik, 1996; Butts, 2001; Granovetter, 1983).

GENDER AND LEADERSHIP. The relationship between gender and leadership has been extensively explored in hundreds of studies. Using meta-analyses, Eagly and associates (see below) have broken down the gender and leadership issue into four areas: emergence, effectiveness, style, and evaluation.

Eagly and Johnson (1990) first looked at the difference of leadership styles by gender. Here, context made a difference. In organizational studies, males and females did not differ in style. In laboratory experiments, however, stereotypical results were obtained; males were more likely to be task oriented and females more likely to be interpersonally oriented in their orientations. One difference consistent with sex-role stereotypes that was found across all settings was that males tended to be more autocratic and females tended to be more democratic.

The question of emergence of leadership was examined in initially leaderless groups (Eagly & Karau, 1991). The results of a survey of studies showed that in general men emerged as leaders more often than women, and this was especially true in short-term task oriented groups. On the other hand, women were slightly more likely to emerge as social leaders. These results are consistent with the tendency in our culture for men to be more task oriented and for women to be more relationally oriented and socially facilitative (Eagly, 1987).

The third meta-analysis by Eagly and her colleagues concerned reactions to and evaluations of male and female leaders (Eagly, Makhijani, & Klonsky, 1992). In the 147 reports investigated, there was a slight tendency for female leaders to be derogated more than male leaders, but again, context and style made a difference. Female leaders who used a masculine style (autocratic, task-oriented) were more likely to be devalued. Female leaders were also more likely to be devalued if they occupied male-dominated roles, or when the evaluators were males. Interestingly, however, ratings by subordinates reversed these evaluations. Male subordinates rated female leaders more positively and female subordinates rated male leaders more positively.

Finally, with respect to the effectiveness of leaders, Eagly and her associates found no overall differences in the effectiveness of male and female leaders (Eagly et al., 1995). However, in particular environments, there were differences with leaders being more effective in gender congruent environments. Additionally, it was found that males were more effective in roles that were numerically dominated by male leaders and subordinates. Not inconsistent with these results, Brown (1979), in a review of 32 female leadership studies, found that in laboratory studies of students compared with managerial studies, female leaders were less effective, suggesting that stereotypes working to the detriment of female leaders may hold more in the laboratory context.

Integration and Cohesion

I now consider the second issue area of group integration and cohesion. Understanding the sources of the degree to which members of a group are attracted to the group, attracted to others in the group, like the other individuals in the group, or want to stay in the group has been a long-standing goal of group researchers. Each of these (attraction, liking, and staying) has been defined as evidence of cohesion by various researchers (Forsyth, 1999). Some researchers have pooled them all together. Schachter (1953), for example, defines cohesion as the "total field of forces acting on members to remain in the group." Hogg and his colleagues, on the other hand, have taken a different tact to distinguish between attraction to others in the group (personal attraction) and attraction to the group (social attraction). They have defined group cohesion uniquely in terms of social cohesion in order to distinguish the group from interpersonal relations (Hogg, 1987).

Several approaches to understanding the sources of group cohesion have been taken over time, including in-group–out-group distinctions, interaction, exchange, and identity processes. Simmel (1955) observed quite early that out-group conflict serves to create in-group cohesion, and the early experiments by Sherif on boys groups at camp verified this quite dramatically (cf. Sherif, 1966). In more recent work based on social identity theory, the mere distinction between an in-group and an out-group, even in the absence of conflict is sufficient to bring some cohesion (Hogg, 1987; Turner, Hogg, Oakes, Reicher, & Wetherell, 1987).

Interaction that is facilitated by a social and physical environment that is conducive to people frequently meeting and interacting with each other brings about a sense of community, cohesiveness, and sharing (Festinger et al., 1950). This, in turn, brings pressures on individuals to share in the group norms and be considered part of the group (Schachter, 1953). The effects of interaction, however, may be seen to vary with the type of interaction and the emotional reactions of members to the interaction. Negative emotions are divisive and positive emotions are integrative (Kemper, 1991). This has been seen very strongly in marital interactions (Gottman, 1993; Gottman, Coan, Carrere, & Swanson, 1998; Tallman, Rotolo, & Gray, 2001).

The notion of positive interaction as a source of group cohesion has been taken up by Lawler and others from an exchange perspective in the theory of relational cohesion (Lawler, 1999, 2000; Lawler & Yoon, 1993, 1996). In this theory, a series of successful exchanges, engaged in over time, leads to positive emotions, which in turn lead to relational cohesion or group commitments. The greater the frequency of exchanges, the greater will be the "emotional buzz" that arises from the exchange process, and the greater will be the degree of cohesion. This theory has been elaborated and extended to build a stronger framework for the role of emotions in not only group cohesion, but also other manifestations of "groupiness" including interpersonal trust, strong norms, and reciprocal typifications (Lawler, 2002).

An identity theory approach to this issue was taken by Burke and Stets (1999) who suggest that it is not the exchange process as such that brings about cohesion and commitment, but the process of self-verification in the group context, or what they term mutual self-verification. They suggest that if, in the process of verifying their own group identities, each person in the group helps to verify the identities of other group members, a mutual dependence comes into existence. The process of mutual verification over time builds trust among the group members who come to rely on each other, and the trust, in turn, builds commitment and positive emotional feelings for the other group members. It is recognized that self-verification may involve exchange behavior as in the theory of relational cohesion, but it goes beyond to involve all social behavior. This theory was supported in a study of marital interaction (Burke & Stets, 1999).

All of the above theories have involved interaction as an important process that builds cohesion. A more cognitive approach involving dissonance was suggested in an early paper by Aronson and Mills (1959). They tested the common observation that people who go through a great deal of trouble or pain to attain something tend to value it more highly. An experimental situation was set up in which some people had to undergo an embarrassing test (two forms that were more [severe condition] and less [mild condition] embarrassing) to obtain membership in an ongoing discussion group, while others did not undergo any test. Afterward, all respondents at this "first meeting" were asked to simply listen to the discussion of the group since they had not yet had a chance to read the material that was to be discussed. The results showed that those who underwent the severe form of the test rated the participants and the discussion much more highly than those who had the mild test or had no test. These results were explained by dissonance theory (Festinger, 1957), suggesting that those in the severe condition paid a high price to belong and adjusted their attitude and feelings about the group to be consistent with the knowledge that they paid a high price.

A cognitive approach is also taken in social identity/self-categorization theory. Knowledge of membership in a group (ingroup) automatically creates an out-group, feelings of being like others in the in-group, and behavior that favors the in-group. This is true even when the in-group is a minimal group, that is, one to which the respondent is randomly assigned, in which there is no interaction and no meeting of other persons in the in-group (or out-group), when in fact there is no group as such. Being named as part of a "group" is sufficient to bring about deindividuation and feelings of belongingness.

Interaction

The study of interaction in groups is the study of the process of individuals acting and reacting to each other over time. As mentioned earlier, this is what the Bales' IPA coding system is designed to capture. One of the early uses of this coding system was to understand the evolution of relationships in a triad (Mills, 1953). Mills was interested in Simmel's hypothesis that triads tend to break into a pair and an "other." He examined the interaction between the most active two members of triads and classified their relationship as *solidary* if each supported the other, otherwise as *conflicting, dominating,* or *contending.* The solidary relationship could be viewed as a coalition of two against one, and when examined over time was the most stable of the relationships. The dominant and contending relationships were the least stable and tended to become conflicting over time. The conflict relationship was of medium stability but tended over time to change to one of the other forms, with more changing to the solidary (coalition) form than either contending or dominant. Thus, the coalition is stable and other forms tend over time to become coalitions of two against one in the triads.

The study of coalitions in the three person group and the conditions under which they would form became an issue that was central for a number of years in social psychology following the methodology initiated by Vinacke and Arkoff (1957) to test some ideas suggested earlier by Caplow (1956). Caplow had analyzed triads and distinguished six basic types, depending upon the relative power of the three members. For example, all members having equal power was type I, or one person having more power than the other two (who are equal, but whose combined power is greater than the first person) was type II, and so on. The relative power of the different members was then used to predict what coalitions would be formed. Vinacke and Arkoff (1957) confirmed most of these predictions and suggested that initial power was the determining factor in the formation of coalitions, with the weaker member more often initiating the formation of coalitions in the manner Simmel predicted with respect to *tertius gaudens.* However, further tests of this question under more strict conditions failed to confirm this finding (Stryker & Psathas, 1960).

Kelley and Arrowood (1960) pointed to another problem with the Vinacke-Arkoff procedure for setting up power differences in the triad. They suggested that several of the triad types were in fact structurally equivalent, even though the assigned power/points were different. By altering the experimental procedure slightly, Kelley and Arrowood showed that, in these structurally equivalent triads, participants learned over time that the point variations in structurally equivalent games were irrelevant and did not need to be considered in dividing up the coalition's profits. The fact that people initially attend to the points indicates the degree to which people look for signs of status and power in our culture.

By the early 1970s a number of theories concerning the formation of coalitions had emerged (Caplow, 1968; Chertkoff, 1971; Gamson, 1961; Laing & Morrison, 1973). One issue in most of these initial studies of coalition formation was that the formation (or not) of coalitions was the only outcome. The process of interaction and negotiation to achieve these outcomes was ignored. As this issue was addressed, there was a shift in the studies to the process of bargaining and exchange (Chertkoff, Skov, & Catt, 1980; Friend, Laing, & Morrison, 1974).

EXCHANGE RESEARCH IN GROUPS. Beginning with the work of Emerson (1972a,b) exchange theory began to study the concept of power. Power was defined as the inverse of the degree to which one person depends upon another in a network of interaction. In this way, power was viewed as emerging from the network of relations and the distribution of resources (Willer, 1999). The earlier work on power and coalitions in the triad can be seen in this network approach. Especially important was that network exchange theory took exchange theory from transactions between persons to the study of transactions between persons embedded in networks. The insight of Emerson was that the power of A over B was in part a function of the alternatives that A has to exchange with persons other than B. When A negotiates with B, she has an advantage if she has an alternative source in C. If A has no alternatives A's power is thereby reduced. This means that it is the structure of the network of relations that is an important determinant of power. This idea was not totally new given the work of Bavelas and Leavitt (Bavelas, 1953; Leavitt, 1951), who showed that the structure of contacts and information flow in a group had a strong impact on leadership and power. Although they looked more at information flow than exchanges, they showed that centrally located persons had more power and were more satisfied with their job than more peripherally located persons, and they had higher evaluations of the job the group completed.

To understand the nature of the relationship between exchange structures and power (in the context of negotiated exchanges in which persons negotiate the distribution of some good), a number of different theories have developed, each trying to increase its scope and predictive accuracy over others. These include power-dependence theory (Cook, Emerson, Gilmore, & Yamagishi, 1983), elementary-relations theory (cf. Willer & Markovsky, 1993), network exchange theory (Markovsky, Willer, & Patton, 1988), expected-value theory (Friedkin, 1992), core-theory (Bienenstock & Bonacich, 1992), and, as extensions to network exchange theory, resistance theory (Heckathorn, 1983; Willer, 1981), and resistance and degree (Lovaglia, 1995a). Such a proliferation of theories can only take place when there is a great deal of research activity and interest in the issues. Some of these are discussed elsewhere in the chapter on Social Exchange Theory in this volume.

Negotiated exchange is not the only kind of exchange, and Molm has engaged in a program of research on non-negotiated exchange that examines not only the distribution of "goods" (positive outcomes such as rewards), but also "bads" (negative outcomes such as punishments) (Molm, 1997). In non-negotiated exchange, people unilaterally give rewards or punishments to others. These may or may not be returned at some point in the future. This is the pattern, for example, in giving birthday gifts. No immediate return is expected, and no negotiation takes place beforehand. By giving out punishments, people exercise what Molm calls coercive power. Coercive power is quite unlike reward power. It is not induced by a coercive power advantage. Rather, it is used purposefully, though sparingly, primarily by people who are disadvantaged in reward power. There is also more individual variability in its use (Molm, 1997).

DEVELOPMENT OF STATUS STRUCTURES. A process orientation was used in more current work on the evolution or development of status structures in groups. One study, following the Bales tradition of studying freely interacting groups, examined the emergence of a status and influence ordering, focusing on total interaction rates (Fisek & Ofshe, 1970). These researchers found that about half the groups differentiated quickly in member participation rates, while the other half went for a long time with nearly equal participation rates among the three members, developing a dominance structure over time. For those that evolved a status structure early, Fiske and Ofshe argued that characteristics of individuals influenced the early development of structure.

In a series of more recent studies, Shelly and Troyer further examine this question of the origins of a status ordering (Shelly & Troyer, 2001a,b). Drawing from expectation states theory, they hypothesize that persons who are initially advantaged with some status characteristic (task skill, status legitimation, or being liked) are likely to emerge quickly as a high contributor in initially leaderless task-oriented groups, and that advantage on more than one dimension should accelerate this process. Compared with a control group, however, only the person with initially advantaged task skill emerged more quickly. Those who had the advantages other than task skill did not emerge as highest contributor more quickly than the highest participator in the control group (with no initial status advantage).

Additionally, being initially advantaged on more than one attribute did not lead to quicker emergence as a high contributor. On the other hand, those advantaged by status or skill tended to take longer turns and were rated as more influential by others in the group (Shelly, Troyer, Munroe, & Burger, 1999). However, when the initial advantage combined status and skill, the combination apparently led to greater legitimacy and the top person did not need to dominate the discussion, so that while influence was high, speeches were shorter (Shelly et al., 1999).

The results of these studies suggest that the process of status emergence is not a simple, straight-forward process. Contrary to Fiske and Ofshe's (1970) expectations that initial status advantage helps the status evolution process, Shelly and Troyer's (2001a) results show that does not always happen. What is happening in the status emergence process in groups of freely interacting individuals remains a topic for future investigation.

Another approach to the evolution of leadership and status structures in freely interacting groups was taken by Riley and Burke (1995) who approached the issue from the point of view of identity processes. They argued that individual behavior is a function of the set of self-meanings that individuals have in roles. People try to portray in their behavior the meanings they hold for themselves in the role, and work to counter disturbances to these self-meanings that arise in the situation—the process of self-verification. They investigated the set of meanings of a task leader identity and found that when group members are able to portray the level of leadership they hold in their identities, and it is confirmed by the reactions of others in the group, they are most satisfied with their performance in the group. When discrepancies occur, they are less satisfied and work to reduce the discrepancy over time. From this we see that the leadership performances are a function not only of the status characteristics individuals hold, but also of individual's identities and the normal identity process of self-verification. Since there is initial variability across group members with respect to the (amount of) task leader identity, there resulted a distribution in task leadership performance and a corresponding status structure.

STATUS STRUCTURES AND EMOTION.   While most of the work examining the relationship between status and emotion looks at the effect of status processes on emotion following the Bales tradition (e.g., that high status persons have more positive emotional responses than low status persons [e.g., Lucas & Lovaglia, 1998]), the reverse connection has begun to be examined. Shelly (1993, 2001; Shelly & Webster, 1997) in a series of experiments has shown that sentiment structures in a group (patterns of liking and disliking) have a small impact on performance expectations of the status ordering in a group. Lovaglia and Houser (1996) have further shown that emotion can strengthen or weaken existing status structures. Through experimental work they showed negative emotions reduce compliance with a high status person, and when emotional reactions are consistent with the existing status structure, they reinforce it, but when the emotional reactions are inconsistent (higher status person showing positive emotion and lower status persons showing negative emotions), status differences are lowered.

Another theory that grows out of expectation states theory goes back to the issue of role-differentiation in that it examines emotional responses to task behavior. Ridgeway and Johnson (1990) develop expectation states theory ideas to incorporate emotional behavior which, as noted, had been excluded from the theory (Berger & Conner, 1974). Ridgeway and Johnson point out that agreements and disagreements, which Bales had considered to be socioemotional behavior, were redefined within the expectation states tradition as instrumental behaviors involving influence. They suggest that there is in fact a dual nature to agreement and disagreement. They have both instrumental and expressive properties, and this plays a key role in group processes. While agreement and disagreement have a task focus as responses to how the task is to be accomplished, reactions to these behaviors are likely to be more emotional.

Drawing on the sociology of emotion literature, Ridgeway and Johnson (1990) suggest that the way in which these emotional reactions play out, however, depends upon the expectation states of the group members. When a person who has lower task expectations for the self than the other experiences a disagreement, he or she is likely to take it as a sign of their lesser ability and react depressively and not express overt emotional behavior. However, when the person has higher task expectations for the self than the other, a disagreement is likely to lead to anger and the expression of negative socioemotional behavior. The result of these processes is to reinforce the status structure by feeding more negative reactions to lower status members.*

Agreements, on the other hand, lead to positive reactions and encourage the person to continue with their contributions to the task, thus reinforcing the emerging structure of task contributions. Because of the correlation between negative reactions and the status structure, positive reactions will tend to go to higher status members because lower status persons will be less inclined to disagree with higher status persons. In this way, socioemotional activity will be also patterned around the status structure and tend to reinforce it.

However, when the status structure is ill-determined, status struggles can lead to more negative socioemotional activity in the group that is contained in part by what Ridgeway and Johnson (1990) term legitimacy dynamics. Here, third persons become important. These other parties may act to reinforce and accept the suggestions of one person rather than another, thus lending legitimacy (and status) to the person whose ideas are accepted. In this way, status structures can emerge through consensual evaluation of the quality of the contributions of different group members.

All of these dynamics, thus, tend to produce and/or reinforce a single status structure based on and supporting the task contributions of members. For this to work, however, there must either be consensus on the initial status rankings or on the relative contributions of different members, with no member pushing the group too hard on the task so as to loose legitimacy. Consistent with the findings of Burke (1974b), this suggests that the legitimacy conditions for leadership when met produce and maintain a single status ordering. What

---

*Work by Stets (1997; Stets & Burke, 1996) showing greater negative interaction from the lower status person to the higher status person seems to contradict this reasoning, suggesting that the process may be more complicated or different in a non-laboratory setting.

Ridgeway and Johnson (1990) do not discuss is what happens when the high task status person uses too much negative behavior to put down contributions and/or challenges by the lower status persons or when the legitimacy conditions for leadership are not met. In this case, a second status ordering may well emerge based on socioemotional contributions (Burke, 1974a).

GROUP POLARIZATION.   Outside the area of status processes, one of the most researched processes in groups has to do with the finding that in making social judgments that involve some level of risk, the decisions of individuals in a group prior to discussion and the decision of the group (or of individuals) after a discussion are quite different (Stoner, 1961). In the initial problems that were given, a shift toward a more risky decision than the average of the individual pre-discussion decisions was noted. Group discussion seemed to intensify people's opinions. Later studies in exploring this phenomenon showed that for some problems there was a shift toward a more conservative decision following discussion. The general phenomenon came to be known as group polarization and was documented in many contexts and cultures (Fraser, Gouge, & Billig, 1971; Gologor, 1977).

Researchers were so captivated by this finding, and the ensuing experiments and theories attempting to explain it, that the number of publications, many of which had only minor variations on the theme, skyrocketed to the point that some journals were threatening a moratorium on publishing any more research on the topic. In spite of this plethora of research, there is still no accepted single explanation. Four different explanations exist, and it may be that all (or none) are an accurate account of the phenomenon. These four explanations, in the order in which they were proposed, are: an extension of Festinger's (1954) social comparison theory, a persuasive arguments theory, social decision theory, and intergroup differentiation theory.

The social comparison theory suggests that on such issues (e.g., in the shift to risk side), people have opinions based on a general culture which supports risk. Each feels that s/he is risky. Only when discussion occurs, however, do people see that they are not as risky as they thought compared to others. This argument has received considerable support (Goethals & Zanna, 1979; Sanders & Baron, 1977).

The persuasive arguments theory focuses on the content of the discussion, and suggests that the more arguments that are presented in one direction (risky) or the other (caution), the more people will move their own opinions in that direction. This is coupled with the ideas that there are more arguments in one direction or the other for a given issue depending upon the culture, and that an individual will not be familiar with all the arguments. As the arguments come out in the group discussion, people are moved in the culturally supported direction. This argument also has received considerable support, some in direct contrast to the social comparison theory (Burnstein & Vinokur, 1977; Vinokur & Burnstein, 1978).

A third argument, based on social decision theory, suggests that groups have implicit rules about how they will make decisions. Groups that generally favor risk taking on an issue seem to adopt a rule that says if only one person favors the risky decision, ignore it. However, if two or more favor the risky decision, then take it. For groups with a more cautious approach, a similar rule applies in the other direction. This approach also has be confirmed (e.g., Davis, Kameda, & Stasson, 1992).

An intergroup relations approach was proposed by Wetherell (1987). She raised two questions that the other theories did not handle: "what makes a persuasive argument persuasive?" and "why are some kinds of extremity desirable?" The approach she suggests draws upon self-categorization theory (Turner, 1985) to argue that group members have an idea of the characteristics of the prototypical group member, and, wanting to be good group members, they emulate the prototypical member. But, prototypicality is, in part, defined by the presence of an out-group (if only implicitly) (Hogg, 1987). Thus, for a group that sees itself as somewhat risky, the prototypical group member would be even more risky to distinguish the in-group from the conservative out-group. Thus, in being good, prototypical group members, they conform to the more extreme prototypical standard. This theory has also received support (Mackie, 1986).

While the principles underlying each of the four current explanations have been confirmed, each also finds some fault with the other explanations. It is possible that each contributes to part of the overall explanation (Isenberg, 1986), or that each holds under certain conditions that are not clear (Brown, 2000). It is also possible that each would be subsumed in a more general theory should that be developed. All of these theories consider each person's initial position as a point on some continuum. However, we also know that there is likely variance around that point—in a sense people's opinions form a probability distribution rather than a point. The shape of this probability distribution may play some role in the dynamics with people finding it easier to change in one direction or another, with some people caring more than others, with some people being influenced more than others, and so on. Clearly, there is more room for work on this issue.

CONCLUSION

Contrary to the worry expressed by Steiner (1974), the study of small groups and small group processes is alive and well. It has become pervasive and diverse, however, across many disciplines and research issues so that it is difficult to see the whole. Indeed, in this brief review I have covered only a small part of the research on groups and group processes.*

What can we make of the current trends? As indicated, much of the research on groups in sociological social psychology is conducted on individual reactions, choices, perceptions, feelings, and so forth in constrained (e.g., limited channels of communication) or artificial (e.g., interacting with a computer simulated other) social situations. And, while this is entirely appropriate for answering certain theoretical issues about particular processes, it does miss phenomena that only occur in the process of interaction. It is not enough to know only what a person sees, feels, or thinks to know how the interaction will pattern itself. As suggested in the emerging field of complexity theory (Gottman, 1991), people adjust and readjust to each other in a dynamic fashion that cannot be replicated in a study of individual reactions and perceptions. The emergence of norms, of roles, of culture, of group development, in short, of what Parsons and Bales called the emerging social system has mostly been ignored. Hopefully, as indicated in some current work, interest in these issues is gaining ascendancy and work will continue to develop.

ACKNOWLEDGMENTS: I wish to thank Jan E. Stets, Lisa Troyer, Michael Lovaglia, and Robert Shelly for comments on an earlier draft.

---

*Indeed, one important area that was not covered was the field study of existing, ongoing groups such as those studied by Thrasher (1927) or Whyte (1955). Included here certainly would be Corsaro's studies of socialization in children's peer groups (e.g., Corsaro, 1992), Anderson's (1978) study of street groups in Chicago, Eder's studies of adolescent girls in school (e.g., Eder, 1983), or Lois' (2001) study of search and rescue teams. Much can be learned from these in-depth studies of ongoing groups.

REFERENCES

Anderson, E. (1978). *A place on the corner.* Chicago: University of Chicago Press.

Aronson, E., & Mills, J. (1959). The effect of severity of initiation on liking for a group. *Journal of Abnormal and Social Psychology, 59,* 177–181.

Asch, S. (1960). Effects of group pressure upon the modification and distortion of judgments. In D. Cartwright & A. Zander (Eds.), *Group dynamics: Research and theory.* Evanston, IL: Row, Peterson.

Back, K. W. (1981). Small groups. In M. Rosenberg & R. H. Turner (Eds.), *Social psychology: Sociological perspectives* (pp. 320–343). New York: Basic Books.

Bales, R. F. (1950). *Interaction process analysis.* Cambridge: Addison-Wesley.

Bales, R. F. (1953). The equilibrium problem in small groups. In T. Parsons, R. F. Bales, & E. A. Shils (Eds.), *Working papers in the theory of action* (pp. 111–161). Glencoe: The Free Press.

Bales, R. F. (1956). Task status and likability as a function of talking and listening in decision-making groups. In L. D. White (Ed.), *The state of the social sciences* (pp. 148–161). Chicago: University of Chicago Press.

Bales, R. F. (1958). Task roles and social roles in problem-solving groups. In E. E. Maccoby, T. M. Newcomb, & E. L. Hartley (Eds.), *Readings in social psychology* (pp. 437–447). New York: Holt, Rinehart & Winston.

Bales, R. F. (1970). *Personality and interpersonal behavior.* New York: Holt, Rinehart & Winston.

Bales, R. F. (1999). *Social interaction systems. Theory and measurement.* New Brunswick: Transaction.

Bales, R. F., & Slater, P. E. (1955). Role differentiation in small decision-making groups. In T. Parsons & R. F. Bales (Eds.), *Family, socialization and interaction process* (pp. 259–306). Glencoe: The Free Press.

Bales, R. F., & Strodtbeck, F. L. (1951). Phases in group problem solving. *Journal of Abnormal and Social Psychology, 46,* 485–495.

Bales, R. F., Strodtbeck, F. L., Mills, T. M., & Roseborough, M. E. (1951). Channels of communication in small groups. *American Sociological Review, 16,* 461–468.

Bavelas, A. (1953). Communication patterns in task-oriented groups. In D. Cartwright & A. Zander (Eds.), *Group dynamics* (pp. 493–506). Evanston, Illinois: Row, Peterson, and Company.

Bennis, W. G., Benne, K. D., & Chin, R. (1961). *The planning of change.* New York: Holt, Rinehart, and Winston.

Berger, J., & Conner, T. L. (1974). Performance expectations and behavior in small groups: A revised formulation. In J. Berger, T. L. Conner, & M. H. Fisek (Eds.), *Expectation states theory: A theoretical research program* (pp. 85–109). Cambridge: Winthrop.

Berger, J., Fisek, M. H., Norman, R. Z., & Zelditch, M., Jr. (1977). *Status characteristics and social interaction: An expectation-states approach.* New York: Elsevier.

Berger, J., Ridgeway, C. L., Fisek, M. H., & Norman, R. Z. (1998). The legitimation and delegitimation of power and prestige orders. *American Sociological Review, 63*(3), 379–405.

Bienenstock, E. J., & Bonacich, P. (1992). The core as a solution to exclusionary networks. *Social Networks, 14*(3–4), 231–243.

Bion, W. R. (1961). *Experiences in groups.* New York: Ballantine Books.

Bird, C. (1950). *Social psychology.* New York: Appleton-Century.

Bonacich, P., & Lewis, G. H. (1973). Function specialization and sociometric judgment. *Sociometry, 36*(1), 31–41.

Borgatta, E. F., & Bales, R. F. (1953a). The consistency of subject behavior and the reliability of scoring in interaction process analysis. *American Sociological Review, 18,* 566–569.

Borgatta, E. F., & Bales, R. F. (1953b). Interaction of individuals in reconstituted groups. *Sociometry, 16,* 302–320.

Borgatta, E. F., & Bales, R. F. (1956). Sociometric status patterns and characteristics of interaction. *Journal of Social Psychology, 43,* 289–297.

Borgatta, E. F., Bales, R. F., & Couch, A. S. (1954). Some findings relevant to the great man theory of leadership. *American Sociological Review, 19,* 755–759.

Borgatta, E. F., & Crowther, B. (1965). *A workbook for the study of social interaction processes; direct observation procedures in the study of individual and group.* Chicago: Rand McNally.

Boring, E. G. (1945). *Psychology for the armed services.* Washington, DC: Infantry Journal.

Brown, R. (2000). *Group processes.* Malden, MA: Blackwell.

Brown, S. M. (1979). Male versus female leaders: A comparison of empirical studies. *Sex Roles, 5*(5), 595–611.

Burke, P. J. (1967). The development of task and social-emotional role differentiation. *Sociometry, 30,* 379–392.

Burke, P. J. (1968). Role differentiation and the legitimation of task activity. *Sociometry, 31,* 404–411.

Burke, P. J. (1971). Task and social-emotional leadership role performance. *Sociometry, 34,* 22–40.

Burke, P. J. (1974a). Leadership role differentiation. In C. G. McClintock (Ed.), *Experimental social psychology* (pp. 514–546). New York: Holt, Rinehart & Winston.

Burke, P. J. (1974b). Participation and leadership. *American Sociological Review, 39,* 822–843.

Burke, P. J., & Stets, J. E. (1999). Trust and commitment through self-verification. *Social Psychology Quarterly,* *62*(4), 347–366.

Burnstein, E., & Vinokur, A. (1977). Persuasive argumentation and social comparison as determinants of attitude polarization. *Journal of Experimental Social Psychology, 13*(4), 315–332.

Burt, R. S., & Janicik, G. A. (1996). Social contagion and social structure. In D. Iacobucci (Ed.), *Networks in marketing* (pp. 32–49). Thousand Oaks, CA: Sage.

Butts, C. T. (2001). The complexity of social networks: Theoretical and empirical findings. *Social Networks, 23*(1), 31–71.

Caplow, T. (1956). A theory of coalitions in the triad. *American Sociological Review, 21,* 489–493.

Caplow, T. (1968). *Two against one: Coalitions in triads.* Oxford, England: Prentice-Hall.

Cartwright, D., & Zander, A. (1953a). Leadership: Introduction. In D. Cartwright & A. Zander (Eds.), *Group dynamics: Research and theory* (pp. 535–550). Evanston, IL: Row, Peterson and Co.

Cartwright, D., & Zander, A. (Eds.). (1953b). *Group dynamics: Research and theory.* Evanston, IL: Row, Peterson and Co.

Chertkoff, J. M. (1971). Coalition formation as a function of differences in resources. *Journal of Conflict Resolution, 15*(3), 371–383.

Chertkoff, J. M., Skov, R. B., & Catt, V. L. (1980). Tests of the Laing and Morrison coalition models under different planning horizons. *Journal of Mathematical Sociology, 7*(2), 241–260.

Cook, K. S., Emerson, R. M., Gilmore, M. R., & Yamagishi, T. (1983). The distribution of power in exchange networks: Theory and experimental results. *American Journal of Sociology, 89,* 275–305.

Cook, K. S., Fine, G. A., & House, J. S. (1995). *Sociological perspectives on social psychology.* Boston: Allyn & Bacon.

Cooley, C. H. (1909). *Social organization.* New York: Scribner.

Corsaro, W. A. (1992). Interpretive reproduction in children's peer cultures. *Social Psychology Quarterly, 55*(2), 160–177.

Davis, J. H. (1996). Small-group research and the steiner questions: The once and future thing. In E. H. Witte & J. H. Davis (Eds.), *Understanding group behavior* (pp. 3–12). Mahwah, NJ: Lawrence Erlbaum.

Davis, J. H., Kameda, T., & Stasson, M. F. (1992). Group risk taking: Selected topics. In J. F. Yates (Ed.), *Risk-taking behavior* (pp. 164–199). Oxford, England: John Wiley and Sons.

Dornbusch, S. M., & Scott, W. R. (1975). *Evaluation and the exercise of authority.* San Francisco: Jossey-Bass.

Eagly, A. H. (1987). *Sex differences in social behavior: A social-role interpretation.* Hillsdale, NJ: LEA.

Eagly, A. H., & Johnson, B. T. (1990). Gender and leadership style: A meta-analysis. *Psychological Bulletin, 108*(2), 233–256.

Eagly, A. H., & Karau, S. J. (1991). Gender and the emergence of leaders: A meta-analysis. *Journal of Personality and Social Psychology, 60*(5), 685–710.

Eagly, A. H., Karau, S. J., & Makhijani, M. G. (1995). Gender and the effectiveness of leaders: A meta-analysis. *Psychological Bulletin, 117*(1), 125–145.

Eagly, A. H., Makhijani, M. G., & Klonsky, B. G. (1992). Gender and the evaluation of leaders: A meta-analysis. *Psychological Bulletin, 111*(1), 3–22.

Eder, D. (1983). Organizational constraints and individual mobility: Ability group formation and maintenance. *Sociological Quarterly, 24*(3), 405–420.

Emerson, R. M. (1972a). Exchange theory, Part 1: A psychological basis for social exchange. In J. Berger, M. Zelditch, Jr., & B. Anderson (Eds.), *Sociological theories in progress, vol. 2* (pp. 38–61). Boston: Houghton-Mifflin.

Emerson, R. M. (1972b). Exchange theory, Part 2: exchange relations and networks. In J. Berger, M. Zelditch, Jr., & B. Anderson (Eds.), *Sociological theories in progress, vol. 2* (pp. 61–83). Boston: Houghton-Mifflin.

Festinger, L. (1954). A theory of social comparison processes. *Human Relations, 7,* 117–140.

Festinger, L. (1957). *A theory of cognitive dissonance.* Stanford: Stanford University Press.

Festinger, L., Schachter, S., & Back, K. W. (1950). *Social pressures in informal groups.* New York: Harper.

Fiedler, F. E. (1978a). The contingency model and the dynamics of the leadership process. In L. Berkowitz (Ed.), *Advances in experimental social psychology* (vol. 11, pp. 59–112). New York: Academic Press.

Fiedler, F. E. (1978b). Recent developments in research on the contingency model. In L. Berkowitz (Ed.), *Group processes.* New York: Academic Press.

Fisek, M. H., & Ofshe, R. (1970). The process of status evolution. *Sociometry, 33*(3), 327–346.

Forsyth, D. R. (1999). *Group dynamics* (3rd ed.). Belmont: Wadsworth.

Fraser, C., Gouge, C., & Billig, M. (1971). Risky shifts, cautious shifts, and group polarization. *European Journal of Social Psychology, 1*(1), 7–30.

French, J. R. P., Jr., & Raven, B. (1960). The bases of social power. In D. Cartwright & A. Zander (Eds.), *Group dynamics: Research and theory* (pp. 607–623). Evanston, IL: Row, Peterson and Co.

Freud, S. (1959). *Group psychology and the analysis of the ego* (J. Strachey, Trans.). New York: Liveright.

Friedkin, N. E. (1992). An expected value model of social power: Predictions for selected exchange networks. *Social Networks, 14*(3–4), 213–229.

Friend, K. E., Laing, J. D., & Morrison, R. J. (1974). Bargaining processes and coalition outcomes. *Personality and Social Psychology Bulletin, 1*(1), 222–224.

Gamson, W. A. (1961). An experimental test of a theory of coalition formation. *American Sociological Review, 26,* 565–573.

Goethals, G. R., & Zanna, M. P. (1979). The role of social comparison in choice shifts. *Journal of Personality and Social Psychology, 37*(9), 1469–1476.

Gologor, E. (1977). Group polarization in a non-risk-taking culture. *Journal of Cross-Cultural Psychology, 8*(3), 331–346.

Gottman, J. M. (1991). Chaos and regulated change in families: A metaphor for the study of transitions. In P. A. Cowan, E. M. Hetherington et al. (Eds.), *Family transitions* (pp. 247–272). Hillsdale, NJ: Lawrence Erlbaum.

Gottman, J. M. (1993). Studying emotion in social interaction. In M. Lewis & J. M. Haviland (Eds.), *Handbook of emotions* (pp. 475–487). New York, NY: Guilford Press.

Gottman, J. M., Coan, J., Carrere, S., & Swanson, C. (1998). Predicting marital happiness and stability from newlywed interactions. *Journal of Marriage and the Family, 60*(1), 5–22.

Gottman, J. M., Markman, H., & Notarius, C. (1977). The topography of marital conflict: A sequential analysis of verbal and nonverbal behavior. *Journal of Marriage and the Family, 39*(3), 461–477.

Granovetter, M. (1983). The strength of weak ties: A network theory revisited. *Sociological Theory,* (1), 201–233.

Hallinan, M. T., & Smith, S. S. (1985). The effects of classroom racial composition on students' interracial friendliness. *Social Psychology Quarterly, 48*(1), 3–16.

Hare, A. P., Borgatta, E. F., & Bales, R. F. (1955). *Small groups: Studies in social interaction.* NY: Alfred A. Knopf.

Heckathorn, D. D. (1983). Extensions of power-dependence theory: The concept of resistance. *Social Forces, 61*(4), 1206–1231.

Heinicke, C., & Bales, R. F. (1953). Developmental trends in the structure of small groups. *Sociometry, 16*, 7–38.

Hogg, M. (1987). Social identity and group cohesiveness. In J. C. Turner, M. A. Hogg, P. J. Oakes, S. D. Reicher, & M. S. Wetherell (Eds.), *Rediscovering the social group* (pp. 89–116). New York: Basil Blackwell.

Hogg, M. A. (1996). Social identity, self-categorization, and the small group. In E. H. Witte & J. H. Davis (Eds.), *Understanding group behavior, Vol. 2: Small group processes and interpersonal relations* (pp. 227–253). Mahwah, NJ: Lawrence Erlbaum.

Hollander, E. P. (1958). Conformity, status, and idiosyncrasy credit. *Psychological Review, 65*, 117–127.

Hollander, E. P. (1993). Legitimacy, power, and influence: A perspective on relational features of leadership. In M. M. Chemers & R. Ayman (Eds.), *Leadership theory and research: Perspectives and directions* (pp. 29–47). San Diego: Academic Press.

Hollander, E. P., & Julian, J. W. (1969). Contemporary trends in the analysis of leadership processes. *Psychological Bulletin, 71*(5), 387–397.

Homans, G. C. (1950). *The human group.* New York: Harpers.

Isenberg, D. J. (1986). Group polarization: A critical review and meta-analysis. *Journal of Personality and Social Psychology, 50*(6), 1141–1151.

Jennings, H. H. (1950). *Leadership and isolation* (2nd ed.). New York: Longmans, Green and Co.

Julian, J. W., Hollander, E. P., & Regula, C. R. (1969). Endorsement of the group spokesman as a function of his source of authority, competence, and success. *Journal of Personality and Social Psychology, 11*(1), 42–49.

Kelley, H. H., & Arrowood, A. J. (1960). Coalitions in the triad: Critique and experiment. *Sociometry, 23*, 231–244.

Kemper, T. D. (1991). Predicting emotions from social relations. *Social Psychology Quarterly, 54*(4), 330–342.

Laing, J. D., & Morrison, R. J. (1973). Coalitions and payoffs in three-person sequential games: Initial tests of two formal models. *Journal of Mathematical Sociology, 3*(1), 3–25.

Lawler, E. J. (1999). Bringing emotions into social exchange theory. *Annual Review of Sociology*(25), 217–244.

Lawler, E. J. (2000). Emotion and group cohesion in productive exchange. *American Journal of Sociology, 106*(3), 616–657.

Lawler, E. J. (2002). Micro social orders. *Social Psychology Quarterly, 65*(1), 4–17.

Lawler, E. J., & Yoon, J. (1993). Power and the emergence of commitment behavior in negotiated exchange. *American Sociological Review, 58*, 465–481.

Lawler, E. J., & Yoon, J. (1996). Commitment in exchange relations: Test of a theory of relational cohesion. *American Sociological Review, 61*, 89–108.

Leavitt, H. (1951). Some effects of certain communication patterns on group performance. *Journal of Abnormal and Social Psychology, 47*, 38–50.

Leik, R. K. (1963). Instrumentality and emotionality in family interaction. *Sociometry, 26*, 134–145.

Lewis, G. H. (1972). Role differentiation. *American Sociological Review, 37*, 424–434.

Lindenberg, S. (1997). Grounding groups in theory: Functional, cognitive, and structural interdependencies. In B. Markovsky, M. Lovaglia, & L. Troyer (Eds.), *Advances in group processes* (vol. 14, pp. 281–331). Greenwich: JAI.

Lippitt, R., & White, R. (1943). The "social climate" of children's groups. In R. G. Barker, J. S. Kounin, & H. F. Wright (Eds.), *Child behavior and development*. New York: McGraw-Hill.

Lois, J. (2001). Managing emotions, intimacy, and relationships in a volunteer search and rescue group. *Journal of Contemporary Ethnography, 30*(2), 131–179.

Lovaglia, M. J. (1995a). Negotiated exchanges in social networks. *Social Forces, 74*(1), 123–155.

Lovaglia, M. J. (1995b). Power and status: Exchange, attribution, and expectation states. *Small Group Research, 26*(3), 400–426.

Lovaglia, M. J., & Houser, J. A. (1996). Emotional reactions and status in groups. *American Sociological Review, 61*(5), 867–883.

Lucas, J. W., & Lovaglia, M. J. (1998). Leadership status, gender, group size, and emotion in face-to-face groups. *Sociological Perspectives, 41*(3), 617–637.

Mackie, D. M. (1986). Social identification effects in group polarization. *Journal of Personality and Social Psychology, 50*(4), 720–728.

Mann, R. D. (1961). Dimensions of individual performance in small groups under task and social–emotional conditions. *Journal of Abnormal and Social Psychology, 62*, 674–682.

Markovsky, B., Willer, D., & Patton, T. (1988). Power relations in exchange networks. *American Sociological Review, 53*, 220–236.

Michener, H. A., & Burt, M. R. (1975). Use of social influence under varying conditions of legitimacy. *Journal of Personality and Social Psychology, 32*(3), 398–407.

Mills, T. M. (1953). Power relations in three-person groups. *American Sociological Review, 18*, 351–357.

Mills, T. M. (1964). *Group transformation*. Englewood Cliffs, NJ: Prentice-Hall.

Molm, L. D. (1997). *Coercive power in exchange*. Cambridge: Cambridge University Press.

Moreno, J. L. (1951). *Sociometry, experimental method and the science of society; An approach to a new political orientation*. Beacon, NY: Beacon House.

Moreno, J. L., & Jennings, H. H. (1960). Statistics of social configurations. In J. L. Moreno (Ed.), *The sociometry reader*. Glencoe, IL: Free Press.

Mullins, N. C., & Mullins, C. J. (1973). *Theories and theory groups in contemporary American sociology*. New York: Harper and Row.

Parsons, T., Bales, R. F., & Shils, E. A. (1953). *Working papers in the theory of action*. New York: Free Press.

Passariello, N. M., & Newnes, C. (1988). The clinical application of a sociometric test in a therapeutic community: A case study. *Journal of Group Psychotherapy, Psychodrama and Sociometry, 40*(4), 169–184.

Patzer, G. L. (1976). An application of sociometric method in business. *Psychology: A Journal of Human Behavior, 13*(3), 52–56.

Ridgeway, C. L. (1991). The social construction of status value: Gender and other nominal characteristics. *Social Forces, 70*(2), 367–386.

Ridgeway, C. L. (2001). The emergence of status beliefs: From structural inequality to legitimizing ideology. In J. T. Jost & B. Major (Eds.), *The psychology of legitimacy: Emerging perspectives on ideology, justice, and intergroup relations* (pp. 257–277). New York: Cambridge University Press.

Ridgeway, C. L., & Berger, J. (1986). Expectations, legitimation, and dominance behavior in task groups. *American Sociological Review, 51*(5), 603–617.

Ridgeway, C. L., & Johnson, C. (1990). What is the relationship between socioemotional behavior and status in task groups? *American Journal of Sociology, 95*(5), 1189–1212.

Ridgeway, C. L., Johnson, C., & Diekema, D. (1994). External status, legitimacy, and compliance in male and female groups. *Social Forces, 72*(4), 1051–1077.

Riedesel, P. L. (1974). Bales reconsidered: a critical analysis of popularity and leadership differentiation. *Sociometry, 37*, 557–564.

Riley, A., & Burke, P. J. (1995). Identities and self-verification in the small group. *Social Psychology Quarterly, 58*(2), 61–73.

Roethlisberger, F. J., & Dickson, W. J. (1970). *Management and the worker; an account of a research program conducted by the Western Electric Company, Hawthorne Works, Chicago*. Cambridge: Harvard University Press.

Sanders, G. S., & Baron, R. S. (1977). Is social comparison irrelevant for producing choice shifts? *Journal of Experimental Social Psychology, 13*(4), 303–314.

Schachter, S. (1953). Deviation, rejection, and communication. In D. Cartwright & A. Zander (Eds.), *Group dynamics: Research and theory*. Evanston, IL: Row, Peterson and Co.

Scheflen, A. (1974). *Communicational structure*. Bloomington, Indiana: Indiana University Press.

Shelly, R. K. (1993). How sentiments organize interaction. In E. J. Lawler, B. Markovsky, & J. O'Brien (Eds.), *Advances in group processes* (vol. 16, pp. 113–132). Greenwich: JAI.

Shelly, R. K. (2001). How performance expectations arise from sentiments. *Social Psychology Quarterly, 64*(1), 72–87.

Shelly, R. K., & Troyer, L. (2001a). Emergence and completion of structure in initially undefined and partially defined groups. *Social Psychology Quarterly, 64*(4), 318–332.

Shelly, R. K., & Troyer, L. (2001b). Speech duration and dependencies in initially structured and unstructured task groups. *Sociological Perspectives, 44*(4), 419–444.

Shelly, R. K., Troyer, L., Munroe, P. T., & Burger, T. (1999). Social structure and the duration of social acts. *Social Psychology Quarterly, 62*(1), 83–95.

Shelly, R. K., & Webster, M., Jr. (1997). How formal status, liking, and ability status structure interaction: Three theoretical principles and a test. *Sociological Perspectives, 40*(1), 81–107.

Sherif, M. (1936). *The psychology of social norms*. New York: Harper.

Sherif, M. (1966). *In common predicament: Social psychology of intergroup conflict and cooperation*. Boston: Houghton Mifflin.

Short, J. F., & Strodtbeck, F. L. (1965). *Group processes and gang delinquency*. Chicago: Chicago University Press.

Simmel, G. (1955). *Conflict and the web of group-affiliations*. Glencoe, IL: Free Press.

Singh, R., Bohra, K. A., & Dalal, A. K. (1979). Favourableness of leadership situations studied with information integration theory. *European Journal of Social Psychology, 9*(3), 253–264.

Slater, P. E. (1955). Role differentiation in small groups. *American Sociological Review, 20*, 300–310.

Steiner, I. D. (1974). Whatever happened to the group in social psychology? *Journal of Experimental Social Psychology, 10*(1), 94–108.

Stets, J. E. (1997). Status and identity in marital interaction. *Social Psychology Quarterly, 60*(3), 185–217.

Stets, J. E., & Burke, P. J. (1996). Gender, control, and interaction. *Social Psychology Quarterly, 59*(3), 193–220.

Stoner, J. A. (1961). *A comparison of individual and group decisions including risk*. Unpublished, MIT, Cambridge.

Strube, M. J., & Garcia, J. E. (1981). A meta-analytic investigation of Fiedler's contingency model of leadership effectiveness. *Psychological Bulletin, 90*(2), 307–321.

Stryker, S., & Psathas, G. (1960). Research on coalitions in the triad: Findings, problems and strategy. *Sociometry, 23*, 217–230.

Tallman, I., Rotolo, T., & Gray, L. N. (2001). Continuity or change? The impact of parents' divorce on newly married couples. *Social Psychology Quarterly, 64*(4), 333–346.

Thibaut, J. W., & Kelley, H. H. (1959). *The social psychology of groups*. New York: John Wiley and Sons.

Thrasher, F. M. (1927). *The gang: A study of 1,313 gangs in Chicago*. Chicago: University of Chicago Press.

Thye, S. R. (2000). A status value theory of power in exchange relations. *American Sociological Review, 65*(3), 407–432.

Turner, J. C. (1985). Social categorization and the self-concept: A social cognitive theory of group behavior. In E. J. Lawler (Ed.), *Advances in Group Processes* (vol. 2, pp. 77–122). Greenwich: JAI.

Turner, J. C., Hogg, M. A., Oakes, P. J., Reicher, S. D., & Wetherell, M. S. (Eds.). (1987). *Rediscovering the social group: A self-categorization theory*. New York: Basil Blackwell.

Verba, S. (1961). *Small groups and political behavior*. Princeton: Princeton University Press.

Vinacke, W. E., & Arkoff, A. (1957). An experimental study of coalitions in the triad. *American Sociological Review, 22*, 406–414.

Vinokur, A., & Burnstein, E. (1978). Novel argumentation and attitude change: The case of polarization following group discussion. *European Journal of Social Psychology, 8*(3), 335–348.

Walker, H. A., Thomas, G. M., & Zelditch, M., Jr. (1986). Legitimation, endorsement, and stability. *Social Forces, 64*(3), 620–643.

Wetherell, M. S. (1987). Social identity and group polarization. In J. C. Turner, M. A. Hogg, P. J. Oakes, S. D. Reicher, & M. S. Wetherell (Eds.), *Rediscovering the social group* (pp. 142–170). Oxford: Blackwell.

Whitaker, D. S., & Lieberman, M. A. (1967). *Psychotherapy through the group process*. New York: Atherton Press.

White, H. C., Boorman, S. A., & Breiger, R. L. (1976). Social structure from multiple networks 1: Blockmodels of roles and positions. *American Journal of Sociology, 81*, 730–780.

White, R., & Lippitt, R. (1953). Leader behavior and member reaction in three "social climates." In D. Cartwright & A. Zander (Eds.), *Group dynamics: Research and theory* (pp. 585–611). Evanston, IL: Row, Peterson and Co.

Whyte, W. F. (1955). *Street corner society*. Chicago: University of Chicago Press.

Willer, D. (1981). Quantity and network structure. In D. Willer & B. Anderson (Eds.), *Networks, exchange, and coercion: The elementary theory and its applications* (pp. 108–127). New York: Elsevier.

Willer, D. (1999). Network exchange theory: Issues and directions. In D. Willer (Ed.), *Network exchange theory* (pp. 1–22). Westport, CT: Praeger.

Willer, D., Lovaglia, M. J., & Markovsky, B. (1997). Power and influence: A theoretical bridge. *Social Forces, 76*(2), 571–603.

Willer, D., & Markovsky, B. (1993). Elementary theory: Its development and research program. In J. Berger & M. Zelditch, Jr. (Eds.), *Theoretical research programs: Studies in the growth of theory* (pp. 323–363). Stanford: Stanford University Press.

Wolff, K. H. (1950). *The sociology of Georg Simmel.* Glencoe, IL: Free Press.

Zelditch, M., Jr. (1969). Can you really study and army in the laboratory? In A. Etzioni (Ed.), *A sociological reader on complex organizations* (pp. 484–513). New York: Holt, Rinehart & Winston.

Zelditch, M., Jr. (2001). Processes of legitimation: Recent developments and new directions. *Social Psychology Quarterly, 64*(1), 4–17.

Zelditch, M., Jr., & Walker, H. A. (1984). Legitimacy and the stability of authority. In E. J. Lawler (Ed.), *Advances in group processes* (pp. 1–27). Greenwich, CT: JAI.

CHAPTER 16

Interaction in Social Networks

DIANE H. FELMLEE

INTRODUCTION

The social network represents a powerful concept for social psychology theory and research, where a social network refers to a set of actors and the ties among them. Thinking in network terms requires branching out from the individual actor to the larger social milieu in which that actor is embedded. Thus, social networks put the "social" into the "psychological."

Another reason that the social network perspective has particular relevance for sociological social psychology is that it places emphasis explicitly on the relationships, or the ties, among actors, rather than on the abstract social nature of behavior. The relational nature of human behavior is not explicit in much of contemporary social psychological work (Felmlee & Sprecher, 2000), where behavior is seen as socially shaped, but not necessarily relationally enacted. Recent theoretical work argues strongly for the need for a major epistemological shift in sociology toward an emphasis on relationships (Emirbayer, 1997; Ritzer & Gindoff, 1992), and network analysis is a research tradition that takes such a perspective. Thus, to see the social world through a network lens is to envision social life in a revolutionary manner. Instead of viewing discrete actors, each with his or her unique characteristics, the world is envisioned as composed of actors with particular relations among them. Such a relational paradigm represents a dramatic departure from a more categorical approach to social interaction.

The network perspective is important for other reasons as well. This approach brings a fundamentally structural perspective to social psychological inquiry, a view in which individuals are seen as linked to one another in a structure of ties. One of the strengths of sociology is its emphasis on social structure, but this focus is not always realized in social psychological work. Finally, a social network perspective aids in bridging the micro–macro gap (Granovetter, 1973). Networks are composed of intimate, micro-level, dyadic ties, as well as

DIANE H. FELMLEE • Department of Sociology, University of California, Davis, CA 95616

Handbook of Social Psychology, edited by John Delamater. Kluwer Academic/Plenum Publishers, New York, 2003.

ties to larger subgroups and societal organizations at the macro-level. For example, both the roles of the family and of the broader community in which individuals live become relevant when examining the issue of social support from a network focus.

The topic of social networks is also unique as compared to many others because it is not a substantive field per se (as are the topics of interpersonal attraction, aggression, or helping behavior), nor is it a distinct social psychological theory. Most commonly, social network characteristics are used as explanatory variables. A social network perspective has been employed in this manner within numerous subareas within psychology, social psychology, and sociology. In other cases, characteristics of social networks themselves are the primary focus of scientific inquiry, but such studies are far fewer in number.

Research regarding social networks has expanded dramatically in recent years, both within social psychology and sociology more generally. In addition, the boundaries between the disciplines of sociology and social psychology begin to blur when considering social network research. In this chapter, I will focus on social network research in which the actors are individuals, rather than organizations, nation states, or other social units, that is, the focus will be on interaction among individuals. I will not, however, review important social psychological work that combines social exchange theory and networks, that is, network exchange theory (e.g., Burke, 1997; Cook & Whitmeyer, 1992), nor other research that synthesizes network models and expectation states theory, that is, "E-state structuralism" (e.g., Skvoretz & Fararo, 1996). Social exchange and expectation states theories are discussed in more detail elsewhere in this volume. Finally, I will focus mainly on recent contributions to the literature within the past decade.

In the first part of this chapter, I elaborate on the principles of a social network perspective, that is, the general statements that can be made about a social network approach to social psychology. Next, I define and illustrate several basic social network concepts. In the following section of the chapter, I summarize some of the main findings from current network research within two particular subareas: (1) groups and collectivities and (2) dyadic relationships. Finally, I discuss an agenda for future research.

Principles of a Social Network Perspective

There are several principles that are key to a social network perspective. These principles point to the unique characteristics of such a perspective (e.g., see Wellman, 1988; Wasserman & Faust, 1994). Here I outline three basic principles, ones that are particularly applicable for network work within social psychology.

1. *A social network perspective emphasizes relations, or ties, among actors.* The basis of these relations could be friendship, work ties, avenues of exchange, kinship, avenues of communication, chains of command, or other social linkages. Social network analysts maintain that social relationships among sets of actors serve as the starting point for social research.

2. *The behavior of actors is interdependent with that of other actors within a social network.* Quantitative work in the social sciences that uses the general linear model generally assumes that one case is independent of the other. However, a fundamental principle of the network perspective is that cases are not independent, that is, one network members' behavior is dependent on the others' behavior.

3. *Individual behavior is influenced by the network environment.* The social network is a basic determinant of an individual's behavior. In many cases, the social capital

inherent in a network provides opportunities, such as when social ties supply job information. In other situations, the network environment may curtail an individual's behavior and provide barriers, rather than opportunities. An example of this would be a family that refuses to allow a member to move to another community with particularly good job openings.

Social Network Concepts

Social network analysis employs a number of unique concepts, such as weak ties, transitivity, and cliques. Although not an exhaustive list, several of the particularly important concepts are briefly described below. For a more detailed discussion of network concepts, ways to measure these concepts, and network methodology, see Wasserman and Faust (1994), Scott (2000), and Galaskiewicz and Wasserman (1993).

In order to illustrate several of these concepts, I will use social network data gathered from the administrative staff of a university department several years ago. To collect these data, I gave a list of administrative staff members to the Chair of the department, John, and to the five members of the secretarial/administrative staff: Nicole, the Administrative Assistant/Head Staff person, Laura, the Graduate Advisor, Rachel, the Undergraduate Advisor, Chris, the Receptionist, and Paul, the Computer Consultant.* I asked each of them if they worked with any of the other administrative staff members on a regular, daily basis. A sociogram that illustrates the responses to this question appears in Figure 16-1. A line between two actors indicates that both members of a particular dyad reported that they worked together on a daily basis, that is, it represents a type of nondirectional tie. Examples of directional ties, represented in a sociogram by arrows rather than lines, would be liking or respect.

SIZE. Size is the number of distinct individuals in a network. Social networks form a web that begins with close connections, then reaches out to acquaintances, and eventually may extend to include those in the wider world. Measuring network size requires a clear definition of what is meant by a particular social network, and thus this concept of network size is not as easily measured as initially might be assumed (Milardo, 1986). One distinction, for example, is between those members of a social network who an individual perceives of as significant, the *psychological network*, and those individuals with whom interaction is regular, the *interactive network* (Surra & Milardo, 1991). Figure 16-1 illustrates an interactive network.

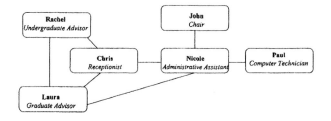

FIGURE 16-1. **Daily work ties among a department's administrative staff.**

*The names, and sometimes gender, are changed to ensure anonymity.

DENSITY.   Density refers to the proportion of network ties to all possible network ties, or in other words, the number of links between actors that do exist, divided by all potential links. In Figure 16-1, the density of the network is 0.47, that is, 47% of all possible ties between the six actors are realized.

TIE STRENGTH.   Ties can vary in strength. Ties between actors that have many links in common are considered "strong," and those with only one or few links are "weak." In mathematical graph theory terms, weak ties are often "bridges," that is, they are the only link between two groups of actors. Figure 16-1 does not contain an example of a "weak tie." However, Paul, the computer assistant, communicated regularly with another group on campus, a group consisting of other computer consultants. If the sample included data from this group of consultants, then the link between the Administrative Assistant, Nicole, and Paul would represent a weak tie between the department's administrative staff and the campus computer consultants.

CLIQUES.   A clique is a collection of actors (at least three) in which all are linked to each other by a tie(s). An example of a clique is the set of actors Rachel, Chris, and Laura in Figure 16-1. Less stringent definitions of cliques, or cohesive subgroups, are commonly used in empirical research, because the absence of just a single tie among actors in a subgroup prevents the subgroup from meeting the formal clique definition.

CENTRALITY.   A central actor is one who is involved in many ties (assuming nondirectional ties). Alternatively, an actor is considered central if the actor lies between many actors, that is, the central actor is located on the shortest path of ties (i.e., geodosics) that link other actors (Freeman, 1979). Nicole is the most central actor in Figure 16-1. For a recent discussion of centrality measures and their importance, see Faust (1997).

TRANSITIVITY.   A triad containing actors A, B, and C, is *transitive* if whenever A has a tie with B, and B has a tie with C, then A also has a tie with C. If A does not have a tie to C, then the triad is *intransitive*. The triad containing actors Rachel, Chris, and Laura is one example of a transitive triad in Figure 16-1. The triad containing actors Rachel, Chris, and Nicole, on the other hand, is intransitive, because Rachel does not have a direct tie to Nicole.

EQUIVALENCE.   Actors are equivalent when they have similar relationships to and from all other actors in a network. Two actors are *structurally equivalent* if they have identical ties to and from all other actors in the network (Burt, 1980). Actors Chris and Laura represent an example of structurally equivalent actors in Figure 16-1.

Note that even a simple social network data set, such as that illustrated here, can offer answers to some interesting questions. For example, to whom would a staff member direct a question about the University's computing facilities? Nicole, the Administrative Assistant, is likely to be a more frequent choice than the Computer Consultant, because she has more routine contact with other staff members and because she is a weak tie from him to other consultants. Who is likely to get together informally? The clique representing Laura, Rachel, and Chris reported informal interaction. Whose job duties changed to encompass some of those of another staff person? The job description of Chris, the receptionist, was upgraded to include some duties of the Graduate Advisor, both of whom occupied equivalent structural positions in the network.

Who was thought by many to be the most powerful person in the department? Nicole, the administrative assistant, was sometimes accused of having more power than the Chair, and she had a good deal of influence in many departmental decisions. Note that Nicole was by far the most central person in the network, which made her the hub of departmental communication, and thus it is not surprising that she was able to exert influence.

In the subsequent year, Nicole received a substantial external job promotion, and the department hired a new administrative assistant. Nicole's pivotal role in the staff network no doubt helped her to obtain such a lucrative promotion. In addition, a new Chair took over as head of the department. It is interesting that the new Chair chose to maintain regular contact with several staff members in addition to the administrative assistant. As a result of these changes, the relative centrality and the relative power of the new administrative assistant was lower, whereas those of the new department head were higher, than in the previous administration. No longer was the administrative assistant believed to "run" the department.

GROUPS AND COLLECTIVITIES

A good deal of interactive social network research is at the small group level, including that involving friendship and transitivity, and this is where the beginnings of network research in social psychology started to take root (e.g., Moreno, 1934). Other work examines more diffuse collectivities, such as communities, or actual extended networks, such as kin networks. Within these research areas, three particularly innovative theoretical breakthroughs were made in the 1970s regarding the following concepts: (1) transitivity or balance, (2) equivalence, and (3) weak ties. The first of these concepts, transitivity, has received the most attention within the subfield of social psychology per se, but the other two concepts have important micro-level implications as well. In this section, I will begin by reviewing these three theoretical developments and then discuss empirical research and more recent network theories in the areas of groups and collectivities.

Foundational Theoretical Concepts

TRANSITIVITY. An important idea to emerge from early social network research is that triads, or subgroups consisting of three people, are noteworthy units of social psychological study that have import for the individuals composing the triad. A theory of structural balance regarding triads was generalized from Heider's (1958) cognitive balance theory, which states that when two people like each other and agree about a topic, such as their feelings about a third person, then cognitive balance occurs. When two people like each other and disagree, however, then imbalance occurs and an unpleasant cognitive state is aroused.

Cartwright and Harary (1956) used mathematical graph theory to formalize Heider's cognitive balance theory, developing a theorem that suggests that social systems will tend to develop into two cliques, with positive ties within each clique and negative ties between members of different cliques. Nevertheless, groups often do not split into exactly two cliques, according to empirical data, and thus subsequent theorists continued to modify balance theory, attempting to provide better fits to data than each previous formalization (e.g., Davis, 1967). The most influential model was based on the transitivity principle for positive relations, as proposed by Holland and Leinhardt (1970): If actor a chooses actor b, and actor b chooses actor c, then actor a chooses actor c. If either of the first two parts of this statement is not true, that is, if a does not choose b, or if b does not choose c, then the cycle is "vacuously transitive," that is, it does not contradict the principle of transitivity. Otherwise, cycles are "intransitive."

Research documents several trends with regard to transitivity in social groups. First, intransitive triads occur less frequently than would be expected by chance (e.g., Hallinan, 1974; Holland & Leinhardt, 1970). The balance theory explanation for this finding is that intransitive triads are cognitively stressful, and thus avoided by individuals. An alternative explanation is that individuals avoid inequality in their dyadic relationships, and in doing so, avoid intransitivity as well (Feld & Elmore, 1982). In addition, it is possible that the relative infrequency of intransitive triads in group data is due to the tendency of people to cognitively impose transitivity onto affiliative interaction patterns that they observe in order to simplify these patterns and make them easier to recall (Freeman, 1992; Krackhardt & Kilduff, 1999).

Second, the absence of intransitive triads is associated with a group network structure that consists of disjoint cliques that are equal or rank ordered (e.g., Davis & Leinhart, 1972). There is a link between the micro-level triadic structure of a group and overall group structure, in other words. Furthermore, research documents differences in intransitivity in several group settings and among various demographic groups. There are race and gender differences in the ways in which school children resolve intransitive friendships, for example, and these patterns are likely to be explained by status differences (e.g., Hallinan & Kubitschek, 1990). Whites demonstrate the exclusive, high-status nature of their friendships in that they tend to prefer decreasing the number of their friends rather than expanding them in response to intransitivity. Black pupils, and Black girls in particular, are more willing to expand their social networks.

Some of the insights provided by this bulk of work include: (1) one individual's tie to another person is influenced by third parties in their network. In other words, even very personal choices on the part of two people, such as whether or not they should be friends, are affected by the network in which they are embedded. Individuals' friendship choices are a function of their friends' friendship choices. (2) There is a link between macro-level group structure and micro-level triadic structure. For example, groups composed of triads that contain no intransitivities have been shown to have a structure that consists of hierarchical cliques (Davis & Leinhardt, 1972). Processes at the micro-level, in which individuals avoid stressful, intransitive triads, result in hierarchy and cliques in the overall group; or vice versa, perhaps it is hierarchy and clique formation processes at the group level that produce a relative lack of intransitivity at the triad level.

STRUCTURAL POSITION. Another major development in social network research began with work in which researchers attempted to place network actors into distinct categories based on structural equivalence (e.g., Lorrain & White, 1971; White, Boorman, & Breiger, 1976). In this approach, actors are grouped into the same category, or position, if they have similar/dissimilar social ties to others in the network. Structurally equivalent actors have the same interlinkages to others in the network, and so are theoretically interchangeable. Two third grade teachers in a primary school teach different students, for example, but they occupy the same position within the school system.

In one application of structural equivalence at the interaction level, Burt (1987) examined data on the diffusion of a medical innovation. He found that structural equivalence was a better explanation of the contagion that occurs in the adoption of a medical innovation than was group cohesion. That is, drug adoption was the result of physicians' perceptions that it represented the proper action for an occupant of their particular position in the social structure rather than adoption being the outcome of conversations with colleagues.

Recent research also demonstrates that this concept of social role, or position, is perceived by people as existing in their social environment if abstract, general definitions of equivalence are used rather than more restrictive definitions, such as structural equivalence (Michaelson & Contractor, 1992). In other words, the general notion of equivalence in social ties is not simply a theoretical abstraction, but it has roots in the minds of social actors as well.

There are at least two noteworthy theoretical contributions from this line of research: (1) One important point is that actors' social positions are determined by the *absence* of ties with other network members as well as the *presence* of ties. Equivalence is a function of the entire pattern of possible ties between and among a set of actors, whether those ties are realized or not. In other words, a set of actors may be considered structurally equivalent when they have no ties to one another. Two third grade teachers in a city's school system may not know each other, but be placed into the same equivalence position because they have a matching pattern of ties to and from others in the school system. (Note that such teachers would not be members of the same clique, however, if they do not know each other.) (2) Another unique contribution of this approach is that social positions are determined on the basis of having similar profiles of social ties across *multiple relationships*, rather than being limited to a *single relationship*. Other network analysis techniques tend to be limited to single relationships. Nevertheless, social positions and roles are likely to be determined not by one type of tie, but by several. Positions in a school system, for example, are apt to be determined by formal authority relationships as well as by more informal connections, such as friendship.

WEAK TIES. In an innovative theoretical contribution that has received a good deal of attention in sociology, Granovetter (1973) proposed that weak ties in a network are an important locale for diffusion of influence and information, opportunities for mobility, and community organization. Individuals with strong, close ties to each other, such as family members and good friends, are likely to possess the same kinds of information, whereas new information is more apt to be obtained from those whose ties are relatively weak and distal. In support of this argument, Granovetter found that individuals were more likely to obtain a new job through contacts they saw occasionally, rather than frequently.

This concept of weak ties is particularly noteworthy for at least two reasons. First, it points to the strength of network links as being worthy of investigation. As a result, it is not uncommon for research today to distinguish network connections by their strength in both theoretical and empirical work (e.g, see Feld & Carter, 1998). Second, Granovetter's theory emphasizes that the strategic location of an individuals' contacts within a network is crucial for the overall flow of information. In other words, network structure plays a fundamental role in interpersonal dynamics.

In addition to these early theoretical contributions to the literature, there have been a number of noteworthy empirical studies, as well as more recent theoretical work, in a variety of subfields within social psychology, including those of friendship, social influence, social support, and computer networks. I begin by discussing friendship network research.

Subareas of Empirical Work

FRIENDSHIP. Two founding network studies in this area are still cited today. In one classic investigation, Festinger, Schachter, and Back (1950) found that proximity was a major determinant of social ties in two new housing complexes, and that residents who lived in less central housing units were more likely to be labelled as deviant. In another influential study, Newcomb (1961) examined the friendship patterns of male college students in a boarding house and found that similarity of age, background, and attitudes influenced mutual liking over time.

In a more recent study on networks, Feld (1991) investigated a particular case of a mathematical "class size paradox," and applied it to friendship groups. In this illustration of the paradox, when individuals compare themselves with their friends, it is likely that most of them will feel relatively inadequate in terms of the number of friends that they have. Empirically, however, most people do have fewer friends than their friends have. This is because mathematically the mean number of friends of friends is always greater than the mean number of friends of individuals. Other research finds, nevertheless, that most individuals employ a self-serving bias when comparing their relative popularity to that of others, and that they subjectively believe that they have more friends than do their own friends (Zuckerman & Jost, 2001).

Current research also examines older adult friendship networks (e.g., Blieszner & Adams, 1992). In one study, for example, three factors were found to underlie the network structure of a sample of adults aged 55 years or older—egalitarianism, sociability, and religiosity (Adams & Torr, 1998). Research also emphasizes the value of similarity in the networks of older adults and finds that widows tend to shift their networks toward greater association with others who have shared this stressful life event (Morgan, Carder, & Neal, 1997).

Recent work examines friendship networks in work organization settings as well. One study finds that the density of friendship networks is inversely related to loneliness, both for males and females (Bell, 1991). Other research finds that informal friendship networks influence organizational effectiveness. More specifically, organizations that have a high proportion of informal friendship networks that cut across work subunits, relative to those friendship ties that exist within subunits, are more effective in the face of a crisis (Krackhardt & Stern, 1988).

Finally, a number of studies find that homophily, the principle that similarity breeds connection, is characteristic of affiliative network systems of various types, including friendship, marriage, support, work, advice, information, and exchange (McPherson, Smith-Lovin, & Cook, 2001). As a result, people's personal networks tend to be homogeneous with regard to several sociodemographic and behavioral characteristics. The strongest barriers to the development of network ties are those of differences in race and ethnicity, followed by differences in age, religion, education, and gender.

SOCIAL INFLUENCE.   Social influence is another group process that is informed by network analyses. Network analysts take a distinctive structural approach to the topic of social influence (Marsden & Friedkin, 1993). The general argument is that the proximity of two network members is associated with the level of interpersonal influence between them, where proximity is either defined by a measure of structural cohesion, which emphasizes network connectivity, or by a measure of equivalence, which stresses similar profiles of interpersonal ties.

One theoretical model that describes the network influence process is the "network effects model," in which actors' opinions are a weighted average of influential opinions of other network members (e.g., Friedkin, 1998). Actor's opinions are not only influenced endogenously by other actors' opinions, but their initial opinions are influenced by a set of exogenous factors. In one application, the network effects model has been used to explain the traditional social psychological topic of shifts in group decisions. Here, Friedkin (1999) demonstrates that choice shifts are a product of a group's social network structure, where certain members have more influence than others when opinions are formed. Pressures in a group cause a group's opinions to converge to a weighted average of members' initial opinions. This explanation is noteworthy because it offers a structural social psychological explanation for group decision shifts, as opposed to other more traditional theories that focus on group norms, decision rules, or persuasive arguments.

SOCIAL SUPPORT.   Another area of social psychological research in which social networks play a major role is that of social support. There is a great deal of evidence that support from a person's social network influences his or her health. A variety of studies, including some that are longitudinal, finds that the presence of social ties is associated with lower levels of stress, and reduced levels of morbidity and mortality (e.g., House, Umberson, & Landis, 1988). Networks also have buffering effects on mental health. A number of studies find that the presence of an intimate confidant, and the perception of support availability, are associated with a reduction in the impact of stressful life events on negative mental health outcomes such as depression and anxiety (e.g., Brown & Harris, 1978; Kessler & McLeod, 1985).

In addition, there is a strong link between network support and life satisfaction, self-esteem, and happiness. For example, a recent meta-analysis of 286 studies on the association between social networks and subjective well-being among older adults finds that networks are positively associated with life satisfaction, self-esteem, and happiness (Pinquart & Sorensen, 2000). Quality of contacts is more highly correlated with well-being than is quantity of contacts, according to the meta-analysis. In addition, quantity of contacts with friends is more important than quantity of contacts with family, presumably because friendships are voluntary and unsatisfactory ones can be dropped. On the other hand, relationships with adult children are important for well-being in old age, too, because quality of ties to adult children is more important for life satisfaction than is quality of ties to friends. Finally, according to the meta-analysis, social network contacts are more closely related to life satisfaction and happiness for women than for men, probably because of the greater importance of social relations for women.

Social support is multifaceted and can be divided into distinct types, such as emotional aid, services, and financial aid, and these various types of support are provided by different network members (Wellman & Worley, 1990). Women, for instance, contribute a great deal of emotional support. In addition, social support located in the community tends to be provided by friends and relatives, rather than by work ties.

The social network opportunity structure also influences the help-seeking process. For example, people who are employed are more likely to use coworkers or friends in addition to physicians when seeking health-related assistance, whereas those that are married are more likely to rely on family members (Pescosolido, 1992). For reviews of additional research on social network support and health, see, for example, House et al. (1988), Pinquart and Sorensen (2000), and Walker, Wasserman, and Wellman (1993).

INTERNET NETWORKS.   A new and promising area for social network research is that of computer assisted networks. The Internet offers a venue for people to form networks that has a number of interesting social psychological characteristics, such as the absence of nonverbal communication, the possibility for relatively egalitarian links (in which people's social demographic characteristics are not necessarily salient), high speed exchanges across great distance, and the development of online small group communities (Wellman et al., 1996). One debate in the field concerns the extent to which the Internet influences individuals' sense of connectedness and satisfaction. One study found that greater use of the Internet was associated with increases in depression and loneliness (Kraut et al., 1998), although others criticize this study and argue that the conclusions are misleading (e.g., McKenna & Bargh, 2000). Some scholars note that the Internet is not a substitute for in-person contact, but that it acts as a complement to existing ties (Koku, Nazer, & Wellman, 2001). Additional research finds that a common misconception is that the Internet results in the seclusion of people, but that on the contrary, the Internet pulls people together by increasing the amount of ties and the maintenance of contacts (Wellman & Hampton, 1999).

The topic of Internet networks is ripe for innovative social psychological work. For example, more studies are needed to address the debates concerning the role of the Internet and people's perceptions of connectedness and satisfaction, especially studies based on empirical data; most of the literature on this topic do not rely on primary data. Structural level research of online networks would also be important (Adams, 1998). For example, we know little about the form of ties that link individuals to one another on the Internet, such as the density of connections, the strength of ties, or the distribution of power and status.

Summary of Groups, Collectivities, and Networks

In sum, network research in these domains has generated innovative theoretical ideas concerning transitivity in triads, positions in group structure, and the role of tie strength. A network perspective also has proven to be beneficial to research within the areas of friendship, social influence, social support, and the Internet. Findings demonstrate the power of the social network to influence the intimate bonds of friendship, shape an individual's opinions, improve a person's mental state, physical health, and life satisfaction, and affect someone's perceptions of connectedness via remote communication.

DYADIC RELATIONSHIPS

A relatively new topic of social psychology inquiry that has been ripe for social network research is that of close dyadic relationships, including courtship and cohabiting alliances as well as marriages. Research finds that social networks widely influence intimate pairs at various relationship stages, including at the initiation of a relationship, during its lifetime, and at its ending (whether due to breakup, divorce, or death). Furthermore, networks affect a close dyad via behavioral, cognitive, and affective channels. Behaviorally, the social network may provide *opportunities* for individuals to be together (see also, Sprecher, Felmlee, Orbuch, & Willett, 2002) or it may erect *barriers* that constrain the likelihood that a particular dyad interacts. On a cognitive level, network members also may provide *information*, either positive or negative, about a potential friend or partner that affects the probability that a dyad may form or, once formed, remain intact. Finally, friends and family members may influence an individual's close relationship on an affective level, by their positive or negative emotional *reactions* to a friend or partner.

Relationship Beginnings

The social environment influences the chance that two people engage in a friendship or a romantic relationship even before they are aware of each other. Societal norms dictate which types of persons are appropriate for an affiliative encounter, and when two people defined by social norms as potential intimate partners meet, cultural values emphasize the primacy of romance over friendship. Furthermore, parents often mold the environment in which their children meet potential friends and courtship partners by choosing to live in particular neighborhoods and by becoming members of certain civic and/or religions institutions. Social network members also directly influence the initiation of close relationships. For example, friends provide an opportunity for partners to meet. Approximately one half of individuals were introduced to their partners by a friend, according to one study of 858 individuals, and two thirds of them had at least one friend in common (Parks & Eggert, 1991).

Relationship Social Roles

In addition to influencing relationship beginnings, the social network may affect the inner dynamics of an intimate liaison once it is established. Networks even may shape social roles in marriages, according to some scholars. Bott (1957, 1971), for example, argued that dense kin networks encourage couples to adopt traditional social norms in their roles as husband or wife. In a study of 20 English families, Bott found that husbands and wives who were in close knit networks, that is, high density networks, were more likely to engage in traditional male–female role segregated activities than couples whose networks were less close knit. Subsequent tests of Bott's hypothesis have sometimes, but not always, found a significant link between network density and role segregation (see review by Milardo & Allan, 1996).

Close Dyads and Change in Network Composition

What happens to a couple's social network as the two members become involved in an intimate relationship? Several studies suggest that a process of "dyadic withdrawal" occurs in which romantic partners tend to withdraw from their social networks to spend time with each other (Huston & Burgess, 1979; Johnson & Leslie, 1982; Slater, 1963). Time spent together as a couple means that there is less time for other friends and family members. Such dyadic withdrawal may act to strengthen a couple's identity as a distinct pair. Nevertheless, research suggests that withdrawal occurs more for acquaintances and intermediate friends, and that couples are less apt to withdraw from close friends and relatives. In other words, "dyadic realignment," may be a better description of changes that occur in networks as couples become closer (Parks, Stan, & Eggert, 1983). As part of their development, couples increase their involvement with mutual friends, seek out couples as friends, continue to interact with relatives, and spend less time with friends who are not close.

As couples grow older, further changes in their networks may occur. According to socioemotional selectivity theory (Carstensen, 1999), as individuals age, they spend less time in trivial relationships and actively select to focus on those that provide meaningful, positive emotional experiences. Thus, a couple's network composition alters both as a couple progresses from dating to a committed relationship and with advances in life stage.

Not surprisingly, a pair's social network also is likely to change following a separation or a divorce. Network size and network density decrease in the aftermath of divorce (Bohannan, 1970; Milardo, 1987; Spanier & Thompson, 1984; Weiss, 1975), and network overlap shrinks as individuals withdraw from a former partner's network members (Rands, 1988).

Relationship Well-Being and Stability

Social networks play a role, too, in relationship satisfaction and the continuance or dissolution of close dyads. Once a relationship has formed, the social network continues to influence close pairs by behavioral (opportunities or barriers), cognitive (positive or negative information), and affective (positive or negative reactions) means.

OPPORTUNITIES/BARRIERS. The social network can act in ways that constrain the ability of a couple to encounter alternative dating or friendship opportunities, and thereby increase couple stability. As a couple becomes more involved, the pair is apt to interact more exclusively with its own network members and less with others (e.g., Johnson & Leslie, 1982). In this situation, interdependence with the network is likely to grow (Milardo, 1982). Increases in network interaction and overlap, however, decrease the opportunity for meeting potential partners because individuals socialize less with new people. Furthermore, a reduction in the chances of meeting others is likely to lower breakup probabilities, because individuals are apt to be hesitant to end a current liaison if they have a limited chance of coming into contact with a viable alternative partner. In one study, for example, individuals who experienced increased network overlap with their partner over a period of 3 months found that their relationship developed over time, whereas those who underwent reductions in overlap experienced relationship deterioration (Milardo, 1982). Greater network overlap between spouses also is associated with marital satisfaction (e.g., Julien & Markman, 1991; Stein, Bush, Ross, & Ward, 1992), particularly if the joint network is balanced in its inclusion of kin from each spouse (Julien, Chartrand, & Bégin, 1999).

On the other hand, in some cases, networks may enhance the opportunities to meet new people and, as a result, be associated with decreased couple stability. For example, friends may invite a member of a pair to join them in situations that increase the chance of meeting a new partner, such as at a party, restaurant, or bar. Friends or relatives also may directly introduce members of a couple to a new partner, either unintentionally or intentionally, by continuing their matchmaking efforts after a match has been cemented. Committed individuals, too, may be viewed by others as particularly acceptable for a platonic friendship, which in turn creates opportunities for romance. Furthermore, significant others themselves may be the source of a new relationship.

Friends and family members also directly provide an opportunity for alternative sources of companionship and intimacy to that offered in an intimate relationship (Felmlee, 2001), and this network substitutability (Marsiglio & Scanzoni, 1995) influences couple satisfaction and stability. For example, when wives had high levels of social interaction with close friends, husbands report lower marital love and greater feelings of ambivalence and conflict (Burger & Milardo, 1995). Furthermore, if an individual's basic needs for intimacy and companionship are readily met by significant others (i.e., high substitutability), then the chances of a breakup are increased. If those intimacy needs are only easily addressed by one's partner (i.e., low substitutability), then breakup probabilities are decreased. A longitudinal study of 290 dating individuals provides support for these arguments (Felmlee, 2001). The closer participants felt to their best friend at the beginning of the study, the greater was the chance that their intimate relationship would break up over a period of 3–5 months, even while controlling for other factors. Presumably possessing a very close friend provides an alternative source of companionship and represents a situation of high network substitutability.

INFORMATION. Positive information from the social network about an intimate partner is apt to increase relationship stability. For instance, communication with a partner's network members provides additional information about that partner and reduces uncertainty. According to the theory of uncertainty reduction (e.g., Berger, 1979), partners attempt to lessen uncertainty about each other by gaining additional information as a relationship progresses, and social networks can facilitate this process. In one study, romantic partners who communicated more frequently with a partner's social network over a 3-month period experienced less uncertainty and were less likely to breakup (Parks & Adelman, 1983).

Network members also may provide couples with negative information that leads to a breakup, although such a possibility has received little attention in the literature. Such information could heighten, rather than lessen, uncertainty about a partner. Family and friends can relay rumors about one partner to the other, for example, or they could offer a negative assessment of a partner's seemingly positive traits. They may provide information, too, about alternative sources of companionship.

REACTIONS. In general, the development of a relationship is enhanced by affective approval from significant others, whereas disapproval aids in undermining the long-term potential of a relationship. According to a symbolic interactionist perspective, the social reactions of others are important because they shape a pair's sense of identity (Lewis, 1973). A pair with a strong sense of "couple identity" (Felmlee & Sprecher, 2000) is more apt to withstand assaults to its viability. In addition, a social network that is approving is likely to provide both emotional support during stressful periods and practical help, such as child care for couples with children.

Marital satisfaction is linked to receiving positive support from the social network or the marriage (Bryant & Conger, 1999). The greater the number of relatives reported to be potentially supportive in time of need, the greater is marital happiness, whereas network disapproval is related to decreased marital satisfaction (Veroff, Douvan, & Hatchett, 1995). The link between marital well-being and connections with kin appears to be stronger for husbands than for wives (Cotton, Antill, & Cunningham, 1993; Milardo & Allan, 1996) and stronger for Black husbands than for their White counterparts (Orbuch, Veroff, & Hunter 1999; Timmer, Veroff, & Hatchett, 1996).

Interaction and support from families appear to be particularly relevant to the well-being of African American marriages, as compared to White marriages (Orbuch et al., 1999; Taylor, Chatters, & Jackson, 1993). Networks are apt to play a crucial role in withstanding the strains of poverty and inequality faced by African Americans in U.S. society. For instance, social networks were critical to the well-being of Black women and their families in an urban ghetto, because of the emotional and practical support provided by network members (Stack, 1974).

The positive social reactions of network members appear to increase stability, for both courtship and marital relationships. One of the strongest predictors of the likelihood of a breakup over a 3-month period is the perception of support from social networks (Parks & Adelman, 1983; Parks et al., 1983). Even when controlling for a number of individual and dyadic predictors, support from a partner's social network decreases the rate of a subsequent breakup over a several month period (Felmlee, Sprecher, & Bassin, 1990). In addition, approval from friends and approval from a partner's family and friends significantly predicts relationship stability over a 3–5-month period (Felmlee, 2001). Furthermore, perceptions of the friends of the female member of a couple are particularly successful in forecasting relationship dissolution, especially for couples who are relatively high in self-disclosure (Agnew, Loving, & Drigotas, 2001). Finally, relatively high levels of support from a female partner's family and friends reduce breakup rates for couples (Sprecher & Felmlee, 1992), even over a lengthy period of 5 years (Sprecher & Felmlee, 2000).

Research also suggests that social networks can serve as a force that aids in keeping married couples together. Greater network support for marriage is associated with a decreased intention to divorce or separate (Bryant & Conger, 1999). In addition, married couples report more network support before and during marriage than do those who divorce (e.g., Thornes & Collard, 1979). Finally, closeness to family significantly predicts marital stability over time for Black couples (e.g., Veroff et al., 1995).

Positive reactions from a social network continue to be important to an intimate dyad even while they are in the process of ending their relationship. An important phase of the breakup process is one in which individuals seek support from their social network for the termination (Duck, 1982). Sprecher and Felmlee (2000) found that couples who broke up reported network support for the dissolution, even in cases in which their networks initially supported the union.

The reactions of the network to a romantic liaison are not necessarily positive; in some cases network members express their opposition. There has been some evidence, although limited, for the "Romeo and Juliet Effect," that is, the argument that couple development is enhanced by opposition, rather than support, from network members. Driscoll, Davis, and Lipetz (1972) were the first to identify this effect in a study in which they found that parental interference, and increases in parental interference over time, were correlated positively with feelings of romantic love for couples. Parks et al. (1983) found that opposition from a partner's family increased the probability of staying together three or more months, but only when slight opposition was compared with a neutral response. Stronger opposition on the part of a partner's family was associated with a lowered likelihood of remaining together. More recent research found that perceptions of support from an individual's family, and overall encouragement to continue dating, were positively and significantly related to subsequent breakup rates (Felmlee, 2001). These effects were only statistically significant, however, in a model that simultaneously controlled for the effects of friend's support and closeness to a best friend.

In sum, to the extent that there is a "Romeo and Juliet Effect" on romantic breakups, it is limited. It appears only from certain network sectors, for example, family members, and in very particular situations, that is, when opposition is slight, and when opposition from parents occurs at the same time that friends are supportive and close.

The Influence of Dyads on Their Social Networks

The causal arrow between close dyads and their social network is not unidirectional. Couples also manipulate their own social environment (Berscheid & Lopes, 1997), intentionally and unintentionally, although there is very little research on this topic. To the extent that couples attempt to influence their network, they are apt to do so on a behavioral (opportunities/barriers), cognitive (positive and negative information), and affective level (positive and negative emotions). In some situations, for instance, individuals may hide a relationship from their network because they anticipate a disapproving reaction (Baxter & Widenmann, 1993), whereas in other cases, they may provide ample opportunity for their friends and family members to meet a partner. In the more extreme case, individuals may terminate relationships with network members who are unsupportive of their partnership, and at the same time foster those that are approving. Moreover, Leslie, Huston, and Johnson (1986) found that most young adults in their study attempted to influence their parents' impression of their relationship by talking about their partner's strengths, that is, providing positive information. Finally, a couple's emotional reaction to a relationship is likely to influence the degree of network approval. Couples who appear to be deeply in love, for instance, are apt to garner more support than those who bicker and fight.

Summary of Relationships and Networks

In sum, the bulk of research suggests that social networks facilitate intimate relationship beginnings, development, well-being, and stability. They do so by providing opportunities to meet and establish a joint identity, by communicating positive information about a partner, and by providing emotional support for the partnership or marriage. In some cases networks play a more disruptive role, but there is little research on this topic and the bulk of studies report a good deal of network support, not opposition, for couples. Couples themselves may aid in producing this supportive reaction by manipulating the information they provide their network, and by eliminating relationships with disapproving network members. In addition, the networks of close dyads tend to change over time. They become more selective at the beginning of a relationship when less close friendships are dropped and once again at a time when couples enter older life stages.

CONCLUSIONS AND FUTURE RESEARCH

Network Structure and Processes

There are many promising directions for future research in this area. One main task is to examine in more detail the network processes and structures that influence these various social psychological phenomena. Most studies reported on here gather data from individuals and rely on respondents' perceptions of network support, density, size, overlap, and so on. Relatively few studies obtain information from network members themselves and thus it is rare for research to examine the dynamic processes by which network effects occur. So, for example, we know that perceptions of support are positively related to psychological well-being as well as couple stability, but we know little about the network processes and structures that produce these effects.

One main reason for the relative lack of research on the underlying social network structures and processes is the exacting data requirements to do such a study. Ideally, information is obtained from every member of a social network. Nevertheless, standard social science studies do not collect data in such a form. There also are problems in accuracy of network data as reported by respondents (e.g., Bernard, Killworth, & Sailor, 1982).

Another reason for the underrepresentation of studies based on network data is the level of technical skills required to undertake network analyses. The statistical and mathematical expertise required to apply and understand some types of network analyses can be demanding, and standard computer packages cannot be used for most complex network analyses. In addition, there are numerous ways of measuring most of the main network concepts, such as density, centrality, cliques, and equivalence, and it is often difficult to distinguish among these different measures. Furthermore, a glance at recently published pieces using a network perspective in social psychology and sociology will reveal that a variety of unique, often esoteric, statistical, and mathematical analyses are used. As a result, the import of the content of the work is likely to elude the average reader. The solution to this problem is not to reduce the sophistication of appropriate network analytic procedures, but it does mean that it is imperative that network analysts elaborate on the implications of their findings for the wider discipline. It also suggests the need for greater consensus among those who study networks about measures and techniques to be used in analyses.

In order to fully investigate network processes, more dynamic studies of networks are needed as well. Change in a social network, rather than the structure of an existing social network at a particular point in time, is likely to have a dramatic influence on individual behavior, and yet dynamic network studies are particularly rare. For example, individuals are likely to become accustomed to the particular level of social network support that they receive in their day to day affairs, and they may learn to adapt to that level, regardless of whether it is relatively low or high, as compared to other people. But when a change in that level of support occurs, such as when a close confidante moves or dies, or when an individual develops a new, close friendship, then the individual's reactions to this new level of network support are apt to be relatively strong.

The Shadow Side of Networks

A good deal of research casts social networks in a very favorable light (Felmlee & Sprecher, 2000). For example, "social support" is one large subfield of research in the social network area. There is no equivalent area of study termed "social neglect" or "social opposition" that would emphasize the deleterious, rather than the beneficial, dimensions of social involvement in mental and physical health. Nevertheless, not all social contact is positively associated with individuals' well-being (e.g., Pagel, Erdly, & Becker, 1987). Uehara (1990), for instance, finds that a subset of women in a sample of low-income African Americans are not satisfied with their own level of social network support; those who tend to be self-reliant, in particular, find their social support to be inadequate. Furthermore, perceptions of the degree of social support one receives strongly correlate with the negative, rather than the positive, aspects of social relationships (Coyne & Downey, 1991), and it is the problematic features of relationships that primarily influence psychological symptoms in individuals (Pagel et al., 1987). Ironically, social support that is positive, but too high in degree, also may be detrimental to well-being; overinvolvement and overprotection on the part of friends and family members may discourage the autonomy necessary for the self-recovery of an ill loved one (Coyne & DeLongis, 1986). Thus, systematic research is needed in the ways in which social networks may detract from, rather than enhance, people's psychological and physical well-being.

"Social capital" often refers to membership in social networks that greatly facilitates the actions of individuals and groups by providing information, influence, power, and solidarity (Adler & Kwon, 2002). Portes (1998), for example, sees social capital as "the ability of actors to secure benefits by virtue of membership in social networks or other social structures." Yet the "shadow side" of social capital receives relatively little attention in the literature (Adler & Kown, 2002; Portes, 1998). Potential difficulties with social capital include the costs associated with creating and maintaining social relationships, overembedding due to excessive network ties, restrictions on freedom placed by network connections, and lower creativity and innovation due to insular group interaction (Adler & Kwon, 2002).

Social networks act as a conduit for information, and as noted earlier, ties that are weak may be a particularly potent source of information transfer (Granovetter, 1973). Yet the content of the messages transmitted via weak or strong network ties may not be accurate. Or such messages could be purposefully misleading and aversive. Gossip and rumor, for instance, which spread through social networks, can be extremely hurtful. "They can steal illusions, wreck relationships, and stir up a cauldron of trouble" (Rosnow, 2001, p. 204). During the Boxer Rebellion, for example, a young Marine, who believed a malicious rumor that circulated about the agonizing tortures in store for captured soldiers, became so agitated and distressed by the rumor that he committed suicide (Rosnow, 2001). Despite their ubiquitous and potent role in human interaction, gossip, rumor, and negative network information transfer more generally, are seldom the focus of sustained social psychological inquiry.

A positivity bias also is seen in research on affiliative networks. Note that although there is an area of research designated "friendship networks," there is no analogous topic of study labeled "enemy networks." Yet individuals develop enemies as well as friends in the course of social interaction within the work place, social groups, and families. Negatively valenced networks are apt to influence the development of subsequent friendships, perceptions of popularity, attitudes, clique formation, as well as power and influence. There are a host of relevant questions that could be raised along these lines, such as to what extent does transitivity apply when enemy relationships, rather than friendships are examined? Under what conditions do negative ties in networks block the flow of information and influence?

Another example of a predilection for the positive is in the area of dyadic romantic relationships (Duck, 1994; Felmlee, 2001; Rook & Pietromonaco, 1987). Here the bulk of research examines the beneficial role of friends and family in increasing relationship stability, for instance. Much less attention has been paid to the ways in which social network members may work to end a couple's alliance. Suppose, for example, that both parents of a young woman disapprove of their daughter's fiance. There are a range of behaviors in which they could engage that might discourage the couple's marriage, including ignoring the fiance, excluding him from family events, conveying disparaging information, and introducing their daughter to alternative, romantic partners. Such tactics even could cross over to the criminal. In one study, a man reported that his girlfriend's mother, who disapproved of his relationship with her daughter: "hired someone to beat me up" (Felmlee, 2001). A more complete treatment of the role of social networks needs to address this "shadow side" of the social environment and the manner in which networks interfere with pairs and act in ways that hasten the demise of an intimate relationship.

Agency: Individuals Influencing their Networks

One long-standing debate among social psychologists is the role of human agency versus that of social structure in influencing individual behavior. A social network perspective represents a quintessential social structural approach to social inquiry, and it is one that could benefit from the inclusion of agency. Although there have been some attempts to develop dynamic, systems approaches in which individuals and their network members mutually influence each other over time (e.g., Felmlee & Greenberg, 1999; Friedkin, 1998), most research focus solely on the role of network structure.

One promising avenue of inquiry along these lines is to examine the ways in which individuals, or groups, work to mold their own networks. For example, as discussed above, people attempt to influence their networks in order to garner support for their intimate relationships by the application of creative information management. They also may drop ties and create new ones in order to maintain a supportive network atmosphere. It is likely that similar processes take place in other social support situations, such as when individuals are in ill health or are facing the death of a loved one. Furthermore, individuals may act in ways that encourage their social ties to provide support or they may hamper aid on the part of others.

A final, important task is to continue to integrate the disparate studies on networks in order to systematically evaluate the state of the field and to develop a unified theoretical perspective. As noted in the introduction, social networks tend to be independent variables in studies, rather than dependent variables, and therefore the main focus of network studies is on topics as varied as individual patterns of help-seeking to interlocking corporate directorates. Moreover, network studies on a range of issues such as the "class size paradox," structural equivalence, and transitivity often are entirely disconnected from each other and their articles seldom cite each other. Thus, there needs to be further work to bring together diverse strands of network research. This is particularly important given the technical sophistication of the field.

In conclusion, a social network perspective has much to offer to social psychological work. As can be seen here, it represents a fundamentally social, relational, and structural lens with which to view social interaction. A growing body of research demonstrates that social networks are useful in furthering our understanding of the structural and relational factors involved in micro-level processes in a wide variety of subfields, such as those of group processes, social support, and close relationships. The potential contributions of this perspective for social psychological theory and research have just begun to be uncovered.

ACKNOWLEDGMENT: I am grateful to John Delamater, Susan Sprecher, and Heather Kohler for their comments on this chapter.

REFERENCES

Adams, R. G. (1998). The demise of territorial determinism: Online friendships. In R. G. Adams & G. Allan (Eds.), *Placing friendship in context* (pp. 153–182). Cambridge, UK: Cambridge University.

Adams, R. G., & Torr, R. (1998). Factors underlying the structure of older adult friendship networks. *Social Networks 20*, 51–61.

Adler, P. S., & Kwon, S. (2002). Social capital: Prospects for a new concept. *Academy of Management Review 27*, 17–40.

Agnew, C. R., Loving, T. J., & Drigotas, S. M. (2001). Substituting the forest for the trees: Social networks and the prediction of romantic relationship state and fate. *Journal of Personality and Social Psychology 81*, 1042–1057.

Baxter, L. A., & Widenmann, S. (1993). Revealing and not revealing the status of romantic relationships to social networks. *Journal of Social and Personal Relationships 10*, 321–337.

Bell, R. A. (1991). Gender, friendship network, density, and loneliness. *Journal of Social Behavior and Personality 6*, 45–56.

Berger, C. R. (1979). Beyond initial interaction: Uncertainty, understanding, and the development of interpersonal relationships. In H. Giles & R. St. Clair (Eds.), *Language and social psychology* (pp. 122–144). Oxford: Basil Blackwood.

Bernard, H. R., Killworth, P. D., & Sailor, L. (1982). Informant accuracy in social network research V: An experimental attempt to predict actual communication from recall data. *Social Policy 46*, 59–60.

Berscheid, E., & Lopes, J. (1997). A temporal model of relationship satisfaction and stability. In R. J. Sternberg & J. Hojjat (Eds.), *Satisfaction in close relationships* (pp. 129–159). New York: Guilford.

Blieszner, R., & Adams, R. G. (1992). *Adult friendship*. Newbury Park, CA: Sage.

Bohannan, P. (1970). The six stations of divorce. In P. Bohannan (Ed.), *Divorce and after* (pp. 33–62). New York: Anchor Books.

Bott, E. (1957, 1971). *Family and social networks*. London: Tavistock.

Brown, G. W., & Harris, T. (1978). *Social origins of depression: A study of psychiatric disorder in women*. New York: Free.

Bryant, C. M., & Conger, R. D. (1999). Marital success and domains of social support in long-term relationships: Does the influence of network members ever end? *Journal of Marriage and the Family 61*, 437–450.

Burger, E., & Milardo, R. M. (1995). Marital interdependence and social networks. *Journal of Social and Personal Relationships 12*, 403–415.

Burke, P. J. (1997). An identity model for network exchange. *American Sociological Review 62*, 134–150.

Burt, R. S. (1980). Models of network structure. *Annual Review of Sociology 6*, 79–141.

Burt, R. S. (1987). Social contagion and innovation: Cohesion versus structural equivalence. *American Journal of Sociology 92*, 1287–1335.

Carstensen, L. L. (1999). Taking time seriously: A theory of socioemotional selectivity. *American Psychologist 54*, 165–181.

Cartwright, D., & Harary, F. (1956). Structural balance: A generalization of Heider's theory. *Psychological Review 63*, 277–292.

Cook, K. S., & Whitmeyer, J. M. (1992). Two approaches to social structure: Exchange theory and network analysis. *Annual Review of Sociology 18*, 109–127.

Cotton, S., Antill, J., & Cunningham, J. (1993). Network structure, network support, and the marital satisfaction of husbands and wives. *Australian Journal of Psychology 45*, 176–181.

Coyne, J. C., & DeLongis, A. (1986). Going beyond social support: The role of social relationships in adaptation. *Journal of Consulting and Clinical Psychology 5*, 454–460.

Coyne, J. C., & Downey, G. (1991). Social factors and psychopathology: Stress, social support, and coping processes. *Annual Review of Psychology 42*, 401–425.

Davis, J. A. (1967). Clustering and structural balance in graphs. *Human Relations 20*, 181–187.

Davis, J. A., & Leinhart, S. (1972). The structure of positive interpersonal relations in small groups. In J. Berger (Ed.), *Sociological theories in progress* (Vol. 2, pp. 218–251). Boston: Houghton Mifflin.

Driscoll, R., Davis, K. E., & Lipetz, M. E. (1972). Parental interference and romantic love: The Romeo and Juliet effect. *Journal of Personality and Social Psychology 24*, 1–10.

Duck, S. W. (1982). A topography of relationship disengagement and dissolution. In S. W. Duck (Ed.), *Personal relationships 4: Dissolving personal relationships*. London and New York: Academic.

Duck, S. W. (1994). Stratagems, spoils, and a serpent's tooth: On the delights and dilemmas of personal relationships. In W. R. Cupach & B. H. Spitzberg (Eds.), *The dark side of interpersonal communication* (pp. 3–24). Hillsdale, NJ: Erlbaum.

Emirbayer, M. (1997). Manifesto for a relational sociology. *American Journal of Sociology 103*, 281–317.

Faust, K. (1997). Centrality in affiliation networks. *Social Networks 19*, 157–191.

Feld, S. L. (1991). Why your friends have more friends than you do. *American Journal of Sociology 96*, 1464–1477.

Feld, S. L., & Elmore, R. (1982). Patterns of sociometric choices: Transitivity reconsidered. *Social Psychology Quarterly 45*, 77–85.

Feld, S. L., & Carter, W. C. (1998) When desegregation reduces interracial contact: A class size paradox for weak ties. *American Journal of Sociology 103(5)*, 1165–1187.

Felmlee, D. (2001). No couple is an island: A social network perspective on dyadic stability. *Social Forces 79(4)*, 1259–1287.

Felmlee, D., Sprecher, S., & Bassin, E. (1990). The dissolution of intimate relationships: A hazard model. *Social Psychology Quarterly 53*, 13–30.

Felmlee, D., & Greenberg, D. (1999). A dynamic systems model of dyadic interaction. *Journal of Mathematical Sociology 22*, 1–26.

Felmlee, D., & Sprecher, S. (2000). Close relationships and social psychology: Intersection and future paths. *Social Psychology Quarterly 63*, 365–376.

Festinger, L., Schachter, S., & Back, K. (1950). *Social pressures in informal groups: A study of human factors in housing.* Stanford, CA: Stanford University Press.

Freeman, L. C. (1979). Centrality in social networks: Conceptual clarification. *Social Networks 1*, 215–239.

Freeman, L. C. (1992). Filling in the blanks: A theory of cognitive categories and the structure of social affiliation. *Social Psychology Quarterly 55*, 118–127.

Friedkin, N. E. (1993). Structural bases of interpersonal influence in groups: A longitudinal case study. *American Sociological Review 58*, 861–873.

Friedkin, N. E. (1998). *A structural theory of social influence.* Cambridge, NY: Cambridge University Press.

Friedkin, N. E. (1999). Choice shift and group polarization. *American Sociological Review 64*, 856–875.

Galaskiewicz, J., & Wasserman, S. (1993). Social network analysis: Concepts, methodology, and directions for the 1990's. *Sociological Methods & Research 22*, 3–22.

Granovetter, M. (1973). The strength of weak ties. *American Journal of Sociology 78*, 1360–1380.

Hallinan, M. (1974). A structural model of sentiment relations. *American Journal of Sociology 80*, 364–378.

Hallinan, M., & Kubitschek, W. N. (1990). The formation of intransitive friendships. *Social Forces 69*, 505–519.

Heider, F. (1958). *The psychology of interpersonal relations.* New York: Wiley.

Holland, P. W., & Leinhardt, S. (1970). A method for detecting structure in sociometric data. *American Journal of Sociology 70*, 492–513.

House, J. S., Umberson, D., & Landis, K. R. (1988). Structures and processes of social support. *Annual Review of Sociology 14*, 293–318.

Huston, T. L., & Burgess, R. L. (1979). The analysis of social exchange in developing relationships. In R. L. Burgess & T. L. Huston (Eds.), *Social exchange in developing relationships* (pp. 3–28). New York: Academic.

Johnson, M. P., & Leslie, L. (1982). Couple involvement and network structure: A test of the dyadic withdrawal hypothesis. *Social Psychology Quarterly 45*, 34–43.

Julien, D., & Markman, H. (1991). Social support and social networks as determinants of individual and marital outcomes. *Journal of Social and Personal Relationships 8*, 549–568.

Julien, D., Chartrand, E., & Bégin, J. (1999). Social networks, structural interdependence, and conjugal adjustment in heterosexual, gay, and lesbian couples. *Journal of Marriage and the Family 61*, 516–530.

Kessler, R. C., & McLeod, J. D. (1985). Social support and mental health in community samples. In S. Cohen & L. Syme (Eds.), *Social support and health* (pp. 219–240). New York: Academic.

Koku, E., Nazer, N., & Wellman, B. (2001). Netting scholars: Online and offline. *American Behavioral Scientist 44*, 1752.

Krackhardt, D., & Stern, R. N. (1988). Informal networks and organizational crises: An experimental simulation. *Social Psychology Quarterly 51*, 123–140.

Krackhardt, D., & Kilduff, M. (1999). Whether close or far: Social distance effects on perceived balance in friendship networks. *Journal of Personality and Social Psychology 76*, 770–782.

Kraut, R., Patterson, M., Lundmark, V., Kiesler, S., Mukopadhayay, T., & Scherlis, W. (1998). Internet paradox: A social technology that reduces social involvement and psychological well-being? *American Psychologist 53*(9), 1017–1032.

Leslie, L. A., Huston, T. L., & Johnson, M. P. (1986). Parental reactions to dating relationships: Do they make a difference? *Journal of Marriage and the Family 48*, 57–66.

Lewis, R. A. (1973). Social reactions and the formation of dyads: An interactionist approach to mate selection. *Sociometry 36*, 400–418.

Lorrain, F., & White, H. C. (1971). Structural equivalence of individuals in social networks. *Journal of Mathematical Sociology 1*, 49–80.

Marsden, P. V., & Friedkin, N. E. (1993). Network studies of social influence. *Sociological Methods & Research 22*, 127–151.

Marsiglio, W., & Scanzoni, J. (1995). *Families and friendships*. New York, NY: HarperCollins.

McKenna, K. Y. A., & Bargh, J. A. (2000). Plan 9 from cyberspace: The implications of the internet for personality and social psychology. *Personality and Social Psychology Review 4*, 57–78.

McPherson, M., Smith-Lovin, L., & Cook, J. M. (2001). Birds of a feather: Homophily in social networks. *Annual Review of Sociology 27*, 415–444.

Michaelson, A., & Contractor, N. S. (1992). Structural position and perceived similarity. *Social Psychology Quarterly 55*, 300–310.

Milardo, R. M. (1982). Friendship networks in developing relationships: Converging and diverging social environments. *Social Psychology Quarterly 45*, 162–172.

Milardo, R. M. (1986). Personal choice and social constraint in close relationships: Applications of network analysis. In V. J. Derlega & B. A. Winstead (Eds.), *Friendship and social interaction* (pp. 145–166). New York: Springer-Verlag.

Milardo, R. M. (1987). Changes in social networks of women and men following divorce. A review. *Journal of Family Issues 8*, 78–96.

Milardo, R. M., & Allan, G. (1996). Social networks and marital relationships. In S. Duck, K. Dindia, W. Ickes, R. Milardo, R. Mills, & B. Saranson (Eds.), *Handbook of personal relationships* (pp. 505–522). London: John Wiley & Sons.

Moreno, J. L. (1934). *Who shall survive? A new approach to the problem of human interrelationships*. Washington, DC: Nervous and Mental Disease.

Morgan, D., Carder, P., & Neal, M. (1997). Are some relationships more useful than others? The value of similar others in the networks of recent widows. *Journal of Social and Personal Relationships 14*, 745–759.

Newcomb, T. M. (1961). *The acquaintance process*. New York: Holt, Rinehart & Winston.

Orbuch, T. L., Veroff, J., & Hunter, A. G. (1999). Black couples, white couples: The early years of marriage. In E. M. Hetherington (Ed.), *Coping with divorce, single-parenting, and remarriage* (pp. 23–46). Hillsdale, NJ: Erlbaum.

Pagel, M. D., Erdly, W. W., & Becker, J. (1987). Social networks: We get by with (and in spite of) a little help from our friends. *Journal of Personality and Social Psychology 53*, 793–804.

Parks, M. R., Stan, C. M., & Eggert, L. L. (1983). Romantic involvement and social network involvement. *Social Psychology Quarterly 46*, 116–131.

Parks, M. R., & Adelman, M. B. (1983). Communication networks and the development of romantic relationships: An expansion of uncertainty reduction theory. *Human Communication Research 10*, 55–79.

Parks, M. R., & Eggert, L. L. (1991). The role of social context in the dynamics of personal relationships. In W. Jones & D. Perlman (Eds.), *Advances in personal relationships* (Vol. 2, pp. 1–34). London: Jessica Kinglsey.

Pescosolido, B. A. (1992). Beyond rational choice: The social dynamics of how people seek help. *American Journal of Sociology 97*, 1096–1138.

Pinquart, M., & Sorensen, S. (2000). Influences of socioeconomic status, social network, and competence on subjective well-being in later life: A meta-analysis. *Psychology and Aging 15*, 18–21.

Portes, A. (1998). Social capital: Its origins and applications in modern sociology. *Annual Review of Sociology 24*, 1024–1047.

Rands, M. (1988). Changes in social networks following marital separation and divorce. In R. M. Milardo (Ed.), *Families and social networks* (pp. 127–146). Newbury Park, CA: Sage.

Ritzer, G., & Gindoff, P. (1992). Methodological relationism: Lessons for and from social psychology. *Social Psychology Quarterly 55*, 128–142.

Rook, K. S., & Pietromonaco, P. (1987). Close relationships: Ties that heal or ties that bind? In W. H. Jones & D. Perlman (Eds.), *Advances in personal relationships* (Vol. 1, pp. 1–35). Greenwich, CN: JAI.

Rosnow, R. L. (2001). Rumor and gossip in interpersonal interaction and beyond: A social exchange perspective. In R. M. Kowalski (Ed.), *Behaving badly: Aversive behaviors in interpersonal relationships* (pp. 203–232). Washington, DC: American Psychological Association.

Scott, J. (2000). *Social network analysis: A handbook* (2nd ed.). Thousands Oaks, CA: Sage.

Skvoretz, J., & Fararo, T. (1996). Status and participation in task groups: A dynamic network model. *American Journal of Sociology 101*, 1366–1414.

Slater, P. E. (1963). On social regression. *American Sociological Review 28*, 339–358.

Spanier, G. B., & Thompson, L. (Eds.). (1984). *Parting: The aftermath of separation and divorce.* Beverly Hills, CA: Sage.

Sprecher, S., & Felmlee, D. (1992). The influence of parents and friends on the quality and stability of romantic relationships: A three-wave longitudinal investigation. *Journal of Marriage and the Family 54*, 888–900.

Sprecher, S., & Felmlee, D. (2000). Romantic partners' perceptions of social network attributes with the passage of time and relationship transitions. *Personal Relationships 7*, 325–340.

Sprecher, S., Felmlee, D., Orbuch, T. L., & Willett, M. C. (2002). Social networks and change in personal relationships. In A. Vangelisti, H. Reis, & M. A. Fitzpatrick (Eds.), *Advances in personal relationships: Vol. 2; Stability and change in relationship behavior* (pp. 257–284). Cambridge.

Stack, C. B. (1974). *All our kin: Strategies for surviving in a black community.* New York: Harper & Row.

Stein, C. H., Bush, E. G., Ross, R. R., & Ward, M. (1992). Mine, yours and ours: A configural analysis of the networks of married couples in relation to marital satisfaction and individual well-being. *Journal of Social and Personal Relationships 9*, 365–383.

Surra, C., & Milardo, R. (1991). The social psychological context of developing relationships: Psychological and interactive networks. In D. Perlman & W. Jones, *Advances in personal relationships* (Vol. 3, pp. 1–36). London: Jessica Kingsley.

Taylor, R. J., Chatters, L. M., & Jackson, J. S. (1993). A profile of familial relations among three-generation black families. *Family Relations 42*, 332–341.

Thornes, B., & Collard, J. (1979). *Who divorces?* London: Routledge & Kegan Paul.

Timmer, S. G., Veroff, J., & Hatchett, S. (1996). Family ties and marital happiness: The different marital experiences of black and white newlywed couples. *Journal of Social and Personal Relationships 13*, 335–359.

Uehara, E. S. (1990). Dual exchange theory, social networks, and informal social support. *American Journal of Sociology 96*, 521–557.

Veroff, J., Douvan, E., & Hatchett, S. J. (1995). *Marital instability: A social and behavioral study of the early years.* Westport, CN: Praeger.

Walker, M. E., Wasserman, S., & Wellman, B. (1993). Statistical models for social support networks. *Sociological Methods & Research 22*, 71–78.

Wasserman, S., & Faust, K. (1994). *Social network analysis: Methods and applications.* New York: Cambridge University Press.

Weiss, R. S. (1975). *Marital separation.* New York: Basic Books.

Wellman, B. (1988). Structural analysis: From method and metaphor to theory and substance. In B. Wellman & S. D. Berkowitz (Eds.), *Social structures: A network approach* (pp. 19–61). New York: Cambridge.

Wellman, B., & Worley, S. (1990). Different strokes for different folks: Community ties and social support. *American Journal of Sociology 96*, 558–588.

Wellman, B., & Hampton, K. (1999). Living networked on and offline. *Contemporary Sociology 28*, 648.

Wellman, B., Salaff, J., Dimitrova, D., Garton, L., Gulia, M., & Haythornthwaite, C. (1996). Computer networks as social networks: Collaborative work, telework, and virtual community. *Annual Review of Sociology 22*, 213–238.

White, H., Boorman, S., & Breiger, R. (1976). Social structures from multiple networks: Blockmodels of roles and positions. *American Journal of Sociology 81*, 731–780.

Zuckerman, E., & Jost, J. (2001). What makes you think you're so popular? Self evaluation maintenance and the subjective size of the "friendship paradox". *Social Psychology Quarterly 64*, 207–223.

CHAPTER 17

Social Structure and Psychological Functioning

Distress, Perceived Control, and Trust

CATHERINE E. ROSS

JOHN MIROWSKY

Psychological functioning includes emotions and cognitions. In this chapter we cover three types of emotions (or feelings)—depression, anxiety, and anger. We call the negative end of the emotion continuum psychological distress, and the positive end, psychological well-being. Cognitions are thoughts, perceptions, or worldviews, including the sense of personal control (versus powerlessness) and trust (versus mistrust), which we cover here. An individual's position in the social structure is indicated here by age; gender; family status, including marital status and parenthood; race; and socioeconomic status (SES), including education, work, and economic resources.

Cognitions link social structure to emotions, as illustrated in Figure 17-1. Distress is generated by objective conditions of disadvantage; but disadvantage must be perceived in order to be felt as emotionally distressing. Research has identified the sense of personal control as an important link between individuals' place in the stratification system and their psychological well-being. Perceived powerlessness is generated by objective conditions of powerlessness and leads to distress. Objective conditions of disadvantage, defined as a lack of social and economic resources, are associated with an inability to achieve goals, or objective powerlessness. These objective conditions shape the *perception* that one is powerless to

CATHERINE E. ROSS • Department of Sociology and Population Research Center, University of Texas, Austin, Texas 78712   JOHN MIROWSKY • Department of Sociology and Population Research Center, University of Texas, Austin, Texas 78712

Handbook of Social Psychology, edited by John Delamater. Kluwer Academic/Plenum Publishers, New York, 2003.

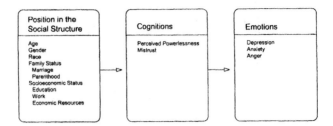

FIGURE 17-1. Theoretical links among social structure, cognitions, and emotions.

achieve desired ends. Despite recent interest in trust, less is known about the structural determinants of trust and whether trust mediates the impact of social structure on psychological
well-being. Theory suggests it does. Theoretically, mistrust is generated by disadvantage,
powerlessness, and threat and leads to distress.

PSYCHOLOGICAL DISTRESS

Defining and Measuring Psychological Distress

DEPRESSION AND ANXIETY.   Distress is an unpleasant subjective emotional state. It takes
two major forms. The first is depression: feeling sad, demoralized, lonely, hopeless, worthless, wishing you were dead, having trouble sleeping, crying, feeling everything is an effort,
and being unable to get going. The second is anxiety: being tense, restless, worried, irritable,
and anxious. Depression and anxiety each take two forms: mood and malaise. Mood refers to
the feelings such as the sadness of depression, or the worry of anxiety. Malaise refers to bodily states, such as the listlessness and distraction of depression or the autonomic ailments
(headaches, stomachaches, dizziness), and restlessness of anxiety. Depression and anxiety—
both mood and malaise—are related in two ways: The maps of their social high and low zones
are very similar, and a person who has one also tends to have the others (although not necessarily at the same time). Table 17-1 shows some examples of symptoms of depression and
anxiety, separating mood and malaise.

   The content of indexes measuring distress has changed over the years. The earliest
community studies, in the late fifties and early sixties, mostly asked about malaise, such as
cold sweats and heart palpitations and other physical symptoms (Gurin, Veroff, & Feld, 1960;
Srole, Langner, Michael, Opler, & Rennie, 1962). One early measure of distress is Langner's
(1962) index, which was the standard in community research for many years. Langner's index
is a check-list of 22 questions that were chosen from a longer list because they best distinguished between people with psychiatric problems and those without. The items are mostly
questions about depression and anxiety, especially the malaise component of anxiety (Do you
feel weak all over much of the time? Are you bothered by acid or sour stomach several times
a week? How often do you suddenly feel hot all over? How often are you troubled with
headaches?). Current studies ask more questions about mood, such as feeling lonely, sad, or
worried. This transition is typified by the contrast between the Gurin index and the Center for
Epidemiologic Studies' Depression Scale (CES-D). In *Americans view their mental health*,
Gurin et al. (1960) measured distress with an index composed entirely of items referring to
malaise such as dizziness, trembling hands, and difficulty getting up in the morning. In contrast, the CES-D includes a number of items about mood, such as feeling depressed, lonely,

TABLE 17-1. Items from Indexes of Depression and Anxiety

Respondents are asked, "How often in the past month have you_____." Responses are recorded as never (0), almost never (1), sometimes (2), fairly often (3), or often (4). Alternatively, respondents are asked, "Now I'm going to read a list of different feelings that people sometimes have. After each one I would like you to tell me on how many days you have felt this way during the last week. On how many days have you____?" (0–7).

Distress
  a. *Depression*
    i. *Mood*
      Felt sad[a]
      Felt lonely[a]
      Felt you couldn't shake the blues[a]
      Felt depressed[b]
      Been bothered by things that don't usually bother you[a]
      Wondered if anything was worthwhile anymore[c]
      Felt that nothing turned out for you the way you wanted it to[c]
      Felt completely hopeless about everything
      Felt worthless
      Thought about taking your own life
    ii. *Malaise*
      Felt that everything was an effort[a]
      Felt you just couldn't get going[a]
      Had trouble keeping your mind on what you were doing[a]
      Had trouble getting to sleep or staying asleep[a]
      Didn't talk to anyone or talked less than usual[b]
      Felt no interest in anything or anybody
      Felt tired all the time
      Had poor appetite
    iii. *Positive affect*
      Enjoyed life[b]
      Felt hopeful about the future[b]
      Felt happy[b]

  b. *Anxiety*
    i. *Mood*
      Worried a lot about little things[c]
      Felt anxious, tense, or nervous[c]
      Felt restless or fidgety[c]
    ii. *Malaise*
      Had dizziness[c]
      Had shortness of breath when you were not exercising or working hard[c]
      Had your hands tremble[c]
      Had your heart beating hard when you were not exercising or working hard[c]
      Suddenly felt hot all over[c]

  c. *Anger*
    i. *Mood*
      Felt annoyed with things or people[d]
      Felt angry[d]
    ii. *Behavioral*
      Yelled at someone[d]

[a]From the short version of the Center for Epidemiological Studies Depression Scale (Modified CES-D) (Mirowsky & Ross, 1990b; Ross & Mirowsky, 1984).
[b]From the CES-D (Radloff, 1977).
[c]Modified version of symptoms from the Langner (1962) index.
[d]From the anger scale (Mirowsky & Ross, 1995, 1996; Ross & Van Willigen, 1996).

Notes: Researchers can use the level of generality or specificity relevant to their research question. At a general level, for example, a distress index can include depression and anxiety, mood and malaise, and positive affect (scored in reverse). At more specific levels, researchers can distinguish between depression and anxiety, and further between depressed (or anxious) mood and malaise.

and sad or not feeling as good as other people, hopeful about the future, or happy, and not enjoying life (Radloff, 1977).

There are a number of reasons for the shift away from indexes composed mostly of physiological indicators of distress. First, researchers discovered that people are far more willing to report their feelings in community surveys than anyone expected. Questions about headaches, sweaty palms, and heart palpitations were used partly to mask the intent of measuring the respondent's emotional state. Second, malaise may indicate physical health problems as well as emotional ones, particularly in aging populations (Johnson & Meile, 1981) or other groups that have unusually high rates of health problems, such as Mexican immigrants to the United States (Wheaton, 1982). The impact of poor health and physical disability on emotional well-being and the impact of emotional well-being on physical health are important issues. The use of physiologic symptoms of distress could bias results in favor of an association (Thoits, 1981). In research on the relationship between physical and psychological well-being, it is best to use purely psychological indicators. In other studies of social patterns of distress "physiogenic bias" is not great and does not account for the major social patterns of distress. Measures of dread, anxiety, sadness, hopelessness, worthlessness, guilt, enervation, and distraction are interrelated. For most purposes they are interchangeable indications of demoralization and distress (Dohrenwend, Shront, Egri, & Mendelson, 1980). Sometimes different types of distress (such as depression and anxiety) have different patterns that provide insight into the nature of a particular social condition (e.g., Mirowsky & Ross, 1984, 1992; Wheaton, 1983), but more often the patterns match and tell the same story about who is distressed and why.

Depression and anxiety are especially useful indicators of the subjective quality of life. Depression and anxiety are highly correlated: People who suffer from one usually also suffer from the other. They are the most common types of psychological problems, experienced by everyone to some degree at some time. Maps of their emotional high and low zones tell us a great deal about the nature of life in different social positions. However, there are other types of emotional distress that have received less attention. One is anger.*

ANGER.   Anger is another unpleasant emotional state also highly correlated with depression. People who feel angry often feel depressed. Weissman and Paykel (1974) first described women who were depressed, partly because of being powerless and dependent vis a vis their husbands. The women got angry at their husbands, took it out on their children, and then felt guilty, which made them even more depressed. Recently a few sociologists have begun to look more systematically at social structure and anger (Ross & Van Willigen, 1996; Schieman, 1999, 2000).

According to the "social structure and psychological distress" paradigm, distress is a consequence of social problems, not the problem itself (Mirowsky & Ross, 1989). Socially

---

*In this chapter, we focus on emotional distress. Cognitive distress, such as schizophrenia, is conceptually distinct from affective problems, such as depression. Anxiety, anger, depression, and lack of positive feelings are basically emotional. Problems such as schizophrenia are basically cognitive—a disorder of the thought processes rather than emotions. Although affective problems have cognitive components, and vice versa, their defining characteristics are different. Cognitive symptoms include seeing things other people don't see, hearing things other people don't hear, believing other people can hear your thoughts, feeling possessed or controlled by forces or beings, thinking you have enemies who want to harm you, being sure everyone is against you, believing you are being plotted against, having nightmares, and having unusual thoughts. Many of these symptoms indicate the delusional thinking of paranoid schizophrenia. Although affective and cognitive problems are conceptually distinct, the same types of people who have a lot of cognitive problems also have a lot of depression and anxiety.

structured inequality, disadvantage, stress, and hardship have broad-reaching consequences for psychological well-being, affecting various types of distress (Aneshensel, Rutter, & Lachenbruch, 1991; Pearlin, 1989). However, most research on the emotional consequences of inequality has used depression as the indicator of distress. By focusing on a particular problem—depression—Aneshensel and her colleagues argue, researchers do not adequately test a sociological model. Conditions of inequality and disadvantage theoretically result in higher levels of all types of distress, including anger (Mirowsky & Ross, 1995).

On the one hand most sociological research ignores anger, and on the other, most research on anger takes a medical model approach. In a medical model, anger is the problem itself. Anger as a health problem has entered the medical literature by way of specification of the components of type A personality. Research indicates that the constellation of behaviors known as type A is not uniformly bad for health: Hostility and anger increase the risk of heart disease, but competitive, hard-driving, goal-oriented behavior does not (Appel, Holroyd, & Gorkin, 1983; Thomas, 1989). In this model, anger is treated a maladaptive emotion with negative health consequences. Thus, people who are "too hostile" are given suggestions to reduce anger like "taking time out," "distracting yourself," and "thought stopping" (Consumer Reports on Health, 1994). The medical model ignores structural strains—the relative risks of anger structured by one's social environment. Nowhere does it suggest that the social situation that produced the anger could be modified, for example, by providing affordable child care to families with children or encouraging fathers to share child care responsibilities with mothers (Ross & Van Willigen, 1996).

This model prevails in spite of the fact that conceptualizations of anger suggest that it is likely caused by social inequality. Anger is a social emotion: It results from the assessment of inequality in social situations or relations, from perceptions of having been unjustly treated, or from perceptions of a violation of a fair social contract (Averill, 1983; Julius, Harburg, Cottington, & Johnson, 1986; Novaco, 1985; Tavris, 1982). Anger, therefore, may be useful in the study of structural determinants of psychological well-being because it may be the result of an individual's assessment of inequality, often as it is played out in interpersonal relations in the family. Theoretically, inequality produces frustration and anger. Studying anger may allow researchers to identify objective conditions perceived as inequitable by individuals. Social patterns of anger may contain a message about patterned social inequalities.

DISTRESS AND WELL-BEING AS OPPOSITE POLES. Well-being and distress are opposite poles on a single continuum: More well-being means less distress and More distress means less well-being. Well-being is a general sense of enjoying life and feeling happy, hopeful about the future, secure, and calm. Lack of these positive feelings is related to depression and anxiety. It is useful to think of a continuum from happy and fulfilled at the well-being end to depressed and anxious at the distress end.

The fact that well-being and distress are opposite poles of the same emotional dimension seems obvious. Yet, some researchers say that positive and negative affect are distinct dimensions of mood, and not just opposite poles (e.g., Bradburn, 1969). The reason given is that the negative correlation between measures of well-being and of distress is not perfect (not -1.0). Depending on how well-being and distress are measured, the estimated correlation ranges from -0.50 (Ross & Mirowsky, 1984a) to near zero (Bradburn, 1969). These correlations seem to suggest that well-being and distress are at least partially independent moods. There are two reasons why the negative correlation between well-being and distress is less than perfect, even though they are opposite poles of a single dimension of mood. The first is random measurement error. There is always a certain amount of randomness in the processes of communicating and recording. By our estimate, the correlation that is corrected for random error is approximately -0.70 (Ross & Mirowsky, 1984).

The second reason the correlation is less than perfect is that some people express their feelings less than others. Differences in expressiveness crosscut differences in mood: The worse a person's mood the less well-being and more distress he or she reports, but the less expressive a person is the less of *both* he or she reports. By our estimate, differences in expressiveness account for 30% of the nonrandom differences in reported well-being and distress. Differences in mood account for the other 70%. Differences in expressiveness are easy to take into account, and investigations show they have little effect on the results of studies (Gove & Geerken, 1977a; Gove, McCorkel, Fain, & Hughes, 1976; Mirowsky & Ross, 1995; Ross & Mirowsky, 1984b). Women are more expressive than men, but this does not account for the higher levels of anxiety and depression reported by women (Mirowsky & Ross, 1995; Ross & Mirowsky, 1984a). Other sociodemographic differences in expressiveness are not as great as that between the sexes, and do not account for the social patterns of distress. Well-being increases and distress decreases with greater education and income, with fewer personal losses and economic hardships, and with marriage. Well-being and distress have opposite sociodemographic patterns because they are opposite ends of the same continuum.

SATISFACTION IS DISTINCT FROM PSYCHOLOGICAL WELL-BEING.   Satisfaction is not a part of psychological well-being. Well-being and distress are the poles of one dimension; satisfaction and discontent are the poles of another. Satisfaction implies a convergence of aspiration and achievement that reflects resignation as much as it does accomplishment. Whereas distress often results from deprivation, dissatisfaction results from deprivation *relative to one's expectations*. Although the two may often go together, the instances in which they do not are important to sociological theory. For example, education increases expected income and thus increases both well-being and satisfaction with one's income; but among people in the *same* income bracket, higher education increases well-being but *de*creases satisfaction with that level of income (Mirowsky, 1987). The most advantaged have the highest expectations, which tends to reduce satisfaction with a given level of achievement, while simultaneously enhancing the sense of well-being (Ross & Van Willigen, 1997).

Social Conditions that Generate Distress

There are five important social patterns of psychological distress: (1) women are more distressed than men; (2) married people are less distressed than the unmarried; (3) parents with children at home are somewhat more distressed than nonparents; (4) the higher one's SES (education, job, and income) the lower one's level of distress; (5) middle-aged people are the least depressed, but older people are least anxious.*

GENDER.   Surveys find that women report higher average levels of depression and anxiety than men (Aneshensel, 1992; Mirowsky & Ross, 1995). Women also rate their health worse and have more physical impairments than men, although they live longer (Ross & Bird, 1994). The evidence that women are more distressed than men seems compelling, yet the pattern has been questioned since the 1970's when it was first uncovered by Walt Gove and his

---

*A sixth pattern—that undesirable life events increase distress—is not included here because these lists of unrelated events are not closely tied to social structure.

colleagues, and it continues to be questioned today (Clancy & Gove, 1974; Dohrenwend & Dohrenwend, 1976, 1977; Rieker & Bird, 2000; Ritchey, LaGory, & Mullis, 1991; Seiler, 1975). Two perspectives question whether women are really more distressed than men. We call them the *response-bias view* and the *gendered-response view* (Mirowsky & Ross, 1995). According to the response-bias view, women are more aware of their emotions, more likely to talk about emotions to others, to be open and expressive, and to think that discussing personal well-being is acceptable rather than stigmatizing. Thus, when women and men are questioned about depression and anxiety, the women report it more. According to the gendered-response theory, women respond to the ubiquitous stress of life with somewhat different emotions than men. In particular, women might feel anxious and depressed where men feel agitated and angry.

As the evidence below will show, women genuinely suffer greater distress than men, and that the difference in distress reflects and reveals women's comparatively disadvantaged social standing. It is not simply that women express their emotions more freely than men, and thus appear more distressed. Nor is it simply that women respond to stressors with different emotions than men, and surveys ask more questions about responses typical of women than about those typical of men. Women do express emotions more freely than men, and women express distress somewhat differently than men. However, expression does not explain the difference in distress. In fact, the more the analyses adjust for differences in expression, the *greater* the gap in distress found between women and men. Furthermore, contrary to gendered-response theory, women feel more angry than men, not less (Conger, Lawrence, Elder, Simmons, & Xiaojia, 1993; Mirowsky & Ross, 1995).

Women are more likely to express their feelings than men by two measures (Mirowsky & Ross, 1995). First, we asked people a direct question about how much they agreed with the statement "I keep my emotions to myself." Men were more likely to agree than women that they keep their emotions to themselves. Second, we used an unobtrusive measure, the tendency to report both positive emotions (happiness) and negative emotions (sadness), using a confirmatory factor method that adjusts for the actual content of happiness and sadness. Women are more likely to express emotions regardless of content. The unobtrusive measure of expressiveness is associated with reports of various types of distress, including depressed mood (sadness), absence of positive mood (happiness), anxiety, anger, and malaise. Contrary to expectations, though, people who say they keep their emotions to themselves actually report more distress of all types, not less. Maybe keeping one's emotions to oneself is distressing in the long run because it precludes supportive responses from other people. Most importantly, adjustment for two measures of expressiveness does not account for sex differences in distress. On the contrary, adjustment for the tendency to express emotions leaves the gender gap intact. In most cases, the gap in distress favoring men increases. Even though women are more expressive than men, their expressiveness does not account for their high reported levels of distress (Gove, 1993; Mirowsky & Ross, 1995).

According to the gendered-response theory, men and women experience the same amount of stress but differ in the nature of their emotional responses to stress (Aneshensel et al., 1991; Dohrenwend & Dohrenwend, 1976, 1977; Rosenfield, 1999). Where men get angry and hostile, women get sad and depressed. Evidence for the gendered-response perspective requires two findings: (1) Women have higher levels of depression; men have higher levels of anger, and (2) people with high levels of anger have low levels of depression. Findings do not support gendered-response theory. First, women are more angry than men, not less (Conger et al., 1993; Ross & Van Willigen, 1996; Weissman & Paykel, 1974; Mirowsky & Ross, 1995). Second, people with high levels of depression are more angry, not less angry. Depression and anger are positively correlated. If men avoided depression by becoming angry, anger and depression would be negatively correlated. Anger does not substitute for depression. Anger accompanies depression.

In fact, all types of distress go together. Depression, anger, anxiety, lack of happiness, and malaise are all positively correlated. Different types of distress do not substitute for one another. Women and men do not face equal levels of frustration, stress, and disadvantage, but simply respond to ubiquitous stress in different ways. Women have more of all types of distress.

Thus far we have focused on distress. Distress is an unpleasant subjective state consisting of emotions and feelings that cause pain and misery. A focus on misery and suffering seems justified on its own, without reference to other values. People would rather not be distressed. It is worse to feel sad, demoralized, lonely, worried, tense, anxious, angry, annoyed, run down, tired, and unable to concentrate or to sleep than to feel happy, hopeful about the future, and to enjoy life. Women are more distressed than men. But what about behaviors like heavy drinking, illegal drug use, or antisocial behavior? Are they substitutes for depression, anxiety, anger, unhappiness, and malaise that women experience? Do men avoid depression by these behaviors?

The distinction between emotional (or affective) problems like depression, anxiety, and anger; and behavioral problems, like heavy drinking, raises the possibility that gendered response may occur across realms of disorder, even though it does not occur within the emotional realm. Women get depressed, anxious, and angry; but men abuse alcohol and illegal drugs, and engage in antisocial behavior more frequently than women (Aneshensel et al., 1991; Ross, 2000). Gove and Tudor (1977) argued that symptoms from different realms should *not* be combined—that they represent inherently distinct phenomena that may be interrelated but should not be confounded. Distress is a problem for the person who suffers it. Antisocial behavior, drinking, and drug use may be correlated with distress, but are not themselves distress. In some cases such as antisocial behavior or alcoholism, the behaviors may be at least as much a problem for other people as for the person himself. However, the question remains whether women feel more distressed than men because the men transform their frustrations into behavioral disorder.

For transrealm gendered response to explain women's greater distress, some type of behavioral disorder must reduce distress. If a behavior does not lower distress, then it cannot account for lower male levels of distress. On this count, there is little or no support for transrealm gendered response. Studies find that depression *in*creases with the level of antisocial behavior, alcoholism, and drug abuse, which are the main problems found more commonly in men than in women (Boyd et al., 1984; Dohrenwend et al., 1980). One study finds that men who drink heavily, use opiates, and smoke cigarettes have higher levels of depression than those who do not, although marijuana use only correlated with depression when it was used to cope with problems (Green & Ritter, 2000). Men and women who drink heavily and engage in behavior that gets them in trouble with the law have higher levels of depression than those who do not (Ross, 2000). Heavy drinking, illegal drug use, and other lawless behavior are not substitutes for depression. Engaging in these behaviors does not protect men from turning stress and frustration inward upon themselves. On the contrary, people who drink and engage in antisocial activities have higher levels of depression than those who do not. When we take heavy drinking and lawless behavior into account the gender gap in depression does not decrease; it increases by about 40% (Ross, 2000). This means that heavy drinking and lawless behavior do not explain why men have lower levels of depression than women. On the contrary, if women drank and engaged in illegal activities as much as men do, women's depression levels would be even higher than they are now. Furthermore, although men use illegal drugs more frequently than women, women are more likely than men to use prescribed psychoactive drugs—over one woman in five compared to less than one man in ten (Verbrugge, 1985). Men's destructive behaviors do not account for their low levels of depression. Depression accompanies illegal activity, use of drugs, and heavy drinking; it does not substitute for it.

Women are more distressed than men. Measured as sadness, demoralization, hopelessness, anxiety, worry, malaise, and anger, women experience distress about 30% more frequently than men (Mirowsky & Ross, 1995). It is not simply that they are more likely to express their feelings. It is not simply that men and women respond differently to the ubiquitous stress of life. Women's and men's lives differ, and this difference puts women at higher risk of distress. Theories of gender inequality or gender-based exposure to social stressors explain women's elevated distress as the consequence of inequality and disadvantage (e.g., Gove & Tudor, 1977; Pearlin, 1989; Ross & Huber, 1985; Ross & Van Willigen, 1996). Different positions in the social structure expose individuals to different characteristic amounts of hardship and constraint. Women's positions at work and in the family disadvantage them compared to men.

Compared with men, women face more economic dependency, restricted opportunities for paid employment, lower earnings, less power at work and at home, more routine and unfulfilling work, more conflict between work and family obligations, and unfairness in the division of household labor (Bianchi, 2000; Budig & England, 2001; Glass & Camarigg, 1992; Glass & Fujimoto, 1994; Mirowsky, 1985; Reskin & Padavic, 1994; Rosenfield, 1989; Ross & Bird, 1994; Ross & Wright, 1998), all of which increase distress. Their greater burden of demands and limitations creates stress and frustration, manifest in higher levels of distress. This idea was first proposed by Gove and his colleagues, who, along with others, found that employed women—whose lives were more like men's—were less distressed than homemakers (Gove & Geerken, 1977; Gove & Tudor, 1973; Kessler & McRae, 1982; Rosenfield, 1980; Ross, Mirowsky, & Ulbrich, 1983). We later found that couples who share both the economic responsibilities and the domestic responsibilities for housework and child care also share much the same level of psychological well-being, and are less distressed than other couples (Ross, Mirowsky, & Huber, 1983). An analysis of the factors that increase the husband's domestic work shows that husbands do more the higher the wife's earnings, and they do *less* the more their own earnings exceed the wife's. Thus, equality in the division of labor at home, which provides psychological benefits to the husband and wife, depends on their economic equality in the work place (Ross, Mirowsky, & Huber, 1983).

Compared with men, women are less likely to be employed, more likely to be employed part-time rather than full-time, having lower earnings, less fulfilling work, and more economic hardship, aspects of SES, which as we discuss next, increase distress. However, young women's levels of education now equal men's (U.S. Bureau of Census, 2000). Since education is the source of SES, the gap between men's and women's levels of distress may close in the future, although thus far evidence for this trend is equivocal (Mirowsky, 1996).

SOCIOECONOMIC STATUS. High SES improves psychological well-being. Low SES increases psychological distress (Glenn & Weaver, 1981; Kessler, 1982; Link, Lennon, & Dohrenwend, 1993; Pearlin, Liebermann, Menaghan, & Muller, 1981; Ross & Huber, 1985; Ross & Van Willigen, 1997). High SES is also associated with good self-reported health, high levels of physical functioning, less chronic disease, and lower mortality (Elo & Preston, 1996; House et al., 1990; Mirowsky, Ross, & Reynolds, 2000; Reynolds & Ross, 1998; Rogers, Hummer, & Nam, 1999; Ross & Wu, 1995; Williams & Collins, 1995). Some people are exposed to more social stressors and fewer resources to deal with them. They are the poor and poorly educated; unemployed, employed part-time, or working at menial and unfulfilling jobs; and living in poor and rundown neighborhoods where crime is a constant threat. Some people have fewer problems and more resources to solve them. They are the well-to-do and well educated, working at challenging and fulfilling jobs and living in pleasant neighborhoods.

SES indicates a person's relative standing in the distribution of opportunity, prosperity, and standing. It broadly refers to one's place in the unequal distribution of socially valued resources, goods, and quality of life. It is typically measured by education, work, and income. People with college educations, employed at good jobs, with high incomes have high SES. Although there is some value in looking at overall standing, there is more value to keeping each component separate. Education, income, and work indicate different underlying concepts. Education indicates the accumulated knowledge, skills, values, and behaviors learned at school (sometimes called human capital), in addition to being a credential that structures employment opportunities. Income and economic hardship indicate economic well-being. Work is productive activity (paid or not). Furthermore, education, employment, and economic resources are not on the same causal level. Education is the key to people's position in the stratification system; it decreases the likelihood of being unemployed, increases the likelihood of full-time employment, and gives people access to good jobs with high incomes. Part of education's effect on psychological well-being is mediated by employment status, work, and economic resources, but some is a direct benefit of schooling (Ross & Van Willigen, 1997).

Employment, especially full-time employment is associated with higher levels of psychological (and physical) well-being (Gore & Mangione, 1983; Pearlin et al., 1981; Reynolds & Ross, 1998; Ross & Mirowsky, 1995; Ross & Van Willigen, 1997). Job qualities also affect psychological well-being. Although some researchers studying stratification look at occupational prestige, this is not really the most important thing about jobs to psychological well-being. The two most important aspects of work to well-being include autonomy and creativity. Work that is autonomous, free from close supervision, and that provides opportunities for workers to make their own decisions; and work that is creative, nonroutine, involves a variety of tasks, and gives people a chance for continued learning and development, decreases distress (Ross & Drentea, 1998; Ross & Wright, 1998). Autonomous and creative work give workers the chance to use their skills in the design and implementation of the their own work; and it gives them the freedom to use thought and independent judgment in doing different things in different ways rather than doing the same thing in the same way in a process designed and controlled by others (Kohn & Schooler, 1982). These qualities of work decrease distress directly and in part by way of boosting people's sense of personal control (Ross & Van Willigen, 1997; Kohn & Schooler, 1982; Kohn, Naoi, Schoenbach, Schooler, & Slomczynski, 1990).

Low income is distressing mostly because it increases economic hardship (Reynolds & Ross, 1998), and economic hardship itself is more than a function of income. Low levels of education, children in the home, and being unmarried all increase economic hardship directly, apart from income (Mirowsky & Ross, 1999), and low levels of education further deprive people of the problem-solving resources needed to cope with the stresses of economic hardship. Ross and Huber (1985) find a synergistic effect on economic hardship of low education and low income, each making the effect of the other worse. Economic hardship increases psychological distress; the chronic strain of struggling to pay the bills and to feed and clothe the children takes its toll in feelings of depression and malaise (Conger et al., 1992; Ge et al., 1992; Krause & Liang, 1993; Pearlin et al., 1981; Ross & Huber, 1985).

MARRIAGE.   Compared to married people, the single, divorced, and widowed have higher levels of depression, anxiety, and other forms of psychological distress (Bowling, 1987; Gove, Hughes, & Style, 1983; Gore & Mangione, 1983; Ross, 1995; Kessler & Essex, 1982; Umberson & Williams, 2000); they have more physical health problems as indicated by acute conditions, chronic conditions, days of disability, and self-reported health (Anson, 1989; Riessman & Gerstel, 1985; Ross, Mirowsky, & Goldsteen, 1990; Umberson, 1987). Compared to married people, the nonmarried have higher death rates from coronary heart disease, stroke, pneumonia, many kinds of cancer, cirrhosis of the liver, automobile accidents, homicide, and suicide, all of which are leading causes of death (Berkman & Breslow, 1983; Kaprio, Koskenuo, & Rita, 1987). (The one exception to the consistent, positive effects of marriage concerns young adults: very young adults who get married do not experience lower depression levels than those who remain single [Horwitz & White, 1991].) The positive effect of marriage on well-being is strong and consistent, and selection of the psychologically healthy into marriage or the psychologically unhealthy out of marriage cannot explain the effect (Booth & Amato, 1991; Horwitz & White, 1991; Menaghan, 1985). Some evidence shows that marriage protects men's psychological well-being more than women's (Gove & Tudor, 1973), although there is also counterevidence which shows men's advantage over women in psychological well-being is as large or larger among the single, divorced, and widowed (Fox, 1980).

Social support and economic resources likely explain why marriage is associated with psychological well-being. Compared to being unmarried, marriage provides emotional support—a sense of being cared about, loved, esteemed, and valued as a person (Ross, 1995). Married people also have higher household incomes and lower levels of economic hardship than the nonmarried. Social support and a lack of economic hardship improve psychological well-being (House, Umberson, & Landis, 1988; Ross et al., 1990).

PARENTHOOD.   Children do not improve parents' psychological well-being, measured as the absence of depression, anxiety, and psychophysiological distress. People with children at home do not have higher levels of well-being than nonparents (Cleary & Mechanic, 1983; Gove & Geerken, 1977; Gore & Mangione, 1983; Kessler & McRae, 1982). In many instances, parents—especially mothers—are more psychologically distressed than nonparents. Children at home either increase psychological distress or have an insignificant effect on well-being (McLanahan & Adams, 1987). The stress of parenthood is felt at home: Kandel and her colleagues, for instance, found that children at home increase depression, but parents whose children have left home are less depressed than the childless of the same age (Kandel, Davies, & Raveis, 1985). Similarly Aneshensel, Frerich's and Clark (1981) found that living with children in the home is the stressful aspect of parenthood.

What are the processes by which children affect parents' distress? Two explanations stand out—economic hardship and the demands of child care. Children in the home lead to economic hardship, increasing depression for both men and women (Ross & Huber, 1985). At the same level of family income, a family with children feels more economic pressure than one without children (Mirowsky & Ross, 1999). The chronic strain of struggling to pay the bills and to feed and clothe the children takes its toll in feelings of depression and anger (Pearlin et al., 1981; Ross & Huber, 1985; Ross & Van Willigen, 1996).

Children greatly increase the total amount of domestic work, especially for women. In the household, mothers do a disproportionate amount of child care—much of it in the form of housework like cooking, cleaning, and doing laundry—which increases depression (Kessler & McRae, 1982; Ross et al., 1983). Furthermore, mothers typically manage the child care arrangements, and thus are further exposed to the difficulties of arranging care for the children while the parents are at work, which also increases depression (Ross & Mirowsky, 1988). Inequity in the distribution of housework and child care is a primary means by which gender inequality is perpetuated in the home, increasing depression and anger among women (Glass & Fujimoto, 1994; Lennon & Rosenfield, 1994; Ross & Van Willigen, 1996). According to the gender inequality perspective, women are not more *vulnerable* to the stressors of parenthood, although some researchers argue that women are more affected by parenthood because the role is more salient to them (Simon, 1992; Thoits, 1984), but rather that women are more *exposed* to the stressors of parenthood than are men.

AGE. Depression starts relatively high in early adulthood, drops to a lifetime low somewhere in the range of 40–60 years-old, and then rises in old age (Mirowsky & Ross, 1992; Schieman, Van Gundy, & Taylor, 2001). Measured in terms of depression, middle-age is the best time of life. The age pattern for anxiety differs somewhat. Anxiety is also very high among the young, but it decreases in a linear fashion with age (Mirowsky & Ross, 1999). It never rises again as does depression. Although it is usually the case that the same people who have high levels of depression also have high levels of anxiety (as among the young), it is not the case among the elderly. They have high levels of depression and low levels of anxiety. (The age pattern for anger mirrors anxiety, with high levels among the young and low levels among the elderly [Schieman, 1999].) Why is depression high among the young, low among the middle-aged, and high again among the elderly? Why is anxiety high among the young, and then decreases for the rest of the life?

Economic resources and work explain some of the pattern. Average personal earnings and household income peak in the 50–59 year-old bracket, about the same time of life when depression reaches its lowest levels. Higher earnings and income reduce an individual's level of depression (Kessler, 1982; Kessler & Cleary, 1980; Mirowsky & Ross, 1989; Wheaton, 1980). Higher earnings and income reduce depression mostly by reducing economic hardship (Ross & Huber, 1985). People find it distressing to have difficulty paying the bills or buying household necessities such as food, clothing, or medicine. Economic hardship threatens one's personal security. Worse than that, it threatens the security of children, partners, and others whom one loves and sustains. Economic hardship generally decreases with older age (Mirowsky & Ross, 1999). Young adults have by far the highest levels of economic hardship. Half say they had difficulty paying bills in the past year. Forty percent report at least one period when they did not have the money to buy food, clothes, or other household necessities. Twenty five percent report a time when they did not have the money for needed medicine or medical care. The levels of economic hardship drop sharply between the ages of 40 and 60. Hardship remains relatively low among those aged 60 and older. Earnings and income are not the only things that determine the risk of economic hardship. The elderly have relatively low rates of hardship despite low earnings and household income for two reasons. First, older adults have fewer children at home, which greatly reduces economic strains. Second, accumulated wealth and government programs such as social security, Medicare, and Medicaid meet many needs. Economic hardship explains some of the elevated depression and anxiety among the young, but cannot account for high depression among the older groups, who experience little economic hardship (Schieman, van Gundy, & Taylor 2001). It could help explain the elderlies' low levels of anxiety, though.

The life cycle of employment generates the rise and fall of earnings and household income. The young and old are least likely to be employed. Employment also improves emotional well-being apart from its impact on household economics. Adults employed full-time enjoy the lowest average depression (Gove & Geerken, 1977; Kessler & McRae, 1982; Kessler,

Turner, & House, 1989; Pearlin et al., 1981; Ross et al., 1983). However, retirees are not significantly more distressed than full-time employees (Ross & Drentea, 1998), so retirement may explain little of the upturn in depression in older age.

Marriage and interpersonal relationships form another major aspect of the adult life cycle that affects well-being (Hughes & Gove, 1981). Middle-aged adults are the ones most likely to be married, and marriage greatly reduces distress, especially compared to widowhood (Umberson, Wortman, & Kessler, 1992). Being single accounts for some of the distress among the young, and widowhood accounts for a lot of the depression among the elderly (Mirowsky & Ross, 1992; Schieman et al., 2001). Social support is also highest in middle-age and lower among the young and old (Turner & Marino, 1994).

Poor health and physical impairment also account for some of the depression among the older groups. As people age they feel less healthy, have more impairments and medical conditions, and expect to live fewer additional years (Mirowsky & Hu, 1996; Ross & Bird, 1994). People find all of these depressing, but physical impairment appears worst possibly because of its large negative impact on perceptions of mastery and control (Mirowsky, 1995; Schieman & Turner, 1998). As people age, work and family situations improve up to a point, after which poor health and a declining sense of control over life counteract the positive trends. Furthermore, as people age, the type of distress seems to change from active (anxiety and anger) to passive (depression).

Age represents cohorts in addition to life course, and one cohort explanation stands out in explaining age patterns of depression—education. Younger generations have higher levels of education than older ones, and education greatly reduces depression (Mirowsky & Ross, 1992; Reynolds & Ross, 1998; Ross & Huber, 1985; Ross & Van Willigen, 1997).

SENSE OF CONTROL

A sense of personal control links social structure to emotional well-being (Mirowsky & Ross, 1989). Perceived control occupies the central position in a three-part model in which social conditions shape perceptions and beliefs, which, in turn, affect emotional well-being. In this section we describe the social causes and emotional consequences of perceived control versus powerlessness. Perceived powerlessness is generated by objective conditions of powerlessness and leads to distress.

Of all the beliefs about self and society that might increase or reduce distress, belief in control over one's own life may be the most important. Seeman placed the sense of powerlessness at the top of his list of types of subjective alienation, defining it as, "the expectancy or probability, held by the individual, that his own behavior cannot determine the occurrence of the outcomes, or reinforcements, he seeks" (Seeman, 1959, p. 784). Alienation is any form of detachment or separation from oneself or from others. Powerlessness is the separation from important outcomes in one's own life; or an inability to achieve desired ends. Perceived powerlessness is the cognitive awareness of this reality. Powerlessness, as a social-psychological variable, is distinct from the objective conditions that may produce it and the distress an individual may feel as a consequence of it.

Defining and Measuring the Sense of Personal Control

The sense of personal control is a learned, generalized expectation that outcomes are contingent on one's own choices and actions (Mirowsky & Ross, 1989; Rotter, 1966; Ross,

Mirowsky, & Cockerham, 1983; Seeman, 1983). People with a high sense of control report being effective agents in their own lives; they believe that they can master, control, and effectively alter the environment. Perceived control is the cognitive awareness of a link between efforts and outcomes. On the other end of the continuum, perceived powerlessness is the belief that one's actions do not affect outcomes. It is the belief that outcomes of situations are determined by forces external to one's self such as powerful others, luck, fate, or chance. People with a sense of powerlessness think that they have little control over meaningful events and circumstances in their lives. As such, perceived powerlessness is the cognitive awareness of a discrepancy between one's goals and the means to achieve them. Perceived control and powerlessness represent two ends of a continuum, with the belief that one can shape conditions and events in one's life on one end of the continuum, and the belief that one's actions cannot influence events and circumstances at the other (Mirowsky & Ross, 1989).

The importance of perceived control is recognized in a number of social and behavioral sciences, where it appears in several forms with various names. In sociology, researchers build on themes of perceived powerlessness versus control. As a result, many of the constructs used by sociologists overlap, and they are not seen as very distinct. Concepts related to personal control appear under a number of different names in addition to perceived powerlessness and control, notably mastery (Pearlin et al., 1981), personal autonomy (Seeman, 1983), the sense of personal efficacy (Downey & Moen, 1987; Gecas, 1989) and instrumentalism (Mirowsky, Ross, & Van Willigen, 1996; Wheaton, 1980), and at the other end of the continuum, fatalism (Wheaton, 1980) and perceived helplessness (Elder & Liker, 1982). In psychology concepts closely related to the sense of personal control include internal locus of control, self-efficacy, and helplessness. Psychologists are more likely than sociologists to focus on differences among related concepts. We briefly define the psychological concepts, saying how the sense of personal control is similar to and different from locus of control, self-efficacy, and helplessness.

LOCUS OF CONTROL.   In cognitive psychology, perceived control appears as locus of control (Rotter, 1966). Belief in an external locus of control is a *learned*, generalized expectation that outcomes of situations are determined by forces external to one's self such as powerful others, luck, fate, or chance. The individual believes that he or she is powerless and at the mercy of the environment. Belief in an internal locus of control (the opposite) is a learned, generalized expectation that outcomes are contingent on one's own choices and actions. Compared to persons with an external locus of control, those with an internal locus of control attribute outcomes to themselves rather than to forces outside of themselves.

Both Rotter (1966) and Seeman (1959) recognized that perceived powerlessness—the major form of subjective alienation—and external locus of control were related concepts. In fact, Rotter derived the concept of locus of control from the sociological concept of alienation, stating "the alienated individual feels unable to control his own destiny" (1966, p. 263). The roots of personal control, described next, are thus found in the work of Seeman and Rotter.

PERSONAL CONTROL.   The sense of personal control (Mirowsky & Ross, 1989, 1992) corresponds to the personal control component of Rotter's locus of control scale, which includes questions like "when I make plans I can make them work" or "I have little influence over the things that happen to me." The concept of personal control refers to *oneself*, not others, and it is *general*, not realm-specific. Thus, unlike Rotter, we exclude beliefs about the control others have over their lives and realm-specific control, like political control, from the concept. For

TABLE 17-2. Mirowsky–Ross Measure of the Sense of Personal Control versus Powerlessness (Mirowsky & Ross, 1991)

Control over Good
  (1) "I am responsible for my own successes"
  (2) "I can do just about anything I really set my mind to"

Control over Bad
  (3) "My misfortunes are the result of mistakes I have made"
  (4) "I am responsible for my failures"

Powerless over Good
  (5) "The really good things that happen to me are mostly luck"
  (6) "There's no sense planning a lot—if something good is going to happen it will"

Powerless over Bad
  (7) "Most of my problems are due to bad breaks"
  (8) "I have little control over the bad things that happen to me"

Notes: To create a mean score perceived control scale, responses to perceived control questions (1 through 4) are coded -2 = strongly disagree, -1 = disagree, 0 = neutral, 1 = agree, 2 = strongly agree, and responses to perceived powerlessness questions (5 through 8) are coded -2 = strongly agree, -1 = agree, 0 = neutral, 1 = disagree, 2 = strongly disagree.

instance, we do not consider questions from the Rotter scale like "the average citizen can have an influence in government decisions" or "there will always be wars" to be measures of the sense of personal control since they do not refer to oneself, and they are realm-specific.

The Mirowsky–Ross measure of the sense of personal control balances statements claiming and denying personal control, and balances statements in which the outcome is positive and negative, as shown in Table 17-2 (Mirosky & Ross, 1991). This eliminates defense, self-blame, and agreement bias from the measure. Defense is the tendency to claim control over good outcomes but deny control over bad outcomes. Self-blame, the opposite, is the tendency to claim control over bad outcomes but not good. Agreement is the tendency to simply say "yes" to survey questions, irrespective of content. Because of our balanced 2×2 design, none of these tendencies biases the measure of personal control.

SELF-EFFICACY. The sense of personal control overlaps to a large extent with self-efficacy despite Bandura's (1986) claim that sense of control and self-efficacy are distinct (although related) concepts. Bandura collectively refers to concepts of locus of control, or sense of control, as outcome-expectancy theories. Self-efficacy, according to Bandura, focuses upon the individual's belief that he or she can (or cannot) effectively perform a specific action, whereas control focuses on the belief that certain actions will ultimately achieve desired goals. According to Bandura, self-efficacy is specific to particular contexts. Thus, the sense of control is a more parsimonious concept than self-efficacy, with more universal application. The degree to which people think they can or cannot achieve their goals, despite the specific nature of the actions required, has applicability to almost all circumstances. More importantly, the sense of personal control may be the root of self-efficacy. A person with a high sense of personal control will likely try other actions if their current repertoire of behaviors is not working. New behaviors may successfully obtain desired goals, which may in turn increase the perceived ability to shape other events and circumstances in life. Therefore, for all intents and purposes, the sense of control may be the foundation of self-efficacy. The conceptual distinction Bandura outlines may well be a largely academic one.

HELPLESSNESS. Another related concept appears in behavioral psychology as learned helplessness. The behavior of learned helplessness results from exposure to inescapable, uncontrollable negative stimuli and is characterized by a low rate of voluntary response and low ability to learn successful behaviors (Seligman, 1975). Although intended as an analog of human depression, it is important to remember that learned helplessness refers to the behavior, not to any cognitive attribution that reinforcements are outside ones control, and not to the imputed emotion of depression. In humans, however, there is a link between an external locus of control (a cognitive orientation) and learned helplessness (a conditioned response): the perception that reinforcement is not contingent on action. Hiroto (1974) found that, compared to subjects with an internal locus of control, those with an external locus of control were less likely to see a connection between behavior and reinforcement, and as a result, learned more slowly.

Heuristics in Psychology and Sociology

The most useful research on the links between social structural conditions, perceptions of control, and emotional outcomes, synthesize the strengths of psychology and sociology—as did Rotter and Seeman—while avoiding the pitfalls. Each discipline has a heuristic, or working assumption, which greatly simplifies reality to provide a base from which to proceed with research. In the extreme, psychology assumes that beliefs come out of people's heads without reference to social conditions, whereas sociology assumes that there is nothing *but* social structure. Sociologists too often discount the ways in which perceptions mediate the effects of social position on well-being; psychologists too often discount the influence of social structure on perceptions. Both links are crucial to understanding the processes by which social position affects psychological well-being.

Sociologists sometimes imply that social structure has consequences for individual behavior or well-being without reference to individual beliefs or perceptions (Braverman, 1974). Erikson (1986) critiques sociologists who think that bringing in social psychological mediating variables somehow makes theory less structural. "There are those," says Erikson (1986), "who argue that one ought to be able to determine when a person is alienated by taking a look at the objective conditions in which she works. The worker exposed to estranging conditions is alienated almost by definition, no matter what she says she thinks or even what she thinks she thinks. That view ... has the effect of closing off sociological investigation rather than the effect of inviting it. Alienation, in order to make empirical sense, has to reside somewhere in or around the persons who are said to experience it." (1986, p. 6). The association between the objective condition and the subjective perception is an important empirical question; one that must be investigated, not assumed (Ross & Mirowsky, 1992; Seeman, 1983).

Some psychologists, on the other hand, discount the effects of social position, instead claiming that perceptions of control are as likely to be illusory as to be based on reality. Levenson says that a belief that one controls important outcomes in one's life is *unrelated* to the belief that others, chance, fate, or luck control the outcomes (Levenson, 1983; see Lachman, 1986, for a review). Brewin and Shapiro (1984) contend that a perceived ability to achieve desirable outcomes is unrelated to a perceived ability to avoid undesirable ones. In both cases, people supposedly fail to see a connection, and the realities of life do not suggest one. Implicitly, these views deny the effects of social structure on the sense of control. Levenson's view suggests that education, prestige, wealth, and power do not shift the locus of real control from others and chance to oneself. Brewin and Shapiro's view suggests that the real resources available for achieving success are useless for avoiding failure. The empirical basis for these claims is small and often insignificant correlations between internal and external control and control over good and bad outcomes. Next we discuss the biases in their scales created by agreement tendencies and defensiveness that produce these results.

CONTROL, DEFENSE, AND ACQUIESCENCE. Responses to questions about personal control capture the concept of interest, and two other cross-cutting concepts—the tendency to agree and self-defense. Some people tend to agree with statements irrespective of content. Agreement tendency can make it appear as if internal and external control are uncorrelated (as in Levenson, above). Some people are more likely to believe that they control the good outcomes in their lives than that they control the bad ones (self-defense); others take more responsibility for their failures than for their successes (self-blame) (as in Brewin and Shapiro above). Agreement tendencies and the tendency toward self-defense or self-blame cross-cut the concept of interest and bias measures unless they balance agreement and defense. Thus, measures of personal control ideally should balance defensiveness and agreement tendencies to achieve unbiased measures. The Mirowsky–Ross measure of the sense of control (Mirowsky & Ross, 1991) is a two-by-two index that balances statements about control with those about lack of control, and statements about success (good outcomes) with those about failure (bad outcomes). It is shown in Table 17-2. Interestingly, Rotter's locus of control scale used a forced-choice format to solve the problem of acquiescence, but his logic apparently was lost when researchers switched to Likert scales. Likert scales are much more efficient in surveys, and are more acceptable to respondents who dislike being forced to choose one of two extremes. Likert scales allow degrees of agreement with each statement. However, Likert scales should balance control and lack of control over good and bad outcomes to ensure validity.

Social Conditions that Generate a Sense of Control

OBJECTIVE POWER AND PERCEIVED CONTROL. Belief in external control is the learned and generalized expectation that one has little control over meaningful events and circumstances in one's life. As such, it is the cognitive awareness of a discrepancy between one's goals and the means to achieve them. Beliefs about personal control are often realistic perceptions of objective conditions. An individual learns through social interaction and personal experience that his or her choices and efforts are usually likely or unlikely to affect the outcome of a situation (Rotter, 1966; Seeman, 1983; Wheaton, 1980). Failure in the face of effort leads to a sense of powerlessness, fatalism, or belief in external control, beliefs that can increase passivity and result in giving up. Through continued experience with objective conditions of powerlessness and lack of control, individuals come to learn that their own actions cannot produce desired outcomes. In contrast, success leads to a sense of mastery, efficacy or belief in internal control, characterized by an active, problem-solving approach to life (Mirowsky & Ross, 1983, 1984; Wheaton, 1980, 1983).

Sociological theory points to several conditions likely to produce a belief in external control. First and foremost is powerlessness. Defined as an objective condition rather than a belief, it is the inability to achieve one's ends or, alternatively, the inability to achieve one's ends when in opposition to others. The second is structural inconsistency, which is a situation in which society defines certain goals, purposes, and interests as legitimate and desirable and also defines the proper procedures for moving toward the objectives but does not provide adequate resources and opportunities for achieving the objectives through legitimate means. The third is alienated labor, a condition under which the worker does not decide what to produce, does not design and schedule the production process, and does not own the product. The fourth is dependency, a situation in which one partner in an exchange has fewer alternative sources of sustenance and gratification than the other. The fifth is role overload, a situation in which expectations of others imply demands that overwhelm the resources and capabilities of the individual. Although these conditions are not exhaustive, they all point to the generative force of various forms of social power. In looking for the sources of perceived powerlessness researchers have looked for variables associated with conditions of powerlessness, structural inconsistency, alienated labor, dependency, and role overload.

Among the major sociodemographic correlates of the sense of personal control are: (1) SES, including education, employment, income; and race, (2) gender, work, and family, including paid and unpaid work, work and family interactions, and marriage and children, and (3) age, generation, and the life course.

SOCIOECONOMIC STATUS. High SES is associated with a sense of personal control. General SES (as measured by an index of family income, occupational prestige of the respondent or breadwinner, and interviewer ratings of the social class of the neighborhood, home, and respondent) is positively related to a sense of mastery and control (Mirowsky & Ross, 1983). Looking at specific components of SES separately, education, employment (especially full-time employment), income, lack of economic hardship, and autonomous and nonroutine work each decrease the sense of powerlessness and increase the sense of control, adjusting for the other components (Downey & Moen, 1987; Mirowsky & Ross, 1983; Ross & Mirowsky, 1989, 1992; Ross et al., 1983; Wheaton, 1980).

Education is the key to a person's place in the stratification system. It shapes the likelihood of being employed at a good job with a high income, and it boosts the sense of control as a direct consequence of schooling. Education raises the sense of personal control because it helps people successfully prevent problems, or solve them if prevention fails, to achieve their goals, and shape their own lives (Mirowsky & Ross, 1989; Pearlin et al., 1981; Ross & Mirowsky, 1992; Wheaton, 1980). Through education, one develops capacities on many levels that increase one's sense of personal control. Schooling builds human capital—skills, abilities, and resources. Education develops the habits and skills of communication: reading, writing, inquiring, discussing, looking things ups, and figuring things out. It develops basic analytic skills such as observing, experimenting, summarizing, synthesizing, interpreting, classifying, and so on. Because education develops the ability to gather and interpret information and to solve problems on many levels, it increases control over events and outcomes in life (Ross & Mirowsky, 1989). Moreover, in education, one encounters and solves problems that are progressively more difficult, complex, and subtle. The process of learning builds problem-solving skills and confidence in the ability to solve problems. Education instills the habit of meeting problems with attention, thought, action, and persistence. Thus, education increases effort and ability, the fundamental components of problem-solving (Wheaton, 1980). For these reasons, high levels of education are associated with a sense of personal control (Pearlin et al., 1981; Ross & Mirowsky, 1992; Wheaton, 1980). Finally, education serves as an avenue to good jobs and high incomes. Thus it marks the social power that helps provide control over circumstances of life (Mirowsky, 1995; Ross & Wu, 1995).

Jobs are important for a number of reasons. Low status jobs produce a sense of powerlessness because the job, and the opportunities and income it provides, are seen as barriers to the achievement of life goals (Wheaton, 1980). Jobs that are substantively complex (especially in work primarily with information and people rather than with things) increase the sense of personal control and psychological self-directedness (Kohn, 1976; Kohn & Schooler, 1982; Ross, 2000). Jobs that provide autonomy—freedom from close supervision and participation in decision-making—increase the sense of personal control (Bird & Ross, 1993; Kohn & Schooler, 1982; Ross & Mirowsky, 1992). Together substantively complex, nonroutine, creative, autonomous work signals control over one's own work, which Kohn and his colleagues call occupational self-direction. Among the employed, occupational self-direction—rather than ownership or control over the labor of others—increases psychological self-direction, which is similar to the sense of personal control (Kohn, 1976; Kohn & Schooler, 1982; Kohn et al., 1990). Job latitude, like occupational self-direction, includes autonomous decision-making and nonroutine work, and it significantly increases perceived control (Seeman, Seeman, & Budros, 1988).

Job disruptions such as being laid off, downgraded, fired, or leaving work because of illness decrease the worker's sense of mastery, partly by lowering income and increasing difficulties in acquiring necessities such as food, clothing, housing, and medical care, or optional but useful items such as furniture, automobiles, and recreation (Pearlin et al., 1981).

In sum, theory strongly predicts a positive relationship between SES and the sense of control, and research strongly supports the prediction. Most aspects of SES, including high levels of education, income, autonomous and creative work, and employment itself are significantly associated with high perceived control. SES may also help explain race and gender differences in perceptions of control.

RACE AND ETHNICITY. Some research finds that minority group members, including Blacks and Mexican Americans, have lower average levels of perceived control than Whites. This is partly due to their lower SES. Lower levels of education and income mediate part of the impact of race on perceived control (Gurin, Gurin, Lao, & Beattie, 1969; Hughes & Demo, 1989). However, the data also show a direct effect of race and ethnicity, even adjusting for education and income, indicating that Blacks and Mexican Americans have a lower sense of control over their lives that is not just due to socioeconomic disadvantage (Ross & Mirowsky, 1989). This could be due to discrimination and restricted opportunities, if barriers based on race frustrate African American's aspirations and lead to a cognitive disconnection between ones efforts and outcomes. In addition to their restricted opportunities in an Anglo-dominated economic system, Mexican Americans also place an emphasis on subordination to the family that may decrease perceived control (Mirowsky & Ross, 1984). Compared to Anglos, persons of Mexican ethnic identity have more of an orientation to family and pseudofamily, whereas Anglos place less emphasis on the mutual obligations of family and friends and more on the individual's personal responsibility for his or her own life. This may generate lower levels of personal control among Mexican Americans, but higher levels of social support.

More research is needed to explain the processes by which race shapes the sense of personal control. According to the theory of personal control, any condition that severs the link between efforts and outcomes reduces the sense of control. Discrimination is an act in which an individual is treated on the basis of race or another ascribed status (like sex or age), rather than on the basis of their own individual achievements, effort, ability, skills, and other "meritocratic" or "performance-based" criteria. If people are treated on the basis of ascribed characteristics over which they have no control, rather than on the basis of achievements over which they do have control, the link between efforts and outcomes is severed. Both negative and positive discrimination produce an uncoupling of what one does and the outcomes of these acts. If a person is hired or promoted on the basis of race, in theory, this will decrease the sense of control. Ironically, correcting past negative discrimination with current positive discrimination, rather than with meritocratic assessments of an individual's own ability to do the job regardless of race, may perpetuate low levels of personal control among African Americans. Only empirical investigation will tell whether this prediction implied by theory is supported.

GENDER, WORK AND FAMILY.   Theory suggests that women have a lower sense of control over their lives than men as a result of economic dependency, restricted opportunities, role overload, and the routine nature of housework and women's jobs. Past evidence indicates that women have a lower sense of control than men (Mirowsky & Ross, 1983, 1984; Thoits, 1987), but often the difference is insignificant (Ross & Bird, 1994; Ross & Mirowsky, 1989). We examine the empirical evidence for expectations based on our theory of personal control. Then we return to the original question of whether women have a lower sense of control over their lives than do men, and the circumstances under which they do and do not.

PAID AND UNPAID WORK.   Women are more likely to do unpaid domestic work; men are more likely to work for pay. Compared to not working for pay, employment is associated with status, power, economic independence, and noneconomic rewards, for both men and women (Bird & Ross, 1993; Gove & Tudor, 1973). For women who are exclusively housewives, domestic work is done without economic rewards, without the opportunity for advancement or promotion for work well done, and, because it is often invisible, devalued, and taken for granted, without psychological rewards (Gove & Tudor, 1973). Theory predicts that people employed for pay have a greater sense of control over their lives than homemakers. Perceived control over one's life is the expectation that one's behavior affects outcomes, and working for pay likely produces a mental connection between efforts and outcomes. In contrast, work done without pay or other rewards produces a sense of disconnection between efforts and outcomes. Effort and skill at housework have few consequences; one does not receive a raise, and one's standard of living is determined by someone else, not by one's abilities at the job. Furthermore, homemakers are economically dependent, which may decrease one's sense of control and increase the perception that powerful others shape one's life. Both economic dependency and the disconnection between work and rewards theoretically decrease perceived control among unpaid domestic workers compared to paid workers. Empirical evidence indicates that employed persons have a higher sense of control than the nonemployed overall (Ross & Mirowsky, 1992), that the employed have a higher sense of control than homemakers specifically (Bird & Ross, 1993; Ross & Drentea, 1998; Ross & Wright, 1998), and that the employed have a greater sense of self-determination than housewives (Ferree, 1976). Elder and Liker (1982) found that elderly women who had taken jobs 40 years earlier, during the Great Depression, had a higher sense of self-efficacy and lower sense of helplessness than women who remained homemakers.

What explains the association between full-time homemaking and low personal control? Bird and Ross (1993) find that, compared to paid work, homemaking is more routine, provides less intrinsic gratification, fewer extrinsic symbolic rewards, and it is unpaid. These differences account for houseworkers' lower sense of control over their lives. Bird and Ross also find that although homemakers are thanked for their work more often than male paid workers, being thanked for work does not significantly affect one's sense of control. However, housework offers one important advantage over the average paid job: higher levels of autonomy. Work autonomy significantly increases the sense of control. Were it not for their autonomy, homemakers would experience an even lower sense of control than is observed.

WORK AND FAMILY INTERACTIONS. Overall, the employed have significantly higher average perceived control than do homemakers. Not all jobs are alike, however; nor are all household contexts of employment. Critical combinations of low pay, nonautonomous working conditions, and heavy family demands (conditions faced disproportionately by women) may negate the positive influence of employment on control. Ross and Mirowsky (1992) find, first, that the difference in perceived control between employed and nonemployed depends on job conditions, including job autonomy and earnings (job authority, promotion opportunities, and job prestige are not significant). As job autonomy and earnings increase among the employed, their sense of control relative to that of the nonemployed increases. Second, household labor modifies the effect of employment on the sense of control. The higher one's responsibility for household work, the less the association between employment and control (Ross & Mirowsky, 1992). Responsibility for household work greatly decreases the sense of control associated with employment. (Household work does not decrease perceived control in itself; among people who are not employed, household work slightly increases the sense of control.) Similarly, Rosenfield (1989) finds that the role overload of mothers who are employed at full-time jobs increases the sense of powerlessness and thus increases depression. Third, the greater the household income from sources other than one's own earnings, the less the association between employment and perceived control (Ross & Mirowsky, 1992). The lower the household income available from other sources, the greater the sense of control associated with having a job compared to not having one. Although other household income increases the sense of control, it decreases the positive effect of one's own employment on the sense of control.

The sense of control predicted for the employed who have low earnings and autonomy (a standard deviation below average) and major responsibility for household chores (a standard deviation above average) is actually lower than the average sense of control than among people who are not employed. At the other extreme, the sense of control predicted for the employed with high earnings and autonomy and low responsibility for household chores is very high, much higher than among the nonemployed.

Job autonomy, earnings, responsibility for household work, and other family income combine to make the association between employment and the sense of control greater for most men than for most women. Men have higher autonomy and earnings, less responsibility for household work, and lower amounts of other household income. Because of the differences in these factors, employment increases the expected sense of control most for married males, followed by nonmarried males, then nonmarried females, and finally married females. For married women, the typical combination of low pay, low autonomy, high responsibility for household chores, and high family income other than personal earnings nearly negates the positive association between employment and the sense of control.

MARRIAGE AND CHILDREN. There is not much research on the ways that family affects women's or men's sense of control over their lives. Ross (1991) finds that marriage has different effects on the sense of control for women than it does for men, and that among women being married increases the expected sense of control in some ways but decreases it in other ways. Adjusting for household income, nonmarried women have a significantly greater sense of control than both men and married women. Ordered from a low to a high sense of control are married females, nonmarried males, married males, and nonmarried females. Everything else being equal, marriage decreases perceived control among women, but not among men. However, everything else is not really equal. Married women have much higher household incomes than do nonmarried women. Thus marriage represents a trade-off for women: It is associated with high household income, which increases perceived control, but it decreases personal control in other ways. The reverse, of course, is true for nonmarried women, who have low household incomes, but otherwise have something (perhaps independence or a lack of subordination) that increases their sense of control. "The economic well-being of married women carries a price, paid in personal control" (Ross, 1991, p. 837). The cost of marriage could be due to direct negative effects on women's autonomy, but some of the negative effect of marriage is due to the circumstances of married women's employment, which is usually combined with heavy responsibilities for household work, as described above.

Theory suggests that the presence of children in the household is associated with low levels of personal control among parents, especially mothers, because children limit freedom, impose constraints, and decrease the ability to maintain an ordered, predictable, and controlled world (Gove & Geerken, 1977). However, there is little evidence of a detrimental effect of children on perceptions of control among women. Overall, the number of children in the household have no significant effect on women's sense of control (Ross, 1991), and have no effect on the sense of control among middle-age Black mothers (Coleman, Antonucci, Adelmann, and Crohan 1987). Children born to mothers under the age of 19 decrease self-efficacy, but children born to women over the age of 19 do not (McLaughlin & Micklin, 1983).

REEXAMINING GENDER. Theory predicts that women have a lower sense of control than men. Adult statuses disadvantage women in terms of objective powerlessness, economic dependence, routine and unfulfilling work, and role overload. Women's positions at work, in households, and in the interactions between the two spheres provide empirical support for explanations of why women would have lower perceived control than men. Women are more likely to be homemakers; and if employed, women's jobs pay less, provide less autonomy, and are frequently combined with household responsibilities that produce role overload. These conditions are associated with low personal control. On the other hand, some research does not find significant differences between men and women in their levels of personal control. These results mean that (1) something else, as yet unidentified, about women's lives offsets the negative conditions, and increases perceived control, (2) under some, as yet unidentified, conditions women have higher levels of control than do men. Identifying these conditions is a fruitful area for research. The fact that nonmarried women who have household incomes on par with married women (an unusual group) have high levels of personal control hints at a route for future research. Another fruitful path relates to age, described next. If younger generations of women have work and education levels more equal to men's, maybe the gap between men and women in perceived is greater among older persons than younger.

AGE. Recent research using large representative samples of persons across the full range of adult ages, from 18 to 90, shows that older adults have a lower sense of control than do younger adults, and that perceived control decreases with age at an accelerating rate (Mirowsky, 1995). Prior studies had produced inconsistent and often contradictory results. In a review, Lachman (1986) concluded that about one third of studies found low levels of control among the elderly, one third found high levels, and one third found no association between age and the sense of control. Rodin (1986) also concluded that there was little evidence that perceived control decreased with age. Inconsistencies in these psychology studies may have resulted from the use of truncated, noncomparable, unrepresentative, and small samples. Many samples contained only elderly, so the comparative data showing higher levels of control among the young and middle-aged was unavailable; and even samples with comparison often used unrepresentative groups of young people (like college students) or elderly (like health plan members). Bias in the measures of perceived control may have also accounted for inconsistencies. Sometimes questions about planning, orderliness, perseverance, self-discipline, achievement, and the like were used to measure perceived control. Although perceived control may be correlated with these things, it is not the same, and many of these things like planning, orderliness, and so on increase with age, and confound associations with perceived control. Finally, indexes that do not account for agreement tendencies obscure the relationship between age and perceived control because older persons are much more likely to agree to statements regardless of content than are younger persons (Mirowsky, 1995; Mirowsky & Ross, 1996).

Why would older persons feel less control over their lives than younger? Rodin (1986a,b) suggests three possible explanations for a negative association between age and the sense of control: loss of meaningful relationships, a deterioration of health and physical functioning, and dependency created and enforced through contact with health professionals that prefer compliant patients. In support of that view, we find that declines in health and physical functioning and widowhood decrease perceptions of control and explain much of the association (Mirowsky, 1995; Mirowsky & Ross, 1999), although Wolinsky and Stump's (1996) test of Rodin's explanations finds little support for any of them. All the researchers conclude that some of the apparent aging effect is really due to cohort differences: Older cohorts have lower levels of education, which explains much of the association between age and the sense of control (Mirowsky, 1995; Wolinsky & Stump, 1996). In addition, older persons are less likely to be employed and more likely to be retired, which decreases perceived control, in part because the daily activities of retirees are comparatively isolated and routine (Ross & Drentea, 1998).

Consequences of the Sense of Personal Control

People with high levels of personal control have low levels of psychological distress (Aneshensel, 1992; Gecas, 1989; Mirowsky & Ross, 1986, 1989; Pearlin et al., 1981; Ross & Mirowsky, 1989; Wheaton, 1980, 1983). Distress tends to be elevated among people who believe they have little influence over the things that happen to them, what is going to happen will happen, we might as well decide what to do by flipping a coin, and success is mostly a matter of getting good breaks. In comparison, distress is low among those who believe that when they make plans they can make them work, misfortunes result from the mistakes they make, there is really no such thing as luck, and what happens to them is their own doing (Wheaton, 1980; Pearlin et al., 1981). A meta-analysis of 97 psychological studies, indicates strong and consistent evidence that a belief in external, as opposed to internal, control is associated with increased distress (Benassi, Sweeney, & Dufour, 1988).

In addition to its direct, demoralizing impact, the sense of not being in control of the outcomes in one's life can diminish the will and motivation to actively solve problems. Wheaton (1983) argues that fatalism decreases coping effort. Belief in the efficacy of environmental rather than personal forces makes active attempts to solve problems seem pointless: "What's the use?" The result is less motivation and less persistence in coping and, thus, less success in solving problems and adapting. Taking Wheaton's arguments a step further, the fatalist has a reactive, passive orientation whereas the instrumentalist has a proactive one. Instrumental persons are likely to search the environment for potentially distressing events and conditions, to take preventive steps, and to accumulate resources or develop skills and habits that will reduce the impact of unavoidable problems (e.g., driving carefully, wearing a seatbelt, and carrying accident insurance). When undesired events and situations occur, the instrumental person is better prepared and less threatened. In contrast, the reactive, passive person ignores potential problems until they actually happen, making problems likely to occur and leaving the person unprepared when they do. Furthermore, passive coping, such as trying to ignore the problem until it goes away, fails to limit the consequences of the problems. Thus, the instrumentalist is constantly getting ahead of problems whereas the fatalist is inevitably falling behind. The theoretical result is a magnification of differences: Fatalists suffer more and more problems, reinforcing their perceived powerlessness and thus producing escalating passivity in the face of difficulties, and more and more distress.

Together, perceived powerlessness and distress negatively impact health. Emotional distress worsens health and poor health in turn is distressing (Aneshensel, Frerichs, & Huba, 1984). Furthermore, perceived control shapes health apart from distress. People with high levels of personal control are effective forces in their own lives. According to the theory of personal control, control's benefit lies in effectiveness (Mirowsky & Ross, 1986, 1989; Ross & Sastry, 1999). Instrumental persons are likely to accumulate resources and to develop skills and habits that prevent avoidable problems and reduce the impact of unavoidable problems. One consequence is better health. The sense of personal control improves health in large part by way of health-enhancing behaviors. Compared to people who feel powerless to control their lives, people with a sense of personal control know more about health, they are more likely to engage in healthy behaviors like quitting smoking, exercising, walking, maintaining a normal weight, and drinking moderately, and, in consequence, they have better self-rated health, better physical functioning, fewer illnesses, and lower rates of mortality (Mirowsky & Ross, 1998; Seeman & Lewis, 1995; Seeman & Seeman, 1983; Seeman et al., 1988).

Next we address some questions about potential modifications of the basic association between perceived control and distress. Is the sense of control over both positive and negative outcomes associated with low distress? Is there such a thing as too much perceived control? What are the interrelationships among perceived control, social support, and distress? Do perceptions of personal control interact with beliefs about the amount of control others have in their effect on distress?

CONTROL OVER GOOD AND BAD OUTCOMES. It is not hard to believe that perceptions of control over good outcomes reduce distress, but does belief in responsibility for one's failures also reduce distress? The answer is "yes." Perceived control over both good and bad outcomes are associated with low levels of depression (Bulman & Wortman, 1977; Krause & Stryker, 1984; Mirowsky & Ross, 1990b). Increases in the belief that "I am responsible for my failures" and "My misfortunes result from the mistakes I have made" have as large and *negative* association with depression as do the beliefs that "I am responsible for my own successes" and "I can do just about anything I set my mind to." Denying responsibility for failure does not protect well-being; it is associated with as much depression as denying responsibility for success. Claiming control of both success and failure is associated with low levels of depression (Mirowsky & Ross, 1990). In contrast there is no measurable benefit from claiming responsibility for success while denying responsibility for failure (self-defense). Furthermore, the perception that positive outcomes are due to chance is as distressing as the perception that negative outcomes are due to chance. The sense that good outcomes are unpredictable, random, and due simply to luck is distressing, probably because it implies that the individual cannot increase the likelihood of his or her own success.

DIMINISHING RETURNS. Is there such a thing as too much perceived control? The idea of a threshold of dysfunction implies that there are diminishing subjective returns to an increasing sense of control, with a limit beyond which it increases distress (Wheaton, 1985b). According to this view, the emotional benefits of a sense of control are largely the consequence of effective action. Effectiveness requires a combination of motivation and realistic appraisal. A greater sense of control implies greater motivation, but an excessive sense of control implies an unrealistic self-appraisal. Distress is minimized by a sense of control that balances motivation and realism. The threshold of dysfunction is the point at which the problems caused by illusory control exactly cancel the benefits from greater motivation (Mirowsky & Ross, 1990a, p. 1516). Wheaton (1985b) found support for this idea in a parabolic model of perceived control (the linear term was significant and negative and the quadratic term was significant and positive), with the minimum depression occurring when perceived control was at about the 80th percentile. Taking this idea a step further, Mirowsky and Ross (1990a) asked whether diminishing benefits to psychological well-being from high levels of control result from illusory control, but not real control. Control perceptions predicted by status (income, education, age, and minority status) are considered realistic; perceptions not attributable to social status are considered illusory. We find that the diminishing returns to high perceived control apply only to the sense of control not attributable to status. There are no diminishing subjective returns to a greater sense of control due to greater status.

SOCIAL SUPPORT AND THE SENSE OF CONTROL.   In addition to perceived control, social support is the other main link between social position and emotional well-being. What are the interrelationships among perceived control, support, and distress? Ross and Mirowsky (1989) describe three views of the relationship between control and support as sources of well-being: *displacement, facilitation*, and *functional substitution*. According to the first view, social support detracts from control and displaces active problem solving. Social support implies a network of reciprocity and mutual obligation that limits instrumental action while fostering dependence. People who solve their own problems have a greater sense of control and self-esteem and are more effective in solving problems than those who turn to others (Brown, 1978). Pearlin and Schooler (1978) conceptualize turning to others as the opposite of self-reliance, and they find that those who rely on themselves to solve their own problems have lower levels of distress than those who turn to others. According to the second view, social support facilitates problem-solving and instrumental action. The importance of support is not that one leans on others in times of trouble, but that perceptions of support give people the courage to act. This perspective would account for the finding that distress is reduced by the perception of available support if needed [perceived support], but not by the actual receipt of support [received support] (Wethington & Kessler, 1986). According to the third view, support and control can substitute for one another to reduce depression. They are alternative means of reducing perceived threat. Control provides confidence in one's ability; support provides confidence in one's worth. Each reduces distress, and each reduces the effect of otherwise stressful conditions (Turner & Noh, 1983). Thus, control is most beneficial—reduces distress the most—when support is low. Similarly, support is most beneficial when control is low. One resource fills the breach if the other is absent. Ross and Mirowsky (1989) find significant negative effects on depression of control and support and a significant positive interaction between control and support. This means that the effect of personal control on depression is not as great at high levels of support as at low levels; and the effect of support on depression is not as great at high levels of perceived control as at low levels. Thus, the functional substitution perspective receives the most empirical support.

PERSONAL AND UNIVERSAL CONTROL.   Personal and universal control significantly interact in their effects on depression. Belief in universal control, the belief that other

Americans control their own lives, is related to a belief in the dominant American ideology of a meritocratic system in which there is ample opportunity for people to succeed if they work hard, on one end of the continuum, compared with a belief that the system is unfair and biased, on the other. Mirowsky et al. (1996) find that people with below-average personal control have lower depression, the more strongly they believe that most Americans control their own lives. People who feel unable to control their own lives are less depressed, not more depressed, if they think *most* Americans control their own lives. This interaction corroborates the view that control in principle is better than no control at all. It contradicts the view suggested by "revised learned helplessness" theory (Abramson, Seligman, & Teasdale, 1978; Peterson & Seligman, 1984) that people feel better about their own powerlessness if they regard it as systemic and universal, excusing themselves from responsibility for a helplessness shared by all. Belief that structural barriers and powerful others hinder achievement for other Americans does not mitigate the depressive effect of personal powerlessness. On the contrary, it exacerbates this effect: Americans who feel powerless find no comfort in the apparent powerlessness of others. Blaming fate or the system does not make people feel better, nor does blaming the successful. These results suggest that it is especially distressing to believe that most people's problems are caused by others who are selfish, greedy, or mean and that the people who have good things do not deserve them.

SUMMARY.   Looking broadly at theory and findings, we see that a sense of mastery and control are associated with achievement, status, education, employment, income, and work that is autonomous, unsupervised, complex, and creative, whereas fatalism and a sense of powerlessness are associated with failure, barriers to achievement, dependence, poverty, disadvantage, economic hardship, poor health and physical impairment, heavy family demands, work overload and work/family conflict, and work that is simple, routine, and closely supervised. People in higher socioeconomic positions tend to have a sense of personal control and people in lower socioeconomic positions a sense of personal powerlessness. This produces socioeconomic, gender, parenthood, and age differences in distress. Patterns of perceived control also help explain some of the beneficial effects of marriage relating to better economic circumstances of the married, but the rest of marriage's beneficial effect is probably due to social support. The sense of powerlessness can be depressing and demoralizing in itself, but worse than that it can undermine the will to seek and take effective action. As a result, the disadvantaged have a triple burden: First, they have more problems to deal with; second, their personal histories are likely to have left them with a sense of powerlessness, and; third, that sense of powerlessness discourages them from martialing whatever energy and resources they do have in order to solve their problems. The result for many is a multiplication of despair.

TRUST

Defining and Measuring Trust and Mistrust

Trust is a belief in the integrity of other people. Trusting individuals expect that they can depend on others (Rotter, 1980). They have faith and confidence in other people. Mistrust, the opposite of trust, is the cognitive habit of interpreting the intentions and behavior of others as unsupportive, self-seeking, and dishonest (Mirowsky & Ross, 1983). Mistrust is an absence of faith in other people based on a belief that they are out for their own good and will exploit or victimize you in pursuit of their goals. Mistrusting individuals believe it is safer to keep their distance from others, and suspicion of other people is the central cognitive component of mistrust (Kramer, 1999). Trust and mistrust express inherently social beliefs about relationships with other people. Trust and mistrust embody learned, generalized expectations about other people's behaviors that transcend specific relationships and situations (Barber, 1983; Gurtman, 1992; Rotter, 1971; Sorrentino, Holmes, Hanna, & Sharp, 1995).

One short mistrust scale sums the number of days in the past week respondents "felt it was not safe to trust anyone," "felt suspicious," and "felt sure everyone was against you" (Mirowsky & Ross, 1983). This scale only asks about the mistrust end of the trust–mistrust continuum, which is a limitation, although it has the advantage of being a likert scale. The GSS includes three forced-choice questions about trust: "Do you think most people would try to take advantage of you if they got a chance, or would they try to be fair?" (Coded take advantage vs. fair) "Would you say that most of the time people try to be helpful, or that they are mostly just looking out for themselves?" (Coded helpful vs. look out for themselves), and "Generally speaking would you say that most people can be trusted or that you can't be too careful in dealing with people?" (Coded can trust vs. can't be too careful) (Brehm & Rahn, 1997; Paxton, 1999). Respondents do not like forced-choice questions, and forced dichotomies also eliminate real variation in beliefs. Likert scales indicate respondents are not very mistrusting, but forced-choice scales indicate that respondents do not endorse statements that others are fair and helpful, either (Mirowsky & Ross, 1983; Paxton, 1999). More work is needed on the development of trust scales. Despite interest in trust and mistrust, little research has been done on the measurement of mistrust, or on the structural causes of mistrust. Recently we developed and tested a theory about social structure and trust, described next (Ross, Mirowsky, & Pribesh, 2001).

Social Conditions that Generate Mistrust: Scarce Resources, Threat, and Powerlessness

Mistrust and trust imply judgments about the likely risks and benefits posed by interaction. How do people make decisions about interaction when it is uncertain whether other people can be trusted? Three things theoretically influence the level of trust: scarce resources, threat, and powerlessness (Ross et al., 2001). Where the environment seems threatening, among those who feel powerless to avoid or manage the threats, and among those with few resources with which to absorb losses, suspicion and mistrust seem well-founded. Mistrust makes sense where threats abound, particularly for those who feel powerless to prevent harm or cope with the consequences of being victimized or exploited. Furthermore, for people with few resources, the consequences of losing what little one has will be devastating. Those with little cannot afford to loose much, and need to be vigilant in defense of what little they have. If so then mistrust will be more common among persons who live in threatening environments; among individuals who feel powerless to prevent or deal with the consequences of harm; and among the disadvantaged, who live in disadvantaged neighborhoods with high levels of threat, and who have few individual resources to make up for any losses.

DISORDER, POWERLESSNESS, AND THE STRUCTURAL AMPLIFICATION OF MISTRUST. Through daily exposure to a threatening environment, where signs of disorder are common, residents come to learn that other people cannot be trusted (Ross et al., 2001). Neighborhoods with high levels of disorder present residents with observable signs and cues that social control is weak (Skogan, 1986, 1990). In these neighborhoods, residents report noise, litter, crime, vandalism, graffiti, people hanging out on the streets, public drinking, run-down and abandoned buildings, drug use, danger, trouble with neighbors, and other incivilities associated with a breakdown of social control. In neighborhoods with a lot of disorder, residents often view those around them with suspicion, as enemies who will harm them rather than as allies who will help them.

Neighborhood disadvantage is associated with mistrust because of the disorder common in these neighborhoods. Residents of disadvantaged neighborhoods—where a high proportion of households are poor and mother-only—have significantly lower levels of trust because these neighborhoods often have high levels of disorder (Ross et al., 2001).

Neighborhood disorder also reinforces a sense of powerlessness that makes the effect of disorder on mistrust even worse (Ross et al., 2001). Perceived powerlessness is the sense that one's own life is shaped by forces outside ones control. It's opposite, the sense of personal control, is the belief that you can and do master, control, and shape your own life. Exposure to uncontrollable, negative events and conditions in the neighborhood in the form of crime, noise, vandalism, graffiti, garbage, fights, and danger promote and reinforce perceptions of powerlessness. In neighborhoods where social order has broken down, residents often feel powerless to achieve a goal most people desire—to live in a clean, safe environment free from threat, harassment, and danger (Geis & Ross, 1998).

The sense of powerlessness reinforced by a threatening environment amplifies the effect of that threat on mistrust, whereas a sense of control would moderate it. At heart, individuals who feel powerless feel awash in a sea of events generated by chance or by powerful others. They feel helpless to avoid undesirable events and outcomes, as well as powerless to bring about desirable ones. Individuals who feel powerless may feel unable to fend off attempts at exploitation, unable to distinguish dangerous persons and situations from benign ones, and unable to recover from mistaken complacency. In contrast those with a sense of personal control may feel that they can avoid victimization and harm and effectively cope with any consequences of errors in judgment. Neighborhood disorder signals the potential for harm. Some people feel they can avoid harm, or cope with it. Neighborhood disorder generates little mistrust among individuals who feel in control of their own lives, but a great deal among those who feel powerless.

Thus mistrust emerges in disadvantaged neighborhoods with high levels of disorder, among individuals with few resources who feel powerless to avoid harm (Ross et al., 2001). Mistrust is the product of an interaction between person and place, but the place gathers those who are susceptible and intensifies their susceptibility. Specifically, disadvantaged individuals generally live in disadvantaged neighborhoods where they feel awash in threatening signs of disorder. Among individuals who feel in control of their own lives, neighborhood disadvantage and disorder produce little mistrust. However, neighborhood disorder impairs residents' ability to cope with its own ill effect by also producing a sense of powerlessness. Neighborhood disorder destroys the sense of control that would otherwise insulate residents from the consequences of disorder. Thus, the very thing needed to protect disadvantaged residents from the negative effects of their environment—a sense of personal control—is eroded by that environment. This is an instance of what we call structural amplification.

STRUCTURAL AMPLIFICATION. Structural amplification exists when conditions undermine the personal attributes that otherwise would moderate their undesirable consequences. The situation erodes resistance to its own ill effect. More generally, it exists when a mediator of the association between an objective condition and a subjective belief or feeling also amplifies the association. The mediator of an undesirable effect is also a magnifier of that effect.

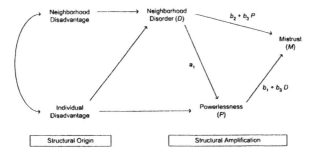

FIGURE 17-2. The structural amplification of mistrust (from Ross et al., 2001).

Mediators link objective social conditions to subjective beliefs and feelings. Mediators are a consequence of an exogenous (or independent) variable and a "cause" of a dependent variable. They explain patterns. Modifiers condition associations between objective conditions and subjective beliefs or feelings, making the associations between exogenous and dependent variables stronger or weaker, depending on their level. Modifiers sometimes moderate effects, lessening the ill effects of disadvantaged or threatening conditions, but in structural amplification, modifiers amplify ill effects, making them worse. Most importantly, in structural amplification, modifiers are also linked to social conditions. Here a sense of powerlessness amplifies the association between neighborhood disorder and mistrust, but the perception of powerlessness does not just come out of people's heads without reference to social conditions. A sense of powerlessness is also a consequence of neighborhood disorder. When modifiers of the association between a social condition and mistrust result from the condition itself, this produces structural amplification (see Figure 17-2).

INDIVIDUAL DISADVANTAGE. Disadvantaged individuals live in disadvantaged neighborhoods, so research on neighborhoods and trust must take into account individual characteristics in order to establish that neighborhoods affect mistrust over and above the characteristics of the individuals who live there. Individual disadvantage also influences mistrust. Older people, Whites, employed persons, those with high household incomes, and the well-educated are more trusting than younger persons, non-Whites, those with low incomes, and those with less education; and in terms of family status, single parents have the highest levels of mistrust, followed by single people without children, married parents, and married persons without children (Ross et al., 2001). Individuals with low incomes, little education, the unemployed, minorities, young people, or single parents may lack the resources that encourage trust. In general individual socioeconomic disadvantage correlates with mistrust, with one exception. Men hold advantaged statuses compared to women, but men are significantly more mistrusting than women (Ross et al., 2001). Why men have lower levels of trust than women despite their more advantaged status is not clear. Possibly, men's relationships are less supportive and more competitive and exploitive than are women's (Turner & Marino, 1994). To the extent that men interact mostly with other men, mistrust may be warranted. In general, disadvantaged individuals are more mistrusting as a consequence of their individual disadvantage and because they live in disadvantaged neighborhoods with high levels of disorder.

Individual disadvantage is also associated with perceived powerlessness. Persons with low incomes, lower levels of education, non-Whites and those who are not married report more personal powerlessness than do people with high incomes, education, Whites, and married persons. Adjustment for perceptions of powerlessness and the way that powerlessness amplifies the harmful effect of neighborhood disorder on mistrust, largely explains the effects of income, education, and race on mistrust. Low household income, minority status, and low educational attainment show the same pattern, which we describe for the case of income: People with low incomes live in neighborhoods with high levels of disorder; they feel a greater sense of personal powerlessness partly as a direct result of their individual disadvantage and partly as a result of the threatening neighborhoods in which they live; and their perceptions of powerlessness make the effect of neighborhood disorder on mistrust even worse. This amplification of disadvantage largely explains the impact of low household income, education, and minority status on mistrust (Ross et al., 2001).

Consequences of Mistrust

The ability to form positive social relationships depends on trust. It allows pairs of individuals to establish cooperative relationships whenever doing so is mutually beneficial (Coleman, 1988, 1990; Rotter, 1980). Coleman emphasizes trust as an element of social capital, because trusting social relationships help produce desired outcomes. Sampson and his colleagues also emphasize trust in their definition of collective efficacy: the mutual trust and social bonds among neighbors that are likely to be effective in decreasing crime (Sampson, Raudenbush, & Earls, 1997). People who trust others form personal ties and participate in voluntary associations more often than do mistrusting individuals (Brehm & Rahn, 1997; Paxton, 1999). Trusting individuals are themselves more trustworthy and honest and are less likely to lie and harm others (Gurtman, 1992; Rotter, 1971, 1980) so that they create and maintain environments of trustworthiness—without which the social fabric cannot hold (Putnam, 1995). Trusting people enter relationships with the presumption that others can be trusted until they have evidence to the contrary. (Given contrary evidence, though, they are not gullible [Rotter, 1971, 1980].) Because trusting individuals can form effective associations with others, the presumption of trust can be an advantageous strategy, despite the fact that expecting people to be trustworthy is risky (Molm, Takahashi, & Peterson, 2000; Orbell & Dawes, 1991; Sullivan & Transue, 1999).

In contrast, the consequences of mistrust can be far-reaching and severe. Mistrust can interfere with the development, maintenance, and use of social support networks. Trust allows pairs of individual to establish cooperative relationships whenever doing so is mutually beneficial. Mistrusting individuals, on the other hand, may not seek social support when in need, may reject offers of such support, and may be uncomfortable with any support that is given. Furthermore, mistrusting individuals help create and maintain the very conditions that seem to justify their beliefs. Their preemptive actions may elicit hostile responses, and their diminished ability to participate in networks of reciprocity and mutual assistance may have several consequences: Without allies they are easy targets of crime and exploitation, when victimized or exploited they cannot share their economic or emotional burden with others, and by not providing aid and assistance to others mistrusting individuals weaken the community's power to forestall victimization and exploitation and to limit its consequences (Mirowsky & Ross, 1983).

Mistrust represents a profound form of alienation, one that has progressed from a sense of separation from others to one of suspicion of others. Furthermore, the cognitive habit of interpreting the intentions and behavior of other people as unsupportive, self-seeking, and dishonest can develop into paranoia, especially under conditions of powerlessness and socioeconomic disadvantage (Mirowsky & Ross, 1983). Paranoia is an even more profound rift with others than is mistrust. Individuals may go from a more general belief that people are manipulative and may harm them in pursuit of goals, to a more specific belief that they have been singled out as a target for persecution. "When other people in one's life have become a hostile army, social alienation is at its deepest" (Mirowsky & Ross, 1983, p. 238). Theory suggests that mistrust is associated with depression and anxiety because it implies severed social relationships.

Conclusion

Some conditions rob people of control over their own lives. Joblessness, dependency, alienated labor, victimization, disadvantage, and disorder ingrain a sense of powerlessness and mistrust that demoralizes and distresses. The most destructive situations hide from people in them the fact that everyone has a choice. However threatening or constricting the situation, it is better to try to understand and solve the problems than it is to avoid or meekly bear them as the inevitable burden of life.

REFERENCES

Abramson, L. Y., Seligman, M. E. P., & Teasdale, J. D. (1978). Learned helplessness in humans: Critique and reformulation. *Journal of Abnormal Psychology, 87*, 49–74.

Aneshensel, Carol. (1992). Social stress: Theory and research. *Annual Review of Sociology, 18*, 15–38.

Aneshensel, Carol, Frerichs, Ralph R., & Clark, Virginia A. (1981). Family roles and sex differences in depression. *Journal of Health and Social Behavior, 22*, 379–393.

Aneshensel, Carol S., Frerichs, Ralph R., & Huba, George J. (1984). Depression and physical illness: A Multiwave, Nonrecursive Causal Model. *Journal of Health and Social Behavior, 25*, 350–371.

Aneshensel, Carol S., Rutter, Carolyn M., & Lachenbruch, Peter A. (1991). Social structure, stress, and mental health: Competing conceptual and analytic models *American Sociological Review, 56*, 166–78.

Anson, Ofra. (1989). Marital status and women's health revisited: The importance of a proximate adult. *Journal of Marriage and the Family, 51*, 185–194.

Appel, Margaret, Holroyd Kenneth, & Gorkin, Larry. (1983). Anger and the etiology and progression of physical illness. In L. Temoshok, C. Van Dyke, & L. Zegans (Eds.), *Emotions in health and illness: Theoretical and research foundations* (pp. 73–85). New York: Grune and Stratton.

Averill, James R. (1983). Studies on anger and aggression: Implications for theories of emotion. *American Psychologist, 38*, 1145–1160.

Bandura, Albert. (1986). *Social foundations of thought and action.* Englewood Cliffs, New Jersey: Prentice-Hall.

Barber, B. (1983). *The logic and limits of trust.* New Brunswick, NJ: Rutgers University Press.

Benassi, Victor A., Sweeney, P. D., & Dufour, C. L. (1988). Is there a relationship between locus of control orientation and depression? *Journal of Abnormal Psychology, 97*, 357–366.

Berkman, Lisa F., & Breslow, Lester. (1983). *Health and ways of living: The Alameda County Study.* NY: Oxford.

Bianchi, Suzanne M. (2000). Maternal employment and time with children: Dramatic change or surprising continuity? *Demography, 37*, 401–414.

Bird, Chloe E., & Ross, Catherine E. (1993). Houseworkers and paid workers: Qualities of the work and effects on personal control. *Journal of Marriage and the Family, 55*, 913–925.

Booth, Alan and Amato, Paul. (1991). Divorce and psychological stress. *Journal of Health and Social Behavior, 32*, 396–407.

Bowling, Ann. (1987). Mortality after bereavement: A review of the literature on survival periods and factors affecting survival. *Social Science and Medicine, 24*, 117–124.

Boyd, Jeffrey H., Burke, Jack D., Gruenberg, Ernst, Holzer, Charles E., Rae, Donald S., George, Linda K., Karno, Marvin, Stolzman, Roger, McEnvoy, Lary, & Nestadt, Gerald. (1984). Exclusion criteria of *DSM-III*: A study of co-occurrence of hierarchy-free syndromes. *Archives of General Psychiatry, 41*, 983–989.

Bradburn, Norman M. (1969). *The structure of psychological well-being.* Chicago: Aldine.

Braverman, H. (1974). *Labor and monopoly capital: The degradation of work in the twentieth century.* New York: Monthly Review Press.

Brehm, John, & Rahn, Wendy. (1997). Individual-level evidence for the causes and consequences of social capital. *American Journal of Political Science, 41*, 999–1023.

Brewin, C. R., & Shapiro, D. A. (1984). Beyond locus of control: Attribution of responsibility for positive and negative outcomes. *British Journal of Psychology, 75*, 43–49.

Brown, Brad B. (1978). Social and psychological correlates of help-seeking behavior among urban adults. *Journal of Community Psychology, 6*, 425–439.

Budig, Michelle J., & England, Paula. (2001). The wage penalty for motherhood. *American Sociological Review, 66*, 204–225.

Bulman, R. J., & Wortman, C. B. (1977). Attributions of blame and coping in the real world: Severe accident victims react to their lot. *Journal of Personality and Social Psychology, 35*, 351–63.

Clancy, Kevin & Gove, Walter R. (1974). Sex differences in mental illness: An analysis of response bias in self-reports *American Journal of Sociology, 80*, 205–215.

Cleary, Paul D., & Mechanic, David. (1983). Sex differences in psychological distress among married people. *Journal of Health and Social Behavior, 24*, 111–121.

Coleman, James S. (1988). Social capital in the creation of human capital. *American Journal of Sociology, 94*, S95–S120.

Coleman, James S. (1990). *Foundations of social theory.* Cambridge, MA: Harvard University Press.

Coleman, L. M., Antonucci, Toni C., Adelmann, Pamela K., & Crohan, Susan E. (1987). Social roles in the lives of middle-aged and older black women. *Journal of Marriage and the Family, 49*, 761–771.

Conger, Rand D., Conger, Katherine J., Elder, Glen H., Lorenz, Frederick O., Simons, Ronald L., & Whitbeck, Les B. (1992). A family process model of economic hardship and adjustment of early adolescent boys. *Child Development, 63*, 526–541.

Conger, Rand D., Lorenz, Frederick O., Elder, Glen H., Simmons, Ronald L., & Ge, Xiaojia. (1993). Husband and wife differences in response to undesirable life events. *Journal of Health and Social Behavior, 34*, 71–88.

Consumer Reports on Health. (1994). Is hostility killing you? *Consumers Union, 6*, 49–50.

Dohrenwend, Bruce P., & Dohrenwend, Barbara S. (1976). Sex differences in psychiatric disorder. *American Journal of Sociology, 82*, 1447–1459.

Dohrenwend, Bruce P., & Dohrenwend, Barbara S. (1977). Reply to Gove and Tudor. *American Journal of Sociology, 82*, 1336–1345.

Dohrenwend, Bruce P., & Shrout, Patrick E. (1985). Hassles in the conceptualization and measurement of life stress variables. *American Psychologist, 40*, 780–785.

Dohrenwend, Bruce P., Shrout, Patrick E., Egri, Gladys G., & Mendelson, Frederick S. (1980). Nonspecific psychological distress and other dimensions of psychopathology. *Archives of General Psychiatry, 37*, 1229–1236.

Downey, G., and Moen, Phyllis. (1987). Personal efficacy, income and family transitions: A longitudinal study of women heading households. *Journal of Health and Social Behavior, 28*, 320–333.

Elder, Glen H., and Liker, Jeffrey K. (1982). Hard times in women's lives: Historical influences across forty years. *American Journal of Sociology, 88*, 241–269.

Elo, Irma T., & Preston, Samuel H. (1996). Educational differentials in mortality: United States, 1979–85. *Social Science and Medicine, 42*, 47–57.

Erikson, Kai. (1986). On work and alienation. *American Sociological Review, 51*, 1–8.

Fox, J. W. (1980). Gove's specific sex-role theory of mental illness. *Journal of Health and Social Behavior, 21*, 260–267.

Ferree, M. M. (1976). Working class jobs: Housework and paid work as sources of satisfaction. *Social Problems, 23*, 431–441.

Ge, Xiaojia, Conger, Rand D., Lorenz, Frederick O., Elder, Glen H., Montague, Ruth B., & Simons, Ronald L. (1992). Linking family economic hardship to adolescent distress. *Journal of Research on Adolescence, 2*, 351–378.

Gecas, Viktor. (1989). The social psychology of self-efficacy. *Annual Review of Sociology, 15*, 291–316.

Geis, Karlyn J., & Ross, Catherine E. (1998). A new look at urban alienation: The effect of neighborhood disorder on perceived powerlessness. *Social Psychology Quarterly, 61*, 232–246.

Glass, Jennifer, & Camarigg, Valerie. (1992). Gender, parenthood and job-family compatibility. *American Journal of Sociology, 98*, 131–151.

Glass, Jennifer, & Fujimoto, Tetsushi. (1994). Housework, paid work, and depression among husbands and wives. *Journal of Health and Social Behavior, 35*, 179–191.

Glenn, Norval D., & Weaver, Charles N. (1981). Education's effects on psychological well-being. *The Public Opinion Quarterly, 45*, 22–39.

Gore, Susan, & Mangione, Thomas W. (1983). Social roles, sex roles, and psychological distress. *Journal of Health and Social Behavior, 24*, 330–312.

Gove, Walter R. (1993). Higher rates of physical symptoms among homeless women do not appear to be due to reporting bias: A comment on Ritchey et al. *Journal of Health and Social Behavior, 34*, 178–181.

Gove, Walter R., & Geerken, Michael R. (1977). The effect of children and employment on the mental health of married men and women. *Social Forces, 56*, 66–76.

Gove, Walter R., & Tudor, Jeannette F. (1973). Adult sex roles and mental illness. *American Journal of Sociology, 78*, 812–835.

Gove, Walter R., & Tudor, Jeannette F. (1977). Sex differences in mental illness: A comment on Dohrenwend and Dohrenwend. *American Journal of Sociology, 82*, 1327–1335.

Gove, Walter R., McCorkel, James, Fain, Terry, & Hughes, Michael D. (1976). Response bias in community surveys of mental health: Systematic bias or random noise? *Social Science and Medicine, 10*, 497–502.

Gove, Walter R., Hughes, Michael M., & Style, Carolyn B. (1983). Does marriage have positive effects on the psychological well-being of the individual? *Journal of Health and Social Behavior, 24*, 122–131.

Green, Brian E., & Ritter, Christian. (2000). Marijuana use and depression. *Journal of Health and Social Behavior, 41*, 40–49.

Gurin, P., Gurin, G., Lao, R. C., & Beattie, M. (1969). Internal–external control in the motivational dynamics of Negro youth. *Journal of Social Issues, 25*, 29–53.

Gurin, Gerald G., Veroff, Joseph, & Feld, Sheila. (1960). *Americans view their mental health.* New York: Basic.

Gurtman, M. B. (1992). Trust, distrust, and interpersonal problems: A circumplex analysis. *Journal of Personality and Social Psychology, 62*, 989–1002.

Hiroto, Donald S. (1974). Locus of control and learned helplessness. *Journal of Experimental Psychology, 102*, 187–193.

Horowitz, Allan & White, Helene Raskin. (1991). Becoming married, depression, and alcohol problems among young adults. *Journal of Health and Social Behavior, 32*, 221–237.

House, James S., Kessler, Ronald C., Herzog, A. Regula, Mero, Richard P., Kinney, Ann M., & Breslow, Martha J. (1990). Age, socioeconomic status, and health. *The Milbank Quarterly, 68*, 383–411.

House, James, Umberson, Debra, & Landis, K. (1988). Structures and processes of social support. *Annual Review of Sociology, 14*, 293–318.

Hughes, Michael, & Demo, David H. (1989). Self-perceptions of Black americans: Self-esteem and personal efficacy. *American Journal of Sociology, 95*, 132–159.

Hughes, Michael M., & Gove, Walter R. (1981). Living alone, social integration, and mental health. *American Journal of Sociology, 87*, 48–74.

Johnson, David Richard, & Meile, Richard L. (1981). Does dimensionality bias in langner's 22-item index affect the validity of social status comparisons? *Journal of Health and Social Behavior, 22*, 415–433.

Julius, Mara, Harburg, Ernest, Cottington, Eric, & Johnson, Ernest. (1986). Anger, coping types, blood pressure and all-cause mortality: A follow-up in Tecumseh, Michigan (1971–1983). *American Journal of Epidemiology, 124*, 220–233.

Kandel, Denise B., Davies, Mark, & Raveis, Victoria H. (1985). The stressfulness of daily social roles for women: Marital, occupational, and household roles. *Journal of Health and Social Behavior, 26*, 64–78.

Kaprio, Jaakko, Koskenuo, Markku, & Rita, Heli. (1987). Mortality after bereavement: A prospective study of 95,647 widowed persons. *American Journal of Public Health, 77*, 283–287.

Kessler, Ronald C. (1982). A disaggregation of the relationship between socioeconomic status and psychological distress. *American Sociological Review, 47*, 752–764.

Kessler, Ronald C., & Cleary, Paul D. (1980). Social class and psychological distress. *American Sociological Review, 45*, 463–478.

Kessler, Ronald C., & Essex, M. (1982). Marital status and depression: The importance of coping resources. *Social Forces, 61*, 484–507.

Kessler, Ronald C., & McRae, James A. (1982). The effect of wives' employment on the mental health of married men and women. *American Sociological Review, 47*, 216–227.

Kessler, Ronald C., Turner, J. Blake, & House, James S. (1989). Unemployment, reemployment and emotional functioning in a community sample. *American Sociological Review, 54*, 648–657.

Kohn, Melvin. (1976). Occupational structure and alienation. *American Journal of Sociology, 82*, 111–130.

Kohn, Melvin, & Schooler, Carmi. (1982). Job conditions and personality: A longitudinal assessment of their reciprocal effects. *American Journal of Sociology, 87*, 1257–1286.

Kohn, Melvin L., Naoi, Atsuhi, Schoenbach, Carrie, Schooler, Carmi, & Slomczynski, Kazimierz M. (1990). Position in the class structure and psychological functioning in the United States, Japan, and Poland. *American Journal of Sociology, 95*, 964–1008.

Kramer, Roderick M. (1999). Trust and distrust in organizations: Emerging perspectives, enduring questions. *Annual Review of Psychology, 50*, 569–598.

Krause, Neil, & Liang, Jersey. (1993). Stress, social support, and psychological distress among the Chinese elderly. *Journals of Gerontology, 48*, P282–p291.

Krause, Neil, & Stryker, Sheldon. (1984). Stress and well-being: The buffering role of locus of control beliefs. *Social Science and Medicine, 18*, 783–790.

Lachman, M. E. (1986). Personal control in later life: Stability, change, and cognitive correlates. In M. M. Baltes & P. B. Baltes (Eds.), *The psychology of control and aging* (pp. 207–236). Hillsdale, NJ: Lawrence Erlbaum.

Langner, Thomas S. (1962). A twenty-two item screening score of psychiatric symptoms indicating impairment. *Journal of Health and Human Behavior, 3*, 269–276.

Lennon, Mary Clare, & Rosenfield, Sarah. (1995). Relative fairness and the division of housework: The importance of options. *American Journal of Sociology, 100*, 506–531.

Lennon, Mary Clare, & Rosenfield, Sarah. (1992). Women and mental health: The interaction of job and family conditions. *Journal of Health and Social Behavior, 33*, 316–327.

Levenson H. (1973). Multidimensional locus of control in psychiatric patients. *Journal of Consulting and Clinical Psychology, 41*, 397–404.

Link, Bruce G., Lennon, Mary Clare, & Dohrenwend, Bruce P. (1993). Socioeconomic status and depression: The role of occupations involving direction, control, and planning. *American Journal of Sociology, 98*, 1351–1387.

McLanahan, Sara, & Adams, Julia. (1987). Parenthood and psychological well-being. In W. Richard Scott & James F. Short (Eds.), *Annual review of sociology* (Vol. 13). Palo Alto, CA: Annual Reviews.

McLaughlin, S. D., & Micklin, M. (1983). The timing of the first birth and changes in personal efficacy. *Journal of Marriage and the Family, 45*, 47–55.

Menaghan, Elizabeth G. (1985). Depressive affect and subsequent divorce. *Journal of Family Issues, 6*, 295–306.

Mirowsky, John. (1985). Depression and marital power: An equity model. *American Journal of Sociology, 91*, 557–592.

Mirowsky, John. (1987). The psycho-economics of feeling underpaid: Distributive justice and the earnings of husbands and wives. *American Journal of Sociology, 92*, 1404–1434.

Mirowsky, John. (1995). Age and the sense of control. *Social Psychology Quarterly, 58*, 31–43.

Mirowsky, John. (1996). Age and the gender gap in depression. *Journal of Health and Social Behavior, 37*, 362–380.

Mirowsky, John, & Hu, Paul Nongzhuang. (1996). Physical impairment and the diminishing effects of income. *Social Forces, 74*, 1073–1096.

Mirowsky, John, & Ross, Catherine E. (1983). Paranoia and the structure of powerlessness. *American Sociological Review, 48*, 228–239.

Mirowsky, John, & Ross, Catherine E. (1984). Mexican culture and its emotional contradictions. *Journal of Health and Social Behavior, 25*, 2–13.

Mirowsky, John, & Ross, Catherine E. (1986). Social patterns of distress. *Annual Review of Sociology, 12*, 23–45.

Mirowsky, John, & Ross, Catherine E. (1989). *Social causes of psychological distress.* New York: Aldine-de Gruyter.

Mirowsky, John, & Ross, Catherine E. (1990a). The consolation prize theory of alienation. *American Journal of Sociology, 95*, 1505–1535.

Mirowsky, John, & Ross, Catherine E. (1990b). Control or defense? Depression and the sense of control over good and bad outcomes. *Journal of Health and Social Behavior, 31*, 71–86.

Mirowsky, John, & Ross, Catherine E. (1991). Eliminating defense and agreement bias from measures of the sense of control: A 2×2 index. *Social Psychology Quarterly, 54*, 127–145.

Mirowsky, John, & Ross, Catherine E. (1992). Age and depression. *Journal of Health and Social Behavior, 33*, 187–205.

Mirowsky, John, & Ross, Catherine E. (1995). Sex differences in Distress: Real or artifact? *American Sociological Review, 60*, 449–68.

Mirowsky, John, & Ross, Catherine E. (1996). Age and the gender gap in depression. *Journal of Health and Social Behavior, 37*, 362–380.

Mirowsky, John, & Ross, Catherine E. (1998). Education, personal control, lifestyle, and health: A human capital hypothesis. *Research on Aging, 20*, 415–449.

Mirowsky, John. (1999). Economic hardship across the life course. *American Sociological Review, 64*, 548–569.

Mirowsky, John, Ross, Catherine E., & Reynolds, John R. (2000). Links between social status and health status. In Chloe E. Bird, Peter Conrad, & Allen M. Freemont (Eds.), *The handbook of medical sociology* (5th ed., pp. 47–67). Upper Saddle River, NJ: Prentice-Hall.

Mirowsky, John, Ross, Catherine E., & Van Willigen, Marieke M. (1996). Instrumentalism in the land of opportunity: Socioeconomic causes and emotional consequences. *Social Psychology Quarterly, 59*, 322–337.

Molm, Linda D., Takahashi, Nobuyuki, & Peterson, Gretchen. (2000). Risk and trust in social exchange: An experimental test of a classical proposition. *American Journal of Sociology, 105,* 1396–1427.

Novaco, Raymond W. (1985). Anger and its therapeutic regulation. In M. A. Chesney & R. H. Rosenman (Eds.), *Anger and hostility in cardiovascular and behavioral disorders.* Hemisphere: New York.

Orbell, John, & Dawes, Robyn M. (1991). A Cognitive Miser Theory of Cooperators' Advantage. *The American Political Science Review, 85,* 515–528.

Paxton, Pamela. (1999). Is social capital declining in the United States? A multiple indicator assessment. *American Journal of Sociology, 105,* 88–127.

Pearlin, Leonard I. (1989). The sociological study of stress. *Journal of Health and Social Behavior, 30,* 241–256.

Pearlin, Leonard I., Lieberman, Morton A., Menaghan, Elizabeth G., & Mullan, Joseph T. (1981). The stress process. *Journal of Health and Social Behavior, 22,* 337–356.

Pearlin, Leonard I., & Schooler, Carmi. (1978). The structure of coping. *Journal of Health and Social Beahvior, 19,* 2–21.

Peterson, Christopher, & Seligman, Martin E. P. (1984). Causal explanations as a risk factor for depression: Theory and evidence. *Psychological Review, 91,* 347–374.

Putnam, Robert D. (1995). Bowling alone: America's declining social capital. *Journal of Democracy, 6,* 65–78.

Radloff, Lenore. (1977). The CES-D scale: A self-report depression scale for research in the general population. *Applied Psychological Measurement, 1,* 385–401.

Reskin, Barbara F., & Padavic, Irene. (1994). *Women and men at work.* Thousand Oaks, CA: Pine Forge Press.

Reynolds, John R., & Ross, Catherine E. (1998). Social stratification and health: Education's benefit beyond economic status and social origins. *Social Problems, 45,* 221–247.

Rieker, Patricia P., & Bird, Chloe E. (2000). Sociological explanations of gender differences in mental and physical health. In Chloe E. Bird, Pater Conrad, & Allen M. Fremont (Eds.), *Handbook of medical sociology* (5th ed., pp. 98–113). NJ: Prentice-Hall.

Riessman, Kohler, Catherine, & Gerstel, Naomi R. (1985). Marital dissolution and health: Do males or females have greater risk? *Social Science and Medicine, 20,* 627–635.

Ritchey, Ferris J., La Gory, Mark, & Mullis, Jeffrey. (1991). Gender differences in health risks and physical symptoms among the homeless. *Journal of Health and Social Behavior, 32,* 33–48.

Rodin, Judith. (1986a). Aging and health: Effects of the sense of control. *Science, 233,* 1271–1276.

Rodin, Judith. (1986b). Health, control, and aging. In Margaret M. Baltes & Paul B. Baltes (Eds.), *The psychology of control and aging* (pp. 139–165). Hillsdale, NJ: Lawrence Erlbaum.

Rogers, Richard G., Hummer, Robert A., & Charles B., Nam. (2000). *Living and dying in the USA: Behavioral, health and social differentials of adult mortality.* San Diego, CA: Academic.

Rosenfield, Sarah. (1980). Sex differences in depression: Do women always have higher rates? *Journal of Health and Social Behavior, 21,* 33–42.

Rosenfield, Sarah. (1989). The effects of women's employment: Personal control and sex differences in mental health. *Journal of Health and Social Behavior, 30,* 77–91.

Rosenfield, Sarah. (1999). Splitting the difference: Gender, the self, and mental health. In Carol S. Aneshensel & Jo C. Phelan (Eds.), *Handbook of the sociology of mental health* (pp. 209–224). NY: Plenum.

Ross, Catherine E. (1991). Marriage and the sense of control. *Journal of Marriage and the Family, 53,* 831–838.

Ross, Catherine E. (1995). Reconceputalizing marital status as a continuum of social attachment *Journal of marriage and the family, 57,* 129–140.

Ross, Catherine E. (2000). Neighborhood disadvantage and adult depression. *Journal of Health and Social Behavior, 41,* 177–187.

Ross, Catherine E., & Bird, Chloe E. (1994). Sex stratification and health lifestyle: Consequences for men's and women's perceived health. *Journal of Health and Social Behavior, 35,* 161–178.

Ross, Catherine E., & Drentea, Patricia. (1998). Consequences of retirement activities for distress and the sense of personal control. *Journal of Health and Social Behavior, 39,* 317–334.

Ross, Catherine E., & Huber, Joan. (1985). Hardship and depression. *Journal of Health and Social Behavior, 26,* 312–327.

Ross, Catherine E., & Mirowsky, John. (1984a). Components of depressed mood in married men and women: The Center for Epidemiologic Studies' Depression Scale. *American Journal of Epidemiology, 119,* 997–1004.

Ross, Catherine E. (1984b). Socially-desirable response and acquiescence in a cross-cultural survey of mental health. *Journal of Health and Social Behavior, 25,* 189–197.

Ross, Catherine E. (1988). Child care and emotional adjustment to wives' employment. *Journal of Health and Social Behavior, 29,* 127–138.

Ross, Catherine E. (1989). Explaining the social patterns of depression: Control and problem-solving—or support and talking. *Journal of Health and Social Behavior, 30,* 206–219.

Ross, Catherine E. (1992). Households, employment, and the sense of control. *Social Psychology Quarterly, 55,* 217–235.

Ross, Catherine E. (1995). Does employment affect health? *Journal of Health and Social Behavior, 36,* 230–243.

Ross, Catherine E., Mirowsky, John, & Cockerham William C. (1983). Social class, Mexican culture, and fatalism: Their effects on psychological distress. *American Journal of Community Psychology, 11,* 383–399.

Ross, Catherine E., Mirowsky, John, & Goldsteen, Karen. (1990). The impact of the family on health: The decade in review. *Journal of Marriage and the Family, 52,* 1059–1078.

Ross, Catherine E., Mirowsky, John, & Huber, Joan. (1983). Dividing work, sharing work, and in-between: Marriage patterns and depression. *American Sociological Review, 48,* 809–823.

Ross, Catherine E., Mirowsky, John, & Pribesh, Shana. (2001). Powerlessness and the amplification of threat: Neighborhood disadvantage, disorder, and mistrust. *American Sociological Review, 66,* 568–591.

Ross, Catherine E., Mirowsky, John, & Ulbrich, Patricia. (1983). Distress and the traditional female role: A comparison of Mexicans and Anglos. *American Journal of Sociology, 89,* 670–682.

Ross, Catherine E., & Sastry, Jaya T. (1999). The sense of personal control: Social structural causes and emotional consequences. In Carol S. Aneshensel & Jo C. Phelan (Eds.), *The handbook of the sociology of mental health and illness* (pp. 369–394). New York, NY: Plenum.

Ross, Catherine E., & Van Willigen, Marieke. (1996). Gender, parenthood and anger. *Journal of Marriage and the Family, 58,* 572–584.

Ross, Catherine E. (1997). Education and the subjective quality of life. *Journal of Health and Social Behavior, 38,* 275–297.

Ross, Catherine E., & Wright, Marylyn P. (1998). Women's work, men's work, and the sense of control. *Work and Occupations, 25,* 333–355.

Ross, Catherine. E., & Wu, Chia-ling. (1995). The links between education and health. *American Sociological Review, 60,* 719–745.

Rotter, Julian B. (1966). Generalized expectancies for internal vs. external control of reinforcements. *Psychological Monographs, 80,* 1–28.

Rotter, Julian B. (1971). Generalized expectancies for interpersonal trust. *American Psychologist, 26,* 443–452.

Rotter, Julian B. (1980). Interpersonal trust, trustworthiness, and gullibility. *American Psychologist, 35,* 1–7.

Sampson, Robert J., Raudenbush, Stephen W., & Earls, Felton. (1997). Neighborhoods and violent crime: A multilevel study of collective efficacy. *Science* 277: 918–924.

Schieman, Scott. (1999). Age and anger. *Journal of Health and Social Behavior, 40,* 273–289.

Schieman, Scott. (2000). Education and the activation, course, and management of anger. *Journal of Health and Social Behavior, 41,* 20–39.

Schieman, Scott, & Turner, Heather A. (1998). Age, disability and the sense of mastery. *Journal of Health and Social Behavior, 39,* 169–186.

Schieman, Scott, Van Gundy, Karen, & Taylor, John. (2001). Status, role, and resource explanations for age patterns in psychological distress. *Journal of Health and Social Behavior, 42,* 80–96.

Seeman, Melvin. (1959). On the meaning of alienation. *American Sociological Review, 24,* 783–791.

Seeman, Melvin. (1983). Alienation motifs in contemporary theorizing: The hidden continuity of classic themes. *Social Psychology Quarterly, 46,* 171–184.

Seeman, Melvin, & Lewis, Susan. (1995). Powerlessness, health and mortality: A longitudinal study of older men and mature women. *Social Science and Medicine, 41,* 517–525.

Seeman, Melvin, & Seeman, Teresa E. (1983). Health behavior and personal autonomy: A longitudinal study of the sense of control in illness. *Journal of Health and Social Behavior, 24,* 144–159.

Seeman, Melvin, Seeman, A. Z., & Budros, A. (1988). Powerlessness, work, and community: A longitudinal study of alienation and alcohol use. *Journal of Health and Social Behavior, 29,* 185–98.

Seiler, Lauren H. (1975). Sex differences in mental illness: Comment on Clancy and Gove's Interpretations. *American Journal of Sociology, 81,* 1458–1462.

Seligman, Martin E. P. (1975). *Helplessness.* San Francisco: Freeman.

Simon, Robin W. (1992). Parental role strains, salience of parental identity and gender differences in psychological distress. *Journal of Health and Social Behavior, 33,* 25–35.

Skogan, Wesley G. (1986). Fear of crime and neighborhood change. In A. J. Reiss & M. Tonry (Eds.), *Communities and Crime* (pp. 203–230) Chicago, IL: University of Chicago Press.

Skogan, Wesley G. (1990). *Disorder and decline.* Berkeley, CA: University of California Press.

Sorrentino, R. M., Holmes, J. G., Hanna, S. E., & Sharp, A. (1995). Uncertainty orientation and trust in close relationships: Individual differences in cognitive styles. *Journal of Personality and Social Psychology, 68,* 314–327.

Srole, Leo, Langner, Thomas S., Michael, S. T., Opler, M. D., & Rennie, T. C. (1962). *Mental health in the metropolis: The midtown Manhattan Study* (Vol. 1). New York: McGraw-Hill.

Sullivan, J. L., & Transue, J. E. (1999). The psychological underpinnings of democracy: A selective review of research on political tolerance, interpersonal trust, and social capital. *Annual Review of Psychology, 50*, 625–650.

Tavris, Carol. (1982). Anger: *The misunderstood emotion.* New York: Simon & Schuster.

Thoits, Peggy A. (1981). Undesirable life events and psychological distress: A problem of operational confounding. *American Sociological Review, 46*, 97–109.

Thoits, Peggy A. (1984). Explaining distributions of psychological vulnerability: Lack of social support in the face of life stress. *Social Forces, 63*, 453–481.

Thoits, Peggy A. (1987). Gender and martial status differences in control and distress. *Journal of Health and Social Behavior, 28*, 7–22.

Thomas, Sandra. (1989). Gender differences in anger expression: Health implications. *Research in Nursing and Health, 12*, 389–398.

Turner, R. Jay, & Noh, Samuel. (1983). Class and psychological vulnerability among women: The significance of social support and personal control. *Journal of Health and Social Behavior, 24*, 2–15.

Turner, R. Jay, & Marino, Franco. (1994). Social support and social structure: A descriptive epidemiology. *Journal of Health and Social Behavior, 35*, 193–212.

Umberson, Debra. (1987). Family status and health behaviors: Social control as a dimension of social integration. *Journal of Health and Social Behavior, 28*, 306–319.

Umberson, Debra, Wortman, Camille B., & Kessler, Ronald C. (1992). Widowhood and depression: Explaining long-term gender differences in vulnerability. *Journal of Health and Social Behavior, 33*, 10–24.

Umberson, Debra and Williams, Kristi. (2000). Family status and mental health. In Carol S. Aneshensel & Jo C. Phelan (Eds.), *Handbook of the sociology of mental health.* (pp. 225–253). NY: Plenum.

U.S. Bureau of the Census. (2000). Profile of the nation's women. www.census.gov

Verbrugge, Lois M. (1985). Gender and health: An update on hypotheses and evidence. *Journal of Health and Social Behavior, 26*, 156–182.

Weissman, Myrna M., & Paykel, Eugene S. (1974). *The depressed woman.* Chicago: University of Chicago Press.

Wethington, Elaine, & Kessler, Ronald C. (1986). Perceived support, received support, and adjustment to stressful life events. *Journal of Health and Social Behavior, 27*, 78–89.

Wheaton, Blair. (1980). The sociogenesis of psychological disorder: An Attributional Theory. *Journal of Health and Social Behavior, 21*, 100–124.

Wheaton, Blair. (1982). Uses and abuses of the Langner index: A reexamination of findings on psychological and psychophysiological distress. In David Mechanic (Ed.), *Psychosocial epidemiology: Symptoms, illness behavior and help-seeking* (pp. 25–53). New Brunswick, NJ: Rutgers University Press.

Wheaton, Blair. (1983). Stress, personal coping resources, and psychiatric symptoms: An investigation of interactive models. *Journal of Health and Social Behavior, 24*, 208–229.

Wheaton, Blair. 1985a. Models for the stress-buffering functions of coping resources. *Journal of Health and Social Behavior, 26*, 352–364.

Wheaton, Blair. 1985b. Personal resources and mental health. In James R. Greenley (Ed.), *Research in community and mental health* (pp. 139–184). Greenwich, CT: JAI.

Williams, David R., & Collins, Chiquita. (1995). US socioeconomic and racial differences in health: Patterns and explanations. *Annual Review of Sociology, 21*, 349–386.

Wolinsky, F. D., & Stump, T. E. (1996). Age and the sense of control among older adults. *Journal of Gerontology: Social Sciences, 51B*, S217–S220.

PART V

THE INDIVIDUAL IN SOCIOCULTURAL CONTEXT

CHAPTER 18

Social Psychological Perspectives on Deviance

HOWARD B. KAPLAN

Social psychological perspectives on deviance refer to discussions of the nature of deviance and explanations of the definition, antecedents, or consequences of deviance that implicate both personal (behavioral or intrapsychic) and social (interpersonal, group, macrosocial) structures and processes. With regard to deviance, social psychological perspectives address any or all of six related questions:

1. What is the nature of deviance? That is, what are the criteria according to which particular attributes or behaviors are defined as deviant?
2. How do particular contextually situated attributes or behaviors come to be defined as deviant while other attributes or behaviors are not so defined?
3. How do people become motivated to engage in ways that are defined as deviant according to a particular set of normative standards, whether those standards are of one's own membership group, or of a group that one neither belongs to nor aspires to belong to?
4. What factors influence the acting out of motivations to deviate?
5. Having acted out initial deviance, what factors influence the (dis)continuity of deviance?
6. What are the consequences of deviance for the individual and the social systems of which the individual is a part?

The state of our understanding of the social psychology of deviance is defined by the answers to these six questions.

HOWARD B. KAPLAN • Department of Sociology, Texas A&M University, College Station, Texas 77843
Handbook of Social Psychology, edited by John Delamater. Kluwer Academic/Plenum Publishers, New York, 2003.

THE NATURE OF DEVIANCE

The very definition of deviant behavior as it is generally understood in contemporary social science is essentially social psychological. Although definitions vary widely, most social psychologists would agree that deviance refers to behaviors or attributes manifested by specified kinds of people in specified circumstances that are judged to violate the normative expectations of a specified group. Shared normative expectations refer to group evaluations regarding the appropriateness or inappropriateness of certain attributes or behaviors when manifested by certain kinds of people in certain circumstances. The term deviance is applied to attributes as well as behaviors. The very terms "disfigured," "obese," "short," and any of a variety of racial epithets connote deviant attributes.

The absence of prescribed (required) behavior or attributes, or the presence of proscribed (forbidden) attributes or behavior violates shared expectations of a specified group that certain kinds of people in certain circumstances will and should manifest certain attributes and behaviors, and will not and should not manifest other specified attributes or behaviors. Violations of normative expectations and the attribution of deviance to the quality or behavior in question, are signified by the application of negative sanctions to the people manifesting the undesirable attributes or behaviors. The presence of deviance, and indeed the degree of deviance, is indicated by the seriousness of the punitive response that is administered. The informal or formal (administered by constituted authorities) sanctions may be relatively mild (shaking of the head, an exchange of glances, or a few days in jail) or severe (ostracism or long periods of incarceration). The administration of more severe sanctions is an indication that the group considers the violations more important. If the sanctions are applied only to certain kinds of people in certain circumstances, then the implication is that the same behavior or attributes may be manifested without punitive responses by other people in other circumstances. If the sanctions are uniformly applied regardless of person or circumstance, then there are no exceptions to the rule.

In general, the rules take into account the abilities of the person to conform to the normative expectations although they need not do so. A person may be stigmatized (negatively sanctioned) for being physically impaired but would not be expected to perform as would non-impaired individuals.

A group that shares a normative system may apply their standards and negatively sanction even non-group members. Indeed, often individuals who do not belong to a group are penalized for that very reason, that is, are stigmatized (e.g., as barbarians or Philistines) by virtue of not being a member of the in-group. Depending upon the group's access to sanctions that are meaningful to the non-group members, the application of negative sanctions may have great adverse impact on the outcomes of non-group members.

The de facto deviation from the expectations of specified normative systems may be motivated or unmotivated. *Motivated deviance* arises from either of two sets of circumstances. In the first set, the person is a member of a group that defines the attributes or behaviors in question as deviant. However, because of a variety of circumstances, the person loses motivation to conform to the normative expectations of the group and becomes motivated to adopt deviant patterns that are expected to satisfy the person's needs better than conventional patterns. In the second set of circumstances, the person is a member of a group in which the attributes or behaviors under consideration are normative though other groups may define the attributes or behaviors as deviant. The person is motivated to conform to the normative prescriptions or proscriptions as one who has been socialized in the group. The person is either unaware or considers it to be irrelevant that another group judges the attributes or behaviors to be deviant. The person's motivation stems from the need to conform to group standards and to evoke approving responses from group members who share these standards for conforming to the group's normative expectations. *Unmotivated deviance* refers to instances of failure to conform to the normative expectations of the person's membership or reference groups, where the failure to conform is contrary to the person's volition. The person would conform if it were possible to do so. However, a variety of circumstances (conflicting role expectations, biogenetically given attributes, inadequate socialization, paucity of social resources) impede the individual from fulfilling the expectations of others.

Social psychological perspectives on deviance are generally aimed at explaining the antecedents and consequences of motivated deviance. Unmotivated deviance is relevant as an explanatory factor, rather than as a dependent variable. The involuntary manifestation of deviant traits and behaviors influences judgments of deviance and the administration of sanctions, as well as the correlates of these phenomena, that in turn influence the voluntary onset or continuation of deviant behaviors.

DEFINING DEVIANCE

A number of perspectives address the question of how and why certain behaviors, attributes, or classes of individuals come to be defined as deviant. This general question encompasses the more specific question of why certain laws are passed and enforced against those who perform the behaviors or display the attributes that are prohibited by the laws in question or that fail to behave in ways or display the attributes that are required by the laws.

Social groups make the rules (including laws that define specific acts performed by specific categories of individuals as deviant) the violation of which constitutes deviant behavior. It is important to understand the processes by which specific behaviors when performed by specified categories of people in specified situations come to be defined as deviant because the process is part of the explanation of the onset, continuity, and consequences of deviant behavior. The fact that certain behaviors are defined as deviant: (1) will serve (under specified conditions) to stimulate or inhibit motivation to perform deviant acts; and, (2) will evoke social responses that (depending upon moderating conditions) influence the (dis)continuity of deviant behavior. If the social definitions of deviance have these effects, it follows that any variable that influences the social definition of behavior as deviant will have indirect effects upon the onset and continuity of deviance. Deviant behavior, in turn, influences the social definition of deviance. As behavior initially defined as deviant becomes increasingly common, greater pressure is exerted to redefine the behavior as within the realm of acceptable responses.

One of the dimensions along which social psychological perspectives vary is the degree to which deviance comes to be defined as violations of consensual norms as opposed to violations of the norms of more influential segments of the population. According to the consensus perspective, in any group, agreement will be observed regarding core values and goals. Any behavior that is recognized as facilitating approximation to those values will be regarded positively and rewarded, while any behaviors or attributes that are regarded as inhibiting approximation of the values will be disvalued and punished. The criteria for the definition of deviance rest upon common recognition of consensual needs, goals, or values (Tittle, 1994). For example, if it is consensually agreed that the family as a basic institution must be protected, then behaviors that are regarded as threatening the stability or functions of this institution will be defined as deviant. Such behaviors might include extramarital intercourse or homosexual behavior (Tittle & Paternoster, 2000). Consistent with the consensus perspective are research studies that observe that widespread agreement exists as to the nature of deviance and the sanctions that should be administered for various degrees of deviance (Rossi, Waite, Bose, & Berk, 1974; Tittle, 1980). Thus, the normative structure may reflect common values as well as, or rather than, the special interests of contending groups.

> Not all legislation and administration of laws stem from compromises and victories by identifiable group interests. The core of criminal law—prohibitions for and sanctions of personal violence, destruction of property, fraud, and other predatory crimes—mirrors and protects the interests of the entire society. This core outlaws offenses that are *mala in se*, wrong in themselves, and that would be abhorred by society even if not condemned by the law. (Akers, 2000, p. 172)

While the consensus perspective focuses on commonalities in values and goals, other perspectives emphasize value differences between groups. Those groups that exercise greater influence, power, or political control are better able to impose definitions of deviance that serve the interests of the more influential groups; and, less powerful groups or segments of the populations are unable to resist the imposition of these definitions. Among the perspectives representing this point of view are the labeling, feminist, and conflict orientations.

From the labeling perspective, deviance is not a quality, a person, act, or attribute. Instead, deviance is the result of the evaluations of others, the applications of sanctions to others, and the labeling of the person, act, or attribute as deviant (Becker, 1963). People who are labeled tend to be those who have less power to resist being labeled. Defining particular acts or attributes as deviant occurs through complex processes involving among others the sponsorship and diffusion of the deviant definitions by "moral entrepreneurs" (Becker, 1963) who have a special interest in achieving widespread acceptance of the definition. A case in point is a study of the process by which marijuana use came to be defined as illegal with the passage of the Marijuana Stamp Tax Act of 1937. The passage of the law was said to be motivated by the felt need of the functionaries of the Federal Bureau of Narcotics to increase their sphere of influence. Passage of the federal felony law was facilitated by a mass media campaign to which the Bureau of Narcotics apparently contributed stories that associated marijuana use with violent behavior.

In a similar vein, various writings loosely categorized as feminist theory argue that more powerful males exercise domination over women. To that end, males define and enforce normative expectations and thereby maintain male domination in society (see Akers, 2000, chapter 10 for a review of these positions). However, research does not consistently support the existence of gender-related disparities in sanctions when important variables such as nature of offense are controlled.

Consistent with these orientations is conflict theory. From this perspective, the enactment of formal laws and the implementation of formal social controls that are legitimized by the political structure function to validate and represent the interests of the more powerful groups in the society (Chambliss, 1974; Quinney, 1970; Turk, 1964; Vold, 1958). Conflict theory addresses the question of why certain laws are passed, that is, why certain acts, attributes, or individuals are defined as criminal while others are not. Although conflict theory focuses on the genesis of laws and their enforcement, the same principles are applicable to the question of why certain normative expectations hold sway and evoke informal sanctions while others do not. That is, in any group those who are more influential by virtue of having greater control over that which is consensually valued influence definitions of right and wrong and have the capacity to coerce conformity through application of sanctions. More powerful segments of society enact laws (define normative expectations) that represent the interests of more powerful segments of the group and apply formal sanctions (or informal sanctions) to those individuals that deviate from the normative expectations that reflect the interests of the dominant or more powerful segments of the group. This position does not receive strong support from research studies that observe for each stage or criminal justice processing that race and class do not play important roles in legal sanctioning when other relevant variables are controlled. However, toward the end of the process, class and race do appear to play a role, perhaps because of accumulated effects of small differences earlier in the process, or perhaps because of the overrepresentation of more powerless groups in the chronic offender category that receive special attention from the criminal justice system (Akers, 2000).

The conflict model may be extended to the small group and interpersonal levels as well. Individuals exercise power over each other and so may require conformity to their expectations to the extent that they have access to resources that the other person requires, regardless of the nature of the resources. To the extent that one person requires affection and the other person is able to dispense it, the latter exercises power over the former. To the extent that each requires affection from the other, both exercise power over the other and they define what is appropriate and inappropriate behavior in the situation accordingly. Insofar as teachers are able to dispense grades, and students require high grades, teachers are in a position to define what is normative and deviant in the context of the classroom. However, to the extent that teachers require the respect of their students and a good reputation, students are in a position to negotiate for definitions of what is acceptable and unacceptable. From these frames of reference, then, the process by which particular behaviors come to be defined as deviant cannot be understood apart from a consideration of such major influences as diversity and political influence. In modern society, different, frequently conflicting, value systems shared by more or less inclusive segments of the population that have in common regional, racial, ethnic, social class, and perhaps maturational (age or stage of development) characteristics, exist side by side. In part, the diversity is the result of the convergence of representatives of different cultures within common geographic limits. In part, the absence of cultural consensus is the result of rapid and uneven rates of cultural change among the different segments of the population, thus ensuring that over time even in a group that initially shared a value system, diversity of value judgments would emerge.

Those segments of the population that differ in the system of values to which each segment subscribes often do not exercise equal influence in the formal institutions whereby rules are implemented and enforced. The segments of the population that are more influential are more likely to successfully implement and enforce rules that reflect their concepts of high priority values and protect their interests. Any behavior that threaten these values, although they may be compatible with the values shared by other less powerful segments of the population, will be defined as deviant. The exercise of undue political influence in the passage of legislation that reflects primarily the values of powerful minorities, is nicely illustrated by an early research report by Lind (1938). The report suggested that Westerners in Honolulu represented a politically powerful minority group that was able to legislate patterns that were contrary to the values of other groups. In particular, the high illegitimacy rate among the Polynesians was consistent with the acceptability of premarital sexual activity in this group that was contrary to the values of politically influential Westerners. Other examples are provided by Sellin's (1938) seminal discussion of the relationship between crime and culture conflict.

If diverse groups exercise equivalent power over each other, they may accommodate each other's expectations. In effect, they agree to disagree and each group conforms to its own socionormative system and regards the other as deviant without attempting to change the existing socionormative frameworks. However, where one group exercises greater influence or power over the other group and where they consider it to be in their collective interest to do so, that group may exercise sanctions that adversely affect the outcomes of the other group and, in doing so, influences at least overt conformity to the socionormative system of the more powerful group. This accommodation is tentative, however, and exists only so long as the less influential group perceives the more dominant group as capable of adversely affecting salient outcomes for the less influential group.

The recognition of the roles of cultural diversity and political influence in the deviance-defining process arguably is most apparent in conflict theory. As Farrell and Swigert summarize this perspective:

> Deviance is the result of social and cultural diversity. Modern society is made up of a proliferation of collectivities, each attempting to satisfy its own needs and promote its standards of value. By gaining access to the institutions of social control, successful competitors are able to establish their norms and interests as the dominant ones and derogate groups that would challenge their position of superiority. Nonconformity, therefore, is intimately related to the socio-political organization of society. Whether because of the cultural differences found among groups or because of the privileges and obligations that accompany the various levels of class, status, and power, minority populations are subject to deviance-defining processes that render their situation and behavior condemnable. (Farrell & Swigert, 1982, pp. 226–227)

It is likely that both consensus and conflict theories are valid in some respects and each contributes to the explanation of why certain things are defined as deviant. Core values relating to the right to be free from capricious physical harm and from theft of one's property might lead to near universal condemnation of the arbitrary taking of life or theft of property. At the same time, individual and group differences may persist in which the interests of the individuals or groups collide. In these instances it is inevitable that different definitions of deviance and morality will arise. Those who are able to exercise greater influence over shared social institutions through the exercise of power will be in a better position to define morality. However, this becomes an issue only when the ability to administer sanctions in support of the definitions of morality is able to influence salient outcomes for other groups. If groups defining deviance in one way are unable to effectively apply meaningful sanctions to other groups who do not define the behavior as deviant, then it becomes irrelevant that different definitions of deviance exist. However, insofar as one group is able to exercise coercive power over another group, then the conflicting definitions of deviance do become an issue. In any case, each group will continue to define as deviant any behavior that threatens their own interests, and will define as normative any behavior that appears to enhance the interests of their group.

MOTIVATION TO DEVIATE

A number of social psychological perspectives address the question of why individuals become motivated to engage in deviant behavior. These perspectives suggest, implicitly or explicitly, that deviant behavior will be performed if it is anticipated, whether consciously or unconsciously, that satisfaction of strongly felt needs will ensue. To say that an individual is disposed or motivated to commit a deviant act is to say that the act symbolizes for the person the achievement of a goal, and therefore, the satisfaction of a need to reach the goal. These perspectives may be divided into two categories: (1) those that address the question of why individuals become motivated to violate the expectations of their own membership group, and (2) those that address the question of why individuals are motivated to engage in behavior that is defined as deviant by other groups although the behavior conforms to the expectations of their own membership group.

Motivation to Deviate from Conventional Norms

Essential to an understanding of deviant behavior is an explanation of why people become motivated to engage in behaviors that deviate from the normative expectations of their membership group(s). Some social psychological perspectives take such motivation for granted and do not attempt to explain it. Thus, in routine activities theory (Cohen & Felson, 1979) the presence of a motivated offender is one of three elements (the other two being suitable targets, and the absence of guardians who might deter the potential offender) that must be present for deviant acts to occur. Hirschi (1969) argues that a motivation to deviate is always present and the focus of theory and research should be to explain the circumstances (namely, the weakening of social bonds) that permit individuals to act out their deviant motivations.

A much larger number of social psychological perspectives, however, address motivation to deviate as a variable to be explained. These theories of deviant behavior focus upon motivations to forestall or assuage strain associated with frustration of the ability to achieve valued ends. Among the earliest of these positions is that espoused by Robert Merton (1938) who observed a disjunction between culturally approved goals and the distribution of the social means to achieve those goals. When individuals are taught to aspire to achieve culturally sanctioned goals but are unable to approximate these goals because of the paucity of resources at their disposal, they experience strain to which they adapt in any of a number of ways. Generally, people will respond to such strain through conformity. The person will accept the culturally approved values and strive to approximate these values through the use of whatever legitimate means are available, and with greater or lesser success. Alternatively, the individual may adapt with any of a number of deviant responses. "Innovation" describes the tendency to accept and strive for culturally approved goals but to do so through the use of illegitimate means. "Rebellion" reflects the rejection of both the legitimacy of the goals and of the means that are socially approved for achieving the goals, while replacing both the goals and means with novel goals and means. "Retreatism" refers to the rejection of socially approved goals and means as this is manifested in such behavioral patterns as forms of mental illness, substance abuse, or vagrancy. "Ritualism" refers to the rejection of conventionally approved goals but maintenance of slavish adherence to the socially approved means for achieving conventional goals (recognizing the implausibility of approximating these values).

The idea that delinquent behaviors reflect responses to the failure to achieve conventional goals through conventional means is apparent in a number of theoretical formulations that might be subsumed under the rubric of subculture theories. These formulations concern the origin and functioning of subcultures in which deviant activities are endorsed. Various students of gang delinquency have suggested different deviant adaptive processes. Implicit in Sutherland's (1937) descriptions of behavior systems of crime, Shaw and McKay's (1942) discussion of criminal traditions in high delinquency areas and Cloward and Ohlin's (1960) identification of criminal subcultures is the proposition that subcultures arose in response to the need to successfully achieve the goals endorsed by the conventional society but through the use of illegitimate means that were the only effective means available to those who formed or joined criminal subcultures. The goals were conventional ones but the patterns used to achieve the goals were illegitimate.

Albert K. Cohen (1955) suggested that the inability of youths to achieve the middle-class values that they had learned in the course of the socialization process and that were reflected in the schools they attended led to a deviant form of adaptation. Rather than accepting the worth of the conventional values and adopting illegitimate means to achieve these values, the youths collectively reject the values and reflect their contempt for the values by engaging in nonutilitarian acts of aggression and vandalism and related forms of deviant behavior. As Kobrin described such a process:

> One of the several adaptive responses available to young males in this situation is to reject the imputation of inferiority and degradation by emphasizing those activities and personal traits which distinguish them from striving, upward mobile persons. The common response inaugurates new norms of conduct out of which develop the distinctive criteria of status in the delinquent group. Thus a coherent social milieu is created in which status is distributed according to success in attacking the symbol of middle-class respectability. Since property represents a central symbol of merit and virtue in the culture of this class, stealing and destructiveness become a principal though not the only form taken by the attack. (Kobrin, 1951, p. 659)

Earlier theories in the tradition tended to focus on the deviance-engendering motivation occasioned by lower class-linked frustrations. Robert Agnew (1992) offers a theory that expands the concept of strain. He distinguishes between three classes of strain that engender deviance. These include the failure to achieve positively valued goals, the removal of positively valued stimuli, and confrontation with negative stimuli. The strain that results from any of these might lead to deviance insofar as the deviant patterns function to avoid or attack the perceived source of strain. In this respect, the theory is similar to that of Kaplan (1972, 1975, 1986) who argues that deviant adaptations to stress may function to permit avoidance of experiences that lead to stressful self-devaluation, attacks upon the conventional normative structure according to the standards of which the individual is caused to devalue himself, and to substitutions of new self-evaluative standards that may more easily be approximated. Research findings are compatible with these perspectives. Thus, a general measure of strain was observed to be related to drug use and delinquency (Agnew & White, 1992); and Kaplan and Peck (1992) reported that self-derogation was related to later theft, violence, and substance use, and that these relations were mediated variously by avoidant (drug use) or aggressive (violence, theft) coping styles.

Numerous other perspectives treat deviant motivation as engendered in similar fashion. Thus, aspects of Tittle's control balance theory are also compatible with the view of deviant behavior as an adaptation to failure to approximate valued goals. A perceived deficit in the ability to exercise control in circumstances where autonomy is valued will dispose the individual to adopt deviant patterns that would permit the individual to alter the balance of control he or she is subject to (Tittle, 1995). For Tittle and Paternoster, "a desire (a) to avoid control, or (b) to exercise more control than one is subject to, constitutes the major compelling force for humans and is implicated especially in criminal or deviant behavior (2000, p. 550)." The theory assumes a predisposing need to exercise control and to escape having control exercised over one's self. A desire for autonomy together with control imbalance (a deficit or surplus of control) and basic human impulses predispose a person to be motivated to engage in deviant behavior. Thus, *deviance can be understood as a maneuver to alter control imbalances and thereby to overcome feelings of humiliation provoked by being reminded of one's unbalanced control ratio.*" (Tittle & Paternoster, 2000, p. 557, emphasis in original.)

Katz (1988) treats the motivation to deviant behavior ("seductions of crime") in terms of needs to protect one's self-esteem, encourage a desired reputation, establish autonomy, demonstrate competence, or other motives (all of which relate to the need to enhance one's self-esteem in one way or another). Similarly, Luckenbill (1977) examined the transactions leading to homicides in terms that reflected the need of individuals to protect their reputation or to attack that of others with whom they were interacting. Both the work of Katz (1988) and Luckenbill (1977) are considered to be instances of interaction analyses in which unique sets of transactions lead to motivated deviant outcomes (Tittle & Paternoster, 2000).

Marxist theories (Quinney, 1980; Taylor, Walton, & Young, 1973) are compatible with Merton's (1938) viewpoint and the perspectives of those who followed him. The Marxist point of view is interpretable as arguing that crime is stimulated by the need to survive under adverse circumstances by using illegitimate means to achieve legitimate goals. In addition to these crimes of accommodation, capitalist systems instigate violent crimes that function to reject a system that is viewed as unjust. Further, Bonger's (1969) version suggests that in the process of capitalism-driven competition, or striving for gain at the expense of others, deviance often reflects the strategy of those who successfully strive as well as the adaptations of those who fail to thrive, that is, those who are deprived. Rational choice theory (Cornish & Clarke, 1986) is also a motivational theory insofar as it focuses on projected benefits of an act as one class of variables affecting the likelihood of behavior.

Implicit in Reckless' containment theory is also the recognition of the important role played by motivation in explaining deviant behavior. He and his colleagues (Reckless, 1961, 1967; Reckless, Dinitz, & Murray, 1956) recognized the relevance of negative emotional responses to the conventional world that is associated with adversity and the attractiveness of deviance (delinquency) as alternative routes to the satisfaction of one's unfulfilled needs. Psychological impulses (dissatisfaction, hostility, and deprivation) that dispose an individual to deviant behavior are called "pushes." The attractions of deviant opportunities are termed "pulls." In a like manner, implicit in Nye's (1958) statements relating to the constraints exercised by internal and external sanctions, is the recognition that deviant behaviors represent alternative ways of meeting personal needs that are unmet with conventional groups (particularly the family).

All of these approaches seem to have in common the premise that deviant behaviors are motivated by needs to forestall or adapt to the psychological distress associated with the need to achieve desirable states that could not be achieved through conventional means. This being the case, it was perhaps inevitable that integrative perspectives would arise that encompass these approaches. Thus, Kaplan (1972, 1975, 1980, 1986, 1995, 1996; Kaplan & Johnson, 2001) argues that in the course of the socialization process, the individual learns to value the possession of certain attributes and the performance of certain behaviors as standards for self-evaluation and positive evaluation by others. In specified circumstances, some individuals may experience chronic failure to approximate valued standards and so experience distressful self-rejecting attitudes and disapproval by valued others. These circumstances motivate the individual to behave in ways that will assuage the distress associated with self-derogation and rejection by others. Although the person may well be motivated to attempt to assuage or forestall further distress through normatively prescribed mechanisms, these may prove to be ineffective in reducing the person's distressful self-attitudes. In these circumstances, the person will be motivated to seek alternative (deviant) response patterns that will function to achieve conventional values, avoid further failure and rejection by others, attack the validity of the conventional standards according to which the person was judged to have failed, and substitute new (deviant) standards that the person finds more easily achievable than the conventional standards and that evoke rewarding attitudes of approval from others in the deviant group.

Kaplan offers a theoretical approach that subsumes all of the specific forms of deviance-engendering stress under the rubric of self-derogating experiences. Motives to engage in deviant behavior whether considered as individual or collective responses are said to reflect the need to avoid self-rejecting attitudes and to maintain or promote positive self-attitudes. Specific motives to attain consensually valued goals by illegitimate means are accounted for by the need to feel positively toward one's self, a prerequisite for which is the achievement of the consensually valued goals. Motivated acts that reflect contempt for the conventional value system and endorsement of values that contradict conventional value systems are intended to function in the service of the self-esteem motive by destroying the validity of the standards by which the person failed and, therefore, which evoked self-devaluing responses. Deviant patterns that appear to be motivated by the need to retreat (whether by decreasing contact with others or by changing one's psychological state) from contact with the conventional value structure function to enhance self-attitudes by (1) avoiding continuing experiences of failure and rejection when measured against conventional standards, or (2) avoiding recognition of such failure and rejection. The attraction of individuals who are socialized according to conventional values to groups that endorse delinquent values in addition to serving any of the foregoing self-enhancing functions, provides a new set of (deviant) standards that the person can adopt, achieve, and, therefore, use as a basis for positive self-evaluation (Kaplan, 1975, 1980, 1982, 1995; Kaplan & Johnson, 2001).

The foregoing perspectives address the emergence of deviant motivations by considering adaptations to the failure to approximate the standards of one's conventional membership groups, and the consequent loss of motivation to conform to and the genesis of motivation to deviate from the conventional standards. Another group of perspectives to which we now turn considers deviant adaptations that account for deviant motivations in terms of needs to conform to the expectations of membership groups that are regarded as deviant by other groups.

Motivation to Conform to Deviant Norms

Frequently people are motivated to behave in ways that conform to the expectations of members of their own groups, but by doing so deviate from the expectations of members of other groups to which they do not belong or to which they do not desire to belong. Arguably, among the most relevant theories for accounting for the development of motivation to engage in such behaviors is social learning theory as is reflected in Sutherland's (1947) differential association perspective and the reformulations of this theory based on principles of social behaviorism (Akers, 1985; Burgess & Akers, 1966). Although Sutherland spoke of criminal behavior, the theory is clearly applicable to the performance of deviant behavior in general. Thus, deviant behavior would be regarded as learned in the course of social interaction. The person learns motives that are favorable to performing the deviant behavior along with supporting rationalizations, attitudes, and techniques for performing the deviant acts. Motivations to engage in the deviant acts depend upon learning attitudes ("definitions") that are favorable to committing the deviant act. If the person is on balance exposed to others' definitions that are favorable to the performance of the deviant behavior, the individual will be motivated to engage in the deviant behavior. Thus, if a person differentially associates with those who communicate favorable attitudes to performance of the deviant behavior, the person is more likely to become motivated to engage in the deviant behavior. This theoretical orientation clearly is applicable to explaining why individuals perform behaviors that are defined as deviant by others from outside their group but are defined favorably from within the group. In brief, differential association theory is interpretable as asserting that motivation to engage in deviant behavior is a function of exposure to norms that endorse the deviant behavior rather than to norms that decry such behavior in the course of membership group interaction (DeFleur & Quinney, 1966). As differential association theory is incorporated in and expanded upon in social learning theory, motivation to engage in particular deviant acts is explained through recourse to differential reinforcement and related principles.

The probability that persons will engage in criminal and deviant behavior is increased and the probability of their conforming to the norm is decreased when they differentially associate with others who commit criminal behavior and espouse definitions favorable to it, are relatively more exposed in-person or symbolically to salient criminal/deviant models, define it as desirable or justified in a situation discriminative for the behavior, and have received in the past and anticipate in the current or future situation relatively greater reward than punishment for the behavior. (Akers, 1998, p. 50)

A great deal of research justifies these conclusions including longitudinal studies of the causes of drinking (Akers, La Greca, Cochran, & Sellers, 1998) and smoking (Akers & Lee, 1996).

The principles of differential association describe well the mechanisms through which deviant groups and subcultures, once they arise, maintain themselves. In the previous section it became apparent that deviant groups may arise as collective adaptations motivated by distressing failure to approximate salient conventional values. Once these groups arise, however, maintenance of the groups depends on mechanisms of socialization and social control that rest on principles of differential association. These principles are suggested in the context of a number of network/subcultural perspectives. Thus, Krohn (1986) notes that social networks might be constructed around deviant activities as well as around conventional activities. Depending upon which of these is in force, behavior might be constrained in the direction of deviant activities as opposed to conventional activities. If the network is organized around deviant activities, the greater the multiplexity (the number of different relationships the actor shares in common with others in the network) and the greater the network density (the ratio of actual social relationships to possible network relationships), the greater will be the constraint to behave in a deviant direction. According to recent research, gang membership appears to stimulate deviant behavior, presumably because normative definitions within the group favor the deviant behavior, that is, behavior that is defined as deviant by other groups (Battin, Hill, Abbott, Catalano, & Hawkins, 1998).

Implicit in a series of studies of the spatial distribution of crime and delinquency and of the writings on social disorganization that grew up around these observation in the 1920s and 1930s in Chicago (Shaw & McKay, 1942) in areas of high delinquency, the residents of the neighborhoods lived under conditions that might be described as stressful characterized as they were by social change, poverty, paucity of resources, and prevalence of deviant patterns. The individual deviant responses to such circumstances may be viewed as adaptations that facilitated adjustment to these distressing circumstances. The individual adaptations to distress that take the form of deviant patterns are socially transmitted and reinforced among the current residents of the neighborhood and are transmitted to newcomers in the neighborhood and to the younger generations that grow up in the neighborhood. Thus, the deviant patterns are explained in part by social learning processes through which people conform to what is in essence a deviant subculture. Residents conform to patterns that are regarded as acceptable within the neighborhood but are regarded as deviant by groups outside of the neighborhood. Consistent with these premises, research by Gottfredson, McNeil, and Gottfredson (1991) reported that indices of social disorganization's relationship to delinquency were mediated by deviant peer associations among other variables.

Once deviant subcultures arise, whether as collective responses to adversity (Cohen, 1955) or otherwise, the collective adaptive responses tend to have a life of their own. These adaptations have the force of morality. Conformity to the rules of the right ways of behaving is rewarded, while deviation from the rules is punished in terms that are valued or disvalued by the group members. If the members of the group ever recognized the origins of the collective responses, they have long since forgotten them. New members who are attracted to the group learn what it takes to be accepted and otherwise rewarded by the group. They adopt the patterns and help pass them on to still other new members of the group. The values attached to the behaviors and the goals of the group are now independent of any values they may once have had and they continued to have in resolving the original needs of the collectivity that gave birth to the subculture.

A person may be born into and reared in a group that views deviant patterns as compatible with traditional group values. The individuals are socialized to recognize the appropriateness of these responses and are motivated to behave accordingly in order to continue to evoke rewarding responses from group members. If any incongruity is noted between the group definition of the behavior as appropriate and the definition by the more inclusive society of the behavior as deviant, then group justifications are provided that neutralize the perceived discrepancy.

An alternative route to the adoption of deviant subcultures is provided by circumstances in which a person who is reared in a more conventional group becomes attracted to, and a member of, a group that defines deviant behaviors as appropriate. The attractiveness of the group is due to the anticipation that important needs will be satisfied by the adoption of the subculture. The satisfactions may be directly tied to the deviant patterns endorsed by the group. For example, vandalism or the very act of affiliation with the subculture that endorses deviant acts may serve to express the person's contempt for conventional standards by the measure of which the person must necessarily judge himself a failure. By rejecting the standards, the person feels it unnecessary to continue to feel unworthy.

However, the performance of the deviant act may be incidental to the gratification achieved from adoption of the subculture. Conforming to the deviant subcultural norms represents ways of earning group approval. That some of the norms happen to require behavior defined as deviant by the inclusive culture is incidental to the group approval that is earned. In any case, whether the person is attracted to the group because of intrinsically satisfying deviant behaviors or because of the potential satisfactions to be gained from group acceptance, the person is motivated to remain a part of the group.

Another set of perspectives addresses the circumstances surrounding the development of dispositions to perform deviant acts that are defined as deviant by other groups but nevertheless conform to the expectations of groups to which the individual belongs or wishes to belong. The deviant behaviors reflect the values of these groups. The individual is motivated to perform those behaviors that reflect group norms in order to gain the satisfaction associated with the behaviors themselves, the approval of other group members for performing the behaviors, and the person's identification with a positive reference group. These perspectives, along with the previously discussed set, address the genesis of motivation to engage in deviant activities. However, not all motives to engage in deviant behavior in fact lead to the expression of deviance. What factors, then, facilitate or impede the acting out of deviant motives?

ACTING OUT DEVIANT MOTIVES

Not all people who are disposed or motivated to behave in deviant fashion actually perform deviant acts. The perspectives that address the question of why individuals who are motivated to engage in deviant acts do or do not actually engage in them, have been classified into two categories (Kaplan, 1984). Whether or not a person acts out the motivation to commit deviant acts is viewed as depending upon (1) the strength of the motives to commit the act as compared to the strength of the motives that dispose a person not to perform the act, that is, counteracting motives, and (2) the situational context and other opportunities to perform the act.

Counteracting Motives

Whether or not a person actually performs the deviant behavior that the person is motivated to perform depends in part upon the strength of counteracting motives to perform the deviant behavior. In the course of the socialization process, the individual learns to need the approval of other people, to conform to the expectations associated with important social identities, to do what is right, and a variety of other motives. If anticipated deviant behavior and the consequences of that behavior appear to threaten the satisfaction of these needs, or if it appears that the needs will be better served by not performing the deviant act, then the person will be somewhat restrained from acting in a deviant fashion.

A variety of social psychological perspectives address the question of why individuals who are motivated to engage in deviant behavior do not act out these motivations. One important class of variables that moderates the acting out of deviant impulses is considered within the context of what some have termed internal and external constraint theories (Tittle & Paternoster, 2000) and others have termed counteracting motives (Kaplan, 1984). Examples of internal constraint theories are those that assert that impulses to deviant behavior are blunted or forestalled by the counteracting effects of a good self-concept (Reckless, 1967), deficiencies in the ability to take into account potential negative consequences of the deviant acts (i.e., impulsivity) (Wilson & Herrnstein, 1985), and inadequacy in learned self-control (Gottfredson & Hirschi, 1990). Examples of external constraint theories include deterrence theory (Zimring & Hawkins, 1973) and social disorganization theory (Sampson & Groves, 1989; Shaw & McKay, 1942). Still other theories focus on both internal and external controls. Such perspectives are traceable to earlier statements of the relevance of internal and external constraints in explaining why people may not act out their motivations to engage in deviant responses (Nye, 1958; Reiss, 1951).

External social controls relate to anticipated informal sanctions by parents or other significant others or to formal sanctions administered by public agencies. Personal or internal controls refer to the threat of an individual's own conscience as an inhibitor of deviant motivations. In any case, virtually all social psychological perspectives on deviance implicitly or explicitly address the role of counteracting motives. A number of these are worthy of consideration.

Just as differential association (Sutherland, 1947) and social learning (Akers, 1985) theories are relevant in explaining why people become motivated to engage in deviant acts that are defined as deviant by groups other than their own, so do these theories become relevant in accounting for why individuals who are motivated to engage in deviant acts fail to actually perform the deviant behavior. It is conceivable that in the course of social interaction they learn normative definitions that are unfavorable to the performance of the deviant acts and are favorable toward conforming to the normative expectations of their group that preclude the performance of such acts. These learned definitions serve as counteracting influences on the performance of the deviant acts that the person might otherwise be disposed to perform. Thus, deviant behavior will occur insofar as "reinforcement, exposure to deviant models, and definitions are not offset by negative formal and informal sanctions and definitions (Akers, 1985, p. 60)."

Deterrence theory speaks to the conditions under which motivations to engage in deviant behavior are acted out insofar as it alleges that the expectation of certain, severe, and swift punishment for engaging in deviant acts administered by formal or informal agents of social control would deter acting out deviant impulses (Tittle, 1980). Earlier theories focused on the deterrent effect of formal (criminal) social sanctions. Later treatments of deterrence theory expanded the concept of deterrence to include the effects of anticipated informal sanctions such as rejecting attitudes from parents, friends, or associates. Presumably, as much research suggests, if individuals anticipated that their deviant behavior would lead to informal sanctions whether in conjunction with or independent of formal sanctions, they would be less likely to actually engage in deviant behaviors (Paternoster, 1985; Zimring & Hawkins, 1973). The deterrent effect of awareness of punishment meted out to others for deviant acts on the part of individuals who have yet to commit a deviant act is called general deterrence (Paternoster, 1985; Zimring, 1971; Zimring & Hawkins, 1973). As we will note later, deterrence theory is also relevant to explaining (dis)continuity of deviant behavior, particularly when focusing on specific deterrents in which the experience of negative social sanctions cause the person who is punished to decrease the likelihood of future deviance.

While deterrence theory focuses on the inhibiting effects of anticipated or actual adverse formal or informal consequences of projected law violations or other forms of deviance, rational choice theory focuses on the anticipated cost/benefit ratio of acting out deviant impulses. A person is more likely to perform the deviant acts that he is disposed to if the individual anticipates the benefits of the act to exceed the cost of performing the act, and will be less likely to perform the act if he perceives that the anticipated costs (imprisonment, rejection by parents and friends, etc.) will exceed projected rewards or benefits (Cornish & Clarke, 1986).

Whether or not someone who is motivated to engage in deviant acts actually performs such acts will depend in part upon the perception that certain costs will be incurred. Such costs include the likelihood of being observed and, consequently, sanctioned for engaging in the deviant act. Thus, in routine activities theory (Cohen & Felson, 1979), the likelihood of deviant acts is greater in the absence of formal or informal guardians who could forestall the deviant act by virtue of the guardian's potential for administering sanctions or causing such sanctions to be administered.

Theories relating to social bonding and social control are arguably the most manifestly relevant approaches to addressing the question of why people act out dispositions to engage in deviant behavior or fail to do so. This is so since these perspectives take for granted that the disposition or motivation to be deviant is present but that circumstances which may impede the disposition are variable. Given the motivation to engage in deviant behavior, acting on those dispositions would be inevitable were it not for countervailing social and personal controls.

On the assumption that individuals are ordinarily disposed to engage in deviant behavior, Hirschi (1969) argues that social bonds to parents, teachers, and others prevent the individual from acting out deviant motives. When these social bonds are weakened, they permit the individual to act on the pre-existing deviant motives. The social bonds consist of four main elements: (1) attachment to others; (2) commitment; (3) involvement; and (4) belief. Attachment to conventional others refers to having close emotional ties to others and caring about meeting their expectations. If one does not care about meeting expectations, then he is more likely to act out deviant impulses. Commitment refers to the investment that a person makes in the conventional normative structure and the rewards that are expected to accrue from conformity with the normative structure. The threat of lost rewards by violating normative expectations decreases the likelihood of acting on deviant impulses. Involvement essentially refers to the amount of time one expends in conventional activities. The more involved one is in conventional activities, the less one is able to act out deviant dispositions. In some sense involvement reflects the lack of opportunity to engage in deviant activities. To the extent that one is not involved in conventional activities, one has the opportunity to engage in the deviant activities to which one is disposed. Belief refers to the approval or acceptance of the conventional normative structure. One conforms to the rules of the social order because they are believed to be right, fitting, and proper. To the extent that the belief in the rightness of the normative order is weakened, the person is enabled to act out any dispositions to deviate that individual is subject to. The elements of social bonding theory may be interpreted as asserting that alternative conventional motives counteract deviant dispositions. That is, individuals learn these motives that have greater affective significance in the hierarchy of values than the deviant behaviors or the goals that can be achieved by deviant behavior.

In general, research findings are consistent with many of the premises of social bonding theory, particularly those relating to attachment, commitment, and belief in the family and other membership groups (Evans, Cullen, Dunaway, & Burton, 1995; Loeber & Stouthamer-Loeber, 1986).

Much of contemporary theory and research on social disorganization focuses upon the impact of social disorganization on diminishing social controls or, in some cases, defines social disorganization in terms of disruption of mechanisms of social control (Bursik, 1988; Gottfredson et al., 1991; Sampson & Groves, 1989; Stark, 1987). Research by Sampson and Groves (1989), for example, observes that the influence of low social class, residential transiency, and broken homes, as well as other such factors (components of social disorganization) on deviance is mediated by indices of community supervision, membership in formal organizations, and the prevalence of friendship networks. In the absence of motives to engage in these conventional networks, dispositions to participate in deviant acts are not counteracted.

Consistent with these perspectives are self-control theory and Marxist theory. Implicit in self-control theory (Gottfredson & Hirschi, 1990) is the premise that individuals will not act out their motivation to engage in deviant acts if they are characterized by higher levels of self-control but will act out deviant inclinations if they lack self-control. Self-control characterizes individuals who received effective socialization in the course of child rearing, and low self-control is the result of ineffective socialization practices. The family is the primary socializing agency although other social institutions such as school contribute as well. Ineffective socialization or low self-control translates into motives to act out pre-existing deviant impulses that are not counteracted by conventional socialization.

Within the context of Marxist conflict theory, motivation to engage in deviant acts is said to be facilitated by the erosion of social controls. This generalization is reflected in the recognition that motivation to succeed at any cost or, if deprived, to survive at any cost, is facilitated by the lack of sympathy for others that is the inevitable outcome of an economic system (capitalism) in which the profit motive is supreme. Moral sentiments that might have forestalled deviant acts are attenuated by capitalism-stimulated selfishness (Bonger, 1969).

A person is unlikely to perform a deviant act if he believes that the act is a violation of a rule that is right. The person is emotionally committed to the rule that to him reflects valued behavior (doing what is right, not doing what is wrong). The performance of the deviant act, however, does not necessarily preclude some moral commitment to the norm. It is possible to commit a deviant act in the face of a moral commitment to a rule that proscribes it if the person is able to justify the act in conventional terms. Sykes and Matza (1957) point out a number of "techniques of neutralization" by which the deviant is able to justify the violation of conventional norms. In fact, it is the apparent need to justify the violation that suggests that there is some degree of commitment to the conventional norms.

Thus, a person may actually perform a deviant act even in the face of learned attitudes that disapprove of such acts if they are able to justify the act in terms that are normatively acceptable such as by normalizing the act, absolving oneself of personal responsibility, blaming the victim, or pointing out that a higher purpose was served by performing the deviant act. The countervailing motives reflected in social bonding and social control perspectives may be neutralized to the extent that individuals who are disposed to perform deviant acts can justify those acts in terms that are conventionally acceptable. Whereas conventional values would ordinarily militate against the individual acting on deviant impulses, techniques of neutralization that justify or excuse performance of the deviant acts would permit the person to act out the deviant disposition (Sykes & Matza, 1957).

Opportunities

Given the motivation to perform a deviant act, circumstances must be such that opportunities to perform the act are present. There cannot be an act of aggression in the absence of an object of aggression, and there cannot be theft without the presence of property that might be purloined. This supposition is reflected in a number of theoretical perspectives including routine activities theory that recognize suitable objects of victimization as being one of three necessary elements for criminal acts to occur, the other two being motivated offenders and the absence of guardians (Cohen & Felson, 1979). The confluence of these items is a function of the "routine activities" that a person engages in. For example, particular patterns of work and play increase or decrease the likelihood that the opportunity to be victimized will present itself. In a later statement of routine activities theory, the significance of opportunities as an explanatory variable is more apparent (Cohen, Kluegel, & Land, 1981). Thus, the probability of criminal victimization is said to depend upon such factors as the attractiveness of, proximity to, and degree of exposure to the object of the deviant acts. Such factors, along with the absence of competent guardians that might increase costs of the act, constitute opportunities to engage in the deviant act.

The role of opportunity related factors is apparent in other social psychological perspectives on deviance as well. As noted above, the opportunity construct is reflected to some extent in the component of social bonding that Hirschi (1969) refers to as involvement, that is, the degree to which one spends time in conventional activities. The more one is involved with conventional activities, the less opportunity (time) one has to engage in any deviant activities to which one is inclined.

Cloward and Ohlin (1960) recognized that the acting out of deviant dispositions depends upon the availability of illegitimate opportunity structures just as the ability to act out deviant motivations depends upon the availability of legitimate opportunity structures. In order to act out delinquent patterns, the potential deviant actors must have available to them illegitimate opportunities in their community. Depending on the social organization of the neighborhoods, illegitimate opportunities of particular kinds will or will not be available to the alienated individual. Cloward and Ohlin (1960) posit the existence of a variety of delinquent subcultures. The "criminal" subculture consisted of norms endorsing illegal money-making activities. The formation of such gangs is facilitated in neighborhoods in which stable adult criminal patterns are observed. "Conflict" gangs are those in which individuals gain prestige through their abilities and willingness to engage in violent activities. In the absence of alternative legitimate or illegitimate opportunities, the availability of such gangs invites participation by alienated youths that seek to enhance their reputation by conforming to violence-endorsing norms. The "retreatist" subculture is organized around patterns of substance abuse. In response to experiences of failure, the youths adapt by retreating from the sources of failure and gain recognition by participation in substance-abusing gangs. In each of these types of gangs, opportunities are presented for the individual to gain status through illegitimate means. Whether or not the individual engages in these activities depends upon the pre-existence of such subcultures.

Other examples are provided by social disorganization and social control perspectives. The hypothesized association between social disorganization and deviant behavior has been linked to increases in opportunities to engage in such behavior that are found in areas characterized by social disorganization (Bursik, 1988; Stark, 1987). From Gottfredson and Hirschi's (1990) perspective, deviant dispositions will eventuate in deviant behavior under conditions of weak self-control. However, although opportunities are said to be plentiful, they must be present for deviant behavior to occur even in the presence of weak self-control. In short, crimes are more likely to occur whenever and wherever opportunities to commit such crimes present themselves. Opportunities refer to both objective reality and subjective perception of situations that facilitate acting out deviant motives.

To summarize, motivation to engage in deviant acts depends upon the absence of countervailing motivation to conform to conventional expectations, and the presence of opportunities to act out pre-existing deviant dispositions. Deviant dispositions are less likely to be acted upon in the presence of countervailing motivations to conform to conventional expectations and in the absence of opportunities to engage in deviant acts.

(DIS)CONTINUATION OF DEVIANT BEHAVIOR

A number of social psychological perspectives address the question of whether the individual, having initiated deviant acts, will continue/increase or discontinue/decrease involvement in deviant activities. Social learning theory is applicable to the question of why people (dis)continue deviant behavior by stating that repetition of deviance occurs because of differential reinforcement by which individuals are rewarded or punished (whether physically or symbolically) for engaging in deviant acts. Past reinforcement, whether actually or vicariously experienced, will lead the individual to desist from or continue the act depending upon whether past experiences were punitive or rewarding in anticipation that similar experiences will ensue (Akers, 1985; Burgess & Akers, 1966). The ability to be conditioned by differential reinforcement may in turn depend upon variability in biogenetically influenced individual traits such as impulsivity which precludes consideration of possible future adverse consequences of the deviant behavior (Wilson & Herrnstein, 1985).

Deterrence theory is relevant to a consideration of factors affecting (dis)continuation of deviant behavior insofar as it is expected that the experience of negative sanctions in response to earlier deviance will have a greater deterrent effect on continuation of deviant behavior than the absence of sanctions in response to early deviance (Paternoster, Saltzman, Waldo, & Chiricos, 1983; Tittle, 1980). Deterrent effects are more or less likely depending upon characteristics of potential negative consequences and of the psychic organization of individuals including the nature of things that people fear, the accuracy with which people perceive the likelihood of undesirable consequences, and whether or not internalized norms make deterrence irrelevant. Additionally, a number of other attributes affect the likelihood of people becoming conditioned as a result of receiving punishment for earlier infractions. Conditionability depends on such features of personality as the ability to anticipate negative consequences and to defer immediate gratification (Tittle & Paternoster, 2000).

The labeling perspective directly addresses the (dis)continuity of deviant behavior. Once a person engages in deviant behavior or is thought to do so, the person evokes negative social sanctions and, frequently as a consequence of being the object of negative social sanctions, develops a deviant identity. The development of a deviant identity increases the likelihood that the individual will become fixed in deviant patterns. That is, the continuity of deviant behavior is increased as a result of being punished for earlier deviant behavior. As Becker notes: "Treating a person as though he were generally rather than specifically deviant produces a self-fulfilling prophecy. It sets in motion several mechanisms which conspire to shape the person in the image people have of him (1963, p. 34)."

The continuity or amplification of deviant behavior in response to negative social sanctions may be thought of as "secondary deviance," that is, behavior that represents an adaptation to the stress experienced as a result of social sanctions to initial deviance (Lemert, 1967). However, continuity of deviant behavior or escalation of such behavior in response to negative social sanctions is not inevitable. Depending upon a number of circumstances, this continuation of deviant behavior as a consequence of mechanisms of social control may or may not occur.

Braithwaite (1989) suggests that whether or not a community attempts to reintegrate a deviant into society following the application of negative social sanctions moderates the relationship between negative social sanctions and continued or increased behavior. If the community attempts to reintegrate the deviant into society following the application of negative social sanctions, the negative social sanctions are not likely to lead to amplification of deviance. However, if the community does not attempt to reintegrate the deviant into society, then negative social sanctions will likely result in an increase or continuation of deviant behavior.

Kaplan (1984) integrates these and several other perspectives within a single theoretical framework. He argues that three sets of factors account for (dis)continuity of deviant behavior. The first category concerns positive reinforcement of the need to perform deviant acts. The positive reinforcement stems from the satisfactions of important needs experienced by the individual as a result of the more or less direct consequences of the deviant behavior. The second set refers to the weakening of counteracting motives or controls that previously deterred the person from performing deviant acts. The third set addresses the availability of opportunities for the performance of deviant behaviors.

Positive Reinforcement of Deviant Behavior

Deviant behavior is self-reinforcing in two respects. First, the performance of deviant behavior may satisfy important needs for an individual. Since the behavior satisfies the needs, as the needs continue or recur, the deviant behavior will continue or be repeated in the expectation that the needs will still or once again be satisfied. Second, regardless of the motivation toward the initial performance of the deviant acts, the deviant behavior creates a need (specifically a need for self-justification) that is satisfied by continuation or repetition of the deviant act. The difference is that in the former instance, a need preceded the deviant behavior that satisfied the need. In the latter case, the deviant behavior created a need that is satisfied by repetition or continuation of the deviant behavior.

DEVIANT ACTS AND NEED SATISFACTION. Frequently, the performance of deviant acts results in the satisfaction of the person's needs. These satisfactions reinforce motives to perform the deviant acts. The various needs that the person experiences have been subsumed under the more general need to feel positively about one's self (Kaplan, 1975, 1980, 1995). It has been argued that deviant acts can satisfy this need in any of several ways. The avoidance of self-devaluing experiences is a consequence of deviant acts insofar as the acts or consequent negative sanctions lead to enforced avoidance of the negative responses of people in the conventional environment. To the extent that a person spends more time with deviant peers, is incarcerated or is otherwise excluded from interacting with conventional others, he will necessarily avoid the negative reactions that he has experienced in the conventional environment in the past.

Deviant acts that involve *attacks* upon conventional institutions may have self-enhancing consequences by causing the individual to express his rejection of the values by which he in the past rejected himself. Deprived of self-acceptance by being unable to approximate conventional standards and, consequently, to earn group approval, the person would find rejection of the standards and of the group that rejected him gratifying. The deviant behavior would signify that the standards by which he formerly rejected himself were invalid.

Deviant activities may provide *substitute* patterns through which the person may more easily evaluate himself in a positive light. By associating with a group that endorses standards that are more easily attainable than those endorsed in the conventional environment, the person may gain gratification from approximating the new standards. Toward the goal of being accepted by the group, the individual behaves in ways that he perceives the group as endorsing and so earns their approval.

Deviant behavior may be positively reinforced as a result of consequences of replacing deviant sources of gratification with conventional ones. For example, deviant activities may give the individual a new sense of power or control over the environment, which leads the person to think of himself as a more effective individual; or, the person may achieve conventional goals (money, prestige) through illicit means.

DELINQUENT ACTS AND SELF-JUSTIFICATION. The initial performance of deviant acts and the negative sanctions evoked by those acts threaten important needs of individuals who are socialized in conventional society, such as the need to perceive one's self as conforming to moral standards and to be accepted by the community as one who conforms to those standards. Among the ways an individual can reduce the resulting distress are: (1) by justifying the act in conventional terms, and (2) by transforming one's identity in ways that justify the behavior as appropriate to the new (deviant) identity. Both self-justifying responses involve the continuation, repetition, or escalation of deviant involvement.

Collective justifications may be provided by the social support of others in deviant subcultures or by employing conventional neutralizing patterns that effectively normalize what would otherwise be regarded as deviant behavior. The justification of the acts in conventional terms required by the individual's socialization experiences facilitates repetition or continuation of earlier deviant acts. The repetition of the deviant behavior, in turn, testifies to the person's belief in the legitimacy of the act.

The consequences of earlier delinquent acts, including rejecting responses by others, frequently lead the person to question his or her self-worth. In order to restore feelings of self-acceptance, the person adopts a deviant identity, reevaluates that identity in positive terms, and conforms to behaviors that validate the identity. In order to accomplish this, the person selectively interacts with deviant peers who respond more positively in support of the deviant activities. The result of this process will be positive experiences associated with the deviant self-image and continued performance of deviant behaviors that are required by the now satisfying (deviant) self-image.

Weakening of Social Controls

The motives that restrain a person from initially performing deviant acts (the need for positive consequences of not performing deviant acts, and fear of the negative consequences that might occur if the deviant acts were performed) frequently are weakened by the consequences of early performance of the act. Thus, the loss of fear of adverse consequences and the weakening of the attraction to the reward of conformity permit continued involvement in the deviant activity.

LIMITED ADVERSE CONSEQUENCES.   As a result of earlier performance of deviant acts, whether or not the acts are detected, the person may observe that few of the anticipated adverse consequences in fact occur. Further, when the initial deviance is observed and harshly responded to, personal and social controls may be weakened as well. In these circumstances, the person is effectively expelled from conventional society, and hence, the interaction between the person and representatives of conventional society is markedly reduced. These acts of expulsion that serve as negative sanctions for the earlier deviance effectively preclude the observation of further wrongdoing and, therefore, the administration of further punishment for the deviant acts. By expelling the person from conventional society, he is removed from the surveillance of those who might prevent future wrongdoing by punishing the deviant acts as they are observed.

DECREASED ATTRACTION TO CONVENTIONAL VALUES.   The experience of negative sanctions in response to initial deviance (informal rejection by family or school, and the stigma associated with being the object of more formal sanctions such as being arrested) reflects both intrinsically distressful experiences and barriers to the achievement of other emotionally significant goals. On the one hand, the shame of being punished for certain infractions leads to a self-defensive rejection of the moral standards. The person is motivated by the need to evaluate himself positively, to create personal justifications for the behavior, and to ally himself with those who can offer collective justifications for the behavior. On the other hand, the rejection of the deviant by members of conventional society deprives the person of access to resources that, aside from being intrinsically valued, are means to the achievement of other valued ends. Such deprivation further alienates the person from the normative order. The person no longer cares what the representatives of the conventional order think about his behavior and so the attitudes of others no longer constrain him from performing a deviant act that he is motivated to perform. Rather, the individual becomes increasingly dependent upon deviant associates for standards of self-evaluation and for the resources for approximating the standards.

Opportunities for Deviance

The early performance of deviant acts has consequences that increase the person's opportunity to perform deviant acts. As a result of the person's rejection of and by conventional society, the person becomes increasingly attracted to deviant associates and increases the amount of social interaction with other deviants. Such increased interaction leads to greater opportunities to observe and learn deviant patterns in addition to being provided with numerous occasions when the enactment of the deviant behavior would be appropriate. As the person becomes symbolically and physically separated from conventional society, he depends upon deviant associates for an increasingly greater proportion of the opportunities to satisfy his own needs. In short, conventional opportunities are foreclosed, while deviant opportunities are increased.

CONSEQUENCES OF DEVIANCE

When patterns of deviance occur, what are the consequences for the individual, the group in which the person holds membership, and society as a whole? Numerous social psychological perspectives address, implicitly or explicitly, these direct and indirect consequences of deviance. In general, the direct responses refer to (1) formal and informal social sanctioning responses to deviant behavior; (2) social functioning; and, (3) social change in the definition and prevalence of patterns of deviant behavior. The perspectives on these phenomena are social psychological in that they implicate such intrapsychic responses as, for example, perceptions of threat to personal and group interests, fear reactions, and perceptions of prevalence of deviance.

Formal and Informal Social Responses

Among the significant social consequences of deviant behavior are the formal and informal responses of community agencies and groups. The occurrence of acts of deviance, when they come to the attention of representatives of the formal institutions of our society, stimulate a programmed series of activities involving the investigation of the crime, arrest of alleged perpetrators, judicial decisions about guilt or innocence of the accused, and, if found guilty, the administration of negative sanctions. Mediating the relationship between patterns of crime and such formal responses are the attitudinal responses of the public (particularly the emotion of fear), the less formal collective responses to the stimulation of fear (including petitions to legislatures, organization of neighborhood watch groups, taking other precautions, and, in rare instances, vigilante action), and the awareness of the crimes that stimulate the fear response. The fear response might be evoked by either direct (personal experience with crime) or second-hand experiences (via mass media and interpersonal communication networks) with crime (Skogan & Maxfield, 1981). The nature of the social responses to the deviant acts depends upon characteristics of the offense, the offender, and the victim.

Social control mechanisms range from informal (gossip, shunning) to formal (systems of adjudication, and consequent responses relating to imprisonment, probation and parole, in-community supervision, psychotherapy, and rehabilitation). Such social control mechanisms arise in response to involuntary as well voluntary deviance. Social policies of ethnic cleansing, apartheid, and genocide represent sanctioning mechanisms in response to undesirable ethnic, racial, or religious attributes.

Whether or not the de facto deviant behavior evokes negative sanctions depends upon the willingness of the observer to define the behavior as deviant. Frequently, observers because of needs of their own or for other reasons, refuse to recognize the behavior as deviant. They either do not recognize that the behavior has occurred, or they define the behavior as within the normal range of expected events (Yarrow, Schwartz, Murphy, & Deasy, 1955). Whether observers choose to recognize the behavior as deviant and to respond with negative social sanctions depends upon a variety of contingencies including the characteristics of the deviant actor. Generally, if the deviant actor is characterized by other undesirable attributes or the actor is powerless to resist the application of the negative social sanctions, the behavior is more likely to be recognized, and the sanctions are more likely to be forthcoming.

The formal and informal societal sanctions frequently are evoked in conjunction with social psychological premises held by the members of the society or surrogates acting on behalf of society. Thus, in response to deviant activities, on the premise that increased severity of punishment would deter deviant activity, society (particularly over the past three decades) has introduced a series of severe criminal justice policies including:

> ... restoration of capital punishment; abolishment of parole and indeterminate sentencing; ending or restricting good time and gain time reductions in sentences for prison inmates; restriction of

judicial sentencing discretion through sentencing guidelines and mandated sentences; longer
prison sentences for drug and violent offenses; "three-strikes-and-you're-out" life sentences for
habitual offenders; direct filing of juvenile offenders to criminal courts; and stricter intermediate
sanctions such as home confinement that controls offenders in the community more than traditional probation does. (Akers, 2000, p. 27)

Deviant acts also evoke responses that are intended to forestall deviance by decreasing
opportunities to engage in deviant acts. Thus, devices such as increased street lighting, self-
locking doors, and providing guards for premises decrease opportunities to engage in certain
kinds of deviant acts. Such precautions are suggested by social psychological assumptions
such as those that are implicit or explicit in orientations such as routine activities theory that
assert opportunity structure to be one of the elements that are the *sine qua non* for the commission of deviant acts (Skogan & Maxfield, 1981).

The negative sanctioning of deviant behavior in turn has its own consequences relating
respectively to deterrence of deviant behavior, escalation of deviance, and affirmation of
moral standards.

CONSEQUENCES FOR DETERRENCE. The future performance of deviant acts may be
influenced by the formal and informal responses to earlier deviance. Part of this influence is
mediated by the effects of the responses with regard to the reaffirmation of the moral code of
the community. More directly, however, these responses, including the administration of more
or less severe punishment and precautionary measures, may deter the individual from acting
out a disposition or limit the opportunities to do so. Perhaps a person otherwise motivated to
perform a deviant act would not do so if swift and sure punishment were anticipated. The
person also would be less likely to act out a disposition to steal if the goods were not easily
available. On the other hand, precautionary tactics that limit opportunity may merely displace
deviant acts onto other areas (Skogan & Maxfield, 1981). These consequences have been considered previously in discussions of deterrence, social control, routine activities, and related
perspectives.

ESCALATION OF DEVIANCE. The administration of negative social sanctions sets in
motion a chain of consequences that under specific conditions leads to the development
of personal and public deviant identities and subsequent negative self-attitudes. Under
conditions whereby the stigmatized individual (1) has experienced attenuation of emotional
ties to the conventional social order, (2) does not have opportunities to pursue conventional
adaptations that permit alleviation of distressful self-attitudes, and (3) is able to justify the
pursuit of alternative deviant adaptations in conventional terms, the stigmatized person will
continue and perhaps escalate involvement in deviant behaviors toward the goal of reducing
the experience of negative self-attitudes that are traceable to being the object of negative social
sanctions (Kaplan, 2001). These conditional consequences are explicated within the context of
the labeling or societal reaction perspective that has been discussed previously. Under mutually exclusive conditions, the negative sanctions will be more likely to have a deterrent effect.

AFFIRMING MORAL STANDARDS AND GROUP SOLIDARITY. In *The Rules of Sociological
Method*, Emile Durkheim introduced the idea that behavior defined as deviant stands in
contrast to collective normative expectations and so functions to define collective normative
standards. Farrell and Swigert expand upon this idea as follows:

Property is valued, for example, not only because respect for it is engendered by institutional
efforts at socialization but also because the propertyless are shamed and the thief imprisoned. In

> much the same way as the moral leader exemplified the cultural ideal, the deviant stands for that to
> which the culture stands opposed. The group derives vitality from repulsion, indignation, and official
> reaction to deviant conduct. By calling attention to the sins, pathologies, and crimes of the outcast,
> the group reinforces its cohesiveness and reaffirms its norms. (Farrell & Swigert, 1982, p. 28)

The visible responses to violations of normative standards serve to communicate that limits are imposed upon behavior and, by implication, the behaviors that are required. Further, the collective responses to deviant behavior (particularly when group cohesiveness is threatened) reinforce a feeling of collective solidarity among the members of the society that (particularly in modern society) is otherwise divided by diverse value systems. The collective response to violation of basic norms reinforces the sense of what commonality the society does possess (Durkheim, 1938; Erikson, 1966).

Social Functioning

Deviant patterns and the social response evoked adversely affect the social functioning of the deviant, of those with whom the deviant would ordinarily interact, and of the victims of the deviance. Additionally, deviant patterns have adverse consequences for the community-wide achievement of social values.

The social functioning of the deviant is disrupted in the sense that among the immediate negative consequences of deviant behavior is the displacement of normative activities by deviant activities. Not only is the performance of current roles lost, but the normal socialization process is interrupted so that the deviant behavior forestalls the learning and performance of adult roles (Hewitt, 1970). The social functioning of others who would ordinarily act as role partners with the deviant is similarly disrupted. The proper performance of one's roles depends upon the proper performance of social roles on the part of those with whom the person interacts in the context of social relationships.

The appropriate performance of social roles on the part of victims is disrupted by the self-protective devices they use to decrease the risk of being a victim. Responses by the potential victim include such personal precautions as walking with others, avoiding dangerous places, and staying home. Such responses in turn place constraints upon the amount of social interaction people may enjoy (Skogan & Maxfield, 1981). Further, less directly, the achievement of social values is hindered both by displacement of resources and by threats to these values posed by the social reactions to deviant behavior in the service of other values. Extensive deviance requires the expenditure of scarce resources in order to protect those who conform to conventional norms. If the resources must be expended in these ways, they cannot be used to achieve other social values.

Social Change

While it may be true that occasional deviance serves the function of reaffirming the values that the deviant behavior contradicts, as deviant behaviors increase, they serve to call into question the worth of these values, and deviant behaviors become stimuli for social change. If deviant behavior is viewed as evoking social responses that reinforce the validity of the social rules that are violated, then such behavior must also be viewed as having the potentially counteracting effect of laying the groundwork for social change in the moral code. Each instance of deviant behavior is a potential stimulus and model for the acting out of pre-existing deviant dispositions. Individuals who are disposed to violate rules may not have acted out their disposition because of the absence of situational stimulus or because of the lack of a conception of what form the acting out might take. When the person who is so stimulated observes a deviant act, he may be stimulated to act out his disposition to commit a deviant act, and at the same time, may be provided with a deviant model that provides the form that the acting out of the deviant tendency might take. In short, one of the social consequences of deviant behavior is the increased likelihood that others will act out the deviant patterns.

Over time, the increased prevalence and visibility of the socially forbidden pattern mitigates the severity of the negative social attitudes and sanctions evoked by the pattern. What was once forbidden slowly becomes an acceptable pattern. Initial violations of a rule indirectly lead to a social change in the acceptability of that pattern. How rapidly this process occurs is, in part, a function of the certainty and severity of punishments and other factors that have been observed to constrain the acting out of deviant impulses. These factors, in turn, presume changing social attitudes. That is, the failure of the legal institutions to respond forcefully to particular violations at any given time indicates that the social attitudes toward the violations have changed. The rules are no longer regarded as sacred, the violations of the rule are no longer abhorrent, and the sanctions are no longer stringent and immediately administered. Social movements which at the outset are regarded as deviant, ultimately become embodiments of respectability.

SOCIAL PSYCHOLOGY OF DEVIANCE: PERSPECTIVES ON THE FUTURE

It was not possible to present in these pages every theoretical perspective that addresses understanding of some aspect of deviant behavior. However, those perspectives that are widely regarded as most productive as well as a representative sample of the range of perspectives that persist in the literature have been presented. These social psychological perspectives on deviant behavior taken together have matured to a point where it is generally recognized that there are many explanations of the antecedents and consequences of deviance. In the past, and to some extent continuing to the present, theories that emphasize one or another factor were pitted against each other. Often one was favored over another when in fact the several theories were addressing different questions, and, in providing answers to those questions, were making separate contributions to the overall understanding of deviant behavior.

For example, as noted above, some perspectives address the questions of how particular behaviors and attributes come to be defined as deviant. Other perspectives address the question of why individuals become motivated to engage in deviant behavior. Still others address the question of what factors facilitate acting out of deviant motivations, or why deviant behavior, once performed, is repeated and escalated rather than stopped or reduced. Finally, some theories focus upon the consequences of deviant behavior. Often, particular social psychological perspectives will deal with some combination but not all of these questions. Even when any one of these questions is addressed, various social psychological perspectives will focus upon one or another explanatory factor. Thus, in explaining why individuals act on deviant motivations, some perspectives will view deviance as adaptations to psychological stress, others will focus upon opportunities to engage in deviance, and still others will focus upon social controls that impede the acting out of deviant motivations.

With increasing frequency it is being recognized that the diverse perspectives that address any one of these questions are compatible or complementary, and that the responses to all or several of these questions may be integrated within an overarching integrative theoretical framework (Akers, 2000; Barak, 1998; Messner, Krohn, & Liska, 1989; Shoemaker, 2000). The best of these address all of these questions and permit translation of constructs into concepts that compose the integrative theory or permit incorporation of research findings stemming from other perspectives within the body of research conducted under the rubric of the integrative theory. Future developments in the social psychology of deviant behavior arguably will bear sweetest fruit by continuing to develop such integrative theories. By way of illustration, Kaplan (1975, 1980, 1995) proposed a general theory that provides a general definition of deviance and addresses the questions regarding how particular traits or behaviors come to be defined as deviant, how people become motivated to engage in deviant behavior, the factors that facilitate the acting out of deviant motivations, influences upon the (dis)continuity of deviant behavior, and the individual and social consequences of deviant behavior. In addressing these questions, Kaplan offers explanations that in effect combine strain theory, labeling theory, control theory, and social learning theory among other perspectives.

Research on deviant behavior must increasingly be guided by such theoretical statements which are, in turn, revised in the face of research findings. Theoretical statements are coming to recognize the complexity of explanations of the antecedents and consequences of deviance. The complexity is reflected in the number of variables that are involved, the indirect as well as direct influences of one variable upon another, the counteracting influences of one variable upon another, and the conditional nature of the relationships between variables. The theoretical structure provides tentative interpretations of research findings and permits the identification of areas where further research is needed.

As theoretical statements become more complex, so must the research activities be more suitable to the task of testing the theories. Increasingly, research on deviant behavior permits analysis of the complex relationships among appropriately large numbers of variables using research designs that permit the determination of the temporal sequences of the variables and analytic methods that are suitable to the estimation of theoretically informed models (Kaplan & Johnson, 2001). For example, primarily through the use of structural equation modeling of multigenerational panel data, Kaplan and his associates have systematically estimated increasingly elaborated, theoretically informed models specifying the direct, indirect, and moderating influences on deviant behavior. To illustrate, in one inclusive model, later deviant behavior was accounted for by the direct and indirect antecedent influences of self-rejection, early deviance, negative social sanctions, disposition to deviance, and deviant peer associations (Kaplan & Johnson, 2001). Deviant adaptations in turn influence self-rejection (Kaplan & Halim, 2000). These linear relationships are moderated by such variables as deviant identity, gender, and race/ethnicity (Kaplan & Halim, 2000; Kaplan & Johnson, 2001; Kaplan & Lin, 2000).

Finally, future social psychological theory and research should attend to the generality of perspectives of deviance when applied in different social psychological settings. Deviant behavior is widely equated with violence, theft, drug use, and other such behaviors. However, the concept of deviance has more general applicability. The concept may refer to the failure of friends or spouses to conform to each other's expectations as when one "cheats" on another. The concept may refer to the failure of an employee to give an employer an "honest day's work for an honest day's pay." Deviant behavior includes the failure of a friend to do a favor for another friend when he or she has no excuse not to do the favor. A good test of the validity of the social psychological perspectives we have been considering is their applicability in a wide variety of interpersonal and group situations that deal with behaviors other than deviance or criminality. Future research should apply the constructs presented within the context of these social psychological perspectives through a wide variety of interpersonal systems including friendship groups, marital dyads, and work groups as well as to behaviors that violate the expectations of the community in general. Arguably one of the greatest benefits of theory and research on deviance is the contribution they make to the study of social psychological processes in general.

ACKNOWLEDGMENT: This work was supported in part by research grants (R01 DA 02497 and R01 DA 10016) and by a Career Scientist Award (K05 DA 00136) to the author from the National Institute on Drug Abuse.

REFERENCES

Agnew, Robert. (1992). Foundation for a general strain theory of crime and delinquency. *Criminology, 30*, 47–87.

Agnew, Robert, & White, Helene Raskin. (1992). An empirical test of general strain theory. *Criminology, 30*, 475–500.

Akers, Ronald L. (1985). *Deviant behavior: A social learning approach* (3rd ed.). Belmont, CA: Wadsworth.

Akers, Ronald L. (1998). *Social learning and social structure: A general theory of crime and deviance.* Boston: Northeastern University Press.

Akers, Ronald L. (2000). *Criminological theories: Introduction, evaluation and application.* Los Angeles: Roxbury.

Akers, Ronald L., La Greca, Anthony J., Cochran, John, & Sellers, Christine. (1989). Social learning theory and alcohol behavior among the elderly, *Sociological Quarterly, 30*, 625–638.

Akers, Ronald L., & Lee, Gang. (1996). A longitudinal test of social learning theory: Adolescent smoking, *Journal of Drug Issues, 26*, 317–343.

Barak, Gregg. (1998). *Integrating criminologies.* Needham Heights, MA: Allyn & Bacon.

Battin, Sara R., Hill, Karl G., Abbott, Robert D., Catalano, Richard E., & Hawkins, David J. (1998). The contribution of gang membership to delinquency beyond delinquent friends. *Criminology, 36*, 93–115.

Becker, Howard S. (1963). *Outsiders: Studies in sociology of deviance.* New York: Free Press.

Bonger, Willem. (1969). *Criminality and economic conditions [1916].* Abridged with an introduction by Austin T. Turk. Bloomington, IN: Indiana University Press.

Braithwaite, John. (1989). *Crime, shame, and reintegration.* Cambridge, MA: Cambridge University Press.

Burgess, Robert L., & Akers, Ronald L. (1966). A differential association-reinforcement theory of criminal behavior. *Social Problems, 14*, 128–147.

Bursik, Robert J. (1988). Social disorganization and theories of crime and delinquency: Problems and prospects. *Criminology, 26*(4), 519–551.

Chambliss, William J. (1969). *Crime and the legal process.* New York: McGraw-Hill.

Chambliss, William J. (1974). The state, the law, and the definition of behavior as criminal or delinquent. In Daniel Glaser (Ed.), *Handbook of criminology* (pp. 7–43). Chicago: Rand McNally.

Cloward, Richard A., & Ohlin, Lloyd E. (1960). *Delinquency and opportunity.* Glencoe, IL: Free Press.

Cohen, Albert K. (1955). *Delinquent boys: The culture of the gang.* Glencoe, IL: Free Press.

Cohen, Lawrence E., & Felson, Marcus. (1979). Social change and crime rate trends: a routine activities approach. *American Sociological Review, 44*, 588–608.

Cohen, Lawrence E., Kluegal, James, & Land, Kenneth. (1981). Social inequality and predatory criminal victimization: An exposition and test of a formal theory. *American Sociological Review, 46*, 505–524.

Cornish, Derek B., & Clarke, Ronald V. (Eds.). (1986). *The reasoning criminal: Rational choice perspectives on offending.* New York: Springer.

DeFleur, Melvin L., & Quinney, Richard. (1966). A reformulation of Sutherland's differential association theory and a strategy for empirical verification. *Journal of Research in Crime and Delinquency, 3*, 1–22.

Durkheim, Emile. (1895/1938). *The rules of sociological method.* New York: The Free Press.

Erikson, Kai T. (1966). *Wayward puritans: A study in the sociology of deviance.* New York: Wiley.

Evans, David T., Cullen, Francis T., Dunaway, R. Gregory, & Burton, Velmer S., Jr. (1995). Religion and crime re-examined: The impact of religion, secular controls, and social ecology on adult criminality. *Criminology, 33*, 195–224.

Farrell, Ronald A., & Swigert, Victoria L. (1982). *Deviance and social control*. Glenview, IL: Scott, Foresman and Company.

Gottfredson, Denise C., McNeill III, Richard J., & Gottfredson, Gary D. (1991). Social area influences on delinquency: A multilevel analysis. *Journal of Research in Crime and Delinquency 28*(2), 197–226.

Gottfredson, Michael, & Travis Hirschi. (1990). *A general theory of crime*. Palo Alto, CA: Stanford University Press.

Hewitt, John P. (1970). *Social stratification and deviant behavior*. New York: Random House.

Hirschi, Travis. (1969). *Causes of delinquency*. Berkeley: University of California Press.

Kaplan, Howard B. (1972). Toward a general theory of psychosocial deviance: The case of aggressive behavior. *Social Science and Medicine, 6*, 593–617.

Kaplan, Howard B. (1975). *Self-attitudes and deviant behavior*. Pacific Palisades, CA: Goodyear.

Kaplan, Howard B. (1980). *Deviant behavior in defense of self*. New York: Academic Press.

Kaplan, Howard B. (1984). *Patterns of juvenile delinquency*. Beverly Hills, CA: Sage.

Kaplan, Howard B. (1986). *Social psychology of self-referent behavior*. New York: Plenum Press.

Kaplan, Howard B. (1995). Drugs, crime, and other deviant adaptations. In H. B. Kaplan (Ed.), *Drugs, crime, and other deviant adaptations: Longitudinal studies* (pp. 3–46). New York: Plenum Press.

Kaplan, Howard B. (1996). Psychosocial stress from the perspective of self theory. In H. B. Kaplan (Ed.), *Psychosocial stress: Perspectives on structure, theory, life-course, and methods* (pp. 175–244). San Diego, CA: Academic Press.

Kaplan, Howard B. (2001). Self-esteem and deviant behavior: A critical review and theoretical integration. In T. J. Owens (Ed.), *Extending self-esteem theory and research: Sociological and psychological currents* (pp. 375–97). New York: Cambridge University Press.

Kaplan, Howard B., & Halim, Shaheen. (2000). Aggression and self-derogation: Moderating influences of gender race/ethnicity, and stage in the life course. *Advances in Life Course Research, 5*, 1–32.

Kaplan, Howard B., & Johnson, Robert J. (2001). *Social deviance: Testing a general theory*. New York: Kluwer Academic/Plenum.

Kaplan, Howard B., & Cheng-hsien Lin. (2000). Deviant identity as a moderator of the relation between negative self-feelings and deviant behavior. *Journal of Early Adolescence, 20*, 150–177.

Kaplan, Howard B., & Peck, B. Mitchell. (1992). Self-rejection, coping style, and mode of deviant response. *Social Science Quarterly, 73*, 903–919.

Katz, Jack. (1988). *Seductions of crime: Moral and sensual attractions to doing evil*. New York: Basic Books.

Kobrin, Solomon. (1951). The conflict of values in delinquency areas. *American Sociological Review 16*, 653–651.

Krohn, Marvin D. (1986). The web of conformity: A network approach to the explanation of delinquent behavior. *Social Problems, 33*, S81–S93.

Lemert, Edwin M. (1967). *Human deviance, social problems, and social control*. Englewood Cliffs, NJ: Prentice Hall.

Lind, A. W. (1938). *Island community: A study of ecological successions in Hawaii*. Chicago: University of Chicago Press.

Luckenbill, David F. (1977). Criminal homicide as a situated transaction. *Social Problems, 25*, 176–186.

Loeber, Rolf, & Stouthamer-Loeber, Magda. (1986). Family factors as correlates and predictors of juvenile conduct problems and delinquency. In Michael Tonry & Norval Morris (Eds.), *Crime and justice* (Vol. 7, pp. 29–149). Chicago: University of Chicago Press.

Merton, Robert K. (1938). Social structure and anomie. *American Social Science Review, 3*, 672–682.

Messner, Steven F., Krohn, Marvin D., & Liska, Allen E. (1989). *Theoretical integration in the study of deviance and crime*. New York: State University of New York Press.

Nye, Ivan F. (1958). *Family relationships and delinquent behavior*. New York: Wiley.

Paternoster, Raymond. (1985). Assessments of risk and behavioral experience: An explanatory study of change. *Criminology, 23*, 417–436.

Paternoster, Raymond, Saltzman, Linda E., Waldo, Gordon P., & Chiricos, Theodore G. (1983). Perceived risk and social control: Do sanctions really deter? *Law and Society Review, 17*, 457–480.

Quinney, Richard. (1970). *The social reality of crime*. Boston: Little, Brown.

Quinney, Richard. (1980). *Class, state, and crime*. New York: Longman.

Reckless, Walter C. (1961). A new theory of delinquency and crime. *Federal Probation, 25*, 42–46.

Reckless, Walter C. (1967). *The crime problem* (4th ed.). New York: Appleton-Century-Crofts.

Reckless, Walter C., Dinitz, Simon, & Murray, Ellen. (1956). Self-concept as an insulator against delinquency. *American Sociological Review, 21*, 744–746.

Reiss, Albert J. (1951). Delinquency as the failure of personal and social controls. *American Sociological Review, 16*, 196–207.

Rossi, Peter H., Waite, Emily, Bose, Christina E., & Berk, Richard E. (1974). The seriousness of crimes: Normative structure and individual differences. *American Sociological Review, 39*, 224–237.

Sampson, Robert J., & Groves, W. Byron. (1989). Community structure and crime: Testing social-disorganization theory. *American Journal of Sociology, 94*(4), 774–802.

Sellin, Thorsten. (1938). Culture conflict and crime. *Social Science Research Council, Bulletin 41*. New York.

Shaw, Clifford, & McKay, Henry D. (1942). *Juvenile delinquency and urban areas*. Chicago: University of Chicago Press.

Shoemaker, Donald J. (2000). *Theories of delinquency: An examination of explanations of delinquent behavior* (4th ed.). New York: Oxford University Press.

Skogan, Wesley G., & Maxfield, Michael G. (1981). *Coping with crime: Individual and neighborhood reactions.* Beverly Hills, CA: Sage.

Stark, Rodney. (1987). Deviant places: A theory of the ecology of crime. *Criminology, 25*, 893–909.

Sutherland, Edwin H. (1937). *The professional thief.* Chicago: University of Chicago Press.

Sutherland, Edwin H. (1947). *Principles of criminology* (4th ed.). Philadelphia: Lippincott.

Sykes, Gresham M., & David Matza. (1957). Techniques of neutralization: A theory of delinquency. *American Journal of Sociology, 22*, 664–670.

Taylor, Ian, Walton, Paul, & Young, Jock. (1973). *The new criminology.* New York: Harper and Row.

Tittle, Charles R. (1980). *Sanctions and social deviance: The question of deterrence.* New York: Praeger.

Tittle, Charles R. (1994). The theoretical basis for inequality in formal social control. In G. S. Bridges & M. A. Myers (Eds.), *Inequality, crime, and social control* (pp. 221–252). Boulder, CO: Westview.

Tittle, Charles R. (1995). *Control balance: Toward a general theory of deviance.* Boulder, CO: Westview.

Tittle, Charles R., & Paternoster, Raymond. (2000). *Social deviance and crime.* Los Angeles: Roxbury.

Turk, Austin T. (1964). Prospects for theories of criminal behavior. *Journal of Criminal Law, Criminology, and Police Sciences, 55*, 454–461.

Vold, George B. (1958). *Theoretical criminology.* New York: Oxford University Press.

Wilson, James Q., & Herrnstein, Richard J. (1985). *Crime and human nature.* New York: Simon and Schuster.

Yarrow, Marian R., Schwartz, Charlotte G., Murphy, Harriet S., & Deasy, Leila C. (1955). The psychological meaning of mental illness in the family. *Journal of Social Issues, 11*(4), 12–24.

Zimring, Franklin E. (1971). *Perspectives on deterrence.* NIMH Monograph Series on Crime and Delinquency Issues. Washington, DC: U.S. Government Printing Office.

Zimring, Franklin, E., & Hawkins, George. (1973). *Deterrence.* Chicago: University of Chicago Press.

CHAPTER 19

Intergroup Relations

Michael A. Hogg

Intergroup relations refers to the way in which people in groups perceive, think about, feel about, and act toward people in other groups. If you replace the word "group" in intergroup with, for example, the words "national" or "ethnic," then what is meant by intergroup relations becomes clear. We all know that international relations refer to how nations view other nations, and how nations act toward and treat one another. We also know that international relations are often fraught with conflict and exploitation, and characterized by intolerance and prejudice. The great challenge for humanity is to reduce conflict and exploitation, and banish intolerance and prejudice, and to replace these with beneficial competition and social harmony. This is an awesome challenge where the stakes are enormously high in terms of human suffering.

In this chapter, I overview what we know about the social psychology of intergroup relations. Although this overview is necessarily selective, I include discussion of personality, self-conception, identity, cognitive processes, motivation, goals, stereotypes, prejudice, disadvantage, stigma, collective action, conflict and harmony, and so forth.

Before beginning we should define the term "intergroup relations." This is not, however, such an easy task. A definition of intergroup relations must of course rest on a definition of "group"—and this is problematic. Within social psychology there are almost as many definitions of a group as there are people who research groups. For example, there are those who believe a group is a small collection of individuals who are interacting with one another in some kind of promotively interdependent manner (e.g., Arrow, McGrath, & Berdahl, 2000), others believe a group exists when people define themselves in terms of the defining attributes of a self-inclusive social category (e.g., Tajfel & Turner, 1986), and yet others believe the group is a nominal fallacy and that "there is no psychology of groups which is not essentially

MICHAEL A. HOGG • School of Psychology, University of Queensland, Brisbane, QLD 4072, Australia

Handbook of Social Psychology, edited by John Delamater. Kluwer Academic/Plenum Publishers, New York, 2003.

and entirely a psychology of individuals" (Allport, 1924, p. 4). Differences in definition often rest on deeper metatheoretical conflicts over the scope and aims of social psychology (see Hogg & Abrams, 1988).

In this chapter I adopt the basically cognitive definition of the social group that underpins the social identity perspective (for recent overviews see Hogg, 2001a, 2003). A group exists psychologically when two or more people define and evaluate themselves in terms of the defining properties of a common self-inclusive category. However it is important to acknowledge that group life involves more than self-definition—it involves social interaction, interdependent goals, emotions, and so forth. Consistent with this definition I adopt Sherif's classic and relatively widely accepted definition of intergroup relations (e.g., Hogg & Abrams, 2001a):

> Intergroup relations refer to relations between two or more groups and their respective members. Whenever individuals belonging to one group interact, collectively or individually, with another group or its members in terms of their group identifications we have an instance of intergroup behavior. (Sherif, 1962, p. 5)

PERSONALITY AND INDIVIDUAL DIFFERENCES

Intergroup behavior tends to be competitive and ethnocentric. In intergroup contexts people generally behave so as to gain or maintain an advantage for their own group over other groups in terms of resources, status, prestige, and so forth (e.g., Brewer & Campbell, 1976). Sumner put it beautifully when he described ethnocentrism as:

> a view of things in which one's own group is the center of everything, and all others are scaled and rated with reference to it .... Each group nourishes its own pride and vanity, boasts itself superior, exalts its own divinities, and looks with contempt on outsiders. Each group thinks its own folkways the only right one .... Ethnocentrism leads a people to exaggerate and intensify everything in their own folkways which is peculiar and which differentiates them from others. (Sumner, 1906, p. 13)

Although intergroup relations are intrinsically enthnocentric, relations between groups can vary widely in their extremity—from harmless generalized images, tolerance, and friendly rivalry to deep-seated hatred, intolerance, and violent conflict.

Because the latter form of intergroup behavior is responsible for the most appalling injustices and inhumanities the study of intergroup relations has tended to focus on this extreme form of intergroup relations—prejudice, discrimination, bigotry, intergroup aggression, and so forth. Social psychologists, like most other people, have wondered whether there may be something "wrong" with people who behave in this way—perhaps these people have dysfunctional personalities, perhaps innate or tied to early childhood experiences, that predispose them to be extremely ethnocentric and intolerant. This perspective has spawned one of social psychology's major and enduring theories of prejudice and intergroup conflict—Adorno, Frenkel-Brunswik, Levinson, and Sanford's (1950) authoritarian personality syndrome (also see, Titus & Hollander, 1957).

Adorno and colleagues adopted a psychodynamic framework to argue that early childhood rearing practices that are harsh, disciplinarian, and emotionally manipulative, produce people who are obsessed by status and authority, intolerant of ambiguity and uncertainty, and hostile and aggressive toward weaker others. These people have an authoritarian personality that predisposes them to extreme forms of intergroup behavior. Research on the authoritarian personality confirms the existence of such a syndrome, but does not provide good evidence for its origins in early childrearing or for its relationship to prejudice and discrimination. People who do not have an authoritarian personality can be prejudiced, and people who do have an authoritarian personality can be free of prejudice. From his classic study of authoritarianism and racism in South Africa and the United States, Pettigrew (1958) concluded that prejudice is less related to personality than it is to socialization within a culture of prejudice that legitimizes prejudice as the background to everyday life. This perspective is now widely accepted by social psychologists who study prejudice and intergroup relations (Billig, 1976; Reynolds, Turner, Haslam, & Ryan, 2001).

Nevertheless, social psychologists have an enduring tendency to develop explanations of extreme and pathological behaviors, such as prejudice, in terms of extreme individuals who have extreme and perhaps pathological personalities. The notion of authoritarianism continues to be popular, but with an emphasis on people's tendency to submit to in-group conventions and authority, and to punish in-group deviants (e.g., Altemeyer, 1994). Another "individual differences" explanation of prejudice is Rokeach's (1960) idea that some people have a dogmatic and closed-minded personality that predisposes them to ethnocentrism, intergroup intolerance, and prejudice. Recently, Sidanius and Pratto and their associates have described a relatively sophisticated, but nonetheless "individual differences," analysis of exploitative power-based intergroup relations, called social dominance theory (e.g., Pratto, Sidanius, Stallworth, & Malle, 1994).

Social dominance theory explains the extent to which people accept or reject societal ideologies or myths that legitimize hierarchy and discrimination, or that legitimize equality and fairness. People who desire their own group to be dominant and superior to out-groups have a high social dominance orientation that encourages them to reject egalitarian ideologies, and to accept myths that legitimize hierarchy and discrimination. These kinds of people are more inclined to be prejudiced than are people who have a low social dominance orientation.

As noted above, social psychologists tend to prefer an account of prejudice that focuses on socialization and cognitive processes, and the role of a culture of prejudice. This is because pure personality and individual differences explanations leave the context specificity, and situational and temporal variability of prejudice, poorly explained. Prejudices can change in form and strength rather faster than personality (i.e., enduring properties of the individual that are largely uninfluenced by context) would be expected to change. Interactionist perspectives that focus on an interaction between personality and social context are more versatile. But then one wonders if the interaction is actually between enduring contextual influences (e.g., ones culture), and immediate situational influences (e.g., an intergroup atrocity)—in which case the notion of personality may not be needed at all.

GOAL RELATIONS AND INTERDEPENDENCE

In contrast to those who emphasize personality and individual differences as an explanation of intergroup behavior—a bottom-up analysis—are those who emphasize the goal relations between groups or individuals—a top-down analysis. A champion of this perspective is Sherif, who maintained that "we cannot extrapolate from the properties of individuals to the characteristics of group situations" (Sherif, 1962, p. 5). Sherif proposed a "realistic conflict" or interdependence theory of intergroup relations (Sherif, 1958), which was predicated on the belief that behavior is driven by goals and by people's perceptions of their relationship to one another with respect to achieving goals. If two groups have the same goal (e.g., prosperity) but the goal is such that one group can only gain at the expense of the other (there is a zero-sum goal relationship, with mutually exclusive goals, and negative interdependence between groups) then intergroup relations will be competitive and dis-harmonious. If two groups have the same goal and the goal is such that it can only be achieved if both groups work together (there is a non-zero-sum goal relationship, with a superordinate goal, and positive interdependence between groups) then intergroup relations will be cooperative and harmonious. At the interpersonal level, mutually exclusive goals lead to interpersonal conflict and group dissolution, whereas superordinate goals lead to interpersonal harmony, group formation, and group cohesion.

This idea was initially tested by Sherif and his associates in a classic series of field experiments at boys' camps in the United States (e.g., Sherif, Harvey, White, Hood, & Sherif, 1961; see Sherif, 1966). In these studies, Sherif manipulated goal relations between individuals and between groups and was able to create cohesive groups, intergroup conflict and hostility, and to some extent intergroup harmony. Variants of the boys' camp paradigm have been used by other researchers (Fisher, 1990). For example, Blake and Mouton (1961) ran 2-week studies with more than 1,000 business executives on management training programs, and others have replicated Sherif's studies in different cultures (e.g., Andreeyva, 1984). The idea that goal relations determine the complexion of intergroup behavior continues to be a powerful theme—for example, in the work of Morton Deutsch (1973), in the field research of Brewer and Campbell (1976), in the research of Insko and associates (Insko et al., 1992), and perhaps most recently in the work of Rabbie in his behavioral interdependence model (e.g., Rabbie, Schot, & Visser, 1989; see Turner & Bourhis's, 1996, critique).

Because realistic conflict theory is a top-down analysis of intergroup relations, it is metatheoretically consistent with more sociological analyses of social behavior. Not surprisingly, it has a substantial legacy in research that traces ethnic and race relations to perceived intergroup threat and to competition over scarce resources (e.g., Bobo & Hutchins, 1996).

Interdependence or realistic conflict approaches to intergroup behavior see conflict arising from situations where other groups threaten in-group goal achievement. There is however another form of threat—out-group actions, or even the existence of an out-group, can pose a threat to the prestige or distinctiveness of one's own group and one's identity as a member of that group. This is a cognitive self-conceptual threat that can provoke a range of actions designed to protect the status of the group and the integrity of the group's boundaries. Some of these reactions include rejection of marginal or deviant in-group members (e.g., Marques, Abrams, Páez, & Hogg, 2001), increased pressures toward in-group uniformity and homogeneity (e.g., Branscombe, Wann, Noel, & Coleman, 1993; Jetten, Spears, & Manstead, 1997), and adoption of strategies designed to consolidate or improve the group's status (e.g., Ellemers, 1993).

SOCIAL CATEGORIZATION

Goals and goal relations play a critical role in intergroup behavior, and are an important component of social psychological explanations of intergroup relations. There is little doubt that groups that can only see themselves as competing over a zero-sum resource are likely to have conflictual intergroup relations, and that this relationship could be improved if those groups could only view themselves as having superordinate goals or non-zero-sum goal relations. However, there may be a more fundamental reason why groups find it difficult to maintain harmonious intergroup relations—perhaps the very existence of separate categories generates competitive behaviors. After all, social categorization is the foundation of intergroup relations—relations between groups can only occur if the social world can be categorized into separate groups (see Hogg, 2001a).

Minimal Groups

This idea was investigated in a series of "minimal group" experiments originally conducted in the late 1960s (e.g., Tajfel, Billig, Bundy, & Flament, 1971), but now replicated countless times (see Diehl, 1990). Minimal group studies are laboratory experiments where people are categorized into two groups ostensibly either randomly or on the basis of some trivial criterion. They then allocate resources (often only points) between anonymous members of their group and anonymous members of the out-group, and complete various other measures about their feelings about themselves, their group, and the other group. The groups have no prior history and no future, there is no interaction, there is no material gain for individuals from membership, and people do not know who is in their group or in the other group. The highly robust finding from these experiments, is that relative to people who are not explicitly categorized, people who are categorized discriminate in favor of their group, show evaluative in-group bias, and indicate that they feel a sense of belonging to their group, and similarity to and liking for their anonymous fellow in-group members.

From the minimal group studies it seemed that competitive intergroup behavior might be an intrinsic feature of the mere existence of a social categorization into in-group and out-group. Competitive goal relations might accentuate the effect or serve as a criterion for the existence of categories, but there was clearly a deeper social-cognitive dynamic at play. This finding and its conceptual implications were a critical catalyst for the development of social identity theory, described below. Subsequent research has identified a number of factors that moderate the minimal intergroup discrimination effect (see below).

Automatic Schema Activation

People cognitively represent physical or social categories as schemas that describe the attributes of the category and the relationships among those attributes. Category schemas vary from concrete exemplars of the category to abstract fuzzy sets of loosely related attributes (prototypes)—for example, Rosch (1978). Categories themselves vary in entitativity—the degree to which they have the properties of a tightly organized, distinctive, and cohesive, unitary construct (e.g., Hamilton & Sherman, 1996).

Social cognition researchers describe how perceptual cues, in particular distinctive visual cues (Zebrowitz, 1996), cause us to categorize people and to imbue them with the properties that are described by our schema of that group (e.g., Fiske & Taylor, 1991; Hamilton & Sherman, 1994). The entire process can be deliberate, but in general it is automatic. Stereotyping of out-group members may be largely an automatic categorization-contingent process that we have little control over (Bargh, 1994; Devine, 1989), although other research suggests that the process may be moderated by a number of factors including the extent to which one is prejudiced (Lepore & Brown, 1997). One controversial line of investigation suggests that if people consciously think about the automatic category–stereotype link, the process paradoxically strengthens the link and increases automatic stereotype activation (Macrae, Bodenhausen, Milne, & Jetten, 1994).

Accentuation and Illusory Correlation Effects

Another effect of social categorization is that it causes us perceptually to accentuate similarities among members of the same category. This appears to be a general consequence of
categorization (Tajfel, 1959), but one that is asymmetrical because we tend to see out-groups
as more homogenous than in-groups (e.g., Judd & Park, 1988). A popular explanation for this
asymmetry is that we are more familiar with the in-group and therefore have more individu-
ating information about in-group than out-group members (Linville, Fischer & Salovey,
1989). Other research has questioned this explanation (e.g., Jones, Wood, & Quattrone, 1981),
with Simon and Brown (1987) showing that relative homogeneity effects may be influenced
by strategic considerations. For example, active minorities often consider themselves to be
relatively more homogenous than the majority out-group—this is clearly quite functional as
such groups need to be consistent and consensual in order to survive and have a chance at
initiating social change (see, Mugny, 1982).

Related to the accentuation effect is the illusory correlation effect (e.g., Hamilton &
Gifford, 1976) in which people associate distinctive behaviors with distinctive categories—
thus laying a foundation for erroneously correlating negative attributes with minority groups.

SELF AND SOCIAL IDENTITY

Social categorization segments the social world into groups, and cognitively represents such
groups in terms of schemas, usually in the form of prototypes. Social categorization profoundly affects person perception, but also, as shown by the minimal group studies described
above, influences how we behave. To fully explore the relationship between social categorization and the entire array of behaviors we associate with groups and intergroup relations
we need to invoke the self-concept. After all, when we categorize other people, perhaps we
also categorize self. The link between social categorization, self-conception, and group and
intergroup behavior is most fully explored by the social identity perspective (e.g., Hogg &
Abrams, 1988; Tajfel & Turner, 1986; Turner, Hogg, Oakes, Reicher, & Wetherell, 1987)—
for recent overviews see Abrams & Hogg (2001), Hogg (2001a, 2003). The social identity
perspective has a number of integrated conceptual components—for example, a focus on the
structure of self and identity (e.g., Turner, 1982), a focus on social comparison processes (see
Hogg, 2000a), a focus on self-enhancement motivation (e.g., Abrams & Hogg, 1988), a focus
on uncertainty-reduction motivation (Hogg, 2000b), a focus on social influence processes
(see Turner, 1991), a focus on the role of beliefs about intergroup relations (Tajfel & Turner,
1986), and a focus on the generative role of the categorization process (Turner et al., 1987).

The social identity perspective argues that people define and evaluate themselves in terms
of the groups to which they belong—groups provide people with a collective self-concept, a
social identity, and people have as many social identities as the groups to which they feel they
belong. Social identity is clearly differentiated from personal identity, which is tied to interpersonal relationships and idiosyncratic personal traits (see Hogg, 2001c; Hogg & Williams, 2000;
cf. Brewer & Gardner, 1996). Because social identities define, prescribe and evaluate who one
is and how one should think, feel and act, people have a strong desire to establish or maintain
the evaluative superiority of their own group over relevant other groups—there is a fierce intergroup struggle for evaluatively positive group distinctiveness. This struggle is, however, tem-
pered by people's understanding of the nature of the relations between their group and relevant
out-groups—their social belief systems. In particular people pay attention to status differences

and the stability and legitimacy of such differences, to the permeability of intergroup boundaries and thus the possibility of passing psychologically from one group to the other, and to the existence of achievable alternatives to the status quo. For social identity theory, group behaviors (conformity, stereotyping, ethnocentrism, in-group favoritism, intergroup discrimination, in-group cohesion, etc.), as distinct from interpersonal behaviors, occur when social identity is the salient basis of self-conceptualization; and the content of group behavior rests on the specific social identity that is salient. Social identity is context-specific in so far as different social identities are salient in different social contexts.

Social identity processes are cognitively generated by social categorization of self and others. People represent groups as prototypes—multidimensional fuzzy sets of attributes that describe and prescribe perceptions, thoughts, feelings, and actions that define the in-group and distinguish it from relevant out-groups. Through a process of metacontrast, prototypes capture the optimal balance between minimization of intragroup differences and maximization of intergroup differences—prototypes strive for maximal entitativity (Hogg, in press). Social categorization perceptually assimilates people to the relevant in-group or out-group prototype and views them, not as unique individual people, but through the lens of category membership—a process of depersonalization occurs. Depersonalization simply refers to a change in the basis of perception, and does not have the negative implications of terms such as "deindividuation" or "dehumanization." Applied to self, social categorization has the same effect as the categorization of other people—it transforms self-conception so that people feel like group members, and it depersonalizes attitudes, feelings, and behaviors such that they conform to the in-group prototype. Thus, self-categorization is responsible for conformity, normative behavior, and the rest of the edifice of group and intergroup behaviors.

The social identity perspective has made a great impact on the social psychology of intergroup relations, and has also contributed significantly to a revival of research on group processes in general (see Moreland, Hogg, & Hains, 1994). Some of the most recent developments in social identity research are covered in the following edited books: Abrams and Hogg (1999), Capozza and Brown (2000), Ellemers, Spears, and Doosje (1999), Hogg and Terry (2001), Worchel, Morales, Páez, and Deschamps (1998).

MOTIVATION AND AFFECT

Motivation

Why do people engage in intergroup behavior, and perhaps more fundamentally why do people identify with groups—what motivates intergroup behavior, and what motivates specific forms of intergroup behavior? One answer is in terms of specific goals that people or groups may want to achieve—goals that can only be achieved by interpersonal or intergroup cooperative interaction (superordinate goals), or goals that are mutually exclusive and can only be achieved by interpersonal or intergroup competition. Functional theories of intergroup relations, such as that proposed by Sherif (e.g., 1958) fall in this camp (see above).

Personality approaches like Adorno et al.'s (1950) authoritarian personality, or Rokeach's (1960) dogmatic personality treat people's need to compartmentalize their social world as a core aspect of authoritarianism or dogmatism. Authoritarian or dogmatic people are therefore strongly motivated to discriminate starkly between groups, and, in the case of authoritarianism, to displace negative feelings onto lower status out-groups (see above). Theories of why people affiliate in the first place have produced a range of motives, of which social reality testing through social comparison is an important one (e.g., Festinger, 1954)—people come together with similar others to obtain validation from individual others for their perceptions, attitudes, and feelings. Terror management is another motive for affiliation (e.g., Greenberg, Solomon, & Pyszczynski, 1997)—people affiliate with others because they fear death. Baumeister and Leary (1995) argue that people simply have a fundamental need to belong that underpins the existence of groups and the way in which groups struggle against one another for survival—the consequences of not belonging, or of being ostracized can be quite extreme (Williams, 2001). Finally, there is a plethora of motivational accounts for why people construe themselves in particular ways (see Sedikides & Strube, 1997).

Social categorization research tends to focus on contextual factors that cause us to categorize ourselves and others in particular ways, and on the consequences of categorizing in that way. One very fundamental motive for social categorization, which also underpins categorization more generally, is a need to structure our subjective environment in contextually meaningful ways that reduce uncertainty and allow us to predict people's behavior, plan our own actions, and locate ourselves relative to other people (e.g., Hogg, 2000b, 2001b). People are more likely to identify with groups when they are faced by self-conceptual uncertainty. When such uncertainty is very high they will seek out totalist groups that are highly orthodox, have simple and consensual prototypes, high entitativity, and strong charismatic leaders, and that engage in extreme forms of intergroup behavior (e.g., Hogg, in press). This analysis allows us to understand why disadvantaged groups may acquiesce in their position rather than struggle for change—change may improve status but it will also introduce uncertainty (also see Jost & Kramer, 2002). It also allows us to understand why groups whose distinctiveness is threatened may react in ways that are aimed, not so much at improving status, but at raising entitativity and cohesion in order to provide a secure and clear social identity (e.g., Hamilton & Sherman, 1996), perhaps through rejection of deviates (e.g., Marques & Páez, 1994).

Another powerful intergroup motive is self-enhancement. According to social identity theory, intergroup behavior is motivated by a struggle between groups to promote or protect their positive distinctiveness from one another, and thus secure a relatively favorable social identity. People engage in this struggle because, at the individual level, group membership mediates self-evaluation via social identity, and people tend to be motivated to feel good about themselves—to have a positive sense of self-esteem (e.g., Sedikides & Strube, 1997). In intergroup contexts self-esteem may motivate social identity processes, but how this is pursued is significantly impacted by social conventions and social belief systems (see Abrams & Hogg, 1988; Rubin & Hewstone, 1998). An alternative view is that self-esteem may not motivate intergroup behavior, but rather act as a psychological monitor, or rather "sociometer," of satisfaction of other motives to do with social connectedness and belonging (e.g., Leary, Tambor, Terdal, & Downs, 1995).

According to Brewer's (1991) theory of optimal distinctiveness people simultaneously strive to be the same as other people (assimilation/inclusiveness) and to be different from other people (differentiation/uniqueness). Because these are contrasting human motives, the equilibrium state is one of optimal distinctiveness. Over-satisfaction of one motive engages the contrasting motive to reinstate optimal distinctiveness. Large groups tend to make people feel insufficiently distinctive, whereas very small groups tend to make people feel too distinctive. Optimal distinctiveness is, therefore, best satisfied by intergroup contexts in which the in-group is not overly large—there is sufficient intergroup and intragroup distinctiveness to balance in-group assimilation.

Generally speaking, there is good evidence that threats to group integrity or group valance, and thus to self-conception and self-evaluation, motivate protective reactions that can, depending on available material and psychological resources, manifest themselves as intergroup conflict, "backlash," more subtle forms of intergroup behavior, or as disidentification (e.g., Branscombe et al., 1993; Ethier & Deaux, 1994). For example, self-affirmation theory (Steele, 1988) describes how people whose identity in one domain is evaluatively threatened, engage in practices that publicly affirm a favorable identity in another domain.

Affect

Perhaps due to the success of social cognition and social categorization perspectives on intergroup relations, there has been a growing tendency for social psychologists to underemphasize the affective aspect of intergroup behavior. This is problematic, given that the most troublesome aspects of intergroup relations are precisely those that involve strong emotions, and powerful affect. There has been a recent resurgence of interest in affective aspects of intergroup relations (Mackie & Smith, 2002), that focuses mainly on intergroup emotions (Mackie, Devos, & Smith, 2000). For example, Branscombe, Doosje, and McGarty (2002) examine the way in which a dominant group experiences collective guilt if members identify strongly with the group, the identity is central to self-conception, and members believe that the group's position of superiority is illegitimate because it rests on the group's violation of a moral value that the group adheres to.

Much of the analysis of intergroup affect and emotion rests on the notion of depersonalization that underpins the social identity perspective (described above). People in salient groups feel other people's emotions as their own because self-categorization merges self and other via prototype-based depersonalization—people experience, or include, the other as part of the self (e.g., Tropp & Wright, 2001; Wright, Aron, & Tropp, 2002). In this way, intergroup feelings (which are often negative) can readily become powerfully consensual collective intergroup feelings. Similarly positive in-group feelings can transform into consensual positive regard and in-group solidarity (e.g., Hogg, 1993).

INTERGROUP ATTITUDES

Stereotyping and Prejudice

Earlier we saw how categories are cognitively represented as schemas or prototypes, and that the link between category cues, categorization, and prototype-based perception of self and others is relatively automatic—the process of stereotyping that we normally associate with out-group perceptions and prejudice. However stereotypes, although held by individuals who apply them to out-groups, need to be understood more broadly as widely shared intergroup attitudes (Tajfel, 1981) that act as theories (e.g., von Hippel, Sekaquaptewa, & Vargas, 1995) or social representations (see Farr & Moscovici, 1984) of the attributes of other groups. Tajfel (1981), in particular, makes a strong case for the various social functions that stereotypes serve. For example, he explains how stereotypes may emerge to justify actions that have been committed or planned by one group against another group—if one group exploits another group it may be useful to justify this action by developing a stereotype of the out-group as unsophisticated and dependent. Stereotypes become more extreme and more resistant to change under conditions of intergroup conflict.

Intergroup attitudes are also affected by the wider normative and legislative environment in which intergroup relations exist. So, for example, racist attitudes may take different forms depending on whether the normative environment is one that inhibits overt racism or one that allows overt racism. A number of researchers have pursued this idea in order to understand modern forms of racism (e.g., Dovidio & Gaertner, 1998; McConahay, 1986)—Swim, Aikin, Hall, and Hunter (1995) provide a similar analysis of modern forms of sexism. In Western societies there is a long history of racism that produces deep-seated racial prejudice, fears, and suspicions. However there is also a tradition of tolerance and egalitarianism that in recent years has become enshrined in social norms and in legislation that suppress racist behavior. For many people, therefore, there is an uncomfortable psychological conflict between two sets of contrasting beliefs. People tend to resolve the conflict by avoiding the racial out-group, avoiding the issue of race, denying the existence of disadvantage, opposing preferential treatment, and so forth. Overt forms of racism have, in many sectors of society, been replaced by this "modern" form. Stereotypes are not simply shared intergroup attitudes, but are intergroup attitudes that take their form from the wider socio-historical context in which a specific intergroup relationship exists.

Social Explanation

Stereotyping also has an attribution dimension (Hewstone & Jaspars, 1982). Pettigrew (1979) draws on classic attribution theory, in particular Ross's (1977) fundamental attribution error (people over-attribute others' behavior to dispositions—and their own behavior to the situation) to describe what he calls the ultimate attribution error. The ultimate attribution error is a group level attribution in which people behave ethnocentrically. Good acts are attributed dispositionally if performed by an in-group member and situationally if performed by an out-group member, and vice versa for bad acts. Research conducted in India (Taylor & Jaggi, 1974) and Malaysia (Hewstone & Ward, 1985) certainly supports this analysis.

A particularly disturbing aspect of intergroup attributions is the tendency to attribute unfavorable outgroup attributes to underlying dispositions or essences. This is a process that transforms intergroup attitudes into immutable properties or essences of outgroups and their members (see Medin & Ortony, 1989). Miller and Prentice (1999) argue that intergroup perceptions that rest on such essentialism create insurmountable category divides than can make it extremely difficult to improve intergroup relations—they cite examples such as the Balkans, Northern Ireland, and the Middle East.

PREJUDICE AND DISCRIMINATION

Intergroup relations are not just about attitudes and explanations. They are about how one group behaves toward another group. The main behavioral feature of intergroup relations is discrimination, which can range from relatively innocuous in-group favoritism, through name-calling and verbal abuse, to systematic intergroup violence and genocide. A key question is what is the relationship between intergroup attitudes and intergroup behavior— a question that is part of the broader attitude–behavior issue.

Attitude–behavior research reveals that people's attitudes and their behavior do not often correspond very closely (see Eagly & Chaiken, 1993). For example, LaPiere's (1934) classic study of attitudes toward Chinese Americans revealed that although a young Chinese

American couple was almost never denied service at hotels and restaurants across the United States, almost all those same establishments subsequently expressed the strong anti-Chinese sentiment that they would not serve Chinese people. The research was conducted mainly in the western United States where, at the time, anti-Chinese sentiment was strongest. As we have seen above, unfavorable intergroup attitudes can be well concealed when a normative environment exists that proscribes prejudice or that mutates it into modern forms (Crosby, Bromley & Saxe, 1980).

Because the absence of overt discrimination may not indicate the absence of underlying negative intergroup sentiments, a great challenge for social psychology is to be able to detect prejudice in environments in which the expression of prejudice is normatively (and often legally) prohibited. The key seems to be to use unobtrusive measures—if people do not know they are being observed or measured then they are more likely to behave in accordance with their attitudes (Crosby, Bromley & Saxe, 1980). Other methods involve the careful analysis of the subtext of what people say in natural conversation (e.g., van Dijk, 1987) or the analysis of behaviors that people have little or no conscious control over (e.g., Fazio, Sanbonmatsu, Powell, & Kardes, 1986; Maass, 1999).

Discriminatory behavior is, however, rather easy to obtain in minimal group studies (Tajfel et al., 1971)—probably because the groups have no history and thus no social norms exist to proscribe discrimination against minimal groups. This research has sometimes been interpreted as leading to the rather gloomy prognosis for humanity that, all things being equal, social categorization per se leads to discrimination. Fortunately, this inference is not completely accurate. Social categorization may be a necessary condition for intergroup discrimination, but it is not sufficient. A series of minimal group experiments by Hogg (2000b) has shown that people need to internalize the social categorization as a context-specific self-definition—people need to self-categorize in order to engage in minimal intergroup discrimination. This research shows that people identify with a minimal categorization if they are in a state of subjective uncertainty—more generally, Hogg (2000b) argues that subjective uncertainty reduction is an important motivation for self-categorization and social identity processes.

Staying with minimal groups, there is another research that shows that whether people discriminate or not is influenced by the available dimension of discrimination. For example, there is a positive–negative asymmetry effect (Otten, Mummendey, & Blanz, 1996). Although people discriminate against out-groups when they are giving rewards, they do not do so when they are giving punishments, unless their group is under threat by being disadvantaged or being in a minority position.

We should also remind ourselves that "real" groups exist in a socio-historical environment that contains wider societal norms that prescribe, proscribe, or direct discriminatory behavior. Furthermore, people have social belief systems relating to status stability and legitimacy, intergroup permeability, and realistic alternatives to the status quo (e.g., Ellemers, 1993; Tajfel & Turner, 1986)—in the pursuit of positive social identity these beliefs influence the form that intergroup behavior takes.

Although discrimination is often viewed unfavorably from the perspective of liberal democratic societies, in-groups generally view it positively—discrimination indicates in-group loyalty and commitment. People seem prepared to accept and even praise unfair or unjust practices when they are directed toward out-groups. However, the story is different when such behavior is directed toward the in-group. Tyler and his colleagues (e.g., Tyler, DeGoey, & Smith, 1996) provide evidence showing that people in groups are not overly concerned about having less than fellow group members (distributive inequality), but they are very concerned about being treated fairly (procedural justice). In-group procedural fairness signifies respect, and is an important influence on members' sense of belonging and thus the extent to which they bond with the group.

One implication of Tyler's analysis is that intergroup discrimination can serve a strategic function. The primary audience for discriminatory behavior may be the in-group—people may overtly discriminate against an out-group in order to bolster their own in-group credentials and standing. For instance, jingoistic rhetoric and overt out-group discrimination on the part of leaders may serve this function (e.g., Reicher & Hopkins, 1986), as does the publicly verifiable nature of delinquent behavior (Emler & Reicher, 1995).

STIGMA AND DISADVANTAGE

The power and status inequalities that almost always exist between groups in society have far-reaching consequences, and are in many ways the essential problem of intergroup relations. If intergroup relations were characterized by groups of equal status and power, disadvantage and all that flows from it would not be present. As it is, intergroup relations are almost always associated with differential status, power, prestige, resources, and so forth. Dominant, majority groups do well out of this arrangement, and their members generally experience a positive sense of identity and esteem. Subordinate, minority groups do not do so well, and their members can carry a stigma that has quite profound effects on self-conception. "Stigmatized individuals possess (or are believed to possess) some attribute, or characteristic, that conveys a social identity that is devalued in a particular social context" (Crocker, Major, & Steele, 1998, p. 505). Stigmas can be visible (race) or concealable (sexual orientation), and can vary in perceived controllability (race has low controllability, whereas obesity has high controllability)—stigma visibility and perceived controllability affect the extent and form of prejudice or discrimination that a member of a stigmatized group suffers.

Because stigmatized groups know exactly the negative stereotypes that others have of them, they experience what Steele and Aronson (1995) have called stereotype threat. Stigmatized individuals are aware that others may judge and treat them stereotypically, and thus, on tasks that really matter to them, they worry that through their behavior they may even confirm the stereotypes. This worry can interfere with and thus impair task performance. Stigmatized people can also suffer attributional ambiguity—they are very sensitive to the causes of others' treatment of them (Crocker & Major, 1989). Stigmatized groups suffer material and social disadvantage, and can find that their goals and aspirations are continually frustrated relative to other groups. A sense of reduced efficacy and motivation can eventually set in, and rather than fight for change, groups can sometimes acquiesce to these conditions— some groups can prefer disadvantage to the uncertainties and dangers of fighting for social change (e.g., Jost & Kramer, 2002).

In general, although some stigmatized individuals are vulnerable to low self-esteem, diminished life satisfaction, and in some cases depression, most members of stigmatized groups are able to weather the assaults and maintain a positive self-image (Crocker & Major, 1989). One way in which this is accomplished is by denying personal disadvantage. Although stigmatized groups are clearly disadvantaged, members of those groups often deny any personal experience of discrimination (e.g., Major, 1994; Taylor, Wright, & Porter, 1994). For example, Crosby (1982) found that employed women who were discriminated against with respect to pay, rarely indicated that they personally had experienced any sex discrimination.

COLLECTIVE ACTION AND
SOCIAL PROTEST

Although disadvantaged or stigmatized groups have an impressive armory of protective or avoidant strategies to redirect energy from direct intergroup conflict, this is not always effective. When deprivation is very acute and a recipe for effective social change is available, disadvantaged groups will eagerly challenge the status quo by political means, or through social protest or other collective behaviors including demonstrations, riots, and uprisings.

Crowds and Riots

According to theories that focus on frustration and relative deprivation, disadvantaged groups will engage in protest only when they actually experience acute frustration. For example, Berkowitz (1972) offered a detailed analysis of how riots may occur. He suggested that in addition to a sense of frustration there needed to be three other conditions: (a) aversive environmental circumstances that would amplify chronic frustration—for example, heat, overcrowding, (b) aggressive environmental cues that would introduce a social learning component—for example, armed police, and (c) social presence that would engage a social facilitation process—for example, many people assembled in the streets. Berkowitz empha- sized the automatic, emotional, and impulsive aspects of collective behavior—he is famous for his "long hot summer" analysis of the late-1960s urban race riots in the United States which mainly occurred during heatwaves.

Reicher (1984, 2001) provides a quite different analysis of the crowd. He adopts a social identity perspective to argue that crowd behavior is a set of deliberate and logical actions that are directly related to the goals and objectives of the group that defines the social identity of the crowd. The apparent volatility of crowd behavior is less extreme than media reports lead one to believe, occurs within limits set by the crowd's identity, and reflects a search for situation-specific behaviors that are consistent with the wider identity of the group.

Collective Action and Social Change

Although disadvantage, particularly acute disadvantage, can translate into riots and demon- strations, it also of course sponsors enduring campaigns for social change; campaigns that can last decades or even centuries. Relative deprivation researchers (e.g., Davis, 1959—see Walker & Pettigrew, 1984) suggest that disadvantage translates into social action when peo- ple suddenly become aware that their expectations and attainments have parted company; in particular, when there is a sudden drop in attainments against a background of rising expectations (Davies, 1969). These conditions have been invoked to explain the rise of anti-semitism in 1930s Europe, the French and Russian revolutions of 1789 and 1917, the American Civil War of the 1860s, and the Black Power movement of the 1960s.

Runciman (1966) introduced an important distinction between fraternalistic (intergroup) relative deprivation (a feeling that one's own group is deprived relative to relevant other groups), and egoistic (interpersonal) relative deprivation (a feeling that oneself is deprived relative to specific other individuals). It is the former that appears to be associated with social protest, whereas the latter is more likely to be associated with acquiescence and depression. For example, racist attitudes in the United States and Britain may be more extreme among skilled blue-collar people than any other group, because this group is most vulnerable to competition from other (e.g., immigrant) groups and thus feels most threatened and fraternalistically most deprived (Vanneman & Pettigrew, 1972; see Esses, Jackson & Armstrong, 1998). Walker and Mann (1987) provide a similar analysis of reactions to unemployment among unemployed Australians.

According to social identity theory disadvantaged groups will engage in direct competition with the dominant group if they perceive intergroup boundaries to be impermeable, and if they perceive their lower status to be illegitimate and unstable, and if they can conceive of a new status quo that is achievable (see Ellemers, 1993; Hogg & Abrams, 1988; Tajfel & Turner, 1986). This analysis attributes protest on the part of disadvantaged groups to a conjunction of social-cognitive factors and social belief systems and ideologies. For example, according to research by Wright, Taylor, and Moghaddam (1990), if members of a disadvantaged group believe that entry to an advantaged group is open, even only slightly open (only a token percentage of people can pass), they shun collective action and instead individually try to gain entry to the advantaged group. Collective action is most likely to be taken when entry to the advantaged group is closed, and then it is only taken by those who believe they were closest to entry, because they feel the strongest sense of relative deprivation. Collective action is only likely to be extreme (e.g., riots, terrorism) when socially acceptable normative means (e.g., peaceful protest, lobbying) are unavailable.

Social Protest and Active Minorities

The study of social protest is the study of how individual discontents or grievances are transformed into collective action: how and why do sympathizers become mobilized as activists or participants (e.g., Klandermans, 1997; Reicher, 2001)? Klandermans (1997) argues that mobilization is a facet of the attitude–behavior relationship—sympathizers hold sympathetic attitudes toward an issue, yet these attitudes do not readily translate into behavior. Participation also resembles a social dilemma. Protest is generally *for* a social good (e.g., equality) or *against* a social ill (e.g., oppression), and as success benefits everyone irrespective of participation but failure harms participants more, it is tempting to "free ride"—to remain a sympathizer rather than become a participant. Social protest can, however, only be fully understood in its wider intergroup context, where there is a clash of ideas and ideologies between groups, and politicized and strategic articulation with other more or less sympathetic organizations.

Social protest is often engaged in by minorities who actively try to change majority attitudes and practices. Research on minority influence suggests that majority and minority groups have access to different influence resources, and may actually influence through different processes (e.g., Maass & Clark, 1984; Wood, Lundgren, Ouellette, Busceme, & Blackstone, 1994). Active minorities need to adopt a particular behavioral style to influence members of a majority group (Mugny, 1982): they need to present a consistent and consensual message, they need to be seen to have made some sacrifice for their cause, they need to be seen to be acting out of principle, and they need to be seen by the majority to be to some extent in-group members. This behavioral style, particularly consistency, creates cognitive conflict in the mind of majority members between majority and minority views—majority members are not immediately influenced, but experience a sudden conversion to the minority point of view at a later time. Consistent minorities have latent, deep-seated, influence over majorities that produces a sudden and enduring conversion effect (Moscovici, 1980; Nemeth,

1986). Minorities that are inconsistent have little impact because their message is easily disregarded. Majorities are taken for granted, and people simply comply with their views without internalizing them or undergoing any deep-seated cognitive change.

Intergroup influence can also involve attitude polarization (e.g., Abrams, Wetherell, Cochrane, Hogg, & Turner, 1990; Mackie, 1986). One or both groups extremitize their normative attitudes to distance themselves further from an out-group or from people not in the in-group. This is particularly likely to occur where groups are in competition, and members identify strongly with their in-group and thus internalize the group norm as their own attitude—the underlying process is self-categorization and depersonalization (see above).

SOCIAL HARMONY AMONG GROUPS

Intergroup Contact

The goal of most intergroup relations researchers is to learn enough about intergroup relations to be able to know, and perhaps advise, how to improve intergroup relations and build social harmony. To this end, a prevalent belief is that close and pleasant interpersonal contact between people from different groups is probably the best way to achieve social harmony—the contact hypothesis (Allport, 1954; also see Amir, 1969; Cook, 1985; Hewstone & Brown, 1986). The idea that appropriate intergroup contact could improve intergroup relations was a central plank in the policy put in place in the United States in 1954 to improve race relations by desegregating the school system. The practice of "busing" children in and out of racially homogenous school districts was partly aimed at increasing inter-racial contact (Schofield, 1991). For contact to be effective it needs to be prolonged and cooperative, it needs to occur within an official and institutional climate that strongly encourages integration, and it needs to be between equal status groups. These conditions are nigh impossible to satisfy; and so contact is notoriously ineffective at changing intergroup attitudes or improving intergroup relations. After all, charged intergroup relations are often associated with groups that are very different—contact simply confirms one's worst fears (Bochner, 1982). In addition, as we have seen above (e.g., Sherif, 1958), intergroup conflict may rest upon real conflicts of interest over scarce resources—until perceived or actual goal relations are changed, contact will simply provide a forum for conflict.

One specific problem is that there can be substantial anxiety associated with intergroup contact, which of course renders the interaction somewhat aversive (Stephan & Stephan, 1985). Intergroup anxiety is a state in which people worry about negative psychological and behavioral consequence for self and negative evaluations of self by both in-group and out-group, as a consequence of intergroup contact. Intergroup anxiety arises out of past experience of contact, intergroup beliefs (stereotypes), and the degree of normative structure of the contact situation. It affects intergroup behavior—intergroup anxiety can produce intergroup avoidance, and stereotype-confirming perceptions, evaluations, and feelings.

Contact, which is not associated with intergroup anxiety can be pleasant; indeed sufficiently pleasant to encourage the development of enduring friendships across group boundaries (Pettigrew, 1998). However, being close friends with people from another group does not guarantee that one has positive attitudes toward that group as a whole (but see Wright, Aron, McLaughlin-Volpe, & Ropp, 1997). Close friendships between members of different groups often do not improve generalized intergroup images. People may like each other as individuals, but they still harbor negative attitudes toward the groups as a whole.

One way to get around this problem is to encourage people in contact situations to de-categorize themselves and treat each other as unique individuals, or to re-categorize themselves as members of a shared superordinate identity. Research by Gaertner and Dovidio and their colleagues (e.g., Gaertner, Dovidio, Anasasio, Bachman, & Rust, 1993; Gaertner, Mann, Murrell, & Dovidio, 1989) shows that both strategies reduce intergroup discrimination, but by different routes: re-categorization improves out-group attitudes, whereas de-categorization worsens in-group attitudes. One problem with re-categorization is that it can, particularly in non-laboratory contexts, represent a threat to the distinctiveness of the separate groups, and associated social identities, that are being encouraged to re-categorize themselves as a single entity. For instance, many organizational mergers fail for precisely these reasons (e.g., Terry, Carey, & Callan, 2001). This problem surfaces at the cultural level in the relative ineffectiveness of assimilationist strategies to forge a single harmonious cultural or national identity out of many cultural groups. Social harmony may be better served by a multicultural strategy that avoids the distinctiveness threat raised by assimilationism (see Hornsey & Hogg, 2000; Prentice & Miller, 1999).

Since re-categorization has a tendency to backfire, perhaps improved generalized intergroup attitudes and relations are more likely to emerge from contact that is framed in intergroup terms. But the problem here, as we have already seen, is that intergroup contact is often sufficiently stressful to render it unpleasant or even hostile. It can be very difficult to produce pleasant intergroup contact, which is a prerequisite for improved generalized images. More generally, it is very difficult to create enduring pluralistic contexts where people identify at the subgroup and at the superordinate group level simultaneously, and thus do not experience identity threat and do not interact in a hostile intergroup manner, but do view each other in group terms that permit generalization.

The main aim of contact is for pleasant interaction to change enduring intergroup images—that is, for generalization to occur through the accumulation of favorable out-group information (bookkeeping), or through a sudden encounter with counter-stereotypic information (conversion), or through the development of a more textured out-group representation (subtyping) (Weber & Crocker, 1983). Research (e.g., Wilder, 1984) shows that people who have pleasant contact with an out-group member who is clearly viewed as being representative or stereotypical of the out-group, do develop improved attitudes toward the out-group as a whole. But generally speaking the relationship between intergroup contact and enduring social harmony is an enormously complex one, which involves a large number of interacting conditions (e.g., Islam & Hewstone, 1993).

Diversity

Intergroup contact is actually extremely prevalent. For example, under the guise of socio-demographic diversity most people work or study in organizations and groups that are socio-demographically diverse in terms of race, gender, ethnicity, religion, and so forth. Such groups act as a crucible for intergroup relations to be played out. Social identity based research tends to show that because roles within such groups tend to correlate with category membership, intergroup relations are highly salient (e.g., Brewer, 1996; Brewer, von Hippel, & Gooden, 1999). If such relations are hostile in society as a whole, then the interactive group accentuates that behavior. Better relations are achieved by cross-cutting roles with category membership (also see Vescio, Hewstone, Crisp, & Rubin, 1999).

This can however be difficult to implement, because of the human tendency to automatically assign leadership roles to people who belong to high status social categories. According to expectation states theory and status characteristics theory (e.g., Berger, Fisek, Norman, & Zelditch, 1977; Ridgeway, 2001), influence within an interactive group is a function of the extent to which a person possesses characteristics that suit him or her to effective task perform-ance (i.e., specific status characteristics), and possesses characteristics that categorize him or her as a member of a high status socio-demographic group (i.e., diffuse status characteristics).

CONCLUDING COMMENTS

In this chapter I have given an overview of the social psychology of intergroup relations. By necessity I have sacrificed some detail in preference for inclusiveness, though the coverage should not be considered encyclopedic. For further or different recent coverage of the social psychology of intergroup relations see Brewer and Brown (1998), Brown and Gaertner (2001), Hogg and Abrams (2001b), and Mackie and Smith (1998).

At the social psychological level, intergroup relations hinge on some very basic social cog-nitive processes. Social categorization segments the world of people into groups, and represents groups schematically, mainly in terms of prototypes. Prototypes of groups are generally shared by people within a group (i.e., they are stereotypes)—they describe and prescribe perceptions, attitudes, behaviors, and feelings that define one group and clearly differentiate that group from other groups. The social categorization process strives to maximize entitativity. The link between category cues, social categorization, and stereotyping is generally relatively automatic.

People define themselves in terms of the groups they belong to—they derive their social identity from group memberships. Because of this, intergroup relations are characterized by a struggle over status and prestige—membership in a prestigious high status group reflects well on self-conception, whereas membership of a low status group is a stigma that is often associ-ated with disadvantage. People are, however, very creative in avoiding the self-evaluative consequences of stigma. Intergroup relations are underpinned by people's need to feel positive about themselves (self-enhancement) and by their need to feel certain about themselves, their place in the world, and how they relate to other people (uncertainty reduction). These motives guide intergroup behavior, but they are moderated by strategic intergroup considerations that rest on people's understanding of the nature of the relations between groups, in terms of the stability and legitimacy of intergroup status differences, the permeability of group boundaries, the goal relations between groups, and so forth.

The relationship between intergroup attitudes and intergroup behavior is a manifestation of the wider issue of attitude–behavior relations—prejudice does not always express itself very obviously in discrimination, and oppressed minorities do not always engage in minority influence, social protest, and collective action.

Finally, because intergroup relations are intrinsically competitive and ethnocentric it is very difficult to improve them. Intergroup contact and diversity only improve relations under very restricted conditions, and attempts to merge groups often backfire because of the identity threat that is usually present. Conditions that respect group differences and affirm iden-tity but reconfigure intergroup relations within a superordinate identity are most promising.

REFERENCES

Abrams, D., & Hogg, M. A. (1988). Comments on the motivational status of self-esteem in social identity and intergroup discrimination. *European Journal of Social Psychology, 18*, 317–334.

Abrams, D., & Hogg, M. A. (Eds.). (1999). *Social identity and social cognition.* Oxford, UK: Blackwell.

Abrams, D., & Hogg, M. A. (2001). Collective identity: Group membership and self-conception. In M. A. Hogg & R. S. Tindale (Eds.), *Blackwell handbook of social psychology: Group processes* (pp. 425–460). Oxford, UK: Blackwell.

Abrams, D., Wetherell, M. S., Cochrane, S., Hogg, M. A., & Turner, J. C. (1990). Knowing what to think by knowing who you are: Self-categorization and the nature of norm formation, conformity, and group polarization. *British Journal of Social Psychology, 29,* 97–119.

Adorno, T. W., Frenkel-Brunswik, E., Levinson, D. J., & Sanford, R. M. (1950). *The authoritarian personality.* New York: Harper.

Allport, F. H. (1924). *Social psychology.* Boston: Houghton-Mifflin.

Allport, G. W. (1954). *The nature of prejudice.* Reading, MA: Addison-Wesley.

Altemeyer, B. (1994). Reducing prejudice in right-wing authoritarians. In M. P. Zanna & J. M. Olsen (Eds.), *The psychology of prejudice: The Ontario symposium* (pp. 131–148). Hillsdale, NJ: Erlbaum.

Amir, Y. (1969). Contact hypothesis in ethnic relations. *Psychological Bulletin, 71,* 319–342.

Andreeva, G. (1984). Cognitive processes in developing groups. In L. H. Strickland (Ed.), *Directions in Soviet social psychology* (pp. 67–82). New York: Springer.

Arrow, H., McGrath, J. E., & Berdahl, J. L. (2000). *Small groups as complex systems: Formation, coordination, development, and adaptation.* Thousand Oaks, CA: Sage.

Bargh, J. A. (1994). The four horsemen of automaticity: Awareness, intention, efficiency, and control in social cognition. In R. S. Wyer, Jr. & T. K. Srull (Eds.), *Handbook of social cognition* (Vol. 1, 2nd ed., pp. 1–40). Hillsdale, NJ: Erlbaum.

Baumeister, R. F., & Leary, M. R. (1995). The need to belong: Desire for interpersonal attachments as a fundamental human motivation. *Psychological Bulletin, 117,* 497–529.

Berger, J., Fisek, M. H., Norman, R. Z., & Zelditch, M. Jr. (1977). *Status characteristics and social interaction.* New York: Elsevier.

Berkowitz, L. (1972). Frustrations, comparisons, and other sources of emotion arousal as contributors to social unrest. *Journal of Social Issues, 28,* 77–91.

Billig, M. (1976). *Social psychology and intergroup relations.* London: Academic Press.

Blake, R. R., & Mouton, J. S. (1961). Reactions to intergroup competition under win/lose conditions. *Management Science, 7,* 420–435.

Bobo, L., & Hutchings, V. L. (1996). Perceptions of racial group competition: Extending Blumer's theory of group position to a multiracial social context. *American Sociological Review, 61,* 951–972.

Bochner, S. (1982). The social psychology of cross-cultural relations. In S. Bochner (Ed.), *Cultures in contact: Studies in cross-cultural interaction.* Oxford, UK: Pergamon.

Branscombe, N. R., Doosje, B., & McGarty, C. (2002). Antecedents and consequences of collective guilt. In D. M. Mackie & E. R. Smith (Eds.), *From prejudice to intergroup emotions: Differentiated reactions to social groups* (pp. 49–66). Philadelphia, PA: Psychology Press.

Branscombe, N. R., Wann, D. L., Noel, J. G., & Coleman, J. (1993). In-group or out-group extremity: Importance of the threatened social identity. *Personality and Social Psychology Bulletin, 19,* 381–388.

Brewer, M. B. (1991). The social self: On being the same and different at the same time. *Personality and Social Psychology Bulletin, 17,* 475–482.

Brewer, M. B. (1996). Managing diversity: The role of social identities. In S. Jackson & M. Ruderman (Eds.), *Diversity in work teams* (pp. 47–68). Washington, DC: American Psychological Association.

Brewer, M. B., & Brown, R. J. (1998). Intergroup relations. In D. T. Gilbert, S. T. Fiske, & G. Lindzey (Eds.), *The handbook of social psychology* (4th ed., Vol. 2, pp. 554–594). New York: McGraw-Hill.

Brewer, M. B., & Campbell, D. T. (1976). *Ethnocentrism and intergroup attitudes: East African evidence.* New York: Sage.

Brewer, M. B., & Gardner, W. (1996). Who is this "we"? Levels of collective identity and self representations. *Journal of Personality and Social Psychology, 71,* 83–93.

Brewer, M. B., von Hippel, W., & Gooden, M. P. (1999). Diversity and organizational identity: The problem of entrée after entry. In D. A. Prentice & D. T. Miller (Eds.), *Cultural divides: Understanding and overcoming group conflict* (pp. 337–363). New York: Russell Sage Foundation.

Brown, R. J., & Gaertner, S. (Eds.) (2001). *Blackwell handbook of social psychology: Intergroup processes.* Oxford, UK: Blackwell.

Capozza, D., & Brown, R. J. (Eds.) (2000). *Social identity processes.* London: Sage.

Cook, S. W. (1985). Experimenting on social issues: The case of school desegregation. *American Psychologist, 40,* 452–460.

Crocker, J., & Major, B. (1989). Social stigma and self-esteem: The self-protective properties of stigma. *Psychological Review, 96*, 608–630.

Crocker, J., Major, B., & Steele, C. (1998). Social stigma. In D. T. Gilbert, S. T. Fiske, & G. Lindzey (Eds.), *The handbook of social psychology* (4th ed., Vol. 2, pp. 504–553). New York: McGraw-Hill.

Crosby, F. (1982). *Relative deprivation and working women.* New York: Oxford University Press.

Crosby, F., Bromley, S., & Saxe, L. (1980). Recent unobtrusive studies of Black and White discrimination and prejudice: A literature review. *Psychological Bulletin, 87*, 546–563.

Davies, J. C. (1969). The J-curve of rising and declining satisfaction as a cause of some great revolutions and a contained rebellion. In H. D. Graham & T. R. Gurr (Eds.), *The history of violence in America: Historical and comparative perspectives* (pp. 690–730). New York: Praeger.

Davis, J. A. (1959). A formal interpretation of the theory of relative deprivation. *Sociometry, 22*, 280–296.

Deutsch, M. (1973). *The resolution of conflict.* New Haven, CT: Yale University Press.

Devine, P. G. (1989). Stereotypes and prejudice: Their automatic and controlled components. *Journal of Personality and Social Psychology, 56*, 5–18.

Diehl, M. (1990). The minimal group paradigm: Theoretical explanations and empirical findings. *European Review of Social Psychology, 1*, 263–292.

Dovidio, J. F., & Gaertner, S. L. (1998). On the nature of contemporary prejudice: The causes, consequences, and challenges of aversive racism. In J. L. Eberhardt & S. T. Fiske (Eds.), *Confronting prejudice: The problem and the response* (pp. 3–32). Thousand Oaks, CA: Sage.

Eagly, A. H., & Chaiken, S. (1993). *The psychology of attitudes.* San Diego, CA: Harcourt Brace Jovanovich.

Ellemers, N. (1993). The influence of socio-structural variables on identity management strategies. *European Review of Social Psychology, 4*, 27–57.

Ellemers, N., Spears, R., & Doosje, B. (Eds.). (1999). *Social identity.* Oxford, UK: Blackwell.

Emler, N., & Reicher, S. D. (1995). *Adolescence and delinquency: The collective management of reputation.* Oxford, UK: Blackwell.

Esses, V. M., Jackson, L. M., & Armstrong, T. L. (1998). Intergroup competition and attitudes towards immigrants and immigration: An instrumental model of group conflict. *Journal of Social Issues, 54*, 699–724.

Ethier, K. A., & Deaux, K. (1994). Negotiating social identity when contexts change: Maintaining identification and responding to threat. *Journal of Personality and Social Psychology, 67*, 243–251.

Farr, R. M., & Moscovici, S. (Eds.). (1984). *Social representations.* Cambridge, UK: Cambridge University Press.

Fazio, R. H., Sanbonmatsu, D. M., Powell, M. C., & Kardes, F. R. (1986). On the automatic activation of attitudes. *Journal of Personality and Social Psychology, 50*, 229–238.

Festinger, L. (1954). A theory of social comparison processes. *Human Relations, 7*, 117–140.

Fisher, R. J. (1990). *The social psychology of intergroup and international conflict resolution.* New York: Springer-Verlag.

Fiske, S. T., & Taylor, S. E. (1991). *Social cognition* (2nd ed.). New York: McGraw-Hill.

Gaertner, S. L., Dovidio, J. F., Anastasio, P. A., Bachman, B. A., & Rust, M. C. (1993). Reducing intergroup bias: The common ingroup identity model. *European Review of Social Psychology, 4*, 1–26.

Gaertner, S. L., Mann, J., Murrell, A., & Dovidio, J. F. (1989). Reducing intergroup bias: The benefits of recategorization. *Journal of Personality and Social Psychology, 57*, 239–249.

Greenberg, J., Solomon, S., & Pyszczynski, T. (1997). Terror management theory of self-esteem and cultural worldviews: Empirical assessments and conceptual refinements. In M. Zanna (Ed.), *Advances in experimental social psychology* (Vol. 29, pp. 61–139). Orlando, FL: Academic Press.

Hamilton, D. L., & Gifford, R. K. (1976). Illusory correlation in interpersonal person perception: A cognitive basis of stereotypic judgments. *Journal of Experimental Social Psychology, 12*, 392–407.

Hamilton, D. L., & Sherman, J. W. (1994). Stereotypes. In R. S. Wyer, Jr. & T. K. Srull (Eds.), *Handbook of social cognition* (Vol. 2, pp. 1–68). Hillsdale, NJ: Erlbaum.

Hamilton, D. L., & Sherman, S. J. (1996). Perceiving persons and groups. *Psychological Review, 103*, 336–355.

Hewstone, M., & Jaspars, J. M. F. (1982). Intergroup relations and attribution processes. In H. Tajfel (Ed.), *Social identity and intergroup relations* (pp. 99–133). Cambridge, UK: Cambridge University Press.

Hewstone. M., & Brown, R. J. (Eds.). (1986). *Contact and conflict in intergroup encounters.* Oxford, UK: Blackwell.

Hewstone, M., & Ward, C. (1985). Ethnocentrism and causal attribution in Southeast Asia. *Journal of Personality and Social Psychology, 48*, 614–623.

Hogg, M. A. (1993). Group cohesiveness: A critical review and some new directions. *European Review of Social Psychology, 4*, 85–111.

Hogg, M. A. (2000a). Social identity and social comparison. In J. Suls & L. Wheeler (Eds.), *Handbook of social comparison: Theory and research* (pp. 401–421). New York: Kluwer/Plenum.

Hogg, M. A. (2000b). Subjective uncertainty reduction through self-categorization: A motivational theory of social identity processes. *European Review of Social Psychology, 11*, 223–255.

Hogg, M. A. (2001a). Social categorization, depersonalization, and group behavior. In M. A. Hogg & R. S. Tindale, (Eds.), *Blackwell handbook of social psychology: Group processes* (pp. 56–85). Oxford, UK: Blackwell.

Hogg, M. A. (2001b). Self-categorization and subjective uncertainty resolution: Cognitive and motivational facets of social identity and group membership. In J. P. Forgas, K. D. Williams, & L. Wheeler (Eds.), *The social mind: Cognitive and motivational aspects of interpersonal behavior* (pp. 323–349). New York: Cambridge University Press.

Hogg, M. A. (2001c). Social identity and the sovereignty of the group: A psychology of belonging. In C. Sedikides & M. B. Brewer (Eds.), *Individual self, relational self, and collective self: Partners, opponents, or strangers.* Philadelphia, PA: Psychology Press.

Hogg, M. A. (2003). Social identity. In M. R. Leary & J. P. Tangney (Eds.), *Handbook of self and identity* (pp. 462–479). New York: Guilford.

Hogg, M. A. (in press). Uncertainty and extremism: Identification with high entitativity groups under conditions of uncertainty. In V. Yzerbyt, C. M. Judd, & O. Corneille (Eds.), *The psychology of group perception: Contributions to the study of homogeneity, entitativity, and essentialism.* Philadelphia, PA: Psychology Press.

Hogg, M. A., & Abrams, D. (1988). *Social identifications: A social psychology of intergroup relations and group processes.* London: Routledge.

Hogg, M. A., & Abrams, D. (2001a). Intergroup relations: An overview. In M. A. Hogg & D. Abrams (Eds.), *Intergroup relations: Essential readings* (pp. 1–14). Philadelphia, PA: Psychology Press.

Hogg, M. A., & Abrams, D. (Eds.). (2001b). *Intergroup relations: Essential readings.* Philadelphia, PA: Psychology Press.

Hogg, M. A., & Terry, D. J. (Eds.). (2001). *Social identity processes in organizational contexts.* Philadelphia, PA: Psychology Press.

Hogg, M. A., & Williams, K. D. (2000). From I to we: Social identity and the collective self. *Group Dynamics: Theory, Research, and Practice, 4*, 81–97.

Hornsey, M. J., & Hogg, M. A. (2000). Assimilation and diversity: An integrative model of subgroup relations. *Personality and Social Psychology Review, 4*, 143–156.

Insko, C. A., Schopler, J., Kennedy, J. F., Dahl, K. R., Graetz, K. A., & Drigotas, S. M. (1992). Individual-group discontinuity from the differing perspectives of Campbell's realistic group conflict theory and Tajfel and Turner's social identity theory. *Social Psychology Quarterly, 55*, 272–291.

Islam, M., & Hewstone, M. (1993). Intergroup attributions and affective consequences in majority and minority groups. *Journal of Personality and Social Psychology, 65*, 936–950.

Jetten, J., Spears, R., & Manstead, A. S. R. (1997). Identity threat and prototypicality: Combined effects on intergroup discrimination and collective self-esteem. *European Journal of Social Psychology, 27*, 635–657.

Jones, E. E., Wood, G. C., & Quattrone, G. A. (1981). Perceived variability of personal characteristics in ingroups and outgroups: The role of knowledge and evaluation. *Personality and Social Psychology Bulletin, 7*, 523–528.

Jost, J. T., & Kramer, R. M. (2002). The system justification motive in intergroup relations. In D. M. Mackie & E. R. Smith (Eds.), *From prejudice to intergroup emotions: Differentiated reactions to social groups* (pp. 227–243). Philadelphia, PA: Psychology Press.

Judd, C. M., & Park, B. (1988). Out-group homogeneity: Judgments of variability at the individual and group levels. *Journal of Personality and Social Psychology, 54*, 778–788.

Klandermans, B. (1997). *The social psychology of protest.* Oxford, UK: Blackwell.

LaPiere, R. T. (1934). Attitudes vs actions. *Social Forces, 13*, 230–237.

Leary, M. R., Tambor, E. S., Terdal, S. K., & Downs, D. L. (1995). Self-esteem as an interpersonal monitor: The sociometer hypothesis. *Journal of Personality and Social Psychology, 68*, 518–530.

Lepore, L., & Brown, R. (1997). Category and stereotype activation: Is prejudice inevitable? *Journal of Personality and Social Psychology, 72*, 275–287.

Linville, P. W., Fischer, G. W., & Salovey, P. (1989). Perceived distributions of the characteristics of in-group and out-group members: Empirical evidence and a computer simulation. *Journal of Personality and Social Psychology, 57*, 165–188.

Maass, A. (1999). Linguistic intergroup bias: Stereotype-perpetuation through language. In M. P. Zanna (Ed.), *Advances in experimental social psychology* (Vol. 31, pp. 79–121). San Diego, CA: Academic Press.

Maass, A., & Clark, R. D. III. (1984). Hidden impact of minorities: Fifteen years of minority influence research. *Psychological Bulletin, 95*, 428–450.

Mackie, D. M. (1986). Social identification effects in group polarization. *Journal of Personality and Social Psychology, 50*, 720–728.

Mackie, D. M., Devos, T., & Smith, E. R. (2000). Intergroup emotions: Explaining offensive action tendencies in an intergroup context. *Journal of Personality and Social Psychology, 79*, 602–616.

Mackie, D. M., & Smith, E. R. (1998). Intergroup relations: Insights from a theoretically integrative approach. *Psychological Review, 105*, 499–529.

Mackie, D. M., & Smith, E. R. (Eds.). (2002). *From prejudice to intergroup emotions: Differentiated reactions to social groups*. Philadelphia, PA: Psychology Press.

Macrae, N., Bodenhausen, G. V., Milne, A. B., & Jetten, J. (1994). Out of mind but back in sight: Stereotypes on the rebound. *Journal of Personality and Social Psychology, 67*, 808–817.

Major, B. (1994). From social inequality to personal entitlement: The role of social comparisons, legitimacy appraisals and group memberships. In M. P. Zanna (Ed.), *Advances in experimental social psychology* (Vol. 26, pp. 293–355). San Diego, CA: Academic Press.

Marques, J. M., Abrams, D., Páez, D., & Hogg, M. A. (2001). Social categorization, social identification, and rejection of deviant group members. In M. A. Hogg & R. S. Tindale, (Eds.), *Blackwell handbook of social psychology: Group processes* (pp. 400–424). Oxford, UK: Blackwell.

Marques, J. M., & Páez, D. (1994). The black sheep effect: Social categorization, rejection of ingroup deviates, and perception of group variability. *European Review of Social Psychology, 5*, 37–68.

McConahay, J. G. (1986). Modern racism, ambivalence, and the modern racism scale. In J. F. Dovidio & S. L. Gaertner (Eds.), *Prejudice, discrimination, and racism* (pp. 91–125). New York: Academic Press.

Medin, D. L., & Ortony, A. (1989). Psychological essentialism. In S. Vosnaidou & A. Ortony (Eds.), *Similarity and analogical reasoning* (pp. 179–195). Cambridge, UK: Cambridge University Press.

Miller, D. T., & Prentice, D. A. (1999). Some consequences of a belief in group essence: The category divide hypothesis. In D. A. Prentice & D. T. Miller (Eds.), *Cultural divides: Understanding and overcoming group conflict* (pp. 213–238). New York: Russell Sage Foundation.

Moreland, R. L., Hogg, M. A., & Hains, S. C. (1994). Back to the future: Social psychological research on groups. *Journal of Experimental Social Psychology, 30*, 527–555.

Moscovici, S. (1980). Toward a theory of conversion behavior. In L. Berkowitz (Ed.), *Advances in Experimental Social Psychology* (Vol. 13, pp. 202–239). New York: Academic Press.

Mugny, G. (1982). *The power of minorities*. London: Academic Press.

Nemeth, C. (1986). Differential contributions of majority and minority influence. *Psychological Review, 93*, 23–32.

Otten, S., Mummendey, A., & Blanz, M. (1996). Intergroup discrimination in positive and negative outcome allocations: Impact of stimulus valence, relative group status, and relative group size. *Personality and Social Psychology Bulletin, 22*, 568–581.

Pettigrew, T. F. (1958). Personality and sociocultural factors in intergroup attitudes: A cross-national comparison. *Journal of Conflict Resolution, 2*, 29–42.

Pettigrew, T. F. (1979). The ultimate attribution error: Extending Allport's cognitive analysis of prejudice. *Personality and Social Psychology Bulletin, 5*, 461–476.

Pettigrew, T. F. (1998). Intergroup contact theory. *Annual Review of Psychology, 49*, 65–85.

Pratto, F., Sidanius, J., Stallworth, L. M., & Malle, B. F. (1994). Social dominance orientation: A personality variable predicting social and political attitudes. *Journal of Personality and Social Psychology, 67*, 741–763.

Prentice, D. A., & Miller, D. T. (Eds.). (1999). *Cultural divides: Understanding and overcoming group conflict*. New York: Russell Sage Foundation.

Rabbie, J. M., Schot, J. C., & Visser, L. (1989). Social identity theory: A conceptual and empirical critique from the perspective of a behavioural interaction model. *European Journal of Social Psychology, 19*, 171–202.

Reicher, S. D. (1984). The St Pauls' riot: An explanation of the limits of crowd action in terms of a social identity model. *European Journal of Social Psychology, 14*, 1–21.

Reicher, S. D. (2001). The psychology of crowd dynamics. In M. A. Hogg & R. S. Tindale (Eds.), *Blackwell handbook of social psychology: Group processes* (pp. 182–208). Oxford, UK: Blackwell.

Reicher, S. D., & Hopkins, N. (1986). Seeking influence through characterising self-categories: An analysis of anti-abortionist rhetoric. *British Journal of Social Psychology, 35*, 297–311.

Reynolds, K. J., Turner, J. C., Haslam, S. A., & Ryan, M. K. (2001). The role of personality and group factors in explaining prejudice. *Journal of Experimental Social Psychology, 37*, 427–434.

Ridgeway, C. L. (2001). Social status and group structure. In M. A. Hogg & R. S. Tindale (Eds.), *Blackwell handbook of social psychology: Group processes* (pp. 352–375). Oxford, UK: Blackwell.

Rokeach, M. (Ed.). (1960). *The open and closed mind*. New York: Basic Books.

Rosch, E. (1978). Principles of categorization. In E. Rosch & B. B. Lloyd (Eds.), *Cognition and categorization* (pp. 27–48). Hillsdale, NJ: Erlbaum.

Ross, L. (1977). The intuitive psychologist and his shortcomings. In L. Berkowitz (Ed.), *Advances in experimental social psychology* (Vol. 10, pp. 174–220). New York: Academic Press.

Rubin, M., & Hewstone, M. (1998). Social identity theory's self-esteem hypothesis: A review and some suggestions for clarification. *Personality and Social Psychology Review, 2*, 40–62.

Runciman, W. G. (1966). *Relative deprivation and social justice*. London: Routledge and Kegan Paul.

Schofield, J. W. (1991). School desegregation and intergroup relations: A review of the literature. In G. Grant (Ed.), *Review of research in education* (Vol. 17, pp. 335–409). Washington, DC: American Education Research Association.

Sedikides, C., & Strube, M. J. (1997). Self-evaluation: To thine own self be good, to thine own self be sure, to thine own self be true, and to thine own self be better. In M. P. Zanna (Ed.), *Advances in experimental social psychology* (Vol. 29, pp. 209–296). New York: Academic Press.

Sherif, M. (1958). Superordinate goals in the reduction of intergroup conflicts. *American Journal of Sociology, 63*, 349–356.

Sherif, M. (Ed.). (1962). *Intergroup relations and leadership*. New York: Wiley.

Sherif, M. (1966). *In common predicament: Social psychology of intergroup conflict and cooperation*. Boston, MA: Houghton-Mifflin.

Sherif, M., Harvey, O. J., White, B. J., Hood, W., & Sherif, C. (1961). *Intergroup conflict and cooperation: The Robbers Cave experiment*. Norman, OK: University of Oklahoma Institute of Intergroup Relations.

Simon, B., & Brown, R. J. (1987). Perceived intragroup homogeneity in minority–majority contexts. *Journal of Personality and Social Psychology, 53*, 703–711.

Steele, C. M. (1988). The psychology of self-affirmation: Sustaining the integrity of the self. *Advances in Experimental Social Psychology, 21*, 261–302.

Steele, C. M., & Aronson, J. (1995). Stereotype vulnerability and the intellectual test performance of African–Americans. *Journal of Personality and Social Psychology, 69*, 797–811.

Stephan, W. G., & Stephan, C. W. (1985). Intergroup anxiety. *Journal of Social Issues, 41*, 157–175.

Sumner, W. G. (1906). *Folkways*. Boston, MA: Ginn.

Swim, J. K., Aikin, K. J., Hall, W. S., & Hunter, B. A. (1995). Sexism and racism: Old fashioned and modern prejudices. *Journal of Personality and Social Psychology, 68*, 199–214.

Tajfel, H. (1959). Quantitative judgement in social perception. *British Journal of Psychology, 50*, 16–29.

Tajfel, H. (1981). Social stereotypes and social groups. In J. C. Turner & H. Giles (Eds.), *Intergroup behaviour* (pp. 144–167). Oxford, UK: Blackwell.

Tajfel, H., Billig, M., Bundy, R. P., & Flament, C. (1971). Social categorization and intergroup behaviour. *European Journal of Social Psychology, 1*, 149–177.

Tajfel, H., & Turner, J. C. (1986). The social identity theory of intergroup behavior. In S. Worchel & W. Austin (Eds.), *Psychology of intergroup relations* (pp. 7–24). Chicago: Nelson-Hall.

Taylor, D. M., & Jaggi, V. (1974). Ethnocentrism and causal attribution in a S. Indian context. *Journal of Cross-cultural Psychology, 5*, 162–171.

Taylor, D. M., Wright, S. C., & Porter, L. E. (1994). Dimensions of perceived discrimination: The personal/group discrimination discrepancy. In M. P. Zanna & J. M. Olson (Eds.), *The psychology of prejudice: The Ontario symposium* (Vol. 7, pp. 233–255). Hillsdale, NJ: Erlbaum.

Terry, D. J., Carey, C. J., & Callan, V. J. (2001). Employee adjustment to an organizational merger: An intergroup perspective. *Personality and Social Psychology Bulletin, 27*, 267–280.

Titus, H. E., & Hollander, E. P. (1957). The California F-scale in psychological research (1950–1955). *Psychological Bulletin, 54*, 47–74.

Tropp, L. R., & Wright, S. C. (2001). Ingroup identification as inclusion of ingroup in the self. *Personality and Social Psychology Bulletin, 27*, 585–600.

Turner, J. C. (1982). Towards a cognitive redefinition of the social group. In H. Tajfel (Ed.), *Social identity and intergroup relations* (pp. 15–40). Cambridge, UK: Cambridge University Press.

Turner, J. C. (1991). *Social influence*. Milton Keynes, UK: Open University Press.

Turner, J. C., Hogg, M. A., Oakes, P. J., Reicher, S. D., & Wetherell, M. S. (1987). *Rediscovering the social group: A self-categorization theory*. Oxford, UK: Blackwell.

Turner, J. C., & Bourhis, R. Y. (1996). Social identity, interdependence and the social group. A reply to Rabbie et al. In W. P. Robinson (Ed.), *Social groups and identities: Developing the legacy of Henri Tajfel* (pp. 25–63). Oxford, UK: Butterworth-Heinemann.

Tyler, T. R., DeGoey, P., & Smith, H. (1996). Understanding why the justice of group procedures matters: A test of the psychological dynamics of the group-value model. *Journal of Personality and Social Psychology, 70*, 913–930.

van Dijk, T. A. (1987). *Communicating racism: Ethnic prejudice in thought and talk*. Newburg Park, CA: Sage.

Vanneman, R. D., & Pettigrew, T. F. (1972). Race and relative deprivation in the urban United States. *Race, 13*, 461–486.

Vescio, T. K., Hewstone, M., Crisp, R. J., & Rubin, J. M. (1999). Perceiving and responding to multiple categorizable individuals: Cognitive processes and affective intergroup bias. In D. Abrams, & M. A. Hogg (Eds.), *Social identity and social cognition* (pp. 111–140). Oxford, UK: Blackwell.

von Hippel, W., Sekaquaptewa, D., & Vargas, P. (1995). On the role of encoding processes in stereotype maintenance. In L. Berkowitz (Ed.), *Advances in experimental social psychology* (Vol. 27, pp. 177–254). New York: Academic Press.

Walker, I., & Mann, L. (1987). Unemployment, relative deprivation, and social protest. *Personality and Social Psychology Bulletin, 13,* 275–283.

Walker, I., & Pettigrew, T. F. (1984). Relative deprivation theory: An overview and conceptual critique. *British Journal of Social Psychology, 23,* 301–310.

Weber, R., & Crocker, J. (1983). Cognitive processes in the revision of stereotypic beliefs. *Journal of Personality and Social Psychology, 45,* 961–977.

Wilder, D. A. (1984). Intergroup contact: The typical member and the exception to the rule. *Journal of Experimental Social Psychology, 20,* 177–194.

Williams, K. D. (2001). *Ostracism: The power of silence.* New York: Guilford.

Wood, W., Lundgren, S., Ouellette, J. A., Busceme, S., & Blackstone, T. (1994). Minority influence: A meta-analytic review of social influence processes. *Psychological Bulletin, 115,* 323–345.

Worchel, S., Morales, J. F., Páez, D., & Deschamps, J.-C. (Eds.). (1998). *Social identity: International perspectives.* London: Sage.

Wright, S. C., Aron, A., McLaughlin-Volpe, T., & Ropp, S. A. (1997). The extended contact effect: Knowledge of cross-group friendships and prejudice. *Journal of Personality and Social Psychology, 73,* 73–90.

Wright, S. C., Aron, A., & Tropp, L. R. (2002). Including others (and groups) in the self: Self-expansion and intergroup relations. In J. P. Forgas & K. D. Williams (Eds.), *The social self: Cognitive, interpersonal and intergroup perspectives* (pp. 343–363). Philadelphia, PA: Psychology Press.

Wright, S. C., Taylor, D. M., & Moghaddam, F. M. (1990). Responding to membership in a disadvantaged group. *Journal of Personality and Social Psychology, 58,* 994–1003.

Zebrowitz, L. A. (1996). Physical appearance as a basis of stereotyping. In C. N. Macrae, C. Stangor, & M. Hewstone, (Eds.), *Stereotypes and stereotyping* (pp. 79–120). New York: Guilford.

CHAPTER 20

Social Psychological Perspectives on Crowds and Social Movements

Deana A. Rohlinger
David A. Snow

Historically, the study of crowds and social movements has been animated by three broad and inclusive questions: What are the conditions underlying the emergence or mobilization of the collective phenomenon in question? Who participates and why some individuals or categories of individuals rather than others? And what are the consequences of the collective phenomena in relation to its targets and for its participants and its broader constituents? Although these are not the only questions that students of crowds and social movements have pursued, they clearly encompass the bulk of the research and writing among scholars of both crowd phenomena and social movements. How has social psychology informed the answers to these focal questions? For the most part, social psychological research and theorization on crowds and social movements has addressed issues and questions relating directly to matters of participation, including the individual-level consequences of participation, thus contributing answers to the second and third questions.

In this chapter, we elaborate these answers and contributions in terms of four theoretical perspectives and four concepts that have currency in both social psychology and the study of social movements and that are relevant to a broad-based understanding of participation in crowds and social movement activities. The four theoretical perspectives include what we call the dispositional perspective, learning and socialization models, the rational choice approach, and social constructionism. The four cornerstone concepts include grievances, symbolization, emotion, and identity. We focus our assessment of each perspective on these four concepts

DEANA A. ROHLINGER AND DAVID A. SNOW • Department of Sociology, University of California-Irvine, Irvine, California 92697

Handbook of Social Psychology, edited by John Delamater. Kluwer Academic/Plenum Publishers, New York, 2003.

because they are fundamental to understanding the precipitants and dynamics of participation, both individually and collectively. Indeed, we contend that a thorough and incisive understanding of the social psychology of participation and related issues requires consideration of grievances, symbolization, emotion, and identity.* After all, however social movements and the crowd activities associated with them are defined,[†] they entail, at the core, a collectivity of individuals engaging in some form of joint action to express their grievances about some matter or issue about which they feel strongly and to which an aspect of their identity is tied. We, thus, proceed by examining and critically assessing what each perspective, and associated research, says about the four concepts, if anything, and the broader, encompassing problem of participation.

Throughout the chapter we draw on two sets of literatures: one pertaining to participation in crowds; the second to participation in social movements. The literatures on the precipitants and dynamics of participation in these two related collective phenomena are quite unbalanced, however, with the literature on social movement participation-related issues being much more extensive. The reason for this imbalance is twofold. One has to do with the association of crowds with collective behavior, and the jettisoning of the so-called collective behavior tradition with the assent and eventual dominance of the resource mobilization and political process (opportunity) perspectives in the 1970s.[‡] The second reason for the imbalance is the failure to recognize empirically and appreciate theoretically, except for among a few scholars (e.g., Oliver, 1989; Turner & Killian, 1987), not only the extent to which some kinds of crowd phenomena and social movements overlap, but the extent to which the theoretical bases for accounting for participation in each are often the same. As a result of this imbalance, our analysis will be informed most heavily by literature on social movements. However, we will draw on relevant literature pertaining to the precipitants and dynamics of participation in the kinds of crowd phenomena most closely related to social movements, such as protest marches and rallies, victory celebrations, and so-called riots.

Three additional features of the organization of the chapter and our subsequent analysis warrant mention. First, our decision to focus on how the four mentioned theoretical perspectives inform understanding of our four focal concepts is based in part on wanting to avoid

---

*Each of these concepts, with the exception of grievances, has a strong footing within social psychology, as reflected in a number of the chapters in this volume. Each of the concepts, including grievances, has considerable contemporary currency in the literature on crowds and social movements as well. But grievances is the least well conceptualized, even though it is widely referred to and often discussed as if it is a necessary condition for constituent mobilization and participation. It is our sense, however, that the concept of grievances is generally used as a cover term for the indignations, resentments, and ill will that derive from a sense of being wronged. Accordingly, grievances can be conceptualized as troublesome and distressing circumstances or conditions felt to be of sufficient magnitude to warrant complaint and remedial action.

[†]For the purpose of this chapter, we employ the conceptualizations of crowds provided by Snow and Oliver (1995, pp. 571–572) and Snow and Paulsen (2000, pp. 553–554), and of social movements by Benford (2000, p. 2717), Snow and Oliver (1995, pp. 571–572), and Turner and Killian (1987, pp. 223–230). These parallel conceptualizations of movements are somewhat broader and more inclusive than those that link movements most closely to the political arena and the state (e.g., Della Porta & Diana, 1999; McAdam, Tarrow, & Tilly, 2001).

[‡]Snow and Davis (1995, p. 191) have called into question the categorization of all scholarship on crowds and social movements prior to the 1970s under the rubric of collective behavior theory because it lumps "together under the same umbrella work emanating from both the Harvard and Chicago (schools), as well as disparate psychologically oriented works." Buechler (2000, p. 40) also has alluded to this questionable categorization, noting that "(w)ith the rise of resource mobilization theory, there was a tendency for all of the versions of the classical model to be collapsed, critiqued, and rejected" and that "this tendency ignored the different theoretical underpinnings of these models and obliterated their subtleties and nuances."

duplicating the previous handbook-like inquiries into the social psychological contributions to the study of crowds and social movements (see Lofland, 1981; Snow & Oliver, 1995; Zurcher & Snow, 1981). Obviously this chapter overlaps with and draws on the earlier ones. Yet it is different in terms of its organizing logic and in terms of the increasing currency and crystallization of the rational choice and constructionist perspectives and the relevance of emotion and identity to the participation process. As well, there are some issues that we do not address. An example is the relevance of social networks and relational connections to mobilization and participation. Our failure to address this issue is due, not to its unimportance, but to our sense that we could add little to what was said about it in the previous handbook discussions (see Snow & Oliver, 1995, pp. 573–577; Zurcher & Snow, 1981, pp. 454–458). Second, in exploring the connections among the anchoring perspectives and concepts, we neither claim nor try to be comprehensive in terms of the literature covered. Rather, we draw selectively on work associated with each perspective that facilitates our examination of their relevance to the four concepts regarded as fundamental to understanding the precipitants and dynamics of participation broadly construed. Finally, in elaborating each perspective, we first present an overview of its application to the focal concepts in the context of crowds and social movements, and then critically assess it empirically and theoretically.

DISPOSITIONAL APPROACH

The dispositional perspective emphasizes the ways in which psychological traits or states render individuals more or less susceptible to participation in crowds and social movement activities. The underlying assumption is that certain personality characteristics and/or cognitive and emotional states are likely to make the appeal of some movements especially attractive, thus predisposing some individuals to participation. Rather than focusing on the material or constructed character of grievances, the dispositional approach focuses attention on the psychological manifestation of or response to grievances, with frustration being the most generic predisposing manifestation or state.* In their review of the dispositional approach (which they call convergence theory), Turner and Killian (1972, pp. 18–21) suggest that frustration emerges from psychological factors or processes that provide a foundation for a common predisposition and collective action. Heightened frustration provides the circumstances by which individuals with similar latent characteristics are brought together and these tendencies are acted out in a larger group.

Early scholars argued that frustration was a result of absolute deprivation, such as a sharp economic decline that affects the quality of life. Because individuals cannot always act collectively against the source of frustration (such as the abstract factors leading to economic decline and the inability of the individual to purchase necessities), it is redirected toward safe and available objects. For example, Dollard, Doob, Miller, Mowrer, and Sears (1939) found a correlation between economic indices and the number of lynchings of African Americans in the Southern states. As cotton prices continued to decline, the level of frustration increased among poor Southern Whites. In turn, Whites redirected their frustration toward African Americans. Thus, the result of this economic deprivation was the increased incidences of lynchings in the South during this timeframe.

---

*Dispositional scholars imply that there is a threshold for grievance aggravation that creates a heightened sense of frustration. However, grievances themselves are by and large taken for granted in this approach.

More recently, scholars have recognized that frustration also arises from relative deprivation. Relative deprivation refers to the paradox that populations that seem to be improving their social and/or economic position or that hold a position of privilege within a larger aggrieved group may also engage in collective action (Snow & Oliver, 1995, pp. 578–579). A sense of deprivation and frustration arises among such populations when there is a gap between what they have and what they want. When this gap becomes intolerable or is seen as unjust, individuals are likely to participate in collective action. Similarly, status inconsistency can be a source of frustration. As the existence and prestige of particular lifestyles are challenged, the individuals committed to these lifestyles become candidates for participation in "status politics" and/or "status crusades" (Gusfield, 1966; Lipset, 1960; Zurcher & Kirkpatrick, 1976).

Heightened frustration, in other words, makes individuals susceptible to movement claims and increases the likelihood that they will participate in collective action. Toch (1965), for example, posited that the potential of the movement to improve the quality of life and/ or offer an avenue for psychological release lures individuals who are suffering from psychological strain to collective action. Along the same lines, Cantril (1941) argued that an individual's basic need to find meaning in the face of a chaotic external environment renders the individual vulnerable to movement ideologies and motivates participation in collective forms. Similarly, social isolation, or a weak or peripheral attachment to existing social networks (Cohn, 1957; Kornhauser, 1959; Lipset, 1950; Nisbet, 1954) and personal powerless (Bell, 1964; Bolton, 1972; Kornhauser, 1959) may cause frustration and increase individual susceptibility to movement claims.

A final source of frustration noted in the literature is the failure of modern society to provide adequate grounding for constituting or maintaining satisfying identities. This is the central theme of Klapp's *Collective Search for Identity* (1969), for example. As well, some scholars argue that movements appeal to individuals with spoiled or stigmatized identities. As Kaplan and Liu (2000, p. 233) contend, "participation in a social movement may represent a personal adaptation to the experience of a spoiled identity."

In addition to frustration and its various sources, numerous scholars have emphasized the presence of particular personality characteristics that increase the likelihood that individuals will act on grievances and participate in collective action. For example, Lipset (1960), drawing on the work of Fromm (1941) and Adorno et al. (1950), has argued that individuals with authoritarian personalities are more likely to participate in extremist movements (also see Hoffer, 1951). He suggested that lower class individuals are more likely to be exposed to punishment, lack of love, and a general atmosphere of tension and aggression since early childhood. These experiences produce a tendency to see politics and personal relationships in "black and white" terms, create a desire for immediate action, and generate impatience for groups that have long-range perspectives. As a result, such individuals are attracted to extremist movements and leaders that offer demonological interpretations of and quick solutions to the "evil forces" disrupting daily life.

Assessment

Dispositional explanations for the emergence of grievances and collective action were largely abandoned in the 1970s because of the lack of empirical support and paradigmatic shifts. First, there was a lack of empirical support for the causal link between individual predispositions, susceptibility, and participation in riots and other collective action (McPhail, 1969, 1991, 1994). This is a function of the tendency of dispositional scholars to over simplify the complexity of human psychology. The bulk of the research examined extreme and often violent behavior of a subset of individuals engaging in such activities as lynchings and riots (Miller & Dollard, 1941). As a result, the relevance of dispositional arguments to more routine and nonviolent forms of collective action, such as vigils and marches, was questionable. Additionally, the presumption of generalized motivations, like intense frustration and spoiled or inadequate identities, contradicts the observation that movement participation is undergrided by a variety of motives (Turner & Killian, 1972; Zurcher & Snow, 1981; Zygmunt, 1972). As well, to postulate that there are generalized movement dispositions is difficult to reconcile with the finding that movement participation frequently transforms existing identities (Hunt & Benford, 1994; Snow & Machalek, 1984).

There were also paradigmatic shifts that decreased the relevance of the dispositional approach. First, participants were increasingly regarded as much more rational than the dispositional approach suggested. Second, scholars became more sensitive to the interactive characteristics of mobilization and participation, which shifted attention to the socially embedded character of action. This focus on social actors renewed scholarly interest in how social and political structures shaped and channeled collective action—phenomena the dispositional approach could not explain since structure presumably did not affect the incidence or intensity of collective action.

The growing recognition of the socially embedded character of collective action also made meaning-making processes and emotion more central to analyses. Whereas the dispositional approach circumvented the need for meaning-making and often conflated irrationality and emotion, scholars increasingly became aware that both were important for understanding the dynamics of collective action. Moreover, these meaning-making processes and affective dimensions were important, as we will discuss, for the explanation of grievance interpretation, participation, and collective form.

These critical observations and paradigm shifts notwithstanding, concern with some psychological predispositions and personality characteristics is not without some merit. If we believe that individuals get involved in collective action that expresses their interests and sentiments, than the personality variables that affect the level and type of participation may be important (Snow & Oliver, 1995). For example, personal efficacy, or the belief that one can make a difference, helps explain why individuals respond to grievances by engaging in collective action (Gamson, 1968; Seeman, 1975).

LEARNING MODELS

In contrast to the dispositional approach, the learning model posits that participation is rooted in learning processes. Two such processes have figured prominently in the literature: behavior modeling and contagion, and socialization. Early learning models argued that participation in collective action was a behavioral response by individuals attempting to satisfy drives. From this perspective, collective action was a learned response that was enacted in and often intensified by the group. Later learning models, however, took a much more sociological approach and focused on the interaction between objective conditions and social background as a way to explain (1) why individuals participate and (2) the form and intensity of collective phenomena. We will discuss each of these approaches in turn.

Behavioral Modeling and Contagion

Early behavioral learning models paralleled dispositional scholars in their conceptualization of participation in collective action. Allport (1920), for example, posited that individual behavior was predisposed by innate or learned responses to satisfy basic drives. But Allport differed from the dispositional thesis in contending that internal drives or dispositions were activated by "social facilitation"—that is, the observation of others doing what one wants or is impelled to do. Thus, the fact that crowd behavior was often aggressive and violent could be explained by social facilitation or contagion.* As individuals join collective gatherings, they watch and hear others in their immediate surroundings and respond in kind. Because social facilitation and/or contagion are reciprocal phenomena, each exchange re-stimulates and heightens the level of group activity (also see Park & Burgess, 1921).

Similarly, Blumer (1939) argued that the disruption of daily routines causes unrest and that this "restlessness" is reciprocal, meaning people respond to and reproduce the behaviors of those around them. Given that individuals have a common disposition to act in particular ways, Blumer argued that the new behaviors spread quickly and often took on a violent character. Miller and Dollard (1941) also suggested that crowd behavior was simply "common mass responses which have [already] been learned by everyone..." (Miller & Dollard, 1941; in McPhail, 1991, p. 36) and that the "circular reaction" processes in crowds increase the intensity of an individual's response and activity. Turner and Killian (1972) discussed contagion in terms of rumor processes. In times of uncertainty, individuals turn to one another to create norms and give direction to the collectivity. However, in contrast to the previous conceptualizations of contagion, which imply that individuals uncritically imitate the behaviors of others, Turner and Killian posited that rumor processes are a "collective problem-solving procedure" and as such "suggestibility takes on a different connotation. It refers to the heightened responsiveness of the individual to cues provided by others when situational anchorages are inadequate" (p. 32) (also see Sherif & Harvey, 1952).

Individuals, then, learn what behaviors to enact in crowds from (1) monitoring the behaviors of others and (2) leaders. The behavioral modeling and contagion approach highlights the notion that if an individual finds that s/he is not engaged in the same behaviors as other crowd members, s/he will typically observe and copy the behavior. However, the impetus for modeling is different. Allport argued that crowd behavior is the escalation of individual predispositions within the group, while Dollard and Miller and Turner and Killian suggested that individuals reproduce the behaviors of those around them in order to reduce anxiety and fit in with the group. Individuals may also model their behavior in line with the suggestions of leaders. Early discussion of the role of leaders suggested that leaders emerge as authority figures that individuals follow because they have the power to reward or punish individuals for compliance or non-compliance respectively (Miller & Dollard, 1941). However, more recent discussions focus on the ability of leaders to interpret events and present positive courses of action in times of uncertainty (Turner & Killian, 1972).

ASSESSMENT. Much like the dispositional approach, the early versions of the learning model encountered two major problems. First, not all crowd participants were continuously

---

*Early scholars such as Le Bon (1895) also discussed contagion as integral to the intensity of crowd behavior. These conceptualizations, however, consider crowd behavior extraordinary. Individuals are transformed by the group experience and individual consciousness disappears altogether. Thus, collective action is less a function of learning processes and more a result of the emergence of an "unconscious personality."

and exclusively engaged in the same behaviors at the same time (see McPhail, 1991; McPhail & Wohlstein, 1983). This undermined the notion that crowd behavior was simply an intensification of learned behavior by the individual. Nor did it fit with the idea that individuals simply copied the behaviors of those around them in an effort to belong to a larger group. Second, because the model was largely used to examine extraordinary and/or violent action, individuals participating in crowds were subject to being characterized as irrational and aberrant, thus making it difficult for learning models to account for nonviolent collective action or sustained participation in collective behavior.

Socialization Models

Sociologists picked up this thread and attempted to explain more sustained participation in collective action through the examination of "activist types." Here the key to understanding differential participation was not in the categorization of psychological characteristics but in the proper contextualization of activism. The socialization approach, in other words, focused attention on the interaction between objective conditions and social background as a way to explain the form and intensity of sustained participation. Although proponents still treated grievances as though they were unproblematic, scholars recognized that the motivation for collective action stemmed from the external environment as well as social location factors and that individuals looked to one another as well as existing social structures to determine the form of collective action.

For example, Mannheim (1970) discussed the problem of generations in which he argued that people of the same age group share a historical location just as individuals of the same class share a social location. Generations, then, represent an objective and taken-for-granted condition, regardless of whether individuals recognize their commonality. While generations may encounter the same historical changes, individuals "work up" the material of these common experiences differently because variations in social background predispose them to interpret events in various ways. Stated differently, individuals are socialized to experience external conditions in particular ways (Berger & Luckmann, 1966).

Proponents of the socialization approach tend to examine how activist values and orientations are transmitted intergenerationally and intragenerationally. *Intergenerational processes* refer to the transmission of activist orientations through childhood socialization. From this perspective, individual participation in activism is a reflection of family values and orientations that encourage political participation (Hyman, 1959). For example, a large number of the student activists of the 1960s came from liberal to left activist families (Bengston, 1970; Flacks, 1972; Westby & Braungart, 1966; Wood & Ng, 1980) and key leaders from the Civil Rights Movement, such as Martin Luther King Jr., had parents that were politically active. Similarly, McAdam (1988) found this process at work in his examination of the Freedom Summer Campaign; those students who volunteered to register Black voters in Mississippi during the summer of 1964 had learned their activist values at home and, thus, were biographically available. Because the students came from largely privileged backgrounds, they had both the time and the energy for activism (also see Flacks, 1972).

Of course, socialization practices vary. In their examination of how socialization practices relate to activism, Block, Haan, and Smith (1972) found that parents whose children were activists tended to stress independence, responsibility, and early maturity while encouraging differentiation and self-expression. Similarly, Flacks (1972) found that parents of activist children were more permissive and lenient in their child-rearing practices and emphasized values other than achievement more than parents of non-activist children. Intergenerational transmission of values from parent to child, however, can be more deliberate. For example, the family is central to maintaining the White Power Movement. Parents actively socialize their children into racist ideologies by naming their children and pets with the symbols of the movement, displaying white power symbols within the home, educating their children at home, and geographically isolating themselves and their children from "the system" (Simi & Futrell, 2002).

Cultural traditions of activism can augment parental socialization and heighten activist values and orientations. African American churches, for instance, have a long history of weaving religion, politics, and resistance together and have served as a seedbed for both social movements and a culture of resistance (Morris, 1984). Similarly, secular and religious Jews, Quakers, and Mennonites have a strong tradition of promoting activist orientations such as pacifism and equality. Children, in other words, may grow up in communities that promote activist values and justify activism and movement participation.

Socialization also occurs intragenerationally. *Intragenerational processes* refer to changes in value orientation or identity that occur (1) as a result of conversion or (2) that change over the life course. Conversion is the relational processes by which the taken-for-granted reality is challenged and alternative worldviews are offered and maintained. In its most extreme form, conversion represents a radical transformation in individual consciousness, lifestyle, and practices.* For example, Klatch (1999) found that for student protestors activism brought a realization of the self and that the social relations among activists dramatically altered, or radicalized, identity. This radicalization increased commitment and solidarity to movement causes, which in turn sustained activist communities despite the high costs of activism (such as government repression and familial strain).

Conversion can also occur through commitment processes, or the processes by which individuals become bound to a group. Unlike the fairly sudden transformations in identity and action described above, commitment entails long-term expenditures of an individual's time and energy and connotes an alignment between individual and group interests (Kanter, 1972). Conversion, however, is not necessarily a static or permanent state. Scholars adopting a role learning approach have argued that conversion occurs in contexts of role and affiliative change that require or create cognitive and behavioral transformations (Balch, 1980; Bromley & Shupe, 1979). For example, after his participant observation of a UFO cult, Balch (1980) concluded that individuals did not undergo a sudden transformation of consciousness. Instead, participants learned roles, which among other things included a special vocabulary. From this perspective, roles that are learned may also be abandoned.

Finally, how one views the world and her/his place in it may vary over the course of a lifetime. In her analysis, Klatch (1999) tracks how activist identities change over the life course. She found that activists on both the Left and Right expressed continuity in core activist values and continued to remain politically active through the 1980s. Klatch (1999) notes:

> The transformative effects of activism continue to shape the daily lives, choices, and pathways of ... [activists. However,] as activists have aged and found meaningful work, become parents, bought homes, and settled down, activism is no longer the master identity of their youth. (p. 328)

McAdam (1988), however, found that while individuals that participated in Freedom Summer in 1964 remain remarkably dedicated to their political vision and are politically active, albeit

---

*See Snow and Machalek (1984) for an elaborated discussion of conversion. It is important to note that the transformative processes often associated with conversion are not always called such. See, for example, Berger and Luckmann's (1966) discussion of secondary socialization and Klatch's (1999) discussion of radicalization.

in different ways, they have also experienced a degree of social isolation as the mainstream becomes increasingly conservative. Similarly, other scholars have noted that activists from this era are different from the mainstream in that they tend to marry less, have fewer children, and are more concentrated in "helping professions" such as social work and teaching (Demerath, Marwell, & Aiken, 1971; Marwell, Aiken, & Demerath, 1987; McAdam, 1988; Whalen & Flacks, 1989).

ASSESSMENT.　　Learning models that made socialization processes central to the explanation of grievances and participation augmented the dispositional approach and behavioral models by examining the transmission of activist orientations during childhood socialization, explaining shifts in identity and worldview that occur over a relatively short period of time, and providing insight into how identity and activist orientations change over the life course. The strength of the socialization approach, in other words, is that it incorporates both social and psychological factors into explanations of participation in collective action. It positions the individual as a social actor who interacts and responds to objective, cultural, social, and relational factors as well as provides an explanation for long-term participation in social and political movements.

However, there has been the tendency for social movement scholars to (1) neglect socialization processes as explanatory factors and (2) discuss socialization processes without identifying them as such. As a result, the approach, as it applies to crowds and social movements, remains underdeveloped. For example, it is unclear how identity meshes with socialization processes. While identity is implied in the analyses, especially as it relates to cognitive transformations or conversions, it is not addressed explicitly in the literature. This raises several questions. Does the malleability of identity vary with the different socialization practices of parents? And how does identity expand to include new experiences and values, especially when they contradict an individual's worldview?

Similarly, the role of emotion is surprisingly absent in the literature. Clearly, activist orientations involve both values and emotions, which motivate collective action and sustain activism over the long haul. A discussion of emotion would also inform the literature on conversion. It is difficult to imagine that conversion involves cognitive transformation only. For example, Klatch (1999) notes that the Left activists that engaged in high-risk activism in the 1960s were committed to their political cause despite the consequences. Undoubtedly, affective dimensions and "emotion-work" are attached to commitment and sustained activism in the face of adversity.

RATIONAL CHOICE APPROACH

The incorporation of rational choice perspectives into the study of crowds and social movements was, in large part, a corrective response to theories that treated participation as irrational and collective phenomena as spontaneous and relatively disorganized. The rational choice approach to crowds and social movements is rooted in Mancur Olson's (1965) microeconomic analysis of participation in various forms of collective action. His orienting postulate is that individuals exercise rational decision-making processes and participate because collective action is either more rewarding or less costly than inaction. In this perspective, individuals are rational decision-makers, meaning that given their "goals and preferences, and their perception of their situations, they act so as to maximize their utility" (Granovetter, 1978, p. 1422). The rational choice approach is grounded in at least three key assumptions regarding decision-making processes. First, individuals possess *relatively* complete information and, therefore, make the best decisions they can in terms of their self-interests. Second, the hierarchy of individual preferences is relatively stable and, therefore, may be used as a starting point for analysis. Third, there are institutional constraints such as social order mechanisms that individuals consider when making decisions about participation (Smelser, 1992). Taken together, these assumptions suggest participation in crowds and social movements is not merely a response to particular grievances, but also a response of individual decisions based on the alignment of collective action with one's perceived interests.

Olson (1965) argued that self-interested and rational individuals would not participate in collective action to achieve group or collective goods. Collective or public goods are goods that benefit all members of a group irrespective of the time and energy expended to obtain them. Because collective goods cannot be feasibly withheld from a portion of the members, such as those members who do not help obtain the benefits in the first place, and individuals seek to obtain benefits while minimizing the costs, individuals will not work to achieve these goods (Oliver, 1980). Stated differently, collective goods and benefits alone are insufficient motivation for participation because "free riding" on the efforts of others provides the same collective good but without the cost of actual participation. The question, then, is what factors play a major role in decision-making processes and prompt individuals to participate in social movement activities?

Some scholars believe that individuals participate in collective action because a cost/benefit "threshold" is met. The threshold is the point where the perceived benefits to an individual exceed the perceived costs. Often this is defined in terms of the proportion of the group an individual would have to see join in collective action before s/he would join in as well. This threshold varies according to norms, preferences, motives, and values of the individual. As Granovetter (1978) suggested is his discussion of threshold models of collective action, someone who is "radical" will have a much lower threshold for engaging in extreme collective forms such as rioting: the benefits of participation are high and the costs of consequences are low. Conversely, a "conservative" individual will have a much higher threshold before s/he engages in rioting: the benefits of participation are low and the costs of consequences are high. The point here is that "different individuals require different levels of safety before entering a riot and also vary in the benefits they derive from rioting" (Granovetter, 1978, p. 1422).

However, political values or orientation are not the only factors that affect thresholds. Threats to other values, resources, and ways of life may be more likely to generate collective action than the promise of benefits because, according to Kahneman and Tversky's (1979) prospect theory, losses are more keenly felt as "disutility" than gains are felt as "utility" (Snow, Cress, Downey, & Jones, 1998). Thus, individuals may differ in a variety of ways, but may still participate in collective action because the threshold has been met. This notion of a threshold is consistent with Oliver and Marwell's (1988, 1992) conceptualization of participation in social movements as a function of "critical mass" in which organizers with limited resources attempt to maximize the total amount of resources within a heterogeneous pool of potential participants.

Gaming approaches constitute another variant of rational choice theorizing. Proponents of this approach posit that individuals select actions with the best payoffs but that these decisions are made relative to others. Much like the threshold model, the potential costs to a given individual decreases as the number of participants increase. Every individual in a crowd, for example, must make a series of decisions. S/he notes the options for action, evaluates the likelihood of success, and considers his/her preferences before selecting the "best" outcome (Berk, 1974).

> Beginning with the *individual* as the unit of analysis, one can postulate that crowd members are engaged in a 'game' in which each 'player's' payoff matrix depends on the actions of others on the scene. Opportunities to be highly satisfied depend on people acting in unison. (Berk, 1974, p. 363, emphasis in original)

These processes depend on group interactions, which are attempts to communicate and influence "individual payoff matrices" and offer alternatives for actions.

Individuals may also make decisions to participate based on their values and expectations. Klandermans (1997), for example, draws on value-expectancy theory, which assumes that an individual's behavior is a function of the value of the expected outcomes that will result from the behavior, and argues that because collective incentives are only indirectly related to individual behavior individuals must make decisions about participation based on her/his expectations of whether or not others will participate. Similarly, Finkel and Muller (1998) posit that an individual's sense of political efficacy may determine participation. Specifically, individuals engage in collective action when they are unhappy with the current provision of collective goods, believe that collective action will be successful, and think that their participation is important to group success.

There may also be incentives for individuals to participate in collective action. Olson (1965) argued "only a *separate and selective incentive* will stimulate a rational individual in a latent group to act in a group-oriented way. ... The incentive must be 'selective' so that those who do not join the organization working for the group's interest, or in other ways contribute to the attainment of the group's interest, can be treated differently from those who do" (in Oliver, 1980, p. 1357, emphasis in original). Selective incentives, then, become part of an individual's cost-benefit analyses and may involve collective and personal identities. For example, individuals may choose to participate on the basis of collective identities when they believe that the benefits of adopting or acting in accordance with a collective identity outweigh the costs, or an individual may have intergenerational investments in particular personal identities that have consequences for the embracement of future collective identities (Laitin, 1998). Additionally, collective identities may be an incentive for individuals who wish to express or affirm their personal identities (Friedman & McAdam, 1992) or because there is congruence between individual values and movement ideology (Klandermans, 1988).

Assessment

Although the rational choice approach has gone a long way toward dispelling the myth of irrational collective action and has strongly influenced the major structural perspectives on movements,* its utility in accounting for participation is limited by its failure to fully

---

*For example, rationality constitutes a cornerstone assumption for both the resource mobilization and political opportunity theories. These approaches emphasize resources, capacities, and opportunities for mobilization (McAdam, 1982, 1999; Tarrow, 1989; Tilly, 1978; Zald & McCarthy, 1987) rather than group and individual level processes that motivate and sustain participation. Grievances generate from objective conditions such as the state, political and social cleavages, and rapid and dramatic economic changes (Piven & Cloward, 1977) and are acted or not acted upon according to the state's capacity to accommodate or repress challengers (Tilly, 1978). Grievances are a response to the structure of power and interests in the state and excluded groups make rational calculations about when they may successfully "grab" power and advance their own interests (McAdam, 1999). As a result, these theories tend to emphasize the role of strategic and rational organizations that mobilize individuals to action.

appreciate the complexity of the motivations and meanings associated with the behaviors in question. A consequence and illustration of this shortcoming is the failure to acknowledge sufficiently the extent to which costs and benefits are subject to differential interpretation both contextually and temporally. While rational choice analyses use social location factors such as age, education, gender, income, and race/ethnicity to predict participation at the individual level, the contexts in which actors are embedded and their subjective experiences, both of which affect how individuals "work up" conceptions of rational action and make decisions (Ferree, 1992), tend to be glossed over. Thus, rational choice approaches are hard pressed to explain why those with a lower socio-economic status contribute more time and more money proportionally than those with high socio-economic status (Verba, Scholzman, & Brady, 1995) or why research that measures costs subjectively have found that it sometimes contradicts the theory. Hirsch (1990), for example, found that campus divestment protestors believed that they paid heavy costs for participation while nonparticipants downplayed these costs arguing that participants received selective benefits (also see Opp, 1988, 1989).

Additionally, rational choice approaches largely reduce motivations for participation to incentives that are extrinsic to the individual rather than values that might override material interests. In fact, values only enter rational choice calculations as a variety of "non-material incentives" (Mueller & Opp, 1986). This conceptualization treats material and non-material incentives as interchangeable parts that logically occur prior, rather than during or after, participation. As a result, attitudes and preferences are treated as "preexisting and stable structures" that predict individual behavior (Ferree, 1992, p. 35). This is clear in the political participation literature that seeks to explain individual participation in politics and collective action by examining the influence of social location variables—such as education, income, gender, political affiliation, ethnicity/race, religion, age, and martial status (Blais, 2000; Verba et al., 1995), resources—such as time, religious and communal organizational affiliation, and social networks (Brady, Verba, & Schlozman, 1995; Rosenstone & Hansen, 1993; Verba et al., 1995), and personal characteristics—such as exposure to politics growing up, political skill, and efficacy (Rosenstone & Hansen, 1993; Verba et al., 1995).

Because rational choice approaches tend to reify costs, benefits, values, and interests, the perspective has difficulty explaining differential action within the same movement. Stated differently, its tendency to treat costs and benefits as unproblematic and its failure to integrate culture, values, socialization, and social interaction into cost-benefit formulas have limited its ability to examine how differential interpretations of grievances create different forms of collective action. Finally, the assumptions that provide the foundation for rational choice approaches ultimately limit the ability of scholars to extend the approach without contradicting its premises. For example, the focus on individual incentives limits the extent to which scholars can discuss the importance of collective identity to mobilization. While collective identity may cause an individual to initially participate in collective action, it is unclear what role

(*Contd.*)

Resource mobilization and political opportunity theory, however, have run into similar criticisms as the rational choice approach. Specifically, these theories are criticized for (1) not offering a plausible account of values, grievances, and ideology; (2) treating rationality as though it were one-dimensional and devoid of meaning-making processes, which make what seems to be irrational behavior to the observer rational in the mind of the individual (Ferree, 1992); (3) as having a structural bias, or emphasizing factors that are relatively stable over time and outside the control of movement actors (Goodwin & Jasper, 1999); (4) for being unable to explain the variation in and the extent to which people share a collective identity which fosters commitment to group goals (Wittier & Taylor, 1992); and (5) devaluing the affective dimensions that motivate and sustain collective action (Polletta & Jasper, 2001).

collective identity plays in sustaining activism, especially in the face of adversity. Similarly, because rational choice tends to associate emotionality with irrationality, it is difficult to incorporate affective dimensions into the discussion of movement emergence and continuity.

In the last few years, however, scholars have made attempts to make rational choice approaches more robust. Hechter and Kanazawa (1997) posit that the rational choice approach should be regarded as a "multilevel enterprise." At the micro analytical level, rational choice contains assumptions regarding individual cognition and behavior. At a macro analytical level, it specifies social structures. "These social structures serve both as the social and material context ... for individual action, and as new structures ... resulting from the actions of individuals whose behavior is described by the lower level assumptions" (p. 193). Additionally, they make distinctions between "thin" and "thick" rational choice models. Thin models are not concerned with the values or goals individuals pursue, and treat values as though they are stable. Thick models, on the other hand, specify individual values and beliefs and recognize that individuals value nonexchangeable goods and that idiosyncratic values may outweigh more common values (although these idiosyncrasies cancel out as the size of the group increases). Finkel and Muller's (1998) examination of participation using panel data is an example of a thick model. They assume that values are not stable over time and in fact that participation itself may create value and attitude changes. In their study they find that participation in collective action is not a "by-product" of selective incentives, but that expectations of social and psychological rewards are the result of past participation.

CONSTRUCTIONIST APPROACH

The constructionist approach, as applied to crowds and social movements, evolved from the realization that grievances could not be taken for granted or as given, as does the resource mobilization approach (McCarthy & Zald, 1994). Rather, grievances were seen as problematic and thus as matters of interpretation and construction. This is not to suggest that grievances could be fabricated whole cloth, but that there is no automatic, determinative relation between material conditions and inequality, for example, and the propensity to engage in movement activity in relation to these conditions. Thus, the constructionist approach, as it initially evolved, focused on the processes through which grievances are interpreted and acted upon, and on the cognitive and ideational factors that motivated and sustained participation (Cohen, 1985; Ferree & Miller, 1985; Gamson, Fireman, & Rytina, 1982; Klandermans, 1984; Snow, Rochford, Worden, & Benford, 1986; Zurcher & Snow, 1981). The constructionist perspective agreed with the rationalist insight that collective action is a rational, purposive, and self-conscious attempt to achieve a given goal. However, it posited that perceptions of grievances, costs and benefits, and the possibility for action are subject to differential interpretation and thus socially constructed. In other words, "what is at issue is not merely the presence or absence of grievances, but the manner in which these grievances are interpreted and the generation and diffusion of those interpretations" (Snow et al., 1986, p. 466).

The constructionist approach, as it as been extended and applied, is relevant not only to the issue of grievance interpretation, but also to matters of emotion and identity as they pertain to constituent mobilization and participation. The orienting or base process for each of these issues is symbolization. Thus, we consider in order symbolization, emotion, and identity.

Symbolization

Foreshadowing the constructionist approach to crowds and social movements was the symbolic interactionist emphasis on the importance of interaction to the creation of norms in times of uncertainty (Sherif, 1936; Sherif & Harvey, 1952; Turner & Killian, 1972). Turner and Killian (1972), for example, posited that when communication is disrupted and the existing norms do not apply in the current situation, individuals turn to one another in order to generate situationally appropriate lines of action. The cues that individuals gather from one another as they communicate determine the course and form of crowd behavior. In other words, normative guidelines emerge through social interaction within specific crowd situations and provide a common understanding of what types of behavior are expected and permitted. Crowd behavior, then, is not characterized by unanimity, but by "differential expression" (Turner & Killian, 1972, p. 22), meaning crowds display a range of behavior because individual participants feel differently about social/political situations, participate in response to different motives and emotions, and ultimately act differently within the crowd situation. What determines the range of behavior deemed acceptable by the group is the "emergent norm(s)" that arises through the process of symbolization.

Symbolization is the process through which events, conditions, artifacts, and people take on particular meaning and become the object of cognitive and affective orientations (Snow & Davis, 1995). It is through the process of symbolization that groups construct a vision of the world and more specifically interpret grievances, develop and communicate claims, select targets of action, construct goals, and develop a course of action. According to Turner and Killian (1972), in times of uncertainty (such as after a natural disaster) individuals turn to one another in order to fill the information gap (also see Shibutani, 1966). This informal communication network, which the authors term rumor, may be quantitatively and qualitatively different from the normal channels of information because individuals seek out others in an effort to confirm and supplement information. As such, individuals may become part of a network that cuts across the typical social and group boundaries. "Strangers who know little about each other, except that they share an interest in the ambiguous situation, interact and become part of an emergent collectivity" (Turner & Killian, 1972, p. 31). Interaction becomes the basis for collective definitions of a problematic situation, a justification for a particular course of action, and the foundation for emergent norms. Thus, it is not particular objects that cause individuals to participate in collective action but the emergence of shared interpretations of an object and the ways in which objects express particular values.

Leaders, then, are crucial to mobilization. Leaders offer an interpretation of grievances in such a way to compel individual action, spread ideas, and foster and maintain loyalty to group goals as well as serve as decision-makers for group action (Gusfield, 1966; Turner & Killian, 1972). In addition to "keynoting" and offering a course of action for collectivities, leaders also interact and respond to groups external to the collectivity (Turner & Killian, 1972). However, publics that are external to the collectivity are also important to symbolization. Bystander publics, for instance, neither support nor oppose collective action. Instead, they are interested publics that witness collective action and only get involved if directly affected by group tactics (Turner, 1970, 1973). Mediating publics, on the other hand, are the primary venue through which collectivities affect change in larger society. Such publics define and evaluate the relevance, goals, and probability of success of collective action. Hence, how such publics perceive particular collectivities and collective action is critical to the development of strategies. Of course, collectivities also respond to opposition and social control agents when formulating the course of collective action. For example, Snow, Zurcher, and Peters (1981) found that the change in police behavior altered the behavior of individuals celebrating the football victories of the University of Texas. During the first crowd event police served more as "supportive viewers than as control agents" (p. 23) and watched the celebration. By the fourth crowd event, however, police changed their behavior and appearance and interfered with the celebrating, specifically in an effort to keep the noise down. This change on the part of the police, which was due primarily to the transformation of the bystander public into a mediating public, affected the behavior of the celebrants and thus the character of the victory celebrations.

More recently, symbolization processes have become central to the framing perspective. Extending earlier work, scholars conceptualized movement actors and organizations as "signifying agents" that are actively engaged in the production and maintenance of meaning for not only constituents but also audiences and bystander publics. In addition, scholars noted that meaning making is a contested process and movement actors must compete with opposition, local government, the state, and mass media to have particular meanings gain ascendance or credibility over others (Gamson, 1992; Snow & Benford, 1988). The verb "framing" denotes this active, ongoing, and continuously evolving process of meaning-making (Snow & Benford, 1992).

One conceptual advantage of the framing perspective over earlier works was that it recognized three different levels of symbolization. First, a movement tries to interpret grievances in such a way that it motivates sympathizers to participate. Because grievance interpretation is a contested process there must be some consensus over the grievances and a course of action before individuals decide to participate in collective action. Second, a movement must negotiate its identity in order to secure continued participation. Finally, a movement must contend with a larger political environment and adjust its meanings to resonate in larger publics in order to gain or maintain credibility. The first level is of interest here.

The products of the framing process are "collective action frames," which are action-oriented sets of meanings and beliefs that both inspire and legitimate collective action (Gamson, 1992; Snow & Benford, 1992). Such frames provide movements with a discourse that supports and justifies movement actions and goals (Zurcher & Snow, 1981). Collective action frames aid in mobilization specifically by (1) identifying a grievance, calling for corrective action, and attributing blame; (2) offering a reasonable and attainable solution for grievance amelioration; and (3) providing a motivation for collective action by aligning individual values and orientations with movement goals, a rationale for participation, and a vocabulary for accounting for actions (Klandermans, 1988; Snow & Benford, 1992). However, attending to these three core framing tasks is not enough to ensure that an individual participates in collective action. Frames must also be sufficiently flexible and inclusive so that they encompass a broad range of social groups. The values involved in framing processes must be central and salient in the culture and/or belief system. If a movement wants to increase its mobilizing potential, it must promote or defend values that are culturally resonant and have high hierarchical salience in the larger belief system (Snow & Benford, 1992).*

Emotion

The treatment of emotions in relation to the processes of symbolization and collective action has changed a great deal over the last 30 years. Early scholars used affective dimensions to

*For a critique and overview of the extensive literature on framing processes in relation to social movements, see Benford (1997) and Benford and Snow (2000).

explain aberrant activity and expression rather than rational, object-directed action. Turner and Killian (1972), for example, used affective dimensions to distinguish acting from expressive crowds. The acting crowd was said to have an object that is external to the crowd, such that crowd actions could be individualistic, as with a riot, or solidaristic, as in the case of a communal organization that organizes disaster relief for its neighbors. An expressive crowd, on the other hand, does not act on an object. Instead, the expressive crowd seeks to change the "mood, the imagery, and the behavior of members themselves ... . The expressive crowd is one that makes behavior sensible that would normally be regarded as eccentric or immoral. It gives significance to subjective sensations which would otherwise be meaningless or disturbing" (pp. 102–103). The expressive crowd provides a setting in which individuals may express feelings freely without the regard for normative social behavior.

Today, it is generally realized that the acting/expressive distinction represents more of a heuristic continuum than distinct types of crowds, which typically have both acting and expressive dimensions. Moreover, scholars have increasingly recognized that emotional considerations are an integral aspect of all crowds and social movements. As Jasper (1998) has emphasized, emotions affect our goals, interests, and actions, and without the flames of passion, there might not be any crowd or social movement activity at all. Additionally, scholars have come to recognize that emotion, like grievances, is to some extent culturally constructed. So while a facial expression may be used the world over, what this expression means and how people respond physically and emotionally may vary across cultures. Emotional response, in other words, varies in part according to an individual's interpretation of a situation, which is informed by culturally based beliefs (Hochschild, 1979). Over the last several years, there have been distinct efforts to bring emotion back into the study of grievance interpretation and initial and sustained participation.

Moral shocks, for example, are often the first step toward participation in some types of social movement activity. Moral shock refers to information that raises such outrage in an individual that s/he recognizes political activity as a solution (Jasper, 1997, 1998; Jasper & Poulsen, 1995). Such shocks may emerge suddenly or over a long period of time and they depend on "preexisting patterns of affect, which channel the interpretation of announcements and revelations" (Jasper, 1998, p. 409). Of course, whether or not an individual participates also depends on symbolization processes. If potential participants do not have a target, a meaningful course of action, or believe that there is a chance to change the situation, than it is unlikely that they will participate in collective action (Snow & Benford, 1988).

Affective dimensions are also pervasive in social networks, which may cause individuals to participate in activism (Nepstad & Smith, 2001) and in personal relationships, which may erode movement participation (Goodwin, 1997). Additionally, emotion is the basis for the commitment processes that bind actors into social systems and sustain activism over the long haul. Commitment is the "willingness of social actors to give their energy and loyalty to social systems, the attachment of personality systems to social relations which are seen as self-expressive" (Kanter, 1968, p. 499). Commitment implies that individual needs and interests align with those of the group, and that individuals will allocate time and energy even in the face of opposition. Affective dimensions and commitment are integral to sustained participation. Kanter (1968), for example, examines the importance of commitment of the residents to the longevity of utopian communities. Gould (2001) illustrates how emotion encouraged resolve among militant AIDs activists and led to the emergence of the organization ACT UP. Barker (2001) examines how emotion sustained the solidarity of shipyard strikers in Gdansk.

Commitment, however, varies by degrees, with particular movements requiring more or less commitment by an individual. Radical or revolutionary movements may involve an encompassing commitment, requiring adherents to choose between a "normal" and "movement" life, as in the case of Hare Krishna or the Symbionese Liberation Army (Turner & Killian, 1972). For movements that are reformative and fit into the normal rhythm of life, commitment may only involve the coordination of roles inside and outside of the movement. In her examination of commitment, Kanter (1968) posits that there are three types of commitment and each has its own object-orientation. Instrumental commitment refers to a calculative or cognitive orientation to the movement and membership roles in the movement. Individuals who maintain participation with an instrumental commitment do so as the result of a utilitarian decision, meaning the line of movement action is consistent with the individual interests. Affective or cohesion commitment refers to the emergence of a positive cathectic orientation to movement members. Here members are bound together emotionally and this provides the basis for cohesion and solidarity as well as the individual gratification. Finally, moral or control commitment refers to the positive evaluation of the movement and its ideology. Commitment here is an expression of norms and functions as the basis for decision-making and cognitive orientation.

Much like commitment, emotion also varies. The fiery and intense passion that motivates participation at the outset of a movement is unlikely to sustain participation over the long haul. In recognition of the variety and depth of emotion that affect the course and form of collective action, Goodwin, Jasper, and Polletta (2001) plot emotions on a two-dimensional scale that is sensitive to temporal variation—how long the feeling lasts, and scope—whether feelings involve a specific object or more generalized feelings about the world. Additionally, they suggest that emotions may be discussed as "nouns" or as "adverbs." When emotions are seen as a "noun," they are regarded as "distinct entities each with its own coherence and behavior implications, at least within a specific cultural setting" (p. 13). This type of emotion is displayed, sometimes consciously, in movement literature, public addresses, and in action, and is not only an expression of feeling but also an attempt to arouse similar feelings in others. When emotions are regarded as an "adverb," they are a "style," "taste," or "tone." This type of emotion is a quality or an identity that is not always easily articulated (Goodwin et al., 2001).

In sum, emotion is pervasive to social life and collective phenomena. It may provide the fiery passion that motivates individuals to get involved or lay the foundation for the commitment work necessary to sustain activism in the face of adversity and over the long haul. However, emotion and the role it plays in these processes varies by (1) the type of emotion expressed, (2) the intensity of the emotion expressed, (3) the length of time the emotion is expressed, and (4) the object orientation involved, which requires different types and depths of emotion.

Identity

A sense of belonging or collective identity is also crucial to the explanation of initial and continued participation in movement activities. Collective identity is the feeling of "we-ness" or "one-ness" among a collectivity that provides a sense of shared agency, which can be an impetus for collective action (Gamson, 1992; Snow & McAdam, 2000; Taylor & Whittier, 1992). More specifically, collective identity may be defined as:

> An individual's cognitive, moral, and emotional connection with a broader community, category, practice or institution. It is a perception of a shared status or relation, which may be imagined rather than experienced directly .... Collective identities are expressed in cultural materials—names, narratives, symbols, verbal styles, rituals, clothing, and so on .... (Polletta & Jasper, 2001, p. 285).

Collective identity is distinct from both personal identity and social identity, although the three types clearly interact. We conceive of personal identities as the attributes and meanings an individual assign to him/herself. Social identities, on the other hand, are those identities that are attributed to others. Social identities may be derived from categorically based membership such as gender or ethnic and national categories or from role incumbency such as "mother" and "teacher" (Snow, 2001). These different identities at times overlap and at other moments diverge.

Nevertheless, collective identities are distinct from social and personal identities in several ways. First, collective identities are not necessarily embedded in existing social identities because they are often emergent rather than rooted in social categories. Second, the shared sense of "we-ness" motivates individuals to act together in the interest of the larger collectivity, which generates a sense of collective agency. Third, the emergence of collective identities suggests that the salience and relevance of social and personal identities has decreased—at least in terms of the object orientation and the corresponding action. Finally, collective identities tend to be more transient than social or personal identities (for further discussion see Snow, 2001). What is at issue here is identity construction. Individuals are social actors who recognize their capacity to create identities and who are aware of the power relations involved in their construction. Hence, groups that are situated differently within a social and economic structure may interpret grievances, mobilize identities, and engage in collective action in very different ways. Collective identity, in other words, is important to (1) the creation of collective claims, (2) recruitment, (3) strategic and tactical decision-making, and (4) movement outcomes (see Polleta & Jasper, 2001, for a review).

Collective identity is both a process and a property of social actors that exists at multiple levels (Gamson, 1995; Snow, 2001). At the level of the group, the lack of recognition by other groups of a particular collective identity, such as "Black" or "homosexual," may generate grievances and serve as a motivation for participation (Cohen, 1985; Melucci, 1995; Touraine, 1981). For example, the socio-historical changes that allowed for the social control of sexuality also created the homosexual collective actor, who pushed for his/her equal rights via the gay liberation movement (D'Emilio, 1983). Similarly, the liberalization of abortion law united some women in moral outrage over the desecration of femininity and lead to participation in the pro-life movement (Ginsburg, 1998). However, the processes, by which these group identities are negotiated do not always take place publicly. Some subordinate groups operate in "havens" or "free social spaces" where they can challenge dominant ideologies, develop alternative meanings, and construct emergent cultural forms away from elites (Fantasia & Hirsch, 1995).

At the level of the organization, collective identity signals the goals and orientations of the organization, which affects with whom it may align, what types of resources it may garner, and what strategies and tactics it may employ (Jensen, 1995). Collective identity at this level must be responsive to both its membership and the larger environment in which it operates. Because collective identities are "invented, created, reconstituted, or cobbled together rather than being biologically preordained or structurally or culturally determined" (Snow, 2001), organizations must maintain collective identities by communicating, negotiating, and making-decisions with its members. This "identity-work" encompasses a range of activities that express who and what a group stands for in contrast to a set of "others" (Schwalbe & Mason-Schrock, 1996; Snow & McAdam, 2000). Types of identity-work include rituals for the expression of solidarity and evocation of shared feelings, identity-talk, the use of songs and slogans that are politically and emotionally evocative, and gestures and symbols that serve as boundary markers of collective differentiation (Eyerman & Jamison, 1998; Hunt & Benford, 1994; Taylor & Whittier, 1992).

Additionally, organizations must maintain collective identities that to some extent resonate within the larger culture. For organizations that want to affect social change, what the organization stands for affects its ability to pursue its goals. Organizations that represent goals that threaten status quo and use tactics that may be construed as dangerous by social control agents or mediating publics are unlikely to garner support let alone successfully change policy or some other aspect of the system (Gamson, 1990). On the other hand, organizations must be careful that its identity is not overly restrictive or it will be unable to respond to a changing political environment (Rohlinger, 2002). In other words, social movement organizations must continually negotiate these various levels of collective identity. Hunt, Benford, and Snow (1994) discuss these multilevel processes in terms of identity fields and framing processes. They posit that there are three socially constructed sets of identities that constitute identity fields that overlap, hang together, and expand and contract across time and space. These identity fields (the protagonist, antagonist, and audience) provide a framework for social movement organizations to negotiate how collective identities relative to other groups, members' needs, and a changing political environment are maintained and expressed.

Assessment

It is arguable that the constructionist approach brings us the furthest in thinking about the range of issues related to participation in crowds and social movements for a number of reasons. First, it assumes an interactive approach, which allows for multiple levels of analysis and a more thorough explanation of the dynamics of participation. Specifically, the constructionist approach acknowledges that grievances may be generated from multiple sources and that how collectivities interpret these grievances help determine the form and course of collective action. Symbolization processes, which involve both affective dimensions and collective identity, are critical in this regard. Symbolization helps to explain (1) how grievances are constructed, (2) why some mobilization efforts succeed and others fail, and (3) how movement strategies, targets, and goals are determined in relation to larger publics.

Second, the constructionist approach recognizes that movements must work hard to maintain participants in collective action over time. Leaders that do not engage in emotion-work and identity-work are likely to lose participants as the passion for action fades and other identities become more salient. Third, a movement must not only maintain a stable number of participants but must also adjust its tactics and goals to align with a larger environment. If, for example, bystander and mediating publics or social control agents regard crowd/movement activities as destructive, criminal, or unreasonable, the chances that these publics will interfere with group activities increases and the chances for group success decline. Because of such considerations, the constructionist approach can stand on it own with respect to some issues, and serve as a useful supplement to other perspectives with respect to other issues relating to the mobilization of constituents and the consequences of participation.

CONCLUSION

In this chapter, we have examined the relevance of four social psychological perspectives to illuminating four cornerstone concepts that are fundamental to understanding the determinants, character, and consequences of participation in crowds and social movements. The four cornerstone concepts include grievances, symbolization, emotion, and identity. In Table 20-1,

TABLE 20-1. Summary Table of the Theoretical Perspectives and the Cornerstone Concepts

Focal concepts	Theoretical perspectives			
	Dispositional	Learning models	Rational choice	Constructionist
Level of analysis	Individual	Individual and Group	Individual	Interactive
Primary assumptions about collective action	Some individuals are predisposed to collective action	(1) is an attempt to satisfy drives or (2) is a function of context	A rational response to interests	Involves affective, cognitive, and ideational dimensions
Grievances	The result of heightened frustration	Result of (1) heightened frustration or (2) socialization processes	Viewed in relation to personal and group interests and the prospect of attaining them	The result of identity, structure, or other constructed grievances
Symbolization	Not discussed	Implied in socialization processes, which develop/change over the life course	Not discussed. People participate because of their attitudes, skills, efficacy and location	Crucial for the explanation of differential participation and forms of collective action
Emotion	Irrational emotionalism	Implied in discussions of conversion	Implied in discussions of selective incentives	A critical resource in initial and continued participation
Identity	Spoiled or inadequate	Subsumed in discussions of activist orientations and conversion processes	Subsumed in discussions of incentives and considered as part of rational calculus	Provides different motives for initial and continued participation

we summarize our observations and highlight the connections between the four theoretical perspectives and the four focal concepts. Arguably, the constructionist approach brings us the furthest in thinking about participation in collective action because it is the most inclusive and emphasizes the interactive nature of participation. However, each of the perspectives facilitates understanding aspects of the social psychology of the participation process. More specifically, initial and continued participation is the result of complex interactions (1) among the four cornerstone concepts and (2) among multiple levels of analysis—the individual, the collectivity, and other groups or organizations that constitute the field of actors relevant to the emergence and operation of social movements and associated crowd activities.

In sum, we think our examination of the theorizing and research pertinent to the corner-stone concepts of grievances, symbolization, emotion, and identity demonstrates the impor-tance of social psychological perspectives for understanding participation in crowd and social movement phenomena. Social psychological perspectives highlight the complex and varied relationships and processes that undergird the articulation of grievances and motivate and sustain participation in crowd and social movement activities. Moreover, because social psy-chological perspectives tend to examine the interactions among individuals and the contexts in which they are embedded, they help contribute to a more thoroughgoing understanding of participation-related issues in relation to crowds and social movements.

REFERENCES

Aberle, D. (1966). *The peyote religion among the Navajo*. Chicago: Aldine.

Allport, F. (1920). The group fallacy in relation to social science. *Journal of Abnormal and Social Psychology, 19*, 60–73.

Barker, C. (2001). Fear, laughter, and collective power: The making of solidarity at the Lenin shipyard in Gdnask, Poland, August 1980. In J. Goodwin, J. Jasper, & F. Polletta (Eds.), *Passionate politics: Emotions and social movements* (pp. 175–194). Chicago: University of Chicago Press.

Bell, D. (1963). *The end of ideology: On the exhaustion of political ideas in the fifties*. New York: The Free Press.

Benford, R. (1997). An insider's critique of the social movement framing perspective. *Sociological Inquiry, 67*, 409–430.

Benford, R., & Snow, D. (2000). Framing processes and social movements: An overview and assessment. *Annual Review of Sociology, 26*, 611–639.

Bengston, L. (1970). The generation gap: A review and typology of social psychological perspectives. *Youth and Society, 25*, 7–32.

Berger, P., & Luckmann, T. (1966). *The social construction of reality: A treatise in the sociology of knowledge*. New York: Anchor Books.

Berk, R. (1974). A gaming approach to crowd behavior. *American Sociological Review, 39*(3), 355–373.

Blais, A. (2000). *To vote or not to vote: The merits and limits of rational choice theory*. Pittsburgh: University of Pittsburgh Press.

Block, J., Haan, N., & Smith, M. B. (1972). Socialization correlates of student activism. In A. Orum (Ed.), *The seeds of politics: Youth and politics in America* (pp. 215–231). Englewood Cliffs, NJ: Prentice-Hall.

Bolton, N. (1972). *The psychology of thinking*. London: Methuen.

Balch, R. (1980). Looking behind the scenes in a religious cult: Implications for the study of conversion. *Sociological Analysis, 41*, 137–143.

Blumer, H. (1939). Collective Behavior. In R. Park (Ed.), *An outline of the principles of sociology* (pp. 221–280). New York: Barnes and Noble.

Brady, H., Verba, S., & Schlozman, K. (1995). Beyond SES: A resource model of political participation. *American Political Science Review, 89*, 271–294.

Bromley, D., & Shupe, A., Jr. (1979). Just a few years seems like a lifetime: A role theory approach to participation in religious movements. In L. Kriesberg (Ed.), *Research in social movements, conflict and change* (pp. 159–185). Greenwich: JAI Press.

Buechler, S. (2000). *Social movements in advanced capitalism: The political economy and cultural construction of social activism*. New York: Oxford University Press.

Cantril, H. (1941). *The psychology of social movements*. New York: John Wiley and Sons.

Cohen, J. (1985). Strategy or identity: New theoretical paradigms and contemporary social movements. *Social Research, 52*, 663–716.

Cohn, N. (1957). *The pursuit of the millennium*. New York: Oxford University Press, Inc.

della Porta, D., & Diana, M. (1999). *Social movements: An introduction*. Oxford, UK: Blackwell.

Demerath, N. J., III, Marwel, G., & Aiken, M. (1971). *Dynamics of idealism: White activists in a Black movement*. San Francisco: Jossey-Bass.

D'Emilio, J. (1983). *Sexual politics, sexual communities*. Chicago: University of Chicago Press.

Dollard, J., Doob, L., Miller, N., Mowrer, H., & Sears, R. (1939). *Frustration and aggression*. New Haven: Yale University Press.

Eyerman, R., & Jamison, A. (1998). *Music and social movements: Mobilizing traditions in the twentieth century*. Cambridge: Cambridge University Press.

Fantasia, R., & Hirsch, E. (1995). Culture in rebellion: The appropriation and transformation of the veil in the Algerian revolution. In H. Johnston & B. Klandermans (Eds.), *Social movements and culture* (pp. 144–159). Minneapolis: University of Minnesota.

Ferree, M. M. (1992). The political context of rationality: Rational choice theory and resource mobilization. In A. Morris & C. Mueller (Eds.), *Frontiers in social movement theory* (pp. 29–52). New Haven: Yale University Press.

Ferree, M. M., & Miller, F. (1985). Mobilization and meaning: Toward an integration of social psychological and resource perspectives on social movements. *Sociological Inquiry, 55*, 38–61.

Finkel, S., & Muller, E. (1998). Rational choice and the dynamics of collective political action: Evaluating alternative models with panel data. *American Political Science Review, 92*(1), 37–49.

Flacks, R. (1972). The liberated generation: An exploration of the roots of student protest. In A. Orum (Ed.), *The seeds of politics: Youth and politics in America* (pp. 353–364). Englewood Cliffs, NJ: Prentice-Hall.

Forward, J. R., & Williams, J. R. (1970). Internal-external control and Black militancy. *Journal of Social Issues, 26*, 75–92.

Friedman, D., & McAdam, D. (1992). Networks, choices, and the life of a social movement. In A. Morris & C. Mueller (Eds.), *Frontiers in social movement theory* (pp. 156–173). New Haven: Yale University Press.

Fromm, E. (1941). *Escape from freedom*. New York: Farrar and Rinehart.

Gamson, W. (1968). *Power and discontent*. Homewood, IL: Dorsey.

Gamson, W. (1990). *The strategy of social protest* (2nd ed.). Belmont, CA: Wadsworth Publishing Company.

Gamson, W. (1992). The social psychology of collective action. In A. Morris & C. Mueller (Eds.), *Frontiers in social movement theory* (pp. 53–76). New Haven: Yale University Press.

Gamson, W. (1995). Constructing social protest. In H. Johnston & B. Klandermans (Eds.), *Social movements and culture* (pp. 53–76). Minneapolis: University of Minnesota Press.

Gamson, W., Fireman, B., & Rytina, S. (1982). *Encounters with unjust authority*. Homewood, IL: Dorsey.

Ginsburg, F. (1998). *Contested lives: The abortion debate in an American community*. Los Angeles: University of California Press.

Goodwin, J. (1997). The libidinal constitution of a high-risk social movement: Affectual ties and solidarity in the Huk rebellion, 1946 to 1954. *American Sociological Review, 62*, 53–69.

Goodwin, J., & Jasper, J. (1999). Caught in a winding, snarling vine: The structural bias of political process theory. *Sociological Forum, 14*(1), 27–54.

Goodwin, J., Jasper, J., & Polletta, F. (2001). Introduction: Why emotions matter. In J. Goodwin, J. Jasper, & F. Polletta (Eds.), *Passionate politics: Emotions and social movements* (pp. 1–24). Chicago: The University of Chicago Press.

Gould, D. (2001). Rock the boat, don't rock the boat, baby: Ambivalence and emergence of militant AIDS activism. In J. Goodwin, J. Jasper, & F. Polletta (Eds.), *Passionate politics: Emotions and social movements* (pp. 135–157). Chicago: University of Chicago Press.

Granovetter, M. (1978). Threshold models of collective behavior. *American Journal of Sociology, 83*(6), 1420–1443.

Gusfield, J. (1963). *Symbolic crusade: Status politics and the American temperance movement*. Urbana, IL: University of Illinois Press.

Gusfield, J. (1966). Functional areas of leadership in social movements. *Sociological Quarterly, 7*, 137–156.

Hechter, M., & Kanazawa, S. (1997). Sociological rational choice theory. *Annual Review of Sociology, 23*, 191–214.

Hirsch, E. (1990). Sacrifice for the cause: The impact of group processes on recruitment and commitment in protest movements. *American Sociological Review, 55*, 243–254.

Hochschild, A. R. (1979). Emotion work, feeling rules, and social structure. *American Journal of Sociology, 85*(3), 551–575.

Hoffer, E. (1951). *The true believer: Thoughts on the nature of mass movements*. New York: Harper and Row.

Hunt, S. (1991). *Constructing collective identity in a peace movement organization*. PhD dissertation. University of Nebraska.

Hunt, S., & Benford, R. (1994). Identity talk in the peace and justice movement. *Journal of Contemporary Ethnography, 22*, 488–517.

Hunt, S., Benford, B., & Snow, D. (1994). Identity fields: Framing processes and the social construction of movement identities. In E. Larana, H. Johnston, & J. Gusfield (Eds.), *New social movements: From ideology to identity* (pp. 185–208). Philadelphia: Temple University Press.

Hyman, H. (1959). *Political socialization*. New York: Free Press.

Jasper, J. (1997). *The art of moral protest: Culture, biography, and creativity in social movements*. Chicago: University of Chicago Press.

Jasper, J. (1998). The emotions of protest: Affective and reactive emotions in and around social movements. *Sociological Forum, 13*(3), 397–424.

Jasper, J., & Poulsen, J. (1995). Recruiting strangers and friends: Moral shocks and social networks in animal rights and anti-nuclear protests. *Social Problems, 42*, 493–512.

Jensen, J. (1995). What's in a name? Nationalist movements and public discourse. In H. Johnston & B. Klandermans (Eds.), *Social movements and culture* (pp. 185–208). Minneapolis: University of Minnesota Press.

Kahneman, D., & Tversky, A. (1979). Prospect theory: An analysis of decision under risk. *Econometrica, 47*, 263–291.

Kanter, R. M. (1968). Commitment and social organization: A study of commitment mechanisms in utopian communities. *American Sociological Review, 33*(4), 99–517.

Kanter, R. (1972). Commitment and community: Communes and utopias in sociological perspective. Cambridge, Massachusetts: Harvard University Press.

Kaplan, H., & Liu, X. (2000). Social movements as collective coping with spoiled personal identities: Intimations from a panel study of changes in the life course between adolescence and adulthood. In S. Stryker, T. Owens, & R. White (Eds.), *Self, identity, and social movements* (pp. 215–238). Minneapolis: University of Minnesota.

Klandermans, B. (1984). Mobilization and participation. *American Sociological Review, 49*, 583–600.

Klandermans, B. (1988). Union action and the free rider dilemma. In L. Kriesberg & B. Misztal (Eds.), *Research in social movements, conflict and change* (pp. 77–92). Greenwich: JAI.

Klandermans, B. (1997). *The social psychology of protest.* Cambridge, MA: Blackwell.

Klapp, O. (1969). *Collective search for identity.* New York: Holt, Rinehart and Winston.

Klatch, R. (1999). *A generation divided: The new left, the new right and the 1960s.* Los Angeles: University of California Press.

Kornhauser, W. (1959). *The politics of mass society.* New York: The Free Press.

Laitin, D. (1998). *Identity in formation: The Russian-speaking populations in the near abroad.* Ithaca, NY: Cornell University Press.

Le Bon, G. (1895). *The crowd: A study of the popular mind.* New York: Viking.

Lipset, S. M. (1950). *Agrarian socialism.* Berkeley: University of California Press.

Lipset, S. M. (1960). *Political man: The social bases of politics.* Baltimore: Johns Hopkins University Press.

Lofland, J. (1981). Collective behavior: The elementary forms. In M. Rosenberg & R. Turner (Eds.), *Social psychology: Sociological perspectives* (pp. 378–446). New York: Basic Books.

Mannheim, K. (1970). Problem of generations. *Psychoanalytical Review, 3*, 378–404.

Marwell, G., Aiken, M., & Demerath, N. J., III. (1987). The persistence of political attitudes among 1960's civil rights activists. *Public Opinion Quarterly, 51*, 383–399.

McAdam, D. (1988). *Freedom summer.* Oxford: Oxford University Press.

McAdam, D. (1999). *Political process and the development of Black insurgency, 1930–1970.* Chicago: University of Chicago Press.

McAdam, D., Tarrow, S., & Tilly, C. (2001). *Dynamics of contention.* Cambridge: Cambridge University Press.

McCarthy, J., & Zald, M. (1994). Resource mobilization and social movements: A partial theory. In M. Zald & J. McCarthy (Eds.), *Social movements in an organizational society: Collected essays* (pp. 15–42). New Brunswick: Transaction Publishers.

McPhail, C. (1969). Student walkout: An examination of elementary collective behavior. *Social Problems, 16*, 441–455.

McPhail, C. (1991). *The myth of the maddening crowd.* New York: Aldine De Gruyter.

McPhail, C. (1994). The dark side of purpose: Individual and collective violence in riots. *Sociological Quarterly, 35*, 1–32.

McPhail, C., & Wohlstein, R. T. (1983). Individual and collective behaviors within gatherings, demonstrations, and riots. *Annual Review of Sociology, 9*, 579–600.

Melucci, A. (1995). The process of collective identity. In H. Johnston & B. Klandermans (Eds.), *Social movements and culture* (pp. 41–63). Minneapolis: University of Minnesota Press.

Miller, N., & Dollard, J. (1941). *Social learning and imitation.* New Haven: Yale University Press.

Morris, A. (1984). *The origins of the civil rights movement: Black communities organizing for change.* New York: Free Press.

Mueller, E., & Opp, K. D. (1986). Rational choice and rebellious collective action. *American Political Science Review, 80*, 471–487.

Nepstad, S. E., & Smith, C. (2001). The social structure of moral outrage in recruitment to the U.S. Central America peace movement. In J. Goodwin, J. Jasper, & F. Polletta (Eds.), *Passionate politics: Emotions and social movements* (pp. 158–174). Chicago: University of Chicago Press.

Nisbet, R. (1954). *The quest for community.* New York: Oxford University Press.

Oliver, P. (1980). Rewards and punishments as selective incentives for collective action: Theoretical investigations. *American Journal of Sociology, 85*(6), 1356–1375.

Oliver, P. (1989). Bringing the crowd back in: The nonorganizational elements of social movements. In L. Kriesburg (Ed.), *Research in social movements, conflict and change* (Vol. 11, pp. 1–30). Greenwich, CT: JAI Press.

Oliver, P., & Marwell, G. (1988). The paradox of group size in collective action. *American Sociological Review, 53*, 1–8.

Oliver, P., & Marwell, G. (1992). Mobilizing technologies for collective action. In A. Morris & C. Mueller (Eds.), *Frontiers in social movement theory* (pp. 251–272). New Haven: Yale University Press.

Olson, M. (1965). *The logic of collective action: Public goods and the theory of* groups. Cambridge: Harvard University Press.

Opp, K. D. (1988). Community integration and incentives for political protest. In B. Klandermans, H. Kriesi, & S. Tarrow (Eds.), *From structure to action: Comparing movement participation across cultures* (pp. 83–103). Greenwich: JAI Press.

Opp, K. D. (1989). *The rationality of political protest*. Boulder, CO: Westview.

Park, R., & Burgess, E. (1921). *Introduction to the science of sociology*. Chicago: University of Chicago Press.

Pinel, E., & Swann, W. (2000). Finding the self through others: Self-verification and social movement participation. In S. Stryker, T. Owens, & R. White (Eds.), *Self, identity, and social movements* (pp. 132–152). Minneapolis: University of Minnesota.

Piven, F. F., & Cloward, R. (1977). *Poor people's movements: Why they succeed, how they fail*. New York: Pantheon Books.

Polletta, F., & Jasper, J. (2001). Collective identity and social movements. *Annual Review of Sociology, 27*, 283–305.

Rohlinger, D. A. (2002). Framing the abortion debate: Organizational resources, media stategies, and movement-countermovement dynamics. *The Sociological Quarterly, 43*, 479–507.

Rosenstone, S. J., & Hansen, J. M. (1993). *Mobilization, participation, and democracy in America*. New York: MacMillan.

Schwalbe, M., & Mason-Schrock, D. (1996). Identity work as group process. *Advances in Group Processes, 13*, 113–147.

Seeman, M. (1975). Alienation studies. *Annual Review of Sociology, 1*, 91–123.

Sherif, M. (1936). *The psychology of social norms*. New York: Harper.

Sherif, M., & Harvey, O. J. (1952). A study in ego functioning: The elimination of stable anchorages in individual and group situations. *Sociometry, 15*, 272–305.

Shibutani, T. (1966). *Improvised news: A sociological study of rumor*. New York: The Bobbs-Merrill Company.

Simi, P., & Futrell, R. (2002, April). *Active abeyance as strategic change in the U.S. White power movement*. Paper presented at the Pacific Sociological Association Meeting April 19–21 2002.

Smelser, N. (1992). The rational choice perspective. *Rationality and Society, 4*(4), 381–410.

Snow, D. (2001). Collective identity and expressive forms. In N. Smelser & P. Baltes (Eds.), *International encyclopedia of the social and behavior sciences* (pp. 2212–2219). London: Elsevier Science.

Snow, D., & Benford, R. (1988). Ideology, frame resonance, and participant mobilization. *International Social Movement Research, 1*, 197–212.

Snow, D., & Benford, R. (1992). Master frames and cycles of protest. In A. Morris & C. Mueller (Eds.), *Frontiers in social movement theory* (pp. 133–155). New Haven: Yale University Press.

Snow, D., Cress, D., Downey, L., & Jones, A. (1998). Disrupting the "quotidian": Reconceptualizing the relationship between breakdown and the emergence of collective action. *Mobilization: The International Journal of Research and Theory about Social Movements, Protest, and Collective Behavior, 3*(1), 1–22.

Snow, D., & Davis, P. (1995). The Chicago approach to collective behavior. In G. Fine (Ed.), *A second Chicago school* (pp. 188–220). Chicago: University of Chicago Press.

Snow, D., & Machalek, R. (1984). The sociology of conversion. *Annual Review of Sociology, 10*, 167–190.

Snow, D., & McAdam, D. (2000). Identity work processes in the context of social movements: Clarifying the identity/movement nexus. In S. Stryker, T. Owens, & R. White (Eds.), *Self, identity, and social movements* (pp. 41–67). Minneapolis: University of Minnesota Press.

Snow, D., & Oliver, P. (1995). Social movements and collective behavior: Social psychological dimensions and considerations. In K. Cook, G. Fine, & J. House (Eds.), *Sociological perspectives on social psychology* (pp. 571–599). Boston: Allyn & Bacon.

Snow, D., & Paulsen, R. (2000). Crowds and riots. *Encyclopedia of sociology* (Vol. 1, 2nd ed., pp. 553–562). New York: Macmillan.

Snow, D., Rochford, B., Jr., Worden, S., & Benford, R. (1986). Frame alignment processes, micromobilization and movement participation. *American Sociological Review, 51*, 464–481.

Snow, D., Zurcher, L., & Peters, R. (1981). Victory celebrations as theater: A dramaturgical approach to crowd behavior. *Symbolic Interaction, 4*, 21–42.

Taylor, V., & Whittier, N. (1992). Collective identity in social movement communities: Lesbian feminist mobilization. In A. Morris & C. Mueller (Eds.), *Frontiers in social movement theory* (pp. 104–129).

Taylor, V., & Whittier, N. (1995). Analytical approaches to social movement culture: The culture of the women's movement. In H. Johnston & B. Klandermans (Eds.), *Social movements and culture* (pp. 163–187). Minneapolis: University of Minnesota.

Tilly, C. (1978). *From mobilization to revolution*. Reading, MA: Addison-Wesley.

Toch, H. (1965). *The social psychology of social movements*. Indianapolis: Bobbs-Merrill.

Touraine, A. (1981). *The voice and the eye*. New York: Cambridge University Press.

Turner, R. (1970). Determinants of social movement strategies. In T. Shibutani (Ed.), *Human nature and collective behavior: Papers in honor of Herbert Blumer* (pp. 145–164). Brunswick: Transaction Books.

Turner, R. (1974). Collective behavior. *Encyclopedia britannica (Vol. 4*, 15th ed., pp. 842–853).

Turner, R., & Killian, L. (1972). *Collective behavior.* Englewood Cliffs, NJ: Prentice-Hall.

Verba, S., Schlozman, K. L., & Brady, H. (1995). *Voice and equality: Civic voluntarism in American politics.* Cambridge: Harvard University Press.

Westby, D., & Braungart, V. (1966). Class and politics in the family backgrounds of student political activists. *American Sociological Review, 31*, 690–692.

Whalen, J., & Flacks, R. (1989). *Beyond the barricades: The sixties generation grows up.* Philadelphia: Temple University Press.

Whittier, N., & Taylor, V. (1992). Collective identity in social movement communities: Lesbian feminist mobilization. In A. Morris & C. Mueller (Eds.), *Frontiers in social movement theory* (pp. 104–129). New Haven: Yale University Press.

Wood, J., & Ng, W. C. (1980). Socialization and student activism: Examination of a relationship. In L. Kriesberg (Ed.), *Research in social movement, conflicts and change* (pp. 21–44). Greenwich, Connecticut: JAI Press.

Zurcher, L., & Kirkpatrick, R. G. (1976). *Citizens for decency: Anti-pornography crusade as status protest.* Austin: University of Texas Press.

Zurcher, L., & Snow, D. (1981). Collective behavior: Social movements. In M. Rosenberg & R. Turner (Eds.), *Social psychology: Sociological perspectives* (pp. 447–482). New York: Basic Book.

Zygmunt, J. (1972). Movements and motives: Some unresolved issues in psychology of social movements. *Human Relations, 25*, 449–467.

CHAPTER 21

Cross-Cultural Social Psychology

Karen Miller-Loessi
John N. Parker

In the last decade or so, cross-cultural issues have received increased attention, and social-psychological research across cultures has proliferated, although unevenly with respect to theoretical and substantive areas. This chapter reviews the basic issues associated with a cross-cultural approach to social psychology, and assesses recent theoretical, methodological, and substantive progress. We first develop a working definition of "culture" and "cross-cultural." We then examine the major motivations for the increase in cross-cultural research at this time in history. We proceed to review some major theoretical issues and empirical work exemplifying different theoretical approaches. Finally, we briefly review methodological issues and practical problems associated with the actual practice of research in different cultures, and conclude with our view of the place of cross-cultural work in social psychology.

WHAT IS "CULTURE"? WHAT IS "CROSS-CULTURAL"?

What is "Culture"?

This is indeed a fundamental question, and one for which there is no one "right" answer. In fact, how best to define culture has been debated for years (Swidler, 1986). Culture is often defined very broadly, more so by anthropologists than sociologists* (De Vos & Hippler, 1969,

*Excerpts from K. Miller-Loessi, Comparative social psychology: Cross-cultural and cross-national in K. S. Cook, G. A. Fine, and J. S. House, (Eds.), *Sociological Perspectives on Social Psychology*, (pp. 397–420), published by Allyn and Bacon, Boston, MA, copyright (c) 1995 by Pearson Education, reprinted by permission of publisher.

Karen Miller-Loessi and John N. Parker • Department of Sociology, Arizona State University, Tempe, AZ 85287
Handbook of Social Psychology, edited by John Delamater. Kluwer Academic/Plenum Publishers, New York, 2003.

p. 323). For example, the noted anthropologists Alfred Kroeber and Clyde Kluckhohn (1952, p. 181) formulated the concept of culture as follows:

> Culture consists of patterns, explicit and implicit, of and for behavior, acquired and transmitted by symbols constituting the distinctive achievement of human groups, including their embodiment in artifacts; the essential core of culture consists of traditional (i.e., historically derived and selected) ideas and especially their attached values; culture systems may, on the one hand, be considered as products of action, on the other as conditioning elements of future action.

This definition is so all-inclusive that it seems to us less useful for social-psychological analysis than the one proposed by James House (House, 1981, p. 542), as follows:

> A *culture* is a set of cognitive and evaluative beliefs—beliefs about what is or what ought to be— that are shared by the members of a social system and transmitted to new members.

Working with House's definition, we note that the cognitive and evaluative beliefs of the group are related to their symbols, their behavior, and to the physical artifacts generated by the social system; however *social structure*, as opposed to culture, is also related to symbols, behavior, and physical artifacts. Social structure is defined by House (1981, p. 542) as "a *persisting* and bounded *pattern* of social relationships (or pattern of behavioral interaction) among the units (that is, persons or positions) in a social system."* Culture may be both a cause and consequence of symbols, behavior, and physical artifacts, just as culture and social structure may reciprocally interact.

An alternative approach to defining culture, proposed by Swidler (1986), deserves mention here. Swidler argues that values should not be considered an inherent component of culture, certainly not with respect to how culture affects action. For Swidler, culture is more usefully conceptualized as a "tool kit" of "symbols, stories, rituals, and world-views"—all embodying meanings—from which people construct "strategies of action" (Swidler, 1986, p. 273). Culture is thus a resource to be used by people in different situations, not by providing valued ends that dictate courses of action, but instead by providing socially meaningful resources from which to choose a line of conduct. Within this framework, she sees a "dynamic interaction between culture and social structure," with culture operating differently under different social structural conditions (Swidler, 1986, p. 283). In this respect, we find parallels to Bourdieu's work on "cultural capital," in which there is a clear reciprocal relationship between cultural capital and structural position (Bourdieu, 1986).

While this line of argument is provocative, it is the case that values are seen as central elements of culture in much of current research comparing the world's cultures. The work of Inglehart, Schwartz, Hofstede, the Chinese Culture Connection, and many others has this focus, as we shall discuss at greater length later.

Whichever definition of culture we choose, there are many complexities in its usage that must be considered. Miller-Loessi (1995, p. 39) notes that at least one, and often more than one, cultural milieu impinges on every concrete instance of a social-psychological phenomenon. Subcultures exist within cultures. Individuals may exist in different cultures over time or at the same time, carrying with them varying residues of each culture they have experienced.

Partly because of these complexities, the nation-state is often the unit of analysis in comparative research; it is a convenient although not precise stand-in for culture. For example, Kohn (1989a) finds it conceptually advantageous to study phenomena across nation-states rather than cultures, because nation-state has a relatively unambiguous meaning, whereas culture does not. In making this distinction, Kohn points out that there can be different cultures

---

*For extended discussions of the distinction between culture and social structure, see Schooler (1996) and Miller-Loessi (1995).

within a nation and different nations can share a similar culture. Often nations can be used to compare cultures, assuming that their cultures make for a useful comparison. (It should be noted that using nation as a "stand-in" for culture makes more sense, the more culturally homogeneous the nation.) Studying nations with similar cultures also can allow one to compare the effects of different political and economic systems—that is, analytically to separate structural from cultural factors as explanatory variables.

What do We Mean by "Cross-Cultural"?

With respect to research, *cross-cultural* normally refers to any explicit *comparison* of cultural differences, such as a cross-cultural study of values in the United States and Japan (Stewart & Bennett, 1991). However, we can also think of research done in any culture other than that of the United States as potentially involving *implicit* comparison to theory and results generated by research in the United States, where the bulk of social-psychological research has been done. Either replication of the U.S.-based research or entirely new insights can be generated by doing research in a culture other than that of the United States. We shall discuss this further in this chapter, particularly in the section on emic research, but our main focus will be explicit comparisons across at least two geographically distinct cultures.

Although comparison among subcultures within the United States or any other country might also be considered *cross-cultural*, it is beyond the scope of this chapter to review such work in any depth. Such comparisons are complicated. One reason is that there is more "contamination" among cultures that coexist in a given geographical area. Another is that there are bound to be factors other than cultural—in particular, socioeconomic differentials—that relate to the beliefs and values of subcultures within broad cultures. Still, there is no question that disentangling these effects yields enormous insights, and we regret that space limitations preclude the consideration that these issues deserve.

WHY TAKE A CROSS-CULTURAL APPROACH?

There are many reasons for the proliferation of cross-cultural social-psychological research in the last decade, and there are reasons why there is a need for even more. Perhaps the first reason is that events in the world increasingly *do* cross cultural boundaries and we need social-psychological insights to help us understand and cope with these changes. Globalization, defined by Robertson (1992, p. 8) as referring to "the compression of the world and the intensification of consciousness of the world as a whole," has been rapidly increasing. Boli and Thomas claim that "technological progress, bureaucratization, capitalist organization, states, and markets are embedded in cultural models, often not explicitly recognized as such, that specify the 'nature of things' and the 'purpose of action' " (Boli & Thomas, 1999, p. 17). Yet although there are consensual elements in these cultural patterns, there still exist enormous differences in cultural paradigms that need to be studied and understood.

Many argue that social psychology can be much more helpful in this regard as it (hopefully) emerges from the exclusively Western, mostly American cultural paradigms that have dominated the discipline since its inception. Comparative research helps to expose bias in social psychology caused by "the blinders and filters of our culture" (Triandis, 1988). After all, social psychology is itself a cultural product, much as religions, political structures, or legal systems are cultural products (Hogan & Emler, 1978; Triandis, 1988). Furthermore, people tend to seek out information that confirms their already established constructions of reality (Swann & Read, 1981), whether these be culturally or otherwise determined, and social psychologists, like other human beings, may operate with unconscious cultural biases. As Hofstede (1980, p. 374) aptly puts it: "If we begin to realize that our own ideas are culturally limited ... we can never be self-sufficient again. Only others with different mental programs can help us find the limitations of our own."

In general, the need for greater cross-cultural understanding is urgent. One reason is that "... the populations of many nations, and of communities within nations, are asserting their distinctiveness more energetically and we need to be able to understand what processes come into play when they meet and interact with one another" (Smith & Bond, 1999, p. 2). Assertion of cultural distinctiveness can be healthy for intergroup relations if accompanied by understanding. However, Stewart and Bennett point out that "deeply critical events facing the world today are rooted in culture ... (yet) many of the national and international tensions, including threats to peace, cannot be addressed at present levels of knowledge and skill" (Stewart & Bennett, 1991, p. ix). It is crucial to bring in the international sphere as a source of important social knowledge (Cole, 1984; Gabrenya, 1988; Galtung, 1990; Malone, 1990). In fact, an understanding of cultural and national differences is one of the main contributions social psychology can make to practical policy makers in today's world (Hofstede, 1980, p. 9). As we interact in an increasingly global environment, cross-cultural and cross-national social psychology have great potential applied usefulness for government, business, and higher education. In sum, we need both knowledge of cultural dynamics in the contemporary world and the imagination to better deal with them.

It is thus our hope that this chapter can efficiently summarize new knowledge useful to the understanding of cross-cultural patterns in major areas of social psychology. Social psychologists have much to contribute to our understanding of each other, in a world in which lack of such understanding grows increasingly deleterious and even dangerous to the harmony, prosperity, and ultimate survival of humanity and of all life on earth.

ETIC VERSUS EMIC APPROACHES

Cross-cultural research can be used to search for differences or similarities in social-psychological processes as they operate in different cultures. Kagitcibasi and Berry (1989), in reviewing research in cross-cultural psychology, identify distinct trends in two opposite directions: the intensive study of psychological phenomena within separate cultures, which is called the indigenous or *emic* approach, and the quest for commonalities across many or all cultures, which is called the universalist or *etic* approach. The terms "emic" and "etic" are taken from linguistic terminology (Berry, 1969; Pike, 1967). The emic approach involves studying behavior from within the system, examining only one culture at a time, discovering rather than imposing structure, and using criteria relative to internal characteristics. The etic approach involves studying behavior from a position outside the system, examining two or more cultures and comparing them, imposing a structure created by the analyst, and using criteria that are considered absolute or universal (Berry, 1969). The emic approach has traditionally been used by anthropologists, in their quest for understanding what is unique to each culture. On the other hand, the thrust of both *sociology* and *psychology* as disciplines has generally been etic, that is, to search for general relationships that transcend particular circumstances. In social psychology, the two approaches to comparative work constitute two different streams of research, with clear and fundamental differences in epistemological assumptions.

The emic approach has historically been the minority view in comparative social psychology, yet it is growing as a significant trend in research, and can be related to more general contemporary theoretical trends such as poststructuralism, postmodernism, and critical theory (see Agger, 1991). It challenges—sometimes radically—the assumptions of the mainstream etic approach. Social-psychological theorists such as Gergen (1973, 1978, 1985; Gergen & Davis, 1985), Sampson (1978, 1985, 1988), Harre (1981), and Kukla (1988) have questioned the positivist, empiricist, modernist epistemology—the belief that knowledge about social-psychological phenomena can be obtained through theoretical analysis and empirical observation aimed at formulating general laws of human behavior—underlying social psychology in general and comparative social psychology in particular. Rather, they have emphasized the contextual, historically bound, socially constructed nature of human psychology. When taken to their logical conclusions, these views lead to radical cultural relativism (Kagitcibasi & Berry, 1989)—the position that there are no social-psychological universals that transcend specific cultures and that universal laws of human behavior cannot be identified. Without necessarily taking this extreme position, a considerable amount of empirical research has been done explicitly arising from, and specific to, particular cultures and nations, which we shall discuss later (see also Backman, 1990; Kagitcibasi & Berry, 1989, for reviews).

The more common, "mainstream" approach in cross-cultural social psychology has been to search for universals (Lonner, 1980). Faucheux (1976) takes the position that unless we define "cultural" as particular, accidental, and contingent, it should theoretically be possible to develop universal theories that incorporate cultural dimensions. This goal, though far from attainment, underlies most comparative research in social psychology.

There appears to be a basic conflict between the emic and the etic approaches, yet Kagitcibasi and Berry (1989) believe that cross-cultural psychology can progress only through a dialectic of the two. And a synthesis of sorts may come about in the recognition that "emic (indigenous) knowledge is necessary for a truly universal psychology, since universals may simply be the common patterns among various emic realities" (Kagitcibasi & Berry, 1989, p. 519). In other words, it may be necessary for social psychology to fully understand diverse realities in order to understand their commonalities, a point more fully developed by Faucheux (1976).

Emic Research in Social Psychology: Some Considerations and Examples

There has been much recent discourse on the value of emic research in social psychology. Emic psychology in general is sometimes referred to as "indigenous psychology" (Kim & Berry, 1993; Sinha, 1997; Smith & Bond, 1999). As background to the emic/indigenous approach, Faucheux (1976, p. 293) asserts that "without others (other cultures, other worldviews) … we might not be able to break out of our cultural 'taken for granted' which is a basic condition for progress in knowledge." Cole (1984) describes how experience in another culture—immersion in its assumptions, relationships, its whole *gestalt*—may give us wholly different ways to think about things. This kind of new perspective may radically alter our theories or even our views of what is important to explain in the first place.

Kim, Park, and Park (2000) identify two types of investigation of such concepts within the indigenous psychology framework. The first is indigenous analysis of psychological concepts, that is, concepts widely studied in the mostly Western psychological literature (such as achievement, the self, and stress). The second is the psychological analysis of indigenous concepts, that is, applying extant psychological theories to indigenous concepts such as *amae*, the Japanese concept of "sweet indulgence," and "face," a typically Asian concept. We will give examples of both types of analysis.

With respect to indigenous analysis of psychological concepts, it may be useful first to offer an analogy demonstrating indigenous analysis of some concrete physical objects. Kim et al. (2000), drawing on Shweder (1991), provide a clear example of how the same object can have different meaning and value in different cultures:

> What is considered a weed in one country (e.g., seaweed, dandelions in France) is considered a vegetable in another (e.g., Korea). What is considered a pest in Korea (e.g., snails) is considered a delicacy in France. If a cabbage grew in a rose garden, we would pluck it out, and if a rose grew in a cabbage patch, we would similarly treat it as a weed (Shweder, 1991). Thus, the distinction between a vegetable and a weed includes the notion of edibility, meaningfulness, and intentionality. (Kim et al., 2000, p. 68)

Although this example is from the physical world, obviously the basic principles operate with respect to social-psychological concepts, which may also vary in their meaning and value in different cultures. Returning to social psychology, we give examples of research on one important concept, the self, as analyzed in three indigenous traditions—India, China, and Russia. Gecas and Burke (1995) argue that social psychology's theoretical paradigms of the *self* have mostly been developed from, and are most applicable to, Western cultures. The dominant paradigm of the self as bounded, independent, and autonomous is challenged by cross-cultural research. The following examples illustrate this point.

Sinha and Naidu (1994) find, among much diversity, a common thread concerning the self in Indian Hindu thought. This is the concept of the Self/Not-Self. Rather than these being a duality, there is continuity between them. Humans are not considered separate from their environment but instead in balance and in harmony—in a sort of symbiotic relationship—with it. Self-development does not consist of acquiring self-referencing concepts and a style that distinguishes the self from the surrounding environment, as in Western thought. Self-development involves "dissolution of the Self or ego and all self and Not-Self distinctions and their attendant cognitive categories" (Sinha & Naidu, 1994, p. 48). In this process, "the essential spiritual unity of all beings is realized" (Sinha & Naidu, 1994, p. 49).

Yu (1994) delineates two sharply contrasting strands of traditional Chinese thought: Confucianism and Taoism. Although they differ from each other, both have powerfully influenced contemporary Chinese thought and both offer sharp contrasts with the Western view of the self. According to Yu (1994, p. 62):

> Deci and Ryan (1991) assert that self-development is instrinsically motivated (is motivated by the needs for competence, autonomy, and relatedness). Development *per se* is not the goal of activity; rather, it is the by-product of activity that emanates from a phenomenal core of one's experience and satisfies one's basic psychological needs. In other words, Deci and Ryan hold that pursuit of external goals or any activities related to such pursuit are of no avail to self-development. In sharp contrast, both Confucians and Taoists emphasize the pursuit of life's ultimate goals as the basis for self-development ... In the process of self-development, whether one's basic psychological needs are met or not is of no importance to either Confucians or Taoists. (Yu, 1994, p. 62)

Confucianism and Taoism offer different goals to strive for, the details of which, though fascinating, are beyond the scope of this chapter. But the point is that, in the Chinese view, self-goals are set by the socially constructed thought system rather than by the "intrinsic" needs of the self. Yu's conclusion is that "exploring and analyzing indigenous Chinese theories and concepts of the self in the 'hundred schools' (*chu-tzu pai-jia*) of pre-Ch'in China" will help map out a "formal theoretical psychology of the Chinese self."

In the former Soviet Union, a tradition of indigenous "folk psychology" was first instigated by the Russian Geographical Society's studies of the Russian peasantry in the 1840s (Bodilova, 1984). In his essay on the self in Soviet social psychology, Igor Kon (1984) discusses the idea of "mythological consciousness" found in the peasantry. In this form of consciousness, "man has not yet separated himself from the surrounding world of nature and has transferred his own qualities to natural objects" (Meletinskii, 1976; quoted in Kon, 1984, p. 34). A. R. Luriia (1974) conducted research with peasants in remote parts of Uzbekhistan in the early 1930s, asking them to describe themselves. The respondents tended to point to events that had occurred in their lives, external factors such as descriptions of their neighbors and evaluations of the group to which they belonged using the pronoun "we" rather than "I." Thus the idea of an individual self separate from either the environment or the collective seemed to be absent among these people, and Western notions of the self simply would not apply.

We turn now to examples of *psychological* analysis of *indigenous* concepts, the second of Kim et al.'s (2000) emic forms of analysis. An example of psychological analysis of an indigenous concept is Smith and Bond's (1999) analysis of Fernandez Dols's (1992) work on "perverse norms." These are norms, common in Spain and some other parts of southern Europe, that are widely held in principle but not often practiced nor enforced. When they are enforced the enforcer is seen as capricious or vindictive, even though everyone agrees with the norm in principle. An example would be that a university candidate is normatively expected to be able to answer even the most obscure questions, but when the questioner asks very obscure questions he or she is seen as (successfully) victimizing the candidate. "Perverse norms" are thus mechanisms of power for those willing to insist on their selective enforcement. Smith and Bond (1999) suggest that perverse norms may be an instance of Triandis's (1988) concept of cultural "looseness" (behavior may deviate considerably from norms) as opposed to cultural "tightness" (behavior must conform exactly to norms). Thus an extant psychological theory may help explain a culturally unique phenomenon.

Another example of psychological analysis of an indigenous concept is Kumagai's (1988) theoretical application of George Herbert Mead's concept of the self integrating the Japanese linguistic term "ki," which identifies "an emotion in the self that hitherto has been bypassed by Western social scientists and locates that emotion (via 'I') unambiguously in the social act" (Kumagai, 1988, p. 177). Kumagai's work raises questions about Mead's exclusion from the self of affective elements and about his view that impulse is passive in social interaction, thus suggesting limitations on the cultural universality of Mead's theory.

All of these findings are instances in which theoretical insight was directly derived from a non-Western cultural context, just as most of the theoretical insights now extant in social psychology were derived from the *Western* cultural context. It can be argued in general that the gradual accumulation of empirical research findings about how things operate in different cultures can contribute to theoretical insight. Those taking a strong deductive stance toward theory construction (such as Faucheux, 1976) might disagree. But if we accept as necessary an interplay between deductive theory construction and inductive reasoning from empirical results, it follows that finding unexpected cross-cultural differences can lead to progress in theory building.

Etic Research: Some Major Streams

RESEARCH ON THE BIOLOGICAL AND THE SOCIAL: DISENTANGLING A COMPLEX RELATIONSHIP. A prime example of etic research—the search for human universals—lies at the juncture of biology and social science. It is through the method of cross-cultural studies that the search for the universal similarities uniting all humans may be most fully realized. We have, as a species, come to realize our common origins. The implications of cross-cultural studies are that, along with the differences in culture that may be found, there is also the possibility of the discovery of universal social and biological features. A more precise understanding of these fundamental biological and cognitive capacities and behaviors could well lead to more complete theories of identity and cognition, as well as to a better articulation of social structures of greater abstraction through the use of these building blocks as heuristic devices. Scholars have attempted through various means to unlock these primary components of our being. The boundaries of our biological and social selves are becoming enmeshed, and several schools of thought in social psychology have begun to address these issues.

Evolutionary social psychology is one area of study that has begun to collect cross-cultural data in search of human universals. This field has attempted to understand why certain social phenomena have come into existence by appealing to the theory of evolution. Behavioral characteristics are understood as contributing to overall *fitness*, that is, the ability of the individual to reproduce and carry on their genetic lineage. Behavioral traits are viewed as being designed by the process of evolution to increase the survival of the individual, and hence their offspring (Kenrick, this volume). Given the universality of the evolutionary framework, the field has attempted to directly investigate what are assumed to be universal sociobiological phenomena using cross-cultural analysis. The study of mate selection strategies has been the area of the most thorough empirical examination. The investigation of Buss (1989) has the most breadth in terms of the greatest inclusion of cultures in the analysis. Samples of respondents ($N = 10,047$) were drawn from thirty-seven cultures with, "37 samples from 33 countries located on six continents and five islands." The study hypothesized that men and women would value different character traits in potential mating partners due to different reproductive strategies used to foster the survival and growth to adulthood of their children. Women were hypothesized to value the potential for status attainment in mates, as this is the area where men contribute the most resources to the offspring, after the child is born and begins entry into the social world. Conversely, men were predicted to value reproductive capacity in potential partners, as this is the area where women contribute the most resources to offspring, in childbirth and child rearing. The study concluded that for all cultures men were more likely to value reproductive capacity in partners than were women, and that women were more likely to value the ability, or potential ability, to obtain resources in a potential partner than were men. Kenrick and Keefe (1992) have also made cross-cultural comparisons of marriage partner preference. This comparison uses data from the United States both contemporarily and historically, in addition to data from Europe, India, and the Philippines. The methodology ranges from content analyses of personal and matrimonial advertisements to the study of marriage statistics. Using the same differential parental investment model they predicted that women would prefer slightly older partners, and that men of all ages would prefer women of ages associated with high fertility. In their cross-cultural analysis this pattern of mate selectivity was supported. It was found that women did prefer slightly older partners, while young men preferred women slightly older than themselves, and older men preferred partners who were younger themselves, this age gap increasing as the men grew older. In this context, both sexes are viewed as attempting to increase the chances of passing on their genes to the next generation. This age\resource selectivity hypothesis has been verified in samples of Southern African pastoralists (Harpending, 1992), and urban Brazilian respondents (Otta, Queiroz, Campos, daSilva, & Silveira, 1999). Evolutionary psychology is one manner in which social psychologists are attempting to understand the intersection of our biological and social selves.

The search for some biological primacy in the social has also led to another area of interest, that of the study of emotions. Given the common genetic heritage that we share the question of which, if any, emotions are common to all humanity arises. This question has been addressed by modern social theorists but has its roots in the work of Charles Darwin and William James. In his book *The Expression of the Emotions in Man and Animals* (1955) Darwin made comparisons between emotional displays in humans and other animals. The study included a cross-cultural analysis based on interviews that Darwin conducted with missionaries, and studies of the universality of the interpretation of facial expressions continue (Ekman et al., 1987). The James–Lange theory (1950) was another early attempt to address the physiological aspects of emotions. This theory postulates that emotions were the result of the interpretation of physiological response to socially stimulating situations.

Modern social psychological theories have also addressed the issue of basic emotions, and there has been a surprising degree of agreement between theory and empirical evidence. The positivist theories of emotion, such as those of Collins (1975, 1990, 1998), Kemper (1987, 1990), and Goffman (1961, 1982) have highlighted the role that emotions play in the interaction process. Kemper (1987) has addressed the issue of basic emotions explicitly. He contends that there are four primary emotions: fear, anger, depression, and satisfaction. These emotions are the product of our autonomic nervous systems, and Kemper argues that which of these primary emotions are felt is the result of social power dynamics. Each of the primary emotions is wed to "specific power-and status-relational outcomes" (1990, p. 45). In this way the primary emotions can be linked to larger societal stratification dynamics. Collins (1990) has joined Kemper in championing this theory. From this perspective emotions "are evolutionarily important, cross-culturally universal, ontogenetically early to emerge, and link up with important outcomes of social relations." While cross-cultural studies that have addressed the question of basic emotions have often found more than these four to be shared by all cultures, all have these components in their lists. Scherer, Wallbott, and Summerfield (1986) found the same four primary emotions to be pan-cultural in their eight-country study of Europe. This study used a questionnaire approach and a sample of 779 university undergraduate respondents. Heider (1991) used a lexical mapping methodology that describes the manner in which emotions are related within a language system in his investigation of three Indonesian cultures. Using translators and informants, he created lists of words related to emotions and mapped their relations to one another through word association. He concluded that among the cultures studied certain emotions were identified as similar in both groups, these include sadness, anger, surprise, love, fear, disgust, and contempt. Heider is careful to say that this should be seen as a descending list, with those emotions at the beginning representing the most widely shared emotions across cultures and those at the end of the list the least. Ekman et al. (1987) in a cross-cultural study of ten cultures with samples ($N = 552$) of university students from Europe, Asia, and the United States used photographs of particular facial expressions and asked respondents to judge what the emotional state of the person in the photograph was experiencing. They found that respondents from all cultures could identify the expression being displayed in the photographs. This agreement on the emotions demonstrated in the photos suggests not only that these emotions (happiness, surprise, sadness, fear, disgust, and anger) are subjectively experienced across these cultures, but that the facial expressions associated with them are also pan-cultural. The question of whether antecedent conditions to emotions are also pan-cultural has been addressed both theoretically and empirically (Boucher & Brandt, 1981; Ellsworth, 1994; Scherer, 1994; Scherer et al., 1986), and at least some of the available evidence suggests that this might be the case. There is opposition to this work, and some constructivist positions on the matter deny the existence of such universal states (Averill, 1982, 1994; Lutz, 1982, 1986). Still, in view of the evidence gathered to date, the existence of some universal emotional antecedent conditions and subjective states seems a tenable position.

Another area of social psychology has also attempted to uncover the basic biological foundations of the social as they are grounded in the face-to-face ecology of the local social psychological situation. This work borrows heavily from the field of human ethology. This is the school of ritual analysis, extending from the social anthropological lineage of Emile Durkheim and Radcliff-Brown to the more contemporary work of Goffman (1961, 1982) and Randall Collins (1975, 1981, 1988, 1998). This body of social psychology has been articulated most comprehensively by Collins (1975, 1981, 1988, 1998). Collins takes the local face-to-face situation, or the interaction ritual, as the primary unit of analysis. He includes in the model basic biological features, such as the ability to manipulate symbols and the propensity to monitor others, as well as universal facial gestures and the micro-synchronization of body rhythms, which are assumed to be present cross-culturally. The interaction ritual is based on an exchange model of emotional energy and cultural capital heavily coupled to these biological processes. Collins (1998) has used this theoretical framework to underpin his examination of philosophical networks historically. In *The Sociology of Philosophies* Collins examines the philosophical networks of Greece, China, Japan, Islam, Christendom, Europe, and India over the last three millennia in his comparative, cross-cultural and transhistorical analysis. The network patterns of philosophers that emerge from his analysis demonstrate the face-to-face ties that lie at the nexus of these networks, and the strong ties between eminent masters, pupils, and contemporaneous rivals. Collins concludes that it is the interaction ritual that is the driver of these groups. The interaction ritual network approach can be used to predict which philosophers (or social actors generally) will become the most eminent, and also, to some extent, the direction of argumentation that they will take. Impressive in scope and ambition, Collins postulates the biologically founded interaction ritual as the universal unit of social analysis, and the basic form from which all things social are derived.

That there are universal human states arising from our shared phylogeny does seem a priori correct, and the empirical data that has been gathered in social psychology that addresses these issues is also suggestive. The question of which elements of the social are shared by all cultures, and to what extent this sharing takes place, is still very much a matter of open debate. We have outlined various branches of social psychology that have made attempts at bridging the gaps in our understanding of the biological and the social through cross-cultural research. These are just some of the areas of social psychology that are attempting to make claims on universal features that are said to be shared with all humanity. These findings remain only tantalizing insights, and the true work of delimiting universals is still ahead. All of these schools of thought suffer from a deficit of large amounts of solid, cross-cultural data, and have a long way to go in proving their positions. Caution needs to be taken in these studies not to conflate the social and the biological, and slow, painstaking work is the only way to proceed. An area of particular methodological importance in making universal claims is in the selection of respondents. Efforts must be made to include not only the widest breadth of cultures in the analyses, but also the greatest diversity of respondents in terms of structural positions within each culture. All too easily may the subjective experiences that similar structural positions

imbue to respondents be misinterpreted as cross-culturally universal. The most salient manifestation of this problem in cross-cultural research has been the reliance upon university
students as sample populations. If true cross-cultural comparisons are to be made, the full
spectrum of social groupings that comprise each culture must be considered. The systematic
search for universal states is one of the most contentious, precarious, and methodologically
demanding areas in social psychology. The challenge and the potential knowledge that may
be gained make the effort worthwhile.

ETIC STUDIES OF THE CENTRAL DIMENSIONS OF CULTURE—ARE THERE UNIVERSAL
VALUES?   Another approach to searching for cross-cultural universals uses surveys to identify modal value-dimensions of cultures. Two general questions motivate research in this vein.
First, are there universal *dimensions* of culture that can be found worldwide? And second,
how do particular cultures rank with respect to modal values on each of these dimensions?

Hofstede (1980) was among the first survey researchers to attempt to identify cultural
dimensions empirically on a massive scale, aiming explicitly to identify major elements of
which cultures are composed. Using survey data from employees of a multinational corporation in forty countries (later expanded to fifty countries [Hofstede, 1983]), he derived using
factor analysis four main dimensions along which dominant value systems in the different
cultures could be ordered. He labeled these dimensions power distance (the extent to which
the less powerful members of groups accept power inequalities); individualism (responsibility for oneself and one's family rather than a larger collective); uncertainty avoidance (the
extent to which people feel threatened by ambiguous situations); and masculinity (the extent
to which the dominant values in society are success, money, and things). Although Hofstede's
focus was on work-related values, he saw the four dimensions that emerged from his analysis as having more general cultural relevance. Although not without its limitations (Triandis,
1982), Hofstede's study has been highly influential, stimulating some to use his factors in
further research and others to attempt to expand or modify his conceptualization.

Among those using Hofstede's work as a starting point is Shalom Schwartz (1994),
whose research program studying values in fifty countries is premised on the assumption that
values are related to three fundamental human needs: biological needs, social coordination
needs, and the survival and welfare needs of groups. Schwartz and colleagues identified
fifty-six values they saw as stemming from these basic needs. They surveyed students and
secondary school teachers in each country as to how much each of the fifty-six values was
"a guiding principle in my life." Analyzing each set of in-country data using smallest space
analysis, a technique that shows statistical relatedness, they found remarkable consistency
across cultures in the clustering of individual values (Sagie & Schwartz, 1996). Analysis of
country means, also using smallest space analysis, yielded a set of culture-level value dimensions that are somewhat related to Hofstede's. Schwartz's dimensions are seven in all, roughly
dichotomized as conservatism versus intellectual autonomy and affective autonomy; mastery
and hierarchy versus egalitarian commitment and harmony.

On a theoretical level, Triandis (1988) explores the question of the likely differential
validity of social-psychological theories in different cultures. He identifies three cultural
dimensions that will likely moderate the generality of social-psychological theories: simplic-
ity versus complexity of the culture, individualism/collectivism, and tightness (behavior must
conform exactly to norms)/looseness (behavior can deviate a good deal from norms). In their
review of recent research in cross-cultural psychology, Kagitcibasi and Berry (1989) confirm
that individualism/collectivism stands out as a universal and important cultural dimension,
affecting many basic psychological processes. For example, attribution processes may operate

somewhat differently in individualistic versus collectivist cultures (Al-Zahrani & Kaplowitz, 1991; Bond, 1983; Bond & Hwang, 1986; Bond, Leung, & Wan, 1982; Crittenden, 1989, 1991; Kashima & Triandis, 1986). These differences may involve even the extent to which attributions are actually made. Bond (1983) points out that the separate person is central to all theories of attribution, and that people in collectivistic cultures, in which the individual personality is not of major concern, may not engage much in attribution because they feel relatively little need to explain individual behavior. To the extent that they do construct explanations for individual behavior, they tend more to attribute behavior to causes *external* to the person (Al-Zahrani & Kaplowitz, 1991; Crittenden, 1989). In contrast, in individualistic cultures, individual action is seen as more problematic and in need of explanation, and behavior is more likely to be attributed to causes *internal* to the individual. While the cultural characteristic of individualism/collectivism may indeed have powerful consequences for a range of social-psychological processes (Bond & Hwang, 1986), Kagitcibasi and Berry (1989) warn that further refinement of the individualism/collectivism concept is needed—for example, it needs to be determined whether these are opposite poles of the same dimension or two independent factors—before further conceptual progress and sophistication can be achieved (see also Leung & Bond, 1989). In subsequent work, Triandis (1990) further reviews and elaborates the individualism/collectivism dimension (see also Oyama, 1990); Schooler (1990a) examines individualism in the historical and social-structural context.

The Chinese Culture Connection (1987) also attempts to abstract important theoretical dimensions from different cultures, but it proceeds from a non-Western, emic premise, unlike most other research in social psychology. That is, the researchers in this group created an instrument based on the Chinese tradition, that is, a survey written in Chinese and reflecting indigenous themes and concerns of Chinese culture. This was then translated to the appropriate language and administered to over 2,000 university students in twenty-two countries representing major geographic and cultural groups of the world. The means for each country were factor-analyzed (as well as analyzed with nonmetric multidimensional scaling to correct for the small N). Four factors emerged: "Integration" (including, e.g., tolerance of others, harmony and solidarity with others, and noncompetitiveness); "Confucian Work Dynamism" (including, e.g., ordering relationships by status and observing this order, thrift, persistence, and having a sense of shame); "Human-Heartedness" (including, e.g., kindness, patience, and courtesy); and "Moral Discipline" (including, e.g., moderation, keeping oneself disinterested and pure, and having few desires). With the exception of Confucian Work Dynamism, the factors correlate well with the four dimensions found by Hofstede (1980). The Chinese Culture Connection considers Integration and Moral Discipline to be forms of collectivism, in that each pits narrow self-seeking against the maintenance of group integrity. They relate human-heartedness to Hofstede's femininity dimension. Finally, the Confucian work dimension differentiates Asian cultures from the rest of the world, and is highly correlated with gross national growth in all countries in the study over the past 20 years. Thus, by using a non-Western instrument, researchers may have identified an important cultural dimension that would not have been discovered with a Western instrument.

Finally, we consider an attempt to map the world on cultural dimensions that is part of a research project stemming from a very different intellectual tradition than any we have so far considered. The project is Ronald Inglehart and colleagues' World Values Survey (Inglehart, Basanez, & Moreno, 1998). Its theoretical starting point is so-called Modernization Theory, which posits that economic development has cultural consequences, roughly described as

---

*For a review and critique of this body of literature, see Miller-Loessi, 1995.

a shift from traditional to modern values and attitudes (Inkeles, 1960; Inkeles & Smith, 1974; Kahl, 1968; Lerner, 1958).* For Inglehart and colleagues, as economic development has increased worldwide, in advanced industrial societies we are seeing a shift from modern to postmodern values. Like Schwartz and colleagues, Inglehart and colleagues see societal values as based on societal needs, and he sees these needs as changing with advanced economic development. The most fundamental change is from material scarcity, still predominant even in early industrialized societies, to material abundance, predominant in advanced industrial societies.

Unlike any of the other cultural-dimension research considered above, the World Values Survey in 1990–1993 collected data from *representative national samples* in forty-three countries representing 70% of the world's population and covering the full range of variation in type of economy, economic development, political system, religious tradition, and geographical location. The surveys cover values and attitudes on a wide range of topics, such as gender roles, political orientations, the importance of the family, religious views, and environmental concerns, to name a few. The total number of respondents was over 60,000.

Out of this impressive array of data, Inglehart and colleagues abstracted via factor analysis country scores on each of the first two factors in a principal components analysis. These two dimensions are:

1. Traditional authority versus Secular-Rational authority. This dimension is based on a large number of items that reflect emphasis on obedience to traditional authority (usually religious authority), and adherence to family and communal obligations, and norms of sharing; or, on the other hand, a secular worldview in which authority is legitimated by rational-legal norms, linked with an emphasis on economic accumulation and individual achievement.
2. Survival values versus Well-being values. This reflects the fact that in post-industrial society, historically unprecedented levels of wealth and the emergence of the welfare states have given rise to shift from scarcity norms, emphasizing hard work and self-denial, to postmodern values emphasizing the quality of life, emancipation of women and sexual minorities and related Postmaterialist priorities such as emphasis on self-expression. (Inglehart et al., 1998, pp. 14–15)

The first dimension seems highly related to the individualism/collectivism dimension found in some form in all the other research we have discussed. The second dimension is less unambiguously related to cultural dimensions found in other research. It appears to be somewhat related to Hofstede's masculinity/femininity dimension, possibly to Triandis' tightness/looseness dimension, and possibly also to Schwartz's mastery and hierarchy versus egalitarian commitment and harmony. Survival values may be analogous to the Chinese Culture Connection's Confucian Work Dynamism, while Well-being may be similar to the Chinese Culture Connection's Integration. This, of course, raises the question of the bipolarity of Inglehart's second factor; the same question has been raised in general about individualism/collectivism (Kagitcibasi & Berry, 1989; Leung & Bond, 1989). Further research is needed to resolve these issues; for now we take the factors as given.

From country scores on the two dimensions, Traditional authority/Secular-Rational authority and Survival values/Well-being values, Inglehart and colleagues generated a cultural map of the forty-three countries showing their relative positions on the two dimensions. One of the many interesting observations one can make from this map concerns the relative power of social structure versus culture in one particular instance, that of East and West Germany. The former West German and East German regions of Germany were still independent states when the World Values surveys were conducted, and were sampled separately. While originating from a common German culture, the two countries experienced massively different political and economic social-structural conditions between 1945 and 1990. Yet, while they did not turn out to be identical on the two value dimensions of the study, they remained very similar to each other—as similar as the United States and Canada. We can interpret this finding as implying that culture is powerfully resistant to social-structural change. This is consistent with the notion proposed by Schooler (1996), that "speed of change generally decreases as we go from psychological to social-structual to cultural levels of phenomena" (Schooler, 1996, p. 324). Another possible interpretation is that the surveys in East and West Germany were conducted in the same language, and thus the questions were subject to less variation in interpretation than questions translated into other languages, no matter how careful the translations. There are undoubtedly other possible interpretations as well. Still, the finding is highly suggestive that culture does resist social-structural change to a great extent. Inglehart and colleagues (1998) also discuss this issue with respect to historically Catholic and historically Protestant countries, and again conclude that culture is remarkably powerful. This is a fascinating finding that invites further thought and research.

CULTURE OR NATION AS CONTEXT: THE VALUE OF CROSS-CULTURAL REPLICATION.
The most common usage of comparative research in social psychology, as noted earlier, is to test the generality or universality of psychological phenomena. Kohn (1989, p. 21) sees cross-national studies that primarily test the generality of findings and interpretations as using the nation as *context*, borrowing Scheuch's (1967) phrase. Most of these studies do not treat different nations as theoretically specified sets of variables, but instead use diverse national settings for tests of the generalizability of hypothesized relationships. Inkeles and colleagues' research on the impact of structural modernization on the psychological modernity of factory workers, urban nonindustrial workers, and cultivators within six nations (Inkeles, 1969; Inkeles & Smith, 1974) fits in this category, as does Form's (1976) study of the impact of technology and work organization on attitudes and beliefs of auto workers in India, Argentina, Italy, and the United States.

Another similar use of culture or nation as context is the cross-cultural replication of results found in only one setting (usually the United States). According to Finifter (1977): "The maturity of an area of empirical investigation can be gauged in part by the amount, probativeness, and informativeness of its replication research" (p. 173). Yet there is a relative scarcity of such studies in social psychology (Finifter, 1977; Sharon & Amir, 1988). One of the reasons for this is that journal editors tend to reject replications, apparently preferring previously untested ideas. This general policy extends to comparative research, such that, at least until recently, there have been relatively few replications of nation- or culture-specific findings in different nations or cultures (Sharon & Amir, 1988; also see Rodrigues, 1982). Yet cross-cultural replications can be very valuable, particularly if they identify cultural dimensions that differ across research sites and that are potentially relevant to the theory being tested (Faucheux, 1976). As posed by Messick (1988a, p. 42), the central question that we must keep before us is this: what is the value of comparative empirical information with regard to understanding the causes of the phenomenon?

Kohn (1989b) argues that cross-national research may force us to revise our interpretations to take account of cross-national differences and inconsistencies that could never be uncovered in single-nation research. This point is exemplified by his own ongoing research, initiated with Carmi Schooler nearly forty years ago in a U.S. survey, and subsequently extended both longitudinally and cross-culturally. This research program is reviewed and critiqued in detail elsewhere (House, 1981; Miller-Loessi, 1995; Mortimer & Lorence, 1995;

Spenner, 1988). We shall briefly overview its major findings here, particularly as they demonstrate the value of replication in cross-cultural research.

In the 1960s Melvin Kohn and Carmi Schooler launched an investigation of the critical intervening role of occupational conditions, particularly opportunities to exercise self-direction on the job, in explaining the relationship of social class and values of U.S. men (Kohn, 1969; Kohn & Schooler, 1969). An early cross-national replication in Italy of a portion of these findings was performed by Leonard Pearlin (Pearlin, 1971; Pearlin & Kohn, 1966). The research was expanded 10 years later to include a follow-up study in the United States, including wives and selected children of the original men (Kohn & Schooler, 1983), and subsequently to cross-national replications and extensions of the research in Poland (Kohn & Slomczynski, 1990; Miller, Slomczynski, & Kohn, 1985; Slomczynski, Miller, & Kohn, 1981) and Japan (Kohn, Naoi, Schoenbach, Schooler, & Slomczynski, 1990; Naoi & Schooler, 1985; Naoi & Schooler, 1990; Schooler & Naoi, 1988). The most recent data collections were a new survey in Poland in 1992, and comparable data collected in the Ukraine in 1992–1993 (Kohn et al., 1997).

Overall, the findings in the United States, Poland, Japan, and the Ukraine confirm the central elements of the theory. People more advantageously located in either the class system or the stratification system of their society are more likely to be intellectually flexible, to be self-directed in their social orientations, and to value self-direction in their children than people who are less advantageously located. Occupational self-direction plays a crucial role in explaining these relationships, with those who do more substantively complex work, those who are less closely supervised, and those who do less routine work being more likely to be located higher in the social-structural hierarchy and also to be more intellectually flexible and self-directed in their orientations and values. All of these findings are cross-nationally consistent, at all time periods during which data were collected.

In contrast, higher social class and more self-direction do *not* have historically or cross-nationally consistent effects on affective states of distress. Affective states of distress include feelings of anxiety and estrangement from self and others, as indicated by indices of anxiety, self-deprecation, lack of self-confidence, distrust of others, and believing that one's ideas differ from those of one's friends, one's relatives, others of one's religious faith, and society in general. In the United States, higher social class and greater occupational self-direction both *decrease* distress, although modestly so. In Japan, as in the United States, managers and employers have relatively low distress, and occupational self-direction per se also leads to lower distress, but in Japan *non*manual workers surpass manual workers in their degree of distress. The pattern for Marxist-Socialist Poland in 1978 was different from either that of the United States or that of Japan; in Poland, as in Japan, nonmanual workers had relatively high levels of distress, but the self-employed were relatively low on distress, Polish managers had markedly *high* levels of distress, and Polish factory workers and nonproduction workers were *less* distressed than members of most other social classes. Moreover, in Poland, occupational self-direction had virtually *no* effect on distress. However, by 1992, in a Poland undergoing market reforms and similarly in a Ukraine undergoing even more radical social change, occupational self-direction affected distress in general negatively—the more self-direction on the job, the less distress, as in the U.S. pattern.

Kohn and Slomczynski (1990, p. 209) and Kohn et al. (1990) saw the cross-national differences among the United States, Poland in 1978, and Japan, as interesting and potentially important for their overall interpretation of the relationships among social structure, self-direction, and psychological functioning. A potentially plausible explanation is that factors other than than self-direction on the job have countervailing effects on distress. For example, in the Poland of 1978, only a particular segment of Polish managers were particularly distressed: those not members of the Polish Communist Party, and therefore subject to unusual uncertainties, risks, and insecurities. The fact that the Polish and Ukrainian surveys conducted after the communist systems of these two nations had collapsed showed results similar to those of the United States is very interesting, but it cannot be capitalism alone that yields this relationship, because in capitalist Japan the work-distress relationship was different. All of this implies a complex relationship between social-structural position and psychological functioning that calls for further research and reflection.

In recent work, Kohn and colleagues (Kohn et al., 2000), in Poland and the Ukraine, have tested the relationship of complexity of activities other than paid employment—household work, looking for work, retirement activities—with the psychological functioning of those engaging in those activities. They have found that the complexity of activities in general, as theorized by Schooler (1984), positively relates to intellectual flexibility and self-directedness of orientation, and negatively to distress. This offers cross-cultural corroboration for a similar relationship found for household work (Schooler, Kohn, Miller, & Miller, 1983; Schooler, Miller, Miller, & Richtand, 1984) in the United States, and suggests the possibility that similar findings for schoolwork and psychological functioning (Miller, Slomczynski, & Kohn, 1985; Miller, Kohn, & Schooler, 1986) might also be interesting to replicate cross-culturally.

Another example of the theoretical value of cross-cultural replication is the work of Yamagishi and his associates on trust and commitment. A theory of trust developed by Yamagishi and Yamagishi (1994) proposes that strong and stable social relations (such as family ties and group ties) provide a sense of security within such relations but endanger trust that extends beyond these relations. This is an explanation for the counterintuitive, but empirically consistent finding that Japanese are less generally "trusting" than Americans. Furthermore, the theory posits that a high level of trust emancipates people from the confines of safe, but closed, relationships. The theory generates two predictions that are supported empirically in experiments in the United States and Japan: (1) social uncertainty promotes commitment formation between particular partners; and (2) high trusters tend to form committed relationships less frequently than low trusters when facing social uncertainty (Yamagishi, Cook, & Watabe, 1998). The experimental results challenge the widely shared view that it is the collectivist "mind" of the Japanese people that makes them go along with the group. For once degree of social uncertainty and the level of general trust are controlled, Americans and Japanese subjects do not exhibit differences in their tendencies to voluntarily form committed relationships. In Japanese society, unlike in an experimental situation, longstanding systems of mutual monitoring and sanctioning are in place within families and groups, thus providing security and generating localized "trust." Furthermore, opportunities for forming new bonds (such as getting a job in a different company) are very limited in Japanese society, although this may be changing. It is these structural factors, Yamagishi et al. (1998) argue—both of which can be controlled in the laboratory—that make "collectivism" appear to be an embedded cultural value. Thus, cross-cultural experimentation can be a powerful tool for explicating the bases for widely assumed cultural differences. However, it also raises questions about behavior in experiments as opposed to values expressed in surveys. Collectivism does tend to be a value commonly expressed in surveys by Japanese respondents, yet when removed from their societal context Japanese subjects do not behave in a particularly collectivist fashion (Yamagishi et al., 1998). A plausible explanation is that Japanese tend to be loyal to existing groups but not interested in forming new ones. Still, this discrepancy in what we would conclude from two different ways of investigating culture is worthy of further consideration.

METHODOLOGICAL ISSUES

As with any social-psychological research, theoretical considerations should dictate methodological decisions in comparative social-psychological research. Ideally, once we determine how our knowledge of social psychology will be advanced by addressing the question or questions of the research, methodological decisions follow.

All researchers, whether comparative or not, face a common set of methodological concerns: issues of planning and funding, measurement of concepts, type of design, sampling, and methods of data analysis. Incorporating a diversity of nations or cultures introduces additional complexities in dealing with these issues, however, and, indeed, there is a large body of literature addressing specifically the problems of comparative research. As Form (1979, p. 3) has noted, "probably no field has generated more methodological advice on a smaller data base with fewer results than has comparative sociology." His point is that, although the numerous methodological caveats in the literature are important to heed, the methodological problems of cross-cultural or cross-national research can be made to seem so formidable that researchers are discouraged from even attempting to find solutions to methodological problems, or they abandon comparative research altogether (see also Kuechler, 1987). As Lincoln and Kalleberg (1990, p. 49) point out: "While the obstacles to careful comparative research are severe, they are hardly unique. In numerous ways, such problems also manifest themselves in studies limited to a single country, though they tend not to attract the attention and concern evoked in the context of comparative work." Comparative research is based on the same principles of scientific method as any research, with the major issues boiling down to issues of validity, reliability, generality, and theoretical consequences (Finifter, 1977).

We agree with Scheuch's comment that "in terms of methodology *in abstracto* and on issues of research technology, most of all that needed to be said has already been published" (Scheuch, 1989, p. 148). For useful, comprehensive discussions of cross-cultural methodology that are relevant to social-psychological research we refer the reader to Triandis and Berry (1980); Lonner and Berry (1986); and van de Vijver and Leung (1997). Among the useful articles on somewhat more specialized methodological topics are those of Kuechler (1987) on the utility of surveys for cross-national research; Archer (1987) and Kuechler (1987) on sources of data for cross-national research; and Finifter (1977) on strategies for evaluating the robustness of cross-cultural findings and for making our knowledge more genuinely cumulative through careful replication and extension in subsequent research.

Two statistical techniques currently receiving widespread attention in sociology and social psychology are highly relevant to comparative research and merit special mention in this chapter. These are the use of confirmatory factor analysis, and hierarchical linear modeling. We also highlight the levels of analysis problem as a particularly important area of confusion in cross-cultural research. Finally, we touch on the exciting possibilities of using the Internet for cross-cultural research.

Confirmatory factor analysis techniques can be extraordinarily useful in addressing one of the central issues in cross-cultural research—the issue of measurement validity. Miller, Slomczynski, and Schoenberg (1981) demonstrate how confirmatory factor-analytic techniques can be used to address the dilemma posed by Berry (1969): that both emic (within-culture) and etic (across-cultures) validity must be considered for overall construct validity, and that these may be in conflict. In other words, the best measurement of a concept in one culture may not be "identical" to the best measurement of that concept in another culture, yet if we wish to claim that we are measuring the "same" concept in the two cultures we need to test the conceptual equivalence of our measures (see Berry, 1980, for discussion). Berry (1969) proposes that the problem can be resolved by an etically derived construct being at first imposed on a given culture, then modified to be valid within that culture. The resulting construct for a given culture would then be composed of both emic (culturally specific) and etic (cross-cultural) elements. Miller et al. (1981) demonstrate in detail how confirmatory factor analysis can be a useful statistical tool for constructing and evaluating such distinct yet overlapping measures of a given concept in different cultures. They illustrate by constructing and testing indices of the concept of authoritarian conservatism in the United States and Poland.

Another problem in cross-cultural research is the levels of analysis problem. According to Smith and Bond (1999), "confusion about levels of analysis is probably the greatest single problem in the current development of cross-cultural psychology" (Smith & Bond, 1999, p. 61). This is also known as the ecological fallacy. The idea is that we cannot draw conclusions about relationships among units at one level from relationships among units at a different level. For example, rich nations tend to have Hofstede's cultural dimension of low power distance, meaning that less powerful members of these societies tend to reject power inequalities. While this may be characteristic of rich nations, that does not mean rich individuals within these societies tend to be egalitarian in their values. Smith and Schwartz (1997) discuss this issue at greater length, but here we simply note that we must take care not to draw erroneous conclusions by inferring from relationships at one level what we would find for relationships at another level of analysis.

Of course, there are many instances in which we want to explicate the effects of cultural dimensions and individual-level variables on some dependent variable. For example, we might want to look at respondents' self-esteem as affected by the individualism of each respondent's values as well as the dominant individualism/collectivism of the culture in which each respondent resides. Hierarchical linear modeling is a relatively recent statistical technique that estimates the separate and joint effects of variables at the different levels (individual and culture) on the dependent variable, in this case self-esteem. Bryk and Raudenbush (1992) describe the technique in detail, with numerous examples including some from cross-national studies. Van de Vijver and Leung (1997) express the hope that cross-cultural researchers will take advantage of this obviously useful technique as new computer applications become available.

Finally, we briefly mention that the Internet offers intriguing possibilities for cross-cultural research. At the time of this writing, these have been little exploited, but with the accelerating pace of technological usage and innovation we suspect that as-yet-unimagined applications will have been realized by the time of this chapter's publication. For now, we report on research by Karr (2000) conducting real-time cross-cultural experimentation using the Internet. She conducted dyadic exchange experiments using subjects physically located in the United States and the Netherlands. In each trial, a subject from the United States was paired with a subject from the Netherlands, and each was aware of this cross-cultural pairing. Despite clear differences between the two societies relevant to the experiment, such as the U.S. emphasis on individual achievement versus the Dutch emphasis on equality and consensus, the exchange outcomes for the subjects were indistinguishable. However, the Americans appeared to have a more aggressive negotiating style—they were significantly more likely than the Dutch to make the first offer of an uneven division of points benefiting themselves—thus supporting the cultural stereotype.

While the results are in themselves interesting, it is also the case that this study demonstrates the feasibility of bringing together subjects from far-flung corners of the world via the Internet, as if they were in the same room. The possibilities of this method for knowledge building are overwhelming and just beginning to be explored.

PROBLEMS AND PROGRESS IN CROSS-CULTURAL RESEARCH

There are a variety of problems associated with cross-cultural research. A number of these are reviewed in detail by Miller-Loessi (1995). These include questions about methodological soundness; researchers' ethnocentric prejudices; extremely high costs in money, time, and energy; political and ethical concerns; and frequently limited generalizability even within nations or cultures.

While these concerns still hold, progress has been made. As we hope this review indicates, a great deal of new and exciting cross-cultural work has been done in social psychology since the early 1990s. One of the concerns expressed in the Miller-Loessi (1995) review was the relatively small number of cross-cultural studies in social psychology. At the time of that writing, cross-cultural research was only a modest proportion of all social-psychological research done (Gabrenya, 1988; Messick, 1988b; Tedeschi, 1988). For example, a search of *Social Psychology Quarterly*, the premier social psychology journal in sociology, for the twelve-year period from 1980 through 1991 yielded only twelve articles (less than 4% of all articles) that were in any way cross-cultural or cross-national. A similar search of the same journal for the period 1992–2001 found twenty-six articles, which constitute almost 11% of all articles published in the journal during that period. While not the "huge outpouring" of recent cross-cultural work in psychology described by Smith and Bond (1999, p. xiii), the change from 4 to 11% between the 1980s and the 1990s still constitutes progress. Innovations such as the Internet may make the coming decade a boom time for cross-cultural research.

THE PLACE OF CROSS-CULTURAL WORK IN SOCIAL PSYCHOLOGY

In concluding this chapter, we turn to Karen Cook's essay, "Advances in the Micro-foundations of Sociology: Recent Developments and New Challenges for Social Psychology" (Cook, 2000). In this essay, she sets forth five major challenges facing social psychology at the turn of the millennium. We see all of these challenges as related in some way to existing or needed cross-cultural research.

1. *The Evolutionary Challenge to Social Psychology.*   In this chapter, we have highlighted the juncture of biology and the social sciences as a crucial one in which important work is being conducted on potentially biological bases of social phenomena. Although Cook cautions, and we reiterate, that we must use extreme caution not to oversimplify the issues, it is also important to proceed with this interdisciplinary work. And examining social processes in widely varying cultures, across space and time, is one of the ways we can address the evolutionary challenge.

2. *The Cross-Cultural Challenge.*   Obviously the cross-cultural challenge is at the heart of this chapter. We note that Cook highlights the notion that to do cross-cultural work most successfully we must engage in joint projects with investigators from different cultures engaged in all phases of the research (see also Miller-Loessi, 1995, p. 417). A recent model for this kind of work is the International Social Justice Project, in which researchers from thirteen different countries worked together over 7 years to develop truly comparative national surveys on social justice issues (Kluegel, Mason, & Wegener, 1995). It is important to recognize that not only is there a gain in general knowledge from this kind of work, but it

is also more likely to provide information relevant to each participating nation's most pressing national concerns. This provides appropriate returns on investment to all participants equally, and encourages further cross-national collaboration.

3. *The Challenge of Understanding Intergroup Conflicts and the Politics of Identity.* This third challenge to social psychology, though not highlighted in this chapter, is an extremely important one to which social psychology can speak. For example, early work by Elizabeth Cohen and Shlomo Sharan in Israel (Cohen & Sharan, 1980) showed that being of Middle-Eastern origin was a lower-status characteristic than being of Western origin, among Israeli youth. In a series of experiments, Middle-Eastern subjects were trained to exhibit a high degree of competence on either academic or nonacademic tasks, whereupon they instructed Western boys in these tasks. Then mixed-ethnic groups engaged in group decision-making tasks. Results of the group interaction showed that both academic and nonacademic training increased the amount of influence wielded by Middle-Eastern subjects in comparison to the control group. This kind of intervention is thus one approach to ameliorating the disparities among different social categories of people. Another approach is suggested by the work of Hamberger and Hewstone (1997), who found that contact *as friends* ameliorated blatant prejudice toward ethnic out-groups in four West European nations. While these and other studies are illuminating, the issue of intergroup understanding and mutual respect are so important and there are so many unanswered questions that more research in this area is urgently needed.

4. *The Challenge of Finding New Modes of Cooperation.* Cook sees a major barrier to meeting this fourth challenge in the growing economic disparities among have and have-not nations in the world. While unbridled global capitalism may be at the center of the problem (see Greider, 1997), our worldviews that support this system also matter. And it is here that social psychology can contribute to solutions. Moving toward greater world cooperation requires structural change as its principal focus, but it is also useful to describe and understand how, as individuals and nations, we envision our place in the world and what might lead us to participate in more equitable and cooperative international efforts. While this is clearly an enormous enterprise, much work has been and is being done to address these issues. As just one example discussed in this chapter, the work of Inglehart and colleagues (Inglehart et al., 1998) on values in the areas of national identity, international trust and cooperation, and economic justice, are relevant to the challenge of creating a world in which nations are willing to work together to solve the problems facing us all.

5. *The Challenge of Envisioning a Larger Worldview.* In sum, we need to apply social psychology in all its methods and forms to understand better the interconnections of people in the world today. This will take resources, energy, and vision. But we conclude with a quote from Robert Malone (1990, p. 168) in his essay on the need for global education: "That we can imagine a cooperative and mutually supportive global society is sufficient for its possibility."

ACKNOWLEDGMENTS: We are indebted to K. Jill Kiecolt for helpful suggestions, and to Heather Shafe, Stephen Sills, Ryan Babcock, Andrea Casir, Sharon Gober, Bart Miles, Felicia Morgan, Charles Nwabeke, Fang Yang, Jennifer Brockel, Rong Wang, Christina Clarke, and Craig Stritar for bibliographic assistance.

REFERENCES

Agger, Ben. (1991). Critical theory, poststructuralism, postmodernism: Their sociological relevance. *Annual Review of Sociology, 17,* 105–131.

Al-Zahrani, Said A., Saad, & Kaplowitz, Stan A. (1993). Attributional biases in individualistic and collectivistic cultures: A comparison of Americans and Saudis. *Social Psychology Quarterly, 56*, 223–233.

Archer, Dane. (1987). "Constructing cross-national data sets: Theoretical issues and practical methods." *Comparative Social Research, 10*, 231–239.

Averill, J. (1980). A constructivist view of emotion. In: Robert Plutchik & Henry Kellerman (Eds.), *Emotion, theory, research, and experience: Vol. 1. Theories of emotion* (pp. 305–339). New York: Academic Press.

Averill, J. (1994). In the eyes of the beholder. In Paul Ekman & Richard Davidson (Eds.), *The nature of emotions: Fundamental questions* (pp. 7–14). New York: Oxford University Press.

Backman, Carl W. (1990). *Advances in European social psychology.* Paper presented at the annual meetings of the American Sociological Association, Washington, DC, August.

Berry, John W. (1969). On cross-cultural comparability. *International Journal of Psychology, 4*, 119–128.

Berry, John W. (1980). Introduction to methodology. In H. C. Triandis & J. W. Berry (Eds.), *Handbook of cross-cultural psychology: Vol. 2. Methodology* (pp. 1–28). Boston: Allyn and Bacon.

Boli, John, & Thomas, George M. (1999). INGOs and the organization of world culture. In John Boli & George M. Thomas (Eds.), *Constructing world culture* (pp. 13–49). Stanford: Stanford University Press.

Bond, Michael Harris (1983). A proposal for cross-cultural studies of attribution. In M. Hewstone (Ed.), *Attribution theory: Social and functional extensions* (pp. 144–157). Oxford: Blackwell.

Bond, Michael Harris, & Hwang, K. K. (1986). The social psychology of the Chinese people. In M. H. Bond (Ed.), *The psychology of the Chinese people* (pp. 213–266). Hong Kong: Oxford University Press.

Bond, Michael Harris, Leung, Kwok, & Wan, Kwok-Choi. (1982). The social impact of self-effacing attribution: The Chinese case. *The Journal of Social Psychology, 118*, 157–166.

Boucher, J., & Brandt, M. (1981). Judgement of emotions: American and Malay antecedents. *Journal of Cross-Cultural Psychology, 12*(3), 272–283.

Bourdieu, Pierre. (1986). The forms of capital. In J. G. Richardson (Ed.), *Handbook of theory and research for the sociology of education* (pp. 241–258). New York: Greenwood.

Bryk, Anthony S., & Raudenbush, Stephen W. (1992). *Hierarchical linear models.* Newbury Park: Sage.

Budilova, Ekaterina A. (1984). On the history of social psychology in Russia. In Lloyd H. Strickland (Ed.), *Directions in soviet social psychology* (pp. 11–28). New York: Springer-Verlag.

Buss, D. M. (1989). Sex differences in human mate preference: Evolutionary hypothesis tested in 37 cultures. *Behavioral and Brain Science, 12*, 1–49.

Chinese Culture Connection. (1987). Chinese values and the search for culture-free dimensions of culture. *Journal of Cross-Cultural Psychology, 18*, 143–164.

Cohen, Elizabeth G., & Sharan, Shlomo. (1980). Modifying status relations in Israeli youth: An application of expectation states theory. *Journal of Cross-Cultural Psychology, 11*, 364–384.

Cole, Michael. (1984). The world beyond our borders: What might our students need to know about it? *American Psychologist, 39*, 998–1105.

Collins, Randall. (1975). *Conflict sociology: Toward an explanatory science.* New York, NY: Academic Press.

Collins, R. (1981). On the microfoundations of macrosociology. *American Journal of Sociology, 86*(5), 984–1014.

Collins, R. (1988). *Theoretical sociology.* San Diego: Harcourt Brace Jovanovich.

Collins, Randall. (1998). *The sociology of philosophies: A global theory of intellectual change.* Cambridge, MA: Harvard University Press.

Cook, Karen S. (2000). Advances in the microfoundations of sociology: Recent developments and new challenges for social psychology. *Contemporary Sociology, 29*, 685–692.

Crittenden, Kathleen S. (1989). Causal attribution in sociocultural context: Toward a self-presentational theory of attribution processes. *The Sociological Quarterly, 30*, 1–14.

Crittenden, Kathleen S. (1991). Asian self-effacement or feminine modesty? Attributional patterns of women university students in Taiwan. *Gender and Society, 5*, 98–117.

Darwin, Charles. [1872] (1955). *The expressions of the emotions in man and animals.* New York: Philosophical Library.

De Vos, George A., & Hippler, Arthur A. (1969). Cultural psychology: Comparative studies of human behavior. In G. Lindzey & E. Aronson (Eds.), *The handbook of social psychology* (2nd ed., vol. 4, pp. 323–417). Reading, MA: Addison-Wesley.

Deci, Edward L., & Ryan, R. M. (1991). A motivational approach to self: Integration in personality. In R. A. Dienstbier (Ed.), *Nebraska symposium on motivation 1990* (pp. 237–288). Lincoln: The University of Nebraska Press.

Eckman et al. (1987). Universals and cultural differences in the judgements of facial expressions of emotion. *Journal of Personality and Social Psychology, 53*(4), 712–717.

Ellsworth, P. (1994). Some reasons to expect universal antecedents of emotions. In Paul Ekman & Richard Davidson (Eds.), *The nature of emotions: Fundamental questions* (pp. 150–154). New York: Oxford University Press.

Faucheux, Claude. (1976). Cross-cultural research in experimental social psychology. *European Journal of Social Psychology, 6*, 269–322.

Fernandez Dols, J. M. (1992). Procesos escabrosos en Psicologia Social: el concepto de norma perversa. *Revista de Psicologia Social, 7*, 243–255.

Finifter, Bernard M. (1977). The robustness of cross-cultural findings. *Annals New York Academy of Sciences, 285*, 151–184.

Form, William H. (1976). *Blue-collar stratification: Autoworkers in four countries.* Princeton, NJ: Princeton University Press.

Form, William H. (1979). Comparative industrial sociology and the convergence hypothesis. *Annual Review of Sociology, 5*, 1–25.

Gabrenya, William K., Jr. (1988). Social science and social psychology: The cross-cultural link. In M. H. Bond (Ed.), *The cross-cultural challenge to social psychology* (pp. 48–66). Newbury Park, CA: Sage.

Galtung, Johan. (1990). Visioning a peaceful world. In Mary E. Clark & Sandra A. Wawrytko (Eds.), *Rethinking the curriculum: Toward an integrated, interdisciplinary college education* (pp. 195–213). New York: Greenwood Press.

Gecas, Viktor, & Burke, Peter J. (1995). Self and identity. In Karen S. Cook, Gary Alan Fine, & James S. House (Eds.), *Sociological perspectives on social psychology* (pp. 41–67). Boston: Allyn and Bacon.

Gergen, Kenneth J. (1973). Social psychology as history. *Journal of Personality and Social Psychology, 26*, 309–320.

Gergen, Kenneth J. (1978). Experimentation in social psychology: A re-appraisal. *European Journal of Social Psychology, 8*, 507–527.

Gergen, Kenneth J. (1985). The social constructionist movement in modern psychology. *American Psychologist, 40*, 266–275.

Gergen, Kenneth J., & Davis, K. (Eds.). (1985). *The social construction of the person.* New York: Springer.

Goffman, Erving. (1961). *Encounters: Two studies in the sociology of interaction.* Indianapolis: Bobbs-Merrill.

Goffman, Erving. (1982). The interaction order: American sociological association, 1982 presidential address. *American Sociological Review, 48*(1), 1–17.

Greider, William. (1997). *One world ready or not: The manic logic of global capitalism.* New York: Simon and Schuster.

Hamberger, Jurgen, & Hewstone, Miles. (1997). Inter-ethnic contact as a predictor of blatant and subtle prejudice: Tests of a model in four West European nations. *British Journal of Social Psychology, 36*, 173–190.

Harpending, H. (1992). Age differences between mates in Southern African Pastoralists. *Behavioral and Brain Sciences, 15*, 102–103.

Harre, R. (1981). Psychological variety. In P. Heelas & A. Lock (Eds.), *Indigenous psychologies: The anthropology of the self* (pp. 79–103). New York: Academic Press.

Heider, K. (1991). *Landscapes of emotion: Mapping three cultures of emotion in Indonesia.* Cambridge, New York: Cambridge University Press.

Hofstede, Geert. (1980). *Culture's consequences: International differences in work-related values.* Beverly Hills, CA: Sage.

Hofstede, Geert. (1983). Dimensions of national cultures in fifty countries and three regions. In Dzuirawiec J. Deregowski & R. Annis (Eds.), *Expiscations in cross-cultural psychology.* Lisse, Netherlands: Swets and Zeitlinger.

Hogan, Robert T., & Emler, Nicholas P. (1978). The biases in contemporary social psychology. *Social Research, 45*, 478–534.

House, James S. (1977). The three faces of social psychology. *Sociometry, 40*, 161–177.

House, James S. (1981). Social structure and personality. In Morris Rosenberg & Ralph H. Turner (Eds.), *Social psychology: Sociological perspectives* (pp. 525–561). New York: Basic Books.

Inglehart, Ronald, Basanez, Miguel, & Moreno, Alejandro. (1998). *Human values and beliefs: A cross-cultural sourcebook.* Ann Arbor: The University of Michigan Press.

Inkeles, Alex. (1960). Industrial man: The relation of status to experience, perception, and value. *American Journal of Sociology, 66*, 1–31.

Inkeles, Alex. (1969). Making men modern: On the causes and consequences of individual change in six developing countries. *American Journal of Sociology, 75*, 208–225.

Inkeles, Alex, & Smith, David H. (1974). *Becoming modern: Individual change in six developing countries.* Cambridge, MA: Harvard University Press.

James, William. [1890] (1890). *The principles of psychology.* New York: Dover.

Kagitcibasi, Cigdem, & Berry, J. W. (1989). Cross-cultural psychology: Current research and trends. *Annual Review of Psychology, 40*, 493–531.

Kahl, Joseph A. (1968). *The measurement of modernism: A study of values in Brazil and Mexico.* Austin: University of Texas Press.

Karr, Linda Bridges. (2000). New horizons in cross-national experimentation. *Current Research in Social Psychology, 5*, 190–205.

Kashima, Yoshihisa, & Triandis, Harry C. (1986). The self-serving bias as a coping strategy: A cross-cultural study. *Journal of Cross-Cultural Psychology, 17*, 83–97.

Kemper, T. D. (1987). How many emotions are there? Wedding the social and autonomic component. *American Journal of Sociology, 93*, 263–289.

Kemper, T. D., & Collins, Randall. (1990). Dimensions of microinteraction. *American Journal of Sociology, 96*, 32–68.

Kenrick, D. T., & Keefe, R. C. (1992). Age preferences in mates reflect sex differences in human reproductive strategies. *Behavioral and Brain Sciences, 15*, 75–133.

Kim, Uichol, & Berry, J. W. (1993). *Indigenous psychologies: Experience and research in cultural context.* Newbury Park, CA: Sage.

Kim, Uichol, Park, Young-Shin, & Park, Donghyun. (2000). The challenge of cross-cultural psychology: The role of the indigenous psychologies. *Journal of Cross-Cultural Psychology, 31*(1), 63–75.

Kluegel, James R., Mason, David S., & Wegener, Bernd. (Eds.). (1995). *Social justice and political change: Public opinion in capitalist and post-communist states.* Hawthorne, New York: Aldine de Gruyter.

Kohn, Melvin L. (1969). *Class and conformity: A study in values.* Homewood, IL: Dorsey Press. (Second edition, University of Chicago Press, 1977.)

Kohn, Melvin L. (1989a). Introduction. In Melvin L. Kohn (Ed.), *Cross-national research in sociology* (pp. 17–31). Newbury Park, CA: Sage.

Kohn, Melvin L. (1989b). Cross-national research as an analytic strategy. In M. L. Kohn (Ed.), *Cross-national research in sociology* (pp. 77–102). Newbury Park, CA: Sage.

Kohn, Melvin L., & Schooler, Carmi. (1969). Class, occupation, and orientation. *American Sociological Review, 34*, 659–678.

Kohn, Melvin L., & Schooler, Carmi. (1983). With the collaboration of Joanne Miller, Karen A. Miller, Carrie Schoenbach, & Ronald Schoenberg. *Work and personality: An inquiry into the impact of social stratification.* Norwood, NJ: Ablex.

Kohn, Melvin L., & Slomczynski, Kazimierz M. (1990). *Social structure and self-direction: A comparative analysis of the United States and Poland.* Cambridge, MA: Basil Blackwell.

Kohn, Melvin L., Naoi, Atsushi, Schoenbach, Carrie, Schooler, Carmi, & Slomczynski, Kazimierz M. (1990). Position in the class structure and psychological functioning in the United States, Japan, and Poland. *American Journal of Sociology, 95*, 964–1008.

Kohn, Melvin L., Slomczynski, K. M., Janicka, K., Khmelko, V., Mach, B. W., Paniotto, V., Zaborowski, W., Gutierrez, R., & Heyman, C. (1997). Social structure and personality under conditions of radical social change: A comparative analysis of poland and the ukraine. *American Sociological Review, 62*(August), 614–638.

Kon, Igor. (1984). The self as a historical-cultural and ethnopsychological phenomenon. In Lloyd H. Strickland (Ed.), *Directions in soviet social psychology* (pp. 29–46). New York: Springer-Verlag.

Kroeber, Alfred L., & Kluckhohn, Clyde. (1952). Culture: A critical review of concepts and definitions. *Papers of the Peabody Museum, 47*(1).

Kuechler, Manfred. (1987). The utility of surveys for cross-national research. *Social Science Research, 16*, 229–244.

Kukla, Andre. (1988). Cross-cultural psychology in a post-empiricist era. In M. H. Bond (Ed.), *The cross-cultural challenge to social psychology* (pp. 141–152). Newbury Park, CA: Sage.

Kumagai, Hisa A. (1988). Ki: The "fervor of vitality" and the subjective self. *Symbolic Interaction, 11*, 175–190.

Lerner, Daniel. (1958). *The passing of traditional society.* Glencoe, IL: Free Press.

Leung, Kwok, & Bond, Michael H. (1989). On the empirical identification of dimensions for cross-cultural comparisons. *Journal of Cross-Cultural Psychology, 20*, 133–151.

Lincoln, James R., & Kalleberg, Arne L. (1990). *Culture, control, and commitment: A study of work organization and work attitudes in the United States and Japan.* Cambridge: Cambridge University Press.

Lonner, Walter J. (1980). The search for psychological universals. In H. C. Triandis & W. W. Lambert (Eds.), *Handbook of Cross-Cultural Psychology: Vol. 1. Perspectives* (pp. 143–204). Boston: Allyn and Bacon.

Lonner, Walter J., & Berry, John W. (Eds.). (1986). *Field methods in cross-cultural research.* Newbury Park, CA: Sage.

Luriia, A. R. (1974). *On the historical development of cognitive processes. (Ob historichescem razvitii poznavatel'nykh protsessov).* Moscow: Nauka.

Lutz, C. (1982). The domain of emotion words on Ifaulk. *American Ethnologist, 9,* 113–128.

Lutz, C., & White, Geoffrey. (1986). The anthropology of emotions. *Annual Review of Anthropology, 15,* 405–436.

Malone, Robert W. (1990). The need for global education. In Mary E. Clark & Sandra A. Wawrytko (Eds.), *Rethinking the curriculum: Toward an integrated, interdisciplinary college education* (pp. 167–179). New York: Greenwood Press.

Meletinskii, E. M. (1976). *Poetics of myth (Poetika mifa).* Moscow: Nauka.

Messick, David M. (1988a). On the limitations of cross-cultural research in social psychology. In M. H. Bond (Ed.), *The cross-cultural challenge to social psychology* (pp. 41–47). Newbury Park, CA: Sage.

Messick, David M. (1988b). Coda. In M. H. Bond (Ed.), *The cross-cultural challenge to social psychology* (pp. 286–289). Newbury Park, CA: Sage.

Miller, Joanne, Slomczynski, Kazimierz M., & Kohn, Melvin L. (1985). Continuity of learning-generalization: The effect of men's intellective process in the United States and Poland. *American Journal of Sociology, 91,* 593–615.

Miller, Joanne, Slomczynski, Kazimierz M., & Schoenberg, Ronald J. (1981). Assessing comparability of measurement in cross-national research: Authoritarian-conservatism in different sociocultural settings. *Social Psychology Quarterly, 44,* 178–191.

Miller, Karen A., Kohn, Melvin L., & Schooler, Carmi. (1985). Educational self-direction and the cognitive functioning of students. *Social Forces, 63,* 923–944.

Miller, Karen A., Kohn, Melvin L., & Schooler, Carmi. (1986). Educational self-direction and personality. *American Sociological Review,* 372–390.

Miller-Loessi, Karen. (1995). Comparative social psychology: Cross-cultural and cross-national. In Karen S. Cook, Gary Alan Fine, & James S. House (Eds.), *Sociological perspectives on social psychology* (pp. 397–420). Boston: Allyn and Bacon.

Mortimer, Jeylan T., & Lorence, Jon. (1995). Social psychology of work. In Karen S. Cook, Gary Alan Fine, & James S. House (Eds.), *Sociological perspectives on social psychology* (pp. 497–523). Boston: Allyn and Bacon.

Naoi, Atsushi, & Schooler, Carmi. (1985). Occupational conditions and psychological functioning in Japan. *American Journal of Sociology, 90,* 729–752.

Naoi, Michiko, & Schooler, Carmi. (1990). Psychological consequences of occupational conditions among Japanese wives. *Social Psychology Quarterly, 53,* 100–116.

Otta, E., Queiroz, R. D. S., Campos, L. D. S., daSilva, M. W. D., & Silveira, M. T. (1998). Age differences between spouses in a Brazilian marriage sample. *Evolution and Human Behavior, 20,* 99–103.

Oyama, Nao. (1990). Some recent trends in Japanese values: Beyond the individual-collective dimension. *International Sociology, 5,* 445–459.

Pearlin, Leonard I. (1971). *Class context and family relations: A cross-national study.* Boston: Little, Brown.

Pearlin, Leonard I., & Kohn, Melvin L. (1966). Social class, occupation, and parental values: A cross-national study. *American Sociological Review, 31,* 466–479.

Pike, Kenneth L. (1967). *Language in relation to a unified theory of the structure of human behavior.* The Hague: Mouton.

Robertson, Roland. (1992). *Globalization: Social theory and global culture.* London: Sage Publications.

Rodrigues, A. (1982). Replication: A neglected type of research in social psychology. *Intra-American Journal of Psychology, 16,* 91–109.

Sagie, G., & Schwartz, Shalom. (1996). National differences in value consensus. In H. Grad, A. Blanco, & J. Georgas (Eds.), *Key issues in cross-cultural psychology.* Lisse: Swets and Zeitlinger.

Sampson, E. E. (1985). The decentralization of identity—toward a revised concept of personal and social order. *American Psychologist, 40,* 1203–1212.

Sampson, E. E. (1988). The debate on individualism: Indigenous psychologies of the individual and their role in personal and societal functioning. *American Psychologist, 43,* 15–22.

Sampson, E. E. (1978). Scientific paradigms and social values: Wanted—a scientific revolution. *Journal of Personality and Social Psychology, 36,* 1332–1343.

Scherer, K. (1994). Evidence for both universality and cultural specificity of emotion and elicitation. In Paul Ekman & Richard Davidson (Eds.), *The nature of emotions: fundamental questions* (pp. 172–75). New York: Oxford University Press.

Scherer, K., Wallbot, H., & Summerfield, A. (1986). *Experiencing emotion: A cross-cultural study.* Cambridge, New York: Cambridge University Press.

Scheuch, Erwin K. (1967). Society as context in cross-cultural comparisons. *Social Science Information, 6,* 7–23.

Schooler, Carmi. (1984). Psychological effects of complex environments during the life span: A review and theory. *Intelligence, 8,* 259–281.

Schooler, Carmi. (1990). Individualism and the historical and social-structural determinants of people's concerns over self-directedness and efficacy. In J. Rodin, C. Schooler, & K. W. Schaie (Eds.), *Self-directedness: Cause and effects throughout the life course* (pp. 19–49). Hillsdale, NJ: Lawrence Erlbaum.

Schooler, C. (1996). Cultural and social-structural explanations of cross-national psychological differences. *Annual Review of Sociology, 22,* 323–349.

Schooler, Carmi, & Naoi, Atsushi. (1988). The psychological effects of traditional and of economically peripheral job settings in Japan. *American Journal of Sociology, 94,* 335–355.

Schooler, Carmi, Kohn, Melvin L., Miller, Karen A., & Miller, Joanne. (1983). Housework as work. In M. L. Kohn & C. Schooler (Eds.), *Work and personality: An inquiry into the impact of social stratification* (pp. 242–260). Norwood, NJ: Ablex.

Schooler, Carmi, Miller, Joanne., Miller, Karen A., & Richtand, Carol. (1984). Work for the household: Its nature and consequences for husbands and wives. *American Journal of Sociology, 90,* 97–124.

Schwartz, Shalom H. (1994). Beyond individualism/collectivism: New dimensions of values. In Uichol Kim, H. C. Triandis, C. Kagitcibasi, S. C. Choi, & G. Yoon (Eds.), *Individualism and Collectivism: Theory, application, and methods.* Newbury Park, CA: Sage.

Sharon, Irit, & Amir, Yehuda. (1988). Cross-cultural replications: A prerequisite for the validation of social-psychological laws. In M. H. Bond (Ed.), *The cross-cultural challenge to social psychology* (pp. 96–108). Newbury Park, CA: Sage.

Shweder, Richard A. (1991). *Thinking through cultures: Expeditions in cultural psychology.* Cambridge, MA: Harvard University Press.

Sinha, Durganand, & Naidu, Radha Krishna. (1994). Multilayered hierarchical structure of the self and not-self: The Indian perspective. In Anne-Marie Bouvy, F. J. R. van de Vijver, Pawel Boski, & Paul Schmitz (Eds.), *Journeys into cross-cultural psychology: Selected papers from the Eleventh International Conference of the International Association for Cross-Cultural Psychology* (pp. 41–49). Lisse: Swets and Zeitlinger.

Sinha, D. (1997). Indigenizing psychology. In J. W. Berry, Y. H. Poortinga, & J. Pandey (Eds.), *Handbook of Cross-Cultural Psychology: Vol. 1. Theory and Method.* Boston: Allyn and Bacon.

Slomczynski, Kazimierz M., Miller, Joanne, & Kohn, Melvin L. (1981). Stratification, work, and values: A Polish-United States comparison. *American Sociological Review, 46,* 720–744.

Smith, Peter B., & Bond, Michael Harris. (1999). *Social psychology across cultures* (2nd ed). Boston: Allyn and Bacon.

Smith, Peter B., & Schwartz, Shalom H. (1997). Values. In J. W. Berry, M. H. Segall, & C. Kagitcibasi (Eds.), *Handbook of cross-cultural psychology* (2nd ed., vol. 3). Boston: Allyn and Bacon.

Spenner, Kenneth I. (1988). Social stratification, work, and personality. *Annual Review of Sociology, 14,* 69–97.

Stewart, Edward C., & Bennett, Milton J. (1991). *American cultural patterns: A cross-cultural perspective.* Yarmouth, Maine: Intercultural Press.

Swann, W. B., & Read, S. J. (1981). Acquiring self-knowledge: The search for feedback that fits. *Journal of Personality and Social Psychology, 41,* 1119–1128.

Swidler, Ann. (1986). Culture in action: Symbols and strategies. *American Sociological Review, 51*(April), 273–286.

Tedeschi, James T. (1988). How does one describe a Platypus? An outsider's questions for cross-cultural psychology. In M. H. Bond (Ed.), *The cross-cultural challenge to social psychology* (pp. 14–28). Newbury Park, CA: Sage.

Triandis, Harry C. (1988). Cross-cultural contributions to theory in social psychology. In M. H. Bond (Ed.), *The cross-cultural challenge to social psychology* (pp. 122–140). Newbury Park, CA: Sage.

Triandis, Harry C. (1990). Cross-cultural studies of individualism and collectivism. In J. Berman (Ed.), *Nebraska symposium on motivation (1989)* (pp. 41–133). Lincoln, NE: University of Nebraska Press.

Triandis, Harry C. (1994). *Culture and social behavior.* New York: McGraw Hill.

Triandis, H. C., & Berry, J. W. (Eds.). (1980). *Handbook of Cross-Cultural Psychology: Methodology (vol. 2).* Boston: Allyn and Bacon.

van de Vijver, Fons, & Leung, Kwok. (1997). *Methods and data analysis for cross-cultural research.* Thousand Oaks, CA: Sage.

Yamagishi, Toshio, & Yamagishi, M. (1994). Trust and commitment in the United States and Japan. *Motivation and Emotion, 18,* 9–66.

Yamagishi, Toshio, Cook, Karen S., & Watabe, Motoki. (1998). Uncertainty, trust, and commitment formation in the United States and Japan. *American Journal of Sociology, 104*(July), 165–194.

Yu, An-Bang. (1994). The self and life goals of traditional Chinese: A philosophical and psychological analysis. In Anne-Marie Bouvy, F. J. R. van de Vijver, Pawel Boski, & Paul Schmitz (Eds.), *Journeys into cross-cultural psychology: Selected papers from the Eleventh International Conference of the International Association for Cross-Cultural Psychology* (pp. 50–67). Lisse: Swets and Zeitlinger.

Index